Lecture Notes in Computer Science 16993

The series Lecture Notes in Computer Science (LNCS), including its subseries Lecture Notes in Artificial Intelligence (LNAI) and Lecture Notes in Bioinformatics (LNBI), has established itself as a medium for the publication of new developments in computer science and information technology research, teaching, and education.

LNCS enjoys close cooperation with the computer science R & D community, the series counts many renowned academics among its volume editors and paper authors, and collaborates with prestigious societies. Its mission is to serve this international community by providing an invaluable service, mainly focused on the publication of conference and workshop proceedings and postproceedings. LNCS commenced publication in 1973.

Lingling Ding · Yannis Manolopoulos ·
Richard Chbeir · Karam Bou-chaaya ·
Schahram Dustdar · Tran Ngoc Tuan
Editors

Web and Big Data

10th Asia-Pacific Web (APWeb) and Web-Age Information Management (WAIM) International Joint Conference, APWeb-WAIM 2026
Danang, Vietnam, September 7–9, 2026
Proceedings, Part I

Springer

Editors
Lingling Ding
Liaoning University
Shenyang, China

Yannis Manolopoulos
University of York
Thessaloniki, Greece

Richard Chbeir
Université de Pau et des Pays de l'Adour
Anglet, France

Karam Bou-chaaya
EXPLEO GROUP
Montigny-le-Bretonneux, France

Schahram Dustdar
TU Wien
Wien, Austria

Tran Ngoc Tuan
FPT University
Ho Chi Minh City, Vietnam

ISSN 0302-9743 ISSN 1611-3349 (electronic)
Lecture Notes in Computer Science
ISBN 978-981-92-5692-1 ISBN 978-981-92-5693-8 (eBook)
https://doi.org/10.1007/978-981-92-5693-8

This Springer imprint is published by the registered company Springer Nature Singapore Pte Ltd.
The registered company address is: 152 Beach Road, #21-01/04 Gateway East, Singapore 189721, Singapore

Preface

This volume (LNCS 16993) and its companion volumes (LNCS 16994 and 16995) contain the proceedings of the 10th Asia-Pacific Web (APWeb) and Web-Age Information Management (WAIM) Joint Conference on Web and Big Data, for short called APWeb-WAIM. The 10th APWeb-WAIM joint conference was held in Da Nang, Vietnam during 7–9 September 2026.

As an Asia-Pacific flagship conference focusing on research, development, and applications related to Web information management, APWeb-WAIM builds on the successes of its ancestor APWeb and WAIM conferences. Previous APWeb events were held in Beijing (1998), Hong Kong (1999), Xi'an (2000), Changsha (2001), Xi'an (2003), Hangzhou (2004), Shanghai (2005), Harbin (2006), Huangshan (2007), Shenyang (2008), Suzhou (2009), Busan (2010), Beijing (2011), Kunming (2012), Sydney (2013), Changsha (2014), Guangzhou (2015), and Suzhou (2016). On the other hand, WAIM events were held in Shanghai (2000), Xi'an (2001), Beijing (2002), Chengdu (2003), Dalian (2004), Hangzhou (2005), Hong Kong (2006), Huangshan (2007), Zhangjiajie (2008), Suzhou (2009), Jiuzhaigou (2010), Wuhan (2011), Harbin (2012), Beidaihe (2013), Macau (2014), Qingdao (2015), and Nanchang (2016). The APWeb-WAIM joint conferences were held in Beijing (2017), Macau (2018), Chengdu (2019), Tianjin (2020), Guangzhou (2021), Nanjing (2022), Wuhan (2023), Jinhua (2024), and Shenyang (2025).

Researchers and practitioners from around the world came together at this leading international forum to share innovative ideas, original research findings, case study results, and practical insights in the areas of the World Wide Web and big data. APWeb-WAIM 2026 received a total of 309 research paper submissions. After a double-blind review process (each paper received at least three review reports), the conference accepted 108 regular research papers, resulting in an acceptance rate less than 35%. In addition, the conference accepted 24 special track papers, 1 industry paper, and 9 demo papers.

Moreover, the following 3 international workshops were organized:

- 9th International Workshop on Knowledge Graph Management and Applications (KGMA), organized by Meng Wang and Xin Wang, and
- 8th International Workshop on Semi-structured Big Data Management and Applications (SemiBDMA), organized by Linlin Ding,
- 1st International Workshop on Natural Resources Survey, Monitoring, and Assessment in the Big Data Era (NRSMA), organized by Xiaohui Huang, Yuewei Wang, Xiaodao Chen, Wei Han, Fan Lei, Yunliang Chen, Jianxin Li, and Lizhe Wang.

The contributed papers address a wide range of topics, such as large language models, knowledge graphs, neural networks and learning, machine learning, time series, tree-enabled processing, prediction, traffic management, community-based issues, recommendation systems, query processing, semantic issues, trajectory management, video and image processing, crowdsourcing, security and privacy, and database engineering.

The high-quality program documented in these proceedings would not have been possible without the authors who chose the APWeb-WAIM joint conference to disseminate their findings.

In addition, the conference program included 3 plenary talks by:

- Gao Cong (Nanyang Technological University, Singapore) entitled: "From AI4DB to Databases for AI: Rethinking Data Systems in the LLM Era",
- Hai Jin (Huazhong University of Science and Technology) entitled: "A Unified Approach of Graph Computing: From Foundations to Systems and Beyond", and
- Xiaofang Zhou (Hong Kong University of Science and Technology) entitled: "Advanced Similarity Query Processing in Vector Databases".

We would like to express our gratitude to all individuals, institutions, and sponsors that supported APWeb-WAIM 2026. We are grateful to all distinguished scientists for their invaluable contributions to the conference program. We are deeply thankful to the Program Committee members for lending their time and expertise to the conference. We also acknowledge the support of the other members of the organizing committee, all of whom helped make APWeb-WAIM 2026 a success.

Special thanks are due to the industry chairs (Dang Van Cuong, Le Quang Dam, and Tran The Hung), workshop chair (Jiajia Li), tutorial chair (Shiyu Yang), demo chairs (Cao Vu Bui, and Vo Quoc Trinh), publicity chairs (Yang Cao, Bohan Li, Nguyen Thi Thu Nga, and Salma Sassi), local organizing committee chairs (Le This My Hahn, Nguyen Dang Nghia, and Luong Vuong Nguyen), CCF TCIS liaison (Xin Wang), and CCF TCDB liaison (Yueguo Chen). Finally, we are grateful to the steering committee representative (Yanchun Zhang) for his guidance and support.

With the ever-growing importance of appropriate methods in these data-rich times and the rapid development of web-related technologies, APWeb-WAIM will continue to be a flagship conference in this field.

Lingling Ding
Yannis Manolopoulos
Richard Chbeir
Schahram Dustdar
Tran Ngoc Tuan
Karam Bou-chaaya

Organization

General Chairs

Richard Chbeir	Université de Pau et Pays de l'Adour, France
Schahram Dustdar	Technical University of Vienna, Austria
Tran Ngoc Tuan	FPT University, Vietnam

Program Chairs

Ding Linlin	Liaoning University, China
Yannis Manolopoulos	University of York, Europe Campus, Greece

Industry Chairs

Dang Van Cuong	University of Da Nang, Vietnam
Le Quang Dam	Marvell Technology, Vietnam
Tran The Hung	FPT Corporation, Vietnam

Tutorials Chair

Shiyu Yang	Guangzhou University, China

Workshop Chair

Jiajia Li	Shenyang Aerospace University, China

Demo Chairs

Cao Vu Bui	FPT University, Vietnam
Vo Quoc Trinh	FPT University, Vietnam

Publicity Chairs

Nguyen This Thus Nga	FPT University, Vietnam
Bohan Li	Nanjing University of Aeronautics and Astronautics, China
Yang Cao	Institute of Science Tokyo, Japan
Salma Sassi	ECE Lyon, France

Publication Chair

Karam Bou-chaaya	Expleo Group, France

Local Organizing Committee Chairs

Le Thi My Hahn	FPT University, Vietnam
Luong Vuong Nguyen	FPT University, Vietnam
Nguyen Dang Nghia	FPT University, Vietnam

CCF TCIS Liaison

Xin Wang	Tianjin University, China

CCF TCDB Liaison

Yueguo Chen	Renmin University of China, China

APWeb-WAIM Steering Committee Representative

Yanchun Zhang	Zhejiang Normal University, China

Program Committee

Sarra Abidi	National School of Computer Science (ENSI), Tunisia
Khloud Al Jallad	Arab International University, Syria

Rui An	Shaanxi Normal University, China
Sauvik Bal	Techno India University, India
Dariusz Barbucha	Gdynia Maritime University, Poland
Emna Ben Abdallah	University of Sfax, Tunisia
Leila Ben Othman	University of Tunis El Manar, Tunisia
Nicola Bena	University of Milan, Italy
Salima Benbernou	University Paris Cité, France
Djamal Benslimane	Claude Bernard University Lyon 1, France
Xin Bi	Northeastern University, China
Ismael Bouassida Rodriguez	University of Sfax, Tunisia
Nizar Bouguila	Concordia University, Canada
Ghizlane Bourahouat	School of Information Sciences, Morocco
Taotao Cai	University of Southern Queensland, Australia
Jinli Cao	La Trobe University, Australia
Yunpeng Chai	Renmin University of China, China
Ameni Chamekh	University of Sfax, Tunisia
Ioannis Chamodrakas	National and Kapodistrian University of Athens, Greece
Tsz Nam Chan	Shenzhen University, China
Jian Chen	Chinese Academy of Sciences, China
Lu Chen	Swinburne University of Technology, Australia
Weitong Chen	Adelaide University, Australia
Xiao Chen	Hong Kong Polytechnic University, China
Zi Chen	Wuhan University of Technology, China
Dickson Chiu	University of Hong Kong, China
Paolo Crippa	Marche Polytechnic University, Italy
Ningning Cui	Chang'an University, China
Alfredo Cuzzocrea	University of Calabria, Italy
Ana da Rocha	Universidade Federal Fluminense, Brazil
Boris Delibasic	University of Belgrade, Serbia
Shizhuo Deng	Northeastern University, China
Linlin Ding	Liaoning University, China
Xiaofeng Ding	Huazhong University of Science and Technology, China
Yuefeng Du	Liaoning University, China
Jide Edu	University of Strathclyde, UK
Mounim El Yacoubi	Télécom SudParis, France
Ichrak Ennaceur	Claude Bernard University Lyon 1, France
Ziquan Fang	Zhejiang University, China
Luigi Gallo	Pegaso University, Italy
Yongfeng Ge	Victoria University, Australia
Xiangyang Gou	Peking University, China

Na Guo	Shenyang Aerospace University, China
Yu Guo	Beijing Normal University, China
Mohammed Haddad	Claude Bernard University Lyon 1, France
Petr Hajek	University of Pardubice, Czech Republic
Akram Hakiri	University of Pau and the Adour Region, France
Sami Hamdi	Jazan University, Saudi Arabia
Nourelhouda Hammouda	University of Sfax, Tunisia
Fei Hao	Shaanxi Normal University, China
Salima Harrat	Higher Normal School of Bouzareah, Algeria
Trong-Minh Hoang	Posts and Telecommunication Institute of Technology, Vietnam
Yang Hongxin	Liaoning University, China
Hao Huang	Wuhan University, China
Shan Huang	Dalian Minzu University, China
Galina Ilieva	Plovdiv University Paisii Hilendarski, Bulgaria
Wissem Inoubli	University of Artois, France
Danwen Ji	Tongji University, China
Hangxu Ji	Northeastern University, China
Ma Ji	Liaoning University, China
Wanting Ji	Liaoning University, China
Dayu Jia	Liaoning University, China
Qinghan Jin	Northeastern University, China
Zhao Jin	Huazhong University of Science and Technology, China
Slim Kallel	University of Sfax, Tunisia
Huhu Kang	Shaanxi Normal University, China
Epaminondas Kapetanios	University of Hertfordshire, UK
Ioannis Karydis	Ionian University, Greece
Aleksandra Klasnja Milicevic	University of Novi Sad, Serbia
Sarah Kohail	Zayed University, UAE
Ferdinand Kpieleh	University of Cincinnati, USA
Kalliopi Kravari	International Hellenic University, Greece
Sabeur Lajili	University of Sousse, Tunisia
Florin Leon	Gheorghe Asachi Technical University of Iaşi, Romania
Hong Va Leong	Hong Kong Polytechnic University, China
Boyang Li	Beijing Institute of Technology, China
Dong Li	Liaoning University, China
Jiajia Li	Shenyang Aerospace University, China
Jianxin Li	Edith Cowan University, Australia
Jiatong Li	Hong Kong Polytechnic University, China

Lei Li	Hong Kong University of Science and Technology (Guangzhou), China
Mo Li	Liaoning University, China
Wei Li	Harbin Engineering University, China
Wentao Li	University of Leicester, UK
Youhuan Li	Hunan University, China
Yuan Li	North China University of Technology, China
Xiang Lian	Kent State University, USA
Kangzheng Liu	Huazhong University of Science and Technology, China
Tingting Liu	Liaoning University, China
Xiaoyi Liu	Arizona State University, USA
Yu Liu	Beijing Jiaotong University, China
Jing Lu	Liaoning University, China
Jiangang Ma	Federation University Australia, Australia
Jie Ma	Xi'an Jiaotong University, China
Ke Ma	Huazhong University of Science and Technology, China
Qiang Ma	Kyoto Institute of Technology, Japan
Yuliang Ma	Northeastern University, China
Elio Masciari	University of Naples Federico II, Italy
Agon Memeti	University of Tetova, North Macedonia
Xiaoye Miao	Zhejiang University, China
Miloud Mihoubi	TÉLUQ University, Canada
Yang-Sae Moon	Kangwon National University, South Korea
Phivos Mylonas	National Technical University of Athens, Greece
Mohamad Nassar	University of New Haven, USA
Thanh Tam Nguyen	Griffith University, Australia
Tiezheng Nie	Northeastern University, China
Alexander Norta	Dymaxion Oy, Estonia
Xiao Pan	Shijiazhuang Tiedao University, China
Dimitrios Panagoulias	University of Piraeus, Greece
Jun Pang	Wuhan University of Science and Technology, China
Sanghyun Park	Yonsei University, South Korea
Yuwei Peng	Wuhan University, China
Nhan Phan	Ho Chi Minh University of Technology, Vietnam
Ahmad Qadeib Alban	Université Paris Dauphine-PSL, France
Yu-Xuan Qiu	Beijing Institute of Technology, China
Pavlo Radiuk	Khmelnytskyi National University, Ukraine
Da Ren	Hong Kong Polytechnic University, China

Boyu Ruan	Hong Kong University of Science and Technology, China
Alexander Ryjov	Lomonosov Moscow State University, Russia
Jarogniew Rykowski	Poznań University of Business and Economics, Poland
Muath Sabha	Arab American University, Palestine
Zaineb Sakhrawi	University of Sfax, Tunisia
Imad Saleh	Paris 8 University, France
Francesco Santini	University of Perugia, Italy
Stefano Sebastio	Collins Aerospace, Ireland
Jiaxing Shen	Lingnan University, China
Han Shi	Liaoning University, China
Tuo Shi	Aalto University, Finland
Yu Shidong	Liaoning University, China
Jiefu Song	IRIT, Toulouse, France
Wei Song	Wuhan University, China
Xiangyu Song	Chang'an University, China
Yumeng Song	Aalborg University, Denmark
Zhen Song	Shandong University, China
Liana Stanescu	University of Craiova, Romania
Yongjiao Sun	Northeastern University, China
Aroua Taamallah	University of Sousse, Tunisia
Chaogang Tang	China University of Mining and Technology, China
Peng Tang	Shandong University, China
Min Tao	Wuzhou University, China
Joe Tekli	Lebanese American University, Lebanon
Yiping Teng	Shenyang Aerospace University, China
Alexandra Vultureanu-Albisi	University of Craiova, Romania
Aina Wang	Liaoning University, China
Beilun Wang	Southeast University, China
Chen Wang	Liaoning University, China
Hongzhi Wang	Harbin Institute of Technology, China
Hua Wang	Victoria University, Australia
Shigang Wang	Heilongjiang University, China
Wenli Wang	Education University of Hong Kong, China
Xiaoyang Wang	University of New South Wales, Australia
Yiqi Wang	Microsoft, Australia
Yishu Wang	Northeastern University, China
Zhaokang Wang	Nanjing University of Aeronautics and Astronautics, China
Zhibin Wang	Nanjing University, China

Shi-ting Wen	NingboTech University, China
Tianxing Wu	Southeast University, China
Zhizhong Wu	Google, USA
Haoran Xu	China University of Geosciences, Beijing, China
Shuai Xu	Nanjing University of Aeronautics and Astronautics, China
Yingwei Xu	Liaoning University, China
Yajun Yang	Tianjin University, China
Yu Yang	Education University of Hong Kong, China
Zhengyi Yang	University of Sydney, Australia
Shanshan Yao	Shanxi University, China
Xin Yao	Northeastern University, China
Zhongming Yao	Aalborg University, Denmark
Shaoyi Yin	University of Toulouse, France
Muhammad Younas	Oxford Brookes University, UK
Jianke Yu	Zhejiang Gongshang University, China
Yonghong Yu	Nanjing University of Posts and Telecommunications, China
Adib Zaman	University of Cincinnati, USA
Yuxiang Zeng	Beihang University, China
Jie Zhang	Hong Kong University of Science and Technology, China
Jilian Zhang	Jinan University, China
Junhua Zhang	Northeastern University, China
Ningyu Zhang	Zhejiang University, China
Xiaohan Zhang	National Supercomputing Shenzhen Center, China
Xiaowang Zhang	Tianjin University, China
Yanfeng Zhang	Northeastern University, China
Yong Zhang	Tsinghua University, China
Chunyan Zhao	East China Normal University, China
Minghao Zhao	East China Normal University, China
Zhigao Zheng	Wuhan University, China
Zixin Zhong	Tongji University, China
Xiangmin Zhou	RMIT University, Australia
Qiang Zhu	University of Michigan – Dearborn, USA
Rui Zhu	Shenyang Aerospace University, China
Yuanxiang Zhu	Liaoning University, China
Zhaonian Zou	Harbin Institute of Technology, China

Sponsors

Springer

Connected Environment & Distributed Energy Data Management Solutions Research Group

The French Chapter of the ACM Special Interest Group on Applied Computing

FPT University Vietnam

Contents

LLM and NLP

Recommendation Systems

Query Processing

Security and Privacy

- C2: Unified Visual Synthesis Mechanism: Unlike existing systems that decouple wallet addresses from real-world identities, our architecture enables the direct rendering of verified administrative data onto the asset's visual interface. This ensures that legal information, such as the owner's full name, is visually persistent and verifiable directly on the digital certificate, eliminating the need for external identity mapping tools.

In this paper, the term 2D data refers specifically to visual digital documents represented on a two-dimensional plane, including scanned land ownership certificates, vehicle registration certificates, engineering drawings, identification cards, and image-based administrative documents. Unlike generic file formats, these documents share two defining characteristics: (i) their visual layout and core content fields are permanently fixed at issuance, and (ii) selected administrative attributes such as the current owner identity must remain updatable over the document lifecycle. The proposed system is designed to manage precisely this class of documents.

2 Related Work

In recent years, the development of blockchain technology combined with decentralized storage mechanisms has driven the emergence of numerous digital data storage systems, particularly for 2D data such as images, documents, and multimedia content. These systems typically employ a hybrid architecture, in which the blockchain handles authentication, transaction recording, and access management, while data is stored off-chain on distributed systems such as IPFS or dedicated storage networks (Benet 2014; Wang et al. 2022). This approach reduces the load on the blockchain, optimizes costs, and improves scalability, making it particularly suitable for large-volume data with high access frequencies (Yaga et al. 2019; Meng and Sun 2022).

Among existing platforms, Filecoin offers decentralized storage via Proof-of-Replication with IPFS integration, but requires re-uploading data on each update (Khalid et al. 2023). Arweave provides permanent one-time-payment storage suited for static data only. Services like NFT.Storage and Pinata support IPFS-based NFT storage but lack version control or dynamic data management (Wang et al. 2021).

At the open-source level, IPFS identifies content by hash-based CIDs, ensuring integrity; any data change produces a new CID. Multiple implementations (Kubo, Helia) and client libraries (ipfs-http-client) facilitate integration (Benet 2014; Trautwein et al. 2022). On the blockchain layer, Ethereum supports smart contracts and NFT standards (ERC-721, ERC-1155) for representing digital assets, while Hardhat enables efficient development and testing (Buterin 2014). Hyperledger Fabric offers permissioned blockchain for enterprise scenarios (Cachin 2016).

Most systems follow a three-layer model (application, blockchain, storage): data is uploaded to IPFS, the CID is stored on-chain via smart contract, and retrieved by CID on demand (Zheng et al. 2017). For dynamic data, version control creates new CIDs per update linked via hash chains (Merkle 1987). Identity systems typically verify off-chain and store hashes on-chain, but this creates a wallet-identity gap in document management (Yaga et al. 2019). Current systems face notable limitations in scalability, transaction latency, 2D data integration depth, and operational costs (Zheng et al. 2017;

Casino et al. 2019; Khalid et al. 2023). Current research trends focus on separating the storage layer from the blockchain layer and applying Layer-2 solutions, though building a comprehensive system managing both static and dynamic data with precise identification remains a highly promising open direction (Khalid et al. 2023; Sariboz et al. 2021). Recently, the paradigm of direct on-chain visualization has been pioneered through the development of the first 3D integrated web-based self-visualization blockchain structure (Ngo-Ho et al. 2026). Building upon this foundational concept of self-visualization, our current study extends the paradigm to the 2D domain, focusing specifically on the complex lifecycle of static and dynamic administrative documents. Overall, the combination of blockchain and distributed storage has laid a solid foundation for 2D data management, but full integration of static-dynamic lifecycle management remains unstandardized (Khalid et al. 2023).

3 System Design

Table 1. Defines the notation used in this section

Symbol	Meaning
u	User wallet address (identity)
c	Certificate or document identifier
n	Current owner name
CID	Content Identifier in IPFS (hash-based)
H()	Keccak-256 hash function

The system uses the Keccak-256 cryptographic hash function, denoted as H = keccak256, which is the standard within the Ethereum Virtual Machine environment. This hash function is modeled as a mapping from a finite bit string space to a fixed-length 256-bit bit-string space (Table 1):

$$H : \{0, 1\}^* \rightarrow \{0, 1\}^{256}$$

To represent the combination of multiple input data points, we define an encoding function:

$$\mathrm{Enc} : \left(\{0, 1\}^*\right)^k \rightarrow \{0, 1\}^*$$

which is a one-to-one encoding function, ensuring that each input tuple is mapped to a unique bit string, eliminating boundary ambiguities. In this case, the multi-argument hash function is normalized:

$$H(x_1, x_2, \ldots, x_k) \cdot H(\mathrm{Enc}(x_1, x_2, \ldots, x_k))$$

In the identity model, each user is represented by a wallet address u, an identifier c, a name n, and IPFS content identifiers f, b. The hash values are defined as:

$$identityHash = H(u, c, n)$$

$$\mathrm{nameHash} = \mathrm{H(n)}$$

$$\mathrm{documentBlockHash} = \mathrm{H(n, c, f, b)}$$

The system uses a two-factor authentication mechanism for the mediator. A secret key $K \in \{0, 1\}^*$ is stored off-chain, while only the commitment value is stored on-chain:

$$\mathrm{mediatorKeyHash} = \mathrm{H(K)}$$

A transaction tx is accepted if and only if:

$$\mathrm{Auth(tx)} = (\mathrm{tx.sender} = \mathrm{mediator}) \wedge \left(\mathrm{H}\left(\mathrm{K}'\right) = \mathrm{mediatorKeyHash}\right)$$

where K' is the key provided by the caller. The probability of violating this condition is bounded above by 2^{-256}.

Each asset is associated with a linear hash chain representing its ownership history. For asset i, the initial value is:

$$\mathrm{h_i(0)} = \mathrm{H}\left(\mathrm{idHash_{owner}}, \mathrm{I_{ipfs}}, \mathrm{t_0}\right)$$

where $\mathrm{I_{ipfs}}$ is the content identifier of the data and $\mathrm{t_0}$ is the creation time. For each transfer step $k \geq 1$

$$\mathrm{h_i(k)} = \mathrm{H(h_i(k-1), idHash_{from}, idHash_{to}, t_k)}$$

This structure forms a linked hash chain, where each element depends directly on the previous one.

After an identity is verified, the system establishes a permanent lock state. At that point, there exists a mapping:

$$\mathrm{u} \mapsto \mathrm{identityHash(u)}$$

which is one-to-one and time-invariant.

The notation $\mathrm{H(x_1, x_2, \ldots)}$ represents the Keccak-256 hash function applied to data encrypted by Enc. The variable t is the timestamp of the current block, and sender is the address calling the function. The revert operation is modeled as an atomic transaction rollback mechanism, ensuring that no intermediate state is recorded if the conditions are not met. Based on these theoretical foundations, the system's core algorithms are described using pseudocode as below:

Algorithm MEDIATE_TRANSFER
Input: id, from, to, key K′
1. if sender ≠ mediator then revert
2. if H(K′) ≠ mediatorKeyHash then revert
3. if id ≥ totalAssets then revert
4. asset ← storageMap[id]
5. if ¬asset.pending then revert
6. newHash ← H(asset.lastTxHash, asset.idHashOwner, idHash(to), now)
7. append provenance (asset.lastTxHash, newHash)
8. update owner, idHash, lastTxHash
9. reset pending state
10. emit AssetTransferred(id, oldOwner, to, newHash)

Algorithm VERIFY_PROVENANCE
Input: provenance list P
1. for each record k from 1 to n do
2. if P[k].prevHash ≠ P[k-1].currentHash then return false
3. expected ← H(P[k-1].currentHash, idHash(from), idHash(to), time)
4. if P[k].currentHash ≠ expected then return false
5. return true

3.1 Visual Integration Mechanism

The visual integration mechanism produces a unified displayed certificate by merging a static IPFS-stored image with dynamically retrieved on-chain ownership metadata, through six steps: (1) fetch the immutable NFT image from IPFS via the on-chain CID, (2) read verified ownership data (owner name, identity hash, timestamp) from the smart contract, (3) resolve the wallet address to a real-world identity via on-chain identity mapping, (4) composite the dynamic metadata as an overlay onto the static image using a client-side HTML5 Canvas renderer—the static IPFS layer is never modified, (5) recompute the image hash and compare against the on-chain CID, rejecting tampered content, (6) render the merged certificate to the user. This pipeline ensures that the static asset remains immutable while ownership information remains current and verifiable without external tools.

The illustration depicts the end-to-end processing workflow of a blockchain-based 2D data storage and verification system, designed with a layered architecture to ensure clear separation between functional components. This structure comprises a user interface and wallet connection layer, a blockchain layer responsible for authentication, a secure data retrieval layer, a client-side integrity verification layer, and an output display layer. This organization allows each layer to perform a distinct role while working closely together to ensure the consistency and reliability of the entire system.

At the user interface layer, users interact via a decentralized web application and a digital wallet to establish a connection, request account access, and generate a digital signature. This process creates an authenticated session based on the wallet address, allowing the system to identify the participating entity without revealing sensitive information. Once verified on the user side, the information is transferred to the blockchain layer, where the smart contract performs identity status checks. This mechanism relies on status flags indicating whether a user has been verified and whether that identity is permanently locked, thereby ensuring that only valid entities can perform asset-related operations.

When the verification conditions are met, the system retrieves data through the distributed storage layer. The smart contract provides the asset's content identifier, allowing the client-side application to query detailed information and download binary data from the off-chain storage system. The use of content-based identification ensures that data cannot be altered without changing the identifier, thereby maintaining the immutability and verifiability of the stored data.

After the data is retrieved, an integrity check is performed on the client side to minimize reliance on third parties. The frontend application recalculates the hash values from the received data and compares them with the values recorded on the blockchain. This comparison mechanism allows for the detection of discrepancies between off-chain stored data and data committed on-chain, thereby ensuring that the displayed content has not been altered or tampered with during transmission or storage.

In the final stage, the browser layer is responsible for displaying the results to the user. When all verification steps are successful, the system provides the full 2D asset along with verified ownership information and the asset's provenance history. Conversely, if any discrepancies are detected during the integrity check or if the data cannot be decrypted, the system will refuse to display the results or issue a warning to protect users from unreliable data.

This architecture clearly demonstrates the combination of blockchain's immutability and the flexibility of off-chain storage. Static data is preserved through immutable CIDs, while dynamic data is managed via a hash-linked version chain. Additionally, the integration of an identity layer enables mapping between wallet addresses and verified user information, laying the foundation for practical applications such as digital document management, where data must ensure immutability while also supporting controlled updates (Fig. 1).

4 Experiments and Results

As there is no unified evaluation standard for hybrid blockchain-IPFS systems, we define metrics across four categories: retrieval performance, throughput, data integrity, and availability.

Within the retrieval performance group, key metrics include average latency and percentiles such as p95 and p99 to reflect performance under normal conditions and worst-case scenarios. Average latency is calculated as:

$$\overline{L} = \frac{1}{N}\sum_{i=1}^{N} L_i$$

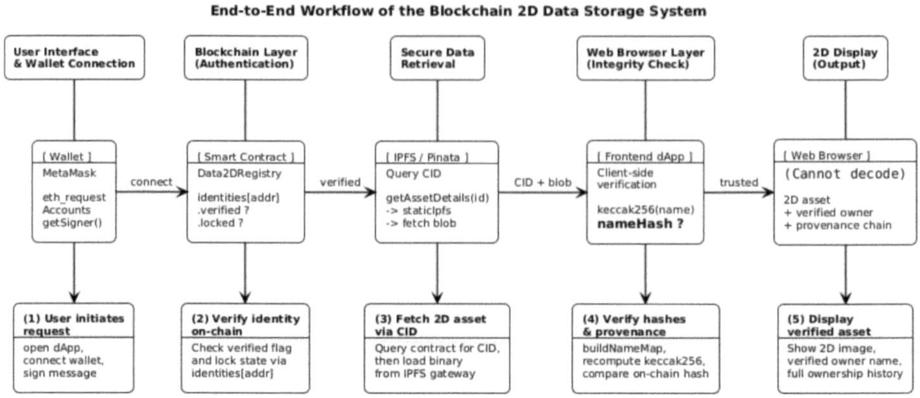

Fig. 1. The end-to-end process of the 2D data storage and verification system on a Blockchain platform

$$\mathrm{TPS} = \frac{N_{tx}}{T}$$

$$I = \frac{N_{verify}}{N_{cid\_match}}$$

where N_{cid_match} is the number of data retrievals with a hash matching the CID stored on the blockchain, and N_{verify} is the total number of checks. The closer the value of I is to 1, the higher the level of data integrity assurance. Additionally, the immutability of the transaction history is evaluated through the hash link integrity metric:

$$\text{Link Integrity} = \frac{H_{total}}{H_{valid}}$$

where H_{valid} is the number of valid hash links and H_{total} is the total number of links. Within the operational cost category, blockchain transaction costs are determined by:

$$\text{Cost} = \text{Gas}_{used} \times \text{Gas}_{price}$$

In addition, off-chain storage costs and data retrieval costs must also be considered when evaluating total operating costs.

The final category is availability and stability, measured by the uptime metric:

$$\text{Availability} = \frac{T_{up}}{T_{total}} \times 100\%$$

where T_{up} is the time the system operates normally and T_{total} is the total observation time. Metrics such as error rates, timeouts, and rollbacks are also used to assess stability.

Evaluation uses scenario-based testing across the full lifecycle, load testing for scalability, and fault injection for resilience.

The system demonstrates strong retrieval performance under moderate load (50 VUs/60 s), with an average latency of about 10.6 ms, indicating fast and stable responses.

Percentile metrics (p50 ≈ 3.02 ms, p90 ≈ 12.46 ms, p95 ≈ 21.46 ms) show most requests are processed efficiently, while peak latency (~354.77 ms) occurs rarely due to network or IPFS delays. The throughput reaches 49.36 requests/s with a 0% error rate, confirming high reliability. Table 2 summarizes key results, including latency, throughput, data integrity, cost, and availability.

Table 2. Performance of the proposed system across evaluation metrics

Metric	Value
Average retrieval latency	10.6 ms
p50/p90/p95	Dynamic 3.02/12.46/21.46
Maximum latency	354.77 ms
Throughput (RPS)	49.36 req/s
Write throughput (TPS)	843.88 tx/s
Read throughput	2288.33 req./s
Transaction latency (avg/p95)	1149.67/1178 ms
Success rate	100%
Data integrity	100%
Cost per transaction	~0.504 USD
Total cost of ownership (TCO)	~50.46 USD
Availability	100%
Error/Timeout/Rollback	0%/0%/0%

The results show that the system achieves high throughput for both read and write operations. Specifically, write throughput reaches 843.88 TPS, reflecting the system's ability to efficiently process blockchain transactions. Meanwhile, read throughput is significantly higher (2288.33 req/s) since no consensus mechanism is required. However, transaction latency remains at ~1.1–1.2 s, a characteristic of blockchain due to the time required for block confirmation, illustrating the trade-off between performance and data immutability.

Regarding data integrity, the system achieves a 100% verification success rate, with all retrieved data matching original values through CID and SHA-256 validation. This confirms the effectiveness of the hybrid architecture combining blockchain and off-chain storage. Nevertheless, verification time remains relatively high due to data retrieval and hash recomputation, illustrating a balance between reliability and efficiency. The total cost of ownership (TCO) has three components: (1) on-chain gas fees averaging $0.504 per transaction (dominant cost), (2) IPFS pinning fees, negligible for small certificate files, and (3) retrieval costs, near-zero via public IPFS gateways. Overall TCO per certificate lifecycle is approximately $0.50, cost-effective versus fully on-chain alternatives, though sensitive to Ethereum gas price volatility.

For availability and stability, under the controlled experimental environment, the prototype achieved 100% uptime with no recorded errors, timeouts, or rollbacks across all evaluated test cases. These results should not be interpreted as guaranteed performance under arbitrary network failures or production-scale load, real-world deployments may be affected by blockchain congestion, IPFS node availability, and network latency. Overall, the system achieves a balance between performance, integrity, and reliability, making it suitable for applications requiring transparency and immutable data, despite limitations in transaction latency and cost.

Table 3 summarizes the hardware and software configuration used across all experiments.

Table 3. Experimental environment configuration

Parameter	Value
Hardware	AMD Ryzen 9/32 GB DDR4 RAM
Blockchain	Ethereum via Hardhat (local node)
IPFS	Kubo (Go-IPFS)
Dataset	500 certificate records
Transactions	5000 blockchain transactions
Load	50 virtual users/60 s

Table 4 compares capability coverage. The proposed system is the only one supporting all four dimensions simultaneously.

Table 4. Feature comparison with existing systems

System	Static 2D	Dynamic data	Identity	Visual integration
NFT.Storage	Yes	No	No	No
Filecoin	Yes	No	No	No
Arweave	Yes	No	No	No
Hyperledger Fabric	Yes	Yes	Yes	No
Proposed System	Yes	Yes	Yes	Yes

The certificate lifecycle is modeled as a state-transition system: Registered → Verified → Pending Transfer → Transferred → Displayed. Each transition is enforced by the smart contract. Five failure cases define system behavior under invalid inputs:

(F1) Broken ownership chain: If $P[k].prevHash \neq P[k-1].currentHash$ for any link, VERIFY_PROVENANCE returns false and the frontend blocks display, protecting users from tampered provenance.

(F2) Invalid CID: If IPFS cannot retrieve content for the stored CID, the retrieval layer returns an error and display is blocked with an explicit user warning.
(F3) Identity mismatch or wrong key: If the caller $\neq$ mediator or $H(K') \neq$ mediatorKeyHash, the smart contract reverts with no state change, preventing unauthorized transfers.
(F4) Duplicate approval: Calling MEDIATE_TRANSFER when asset.pending is already false triggers a revert, preventing double-spending of ownership rights.
(F5) Unverified target identity: If idHash(to) is absent from the on-chain identity mapping, the transfer is rejected before any state is modified.

The current system models ownership history as a linear hash chain, which is sufficient for sequential one-to-one transfers. However, real-world administrative records can involve more complex events. Co-ownership (multiple holders of a single asset), inheritance (transfer upon owner death), revocation (government cancellation of a certificate), dispute resolution (contested ownership), and rollback (correction of an erroneous transfer) all require provenance structures beyond a simple chain. These cases are better modeled as a provenance graph. Extending the system to support such events while maintaining on-chain verifiability and visual integration remains an important direction for future work.

5 Conclusion

This paper has presented a blockchain architecture that addresses the disconnect between static NFT assets and dynamic administrative metadata. Traditional decentralized models secure immutable content but fail to reflect real-world ownership changes in a visually intuitive manner for documents such as land titles and vehicle registrations. The primary contribution lies in the Programmable Block Ownership framework: a hybrid IPFS-Blockchain architecture with a linked hash chain that keeps core asset attributes immutable while allowing ownership identity to evolve under strict regulatory control. Crucially, the system enables direct visual synthesis of verified real-world identities onto the displayed certificate, eliminating the wallet-identity gap without requiring external lookup tools. Experimental evaluations demonstrated 100% data integrity and high availability under the evaluated controlled conditions, demonstrating the system's practical viability. Future work will explore zero-knowledge proofs for identity privacy, support for complex provenance graphs (co-ownership, inheritance, revocation), and optimizing real-time visual synthesis overhead.

References

Alharby, M., van Moorsel, A.: Blockchain-Based Smart Contracts: A Systematic Mapping Study. arXiv: https://arxiv.org/abs/1710.06372 (2017)

Benet, J.: IPFS–Content Addressed, Versioned, P2P File System. arXiv: https://arxiv.org/abs/1407.3561 (2014)

Buterin, V.: A Next-Generation Smart Contract and Decentralized Application Platform. Ethereum Foundation. https://ethereum.org/en/whitepaper/ (2014)

Cachin, C.: Architecture of the hyperledger blockchain fabric. In: Proceedings of the Workshop on Distributed Cryptocurrencies and Consensus Ledgers. https://arxiv.org/abs/1601.04236 (2016)

Casino, F., Dasaklis, T.K., Patsakis, C.: A systematic literature review of blockchain-based applications. Telematics Inform. **36**, 55–81 (2019). https://doi.org/10.1016/j.tele.2018.11.006

Chen, L., Zhang, X., Sun, Z.: Scalable blockchain storage model based on DHT and IPFS. KSII Trans. Internet Inf. Syst. (2022). https://doi.org/10.3837/tiis.2022.07.009

Christidis, K., Devetsikiotis, M.: Blockchains and smart contracts for the internet of things. IEEE Access **4**, 2292–2303 (2016) https://ieeexplore.ieee.org/document/7467408

Dorri, A., Kanhere, S.S., Jurdak, R.: Blockchain in Internet of Things: Challenges and Solutions. arXiv: https://arxiv.org/abs/1608.05187 (2016)

Dwork, C., Naor, M.: Pricing via processing or combatting junk mail. In: Advances in Cryptology, CRYPTO'92, pp. 139–147. Springer (1992). https://doi.org/10.1007/3-540-48071-4_10

Kang, P., Yang, W., Zheng, J.: Blockchain private file storage-sharing method based on IPFS. Sensors **22**(14), 5100 (2022). https://doi.org/10.3390/s22145100

Khalid, M.I., et al.: A comprehensive survey on blockchain-based decentralized storage networks. IEEE Access (2023) https://ieeexplore.ieee.org/document/10026822

Kuzlu, M., Pipattanasomporn, M., Gurses, L., Rahman, S.: Performance analysis of a hyperledger fabric blockchain framework. In: IEEE Conference Proceedings (2019). https://ieeexplore.ieee.org/document/8946222

Meng, L., Sun, B.: Research on decentralized storage based on blockchain. Sustainability **14**(20), 13060 (2022). https://doi.org/10.3390/su142013060

Merkle, R.C.: A digital signature based on a conventional encryption function. In: Advances in Cryptology, CRYPTO'87, pp. 369–378. Springer (1987). https://doi.org/10.1007/3-540-48184-2_32

Nakamoto, S.: Bitcoin: A Peer-to-Peer Electronic Cash System. https://bitcoin.org/bitcoin.pdf (2008)

Ngo-Ho, A.-K., Thach, H.-D., & Ngo-Ho, A.-K.: The first 3D integrated web-based self-visualization blockchain structure. In: Proceedings of the 10th APWeb-WAIM International Joint Conference on Web and Big Data (APWeb-WAIM 2026). Springer (2026)

Trautwein, D., et al.: Design and Evaluation of IPFS: A Storage Layer for the Decentralized Web. arXiv: https://arxiv.org/abs/2205.01728 (2022)

Yaga, D., Mell, P., Roby, N., Scarfone, K.: Blockchain Technology Overview (NIST IR 8202). National Institute of Standards and Technology (2019). https://doi.org/10.6028/NIST.IR.8202

Zheng, Z., Xie, S., Dai, H., Chen, X., Wang, H.: An overview of blockchain technology. In: 2017 IEEE International Congress on Big Data, pp. 557–564. IEEE (2017). https://doi.org/10.1109/BigDataCongress.2017.85

DAPU: Dynamic Attribute and Policy Updating Attribute-Based Access Control for Cloud Data Sharing

Zhaoyu Chen[1], Zinan Shen[1], Wu Xin[1(✉)], Zhangti Li[2], Yahui Zhao[2(✉)], Cong Li[1], and Zhonghai Wu[1]

[1] Peking University, Beijing, China
chenzhaoyu@stu.pku.edu.cn, {sznnzs,xinwu,li.cong,wuzh}@pku.edu.cn
[2] China Unicom Software Research Institute, Beijing, China
{lizt21,zhaoyh99}@chinaunicom.cn

Abstract. With the emergence of diverse data-driven services, such as personalized recommendation, cross-organizational data analytics, and model training, data are increasingly shared among different users and organizations. Such sharing can improve service quality and user experience, but it also raises serious concerns about the confidentiality of sensitive data. Ciphertext-policy attribute-based encryption (CP-ABE) provides a promising cryptographic foundation for enforcing expressive access control over outsourced data. Practical cloud data sharing is dynamic, requiring both access policy updates and user revocation. However, existing CP-ABE-based solutions cannot address these two requirements simultaneously. Revocable CP-ABE schemes often assume static access policies and require costly data re-encryption when policies change, whereas policy-updatable CP-ABE schemes commonly lack efficient attribute revocation or rely on coarse-grained user exclusion. Moreover, approaches based on attribute-based proxy re-encryption may introduce unauthorized re-delegation risks if proxy operations are not strictly controlled by data owners. To address these challenges, we propose DAPU, a dynamic attribute and policy updating access control scheme for secure cloud data sharing. DAPU enables encrypted access privileges to evolve efficiently by allowing data owners to outsource policy-update operations to the cloud server, thereby reducing owner-side computation overhead without exposing plaintext data. Meanwhile, DAPU supports direct and fine-grained attribute revocation, ensuring that revoked users cannot regain access through subsequent policy updates. We formally analyze the security of DAPU and prove its selective security under the defined threat model. Experimental results show that DAPU scales linearly with the number of attributes while maintaining constant-time revocation overhead.

Keywords: Cloud data sharing · Data security · CP-ABE · Attribute revocation · Dynamic policy updating

---

Zhaoyu Chen and Zinan Shen are contributed equally to this work.

L. Ding et al. (Eds.): APWeb-WAIM 2026, LNCS 16993, pp. 15–31, 2027.
https://doi.org/10.1007/978-981-92-5693-8_2

1 Introduction

With the emergence of diverse data-driven services, such as personalized recommendation, cross-organizational data analytics, and model training, data are increasingly shared among different users and organizations to improve service quality and user experience. Meanwhile, the rapid proliferation of cloud computing has made cloud servers a common infrastructure for storing and managing massive volumes of sensitive information, ranging from enterprise records to personal data [1,4]. Although cloud-assisted data sharing improves scalability and accessibility, it also raises serious concerns about the security and privacy of outsourced sensitive data in dynamic cloud environments [12,13,15]. To achieve flexible and fine-grained access control while preserving data confidentiality, ciphertext-policy attribute-based encryption (CP-ABE) [2] has emerged as a foundational cryptographic mechanism.

Although CP-ABE provides robust access control, traditional static schemes struggle with the dynamic demands of cloud data sharing. Owners frequently need to update access policies due to evolving business or regulatory requirements. Moreover, dynamic user attributes require timely updates or immediate key revocation upon role or context changes. For instance, in a collaborative data platform, an access policy might be defined as ((“Role = Researcher” AND “Project = Genome”) OR “Director”). If a researcher leaves the project, their data access must be revoked immediately. To address these challenges, enhanced CP-ABE schemes support user revocation and policy updates. As summarized in Table 1, legacy revocation schemes primarily support user- or attribute-level revocation, whereas policy-update schemes dynamically modify access structures via ciphertext transformation. Specifically, revocation schemes [6,7,14,16,18] embed a revocation list in ciphertexts or periodically re-key non-revoked users. Meanwhile, policy-update approaches [8,10,17,19] generate re-encryption keys to delegate ciphertext transformation to cloud servers, modifying privileges without exposing plaintext. Nevertheless, current schemes rarely support fine-grained revocation and efficient policy updates simultaneously. Relying solely on policy updates for user revocation causes policy expansion, triggering heavy storage and performance overhead while forcing owners to remain online. To achieve both goals, subsequent studies [5,9,11] integrated revocation into attribute-based proxy re-encryption (AB-PRE). However, in AB-PRE models, authorized users can misuse re-encryption capabilities to transfer access privileges to unauthorized parties without owner consent.

In this paper, we propose DAPU, an attribute-based access control scheme featuring dynamic attribute revocation and policy updating for secure cloud data sharing. To mitigate large-scale dataset processing overhead, we design a secure, outsourced policy update mechanism that delegates intensive ciphertext transformation workloads to the cloud server. Specifically, we introduce an attribute versioning mechanism that assigns an independent version number to each attribute. For frequently changing attributes, the system merely refreshes corresponding cloud-side ciphertext components to instantly update or revoke access privileges. This decoupled approach enables non-revoked users to

Table 1. Comparison of revocation and policy update mechanisms (m: number of policy attributes, n: number of users, r: revocation list size, $\times$: unsupported)

Scheme	Revocation Granularity	Key Update Cost Parameter	CT Update Cost Parameter	Policy Update
Xue et al. [14]	Attribute-level	1	1	$\times$
Han et al. [7]	User-level	$\times$	$\log n$	$\times$
Yin et al. [18]	User-level	$\times$	r	$\times$
Yang et al. [16]	Attribute-level	1	1	$\times$
Li et al. [8]	Policy-level	m	m	✓
Yang et al. [17]	Policy-level	m	m	✓
Zhao et al. [19]	Policy-level	$n \cdot m$	m	✓
Liang et al. [10]	Policy-level	m	m	✓
Ours	**Attribute-level**	**1**	**1**	✓

seamlessly update keys while effectively preventing revoked users from accessing shared data. Furthermore, to adjust the overall access policy, the data owner simply releases specific update keys, authorizing the cloud server to smoothly transform ciphertexts from the old policy to the new one without disclosing plaintext throughout the operational lifecycle.

The main contributions of this paper are summarized as follows:

- We propose a novel CP-ABE scheme (DAPU) that supports dynamic attribute revocation and policy evolution for secure cloud data sharing. By introducing an attribute versioning mechanism, our scheme enables efficient, owner-controlled attribute revocation without requiring modifications to existing access policies or expanding the policy size.
- We design a secure outsourced policy update algorithm that leverages update keys to delegate computationally intensive ciphertext transformation tasks to the cloud server. This approach achieves dynamic access management without decrypting the underlying data, effectively eliminating the high communication overhead typical of the traditional "retrieve–decrypt–re-encrypt–upload" paradigm.
- We conduct an evaluation using local cryptographic benchmarks and cloud deployment. The results show that encryption and decryption costs scale linearly with the number of attributes, while the revocation overhead remains constant. Dynamic operations also remain within milliseconds for policies with up to 30 attributes, indicating practical efficiency in cloud data sharing.

2 Preliminary

2.1 System Model

As illustrated in Fig. 1, the system model consists of the following entities:

Authority: The authority manages issuing keys and revoking users. The authority generates secret keys (SK) for users. When a user's attributes are revoked, the authority generates a revocation key to update the ciphertext in the cloud and update non-revoked users' SK. The authority is fully trusted to execute setup, key generation, and revocation correctly.

Cloud Server: The cloud server stores encrypted data and processes update keys to refresh ciphertexts upon policy changes or attribute revocations. It is assumed semi-honest: it follows prescribed update procedures but is curious about the outsourced ciphertexts and update information it handles.

Data Owner: Data owners encrypt the data under access policies and upload it to the cloud server. They also request the cloud server to update the ciphertexts when access policies change or request the authority to revoke users.

User: Each user is assigned a set of attributes. Users can retrieve ciphertext from the cloud server, but they can decrypt the data only if their attributes satisfy the access policy embedded in the ciphertext. Users may collude, but collusion does not enable decryption unless the queried or updated secret key corresponds to an attribute set that satisfies the access policy.

Running Scenario: Consider a collaborative health-data platform where a data owner encrypts a clinical dataset under an initial policy P_1, such as "Researcher in the Genome project or Director", and uploads the ciphertext to the cloud server. A researcher whose attributes satisfy P_1 can decrypt the data, while other users cannot. If the researcher leaves the Genome project, the authority revokes the corresponding project attribute by refreshing its version number. The cloud server then updates only the ciphertext components associated with this attribute, and non-revoked users update the affected secret-key component through the authority. Later, if the data owner changes the access rule to a new policy P_2, the owner generates a policy update key and asks the cloud server to transform the ciphertext from P_1 to P_2 without downloading, decrypting, or re-encrypting the data locally. This scenario illustrates how attribute revocation and outsourced policy updating are coordinated among the entities in Fig. 1.

2.2 Bilinear Pairing

Let G and G_T be multiplicative cyclic groups of prime order p with generator g. A bilinear pairing is a map $e : G \times G \rightarrow G_T$ with the following properties: (1) Bilinearity: for all $u, v \in \mathbb{Z}_p$, $e(g^u, g^v) = e(g, g)^{uv}$; (2) Non-degeneracy: $e(g, g) \neq 1$; and (3) Computability: $e(g, h)$ can be computed in polynomial time.

2.3 Linear Secret-Sharing Scheme (LSSS)

An LSSS allows a secret s to be shared among a set of attributes so that only subsets satisfying an access structure can reconstruct s. The access structure is represented by a matrix M and a mapping ρ from matrix rows to attributes. Given a random vector $\boldsymbol{v} = (s, y_2, \dots, y_n)$, the shares are obtained by matrix multiplication. LSSS is widely used to represent policies in CP-ABE.

3 The Construction of DAPU

3.1 The Underlying CP-ABE Scheme

In this section, we present the concrete construction of our underlying CP-ABE scheme. It consists of four algorithms: Setup, KeyGen, Encrypt and Decrypt. Following the running scenario in Sect. 2.1, these algorithms are first used to initialize the system, issue user keys, encrypt data under the initial policy P_1, and allow only users whose attributes satisfy P_1 to recover the plaintext.

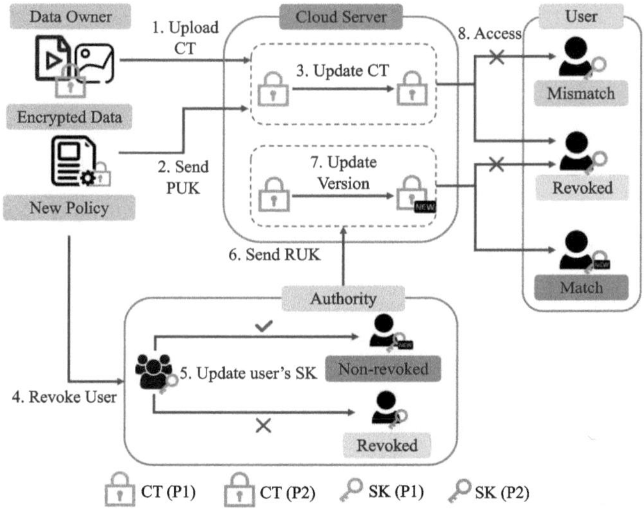

Fig. 1. Workflow of the secure cloud data sharing scheme with policy update and user revocation. CT denotes ciphertext, SK denotes users' secret key, P1 and P2 represent the two different access policies, PUK denotes policy update key, and RUK denotes revocation update key.

• Setup $(1^\lambda) \rightarrow (msk, PP, \{PK_x\}, \{VK_x\})$: The setup algorithm takes as inputs the security parameter λ. It picks a secure hash function $H : \{0,1\}^* \rightarrow \mathbb{G}$. Then it randomly selects $g \in \mathbb{G}$ and $\alpha, \beta, \gamma, a \in \mathbb{Z}_p$, and outputs the master secret key msk and the public parameters PP as:

$$msk = (\alpha, \beta, \gamma, a), \; PP = (g, g^a, g^{\frac{1}{\beta}}, g^\beta, e(g,g)^\alpha).$$

For each attribute x, the algorithm randomly selects $v_x \in \mathbb{Z}_p$ as the initial attribute version number $VK_x = v_x$. It computes and outputs the public attribute key PK_x as:

$$PK_x = (PK_{1,x} = H(x)^{v_x}, PK_{2,x} = H(x)^{v_x \gamma}).$$

The public parameters PP and the public attribute keys PK_x are then published to all system users.

- KeyGen $(msk, S, \{VK_x\}_{x\in S}) \rightarrow SK$: The secret key generation algorithm takes as inputs the master secret key msk, a set of attributes S that describe the user, and the corresponding set of attribute version numbers $\{VK_x\}_{x\in S}$. The algorithm randomly selects $t \in \mathbb{Z}_p$, and generates the user's secret key as:
$$SK = \left(K = g^{\frac{\alpha}{\beta}} \cdot g^{\frac{at}{\beta}}, L = g^t, \forall x \in S : K_x = g^{t\beta^2} \cdot H(x)^{v_x t\beta}\right).$$
- Encrypt $(PP, \{PK_x\}, m, (\mathcal{M}, \rho)) \rightarrow CT$: The encryption algorithm takes as inputs the public parameters PP, the set of public attribute key $\{PK_x\}$, the message m and an $n \times l$ LSSS matrix $\mathcal{M}$ with ρ mapping its rows to attributes. The data owner first selects a random encryption exponent $s \in \mathbb{Z}_p$ and a random vector $\boldsymbol{v} = (s, y_2, \ldots, y_n) \in \mathbb{Z}_p^n$. Then the data owner stores the encryption information $\mathsf{EncInfo}_m = \boldsymbol{v}$. This information is sensitive owner-side metadata rather than part of the outsourced ciphertext. It consists of n elements in $\mathbb{Z}_p$, so the per-ciphertext storage overhead is $n\lceil\log_2 p\rceil$ bits, or equivalently n serialized field elements, and grows linearly with the dimension of the sharing vector. The data owner stores $\mathsf{EncInfo}_m$ locally, or in an owner-controlled key-management component, and does not disclose it to the cloud server or users. For $i \in \{1, \ldots, l\}$, it computes $\lambda_i = \boldsymbol{v} \cdot \mathcal{M}_i$, where $\mathcal{M}_i$ is the i-th row of the matrix $\mathcal{M}$. Next, the algorithm randomly selects $r_1, r_2, \ldots, r_l \in \mathbb{Z}_p$ and generates the ciphertext as:

$$CT = \Big(C = m \cdot e(g,g)^{\alpha s},\ C' = g^{\beta s}, C_i = g^{a\lambda_i}(g^{\beta})^{-r_i} H(\rho(i))^{-r_i v_{\rho(i)}},$$
$$D_{1,i} = H(\rho(i))^{v_{\rho(i)} r_i \gamma}, D_{2,i} = g^{\frac{r_i}{\beta}} (i = 1, \ldots, l)\Big).$$

- Decrypt $(CT, (\mathcal{M}, \rho), SK) \rightarrow m$: The decryption algorithm takes as inputs the ciphertext CT, the LSSS structure $(\mathcal{M}, \rho)$ and the user's secret key SK for a set of attributes S. Suppose the user's attribute set S satisfies the access structure and let $I \subset \{1, 2, \ldots, l\}$ be defined as $I = \{i : \rho(i) \in S\}$. Then the algorithm computes the set of constants $\{w_i \in \mathbb{Z}_p\}_{i\in I}$ to reconstruct the encryption exponent $s = \Sigma_{i\in I} w_i \lambda_i$. It computes:

$$\frac{e(C', K)}{\Pi_{i\in I}\left(e(C_i, L)\, e(D_{2,i}, K_{\rho(i)})\right)^{w_i}} = e(g,g)^{\alpha s}.$$

It can then compute the decrypted message as $m = C/e(g,g)^{\alpha s}$.

3.2 Efficient Attribute Revocation

In this section, we describe the construction of our attribute revocation scheme. Suppose an attribute x' is revoked from a user μ. Our scheme consists of three algorithms: RUKeyGen, SKUpdate, and RCTUpdate.

- RUKeyGen $(msk, VK_{x'}) \rightarrow (RUK_{x'}, \widetilde{VK}_{x'}, \widetilde{PK}_{x'})$: The revocation update key generation algorithm takes as inputs the master secret key msk and the current version number $VK_{x'}$ of the revoked attribute x'. The algorithm generates a new attribute version number $\widetilde{VK}_{x'}$ by randomly selecting $\widetilde{v}_{x'} \in \mathbb{Z}_p(\widetilde{v}_{x'} \neq v_{x'})$ and setting $\widetilde{VK}_{x'} = \widetilde{v}_{x'}$. Then, the authority computes the revocation update key as:

$$RUK_{x'} = \left(RUK_{1,x'} = \frac{\widetilde{v}_{x'}}{v_{x'}}, RUK_{2,x'} = \frac{v_{x'} - \widetilde{v}_{x'}}{v_{x'}\gamma} \right).$$

  It sends $RUK_{x'}$ to the cloud server via secure channels. The authority also updates the public attribute key of the revoked attribute x' as:

$$\widetilde{PK}_{x'} = (\widetilde{PK}_{1,x'} = H(x')^{\widetilde{v}_{x'}}, \widetilde{PK}_{2,x'} = H(x')^{\widetilde{v}_{x'}\gamma}).$$

  It broadcasts a message to all the users that the public attribute key of x' has been updated. All the users can obtain the new public attribute key from the public bulletin board of the authority.
- SKUpdate $(msk, L, K_{x'}, RUK_{x'}) \rightarrow \widetilde{SK}$: The secret key update algorithm takes as inputs the master secret key msk, two secret key components L and $K_{x'}$ of the non-revoked user, and the revocation update key $RUK_{x'}$. In this process each non-revoked user submits the secret components $L = g^t$ and $K_{x'} = g^{t\beta^2} \cdot H(x')^{v_{x'}t\beta}$ to the authority. The authority computes the new component $\widetilde{K}_{x'}$ associated with the revoked attribute x' as:

$$\widetilde{K}_{x'} = \left(\frac{K_{x'}}{L^{\beta^2}} \right)^{RUK_{1,x'}} \cdot L^{\beta^2} = g^{t\beta^2} \cdot H(x')^{\widetilde{v}_{x'}t\beta}.$$

  Then, the authority returns $\widetilde{K}_{x'}$ to the non-revoked user. The user updates its secret key by replacing the component $K_{x'}$ with the new one $\widetilde{K}_{x'}$:

$$\widetilde{SK} = (K, L, \widetilde{K}_{x'}, \forall x \in S/\{x'\} : K_x).$$

- RCTUpdate $(CT, RUK_{x'}) \rightarrow \widetilde{CT}$: The ciphertext update algorithm takes as inputs the ciphertext CT associated with the revoked attribute x' and the revocation update key $RUK_{x'}$. The algorithm updates the ciphertext associated with x' as:

$$\begin{aligned}\widetilde{CT} = \Big(& \widetilde{C} = C, \widetilde{C'} = C', \forall i = 1, \ldots, l : \widetilde{D}_{2,i} = D_{2,i}, \\ & if\ \rho(i) \neq x' : \widetilde{C}_i = C_i, \widetilde{D}_{1,i} = D_{1,i}, \\ & if\ \rho(i) = x' : \widetilde{C}_i = C_i \cdot (D_{1,i})^{RUK_{2,x'}}, \widetilde{D}_{1,i} = (D_{1,i})^{RUK_{1,x'}} \Big).\end{aligned}$$

Revocation workflow. In a large user population, a revocation event is processed with respect to the affected attribute x' rather than by re-encrypting data for every user. The authority first refreshes the version of x' and releases $RUK_{x'}$ to the cloud server, which updates only the ciphertext rows labeled with x'. Users whose attribute sets do not contain x' are not involved. Among users holding x', only non-revoked users that still need this attribute contact the authority to update the corresponding key component; the revoked user is not issued the new component. During SKUpdate, the submitted components L and $K_{x'}$ should be transferred over authenticated and encrypted channels, and the authority returns only $\widetilde{K}_{x'}$. Although these values are not a complete secret key, they are still sensitive key material and should not be exposed on unauthenticated channels. Batch revocation can be handled by grouping revocation requests by affected attributes and executing the same version-update procedure for each attribute. Offline non-revoked users do not block cloud-side ciphertext updates; they can obtain $\widetilde{K}_{x'}$ when they reconnect, but before doing so they cannot decrypt ciphertexts that require the new version of x'.

3.3 Dynamic Policy Updating

In this section, we describe the construction of our policy updating scheme. Suppose the data owner wants to convert an LSSS structure $(\mathcal{M}, \rho)$ to $(\widetilde{\mathcal{M}}, \widetilde{\rho})$. Our scheme consists of two algorithms: PUKeyGen and PCTUpdate.

- $\mathsf{PUKeyGen}(\mathsf{EncInfo}_m, (\mathcal{M}, \rho), (\widetilde{\mathcal{M}}, \widetilde{\rho})) \rightarrow PUK_m$: The policy update key generation algorithm takes as inputs the encryption information $\mathsf{EncInfo}_m = \boldsymbol{v}$ of the message m, the previous LSSS structure $(\mathcal{M}, \rho)$ and the new LSSS structure $(\widetilde{\mathcal{M}}, \widetilde{\rho})$. The data owner needs to retain $\mathsf{EncInfo}_m$ only while future policy updates for the corresponding ciphertext are expected. Once the ciphertext is deleted, re-encrypted under a fresh policy, or no longer requires policy evolution, the owner can erase the old $\mathsf{EncInfo}_m$. Since $\boldsymbol{v}$ contains the encryption secret s, compromise of $\mathsf{EncInfo}_m$ would weaken the confidentiality of the corresponding ciphertext and may allow unauthorized generation of policy update material. Therefore, $\mathsf{EncInfo}_m$ should be protected with the same care as cryptographic secret state, for example by encrypted owner-side storage, access-controlled key management, or hardware-backed protection. Suppose $\mathcal{M}$ is an $n \times l$ matrix and $\widetilde{\mathcal{M}}$ is an $\widetilde{n} \times \widetilde{l}$ matrix.

The algorithm first calls the PolicyCompare algorithm and outputs three sets of row indexes $I_{1,\widetilde{\mathcal{M}}}, I_{2,\widetilde{\mathcal{M}}}, I_{3,\widetilde{\mathcal{M}}}$ of $\widetilde{\mathcal{M}}$. Then it randomly selects a vector $\widetilde{\boldsymbol{v}} = (s, \widetilde{y}_2, \ldots, \widetilde{y}_n) \in \mathbb{Z}_p^n$, where s is the encryption secret in the previous ciphertext. It computes $\lambda_i = \boldsymbol{v} \cdot \mathcal{M}_i$ and $\widetilde{\lambda}_i = \widetilde{\boldsymbol{v}} \cdot \mathcal{M}_i$, and lets $I_{\mathcal{M}} = \{1, \ldots, l\}$ be the set of row indexes in $\mathcal{M}$.

Then, for each $j \in [1, \widetilde{l}]$:

(a) If $(j, i) \in I_{1,\widetilde{\mathcal{M}}}$ (Type 1), the algorithm computes the policy update key as:

$$PUK_{j,i,m} = \left(PUK_{j,i,1}^{(1)} = g^{a(\widetilde{\lambda}_j - \lambda_i)} \right).$$

Algorithm 1. PolicyCompare

Input: New policy $\left(\widetilde{\mathcal{M}}, \widetilde{\rho}\right)$ with $\widetilde{l} \times \widetilde{n}$ matrix.
Input: Previous policy $(\mathcal{M}, \rho)$ with $l \times n$ matrix.
Output: Subsets of row indexes in $\widetilde{\mathcal{M}}$: $I_{1,\widetilde{\mathcal{M}}}, I_{2,\widetilde{\mathcal{M}}}, I_{3,\widetilde{\mathcal{M}}}$.

```
I_M̃ ←index set of rows in M
for j = 1 to l do
    if ρ̃(j) appears in M then
        if I_M ≠ ∅ and ∃i ∈ I_M s.t. ρ(i) = ρ̃(j) then
            add (j, i) to I_{1,M̃}
            delete i from I_M
        else
            find any i ∈ [1, l] s.t. ρ(i) = ρ̃(j)
            add (j, i) to I_{2,M̃}
        end if
    else
        add (j, 0) to I_{3,M̃}
    end if
end for
```

(b) If $(j, i) \in I_{2,\widetilde{\mathcal{M}}}$ (Type 2), the algorithm randomly selects $x_j \in \mathbb{Z}_p$ and computes the policy update key as:

$$PUK_{j,i,m} = (x_j, PUK_{j,i,1}^{(2)} = g^{a(\widetilde{\lambda}_j - x_j \lambda_i)}).$$

(c) If $(j, i) \in I_{3,\widetilde{\mathcal{M}}}$ (Type 3), the algorithm randomly selects $\widetilde{r}_j \in \mathbb{Z}_p$ and computes the policy update key as:

$$PUK_{j,i,m} = \Big(PUK_{j,i,1}^{(3)} = g^{a\widetilde{\lambda}_j} \left(g^{\beta}\right)^{-\widetilde{r}_j} H\left(\rho\left(j\right)\right)^{-\widetilde{r}_j v_{\rho(j)}},$$
$$PUK_{j,i,2}^{(3)} = H\left(\rho\left(j\right)\right)^{v_{\rho(j)} \widetilde{r}_j \gamma}, PUK_{j,i,3}^{(3)} = g^{\frac{\widetilde{r}_j}{\beta}}\Big).$$

Finally, the algorithm outputs the policy update key as:

$$PUK_m = \Big(\left(Type\ 1, \{PUK_{j,i,m}\}_{(j,i) \in I_{1,\widetilde{\mathcal{M}}}}\right),$$
$$\left(Type\ 2, \{PUK_{j,i,m}\}_{(j,i) \in I_{2,\widetilde{\mathcal{M}}}}\right),$$
$$\left(Type\ 3, \{PUK_{j,i,m}\}_{(j,i) \in I_{3,\widetilde{\mathcal{M}}}}\right) \Big).$$

PCTUpdate(PUK_m, CT): The ciphertext update algorithm takes as inputs the policy update key PUK_m and the previous ciphertext CT. For each $j \in [1, \widetilde{l}]$,

1. If Type 1 ($(j,i) \in I_{1,\widetilde{\mathcal{M}}}$), the algorithm computes the new ciphertext component as:

$$\widetilde{C}_j = C_i \cdot PUK^{(1)}_{j,i,1} = g^{a\widetilde{\lambda}_j} \left(g^{\beta}\right)^{-r_i} H\left(\rho\left(i\right)\right)^{-r_i v_{\rho(i)}},$$

$$\widetilde{D}_{1,j} = D_{1,i}, \widetilde{D}_{2,j} = D_{2,i}.$$

2. If Type 2 ($(j,i) \in I_{2,\widetilde{\mathcal{M}}}$), the algorithm computes the new ciphertext component as:

$$\widetilde{C}_j = C_i^{x_j} \cdot PUK^{(2)}_{j,i,1} = g^{a\widetilde{\lambda}_j} \left(g^{\beta}\right)^{-r_i} H\left(\rho\left(i\right)\right)^{-r_i v_{\rho(i)}},$$

$$\widetilde{D}_{1,j} = \left(D_{1,i}\right)^{x_j}, \widetilde{D}_{2,j} = \left(D_{2,i}\right)^{x_j}.$$

3. If Type 3 ($(j,i) \in I_{3,\widetilde{\mathcal{M}}}$), the algorithm computes the new ciphertext component as:

$$\widetilde{C}_j = PUK^{(3)}_{j,i,1}, \widetilde{D}_{1,j} = PUK^{(3)}_{j,i,2}, \widetilde{D}_{2,j} = PUK^{(3)}_{j,i,3}.$$

Finally, the algorithm outputs the new ciphertext as:

$$\widetilde{CT} = \left(C, C', \widetilde{C}_j, \widetilde{D}_{1,j}, \widetilde{D}_{2,j}\left(j = 1, \ldots, \widetilde{l}\right)\right).$$

4 Security Analysis

4.1 Security Model

In this security model, the challenger captures a fully trusted authority, the cloud server is semi-honest, and the adversary may coordinate colluding users but still cannot obtain decryption capability unless a queried attribute set satisfies the challenged access structure. To capture the security of DAPU, we define the following interactive games between a challenger $\mathcal{C}$ and the adversary $\mathcal{A}$.

Dynamic leakage. For revocation updates, we define the admissible leakage as $\mathcal{L}_{\mathsf{RCTUpdate}} = (x', \{i \mid \rho(i) = x'\}, RUK_{x'}, \widetilde{PK}_{x'})$, namely the revoked attribute label, the ciphertext rows associated with this attribute, the update token, and the updated public attribute key. For policy updates, we define $\mathcal{L}_{\mathsf{PCTUpdate}} = ((\mathcal{M}, \rho), (\widetilde{\mathcal{M}}, \widetilde{\rho}), I_{1,\widetilde{\mathcal{M}}}, I_{2,\widetilde{\mathcal{M}}}, I_{3,\widetilde{\mathcal{M}}}, PUK_m)$, namely the old and new public access structures, the row type/index mapping generated by PolicyCompare, and the policy update token. These leakage functions expose the metadata needed by the cloud to perform ciphertext transformation, but they do not reveal the plaintext, the encryption secret s, the master secret key, or any complete user secret key.
Init: $\mathcal{A}$ outputs the challenge access structures $\left\{(\mathcal{M}_1^*, \rho_1^*), \ldots, (\mathcal{M}_q^*, \rho_q^*)\right\}$.
Setup: $\mathcal{C}$ calls the setup algorithm and generates the public parameters PP and the master secret key msk. $\mathcal{C}$ returns PP to $\mathcal{A}$.

Phase 1: $\mathcal{A}$ is given a polynomial bounded number of oracle access to the secret key SK that corresponds to a set of attributes S and the revocation update key RUK, with the constraint that: 1) none of the secret key queries can satisfy the access structures; 2) none of the updated secret keys $\widetilde{SK}$ generated by the queried secret keys SK and revocation update keys RUK can satisfy the access structures. The view obtained from each revocation update query is bounded by $\mathcal{L}_{\mathsf{RCTUpdate}}$, and the query is not allowed to create a non-revoked key that satisfies the challenged access structure.
Challenge: $\mathcal{A}$ submits two equal-length challenge messages m_0^* and m_1^*. $\mathcal{C}$ randomly selects a bit $b \in \{0, 1\}$, and calls the encryption algorithm to get the challenge ciphertexts $\{CT_1^*, \ldots, CT_q^*\}$ under the challenge access structures. Finally $\mathcal{C}$ returns $\{CT_1^*, \ldots, CT_q^*\}$ to $\mathcal{A}$.
Phase 2: $\mathcal{A}$ continues to make queries as in **Phase 1**. It can also make policy update key queries by submitting the pair $(\mathcal{M}_i^*, \rho_i^*)$, $(\mathcal{M}_j^*, \rho_j^*)$. $\mathcal{C}$ returns the corresponding policy update key PUK. The information revealed by a policy update query is bounded by $\mathcal{L}_{\mathsf{PCTUpdate}}$: the adversary may learn how old policy rows are matched, reused, split, or newly generated, but it does not learn the message or the secret sharing vector beyond the masked group elements contained in PUK.
Guess: $\mathcal{A}$ outputs its guess $b' \in \{0, 1\}$ for b and wins the game if $b' = b$.

Definition 1. The advantage of $\mathcal{A}$ in the game is defined as follows:

$$\mathrm{Adv}_{\mathcal{A},\mathrm{DAPU}}(\lambda) = \left| \Pr[b = b'] - \frac{1}{2} \right|.$$

DAPU is secure if $\mathrm{Adv}_{\mathcal{A},\mathrm{DAPU}}(\lambda)$ is negligible for any probabilistic polynomial time (PPT) adversary $\mathcal{A}$ in the above game.

Correctness under dynamic updates. Revocation update and policy update affect different parts of the ciphertext/key state. $\mathsf{RCTUpdate}$ changes only the components associated with the revoked attribute version, and $\mathsf{SKUpdate}$ gives only non-revoked users the matching new key component. $\mathsf{PCTUpdate}$ keeps the encryption secret s unchanged and transforms the ciphertext shares from $(\mathcal{M}, \rho)$ to $(\widetilde{\mathcal{M}}, \widetilde{\rho})$. Therefore, after a revocation followed by a policy update, any non-revoked user whose updated attributes satisfy the new policy can reconstruct the same secret s and decrypt, whereas a revoked user lacks the new version component for x' and cannot recover access from PUK_m alone.

4.2 Proof of Security for Our Scheme

We conclude the security analysis with the following theorem.

Definition 2. Let $\mathbb{G}$ be a group of prime order p, g be a generator of $\mathbb{G}$ and $a, s, b_1, \ldots, b_q \in \mathbb{Z}_p$ be chosen at random. Given $T \in \mathbb{G}_T$ and a vector $\boldsymbol{y} =$

$$g, g^s, g^a, \ldots, g^{a^q}, g^{a^{q+2}}, \ldots, g^{a^{2q}},$$

$$\forall_{1\le j\le q}, g^{s\cdot b_j}, g^{a\cdot b_j}, \dots, g^{a^q\cdot b_j}, g^{a^{q+2}\cdot b_j}, \dots, g^{a^{2q}\cdot b_j},$$
$$\forall_{1\le j,k\le q, j\ne k}, g^{a\cdot s\cdot b_k/b_j}, \dots, g^{a^q\cdot s\cdot b_k/b_j}$$

the q-parallel BDHE assumption is that it is difficult for any PPT algorithm to determine whether $T = e(g,g)^{a^{q+1}s}$ or $T \in_R \mathbb{G}_T$.

Theorem 1. *If the decisional q-parallel BDHE assumption holds, DAPU is secure against PPT adversaries.*

Proof.. Suppose we have a PPT adversary $\mathcal{A}$ with non-negligible advantage $adv_{\mathcal{A}}$ in the selective security game against our construction and suppose it chooses a challenge matrix M^* with at most q columns. We can build a simulator $\mathcal{B}$ that plays the decisional q-parallel BDHE problem with non-negligible advantage.
Init: $\mathcal{B}$ takes in a q-parallel BDHE challenge $\boldsymbol{y}, T$. The adversary gives the algorithm the challenge access structure (M^*, ρ^*), where M^* has n^* columns.
Setup: $\mathcal{B}$ randomly chooses $\beta, \gamma, \alpha' \in \mathbb{Z}_p$ and implicitly set $\alpha = \alpha' + a^{q+1}$. It computes $e(g,g)^\alpha = e(g,g)^{\alpha'} \cdot e(g^a, g^{a^q})$. For attribute x, it randomly selects v_x and computes $H(x) = g^{z_x} \prod_{i\in X} \left(g^{aM^*_{i,1}/b_i} \cdot g^{a^2 M^*_{i,2}/b_i} \dots g^{a^{n^*} M^*_{i,n^*}/b_i} \right)$, where X denotes the set of indices i such that $\rho^*(i) = x$. Note that PP and $\{PK_x\}$ can all be computed using provided items.
Phase 1: In this phase $\mathcal{B}$ answers revocation update key queries and private key queries. For RUK queries, it randomly selects $\tilde{v}_{x'}$ and computes $RUK_{x'}$ using RUKeyGen. For secret key queries, it first finds a vector $\boldsymbol{w} = (w_1, \dots, w_{n^*}) \in \mathbb{Z}_p^{n^*}$ such that $w_1 = -1$ and $\boldsymbol{w} \cdot M^*_i = 0$. By the definition of LSSS such a vector must exist. Then it randomly selects $r \in \mathbb{Z}_p$ and implicitly sets $t = r + w_1 a^q + w_2 a^{q-1} \dots + w_{n^*} a^{q-n^*+1}$. It computes

$$K = g^{\frac{\alpha'}{\beta}} g^{\frac{ar}{\beta}} \prod_{i=2,\dots,n^*} (g^{a^{q+2-i}})^{\frac{w_i}{\beta}}, L = g^r \prod_{i=1,\dots,n^*} (g^{a^{q+1-i}})^{w_i}.$$

Next, for $\forall x \in S$, if there is no i such that $\rho^*(i) = x$ we simply let $K_x = L^{\beta^2 + z_x v_x \beta}$; otherwise it can also computes K_x as:

$$K_x = L^{\beta^2} \left(L^{z_x} \prod_{i\in X} \prod_{j=1,\dots,n^*} \left(g^{(a^j/b_i)r} \cdot \prod_{k=1,\dots,n^*, k\ne j} \left(g^{a^{q-k+1+j}/b_i} \right)^{w_k} \right)^{M^*_{i,j}} \right)^{v_x \beta}.$$

Challenge: $\mathcal{B}$ first flips a coin b and computes

$$C = m_b T \cdot e(g^s, g^{\alpha'}), C' = (g^s)^\beta.$$

It randomly selects $r'_1, \dots, r'_l, y'_2, \dots, y'_{n^*}$, then implicitly set $r_i = \frac{sb_i}{v_{\rho^*(i)}} - r'_i$ and the vector $\boldsymbol{v} = (s, sa + y'_2, \dots, sa^{n^*-1} + y'_{n^*})$. It computes $\lambda_i = \boldsymbol{v} \cdot M_i$. For each $i \in [l]$, we define R_i as the set of all k such that $i \ne k$ and $\rho^*(i) = \rho^*(k)$, the challenge ciphertext components are then generated as:

$$C_i = g^{-\beta r_i} \cdot H(\rho^*(i))^{r_i' v_{\rho^*(i)}} \cdot (g^{b_i s})^{-z_{\rho^*(i)}} \cdot \left(\prod_{j=2,\ldots,n^*} (g^a)^{M^*_{i,j} y'_j} \right)$$
$$\cdot \left(\prod_{k \in R_i} \prod_{j=1,\ldots,n^*} (g^{-a^j \cdot s \cdot (b_i/b_k) M^*_{k,j}}) \right),$$
$$D_{1,i} = H(\rho^*(i))^{r_i' v_{\rho^*(i)} \gamma} \cdot \left(\prod_{k \in R_i \cup \{i\}} \prod_{j=1,\ldots,n^*} (g^{-a^j \cdot s \cdot (b_i/b_k) M^*_{k,j}}) \right),$$
$$D_{2,i} = g^{\frac{-r_i'}{\beta}} g^{-\frac{s b_i}{\beta v_{\rho^*(i)}}}.$$

Phase 2: $\mathcal{A}$ continues to make queries as in Phase 1. It can also make policy update key queries. $\mathcal{B}$ randomly selects $y'_2, \ldots, y'_{n^*} \in \mathbb{Z}_p$, set $\tilde{\boldsymbol{v}}_0 = s$ and $\tilde{\boldsymbol{v}}_i = sa^{j-1} - \frac{sa^{j-1} M_j}{M'_i} + y'_i)$ for Type 1, $\tilde{\boldsymbol{v}}_i = sa^{j-1} - \frac{sa^{j-1} M_j x_j}{M'_i} + y'_i)$ for Type 2, $\tilde{\boldsymbol{v}}_i = sa^{i-1} + y'_i$ for Type 3 and computes PUK_m using PUKeyGen. Note that we can compute PUK_m since it does not contain the unknown term $g^{a^{q+1}}$. For revocation queries, $RUK_{x'}$ only provides conversion factors for the attribute version of x'; even a curious cloud learns the affected attribute and rows but not $v_{x'}$, $\widetilde{v}_{x'}$, γ, or the user randomness t. For policy update queries, the Type 1, Type 2, and Type 3 components reveal the row correspondence and update type, while their group elements are masked by the fresh sharing randomness and do not expose s or the plaintext. Thus, the simulated dynamic-update view is exactly the leakage specified by $\mathcal{L}_{\mathsf{RCTUpdate}}$ and $\mathcal{L}_{\mathsf{PCTUpdate}}$.
Guess: $\mathcal{B}$ outputs 0 to guess that $T = e(g,g)^{sa^{q+1}}$ if $b = b'$ and otherwise outputs 1. Note that $\mathcal{B}$'s advantage equals $\mathcal{A}$'s advantage.

When $T = e(g,g)^{a^{q+1}s}$, $\mathcal{B}$ gives a perfect simulation so we have that:

$$\mathsf{Pr}[\mathcal{B}(\boldsymbol{y}, T = e(g,g)^{a^{q+1}s}) = 0] = \frac{1}{2} + \mathsf{Adv}_{\mathcal{A}}.$$

When T is a random group element, the message m_b is completely hidden from $\mathcal{A}$, so we have $\mathsf{Pr}[\mathcal{B}(\boldsymbol{y}, T) = 0] = \frac{1}{2}$. Therefore, $\mathcal{B}$ can solve the decisional q-parallel BDHE problem with non-negligible advantage.

5 Evaluation

Experiment Setup. We conduct the experiments by measuring two dimensions: time cost and storage/communication cost. We vary the number of attributes involved in the access policy from 5 to 30, covering cloud data-sharing policies from simple role-based rules to moderately complex combinations of department, project, data type, and permission attributes. This controlled range allows us to evaluate how increasing policy complexity affects the major cryptographic operations while keeping other factors fixed. In addition, five PBC pairing-parameter profiles ("secp192r1", "secp224r1", "secp256r1", "secp384r1" and "secp512r1") [3] are tested to evaluate the impact of stronger implementation parameter sizes on system performance. These labels denote the parameter profiles used in our implementation and should not be interpreted as claiming that ordinary NIST prime curves are directly used as pairing curves; the security claim remains based on the decisional q-parallel BDHE assumption over bilinear groups. All schemes are implemented with the PBC (Pairing-Based Cryptography) library. To minimize environmental fluctuations and operating system scheduling noise, each cryptographic operation in our experiments is executed independently for 100 iterations. The empirical results reported in this section represent the arithmetic mean of these sequential runs, thereby ensuring statistical stability and reproducibility.

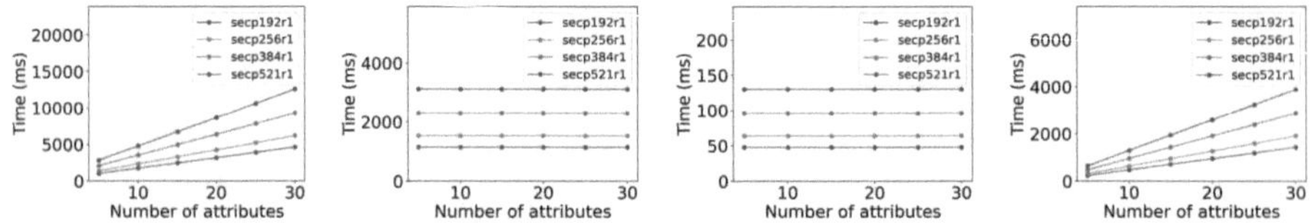

Fig. 2. Storage and communication overhead of keys and ciphertexts under varying policy sizes. While the ciphertext and user secret key sizes grow linearly as expected, the revocation update key (RUK) size is strictly constant, demonstrating minimal communication cost for frequent attribute revocations.

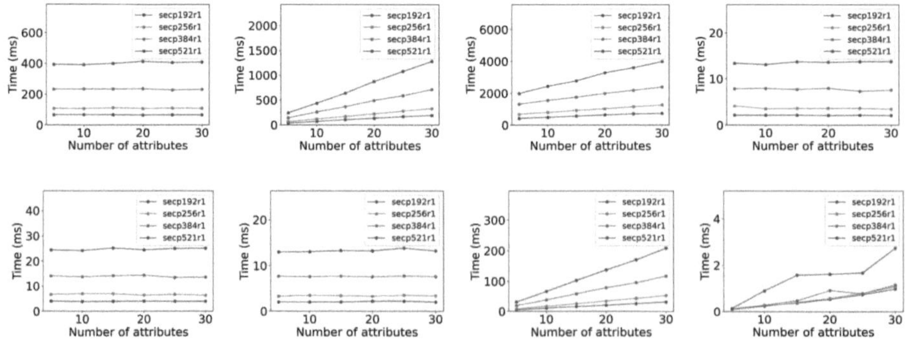

Fig. 3. Computation cost of cryptographic operations versus policy size. As shown, the key generation and encryption costs scale linearly with the number of attributes, while dynamic operations such as revocation key generation and ciphertext update remain lightweight and practically constant, confirming the efficiency of our outsourced design.

Impact of Policy Size. We first evaluate how the number of attributes affects the computation cost of the proposed scheme, as shown in Fig. 2 and Fig. 3.

The experimental environment is Ubuntu 22.04 LTS Desktop with an Intel(R) Core(TM) i5-12500H and 8GB RAM. As expected, encryption and key generation costs grow monotonically with the policy size. This trend is consistent across all tested security parameters.

In contrast, dynamic management operations (policy updates, revocation key, and ciphertext updates) remain highly efficient, staying within a few milliseconds even at 30 attributes, eliminating costly data re-encryption.

Impact of Security Parameters. Next, we analyze the impact of increasing pairing parameters on system performance. The experimental results show that stronger security parameters naturally lead to higher computation costs for pairing-based operations such as encryption and decryption.

Nevertheless, the update-related procedures scale favorably with the security parameter. In particular, revocation key generation and ciphertext update operations remain efficient even under the largest tested parameter setting. This confirms that the proposed scheme maintains practical efficiency while providing enhanced security.

Table 2. Length of keys/ciphertexts (in bytes) and the running time (in milliseconds) of each phase with different policy sizes (varying number of attributes). The columns SK, CT, RUK, and PUK indicate the length of the user secret key, ciphertext, revocation update key, and policy update key respectively. KeyGen, Encrypt, and Decrypt indicate the running time of key generation, encryption, and decryption. The "Revocation" time represents the total time required for updating the secret key of a non-revoked user and updating a ciphertext during the revocation of a single attribute. "Policy Updating" represents the time cost of the policy updating process.

<table>
<tr><th rowspan="2">Num. of attrs.</th><th rowspan="2">SK</th><th rowspan="2">KeyGen</th><th rowspan="2">CT</th><th rowspan="2">Encrypt</th><th rowspan="2">Decrypt</th><th colspan="2">Revocation</th><th colspan="2">Policy Updating</th></tr>
<tr><th>RUK</th><th>Time(ms)</th><th>PUK</th><th>Time(ms)</th></tr>
<tr><td>5</td><td rowspan="6">1536</td><td rowspan="6">43.5</td><td>1408</td><td>27.9</td><td>244.9</td><td rowspan="6">64</td><td rowspan="6">5.6</td><td>320</td><td>3.7</td></tr>
<tr><td>10</td><td>2368</td><td>50.3</td><td>286.2</td><td>640</td><td>7.5</td></tr>
<tr><td>15</td><td>3328</td><td>72.7</td><td>327.3</td><td>960</td><td>11.4</td></tr>
<tr><td>20</td><td>4288</td><td>95.1</td><td>368.6</td><td>1280</td><td>15.2</td></tr>
<tr><td>25</td><td>5248</td><td>117.5</td><td>409.9</td><td>1600</td><td>19.0</td></tr>
<tr><td>30</td><td>6208</td><td>140.1</td><td>451.9</td><td>1920</td><td>22.9</td></tr>
</table>

Cloud Deployment Case Study. The test results of DAPU in a cloud deployment case study are shown in Table 2. We deploy the experiment on an Aliyun ecs.c7t.xlarge instance with 4 vCPUs and 8 GiB of memory. The PBC pairing-parameter profile labeled "secp256r1" is used in this case study. We fix the size of user's attribute set as 10 and vary the number of attributes involved in the access policy from 5 to 30. The fixed user attribute set isolates the effect of access-policy size, while the Aliyun instance reflects the virtualized cloud environment in which outsourced ciphertext updates are expected to run. Thus, the case study is intended to evaluate practical cloud-side execution under controlled policy-complexity settings. The KeyGen algorithm for a user costs 43.5 milliseconds, while the costs of Encrypt and Decrypt scale linearly with the number of attributes. The time cost and communication costs of the revocation process remain constant, as the revocation algorithm only involves the single component associated with the revoked attribute. In contrast, both the time cost and the update key length of the policy updating algorithm increase linearly with the size of the policy.

Comparative Discussion. DAPU achieves constant ($O(1)$) revocation overhead (64-byte RUK, 5.6 ms), while Han [7] and Yin [18] scale with user size ($\log n$) or revocation list (r). For policy updates, DAPU transforms a 30-attribute policy in 22.9 ms, avoiding the $n \cdot m$ complexity of Zhao [19]. DAPU also eliminates the re-delegation risks inherent in AB-PRE schemes [5,9,11] while matching or exceeding their efficiency.

6 Conclusion

In this paper, we presented DAPU, an attribute-based access control scheme with dynamic attribute and policy updating for secure cloud data sharing. By unifying user revocation, key update, and policy update within a single ABE framework, our scheme supports fine-grained and long-term access control without requiring ciphertext re-encryption or complete key redistribution. Ciphertext update operations are efficiently delegated to the cloud through lightweight computations, while preserving data confidentiality and access correctness for legitimate users. The evaluation results indicate that our scheme is practical for cloud data sharing settings with frequently changing users and access policies.

Acknowledgments. This work was supported by China Unicom Software Research Institute.

References

1. Bacis, E., di Vimercati, S.D.C., Foresti, S., Paraboschi, S., Rosa, M., Samarati, P.: Securing resources in decentralized cloud storage. IEEE Trans. Inf. Forensics Secur. **15**, 286–298 (2019)
2. Bethencourt, J., Sahai, A., Waters, B.: Ciphertext-policy attribute-based encryption. In: IEEE Symposium on Security and Privacy, pp. 321–334. IEEE (2007)
3. Chen, L., Moody, D., Regenscheid, A., Randall, K.: Recommendations for discrete logarithm-based cryptography: elliptic curve domain parameters. Technical Report. NIST (2019)
4. Chen, Y., Liu, X., Zhang, Z.: Dynamic access control and privacy-preserving data sharing in cloud environments. In: International Conference on Web-Age Information Management, pp. 112–126. Springer (2025)
5. Ge, C., Susilo, W., Liu, Z., Baek, J., Luo, X., Fang, L.: Attribute-based proxy re-encryption with direct revocation mechanism for data sharing in clouds. IEEE Trans. Dependable Secure Comput. **21**(2), 949–960 (2024)

6. Goyal, V., Pandey, O., Sahai, A., Waters, B.: Attribute-based encryption for fine-grained access control of encrypted data. In: ACM Conference on Computer and Communications Security, pp. 89–98. ACM (2006)
7. Han, D., Pan, N., Li, K.C.: A traceable and revocable ciphertext-policy attribute-based encryption scheme based on privacy protection. IEEE Trans. Dependable Secure Comput. **19**(1), 316–327 (2020)
8. Li, J., Wang, S., Li, Y., Wang, H., Wang, H., Wang, H., Chen, J., You, Z.: An efficient attribute-based encryption scheme with policy update and file update in cloud computing. IEEE Trans. Industr. Inf. **15**(12), 6500–6509 (2019)
9. Li, X., Xie, Y., Peng, C., Luo, E., Li, X., Zhou, Z.: EPREAR: an efficient attribute-based proxy re-encryption scheme with fast revocation for data sharing in AIoT. IEEE Trans. Mob. Comput. **24**(10), 11005–11018 (2025)
10. Liang, X., Weng, J., Yang, A., Yao, L., Jiang, Z., Wu, Z.: Attribute-based conditional proxy re-encryption in the standard model under LWE. In: European Symposium on Research in Computer Security, pp. 147–168. Springer (2021)
11. Luo, J., Zeng, P., Wang, X.: Bilateral privacy-aware proxy re-encryption with traceability and revocation for IoMT. IEEE Internet Things J. **12**(24), 52794–52806 (2025)
12. Ning, J., Cao, Z., Dong, X., Liang, K., Ma, H., Wei, L.: Auditable $sigma$-time outsourced attribute-based encryption for access control in cloud computing. IEEE Trans. Inf. Forensics Secur. **13**(1), 94–105 (2017)
13. Wang, H., Li, J., Zhao, F.: A survey on secure cloud data sharing and fine-grained access control. IEEE Trans. Cloud Comput. **12**(3), 2300–2315 (2024)
14. Xue, L., Yu, Y., Li, Y., Au, M.H., Du, X., Yang, B.: Efficient attribute-based encryption with attribute revocation for assured data deletion. Inf. Sci. **479**, 640–650 (2019)
15. Xue, Y., Xue, K., Gai, N., Hong, J., Wei, D.S., Hong, P.: An attribute-based controlled collaborative access control scheme for public cloud storage. IEEE Trans. Inf. Forensics Secur. **14**(11), 2927–2942 (2019)
16. Yang, K., Jia, X., Ren, K.: Attribute-based fine-grained access control with efficient revocation in cloud storage systems. In: ACM SIGSAC Symposium on Information, Computer and Communications Security, pp. 523–528. ACM (2013)
17. Yang, K., Jia, X., Ren, K., Xie, R., Huang, L.: Enabling efficient access control with dynamic policy updating for big data in the cloud. In: IEEE Conference on Computer Communications, pp. 2013–2021. IEEE (2014)
18. Yin, H., Li, J., Zhu, Y., Zhang, L., Qiao, B.: A traceable CP-ABE scheme supporting dynamic revocation and efficient decryption for medical data sharing. IEEE Internet Things J. **12**(24), 53610–53622 (2025)
19. Zhao, F., Weng, J., Xie, W., Li, M., Weng, J.: HRA-secure attribute-based threshold proxy re-encryption from lattices. Inf. Sci. **655**, 119900 (2024)

DCS-HTLC: An Environment-Aware Adaptive Protocol for Cross-Chain Atomic Swaps

Guoqiong Liao[1,2], Linfeng Huang[1(✉)], Wei Yu[1], Jingyu Xu[1], Hongyang Chen[1], and Liangqiu He[1]

[1] Modern Industry School of Virtual Reality, Jiangxi University of Finance and Economics, Nanchang 330032, China
liaoguoqiong@163.com, yellow_hlf@foxmail.com

[2] Jiangxi Tourism and Commerce Vocational College, Nanchang 330100, China

Abstract. As the blockchain ecosystem becomes increasingly heterogeneous, "value silos" have emerged as the primary bottleneck restricting the interoperability of decentralized assets. Classical Hash Time-Locked Contracts (HTLCs) adopt a static timing design, rendering them vulnerable to time-mismatch and free option attacks under network congestion and price volatility, which undermines atomicity and fairness. To address these issues, this paper proposes DCS-HTLC, an environment-aware adaptive cross-chain atomic swap protocol. The protocol employs a Dynamic Time-Lock (DTL) mechanism to sense the congestion coefficient ρ and compensate for physical delays, utilizes a Collateral Penalty (CP) mechanism based on asset volatility σ to suppress arbitrage, and leverages Full-link State Control (FSC) to achieve state alignment. Under the assumption of a partially synchronous network, we model the cross-chain transaction as an extensive-form game and formally prove that the protocol satisfies adaptive liveness, incentive compatibility, and complete atomicity. Experimental evaluations demonstrate that under network congestion environments, the protocol achieves a transaction success rate of 95.8% with a state control overhead of only 4.0%, rendering the attacker's expected payoff strictly negative. Under the premise of guaranteeing complete atomicity, DCS-HTLC effectively enhances the liveness of cross-chain transactions and the incentive compatibility of the protocol.

Keywords: Atomic Swap · Hash Time-Locked Contract · Dynamic Time-Lock · Collateral Penalty · State Control

1 Introduction

The current decentralized network has rapidly evolved beyond the early peer-to-peer payment model into a highly complex ecosystem where multiple heterogeneous chains coexist (e.g., Ethereum, Polkadot, and Cosmos). In recent years,

L. Ding et al. (Eds.): APWeb-WAIM 2026, LNCS 16993, pp. 32–48, 2027.
https://doi.org/10.1007/978-981-92-5693-8_3

diverse public chains and Layer 2 scaling solutions have emerged, demonstrating a booming market scale and driving massive cross-domain interaction demands [3]. As decentralized finance (DeFi) and Web3 applications proliferate, users frequently need to transfer value across different ledger boundaries. Behind this prosperity, however, different blockchains are inherently logically fragmented due to fundamental differences in underlying consensus mechanisms, cryptographic primitives, and ledger structures. This phenomenon, widely known as "Value Silos" [1,7], has become the primary bottleneck restricting the large-scale interoperability and liquidity pooling of decentralized assets. Cross-chain technology serves as the core method to break the barriers of these blockchain ecological silos. Although mainstream cross-chain schemes, such as Notary Schemes and wrapped-asset Sidechains, successfully facilitate data and asset interactions, they fundamentally rely on external trust dependencies and centralized federations [1,19]. Recent high-profile exploits on centralized cross-chain bridges—resulting in billions of dollars in losses—have made the industry profoundly aware of the critical vulnerabilities inherent in multi-signature "honeypot" architectures [20]. Consequently, trustless cross-chain atomic swaps, characterized by their complete decentralization, non-custodial properties, and native cryptographic security, are increasingly recognized as the definitive technical path for decentralized interoperability [9].

As the classic paradigm for atomic swaps, the Hash Time-Locked Contract (HTLC) utilizes a hash-lock for transaction intent synchronization and a time-lock for handling abnormal refunds. This dual-lock design theoretically establishes an "all-or-nothing" atomicity guarantee mechanism for cross-chain exchanges [9]. However, when deployed in realistic partially synchronous network environments and subjected to complex rational game scenarios, classical HTLCs face three critical challenges:

- **Parameter Mismatch in Physical Environments.** Existing protocols rely on static time-locks to ensure timing security. In partially synchronous networks, severe throughput fluctuations render static windows obsolete. Excessive windows needlessly freeze capital, driving up opportunity costs [6]; conversely, insufficient windows cause legitimate transactions to be forcibly rolled back during network congestion, leading to involuntary liveness failures.
- **Game Unfairness in Rational Environments.** Asymmetric time-lock settings inherently grant the transaction initiator an arbitrage space, effectively creating a "free option" [8]. During significant exchange rate volatility, this asymmetry incentivizes rational nodes to execute Griefing Attacks [2,13,15,17], trapping the honest party's funds without compensation and fundamentally undermining the economic fairness of the protocol.
- **State Inconsistency in Distributed Environments.** Traditional schemes focus primarily on financial value equivalence, often neglecting the synchronization of the underlying distributed state machines [4]. If network partitions or localized node downtime occur, the system fails to achieve deterministic state rollback, leaving transactions in a "half-deadlock". Without forced cross-

chain state alignment, the system is directly exposed to double-spending vulnerabilities and permanent asset loss [18].

In summary, how to simultaneously satisfy efficient execution, game fairness, and complete atomicity for cross-chain transactions over dynamic heterogeneous networks remains an urgent problem to be solved. To systematically address these vulnerabilities, this paper proposes DCS-HTLC, an environment-aware adaptive cross-chain atomic swap protocol. Based on a multi-dimensional dynamic interoperable architecture, this protocol achieves the deep integration of underlying physical environment perception, logic-layer game decision-making, and full-link state control, forming a resilient, adaptive collaborative mechanism that covers the entire lifecycle of cross-chain transactions.

The main contributions of this paper are summarized as follows:

- We propose a Dynamic Time Lock (DTL) mechanism, which dynamically adjusts the lock window based on a non-linear optimization model of the transaction environment, amount, and node credit to ensure the liveness of cross-chain transactions.
- We design a Collateral Penalty (CP) mechanism, which utilizes a dynamic deposit model to sense the price volatility of the underlying asset and potential arbitrage space, reshapes the Nash equilibrium, anchors "honest performance" as the unique optimal strategy for rational participants, and economically suppresses the free option attack.
- We construct a Full-Link State Control (FSC) mechanism. By utilizing lightweight state vector synchronization and cross-chain snapshot proofs, the system can forcefully align the global state under abnormal environments, ensuring that cross-chain transactions satisfy complete atomicity.
- Experimental results demonstrate that DCS-HTLC achieves a 95.8% transaction success rate under severe network congestion with a minimal state control overhead of only 4.0%, effectively enhancing the robustness of cross-chain swaps. Furthermore, the protocol strictly suppresses the attacker's expected payoff to negative values, guaranteeing incentive compatibility.

The remaining parts of this paper are arranged as follows: Sect. 2 reviews related work regarding cross-chain liveness, fairness, and atomicity. Section 3 establishes the system model and formalizes the security properties under a partially synchronous environment. Section 4 elaborates on the mechanism design of DCS-HTLC, including the dynamic protocol transitions and core sensing-execution logic. Section 5 provides the correctness analysis and formal proofs for incentive compatibility and liveness. Section 6 presents the comprehensive experimental evaluation, highlighting the protocol's robustness under network congestion. Finally, Sect. 7 concludes the paper.

2 Related Work

The Hash Time-Locked Contract (HTLC) [9] establishes the underlying paradigm for current cross-chain protocols, yet ensuring transaction liveness under dynamic network conditions remains a significant hurdle. To improve execution efficiency, recent works explored cryptographic primitives, such as universal atomic swaps via adaptor signatures [12] and PipeSwap [11], alongside architectural adjustments like parallel processing in Lilac [5]. Nevertheless, these static solutions struggle with the severe throughput fluctuations inherent in partially synchronous networks. To address this, dynamic optimization methods like RL-ABO [10] and reputation-based reallocation [16] adapt to heterogeneous environments, but integrating real-time environmental sensing directly into the HTLC execution logic requires further exploration.

Beyond physical liveness, traditional HTLCs' sequential execution creates a structural game imbalance. Han et al. [8] and Xu et al. [17] theoretically revealed the "free option" vulnerability, proving that rational nodes will inevitably launch Griefing Attacks [2] during severe exchange rate volatility. To reshape the Nash equilibrium, various economic deterrence mechanisms emerged. Tsabary et al. [13] introduced MAD-HTLC based on mutual destruction, though it faces reverse bribery risks [14]. Similarly, credit-based models like DPC-HTLC [15] constrain rational deviations via economic deposits. However, these models rely on static penalty parameters, failing to dynamically calibrate the deterrence force against real-time market fluctuations.

Even with liveness and fairness guaranteed, maintaining complete atomicity across isolated ledgers remains challenging. At the distributed state level, cross-chain interactions face severe state inconsistency risks during localized network partitions [18]. A local timeout without synchronized state awareness can lead to fatal asymmetric commits, exposing the system to double-spending. While protocols like XCLAIM [19] and layered state commitments [4] improve atomicity via relay-backed proofs, they incur heavy on-chain verification overhead. Unlike these static, heavy, or single-dimensional solutions, our DCS-HTLC protocol seamlessly integrates dynamic time-locks, market-aware collateral, and lightweight state proofs. This multi-dimensional approach effectively breaks existing performance bottlenecks, achieving an optimal balance among adaptive liveness, game fairness, and complete atomicity.

3 Problem Definition

To rigorously characterize the execution boundaries of the DCS-HTLC protocol under high uncertainty and support its security proofs, this section constructs a cross-chain transaction system model covering physical topology, multi-dimensional environmental parameters, distributed state machines, and eventual consistency specifications.

Participants P_i drive interactions by deploying smart contracts SC_i on underlying heterogeneous chains. The cryptographic security is guaranteed by the high-entropy property of the secret preimage and the collision resistance of the one-way hash function $H(\cdot)$. This paper adopts a partially synchronous network model, assuming an unknown global stabilization time and a transmission delay upper bound. Our threat model assumes two main adversary types: network-level attackers manipulating message commit orders, and profit-driven rational Byzantine nodes adopting malicious default strategies to maximize returns.

To characterize this dynamic environment, the protocol perceives multi-dimensional parameters in real-time, formally defined as follows:

Definition 1 (Dynamic Time-Lock). In the physical timing dimension, let ρ be the network's current congestion coefficient and δ be the expected physical delay. The protocol uses ρ as an adaptive feedback factor to deduce and generate a resilient time window capable of covering the actual confirmation delay t_a of a transaction, denoted as the dynamic time-lock Δ_{lock}.

Definition 2 (Performance Deposit). In the economic game dimension, let ν be the value of the exchanged assets, and σ be the market asset exchange rate volatility. Exchange rate fluctuations will spawn a "free option attack" arbitrage gain G_{opt} to be captured by malicious nodes. To hedge against this potential risk, the symmetric economic penal constraint forcefully imposed by the protocol on both parties is denoted as the performance deposit d.

Definition 3 (Global Joint State). Let $i \in \{A, B\}$ be the underlying chain index, and $st_i \in \{\mathbb{I}, \mathbb{L}, \mathbb{R}, \mathbb{A}\}$ be the local contract state of the chain. To reflect the distributed full picture of the transaction, the full-link state is represented by a vector composed of the dual-chain local states, denoted as $\mathcal{V} = \langle st_A, st_B \rangle$. Here, $\mathbb{I}$ is the initialized state of the contract; $\mathbb{L}$ is the readiness and game period of dual freezing of assets and deposits, serving as the critical zone of risk confrontation; $\mathbb{R}$ represents the positive execution final state of cross-chain asset confirmation and transfer after the preimage is validly verified; and $\mathbb{A}$ represents the negative rollback final state triggered by a timeout or explicit default.

Based on these definitions, the challenges faced by existing protocols can be formalized: When $\rho \to 1$ or $\sigma \gg 0$, a fixed time window will cause the actual confirmation delay t_a of honest transactions to breach the security time limit, or cause the default arbitrage gain G_{opt} to exceed the penalty cost. This ultimately leads to a utility inversion in the expected utility u_i of participant P_i, driving them to initiate an attack, which in turn causes the global state $\mathcal{V}$ to fall into an asymmetric final state.

Therefore, the DCS-HTLC protocol is required to satisfy the following three core security properties:

Property 1 (Adaptive Liveness). In a partially synchronous network, let ϵ be the security redundancy. If the Δ_{lock} generated by the protocol possesses a non-linear expansion capability, ensuring that the timing constraint relationship $\Delta_{lock} > \delta + \epsilon \geq t_a$ always holds, then the protocol is said to satisfy adaptive liveness.

Property 2 (Incentive Compatibility). Let $\mathcal{S} = \{C, D\}$ be the strategy space of cross-chain nodes, where C is honest performance and D is malicious default. For any participant P_i, if the protocol ensures that their utility function satisfies $u_i(C) > u_i(D)$ under any σ environment, then the protocol is said to satisfy incentive compatibility.

Property 3 (Complete Atomicity). If the global joint state $\mathcal{V}$ of a cross-chain transaction can deterministically converge to a consistent symmetric state set within a finite time, that is, the final valid state always satisfies $\mathcal{V} \in \{\langle\mathbb{R},\mathbb{R}\rangle, \langle\mathbb{A},\mathbb{A}\rangle\}$, then the protocol is said to satisfy complete atomicity.

4 Mechanism Design

4.1 Protocol Overview and State Transitions

To support adaptive cross-chain interoperability, DCS-HTLC integrates real-time environmental sensing directly with on-chain execution logic. The protocol operates through a core decision hub that aggregates the Dynamic Time-Lock (DTL), Collateral Penalty (CP) and Full-link State Control (FSC) modules to optimize asset and control flows. By utilizing oracle clusters and relayers, the protocol captures physical network contexts (e.g., congestion ρ, volatility σ) and cryptographic proofs to execute adaptive logic across heterogeneous chains.

Driven by the core decision hub, the interaction sequence centers on the evolution of the global state vector $\mathcal{V} = \langle st_A, st_B\rangle$. As illustrated in Fig. 1, the process is divided into four key phases:

1. **Negotiation and Parameter Initialization.** P_A and P_B reach an off-chain consensus on assets ν_A and ν_B. The DTL and CP modules are triggered to calculate adaptive time-locks Δ^i_{lock} and performance deposit d based on real-time congestion ρ and volatility σ. At this stage, the system remains in the initial state $\mathcal{V} = \langle\mathbb{I},\mathbb{I}\rangle$.
2. **Bidirectional Lock and Game Readiness.** P_A deploys contract SC_A, locking ν_A and d with Δ^A_{lock} to transition $st_A \leftarrow \mathbb{L}$. Subsequently, P_B monitors this event and deploys SC_B on Chain B using the same hash $y = H(x)$, locking ν_B and d ($st_B \leftarrow \mathbb{L}$). The global state vector thus converges to the critical game state $\mathcal{V} = \langle\mathbb{L},\mathbb{L}\rangle$, where the deposit d effectively suppresses any free option arbitrage payoff.
3. **Preimage Revelation and Asset Confirmation.** P_A proactively submits preimage x to SC_B to redeem ν_B, causing $st_B \leftarrow \mathbb{R}$. P_B swiftly captures x from Chain B and submits it to SC_A to extract ν_A ($st_A \leftarrow \mathbb{R}$). Finally, the global state vector converges to the symmetric complete atomicity final state $\mathcal{V} = \langle\mathbb{R},\mathbb{R}\rangle$, successfully concluding the cross-chain transaction.
4. **Abnormal Timeout and Full-Link State Control.** If network partitions or malicious downtime trigger a local timeout (e.g., $st_A \leftarrow \mathbb{A}$) while the counterparty has completed revelation ($st_B \leftarrow \mathbb{R}$), the FSC mechanism intervenes. By submitting a cross-chain SPV proof π_{SPV}, FSC forcefully aligns the state (e.g., $st_A \leftarrow \mathbb{R}$) via a cryptographic interrupt, ensuring deterministic convergence to $\mathcal{V} = \langle\mathbb{R},\mathbb{R}\rangle$.

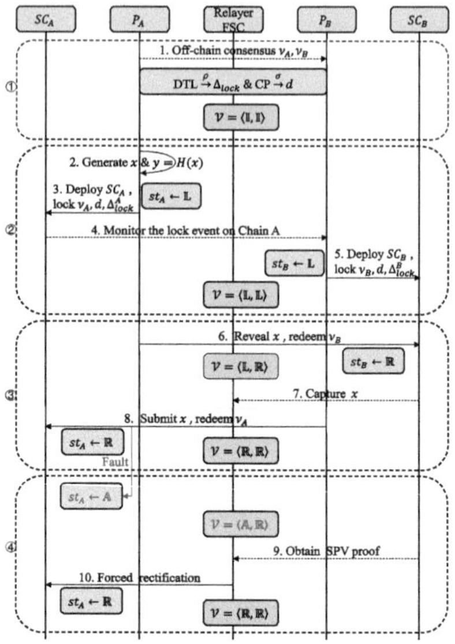

Fig. 1. The interaction sequence and state evolution of the cross-chain transaction.

4.2 Dynamic Time-Lock (DTL) Mechanism

In traditional HTLCs, static time-locks often trigger critical time-mismatches during network congestion, leading to involuntary rollbacks. To address this, DCS-HTLC integrates the **Dynamic Time-Lock (DTL)** mechanism, an adaptive control algorithm that calibrates timing parameters through two phases: *asynchronous delay perception* and *multi-dimensional window calculation.*

Asynchronous Delay Perception. DTL captures physical queuing delays by sampling the Mempool states of target chains through oracle clusters. We model the transaction packing process as a classical $M/M/1$ queuing system. Let λ be the average arrival rate and η be the service rate derived from block constraints. The real-time congestion coefficient is defined as $\rho = \lambda/\eta \in [0, 1)$. According to queuing theory, the expected physical delay δ is:

$$\delta = \frac{\delta_0}{1-\rho}, \tag{1}$$

where δ_0 is the baseline delay. This model ensures the time-lock possesses non-linear expansion capability as $\rho \to 1$, preventing premature timeouts during surges.

Multi-dimensional Lock Window Calculation. DTL further introduces dual regulatory factors—risk premium and credit discount—to output the final dynamic window:

- **Risk Premium Factor (μ):** To explicitly quantify the exposure to market fluctuations, μ is formulated as $\mu = 1+\tau \cdot \hat{\nu} \cdot e^{\sigma} > 1$, where $\hat{\nu}$ is the normalized transaction asset value and τ is a systemic sensitivity coefficient. High asset value or severe exchange rate volatility ($\sigma \gg 0$) exponentially amplifies μ, forcing high-risk transactions to dynamically acquire wider safety margins.
- **Credit Discount Factor (ω):** The discount is mathematically mapped via a decay function $\omega = 1 - e^{-\xi \cdot Cr} \in [0, 1)$, where the credit score $Cr = \alpha \cdot \kappa + (1 - \alpha) \cdot f(l)$ integrates the node's historical transaction success rate κ and normalized stake longevity $f(l)$ with weight α. Reputable nodes with a proven track record receive an ω close to 1, effectively minimizing the security redundancy ϵ. Conversely, newly generated or malicious identities strictly default to $\omega \to 0$ to maximize their time-lock costs.

The final time-lock Δ^i_{lock} for contract SC_i on chain i is formulated as:

$$\Delta^i_{lock} = \delta_i + \mu(1 - \omega)\epsilon. \tag{2}$$

During preparation, the DTL engine injects these optimized parameters into the contract logic and satisfies Adaptive Liveness.

4.3 Collateral Penalty (CP) Mechanism

During the cross-chain two-phase commit process, the lock window Δ_{lock} grants the initiator a call/put option. Significant exchange rate fluctuations may incentivize rational nodes to withhold the preimage x for arbitrage, a "free option" vulnerability that undermines fairness. To eradicate this, DCS-HTLC introduces the **Collateral Penalty (CP)** mechanism to reshape the game payoff matrix.

Option-Based Arbitrage Modeling. The CP mechanism quantifies the maximum default payoff triggered by volatility during Δ_{lock}. Using quantitative finance logic, the maximum arbitrage gain G_{opt} within the dual-chain lock window Δ^{max}_{lock} is expressed as:

$$G_{opt} = \nu \cdot \max\left(0, e^{\sigma\sqrt{\Delta^{\max}_{lock}}} - 1\right). \tag{3}$$

The arbitrage space increases monotonically with volatility σ and window size Δ^{max}_{lock}, requiring the penalty intensity to adapt accordingly.

Dynamic Deposit Configuration. To ensure the system satisfies formal security constraints, participants must post a symmetric performance deposit d during the preparation phase. This value is collateralized via native assets on respective chains to construct a symmetric game boundary:

$$d = G_{opt} + p_{base}, \tag{4}$$

where p_{base} covers Gas consumption and FSC relay bounties.

State-Driven Execution Logic. The penalty actions are governed by the local state st_i through two deterministic paths:

- **Confirmation and Refund Phase.** If node P_i acts honestly (C) and submits a valid preimage before Δ^i_{lock} expires ($st_i \leftarrow \mathbb{R}$), the CP module unconditionally refunds the deposit d.
- **Timeout and Slashing Phase.** If node P_i defaults (D), causing a local timeout ($st_i \leftarrow \mathbb{A}$), the deposit d is permanently forfeited and liquidated to compensate the victim.

Through these constraints, the CP mechanism establishes the absolute inequality $u_i(C) > u_i(D)$, effectively suppressing any motivation for rational deviation. By ensuring that the expected payoff of an attack is strictly negative, the protocol formally satisfies Incentive Compatibility.

4.4 Full-Link State Control (FSC) Mechanism

The FSC mechanism is designed to mitigate global state asymmetry caused by network partitions, localized censorship, or malicious withholding of the preimage x. In traditional HTLCs, if the preimage is revealed on Chain B but fails to propagate to Chain A before Δ^A_{lock} expires, the system falls into a "half-deadlock" state $\mathcal{V} = \langle \mathbb{A}, \mathbb{R} \rangle$. To prevent this, FSC introduces a stateless relay network combined with on-chain Simplified Payment Verification (SPV) to ensure deterministic state alignment.

Cross-Chain Evidence Collection and Verification. When P_A redeems assets on Chain B, the preimage x is inscribed into the transaction receipt R. If Δ^A_{lock} approaches expiration without SC_A receiving x, independent relayers capture R and construct an SPV proof $\pi_{SPV} = (Header_B, MerklePath, R)$. The SC_A contract executes a multi-stage verification process as follows:

- **Header and Consensus Validation.** The contract verifies $Header_B$ against the synchronized light-client root. This ensures that the evidence originates from a valid and finalized block on the source chain, preventing spoofing attacks.
- **Inclusion and Merkle Proof.** The contract validates the existence of the transaction receipt R within the block through the provided Merkle Path. This step guarantees the integrity and non-tamperability of the revealed preimage x.
- **Semantic Alignment and Execution.** The contract performs a final check to ensure $H(x) == y$. Upon success, FSC executes a cryptographic interrupt to halt the timeout, updating the state to $st_A \leftarrow \mathbb{R}$ and ensuring the global state converges to $\mathcal{V} = \langle \mathbb{R}, \mathbb{R} \rangle$.

Incentive Compatibility and Security Reinforcement. To ensure the robustness of the relay network under adversarial environments, FSC incorporates the following security and economic constraints (the detailed theoretical analysis regarding FSC's economic resilience against advanced adversarial threats is deferred to the security discussion in Sect. 5.4):

- **Profit-Driven Relayer Bounty.** Upon successful state alignment, the defaulting party's deposit d is partially slashed to reward the relayer. This covers Gas consumption and incentivizes rational relayers to maintain high availability.
- **Anti-MEV Address Binding.** To prevent front-running attacks, SC_A is designed to release assets ν_A strictly to the predefined address of P_B. This ensures that intercepted proofs or preimages cannot be exploited by malicious third parties.

The complete execution logic of the FSC mechanism is detailed in Algorithm 1, which formally guarantees that DCS-HTLC satisfies Complete Atomicity.

Algorithm 1. Full-Link State Forced Rectification based on SPV Evidence

Input: Reveal operation R, preimage hash y, relay node address $addr$
Output: Updated global state $\mathcal{V}$, reassigned state of assets and bounties

procedure CAPTEVIDENCE(R, y)
$x \leftarrow R.preimage$
if $H(x) \neq y$ **then**
  return Error
end if
$\pi_{SPV} \leftarrow (Header_B, MerklePath, R)$
SUBMITTOCHAINA($\pi_{SPV}, x, addr$)
end procedure
procedure OVERSTATE($\pi_{SPV}, x, addr$)
if $st_A == \mathbb{A}$ **or** VERIFY(π_{SPV}) $==$ **False or** $H(x) \neq y$ **then**
  return Revert
end if
$st_A \leftarrow \mathbb{R}$; RELEASEASSET($\nu_A, P_B$)
$d_{slash} \leftarrow$ SLASHDEPOSIT(P_A)
TRANSFERBOUNTY($d_{slash} \cdot \beta, addr$); $\mathcal{V} \leftarrow \langle \mathbb{R}, \mathbb{R} \rangle$
return $\mathcal{V}$
end procedure

5 Correctness Analysis

5.1 Proof of Adaptive Liveness

Theorem 1. For any honest transaction, the timing relationship $\Delta_{lock} > \delta + \epsilon \geq t_a$ specified in **Property 1** always holds.

Proof: In traditional HTLCs, static time-locks fail to cover t_a when $\rho \to 1$. In DCS-HTLC, the DTL mechanism calculates δ using the M/M/1 model (Eq. 1), ensuring δ possesses the same non-linear expansion capability as the network congestion. By injecting this into Eq. 2, the generated Δ_{lock} inherently sets the physical expected delay δ as its lower bound. Since the security redundancy $\mu(1-\omega)\epsilon$ is non-negative and adaptively compensates for the probabilistic fluctuation γ of block generation ($t_a = \delta + \gamma$), the protocol guarantees $\Delta_{lock} > \delta + \epsilon \geq t_a$. This satisfies the timing coverage required by **Property 1**, ensuring transaction liveness under any $\rho \in [0, 1)$. □

5.2 Proof of Incentive Compatibility

Theorem 2. For any rational node P_i, the utility function satisfies $u_i(C) > u_i(D)$ under any volatility σ, satisfying **Property 2**.

Proof: We map the game outcomes to the utility definitions in Sect. 3. Under the honest strategy C, the swap succeeds and the deposit d is refunded, resulting in $u_i(C) = 0$. Under the malicious default strategy D, the node captures an arbitrage gain G_{opt}, but the state transition $st_i \leftarrow \mathbb{A}$ triggers the CP mechanism to slash the deposit d. According to Eq. 4, the protocol forces $d = G_{opt} + p_{base}$. Thus, $u_i(D) = G_{opt} - d = -p_{base}$. Since $p_{base} > 0$ represents the strictly positive base penalty cost, the inequality $u_i(C) > u_i(D)$ holds regardless of the value of σ. This anchors strategy C as the unique Nash Equilibrium, satisfying **Property 2.** □

5.3 Proof of Complete Atomicity

Theorem 3. The global joint state $\mathcal{V}$ eventually converges to the set $\{\langle\mathbb{R}, \mathbb{R}\rangle, \langle\mathbb{A}, \mathbb{A}\rangle\}$, satisfying **Property 3**.

Proof: Assume an asymmetric final state $\mathcal{V} = \langle\mathbb{A}, \mathbb{R}\rangle$ exists, where $st_B = \mathbb{R}$ implies a valid preimage x is inscribed on Chain B. Property 1 ensures that before st_A triggers a local timeout rollback, there exists a security redundancy window T for evidence collection. Within T, the profit-driven FSC relayers capture the state fact of Chain B and construct π_{SPV}. According to the FSC rectification logic, the Chain A contract verifies π_{SPV} and forcefully executes the state transition $st_A \leftarrow \mathbb{R}$ via a cryptographic interrupt. This forces the state vector to converge to $\langle\mathbb{R}, \mathbb{R}\rangle$ and blocks the path to any asymmetric state $\mathcal{V} \notin \{\langle\mathbb{R}, \mathbb{R}\rangle, \langle\mathbb{A}, \mathbb{A}\rangle\}$. Thus, complete atomicity as defined in **Property 3** is achieved. □

5.4 Security Discussion Under Complex Adversarial Threats

Beyond the primary security properties proved above, the practical deployment of cross-chain protocols in wild decentralized environments demands robust resilience against complex malicious exploits, particularly targeting the FSC relay layer.

- **Sybil and Collusion Resistance.** The decentralized state alignment in FSC heavily relies on independent relayers. A critical vulnerability in naive relay networks is that an adversary can launch a Sybil attack by creating thousands of virtual identities to manipulate SPV evidence or forge state synchronization. To systematically neutralize this threat, DCS-HTLC restricts pool entry via a stake-weighted mechanism where prospective relayers must lock up a verifiable collateral bond on the source chain. Malicious submissions or collusive behaviors automatically trigger contract-level slashing. By securely tying validation influence to physical capital, the cost of staging a Sybil attack is rendered prohibitively high, enforcing honesty among rational profit-driven relayers.
- **Anti-MEV and Front-running Resilience.** Public blockchain mempools represent a highly adversarial environment where execution-ordering manipulation can destroy transaction fairness. If a relayer broadcasts an SPV proof π_{SPV} and its corresponding preimage x, a predatory MEV searcher bot could front-run the transaction to hijack either the underlying asset ν_A or the relayer bounty. Our protocol structurally mitigates this vector via cryptographic address binding: SC_A hardcodes the asset recipient to P_B at initialization, meaning the SPV proof serves strictly as a state-transition trigger rather than a spend permission. Furthermore, the contract binds the bounty distribution exclusively to the authenticated `msg.sender` of the registered relayer, mathematically zeroing out the expected payoffs for front-running replays.

6 Evaluation

6.1 Experimental Setup

We implement the core smart contracts of DCS-HTLC in Solidity v0.8.20. The heterogeneous testbed integrates a private Ethereum chain (via Geth) and a Hyperledger Fabric consortium chain. Off-chain modules, including the DTL engine and FSC relayers, operate as proxy services to collect real-time network states and synchronize them to on-chain contracts. To simulate asynchronous network congestion, we inject controllable delays into node communication links, dynamically decaying throughput from 50 TPS to 5 TPS. We systematically compare DCS-HTLC against three baselines: Standard HTLC [9], MAD-HTLC [13], and DPC-HTLC [15], evaluating its overall performance and effectiveness across multiple dimensions.

6.2 On-Chain Overhead Analysis

As shown in Fig. 2, the cumulative dual-chain Gas overhead of DCS-HTLC is approximately 250k. By offloading core DTL and FSC computations to an off-chain proxy, their on-chain state anchoring consumes only ~10k Gas, accounting for merely 4.0% of the total. While this introduces an 18.2% overhead increase over Standard HTLC, it successfully suppresses the attack payoff to a negative value. Furthermore, compared to MAD-HTLC, DCS-HTLC achieves equivalent penal deterrence while reducing on-chain resource consumption by 19.3%, demonstrating a highly cost-effective and balanced architecture.

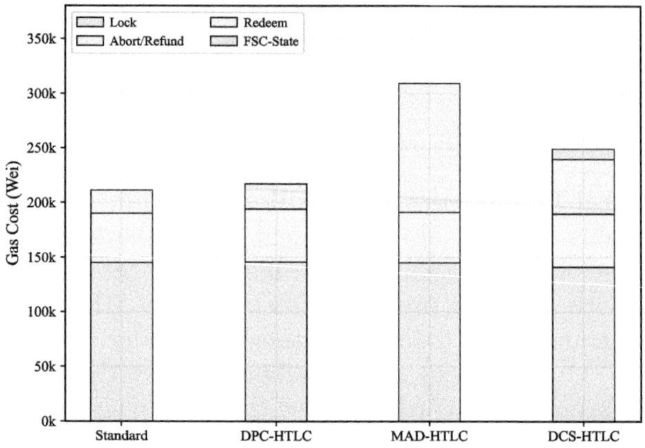

Fig. 2. The stacked distribution of Gas consumption for each protocol.

6.3 Adaptive Liveness Evaluation

The experimental results in Fig. 3 demonstrate that under a high-load phase (5 TPS), the static time-locks of Standard HTLC and MAD-HTLC fail to perceive network delays, causing their Transaction Success Rate (TSR) to plummet below 30%, while DPC-HTLC drops to 40%. In contrast, DCS-HTLC exhibits a unique "self-healing" capability. Although the TSR initially drops to 81.6% at the onset of congestion, the DTL mechanism rapidly recalibrates the time-lock parameters based on real-time sensing. This enables the success rate to rebound and stabilize at 95.8%, effectively hedging against network asynchronous risks by resiliently extending state lock periods.

6.4 Incentive Compatibility Analysis

To evaluate economic fairness, Fig. 4 tracks the attacker's expected net payoff under varying exchange rate volatility (σ). Traditional protocols (Standard HTLC, DPC-HTLC) breach the zero-profit baseline at a mere $\sigma = 0.5\%$, enabling risk-free option arbitrage. While MAD-HTLC delays this vulnerability, its fixed penalty is still breached when $\sigma > 5\%$. Conversely, DCS-HTLC consistently suppresses the attacker's payoff below zero (stabilizing around -0.1284 ETH) with minimal sensitivity to volatility spikes. This demonstrates that the CP mechanism effectively eradicates the "free option" exploit, ensuring strict incentive compatibility.

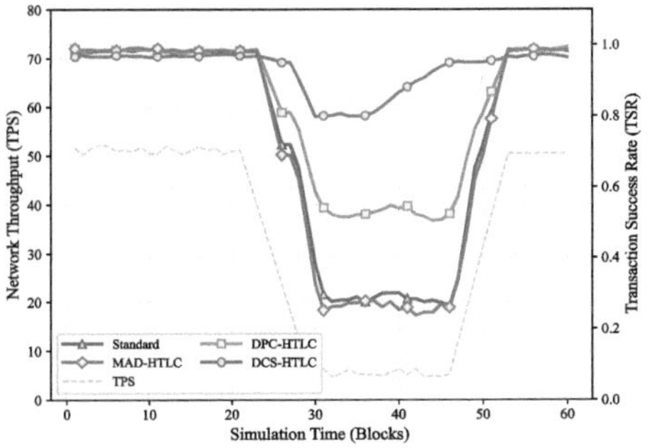

Fig. 3. The Transaction Success Rate under varying network throughput.

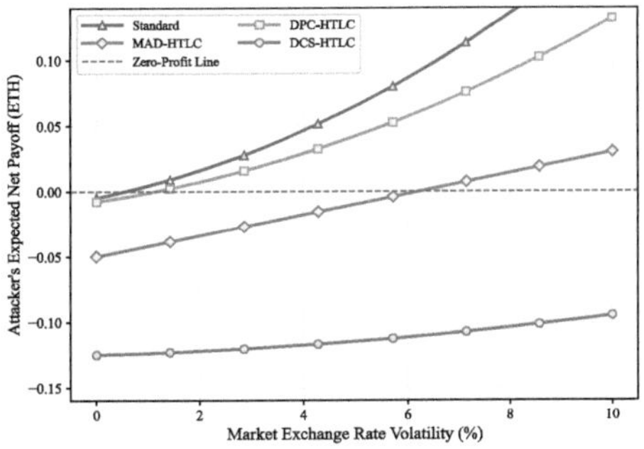

Fig. 4. The attacker's expected net payoff under varying volatility.

6.5 Capital Efficiency and Liquidity Lock-up Profiling

We evaluate cumulative liquidity lock-up overhead to quantify capital efficiency. As shown in Fig. 5, static-window baselines (Standard HTLC, MAD-HTLC, DPC-HTLC) suffer exponential freezes of 13.6k, 10.1k, and 6.8k units under 1,000 concurrent swaps. DCS-HTLC dynamically mitigates this via the credit factor ω. Low-reputation nodes ($Cr \to 0$) face a defensive linear window ($\omega \to 0$) locking 5.2k units. Conversely, high-reputation nodes ($Cr \to 1$) compress safety redundancy ($\mu(1-\omega)\epsilon \to 0$) to merely 1.5k units, achieving 89.0% and 78.1% liquidity optimizations over Standard and DPC-HTLC and securely maximizing capital velocity.

6.6 FSC Relayer Network Scalability Profiling

We evaluate the Full-Link State Control (FSC) scalability by stress-testing the stateless relayer pool under up to 500 concurrent cross-chain anomalies. As shown in Fig. 6, dispatching overhead scales linearly without secondary congestion. Under peak stress (500 faults), the average SPV queuing delay remains below 0.5 block intervals, ensuring rapid state rectification. Concurrently, bandwidth consumption peaks at a negligible 50 KB/s. This proves the lightweight SPV evidence imposes trivial communication overhead, confirming the FSC control plane's high availability and robustness.

6.7 Ablation Study Analysis

Table 1 evaluates the independent contributions of DCS-HTLC's core modules to the overall security properties. Removing the **DTL** mechanism causes the Transaction Success Rate (TSR) under congestion to plummet from 95.8% to 28.5%, proving its necessity for adaptive liveness despite a marginal 4k Gas overhead. Ablating the **CP** module shifts the attacker's expected payoff from −0.1284 to

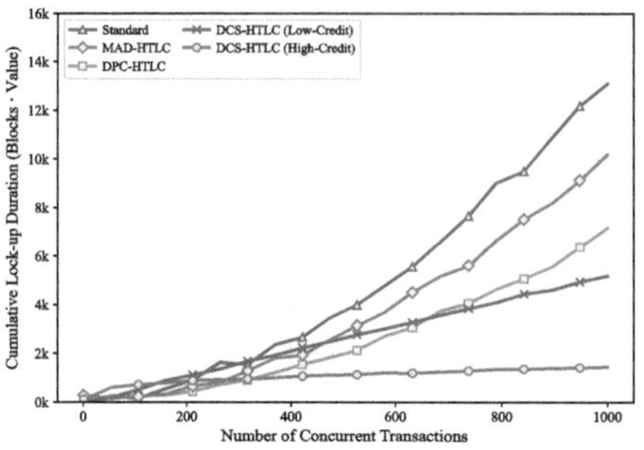

Fig. 5. Liquidity lock-up duration under concurrent workloads.

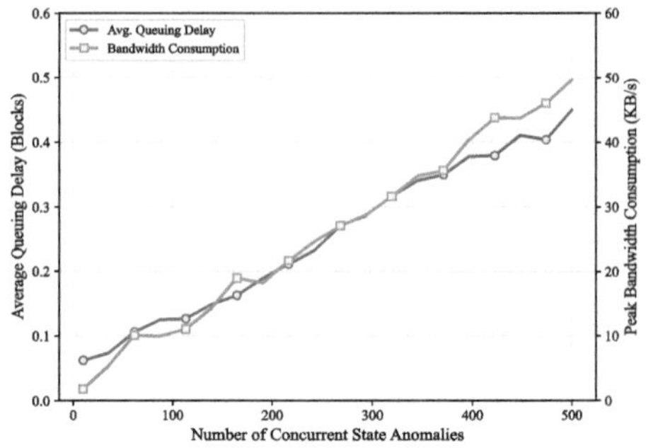

Fig. 6. FSC relayer queuing delay and bandwidth under concurrent anomalies.

+0.0156 ETH, validating its economic deterrence against free option attacks at a cost of ∼31k Gas. Finally, without **FSC**, the state Violation Rate surges from $< 0.1\%$ to 12.5%, highlighting its critical role in guaranteeing complete atomicity with only a lightweight ∼9k Gas overhead. These results confirm that the organic coupling of all three components is indispensable for balancing efficiency, fairness, and security.

Table 1. Ablation analysis of different components.

Configuration	TSR	Violation rate	Attacker payoff	Gas cost
DCS-HTLC (Full)	95.8%	$< 0.1\%$	−0.1284	146k
w/o DTL	28.5%	$< 0.1\%$	−0.1250	142k
w/o CP	96.2%	$< 0.1\%$	+0.0156	115k
w/o FSC	88.2%	12.5%	−0.0910	137k

7 Conclusion

This paper proposes DCS-HTLC, an environment-aware adaptive protocol to address the challenges of atomic swaps across heterogeneous blockchains. By integrating Dynamic Time-Lock (DTL), Collateral Penalty (CP), and Full-Link State Control (FSC), the system achieves an optimized balance among adaptive liveness, incentive compatibility, and complete atomicity. Theoretical analysis confirms that DCS-HTLC anchors the honest strategy as the unique Nash Equilibrium while ensuring deterministic state convergence under partial synchrony. Experimental evaluations demonstrate that DCS-HTLC maintains a stable 95.8% transaction success rate under severe congestion, significantly outperforming static baselines. The protocol effectively suppresses the "free option" arbitrage payoff to negative values with only 4.0% additional overhead for state control. While evaluations on private testbeds validate our theoretical model, we acknowledge the inherent limitations of simulated environments. Production-grade deployments face unpredictable variables, including massive concurrent transactions and active MEV searcher bots. Therefore, our future work will focus on deploying DCS-HTLC on public testnets to empirically evaluate its scalability and robustness against real-world MEV exploits. Additionally, we plan to explore the integration of Zero-Knowledge Proofs (ZKP) to further enhance privacy protection and optimize the compression efficiency of cross-chain state anchoring.

Acknowledgment. This work is supported by the National Natural Science Foundation of China Project (No. 62272207) and the Jiangxi Natural Science Foundation Project (No. 20224ACB202009).

References

1. Belchior, R., Vasconcelos, A., Guerreiro, S., Correia, M.: A survey on blockchain interoperability: past, present, and future trends. ACM Comput. Surv. **54**(8), 1–41 (2021)
2. Belotti, M., Moretti, S., Potop-Butucaru, M., Secci, S.: Game theoretical analysis of cross-chain swaps. In: 40th IEEE ICDCS, pp. 485–495. IEEE (2020)
3. Binance Research: Full-Year 2025 & Themes for 2026. https://www.binance.com/en/research/analysis/full-year-2025-and-themes-for-2026. Last accessed 27 Jan 2026
4. Cai, Y., Cheng, R., Zhou, Y., Zhang, S., Xiao, J., Jin, H.: Enabling complete atomicity for cross-chain applications through layered state commitments. In: 43rd IEEE SRDS, pp. 248–259. IEEE (2024)
5. Ding, D.: Lilac: Parallelizing atomic cross-chain swaps. In: 27th IEEE ISCC, pp. 1–8. IEEE (2022)
6. Duan, T., et al.: PieBridge: an on-demand scalable cross-chain architecture. J. Comput. Res. Dev. **60**(11), 2520–2533 (2023). (in Chinese)
7. Duan, T., et al.: A review of blockchain interoperability technology. J. Softw. **35**(2), 800–827 (2024). (in Chinese)
8. Han, R., Lin, H., Yu, J.: On the optionality and fairness of atomic swaps. In: 1st ACM AFT, pp. 62–75. ACM (2019)
9. Herlihy, M.: Atomic cross-chain swaps. In: 37th ACM PODC, pp. 245–254. ACM (2018)
10. Li, Y., Miao, S., Zhang, Z., Xu, X., Qiu, W., Zheng, Z.: RL-ABO: Adaptive blockchain control parameter optimization method based on reinforcement learning. In: APWeb-WAIM 2025. LNCS, vol. 16115, pp. 649–663. Springer (2025)
11. Ni, P., Tian, A., Xu, J.: Warning! the timeout T cannot protect you from losing coins: PipeSwap. In: 46th IEEE SP, pp. 1566–1583. IEEE (2025)
12. Thyagarajan, S., Malavolta, G., Moreno-Sanchez, P.: Universal atomic swaps: Secure exchange of coins across all blockchains. In: 43rd IEEE SP, pp. 1299–1316. IEEE (2022)

13. Tsabary, I., Yechieli, M., Manuskin, A., Eyal, I.: MAD-HTLC: Because HTLC is crazy-cheap to attack. In: 42nd IEEE SP, pp. 1230–1248. IEEE (2021)
14. Wadhwa, S., Stoeter, J., Zhang, F., Nayak, K.: He-HTLC: Revisiting incentives in HTLC. In: 30th NDSS. Internet Society (2023)
15. Wang, K., Wang, D., Zhi, H., Chen, Y., Zhang, X.: Hash time lock with dynamic premium based on credit in cross-chain transaction. In: 7th IEEE Blockchain, pp. 123–130. IEEE (2024)
16. Wang, Z., Qiu, X., Zhao, H., Zhang, A., Yuan, Y.: Reputation-based blockchain node reallocation in heterogeneous networks. In: APWeb-WAIM 2025. LNCS, vol. 16116, pp. 3–18. Springer (2025)
17. Xu, J., Ackerer, D., Dubovitskaya, A.: A game-theoretic analysis of cross-chain atomic swaps with HTLCs. In: 41st IEEE ICDCS, pp. 584–594. IEEE (2021)
18. Zakhary, V., Agrawal, D., El Abbadi, A.: Atomic commitment across blockchains. In: 46th VLDB, pp. 1319–1331 (2020)
19. Zamyatin, A., Harz, D., Lind, J., Panayiotou, P., Gervais, A., Knottenbelt, W.: XCLAIM: Trustless, interoperable, cryptocurrency-backed assets. In: 40th IEEE SP, pp. 193–210. IEEE (2019)
20. Zhang, M., Zhang, X., Zhang, Y., Lin, Z.: Security of cross-chain bridges: attack surfaces, defenses, and open problems. In: 27th RAID, pp. 298–316. ACM (2024)

DCSM: Dynamic Controller–Switch Mapping for SDN Controller Load Balancing

Firas Zobary(✉)

Wuhan University of Technology, Wuhan, Hubei, China
firas_zobary@hotmail.com

Abstract. Efficient load balancing in distributed Software-Defined Networking (SDN) control planes is critical for ensuring scalability, low latency, and reliable network performance under dynamic traffic conditions. Traditional approaches often rely on reactive strategies, single-metric assessments, or independent selection of switches and controllers, which can result in suboptimal load distribution, high migration cost, and unstable control-plane behavior. This paper proposes a Dynamic Controller-Switch Mapping (DCSM) framework for adaptive, cost-aware load balancing in multi-controller SDN environments. DCSM integrates multi-metric load evaluation—combining controller resource utilization and traffic demand—with a joint optimization mechanism for selecting both candidate switches and destination controllers. A formal migration cost model is incorporated to balance the benefits of load redistribution against communication and control overhead. Furthermore, post-migration evaluation ensures stability and prevents load oscillation. Extensive experiments on real-world network topologies demonstrate that DCSM significantly outperforms state-of-the-art approaches, including SMCLBRT, DHA, and DLBMT, across multiple performance metrics: balance index, controller response time, load balancing rate, migration cost, and communication overhead. The framework shows consistent superiority in both small and large-scale topologies, highlighting its scalability and robustness under high traffic conditions. The results confirm that DCSM provides an effective and practical solution for dynamic load balancing, enabling high control-plane efficiency, low latency, and stable network operation in large-scale SDN deployments.

Keywords: SDN · Load Balancing · Switch Migration

1 Introduction

Software-Defined Networking (SDN) has emerged as a transformative paradigm that decouples the control plane from the data plane, enabling centralized network intelligence and programmable management [1]. By delegating forwarding decisions to logically centralized controllers, SDN significantly enhances network flexibility, simplifies configuration, and supports rapid innovation. However, this architectural centralization introduces critical scalability and reliability challenges, particularly in large-scale and

L. Ding et al. (Eds.): APWeb-WAIM 2026, LNCS 16993, pp. 49–63, 2027.
https://doi.org/10.1007/978-981-92-5693-8_4

dynamic network environments [2]. A single controller can become a performance bottleneck due to excessive control requests, leading to increased latency, degraded Quality of Service (QoS), and potential single points of failure [3].

To address these limitations, distributed SDN control plane architectures have been widely adopted, where multiple controllers collaboratively manage the network [4]. While such architectures improve fault tolerance and scalability, they introduce a new challenge: load imbalance among controllers. Due to the dynamic and unpredictable nature of traffic, certain controllers may become overloaded with Packet-in requests, while others remain underutilized. This imbalance negatively impacts flow setup latency, controller responsiveness, and overall network performance.

Dynamic load balancing has therefore become a fundamental research problem in distributed SDN environments [5]. A widely adopted approach to achieve load balancing is switch migration, where switches are reassigned from overloaded controllers to underloaded ones. Despite extensive research in this area, existing approaches suffer from several key limitations. First, many rely on simplistic or single-metric load models, failing to capture the multidimensional nature of controller load. Second, the selection of switches and destination controllers is often treated independently, leading to suboptimal or even counterproductive migration decisions. Third, migration cost is frequently overlooked, resulting in excessive overhead or oscillatory behavior that destabilizes the system.

To overcome these challenges, this paper proposes a Dynamic Controller-Switch Mapping (DCSM) framework for efficient and stable load balancing in distributed SDN control planes. The proposed approach adopts a holistic and coordinated strategy that integrates multi-metric load assessment, joint optimization of switch and controller selection, and cost-aware migration decisions. Specifically, DCSM evaluates controller load using a combination of resource utilization (CPU and memory), Packet-In rates, and controller processing capacity, providing a comprehensive view of system dynamics.

Unlike existing methods, DCSM tightly couples the selection of migration candidates with destination controller decisions through a unified optimization framework. Furthermore, it incorporates an explicit migration cost model, capturing both signaling overhead and control path reconfiguration impact. By combining these factors into a unified decision-making process, DCSM ensures that each migration improves global load distribution while minimizing operational overhead.

The main contributions of this paper can be summarized as follows:

1. A multi-metric load assessment and imbalance detection mechanism that accurately captures controller load dynamics and triggers migration only when necessary.
2. A jointly optimized switch and destination controller selection strategy that evaluates post-migration system states to ensure effective load redistribution.
3. A cost-aware migration model that integrates signaling cost and control load transfer cost, enabling efficient and stable migration decisions.
4. A comprehensive evaluation demonstrates that DCSM significantly outperforms existing approaches in terms of load balance, response time, migration cost, and communication overhead.

Unlike prior approaches that independently optimize switch migration or destination controller selection, DCSM introduces a coordinated post-migration evaluation framework that jointly considers: (1) multi-metric controller load, (2) migration efficiency, (3) residual controller utilization, and (4) migration cost, within a unified decision process. In contrast to reactive or greedy migration schemes, DCSM evaluates the global post-migration system state to reduce oscillation and avoid problem-shifting.

The remainder of this paper is organized as follows: Sect. 2 presents the related works. Section 3 describes the proposed DCSM framework in detail. Section 4 provides performance evaluation and experimental results. Finally, Sect. 5 concludes the paper.

2 Related Works

Dynamic load balancing is a fundamental requirement in SDN due to the inherently dynamic and unpredictable nature of network traffic [6, 7]. As SDN applications continue to expand across diverse domains, including smart environments and industrial systems, maintaining efficient and scalable control-plane operations has become increasingly critical. To address this challenge, a wide range of load-balancing strategies have been proposed, which can be broadly categorized into reactive switch migration mechanisms, traffic-aware and AI-based approaches, migration-based redistribution strategies, and optimization-driven methods.

Switch migration is one of the most widely adopted techniques for mitigating controller overload in distributed SDN environments. This approach redistributes control-plane load by transferring switches from overloaded controllers to underutilized ones, thereby improving resource utilization. For instance, Hu et al. [8] proposed an Efficiency-Aware Switch Migration (EASM) mechanism that triggers migration when control-plane traffic exceeds a predefined threshold. The method employs a greedy algorithm to select the destination controller, ensuring low computational complexity. Despite its efficiency, reactive migration strategies suffer from inherent limitations. Since migration is triggered only after overload conditions occur, temporary performance degradation is often unavoidable during detection and migration phases. Furthermore, greedy-based selection methods may lead to suboptimal global load distribution, particularly in large-scale or highly dynamic networks.

To improve adaptability, traffic-aware load balancing strategies have been developed to respond to real-time traffic variations. Prior studies as in [9, 10] have introduced mechanisms that dynamically adjust controller assignments based on traffic conditions, thereby enhancing Quality of Service (QoS) and system robustness. More recently, in [11], Artificial Intelligence (AI) and Machine Learning (ML) techniques have been incorporated to enable predictive load balancing through traffic forecasting and proactive resource allocation.

While these approaches improve responsiveness and prediction accuracy, they often focus primarily on traffic estimation rather than migration decision stability. In particular, many AI-based methods do not adequately address the coordination between switch selection and destination controller assignment, nor do they consider the long-term impact of migration decisions, such as load oscillation and system instability.

Several studies have explored switch migration mechanisms to redistribute controller workloads more effectively. Early work by Dixit et al. [12] demonstrated the benefits of reassigning switches from heavily loaded controllers to neighboring controllers with available capacity. However, this approach does not consider propagation delay between switches and controllers, limiting its applicability in wide-area network (WAN) environments.

Subsequent research introduced more advanced migration mechanisms. Zhou et al. [13] proposed a distributed control framework capable of maintaining low response times under increasing Packet-In traffic and supporting dynamic controller scalability. However, their method relies on random switch selection, which neglects the impact of migration on the target controller and may lead to unstable load conditions. Similarly, Wang et al. [14] developed a migration efficiency model that incorporates migration cost into decision-making. Although this approach improves cost-awareness, it does not sufficiently address load oscillation caused by frequent and unstable migrations.

In addition to migration-based techniques, architectural and optimization-driven approaches have been proposed to improve load distribution. Hierarchical control plane architectures provide structured load distribution by organizing controllers into multiple layers. For example, Lan et al. [15] introduced a hierarchical mapping strategy for static load balancing. However, this approach relies on proximity-based controller selection and does not consider controller utilization, potentially leading to inefficient resource allocation.

Metaheuristic optimization techniques have also been applied to enhance load balancing decisions. Guo and Ye [16] proposed a hybrid Genetic-Bird Swarm Optimization (GBSO) algorithm that combines evolutionary and swarm intelligence principles to optimize switch migration. While effective in improving load distribution, such methods often incur high computational complexity and require parameter tuning, limiting their scalability in large and dynamic network environments.

In summary, existing dynamic load-balancing approaches exhibit several limitations. Reactive methods suffer from delayed response to traffic fluctuations, while traffic-aware and AI-based approaches often overlook migration stability and coordination. Migration-based strategies may rely on random or greedy decisions, leading to suboptimal load distribution and potential oscillation. Meanwhile, optimization-based methods can introduce significant computational overhead.

A key limitation across many existing works is the decoupled decision-making process, where the selection of switches and destination controllers is handled independently. This often results in myopic decisions that fail to consider global system impact, leading to problem-shifting and instability. To address these challenges, this paper proposes a DCSM framework. The proposed approach introduces a holistic and coordinated migration strategy that jointly optimizes switch selection and controller assignment while incorporating a formal migration cost model. By explicitly considering post-migration load distribution and system stability, DCSM enables efficient, scalable, and sustainable load balancing in distributed SDN environments.

3 Proposed DCSM for Dynamic Load Balancing

3.1 System Architecture of DCSM

The proposed DCSM architecture, illustrated in Fig. 1, operates as a distributed module deployed on each SDN controller within the control plane, enabling coordinated load balancing through dynamic switch migration.

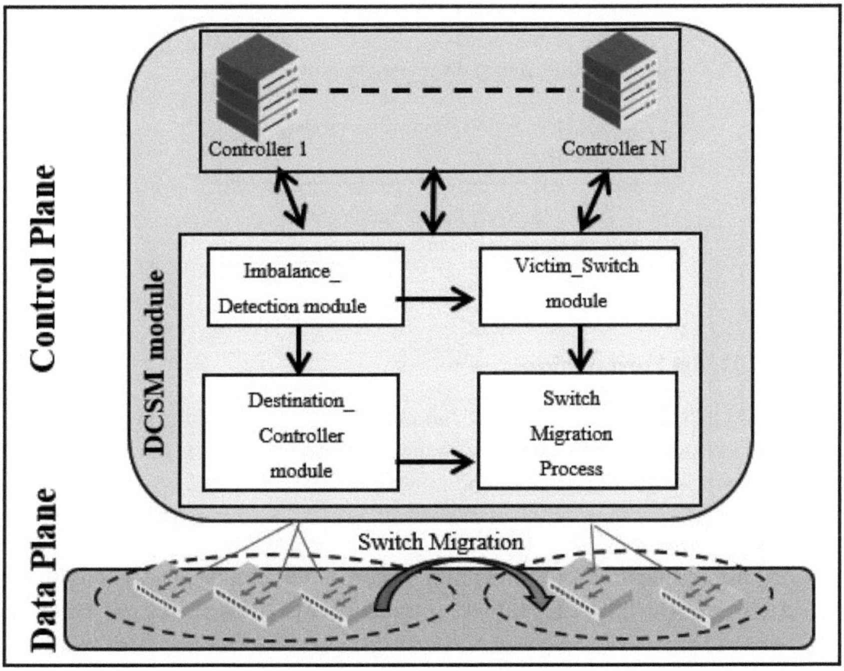

Fig. 1. DCSM system architecture

The main algorithm is described in DCSM_Main (Algorithm 1) in which each controller maintains a consistent global network view by aggregating its own load statistics with those of peer controllers to compute real-time load ratios and mean load values.

Algorithm 1 DCSM_Main

```
Input: G = (V, E), Controller Load Threshold TH
Output: Load Balancing Achieved
for each node v_i ∈ V do
if (Controller Load > TH) then
    Generate X matrix
    Call Imbalance_Detection module ()
    Call Victim_Switch module ()
    Call Destination_Controller module ()
    Start Migration
else
    The Controllers are in Stable Mode
return Load Balancing Achieved
```

3.2 DCSM Model Formulation

The proposed DCSM approach employs an undirected, connected graph $G = (V, E)$ to represent its network topology, where V is the set of nodes and E is the set of links. The node set V comprises both switches and controllers, denoted as $S = \{S_1, S_2, \cdots, S_m\}$ and $C = \{C_1, C_2, \cdots, C_n\}$, respectively. Here, C_i refers to the ith controller. All the notations are illustrated in Table 1.

In SDN, the association between the ith switch and the jth controller is defined by a binary variable x_{ij} which denotes if there is a link between this switch and controller.

$$x_{ij} = \begin{cases} 1, & \text{if the switch } v_i \text{ is controlled by the controller } C_j \\ 0, & \text{Otherwise} \end{cases} \tag{1}$$

The X matrix represents the controller-switch association state. A surge in *Packet-In* messages that overloads a controller will automatically trigger the switch migration process. The system employs a multi-metric approach to assess controller load, incorporating network resource utilization, *Packet-In* request rates, and individual controller capacity, rather than relying on simplistic load adjustments.

The DCSM modules will be explained in detail as follows:

1. Imbalance_Detection Module

The Imbalance Detection module identifies load imbalance by computing the real-time load ratio of each controller based on both resource utilization and traffic demand. Specifically, controller load is modeled using a weighted combination of CPU and memory utilization, normalized by controller capacity:

$$L_i = w_1 \cdot \frac{S_{cpu}}{Q'_i} + w_2 \cdot \frac{S_{memory}}{Q''_i} \tag{2}$$

Table 1. Notation used in DCSM

Notation	Description
TH	Controller threshold
L_i	Resource utilization ratio of controller C_i
L_i^{real}	Real time load of controller C_i
L_{mean}^{real}	Mean real time load ratio
ρ_i	Controller processing capacity of C_i
BI	Balance index
$BI_{(i,j)}$	Balance index after migration from C_i to C_j
S^{req}	Switch request rate message
φ	Migration triggering factor
$h_{ci}^{S_m}$	Hop counts from switch to controller
δ	Migration efficiency value
λ_m	Average flow request rate of switch S_m

where S_{cpu} and S_{memory} denote CPU and memory usage, Q_i' and Q_i'' represent resource capacities, and $\sum w_i = 1$. Unless otherwise stated, equal weighting ($w_1 = w_2 = 0.5$) is adopted to avoid bias toward specific metrics and ensure balanced consideration of resource utilization and traffic dynamics. The weighting mechanism can be adjusted according to deployment requirements and network priorities. The real-time load ratio is then defined as:

$$L_i^{real} = \frac{1}{\rho_i} \sum_{S \in C_i} \left[L_i \cdot S^{req} \right] \tag{3}$$

where ρ_i denotes controller processing capacity. The system-wide average load is computed as:

$$L_{mean}^{real} = \frac{1}{K} \sum_{i=1}^{K} L_i^{real} \tag{4}$$

To quantify load imbalance, the Balance Index (BI) is defined as the normalized standard deviation of controller load ratios, where a lower value indicates better load distribution as follows:

$$BI = \frac{\frac{1}{K}\sqrt{\sum_{i=1}^{K} \left(L_i^{real} - L_{mean}^{real} \right)^2}}{L_{mean}^{real}} \tag{5}$$

The Balance Index is equivalent to the coefficient of variation of controller loads. Finally, a triggering factor is introduced to classify controller states:

$$\varphi_{C_i} = \frac{L_i^{real}}{L_{mean}^{real}} \tag{6}$$

To avoid unnecessary migrations caused by minor fluctuations around the mean load, migration decisions are triggered only when the imbalance persists beyond the predefined controller load threshold TH. Based on this factor, controllers are categorized as is overloaded ($\varphi_{C_i} > 1$), underloaded ($\varphi_{C_i} < 1$), or operating in a stable state ($\varphi_{C_i} = 1$).

2. Victim Switch Selection Module

The Victim Switch Selection module identifies the most suitable switch for migration from overloaded controllers. Each candidate switch is evaluated using a migration efficiency metric and its impact on the post-migration Balance Index ($BI^{'}$), ensuring that migration improves overall load distribution. Candidate switches are ranked according to migration efficiency and post-migration $BI^{'}$ reduction.

Migration efficiency is defined as the ratio between the switch traffic load and migration cost (measured by hop distance):

$$\delta_{S_{m,ci}} = \frac{S_m^{req}}{h_{ci}^{S_m}} \tag{7}$$

To assess the effectiveness of migration, the controller loads are updated after migrating switch S_m, and the corresponding post-migration Balance Index is computed. Only switches that reduce the balance index are considered valid candidates. Among these candidates, the switch with the highest migration efficiency is selected for migration. This joint evaluation ensures that the selected switch not only maximizes load reduction but also contributes to improved global load balance.

3. Destination Controller Selection Module

After selecting the candidate switch, the Destination Controller Selection module determines the most suitable target controller for migration. Destination controllers are evaluated using residual capacity and migration cost before migration approval. Unlike conventional approaches that select the least-loaded controller, the proposed method formulates this step as a multi-objective optimization problem. First, the migration cost is modeled to capture the overhead of switch reassignment. It consists of two components: (i) signaling cost (SC), which depends on the switch request rate and hop distance, and (ii) control load transfer cost ($CLTC$), which reflects the impact of path changes on control traffic. These components are combined into a unified cost metric and formulated as follows:

$$SC = S_m^{req} \times \min\left(h_{cj}^{S_m}\right) \tag{8}$$

$$CLTC = \lambda_m \times \left(h_{cj}^{S_m} - h_{ci}^{S_m}\right) \tag{9}$$

$$MC_{i,j} = w^1 \cdot SC + w^2 \cdot CLTC \tag{10}$$

After that, the migration efficiency of moving the switch from controller c_i to c_j is calculated as:

$$\delta_{ij} = \frac{\left|BI'_{(i,j)} - BI_{(i,j)}\right|}{MC_{i,j}} \tag{11}$$

Next, the framework evaluates the remaining capacity of candidate controllers to ensure that migration does not create secondary overload conditions.

$$RU_j = \frac{\rho_j - L_j^{real}}{\rho_j} \tag{12}$$

RU_j yields a value between 0 and 1 where a value closer to 1 indicates a highly underutilized system with ample room for load acceptance, while a value closer to 0 suggests the underloaded controller is nearing its capacity limits. To evaluate the suitability of a specific switch-controller pair, we define a Valuation Function ($\xi_{m,j}$). This function integrates the switch's load profile, the controller's remaining capacity, and the network path cost into a single score:

$$\xi_{m,j} = \frac{\lambda'_m \times RU_j}{h'_{mj}(1 - RU_j)} \tag{13}$$

where λ'_m represents the average load to be migrated, and h'_{mj} is the average hop counts between the candidate switch and a potential target controller. Higher residual utilization and lower hop distance increase controller suitability. Finally, the combination of the remaining utilization and the migration efficiency are aggregated as follows:

$$\psi_j = w^1 \cdot \xi_{m,j} + w^2 \cdot \delta_{ij} \tag{14}$$

The higher ψ_j value, the more chance for controller j to be selected as target controller. Preliminary experiments showed that balanced weights provide stable performance across different topologies without over-prioritizing migration efficiency or residual capacity.

4. Switch Migration Process

The switch migration process transfers control of a switch from an overloaded controller (old master) to an underutilized controller (new master) with minimal disruption to data-plane operations. This process is executed in three phases:

- **Initiation and Negotiation:**

When a controller becomes overloaded, it selects candidate switches and a target controller. A migration request is sent to the destination controller, which evaluates its available capacity and responds with acceptance or rejection using standard control messages (e.g., OpenFlow role negotiation).

- **Reconfiguration and Handover:**

Upon approval, the destination controller synchronizes with the switch (e.g., collecting state information). The old master then issues a role change command, promoting the destination controller to master. The switch updates its control association and confirms the role transition.

- **Post-migration Update:**

After handover, both controllers update the global network state to reflect the new mapping. The old master releases or downgrades its connection, while the new master assumes full control of the switch.

This coordinated procedure ensures seamless migration without interrupting ongoing traffic, while enabling effective redistribution of control-plane load.

The computational complexity of DCSM mainly depends on victim switch evaluation and destination controller selection. Assuming m switches and n controllers, imbalance detection requires $O(n)$, victim switch evaluation requires $O(m)$, and destination controller evaluation requires $O(n)$. Therefore, the overall migration decision complexity is approximately $O(m + n)$ per migration cycle. Since migration is triggered only under imbalance conditions, the framework remains computationally efficient for dynamic SDN environments.

4 Performance Evaluation

4.1 Experimental Setup

The proposed DCSM framework is evaluated using the Mininet emulation platform, which provides a realistic and flexible environment for SDN experimentation. The control logic is implemented on the Ryu controller due to its extensibility and support for OpenFlow-based applications. Experiments are conducted on a Linux-based system (Ubuntu 20.04) with an Intel Core i5 processor and 16 GB RAM. Network traffic is generated using the IPerf tool, where each new flow triggers a Packet-In event, allowing accurate measurement of controller workload and resource utilization. To validate scalability and robustness, experiments are performed on multiple real-world network topologies obtained from the Internet Topology Zoo, including Atmnet, ARN, BellCanada, and Interroute. These topologies represent increasing network sizes and complexities, enabling comprehensive evaluation under diverse conditions. The topologies environment specifications are listed in Table 2.

Table 2. Network topologies specifications

Topology	Atmnet	ARN	BellCanada	Interroute
Nodes	21	30	48	110
Edges	22	29	65	158
Controller number	3	4	5	7
Threshold	1k	1.2k	1.5k	2k

4.2 Experimental Results and Analysis

Balance Index Evaluation

The performance of the proposed DCSM framework is evaluated against SMCLBRT, DHA, and DLBMT across four topologies (Atmnet, ARN, BellCanada, and Interroute) using the Balance Index (BI), where lower values indicate better load distribution. As shown in Fig. 2, DCSM consistently achieves the lowest BI under all traffic conditions and topologies, maintaining values below 0.37. This performance is attributed to its joint optimization strategy, which combines migration efficiency with post-migration BI evaluation and considers controller residual capacity to prevent imbalance.

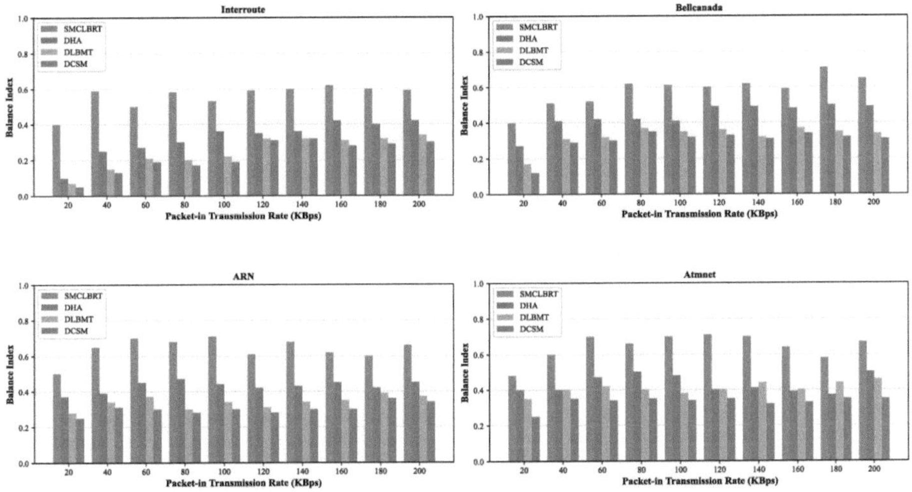

Fig. 2. Balance index among different topologies

Quantitatively, DCSM significantly reduces BI compared to competing methods. In the Interroute topology, BI is reduced by 60.1%, 30.9%, and 9.3% relative to SMCLBRT, DHA, and DLBMT, respectively. Similar improvements are observed across ARN, BellCanada, and Atmnet. These results demonstrate that DCSM effectively avoids problem-shifting and achieves more stable and efficient load balancing than existing approaches.

Controller Average Response Time Evaluation.

Load imbalance increases controller response time due to resource contention and queuing delays. Effective load balancing reduces latency by distributing workload more evenly. As shown in Fig. 3, DCSM consistently achieves the lowest average response time across all topologies, with 177 ms (Atmnet), 154 ms (ARN), 217 ms (BellCanada), and 352 ms (Interroute). Compared to SMCLBRT, DCSM reduces response time by up to 40.7% in Interroute, highlighting the limitations of reactive approaches. Although DLBMT performs competitively, DCSM still achieves an additional 4.9–6.8% improvement due to its joint optimization and post-migration evaluation. The performance gain becomes more significant in larger topologies, confirming the scalability and effectiveness of DCSM in dynamic environments.

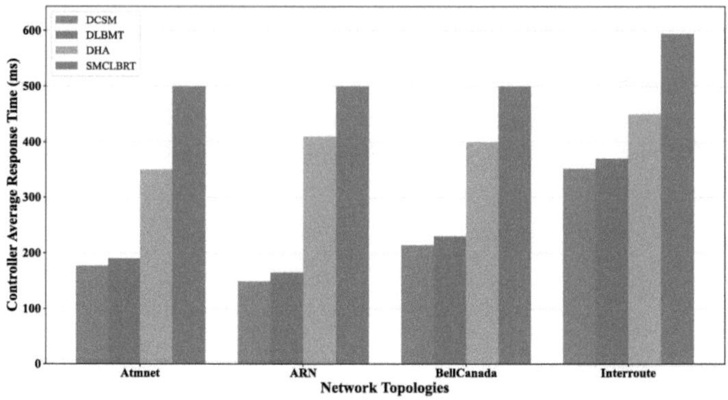

Fig. 3. Controller average response time evaluation

Load Balancing Rate Evaluation

The Load Balancing Rate (LBR) measures the stability of load distribution across controllers, defined as:

$$LBR = \left[1 - \frac{std(C_{Load})}{L_{mean}^{real}}\right] \times 100 \tag{15}$$

where higher values indicate better balance.

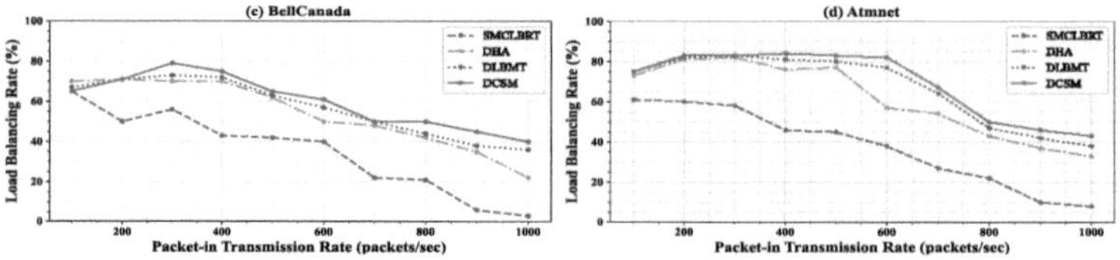

Fig. 4. Load balancing rate evaluation

As shown in Fig. 4, DCSM consistently achieves the highest LBR across all topologies and traffic conditions. The advantage is most significant at high traffic rates (600–1000 packets/s), where DCSM maintains 40–60% LBR in the Interroute topology, while SMCLBRT drops to 3–40%. Overall, DCSM outperforms all methods, exceeding DLBMT by 5–15% at peak loads and showing substantially better stability than DHA and SMCLBRT. While all approaches degrade with increasing traffic, DCSM maintains the most stable performance, demonstrating its ability to prevent load oscillation and sustain efficient operation in large-scale and high-load environments. The consistently higher LBR under increasing traffic demonstrates that DCSM maintains stable controller load distribution over time and effectively mitigates oscillatory migration behavior.

Communication Overhead Evaluation

Communication overhead is evaluated in terms of switch–controller (SC) and controller–controller (CC) message exchanges to assess scalability. As shown in Fig. 5, DCSM consistently achieves the lowest SC overhead among distributed approaches, reducing it by up to 19.8% (Atmnet), 12.2% (ARN), 7.7% (BellCanada), and 10.1% (Interroute) compared to DLBMT, with similar improvements over DHA. For CC overhead, DCSM also outperforms competing methods, achieving reductions of up to 19% (Atmnet), 24% (ARN), 18.2% (BellCanada), and 16.9% (Interroute) relative to DHA and DLBMT. Although SMCLBRT avoids inter-controller communication, it incurs significantly higher SC overhead, indicating that minimizing CC traffic alone is insufficient. Overall, DCSM achieves the best trade-off between CC and SC overhead, reducing coordination cost without increasing communication burden, thereby ensuring scalability in large-scale SDN environments.

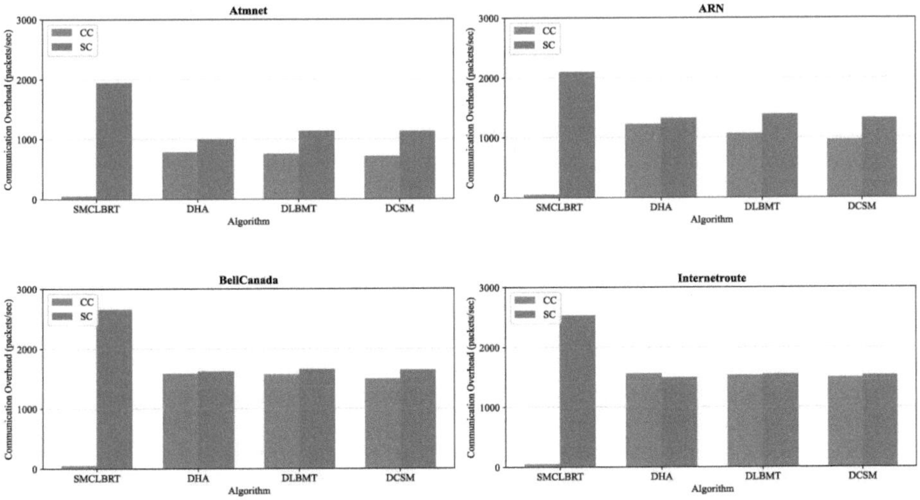

Fig. 5. Communication overhead evaluation

5 Conclusion

This paper presented a Dynamic Controller-Switch Mapping (DCSM) framework for efficient and stable load balancing in distributed SDN control planes. Unlike existing approaches, DCSM adopts a holistic strategy that integrates multi-metric load assessment, joint optimization of switch and controller selection, and a cost-aware migration model. By explicitly evaluating post-migration system states, the proposed framework effectively avoids load oscillation and problem-shifting, ensuring sustainable load distribution. Extensive experiments conducted on real-world network topologies demonstrate that DCSM consistently outperforms state-of-the-art methods, including SMCLBRT, DHA, and DLBMT. The results show significant improvements in key performance metrics, including reduced Balance Index, lower response time, higher load balancing rate, minimized migration cost, and reduced communication overhead. In addition, since migration cost in DCSM consists of signaling overhead and control-load transfer overhead, the reduced SC and CC communication overhead directly reflects lower migration cost. Moreover, the performance gains become more pronounced in large-scale and high-traffic scenarios, confirming the scalability and robustness of the proposed approach. Overall, DCSM provides an effective and practical solution for dynamic load balancing in modern SDN environments, enabling improved control-plane efficiency and network performance. Future work will focus on integrating predictive traffic models and extending the framework to support heterogeneous and geo-distributed SDN architectures.

Acknowledgements. No funding was received to support this work.

Disclosure of Interests. The authors declare no competing interests

References

1. Li, P., Wang, J.: Rethinking networks for the digital age: the rise and impact of software-defined networking. In: 2025 IEEE International Symposium on Broadband Multimedia Systems and Broadcasting (BMSB), pp. 1–6. IEEE, Ireland (2025)
2. Bouchmal, O., Cimoli, B., Stabile, R., Vegas Olmos, J.J., Tafur Monroy, I.: From classical to quantum machine learning: survey on routing optimization in 6G software defined networking. Front. Commun. Netw. **4**, 1220227 (2023)
3. Shaik, K.M.N.: Securing inter-controller communication in distributed SDN networks. Int. J. Technol. Manag. Human. **10**(4), 28–48 (2024)
4. Tivig, P.-T., Brumaru, A., Obreja, S.G.: Creating scalable distributed control plane in SDN to rule out the single point of failure. In: 2022 14th International Conference on Communications (COMM), pp. 1–6. IEEE, Bucharest (2022)
5. Beissenova, G., et al.: Load balancing in DCN servers through software defined network machine learning. Int. J. Adv. Comput. Sci. Appl. **15**(2), 509–519 (2024)
6. Liu, Y., Gu, H., Yan, F., Calabretta, N.: Highly-efficient switch migration for controller load balancing in elastic optical inter-datacenter networks. IEEE J. Sel. Areas Commun. **39**(9), 2748–2761 (2021)
7. Babbar, H., Rani, S., Gupta, D., Aljahdali, H.M., Singh, A., Al-Turjman, F.: Load balancing algorithm on the immense scale of internet of things in SDN for smart cities. Sustainability **13**(17), 9587 (2021)
8. Hu, T., Lan, J., Zhang, J., Zhao, W.: EASM: efficiency-aware switch migration for balancing controller loads in software-defined networking. Peer Peer Netw. Appl. **12**(2), 452–464 (2019)
9. Lakhani, G., Kothari, A.: Fault administration by load balancing in distributed SDN controller: a review. Wirel. Pers. Commun. **114**(4), 3507–3539 (2020)
10. Beiruti, M.A., Ganjali, Y.: Load migration in distributed sdn controllers. In: NOMS 2020–2020 IEEE/IFIP Network Operations and Management Symposium, pp. 1–9. IEEE, Budapest (2020)

11. Belgaum, M.R., Ali, F., Alansari, Z., Musa, S., Alam, M.M., Mazliham, M.S.: Artificial intelligence based reliable load balancing framework in software-defined networks. CMC—Comput. Mater. Contin. **70**, 251–266 (2022)
12. Dixit, A., Hao, F., Mukherjee, S., Lakshman, T.V., Kompella, R.: Towards an elastic distributed SDN controller. ACM SIGCOMM Comput. Commun. Rev. **43**(4), 7–12 (2013)
13. Zhou, Y., et al.: A load balancing strategy of SDN controller based on distributed decision. In: 2014 IEEE 13th International Conference on Trust, Security and Privacy in Computing and Communications, pp. 851–856. IEEE, Beijing (2014)
14. Wang, C., Hu, B., Chen, S., Li, D., Liu, B.: A switch migration-based decision-making scheme for balancing load in SDN. IEEE Access **5**, 4537–4544 (2017)
15. Lan, W., Li, F., Liu, X., Qiu, Y.: A dynamic load balancing mechanism for distributed controllers in software-defined networking. In: 2018 10th International Conference on Measuring Technology and Mechatronics Automation (ICMTMA), pp. 259–262. IEEE, Changsha (2018)
16. Guo, F., Ye, A.: The application and performance optimization of multi-controller-based load balancing algorithm in computer networks. Egypt. Inf. J. **30**, 100678 (2025)

Group Distillation for Semi-supervised Federated Learning in Heterogeneous Edge Computing

Yibing Wang, Xingjian Lu(✉), and Xiaoying Tu

East China Normal University, Shanghai 200062, China
xjlu@cs.ecnu.edu.cn

Abstract. In federated learning, multiple clients collaboratively train a global model. However, statistical heterogeneity across client data often detrimentally affects model performance. Most existing approaches assume the availability of labeled data on clients; yet in real-world scenarios, the real-time data acquired by edge devices are typically unlabeled, rendering such methods inapplicable. Furthermore, these approaches are predominantly based on model parameter aggregation, which imposes the requirement that the server and clients share identical model architectures, further limiting their practical applicability. In this paper, we propose GKD-SSFL, a novel semi-supervised federated learning framework designed for the scenario where clients possess abundant unlabeled data while the server holds limited labeled data, which effectively overcomes the above limitations. It leverages client grouping and knowledge distillation to effectively guide the learning of global model. Specifically, it first estimates the data distribution across clients, then partitions them into groups, and extracts knowledge from each group. The server then aggregates knowledge from all groups for global model training. For clients, we devise a round-adaptive training strategy that dynamically adjusts their local training objectives throughout rounds. Extensive experiments under various configurations demonstrate that our method outperforms existing methods.

Keywords: Federated Learning · Knowledge Distillation · Edge Computing

1 Introduction

With the widespread adoption of the Internet of Things (IoT) and intelligent terminals, edge computing has gradually emerged as a critical computing paradigm to meet the demands for low latency, high bandwidth, and data privacy protection. In edge computing environments, massive amounts of data are generated by a large number of devices, posing a critical challenge in efficiently and securely harnessing these data for intelligent model training. To address this challenge,

L. Ding et al. (Eds.): APWeb-WAIM 2026, LNCS 16993, pp. 64–79, 2027.
https://doi.org/10.1007/978-981-92-5693-8_5

Federated Learning (FL) [1,2] has attracted considerable attention for its ability to collaboratively train a global model across multiple edge devices while preserving data privacy. By training models locally on clients and sharing only model parameters, FL effectively avoids the privacy risks associated with centralized data transmission, aligning well with the distributed and privacy-sensitive nature of edge computing.

However, conventional FL methods presuppose that clients have access to labeled data. In practice, the data collected by edge devices are largely unlabeled, and manual annotation is often prohibitively expensive, thereby limiting the applicability of such methods. To address this bottleneck, Semi-Supervised Federated Learning (SSFL) [3] has been proposed, which leverages unlabeled client data alongside limited labeled data to facilitate model training. By combining the privacy guarantees of FL with the unlabeled data utilization capability, SSFL is ideally suited for typical edge settings where labeled data exist only on the server and clients possess solely unlabeled data. The server's supervised training guides clients' unsupervised learning, enabling SSFL to enhance both model generalization and training efficiency without compromising privacy.

While SSFL exhibits strong theoretical promise, its practical application is nevertheless confronted with critical challenges. On one hand, statistical heterogeneity leads to significant variations in data distributions across clients, with each client's data deviating substantially from the global distribution. This disparity exacerbates the challenge of model aggregation, adversely affecting convergence speed and often resulting in performance fluctuations or even degradation of the global model. Some methods [4] attempt to mitigate this issue by enforcing label consistency among clients, yet this often comes at the cost of the global model's final performance. Other approaches [5] rely on the global model to generate pseudo-labels for unlabeled client data; however, the quality of these pseudo-labels is intrinsically tied to the model's predictive accuracy. When the model performs poorly, the resulting pseudo-labels become unreliable, thereby negatively impacting the subsequent training process. On the other hand, model heterogeneity introduces additional complexity to SSFL. In practical environments, clients often have varying computational capabilities and storage resources, which naturally leads to differences in their model architectures. Such diversity impedes the deployment of standard aggregation protocols and necessitates more adaptive training frameworks.

In this paper, we present GKD-SSFL, a novel SSFL framework that addresses the aforementioned challenges through an "Estimation-Grouping-Distillation" process, which integrates client grouping with knowledge distillation (KD) [6]. First, the framework estimates the underlying data distribution of each client and strategically groups them to achieve a relatively balanced distribution across different groups. Subsequently, knowledge is extracted from each group, and these group-level knowledge representations are aggregated and integrated to train a robust global model, thereby overcoming the barrier posed by model heterogeneity. For client models, we design a round-adaptive training strategy that dynamically adjusts their training objectives to align with global model training while improving their own performance. The main contributions of this paper are summarized as follows:

- It groups clients by evaluating the relative composition of each client's data distribution across classes at the current round, ensuring that each group has relatively balanced prediction performance, which helps mitigate the impact of statistical heterogeneity.
- Each group extracts and integrates its internal knowledge, and the knowledge from multiple groups is then collectively used to train the global model, thereby mitigating the impact of model heterogeneity.
- We propose a general, modular SSFL framework by following "Estimation-Grouping-Distillation" process where each component is replaceable, and evaluate it on three benchmark datasets across various configurations. The results indicate that GKD-SSFL exhibits superiority in highly heterogeneity, outperforming existing methods.

2 Related Work

2.1 Semi-supervised Federated Learning

SSFL can generally be divided into three representative settings [7,8]: (1) each client possesses its own private dataset, but some clients have labeled data while others have unlabeled data; (2) every client contains both labeled and unlabeled data, and the server does not hold any data; and (3) the server possesses labeled data, whereas all data on the clients are unlabeled. This paper concentrates on the third scenario.

A straightforward approach is to integrate existing semi-supervised learning (SSL) methods (e.g., FixMatch [9], UDA [10]) with standard federated learning algorithms (e.g., FedAvg). However, such integration not only fails to address the heterogeneity issue, but also underutilizes the diverse knowledge embedded in client models. FedMatch [4] represents a state-of-the-art SSFL framework that leverages inter-client consistency loss and disjoint learning to enhance the performance over naive combinations of FL and SSL approaches. SemiFL [5] orchestrates training by alternating between supervised learning on server and unsupervised learning on clients, ensuring pseudo-labels are generated by the global model and producing reliable labels consistently throughout training. However, these methods remain constrained by the standard FL framework, rendering them incompatible with scenarios involving heterogeneous models. Moreover, they often neglect the inherent heterogeneity among clients. By enforcing inter-client consistency to boost performance, these methods risk underutilizing the unique samples available on each client. Our approach addresses heterogeneity by effectively utilizing the strengths of different client models, leading to enhanced model performance.

2.2 Federated Distillation

FD [11,12] is a distributed learning framework that combines FL and KD, supporting model heterogeneity while alleviating the impact of statistical heterogeneity. Instead of uploading model parameters or gradients, each client sends soft predictions to the central server for model updates, thus significantly reducing communication costs. Currently, FD is widely used to deal with the problem of statistical heterogeneity.

FedBR [13] incorporates block-wise regularization and KD into the FedAvg to effectively alleviate statistical heterogeneity during local training. DS-FL [14] aggregates client logits via an entropy-reduction method, reducing predictive uncertainty to obtain a more certain global model. FedSND [15] employs local self-distillation on clients and incorporates a pseudo-sample generation module on the server, collectively improving model accuracy and communication efficiency. However, these methods target supervised settings where client data are labeled. When applied to unlabeled client data, the locally generated knowledge becomes inherently unverifiable, limiting its contribution to the global model. Our method primarily targets semi-supervised learning scenarios. By grouping clients, our method leverages the strengths of each client, filters out effective knowledge, enhances the quality of knowledge, and thereby improves the global model's training.

3 Proposed Method

Assume that K clients work together to train a global model. Each client k possesses an unlabeled local dataset $\boldsymbol{D}_k = \{(x^{(i)})\}_{i=1}^{N_k}$, where N_k denotes the total number of samples owned by client k. The server hosts a small, labeled public dataset $\boldsymbol{D}_p = \{(x^{(i)}, y^{(i)})\}_{i=1}^{N_p}$, which is used to train the global model ϕ_{glob}, where N_p denotes the total number of samples on the server. Let $f(\cdot)$ denote the model computation, and $f(x;\phi)$ represent the prediction of model ϕ on input sample x. Thus, the global training loss $\mathcal{L}_{Glob}$ can be formulated as:

$$\mathcal{L}_{Glob} = \sum_{(x^{(i)},y^{(i)})\in \boldsymbol{D}_p} \mathcal{L}_{CE}\left(y^{(i)}, f(x^{(i)};\phi_{glob})\right) + \beta \cdot \mathcal{L}_{KL}\left(z_t^{(i)}, z_{glob}^{(i)}\right), \tag{1}$$

$$\mathcal{L}_{KL}(z_t^{(i)}, z_{glob}^{(i)}) = \tau^2 \cdot KL(softmax(\frac{z_t^{(i)}}{\tau})||softmax(\frac{z_{glob}^{(i)}}{\tau})). \tag{2}$$

where $z_{glob}^{(i)}$ denotes the output logits of the global model ϕ_{glob}, and $z_t^{(i)}$ represents the teacher knowledge that guides the training of the global model. $\mathcal{L}_{CE}$ denotes the cross-entropy loss and $\mathcal{L}_{KL}$ represents the Kullback-Leibler (KL) divergence loss. τ is a hyperparameter used to adjust the sharpness of the output distribution [16], and β is also a hyperparameter that controls the relative contribution of the two components in the overall loss function.

3.1 Collaborative Training via Estimation, Grouping, and Distillation

Statistical heterogeneity poses a core challenge to building a performant global model, as directly averaging the outputs of clients to guide global model training may introduce noise and bias, thereby undermining the training process. As shown in Fig. 1, in GKD-SSFL, we would like to group all clients such that the overall data distribution within each group becomes approximately homogeneous, thereby enabling the knowledge generated within a group to better align with that produced under a balanced distribution. Subsequently, the global model is trained using this knowledge, allowing it to effectively leverage diverse signals for robust generalization.

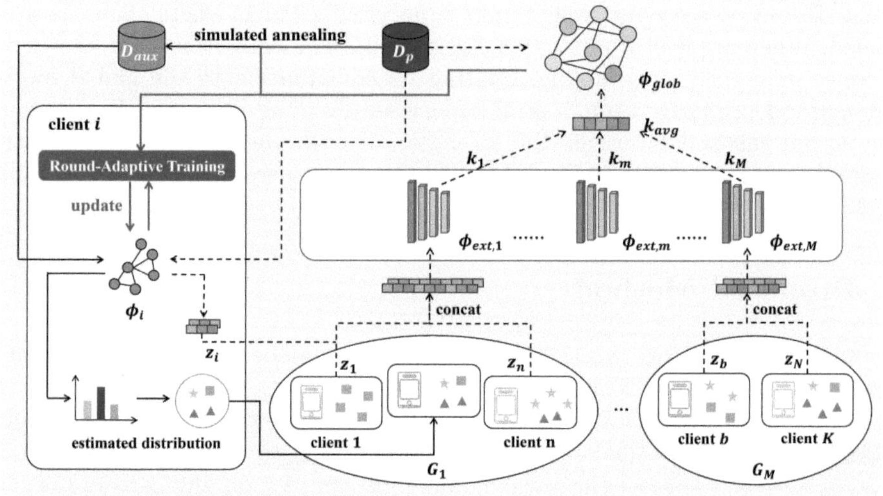

Fig. 1. Collaborative training via estimation, grouping, and distillation.

Data Distribution Estimation. Since the local data of clients are unlabeled, it is not possible to know the exact data distribution of each client. Thus, GKD-SSFL infers the local data distribution of each client by evaluating the client model's predictive performance on samples from various classes.

We construct an auxiliary dataset $\boldsymbol{D}_{aux}$ by performing stratified sampling on $\boldsymbol{D}_p$ for efficient estimation, eliminating the need for ground-truth labels. Specifically, For class j, stratified sampling produces a subset $\boldsymbol{D}^j_{aux} = \{(x^{(i)}, y^{(i)}) \in \boldsymbol{D}_p | i \in I_j\}$, where I_j denotes a set of indices randomly sampled from class j and $|\boldsymbol{D}^j_{aux}| = U$. Subsequently, the subsets from each class are merged into a unified representative set, forming the final dataset $\boldsymbol{D}_{aux} = \sum_{j=1}^{C} \boldsymbol{D}^j_{aux}$ where C denotes the total number of classes. $\boldsymbol{D}_{aux}$ is a balanced set of U samples per class, which enables an accurate assessment of the client's predictive performance on each class, thereby facilitating the inference of the client's latent data distribution.

For classification tasks, the dimensionality of model's final layer corresponds to the number of classes. Assume $W = [w_1, w_2, \ldots, w_C]$ represents the weight matrix of the output layer. Existing work [17] has demonstrated that the squared expectation of the gradient exhibits a correlation with the number of samples per class, as follows:

$$\frac{E||\nabla L_{aux}(w_i)||^2}{E||\nabla L_{aux}(w_j)||^2} \approx \frac{n_i^2}{n_j^2}, \tag{3}$$

where $\nabla L(w_i)$ denotes the gradient with respect to the weights of the i-th neuron, and n_i is the number of training samples belonging to class i. Therefore, the data distribution of each client can be approximately inferred by leveraging this relationship.

For each model, the gradient vector $\{\nabla L_{aux}(w_1), \nabla L_{aux}(w_2), \ldots, \nabla L_{aux}(w_C)\}$ can be computed during its training on $\boldsymbol{D}_{aux}$. Then, for class i, the class ratio R_i can be estimated as:

$$R_i = \frac{e^{\frac{\theta}{||\nabla L_{aux}(w_i)||^2}}}{\sum_j e^{\frac{\theta}{||\nabla L_{aux}(w_j)||^2}}}. \tag{4}$$

where θ is a hyperparameter that controls the normalization among classes, experimentally set to 5. Following this procedure, we can derive the composition vector $R = [R_1, ..., R_C]$ that reflects the client data distribution.

As shown in Fig. 2, the estimated distribution closely aligns with the actual distribution. In a heavily skewed distribution where one class is particularly dominant, our method accurately identifies and emphasizes this majority class. Furthermore, in more balanced scenarios, it not only correctly recognizes the major classes but also reliably estimates non-negligible probabilities for minority classes, demonstrating the validity of our distribution estimation approach.

As clients incorporate additional knowledge during training, the data distribution evolves dynamically. GKD-SSFL dynamically assesses the evolving data distribution throughout the training process. This capability to track distributional shifts provides fine-grained guidance, which in turn enables more accurate and effective client grouping.

Client Grouping. After obtaining the estimation of clients' data distribution, we group them to ensure that the overall data distribution across the groups is relatively balanced. In our work, we use simulated annealing [18,19] to achieve it.

Initially, each client forms a singleton group, such that we have N initial groups $G = \{G_1, G_2, ..., G_N\}$ with $|G_n| = 1 (1 \leq n \leq N)$. Subsequently, client assignments are iteratively adjusted to minimize the total variance across all groups.

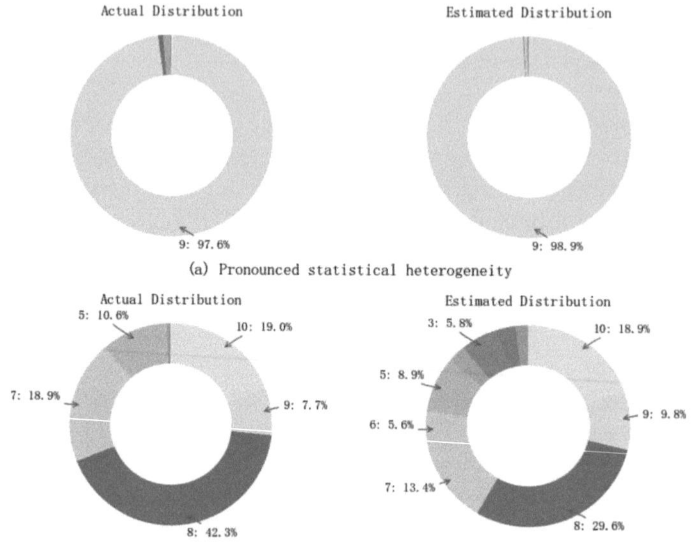

(a) Pronounced statistical heterogeneity

(b) Moderate statistical heterogeneity

Fig. 2. Comparison of the actual distribution and the estimated distribution on CIFAR-10 under two different data distributions.

In each iteration, a new client grouping is generated by stochastically applying one of two following operations: (1) randomly select two groups and merge the clients within them; (2) randomly select a group, and if the group contains more than two clients, split it into two groups. After completing the operation, empty groups are removed and a new grouping $G = \{G_1, G_2, ..., G_M\}(M \leq N)$ is obtained. To minimize inter-group differences, we compute an overall divergence metric across all groups and compare the value between the original and the new grouping, where a smaller value indicates a better grouping. If the new solution is superior, it is accepted unconditionally; otherwise, it is accepted with a certain probability to avoid getting stuck in local optima. The process continues iteratively until no better solution is found over a number of consecutive rounds.

To speed up training, we regroup clients every T rounds. When T is too large, the ongoing training of client models may lead to inaccuracies in current groupings, thereby harming the quality of knowledge used to train the global model. Conversely, if T is too small, it will lead to higher resource expenditure on the server and fail to sufficiently learn the knowledge of clients within that group. Therefore, it is crucial to select an appropriate T. Subsequent experiments also verify that T affects model performance.

Feature Extraction. For each group G_j, the number of clients typically exceeds one, and multiple models within a group may contain redundant or irrelevant information. Therefore, a key challenge is how to effectively aggregate knowledge from multiple clients to extract useful information to guide the training of the global model. GKD-SSFL chooses to train a feature extractor to compress the knowledge from multiple clients within a group.

Since the knowledge output by the client model is already highly distilled, and this operation is relatively straightforward, we just use a Multilayer Perceptron (MLP) as the model, denoted as $\phi_{ext,j}$ for G_j. Due to its limited number of parameters, $\phi_{ext,j}$ only requires a small amount of data for pre-training. Having obtained the clients output on $\boldsymbol{D}_{aux}$, in addition to being used for clients grouping, we concatenate the outputs of all members in G_j to get $GK_j = \{z_{j_0}; z_{j_1}; ...\}$, where z_{j_i} is the output of i-th member. GK_j is the input of $\phi_{ext,j}$, and its output layer shares the same dimensionality as that of the global model. The extraction model is trained for R_e times in each round, using a supervised loss:

$$\mathcal{L}_{ext,j} = -\frac{1}{C \times U} \sum_{c=1}^{C} \sum_{i=1}^{U} y^{(c,i)} log(f(GK_j^{(c,i)}; \phi_{ext,j})), \tag{5}$$

where C is the total number of classes and U is the number of samples per class. $GK_j^{(c,i)}$ denotes the input for the i-th sample belonging to class c, and $y^{(c,i)}$ is the corresponding label. Based on this approach, we aim to capture the essential information contained in diverse client features, thereby providing more effective guidance for global model training.

Global Knowledge Distillation. After training the feature extractors for each group, we compute the combined output k_j of group G_j on $\boldsymbol{D}_p$. Then the group knowledge will be averaged and utilized for global model training:

$$k_{avg} = \frac{1}{M} \sum_{i=1}^{M} k_i, \tag{6}$$

where M is the total number of groups. The update is performed according to (1), and $\mathcal{L}_{KL}$ can be formulated as:

$$\mathcal{L}_{KL} = \tau^2 \cdot KL(softmax(\frac{k_{avg}}{\tau})||softmax(\frac{z_{glob}}{\tau})). \tag{7}$$

where z_{glob} is the output of global model.

3.2 Round-Adaptive Training

Each client k possesses a local unlabeled dataset $\boldsymbol{D}_k$, and its local model ϕ_k is trained using data augmentation to effectively leverage the limited informational content of the unsupervised data.

The local dataset is partitioned into multiple batches, and let $\mathcal{B}$ denote a single batch. For each sample $x^{(i)} \in \mathcal{B}$, we apply augmentation to obtain $\tilde{x}^{(i)}$, forming an augmented batch $\tilde{\mathcal{B}}$. The output of client k can be written as $f_k(x^{(i)}; \phi_k)$ and $f_k(\tilde{x}^{(i)}; \phi_k)$ respectively. So the contrastive loss can be written as:

$$\mathcal{L}_{cl} = -log \frac{exp(\frac{sim(f(x^{(i)};\phi_k), f(\tilde{x}^{(i)};, \phi_k))}{\tau_{local}})}{\sum_{x^{(j)} \in (\mathcal{B} \cup \tilde{\mathcal{B}} - \{x^{(i)}\})} exp(\frac{sim(f(x^{(i)};\phi_k), f(x^{(j)};\phi_k))}{\tau_{local}})}. \tag{8}$$

For an anchor sample, it has a positive sample and $2|\mathcal{B}| - 2$ negative samples. τ_{local} is a hyperparameter used to adjust the sharpness of the distribution [16]. When τ_{local} is relatively low, the probability distribution becomes sharper, causing the model focus primarily on the maximum value in the logits. And as τ_{local} gradually increases, the distribution smooths out, blurring the boundaries between sample classes and capturing relative information between different classes.

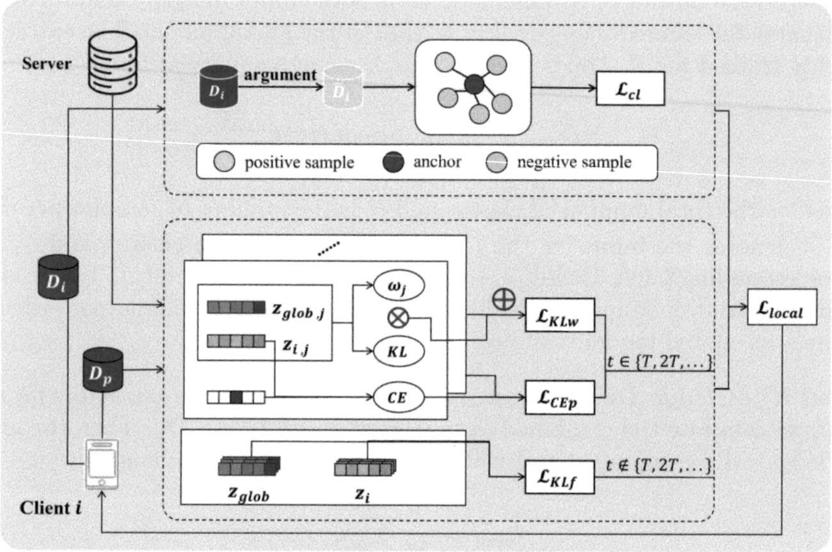

Fig. 3. Round-adaptive training.

Furthermore, due to the lack of task-specific supervision signals on clients, the locally trained models tend to contain substantial redundant information. In contrast, the global model not only aggregates knowledge from multiple clients but also undergoes supervised learning on a public dataset, enabling it to serve as a knowledge source to guide the training of local client models. Since client grouping is performed every T rounds, it is critical to ensure that the data distribution on clients remains relatively consistent during the intermediate rounds. At the same time, our method seeks to enhance the performance of client models. Therefore, we propose round-adaptive training strategy illustrated in the Fig. 3.

From round $nT+1$ to $(n+1)T-1$, we utilize the knowledge from the global model to fine-tune the update of client models by introducing KL loss:

$$\mathcal{L}_{KLf}(z_{glob}, z_i) = \tau_{local}^2 \cdot KL(softmax(\frac{z_{glob}}{\tau_{local}})||softmax(\frac{z_i}{\tau_{local}})), \quad (9)$$

where z_{glob} and z_i represent the outputs of the global model and local model respectively. And at round $t = nT$, by not having to consider changes in client data distribution, GKD-SSFL employs the samples on $\boldsymbol{D}_p$ for supervised training and dynamically adjusts the strength of knowledge transfer from the global model according to its performance improvement over the local model.

For sample $(x^{(j)}, y^{(j)}) \in \boldsymbol{D}_p$, we compute the divergence between global model and local model to determine the weight w_j:

$$w^{(j)} = \sigma(\mathcal{L}_{CE}(y^{(j)}, f(x^{(j)}; \phi_i)) - \mathcal{L}_{CE}(y^{(j)}, f(x^{(j)}; \phi_{glob}))), \tag{10}$$

where $\sigma(\cdot)$ is used to keep the weight within the range of 0–1. And the KL loss is calculated by the weighted sample summation based on the obtained values:

$$\mathcal{L}_{KLw}(z_{glob}, z_i) = \tau_{local}^2 \sum_{j=1}^{|\boldsymbol{D}_p|} w^{(j)} \cdot < softmax(\frac{z_{glob}^{(j)}}{\tau_{local}}), softmax(\frac{z_i^{(j)}}{\tau_{local}}) > . \tag{11}$$

4 Experiment

4.1 Experiment Settings

Datasets. To evaluate our method, we conduct experiments with FMNIST (FMNIST) [20], CIFAR-10 [21], and CIFAR-100 [21],using the Dirichlet distribution function $Dir(\gamma)$ [22] to partition the original dataset, generating varied distributions for different clients. Here, γ controls the degree of heterogeneity, with smaller values indicating higher levels of heterogeneity. We set γ to 0.1 (severe heterogeneity) and 0.5 (reduced heterogeneity) for the experiments. As γ decreases, the differences in data distribution among the clients become increasingly pronounced, making global model training more challenging.

Moreover, the size of the public dataset plays a crucial role in influencing the performance of the global model. To thoroughly evaluate the robustness and generalizability of our proposed method, we conduct experiments using two different sizes of public datasets $|\boldsymbol{D}_p|$ for each benchmark dataset.

Baselines. We compare GKD-SSFL against two categories of approaches:

1. Incorporating SSL methods (e.g. UDA [10] and FixMatch [9]) into client model training in traditional FL algorithms (e.g., FedAvg [1], FedProx [23]);

2. Existing SSFL methods, including: (1) FedMatch [4] decomposes model parameters into dense supervised and sparse unsupervised components to separate training on labeled and unlabeled data. (2) SemiFL [5] improves pseudo-label quality by alternating training, fine-tuning the global model and generating pseudo-labels exclusively from the global model. (3) FedFAME [24] performs local training based on model contrast loss and distillation loss, and then combines it with labeled data from the server side for supervised fine-tuning.

4.2 Model Accuracy

To evaluate the effectiveness of GKD-SSFL, we compared its performance with that of global models obtained using different methods. The experiments, which involve varying degrees of statistical heterogeneity and public datasets of different sizes, have results shown in Table 1. Overall, GKD-SSFL achieves consistent and substantial performance gains across all experimental settings.

Two categories of methods are compared, and it's found that existing SSFL methods do not show a significant performance improvement, and often exhibit a decline in performance. However, GKD-SSFL consistently maintains a stable performance improvement. Compared to the second-best method, it achieves performance gains of up to 0.85%, 5.06%, and 6% on the FMNIST, CIFAR-10 and CIFAR-100 datasets, respectively. This indicates that as task difficulty increases, the advantages of GKD-SSFL become more pronounced, leading to more significant performance improvements. Furthermore, in most cases, the performance of global models decreases as the size of the public dataset decreases. Among these, our method exhibits the least performance degradation, indicating that it possesses superior generalization capabilities compared to other methods.

Table 1. Model accuracy on three datasets

	$\|D_p\|$	γ	FedAvg		FedProx		Fed	Semi	Fed	GKD-
			UDA	FixMatch	UDA	FixMatch	Match	FL	FAME	SSFL
FMNIST	2100	0.1	89.94	89.92	89.95	89.92	89.9	90.2	83.74	**91.01**
		0.5	87.51	87.34	87.46	87.28	87.47	88.26	82.86	**89.11**
	700	0.1	82.61	82.19	82.59	82.12	81.1	83.89	76.92	**84.51**
		0.5	84.24	84.05	84.35	84.07	83.19	85.51	80.74	**86.27**
CIFAR-10	2100	0.1	45.02	43.92	44.89	43.74	46.61	50.07	43.69	**50.91**
		0.5	43.91	43.08	43.9	43.3	44.74	47.72	41.93	**50.02**
	700	0.1	34.22	31.58	34.23	31.29	36.56	39.05	38.64	**42.64**
		0.5	33.87	30.95	33.68	31.08	34.61	37.54	37.8	**42.86**
CIFAR-100	2100	0.1	10.72	13.98	10.8	14.35	18.84	13.02	9.02	**25.05**
		0.5	9.9	12.65	9.96	12.46	18.53	12.8	7.7	**23.33**
	700	0.1	10.64	12.72	10.8	12.37	12.11	-	7.9	**18.82**
		0.5	9.02	11.52	8.88	11.54	11.26	10.48	8.83	**17.26**

4.3 Model Heterogenity

GKD-SSFL employs KD to address the inherent model heterogeneity in FL. Generally, larger models typically achieve superior performance by capturing more complex knowledge with their greater representational capacity. This study systematically examines how model performance varies with different settings of global and client models. We evaluate two model types (ResNet9 and two-layer CNNs) across two settings on CIFAR-100, with results presented in Table 2.

While the homogeneous use of large models yields better performance, our method in the heterogeneous setting effectively harnesses knowledge from smaller models to narrow the performance gap, thus establishing performance parity for the global model. As the size of the public dataset increases, the performance gap between the two cases gradually diminishes. This indicates that with sufficient data for information exchange among client models, the deficiency in feature extraction of client models can be overcome, leading to excellent performance. The experiments validate the effectiveness of GKD-SSFL.

Table 2. Experiments on model heterogeneity with CIFAR-100

Server	Clients	$\|\boldsymbol{D}_p\|$=6000		$\|\boldsymbol{D}_p\|$=3600		$\|\boldsymbol{D}_p\|$=1800	
		γ=0.1	γ=0.5	γ=0.1	γ=0.5	γ=0.1	γ=0.5
ResNet9	CNNs	30.72	27.72	23.72	21.72	15.58	15.43
ResNet9	ResNet9	30.47	27.87	25.05	23.33	18.82	17.26

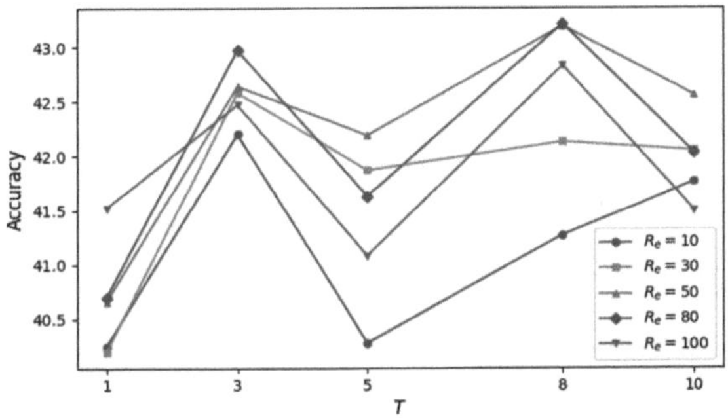

Fig. 4. Effect of hyperparameters R_e and T on CIFAR-10 with $\gamma = 0.1$.

4.4 Hyperparameter Study

Effect of hyperparameters R_e and T. GKD-SSFL trains one feature extractor per group to compress the features of individual clients and obtain higher-quality knowledge. We achieve this objective using the auxiliary dataset; however, given its limited size, we must carefully regulate the number of training epochs R_e to prevent overfitting. Furthermore, the grouping frequency T must also be set to an appropriate value to prevent performance degradation caused by either excessive regrouping or overly rigid client partitions. Therefore, we conduct experiments on these two hyperparameters with the results presented in Fig. 4. As R_e increases, model performance first improves steadily by acquiring more knowledge through additional training, peaks at an optimum, and then gradually declines, because further training causes the model to overfit to noise and interference rather than useful patterns. Regarding hyperparameter T, the performance of most models attains a local optimum at T is 3 or 8. Overall, when R_e is relatively small, model performance peaks at $T = 3$, whereas with larger R_e, the peak occurs at $T = 8$. Taken together, the optimal solution corresponds to a smaller R_e as T gets larger.

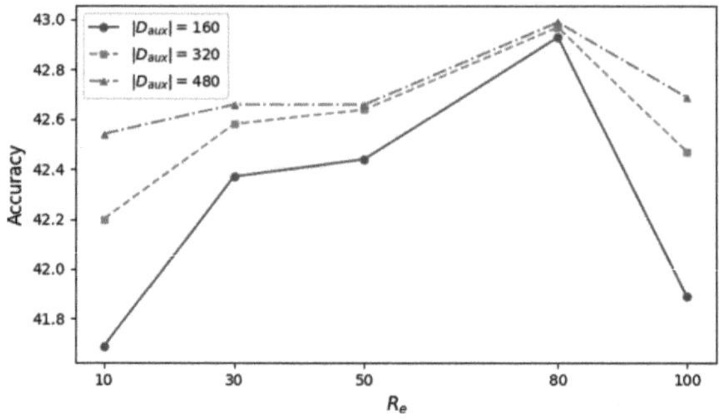

Fig. 5. Effect of hyperparameter $|\boldsymbol{D}_{aux}|$ on CIFAR-10 with $\gamma = 0.1$.

Effect of hyperparameter $|\boldsymbol{D}_{aux}|$. $\boldsymbol{D}_{aux}$ is used for grouping as well as the training of feature extractors. In general, this dataset will be small in size, therefore, we want to explore the effect of the size of $\boldsymbol{D}_{aux}$ on the model performance, and it is investigated on the CIFAR-10 dataset of $p = 0.1$. As shown in Fig. 5, the model's performance improves with increasing auxiliary dataset size, demonstrating that a larger dataset enables more precise client grouping and richer knowledge extraction. However, as $\boldsymbol{D}_{aux}$ expands, The performance gains gradually diminish, because the size of $\boldsymbol{D}_{aux}$ is already sufficient to fully capture the data distribution; further increases in the dataset will have no impact on the prediction results. Furthermore, the feature extractor has already learned to capture most of the relevant information, and the additional insights that can be gleaned from subsequent data additions become limited.

Table 3. Ablation Studies on Different Components Across Three Datasets.

CG	RAT	FMNIST				CIFAR-10				CIFAR-100			
		$\|\boldsymbol{D}_p\|$=2100		$\|\boldsymbol{D}_p\|$=700		$\|\boldsymbol{D}_p\|$=1800		$\|\boldsymbol{D}_p\|$=600		$\|\boldsymbol{D}_p\|$=3600		$\|\boldsymbol{D}_p\|$=1800	
		γ=0.1	γ=0.5	γ=0.1	γ=0.5	γ=0.1	γ=0.5	γ=0.1	γ=0.5	γ=0.1	γ=0.5	γ=0.1	γ=0.5
✓	✓	**91.01**	**89.11**	**84.51**	**86.27**	**50.91**	**50.02**	**42.64**	**42.86**	**25.05**	**23.33**	**18.82**	**17.26**
✓		90.54	88.82	84.43	86.24	49.79	49.25	39.51	39.04	23.99	22.03	18.77	16.72
	✓	90.63	88.9	84.18	85.95	49.94	49.34	41.55	41.49	23.41	22.75	18.67	16.87
		90.43	88.24	84.03	85.92	49.63	49.28	38.78	38.71	23.12	21.91	18.57	16.49

4.5 Ablation Study

In GKD-SSFL, data distribution estimation serves as a prerequisite for client grouping, while knowledge distillation is adopted to transfer the group knowledge to the global model. These components are tightly coupled, forming a complete pipeline that aims to fully exploit the knowledge embedded in individual clients, with client grouping being the core step of the framework. Meanwhile, clients employ round-adaptive training strategy to align with the server's training process, improving their own performance while providing useful knowledge to the global model. In this section, we conduct ablation experiments to validate the effectiveness of these two modules. Without client grouping (CG) is equivalent to treating each client as an independent group, and similarly, the absence of round-adaptive training (RAT) corresponds to clients training their own models using an identical objective in each round. The results in Table 3 indicate that disabling either module individually results in a decrease in accuracy, while removing both incurs larger penalty. It achieved a maximum reduction of 0.87% on FMNIST, and reductions of 4.15 and 1.93% on CIFAR-10 and CIFAR-100, respectively. The variation in model performance across different settings clearly demonstrates the effectiveness of these two modules in GKD-SSFL.

Table 4. Experiments with different feature extractors on CIFAR-10

Feature extractor	$\|\boldsymbol{D}_p\|$=1800		$\|\boldsymbol{D}_p\|$=600	
	γ=0.1	γ=0.5	γ=0.1	γ=0.5
Weighted aggregation	50.24	47.75	40.51	40
Attention	49.81	46.99	41.82	41.19
One layer	49.23	**50.43**	**43.19**	41.55
Two layers	**50.91**	50.02	42.64	**42.86**

After all clients have been grouped, each group trains a feature extractor to integrate the knowledge of its members and extract useful information. In GKD-SSFL, we employ linear layers for this purpose. Table 4 compares our method against other feature extraction approaches. The results show that the best performance is consistently obtained using either a single linear layer or two. Our method outperforms existing approaches, achieving gains of up to 3.44% over attention mechanisms and 2.86% over weighted aggregation. This indicates that our simple linear architecture effectively aggregates distributed client knowledge into unified representations for model training, confirming the soundness of our design.

5 Conclusion

In this paper, we propose GKD-SSFL, a novel SSFL framework that effectively addresses the challenge of global model training in heterogeneous settings. It constructs an "Estimation-Grouping-Distillation" process, which first estimates client distributions, then forms homogeneous groups, and finally enables efficient knowledge fusion. For the clients, it also develops a round-adaptive training strategy specifically. The framework is highly flexible and extensible, with replaceable components. We conduct comprehensive evaluations of GKD-SSFL on three recognized benchmark datasets across various configurations, demonstrating its marked improvements over alternative baselines. While our method benefits from a public dataset, such data may be unavailable in practice under some circumstances, so overcoming this requirement will be an important direction for future work.

Acknowledgments. This work was supported by Natural Science Foundation of Shanghai (No. 25ZR1401100).

References

1. McMahan, B., Moore, E., Ramage, D., et al.: Communication-efficient learning of deep networks from decentralized data. In: Artificial intelligence and statistics. pp. 1273–1282. PMLR (2017)
2. Chan, Y.H., Ngai, E.C.: Exploiting features and logits in heterogeneous federated learning. Comput. Netw. **264**, 111271 (2025)
3. Song, Z., Yang, X., Zhang, Y., Fu, X., Xu, Z., King, I.: A systematic survey on federated semi-supervised learning. In: IJCAI. vol. 16, p. 18 (2024)
4. Jeong, W., Yoon, J., Yang, E., et al.: Federated semi-supervised learning with inter-client consistency and disjoint learning. In: ICLR (2021)
5. Diao, E., Ding, J., Tarokh, V.: Semifl: semi-supervised federated learning for unlabeled clients with alternate training. Adv. Neural. Inf. Process. Syst. **35**, 17871–17884 (2022)
6. Hinton, G., Vinyals, O., Dean, J.: Distilling the knowledge in a neural network (2015). arXiv:1503.02531 arXiv preprint
7. Bai, S., Li, S., Zhuang, W., Zhang, J., Yang, K., Hou, J., Yi, S., Zhang, S., Gao, J.: Combating data imbalances in federated semi-supervised learning with dual regulators. In: Proceedings of the AAAI Conference on Artificial Intelligence, vol. 38, pp. 10989–10997 (2024)
8. Shen, N., Xu, T., Huang, S., Chen, Z., Li, J.: Dynamic client distillation for semi-supervised federated learning in a realistic scenario. IEEE Trans. Med. Imaging (2025)
9. Sohn, K., Berthelot, D., Carlini, N., et al.: Fixmatch: simplifying semi-supervised learning with consistency and confidence. Adv. Neural. Inf. Process. Syst. **33**, 596–608 (2020)
10. Xie, Q., Dai, Z., Hovy, E., et al.: Unsupervised data augmentation for consistency training. Adv. Neural. Inf. Process. Syst. **33**, 6256–6268 (2020)

11. Xu, B., Cheng, L., Wen, Q., Zou, Z., Hu, X., Dong, Z., Qi, J.: Heterogeneous federated learning driven by multi-knowledge distillation. IEEE Trans. Mob. Comput. (2025)
12. Yao, D., Pan, W., Dai, Y., et al.: Fedgkd: toward heterogeneous federated learning via global knowledge distillation. IEEE Trans. Comput. **73**(1), 3–17 (2023)
13. Liu, J., Zeng, Q., Xu, H., et al.: Adaptive block-wise regularization and knowledge distillation for enhancing federated learning. IEEE/ACM Trans. Network. **32**(1), 791–805 (2023)
14. Itahara, S., Nishio, T., Koda, Y., et al.: Distillation-based semi-supervised federated learning for communication-efficient collaborative training with non-iid private data. IEEE Trans. Mob. Comput. **22**(1), 191–205 (2021)
15. Zheng, X., Ying, S., Zheng, F., et al.: Federated learning on non-iid data via local and global distillation. In: ICWS. pp. 647–657. IEEE (2023)
16. Chandrasegaran, K., Tran, N.T., Zhao, Y.: Revisiting label smoothing and knowledge distillation compatibility: What was missing? In: International Conference on Machine Learning, pp. 2890–2916 (2022). PMLR
17. Yang, M., Wang, X., Zhu, H., et al.: Federated learning with class imbalance reduction. In: EUSIPCO, pp. 2174–2178. IEEE (2021)
18. Van, P.J.M.L., Aarts, E.H.L.: Simulated Annealing: Theory and Applications. D.Reidel Publishing Company (1987)
19. Solat, F., Patni, S., Lim, S.: Heterogeneous privacy level-based client selection for hybrid federated and centralized learning in mobile edge computing. IEEE Access (2024)
20. Xiao, H., Rasul, K., Vollgraf, R.: Fashion-mnist: a novel image dataset for benchmarking machine learning algorithms (2017). arXiv:1708.07747 arXiv preprint
21. Krizhevsky, A., Hinton, G.: Learning multiple layers of features from tiny images (2009)
22. Zhao, Y., Li, M., Lai, L., et al.: Federated learning with non-iid data. Neurocomputing **465**, 371–380 (2021)
23. Li, T., Sahu, A.K., Zaheer, M., et al.: Federated optimization in heterogeneous networks. Proc. Mach. Learn. Syst. **2**, 429–450 (2020)
24. Malaviya, S., Shukla, M., Korat, P.: Fedfame: A data augmentation free framework based on model contrastive learning for federated semi-supervised learning. In: Proceedings of the 38th ACM/SIGAPP Symposium on Applied Computing, pp. 1114–1121 (2023)

Database Engineering

AptMem: Adaptive Page Profiling and Placement for Heterogeneous Memory Systems

Shan Liu[1], Hong Gao[1(✉)], Lina Chen[1], and Jinbao Wang[2]

[1] College of Computer Science and Technology, Zhejiang Normal University, Jinhua, China
honggao@zjnu.edu.cn
[2] Faculty of Computing, Harbin Institute of Technology, Weihai, China

Abstract. With the rapid development of memory-intensive applications, traditional DRAM–SSD systems face a contradiction between capacity constraints and access performance. Although NVM bridges the gap between the two in terms of capacity and latency, its higher access latency and write overhead limit its ability to directly replace DRAM. Consequently, existing research seeks a trade-off between capacity expansion and access performance by constructing DRAM–NVM hybrid memory systems. However, as these systems rely heavily on page management strategies, improper data placement and migration can degrade performance and increase NVM write overhead. To address this, we propose AptMem, an adaptive page management mechanism for horizontal DRAM–NVM hybrid memory. AptMem achieves hot/cold page identification by jointly modeling short-term access behavior and long-term activity of pages. It employs a dirty-page-aware asymmetric hot page promotion strategy, ensuring write-intensive pages preferentially reside in DRAM while read-intensive pages follow a conservative migration path, thereby reducing NVM write pressure and invalid migrations. Furthermore, AptMem introduces a threshold self-adaptation mechanism based on runtime cost feedback, allowing hot/cold page determination to dynamically adapt to workload changes. Experimental results based on YCSB workloads show that AptMem enables more effective hot/cold page identification and cross-tier migration management, achieving a better balance between system performance and storage overhead under dynamic workloads.

Keywords: Hybrid memory systems · NVM · Page management · Hot/cold page identification · Adaptive systems

1 Introduction

With the rapid development of memory-intensive applications, modern computing systems face increasingly prominent contradictions between capacity and

L. Ding et al. (Eds.): APWeb-WAIM 2026, LNCS 16993, pp. 83–98, 2027.
https://doi.org/10.1007/978-981-92-5693-8_6

performance within the memory-storage hierarchy [1]. In traditional DRAM–SSD architectures, limited DRAM capacity and lower SSD access performance make frequent data swapping a major system bottleneck [2]. To alleviate these issues, emerging NVM [3,4] has been introduced, offering byte-addressability and a trade-off between capacity and performance. However, its high write overhead and limited write endurance make it difficult to directly replace DRAM [5,6]. Therefore, constructing an efficient DRAM–NVM hybrid memory system is key to achieving high-performance and large-capacity main memory [7].

Regarding the organization of DRAM–NVM hybrid memory systems, existing research primarily adopts either cached vertical architectures or flat horizontal architectures. The former treats DRAM as a cache for NVM to reduce access latency through cache hits, but its performance depends heavily on the hit rate, making it difficult to consistently avoid high-latency access under dynamic workloads. Consequently, the latter treats DRAM and NVM as parallel main memory resources, with system software explicitly managing data placement, providing greater flexibility for page allocation and migration. However, the performance of this architecture relies on the effectiveness of hot/cold page identification and migration strategies. Existing methods mostly rely on fixed or single access features, which are prone to misjudgment and introduce additional migration and write overheads, thereby limiting overall performance gains.

To address these issues, this paper proposes AptMem, an adaptive page management mechanism for horizontal DRAM–NVM heterogeneous memory. Unlike traditional migration strategies based on single observations, AptMem transforms page management from instantaneous decision-making into a dynamic process driven by multi-stage verification and feedback. By jointly characterizing short-term activity and long-term residency features of pages, AptMem employs a progressive cold page demotion strategy and a dirty-page-aware asymmetric hot page promotion strategy. Combined with a runtime cost-feedback mechanism for adaptive threshold adjustment, AptMem reduces NVM write pressure while improving system stability and resource utilization efficiency. The main contributions of this paper are as follows:

(1) AptMem Framework: We propose an adaptive DRAM–NVM framework using progressive demotion and dirty-aware promotion to filter transient hotspots and reduce migration and write overhead.

(2) Threshold Adaptation: We design a cost-feedback mechanism to dynamically adjust hot/cold boundaries, achieving a stable balance between performance and overhead under varying workloads.

2 Background and Related Work

2.1 Hybrid Memory Architectures

As discussed in the introduction, the significant disparities in latency and capacity among DRAM, NVM, and SSD have driven researchers to develop multi-tiered hybrid memory systems to balance performance and capacity. In this context, existing DRAM–NVM hybrid memory architectures are primarily categorized into two types: cached vertical and flat horizontal architectures.

(a) Vertical architecture (b) Horizontal architecture

Fig. 1. Comparison of hybrid memory architectures

Cache-Mode Vertical Architecture. The Cache-mode Vertical Architecture (Fig. 1a) treats DRAM as a cache for NVM. Data placement and replacement are managed by hardware or memory controllers, expanding main memory capacity without modifying the software stack while leveraging DRAM's low latency [8–10]. However, its performance is highly dependent on the cache hit rate. Upon a DRAM cache miss, the processor must retrieve data via high-latency NVM accesses and promote it to DRAM, which extends the critical access path [8,9]. Recent studies have explored optimizing DRAM cache policies, such as introducing prefetching mechanisms to improve efficiency [11]. Nevertheless, these solutions mitigate latency gaps through caching mechanisms rather than directly addressing NVM's inherent access latency and endurance limitations.

Flat-Mode Horizontal Architecture. Unlike the Cache-mode Vertical Architecture,the Flat-mode Horizontal Architecture organizes DRAM and NVM within a unified address space (Fig. 1b). The operating system or runtime system manages data placement and migration, allowing for dynamic layout adjustments based on workloads. The core objective is to migrate hot data to DRAM to reduce latency while designing migration policies to minimize NVM writes, thereby enhancing both performance and endurance. To this end, various page management mechanisms have been proposed, including write-aware replacement policies [15], access-history-based placement [16], and fine-grained data migration methods [12,17,18]. For instance, APP-LRU [14] performs page placement based on access history but only triggers migration during replacement, making it difficult to respond timely to write-intensive NVM pages and thus increasing NVM write overhead. CLOCK-DWF [15] forces modified pages to reside in DRAM to reduce NVM writes. However, since it only passively evicts cold pages when DRAM is full, it often triggers frequent invalid migrations between media, leading to additional NVM write costs. Furthermore, some works attempt to reduce the cost of individual writes through fine-grained migration. MiniPage [12] employs cache-line-grained migration and a tier-by-tier promotion strategy to lower write overhead, though this may degrade cache efficiency in large-scale scenarios. Spitfire [13] introduces a lightweight learning mechanism for adaptive migration, yet it may still suffer from frequent migrations due to over-sensitive policies, resulting in extra NVM writes.

2.2 Hot/Cold Page Identification

In DRAM–NVM hybrid architectures, hot/cold page identification serves as the foundation for page migration decisions. Existing research primarily focuses on vertical tiering, generally categorized into two types. One category relies on hardware sampling. For instance, HeMem [19] and Memtis [20] utilize PEBS to collect access frequencies and determine hot/cold pages based on fixed or statistical thresholds, with Memtis further adjusting thresholds dynamically according to access distributions. While these methods accurately reflect access intensity, they are hardware-dependent and struggle to capture temporal variations in access behavior. Another category is software-triggered: TPP [21] and FlexMem [22] leverage page fault exceptions to trigger access recording, while Multi-Clock [23] scans page table access bits and uses multi-level clock-based lists for differentiation. However, their accuracy is constrained by fixed scanning windows and decay rules, often leading to decision lag under dynamic workloads. Additionally, AutoNUMA [24] maintain access states across multiple time windows to approximate frequency, yet their heat models remain limited by empirical parameters and static or semi-dynamic thresholds.

Existing hot/cold page identification either rely on single metrics failing to capture long-term data evolution, or depend on static thresholds imprecise under dynamic workloads. In flat-mode architectures, where hot/cold page identification dictates data placement, such limitations exacerbate performance fluctuations and hinder the trade-off between throughput and NVM endurance.

3 AptMem Architecture

3.1 Architecture Overview

Figure 2 illustrates the overall architecture of AptMem, designed for DRAM–NVM horizontal heterogeneous memory to balance performance, migration overhead, and device endurance. In practice, page management faces three primary challenges: Firstly, short-term access fluctuations often lead to misjudgments and frequent page thrashing. Secondly, the asymmetric read/write costs of NVM require migration strategies to be access-type aware to mitigate device wear. Thirdly, fixed management thresholds fail to adapt to dynamic workloads, resulting in sub-optimal system performance.To address these, AptMem employs a unified framework based on multi-stage verification and feedback. Decisions rely on temporal accumulation rather than instantaneous observations, reducing noise interference. The process consists of three collaborative modules: (1) Progressive Cold Page Demotion, transforming identification into a multi-stage validation, (2) Dirty-Page-Aware Asymmetric Promotion, balancing performance and write amplification via access-type differentiation, (3) Cost-Feedback Threshold Adaptation, dynamically adjusting hot/cold boundaries. Specifically, Age_high and

Age_low serve as asymmetric thresholds for DRAM cold-page identification and NVM hot-page filtering, respectively.

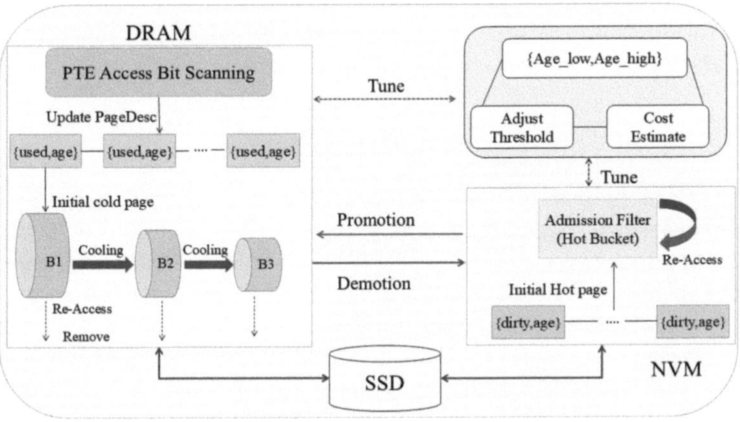

Fig. 2. AptMem overall design framework.

3.2 Dual-Dimensional Hotness Profiling

Page hotness modeling serves as the foundation for migration decisions. However, dynamic workloads make it challenging for a single dimension to accurately characterize page behavior. Frequency-based methods respond quickly but often misidentify transient bursts as stable hotspots. Conversely, methods based on historical accumulation or temporal decay reflect long-term trends but respond sluggishly to workload shifts. This inherent contradiction makes it difficult for single-dimensional approaches to balance accuracy and stability.To address this, AptMem employs a dual-dimensional hotness model, characterizing page behavior through short-term activity and long-term residency features. The short-term dimension approximates the instantaneous access state using the page table's used bit combined with periodic scanning, without introducing overhead to the critical path. The long-term dimension utilizes logical age to represent the time interval since the last access:

$$age(p) = t_{now} - t_{last\_access}(p) \tag{1}$$

where p denotes the current page, t_{now} represents the current logical time of the system, and $t_{last\_access}(p)$ is the time of the most recent access to page p. In the DRAM tier, the system increments page age through periodic scanning. Given the large capacity of NVM and the high cost of full-range scanning, AptMem adopts a partitioned sampling strategy. The NVM space is divided into multiple logical regions, and age growth is approximated by the number of logical regions traversed by the scanning pointer, thereby reducing scanning overhead.

The system maintains only lightweight page metadata, including t_{last_access}, age, and Bucket_id (detailed in Sects. 3.3 and 3.4), ensuring constant-space overhead. Notably, hotness does not directly trigger migration. Instead, it serves as input for subsequent multi-stage mechanisms. Through progressive demotion and candidate verification, transient behaviors are filtered to prevent misjudgments from escalating into unnecessary migration overhead.

3.3 Progressive Cold-Page Demotion Strategy

In DRAM–NVM hybrid memory systems, the goal of cold page demotion is to migrate low-value pages from DRAM to NVM, thereby reclaiming high-performance memory space. However, if demotion decisions rely on single observations, the system inevitably misidentifies briefly dormant hot pages as cold, leading to premature eviction. Such misjudgments directly increase cross-layer migration overhead and cause pages to oscillate between DRAM and NVM, resulting in migration thrashing that significantly degrades system stability and overall performance. To prevent transient behaviors from directly triggering migrations, AptMem proposes a progressive cold page demotion mechanism based on multi-stage verification, transforming cold page determination from a one-time decision into a gradual confirmation process. In this mechanism, the system maintains a staged coldness structure for candidate cold pages in DRAM:

$$ColdBucket = \{B_1, B_2, \ldots, B_K\} \tag{2}$$

where B_i represents the i-th coldness level bucket. Transitions between different levels involve only updates to the bucket index without triggering data movement, thereby decoupling logical state evolution from physical migration. During execution, when a page in DRAM remains unaccessed within a scanning cycle and its logical age exceeds the threshold Age_high, the system does not immediately migrate it to NVM. Instead, it marks the page as an initial cold page and inserts it into the lowest-level bucket B_1. In subsequent cycles, the page progresses toward higher levels only if it remains continuously unaccessed. If it is re-accessed, its state is immediately reset, and it exits the structure. Only when a page undergoes multi-stage verification and reaches the highest level B_K is it considered a stable cold page and becomes a candidate for demotion.

However, while progressive determination improves identification accuracy, it may introduce delays in releasing cold pages, affecting system throughput under high memory pressure. To address this, AptMem introduces a watermark-based migration mechanism. When the available DRAM space falls below the threshold W_{min}, the system enters pressure mode and prioritizes demoting pages from high-coldness buckets, ensuring space reclamation efficiency while maintaining determination accuracy. Each bucket is organized as a FIFO queue, allowing the system to evict pages that have stayed longest in the current level with constant-order $O(1)$ overhead, avoiding complex global sorting or scanning.

3.4 Dirty-Page-Aware Asymmetric Hot Page Promotion Strategy

In hybrid memory, hot page promotion aims to migrate high-value NVM pages to DRAM to optimize latency and write overhead. However, promotion strategies are easily disturbed by access fluctuations and affected by NVM read-write asymmetry. A uniform strategy is often suboptimal: failing to prioritize write-intensive pages creates continuous write pressure, while aggressively promoting all hotspots can lead to DRAM being occupied by transient accesses, reducing its utilization. Therefore, hot page promotion must, while identifying hotspots, also consider the system impact of different access types.To address this, AptMem introduces a dirty-page-aware asymmetric strategy, extending migration decisions from uniform rules to a differentiated mechanism based on write sensitivity. In this design, write-intensive pages are prioritized as high-value objects, while read-intensive pages must satisfy stricter screening criteria to prevent transient accesses from occupying DRAM resources. Whether a page enters the candidate set is determined by its logical age and the threshold Age_low, with the decision threshold dynamically adjusted based on the page's write characteristics:

$$T(p) = \begin{cases} m \cdot Age\_low, & p.dirty = 1 \\ Age\_low, & p.dirty = 0 \end{cases} \tag{3}$$

where $m > 1$ is to relax the admission criteria for dirty pages. This allows write-intensive pages to enter the candidate set at lower access intensities, prioritizing their migration to DRAM to absorb subsequent write operations. Conversely, clean pages must meet stricter conditions to avoid occupying DRAM space with short-term accesses. This asymmetric design enables the system to achieve an optimal trade-off between write amplification control and performance.

However, threshold adjustment alone cannot entirely eliminate the risk of misjudgment caused by transient hotspots. Therefore, AptMem further transforms page promotion from a direct trigger into a candidate verification process. The system constructs a flat logical verification structure in NVM:

$$HotBucket = \{P_{candidate}\} \tag{4}$$

where $P_{candidate}$ represents the set of hot page candidates. Once a page reaches the promotion threshold, it is temporarily stored in the $HotBucket$ rather than being migrated immediately. During the candidate stage, cross-layer migration is triggered only if the page is accessed again and DRAM has sufficient available space. While this verification mechanism improves identification accuracy, it may lead to candidate set expansion and increased management overhead. To prevent the HotBucket from expanding rapidly under high concurrency and becoming a performance bottleneck, AptMem implements a dynamic constraint mechanism based on system status rather than a fixed capacity limit:

$$\begin{cases} |HotBucket| \leq F_{dram} \\ \Delta|HotBucket| > 0 \text{ only if } F_{dram} > W_{min} \end{cases} \tag{5}$$

where F_{dram} represents the current available DRAM space. This constraint ensures that the candidate set size does not exceed the system's carrying capacity and allows growth only when sufficient space is available. When the system approaches a pressure state, the HotBucket stops accepting new candidates and naturally shrinks through page promotions or evictions. In implementation, the HotBucket utilizes a lightweight index structure that maintains only necessary information, such as page identifiers and logical ages, and employs a FIFO strategy to evict older entries when the capacity limit is reached, ensuring structural stability.

3.5 Cost-Feedback-Based Threshold Self-adaptation Mechanism

AptMem controls migrations via progressive demotion and dirty-aware promotion, yet performance relies on thresholds Age_high and Age_low. Determining DRAM coldness and identifying NVM hotspots, these thresholds dictate the trade-off between hotspot retention and migration overhead. However, static thresholds lack stability under dynamic workloads, local optimal configurations fail as access patterns, read/write ratios, and memory pressure fluctuate. For instance, a low Age_low accelerates hotspot capture during read-intensive phases but triggers excessive migrations under write-heavy or high-pressure scenarios. Without adaptation, persistent threshold mismatch leads to frequent migrations and degraded hit ratios, eventually compromising performance.

Consequently, static or offline tuning fails to handle dynamic workloads, necessitating continuous parameter adjustment. To this end, AptMem transforms threshold selection into a feedback-driven online optimization via local exploration. A key challenge is the coupling effect: Age_high and Age_low act on demotion and promotion paths, respectively, with their changes cross-influencing the system through page flow. Simultaneous adjustments can trigger policy oscillation or prevent convergence. To ensure robustness, AptMem adopts a single-dimension alternating optimization strategy, adjusting one threshold per round. This decomposes multi-parameter searching into stable one-dimensional steps, significantly reducing complexity. To evaluate threshold configurations, AptMem constructs a unified cost function to quantify the system's operational state:

$$Cost = \frac{\alpha \cdot R_{ssd} - \beta \cdot H_{nvm} + \gamma \cdot M_{dram \leftrightarrow nvm}}{T} \tag{6}$$

This function integrates SSD access pressure (R_{ssd}), NVM hit gain (H_{nvm}), cross-layer migration overhead ($M_{dram \leftrightarrow nvm}$), and system throughput (T). By normalizing these metrics against throughput, the system eliminates dimensional differences. Weight coefficients (α, β, γ) are used to establish a unified evaluation standard balancing performance gain and resource consumption.

The threshold update process is organized as a closed loop of trial, evaluation, and selection. If a local adjustment reduces the cost, the system continues exploring in that direction. If the cost increases, the system does not revert but accepts the change with a certain probability to avoid converging prematurely to a local optimum. This balance between exploitation and exploration allows the system to improve parameter configurations in dynamic environments.

However, relying solely on short-term observations for feedback introduces instability. Due to the phased and bursty nature of page accesses, statistical results within narrow time windows fluctuate significantly. Direct adjustments based on such noise can lead to frequent switching between configurations, causing policy thrashing. Therefore, AptMem introduces a dynamic observation window mechanism. In the early stages of operation, a shorter window is used to accelerate parameter exploration. As the system stabilizes, the window expands to incorporate longer-term statistical information, smoothing out short-term fluctuations. This adaptive transition from rapid exploration to stable decision-making achieves a balance between convergence speed and decision stability.

4 Experimental Evaluation

4.1 Experimental Setup

The experimental environment is built on a multi-tiered storage server. The core hardware configuration consists of two Intel Xeon Gold 6330 processors and a memory subsystem comprising 8×16GB DDR4 DRAM and 8×256GB Intel Optane PMEM, with PMEM configured in App Direct mode. Workloads are built using YCSB by varying dataset size (K), skewness (z), write ratio (u), and DRAM/NVM capacity. Key metrics are throughput and three normalized overheads: SSD Read/TP (access pressure), Migration/TP (DRAM-NVM migration overhead), and NVM Writes/TP (write amplification).To ensure a fair comparison, all schemes are implemented within the unified Spitfire framework. We evaluate five configurations: Spitfire-Fixed and Spitfire-Prob serve as the original migration policies in Spitfire, utilizing fixed-threshold and probabilistic migration strategies, respectively. SIEVE [25] is integrated into Spitfire as an alternative hot/cold identification mechanism based on its cache replacement logic while preserving the same migration pipeline. AptMem-Fixed isolates the benefits of our adaptive hot/cold page identification under fixed migration, while AptMem-Prob further combines adaptive identification with probabilistic migration to demonstrate overall system-level gains.

4.2 Effectiveness Analysis and Validation

This section evaluates AptMem's progressive cold page demotion, dirty-aware asymmetric hot page promotion, and cost-feedback adaptation mechanisms. Following Spitfire's official implementation and common hybrid storage practices, the default experimental parameters are fixed as follows: data skewness $z = 0.6$, write ratio $u = 0.05$, working set size $K = 512$, and capacity ratio DRAM:NVM = 1:2. This configuration establishes a controlled, moderately skewed workload baseline to objectively assess the performance benefits of our strategies.

Evaluating Core Threshold Sensitivity in AptMem. This section evaluates the parameter sensitivity of AptMem's cold page demotion and hot page promotion strategies. To isolate their effects, we vary only Age_high for demotion and only Age_low for promotion under a unified baseline workload. The resulting throughput and media pressure fluctuations are shown in Fig. 3.

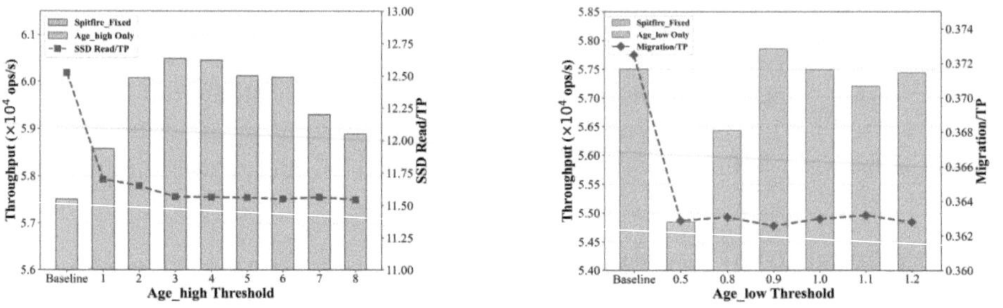

(a) Age_high (b) Age_low

Fig. 3. Impact of thresholds on system throughput and performance

Firstly, we evaluate cold page demotion by sweeping Age_high within $[1, 8]$ (Fig. 3a). Throughput peaks when $Age\_high \in [3, 4]$, outperforming Spitfire by 5.2%. Accompanied by decreased SSD reads, this confirms that an optimal threshold accurately evicts truly cold pages, freeing DRAM for high-frequency accesses. However, an excessively large Age_high retains stale cold pages in DRAM, which squeezes out hot spots, causes cache pollution, and degrades throughput. Secondly, we assess dirty-aware asymmetric promotion by varying Age_low within $[0.5, 1.2]$ (Fig. 3b). The system achieves an optimal balance at $Age\_low = 0.9$, maximizing throughput while minimizing migration overhead. By tightening the promotion standard, the system filters out read-burst-induced pseudo-hotspots, averting invalid migrations. Yet, this benefit is restricted to a narrow interval, deviating from 0.9 causes rapid throughput drops and migration overhead rebounds. In summary, while static hot/cold identification strategies improve performance, their optimal ranges are sensitive and impractically narrow. Because real-world workload characteristics evolve dynamically, static thresholds inevitably fail to maintain global optimality due to real-time parameter drift. This limitation empirically underscores the necessity of a cost-feedback adaptive regulation mechanism.

Effectiveness and Stability of Adaptive Mechanism. This section evaluates the comprehensive performance of AptMem integrated with the cost-feedback adaptive mechanism. The experiment compares the baseline Spitfire-Fixed, the static AptMem-Fixed(Static) with near-optimal thresholds, and the adaptive AptMem-Fixed to verify the system's automatic optimization capability in dynamic environments. Figure 4a shows that both AptMem versions

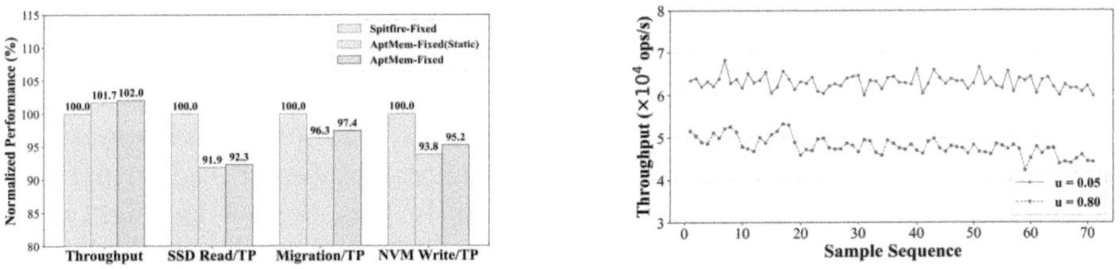

(a) Performance comparison (b) Adaptive Throughput Fluctuation

Fig. 4. Effectiveness and stability of the adaptive mechanism

comprehensively outperform Spitfire. Compared to the optimal static version equipped with prior knowledge, the adaptive version incurs only marginal exploration overhead in SSD reads, cross-tier migrations, and NVM writes. In exchange, the adaptive mechanism successfully captures runtime workload variations, further boosting overall throughput to 102.0%. This indicates that AptMem can closely approach the theoretical static optimum in core performance without manual intervention. Furthermore, Fig. 4b verifies the long-term stability of the adaptive mechanism. During the initial phase, the system achieves fast convergence through aggressive exploratory adjustments, causing brief throughput fluctuations. In later stages, the parameters converge to the optimal interval, and the fluctuations narrow significantly. Occasional jumps in the curve represent precise real-time corrections to local workload shifts rather than system oscillations. This demonstrates that the mechanism can achieve rapid response to underlying workload changes and maintain long-term high resilience at the cost of minimal fluctuations.

4.3 Impact of Environmental Factors on Performance

Impact of Access Skewness. This section evaluates the comprehensive performance of AptMem across different data skewness levels. Keeping other parameters identical to those in Sect. 4.2, we vary the Zipfian skewness z among 0.6, 0.8, and 0.9. The results are shown in Fig. 5.

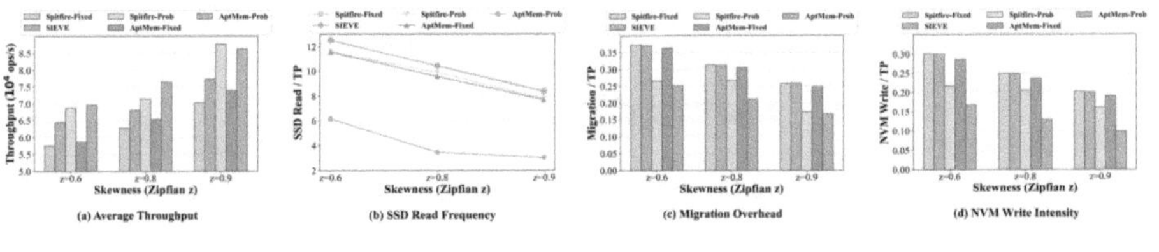

Fig. 5. Impact of access skewness.

Under moderate skewness ($z \leq 0.8$), AptMem exhibits a significant comprehensive advantage. Its multi-stage candidate verification and dirty-aware migration mechanisms effectively intercept transient access fluctuations, drastically reducing invalid cross-tier migrations and NVM write pressure. Because of this precise data retention in the memory tier, the probability of erroneously evicting high-frequency hot pages decreases significantly, which in turn alleviates the underlying SSD access overhead. Within this range, AptMem-Fixed outperforms Spitfire-Fixed in throughput, although it slightly lags behind the lightweight SIEVE algorithm in pure throughput due to the computational overhead of fine-grained management, it maintains an overwhelming advantage in reducing media wear and migration volume.When the skewness reaches an extreme level ($z = 0.9$), the vast majority of hot pages stably reside in the memory tier, shifting the system bottleneck from SSD I/O to CPU management overhead. In this low-I/O-pressure scenario, the verification and computational costs introduced by AptMem-Prob to maintain high-precision tiering become apparent, allowing the lighter-weight Spitfire-Prob to achieve a slight throughput advantage.In summary, AptMem is highly suitable for typical workloads with relatively dispersed hot and cold distributions, effectively balancing throughput and media interaction overhead. In extreme hotspot scenarios, the slight throughput degradation is essentially a deliberate trade-off, exchanging minor computational overhead for reduced media wear, which is crucial for extending the endurance of underlying non-volatile storage devices.

Impact of Write Ratio. This section aims to evaluate the performance and media overhead of AptMem under varying read-write mixed workloads, and to verify its dynamic regulation capability in high write-pressure scenarios. Keeping other system parameters constant, we progressively increase the write request ratio u in the workload from 0.05 to 0.8 to simulate various application scenarios ranging from read-intensive to write-intensive. The experimental results are shown in Fig. 6.

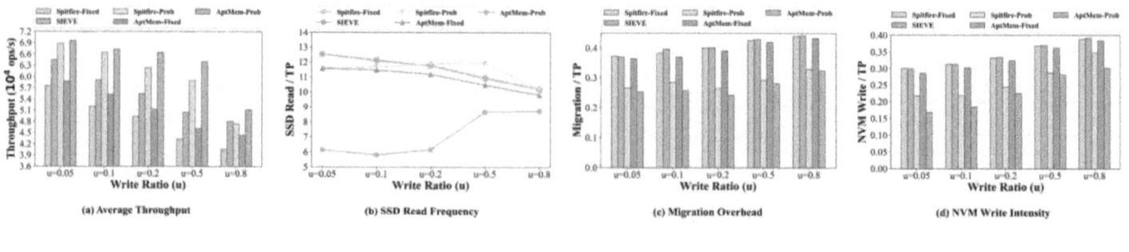

Fig. 6. Impact of write ratio

As the write ratio u increases from 0.05 to 0.8, the throughput of all systems declines due to the heavier I/O workload. AptMem-Prob consistently achieves optimal performance across all ratios, leveraging the synergy between Dirty-Page-Aware Asymmetric Hot Page Promotion and threshold adaptation to maintain low NVM write intensity and migration overhead. Notably, unlike other schemes, AptMem-Prob's SSD read frequency experiences a slight increase after

$u > 0.1$. This reflects the regulatory role of the mechanism: as the proportion of dirty pages increases, the Cost-Feedback-Based Threshold Self-Adaptation module detects NVM pressure and tightens hot/cold determination criteria. Consequently, the system selectively retains core hot data instead of promoting all accessed pages from SSD to memory tiers. Although this forces some sub-hot requests to be serviced through the SSD I/O path, it strategically trades a marginal increase in read I/O for reductions in NVM write load and migration volume. By reducing NVM write congestion, AptMem-Prob preserves bandwidth for high-frequency write requests, maintaining performance leadership.

Impact of DRAM:NVM Capacity Ratio. This section evaluates the system's performance and media overhead under varying heterogeneous memory capacity ratios to verify AptMem's dynamic regulation capability in scenarios with constrained DRAM resources and expanded NVM space. Keeping other baseline workload parameters constant, we set the DRAM:NVM capacity ratio as the sole independent variable, progressively scaling it from 1:1 to 1:7. The experimental results are shown in Fig. 7.

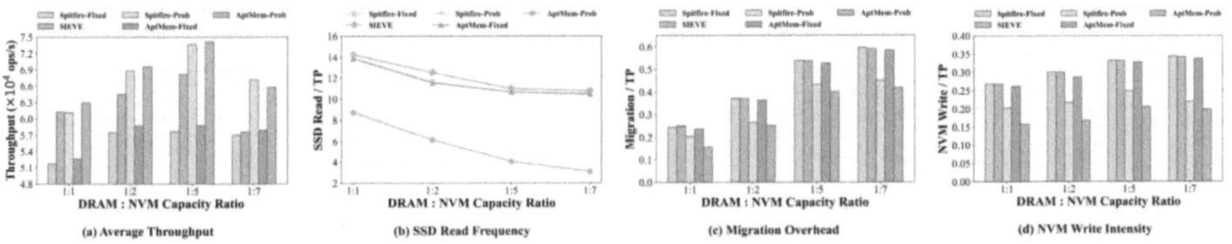

Fig. 7. Impact of DRAM:NVM capacity ratio

As the DRAM–NVM ratio scales from 1:1 to 1:7, throughput initially improves as larger NVM reduces SSD access pressure. However, diminishing returns emerge under severe DRAM constraints due to escalating inter-medium migrations and NVM writes, proving sufficient DRAM remains indispensable. Driven by cost-feedback adaptation, AptMem-Prob mitigates this by tightening Age_high to retain high-value pages in shrinking DRAM. Meanwhile, adaptive Age_low and dirty-aware promotion stabilize hot-page residency. Conversely, lacking adaptive control, Spitfire-Fixed and SIEVE experience rapidly increasing migration overhead. Under the extreme 1:7 ratio, the space for adaptive optimization shrinks, making metadata and candidate verification overheads visible, allowing the lightweight Spitfire-Prob to achieve slightly higher throughput. AptMem trades this marginal throughput loss under highly constrained DRAM for consistently lower migration overhead and reduced NVM write pressure.

Impact of Data Scale. This section evaluates the system's performance and resource scheduling capabilities under expanding dataset sizes to verify AptMem's scalability and cache management resilience for large-scale working sets.

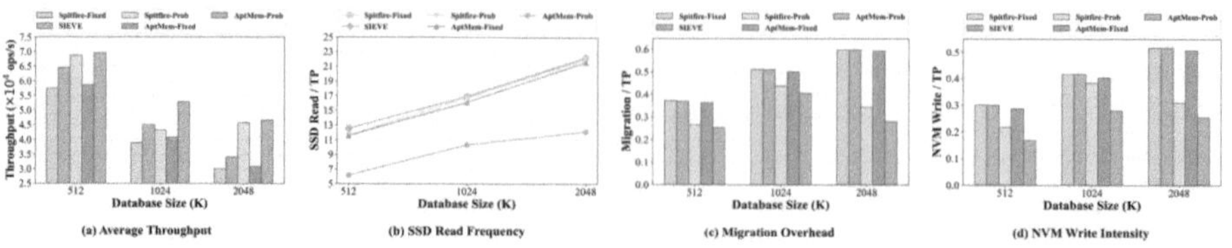

Fig. 8. Impact of data scale

Keeping other baseline workload parameters constant, we set the working set size k as the sole independent variable, progressively scaling it from 512 to 2048 to simulate severe scenarios with increasingly constrained cache capacity. The experimental results are shown in Fig. 8. As the workload size scales from 512K to 2048K, the throughput of all systems declines due to the shrinking cache-to-dataset ratio. Under such high-pressure workloads, AptMem-Prob demonstrates superior scalability, maintaining a lower growth rate in SSD read frequency by dynamically tuning Age_high and Age_low to lock onto core hot spots. Notably, in the 2048K scenario, systems like Spitfire-Fixed and SIEVE suffer from excessive migration overhead due to static identification strategies. In contrast, AptMem-Prob's migration overhead shows a slight decline. This counter-intuitive optimization stems from the synergy between progressive demotion and dirty-aware promotion: the cost-feedback mechanism tightens promotion thresholds by evaluating the benefit-to-cost ratio of NVM writes versus SSD reads. This on-demand migration strategy effectively reduces performance degradation caused by NVM write saturation, proving that AptMem maintains high I/O efficiency and resource conservation even as the data scale expands.

5 Conclusion

This paper presents AptMem, an adaptive page management mechanism for horizontal DRAM–NVM hybrid memory. By integrating short-term access flags with logical age, AptMem achieves fine-grained hot/cold profiling through dual-dimensional modeling. It employs progressive demotion and dirty-aware asymmetric promotion to minimize migration overhead, with a cost-feedback mechanism enabling dynamic threshold adjustment. Experimental results demonstrate that, rather than pursuing peak throughput under all conditions, AptMem effectively maintains robust performance in write-intensive scenarios by prioritizing the mitigation of practical deployment bottlenecks: costly cross-tier accesses and NVM write amplification. In our future work, we plan to explore fine-grained media characterization between DRAM and NVM. We aim to shift from the uniform page-level management to a finer-grained control mode, incorporating sub-page level access monitoring to precisely capture the write asymmetry of NVM and enhance its physical endurance.

Acknowledgment. This work is supported by the Key R & D Program of National Ministry of Science and Technology under Grant No. 2023YFB4503602.

References

1. Mutlu, O., Meza, J., Subramanian, L.: The main memory system: challenges and opportunities. Commun. Korean Inst. Inf. Sci. Eng. **33**(2), 16–41 (2015)
2. Koh, S., Jang, J., Lee, C.: Faster than flash: an in-depth study of system challenges for emerging ultra-low latency SSDs. In: Proceedings of IISWC, pp. 216–227. IEEE (2019)
3. Koutsoukos, D., Bhartia, R., Friedman, M.: NVM: is it not very meaningful for databases? PVLDB **16**(10), 2444–2457 (2023). https://doi.org/10.14778/3603581.3603586
4. Boukhobza, J., Rubini, S., Chen, R., et al.: Emerging NVM: a survey on architectural integration and research challenges. ACM TODAES **23**(2), 1–32 (2017)
5. Kargar, S., Nawab, F.: Challenges and future directions for energy, latency, and lifetime improvements in NVMs. Distrib. Parallel Databases **41**(3), 163–189 (2023)
6. Koshiba, A., Hirofuchi, T., Takano, R., et al.: A software-based NVM emulator supporting read/write asymmetric latencies. IEICE Trans. Inf. Syst. **102**(12), 2377–2388 (2019)
7. Arulraj, J., Pavlo, A., Malladi, K.T.: Multi-tier buffer management and storage system design for non-volatile memory (2019). arXiv:1901.10938 arXiv preprint
8. Meza, J., Chang, J., Yoon, H.B., et al.: Enabling efficient and scalable hybrid memories using fine-granularity DRAM cache management. IEEE Comput. Archit. Lett. **11**(2), 61–64 (2012)
9. Qureshi, M.K., Srinivasan, V., Rivers, J.A.: Scalable high performance main memory system using phase-change memory technology. In: Proceedings of ISCA, pp. 24–33 (2009)
10. Yoon, H.B., Meza, J., Ausavarungnirun, R.: A memory controller with row buffer locality awareness for hybrid memory systems (2018). arXiv:1804.11040 arXiv preprint
11. Subisha, V., Gohil, V., Ujjainkar, N.: Prefetching in hybrid main memory systems. In: Proceedings of HotStorage (2020)
12. Van Renen, A., Leis, V., Kemper, A.: Managing non-volatile memory in database systems. In: Proceedings of SIGMOD, pp. 1541–1555 (2018)
13. Zhou, X., Arulraj, J., Pavlo, A.: Spitfire: a three-tier buffer manager for volatile and non-volatile memory. In: Proceedings of SIGMOD, pp. 2195–2207 (2021)
14. Wu, Z., Jin, P., Yang, C., et al.: APP-LRU: a new page replacement method for PCM/DRAM-based hybrid memory systems. In: IFIP International Conference on Network and Parallel Computing, pp. 84–95. Springer, Berlin, Heidelberg (2014)
15. Lee, S., Bahn, H., Noh, S.H.: CLOCK-DWF: a write-history-aware page replacement algorithm for hybrid PCM and DRAM memory architectures. IEEE Trans. Comput. **63**(9), 2187–2200 (2013)
16. Liu, E., Hashemi, M., Swersky, K.: An imitation learning approach for cache replacement. In: International Conference on Machine Learning, pp. 6237–6247 (2020) PMLR
17. Wang, X., Jin, P., Luo, Y., et al.: Cooperative buffer management with fine-grained data migrations for hybrid memory systems. IEEE TCAD **42**(6), 1838–1851 (2022)
18. Chi, Y., Yue, J., Liao, X., et al.: A hybrid memory architecture supporting fine-grained data migration. Front. Comput. Sci. **18**(2), 182103 (2024)
19. Raybuck, A., Stamler, T., Zhang, W.: HeMem: scalable tiered memory management for big data applications and real NVM. In: Proceedings of SOSP, pp. 392–407 (2021)

20. Lee, T., Monga, S.K., Min, C.: Memtis: Efficient memory tiering with dynamic page classification and page size determination. In: Proceedings of SOSP, pp. 17–34 (2023)
21. Maruf, H.A., Wang, H., Dhanotia, A.: TPP: transparent page placement for CXL-enabled tiered-memory. In: Proceedings of ASPLOS, vol. 3, pp. 742–755 (2023)
22. Xu, D., Ryu, J., Shin, K.: FlexMem: adaptive page profiling and migration for tiered memory. In: Proceedings of USENIX ATC, pp. 817–833 (2024)
23. Maruf, A., Ghosh, A., Bhimani, J.: Multi-clock: dynamic tiering for hybrid memory systems. In: Proceedings of HPCA (2022)
24. van Riel, R., Chegu, V.: Automatic NUMA balancing. Red Hat Summit, pp. 521–534 (2014)
25. Zhang, Y., Yang, J., Yue, Y.: SIEVE is simpler than LRU: an efficient Turn-Key eviction algorithm for web caches. In: 21st USENIX Symposium on Networked Systems Design and Implementation (NSDI 24), pp. 1229–1246. USENIX Association (2024)

DSEBench: A Test Collection for Explainable Dataset Search with Examples

Qing Shi[1], Jing He[1], Qiaosheng Chen[1], Kongfa Hu[2,3], and Gong Cheng[1,4(✉)]

[1] State Key Laboratory of Novel Software Technology, Nanjing University, Nanjing 210023, China
{qingshi,522024330021,qschen}@smail.nju.edu.cn, gcheng@nju.edu.cn
[2] School of Artificial Intelligence and Information Technology, Nanjing University of Chinese Medicine, Nanjing 210023, China
kfhu@njucm.edu.cn
[3] Jiangsu Collaborative Innovation Center of Traditional Chinese Medicine in Prevention and Treatment of Tumor, Nanjing 210023, China
[4] NJU-ZZX Joint Institute for Data Science, Nanjing 210000, China

Abstract. With rapidly growing open datasets in heterogeneous formats on the Web, dataset search has been a well-established task in the Web and information retrieval research. Current approaches retrieve datasets either based on keyword queries or by identifying datasets similar to a given target dataset. These paradigms fail when the information need involves both keywords and target datasets. To address this gap, we investigate a generalized task, Dataset Search with Examples (DSE), and extend it to Explainable DSE (ExDSE), which further requires identifying relevant fields of the retrieved datasets. We construct DSEBench, the first test collection that provides high-quality dataset-level and field-level annotations to support the evaluation of DSE and ExDSE, respectively. In addition, we employ a large language model to generate extensive annotations for training purposes. We establish comprehensive baselines on DSEBench by adapting and evaluating a variety of lexical, dense, and LLM-based retrieval, reranking, and explanation methods to advance dataset search research on the Web and over big data. Our data and code are on GitHub: https://github.com/nju-websoft/DSEBench.

Keywords: Dataset search · Dataset discovery · Explainable information retrieval

1 Introduction

The Web has witnessed an explosive growth of openly available datasets in diverse formats, including RDF data, CSV files, and many others, which have become an important source of big data. This trend creates urgent opportunities and challenges for Web data management and retrieval research [20].

Qing Shi and Jing He contributed equally to this work.

L. Ding et al. (Eds.): APWeb-WAIM 2026, LNCS 16993, pp. 99–115, 2027.
https://doi.org/10.1007/978-981-92-5693-8_7

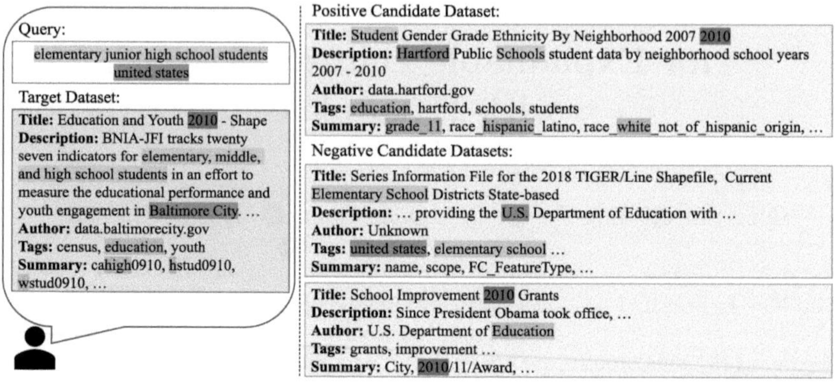

Fig. 1. An example of ExDSE. Left: The user submits a query and a target dataset. Right: The system aims to return positive candidate datasets that exhibit both relevance to the query (highlighted in yellow and green) and similarity to the target dataset (highlighted in magenta, cyan, and gray), as opposed to negative ones that are only relevant to the query or only similar to the target dataset. These judgments are supported by specific metadata and content fields.

Motivation. Efficiently and accurately finding required datasets from massive Web data repositories is a shared challenge for Web technologies and data management. Existing research follows two paradigms [20]: keyword-based search [2] that retrieves datasets *relevant to a query*, or similarity-based discovery [3] that finds datasets *similar to a target dataset*. For ordinary Web users and data scientists, describing complex data needs using keywords alone is often insufficient; providing an example dataset as a known target is a powerful and complementary way to express search intent. Indeed, the recent nlcTables [7] has demonstrated the value of this combination, but it is limited to tabular datasets. Moreover, while explainable information retrieval (IR) is trending, *explainability in dataset search* remains underexplored. Current systems provide insufficient justifications, leaving users without insight into the factors driving retrieval decisions.

To address these limitations, Fig. 1 anticipates a combined scenario. A user poses a query "elementary junior high school students united states" while providing a target dataset "Education and Youth 2010" to imply specific preferences (e.g., student indicators in 2010). A positive candidate dataset aligns with both inputs, while negative ones may match either input, but not both. Moreover, the specific fields driving these relevance and similarity judgments are pinpointed.

Task Definition. We formulate the above scenario as a generalization of established paradigms, termed *Dataset Search with Examples* (**DSE**). Given a keyword query q and a set of target datasets D_t, the task is to retrieve a list of candidate datasets D_c that are most relevant to q and, simultaneously, similar to the datasets in D_t. As an extension, *Explainable DSE* (**ExDSE**) requires identifying, for each candidate dataset $d \in D_c$, a subset of its metadata or content fields F_d that indicate d's relevance to q or similarity to D_t.

Contributions. Progress in DSE research is hindered by the lack of test collections. Existing test collections [5,13,16] are primarily designed for keyword-only inputs, while nlcTables [7] incorporates target datasets but focuses on tabular datasets; none of them provides field-level annotations for explainable dataset search. To fill this gap, **DSEBench** delivers a unified benchmark for DSE and ExDSE and establishes a research basis for the community:

- It provides high-quality human annotations for query relevance and target similarity to enable DSE evaluation, fine-grained field-level annotations for ExDSE evaluation, and synthetic annotations for training.
- We adapt a variety of retrieval, reranking, and explanation methods and evaluate them on DSEBench to establish a performance baseline.

2 Related Work

Dataset Search Benchmarks. Dataset search research broadly follows three paradigms. Relevance-based approaches retrieve datasets based on textual relevance to a query, including general-purpose systems like Google Dataset Search [2]. Their evaluation is based on established test collections including NTCIR [13], ACORDAR [5,16], and WTR [6]. Similarity-based discovery, particularly popular in the database community, aims to find datasets similar to an input dataset [20]. Test collections like LakeBench [8] provide ground truth for relational data tasks, not applicable to generalized dataset search where metadata plays a key role and data formats vary. Combined approaches such as Aurum [10] integrate keyword search with similarity-based navigation. However, Aurum itself does not provide a public test collection for systematic evaluation. A recent benchmark, nlcTables [7], introduces natural-language-conditional table discovery by combining a query table with natural-language requirements. However, it is limited to tabular datasets and does not provide field-level annotations for the evaluation of explainability. For the broader DSE setting on heterogeneous datasets, there is still no public test collection to evaluate this composite task. *Our DSEBench fills this critical gap and provides the first performance baseline for DSE.*
Explainable Dataset Search. Existing explainability research in this domain focuses on the generation of data snippets to summarize dataset content [30]. Although effective for content understanding, ExDSE further requires identifying the specific metadata fields that indicate query relevance and target similarity. This can be framed as a feature attribution problem. Following the taxonomy of explainable IR [1], post hoc methods such as LIME [21] and SHAP [17] are applicable to quantify field contributions. *Our DSEBench is among the first to provide field-level ground truth to evaluate ExDSE.*
Relevance Feedback. Relevance Feedback (RF) refines queries using user judgments on retrieved documents [22]. DSE is conceptually similar to RF: both leverage user-provided examples to guide the search process. Despite this high-level similarity, *there are fundamental differences between DSE and RF.* First,

DSE processes the query and target datasets as an initial input, unlike the iterative interaction in RF. Second, the target datasets in DSE define a desired semantic profile (e.g., specific provenance or context) that complements topicality. To capture it, directly adapting RF methods to DSE is suboptimal, as revealed by our evaluation, reflecting the unique challenges of DSE.

3 Construction of DSEBench

We constructed DSEBench by extending the English subset of NTCIR [13], a popular test collection for keyword-based dataset search. The original collection offers 46,615 datasets, 92,930 data files, and associated relevance judgments.

3.1 Dataset Preprocessing

The NTCIR datasets offer semi-structured metadata and text-rich data files. The latter contains a wealth of information that is not covered by metadata and is crucial for effective search, necessitating their inclusion in our test collection.

Dataset Fields. We define a dataset by five fields: four standard *metadata fields* provided by the publisher (`title`, `description`, `tags`, `author`) and a *content field* (`summary`) extracted from the data files to compactly describe their content. When we refer to a dataset in this paper, we indicate its five fields.

Table 1. Format distribution of data files

Format	#Files	%
PDF	47,413	51.02%
TXT	12,531	13.48%
HTML	9,298	10.01%
CSV	7,577	8.15%
XML	4,549	4.90%
JSON	1,940	2.09%
RDF	1,484	1.60%
XLSX, XLS	1,466	1.58%
DOCX, DOC	453	0.49%
Others	6,219	6.69%

Content Summary. The `summary` field is essential because raw data files are challenging to process directly due to their diverse formats and large sizes. As shown in Table 1, file formats range from unstructured PDF to structured CSV and RDF. Direct use of data files in search is hindered by readability issues (e.g., machine-readable RDF) and excessive length. To address this, we generate content summaries for quick comprehension, ensuring that the content is usable for retrieval and readable for human annotators. Their effectiveness in improving retrieval accuracy has been demonstrated [30].

The data formats offered by NTCIR are not always accurate. We detected the real format of each data file using `python-magic`. *Format-specific content summaries* are defined as follows. For tabular files (CSV, XLSX, XLS), we extracted all table headers to provide a concise description of the data structure and attributes. For textual files (PDF, TXT, HTML, DOCX), we generated an abstract to distill key ideas and topics from the text. For structured files (JSON, XML, RDF), we extracted all keys, tags, or predicates to compactly represent

the data organization and schema. For other files (HDF, etc.), their summaries were left empty.
Summary Generation. For tabular files, we applied heuristic rules to extract headers from CSV, achieving an accuracy of 92% on a random sample of 50 test files. For complex XLSX/XLS structures, we exploited their inherent features [9], achieving an accuracy of 91% in 100 test samples. For textual files, we performed optical character recognition on PDF and removed HTML tags. We then used `bart-large-cnn` to generate abstracts cost-effectively, truncating the input text to 1,024 tokens and generating up to 300 tokens. For structured files, we extracted keys, tags, and predicates from JSON, XML, and RDF using `json`, `xml`, and `rdflib`, respectively.

3.2 Test and Training Cases

Recall that the input of DSE consists of a query q and a set of target datasets D_t. We adapted NTCIR's query-dataset pairs to DSE as follows.
Test and Training Split. We adapted the 141 query-dataset pairs annotated as highly relevant in NTCIR to form our *test cases* where the query and the dataset became q and a singleton set D_t of target datasets, respectively. For quality considerations, the 1,434 query-dataset pairs annotated as partially relevant in NTCIR were similarly adapted to our *training cases*; to avoid train-test overlap, we filtered out any pairs that involved queries or datasets present in the test cases, resulting in 672 training cases.
Synthetic Training Cases. Since 672 training cases would be insufficient for fine-tuning large models, we synthesized a larger number of training cases from 45,472 datasets in NTCIR that are not annotated relevant to any query. Specifically, we fine-tuned a `T5-base` model to cost-effectively generate a query q from the title and description of each dataset, so that the input dataset served as D_t. The model was fine-tuned on the $141 + 1,434$ pairs mentioned above with an 80/20 train/valid split.

To improve the quality of synthetic queries, we applied rigorous filtering to remove trivial queries that duplicated the title of the dataset, verbose queries with excessive repetition of words, and vague queries that were too broad and lacked concrete search intent. We also ensured that the generated queries did not overlap with the test cases. This yielded 3,810 distinct queries generated from 5,065 datasets, bringing the total number of training cases from 672 to 5,737.

3.3 Pooling

It would be impractical to manually judge the relevance and similarity of 46,615 datasets to 141 test and 5,737 training queries. Following common practices in IR evaluation, we used the pooling method to reduce the number of judgments.
Retrievers. We adapted four popular retrievers, including two lexical models (BM25, TF-IDF) and two dense models (`BGE-large-en-v1.5` [26], `GTE-large` [14]).

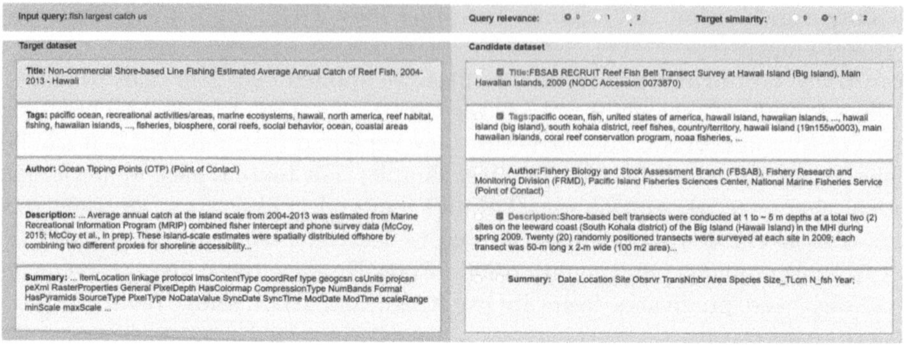

Fig. 2. A screenshot of our tool for human annotation. Left: An input of DSE, including a query and a target dataset. Right: A candidate dataset with annotation options. In this example, the candidate dataset is annotated partially similar to the target dataset. Accordingly, the second column of checkboxes are enabled, and three fields of the candidate dataset are annotated indicators of its similarity. However, the candidate dateset is annotated irrelevant to the query, so the first column of checkboxes representing indicators of relevance are disabled.

Implementation. We concatenated all fields of a dataset to construct a pseudo-document. Given an input (q, D_t), since DSE requires finding datasets relevant to both q and D_t, we concatenated q with the pseudo-document of each target dataset $d_t \in D_t$ into an expanded query to retrieve candidate datasets.[1]
Results. We collected 20 candidate datasets with the highest rank from each retriever, resulting in 7,415 (q, D_t, d_c) triples for test cases and 337,976 triples for training cases, where d_c indicates a candidate dataset to be annotated. To balance between quality and cost of annotation, we invited human experts to annotate test cases and used a large language model (LLM) for training cases.

3.4 Human Annotation of Test Cases

We recruited 24 graduate or undergraduate computer science students with experience in dataset search to annotate 7,415 (q, D_t, d_c) triples in test cases.
Dataset-Level Judgments. Given a triple (q, D_t, d_c), following the task definition of DSE, an annotator judged how much the candidate dataset d_c is *relevant to the query* q, and how much d_c is *similar to the target datasets* in D_t. In accordance with NTCIR, the judgments were scored using a graded scale: 0 for irrelevant or dissimilar, 1 for partially relevant or partially similar, and 2 for highly relevant or highly similar.
Field-Level Judgments. For each partially or highly relevant/similar dataset, the annotator was further required to identify in the candidate dataset *which fields indicate its relevance/similarity*, to be used in the evaluation of ExDSE.

[1] To prevent short but important fields from being overlooked, we followed [25] to repeat the query, `tags`, and `author` fields 100 times during concatenation.

Table 2. Distribution of dataset-level judgments

	#Cases	#Triples	Judgment	Query Relevance	Target Similarity
Test cases	141	7,415	0	5,056 (68.19%)	3,891 (52.47%)
			1	1,622 (21.87%)	2,474 (33.36%)
			2	737 (9.94%)	1,050 (14.16%)
Training cases	5,699	122,585	0	67,541 (55.10%)	58,592 (47.80%)
			1	41,290 (33.68%)	52,590 (42.90%)
			2	13,754 (11.22%)	11,403 (9.30%)

Table 3. Distribution of field-level judgments

	Query relevance		Target similarity	
	#Triples	Indicator field	#Triples	Indicator field
Test cases	2,359	title: 2,086 (88.43%)	3,524	2,941 (83.46%)
		description: 2,132 (90.38%)		2,818 (79.97%)
		tags: 1,135 (48.11%)		2,206 (62.60%)
		author: 153 (6.49%)		1,916 (54.37%)
		summary: 373 (15.81%)		882 (25.03%)
Training cases	55,044	title: 53,233 (96.71%)	63,993	18,273 (28.55%)
		description: 41,666 (75.70%)		18,791 (29.36%)
		tags: 35,141 (63.84%)		42,428 (66.30%)
		author: 13,540 (24.60%)		25,504 (39.85%)
		summary: 8,950 (16.26%)		23,902 (37.35%)

Annotation Tool. Annotation was performed using a Web tool illustrated in Fig. 2. To avoid position bias, the fields were displayed in random order.

Task Assignment. To obtain high-quality annotations, we assigned each of the 7,415 (q, D_t, d_c) triples from test cases to *two independent annotators*. When they provided the same score, it was accepted as the final score. Otherwise, we assigned the triple to a *third annotator*, and the final score was determined on the basis of a majority vote, that is, by the third annotator. However, when three scores differed from each other, we took their mean value (i.e., 1) as the final score. Field-level disagreements were resolved analogously.

Results. Table 2 presents the distribution of the judgments made at the dataset level. As shown in the upper half of the table, more than two thirds (68.19%) of the candidate datasets are irrelevant to the query and more than half (52.47%) are dissimilar to the target datasets. The highly relevant and similar datasets account for 9.94% and 14.16%, respectively.

Table 3 presents the distribution of the judgments made at the field level. As shown in the upper half of the table, two popular indicator fields are `title` and `description`. Although `author` is rarely selected as an indicator field for query relevance (6.49%), it often indicates target similarity (54.37%). Another fairly useful field is `summary` (15.81%–25.03%).

Fig. 3. Inter-annotator agreements on dataset-level judgments for the test cases.

Fig. 4. Inter-annotator agreements on field-level judgments for the test cases.

Inter-Annotator Agreement. Figure 3 shows the distribution of inter-annotator agreements on the dataset-level judgments. Two annotators reach a consensus on the query relevance and target similarity for more than 69% and 68% of the triples, respectively. Only for less than 3% of the triples, a third annotator is introduced but the three judgments are still divergent, so their mean value must be taken. We calculated Krippendorff's α, a statistical measure of the agreement achieved. The results $\alpha = 0.51$ for query relevance and $\alpha = 0.52$ for target similarity represent *a moderate degree of agreement between the annotators*, higher than $\alpha = 0.44$ reported on NTCIR [13].

Figure 4 shows the distribution of inter-annotator agreements on the field-level judgments. Two annotators reach a consensus for more than 65% and 55% of the judgments of indicator field for query relevance and target similarity, respectively. Their disagreements are resolved by introducing a third annotator.

3.5 LLM Annotation of Training Cases

We prompted a popular and cost-effective LLM, GLM-3-Turbo [27], to annotate 337,976 (q, D_t, d_c) triples in training cases. In accordance with human annotation, we collected dataset-level and field-level judgments from LLM outputs.

Quality Control. We found that LLM provided many superficially inaccurate dataset-level judgments, so we applied heuristic filtering. For query relevance, we removed the cases where the occurrence of query keywords in candidate datasets was either implausibly low despite being labeled relevant or implausibly high despite being labeled irrelevant. For target similarity, we removed the cases where the overlap between the candidate dataset and the target dataset was inconsistent with the label, e.g., for a dissimilar pair, the string similarity of their fields was too high or they shared an excessive number of tags.

Although these heuristics might also mistakenly filter out high-quality judgments, we checked the results and, in general, observed *substantially improved quality*. The accuracy for query relevance and target similarity judgments increased from 73% and 69%, respectively, to more than 85% based on a manual check of 3,378 triples sampled. Given this satisfactory quality and large size of LLM annotations, they form useful training cases for weak supervision.

We did not filter field-level judgments because our investigation revealed their relatively high accuracy but complex error patterns that are hard to detect.

Results. Finally, we kept 122,585 triples with complete annotations (i.e., no judgment discarded) from 5,699 training cases. The lower half of Tables 2 and 3 present their distributions of dataset-level and field-level judgments, respectively, generally resembling the distributions in the test cases.

4 Evaluation of DSE

A typical IR pipeline consists of *first-stage retrieval* and *reranking*. Following this convention, we used DSEBench to separately evaluate retrieval and reranking models. All experiments were conducted on an Intel Xeon Gold 5222 CPU with four NVIDIA GeForce RTX 3090 GPUs. Our code is on GitHub.

4.1 Training, Validation, and Test Sets

DSEBench provides 141 test cases and 5,699 training cases. To ensure comparability, we provide two official splits:

- **Five-Fold Split:** We randomly partitioned 141 test cases into five nearly equal-sized folds for cross-validation (3/1/1 for training/validation/test). Performance should be averaged over five runs.

- **Annotator Split:** We divided the 5,699 training cases into 80% for training and 20% for validation, using the 141 test cases strictly for testing.

4.2 Evaluation Metrics

Standard IR evaluation metrics were used on the test set: MAP@5, NDCG@5, Recall@5 (R@5), MAP@10, NDCG@10, and Recall@10 (R@10), where NDCG@10 was also used for the selection of hyperparameters on the validation set. All metrics were calculated using `pytrec-eval-terrier`.

These metrics rely on gold-standard labels. Recall that each triple (q, D_t, d_c) annotated in DSEBench is associated with two dataset-level judgments: the relevance of the candidate dataset d_c to the query q and the similarity of d_c to the target datasets in D_t, both in the range of $\{0, 1, 2\}$. Following the task definition of DSE, since query relevance and target similarity are indispensable, their product was taken as the gold-standard graded label of (q, D_t, d_c) in the range of $\{0, 1, 2, 4\}$ to ensure that d_c receives a high overall score only if it is highly relevant to q *and* highly similar to D_t; a low score in either aspect would significantly penalize the overall score. Note that query relevance and target similarity can also be combined in other reasonable ways, such as their harmonic mean.

4.3 Benchmarking Retrieval Models

Retrievers. We adapted and evaluated seven representative retrieval models:

- unsupervised models, including lexical models **BM25** and **TF-IDF**, and dense models **BGE** (`bge-large-en-v1.5`) [26] and **GTE** (`gte-large`) [14];
- supervised models, including **DPR** [12] (bi-encoder), **ColBERTv2** [23] (late interaction), and **coCondenser** [11] (specialized pre-training).

We also evaluated a classic RF method by adapting it to the DSE task:

- Rocchio [22] uses target datasets as positive feedback (**Rocchio-P**) or also infers negative feedback from non-target datasets (**Rocchio-PN**).

Implementation Details. Following the implementation in Sect. 3.3, we concatenated all fields to construct pseudo-documents as dataset representations. The query was expanded with the pseudo-documents of target datasets.

The supervised models were evaluated in three configurations: **not fine-tuned**, **fine-tuned with the five-fold split**, and **fine-tuned with the annotator split**, as defined in Sect. 4.1. Gold-standard graded scores were reduced to binary labels (positive or zero) to facilitate fine-tuning. Other implementation details are documented in our GitHub repository.

Evaluation Results. We evaluated the highest-ranked datasets retrieved by each model from the full corpus of 46,615 datasets. Table 4 presents the results. Among unsupervised models, dense models (BGE and GTE) outperform lexical models (BM25 and TF-IDF). For supervised models, fine-tuning yields substantial gains. The performance difference between the five-fold and annotator

Table 4. Evaluation results of retrieval Models

	MAP@5	@10	NDCG@5	@10	R@5	@10
Unsupervised models						
BM25	0.0982	0.1739	0.3059	0.3416	0.1705	0.2769
TF-IDF	0.0921	0.1615	0.2971	0.3227	0.1572	0.2576
BGE	0.1045	0.1834	0.3233	0.3598	0.1756	0.2887
GTE	0.1104	0.1921	0.3267	0.3649	0.1820	0.2983
Supervised models (not fine-tuned)						
DPR	0.1072	0.1757	0.3248	0.3472	0.1706	0.2695
ColBERTv2	0.1072	0.1799	0.3206	0.3510	0.1687	0.2720
coCondenser	0.1029	0.1671	0.3142	0.3326	0.1597	0.2525
Supervised models (fine-tuned with the five-fold split)						
DPR	0.1204	0.1929	0.3574	0.3769	0.1833	0.2967
ColBERTv2	0.1247	0.2052	0.3449	0.3779	0.1909	0.3066
coCondenser	**0.1387**	**0.2286**	**0.3784**	**0.4147**	**0.2110**	**0.3401**
Supervised models (fine-tuned with the annotator split)						
DPR	0.1194	0.1936	0.3551	0.3757	0.1851	0.2914
ColBERTv2	0.1109	0.1925	0.3360	0.3760	0.1800	0.3033
coCondenser	<u>0.1286</u>	<u>0.2238</u>	<u>0.3656</u>	<u>0.4136</u>	<u>0.1979</u>	<u>0.3367</u>
RF Methods						
Rocchio-P	0.1033	0.1782	0.3139	0.3452	0.1713	0.2837
Rocchio-PN	0.1023	0.1773	0.3125	0.3441	0.1696	0.2828

splits is minimal, suggesting that *the large-scale LLM annotations in DSEBench are almost as effective as human annotations for training.* RF methods slightly improve on the vanilla TF-IDF, but remain inferior to other approaches, highlighting that *adapting RF is insufficient for addressing the complex DSE task.*

4.4 Benchmarking Reranking Models

Rerankers. We adapted and evaluated six representative reranking models:

- text-based models, including the state of the art on MTEB's reranking leaderboard such as **SFR**-`Embedding-Mistral` [19] and **Stella**-`en-1.5B-v5` [28], and **BGE-reranker**-`v2-minicpm-layerwise` [4], a supervised cross-encoder model specifically designed for reranking tasks;
- structure-based models, including **HINormer** [18], a popular heterogeneous Graph Neural Network (GNN), and the state-of-the-art **HHGT** [31], both employing a graph structure representing relationships between datasets [15];

- **LLM**, specifically `GLM-4-Plus` [27], which supports a large context length.

Implementation Details. For text-based models, textual representations were constructed identically to Sect. 4.3. We evaluated BGE-reranker under the same fine-tuning splits, while SFR and Stella were evaluated directly without fine-tuning. For structure-based models, we constructed a graph based on dataset relationships [15]. Reranking scores were predicted using a multi-layer perceptron processing the GNN-enhanced node representation alongside the mean representation of the top-20 textually similar nodes. LLMs were evaluated in zero-shot, one-shot, ListwiseRankLLM [24], and multi-layer configurations [29]. Full implementation details on hyperparameter settings, GNN configurations, and LLM prompting strategies are documented in our GitHub repository.

Table 5. Evaluation results of reranking Models

	MAP@5	@10	NDCG@5	@10	R@5	@10
Supervised Models (not fine-tuned)						
Stella	0.1180	0.2106	0.3509	0.3981	0.1938	0.3307
SFR	0.1184	0.2090	0.3488	0.3920	0.1940	0.3225
BGE-reranker	0.1170	0.2032	0.3470	0.3877	0.1930	0.3163
Supervised Models (fine-tuned with the five-fold split)						
BGE-reranker	0.1178	0.2085	0.3464	0.3956	0.1914	0.3273
HINormer	0.1009	0.1734	0.3112	0.3407	0.1313	0.2643
HHGT	0.0874	0.1550	0.2781	0.3090	0.1139	0.2333
Supervised Models (fine-tuned with the annotator split)						
BGE-reranker	<u>0.1249</u>	<u>0.2146</u>	<u>0.3665</u>	<u>0.4099</u>	<u>0.1985</u>	<u>0.3347</u>
HINormer	0.0876	0.1617	0.2682	0.3089	0.1142	0.2339
HHGT	0.0816	0.1449	0.2658	0.2977	0.1215	0.2342
LLMs						
LLM (zero-shot)	0.1144	0.1748	0.3130	0.3360	0.1691	0.2652
LLM (one-shot)	0.1154	0.1776	0.3058	0.3327	0.1691	0.2729
LLM (RankLLM)	0.1191	0.2011	0.3506	0.3804	0.1735	0.2910
LLM (multi-layer)	**0.1468**	**0.2398**	**0.4071**	**0.4451**	**0.2093**	**0.3608**

Evaluation Results. We evaluated the highest-ranked datasets after reranking the union of the top-10 datasets retrieved by the models evaluated in Sect. 4.3. Table 5 presents the results. Among supervised models, BGE-reranker performs better after fine-tuning, particularly with the annotator split, *reinforcing the value of the LLM annotations in DSEBench.* The structure-based models (HINormer and HHGT) generally underperform compared to BGE-reranker, suggesting that while semantic relationships between datasets may be useful, textual representations remain the dominant signal for DSE. For LLMs, the multi-layer setting achieves the highest scores across all metrics, likely thanks to the robustness of ensemble voting and reduced context length per inference.

5 Evaluation of ExDSE

Building on DSE, ExDSE further requires identifying the indicator fields for query relevance and target similarity. We used the test cases in DSEBench to evaluate the explanation methods.

Evaluation Metric. The F1 score was used to compare the set of indicator fields identified by an explanation method with the gold standard in DSEBench.

Explainers. We adapted and evaluated four post hoc explainers:

- **Feature Ablation**, assessing the importance of a field based on the change in ranking scores after its removal;
- surrogate models, including two popular implementations **LIME** [21] and **SHAP** [17], which train proxy models to estimate field contributions;
- **LLM**, specifically `GLM-4-Air` [27], directly generating indicator fields.

Implementation Details. Explanation methods were coupled with the retrieval models evaluated in Section 4.3 (excluding the incompatible RF method). Feature Ablation identified indicator fields based on ranking score degradation after field exclusion. LIME used an SVM proxy model trained on perturbed samples to estimate field contributions. SHAP used a partition explainer. LLMs were evaluated in zero-shot and few-shot configurations. Thresholds, sample sizes, and other implementation details are documented in our GitHub repository.

Table 6. Evaluation results (F1) of explanation methods

	Query relevance				Target similarity			
	BM25	DPR	coCond. (f.-f.)	coCond. (ann.)	BM25	DPR	coCond. (f.-f.)	coCond. (ann.)
Feature ablation	0.4819	0.2806	0.4754	0.4193	0.4750	0.3216	0.3675	0.3351
LIME	0.6325	0.6943	0.6960	0.7100	0.7562	0.7650	0.7761	0.7529
SHAP	0.6507	0.6718	0.6761	0.6894	**0.7835**	**0.8201**	**0.8007**	**0.7899**
LLM (zero-shot)	0.6455	0.6492	0.6351	0.6334	0.7315	0.7450	0.7264	0.7121
LLM (few-shot)	**0.7246**	**0.7316**	**0.7218**	**0.7239**	0.7647	0.7757	0.7637	0.7508

Note DPR = DPR (not fine-tuned); coCond. (f.-f.) = coCondenser (fine-tuned with the five-fold split); coCond. (ann.) = coCondenser (fine-tuned with the annotator split)

Evaluation Results. Among the top-20 datasets retrieved by a retrieval model, we applied each explanation method to all datasets that have at least one annotated indicator field in DSEBench. Table 6 presents the evaluation results averaged over all such datasets, obtained in a variety of retrieval model and configuration settings: unsupervised BM25, DPR not fine-tuned, coCondenser fine-tuned with the five-fold split, and coCondenser fine-tuned with the annotator split. The results with other retrieval models or configurations exhibit similar patterns, and thus are omitted.

Feature Ablation consistently performs worst, suggesting that simple field exclusion is ineffective for ExDSE. Between surrogate models, SHAP outperforms LIME (and all others) in identifying indicator fields for target similarity, likely because of the robustness of its Shapley value theory compared to LIME's sampling mechanism. LLM performs significantly better in the few-shot setting, exceeding other methods in identifying indicator fields for query relevance.

Table 7. General field preferences of explanation methods

	Field preferences by frequency
Feature ablation	`description` > `title` > `summary` > `tags` > `author`
LIME	`description` > `tags` > `title` > `summary` > `author`
SHAP	`description` > `summary` > `title` > `tags` > `author`
LLM (zero-shot)	`description` > `tags` > `summary` > `title` > `author`
LLM (few-shot)	`description` > `tags` > `title` > `summary` > `author`

Table 7 shows the general field preferences of each explanation method, where the fields are ordered by their frequency of being identified as an indicator field. All methods prioritize `description`, likely due to its rich information. In contrast, `author` is rarely selected. In particular, the extracted content `summary` has a selection frequency comparable to key metadata such as `title` and `tags`, *confirming the utility of content summaries in ExDSE.*

6 Conclusions

This paper investigates DSE, a composite IR task that generalizes two established dataset search paradigms: keyword-based search and similarity-based discovery. To advance research in this area, we release DSEBench, the first dedicated test collection for DSE, comprising high-quality human-annotated test cases along with a large set of LLM-annotated training cases, supporting the evaluation of unsupervised and supervised methods. The annotations encompass not only query relevance and target similarity of datasets in DSE, but also indicator fields that serve as explanations to support ExDSE evaluation. Using DSEBench, we evaluate a variety of adapted retrieval, reranking, and explanation methods to establish comprehensive baselines for future comparative research.

Limitations and Future Work. First, DSEBench is constructed from a single test collection for dataset search, the English version of NTCIR, where the datasets mainly offer government data. There are datasets in other domains and languages, such as academic datasets, which will be considered in the next version of DSEBench. Second, the current inputs in DSEBench contain a singleton set of target datasets. A more general setting is to consider multiple target datasets with a query. However, this requires a larger number of datasets that are known to be relevant to the query as the target datasets, which will reduce the number of test cases that can be generated. Third, in our evaluation, the query and the fields of the target datasets are concatenated in a straightforward way into an expanded query. It might be an idea to consider models that can directly exploit such structured inputs.

Acknowledgments. This study was funded by the Noncommunicable Chronic Diseases-National Science and Technology Major Project (2025ZD0544900) and the Fundamental Research Funds for the Central Universities (No. 2026300429).

Disclosure of Interests. The authors have no competing interests to declare that are relevant to the content of this article.

References

1. Anand, A., Lyu, L., Idahl, M., Wang, Y., Wallat, J., Zhang, Z.: Explainable information retrieval: a survey. CoRR **abs/2211.02405** (2022)
2. Brickley, D., Burgess, M., Noy, N.F.: Google dataset search: building a search engine for datasets in an open web ecosystem, pp. 1365–1375. WWW (2019)
3. Castelo, S., Rampin, R., Santos, A.S.R., Bessa, A., Chirigati, F., Freire, J.: Auctus: a dataset search engine for data discovery and augmentation. PVLDB **14**(12), 2791–2794 (2021)
4. Chen, J., Xiao, S., Zhang, P., Luo, K., Lian, D., Liu, Z.: Bge m3-embedding: multi-lingual, multi-functionality, multi-granularity text embeddings through self-knowledge distillation (2023)
5. Chen, Q., Luo, W., Huang, Z., Lin, T., Wang, X., Soylu, A., Ell, B., Zhou, B., Kharlamov, E., Cheng, G.: ACORDAR 2.0: a test collection for ad hoc dataset retrieval with densely pooled datasets and question-style queries. In: SIGIR, pp. 303–312 (2024)
6. Chen, Z., Zhang, S., Davison, B.D.: WTR: a test collection for web table retrieval. In: SIGIR, pp. 2514–2520 (2021)
7. Cui, L., Li, H., Chen, K., Shou, L., Chen, G.: nlctables: a dataset for marrying natural language conditions with table discovery. In: SIGIR, pp. 3638–3647. ACM (2025)
8. Deng, Y., Chai, C., Cao, L., Yuan, Q., Chen, S., Yu, Y., Sun, Z., Wang, J., Li, J., Cao, Z., Jin, K., Zhang, C., Jiang, Y., Zhang, Y., Wang, Y., Yuan, Y., Wang, G., Tang, N.: Lakebench: a benchmark for discovering joinable and unionable tables in data lakes. PVLDB **17**(8), 1925–1938 (2024)
9. Fang, J., Mitra, P., Tang, Z., Giles, C.L.: Table header detection and classification, pp. 599–605. AAAI (2012)
10. Fernandez, R.C., Abedjan, Z., Koko, F., Yuan, G., Madden, S., Stonebraker, M.: Aurum: a data discovery system. In: ICDE, pp. 1001–1012 (2018)
11. Gao, L., Callan, J.: Unsupervised corpus aware language model pre-training for dense passage retrieval, pp. 2843–2853. ACL (2022)

12. Karpukhin, V., Oguz, B., Min, S., Lewis, P., Wu, L., Edunov, S., Chen, D., Yih, W.T.: Dense passage retrieval for open-domain question answering. EMNLP, pp. 6769–6781 (2020)
13. Kato, M.P., Ohshima, H., Liu, Y.H., Chen, H.L.: A test collection for ad-hoc dataset retrieval. In: SIGIR, pp. 2450–2456 (2021)
14. Li, Z., Zhang, X., Zhang, Y., Long, D., Xie, P., Zhang, M.: Towards general text embeddings with multi-stage contrastive learning. arXiv preprint arXiv:2308.03281 (2023)
15. Lin, K., Alrashed, T., Noy, N.F.: Relationships are complicated! an analysis of relationships between datasets on the web. ISWC **15231**, 47–66 (2024)
16. Lin, T., Chen, Q., Cheng, G., Soylu, A., Ell, B., Zhao, R., Shi, Q., Wang, X., Gu, Y., Kharlamov, E.: ACORDAR: a test collection for ad hoc content-based (RDF) dataset retrieval. In: SIGIR, pp. 2981–2991 (2022)
17. Lundberg, S.M., Nair, B., Vavilala, M.S., Horibe, M., Eisses, M.J., Adams, T., Liston, D.E., Low, D.K.W., Newman, S.F., Kim, J., et al.: Explainable machine-learning predictions for the prevention of hypoxaemia during surgery. Nat. Biomed. Eng. **2**(10), 749 (2018)
18. Mao, Q., Liu, Z., Liu, C., Sun, J.: Hinormer: representation learning on heterogeneous information networks with graph transformer. In: WWW, pp. 599–610 (2023)
19. Meng, R., Liu, Y., Joty, S.R., Xiong, C., Zhou, Y., Yavuz, S.: Sfr-embedding-mistral:enhance text retrieval with transfer learning. Salesforce AI Res. Blog (2024)
20. Paton, N.W., Chen, J., Wu, Z.: Dataset discovery and exploration: a survey. CSUR **56**(4), 102:1–102:37 (2024)
21. Ribeiro, M.T., Singh, S., Guestrin, C.: "why should I trust you?": explaining the predictions of any classifier. In: KDD, pp. 1135–1144 (2016)
22. Rocchio Jr, J.J.: Relevance feedback in information retrieval. In: The SMART Retrieval System: Experiments in Automatic Document Processing (1971)
23. Santhanam, K., Khattab, O., Saad-Falcon, J., Potts, C., Zaharia, M.: Colbertv2: effective and efficient retrieval via lightweight late interaction. In: NAACL, pp. 3715–3734 (2022)
24. Sharifymoghaddam, S., Pradeep, R., Slavescu, A., Nguyen, R., Xu, A., Chen, Z., Zhang, Y., Chen, Y., Xian, J., Lin, J.: Rankllm: A python package for reranking with llms. In: SIGIR, pp. 3681–3690 (2025)
25. Wang, L., Yang, N., Wei, F.: Query2doc: query expansion with large language models. EMNLP, pp. 9414–9423 (2023)
26. Xiao, S., Liu, Z., Zhang, P., Muennighoff, N.: C-pack: packaged resources to advance general chinese embedding (2023)
27. Zeng, A., Xu, B., Wang, B., Zhang, C., Yin, D., Rojas, D., Feng, G., Zhao, H., Lai, H., Yu, H., Wang, H., Sun, J., Zhang, J., Cheng, J., Gui, J., Tang, J., Zhang, J., Li, J., Zhao, L., Wu, L., Zhong, L., Liu, M., Huang, M., Zhang, P., Zheng, Q., Lu, R., Duan, S., Zhang, S., Cao, S., Yang, S., Tam, W.L., Zhao, W., Liu, X., Xia, X., Zhang, X., Gu, X., Lv, X., Liu, X., Liu, X., Yang, X., Song, X., Zhang, X., An, Y., Xu, Y., Niu, Y., Yang, Y., Li, Y., Bai, Y., Dong, Y., Qi, Z., Wang, Z., Yang, Z., Du, Z., Hou, Z., Wang, Z.: Chatglm: a family of large language models from GLM-130B to GLM-4 all tools. CoRR **abs/2406.12793** (2024)
28. Zhang, D., Li, J., Zeng, Z., Wang, F.: Jasper and stella: distillation of sota embedding models (2025)
29. Zhang, W., Gui, L., Procter, R., He, Y.: Multi-layer ranking with large language models for news source recommendation. In: SIGIR, pp. 2537–2542 (2024)

30. Zhou, X., Chen, Q., Chen, J., Cheng, G.: μds: multi-objective data snippet extraction for dataset search. In: SIGIR, pp. 116–126 (2025)
31. Zhu, Q., Zhang, L., Xu, Q., Liu, K., Long, C., Wang, X.: HHGT: hierarchical heterogeneous graph transformer for heterogeneous graph representation learning. WSDM, pp, 318–326 (2025)

GMVCC: A Multi-version Concurrency Control Framework for GPU-Accelerated Transaction Processing

Haodong Lv(✉), Jianpeng Wei, Xiangting Chen, Fangfang Li, Xiaohua Li, Yu Gu, and Ge Yu

Northeastern University, Shenyang, China
{2301927,2310745,2401811}@stu.neu.edu.cn,
{lifangfang,lixiaohua,guyu,yuge}@mail.neu.edu.cn

Abstract. We present GMVCC, a GPU-accelerated in-memory OLTP system designed to exploit massive parallelism for transaction processing. To address the limitations of single-version storage in existing GPU-accelerated OLTP systems, GMVCC implements a multi-version storage model on the GPU during transaction execution. It further incorporates a transactional repair technique to mitigate the high abort rates inherent in multi-version optimistic concurrency control. Additionally, we propose several GPU-specific optimizations tailored for efficient multi-version storage and access. The experimental results based on TPC-C and YCSB show that the throughput of GMVCC achieves up to a 1.3× improvement over the current state-of-the-art GPU-based OLTP systems under write-intensive workloads.

Keywords: Deterministic Concurrency Control · Transaction Processing · GPU Acceleration

1 Introduction

General-Purpose Graphics Processing Units (GPUs) combine massive parallelism with ultra-high memory bandwidth and have become key accelerators in high-performance computing. In database systems, due to the implicit parallelism of numerous independent short transactions in batch-mode Online Transaction Processing (OLTP) workloads being exploited by GPU, GPU acceleration has gradually expanded from Online Analysis Processing (OLAP) type systems to research on OLTP type acceleration. Recent systems such as Gacco [3] and LTPG [21] demonstrate that GPU-driven OLTP can be a cost-effective alternative to expensive multi-core CPU platforms. This trend is further accelerated by the rise of autonomous AI agents, whose machine-speed, high-frequency transaction bursts align perfectly with the GPU's computational density. However, these agentic workloads frequently rely on shared states for collaborative decision-making, intensifying data contention. Under such modern workloads, traditional

L. Ding et al. (Eds.): APWeb-WAIM 2026, LNCS 16993, pp. 116–131, 2027.
https://doi.org/10.1007/978-981-92-5693-8_8

single-version storage models frequently encounter severe serialization or high abort rates, posing significant challenges for maintaining both throughput and reliability in agent-centric environments.

Deterministic concurrency control (DCC) has made substantial progress on CPUs, where advances in multi-version concurrency control algorithms (MVCC) [7,14,17,19,20] have led to performance surpassing that of traditional single-version approaches [13,18] under high contention scenarios. By contrast, GPU-based transaction processing systems [3,10,11,21] largely remain single-version because of hardware and memory-architecture constraints. Specifically, the limited on-device memory capacity and the high cost of pointer-chasing in linked-list version chains—which often triggers memory divergence—pose significant hurdles for GPU-based MVCC. This design choice forgoes an important opportunity: multi-version storage naturally alleviates write-after-write (WAW) and write-after-read (WAR) conflicts, potentially increasing concurrency on massively parallel architectures such as GPUs [15,22]. Consequently, exploring multi-version storage on GPUs is both novel and challenging. It also raises several distinct challenges:

Challenge 1: Version-Chain Traversal Overhead. Pointer-based version chains trigger severe memory divergence and fragmented bandwidth utilization on GPUs due to non-coalesced accesses and unequal chain lengths. This results in fragmented bandwidth utilization and significant warp stalls, making traditional linked-list traversal a primary bottleneck for GPU throughput. To address this, we propose a **metadata-data separation storage scheme** that enables coalesced memory access and improves traversal efficiency.

Challenge 2: Concurrency-Visibility Trade-off. Maintaining correct version visibility in a massively parallel SIMT execution requires frequent global synchronizations or high-contention atomic operations. These mechanisms, while ensuring consistency, often lead to warp stalls and significant hardware underutilization, negating the throughput benefits of GPU-based concurrency. We employ a **deterministic optimistic concurrency control (DOCC)** scheme coupled with a **repair phase** that leverages multi-version metadata to mitigate aborts and avoid costly full re-executions.

Challenge 3: Garbage Collection Complexity. Managing multiple versions per record demands efficient reclamation. We adopt a **lightweight inter-batch garbage collection** strategy to minimize GPU-side overhead.

We summarize our contributions as follows.

- We present GMVCC, a GPU multi-version optimistic concurrency control system. Unlike prior GPU-based systems, GMVCC reexamines storage design and enables multi-version execution on GPU architectures.
- We propose two GPU-oriented techniques for multi-version batch transaction processing: (i) a low-contention multi-version data-access mechanism, and (ii) a repair phase for batches that leverages static analysis and data reuse to mitigate the cost of re-executing aborted transactions; this phase also redistributes tasks to lower abort rates.

- We evaluate GMVCC on TPC-C [1] and YCSB [5] benchmarks. Results show up to 1.3× higher transaction throughput than state-of-the-art GPU-based OLTP systems and better performance under write-intensive workloads.

The remainder of this paper is organized as follows. Section 2 reviews background and related work. Section 3 presents the system design and storage optimizations. Section 4 details the execution model and optimization techniques. Section 5 reports experimental results (Table 1).

Table 1. Comparison of existing GPU transaction processing systems

System	CC	Scene	Limitation
Gacco [3]	DPCC	Low-frequency hybrid transactions	Preprocessing overhead homogeneous transaction batches
LTPG [21]	DOCC	High-throughput mixed workloads	Requires additional optimization logic under high contention
GPUTx [11]	Dependency graph scheduling	Predefined r/w set transactions	Poor adaptability to dynamic workloads, performance degradation under high contention

2 Background and Motivation

2.1 GPU Transaction Processing Systems

While the massive parallelism of GPUs offers substantial potential for accelerating main-memory database transactions, their distinctive architecture calls for tailored system designs. In particular, differences from CPUs, most notably the Single-Instruction Multi-Threads (SIMT) execution model and complex memory hierarchies [8,16,24], complicate the design of efficient systems. We therefore analyze the current landscape of GPU-based transaction processing, with an emphasis on concurrency control mechanisms, storage models, and the primary performance bottlenecks.

2.2 Analysis of Existing Technology

GPU Transaction Architectures. Current systems mainly adopt two architectures. *Pure GPU architectures* (e.g., GPUTx [11], GPU-TPS [10]) deploy the entire pipeline on the GPU to maximize parallelism via batch processing (e.g., conflict-free k-sets). However, they are limited by VRAM capacity and dependency-graph overhead, making them suitable only for low-conflict workloads. Conversely, *CPU-GPU heterogeneous architectures* (e.g., GalOP [2], GaccO [3], LTPG [21]) achieve resource synergy via task partitioning. They offload high-frequency transactions to the GPU while keeping others on the CPU, utilizing pipelined execution or multi-phase conflict resolution (e.g., dynamic hash buckets) to handle high-contention scenarios more effectively.

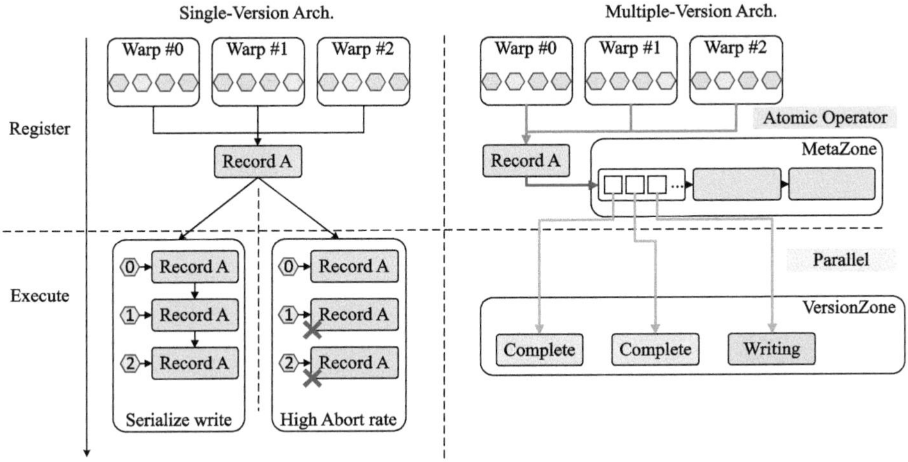

Fig. 1. Comparison on storage scheme

2.3 Deterministic Concurrency Control Mechanisms

On GPUs, the design of concurrency control is shaped by architectural constraints, and existing solutions fall into pessimistic and optimistic families.

Pessimistic concurrency control has proven ill-suited for the GPU's massively parallel model. Traditional two-phase locking (2PL) either serializes execution with coarse-grained locks or incurs high overhead and contention-including starvation-with fine-grained locks [9], yielding suboptimal performance in systems such as GPUTx [11] and GPU-TPS[10]. Alternatively, dependency graph scheduling is limited by its reliance on static analysis, rendering it impractical for dynamic workloads.

Optimistic concurrency control (OCC) aligns better with the GPU, deferring conflict detection to a validation phase that can be efficiently parallelized on the GPU. Systems such as LTPG [21] demonstrate this by using optimized validation kernels to handle high contention effectively.

2.4 Storage Scheme

The prevalent use of single-version storage in GPU transaction-processing systems reflects pragmatic constraints-limited VRAM capacity and the overhead of traversing version chains in multi-version designs. However, this choice constrains concurrency control: under write contention, single-version schemes must either serialize writes, undermining GPU parallelism, or rely on OCC with elevated abort rates. Although ad-hoc optimizations provide partial mitigation, multi-version storage inherently removes this trade-off, as shown in Fig. 1.

2.5 Transaction Healing

Transaction repair/re-execution techniques mitigate the cost of conflicts by avoiding full abort-and-restart [4,6]. They reduce resource waste under high contention [12] and improve throughput and scalability by performing fine-grained, operation-level repair instead of restarting entire transactions. In distributed settings, Hackwrench [6] addresses cross-node communication and batched-commit conflicts with a repair strategy that couples batched commits with dependency chains. For multi-core, in-memory databases using OCC, Transaction Healing [23] implements operation-level repair via static analysis and runtime caching.

3 System Design

3.1 Architecture Design

Our proposed system, GMVCC, accelerates GPU transaction processing by introducing a batch-level MVCC scheme. As depicted in Fig. 1, this approach emulates a multi-version environment within each batch while maintaining a single-version storage model for the global state. Initially, single-version data snapshots are transferred to the GPU, where the pre-allocated "*Buffer Zone*" and an auxiliary "*version array buffer*" manage transaction-local versions. After the batch is completed, GMVCC's garbage collection consolidates these versions into a new single-version snapshot, and both the snapshot and the transaction outcomes are returned to the CPU.

3.2 Storage Design

To minimize the overhead associated with data transfer control, the table data transmitted between the CPU and GPU are maintained as single-version snapshots, while multi-version processing is implemented only on the GPU. Data versions are stored in pre-allocated buffers to avoid the inherent performance bottlenecks of dynamic memory allocation on the GPU. The size of this buffer is determined by the potential maximum VRAM occupancy required for processing the transactional batch.

Traditional chain-based storage suffers from two GPU-specific bottlenecks: (1) **Synchronization Overheads**, where locking or atomic chain updates trigger severe warp divergence; and (2) **Memory Access Inefficiency**, as sequential pointer-chasing across discrete nodes breaks memory coalescing, significantly increasing latency.

To address these issues, we propose decoupling version metadata from payload storage. As depicted in Fig. 2, each version logically consists of a **Metadata Zone** (containing *version_id*, *status*, *next_ptr*) and a **Data Zone** (containing the payload). By packing control details into a fixed-size Version Array, metadata traversal becomes independent of payload data. This allows threads to locate or insert versions via coalesced metadata access, while concurrent payload writes do not interfere with metadata-level operations. Furthermore, due to the characteristics of deterministic batch processing, the *version_id* to be read is predetermined. Consequently, we omit traditional timestamps, retaining only the *version_id* and a *status* flag (locked or committed). Such separation effectively transforms irregular pointer-chasing into predictable memory patterns, yielding a concurrency model optimized for the GPU's SIMT execution. Under this storage schema, read and write operations are structured as follows.

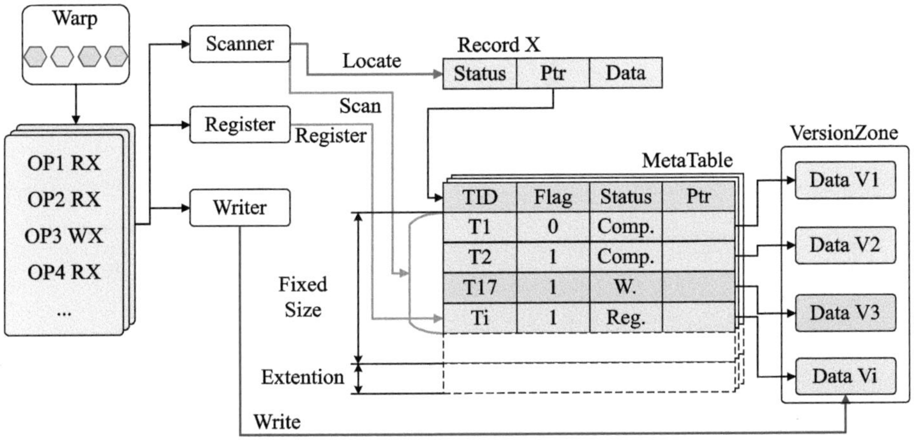

Fig. 2. Logic storage scheme

Write operations. Sub-transactions reserve version slots using a single *atomicAdd* on the Version Array's counter, ensuring contention-free indexing within a warp. If the array is full, a lock is temporarily acquired to link a new Version Array, ensuring safe metadata expansion while allowing concurrent reads to proceed. Following reservation, the thread initializes control metadata (e.g., payload pointer and status flags) in the contiguous Version Array and writes the data payload into a separate Version Buffer. Memory for the payload is managed via global atomic offsets, which avoids expensive global synchronization and ensures that version creation remains a lightweight, metadata-driven process.

Read operations. Instead of sequential pointer-chasing, a read operation performs a coalesced scan of the contiguous Version Array to identify the latest visible version based on metadata status flags. Once the target version is located, the thread directly retrieves the data payload from the referenced buffer location. This design transforms irregular chain traversals into predictable, high-bandwidth memory access patterns, significantly reducing warp stalls and memory latency during the execution phase.

4 Execution Model and Optimization Strategies

4.1 Execute Schema Design

The execution of GMVCC follows a multi-round batch processing model, designed to maximize GPU utilization while minimizing synchronization overhead. The concurrency control of this system follows a phased execution model:

Execution (Repair) - Validation - Commit, as shown in Fig. 3, with synchronization between phases ensured by barriers. The system uses the order of transaction arrival as the deterministic scheduling outcome.

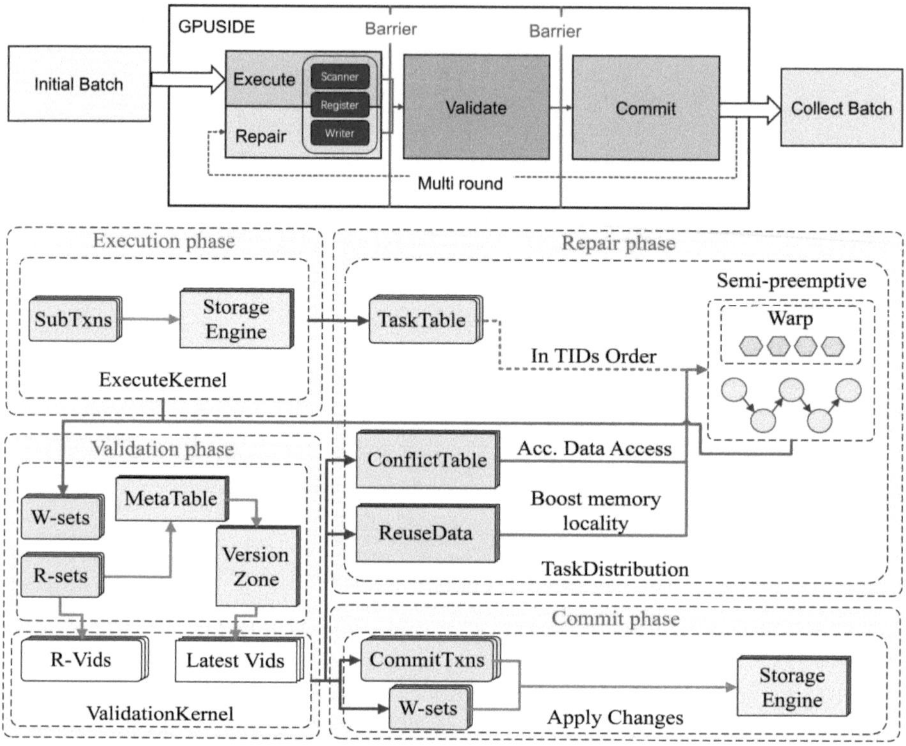

Fig. 3. Execution scheme

Execution phase. Transactions are statically analyzed and pre-divided into independent sub-transactions, which are mapped to GPU threads in a one-to-one relationship. Transactions of the same type are mapped to the same warp to minimize execution divergence within warps. During this phase, write operations insert new versions into designated version slots following the method described earlier. Creation of version metadata is managed by a per-version version array to ensure minimal-wait writing. When version metadata is created, it is marked as "Writing". Once the complete payload is written to the version buffer, the metadata is updated to "Readable", making the version visible to other threads.

Sub-transactions collectively maintain the read set accessed during execution. They follow the reading protocol defined in the execution model to access the latest visible version of the target data and record the version read during the execution phase.

Validation phase. As shown in Algorithm 1, Validation proceeds at the granularity of individual read operations. For each recorded read, a GPU thread

Algorithm 1 Validation phase

```
Input: Transactions set T, Device multiversion buffers B, Transaction ID T_id
Output: Verification results VR_res
Function GetLatestVisibleVersion(x, T_id)
  version_list ← GetVersionList(x)
  max_valid_version ← 0
  for all v in version_list do
    if v.creator_id < T_id ∧ v.creator_id > max_valid_version then
      max_valid_version ← v.creator_id
    end if
  end for
  return max_valid_version
Function ValidKernel(T, S, B)
  for each thread in Warp do
    validationPassed ← true
    RTS ← GetRTS(thread, T)
    V_lv ← GetLatestVisibleVersion(T, B)
    if RTS ≠ V_lv then
      validationPassed ← false
    end if
  end for
```

re-reads the latest visible version determined by the visibility rules for the corresponding sub-transaction. Due to the synchronization barrier between the validation and execution phases, all write operations have already created version metadata tagged with the original transaction IDs at this point. If the re-read latest visible version matches the version recorded in the read set during the execution phase, the sub-transaction is considered validated. However, validation mark is only applied at the sub-transaction level; the entire transaction remains uncommitted at this stage.

Commit phase. To ensure deterministic execution outcomes, the commit phase only allows the submission of a contiguous sequence of validated transactions from the head of the batch. If there exists a non-validated transaction between two validated transactions, the latter cannot be committed in this round. This policy prevents potential cascading aborts induced by the unresolved transaction. To avoid expensive rollback overhead, this phase enforces a strict deterministic protocol, as shown in Algorithm 2.Âă

Repair phase. Given the GPU's massive parallelism, transactions execute concurrently during the execution phase, and scheduling is handled entirely by the CUDA scheduling mechanism. The strict commit protocol requiring a contiguous sequence of validated transactions leads to significant performance volatility. Avoiding costly transaction aborts typically involves substantial overhead, including garbage collection, data copying, and internal batch reorganization, which increases inter-batch latency.

To address this, we introduce a bounded-iteration repair phase, designed to leverage useful information retained in GPU memory from the multi-version execution process, such as precomputed indices and pointers to version-metadata

Algorithm 2 Commit phase

```
Input: Status bitmap array status, Transaction IDs T_id
Output: Final commit decision CD_res
// Each 64-bit bitmap word stores the validation results of 64 consecutive transactions.
// Bit = 1/0 indicates validation success/failure;
// FULL_MASK = 0xffffffffffffffff.
Function CommitTransactions(batch)
  status ← AllValidateStatus(T)
  for all thread in Warp do
    for all i in [0, Tid/64)
      if status[i] ≠ FULL_MASK then
        commit ← false
        return
      end if
    end for
    // Prefix mask covering all transactions
    // from the beginning of the current
    // bitmap segment to transaction Tid.
    mask ← (1 ≪ (Tid mod 64 + 1)) − 1
    if (status[i]&mask) == mask then
      commit ← true
    end if
  end for
```

entries, as illustrated in Algorithm 3. By reusing this information, the computational overhead of the repair process is minimized. Crucially, the repair phase does not create new versions. Instead, it performs in-place updates to existing ones. Compared to aborting and re-executing transactions, this lightweight repair phase reduces the number of instructions that need to be re-executed. Furthermore, transactions already committed during the repair phase can be directly skipped.

Garbage collection. Implementing a standalone garbage collector on GPUs is nontrivial, so we adopt a simplified scheme based on single-version-to-multiversion snapshot transfer. During the transaction commit phase, we write data back to the single-version snapshot, while the versioned data of the current batch residing in GPU memory is directly cleared. As a result, the multiversion state is ephemeral: it is effective only during the execution and repair iterations of the current batch and remains invisible to subsequent batches.

4.2 Theoretical Analysis

To quantify the efficiency of GMVCC, we establish a cost model focused on its core execution phases. Let T be the initial batch size, U_i the uncommitted transactions in round i, c_r the conflict probability, and k the GPU parallelism capacity. The total cost is defined as $C_{total} = \sum_{i=1}^{r} C_{round\_i} + C_{gc}$.In the first round, the execution cost C_{exec} accounts for both metadata and payload operations. To reflect our optimization, we introduce an improvement coefficient α for metadata-payload separation. The overhead is modeled as:$C_{exec} =$

Algorithm 3 Repair Phase

```
Input: Transaction Set T, Snapshot S, Multi-version Buffer B
Output: Updated Metadata M', Repair Results RR_res
Function RepairTransactions(T, S, B)
  for each subTransaction in T do
    if subTransaction.committed then
      continue
    end if
    if NeedRepair(subTransaction, B) then
      exec(SubTxnInst)
//updates version references and visibility metadata using existing version
// entries without allocating new versions.
      RelinkingMetaData()
    end if
  end for
```

$\alpha \cdot T \cdot W \cdot \left[\frac{t_{data}}{k} + t_{meta} \cdot \left(c_r \cdot p + \frac{1-c_r \cdot p}{k}\right)\right]$ where p represents the probability of atomic coordination for concurrent writes.For subsequent rounds ($r \geq 2$), GMVCC replaces the full execution phase with a Repair Phase. Its cost C_{rep} follows a similar structure to C_{exec} but utilizes a reduced metadata overhead t_{meta-r}, reflecting the efficiency of salvaging partial results. Combined with the validation (C_{val}) and commit (C_{commit}) overheads—both of which scale with U_i and the hardware limit k—the model demonstrates that GMVCC minimizes C_{total} by reducing both the number of re-executed transactions and the per-transaction synchronization penalty on the GPU.

4.3 Optimization Strategies

While adaptive warp partitioning maximizes utilization, it fails to prevent repeated aborts due to nondeterministic re-scheduling. Informed by contention data from the initial execution, we introduce a conflict-aware task distribution for the repair phase. This hybrid approach steers repair more effectively while retaining high utilization during the initial execution.

Task distribution.

The task distribution mechanism spans the validation and repair phases to enable informed scheduling. During validation, per-item contention is recorded in metadata and a global task table, which is then sorted by (transaction ID, item ID). Threads retrieve repair tasks from the resulting queue, prioritizing transactions with smaller IDs within the same warp to minimize potential conflicts. The execution is semi-preemptive: if a larger-ID transaction is scheduled ahead of competing smaller-ID tasks, the thread detects the conflict during metadata scanning and attempts a task re-retrieval. Regardless of the re-retrieval outcome, the thread completes its current task to maintain high hardware utilization. This mechanism approximates an internal priority-based schedule within the repair phase, avoiding the high abort rates of unordered parallel execution without resorting to serial execution, which would otherwise fail to exploit GPU's massive thread parallelism.

Data reuse. GMVCC employs a change bit in the control-metadata region to accelerate scans. For reads issued in the repair phase, if the change bit is unset-meaning the control metadata has not been updated since the prior read-the system reuses the previously computed read result. This avoids redundant metadata traversal and memory accesses, directly reducing read latency in the repair phase. In addition, GMVCC caches immutable artifacts (e.g., base-row indices and pointers into the metadata region) in each transaction's data region. By retaining these values locally, the repair phase can access them via direct lookups, eliminating repeated index construction and pointer resolution.

5 Experiment Study

In this section, we present a comprehensive evaluation of GMVCC. We first describe the experimental setup, then conduct three experiments: (i) end-to-end performance relative to state-of-the-art baselines, (ii) GPU-side batch-execution characteristics, and (iii) effectiveness of the core optimizations. Across all experiments, we report throughput, commit rate, and latency, and relate the findings to GMVCC's core design principles.

5.1 Experimental Setup

Benchmarks. We use two standard benchmarks: TPC-C [1] (executing the dominant NewOrder and Payment mix, ≈90% of the full workload) and YCSB [5] (evaluating throughput and scalability under various read/write ratios).
Hardware environment. Experiments are conducted on a server equipped with an NVIDIA RTX A6000 GPU and 30-core Intel Xeon CPUs (768 GB RAM). We compare the GPU-based system (1 GPU) against the CPU-based system (30 cores) within a single NUMA region. Notably, the acquisition costs of these two setups are comparable, ensuring a fair performance-per-dollar evaluation.
Comparison systems. We compare GMVCC against representative CPU-based baselines (DBx1000 [24], Bohm [7], Aria [13]) and state-of-the-art GPU-accelerated systems (GPUTx [11], Gacco [3], LTPG [21]).

Our experiments were conducted using the official code for open-source CPU systems and our own re-implementations of the non-open-source GPU systems.

5.2 Overall Performance Acceleration

For mixed workloads (50% NewOrder and 50% Payment), GMVCC achieves throughput values close to the leading baseline systems, as shown in Table 2. Specifically, its throughput reaches 2.33×10^6 TX/s (1 warehouse), 19.16×10^6 TX/s (16 warehouses), 18.09×10^6 TX/s (32 warehouses), and 16.94×10^6 TX/s (64 warehouses)-a performance that is only 5–8% lower than LTPG [21], the top-performing GPU-based system for mixed workloads. This small performance gap can be attributed to GMVCC's multi-version design. In mixed workloads, the diversity and unpredictability of data access patterns limit the effectiveness of GMVCC's transaction repair mechanism in mitigating conflict-induced performance degradation. When access patterns vary, the repair mechanism may struggle to resolve conflicts efficiently, resulting in suboptimal GPU parallelism and

Table 2. Comparison of existing transaction processing systems (10^6 TX/S)

System	0_1^1	0_{16}	0_{32}	0_{64}	50_1	50_{16}	50_{32}	50_{64}	100_1	100_{16}	100_{32}	100_{64}
DBx1000 [24]	0.11	3.82	7.09	9.98	0.83	2.62	2.59	2.21	0.17	1.63	1.37	1.12
Bohm [7]	0.005	0.01	0.02	0.03	0.004	0.02	0.03	0.04	0.10	0.06	0.08	0.11
Aria [13]	0.07	0.19	0.44	0.77	0.19	0.60	0.77	0.98	0.12	1.00	1.08	1.12
GPUTx [11]	0.06	0.67	0.53	0.41	0.02	0.02	0.01	0.09	0.01	0.09	0.06	0.04
Gacco [3]	84.85	84.40	85.12	94.98	1.63	15.78	15.52	15.27	1.37	13.10	12.73	12.63
LTPG [21]	1.89	17.38	16.62	15.83	2.01	18.43	18.61	17.92	1.96	18.63	23.05	22.96
GMVCC	2.20	19.69	19.93	20.88	2.33	19.16	18.09	16.94	2.20	24.17	27.37	28.49

We donate a_b as a percentage neworder transactions in b warehouses

reduced performance. Additionally, the presence of multiple transaction types complicates data access patterns, causing uneven hot-spot data distribution and increasing challenges in version management and transaction scheduling.

In single-transaction workloads (100% NewOrder), GMVCC outperforms all baselines: 24.17×10^6 TX/s (16 warehouses), 27.37×10^6 TX/s (32 warehouses), and 28.49×10^6 TX/s (64 warehouses), exceeding LTPG by 12.3–29.7%. We attribute this advantage to GMVCC's GPU-optimized multiversion design-specifically, metadata-payload separation and the intra-batch repair phase. These mechanisms operate exceptionally well in single-transaction scenarios, ensuring high throughput.

5.3 GPU-Side Batch Execution Characteristics

This section evaluates GMVCC's GPU-side batch execution using TPC-C and a range of YCSB workloads. All reported results include host-device data-transfer overheads.

Processing performance on TPC-C. We study how transaction-batch size and dataset scale affect throughput, commit rate, and latency under a 100% NewOrder workload.

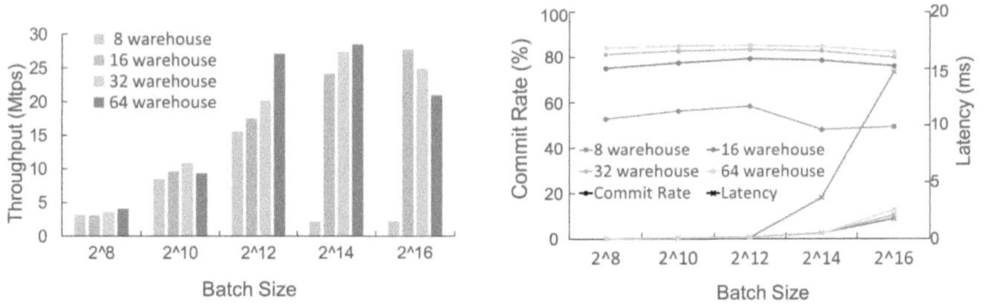

(a) Throughput of GMVCC (b) Commit Rate/Latency of GMVCC

Fig. 4. Processing performance of GMVCC

The results of this experiment are shown in Fig. 4(4). Under appropriate batch sizes $2^{12} - 2^{14}$, GMVCC's core designs fully leverage GPU multi-core scalability, achieving throughputs of 24.177×10^6-28.493×10^6 TX/s, commit rates of 78.8–84.8%, and latencies of 0.487–0.534 ms for 16–64 Warehouses. Under extreme contention (8 Warehouse), GMVCC exhibits significant performance degradation. Data concentration leads to frequent transaction conflicts that exceed the mitigation capacity of the transaction repair mechanism, resulting in underutilized GPU parallelism. As shown in Fig. 4(b), throughput peaks at a moderate batch size and then drops sharply, while latency rises drastically as batch size increases, as to maintain the commit rate, the latency increases significantly. For extra-large batches (exceeding 2^{14}), GMVCC's performance also declines. Although data dispersion in large batches helps slightly improve execution phase commit rates by reducing local hot-spot conflicts, this gain is insufficient to offset the latency overhead introduced by GMVCC's multi-version design. The fragmentation of the metadata region disrupts GPU-optimized coalesced memory access, and accumulated overhead from version creation and data transfer further drives down overall performance.

Processing performance on YCSB. In this section, with the batch size fixed at 10^4, we investigated the system throughput of different data sizes under various YCSB workloads. A Zipfian distribution with parameter $\alpha = 2.5$ was used to simulate skewed data access. Among these workloads, "100% Read" represents the Read-Only workload, "20% Write-80% Read" represents the Read-Heavy workload, "20% Read-80% Write" represents the Write-Heavy workload, and the Read-Latest workload was also tested. We use LTPG [21], the state-of-the-art single-version GPU transaction processing system, as the comparison baseline.

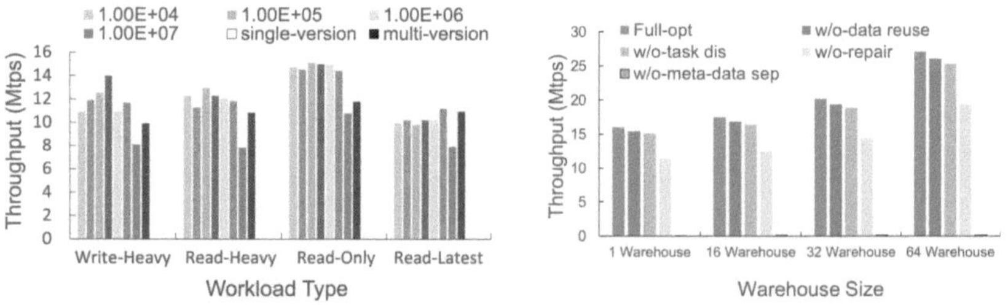

(a) System performance on YCSB (b) The impact of core optimization

Fig. 5. YCSB experiment results and ablation study results

The results are shown in Fig. 5(a). In single-workload configurations that include writes, GMVCC's throughput exhibits an increase-then-decrease pattern as the dataset scales, driven by its multi-version design (metadata-payload separation) and GPU memory-access characteristics. With small datasets, the metadata region maintains strong locality, enabling efficient scans; as the dataset grows, hot spots are dispersed while metadata remains centralized, further increasing throughput. Beyond a size threshold, however, table growth fragments the metadata region, disrupting coalesced memory accesses and raising thread scan latency; in addition, host-device transfers and version-creation costs accumulate with scale. Although larger datasets continue to reduce contention, these combined overheads outweigh the benefit, causing throughput to decline.

In **read-only workloads**, GMVCC and LTPG [21] maintain performance within the same order of magnitude, with no substantial gap. GMVCC leverages a CPU-GPU single-version snapshot transfer mechanism to reuse single-version data initially synchronized to the GPU, eliminating the overhead of multi-version metadata traversal. Because read-only workloads create no new versions, only minimal checks of the control-metadata region are required. Consequently, the performance gap remains within 5%, and GMVCC exhibits no notable performance loss. In **mixed workloads with low write ratios**, the relative performance of GMVCC and LTPG is contingent on the data size. For small to medium-sized datasets, LTPG maintains a slight performance edge. The low write ratio minimizes contention, allowing its lightweight, single-version architecture to operate with high efficiency. In contrast, GMVCC incurs a minor overhead from version creation, even with few writes, which leads to marginally lower performance than LTPG in these scenarios. However, as the data size increases to 10^6 or more, the architectural benefits of GMVCC begin to offset this overhead, allowing it to outperform LTPG.In **write-heavy workloads**, GMVCC consistently outperforms LTPG, with its performance advantage widening as the data size increases. This is driven by GMVCC's native support for parallel version creation, which eliminates the write serialization bottlenecks inherent in LTPG. Furthermore, the transaction repair mechanism effectively minimizes the re-execution overhead of aborted transactions, significantly boosting throughput in high-contention scenarios. As the dataset scales, this combination of advantages allows GMVCC's performance lead to expand to 20–30%.

5.4 Effects of Core Optimizations

In this section, we quantify the contribution of GMVCC's optimization mechanisms via ablation: we disable each mechanism in isolation and measure the resulting throughput degradation.We evaluate four mechanisms in Fig. 5(b): metadata-payload separation, intra-batch repair, task redistribution, and data reuse. The repair phase is the principal performance driver, accounting for approximately 40% of the overall gain. Task redistribution yields a slightly larger benefit than data reuse: disabling the former reduces throughput by an additional 1%-2% relative to disabling the latter. The redistribution mechanism enhances the adaptability of parallel scheduling under high contention by redistributing tasks, whereas data reuse mainly removes local redundant accesses. Metadata-payload separation serves as a foundational prerequisite for the other mechanisms.

6 Conclusion

We present GMVCC, a GPU-based transaction processing system built around multiversion optimistic concurrency control. GMVCC revisits the design space for GPU-based OLTP under multi-version storage and reduces overhead via metadata-payload separation and an intra-batch repair phase. We further introduce optimizations that exploit multi-version information to lower in-batch aborts. In experiments on TPC-C, GMVCC delivers up to 1.3× higher throughput than state-of-the-art GPU OLTP systems and maintains superior performance under write-heavy workloads.

Acknowledgments. This work was supported by the National Natural Science Foundation of China (U23B2019).

References

1. TPC Benchmark C. (2010). http://www.tpc.org/tpcc/
2. Boeschen, N., Binnig, C.: Galop: Towards a gpu-accelerated OLTP DBMS. In: DaMoN, pp. 9:1–9:3 (2021)
3. Boeschen, N., Binnig, C.: Gacco - A gpu-accelerated OLTP DBMS. In: SIGMOD, pp. 1003–1016 (2022)
4. Burke, M., Suri-Payer, F., Helt, J., Alvisi, L., Crooks, N.: Morty: scaling concurrency control with re-execution. EuroSys, pp. 687–702 (2023)
5. Cooper, B.F., Silberstein, A., Tam, E., Ramakrishnan, R., Sears, R.: Benchmarking cloud serving systems with YCSB. SoCC, pp. 143–154 (2010)
6. Dong, Z., Wang, Z., Zhang, X., Xu, X., Zhao, C., Chen, H., Panda, A., Li, J.: Fine-grained re-execution for efficient batched commit of distributed transactions. Proc. VLDB Endow. **16**(8), 1930–1943 (2023)
7. Faleiro, J.M., Abadi, D.J.: Rethinking serializable multiversion concurrency control. Proc. VLDB Endow. **8**(11), 1190–1201 (2015)
8. Gao, L., Wang, J., Zhang, W.: Adaptive contention management for fine-grained synchronization on commodity gpus. ACM Trans. Archit. Code Optim. **19**(4), 58:1–58:21 (2022)
9. Gao, L., Xu, Y., Wang, R., Luan, Z., Yu, Z., Qian, D.: Thread-level locking for SIMT architectures. IEEE Trans. Parallel Distributed Syst. **31**(5), 1121–1136 (2020)
10. Gao, L., Xu, Y., Wang, R., Yang, H., Luan, Z., Qian, D.: Accelerating in-memory transaction processing using general purpose graphics processing units. Future Gener. Comput. Syst. **97**, 836–848 (2019)
11. He, B., Yu, J.X.: High-throughput transaction executions on graphics processors. Proc. VLDB Endow. **4**(5), 314–325 (2011)
12. Cooper, B.F., Silberstein, A., Tam, E., Ramakrishnan, R., Sears, R.: Benchmarking cloud serving systems with YCSB. SoCC, pp. 143–154 (2010)
13. Lu, Y., Yu, X., Cao, L., Madden, S.: Aria: a fast and practical deterministic OLTP database. Proc. VLDB Endow. **13**(11), 2047–2060 (2020)
14. Qin, D., Brown, A.D., Goel, A.: Caracal: contention management with deterministic concurrency control. SOSP, pp. 180–194 (2021)

15. Riegger, C., Vinçon, T., Petrov, I.: Multi-version indexing and modern hardware technologies: a survey of present indexing approaches. iiWAS, pp. 266–275 (2017)
16. Rosenfeld, V., Breß, S., Markl, V.: Query processing on heterogeneous CPU/GPU systems. ACM Comput. Surv. **55**(2), 11:1–11:38 (2023)
17. Sui, Y., Yang, X., Wang, B., Zhang, Y., Zheng, B.: Wait and see: A delayed transactions partitioning approach in deterministic database systems for better performance. Proceedings of the ACM on Management of Data **3**, 1–27 (2025)
18. Thomson, A., Diamond, T., Weng, S., Ren, K., Shao, P., Abadi, D.J.: Calvin: fast distributed transactions for partitioned database systems. In: SIGMOD, pp. 1–12 (2012)
19. Wang, X., Peng, Y., Huang, H.: Gria: an efficient deterministic concurrency control protocol. Front. Comput. Sci. **18**(4) (2024)
20. Wang, X., Peng, Y., Huang, H., Li, X.: Dodo: a scalable optimistic deterministic concurrency control protocol. Future Gener. Comput. Syst. **159**, 15–26 (2024)
21. Wei, J., Gu, Y., Li, T., Qi, J., Li, C., Zhang, Y., Jensen, C.S., Yu, G.: LTPG: large-batch transaction processing on gpus with deterministic concurrency control. In: ICDE, pp. 3865–3877 (2024)
22. Wu, Y., Arulraj, J., Lin, J., Xian, R., Pavlo, A.: An empirical evaluation of in-memory multi-version concurrency control. Proc. VLDB Endow. **10**(7), 781–792 (2017)
23. Wu, Y., Chan, C.Y., Tan, K.: Transaction healing: Scaling optimistic concurrency control on multicores. In: SIGMOD. pp, pp. 1689–1704. (2016)
24. Yu, X., Bezerra, G., Pavlo, A., Devadas, S., Stonebraker, M.: Staring into the abyss: an evaluation of concurrency control with one thousand cores. Proc. VLDB Endow. **8**(3), 209–220 (2014)

TabDitFlow: Flow Matching with Diffusion Transformer for Tabular Data Generation

Yangchen Ou[1,2], Jun Fang[1,2(✉)], and Enyu Cui[1,2]

[1] School of Information, North China University of Technology, Beijing, China
fangjun@ncut.edu.cn
[2] Beijing Key Laboratory on Integration and Analysis of Large-Scale Stream Data, North China University of Technology, Beijing, China

Abstract. Generating high-fidelity synthetic tabular data is an important and challenging problem. The main difficulty lies in the heterogeneous nature of tabular features and the complex dependencies across columns. Although recent diffusion-based methods have shown promising results, they often rely on stochastic sampling trajectories, which can reduce sampling efficiency, and may struggle to capture feature interactions effectively. In this paper, we propose TabDitFlow, a generative method that combines conditional flow matching based on a linear interpolation path with a diffusion Transformer tailored to tabular data. By training with straight-line conditional flow matching paths, TabDitFlow provides a deterministic ODE-based generation process as an alternative to stochastic diffusion sampling. We further adopt a column-wise tokenization scheme and incorporate the AdaLN-Zero conditioning mechanism in the Transformer backbone, enabling the model to better capture dependencies across features and handle mixed-type tabular data within a unified feature space. Experiments on multiple real-world benchmark datasets show that TabDitFlow achieves strong and competitive performance in both statistical fidelity and downstream utility.

Keywords: tabular data generation · conditional flow matching · diffusion Transformer

1 Introduction

Tabular data is one of the most important data forms in machine learning. It is widely used in finance, healthcare, public administration and education [5,6,11,20]. Unlike images and text, tabular data usually contains both numerical and categorical features. Different columns often have different data types, value ranges and semantic meanings. This gives tabular data an inherently heterogeneous structure.

In real-world applications, high-quality tabular data is often difficult to obtain. Privacy regulations such as the EU General Data Protection Regulation [19] and the US Health Insurance Portability and Accountability Act [1]

L. Ding et al. (Eds.): APWeb-WAIM 2026, LNCS 16993, pp. 132–146, 2027.
https://doi.org/10.1007/978-981-92-5693-8_9

impose strict constraints on the collection, storage and sharing of sensitive data. In many domains, data collection is also slow and costly. Real-world datasets often suffer from limited sample sizes and severe class imbalance. Meanwhile, the heterogeneous nature of tabular data makes high-quality tabular generation particularly challenging. On this background, tabular data generation has attracted increasing attention, because it aims to produce substitute data that preserve reasonable structure and statistical characteristics while reducing the direct exposure of sensitive records [23].

To address this problem, researchers have proposed many deep generative methods for tabular data. These methods include GAN-based models [9], VAE-based models [12], large-language-model-based methods [4] and diffusion-based methods [10]. Although these methods have advanced the field, they still face clear limitations on complex tabular data. Existing methods often struggle to capture heterogeneous feature semantics and complex cross-column dependencies. They may also fail to preserve the joint distribution of real data. Diffusion models, in particular, show strong distribution modeling ability and stable training behavior. However, their generation process relies on stochastic diffusion paths. These paths are often indirect and usually require many sampling steps. This leads to high inference cost and limits efficiency in large-scale tabular generation.

Flow matching [15] provides a promising alternative to diffusion-based generation. Traditional diffusion models learn a stochastic reverse process from noise to data. In contrast, flow matching learns a deterministic ordinary differential equation that transports samples from a simple prior distribution to the target data distribution. In particular, conditional flow matching with a linear interpolation path constructs intermediate states between a noise sample and a real sample. This makes probability transport more direct and simplifies the learning objective. However, flow matching mainly provides a deterministic generative framework. Its final performance still depends on the expressive power of the velocity network. For mixed-type tabular data, insufficient modeling of heterogeneous features and cross-column dependencies can still limit generation quality.

Motivated by this, we propose TabDitFlow for tabular data generation. TabDitFlow combines conditional flow matching based on a linear interpolation path with a diffusion Transformer [18]. It uses conditional flow matching as the generative foundation and adopts a Transformer backbone tailored for tabular data. Specifically, TabDitFlow maps numerical features into a standard normal space through quantile transformation to better align them with the Gaussian prior. It then applies column-wise tokenization so that each column is represented as an independent Transformer token. This design strengthens the modeling of heterogeneous features and cross-column dependencies. For classification tasks, TabDitFlow adopts AdaLN-Zero modulation to inject continuous time information and class-label conditioning into each layer. For regression tasks, the target value is treated as an additional numerical column rather than an external condition. TabDitFlow provides a deterministic ODE-based generation framework and strengthens the modeling of cross-column dependencies.

The main contributions of this paper are summarized as follows:

1. We propose TabDitFlow, a flow matching based method for tabular data generation. By combining conditional flow matching based on a linear interpolation path with a structured DiT backbone, TabDitFlow provides a deterministic ODE-based generation framework and strengthens the modeling of cross-column dependencies.
2. We develop a tabular-oriented modeling scheme for mixed-type data. It includes numerical distribution alignment, column-wise tokenization and task-specific conditioning strategies. These designs help preserve heterogeneous feature semantics and improve the quality of generated samples.
3. Extensive experiments on five real-world tabular datasets demonstrate that TabDitFlow achieves competitive performance in both downstream utility and statistical fidelity. It also shows competitive performance in preserving numerical correlation structures and representative bivariate distributions.

2 Related Work

Tabular data generation has become an important topic in generative modeling [22]. Due to the heterogeneous feature types and complex column dependencies in tabular data, generation requires accurate modeling of both marginal distributions and joint data structures. Existing methods can be broadly grouped into GAN-based methods, VAE-based methods, language-model-based methods [7], diffusion-based methods [14] and flow-matching-based methods.

Early representative methods include CTGAN [24] and TVAE [17]. CTGAN introduces conditional adversarial learning and feature-specific normalization for mixed-type tabular data. However, adversarial training is often unstable, and its ability to capture complex joint distributions can be limited. TVAE applies variational autoencoders to tabular generation and provides more stable training, but its generation quality is constrained by the latent distribution assumption and the decoding process. GReaT [3] transforms each table row into a text sequence and fine-tunes a language model to generate tabular records autoregressively. Although this provides a new perspective for tabular generation, sequential text generation may suffer from limited efficiency and format inconsistency on complex tables.

Diffusion models have recently achieved competitive performance in tabular data generation. TabDDPM [13] introduces denoising diffusion probabilistic models into tabular generation and shows clear advantages over earlier GAN- and VAE-based methods. TabDiff [21] further develops a unified diffusion framework for mixed-type tabular data, using feature-wise diffusion processes and a Transformer-based denoising network to model different feature types and column relationships. Nevertheless, diffusion-based methods usually rely on stochastic diffusion paths and multi-step iterative sampling, which increases inference cost [2].

Flow matching provides another promising direction for generative modeling [16]. Instead of learning a stochastic denoising process, flow matching learns a deterministic velocity field that transports samples from a simple prior distribution to the data distribution. Recently, RecTable [8] applies rectified flow to tabular generation and demonstrates the potential of flow-based methods for efficient sample generation. However, existing flow matching based tabular methods still face challenges in modeling heterogeneous feature semantics, complex column dependencies and real data distributions. This motivates our proposed TabDitFlow, which combines conditional flow matching with a tabular-oriented diffusion Transformer backbone.

3 Problem Definition

Given a tabular dataset $D = \{(\mathbf{x}^{(i)}, y^{(i)})\}_{i=1}^{N}$, $\mathbf{x}^{(i)}$ denotes the feature vector of the i-th sample and contains numerical and categorical features. $y^{(i)}$ denotes the corresponding target variable. After preprocessing, each sample is mapped into a vector $\mathbf{z}^{(i)}$ in a unified feature space. The distribution of real data in this space is denoted by $p_{\text{real}}(\mathbf{z})$.

The goal of tabular data generation is to learn a generative model and produce a synthetic dataset $\tilde{D} = \{\tilde{\mathbf{z}}^{(i)}\}_{i=1}^{M}$. The synthetic data should be as close as possible to the real data distribution in a statistical sense. It should also preserve the marginal distributions of heterogeneous columns and the dependencies among columns as much as possible.

For regression tasks, the target value is treated as an additional numerical column and is modeled together with the other feature columns. In this case, the problem is to learn a synthetic distribution $p_{\text{syn}}(\mathbf{z})$ that is close to the real data distribution $p_{\text{real}}(\mathbf{z})$, that is,

$$\min \ \text{dist}\big(p_{\text{syn}}(\mathbf{z}), p_{\text{real}}(\mathbf{z})\big). \tag{1}$$

For classification tasks, the class label y is used as conditional information. The model learns the data distribution under a given class condition and generates samples that match the specified class. In this case, the problem is to learn a conditional synthetic distribution $p_{\text{syn}}(\mathbf{z} \mid y)$ that is close to the conditional real data distribution $p_{\text{real}}(\mathbf{z} \mid y)$, that is,

$$\min \ \text{dist}\big(p_{\text{syn}}(\mathbf{z} \mid y), p_{\text{real}}(\mathbf{z} \mid y)\big). \tag{2}$$

Here, $\text{dist}(\cdot, \cdot)$ denotes the discrepancy between the synthetic distribution and the real distribution.

4 Preliminaries

Flow matching is a continuous-time generative modeling method that learns a velocity field to transport samples from a simple prior distribution to a target data distribution. Instead of constructing a stochastic denoising process, flow matching defines a continuous probability path between the source distribution and the target distribution and trains a neural network to predict the corresponding velocity along this path. Once the velocity field is learned, new samples can be generated by solving the associated ordinary differential equation from the prior distribution to the data distribution.

Let $\mathbf{z}_0 \sim \pi$ be a sample drawn from a simple prior distribution and let $\mathbf{z}_1 \sim q$ be a sample drawn from the target data distribution. A commonly used probability path between them is defined by linear interpolation:

$$\mathbf{z}_t = \psi_t(\mathbf{z}_0, \mathbf{z}_1) = (1-t)\mathbf{z}_0 + t\mathbf{z}_1, \quad t \in [0, 1]. \tag{3}$$

Here, t denotes the continuous time variable. When $t = 0$, the sample lies at the source point $\mathbf{z}_0$ and when $t = 1$, it reaches the target point $\mathbf{z}_1$. Therefore, $\mathbf{z}_t$ describes a continuous trajectory that connects the prior distribution and the target distribution.

The target velocity along this path is obtained by differentiating $\mathbf{z}_t$ with respect to t:

$$\mathbf{u}_t(\mathbf{z}_t \mid \mathbf{z}_0, \mathbf{z}_1) = \frac{d\mathbf{z}_t}{dt} = \mathbf{z}_1 - \mathbf{z}_0. \tag{4}$$

Under the linear interpolation path, the target velocity is constant with respect to t. This property makes the learning objective simple and stable, since the network only needs to match the displacement vector from the source point to the target point along the path.

Flow matching learns a parametric velocity field $v_\theta(\mathbf{z}_t, t)$ by regressing the target velocity along the interpolation path. The standard objective is

$$\mathcal{L}_{\mathrm{FM}}(\theta) = \mathbb{E}_{t \sim U(0,1),\, \mathbf{z}_0 \sim \pi,\, \mathbf{z}_1 \sim q} \left[\left\| v_\theta(\psi_t(\mathbf{z}_0, \mathbf{z}_1), t) - (\mathbf{z}_1 - \mathbf{z}_0) \right\|_2^2 \right]. \tag{5}$$

This objective samples a time point t uniformly from $[0, 1]$ and minimizes the discrepancy between the predicted velocity and the target velocity at the corresponding intermediate state $\mathbf{z}_t$. In this way, the network is trained to approximate the velocity field over the entire transport path rather than at a single endpoint.

After training, generation is performed by solving the ordinary differential equation associated with the learned velocity field. Starting from a sample drawn from the prior distribution, the learned flow transports it continuously toward the target data distribution.

5 Methodology

TabDitFlow is a conditional flow matching method for mixed-type tabular data generation. As shown in Fig. 1, its pipeline consists of three stages. First, numerical and categorical features are transformed into a unified feature space. Second, intermediate samples are tokenized column by column and processed by a DiT backbone to predict the velocity field. Finally, synthetic samples are generated by solving the corresponding ODE and applying inverse preprocessing.

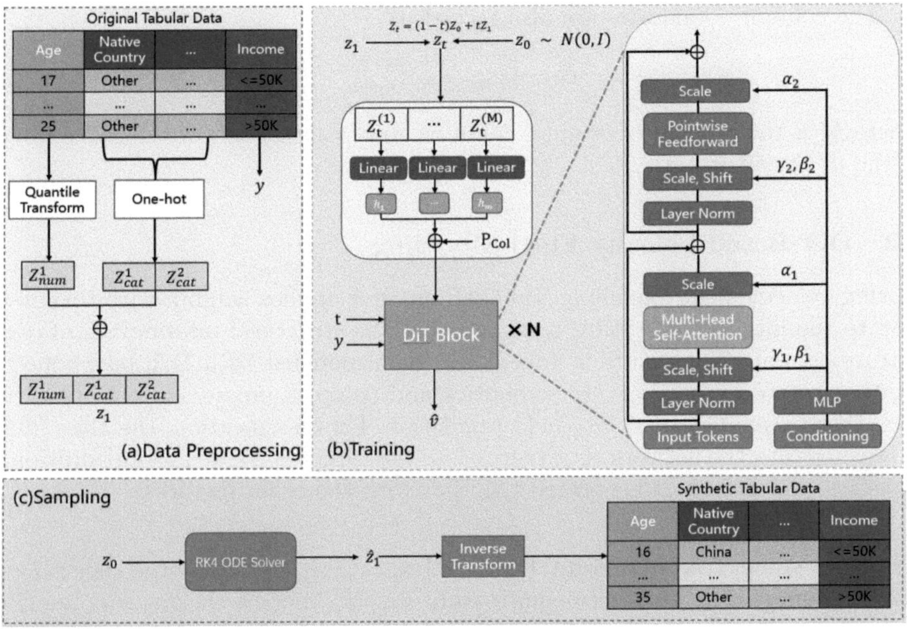

Fig. 1. Overview of TabDitFlow. The framework includes data preprocessing, conditional flow matching training and ODE-based sampling. Column-wise tokens are fed into a DiT-based velocity network, and synthetic samples are obtained through velocity-field integration and inverse preprocessing.

5.1 Data Preprocessing

Tabular data contains numerical and categorical features. Flow matching works in a continuous Euclidean space. Each feature is therefore mapped into a unified vector representation.

For a numerical feature x_j, a quantile transform is applied:

$$z_j = \Phi^{-1}\big(\hat{F}_j(x_j)\big), \tag{6}$$

where $\hat{F}_j$ is the empirical cumulative distribution function of the j-th feature and Φ^{-1} is the inverse cumulative distribution function of the standard normal distribution.

For a categorical feature c_k, one-hot encoding is used:

$$\mathbf{z}_k = \mathrm{OneHot}(c_k) \in \{0,1\}^{K_k}, \tag{7}$$

where K_k is the number of categories in the k-th feature.

All processed features are concatenated into a unified vector:

$$\mathbf{z} = \mathrm{Concat}\big(z_1, \ldots, z_{M_n}, \mathbf{z}_1, \ldots, \mathbf{z}_{M_c}\big) \in \mathbb{R}^D, \tag{8}$$

where M_n and M_c denote the numbers of numerical and categorical features and D is the total dimension after concatenation.

The column boundaries are also recorded:

$$\mathcal{S} = \{(s_m, e_m)\}_{m=1}^{M}, \tag{9}$$

where M is the number of original columns and (s_m, e_m) denotes the slice range of the m-th column in $\mathbf{z}$.

5.2 DiT-Based Velocity Field Modeling

During velocity field modeling, TabDitFlow first applies column-wise tokenization to the intermediate state z_t to preserve the structural information of each feature column. The resulting tokens are then modeled by a DiT backbone to capture heterogeneous feature semantics and complex cross-column dependencies, thereby enabling velocity field prediction. For classification, the class label is injected into the network. For regression, the target is treated as an additional numerical column. It is generated together with the other features.

Column-Wise Tokenization. Let $\mathcal{S} = \{(s_m, e_m)\}_{m=1}^{M}$ denote the slice ranges of all columns. For an intermediate state $\mathbf{z}_t$, the slice of the m-th column is written as $\mathbf{z}_t^{(m)}$. A column-wise token is then constructed by

$$\mathbf{h}_m = \mathbf{W}_{\text{in}}^{(m)} \mathbf{z}_t^{(m)} + \mathbf{b}_{\text{in}}^{(m)} + \mathbf{P}_{\text{col}}^{(m)}. \tag{10}$$

Here $\mathbf{W}_{\text{in}}^{(m)}$ and $\mathbf{b}_{\text{in}}^{(m)}$ are learnable projection parameters for the m-th column. $\mathbf{P}_{\text{col}}^{(m)}$ is a learnable column embedding.

The token sequence is

$$\mathbf{H} = [\mathbf{h}_1, \mathbf{h}_2, \ldots, \mathbf{h}_M]. \tag{11}$$

This sequence preserves column boundaries and column identities. It also provides a structured input for later dependency modeling.

DiT-Based Velocity Prediction. The token sequence $\mathbf{H}$ is fed into a DiT backbone. The backbone models interactions across columns through self-attention.

For classification, the time step t and the class label y are encoded and fused as

$$\mathbf{c} = \text{MLP}\big(\text{Sin}(t) + \text{Emb}(y)\big). \tag{12}$$

Here $\text{Sin}(t)$ is the sinusoidal time embedding and $\text{Emb}(y)$ is the label embedding.

For regression, no label embedding is used. The modulation input only contains the time embedding.

AdaLN-Zero style modulation is used in each DiT block. The modulation parameters are

$$(\gamma_1, \beta_1, \alpha_1, \gamma_2, \beta_2, \alpha_2) = \text{Split}\big(\text{Linear}(\text{SiLU}(\mathbf{c}))\big). \tag{13}$$

Given the input token sequence $\mathbf{H}$, one DiT block is defined as

$$\mathbf{H}_{\text{norm1}} = \text{LayerNorm}(\mathbf{H}) \odot (1 + \gamma_1) + \beta_1, \tag{14}$$

$$\mathbf{H}_{\text{attn}} = \mathbf{H} + \alpha_1 \odot \text{MHSA}(\mathbf{H}_{\text{norm1}}), \tag{15}$$

$$\mathbf{H}_{\text{norm2}} = \text{LayerNorm}(\mathbf{H}_{\text{attn}}) \odot (1 + \gamma_2) + \beta_2, \tag{16}$$

$$\mathbf{H}_{\text{out}} = \mathbf{H}_{\text{attn}} + \alpha_2 \odot \text{FFN}(\mathbf{H}_{\text{norm2}}). \tag{17}$$

Here MHSA($\cdot$) denotes multi-head self-attention, FFN($\cdot$) denotes the feed-forward network and $\odot$ denotes element-wise multiplication.

After several DiT blocks, the output sequence is mapped back to the unified space. This gives the predicted velocity field.

5.3 Sampling

During sampling, generation is formulated as an initial value problem of an ordinary differential equation (ODE). We first sample an initial noise vector $\mathbf{z}_0 \sim \mathcal{N}(\mathbf{0}, \mathbf{I})$ and then integrate the learned probability flow. For classification tasks, sampling is conditioned on the specified class label y, while for regression tasks the target value is generated jointly with the feature columns because it is included in the tabular representation itself.

For classification tasks, the sampling process is governed by

$$d\mathbf{z}_t = v_\theta(\mathbf{z}_t, t, y)\, dt \tag{18}$$

In practice, we solve this ODE using the fourth-order Runge–Kutta (RK4) solver. The step size is set as $h = 1/S$, where S denotes the number of sampling steps.

After ODE integration, the generated vector is mapped back to the original tabular space through inverse preprocessing. Numerical features are restored by inverse quantile transformation, while categorical features are converted back from their encoded form to the corresponding category labels.

6 Experiments

6.1 Experimental Setup

Datasets. We conduct experiments on five real-world tabular datasets: Adult, Default, Churn2, California Housing, and Abalone. Adult, Default, and Abalone are obtained from the UCI Machine Learning Repository, while Churn2 and California Housing are obtained from Kaggle. These datasets cover financial risk control, customer churn prediction in banking, house price estimation, and biological regression tasks. They include both binary classification and regression problems. This setting allows a broad evaluation of the proposed method across domains and downstream tasks and tests the ability to fit different data distributions. Detailed statistics are reported in Table 1. For each dataset, we split the real data into a training set D_{train}, a validation set D_{val}, and a test set D_{test} with an 8:1:1 ratio (Table 1).

Table 1. Detailed statistics of the datasets used in our experiments.

Dataset	#Samples	Task	#Numerical	#Categorical
Adult	48842	Classification	6	8
Default	30000	Classification	14	9
Churn2	10000	Classification	4	6
California housing	20640	Regression	8	1
Abalone	4177	Regression	7	1

Baselines. In the experiments, we compare TabDitFlow with several representative tabular data generation methods, including CTGAN, TVAE, GReaT, TabDiff and RecTable. CTGAN and TVAE are included as representative GAN-based and VAE-based methods, respectively. GReaT is used as a large-language-model-based method, TabDiff is included as a diffusion-based method and RecTable is adopted as a flow matching based method.

Evaluation Metrics Downstream Task Performance. We evaluate downstream utility by training an XGBoost model on synthetic data D_{synth} and evaluating it on the real test set D_{test}. For classification tasks, we report AUC. For regression tasks, we report R^2.

Statistical fidelity. We compute several metrics to measure distribution similarity between synthetic and real data [25]. KSComplement evaluates marginal fitting for numerical columns. TVComplement evaluates distribution fitting for categorical columns. JS Divergence measures overall distribution discrepancy. CorrelationSimilarity measures how well cross-column correlation structure is preserved.

6.2 Experimental Settings

We implement TabDitFlow in PyTorch 2.6.0 with CUDA 12.4. The DiT-based velocity network uses a hidden dimension of 128, 4 attention heads and 3 AdaLN blocks. The learning rate is set to 10^{-3} and the weight decay is set to 10^{-4}. TabDitFlow is trained for 200 epochs with a batch size of 256 using the mean squared error loss. To stabilize training, we apply an exponential moving average with decay 0.999 and clip the gradient norm to 1.0. For numerical features, we apply QuantileTransformer with the output distribution set to normal. Categorical features are encoded using one-hot encoding. During generation, we solve the learned ODE using a fourth-order Runge–Kutta solver with 50 integration steps. For each dataset, all experiments are repeated five times under different random seeds and the results are reported as mean $\pm$ standard deviation. For baseline methods, we use their official implementations from publicly available GitHub repositories.

6.3 Main Results

Table 2 reports the downstream utility results on all datasets. Original denotes the real-data setting, where the downstream model is trained on the real training set and evaluated on the real test set. For synthetic-data-based methods, the downstream model is trained on the generated training data and evaluated on the real test data. Among these methods, TabDitFlow ranks first on three of the five datasets. It obtains 0.821 on Churn2, 0.779 on California Housing, and 0.451 on Abalone. On Default, TabDitFlow obtains 0.746, which is close to TabDiff with 0.747. On Adult, it reaches 0.903, lower than GReaT with 0.911 and TabDiff with 0.910.

For the two regression datasets, TabDitFlow obtains the highest R^2 among synthetic-data-based methods. On California Housing, it reaches 0.779. TabDiff obtains 0.728, while TVAE and GReaT obtain 0.616 and 0.542. CTGAN obtains 0.285, and RecTable gives a negative score of −0.178. On Abalone, TabDitFlow obtains an R^2 score of 0.451. It is slightly higher than TabDiff with 0.448. It also exceeds GReaT, TVAE, and CTGAN, whose scores are 0.373, 0.309, and 0.234, respectively.

Table 2. Main results on all datasets. For classification datasets, each entry is reported as AUC. For regression datasets, each entry is reported as R^2. Higher is better for both. The best results among synthetic-data-based methods are shown in **bold** and the second-best results are underlined.

Method	Adult (C)	Default (C)	Churn2 (C)	California Housing (R)	Abalone (R)
Original	.925±.005	.752±.007	.834±.013	.835±.010	.472±.043
CTGAN	.882±.003	.690±.024	.672±.026	.285±.018	.234±.043
TVAE	.874±.003	.731±.006	.763±.025	.616±.026	.309±.095
GReaT	**.911**±.004	.739±.012	<u>.813</u>±.015	.542±.055	.373±.025
TabDiff	<u>.910</u>±.006	**.747**±.006	.802±.018	<u>.728</u>±.011	<u>.448</u>±.053
RecTable	.480±.069	.492±.046	.482±.037	−.178±.062	−.268±.105
TabDitFlow (Ours)	.903±.005	<u>.746</u>±.008	**.821**±.008	**.779**±.007	**.451**±.051

6.4 Statistical Fidelity Results

Table 3 reports the statistical fidelity results on all datasets. TabDitFlow obtains the best CorrelationSimilarity on four datasets, including Default, Churn2, California Housing, and Abalone. On Default, it achieves 0.984. The corresponding scores of TabDiff and CTGAN are 0.982 and 0.936. On Churn2, TabDitFlow reaches 0.991. GReaT and TabDiff follow with 0.990 and 0.989.

For marginal distribution metrics, TabDitFlow ranks near the top on most datasets. On Default, it obtains 0.992 KSComplement, 0.995 TVComplement, and 0.016 JS Divergence. On Churn2, it ranks first on all four fidelity metrics.

The scores are 0.988 for KSComplement, 0.994 for TVComplement, 0.022 for JS Divergence, and 0.991 for CorrelationSimilarity. On California Housing, TabDitFlow reaches 0.991 KSComplement and 0.994 TVComplement. Its JS Divergence is 0.033.

The correlation scores are in line with the utility results on the regression datasets. On California Housing, TabDitFlow obtains 0.995 CorrelationSimilarity. TabDiff obtains 0.992, while TVAE, CTGAN, and GReaT obtain 0.953, 0.892, and 0.839. On Abalone, TabDitFlow reaches 0.988. TabDiff, GReaT, and CTGAN obtain 0.964, 0.806, and 0.801 respectively.

Table 3. Statistical fidelity comparison across all datasets.

Dataset	Metric	CTGAN	TVAE	GReaT	TabDiff	RecTable	TabDitFlow
Adult	KS ↑	.788±.019	.832±.020	.903±.001	.993±.001	.993±.001	**.994**±.001
	TV ↑	.903±.005	.940±.011	.721±.002	**.993**±.001	.350±.002	**.993**±.001
	JS ↓	.135±.003	.135±.009	.253±.008	**.020**±.000	.383±.001	.022±.001
	Corr ↑	.970±.009	.967±.007	.969±.004	**.995**±.000	.947±.002	.995±.001
Default	KS ↑	.890±.003	.877±.009	.759±.011	.986±.001	.988±.002	**.992**±.001
	TV ↑	.948±.013	.907±.012	.644±.014	.992±.001	.524±.001	**.995**±.001
	JS ↓	.082±.002	.115±.009	.166±.004	.020±.000	.199±.001	**.016**±.000
	Corr ↑	.936±.004	.904±.024	.794±.028	.982±.001	.727±.002	**.984**±.003
Churn2	KS ↑	.859±.019	.771±.022	.918±.004	.986±.001	.979±.002	**.988**±.001
	TV ↑	.910±.012	.730±.038	.938±.003	.993±.001	.843±.002	**.994**±.001
	JS ↓	.128±.006	.314±.025	.052±.008	.024±.001	.129±.002	**.022**±.001
	Corr ↑	.970±.006	.898±.024	.990±.004	.989±.003	.987±.004	**.991**±.002
California Housing	KS ↑	.926±.006	.930±.003	.658±.003	.988±.002	.970±.001	**.991**±.002
	TV ↑	.755±.004	.956±.023	.504±.004	.992±.002	.791±.003	**.994**±.001
	JS ↓	.162±.008	.144±.004	.278±.046	.036±.001	.103±.001	**.033**±.001
	Corr ↑	.892±.013	.953±.006	.839±.033	.992±.001	.724±.002	**.995**±.001
Abalone	KS ↑	.859±.014	.944±.008	.940±.002	**.982**±.004	.950±.003	.977±.004
	TV ↑	.972±.007	.880±.034	.965±.007	**.992**±.004	.734±.012	.991±.002
	JS ↓	.191±.019	.134±.008	.111±.012	.071±.006	.149±.002	**.056**±.005
	Corr ↑	.801±.027	.957±.006	.806±.105	.964±.008	.236±.005	**.988**±.014

For KSComplement, TVComplement and CorrelationSimilarity, higher is better. For JS Divergence, lower is better. The best results are shown in **bold** and the second-best results are underlined

6.5 Ablation Study

Table 4 compares TabDitFlow with two backbone variants. The MLP variant removes the TabDiT backbone and column-wise tokenization. The Transformer variant replaces TabDiT with a standard Transformer. The MLP variant gives the lowest utility on all five datasets. On Default, Churn2, California Housing, and Abalone, its utility scores are 0.662, 0.679, 0.697, and 0.319. TabDitFlow improves them to 0.746, 0.821, 0.779, and 0.451.

Compared with the Transformer variant, TabDitFlow gives better results on most datasets. On Abalone, TabDitFlow improves Utility from 0.418 to 0.451. CorrelationSimilarity also increases from 0.983 to 0.988. On Churn2, Utility increases from 0.815 to 0.821, and JS Divergence decreases from 0.024 to 0.022. On California Housing, TabDitFlow improves Utility from 0.776 to 0.779 and CorrelationSimilarity from 0.994 to 0.995.

Table 4. Ablation study on backbone design. Utility denotes AUC for classification datasets and R^2 for regression datasets. For Utility, KS, TV and Corr, higher values are better. For JS, lower values are better. The best result is shown in **bold** and the second-best result is underlined.

Dataset	Variant	Utility	KS ↑	TV ↑	JS ↓	Corr ↑
Adult	MLP	.868±.004	.975±.001	.650±.002	.223±.002	.977±.001
	Transformer	.902±.006	.994±.000	**.994**±.001	.022±.000	.994±.001
	TabDitFlow	**.903**±.005	**.994**±.001	.993±.001	**.022**±.001	**.995**±.001
Default	MLP	.662±.010	.941±.002	.768±.009	.155±.006	.845±.002
	Transformer	.744±.009	.992±.002	.994±.002	.016±.001	.982±.001
	TabDitFlow	**.746**±.008	**.992**±.001	**.995**±.001	**.016**±.000	**.984**±.003
Churn2	MLP	.679±.015	.957±.003	.932±.009	.078±.007	.989±.003
	Transformer	.815±.011	.985±.002	.993±.001	.024±.001	.990±.001
	TabDitFlow	**.821**±.008	**.988**±.001	**.994**±.001	**.022**±.001	**.991**±.002
California Housing	MLP	.697±.010	.987±.001	.968±.003	.037±.001	.982±.002
	Transformer	.776±.009	.990±.001	.993±.004	.033±.003	.994±.002
	TabDitFlow	**.779**±.007	**.991**±.002	**.994**±.001	**.033**±.001	**.995**±.001
Abalone	MLP	.319±.054	.974±.004	.970±.013	.063±.007	.729±.015
	Transformer	.418±.085	.975±.007	.986±.008	.060±.003	.983±.010
	TabDitFlow	**.451**±.051	**.977**±.004	**.991**±.002	**.056**±.005	**.988**±.014

6.6 Visualization Analysis

To further evaluate the quality of the generated tabular data, qualitative visualizations are provided from two perspectives. First, the joint distributions of representative feature pairs are compared between real and synthetic data. Second, the correlation structures preserved by different methods are analyzed.

Bivariate Joint Distribution Comparison. Figure 2 compares the bivariate densities of real data and synthetic data on three representative feature pairs from the Adult dataset: age–hours-per-week, age–education-num, and age–capital-gain. Overall, TabDitFlow produces joint distributions close to the real data. It preserves the main high-density regions and maintains the overall contour shapes across different feature pairs.

For age–hours-per-week, TabDitFlow reproduces the concentration around standard working hours and keeps the horizontal density bands observed in the real data. For age–education-num, it captures the major bands corresponding to common education levels. For age–capital-gain, most density mass remains near zero capital gain, while the spread along the age axis is still preserved. Compared with the baselines, TabDitFlow shows fewer fragmented modes and less over-smoothed density patterns.

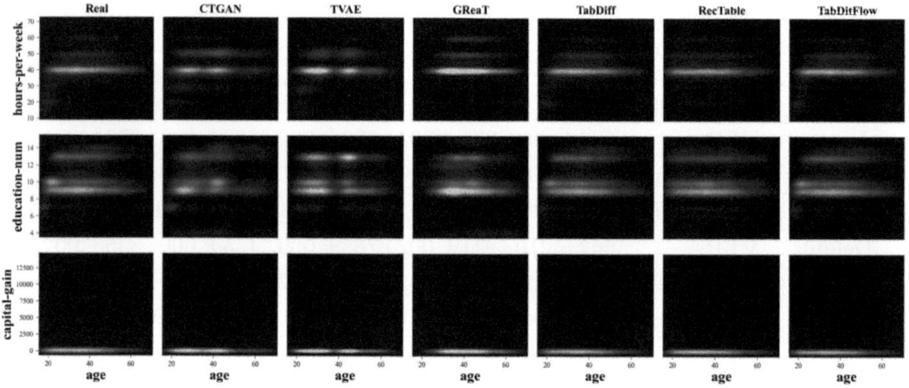

Fig. 2. Bivariate density comparisons between real data and synthetic data generated by different methods on representative feature pairs from the Adult dataset. The three rows correspond to age paired with hours-per-week, education-num, and capital-gain, respectively.

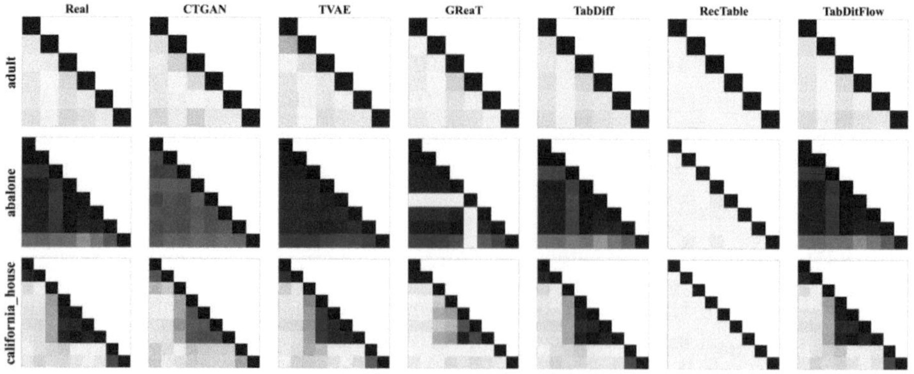

Fig. 3. Correlation heatmaps of numerical features for real data and synthetic data generated by different methods across three datasets.

Correlation Structure Analysis. Figure 3 shows the correlation matrices of real and synthetic data on three representative datasets. Only numerical features are used. TabDitFlow produces heatmaps that are close to the real data. It keeps the sparse correlation pattern on Adult. It also preserves the dense dependency patterns on Abalone and California Housing.

TabDiff also performs well in preserving correlation structures. Its results are close to the real heatmaps on Abalone and California Housing. Compared with the other baselines, TabDitFlow shows more stable visual alignment with the real data. This indicates that TabDitFlow can effectively preserve cross-feature correlation structures.

7 Conclusion

In this paper, we propose TabDitFlow for heterogeneous tabular data generation. It combines flow matching and a diffusion Transformer while using label conditioning for classification tasks. Experimental results show that TabDitFlow achieves competitive performance in statistical fidelity and downstream task utility.

Acknowledgments. This work was supported by the National Key R&D Program: the Research and development of key technologies for intelligent meteorological navigation of ocean-going ships (2023YFC3107900).

References

1. Act, A., et al.: Health insurance portability and accountability act of 1996. Public Law **104**(191), 1–16 (1996)
2. Albergo, M., Boffi, N.M., Vanden-Eijnden, E.: Stochastic interpolants: a unifying framework for flows and diffusions. J. Mach. Learn. Res. **26**(209), 1–80 (2025)
3. Borisov, V., Sessler, K., Leemann, T.: Language models are realistic tabular data generators. In: The Eleventh International Conference on Learning Representations (2023)
4. Brown, T.B., Mann, B., Ryder, N.: Language models are few-shot learners. In: Proceedings of the 34th International Conference on Neural Information Processing Systems. NIPS '20, Curran Associates Inc, Red Hook, NY, USA (2020)
5. Cao, L.: AI in finance: challenges, techniques, and opportunities. ACM Comput. Surv. (CSUR) **55**(3), 1–38 (2022)
6. Combrink, H.M., Marivate, V., Rosman, B.: Comparing synthetic tabular data generation between a probabilistic model and a deep learning model for education use cases (2022). arXiv:2210.08528 arXiv preprint
7. Fang, X., Xu, W., Tan, F.A., Zhang, J., Hu, Z., Qi, Y., Nickleach, S., Socolinsky, D., Sengamedu, S., Faloutsos, C.: Large language models (llms) on tabular data: Prediction, generation, and understanding-a survey (2024). arXiv:2402.17944 arXiv preprint
8. Fuchi, M., Takagi, T.: Rectable: fast modeling tabular data with rectified flow (2025). arXiv:2503.20731 arXiv preprint

9. Goodfellow, I.J., Pouget-Abadie, J., Mirza, M., et al.: Generative adversarial nets. In: Ghahramani, Z., Welling, M., Cortes, C., Lawrence, N., Weinberger, K.Q. (eds.) Advances in Neural Information Processing Systems, vol. 27. Curran Associates, Inc. (2014)
10. Ho, J., Jain, A., Abbeel, P.: Denoising diffusion probabilistic models. Adv. Neural. Inf. Process. Syst. **33**, 6840–6851 (2020)
11. Jeong, C., Kim, S., Park, J.: Customs import declaration datasets (2022). arXiv:2208.02484 arXiv preprint
12. Kingma, D.P., Welling, M.: Auto-encoding variational bayes. CoRR abs/1312, p. 6114 (2013)
13. Kotelnikov, A., Baranchuk, D., Rubachev, I.: Tabddpm: modelling tabular data with diffusion models. In: International Conference on Machine Learning, pp. 17564–17579 (2023) PMLR
14. Li, Z., Huang, Q., Yang, L., Shi, J., Yang, Z., van Stein, N., Bäck, T., van Leeuwen, M.: Diffusion models for tabular data: challenges, current progress, and future directions. arXiv preprint arXiv:2502.17119 (2025)
15. Lipman, Y., Chen, R.T.Q., Ben-Hamu, H.: Flow matching for generative modeling. In: The Eleventh International Conference on Learning Representations (2023)
16. Nasution, B.I., Eijkelboom, F., Elliot, M., Allmendinger, R., Naesseth, C.A.: Flow matching for tabular data synthesis. Trans. Mach. Learn. Res. (2026)
17. Patki, N., Wedge, R., Veeramachaneni, K.: The synthetic data vault. In: 2016 IEEE International Conference on Data Science and Advanced Analytics (DSAA), pp. 399–410 (2016). 10.1109/DSAA.2016.49
18. Peebles, W., Xie, S.: Scalable diffusion models with transformers. In: 2023 IEEE/CVF International Conference on Computer Vision (ICCV), pp. 4172–4182 (2023). 10.1109/ICCV51070.2023.00387
19. Regulation, P.: Regulation (eu) 2016/679 of the european parliament and of the council. Regulation (eu) **679**(2016), 10–3 (2016)
20. Shailaja, K., Seetharamulu, B., Jabbar, M.A.: Machine learning in healthcare: a review. In: Proceedings of the 2018 Second International Conference on Electronics, Communication and Aerospace Technology (ICECA), pp. 910–914. IEEE (2018)
21. Shi, J., Xu, M., Hua, H., Zhang, H., Ermon, S., Leskovec, J.: Tabdiff: a mixed-type diffusion model for tabular data generation (2024). arXiv:2410.20626 arXiv preprint
22. Shi, R., Wang, Y., Du, M., Shen, X., Chang, Y., Wang, X.: A comprehensive survey of synthetic tabular data generation. arXiv preprint arXiv:2504.16506 (2025)
23. Stoian, M.C., Giunchiglia, E., Lukasiewicz, T.: A survey on tabular data generation: Utility, alignment, fidelity, privacy, and beyond (2025). arXiv:2503.05954 arXiv preprint
24. Xu, L., Skoularidou, M., Cuesta-Infante, A.: Modeling tabular data using conditional gan. Adv. Neural. Inf. Process. Syst. **32** (2019)
25. Yang, S.C.H., Eaves, B., Schmidt, M., Swanson, K., Shafto, P.: Structured evaluation of synthetic tabular data (2024). arXiv:2403.10424 arXiv preprint

Task-Oriented Subtable Construction for Column Annotation on Large Tables

Changlong Wang, Pengjuan Lu(✉), Zhixiong Yin, Wenhao Zhao, and Huimei Tian

Northwest Normal University, Lanzhou, China
wchlong@nwnu.edu.cn, 2863109266@qq.com

Abstract. Tabular data are widely used in applications such as data management, information retrieval, and knowledge discovery. Column Type Annotation (CTA) and Column Property Annotation (CPA) are two fundamental tasks in table semantic understanding. However, for large-scale tables, existing approaches are often limited by the token length of pre-trained language models, which makes it difficult to fully exploit tabular contextual information. In addition, conventional strategies, such as direct truncation and random sampling, often lead to context loss and structural disruption. To address this issue, this paper proposes a task-oriented subtable construction approach for column annotation on large tables. Specifically, the proposed approach produces final predictions for the original table through task-oriented column clustering, row-window partitioning, and subtable-level prediction fusion, thereby preserving more task-relevant context and local table structure under input length constraints. Furthermore, considering the different contextual requirements of CTA and CPA, differentiated subtable construction strategies are designed for the two tasks. Experimental results on multiple datasets show that the proposed approach outperforms direct truncation and random subsampling baselines, while remaining competitive with representative approaches under comparable settings. In particular, the proposed approach gives especially strong improvements for CPA.

Keywords: Column Type Annotation · Column Property Annotation · Large Tables · Subtable Construction

1 Introduction

Tables are a fundamental form of structured data, and modeling column semantics and inter-column relations is central to table understanding. To support downstream applications such as retrieval, alignment, integration, and reuse, tables typically require semantic annotation [1]. Among these tasks, Column Type Annotation (CTA) and Column Property Annotation (CPA) are two core problems: the former aims to identify the semantic type of an individual column, while the latter focuses on inferring the relation between two columns.

L. Ding et al. (Eds.): APWeb-WAIM 2026, LNCS 16993, pp. 147–163, 2027.
https://doi.org/10.1007/978-981-92-5693-8_10

In practical applications, large tables are widely found in open data portals, enterprise data lakes, and Web tables. For example, government open data often contains statistical tables involving cities, population, area, and fiscal revenue, while enterprise data lakes commonly include business tables related to products, orders, customers, and transactions. Such tables typically contain a large number of rows and columns, concise or underspecified headers, and heterogeneous value types. As a result, accurate CTA and CPA cannot rely solely on the target column itself; instead, they require the comprehensive use of contextual information, including headers, cell values, neighboring columns, semantically related columns, and local table structures.

In recent years, pre-trained language models (PLMs) and large language models (LLMs) have substantially improved the modeling of table headers, cell values, and intra-table context. However, column annotation on large tables remains challenging. Conventional PLMs are constrained by input length and often fail to capture sufficient context, while LLMs still suffer from high inference cost, limited long-context utilization, and unstable outputs. Under input length constraints, existing approaches typically rely on direct table truncation [2] or random row–column subtable sampling [3]. Yet these strategies often discard contextual and structural information that is important for prediction. As a result, the key challenge is not simply to compress the input, but to preserve as much task-relevant semantic and structural information as possible under limited token budgets.

To address this issue, we propose a task-oriented subtable construction approach for column annotation on large tables. Instead of applying task-agnostic compression, the proposed approach constructs subtables according to the contextual requirements of specific tasks and derives table-level predictions through fusion. In particular, we design different construction strategies for CTA and CPA. For CTA, the approach groups semantically related columns and preserves local structure through continuous row windows. For CPA, it organizes target-column contexts around the main column and incorporates semantic context, local neighborhood context, and half-overlapping row windows for relation prediction. The main contributions of this paper are summarized as follows:

1. We propose a task-oriented subtable construction approach for column annotation on large tables. Under restricted token budgets, the approach aims to preserve task-relevant context through task-aware column selection, local row-context organization, and table-level prediction fusion.
2. To address the different context requirements of CTA and CPA, we design a continuous multi-window subtable construction strategy for CTA, as well as a relation-oriented subtable construction strategy for CPA that organizes semantically related columns and local neighborhood columns around the main column.
3. We conduct extensive experiments on nine public datasets. The results show that the proposed approach is more effective than direct truncation and random subsampling, and remains competitive compared with representative baselines, especially on the CPA task.

2 Related Work

Existing studies on column annotation can generally be grouped into three lines of work: context- and knowledge-enhanced approaches, LLM-based approaches, and approaches for annotation on large tables through input organization and decomposition. The first two directions mainly improve semantic representation and inference, whereas the third focuses on adapting column annotation on large tables to input-length constraints.

Early studies improved column annotation by exploiting intra-table context or external knowledge. Representative examples include Sato [4] and C_2 [5], which rely on signals such as value distributions, headers, topic features, or knowledge graphs to infer column semantics. More recently, PLMs have become a dominant paradigm for semantic table understanding, with representative approaches including TURL [6], RECA [7], and Doduo [2]. Although these approaches substantially improve semantic representation quality, their effectiveness on large tables is still limited by input length constraints and incomplete context coverage.

Another line of work applies LLMs to column annotation tasks, including both CTA and CPA [8,9]. Owing to their strong contextual understanding and few-shot generalization ability, these approaches provide considerable flexibility in zero-shot and few-shot settings. However, for large tables with many columns and rows, they remain expensive at inference time and often fail to fully exploit long-context information.

Recent work has also addressed annotation on large tables from the perspective of input construction. Watchog [10] improves column annotation by reorganizing table inputs and constructing training instances. TorchicTab [3] generates subtables through random row and column sampling. Retrieve-and-Verify [11] removes irrelevant noisy columns in wide tables through a retrieve-and-verify framework, while CENTS [12] selects more representative table subsets under token budget constraints. Although these approaches alleviate input-length issues to some extent, they primarily focus on selection or compression rather than explicitly preserving task-relevant context together with its local structure.

Overall, existing approaches still struggle to preserve both task-relevant context and local structural integrity in large-table settings.

3 Proposed Approach

3.1 Problem Formulation

Let T be a relational table with column set $C(T) = \{c_1, c_2, \ldots, c_n\}$ and row set $R(T) = \{r_1, r_2, \ldots, r_m\}$, where c_j denotes the j-th column and r_i denotes the i-th row. The cell value at row i and column j is denoted by v_{ij}. Let $\mathcal{L}^{\text{type}} = \{\ell_1^{\text{type}}, \ell_2^{\text{type}}, \ldots, \ell_a^{\text{type}}\}$ be the set of column type labels, and let $\mathcal{L}^{\text{rel}} = \{\ell_1^{\text{rel}}, \ell_2^{\text{rel}}, \ldots, \ell_b^{\text{rel}}\}$ be the set of relation labels for CPA.

Definition 1. (Column Type Annotation) Given a table T and its column set $C(T)$, the goal of CTA is to assign each target column $c_j \in C(T)$ a type label $t_j \in \mathcal{L}^{\text{type}}$ that best characterizes the semantic category of the column.

Definition 2. (Column Property Annotation) Given a table T, a main column $c_k \in C(T)$, and a target column $c_j \in C(T)$ with $k \neq j$, the goal of CPA is to predict a relation label $re_{k,j} \in \mathcal{L}^{\text{rel}}$ that captures the semantic relation between c_k and c_j.

Example. Figure 1 illustrates examples of CTA and CPA tasks. For the CTA task, the columns *person, location*, and *sports_team* correspond to different semantic types. For the CPA task, when *person* is treated as the main column, the column pair (*person, location*) corresponds to the relation *place_of_birth*, while the column pair (*person, sports_team*) corresponds to *team_roster*.

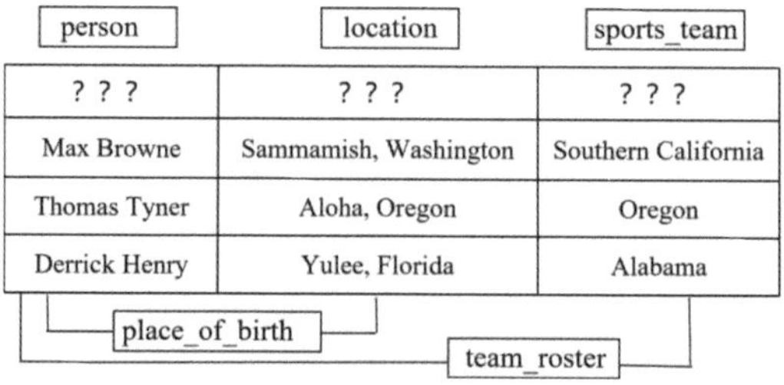

Fig. 1. Examples of CTA and CPA tasks.

3.2 Framework Overview

Based on the above analysis, we propose a task-oriented subtable construction approach from the perspective of input organization and data construction, while keeping the backbone predictor unchanged. The core idea is to select task-relevant contexts according to the prediction targets of different annotation tasks under the input length constraint, rather than simply truncating or randomly compressing the original table. Specifically, CTA targets individual columns and therefore focuses on preserving semantically related columns and local distributions reflected by contiguous rows. CPA targets column pairs and thus focuses on organizing contexts around the main and target columns while preserving inter-column semantic associations and layout proximity. Thus, task-oriented subtable construction selects semantic and structural contexts centered on task-specific prediction targets within the input budget.

As shown in Fig. 2, the proposed approach consists of four stages: column representation learning, task-oriented subtable construction, subtable-level prediction, and table-level prediction fusion. First, column-level semantic representations are learned and used to construct subtables for CTA and CPA under the input length constraint. Then, the backbone predictor is applied to perform local prediction on the generated subtables. Finally, multiple predictions associated with the same original column or column pair are fused to obtain table-level annotation results.

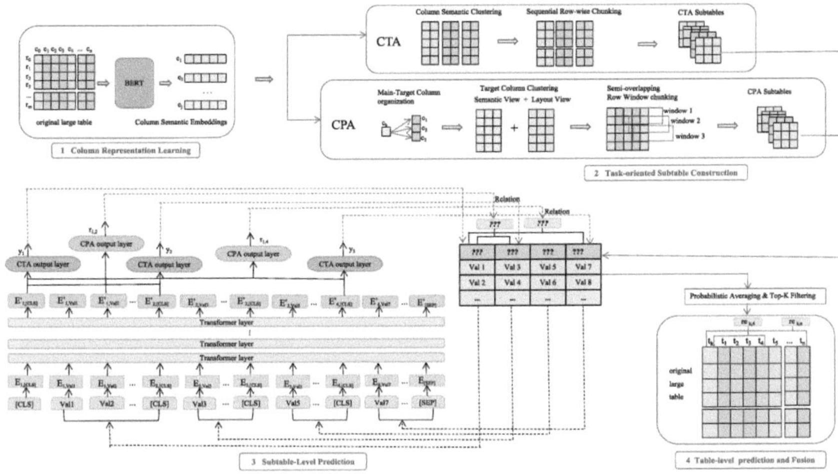

Fig. 2. Framework of the proposed task-oriented subtable construction approach for column annotation on large tables.

Column Representation Learning. To support subsequent task-oriented subtable construction, we first construct a textual sequence for each column. Given the j-th column c_j in table T, let h_j denote its header and $\{v_{1,j}, v_{2,j}, \ldots, v_{m,j}\}$ denote its cell values in row order. We concatenate the header and column values in order as

$$x_j = h_j \oplus [\text{SEP}] \oplus v_{1,j} \oplus [\text{SEP}] \oplus \cdots \oplus [\text{SEP}] \oplus v_{\sigma,j}, \quad 1 \leq \sigma \leq m \tag{1}$$

where $\oplus$ denotes text concatenation, [SEP] is a special token separating the header and cell values, and σ is the number of retained cell values under the token budget. We then introduce a pretrained BERT model [13] as the text encoder. For a given column sequence x_j, it is first converted into the model input format by the tokenizer, and contextualized feature representations are then obtained through bidirectional Transformer layers. We take the final-layer hidden vector of the [CLS] token as the semantic representation $\mathbf{e}_j$ of the column:

$$\mathbf{e}_j = \text{BERT}(\text{Tok}(x_j))_{[\text{CLS}]}, \quad \mathbf{e}_j \in \mathbb{R}^d \tag{2}$$

where Tok$(\cdot)$ denotes tokenization and encoding, and d is the hidden feature dimension of BERT. The semantic representations of all columns in table T are denoted by $E(T) = [\mathbf{e}_1, \mathbf{e}_2, \ldots, \mathbf{e}_n]$.

Task-Oriented Subtable Construction. This stage aims to construct effective subtables under model input constraints by adapting the construction strategy to the objectives and contextual requirements of CTA and CPA.

CTA Subtable Construction. For CTA, where the prediction target is an individual column, we construct subtables by combining semantic column clustering with continuous row-window partitioning. Given the column embeddings $E(T)$ of table T, we first apply K-Means to cluster the columns in the table, obtaining a set of column clusters denoted by $G = \{g_1, g_2, \dots, g_w\}$, where w is the number of clusters and g_i denotes the i-th column cluster. In practice, the initial value of w is set according to a preset maximum number of columns per group, and any oversized cluster is further split sequentially if necessary. Given w, the clustering is performed by minimizing the within-cluster squared error between column embeddings and their corresponding centroids:

$$G^* = \arg\min_G \sum_{i=1}^{w} \sum_{c_j \in g_i} \|\mathbf{e}_j - \boldsymbol{\mu}_i\|_2^2 \tag{3}$$

where $\boldsymbol{\mu}_i$ denotes the centroid of the i-th cluster. The final clustering result is denoted by $G^* = \{g_1^*, g_2^*, \dots, g_w^*\}$.

After column clustering, each cluster is further partitioned along the row dimension to form multiple subtables. Since different column clusters may vary in both the number of columns and the length of cell content, we dynamically determine the window size under the model token budget according to the average number of tokens per row in the current cluster. Let τ denote the maximum number of input tokens allowed by the model, let $\bar{n}_{\text{row}}$ denote the average number of tokens per row in the current cluster, and let N_{row} denote the total number of rows in the current block. The row-window size is defined as:

$$w_{\text{row}} = \min\left(N_{\text{row}}, \max\left(1, \left\lfloor \frac{\tau}{\bar{n}_{\text{row}}} \right\rfloor\right)\right) \tag{4}$$

To reduce the effect of row-order disruption, each subtable preserves local continuity along the row dimension, and continuous subtable blocks are generated by sequential scanning.

CPA Subtable Construction. For CPA, we construct subtables around the main column by combining semantic-cluster-view blocks and layout-neighborhood-view blocks, together with row-window partitioning and validity filtering.

The goal of CPA is to predict the relation label between a main column and a target column, and the prediction target is therefore a column pair rather than a single column. Accordingly, instead of uniformly partitioning the entire table, our approach organizes candidate column pairs around the main column. For a given main column c_k, let the set of target columns paired with c_k in table T be defined as

$$Y_k = \{c_j \mid (c_k, c_j) \in Q(T)\} \tag{5}$$

where $Q(T)$ denotes the set of column pairs in table T that require relation prediction. Based on the semantic representations of the target columns in Y_k, we first perform clustering and obtain a set of semantic groups, denoted by $\mathcal{G}_k = \{g_{k,1}, g_{k,2}, \ldots, g_{k,t}\}$, where t is the number of semantic groups associated with the main column c_k. In practice, the initial value of t is set according to the same preset maximum number of columns per group as in CTA, and any oversized group is further split when necessary.

To jointly preserve semantic relations and structural cues, we design two complementary contextual views. The first is the semantic-cluster view. For each target-column group $g_{k,s} \in \mathcal{G}_k$, we construct a core column set $\mathcal{B}_{k,s} = \{c_k\} \cup g_{k,s}$, where c_k is the main column. Let $\mathbf{e}_q$ denote the semantic representation of the q-th column. The local block center is then defined as

$$\mathbf{e}^*_{\mathcal{B}_{k,s}} = \mathrm{Norm}\left(\frac{1}{|\mathcal{B}_{k,s}|} \sum_{c_q \in \mathcal{B}_{k,s}} \mathbf{e}_q\right) \tag{6}$$

where $\mathrm{Norm}(\cdot)$ denotes ℓ_2 normalization. We then rank the remaining columns in $C(T) \setminus \mathcal{B}_{k,s}$ according to their cosine similarity to $\mathbf{e}^*_{\mathcal{B}_{k,s}}$, and select at most m_{ctx} columns as background context, denoted by C_{ctx}, where $C(T)$ is the original column set of table T. Accordingly, the semantic-cluster view block is written as $H_{\mathrm{sem}} = \mathcal{B}_{k,s} \cup C_{\mathrm{ctx}}$.

The second is the layout-neighborhood view, which is intended to capture local structural dependencies around the main column. Specifically, taking c_k as the center, we select neighboring columns within a column distance of at most δ on both sides in the original table as local context, denoted by $N_r(c_k)$. If $N_r(c_k)$ contains any target column paired with the main column c_k, we construct the layout-neighborhood view block as $H_{\mathrm{lay}} = \{c_k\} \cup N_r(c_k)$. Therefore, for CPA, the approach does not produce only a single type of block; instead, it constructs semantic-cluster view blocks and layout-neighborhood view blocks in parallel, so as to preserve both semantic relation information and local structural information.

Along the row dimension, we determine the admissible number of rows for each block under the token budget, with the row-window size computed in the same way as in Eq. (4), and generate multiple local row blocks using a half-overlapping window strategy, where adjacent windows share approximately 50% of their rows. This allows the same column pair to be observed under multiple local contexts, thereby improving prediction stability.

We further apply a validity filter to each row block. If a target column contains no usable text within the current window, it is removed from the block. If no supervised target column remains in the current subtable after filtering, the subtable is discarded. When the main column is empty, a placeholder token is used instead.

Subtable-Level Inference. After task-oriented construction, the original large table is transformed into a collection of subtables that satisfy the input-length constraint of the backbone model. Each subtable is fed independently into the predictor for local inference. For CTA, the model outputs type predictions for the target columns in the subtable. For CPA, it outputs relation predictions for the main–target column pairs contained in the block. Because the same original column or column pair may appear in multiple subtables, the outputs obtained at this stage are subtable-level predictions based on local contexts. Therefore, the predictions from different subtables must be further fused to produce the final global annotation for the original table.

Table-Level Prediction Fusion. The goal of this stage is to map subtable-level predictions back to the original columns or column pairs and then perform table-level selection and fusion.

We compare three fusion strategies, namely majority voting, logit averaging, and probability averaging. Majority voting selects the label predicted most frequently across different subtables as the final output. Logit averaging computes the element-wise average of the output logits and then selects the label with the largest averaged logit. Probability averaging first converts logits into probability distributions over labels and then aggregates them. Experimental results show that probability averaging performs best. To further reduce the influence of low-confidence noise, we introduce a confidence-based filtering mechanism on top of probability averaging.

Specifically, let $z_j^{(u)}$ denote the logits produced by the u-th subtable for the original column c_j. Its probability distribution over labels is computed by

$$p_j^{(u)} = \text{softmax}(z_j^{(u)}) \tag{7}$$

We define the maximum probability in this distribution as the confidence of the corresponding subtable prediction. Let d denote the label index. Then the confidence of the u-th subtable prediction is given by $\max_d p_{j,d}^{(u)}$. To ensure the quality of fusion, we retain only the top-K subtable predictions with the highest confidence for aggregation. Let the indices of the retained subtables form the set $\mathcal{S}_j$. The fused probability $\bar{p}_j$ and the final predicted label $\hat{y}_j$ for the original column c_j are then computed as

$$\bar{p}_j = \frac{1}{|\mathcal{S}_j|} \sum_{u \in \mathcal{S}_j} p_j^{(u)}, \qquad \hat{y}_j = \arg\max_d \bar{p}_{j,d} \tag{8}$$

Table 1. Statistics of the datasets used in our experiments.

Dataset	Tables	Types	Mean/Median cols	Mean/Median rows
sotab-cta	59,548	91	8/7	182/33
sotab-cpa	51,334	176	9/8	236/42
sotab-round1-sch-cta	56,547	40	7/6	179/30
sotab-round1-sch-cpa	53,722	50	8/8	197/33
sotab-round2-dbp-cta	86,973	46	8/7	178/31
sotab-round2-dbp-cpa	64,052	49	9/8	225/38
gittablessc-cta	2,853	53	13/9	–
sotab-round3-cta	24,275	91	8/7	–
sotab-round3-cpa	20,686	176	9/8	–

For CPA, the same fusion strategy is adopted, except that the fusion object is changed from the original column c_j to the original column pair (c_k, c_j). In this way, predictions from multiple local contexts are aggregated to produce more stable table-level annotations while suppressing low-confidence noise. The parameter K is selected on the validation set, and we use $K = 5$ in the final setting.

4 Experiments

4.1 Experimental Setup

Datasets. We conduct experiments on two public table corpora designed for large-table scenarios: SOTAB [14] and GitTables [15]. The former contains many wide tables with complex semantic annotations, while the latter is collected from real-world tables in open-source repositories and exhibits larger row scales and more diverse content distributions. From these two corpora, we construct nine experimental subsets for CTA and CPA. Their statistics are reported in Table 1.

Baselines. To evaluate the proposed approach in large-table scenarios, we compare it with two categories of baselines. The first category consists of basic context-compression approaches, including the fixed-token truncation strategy Doduo [2] and the random row–column subtable sampling strategy TorchicTab [3]. The second category includes advanced table understanding models, namely RECA [7], Watchog [10], REVEAL [11], and CENTS [12]. These approaches address context compression and information preservation in large-table settings from different perspectives, including cross-table enhancement, local subtable construction, retrieval-based context selection, and representative subset extraction under budget constraints.

Comparison protocol. Considering that some baselines differ in terms of public implementation, test-label availability, data splits, and evaluation protocols, we divide the reported comparisons into two categories. Approaches that can be reproduced or aligned under the same datasets, label schemes, and evaluation metrics are treated as comparisons under unified settings and used to support the main conclusions. Approaches that are difficult to fully reproduce or follow inconsistent protocols are reported only as reference comparisons, providing a performance reference for the proposed approach with respect to existing work. Specific limitations are discussed in the corresponding experimental subsections.

Evaluation Metrics. Following common evaluation practice in table understanding and prior work [2,11], we adopt Micro-F1 as the primary evaluation metric for both CTA and CPA, while Macro-F1 is reported as a supplementary metric to reflect performance across classes.

Hyperparameter Settings. We adopt Doduo [2] as the backbone predictor. The maximum input length is set to 512 tokens. The preset maximum number of columns per cluster/group is set to 16. For CPA, the neighborhood radius is set to $\delta = 2$, and the number of background context columns is set to $m_{\text{ctx}} = 3$.

4.2 Main Results

We evaluate the proposed approach from three perspectives: the necessity of splitting compared with full-table truncation, the advantage of task-oriented subtable construction over random subsampling, and the overall performance compared with representative baselines.

Necessity of Structured Splitting. To verify the necessity of subtable construction itself, we compare the proposed approach with Doduo, which applies direct truncation to the full table without constructing subtables. The two approaches use the same datasets, label schemes, evaluation metrics, and backbone predictor, and differ only in input organization.

As shown in Table 2, compared with Doduo, the proposed approach achieves higher Micro-F1 scores on both *sotab-cta* and *sotab-cpa*. This suggests that, in large-table settings, task-oriented subtable construction can be more effective than naive direct truncation, as it preserves more local evidence relevant to the target columns and alleviates context loss caused by overlong inputs.

Table 2. Comparison between Doduo and our approach on *sotab-cta* and *sotab-cpa*.

Dataset	Approach	Micro-F1
sotab-cta	Doduo	84.82
	Ours	**93.60**
sotab-cpa	Doduo	79.96
	Ours	**84.85**

Effectiveness of the Splitting Strategy. The test-set results of TorchicTab [3] are obtained through the official SemTab evaluation server, under which the test labels are typically not released to participants. Therefore, to ensure a fair and comparable evaluation, we compare our approach with TorchicTab on the official validation sets using the same metrics.

As shown in Table 3, our approach consistently outperforms TorchicTab on both tasks. These results indicate that, compared with random row–column subsampling, the proposed subtable construction strategy is better at preserving inter-column semantic associations and local structural information, and can thus achieve stable performance gains under different ontology definitions and label schemes.

Table 3. Comparison between TorchicTab (random) and our approach (split) on four datasets.

Dataset	Approach	Macro-F1 (Valid)	Micro-F1 (Valid)
sotab-round1-sch-cta	TorchicTab	92.76	94.14
	Ours	**94.30**	**95.81**
sotab-round1-sch-cpa	TorchicTab	94.51	94.96
	Ours	**97.88**	**98.02**
sotab-round2-dbp-cta	TorchicTab	91.25	92.34
	Ours	**92.77**	**93.16**
sotab-round2-dbp-cpa	TorchicTab	91.69	92.72
	Ours	**93.13**	**93.51**

Comparison with Representative Baselines. Given the differences in model paradigms, public implementations, and evaluation settings among competing approaches, we divide the comparison into two parts: comparisons under unified settings for reproducible PLM-based baselines, and reference comparisons for LLM-based approaches following different technical paradigms.

Table 4 reports the results against RECA, Watchog, and REVEAL. Overall, our approach remains competitive in large-table settings. Compared with RECA and Watchog, it consistently achieves better performance on all reported metrics. Compared with REVEAL, our approach achieves higher Micro-F1 on CTA, although its Macro-F1 is slightly lower, and outperforms REVEAL on all metrics for CPA. This suggests that the proposed approach is effective for column annotation on large tables under limited input budgets. Unlike cross-table retrieval or generic subtable construction, our approach reconstructs subtables around the target task and therefore covers key local information for column-level and column-pair-level prediction more effectively under limited token budgets.

Table 5 presents a reference comparison with the LLM-based approach CENTS. Although the two approaches are not fully aligned in terms of data splits and evaluation protocol, the results still provide a useful reference for understanding their relative performance under different technical settings. Under this comparison setting, our approach achieves higher Micro-F1 scores than CENTS on both CTA and CPA.

Although the proposed approach alleviates the input-length constraints in large-table scenarios through task-oriented subtable construction, its performance may still be affected by several challenging cases. For CTA, when columns have similar value distributions, or when numeric and date columns lack explicit units, the model may require richer contextual evidence to distinguish semantically close types. For CPA, when the main column is semantically related to multiple candidate columns, or when different relations involve similar subject and object types, relation labels may still be difficult to distinguish. These observations suggest that richer contextual signals, such as unit information, table captions, or stronger column representations, may further improve robustness in complex table scenarios.

5 Ablation Analysis

We conduct ablation experiments to evaluate the contribution of each component to the overall performance. Except for the removed component, all other settings are kept identical to those of the full model. Unless otherwise specified, the ablation experiments for CTA and CPA are conducted on *sotab-round3-cta* and *sotab-round3-cpa*, respectively. To reduce computational cost, all variants are evaluated on the same fixed 50% subset of the corresponding data split. This subset is used only for relative comparison among ablation variants and not for

Table 4. Comparison with representative PLM-based baselines under unified settings.

Approach	gittablessc-cta		sotab-round3-cta		sotab-round3-cpa	
	Macro-F1	Micro-F1	Macro-F1	Micro-F1	Macro-F1	Micro-F1
RECA	35.10	64.52	68.21	68.52	47.56	54.31
Watchog	36.06	65.24	84.19	86.23	72.60	76.52
REVEAL	<u>41.98</u>	69.26	<u>87.60</u>	88.35	77.81	80.45
Ours	**41.58**	**69.57**	**86.36**	**90.05**	**78.68**	**80.65**

Table 5. Reference comparison with the LLM-based approach CENTS under different evaluation settings.

Dataset	Approach	Micro-F1
sotab-cta	CENTS	80.4
	Ours	**93.60**
sotab-cpa	CENTS	79.1
	Ours	**84.85**

reporting the final performance of the full model. In addition, Figs. 3(a) and 3(b) compare different fusion strategies on *sotab-round1-sch-cta* and *sotab-round3-cpa*, respectively.

5.1 Ablation on CTA

Table 6 shows that the main performance gain for CTA comes from contiguous multi-window coverage. Compared with the full approach, removing K-Means clustering leads to only a small performance drop, indicating that K-Means-based semantic grouping can further improve the semantic compactness of local column context, but is not the dominant factor. The very small drop for the Random Row Subsampling variant suggests that preserving row continuity is only mildly helpful, whereas the main gain comes from multi-window coverage. In contrast, the *Single Window* variant exhibits the most severe degradation, especially a drop of 10.3 points in Macro-F1, indicating that in large-table settings, a single window is insufficient to cover enough evidence for reliable type prediction.

Table 6. Ablation results of different components for CTA.

Approach/Variants	Macro-F1	Micro-F1
Ours (full)	**80.27**	**86.83**
w/o clustering	79.35 (↓0.92)	85.79 (↓1.04)
Random row subsampling	80.18 (↓0.09)	86.64 (↓0.19)
Single window	69.97 (↓10.3)	83.85 (↓2.98)

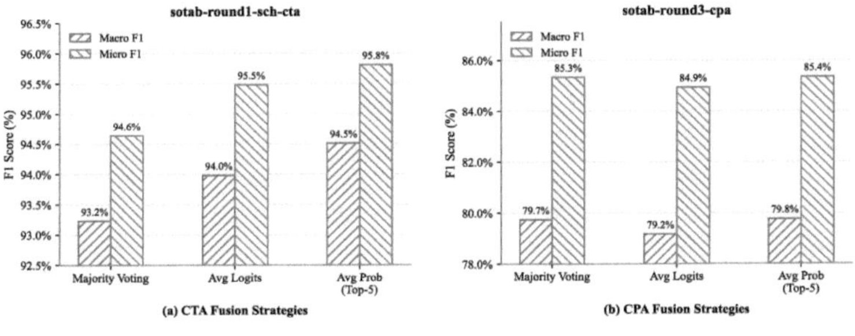

Fig. 3. Performance under different fusion strategies for (a) CTA and (b) CPA.

Figure 3(a) compares different table-level prediction fusion strategies. On CTA, probability averaging outperforms majority voting and achieves the best performance at $K = 5$ (Top-5). This indicates that CTA is relatively sensitive to the confidence information carried by predictions from different windows, and that probability averaging can make better use of the discriminative strength of different local contexts, thereby producing more stable column-level predictions.

5.2 Ablation on CPA

Table 7 shows that the components for CPA are complementary, although their contributions differ. The *Layout Only* variant leads to the largest performance drop, showing that structural neighborhood information alone is insufficient for relation recognition, and that organizing semantically related target columns around the main column remains the primary basis for CPA. The performance drop of *Semantic Only* further confirms that layout-neighborhood information provides indispensable structural cues. Additional experiments show that removing background context columns from the semantic view and disabling semi-overlapping chunking also degrade performance. This suggests that highly similar background columns help enrich local relational context, while semi-overlapping windows improve repeated observation opportunities and prediction consistency for the same column pair under different local contexts. Overall, the performance gains mainly come from the close coupling of semantic and layout views, together with the stability improvements brought by background context and overlapping chunking.

Table 7. Ablation results of different components for CPA.

Approach/Variants	Macro-F1	Micro-F1
Ours (full)	**79.17**	**84.94**
Semantic only	78.50 (↓0.67)	84.65 (↓0.29)
Layout only	75.19 (↓3.98)	81.48 (↓3.46)
w/o context columns	78.14 (↓1.03)	84.16 (↓0.78)
w/o semi-overlap chunking	78.16 (↓1.01)	84.36 (↓0.58)

Figure 3(b) shows that CPA is noticeably less sensitive to the fusion strategy than CTA, as the performance gap between majority voting and probability averaging remains small. This suggests that, under the current subtable construction scheme, different subtables already yield consistent predictions for the same column pair, thereby reducing the reliance of CPA on fine-grained probability weighting.

5.3 Efficiency and Overhead Analysis

Table 8 reports the component-level overhead of two subtable construction strategies on *SOTAB-round3-CTA*. For a fair comparison, both approaches process the same number of tables and generate the same number of subtables. The proposed approach takes approximately 2.03× and 1.44× the running time of random subsampling on the validation and test sets, respectively. The additional overhead mainly comes from column representation learning, column clustering, and subtable writing, but it can be further mitigated through caching and parallel processing. Overall, the proposed approach achieves broader task-relevant

Table 8. Component-level overhead comparison between the task-oriented subtable construction strategy and random subsampling.

Split	Strategy	Tables	Total blocks	Rep.	Clust.	Win.	Save	Total
valid	Ours	1000	19221	27.33	4.07	33.13	88.89	153.42
	Random	1000	19221	0.00	0.00	29.93	45.69	75.62
test	Ours	2000	37480	57.65	9.73	87.13	140.55	295.06
	Random	2000	37480	0.00	0.00	59.74	145.30	205.04

Note: Rep., Clust., Win., and Save denote the time costs of column representation learning, column clustering, window partitioning with subtable generation, and writing generated subtables to disk, respectively. Total denotes the total time of the subtable construction stage, excluding raw table loading time. All time costs are measured in seconds

context coverage and higher annotation performance with controllable construction overhead.

6 Conclusion

This paper presents a task-oriented subtable construction approach for column annotation on large tables. Under model input length constraints, the proposed approach organizes task-relevant local context more effectively and provides a unified input-construction strategy for both CTA and CPA. Experimental results show that the proposed approach achieves clear overall advantages on multiple datasets and exhibits good robustness across different ontology definitions and label schemes. These results demonstrate that the proposed strategy effectively alleviates the conflict between limited model input windows and the need for sufficient contextual information.

Meanwhile, the generalizability of the experimental conclusions is still subject to several factors. First, this work mainly adopts Doduo as the backbone predictor. Although the proposed approach does not modify the model architecture and can be transferred to other table encoders, validation across different backbone models is left for future work. Second, several components, including column clustering, window partitioning, and prediction fusion, involve empirical design choices, and their parameter settings may vary across datasets and tasks. In addition, the efficiency analysis shows that although the task-oriented subtable construction strategy introduces additional subtable generation overhead, the resulting gains in local contextual information significantly improve model performance. Future work will focus on exploring adaptive splitting strategies and lightweight inference mechanisms, with the aim of reducing processing costs in large-scale table scenarios while maintaining strong performance.

Acknowledgment. This work was supported by the National Natural Science Foundation of China under Grant Nos. 62362060 and 72364033.

References

1. Nazari, A.B.K., Rafiei, D., Nascimento, M.A.: MixedSAND: Semantic annotation of mixed-unit numeric data. In: Proceedings of the ACM Web Conference 2025, pp. 178–187. (2025)
2. Suhara, Y., Li, J., Li, Y., Zhang, D., Demiralp, Ç., Chen, C., Tan, W.-C.: Annotating columns with pre-trained language models. In: Proceedings of the 2022 International Conference on Management of Data, pp. 1493–1503 (2022)
3. Dasoulas, I., Yang, D., Duan, X., Dimou, A.: TorchicTab: semantic table annotation with Wikidata and language models. In: Proceedings of the Semantic Web Challenge on Tabular Data to Knowledge Graph Matching. CEUR Workshop Proceedings, vol. 3557, pp. 21–37 (2023)
4. Zhang, D., Suhara, Y., Li, J., Hulsebos, M., Demiralp, Ç., Tan, W.-C.: Sato: contextual semantic type detection in tables. Proc. VLDB Endow. **13**, 1835–1848 (2020). https://doi.org/10.14778/3407790.3407793
5. Khurana, U., Galhotra, S.: Semantic concept annotation for tabular data. In: Proceedings of the 30th ACM International Conference on Information & Knowledge Management, pp. 844–853 (2021)
6. Deng, X., Sun, H., Lees, A., Wu, Y., Yu, C.: TURL: table understanding through representation learning. ACM SIGMOD Rec. **51**(1), 33–40 (2022). https://doi.org/10.1145/3542700.3542709
7. Sun, Y., Xin, H., Chen, L.: RECA: Related tables enhanced column semantic type annotation framework. Proc. VLDB Endow. **16**(6), 1319–1331 (2023). https://doi.org/10.14778/3583140.3583149
8. Feuer, B., Liu, Y., Hegde, C., Freire, J.: ArcheType: a novel framework for open-source column type annotation using large language models. Proc. VLDB Endow. **17**(9), 2279–2292 (2024). https://doi.org/10.14778/3665844.3665857
9. Korini, K., Bizer, C.: Column property annotation using large language models. In: The Semantic Web: ESWC 2024 Satellite Events. Lecture Notes in Computer Science, vol. 15344, pp. 61–70. Springer, Cham (2025). https://doi.org/10.1007/978-3-031-78952-66
10. Miao, Z., Wang, J.: Watchog: a light-weight contrastive learning based framework for column annotation. Proc. ACM Manag. Data **1**(4), 272:1–272:24 (2023). https://doi.org/10.1145/3626766
11. Ding, Z., Sun, Y., Shi, J.: Retrieve-and-verify: a table context selection framework for accurate column annotations. Proc. ACM Manag. Data **3**(6), 1–27 (2025). https://doi.org/10.1145/3769823
12. Xiao, G., He, D., Wang, J., Balazinska, M.: CENTS: a flexible and cost-effective framework for LLM-based table understanding. Proc. VLDB Endow. **18**(11), 4574–4587 (2025). https://doi.org/10.14778/3749646.3749714
13. Devlin, J., Chang, M.-W., Lee, K., Toutanova, K.: BERT: pre-training of deep bidirectional transformers for language understanding. In: Proceedings of the 2019 Conference of the North American Chapter of the Association for Computational Linguistics: Human Language Technologies, Volume 1 (Long and Short Papers), pp. 4171–4186 (2019). https://doi.org/10.18653/v1/N19-1423

14. Korini, K., Peeters, R., Bizer, C.: SOTAB: the WDC Schema.org table annotation benchmark. In: Proceedings of the Semantic Web Challenge on Tabular Data to Knowledge Graph Matching. CEUR Workshop Proceedings, vol. 3320, pp. 14–19 (2022)
15. Hulsebos, M., Demiralp, Ç., Groth, P.: GitTables: a large-scale corpus of relational tables. Proc. ACM Manag. Data **1**(1), 30:1–30:17 (2023). https://doi.org/10.1145/3588710

Enterprise and Education Applications

A Chain-of-Thought Guided Framework for Identity Preservation Video Generation in Education

Junda Wang, Li Li(✉), and Jiwei Li

College of Computer and Information Science, Southwest University, Chongqing 400715, China
1750263541@qq.com, lily@swu.edu.cn

Abstract. Maintaining identity consistency in AI-generated educational videos is critical for virtual teacher-learner interaction. However, existing frameworks suffer from severe identity drift and lack explicit pedagogical reasoning during long-sequence synthesis. We propose **Baize**, a pedagogically aligned multimodal generation framework for identity-preserving educational video synthesis. The framework integrates three components: (1) a Faster-Whisper perception module for robust speech understanding (7.82% CER at 5dB noise); (2) a Chain-of-Thought (CoT) guided reasoning module transforming student states into pedagogical feedback; and (3) a two-stage generation strategy combining LoRA-enhanced Stable Diffusion (MCS = 0.9513) with image-to-video expansion for temporally coherent synthesis. The proposed method is trained on a dataset of 40,000 instructional dialogues annotated with teaching reasoning chains. Experimental results demonstrate that our framework achieves encouraging pedagogical alignment and favourable identity consistency, reducing long-sequence identity drift compared to traditional end-to-end baselines. This work provides a practical paradigm for pedagogically grounded multimodal educational content generation.

Keywords: Multimodal Generation · Pedagogical Reasoning · Identity Preservation · Chain-of-Thought · Personalized Education

1 Introduction

Recent advances in generative AI have enabled the emergence of virtual educational agents capable of producing multimodal instructional content [1,2]. In intelligent tutoring scenarios, feedback quality plays a central role in maintaining student engagement, emotional stability, and learning continuity [3]. However, most existing educational systems still rely on static text or template-based audio responses [4], limiting their ability to deliver immersive and emotionally coherent learning experiences.

The above limitations become particularly severe in emotionally sensitive educational settings such as early childhood learning, where stable teacher identity and affective interaction are essential for sustaining learner attention and

L. Ding et al. (Eds.): APWeb-WAIM 2026, LNCS 16993, pp. 167–182, 2027.
https://doi.org/10.1007/978-981-92-5693-8_11

trust. Existing unimodal feedback mechanisms often fail to establish long-term emotional consistency, resulting in fragmented interactions and reduced pedagogical immersion.

Recent breakthroughs in Large Language Models (LLMs) and Diffusion Models have opened promising pathways for constructing virtual teachers capable of visual representation, linguistic expression, and emotional feedback. However, directly applying these models to dynamic educational content generation faces three key challenges:

- **Lack of Pedagogically Grounded Reasoning**: Existing LLM-based educational agents can generate fluent responses but often fail to perform explicit pedagogical reasoning, such as diagnosing misconceptions, selecting instructional strategies, or adapting feedback according to student emotional states.
- **Identity Drift in Long-Sequence Video Generation**: Current text-to-video generation frameworks struggle to preserve stable character identity across frames, leading to inconsistent facial structure, appearance, and teaching persona during educational interactions.
- **Weak Cross-Modal Coordination**: Existing multimodal educational systems lack unified coordination mechanisms between language reasoning and visual generation, resulting in semantically inconsistent or pedagogically misaligned outputs [5].

The four contributions address the three challenges respectively: Chain-of-Thought guided fine-tuning and feature extraction solve the problem of lacking pedagogical reasoning capability; the two-stage generation strategy solves the identity drift problem; and the end-to-end architecture solves the problem of weak cross-modal coordination. The four contributions are as follows:

- We propose Baize, a pedagogically aligned multimodal framework for identity-preserving educational video generation.
- We introduce a Chain-of-Thought guided pedagogical reasoning mechanism, which fine-tunes a DeepSeek-R1-Distill-Qwen-7B model [6] using LoRA [7] on a dataset of 40,000 pedagogically annotated examples (constructed by Lior Shani et al.) [8]. This approach enables the large language model to generate educationally appropriate feedback by performing explicit reasoning steps.
- We propose a two-stage identity-preserving generation strategy that significantly mitigates identity drift in long-sequence educational video synthesis.
- Extensive experiments demonstrate that the proposed framework achieves encouraging pedagogical alignment and robust identity consistency.

2 Related Work

2.1 Generative AI in Education

Recent advancements in Large Language Models (LLMs) have shown strong potential for generating educational content and providing personalized feedback [1]. However, most existing educational systems still rely on unimodal interaction forms such as static text or templated audio, limiting emotional engagement and immersive learning experiences, especially in early childhood education.

Recent studies have explored reinforcement learning from human feedback (RLHF) for improving multi-turn instructional dialogue quality [8]. While these approaches improve conversational coherence, they mainly focus on general dialogue optimization rather than explicit pedagogical reasoning.

2.2 Pedagogical Reasoning and Efficient Fine-Tuning

Chain-of-Thought (CoT) prompting [5] has significantly improved reasoning capabilities in LLMs by introducing intermediate reasoning steps before generating final responses. Although CoT has achieved strong performance in mathematical and commonsense reasoning tasks, its application to pedagogical dialogue generation remains underexplored. Educational interactions require reasoning about student understanding, misconception diagnosis, and adaptive instructional strategies rather than only producing correct answers.

To efficiently adapt large models to domain-specific tasks, recent work has adopted Low-Rank Adaptation (LoRA) [7], which injects trainable low-rank matrices into model parameters while preserving the general capabilities of foundation models. Such efficient adaptation is particularly suitable for educational applications requiring rapid deployment and iterative optimization.

2.3 Multimodal Generation and Identity Consistency

Recent progress in diffusion models has enabled high-quality multimodal generation across text, image, and video domains [9]. However, existing video generation frameworks often suffer from *identity drift*, where character appearance becomes inconsistent across frames.

Several approaches attempt to preserve visual consistency through conditional control or personalized generation [10, 11]. Nevertheless, maintaining stable character identity during long-sequence video synthesis remains challenging, particularly in educational scenarios that require coherent virtual teacher personas.

To address this issue, our framework adopts a two-stage generation strategy that first anchors character identity using LoRA-enhanced Stable Diffusion and then performs motion synthesis through image-to-video generation.

2.4 Summary and Open Challenges

Although prior work has achieved substantial progress in educational dialogue systems, reasoning-enhanced LLMs, and identity-preserving generation, several challenges remain unresolved:

- Existing educational dialogue systems rarely incorporate explicit pedagogical reasoning chains.

- Large-scale CoT-annotated instructional dialogue datasets remain limited.
- Identity-preserving video generation has not been effectively integrated with pedagogical feedback generation.

To address these limitations, we propose a multimodal framework that combines CoT-guided pedagogical fine-tuning, LoRA-based efficient adaptation, and a two-stage identity-preserving video generation pipeline.

3 Methodology

3.1 Problem Formulation

Given a student speech input S_{in}, the objective of the proposed framework is to generate pedagogically appropriate and identity-consistent multimodal feedback:

$$\mathcal{G} : S_{in} \rightarrow \{E, A_{out}, V_{out}\} \tag{1}$$

where E denotes the generated educational feedback text, A_{out} represents synthesized speech audio, and V_{out} denotes the generated instructional video.

The framework aims to simultaneously optimize three objectives:

- **Pedagogical Alignment**: ensuring that generated feedback follows appropriate instructional reasoning;
- **Identity Consistency**: preserving stable visual identity across generated frames;
- **Cross-Modal Coherence**: maintaining semantic consistency between language, audio, and visual outputs.

The overall optimization objective can be formulated as:

$$\mathcal{L}_{total} = \lambda_1 \mathcal{L}_{ped} + \lambda_2 \mathcal{L}_{identity} + \lambda_3 \mathcal{L}_{coherence} \tag{2}$$

where $\mathcal{L}_{ped}$ measures pedagogical reasoning quality, $\mathcal{L}_{identity}$ constrains character consistency, and $\mathcal{L}_{coherence}$ enforces multimodal semantic alignment.

3.2 System Architecture Overview

The proposed framework adopts a hierarchical multimodal reasoning-and-generation architecture that progressively transforms raw student speech into pedagogically aligned audio-visual instructional feedback, as illustrated in Fig. 1.

Perception Layer. This layer employs Faster-Whisper [12] for noise-robust speech transcription, providing the textual foundation T_{in} for subsequent reasoning. The model maintains a low Character Error Rate of 7.82% even under extreme 5dB noise conditions.

Reasoning Layer. The reasoning layer serves as the semantic decision center of the framework, transforming low-level perceptual signals into pedagogically grounded multimodal generation instructions:

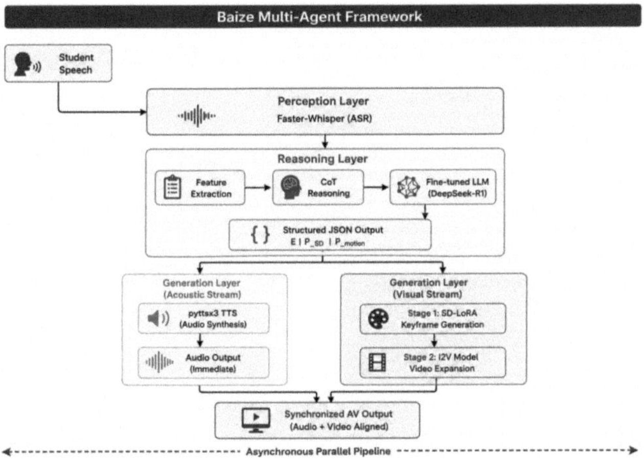

Fig. 1. Overall architecture of the Baize multimodal framework. The framework consists of three layers: (1) Perception Layer: Faster-Whisper transcribes student speech into text. (2) Reasoning Layer: A feature extraction module processes the transcript, followed by Chain-of-Thought reasoning and a fine-tuned LLM that generates structured JSON outputs. (3) Generation Layer: Two parallel streams execute asynchronously—the acoustic stream synthesizes audio feedback via pyttsx3, while the visual stream first generates identity-preserving keyframes via SD-LoRA and then expands them into video via an image-to-video model. The two streams are synchronized for final audio-visual output.

- **Feature Extraction**: A lightweight module extracts five pedagogical dimensions (correctness, error type, confidence, urgency, emotional tone) from the transcript.
- **CoT Reasoning**: The extracted features and transcript are fed into a fine-tuned LLM that generates explicit pedagogical reasoning chains—diagnosing student understanding, selecting instructional strategies, and formulating encouraging feedback.
- **Instruction Generation**: The model outputs JSON-constrained instructions including feedback text E, visual prompts P_{SD}, and motion instructions P_{motion}.

The backbone DeepSeek-R1-Distill-Qwen-7B [6] is fine-tuned via LoRA [7] on 40,000 CoT-annotated instructional dialogues.

Generation Layer. This layer executes a decoupled multimodal output strategy with two parallel streams:

- **Acoustic Stream**: Synthesizes feedback text E into natural speech via pyttsx3 with zero latency.
- **Visual Stream**: First generates an identity-preserving keyframe I_{key} via self-trained SD-LoRA, then expands it into a coherent video segment V_{out} using MiniMax-I2V-01-Live [13].

The three layers operate asynchronously—audio synthesis and video rendering execute in parallel on separate threads, ensuring real-time responsiveness without blocking audio feedback.

3.3 Pedagogical Reasoning via Chain-of-Thought Fine-Tuning

To ensure professional instructional quality and transparent reasoning, we adopt a Chain-of-Thought (CoT) guided fine-tuning approach on the DeepSeek-R1-Distill-Qwen-7B model.

Dataset. The dataset used in this paper serves as a benchmark resource for evaluating multi-turn dialogue algorithms, with its construction process simulating real-world teacher-student interaction scenarios. The dataset was generated by prompting the advanced large language model Gemini Ultra, and it contains complete dialogues in which a teacher teaches a specific topic to a student. It also records metadata such as the teacher's teaching preferences, the student's learning preferences, and the reactions of both parties when interactions do not align with their preferred styles. The dataset comprises a total of **40,000 training examples** and **7,234 validation examples**, with each sample consisting of a complete teacher-student dialogue.

Pedagogical Feature Extraction. To ground CoT reasoning in observable student states, we extract five features from each ASR transcript, shown in Table 1.

Table 1. Pedagogical feature set

Feature	Example values
Correctness flag	{correct, partial, incorrect}
Error type	{none, factual, procedural, conceptual}
Confidence score	[0.0, 1.0]
Urgency level	{low, medium, high}
Emotional tone	{positive, neutral, frustrated}

LoRA Fine-Tuning with CoT. The pedagogical reasoning process consists of three sequential stages:

1. **Student State Diagnosis**: identifying correctness, misconception type, confidence level, and emotional state;
2. **Instructional Strategy Selection**: determining appropriate pedagogical strategies such as encouragement, correction, scaffolding, or elaboration;

3. **Response Formulation**: generating multimodal instructional feedback aligned with the selected teaching strategy.

We employ LoRA [7] to fine-tune DeepSeek-R1-Distill-Qwen-7B on our dataset. The training minimizes cross-entropy loss:

$$\mathcal{L}_{\text{COT}} = -\sum_{t=1}^{T} \log P(y_t \mid y_{<t}, T_{\text{in}}, f_{\text{ped}}) \tag{3}$$

where f_{ped} is the feature vector. The mapping function $\mathcal{F}$ transforms inputs into structured instructions:

$$\mathcal{F}(T_{\text{in}}, f_{\text{ped}}, K_{\text{edu}}) \rightarrow \{E, P_{\text{SD}}, P_{\text{motion}}\} \tag{4}$$

3.4 Identity-Preserving Content Synthesis

Real-Time Acoustic Feedback. The feedback text E generated by the reasoning layer is synthesized into natural speech via the pyttsx3 engine, providing low-latency audio output that simulates an encouraging teacher persona.

Two-Stage Decoupled Visual Generation. To mitigate identity drift in long-sequence video synthesis, we adopt a two-stage decoupled generation strategy based on Stable Diffusion (SD) [14].

Stage 1: Identity-Anchored Keyframe Generation.

We employ LoRA fine-tuning on a pre-trained Stable Diffusion model to generate identity-consistent keyframes of the virtual teacher "Baize". The diffusion model follows the standard denoising objective:

$$\mathcal{L}_{\text{SD}} = \mathbb{E}_{z,\epsilon,t}\left[\|\epsilon - \epsilon_\theta(z_t, t, c)\|_2^2\right] \tag{5}$$

LoRA introduces trainable low-rank matrices into the cross-attention layers:

$$W' = W + BA \tag{6}$$

where W is the original weight matrix and A, B are trainable low-rank parameters. During fine-tuning, only A and B are updated while the original SD parameters remain frozen. This process produces an identity-preserving keyframe I_{key} with stable facial appearance and visual style.

Stage 2: Temporal Video Expansion.

Given the anchored keyframe I_{key} and motion instruction P_{motion}, an image-to-video model synthesizes temporally coherent video sequences. Since identity information is already established during the keyframe generation stage, the video model primarily focuses on motion synthesis, thereby significantly reducing identity drift.

Compared with direct end-to-end text-to-video generation, the proposed decoupled strategy separates identity modeling from temporal dynamics, resulting in more stable character consistency across generated frames.

Asynchronous Pipeline Integration. To ensure real-time responsiveness, the framework adopts an asynchronous parallel pipeline. When the reasoning layer outputs structured instructions, the system simultaneously triggers two independent threads: an acoustic thread for immediate audio playback and a visual thread for video generation. This design ensures students hear verbal feedback without delay. Once video generation completes, the system synchronizes the video with ongoing audio playback, achieving seamless audio-visual alignment.

4 Experiments and Results

This section evaluates the proposed Baize framework from three perspectives:

- **Perception Robustness**: evaluating the robustness of the ASR module under noisy educational environments;
- **Pedagogical Reasoning Quality**: evaluating whether the CoT-guided LLM can generate semantically aligned and pedagogically appropriate instructional feedback;
- **Identity Preservation**: evaluating the effectiveness of the proposed two-stage generation strategy in mitigating identity drift during long-sequence video synthesis.

We further conduct ablation studies to analyze the contribution of each core component within the proposed framework.

4.1 Perception Robustness Analysis

To evaluate the perception layer's performance under noise, we constructed a benchmark dataset containing 500 instructional commands (1–4 s each). We injected Additive White Gaussian Noise (AWGN) at three SNR levels (Clean, 15dB, 5dB) and used Character Error Rate (CER) as the evaluation metric:

$$\text{CER} = \frac{S + D + I}{N} \times 100\% \tag{7}$$

where S, D, I are substitutions, deletions, and insertions, respectively, and N is the total characters. We compare Faster-Whisper against the original Whisper architecture to evaluate whether optimized inference and decoding strategies can improve robustness under noisy educational scenarios. The results are shown in Table 2.

Table 2. CER performance under different noise conditions

Model	Clean	15dB	5dB
Standard Whisper	3.52%	8.41%	15.63%
Faster-Whisper	**1.24%**	**3.15%**	**7.82%**

Faster-Whisper maintains a low CER of 7.82% even under 5dB extreme noise, outperforming the baseline by 49.9%. This robustness ensures reliable semantic input for subsequent reasoning and generation within the multimodal pipeline [15].

4.2 Reasoning Adaptation

To evaluate the effectiveness of our Chain-of-Thought guided fine-tuning approach, we conducted experiments on the validation set comprising **7,234** instructional dialogue examples. The model was fine-tuned using LoRA (r=16 $\alpha = 32$) on **40,000** training examples for 3 epochs.

Training Convergence. The training process exhibited stable convergence, with the loss function decreasing consistently over three epochs. Figure 2 shows the training loss curve of DeepSeek-R1-Distill-Qwen-7B during pedagogical fine-tuning.

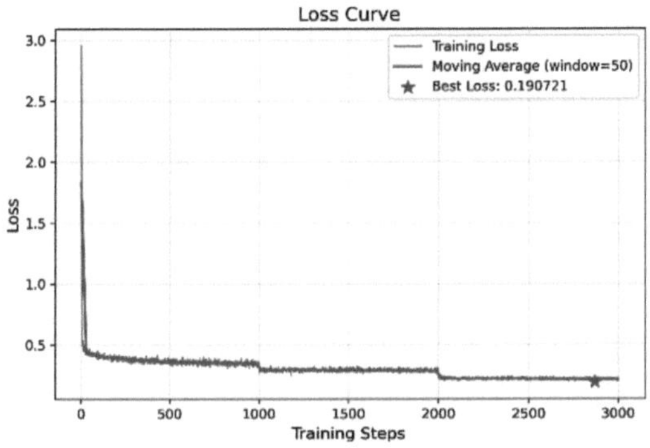

Fig. 2. Training loss curve of DeepSeek-R1-Distill-Qwen-7B during pedagogical fine-tuning.

The final validation loss reached 0.213, indicating successful knowledge anchoring. The continuous reduction in loss confirms the stability of the fine-tuning process [16].

Output Quality Evaluation. We evaluated the model's output quality on 7,234 validation examples. Due to the inherent flexibility of natural language generation, exact string matching often underestimates model performance. Therefore, we adopted **semantic similarity** as the primary evaluation metric, using Sentence-BERT embeddings to measure the semantic alignment between generated and expected responses.

As shown in Table 3, the model achieves an average semantic similarity of **0.72** with ground truth responses. Over 85% of generated responses exhibit

Table 3. Semantic similarity distribution on validation set

Metric	Value
Average semantic similarity	0.72
Proportion with similarity > 0.6	71.4%
Proportion with similarity > 0.5	85.7%

semantic similarity above 0.5, indicating that the model successfully learns pedagogical response patterns despite surface-level lexical differences.

Qualitative Analysis. We manually examined the model's outputs across diverse topics. Representative examples are presented in Table 4.

Table 4. Example model outputs vs. expected responses

Student input	Expected response	Model generated
"I am! This is a great way to learn"	"I'm glad you're enjoying it"	"I'm glad you're enjoying it. Let's continue exploring"
"Teacher, what is buoyancy?"	"Buoyancy is the upward force..."	"It's the upward force exerted on an object in a fluid"

The qualitative analysis reveals that while the model's outputs may differ lexically from the ground truth, they consistently capture the **semantic intent** and **pedagogical appropriateness**. For instance, when a student expresses understanding, the model appropriately affirms the response; when a student asks for a definition, the model provides a correct scientific explanation.

4.3 Identity Consistency

The core challenge in the generation layer is maintaining the visual identity of the virtual teacher"Baize" across dynamic outputs.

To construct the identity-preserving visual dataset, we first collected the original virtual teacher design and employed Gemini [17] to generate 50 identity-consistent reference images under different viewpoints, poses, and environmental conditions. These images were manually filtered and annotated before being used for LoRA fine-tuning.

Similarity Metric. To quantitatively evaluate the consistency between the generated frames V_{gen} and the target character V_{target}, we employ the Mean Cosine Similarity (MCS) based on Contrastive Language-Image Pre-training

(CLIP) feature embeddings [18] as the primary evaluation metric. We adopt CLIP embeddings due to their strong capability in measuring semantic-level visual consistency across generated character images. The cosine similarity is defined as:

$$S_c(V_{\text{gen}}, V_{\text{target}}) = \frac{V_{\text{gen}} \cdot V_{\text{target}}}{||V_{\text{gen}}||\,||V_{\text{target}}||} \tag{8}$$

where V_{gen} and V_{target} denote the high-dimensional vector representations of the generated image and the target template image in the CLIP latent space, respectively. The similarity score S_c ranges from $[-1, 1]$, where a value closer to 1 indicates a higher degree of alignment in terms of overall character persona.

During the experimental phase, we conducted batch sampling of the generated instructional keyframes and calculated their MCS values to verify the stability of the LoRA-enhanced diffusion model in maintaining virtual identity consistency. The experimental results demonstrate that the significant improvement in this metric directly reflects the system's ability to effectively mitigate the "identity drift" problem during long-sequence generation [11], thereby ensuring a coherent visual feedback experience for learners.

Statistical Analysis of Stability. By integrating self-trained LoRA weights (trigger word: baize_sks), the system anchors the teacher's visual identity. Table 5 presents the statistical dispersion of identity consistency across 500 generated keyframes.

Table 5. Statistical analysis of character identity consistency across generated keyframes

Metric	Value
Mean cosine similarity (MCS) ↑	**0.9513**
Variance (σ^2) ↓	**0.0011**
Standard deviation (σ) ↓	**0.0339**

The high MCS of 0.9513 combined with an extremely low variance of 0.0011 provides empirical evidence of the system's high cohesion. This demonstrates robust anti-drift capability, ensuring that facial features remain invariant even with varying viewpoint prompts or different environmental prompts.

4.4 Qualitative Visualization Comparison

To qualitatively evaluate the effectiveness of the proposed identity-preserving generation strategy, we compare our two-stage framework with direct end-to-end text-to-video generation.

Existing end-to-end text-to-video models struggle to maintain stable character identity across frames when only textual prompts are provided. In educational scenarios, such instability can disrupt learners' visual continuity and weaken emotional engagement.

In contrast, the proposed framework first generates an identity-anchored keyframe using SD-LoRA and subsequently performs motion expansion via an image-to-video model. This decoupled strategy separates identity modeling from temporal synthesis, thereby significantly reducing appearance drift.

Figure 3 presents the generated identity-preserving keyframe compared with the original virtual teacher design. Figure 4 further illustrates representative video frames generated from the anchored keyframe. The visual results demonstrate that the proposed framework maintains stable facial features, hairstyle, and clothing attributes across dynamic motion sequences.

Fig. 3. Comparison between the original virtual teacher design (left) and the identity-preserving keyframe generated by SD-LoRA (right).

Fig. 4. Representative video frames synthesized from the identity-anchored keyframe using the image-to-video generation model.

4.5 Ablation Study

To quantitatively evaluate the contribution of each component in the proposed Baize framework, we conduct a comprehensive ablation study by progressively removing or replacing key modules. We focus on three core aspects of the system: (1) Pedagogical Reasoning Quality, (2) Identity Consistency, (3) Generation Stability. We evaluate four degraded variants of the framework:

- **w/o CoT**: Removes Chain-of-Thought reasoning and directly generates feedback responses.
- **w/o Feature Extraction**: Removes pedagogical feature extraction and uses only raw ASR transcripts.
- **w/o LoRA**: Uses the original Stable Diffusion model without identity-specific LoRA fine-tuning.
- **End-to-End T2V**: Replaces the proposed two-stage generation strategy with direct text-to-video synthesis.

Pedagogical Reasoning Evaluation. We first analyze the impact of pedagogical reasoning modules on response quality. Following the evaluation protocol in Sect. 4.2, semantic similarity is adopted as the primary metric (Table 6).

Table 6. Ablation study on pedagogical reasoning quality

Method	Semantic similarity	Responses > 0.5
Full Baize framework	**0.72**	**85.7%**
w/o CoT	0.61	73.4%
w/o feature extraction	0.65	78.9%

The results indicate that explicit Chain-of-Thought reasoning improves pedagogical response quality. Removing CoT leads to a substantial decrease in semantic similarity, suggesting that intermediate reasoning steps are essential for generating contextually appropriate educational feedback.

Similarly, removing pedagogical feature extraction reduces the model's ability to adapt responses according to student emotional states and confidence levels.

Identity Consistency Evaluation. We further evaluate the contribution of LoRA fine-tuning and the proposed two-stage generation strategy on identity preservation. The results are shown in Table 7.
The experimental results demonstrate that LoRA fine-tuning substantially improves character identity consistency. Without LoRA adaptation, the generated teacher images exhibit noticeable variations in facial structure and visual style.

Furthermore, replacing the proposed decoupled generation pipeline with direct end-to-end text-to-video synthesis increases identity drift. This validates the effectiveness of the proposed identity-anchored keyframe generation strategy.

Table 7. Ablation study on identity consistency

Method	MCS ↑	Variance ↓
Full Baize framework	**0.9513**	**0.0011**
w/o LoRA	0.5864	0.0487
End-to-End T2V	0.4219	0.0724

Discussion. The ablation study confirms that all proposed components contribute positively to the overall framework performance. In particular:

- Chain-of-Thought reasoning improves pedagogical coherence and contextual appropriateness.
- Pedagogical feature extraction enhances adaptive feedback generation.
- LoRA fine-tuning is critical for maintaining stable character identity.
- The two-stage generation strategy effectively mitigates long-sequence identity drift.

These findings collectively validate the necessity of integrating reasoning-aware educational modeling with identity-preserving multimodal generation.

5 Conclusion

This paper presented Baize, a pedagogically aligned multimodal framework for identity-preserving educational video generation. Baize integrates three components: a Faster-Whisper perception module for robust speech understanding, a Chain-of-Thought reasoning module for pedagogically appropriate feedback, and a two-stage visual synthesis strategy combining LoRA-enhanced Stable Diffusion with image-to-video expansion.

Experimental results show that Baize achieves encouraging noise robustness, semantically aligned feedback, and improved identity consistency in long-sequence video synthesis. The decoupled generation strategy effectively mitigates identity drift compared to end-to-end text-to-video approaches.

There are some limitations. First, the visual generation pipeline incurs high latency: while SD-LoRA keyframe generation takes only seconds per image on an NVIDIA RTX 3090 (12GB VRAM), the subsequent image-to-video synthesis remains time-consuming. Although the asynchronous pipeline enables immediate audio feedback, the visual latency still hinders fully real-time classroom deployment. Second, long-term pedagogical effectiveness in real classrooms has not been systematically validated. Furthermore, our evaluation currently focuses on a single virtual teacher character; although the LoRA-based framework can be readily extended to new personas by retraining on new data, generalization to diverse teacher identities requires further investigation.

Future work will focus on improving real-time efficiency via lightweight synthesis and model acceleration, expanding the dialogue dataset to more diverse scenarios, and incorporating human preference optimization and reinforcement learning to enhance pedagogical quality and emotional interaction. We also plan to investigate advanced identity-preserving methods for long-horizon interaction.

Overall, this work demonstrates the potential of combining pedagogical reasoning with identity-preserving generation to build emotionally coherent and educationally reliable virtual agents.

Acknowledgments. Li Li is the corresponding author for the paper. This work was supported by Student Innovation Fund from Southwest University (Grant No. SWUS26109).

References

1. Brown, T., Mann, B., Ryder, N., Subbiah, M., Kaplan, J.D., Dhariwal, P., Neelakantan, A., Shyam, P., Sastry, G., Askell, A., et al.: Language models are few-shot learners. Adv. Neural. Inf. Process. Syst. **33**, 1877–1901 (2020)
2. Vaswani, A., Shazeer, N., Parmar, N., Uszkoreit, J., Jones, L., Gomez, A.N., Kaiser, Ł., Polosukhin, I.: Attention is all you need. AAdv. Neural Inf. Process. Syst. **30** (2017)
3. Hattie, J., Timperley, H.: The power of feedback. Rev. Educ. Res. **77**(1), 81–112 (2007)
4. Supentri, S., Isjoni, I., Caska, C., Erlinda, S.: Redesigning pancasila education for generation Z: a mixed-methods needs analysis of pedagogical mismatch and interactive civic E-module design in Indonesian higher education. F1000Research **15**, 707 (2026). 10.12688/f1000research.180069.1
5. Wei, J., Wang, X., Schuurmans, D., Bosma, M., Ichter, B., Xia, F., Chi, E., Le, Q., Zhou, D.: Chain-of-thought prompting elicits reasoning in large language models. In: Advances in Neural Information Processing Systems (NeurIPS), vol. 35, pp. 24824–24837. Curran Associates, Inc (2022)
6. Guo, D., Yang, D., Zhang, H., Song, J., Wang, P., Zhu, Q., Xu, R., Zhang, R., Ma, S., Bi, X., et al.: DeepSeek-R1 incentivizes reasoning in LLMs through reinforcement learning. Nature **645**(8081), 633–638 (2025). https://doi.org/10.1038/s41586-025-09422-z
7. Hu, E.J., Shen, Y., Wallis, P., Allen-Zhu, Z., Li, Y., Wang, S., Wang, L., Chen, W.: LoRA: Low-rank adaptation of large language models. In: International Conference on Learning Representations (ICLR) (2022)
8. Shani, L., Rosenberg, A., Cassel, A., Lang, O., Calandriello, D., Zipori, A., Noga, H., Keller, O., Piot, B., Szpektor, I., Hassidim, A., Matias, Y., Munos, R.: Multi-turn reinforcement learning with preference human feedback. In: Advances in Neural Information Processing Systems (NeurIPS), vol. 37, pp. 118953–118993. Curran Associates, Inc (2024). https://doi.org/10.52202/079017-3779
9. Ho, J., Salimans, T.: Classifier-free diffusion guidance (2022). arXiv:2207.12598 arXiv preprint
10. Zhang, L., Rao, A., Agrawala, M.: Adding conditional control to text-to-image diffusion models. In: Proceedings of the IEEE/CVF International Conference on Computer Vision, pp. 3836–3847 (2023)
11. Gal, R., Alaluf, Y., Atzmon, Y., Patashnik, O., Bermano, A.H., Chechik, G., Cohen-Or, D.: An image is worth one word: Personalizing text-to-image generation using textual inversion (2022). arXiv:2208.01618 arXiv preprint

12. Radford, A., Kim, J.W., Xu, T., Brockman, G., McLeavey, C., Sutskever, I.: Robust speech recognition via large-scale weak supervision. In: International Conference on Machine Learning, pp. 28492–28518. PMLR (2023)
13. Li, A., Gong, B., Yang, B., Shan, B., Liu, C., Zhu, C., Zhang, C., Guo, C., Chen, D., Li, D., et al.: Minimax-01: scaling foundation models with lightning attention. arXiv preprint arXiv:2501.08313 (2025)
14. Rombach, R., Blattmann, A., Lorenz, D., Esser, P., Ommer, B.: High-resolution image synthesis with latent diffusion models. In: Proceedings of the IEEE/CVF Conference on Computer Vision and Pattern Recognition, pp. 10684–10695 (2022)
15. Watanabe, S., Hori, T., Karita, S., Hayashi, T., Nishitoba, J., Unno, Y., Soplin, N.E.Y., Heymann, J., Wiesner, M., Chen, N.: ESPnet: end-to-end speech processing toolkit (2018). arXiv:1804.00015 arXiv preprint
16. He, K., Zhang, X., Ren, S., Sun, J.: Deep residual learning for image recognition. In: Proceedings of the IEEE Conference on Computer Vision and Pattern Recognition, pp. 770–778 (2016)
17. Team, G.: Gemini: a family of highly capable multimodal models (2023). arXiv:2312.11805 arXiv preprint
18. Radford, A., Kim, J.W., Hallacy, C., Ramesh, A., Goh, G., Agarwal, S., Sastry, G., Askell, A., Mishkin, P., Clark, J.: Learning transferable visual models from natural language supervision. In: International Conference on Machine Learning, pp. 8748–8763. PMLR (2021)

TRUST-ESD: A Risk-Calibrated and Governance-Aware AI Framework for Enterprise Strategic Decision Support Under Uncertainty

Tian Qiu[1], Li Yan[1], Mahabubur Rahman Miraj[2(✉)], Shanqin Yi[3], Md Intekhab Rahman Galib[4], and Jahid Hasan[5]

[1] School of Economics and Management, Xinyu University, Xinyu, China
[2] College of Computer Science, Chongqing University, Chongqing, China
miraj@stu.cqu.edu.cn
[3] School of Economics and Business Administration, Chongqing University, Chongqing, China
[4] School of Management, Xi'an Jiaotong University, Xi'an, China
[5] School of Law and Public Administration, China Three Gorges University, Yichang, China

Abstract. Enterprise strategic decision support requires AI systems that are not only accurate, but also uncertainty-aware, risk-calibrated, explainable, and governance-compliant. This paper proposes TRUST-ESD, a risk-calibrated and governance-aware framework for enterprise decision support under uncertainty. TRUST-ESD evaluates feasible counterfactual strategies through predictive utility estimation, conformal uncertainty calibration, CVaR-based downside-risk scoring, risk-memory retrieval, policy-as-code governance, explainability, and human oversight. Unlike prediction-only methods that select actions by maximum expected utility, TRUST-ESD recommends strategies that balance value, reliability, risk exposure, and compliance. Experimental results show that TRUST-ESD improves risk-adjusted utility by 7.95%, reduces risk exposure by 23.22%, reduces CVaR by 23.78%, lowers calibration error by 13.89%, improves explanation fidelity by 10.90%, and increases governance compliance by 9.76% compared with strong uncertainty-aware baselines, while maintaining competitive predictive accuracy. Ablation and case-study analyses further confirm that uncertainty calibration, downside-risk scoring, risk memory, explainability, and governance validation jointly improve trustworthy enterprise decision-making.

Keywords: Trustworthy AI · Enterprise Decision Support · Conformal Prediction · Risk Memory · Policy-as-Code Governance

1 Introduction

Artificial intelligence is increasingly used for enterprise strategic decision-making, where organizations must choose actions under market volatility, operational

L. Ding et al. (Eds.): APWeb-WAIM 2026, LNCS 16993, pp. 183–198, 2027.
https://doi.org/10.1007/978-981-92-5693-8_12

uncertainty, resource constraints, and governance requirements [3,7]. However, prediction accuracy alone is insufficient for such settings, since conventional evaluation metrics do not fully capture decision risk, policy feasibility, or downstream business consequences [1]. A strategy with high expected utility may still be unsuitable if it is uncertain, exposed to severe downside risk [24], difficult to justify through explainable evidence [8], or inconsistent with enterprise policy constraints [3,10]. Thus, enterprise decision support requires AI systems that are not only predictive, but also risk-calibrated [24], explainable [8], auditable, and governance-aware [2,6].

Existing AI-based decision-support methods are largely prediction-centered: they estimate future outcomes and select the option with the highest expected value. This approach is limited in strategic enterprise scenarios, where actions such as pricing adjustment, inventory expansion, resource allocation, or market entry may appear beneficial under point prediction but become fragile under demand fluctuation, financial exposure, operational instability, or regulatory constraints [3,7]. Although prior work on trustworthy AI emphasizes human oversight [2], transparency and accountability [4,6], fairness in predictive systems [5], explainability for black-box models [8], and cybersecurity-aware governance [10], these aspects are rarely integrated into a unified quantitative decision pipeline.

To address this gap, we propose TRUST-ESD, a risk-calibrated and governance-aware framework for enterprise strategic decision support under uncertainty. TRUST-ESD evaluates feasible counterfactual strategies by estimating predictive utility, calibrating uncertainty with conformal intervals, measuring downside risk using CVaR, incorporating historical risk memory, and enforcing policy-as-code governance with human oversight. Instead of selecting the action with the highest predicted utility, TRUST-ESD recommends the strategy that best balances value, reliability, risk control, explainability, and compliance.

The main contributions are as follows:

- We formulate enterprise decision support as a risk-calibrated and governance-constrained recommendation problem.
- We propose TRUST-ESD, integrating counterfactual strategy generation, conformal uncertainty calibration, CVaR risk scoring, risk memory, policy governance, explainability, and human oversight.
- We design a composite decision objective that jointly balances utility, uncertainty, downside risk, governance compliance, and hard-policy constraints.
- We evaluate TRUST-ESD against prediction-only, uncertainty-aware, and decision-aware baselines using predictive, decision, risk, calibration, explainability, and governance metrics.

2 Related Work

Enterprise decision-support research has largely focused on predictive modeling over structured business data. Classical models such as Linear and Logistic Regression [15] and Random Forest [17] provide transparent or ensemble-based prediction, while more advanced machine learning models such as XGBoost [16], LightGBM [19], CatBoost [16], TabNet, and FT-Transformer [20] offer stronger nonlinear and tabular representation learning. Comparative machine learning studies further show that model integration and advanced learners can improve predictive performance across complex structured-data tasks [18]. Uncertainty-aware methods such as NGBoost [16], Quantile LightGBM [19], and Deep Ensembles [22] improve confidence estimation, but they do not inherently support counterfactual strategy evaluation, CVaR-based downside-risk control [24], risk memory, policy governance, or human oversight [2,3]. As shown in Table 1, decision-aware variants partially address utility, uncertainty, risk, or policy filtering, yet they still lack a unified trustworthy decision pipeline. TRUST-ESD addresses this gap by integrating predictive modeling, calibrated uncertainty, counterfactual strategy evaluation, CVaR risk scoring [24], risk-memory retrieval, policy-as-code governance [3,7], explainability [8], and human oversight [2,6] into a single enterprise decision-support framework.

Table 1. Comparison of representative baselines with TRUST-ESD framework.

Method	Predictive Modeling	Uncertainty Calibration	Counterfactual Strategy	CVaR Risk	Risk Memory	Policy Governance	Explainability Support	Human Oversight
Linear / Logistic Regression	✓	✗	✗	✗	✗	✗	✓	✗
Random Forest	✓	△	✗	✗	✗	✗	△	✗
XGBoost	✓	✗	✗	✗	✗	✗	△	✗
LightGBM	✓	△	✗	✗	✗	✗	△	✗
CatBoost	✓	✗	✗	✗	✗	✗	△	✗
TabNet	✓	✗	✗	✗	✗	✗	✓	✗
FT-Transformer	✓	✗	✗	✗	✗	✗	△	✗
NGBoost	✓	✓	✗	✗	✗	✗	△	✗
Quantile LightGBM	✓	✓	✗	✗	✗	✗	△	✗
Deep Ensembles	✓	✓	✗	△	✗	✗	△	✗
Utility-Only Decision	✓	✗	✓	✗	✗	✗	△	✗
Uncertainty-Penalized Decision	✓	✓	✓	✗	✗	✗	△	✗
CVaR-Risk Decision	✓	✓	✓	✓	✗	✗	△	✗
Policy-Filtered Decision	✓	✓	✓	△	✗	✓	△	△
TRUST-ESD w/o Risk Memory	✓	✓	✓	✓	✗	✓	✓	✓
Full TRUST-ESD	✓	✓	✓	✓	✓	✓	✓	✓

✓ indicates explicit support, △ indicates partial, and × indicates no explicit support

3 TRUST-ESD: Problem Formulation and Framework

3.1 Problem Setup and Decision Objective

Enterprise strategic decision support aims to select an action that is not only valuable, but also reliable, risk-aware, explainable [8], and policy-compliant [3,7]. At decision time t, the enterprise state is represented as

$$x_t = \{x_t^b, x_t^m, x_t^o, x_t^e\}, \tag{1}$$

where x_t^b, x_t^m, x_t^o, and x_t^e denote business data, market signals, operational indicators, and external constraints. The state is mapped into a decision representation

$$z_t = \phi(x_t) \in \mathbb{R}^d. \tag{2}$$

Given a candidate strategy set $A_t = \{a_1, \ldots, a_K\}$, TRUST-ESD constructs a state–action representation

$$\xi_{t,k} = \Gamma(z_t, a_k), \tag{3}$$

and assigns each strategy a risk-calibrated score:

$$S_{t,k} = \alpha \bar{u}_{t,k} - \beta \bar{\sigma}_{t,k} - \gamma \bar{R}_{t,k} + \omega G_{t,k} - \mu V_{t,k}, \tag{4}$$

where $\bar{u}_{t,k}$, $\bar{\sigma}_{t,k}$, and $\bar{R}_{t,k}$ denote normalized utility, uncertainty, and risk, while $G_{t,k}$ and $V_{t,k}$ denote governance compliance and hard-policy violation. The selected strategy is

$$a_t^* = \arg \max_{a_k \in A_t^{\text{feas}}} S_{t,k}, \qquad \text{s.t. } p_j(z_t, a_k) = 1,\ \forall p_j \in P_{\text{hard}}. \tag{5}$$

Thus, TRUST-ESD prevents high-utility but risky or non-compliant strategies from being selected.

3.2 Framework Overview

Figure 1 shows the overall TRUST-ESD pipeline. Enterprise inputs are first transformed into a decision-ready state representation, after which feasible counterfactual strategies are generated and evaluated through predictive utility estimation, conformal uncertainty calibration, CVaR-based risk scoring [24], explainability [8], governance validation [3,7], and human oversight [2].

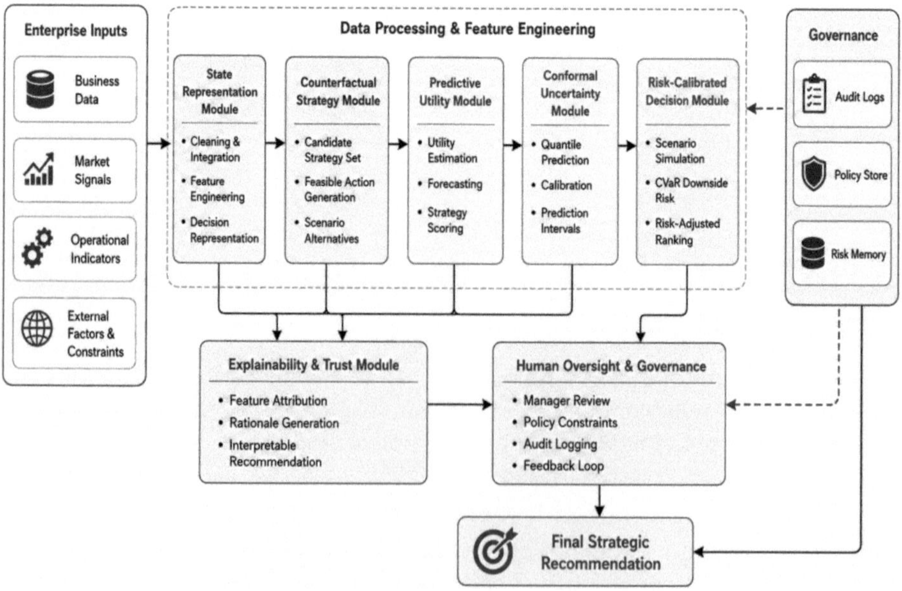

Fig. 1. TRUST-ESD framework for risk-aware enterprise decision support.

The end-to-end process is summarized as

$$x_t \rightarrow z_t \rightarrow A_t^{\text{feas}} \rightarrow \hat{u}_{t,k} \rightarrow PI_{t,k}^{\text{conf}} \rightarrow R_{t,k} \rightarrow S_{t,k} \rightarrow y_t^*. \tag{6}$$

The final output is a governance-aware recommendation:

$$y_t^* = \{a_t^*, \psi_t^*, c_t^*, \ell_t^*\}, \tag{7}$$

where ψ_t^* is the explanation, c_t^* the compliance report, and ℓ_t^* the audit record.

3.3 Counterfactual Strategy Generation and Utility Estimation

TRUST-ESD evaluates multiple feasible strategies rather than producing a single prediction. Each strategy is represented as

$$a_k = [\Delta q_k, \Delta p_k, \Delta b_k, \Delta c_k], \tag{8}$$

corresponding to resource, pricing, budget, and capacity adjustments. Feasible actions are obtained by

$$A_t^{\text{feas}} = \{a_k \in A_t \mid c_j(z_t, a_k) = 1,\ \forall c_j \in C_{\text{hard}}\}. \tag{9}$$

For each feasible strategy, the predictive utility model estimates

$$\hat{u}_{t,k} = g_\theta(\xi_{t,k}). \tag{10}$$

The realized utility is computed as

$$U_{t,k} = U(z_t, a_k, d_t), \tag{11}$$

where d_t is the observed outcome. For inventory-oriented decisions, this can be instantiated as

$$U_{t,k} = p_t \min(q_{t,k}, d_t) - c_t q_{t,k} - h_t(q_{t,k} - d_t)^+ - s_t(d_t - q_{t,k})^+ - C(a_k), \tag{12}$$

where $(x)^+ = \max(x, 0)$.

3.4 Conformal Uncertainty and CVaR Risk Scoring

To avoid overconfident recommendations, TRUST-ESD estimates calibrated uncertainty for each strategy, supporting reliable and trustworthy decision-making [2,6]. Given lower, median, and upper utility quantiles

$$\hat{q}_{\tau_l}(\xi_{t,k}), \quad \hat{q}_{0.5}(\xi_{t,k}), \quad \hat{q}_{\tau_u}(\xi_{t,k}), \tag{13}$$

the predicted utility is $\hat{u}_{t,k} = \hat{q}_{0.5}(\xi_{t,k})$. The conformal prediction interval is

$$PI_{t,k}^{\text{conf}} = [\hat{q}_{\tau_l}(\xi_{t,k}) - \Delta_\alpha, \hat{q}_{\tau_u}(\xi_{t,k}) + \Delta_\alpha], \tag{14}$$

and the uncertainty score is

$$\hat{\sigma}_{t,k} = \text{Upper}(PI_{t,k}^{\text{conf}}) - \text{Lower}(PI_{t,k}^{\text{conf}}). \tag{15}$$

For downside-risk estimation, utility scenarios are sampled from the calibrated interval:

$$\tilde{u}_{t,k}^{(s)} \sim PI_{t,k}^{\text{conf}}, \qquad L_{t,k}^{(s)} = -\tilde{u}_{t,k}^{(s)}. \tag{16}$$

The tail risk is measured by

$$\text{CVaR}_\tau(a_k) = \mathbb{E}[L_{t,k}^{(s)} \mid L_{t,k}^{(s)} \geq \text{VaR}_\tau(a_k)]. \tag{17}$$

The model-based risk score is

$$R_{t,k}^{\text{model}} = \lambda_1 \,\text{CVaR}_\tau(a_k) + \lambda_2 \Pr(L_{t,k} > 0) + \lambda_3 \Pr(Viol_{t,k} = 1). \tag{18}$$

3.5 Risk Memory and Policy-as-Code Governance

TRUST-ESD stores previous decisions in a risk memory

$$\mathcal{M} = \{(z_i, a_i, \hat{u}_i, u_i, R_i, V_i, H_i)\}_{i=1}^{N}, \tag{19}$$

where u_i, R_i, V_i, and H_i denote realized utility, realized risk, policy violation, and human override status. For a new strategy, similar historical cases are retrieved as

$$\mathcal{N}_{t,k} = \text{TopM}(\text{sim}((z_t, a_k), (z_i, a_i)), \mathcal{M}). \tag{20}$$

The memory-based risk is

$$R_{t,k}^{\text{mem}} = \frac{1}{|\mathcal{N}_{t,k}|} \sum_{i \in \mathcal{N}_{t,k}} [\eta_1 (\hat{u}_i - u_i)^+ + \eta_2 R_i + \eta_3 V_i + \eta_4 H_i]. \tag{21}$$

The final risk estimate is

$$R_{t,k} = \delta R_{t,k}^{\text{model}} + (1 - \delta) R_{t,k}^{\text{mem}}. \tag{22}$$

Governance is implemented through policy-as-code rules $P = \{p_1, \dots, p_J\}$ to support regulatory and organizational compliance [3], where

$$p_j(z_t, a_k, \hat{u}_{t,k}, \hat{\sigma}_{t,k}, R_{t,k}) \in \{0, 1\}. \tag{23}$$

The governance compliance score and hard-violation indicator are

$$G_{t,k} = \frac{1}{J} \sum_{j=1}^{J} p_j(z_t, a_k, \hat{u}_{t,k}, \hat{\sigma}_{t,k}, R_{t,k}), \tag{24}$$

$$V_{t,k} = \mathbb{I}[\exists p_j \in P_{\text{hard}} : p_j(z_t, a_k, \hat{u}_{t,k}, \hat{\sigma}_{t,k}, R_{t,k}) = 0]. \tag{25}$$

3.6 Explainability, Human Oversight, and Audit Logging

TRUST-ESD explains the selected strategy at the decision-score level [8]:

$$\psi_t^* = e(z_t, a_t^*, S_{t,k}). \tag{26}$$

A generic score decomposition is

$$S_{t,k} = S_0 + \sum_{r=1}^{d} \Phi_r^u - \sum_{r=1}^{d} \Phi_r^\sigma - \sum_{r=1}^{d} \Phi_r^R + \Phi^G, \tag{27}$$

where the terms represent utility, uncertainty, risk, and governance contributions. The final recommendation is validated through

$$y_t^* = h(a_t^*, \psi_t^*, G_{t,k}, R_{t,k}, M_t), \tag{28}$$

where $M_t \in \{\text{accept}, \text{revise}, \text{override}\}$ denotes managerial review. Each decision creates an audit record

$$\ell_t = \{x_t, A_t, a_t^*, S_{t,k}, \hat{u}_{t,k}, \hat{\sigma}_{t,k}, R_{t,k}, G_{t,k}, \psi_t^*, M_t\}, \tag{29}$$

which is stored for accountability and used to update the risk memory:

$$\mathcal{M} \leftarrow \mathcal{M} \cup \{\ell_t\}. \tag{30}$$

Algorithm 1 summarizes the end-to-end TRUST-ESD pipeline from enterprise state representation to governance-aware recommendation.

Algorithm 1. TRUST-ESD Risk-Calibrated Governance-Aware Decision

Require: Enterprise state x_t, candidate strategies A_t, policy set P, risk memory $\mathcal{M}$
Ensure: Final recommendation y_t^*

```
Construct enterprise representation z_t = φ(x_t)
Generate feasible strategies A_t^feas using operational constraints
for each strategy a_k ∈ A_t^feas do
    Construct state–action representation ξ_{t,k} = Γ(z_t, a_k)
    Estimate predicted utility û_{t,k} = g_θ(ξ_{t,k})
    Compute conformal interval PI_{t,k}^conf and uncertainty σ̂_{t,k}
    Simulate utility scenarios and estimate R_{t,k}^model using CVaR
    Retrieve similar historical cases from M
    Compute memory-based risk R_{t,k}^mem
    Combine risks R_{t,k} = δ R_{t,k}^model + (1 − δ) R_{t,k}^mem
    Evaluate governance compliance G_{t,k} and violation indicator V_{t,k}
    Compute TRUST-ESD score S_{t,k}
    Generate explanation ψ_{t,k}
end for
Select a_t^* = arg max_{a_k ∈ A_t^feas} S_{t,k} subject to hard policy satisfaction
Validate recommendation through human review if required
Generate final recommendation y_t^* = {a_t^*, ψ_t^*, c_t^*, ℓ_t^*}
Update audit log and risk memory M
return y_t^*
```

4 Experimental Process

4.1 Datasets and Training Processes

TRUST-ESD is evaluated in an enterprise decision-support setting where the goal is to select risk-calibrated and governance-compliant strategies, following the full pipeline from state representation and strategy generation to uncertainty calibration, CVaR risk scoring [24], policy validation [3, 7], explanation [8], and human oversight [2].

Given an enterprise state x_t and a feasible strategy set

$$A_t^{\text{feas}} = \{a_1, a_2, \ldots, a_K\}, \tag{31}$$

each method produces a recommendation by ranking candidate strategies. Prediction-only baselines select

$$a_t^{\text{pred}} = \arg \max_{a_k \in A_t^{\text{feas}}} \hat{u}_{t,k}, \tag{32}$$

whereas TRUST-ESD selects

$$a_t^* = \arg \max_{a_k \in A_t^{\text{feas}}} S_{t,k}, \tag{33}$$

where $S_{t,k}$ jointly accounts for predicted utility, calibrated uncertainty, downside risk [24], risk memory, and governance compliance [3, 6].

The experimental benchmark is built from enterprise-oriented retail tabular data, using *Rossmann Store Sales* [12] and *M5 Forecasting* [11] to simulate strategic decision support. Each instance represents a store–item–time state, where candidate strategies include conservative replenishment, aggressive replenishment, promotion, cost-saving, risk-control, and capacity expansion. Realized utility, downside risk, and policy compliance are computed using observed demand or sales. The data are chronologically split into training, validation, calibration, and test sets for model fitting, hyperparameter tuning, conformal calibration, and final evaluation, respectively, with all preprocessing fitted only on the training set to avoid information leakage.

4.2 Baseline Models

TRUST-ESD is evaluated against prediction-only, uncertainty-aware, and decision-aware baselines. The prediction-only group includes Linear Regression [15], Random Forest [17], XGBoost [16], LightGBM [19], CatBoost [16], TabNet, and FT-Transformer [20], which select strategies by maximizing predicted utility. Comparative machine learning studies further support the use of integrated and nonlinear models for complex prediction tasks [18]. The uncertainty-aware group includes NGBoost [16], Quantile LightGBM [19], and Deep Ensembles [22], which additionally estimate predictive uncertainty but do not directly optimize downside risk [24] or governance compliance [3]. The decision-aware group includes Utility-Only, Uncertainty-Penalized, CVaR-Risk [24], Policy-Filtered [3, 7], TRUST-ESD variants enable controlled comparison of utility, uncertainty, risk, policy filtering, memory, and the full framework.

4.3 Evaluation Metrics

The evaluation covers prediction quality, decision quality, risk control, calibration, explainability, and governance. Predictive performance is measured using RMSE, MAE, and R^2 for regression tasks [21], and Accuracy [16,23], F1-score [16,25], and AUC [21,25]for classification tasks.

Decision quality is evaluated using Average Utility and Risk-Adjusted Utility:

$$AU = \frac{1}{N}\sum_{t=1}^{N} U_{t,a_t}, \tag{34}$$

$$RAU = \frac{1}{N}\sum_{t=1}^{N} \left(U_{t,a_t} - \rho R_{t,a_t}\right), \tag{35}$$

where U_{t,a_t} is the realized utility of the selected strategy and R_{t,a_t} is its risk score.

Risk-control performance is measured using Average Risk Exposure, Downside Loss, and CVaR [24]:

$$DL = \frac{1}{N}\sum_{t=1}^{N} \max(0, -U_{t,a_t}). \tag{36}$$

Uncertainty reliability is evaluated using Prediction Interval Coverage Probability and Mean Prediction Interval Width, which assess whether calibrated prediction intervals provide reliable uncertainty estimates:

$$PICP = \frac{1}{N}\sum_{t=1}^{N} \mathbb{I}[u_t \in PI_t^{\text{conf}}], \tag{37}$$

$$MPIW = \frac{1}{N}\sum_{t=1}^{N} \left(Upper(PI_t^{\text{conf}}) - Lower(PI_t^{\text{conf}})\right). \tag{38}$$

Governance performance is measured using Governance Compliance Rate, Policy Violation Rate, Human Review Rate, Human Override Rate, and Audit Completeness, reflecting trustworthy AI requirements for oversight [2], accountability [4,6], regulatory compliance [3,7], and secure machine learning deployment [10]:

$$GCR = \frac{\#\text{compliant recommendations}}{\#\text{total recommendations}}, \qquad PVR = 1 - GCR. \tag{39}$$

Explainability is measured by Fidelity and Attribution Stability to evaluate whether TRUST-ESD provides reliable and interpretable strategic recommendations [8].

4.4 Candidate Strategy Construction and Implementation Details

To convert predictive outputs into decision-support instances, each test sample is paired with the same finite candidate strategy set as in Table 2. In the retail decision setting, based on demand-forecasting benchmarks such as *Rossmann Store Sales* [12] and *M5 Forecasting* [11], each strategy defines an operational quantity $q_{t,k}$ using the predicted demand $\hat{d}_t$ and the calibrated prediction interval $PI_t^{\mathrm{conf}} = [l_t, u_t]$. This ensures fair evaluation under identical actions, outcomes, and constraints.

Table 2. Candidate strategy definitions used for decision evaluation.

Strategy	Action rule	Main risk source
Conservative	$q_{t,k} = 1.05\hat{d}_t$	Mild overstock
Aggressive	$q_{t,k} = 1.25\hat{d}_t$	High holding cost
Cost-saving	$q_{t,k} = 0.90\hat{d}_t$	Stockout risk
Promotion	$q_{t,k} = 1.15\hat{d}_t$	Promotion cost
Risk-control	$q_{t,k} = u_t$	Higher inventory cost
Capacity expansion	$q_{t,k} = \min(1.30\hat{d}_t, q_{\max})$	Fixed expansion cost

For each selected strategy, realized utility is computed using the observed outcome d_t, enabling evaluation beyond prediction error through decision utility, downside loss, CVaR-based risk control [24], calibration quality, and policy compliance [3,7]. All models use the same preprocessing, training, calibration, and test protocol to ensure a fair comparison: hyperparameters are tuned on the validation set, Δ_α is estimated on the calibration set, and the test set is used only for final reporting. The TRUST-ESD coefficients $\alpha, \beta, \gamma, \omega, \mu$, scenario number S, CVaR level τ [24], and memory size M are selected by validation performance under hard policy constraints. Governance rules are implemented as deterministic constraints aligned with trustworthy AI oversight [2], accountability-oriented AI governance [4,6], and secure machine learning deployment principles [10], while results are reported as mean values with standard deviations over repeated runs.

5 Results and Analysis

5.1 Overall Performance

Full TRUST-ESD achieves the strongest overall decision-support performance while maintaining competitive predictive accuracy. As shown in Table 3, Deep Ensembles obtains the best RMSE and MAE, but its decision quality and trustworthiness metrics are weaker than those of the proposed framework. Full TRUST-ESD reaches the highest RAU of 0.815, lowest risk exposure of 0.162, lowest CVaR of 0.218, lowest ECE of 0.031, highest PICP of 0.939, highest

Fidelity of 0.834, and highest GCR of 0.967. Compared with Deep Ensembles, TRUST-ESD improves RAU by 7.95%, reduces risk exposure by 23.22%, reduces CVaR by 23.78%, lowers ECE by 13.89%, improves PICP by 1.19%, improves explanation fidelity by 10.90%, and improves governance compliance by 9.76%.

Table 3. Overall performance results.

Model	RMSE↓	MAE↓	Utility↑	RAU↑	Risk Exp.↓	CVaR↓	ECE↓	PICP↑	Fidelity↑	GCR↑
Linear Regression	0.168	0.124	0.701	0.612	0.318	0.421	0.091	0.812	0.642	0.804
Random Forest	0.143	0.105	0.742	0.651	0.292	0.384	0.076	0.845	0.681	0.823
XGBoost	0.129	0.094	0.781	0.692	0.263	0.352	0.063	0.872	0.713	0.841
LightGBM	0.124	0.091	0.804	0.711	0.248	0.336	0.058	0.884	0.729	0.852
CatBoost	0.122	0.089	0.811	0.718	0.241	0.327	0.056	0.887	0.736	0.858
TabNet	0.135	0.098	0.776	0.684	0.257	0.348	0.066	0.864	0.754	0.846
FT-Transformer	0.121	0.088	0.817	0.731	0.232	0.314	0.052	0.891	0.768	0.867
NGBoost	0.131	0.095	0.795	0.734	0.226	0.301	0.041	0.915	0.724	0.861
Quantile LightGBM	0.126	0.092	0.806	0.746	0.219	0.294	0.038	0.923	0.731	0.873
Deep Ensembles	**0.119**	**0.086**	0.823	0.755	0.211	0.286	0.036	0.928	0.752	0.881
Utility-Only	0.122	0.089	**0.836**	0.704	0.284	0.369	0.057	0.866	0.741	0.812
Uncertainty-Penalized	0.122	0.089	0.821	0.758	0.224	0.302	0.039	0.921	0.749	0.846
CVaR-Risk	0.123	0.090	0.812	0.781	0.196	0.263	0.038	0.919	0.755	0.867
Policy-Filtered	0.123	0.090	0.804	0.776	0.188	0.257	0.039	0.918	0.762	0.932
TRUST-ESD w/o Risk Memory	0.123	0.090	0.814	0.793	0.179	0.241	0.035	0.931	0.811	0.944
Full TRUST-ESD	0.124	0.091	0.818	**0.815**	**0.162**	**0.218**	**0.031**	**0.939**	**0.834**	**0.967**

Best in **bold**, and second-best in underlined

5.2 Decision Utility and Risk-Adjusted Utility

The Utility-Only baseline achieves the highest raw utility of 0.836, whereas Full TRUST-ESD obtains a slightly lower raw utility of 0.818, corresponding to only a 2.15% reduction. However, after risk adjustment, TRUST-ESD improves RAU from 0.704 to 0.815 over Utility-Only, yielding a 15.77% gain in risk-adjusted decision quality. This trade-off is visualized in Fig. 2, where its preserves high utility while substantially improving risk-adjusted value. Compared with CVaR-Risk and Policy-Filtered baselines, TRUST-ESD further improves RAU by 4.35% and 5.03%, respectively, demonstrating that the full framework provides a stronger balance between expected value, uncertainty, risk, and governance.

5.3 Risk Exposure and CVaR Analysis

TRUST-ESD provides the strongest downside-risk control. It achieves the lowest risk exposure of 0.162 and the lowest CVaR of 0.218, indicating that its selected strategies are less vulnerable to adverse outcomes. Compared with Policy-Filtered, TRUST-ESD reduces risk exposure by 13.83% and CVaR by 15.18%; compared with CVaR-Risk, it reduces risk exposure by 17.35% and CVaR by 17.11%. The advantage becomes more substantial against Utility-Only, where TRUST-ESD reduces risk exposure by 42.96% and CVaR by 40.92%. Figure 3 shows that TRUST-ESD achieves the best risk–utility trade-off.

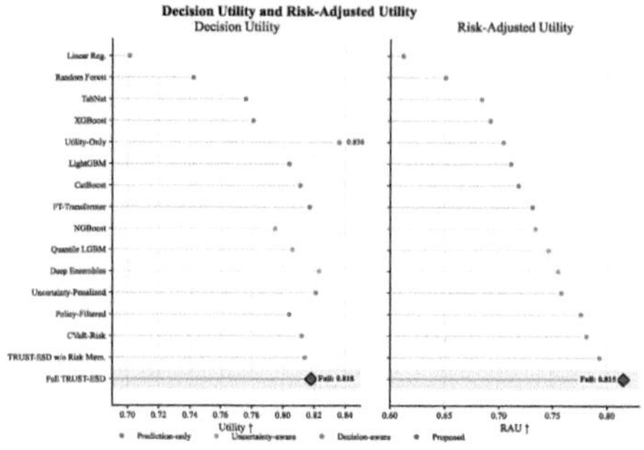

Fig. 2. Decision and risk-adjusted utility.

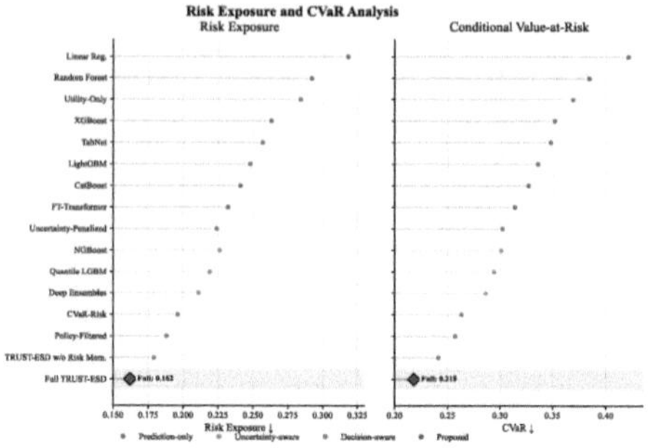

Fig. 3. Risk exposure and CVaR trade-off.

5.4 Calibration Analysis

Reliable uncertainty estimation is essential because overconfident recommendations can lead to costly enterprise decisions. TRUST-ESD achieves the lowest ECE of 0.031 and the highest PICP of 0.939, indicating both stronger calibration and better interval coverage. The calibration comparison in Fig. 4 shows that conformal uncertainty calibration improves reliability over strong uncertainty-aware baselines. Compared with Quantile LightGBM, TRUST-ESD reduces ECE by 18.42% and improves PICP by 1.73%; compared with Deep Ensembles, it reduces ECE by 13.89% and improves PICP by 1.19%.

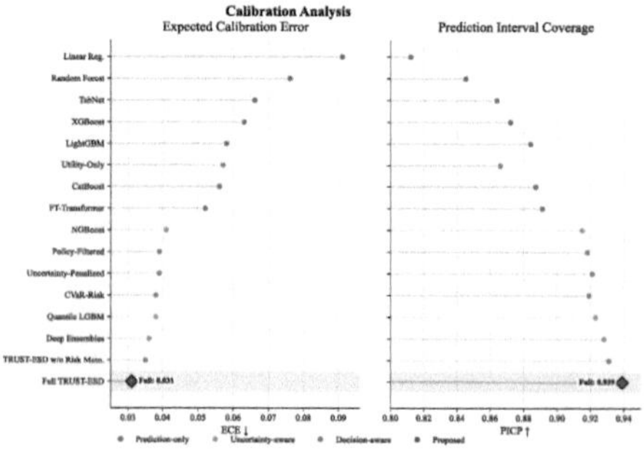

Fig. 4. Calibration performance.

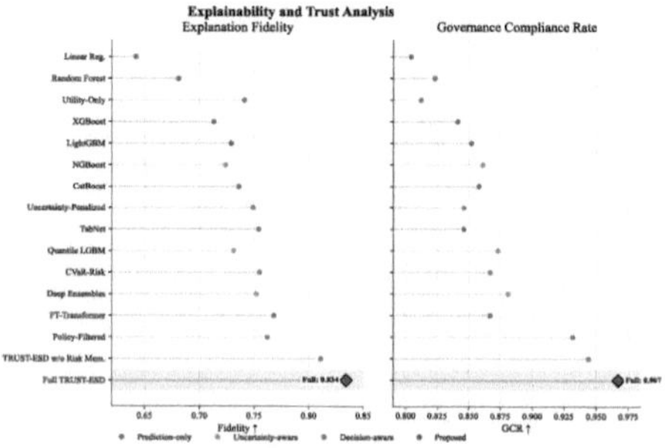

Fig. 5. Explainability and trust analysis.

5.5 Explainability and Trust Analysis

Full TRUST-ESD obtains the highest explanation fidelity of 0.834, outperforming FT-Transformer by 8.59%, Policy-Filtered by 9.45%, and Deep Ensembles by 10.90%. This improvement is important because TRUST-ESD explains the final strategic score, not only the predictive utility estimate. As reported in Fig. 5, the proposed method provides stronger explainability and trust performance than both prediction-only and uncertainty-aware baselines. The ablation results further support this finding: removing the explainability module reduces fidelity from 0.834 to 0.684, corresponding to a 17.99% degradation.

5.6 Governance Compliance Analysis

Governance validation substantially improves deployment suitability under enterprise policy constraints. Full TRUST-ESD achieves the highest GCR of 0.967, improving over Policy-Filtered by 3.76%, Deep Ensembles by 9.76%, and Utility-Only by 19.09%. In terms of policy violation rate, TRUST-ESD reduces violations from 0.068 to 0.033 compared with Policy-Filtered, a 51.47% reduction, and from 0.188 to 0.033 compared with Utility-Only, an 82.45% reduction. These results, summarized visually in Fig. 6, show that policy-as-code validation and human-governance routing help convert model outputs into safer and more compliant enterprise recommendations.

5.7 Ablation Study

The ablation results confirm that each TRUST-ESD component contributes to a distinct dimension of trustworthy decision support. Removing CVaR risk scoring causes a 9.08% RAU degradation and increases risk exposure by 56.79%, showing that downside-risk modeling is central to robust strategy selection. Removing conformal calibration causes a 5.77% RAU drop, increases ECE by 96.77%, and reduces PICP by 8.20%, confirming the importance of calibrated uncertainty. Risk memory also contributes meaningfully: removing it reduces RAU by 2.70% and increases CVaR by 10.55%. As shown in Table 4, removing policy governance mainly reduces GCR by 9.82%, while removing explainability sharply lowers fidelity. The Utility-Only variant achieves the highest raw utility but suffers the largest RAU degradation of 13.62%, with 75.31% higher risk exposure and 69.27% higher CVaR than Full TRUST-ESD.

5.8 Case Study

The case-level analysis shows how TRUST-ESD avoids aggressive but fragile strategies. The Aggressive strategy achieves the highest raw utility of 0.812, but its high uncertainty penalty of 0.156, high risk penalty of 0.241, and lower governance score of 0.781 reduce its final score to 0.524. In contrast, the Risk-Control strategy has a slightly lower utility of 0.742, but it reduces the uncertainty penalty by 66.67%, reduces the risk penalty by 70.54%, improves governance

Table 4. Ablation analysis.

Variant	Utility↑	RAU↑	ΔRAU↓	Risk Exp.↓	CVaR↓	ECE↓	PICP↑	Fidelity↑	GCR↑
TRUST-ESD w/o conformal calibration	0.812	0.768	5.77%	0.191	0.259	0.061	0.862	0.819	0.948
TRUST-ESD w/o CVaR risk	0.826	0.741	9.08%	0.254	0.338	0.036	0.928	0.821	0.951
TRUST-ESD w/o risk memory	0.814	<u>0.793</u>	<u>2.70%</u>	<u>0.179</u>	<u>0.241</u>	<u>0.035</u>	<u>0.931</u>	<u>0.811</u>	<u>0.944</u>
TRUST-ESD w/o policy governance	0.822	0.776	4.79%	0.185	0.249	0.034	0.930	0.823	0.872
TRUST-ESD w/o explainability	0.820	0.786	3.56%	0.174	0.232	0.033	0.936	0.684	0.938
TRUST-ESD utility-only scoring	**0.836**	0.704	13.62%	0.284	0.369	0.057	0.866	0.741	0.812
Full TRUST-ESD	<u>0.818</u>	**0.815**	**0.00%**	**0.162**	**0.218**	**0.031**	**0.939**	**0.834**	**0.967**

Best in **bold**, and second-best in <u>underlined</u>

compliance by 24.33%, and increases the final decision score by 33.21% compared with the Aggressive strategy. Figure 7 shows that TRUST-ESD selects the most balanced strategy, not merely the highest-utility one.

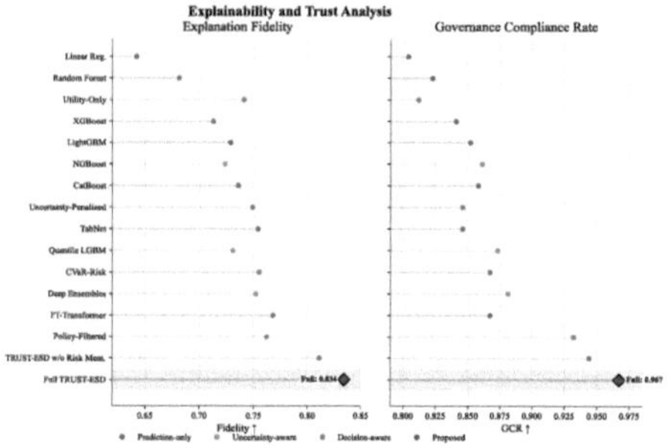

Fig. 6. Governance compliance analysis.

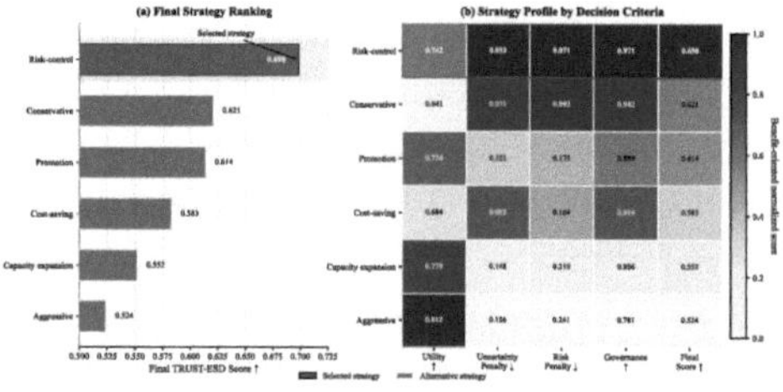

Fig. 7. Case-level strategy analysis.

6 Conclusion

This paper presented TRUST-ESD, a risk-calibrated and governance-aware framework for enterprise strategic decision support under uncertainty. By integrating predictive utility estimation, conformal uncertainty calibration, CVaR-based downside-risk scoring, risk-memory retrieval, policy-as-code governance, explainability, and human oversight, TRUST-ESD moves beyond prediction-only recommendation toward trustworthy strategic decision-making. Experimental results show that the proposed framework improves risk-adjusted utility, reduces risk exposure and CVaR, strengthens calibration, and improves explanation fidelity and governance compliance while maintaining competitive predictive accuracy. The ablation and case-study analyses further confirm that each component contributes to robust, interpretable, and policy-compliant decision support. Future work will extend TRUST-ESD to dynamic enterprise environments, adaptive governance policies, and real-world human feedback settings.

References

1. AI, T.B.: Artificial Intelligence (AI) for Energizing the E-commerce (2022)
2. High-Level Expert Group on AI: Ethics guidelines for trustworthy AI. European Commission (2018). https://digital-strategy.ec.europa.eu/en/library/ethics-guidelines-trustworthy-ai
3. European Union: AI Act. European Parliament (2023). https://www.europarl.europa.eu/news/en/headlines/society/20230601STO93804/eu-ai-act-first-regulation-on-artificial-intelligence
4. Barletta, V.S., Caivano, D., Gigante, D., Ragone, A.: A rapid review of responsible AI frameworks: how to guide the development of ethical AI. In: Proceedings of the 27th International Conference on Evaluation and Assessment in Software Engineering, EASE '23, pp. 358–367. Association for Computing Machinery, New York, NY, USA (2023). https://doi.org/10.1145/3593434.3593478
5. Chouldechova, A.: Fair prediction with disparate impact: a study of bias in recidivism prediction instruments. Big Data **5**(2), 153–163 (2016)
6. Jobin, A., Ienca, M., Vayena, E.: The global landscape of AI ethics guidelines. Nat. Mach. Intell. **1**(9), 389–399 (2019). https://doi.org/10.1038/s42256-019-0088-2
7. European Parliament and Council of the European Union: Regulation (EU) 2016/679 of the European Parliament and of the Council. Off. J. Eur. Union (2016). https://data.europa.eu/eli/reg/2016/679/oj
8. Kenny, E.M., Ford, C., Quinn, M., Keane, M.T.: Explaining black-box classifiers using post-hoc explanations-by-example: the effect of explanations and error-rates in XAI user studies. Artif. Intell. **294**, 103459 (2021)
9. Baldassarre, M.T., Caivano, D., Fernandez Nieto, B., Gigante, D., Ragone, A.: The social impact of generative AI: an analysis on ChatGPT. In: Proceedings of the 2023 ACM Conference on Information Technology for Social Good, GoodIT '23, pp. 363–373. Association for Computing Machinery, New York, NY, USA (2023)
10. ENISA: Securing Machine Learning Algorithms. European Union Agency for Cybersecurity (2021). https://www.enisa.europa.eu/publications/securing-machine-learning-algorithms
11. Howard, A., inversion, Makridakis, S., Vangelis: M5 Forecasting - Accuracy. Kaggle (2020). https://kaggle.com/competitions/m5-forecasting-accuracy
12. FlorianKnauer, Cukierski, W.: Rossmann Store Sales. Kaggle (2015). https://kaggle.com/competitions/rossmann-store-sales
13. Corporación Favorita, inversion, Elliott, J., McDonald, M.: Corporación Favorita Grocery Sales Forecasting. Kaggle (2017). https://kaggle.com/competitions/favorita-grocery-sales-forecasting
14. Cao, Y.: IEEE-CIS Fraud Detection. IEEE Dataport (2026). https://doi.org/10.21227/y5e7-wp63
15. Tripepi, G., Jager, K.J., Dekker, F.W., Zoccali, C.: Linear and logistic regression analysis. Kidney Int. **73**(7), 806–810 (2008)
16. Miraj, M.R., Huang, H., Yang, T., Zhao, J., Mu, N., Lei, X.: GK-SMOTE: A hyperparameter-free noise-resilient Gaussian KDE-based oversampling approach. In: Asia-Pacific Web and Web-Age Information Management Joint International Conference on Web and Big Data, pp. 197–212. Springer Nature Singapore, Singapore (2025)

17. Salman, H.A., Kalakech, A., Steiti, A.: Random forest algorithm overview. Babylon. J. Mach. Learn. **2024**, 69–79 (2024)
18. Zhao, P., Li, K., Zhou, N., Chen, Q., Zhou, M., Qi, C.: Enhanced prediction of occurrence forms of heavy metals in tailings: a systematic comparison of machine learning methods and model integration. Int. J. Miner. Metall. Mater. **32**(10), 2406–2417 (2025)
19. Tyralis, H., Papacharalampous, G., Doulamis, N., Doulamis, A.: Merging satellite and gauge-measured precipitation using LightGBM with an emphasis on extreme quantiles. IEEE J. Sel. Top. Appl. Earth Obs. Remote. Sens. **16**, 6969–6979 (2023)
20. Mota, M.B., de Oliveira, A.B., Bof, P., Barone, D.A.C.: A comparative analysis of ANN, TabNet and FT-Transformer models in EEG classification of neuropsychiatric disorders. In: Latin American Workshop on Computational Neuroscience, pp. 37–45. Springer Nature Switzerland, Cham (2025)
21. Yang, T., Miraj, M.R., Lei, X., Mu, N., Huang, H.: DeadMap: open yet locked–key-controlled dataset protection with feature-level collisions. J. Mach. Learn. Inf. Secur. **2**(1), 5 (2026)
22. Abe, T., Buchanan, E.K., Pleiss, G., Zemel, R., Cunningham, J.P.: Deep ensembles work, but are they necessary? Adv. Neural. Inf. Process. Syst. **35**, 33646–33660 (2022)
23. Zhao, J., Huang, H., Miraj, M.R.: Covert backdoor attacks to pre-trained encoders in self-supervised learning. In: 2025 International Joint Conference on Neural Networks, IJCNN, pp. 1–8. IEEE (2025)
24. Moghimi, M., Ku, H.: Beyond CVaR: leveraging static spectral risk measures for enhanced decision-making in distributional reinforcement learning (2025). arXiv:2501.02087 arXiv preprint
25. Yang, T., Zhao, J., Lei, X., Huang, H., Mu, N., Zhou, X., Miraj, M.R.: Entity backdoor attacks against fine-tuned models. In: International Conference on Intelligent Computing, pp. 338–349. Springer Nature Singapore, Singapore (2025)

Managing Curriculum Knowledge Graphs for Trustworthy Educational Question Answering via Adaptive-Critic RAG

Yanli Liu(✉), Bin Yang, and Heng Zhang

School of Artificial Intelligence and Data Science, Shanghai Dianji University, Shanghai, China
{liuyl,zhangheng}@sdju.edu.cn, 24600003160319@st.sdju.edu.cn

Abstract. Retrieval-augmented generation (RAG) is pivotal for deploying large language models in knowledge-intensive domains; however, educational question answering (QA) systems remain hindered by hallucinations, incomplete knowledge coverage, and inconsistent evidence utilization. To address these issues, we propose *Adaptive-Critic Graph RAG*, an evaluation-driven framework that couples adaptive retrieval with curriculum knowledge graph (KG) reasoning for smart classroom scenarios. Methodologically, we design a three-dimensional critic model—fine-tuned on DeepSeek-LLM-7B via LoRA using DeepSeek-V3-assisted annotations—to evaluate retrieval necessity, answer accuracy, and knowledge coverage through reflective tokens. We further construct a curriculum-aligned KG from anonymized pedagogical materials, classroom transcripts, and course resources, and introduce relation-strength scores to support interpretable graph traversal and evidence fusion. The generator is trained to co-produce answers and reflective tokens, enabling dynamic retrieval control during decoding. Experiments on real-world classroom recordings from the Zhike Smart Course platform show consistent improvements over representative RAG baselines. Our framework achieves 44.1% strict answer accuracy, 52.7% knowledge coverage, and 72.8% citation consistency, while reducing retrieved chunks by 27% and inference latency by 12%. These results suggest that combining multi-dimensional critic signals with curriculum-anchored graph evidence can improve evidence traceability and retrieval efficiency in educational QA, although further expert evaluation and cross-domain validation remain necessary.

Keywords: large language model · information retrieval · adaptive retrieval · graph data management · trusted AI · educational question-answering

1 Introduction

As large language models (LLMs) increasingly permeate conversational tutoring, intelligent classroom response systems show immense promise in delivering scal-

L. Ding et al. (Eds.): APWeb-WAIM 2026, LNCS 16993, pp. 199–213, 2027.
https://doi.org/10.1007/978-981-92-5693-8_13

able, context-aware pedagogical feedback [4,12]. However, educational environments are high-stakes domains where instructional precision is non-negotiable. Generative models relying solely on parametric memory frequently hallucinate, omit critical prerequisite concepts, and exhibit false confidence when confronted with multi-step disciplinary reasoning [1]. Such inconsistent evidence utilization severely misguides students' comprehension of core knowledge and erodes educators' trust, critically bottlenecking the deployment of LLM-based assistants in rigorous teaching scenarios [21].

While Retrieval-Augmented Generation (RAG) and knowledge graph (KG) augmentations offer pathways to mitigate these factual inaccuracies, existing paradigms exhibit fundamental pedagogical limitations [5,14]. First, traditional RAG employs static retrieval strategies, failing to dynamically assess the necessity and depth of retrieval; this inevitably yields either excessive informational noise or insufficient knowledge coverage. Second, current Graph RAG approaches primarily target open-domain corpora [3]. They lack the rigorous structural alignment with curriculum standards and prerequisite dependencies essential for semantically coherent, multi-hop pedagogical reasoning. Third, and most critically, existing evaluative mechanisms rely on coarse, singular signals [1,9]. They fail to simultaneously differentiate distinct failure modes—such as unnecessary retrieval, factual inaccuracy, and insufficient coverage—thereby precluding fine-grained orchestration of the retrieval-generation loop. Consequently, an open challenge lies in constructing a multi-dimensional, judgment-driven framework that seamlessly fuses curriculum-constrained KGs with multi-source evidence into a traceable, closed-loop cognitive architecture [16].

To bridge this critical gap, this paper introduces Adaptive-Critic Graph RAG, an evaluation-driven framework for trustworthy educational Q&A, comprehensively designed and validated on large-scale, real-world classroom transcripts from the Zhike Smart Course platform. Operating through a closed-loop "evaluation-decision-retrieval-generation" process, this system systematically balances answer correctness, coverage completeness, and evidence traceability.

The principal contributions of this paper are summarized as follows:

1. Multi-dimensional adaptive critic mechanism. We design a 3D evaluation space capturing retrieval necessity, answer accuracy, and knowledge coverage. This explicitly decouples error types and provides interpretable, reflective control signals for dynamic retrieval triggering and generative refinement.
2. Curriculum-Aligned Knowledge Graph. Strictly guided by formal syllabi, we construct a pedagogical KG that models "knowledge-relationship-concept" dependencies. By introducing relation-strength scoring, we ensure graph retrieval possesses explicit educational interpretability and enhances multi-hop reasoning aligned with course semantics.
3. Hierarchical Evidence Fusion Architecture. We propose a layered fusion pipeline to align structured graph data with unstructured textual chunks. This module performs conflict detection and weighted arbitration to produce traceable evidence chains directly usable for generation and explanation.

4. Closed-loop Systemic Validation. We implement the reflective framework using authentic classroom data. The results show that the proposed method improves evidence-related metrics, especially citation consistency and retrieval efficiency, compared with representative RAG baselines under the same evaluation protocol.

The remainder of this paper is organized as follows: Sect. 2 reviews prior work, Sect. 3 details the proposed methodology, Sect. 4 presents the experimental setup and results, and Sect. 5 concludes with a discussion of future directions.

2 Related Work

Retrieval-Augmented Generation (RAG) bridges neural text generation with information retrieval, enabling language models to anchor their outputs to external knowledge sources [10, 19]. Centering on the proposed Adaptive-Critic Graph RAG, we contextualize our approach within three highly relevant technical paradigms. Table 1 summarizes the functional distinctions between our method and representative baselines.

2.1 Adaptive RAG and Self-reflection

Traditional RAG paradigms typically employ static retrieval strategies. While improving factuality, fixed-k retrieval frequently generates redundant evidence for simple queries (increasing latency) or fails to cover critical knowledge for complex reasoning (yielding plausible but incomplete responses) [14]. To address these limitations, recent research integrates adaptive retrieval control and self-reflective evaluators, orchestrating "draft-evaluate-revise" loops through independent critics or uncertainty estimation [8, 9, 18].

Despite these advances, existing adaptive frameworks rely predominantly on one-dimensional scalar signals (e.g., confidence or entropy) or coarse-grained labels. Consequently, they struggle to decouple distinct failure modes—such as unnecessary over-retrieval, factual inaccuracies, and insufficient knowledge coverage—precluding fine-grained orchestration of retrieval intensity and answer refinement [6, 7, 17]. In contrast, our Adaptive-Critic Graph RAG explicitly structures the evaluation space into three distinct pedagogical dimensions. This multidimensional signal acts as a trainable control variable, enabling the system to execute adaptive decisions grounded in specific error types rather than generalized uncertainty [1].

2.2 Graph-Augmented RAG

To support multi-hop reasoning and contextual aggregation, graph-augmented RAG elevates retrieval units from fragmented text to coherent subgraphs, mitigating the logical discontinuities inherent in dense vector search [2, 11, 23]. However, conventional knowledge graphs (KGs) are primarily constructed around generic entities or document fragments targeting open-domain corpora. They critically lack structural alignment with formal curriculum standards, knowledge hierarchies, and prerequisite dependencies [25].

Our method distinguishes itself by introducing a curriculum-aligned KG. By organizing course structures into "knowledge-relationship-concept" triples and assigning relation-strength scores to edges, our framework quantifies knowledge dependencies. This design ensures that graph retrieval outputs possess explicit pedagogical interpretability, naturally facilitating path-level evidence tracing within educational contexts [13,15].

2.3 Curriculum-Aligned Generation in Education

Educational question-answering demands rigorous curriculum consistency, structural interpretability, and comprehensive coverage. While existing educational KGs and adaptive learning systems excel in pedagogical analytics or resource recommendation, they remain largely disconnected from modern RAG architectures. Conversely, standard text-based educational QA directly grounded in course materials often neglects conceptual hierarchies, struggling to form stable reasoning chains for complex queries [20].

Therefore, the critical research gap lies not in choosing between KGs and RAG [19], but in unifying course-aligned structured knowledge, unstructured textual evidence, and adaptive evaluation signals. By coupling a 3D critic-driven retrieval mechanism with a hierarchical evidence fusion framework [22,24], our architecture offers a curriculum-grounded and traceable solution for educational QA in real-world intelligent classroom settings [4].

Table 1. Functional comparison of our-RAG with representative retrieval methods.

Method	Adaptive retrieval	Graph/KG	Critic/reflection	Multi-dimensional evaluation
Self-RAG	Yes	No	Yes (single signal)	No
DRAGIN	Yes (info need)	No	No	No
GraphRAG	Yes (graph-based)	Yes	No	No
Our-RAG	**Yes (3D signals)**	**Yes**	**Yes (critic + tags)**	**Yes**

3 Methodology

3.1 Overview of the Overall Framework

The proposed Adaptive-Critic Graph RAG employs a three-tiered collaborative architecture to establish a holistic, closed-loop cognitive system for educational question-answering, encompassing evaluation, decision-making, retrieval, and generation.

As illustrated in Fig. 1, the system comprises three core layers:

1. **Retrieval and QA Layer**: This layer manages the online reasoning process. Upon receiving user queries, the system generates preliminary responses, which are then guided by evaluative signals from the 3D Critic Model to drive adaptive retrieval decisions and answer refinement.
2. **Course KG Construction Layer**: Acting as the foundational knowledge base, it organizes textbooks, syllabi, and classroom records into a dual-form foundation that supports both natural language evidence retrieval and structured path-based access.
3. **Entity-Relationship Fusion Layer**: Positioned between the retrieval module and the knowledge base, it performs unified integration and consistency coordination for candidate evidence from both retrieval channels.

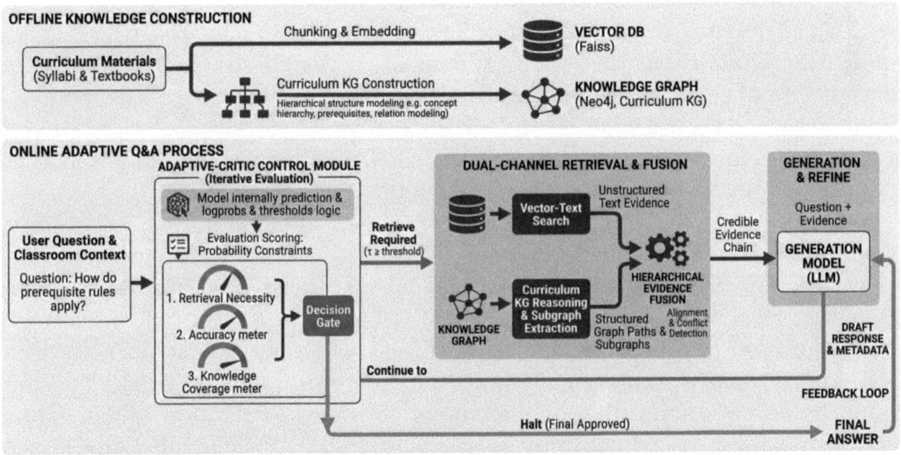

Fig. 1. Adaptive-critic graph RAG system mechanism overview.

3.2 Curriculum Knowledge Graph Construction

To enhance semantic representation and curriculum-aware reasoning, we construct a curriculum-aligned knowledge graph (KG) from anonymized pedagogical materials, including textbooks, syllabi, lesson plans, classroom transcripts, and exercise-oriented resources. The KG is designed to explicitly represent course concepts, topic hierarchies, prerequisite dependencies, procedural steps, and evidence links. DeepSeek-V3 is used as an assisted extractor with task-specific prompts, followed by schema normalization, duplicate merging, and manual spot checking. The final KG contains 12,450 nodes and 38,200 edges and is stored in Neo4j for efficient graph traversal and evidence retrieval.

The source documents include textbooks and teaching materials for concept and definition extraction, syllabi and curriculum standards for topic hierarchy and prerequisite constraints, lesson plans for procedural knowledge, classroom transcripts for teacher–student interactions and misconceptions, and exercises for application-oriented evidence alignment.

The KG schema contains several entity types, including Course, Topic, Concept, Formula, Procedural Step, Question, Example, and Evidence Chunk. The main relation types include belongs-to, part-of, prerequisite-of, explains, applies-to, evidence-for, and co-occurs-with. These relation types allow the graph retrieval module to return not only isolated nodes but also interpretable curriculum paths.

For each extracted triple (h, r, t), we assign a normalized relation-strength score:

$$w(h, r, t) = \text{Normalize}\left(\lambda_1 c_{\text{LLM}} + \lambda_2 c_{\text{source}} + \lambda_3 c_{\text{freq}} + \lambda_4 c_{\text{curr}}\right), \tag{1}$$

where c_{LLM} denotes the extraction confidence estimated by the LLM, c_{source} denotes the reliability of the source document, c_{freq} denotes the normalized co-occurrence frequency across teaching materials and classroom records, and c_{curr} denotes whether the relation is explicitly supported by the syllabus or curriculum hierarchy. In our implementation, the coefficients are empirically set on the validation set as $\lambda_1 = 0.35$, $\lambda_2 = 0.25$, $\lambda_3 = 0.20$, and $\lambda_4 = 0.20$.

Representative triples include Topic–Concept, Concept–Prerequisite, Formula–Exercise, and Evidence–Answer links, illustrating how the KG connects conceptual hierarchy, prerequisite structure, and answer-level evidence.

To improve KG quality, we perform three-stage quality control. First, rule-based filters remove malformed triples and merge duplicate entities. Second, schema mapping standardizes synonymous entities and relation labels. Third, a sampled subset of triples and prerequisite paths is manually checked by domain-aware annotators to assess entity correctness, relation correctness, and path validity. Disagreements are resolved through discussion. This process helps reduce extraction noise and improves the reliability of graph-based evidence retrieval.

3.3 Adaptive 3D Critic Model

To achieve controllable retrieval and trustworthy generation, we construct a three-dimensional evaluator (Critic). As illustrated in Fig. 2, it employs a unified assessment space defined by "retrieval necessity, answer accuracy, and knowledge coverage". This design explicitly decouples risks such as over-retrieval, factual bias, and insufficient coverage.

The Critic model is based on DeepSeek-LLM-7B and fine-tuned via LoRA with a rank $r = 16$, a scaling factor $\alpha = 32$, and a dropout rate of 0.05 [1]. The critic is trained to predict reflective labels in a three-dimensional label space. DeepSeek-V3 is used to generate initial labels, and a manually audited subset is used to check the reliability of the automatic annotation process.

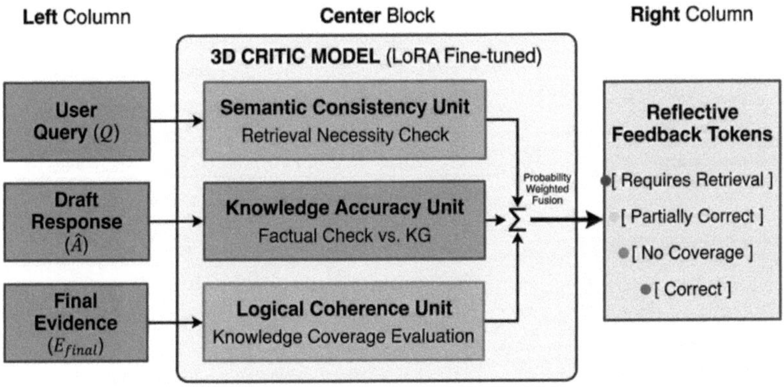

Fig. 2. Operational mechanism diagram of the three-dimensional critic model.

The critic predicts reflective labels in three dimensions: Retrieval Necessity (Retrieve/No Retrieve), Answer Accuracy (Correct/Partially Correct/Incorrect), and Knowledge Coverage (Full/Most/Small/No Coverage). These labels respectively control evidence triggering, factual verification, and curriculum knowledge completeness.

The annotation data are divided into training, validation, and test subsets with a 70/10/20 split. The validation set is used for threshold selection and probability calibration, while the test set is held out for evaluating the critic's predictive behavior. To reduce model-specific annotation bias, two domain-aware annotators independently review a random subset of automatically labeled samples. They check whether the reflective labels are consistent with the question, reference answer, and evidence chain. Disagreements are resolved through discussion, and the audited subset is used as a quality-control reference rather than as additional training data.

Given a question x, candidate answer y, and reflection label r, we optimize the Critic parameters by maximizing the conditional likelihood:

$$\max_{C} \mathbb{E}_{((x,y),r)\sim D_{critic}} \log P_C(r|x,y). \tag{2}$$

3.4 Unified Hierarchical Fusion Architecture

To reconcile structured graph evidence with unstructured textual chunks, we propose a hierarchical evidence fusion architecture. As shown in Fig. 3, it integrates two layers:

- **Layer 1 (Data Alignment and Standardization)**: Converges dual-track inputs into a unified semantic space by addressing expression heterogeneity.
- **Layer 2 (Conflict Resolution and Intelligent Weighting)**: Detects unit-level contradictions and performs arbitration by integrating relation strength scores with source reliability.

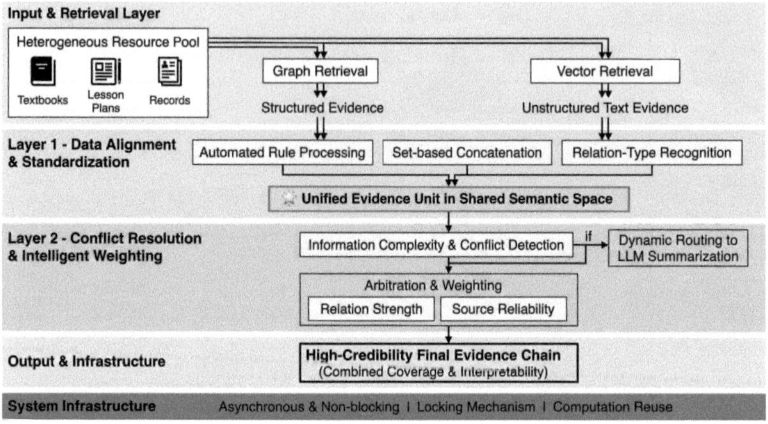

Fig. 3. Unified hierarchical fusion architecture diagram.

3.5 Adaptive Control and Scoring Mechanism

The framework converts the log probabilities of reflective tokens into normalized label probabilities. For a label l in a label set $\mathcal{L}$, its probability is computed as:

$$p(l) = \frac{\exp(\ell_l)}{\sum_{l' \in \mathcal{L}} \exp(\ell_{l'})}, \tag{3}$$

where ℓ_l denotes the token log probability assigned to label l. This normalization allows the three reflective dimensions to be used as comparable control signals.

For retrieval triggering, the system evaluates the normalized retrieval probability:

$$p_{\text{retrieve}} = \frac{p(\text{Retrieve} = \text{Yes})}{p(\text{Retrieve} = \text{Yes}) + p(\text{Retrieve} = \text{No})} > \delta, \tag{4}$$

where δ is set to 0.55 according to validation-set performance. This threshold is selected to balance retrieval precision, knowledge coverage, and inference latency.

To enforce generation refinement, the Answer Accuracy score $s(ACC)$ and Knowledge Coverage score $s(KC)$ are computed by weighting categorical labels:

$$s(\text{ACC}) = \frac{p(\text{ACC} = \text{Correct}) + 0.5p(\text{ACC} = \text{Partially})}{S_{\text{ACC}}}, \tag{5}$$

where

$$S_{\text{ACC}} = p(\text{ACC} = \text{Correct}) + p(\text{ACC} = \text{Partially}) + p(\text{ACC} = \text{Incorrect}). \tag{6}$$

Similarly, the knowledge coverage score is defined as:

$$s(\text{KC}) = \frac{p(\text{KC} = \text{Full}) + 0.6p(\text{KC} = \text{Most}) + 0.2p(\text{KC} = \text{Small})}{S_{\text{KC}}}, \tag{7}$$

where

$$S_{\text{KC}} = p(\text{KC} = \text{Full}) + p(\text{KC} = \text{Most}) + p(\text{KC} = \text{Small}) + p(\text{KC} = \text{None}). \quad (8)$$

If $p_{retrieve}$ exceeds the threshold or either $s(ACC)$ or $s(KC)$ falls below the refinement threshold, the system continues retrieval or answer revision; otherwise, the generation process is halted and the current answer is returned.

4 Experiments

4.1 Dataset

Raw experimental data were obtained from the classroom teaching recording system of the *Zhike Smart Course* platform. This system utilizes advanced speech recognition to document real-time teacher-student interactions. Throughout each 45-minute lesson, the platform captures comprehensive audio content—including instructional explanations, student inquiries, and collaborative discussions—and converts it into structured text via natural language processing algorithms. This corpus precisely preserves speaker identities and temporal features, such as dialogue timestamps and sentence intervals, forming a continuous dialogue dataset spanning 100 real-world lessons (approximately 75 h) of instructional content.

4.2 Experimental Setup

From the classroom recordings, we construct an evaluation set of $N = 5000$ instructional QA items. Specifically, each 45-min lesson is first cleaned to remove non-instructional utterances, ASR noise, classroom management dialogue, and device-related interruptions. Then, the transcript is segmented according to topic continuity, speaker turns, timestamps, and keyword changes. Consecutive segments discussing the same pedagogical topic are merged to preserve semantic completeness. Finally, an LLM-based extraction prompt is used to select 50 core instructional data points from each lesson, covering concept explanation, student question, teacher response, example-based reasoning, and summary-style knowledge points.

Each evaluation item is serialized into a structured JSON schema containing a unique identifier, question, reference answer, speaker role, timestamp, keywords, target knowledge points, and aligned evidence. The aligned evidence consists of both unstructured textual chunks and structured KG paths when available. This design ensures that answer accuracy, knowledge coverage, and citation consistency can be evaluated against explicit reference evidence rather than only against free-form model judgments.

The retrieval system uses a dual-source design. The primary evidence sources are the curriculum corpus and the curriculum KG. The curriculum corpus is indexed as textual chunks for vector and lexical retrieval, while the curriculum KG is stored in Neo4j and queried through Cypher/APOC-based graph traversal. Chinese Wikipedia is used only as an auxiliary open-domain background source and for baseline comparison when general factual context is required. Therefore, the reported Our-RAG results mainly reflect the contribution of curriculum-aligned textual evidence and graph evidence, rather than relying solely on open-domain Wikipedia retrieval.

For text retrieval, we combine TF-IDF-based lexical matching with dense semantic similarity. For graph retrieval, the system expands curriculum nodes through prerequisite and topic-level relations and ranks candidate paths according to relation strength and source reliability. The final evidence pool is obtained by hierarchically fusing retrieved text chunks and KG paths. All experiments are conducted on a single NVIDIA A100 Tensor Core GPU with 80GB VRAM under Ubuntu 22.04.

For fair comparison, all baselines are evaluated on the same 5000 instructional QA items, the same curriculum corpus, the same preprocessing and chunking pipeline, and the same evaluation protocol. Unless required by the original baseline design, the generator backbone and maximum evidence budget are kept comparable across methods. Chinese Wikipedia is used only as auxiliary background knowledge or for baseline comparison, while the reported Our-RAG results mainly rely on curriculum-aligned textual evidence and KG paths.

The main evaluation metrics are operationally defined as follows. Answer Accuracy is the proportion of answers judged correct under a strict reference-answer and evidence-alignment criterion. Knowledge Coverage measures the overlap between generated and reference curriculum knowledge points. Citation Consistency is the proportion of cited evidence units that directly support the corresponding answer statements. Evidence Precision, Recall, and Knowledge F1 are computed by comparing retrieved evidence units with the reference evidence set. Invalid Retrieval Rate denotes the proportion of retrieval calls that fail to return useful evidence, and Match Score denotes the average semantic similarity between generated and reference answers.

4.3 Collection of Special Annotations

To establish supervised signals for adaptive retrieval, we employ DeepSeek-V3 to generate initial reflective annotations for the raw data. The annotation process covers three dimensions:

1. **Retrieval Necessity**: Distinguishes whether a query can be answered from parametric knowledge alone or requires external evidence.
2. **Knowledge Coverage**: Evaluates whether the answer covers the required curriculum knowledge points and prerequisite concepts.
3. **Answer Accuracy**: Checks whether the generated answer is factually consistent with the reference answer and aligned evidence.

To reduce the risk of model-specific labeling bias, we conduct a human audit on a sampled subset of the automatically annotated data. Two domain-aware annotators independently review the reflective labels by comparing the question, candidate answer, reference answer, and evidence chain. The review focuses on whether the label is pedagogically reasonable, factually grounded, and aligned with the expected curriculum objective. Disagreements are resolved through discussion. Detailed prompt templates and exemplary cases for these annotations are organized in the Appendix for reproducibility.

4.4 Model Fine-Tuning and Ablation Experiments

We utilized the LoRA (Low-Rank Adaptation) method to fine-tune the DeepSeek-7B-chat base model. LoRA parameters were set to a rank $r = 16$, a scaling factor $\alpha = 32$, and a dropout rate of 0.05, significantly reducing computational overhead while maintaining high task adaptation. The system adopts a staged Critic-Generator architecture: the Critic model first learns to predict introspective tokens, providing supervisory signals that the Generator subsequently internalizes to autonomously execute reflective logic during decoding [1].

Preliminary performance metrics for the fine-tuned Our-RAG model are summarized in Table 2. The Match Score denotes the average semantic similarity between generated answers and reference answers. Retrieval calls per 100 queries indicate the average number of retrieval operations triggered by the adaptive controller, rather than the number of final evidence chunks.

Table 2. Fine-tuned our-RAG model performance metrics.

Metric	Value
Match score	0.55
Retrieval calls per 100 queries	174.87

To validate the contribution of each module, we conducted ablation studies (see Fig. 4). The complete model achieved an accuracy of 44.1%. Removing the Retrieval Module reduced accuracy to 27.6%, confirming the necessity of external knowledge in specialized educational contexts. Eliminating the Accuracy Assessment Module reduced accuracy to 28.4%, with a corresponding decline in citation consistency, highlighting its role as a quality-control gate. Ablation of the Knowledge Coverage Module resulted in a drop to 42.5% accuracy and marked deterioration in answer completeness, often yielding "partially correct" responses unsuitable for pedagogical depth.

4.5 Results Analysis

The overall performance comparison in Table 3 shows that Our-RAG achieves the best results on knowledge coverage and citation consistency among the compared methods. The gain in strict answer accuracy over the strongest baselines is modest, while the improvement in citation consistency is more pronounced.

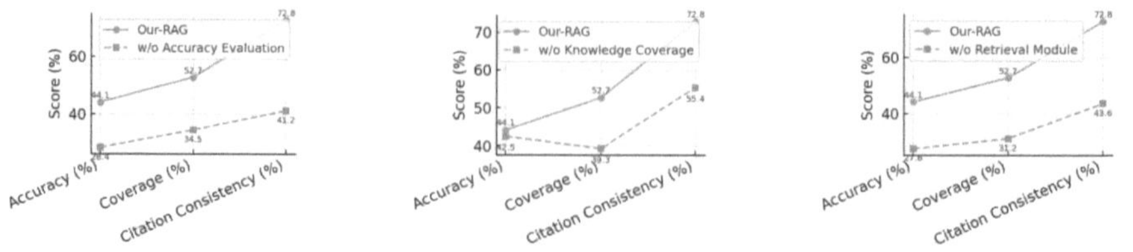

(a) w/o Accuracy Evaluation (b) w/o Knowledge Coverage (c) w/o Retrieval Module

Fig. 4. Ablation results of Our-RAG under different module configurations.

Specifically, Our-RAG achieves a citation consistency of 72.8%, compared with 64.5% for FLARE and 66.1% for Self-RAG. This suggests that the main advantage of the proposed 3D evaluation mechanism lies in improving evidence alignment and constraining generated answers to traceable evidence.

Table 3. Overall performance comparison across different RAG architectures.

Model	Accuracy (%)	Knowledge coverage (%)	Citation consistency (%)
Zero-shot LLM	26.8	24.1	34.2
Naive RAG	38.7	41.3	57.2
Graph RAG	41.5	44.8	61.0
Light-RAG	42.7	47.1	63.4
Self-RAG	43.2	49.5	66.1
FLARE	43.8	50.3	64.5
Our-RAG	**44.1**	**52.7**	**72.8**

Table 4. Evidence retrieval and knowledge utilization metrics.

Model	Precision (%)	Recall (%)	Knowledge F1 (%)	Retrieved chunks
Naive RAG	61.2	58.7	59.9	8.4
Graph RAG	64.0	62.3	63.1	9.1
Light-RAG	66.8	65.1	65.9	7.8
Self-RAG	69.4	67.2	68.3	7.5
FLARE	67.3	66.1	66.7	7.2
Our-RAG	**78.2**	**75.4**	**76.8**	**6.1**

In terms of knowledge utilization (Table 4), Our-RAG achieves an Evidence Precision of 78.2% and a Knowledge F1 of 76.8%, outperforming all other models. This indicates that critic-guided retrieval is more effective at selecting useful pedagogical evidence while reducing irrelevant retrieved chunks.

Table 5. Overall system efficiency and operational metrics.

Model	Latency (ms)	Throughput (req/min)	Invalid retrieval rate (%)
Naive RAG	1895	31	21.4
Graph RAG	2011	29	18.7
Light-RAG	1763	34	17.3
Self-RAG	1820	32	15.9
FLARE	1754	33	14.7
Our-RAG	**1540**	**38**	**9.3**

Finally, system efficiency results (Table 5) show that our adaptive strategy reduces retrieved fragments to 6.1 (a 27% reduction vs. Naive RAG) and decreases system latency by 12% to 1540 ms. These efficiency gains, coupled with high throughput (38 requests/min), demonstrate the framework's practical viability for real-time intelligent classroom deployment.

5 Conclusion

This paper presented Adaptive-Critic Graph RAG, an evaluation-driven retrieval augmentation framework for educational QA. By combining a three-dimensional critic, a curriculum-aligned KG, and hierarchical evidence fusion, the framework supports adaptive retrieval and traceable answer generation. Experiments on real-world classroom transcripts show improvements in knowledge coverage, citation consistency, and retrieval efficiency over representative RAG baselines. Although the gain in strict answer accuracy is modest, the stronger evidence alignment suggests that curriculum-aware graph reasoning and critic-guided control are useful for improving the transparency of educational QA systems.

This study still has limitations. The current validation is based on classroom data from the Zhike platform and may not fully represent other subjects, grade levels, or teaching styles. The reflective labels are initially generated by DeepSeek-V3 and may inherit model-specific preferences, although a sampled subset is manually audited. Future work will expand expert-labeled data, report more detailed inter-annotator agreement, incorporate pedagogical evaluation signals such as student learning outcomes, and explore incremental KG maintenance for rapidly changing curriculum resources.

References

1. Asai, A., Wu, Y., Ma, X.: Self-rag: learning to retrieve, generate, and critique through self-reflection. In: Proceedings of the International Conference on Learning Representations (2024). arXiv:2310.11511
2. Edge, D., et al.: From local to global: a graph rag approach to query-focused summarisation. arXiv:2401.03568 (2024)

3. Fang, J., Meng, Z., Macdonald, C.: Trace the Evidence: Constructing Knowledge-Grounded Reasoning Chains for Retrieval-Augmented Generation, vol. 11460, pp. 8472–8494 (2024). https://doi.org/10.48550/arxiv.2406.11460
4. Garzón, J., Patiño, E., Marulanda, C.: Systematic review of artificial intelligence in education: trends, benefits, and challenges. Multimodal Technol. Interact. **9**(8), 84 (2025). https://doi.org/10.3390/mti9080084
5. Guo, Y., Wang, X., Zhang, W.: Lightrag: simple and fast retrieval-augmented generation for large language models. arXiv:2410.05779 (2024)
6. Hei, Z., Liu, W., Ou, W., et al.: Dr-rag: applying dynamic document relevance to retrieval-augmented generation for question-answering. arXiv abs/2406.07348 (2024). https://doi.org/10.48550/arxiv.2406.07348
7. Huang, J., Wang, M., Cui, Y., et al.: Layered query retrieval: an adaptive framework for retrieval-augmented generation in complex question answering for large language models. Appl. Sci. (2024). https://doi.org/10.3390/app142311014
8. Jeong, M., Sohn, J., Sung, M., et al.: Improving medical reasoning through retrieval and self-reflection with retrieval-augmented large language models. Bioinformatics **40**, i119–i129 (2024). https://doi.org/10.1093/bioinformatics/btae238
9. Jeong, S., Baek, J., Cho, S.: Adaptive-rag: learning to adapt retrieval-augmented large language models through question complexity. arXiv abs/2403.14403, pp. 7036–7050 (2024). https://doi.org/10.48550/arxiv.2403.14403
10. Jiang, Z., Gu, Y., Han, X.: Active retrieval augmented generation. In: Proceedings of the 2023 Conference on Empirical Methods in Natural Language Processing (2023)
11. Jin, W., Zhao, B., Yu, H., et al.: Improving embedded knowledge graph multi-hop question answering by introducing relational chain reasoning. Data Min. Knowl. Disc. **37**, 255–288 (2021). https://doi.org/10.1007/s10618-022-00891-8
12. Kasneci, E., Seßler, K., Küchemann, S., et al.: ChatGPT for good? opportunities and challenges of large language models in education. Learn. Individ. Differ. **103**, 102274 (2023). https://doi.org/10.1016/j.lindif.2023.102274
13. Knollmeyer, S., Caymazer, O., Grossmann, D.: Document GraphRAG: knowledge graph enhanced retrieval-augmented generation for document-question answering within the manufacturing domain. Electronics (2025). https://doi.org/10.3390/electronics14112102
14. Lewis, P., Perez, E., Piktus, A.: Retrieval-augmented generation for knowledge-intensive NLP tasks. In: Advances in Neural Information Processing Systems, vol. 33 (2020)
15. Linders, J., Tomczak, J.: Knowledge graph-extended retrieval augmented generation for question answering. arXiv abs/2504.08893 (2025). https://doi.org/10.48550/arxiv.2504.08893
16. Pan, S., Luo, L., Wang, Y., et al.: Unifying large language models and knowledge graphs: a roadmap. IEEE Trans. Knowl. Data Eng. **36**, 3580–3599 (2023). https://doi.org/10.1109/tkde.2024.3352100
17. Sarmah, B., Mehta, D., Hall, B., et al.: HybridRAG: integrating knowledge graphs and vector retrieval augmented generation for efficient information extraction. In: Proceedings of the 5th ACM International Conference on AI in Finance (2024). https://doi.org/10.1145/3677052.3698671
18. Su, W., Tang, Y., Ai, Q.: DRAGIN: dynamic retrieval augmented generation based on the real-time information needs of large language models. arXiv:2403.10081 (2024)
19. Wang, S.: Large language models for education: a survey and outlook. Comput. Educ.: Artif. Intell. (2024). arXiv:2403.18105

20. Wu, Y., Han, X., Song, W., et al.: MindMap: constructing evidence chains for multi-step reasoning in large language models. In: Proceedings of the AAAI Conference on Artificial Intelligence, pp. 19270–19278 (2024). https://doi.org/10.1609/aaai.v38i17.29896
21. Yan, L., Sha, L., Zhao, L., et al.: Practical and ethical challenges of large language models in education: a systematic scoping review. Br. J. Educ. Technol. **55**, 90–112 (2023). https://doi.org/10.1111/bjet.13370
22. Yuan, X., Di, S., Tang, J.: Towards self-cognitive exploration: metacognitive knowledge graph retrieval augmented generation (2025). Preprint
23. Zhang, Q., Chen, S., Bei, Y., et al.: A survey of graph retrieval-augmented generation for customised large language models. arXiv abs/2501.13958 (2025). https://doi.org/10.48550/arxiv.2501.13958
24. Zhang, Q., Xiang, Z., Xiao, Y., Wang, L., Li, J., Wang, X., Su, J.: FaithfulRAG: fact-level conflict modeling for context-faithful retrieval-augmented generation. In: Proceedings of the 63rd Annual Meeting of the Association for Computational Linguistics (Volume 1: Long Papers), pp. 21863–21882 (2025)
25. Zhu, Y.: A knowledge graph and BiLSTM-CRF-enabled intelligent adaptive learning model and its potential application. Alex. Eng. J. (2024). https://doi.org/10.1016/j.aej.2024.02.011

EG-CM: An End-to-End Generative Reasoning Framework for Detecting and Explaining Chinese Harmful Memes

Xinze Wu, Yaru Zhao, Tingyue Guan, Xueyao Zhang, Yan Li, and Binyang Li(✉)

University of International Relations, Beijing, China
{xzwu,zhaoyaru,gtyyy0314,xyzhang,liyan,byli}@uir.edu.cn

Abstract. Internet memes are widely used in online communication and often combine images and text. Some memes contain harmful content and may spread hate or discrimination. Detecting harmful memes in Chinese is difficult because harmful intent is often implicit and depends on linguistic features, cultural references, and subtle relations between images and text. Existing knowledge-enhanced methods usually follow a two-stage process where a large language model produces external knowledge and a separate classifier uses this knowledge. This process produces static information and does not support joint optimization of cross-modal understanding and reasoning. To address these limitations, we propose EG-CM, an end-to-end generative reasoning framework for Chinese harmful meme detection. EG-CM reformulates the task as conditional text generation and uses an instruction-tuned multimodal large model to generate fine-grained labels and structured explanations from meme inputs. The framework supports integrated learning of visual, textual, and cross-modal features and encourages the model to form clear reasoning before classification. Experiments on public datasets show that EG-CM improves the F1 score by 8.7% compared with state-of-the-art methods. The results indicate that generative reasoning is effective for detecting and explaining harmful memes in Chinese. Our code is available at https://anonymous.4open.science/status/Explain-M3-2C76.

Keywords: Chinese Harmful Memes · Multimodal Large Models · Conditional Text Generation · Instruction Fine-tuning

1 Introduction

Internet memes are multimodal units that contain images and text. They have become a common way for users to express ideas, attitudes, and emotions in online communication [1]. The short format and flexible structure of memes make them suitable for rapid sharing on social platforms. Memes often rely on humor, symbolic images, or short phrases to communicate a message, and these features give memes a strong ability to attract attention and influence public opinion.

L. Ding et al. (Eds.): APWeb-WAIM 2026, LNCS 16993, pp. 214–230, 2027.
https://doi.org/10.1007/978-981-92-5693-8_14

However, the same properties that make memes appealing also introduce risks. Some memes contain harmful content that promotes hate, discrimination, or toxic views [2,3]. Harmful memes may influence social discourse in subtle ways, and they may affect groups or individuals who are exposed to them. These risks make harmful meme detection an important problem for maintaining a healthy online environment and reducing potential social conflicts.

Chinese harmful meme detection presents additional challenges that are not fully addressed by current methods. Harmful intent in Chinese memes is often implicit. It may appear through linguistic features such as polysemy, wordplay, or indirect expressions. It may also depend on cultural references or humor that require background knowledge. Chinese memes often use symbolic images or short text segments to imply ideas that are not directly stated. The relation between images and text may carry the harmful meaning. These characteristics make harmful content difficult to detect with simple labels or surface features. A binary distinction between harmful and harmless content cannot describe the range of harmful meme types that appear in real data. Effective detection requires models that can understand cross-modal signals, process semantic information in both modalities, and form stable reasoning about cultural and contextual cues.

Recent studies propose knowledge-enhanced frameworks to improve harmful meme detection. The MKE model [4] is a representative example. MKE uses a two-stage process. A fixed large language model produces external knowledge for each meme. A separate classifier then uses this knowledge to support training. This design helps the model include background information and improves its ability to understand complex or implicit semantics. However, the two-stage structure introduces clear limits. The knowledge and the classifier operate independently. The classifier cannot influence how the knowledge is generated. The static knowledge cannot change during training and cannot adapt to specific meme features. The model cannot update visual and textual understanding in a unified way because the two components are not linked. The static information may also miss subtle, ambiguous, or context-dependent harmful cues. These limits reduce the ability of the model to handle fine-grained harmful content and reduce performance on diverse meme types.

We propose EG-CM to address these problems. EG-CM is an end-to-end explanation-generative framework for Chinese harmful meme detection. EG-CM reformulates the task as conditional text generation. This design replaces the two-stage process with a single model that produces both a label and a structured explanation for each meme input. EG-CM uses an instruction-tuned multimodal large model that receives the meme as input and outputs the label and explanation through one sequence. The end-to-end design allows the model to learn visual, textual, and cross-modal features together. The model can update these features throughout training. The requirement to generate explanations encourages the model to form explicit reasoning rather than rely on surface patterns [5]. This structure helps the model address implicit harmful intent and improves generalization across different meme types. The combination of end-to-end learning and explanation generation provides a stable way to understand complex multimodal signals and cultural cues. The contributions of this work are as follows.

- We propose EG-CM, an end-to-end explanation-generative framework that reformulates harmful meme detection as conditional text generation and supports both fine-grained classification and explanation generation.
- We apply instruction tuning to a multimodal large model with culturally aware prompts, enabling the model to generate labels and structured explanations that reflect the implicit linguistic and cultural cues in Chinese memes.
- We introduce explanation generation as an auxiliary training signal, which improves the model's reasoning ability and leads to a 8.7% F1 improvement over state-of-the-art methods, confirming the effectiveness of our approach.

2 Related Work

2.1 Conventional Harmful Meme Detection Methods

Early research on harmful content detection mainly focused on building benchmark datasets and modeling single-modality text. Hate Speech [6] and HateXplain [7] provided sentence-level and fine-grained annotations for hate speech, which helped establish BERT [8] and RoBERTa [9] as standard baselines for text-based detection tasks. For image-based modeling, feature extraction commonly relied on ResNet [10] and ViT [11]. CLIP [12] supported cross-modal alignment and influenced later multimodal studies. Based on CLIP, HateCLIPper [13] and VisualBERT [14] further explored joint modeling of images and text. These studies mainly targeted English data and their findings cannot be directly transferred to Chinese. Chinese harmful content detection has remained mostly text-centric, as shown by COLD [15] and CDIAL-BIAS [16], where single-modality text is the primary input. This setting is not sufficient for detecting multimodal hate speech on social media. Recently, multimodal Chinese harmful meme datasets such as ToxiCN_MM [4] and CMMHS [17] have begun to address this limitation. Existing multimodal approaches still struggle with semantic features common in Chinese memes, including implicit metaphors, cultural references, and homophonic wordplay, and the lack of deep reasoning ability remains a major factor that limits accuracy and generalizability.

2.2 Knowledge-Augmented Harmful Meme Detection Methods

Recent studies have explored using external knowledge to improve deep semantic reasoning in harmful meme detection. The multimodal hate speech detection framework MHSDF [18] integrates convolutional neural networks and recurrent neural networks to process text, image, audio, and video data, and uses attention mechanisms to fuse multimodal features for multi-class classification. KMTCH [17] incorporates knowledge augmentation, including Chinese hate lexicons and background information generated by large language models, and uses a multimodal Transformer for five-category classification, which improves Chinese semantic understanding and cross-modal alignment. Among existing methods, the MKE model [4] is a representative approach. MKE uses a two-stage process. A fixed large language model such as GPT-4 first generates descriptive or analytical knowledge from the meme's image and text. The generated knowledge is then combined with the original meme content and passed to a trainable detector. Injecting LLM-generated linguistic and common-sense knowledge improves detection for complex memes. However, pipeline-based methods have a key limitation. Knowledge generation and knowledge use are completely separate. The detector cannot influence what knowledge is produced during training and cannot adjust the generated information according to sample difficulty. This static and unidirectional knowledge injection treats the LLM as a fixed feature extractor and restricts the upper bound of the framework's performance.

3 Methodology

3.1 Problem Statement

We formalize the harmful meme detection task as a conditional text generation problem based on multimodal inputs. Let the input space be $\mathcal{X} = \mathcal{I} \times \mathcal{T}$, where $\mathcal{I}$ denotes the image space ($\mathbb{R}^{H\times W\times C}$) and $\mathcal{T}$ represents the text space associated with the image. Each input instance can be represented as a tuple $x_i = (img_i, txt_i) \in \mathcal{X}$, consisting of an image, its corresponding text and explanation.

Our objective is to learn a mapping function $\mathcal{M} : \mathcal{X} \to \mathcal{Y}$, where $\mathcal{Y}$ is a natural language text space containing structured information. Specifically, for each input x_i, the model is required to generate a textual output $y_i \in \mathcal{Y}$ that includes both a clear classification label (e.g., "Targeted Harmful") and an explanatory rationale supporting the decision, thereby unifying classification and explanation.

To this end, we employ a pretrained multimodal large model M_θ as the backbone, with parameters θ. The model is formulated as a conditional autoregressive language model, parameterizing the probability distribution of generating an output text sequence y given a multimodal input x:

$$p_\theta(y|x) = \prod_{t=1}^{|y|} p_\theta(y_t|y_{<t}, x)$$

where y_t denotes the token at time step t in the output sequence y, and $y_{<t}$ represents all previously generated tokens before step t. This formulation enables the model to generate explanatory text progressively in a cross-modal context, thereby facilitating joint understanding and reasoning over image-text memes.

3.2 Two-Stage Annotation Pipeline

To construct the instruction fine-tuning dataset D_{inst} for EG-CM, we apply a two-stage annotation pipeline to the ToxiCN_MM dataset: automatic generation by a multimodal large model followed by manual verification and correction.

In the automatic stage, we use the open-source multimodal large model **Qwen-VL-plus** (used exclusively for annotation and distinct from the backbone model employed for training) to generate initial explanations for each meme. During the manual verification stage, a team of four annotators reviews all generated explanations. We required that each explanation comprehensively analyze the harmfulness of the meme by integrating both image and text content. To prevent label leakage, we explicitly instructed annotators not to directly use category names in the explanation text, and conducted simple keyword spot-checks for verification; no label leakage was found in the final dataset. In cases of disagreement, the final explanation is determined by majority vote. Explanations that fail to meet the standards are corrected; all samples were retained after revision, and no instance was discarded. This two-stage process ensures that the resulting instruction fine-tuning dataset is of high quality, semantically accurate, free of overly templatized phrasing, and well-suited for model training.

3.3 Model Overview

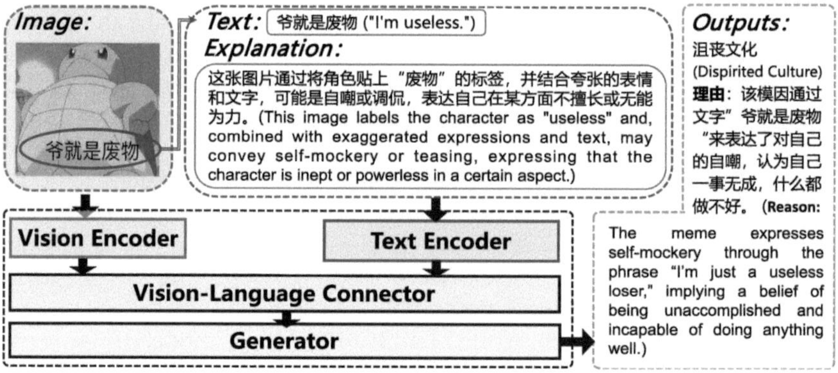

Fig. 1. Overview of the proposed EG-CM architecture.

Figure 1 illustrates the overall architecture of the proposed end-to-end harmful meme detection framework, EG-CM. EG-CM first extracts high-dimensional visual features from the input image using the Vision Encoder, while the Text Encoder encodes the embedded text and related contextual information. Subsequently, the Vision-Language Connector maps the visual features into the same semantic space as the text embeddings, enabling cross-modal alignment and information fusion. Finally, the Generator autoregressively produces a natural language output based on the fused multimodal representation, which includes both a precise classification label and a structured explanation supporting the decision.

In terms of implementation details, we insert low-rank adaptation (LoRA) modules into the query, key, value, and output projection matrices of all self-attention layers in both the visual encoder and the text module of Qwen2-VL. Our inputs are constructed following the ChatML conversation template, and the system instruction explicitly prescribes a fixed output format, thereby ensuring structural consistency and parsability of the generated results. Moreover, a two-layer MLP projects the visual features into the text embedding space; the projected visual tokens are then directly concatenated with the text token sequence and fed into the Transformer layers of Qwen2-VL, where deep interaction between visual and linguistic information is achieved through joint self-attention, unifying the entire cross-modal reasoning process within a single end-to-end architecture.

3.4 Instruction Fine-Tuning for Generative Explanation

To enable harmful meme detection, we adopt an **instruction fine-tuning** strategy that unifies multimodal reasoning with generative explanation. The framework integrates a vision encoder, a text encoder, a vision-language connector, and a generator into a single end-to-end architecture.

First, the **vision encoder** E_V extracts high-level visual features from the input image img_i, capturing both semantic content and visual cues. We adopt an advanced Vision Transformer (ViT) architecture, which represents the image as a sequence of patch embeddings and applies self-attention to capture global contextual information. Simultaneously, the **text encoder** E_T, based on a powerful decoder-only Transformer, encodes the textual content txt_i embedded in the meme, preserving fine-grained semantic and syntactic information.

Next, the **vision-language connector** P_C aligns visual and textual representations into a shared embedding space. This alignment can be achieved via cross-attention or multi-layer perceptron (MLP) projections. In our framework, we adopt Qwen2-VL as the backbone, which integrates a vision encoder with an MLP projector to map visual features to the text embedding space, followed by cross-attention layers in the language model to enable deep multimodal fusion. Both components are fine-tuned via LoRA to adapt to the harmful meme detection task. This design enables effective cross-modal interaction and ensures that visual cues inform textual reasoning and vice versa.

To guide the model's reasoning, we design a **prompt template function** $f_{prompt} : \mathcal{X} \rightarrow \mathcal{V}^*$, which converts each multimodal instance $x_i = (img_i, txt_i)$ into a natural language instruction. Concurrently, a **target response function** $f_{target} : \mathcal{L} \times \mathcal{R} \rightarrow \mathcal{V}^*$ generates a structured sequence combining the classification label lbl_i and an explanatory rationale rsn_i. The original dataset D is thus transformed into an instruction fine-tuning dataset $D_{inst} = \{(prompt_i, answer_i)\}_{i=1}^{N}$, where $prompt_i = f_{prompt}(x_i)$, $answer_i = f_{target}(lbl_i, rsn_i)$. Special visual tokens $<vision_start| >< |image_pad| >< |vision_end| > |$ are inserted to indicate the image content position within the text input.

Prompt design plays a critical role in model performance and output quality. In our work, we ensure:

- **Clear role definition**: The prompt defines the model as a "harmful meme classification assistant," providing explicit task context.
- **Task-specific guidance**: Prompts explicitly enumerate all five classification categories, reducing ambiguity in label generation.
- **Output format constraint**: The output strictly follows "label. Reason: explanation," avoiding additional or missing content and ensuring consistency across examples.

Finally, the **generator** G_θ produces the output y_i, which jointly contains the classification label and the explanation:

$$y_i = G_\theta(E_V(img_i), E_T(txt_i), P_C(E_V(img_i), E_T(txt_i)))$$

By integrating instruction fine-tuning with the multimodal backbone, the model learns to reason across image and text, generating explanations that enhance transparency and robustness in Chinese harmful meme detection.

3.5 Training and Inference

Training. The model is trained end-to-end using a token-level cross-entropy loss over the generated sequence:

$$\mathcal{L}(\theta; D_{\text{inst}}) = -\sum_{i=1}^{N} \log p_\theta(\text{answer}_i \mid \text{prompt}_i),$$

Because Qwen2-VL is an autoregressive generative model, it generates the label and explanation as a unified sequence; therefore, the standard token-level cross-entropy loss naturally provides supervision for both parts without requiring any auxiliary classification head. To explicitly optimize both classification accuracy and explanation quality, we adopt a joint loss formulation:

$$\mathcal{L}_{\text{joint}} = \lambda_1 \mathcal{L}_{\text{cls}}(y_{\text{true}}, \hat{y}) + \lambda_2 \mathcal{L}_{\text{gen}}(\text{exp}_{\text{true}}, \widehat{\text{exp}}),$$

where $\mathcal{L}_{\text{cls}}$ denotes the cross-entropy summed over the label tokens in the output sequence, $\mathcal{L}_{\text{gen}}$ denotes the cross-entropy summed over the explanation tokens, and we set $\lambda_1 = 1.0$ and $\lambda_2 = 0.5$ to balance the two objectives.

Inference. Since the model output is natural language, we define a deterministic parsing function $f_{\text{parse}} : \mathcal{Y} \rightarrow \mathcal{L}$ to extract the final classification label $\hat{l} \in \mathcal{L}$ from the generated response using keyword matching or regular expressions. This enables quantitative evaluation of classification performance. We design a two-stage parsing function to extract the label. In the first stage, exact matching is performed: the generated text is searched for the complete pattern consisting of one of the five harmful category names followed by the evidence and explanation segments, as specified in the instruction. When the format is incorrect, the second stage falls back to a more relaxed regular expression that only captures one of the five category keywords appearing at the beginning of the output, optionally followed by punctuation. If both stages fail to produce a valid label, the sample is marked as invalid and excluded from the computation of classification metrics. Thanks to strict instruction fine-tuning, the model almost never outputs words outside the five harmful categories; therefore, synonym substitutions or mixed-language outputs do not occur in practice. This two-stage strategy ensures both parsing reliability and evaluation transparency.

4 Experiments

In this section, we conduct a series of experiments to evaluate the effectiveness of the proposed end-to-end explainable detection framework, **EG-CM**, focusing on the following core research questions (RQs):

- **RQ1**: Compared with existing mainstream baseline models, including pipeline-based and feature-fusion methods, does our end-to-end generative framework achieve superior performance in multi-class harmful content classification?
- **RQ2**: Does enforcing the model to generate explanatory rationales during training improve the accuracy of its classification decisions?
- **RQ3**: For which types of harmful memes, particularly those relying on deep cultural context and complex image-text interactions, does the model demonstrate strengths, and what are its limitations?

4.1 Settings

Datasets. We conduct all experiments on the publicly available ToxiCN_MM dataset, the largest and most finely annotated benchmark for Chinese harmful meme detection, which contains 12,000 samples. To the best of our knowledge, ToxiCN_MM is currently the only publicly available dataset that provides both multi-class harmful labels and rich multimodal content specifically for Chinese memes, making it the most suitable choice for evaluating our approach. We systematically annotate explanation fields for each meme based on this dataset. Following the official data split, we assign 9,600 samples to the training set and 2,400 samples to the validation and test sets. We evaluate model performance on two subtasks: (1) Harmful Type Identification, which covers one harmless category and four harmful categories, and (2) Explanation Generation.

Baselines. We compare EG-CM against text models (GPT-3.5/4, RoBERTa [9]), image models (ResNet [10], ViT [11]), and multimodal models (GPT-4, VisualBERT [14], Hate-CLIPper [13], CLIP [12], and MKE variants [4]). These baselines cover standard benchmarks for language understanding, visual feature extraction, and cross-modal alignment. We select baselines spanning diverse modeling paradigms for comprehensive comparison. Text-only models (GPT-3.5, GPT-4, RoBERTa) serve as strong unimodal baselines to capture the linguistic features of memes, while image-only models (ResNet, ViT) evaluate the standalone contribution of visual features. For multimodal approaches, we include: (1) VisualBERT: Classic cross-attention-based early vision-language fusion model. (2) Foundational cross-modal model, tested as feature extractor and zero-shot classifier. (3) GPT-4: Large general-purpose multimodal LLM for benchmarking. (4) MKE: A state-of-the-art knowledge-enhanced method with a two-stage pipeline (GPT-4 generates external knowledge, followed by a classifier for detection). We evaluate both its CLIP-based (MKE-CLIP) and fusion-based (MKE-Fusion) variants.

Evaluation Metrics. For the multi-class harmful type identification task, we adopt standard classification metrics used in prior work, including Precision (P), Recall (R), F1 score, and per-class F1 scores. To evaluate the quality of the generated explanations, we employ widely-used natural language generation metrics: BLEU, METEOR, and BERTScore, which measure the similarity between the model-generated explanations and human-annotated rationales, thereby quantifying the quality of the model's explanation generation.

Implementation Details. We build EG-CM on top of the open-source multimodal large model **Qwen2-VL-7B** (the 7-billion parameter variant), using Qwen2VLProcessor to handle multimodal inputs. To reduce computational costs, we adopt parameter-efficient fine-tuning (PEFT) with Low-Rank Adaptation (LoRA). In our setup, the rank r is set to 16, and the α parameter is 32. These values are selected based on the official recommendation for Qwen2-VL and further validated through preliminary experiments on the validation set, where we compared ranks $r \in \{8, 16, 32\}$ and found that $r = 16$ with $\alpha = 32$ achieves the best trade-off between performance and parameter efficiency. LoRA is applied to projection matrices in both text and vision modules, including the query, key, and value projections in self-attention layers, as well as certain layers of the visual encoder. This allows the model to efficiently adapt to harmful meme detection while preserving pretrained knowledge. We train using the AdamW optimizer with an initial learning rate of 3×10^{-5}, employing a cosine decay scheduler with warm-up. Experiments are conducted on 4 NVIDIA A100 GPUs. Each device uses a batch size of 8 with gradient accumulation steps of 4, resulting in an effective global batch size of $8 \times 4 \times 4 = 128$. Hyperparameters for baseline models follow the original papers or are determined via grid search on the validation set.

4.2 Experimental Results

Harmful Type Identification. Based on the results reported in Table 1, several important observations can be made regarding the performance of our proposed EG-CM.

First, when comparing across modalities, text-only models (GPT-3.5, GPT-4, RoBERTa) achieve moderate F1 scores, with RoBERTa performing best among them (F1 = 55.85%), but they still struggle with certain categories such as *Sexual*

Table 1. Main experimental results on the ToxiCN_MM test set.

Modality	Model	Multi-class harmful type identification						
		P	R	F1	$F1_{Tg.}$	$F1_{Sex.}$	$F1_{Off.}$	$F1_{Disp.}$
Text	GPT3.5	36.93	32.60	32.45	27.42	10.52	29.01	14.63
	GPT4	58.29	41.81	44.86	11.43	32.26	62.22	34.15
	RoBERTa	53.24	60.06	55.85	48.79	42.70	71.81	29.23
Image	ResNet	35.66	36.23	36.46	16.67	20.93	51.28	12.28
	ViT	43.38	37.86	39.10	24.17	34.32	54.57	9.01
Multimodal	GPT-4	58.87	41.77	43.89	23.53	55.74	32.56	23.53
	VisualBERT	69.37	72.29	70.42	36.8	29.25	65.85	3.88
	Hate-CLIPper	68.02	72.41	69.02	5.91	21.06	50.33	1.99
	CLIP	54.85	64.95	57.85	49.58	49.64	74.65	26.92
	MKE (CLIP)	60.38	63.52	61.47	51.52	57.14	77.19	33.33
	MKE (fusion)	62.41	62.08	62.17	**53.27**	56.10	74.54	39.24
	EG-CM (ours)	**79.16**	**78.92**	**78.74**	49.41	**57.14**	**74.96**	**47.2**

All scores are reported in percentages (%). The best results are highlighted in bold

and *Disparagement*, reflecting the limitations of relying solely on textual cues. Image-only models (ResNet, ViT) perform worse overall, particularly on categories requiring deeper semantic understanding, highlighting the insufficiency of visual information alone for harmful meme detection.

Multimodal models generally outperform unimodal baselines, demonstrating the importance of integrating both text and visual cues. Among multimodal baselines, VisualBERT and CLIP-based methods improve F1 scores across several categories, while MKE variants further enhance performance through knowledge-enhanced fusion.

EG-CM significantly surpasses all baselines with a macro F1 of 78.74%, showing substantial gains in both precision and recall. Notably, EG-CM achieves the highest per-category F1 scores in *Sexual* (57.14%) and *Disparagement* (47.2%), indicating its superior ability to handle categories that require nuanced cross-modal understanding and cultural context. This improvement can be attributed to our end-to-end generative framework, which jointly optimizes classification and explanation generation, enabling the model to learn richer semantic representations that enhance its decision-making capability.

Overall, these results confirm that EG-CM effectively leverages multimodal information and interpretable training signals, outperforming both unimodal and existing multimodal baselines across almost all harmful meme categories. We note that on the Targeted Harmful category, EG-CM trails behind MKE-Fusion (49.41% vs. 53.27%), a limitation we analyze in detail in Sect. 4.6.

Explanation Generation Evaluation. Table 2 presents the quality of the explanations generated by EG-CM, measured by BLEU, METEOR, and

BERTScore. The results indicate that our model produces explanations that are both fluent and semantically aligned with human annotations.

BLEU and METEOR scores. BLEU-1 to BLEU-4 scores show a reasonable n-gram overlap between generated and reference explanations, with BLEU-4 reaching 14.83%. While these scores may appear moderate, they are typical for open-ended text generation tasks where multiple valid explanations exist. The METEOR score of 37.47% further confirms that the generated explanations capture key lexical and semantic elements, as METEOR accounts for synonyms and stemming, making it more robust than BLEU for evaluating explanatory text.

BERTScore. The BERTScore F1 of 74.56% demonstrates a high level of semantic similarity between generated and reference explanations, even when surface forms differ. This indicates that EG-CM's explanations are not merely copying training patterns but are genuinely reasoning about the meme content. The consistent BERT precision (73.78%) and recall (75.48%) suggest that the model balances between generating relevant content and covering all important aspects of the reference.

Overall, these results validate that EG-CM can generate informative, faithful explanations that align closely with human judgments, fulfilling the dual goal of detection and interpretability.

Table 2. Explanation generation results.

Model	Explanation generation							
	B-1	B-2	B-3	B-4	METEOR	BERT_P	BERT_R	BERT_F1
EG-CM	40.02	26.87	19.83	14.83	37.47	73.78	75.48	74.56

All scores are in percentage (%)

4.3 Human Evaluation Results

Although automatic metrics such as BLEU and METEOR are convenient for quantitative comparison, they may not fully reflect the actual quality of generated explanation text. Following established practices for human evaluation of generated explanations, we recruited three raters, none of whom had participated in the previous annotation work, to conduct a manual assessment of the generated explanations. We randomly sampled 200 instances from the ToxiCN_MM test set, covering all five categories with at least 20 samples per category. For each sample, the raters were presented with the original meme and the complete model output. They rated each explanation on the following three criteria using a 1-to-5 Likert scale (1 = unacceptable, 5 = excellent):

- Factual CorrectnessïijŽwhether the explanation accurately identifies the harmful elements present in the meme, considering both the image and the text.

- Reasoning Completeness: whether the explanation provides a sufficient and logically coherent reasoning chain to support its classification conclusion.
- Helpfulness: whether the explanation helps a reader understand why the meme is considered harmful.

Prior to the formal evaluation, the raters underwent a calibration session using 10 held-out samples to align their understanding of the criteria. During the formal evaluation, all ratings were conducted independently. We used the intraclass correlation coefficient (ICC(3,1)) to assess the agreement among the three raters, with detailed results presented in Table 3. The model achieved average scores of 3.34, 3.16, and 3.26 on factual correctness, reasoning completeness, and helpfulness, respectively. The intraclass correlation coefficients (ICC(3,1)) ranged from 29.63% to 32.47%, indicating fair to moderate inter-rater reliability.

Table 3. Human evaluation results.

Criterion	Human evaluation		
	Mean	Std	ICC(3,1) (%)
Factual correctness	3.34	1.25	32.47
Reasoning completeness	3.16	1.28	29.63
Helpfulness	3.26	1.32	31.15

4.4 Ablation Study

To verify the effectiveness of the key design in our framework, namely explanation generation, we conducted an ablation study (addressing RQ2). We designed a variant model, *w/o Explanation*, which removes the task constraint of generating explanatory rationales. All other components of the model, including the backbone network and training hyperparameters, remain unchanged.

Table 4. Ablation study results.

Model	Multi-class harmful type identification		
	P	R	F1
EG-CM (Full)	**79.16**	78.92	**78.74**
w/o Explanation	57.49	68.92	56.49
w/o Text	51.92	65.62	57.11
w/o Image	78.46	**79.96**	78.09

All scores are in percentage (%)

As shown in Table 4, the full model significantly outperforms the variant without explanation generation. This result strongly demonstrates that enforcing the model to generate explanatory rationales does more than provide interpretability. It acts as a form of "learning constraint" or a chain-of-thought-like guidance, encouraging the model to learn more robust and generalizable features, thereby enhancing the performance on the main task (classification).

To further validate the choice of LoRA rank, we conduct a sensitivity analysis by varying the rank$r$while keeping other hyperparameters fixed. As shown in Table 5, increasing the LoRA rank from 8 to 16 improves the F1 score from 78.20% to 78.74%. However, further increasing to 32 yields a slight decrease to 78.25%, likely due to overfitting or optimization challenges with larger rank. Therefore, we select $r = 16$ as it achieves the best trade-off between performance and parameter efficiency.

Table 5. Performance comparison with different LoRA ranks (%).

Rank	Multi-class harmful type identification		
	P	R	F1
8	78.96	**79.54**	78.20
16	79.16	78.92	**78.74**
32	**79.84**	79.17	78.25

We also experimented with keeping $\alpha = 2r$ (i.e., $\alpha = 16, 32, 64$ for $r = 8, 16, 32$) and observed a similar trend, with $r = 16$ still performing the best. For simplicity and to isolate the effect of rank, we report results with fixed $\alpha = 32$.

4.5 Qualitative Analysis and Case Study

To intuitively understand the model's behavior patterns and limitations (addressing RQ3), we conducted a case study. We selected two representative examples of Chinese internet memes to further validate the model's multi-scenario recognition capability, with detailed case information and comparative analysis presented in Table 6. Through cross-modal semantic fusion, the model can identify potentially offensive meanings embedded in pinyin abbreviations and capture the interaction between image expressions and accompanying text. These cases demonstrate that EG-CM, leveraging cross-modal reasoning and cultural knowledge integration, can accurately detect implicit harmful content while also understanding the emotional nuance of memes, showing strong adaptability in the complex context of Chinese internet memes.

Table 6. Case study.

Type	(a)	(b)
Meme		
Text	"MDZZ"	"我真的太难了"
Explanation	(a) 这张图片通过将猫贴上"MDZZ"的标签，是文字"妈的智障"的拼音缩写，常用来表示对他人的不满或鄙视。 This image labels the cat with 'MDZZ,' which is the pinyin abbreviation for the phrase ' 妈的智障' (literally 'mom's idiot'), commonly used to express dissatisfaction or contempt towards someone. (b) 这张图片通过描述角色"我真的太难了"，表达了说话者的无奈和困境，可能是遇到了某种难以解决的问题或挑战。 This image expresses the speaker's helplessness and predicament by depicting the character saying 'I'm really having a hard time,' possibly indicating that they are facing some kind of difficult problem or challenge.	
Output	(a) 一般性有害。理由：这张图片通过将"mdzz"谐音"妈的智障"，是一句网络用语，含有侮辱性质，表示对某人或某事的不满或鄙视。 Generally harmful. Reason: This image uses the homophonic pun 'mdzz' for ' 妈的智障' (damn idiot), which is an online slang term with an insulting nature, expressing dissatisfaction or contempt towards someone or something. (b) 沮丧文化。理由：这张图片通过描述一只小龟龟委屈的表情，结合文字"我真的太难了"，表达了说话者遇到了很大的困难和压力，感到非常艰难。 Frustration culture. Reason: This picture conveys the speaker's great difficulty and stress through the depiction of a small turtle's distressed expression, combined with the text 'I'm really having a hard time,' expressing a sense of struggle and hardship.	

4.6 Discussion

Analysis on Targeted Harmful Category. While EG-CM achieves state-of-the-art performance on most categories, its F1 score on the "Targeted Harmful" category (49.41%) is lower than that of MKE-Fusion (53.27%). We analyze the core causes of this gap via misclassified sample inspection and annotation comparison.

First, targeted harmful memes typically carry explicit attacks on specific individuals, organizations or social groups, whose harmful intent identification relies heavily on external knowledge of the target entity (e.g., background, associated stereotypes). MKE explicitly incorporates GPT-4 generated external knowledge for this task, while EG-CM only depends on pretrained internal knowledge, which has insufficient coverage for niche or emerging entities, leading to misclassifications.

Second, the structured explanation generation objective may introduce noise. When visual-textual cues are ambiguous, the model may prioritize coherent explanation generation over accurate label prediction. Manual inspection confirms that some misclassified samples correctly identify harmful elements in the explanation, but are assigned to wrong related categories (e.g., "General Offense" instead of "Targeted Harmful"), indicating the explanation task occasionally overrides the classification objective.

Our analysis summarizes two main error types: (1) category confusion between harmful types with overlapping characteristics; (2) misinterpretation of the image-text semantic interaction, such as missing visual cues that specify the attack target. To address these limitations, we plan to introduce counterfactual consistency into training. By maintaining coherent predictions and explanations under counterfactual perturbations, the model can enhance reasoning robustness and better differentiate closely related harmful categories.

Analysis on Modality Reliance and Dataset Characteristics. The ablation study in Sect. 4.3 shows that removing the image branch only causes a 0.65% performance drop, indicating EG-CM relies heavily on textual cues. To investigate whether the model will underperform on vision-dominant memes where harmful intent is mainly conveyed by visual content, we construct a vision-dominant subset (defined as memes with fewer than three Chinese characters or only non-semantic symbols like emojis) from the 2,400 test samples, and only identify 47 such samples (1.96% of the test set).

Manual inspection of these 47 samples reveals that their short text already contains direct harmful expressions (e.g., offensive words), which alone provide sufficient evidence for harmfulness judgment, while the image only plays a role. These are not genuine vision-dominant memes, which reveals an inherent characteristic of the ToxiCN_MM dataset: almost all samples include independently harmful text, and purely image-based harmful memes are extremely rare. This text-dominant nature explains the minimal performance drop after removing the image branch, as the model can already make accurate predictions via text alone.

This limitation means the current dataset cannot directly assess EG-CM's capability on genuine vision-dominant memes, highlighting the need for more visually diverse benchmarks in future research. To enhance the model's visual reasoning ability, we plan to introduce stronger visual encoders, explicit visual grounding mechanisms and vision-centric pre-training objectives, and evaluate the model on datasets with a higher proportion of image-centric harmful memes.

4.7 Conclusion

In this work, we presented EG-CM, an end-to-end instruction-tuned multimodal framework for Chinese harmful meme detection with explanation generation. Our experiments show that EG-CM improves multi-category classification performance and produces stable explanatory rationales, indicating that explanation supervision is an effective learning signal. The framework also handles implicit expressions and cultural features in Chinese memes, which suggests its usefulness in real-world content safety applications.

However, we also identify limitations: EG-CM underperforms on the "Targeted Harmful" category compared to knowledge-enhanced methods, and the

ToxiCN_MM dataset is predominantly text-driven, making it difficult to assess the model's performance on genuinely vision-dominant memes. Future work will focus on integrating external knowledge (e.g., entity linking, knowledge graphs) to improve targeted harmful detection, and enhancing visual understanding through stronger visual encoders and explicit grounding mechanisms. We also plan to validate EG-CM on more visually diverse datasets as they become available.

Acknowledgments. Beijing Natural Science Foundation (Grant number: 4262075), Research Funds for NSD Construction, University of International Relations (Grant numbers: 3262026T23)

References

1. Shifman, L.: Memes in Digital Culture. The MIT Press (2013)
2. Kiela, D., Firooz, H., Mohan, A., Goswami, V., Singh, A., Ringshia, P., Testuggine, D.: Detecting hate speech in multimodal memes. The hateful memes challenge (2021)
3. Pramanick, S., Dimitrov, D., Mukherjee, R., Sharma, S., Shad Akhtar, M., Nakov, P., Chakraborty, T.: Detecting harmful memes and their targets. In: Zong, C., Xia, F., Li, W., Navigli, R. (eds.) Findings of the Association for Computational Linguistics: ACL-IJCNLP 2021, pp. 2783–2796. Association for Computational Linguistics (2021), Online
4. Lu, J., Xu, B., Zhang, X., Wang, H., Zhu, H., Zhang, D., Yang, L., Lin, H.: Towards comprehensive detection of Chinese harmful memes (2024)
5. Liu, H., Li, C., Wu, Q., Lee, Y.J.: Visual instruction tuning (2023)
6. de Gibert, O., Perez, N., García-Pablos, A., Cuadros, M.: Hate speech dataset from a white supremacy forum. In: Fišer, D., Huang, R., Prabhakaran, V., Voigt, R., Waseem, Z., Wernimont, J. (eds.) Proceedings of the 2nd Workshop on Abusive Language Online (ALW2), Brussels, Belgium, pp. 11–20. Association for Computational Linguistics (2018)
7. Mathew, B., Saha, P., Yimam, S.M., Biemann, C., Goyal, P., Mukherjee, A.: Hatexplain: a benchmark dataset for explainable hate speech detection (2022)
8. Devlin, J., Chang, M.W., Lee, K. and Toutanova, K.: BERT: pre-training of deep bidirectional transformers for language understanding. In: Burstein, J., Doran, C., Solorio, T. (eds.) Proceedings of the 2019 Conference of the North American Chapter of the Association for Computational Linguistics: Human Language Technologies, Volume 1 (Long and Short Papers), Minneapolis, Minnesota, pp. 4171–4186. Association for Computational Linguistics (2019)
9. Zhuang, L., Wayne, L., Ya, S. and Jun, Z.: A robustly optimized BERT pre-training approach with post-training. In: Li, S., Sun, M., Liu, Y., Wu, H., Liu, K., Che, W., He, S., Rao, G. (eds.) Proceedings of the 20th Chinese National Conference on Computational Linguistics, Huhhot, China, pp. 1218–1227, August 2021. Chinese Information Processing Society of China
10. He, K., Zhang, X., Ren, S., Sun, J.: Deep residual learning for image recognition (2015)

11. Dosovitskiy, A., Beyer, L., Kolesnikov, A., Weissenborn, D., Zhai, X., Unterthiner, T., Dehghani, M., Minderer, M., Heigold, G., Gelly, S., Uszkoreit, J., Houlsby, N.: An image is worth 16x16 words: Transformers for image recognition at scale (2021)
12. Radford, A., Kim, J.W., Hallacy, C., Ramesh, A., Goh, G., Agarwal, S., Sastry, G., Askell, A., Mishkin, P., Clark, J., Krueger, G., Sutskever, I.: Learning transferable visual models from natural language supervision (2021)
13. Kumar, G.K., Nandakumar, K.: Hate-CLIPper: multimodal hateful meme classification based on cross-modal interaction of CLIP features. In: Biester, L., Demszky, D., Jin, Z., Sachan, M., Tetreault, J., Wilson, S., Xiao, L., Zhao, J. (eds.) Proceedings of the Second Workshop on NLP for Positive Impact (NLP4PI), Abu Dhabi, United Arab Emirates (Hybrid), pp. 171–183. Association for Computational Linguistics (2022)
14. Li, L.H., Yatskar, M., Yin, D., Hsieh, C.-J., Chang, K.-W.: Visualbert: a simple and performant baseline for vision and language (2019)
15. Deng, J., Zhou, J., Sun, H., Zheng, C., Mi, F., Meng, H., Huang, M.: Cold: a benchmark for Chinese offensive language detection (2022)
16. Zhou, J., Deng, J., Mi, F., Li, Y., Wang, Y., Huang, M., Jiang, X., Liu, Q., Meng, H.: Towards identifying social bias in dialog systems: framework, dataset, and benchmark. In: Goldberg, Y., Kozareva, Z., Zhang, Y. (eds.) Findings of the Association for Computational Linguistics: EMNLP 2022, Abu Dhabi, United Arab Emirates, pp. 3576–3591. Association for Computational Linguistics (2022)
17. Huang, Q., Li, P., Wang, W., Zhang, X., Chen, S., Cheng, H., Liu, Z.: Knowledge-enhanced Chinese multimodal hate speech detection. Expert Syst. Appl. **299**, 129906 (2026)
18. Prabhu, R., Seethalakshmi, V.: A comprehensive framework for multi-modal hate speech detection in social media using deep learning. Sci. Rep. **15**(1), 13020 (2025)

Prediction

Dyna-CLIM: Dynamic Cross-Layer Attention for Influence Prediction in Multiplex Networks

Weilan Yan[1], Guohua Chen[1], Shuangjiao Tang[1], Chengzhe Yuan[2(✉)], Ronghua Lin[1], Chengjie Mao[1], and Yong Tang[1,3]

[1] School of Computer Science, South China Normal University, Guangzhou, China
{buleyan,chengh,tangshuangjiao,rhlin,ytang}@m.scnu.edu.cn, maochj@qq.com
[2] School of Electronics and Information, Guangdong Polytechnic Normal University, Guangzhou, China
ycz@gpnu.edu.cn
[3] Institute of Data Intelligence, Guangdong University of Science and Technology, Dongguan, China

Abstract. Identifying influential nodes in multiplex social networks is crucial for influence-aware seed selection, where heterogeneous relation layers jointly shape diffusion dynamics. Existing methods often struggle to suppress noisy intra-layer aggregation, align semantically diverse layers, and model node-specific cross-layer coupling without fixed global transition assumptions. To address these limitations, this paper proposes Dyna-CLIM, a dynamic cross-layer influence modeling framework for efficient node influence prediction. Dyna-CLIM encodes each relation layer with a GIN-based module enhanced by an adaptive damping gate, and then employs contrastive heterogeneous alignment to reduce semantic discrepancies across layers. A directed node-specific cross-layer attention mechanism further provides representation-level soft routing as a learned proxy for asymmetric coupling tendencies among relation layers. The fused representations are finally fed into a pseudo-regression predictor for ranking-based Top-k seed selection. Experiments on multiple real-world multiplex social network datasets show that Dyna-CLIM consistently achieves stronger diffusion performance and more dispersed seed selection than representative baselines, while providing interpretable cross-layer attention patterns.

Keywords: Influence Prediction · Multiplex Social Networks · Cross-layer Attention · Graph Neural Networks

1 Introduction

Multiplex social networks provide a more faithful abstraction of real social interaction than single-layer graphs because the same individuals may be connected through multiple types of relations, such as friendship, collaboration, advice

L. Ding et al. (Eds.): APWeb-WAIM 2026, LNCS 16993, pp. 233–249, 2027.
https://doi.org/10.1007/978-981-92-5693-8_15

seeking, co-learning, or organizational communication. Practical academic social platforms such as SCHOLAT[1] also exhibit this multiplex nature, where scholars may be associated through heterogeneous academic and social relations. These relations usually encode different interaction semantics, structural densities, and propagation preferences. Such systems are naturally modeled as multilayer networks with a shared node set and heterogeneous relation layers, and empirical studies show that their structural properties cannot be fully captured by a single aggregated graph [1,2].

Influence maximization in multiplex networks aims to identify a small group of seed nodes that can trigger the largest possible diffusion cascade across coupled relation layers. Classical single-layer IM and scalable sampling-based approximations established the algorithmic foundation for seed selection in large graphs [3,4]. However, multiplex IM is more challenging because influence may propagate not only through intra-layer edges but also through cross-layer identity coupling. In this paper, the research problem is defined as learning an influence scoring function for multiplex networks that ranks nodes according to their expected diffusion capability under a given seed budget, while avoiding expensive online diffusion simulation during seed selection.

Existing IM methods, however, still exhibit limitations in scalability and representation capacity when transferred to multiplex networks. Topology-based heuristics, such as degree centrality [5], modified degree-based ranking [6], and local fuzzy information centrality [7], provide efficient node-ranking criteria, but they mainly rely on static structural indicators and therefore cannot fully characterize cascade dynamics or cross-layer propagation effects. Learning-based approaches such as DeepInf [8] and reinforcement-learning-based methods such as PIANO [9] improve influence estimation or formulate seed selection as sequential decision-making; nevertheless, most of these methods are developed for single-layer graphs, as also observed in recent surveys [10]. For multiplex IM, existing studies have considered heterogeneous diffusion models [11], clique-based search [12], swarm optimization [13], and learning-based reasoning [14]. Nevertheless, many of them still depend on static layer-level fusion, predefined inter-layer coupling, or globally shared transition assumptions, which restricts their ability to model node-specific and direction-sensitive spreading patterns.

A central challenge is to obtain reliable node representations while preserving both intra-layer specificity and cross-layer consistency. Different layers often exhibit distinct densities, semantics, and neighborhood structures. Direct message passing may amplify noisy neighbors, while naive concatenation or averaging across layers may ignore semantic shifts among relation types. Although HAN and MAGNN show that attention and metapath-based aggregation can model relation-dependent semantics in heterogeneous graphs [15,16], multiplex influence prediction further requires dynamic coupling estimation at the node level. In particular, a node influential in one relation layer may not be equally influential in another layer, and the propagation evidence between two layers may be asymmetric.

[1] https://www.scholat.com/.

To address these issues, this paper proposes Dyna-CLIM, a dynamic cross-layer influence modeling framework for multiplex node influence prediction. Rather than treating cross-layer transitions as explicit simulation-time operations, Dyna-CLIM learns representation-level soft routing that acts as a proxy for cross-layer coupling tendencies. Specifically, it first extracts layer-specific node representations through a GIN-based encoder with an adaptive damping gate, then applies contrastive heterogeneous alignment to improve cross-layer representation consistency, and finally learns directed node-specific cross-layer attention weights for feature-space routing. In this way, Dyna-CLIM supports efficient Top-k seed ranking while retaining interpretable cross-layer coupling patterns. The main contributions of this paper are summarized as follows:

- We propose Dyna-CLIM, an end-to-end dynamic cross-layer influence modeling framework that models layer-to-layer coupling through learnable feature-space routing for efficient Top-k seed selection.
- We develop a noise-aware intra-layer encoding module that combines GIN-based message passing with a learnable damping gate to balance structural aggregation and node-specific information.
- We design a heterogeneity-consistent cross-layer routing mechanism that integrates contrastive alignment with directed node-specific attention to estimate asymmetric inter-layer coupling strengths.
- Extensive experiments on four real-world multiplex datasets demonstrate that the proposed model consistently outperforms representative baselines under multiple diffusion-oriented evaluation metrics.

2 Related Work

2.1 Influence Maximization

Influence maximization (IM) in single-layer networks seeks to select a limited number of seed nodes that maximize the expected diffusion spread under a given propagation model. Classical IM and reverse influence sampling provide the algorithmic foundation for cascade-based seed selection and scalable approximation [3,4]. Topology-driven heuristics, including degree, closeness, betweenness, K-shell, MDER, and LFIC, provide efficient node ranking criteria based on structural importance [5–7,17]. These methods are computationally attractive and easy to deploy on large graphs, but they generally rely on static structural proxies. As a result, they may fail to characterize stochastic cascade behavior and tend to select seeds with highly overlapping influence regions.

- Learning-based IM methods improve influence estimation by introducing graph representation learning or sequential decision-making into seed selection. Representative GNN-based and deep optimization methods learn influence-oriented node representations, while reinforcement learning methods formulate seed selection as a graph decision process [8,9,18]. By learning from simulated or observed diffusion outcomes, these methods can reduce the dependence on handcrafted centrality indicators and improve ranking flexibility. However, most of them are mainly designed for single-topology settings, where all relations are represented by one graph, and their assumptions do not directly capture relation heterogeneity or cross-layer interaction in multiplex networks.

- Multilayer and multiplex IM extends the single-layer setting by allowing influence to propagate both within individual layers and across multiple coupled relation layers. Existing studies have explored heterogeneous diffusion models, clique-based multilayer heuristics, swarm optimization, and learning-based reasoning frameworks [11–14]. These studies demonstrate the importance of modeling layer-aware propagation, but many existing multilayer or multiplex methods still depend on global layer-level fusion, predefined inter-layer coupling, or static transition assumptions. Such designs limit their ability to characterize node-specific and direction-sensitive propagation patterns, especially when different relation layers exhibit distinct semantics and diffusion strengths.

2.2 Attention Mechanisms

Attention mechanisms assign adaptive importance weights to different information sources. The Transformer demonstrates the effectiveness of self-attention for dependency modeling, and Graph Attention Networks extend this idea to graph neighborhoods through learned neighbor weights [19,20]. These mechanisms improve the flexibility of message passing by avoiding uniform aggregation over all inputs and provide interpretable weights that indicate the relative contribution of different neighbors or features.

Attention is also important for heterogeneous and multiplex graph learning, where different neighbors, relations, and semantic paths may contribute unequally to node representations. HAN and MAGNN employ hierarchical attention or metapath-based contextual aggregation to model relation-dependent semantics in heterogeneous graphs [15,16]. However, most existing attention mechanisms focus on neighborhood aggregation, semantic-path weighting, or static relation importance, rather than explicitly learning directed node-specific coupling between relation layers for multiplex influence prediction. In this task, cross-layer attention should reflect how the representation of a node in one layer contributes to its diffusion potential in another layer, rather than only providing an averaged layer preference. Different from prior work, Dyna-CLIM uses dynamic cross-layer attention to estimate asymmetric layer-to-layer routing strengths at the node level and combines this mechanism with heterogeneous contrastive alignment for influence-oriented representation learning.

3 Preliminaries

3.1 Problem Definition

Definition 1 (*Multiplex network*). A multiplex network with L relation layers is denoted as $\mathcal{G} = \{G^{(\ell)}\}_{\ell=1}^{L}$. The ℓ-th layer is $G^{(\ell)} = (V, E^{(\ell)}, X^{(\ell)})$, where V is the shared node set, $|V| = n$, $E^{(\ell)}$ is the edge set of layer ℓ, and $X^{(\ell)}$ denotes the initial node feature matrix in that layer.

Definition 2 (*Node influence*). For a node v, its influence is defined as the expected number of nodes activated by a multiplex diffusion process when v is used as the only initial seed:

$$I(v) = \mathbb{E}\left[|A_\infty(\{v\})|\right], \tag{1}$$

where $A_\infty(\{v\})$ denotes the final activated node set.

Multiplex influence maximization seeks a seed set S^* with at most k nodes that maximizes the expected diffusion range under a multiplex diffusion model $\mathcal{M} = \{\mathcal{M}_1, \mathcal{M}_2, \ldots, \mathcal{M}_L\}$:

$$S^* = \arg \max_{S \subseteq V,\ |S| \leq k} \sigma_{\mathcal{M}}(S). \tag{2}$$

Exact influence evaluation under independent cascade or linear threshold models is computationally hard. In multiplex networks, the state space grows rapidly because of layer coupling. This work therefore learns node-level influence scores for efficient ranking-based approximate seed selection rather than directly solving the exact set optimization problem in Eq. (2). The ranking-based formulation is computationally efficient, but it does not explicitly optimize the marginal gain of a seed set during selection.

3.2 Diffusion and Learning Setup

Dyna-CLIM uses diffusion models for both offline pseudo-label generation and final seed evaluation. Multi-IC, Multi-SIR, and Multi-LT extend cascade-style, epidemic-style, and threshold-style diffusion processes to multiplex settings by allowing propagation over layer-specific edges or states [3,21–23]. In the experiments, Multi-SIR is used to generate supervision labels, while Multi-SIR, Multi-IC, and Multi-LT are used to evaluate the selected Top-k seeds under different diffusion assumptions. The purpose of this cross-model evaluation is not to claim that SIR labels are equivalent to IC or LT dynamics, but to test whether the learned structural influence signals transfer across related multiplex diffusion protocols.

To reduce semantic gaps among relation layers, Dyna-CLIM adopts contrastive learning to align compatible cross-layer representations. Following the InfoNCE principle [24], representations of the same node across two layers are treated as positive pairs, while representations of different nodes are treated as negative pairs. This objective encourages transferable cross-layer diffusion evidence to be mapped into a more consistent feature space while suppressing noisy or irrelevant layer-specific signals.

Because directly optimizing discrete seed combinations or repeatedly performing online diffusion simulation is expensive, Dyna-CLIM formulates influence prediction as a pseudo-regression task. A nonlinear mapping $f_\Theta(\cdot)$ learns to approximate proxy influence labels generated by offline diffusion simulation, and the predicted score is then used for ranking-based Top-k seed selection. During online inference, the model only requires one neural forward pass and a descending sort over predicted influence scores.

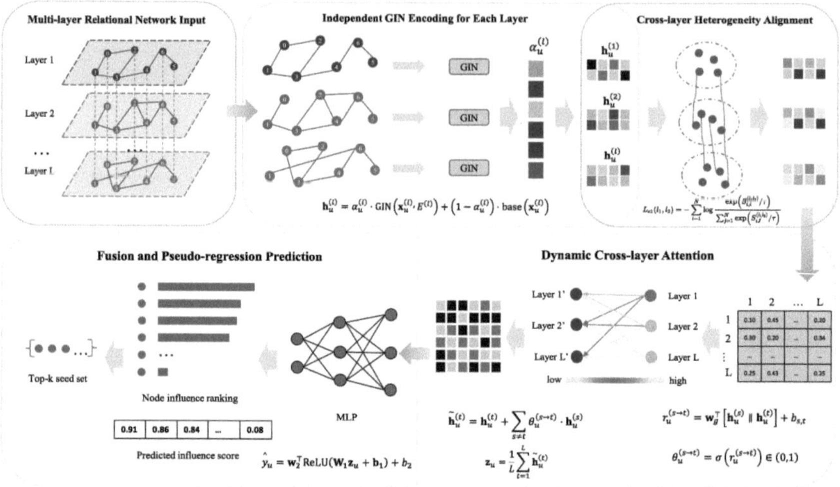

Fig. 1. Vector overview of Dyna-CLIM from multiplex network input to Top-k candidate seed output.

4 The Dyna-CLIM Framework

The core idea of Dyna-CLIM is to estimate cross-layer coupling tendencies with learnable soft routing in the representation space. As shown in Fig. 1, the pipeline starts from a multi-layer relational network input, applies independent GIN encoding per layer, performs cross-layer heterogeneity alignment, computes dynamic cross-layer attention, and fuses representations for pseudo-regression-based influence ranking and Top-k candidate seed selection.

4.1 Intra-layer Feature Extraction

To obtain clean single-layer semantics, Dyna-CLIM first encodes each relation layer independently. A GIN-based encoder is adopted because of its strong graph representation capacity [25]. The adaptive damping gate aggregates intra-layer information only from neighbors in the same layer. For node u in layer ℓ, the adaptive damping coefficient is

$$\alpha_u^{(\ell)} = \sigma\left(\mathbf{w}_d^\top \mathbf{x}_u^{(\ell)} + b_d\right), \quad \alpha_u^{(\ell)} \in (0, 1), \tag{3}$$

where $\sigma(\cdot)$ is the sigmoid function, and $\mathbf{w}_d$ and b_d are learnable parameters. To maintain dimensional consistency in residual paths, a projection basis is defined as

$$\text{base}\left(\mathbf{x}_u^{(\ell)}\right) = \begin{cases} \mathbf{P}\mathbf{x}_u^{(\ell)}, & F \neq D, \\ \mathbf{x}_u^{(\ell)}, & F = D, \end{cases} \tag{4}$$

where F is the input feature dimension, D is the hidden dimension, and $\mathbf{P}$ is a linear projection matrix. The final intra-layer representation is obtained by damping the GIN aggregation and the projected node basis:

$$\mathbf{h}_u^{(\ell)} = \alpha_u^{(\ell)} \cdot \text{GIN}\left(\mathbf{x}_u^{(\ell)}, E^{(\ell)}\right) + \left(1 - \alpha_u^{(\ell)}\right) \cdot \text{base}\left(\mathbf{x}_u^{(\ell)}\right). \tag{5}$$

This design captures relation-specific structure-feature semantics without introducing cross-layer noise. The damping coefficient is computed from the node features in the current implementation. This design keeps the gate lightweight, while more structure-aware variants could additionally incorporate degree or neighborhood statistics when richer local structural signals are available.

4.2 Cross-Layer Heterogeneous Alignment

After intra-layer encoding, representations from different layers still lie in different semantic spaces. Given two layer embedding matrices $\mathbf{H}^{(\ell_1)}$ and $\mathbf{H}^{(\ell_2)} \in \mathbb{R}^{N \times D}$, their normalized forms $\widetilde{\mathbf{H}}^{(\ell)}$ are used to build the inter-layer similarity matrix:

$$\mathbf{S}^{(\ell_1,\ell_2)} = \widetilde{\mathbf{H}}^{(\ell_1)} \left(\widetilde{\mathbf{H}}^{(\ell_2)}\right)^{\top} \in \mathbb{R}^{N \times N}. \tag{6}$$

With temperature $\tau > 0$, the cross-layer contrastive loss is

$$\mathcal{L}_{\text{cl}}^{(\ell_1,\ell_2)} = -\sum_{i=1}^{N} \log \frac{\exp\left(S_{i,i}^{(\ell_1,\ell_2)}/\tau\right)}{\sum_{j=1}^{N} \exp\left(S_{i,j}^{(\ell_1,\ell_2)}/\tau\right)}. \tag{7}$$

The positive pair is the representation of the same node across two layers, and negative pairs are cross-layer representations of different nodes. In this work, a learnable matrix $C \in \mathbb{R}^{L \times L}$ is transformed into row-wise softmax weights, and the losses over all layer pairs are aggregated as

$$\mathcal{L}_{cl} = \sum_{\ell_1=1}^{L} \sum_{\ell_2 \neq \ell_1} w_{\ell_1,\ell_2} \cdot \mathcal{L}_{\text{cl}}^{(\ell_1,\ell_2)}, \quad w_{\ell_1,\ell_2} = \frac{\exp(C_{\ell_1,\ell_2})}{\sum_{r \neq \ell_1} \exp(C_{\ell_1,r})}. \tag{8}$$

The adaptive weights avoid forcing all layer pairs to contribute equally to the alignment objective. This is useful because relation layers may differ in density, semantics, and noise level, so uniformly averaging all pairwise losses can overemphasize weakly related or noisy layer pairs. For very small datasets, the number of in-batch negative samples is limited; memory banks or cross-batch negatives are possible extensions when stronger contrastive signals are required.

4.3 Dynamic Cross-Layer Attention

Conventional multiplex models often use static cross-layer probabilities. Dyna-CLIM instead learns node-specific and directed cross-layer attention weights. For a source layer s and a target layer t with $s \neq t$, the migration score of node u is

$$r_u^{(s \to t)} = \mathbf{w}_g^\top \left[\mathbf{h}_u^{(s)} \| \mathbf{h}_u^{(t)}\right] + b_{s,t}, \tag{9}$$

where $[\cdot\|\cdot]$ denotes vector concatenation and $b_{s,t}$ is a layer-pair-specific bias. The dynamic cross-layer attention weight is

$$\theta_u^{(s \to t)} = \sigma\left(r_u^{(s \to t)}\right) \in (0, 1). \tag{10}$$

This weight describes how strongly the representation of node u in layer s is routed to its identity state in layer t in the learned feature space. The mechanism is asymmetric because $\theta_u^{(s \to t)}$ and $\theta_u^{(t \to s)}$ are not generally equal. These weights are learned coupling indicators rather than causal evidence of real-world propagation.

4.4 Aggregation and Pseudo-Regression Prediction

Given dynamic cross-layer attention weights, Dyna-CLIM performs soft-routing aggregation. For target layer t, the fused representation is

$$\widetilde{\mathbf{h}}_u^{(t)} = \mathbf{h}_u^{(t)} + \sum_{s \neq t} \theta_u^{(s \to t)} \cdot \mathbf{h}_u^{(s)}. \tag{11}$$

The final global representation is obtained by averaging fused representations over all layers:

$$\mathbf{z}_u = \frac{1}{L} \sum_{t=1}^{L} \widetilde{\mathbf{h}}_u^{(t)}. \tag{12}$$

The global representation is fed into a two-layer MLP regression head to obtain the continuous influence score:

$$\hat{y}_u = \mathbf{w}_2^\top \mathrm{ReLU}\left(\mathbf{W}_1 \mathbf{z}_u + \mathbf{b}_1\right) + b_2. \tag{13}$$

Compared with discrete ranking, pseudo-regression captures fine-grained differences in spreading range and provides a numerical basis for ranking-based candidate seed selection.

4.5 Joint Loss Optimization

Dyna-CLIM is trained end to end. To improve influence fitting while maintaining cross-layer consistency, the total loss combines a supervised score-fitting loss and the contrastive alignment loss:

$$\mathcal{L} = \mathcal{L}_{\text{fit}} + \lambda \cdot \mathcal{L}_{\text{cl}}, \tag{14}$$

where the score-fitting loss is

$$\mathcal{L}_{\text{fit}} = \frac{1}{|\mathcal{I}_{\text{tr}}|} \sum_{u \in \mathcal{I}_{\text{tr}}} (\hat{y}_u - y_u)^2. \tag{15}$$

Here y_u is the offline diffusion label, $\mathcal{I}_{\text{tr}}$ denotes the training node set, and λ controls the contrastive constraint. The efficiency gain mainly refers to online inference: after offline training, Dyna-CLIM uses a forward pass and Top-k sorting instead of repeated diffusion simulation. The offline cost consists of pseudo-label simulation and model training, whereas seed selection no longer requires repeated diffusion evaluation for each candidate set. The learned attention weights $\theta_u^{(s \to t)}$ can also be extracted for interpreting layer-to-layer coupling patterns.

5 Experiments

5.1 Datasets

Four real multiplex social network datasets are used to evaluate effectiveness. TailorShop records social interaction patterns among employees in a tailor shop and is commonly used in multilayer network studies [1]. LazegaLawyers is derived from a sociological survey of a law firm and contains coworking, advice, and friendship relations [26]. CKM describes medical innovation diffusion among physicians through consultation, discussion, and friendship relations [27]. SCHOLAT[2] is a large-scale academic social network containing 2,302 scholar nodes and released as an open multiplex network dataset. Dataset statistics are reported in Table 1.

The layer-wise density and critical propagation probability are defined as

$$\rho_\ell = \frac{2|E_\ell|}{|V|(|V|-1)}, \quad p_\ell^{\text{crit}} = \frac{1}{(|V|-1)\rho_\ell}. \tag{16}$$

5.2 Baselines

Following prior multi-layer IM comparisons, we categorize the compared methods into single-layer and multi-layer baselines. Single-layer baselines are first applied to a union graph constructed by merging all relation layers, while multi-layer baselines follow their original multilayer settings. The seed sets selected by all methods are then evaluated under the same Multi-SIR, Multi-IC, and Multi-LT simulators.

- DC selects seed nodes according to degree centrality [28].
- CC ranks nodes by closeness centrality over reachable paths [29].
- BC measures node importance by shortest-path betweenness [30].
- ISBC enhances betweenness-based ranking with isolation-aware influence measurement [31].

[2] https://www.scholat.com/research/opendata/#multiplex_network.

Table 1. Statistics of the experimental datasets.

Dataset	Layer	Nodes	Edges	ρ_ℓ	p_ℓ^{crit}
TailorShop	1	39	158	0.2130	0.123
	2	39	223	0.3010	0.087
	3	39	76	0.1030	0.257
	4	39	95	0.1280	0.205
LazegaLawyers	1	71	717	0.2890	0.050
	2	71	399	0.1610	0.089
	3	71	378	0.1520	0.094
CKM	1	241	449	0.0155	0.268
	2	241	498	0.0172	0.242
	3	241	423	0.0146	0.285
SCHOLAT	1	2302	11,393	0.00430	0.101
	2	2302	139,004	0.0525	0.008
	3	2302	70,226	0.0265	0.016

- K-Shell ranks nodes according to their core positions in the network hierarchy [17].
- IM-ELPR combines extended H-index ranking, label propagation, and community refinement [32].
- KSN is a knapsack-based multilayer IM heuristic using layer-wise decomposition [11].
- ISF is a greedy multilayer IM strategy under heterogeneous diffusion settings [11].
- CIM selects influential nodes based on clique structures in multilayer networks [12].
- DPSOMIM applies discrete particle swarm optimization to multilayer IM [13].
- MIM-Reasoner supports multiplex IM through learning-based reasoning with theoretical guarantees [14].

5.3 Experimental Setup

All multiplex layers are aligned by shared node identities and converted into unweighted undirected graphs after removing duplicate edges and self-loops. Since external attributes are unavailable, nodes are initialized by identity indicators and projected into a dense feature space. Dyna-CLIM is trained with Adam using a learning rate of 10^{-3}, weight decay of 5×10^{-4}, hidden dimension of 64, contrastive temperature $\tau = 0.1$, and alignment weight $\lambda = 0.2$. Ten percent of nodes are used for supervised pseudo-label training, while all nodes are ranked as candidates under a transductive influence-ranking protocol.

Pseudo labels are generated by 1,000 single-source Multi-SIR simulations, and the average final infected-or-recovered size is used as the target influence score [22]. This supervision may favor SIR-like diffusion behavior, so Multi-IC and Multi-LT are included as cross-model evaluation settings to examine whether the learned rankings capture more general structural influence potential. The selected Top-k seeds are evaluated under Multi-SIR, Multi-IC, and Multi-LT. For Multi-SIR, the layer-wise infection probability is set to p_ℓ^{crit} in Table 1 and the recovery probability is fixed to 1. For Multi-IC, each newly activated node has one chance to activate each inactive neighbor with probability p_ℓ^{crit}. For Multi-LT, node thresholds are sampled uniformly from $(0, 1)$, and activation depends on normalized cumulative influence from activated neighbors [3]. The maximum propagation depth is set to step $= 5$, and each evaluation is repeated 1,000 times. TailorShop and LazegaLawyers use $k = 10$, while CKM and SCHOLAT use 10% of nodes as the seed budget.

All experiments are conducted on a workstation equipped with an Intel Xeon Silver 4210R CPU, 64 GB RAM, and one NVIDIA RTX 3090 GPU with 24 GB memory. The implementation is based on PyTorch and PyTorch Geometric. To substantiate the efficiency claim, Table 2 reports the training time, inference time, peak GPU memory, and offline diffusion-simulation budget. Training time covers representation learning, contrastive alignment, and pseudo-regression optimization. Inference time denotes one forward pass over all nodes plus Top-k ranking. Dyna-CLIM remains lightweight across the four datasets; after offline training, online seed selection only requires a single forward pass and sorting operation, avoiding repeated diffusion simulation during seed selection.

Table 2. Efficiency statistics of Dyna-CLIM on four multiplex datasets.

Dataset	Train time (s)	Inference time (ms)	Peak memory (MB)	Simulation budget
TailorShop	7.8	1.6	312	39×1000 runs
LazegaLawyers	10.4	2.3	336	71×1000 runs
CKM	14.9	3.8	371	241×1000 runs
SCHOLAT	68.5	24.7	824	2302×1000 runs

Training time is reported for one complete training run. Inference time denotes one forward pass over all nodes plus top-k ranking

5.4 Evaluation Metrics

The Top-k nodes ranked by predicted score are selected as seeds and evaluated under multiplex diffusion simulation. The mean activated size over 1,000 simulation runs is reported as $N(k)$, which measures the diffusion range of the selected seed set under Multi-SIR, Multi-IC, and Multi-LT. To measure redundancy among selected seeds, the structural dispersion metric is computed on the union graph:

$$D_{\mathrm{avg}} = \frac{\sum_{u,v \in S,\ u \neq v} D_{u,v}}{k(k-1)}, \tag{17}$$

where $D_{u,v}$ is the shortest-path distance between two selected seeds in the union graph. A larger D_{avg} indicates more dispersed seeds and lower diffusion overlap.

This metric provides an indirect check on redundancy among selected seeds, although it does not replace explicit marginal-gain optimization.

5.5 Performance Analysis

Table 3 reports the influence range $N(k)$ under Multi-SIR, Multi-IC, and Multi-LT. As shown in the table, Dyna-CLIM obtains the best value in all twelve dataset–diffusion settings and improves over the strongest remaining baseline by about 9.60% on average. The comparison suggests that dynamic cross-layer attention is associated with consistent gains under different diffusion assumptions, especially on SCHOLAT with friendship, team, and course layers. Since the model is trained with Multi-SIR pseudo labels, the gains under Multi-IC and Multi-LT indicate cross-protocol robustness rather than direct supervision under those two models (Table 4).

Table 3. Influence range $N(k)$ of different methods under Multi-SIR, Multi-IC, and Multi-LT.

Model	TailorShop			LazegaLawyers			CKM			SCHOLAT		
	Multi-SIR	Multi-IC	Multi-LT	Multi-SIR	Multi-IC	Multi-LT	Multi-SIR	Multi-IC	Multi-LT	Multi-SIR	Multi-IC	Multi-LT
DC [28]	33.7	32.8	37.7	54.2	48.8	59.3	158.1	146.8	47.0	1255.1	1198.9	497.7
CC [29]	33.7	32.6	37.7	54.6	49.1	59.3	89.1	85.3	42.9	1301.1	1243.1	1209.8
BC [30]	34.1	32.9	37.7	54.9	49.6	57.9	122.4	115.1	48.1	1406.8	1343.5	1494.4
ISBC [31]	33.8	32.6	37.9	52.9	45.7	12.8	100.2	94.1	35.7	1331.8	1265.3	1225.9
K-Shell [17]	32.4	30.7	31.8	52.6	45.8	20.1	89.3	83.9	37.3	1222.6	1153.1	345.8
IM-ELPR [32]	33.6	32.1	36.4	54.8	48.2	13.1	167.2	153.7	42.3	1394.4	1321.5	360.2
KSN [11]	33.3	34.2	16.0	53.5	53.0	11.7	125.2	149.4	83.9	1482.2	1530.7	246.8
ISF [11]	31.8	32.8	25.2	53.2	51.3	17.8	158.4	174.7	43.3	1457.4	1484.8	1157.7
CIM [12]	31.7	33.0	24.9	54.1	53.0	54.7	152.0	165.1	52.2	1376.9	1404.2	332.4
DPSOMIM [13]	34.3	34.6	37.8	54.8	53.7	21.2	162.9	178.0	85.9	1526.2	1534.5	1538.2
MIM-Reasoner [14]	33.1	33.9	13.7	52.8	51.4	12.1	144.1	172.3	36.3	1507.2	1526.2	421.3
Dyna-CLIM	**35.2**	**35.7**	**38.5**	**63.4**	**60.8**	**63.8**	**179.2**	**193.6**	**115.2**	**1628.7**	**1679.5**	**1620.4**

The best result in each column is highlighted in bold, and the second-best result is underlined

Table 4. Average seed distance D_{avg} on four datasets.

Model	TailorShop	LazegaLawyers	CKM	SCHOLAT
DC [28]	1.11	1.09	3.09	1.08
CC [29]	1.17	1.10	1.95	1.48
BC [30]	1.22	1.16	2.51	1.87
ISBC [31]	1.40	1.58	2.52	1.84
K-Shell [17]	1.09	1.24	2.18	1.03
IM-ELPR [32]	1.53	1.89	3.97	2.31
KSN [11]	1.71	1.73	4.07	2.11
ISF [11]	1.20	1.33	4.16	1.90
CIM [12]	1.11	1.02	3.29	1.02
DPSOMIM [13]	1.51	1.62	3.53	2.29
MIM-Reasoner [14]	1.77	1.58	4.27	2.71
Dyna-CLIM	**1.86**	**1.91**	**4.45**	**3.05**

The best result in each column is highlighted in bold, and the second-best result is underlined

Dyna-CLIM also achieves the highest D_{avg} on all datasets, suggesting that its selected candidate seeds are more structurally dispersed.

5.6 Ablation Study

To verify the contribution of each component, three variants are tested: w/o CL removes InfoNCE alignment by setting $\lambda = 0$; Fixed Attention replaces node-specific cross-layer attention with static mean fusion; w/o Damping fixes the damping coefficient to 1 and degenerates to standard GIN aggregation. The ablation results are visualized in Fig. 2, where the upper panel reports normalized $N(k)$ and the lower panel reports D_{avg}.

As shown in Fig. 2, removing contrastive alignment, dynamic attention, or damping weakens performance under Multi-SIR, suggesting that the three components are complementary.

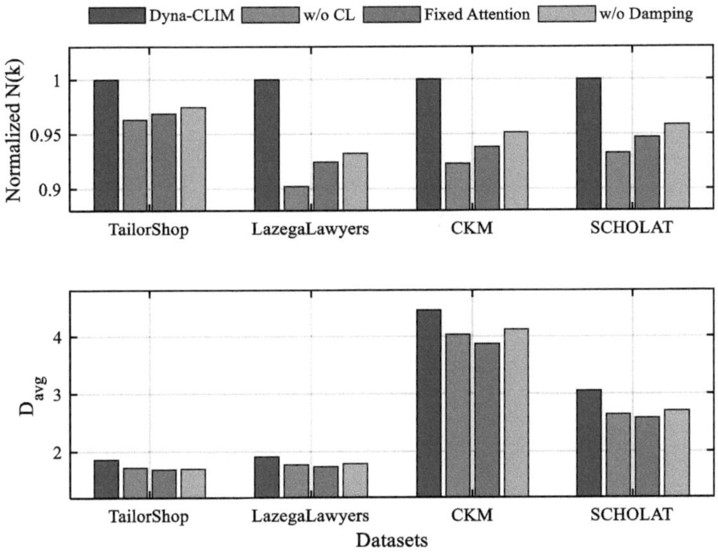

Fig. 2. Ablation visualization under Multi-SIR. The upper panel reports normalized influence range $N(k)$, and the lower panel reports seed dispersion D_{avg} across four datasets.

5.7 Interpretability Analysis

Dynamic cross-layer attention provides an interpretable view of learned coupling tendencies. Table 5 reports the average attention weights of the Top-10% high-influence nodes in SCHOLAT.

The attention matrix exhibits clear asymmetry. The weight from friendship to team is the largest, indicating a stronger learned coupling tendency in the model representation. The course layer has lower outward weights for the high-influence nodes considered here. These weights provide interpretable cross-layer coupling signals.

Table 5. Average cross-layer attention weights on SCHOLAT; diagonal entries are omitted because only $s \neq t$ transitions are modeled.

Source/target	Friendship	Team	Course
Friendship	–	0.68	0.53
Team	0.61	–	0.42
Course	0.38	0.47	–

5.8 Hyperparameter Sensitivity

We examine the maximum propagation depth step used in offline diffusion simulation. As shown in Fig. 3, performance generally improves from step = 0 to step = 5, indicating that deeper diffusion captures more valid cascade paths. At step = 10, small datasets degrade due to distant noise, while SCHOLAT shows only marginal additional gains.

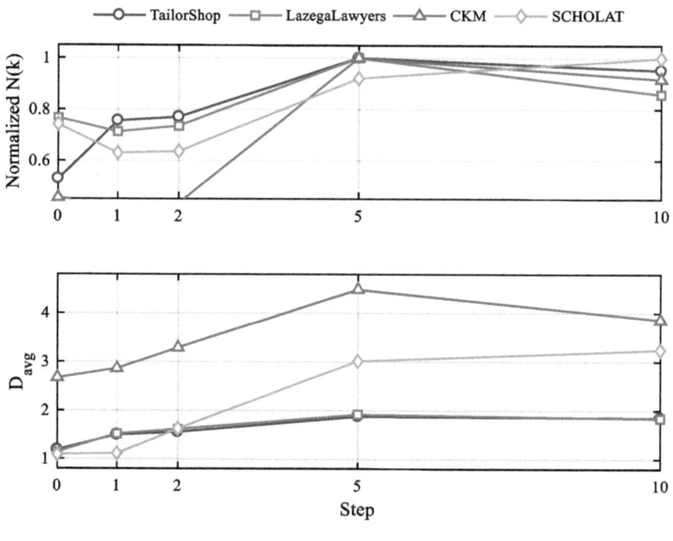

Fig. 3. Step sensitivity visualization under Multi-SIR. The upper panel shows normalized influence range $N(k)$ for different step values, and the lower panel shows the corresponding seed dispersion D_{avg}.

5.9 Limitations and Discussion

Dyna-CLIM focuses on efficient influence-aware ranking rather than exact combinatorial influence maximization. Therefore, the current Top-k selection procedure does not explicitly model marginal spread gain or audience overlap among already selected seeds. The seed dispersion metric partially evaluates this issue, but future work can combine the learned scores with diversity-aware or submodular re-ranking strategies.

The learned cross-layer attention weights should also be interpreted as representation-level coupling indicators, not as calibrated probabilities of real diffusion transitions. Their value is to expose asymmetric layer-to-layer dependencies useful for influence prediction, while a formal equivalence between attention weights and a specific diffusion model would require additional theoretical assumptions. Finally, the present experiments report mean performance over repeated diffusion simulations; repeated model training with confidence intervals or significance tests would provide a stronger assessment of statistical robustness.

6 Conclusion and Future Work

This paper presented Dyna-CLIM, a dynamic cross-layer attention model for node influence prediction in multiplex networks. The method models cross-layer coupling tendencies with representation-level soft routing and integrates intra-layer feature extraction, cross-layer heterogeneous alignment, node-specific directed attention, and pseudo-regression prediction. Experiments on multiple real multiplex social networks demonstrate that Dyna-CLIM improves diffusion spread and structural seed dispersion compared with representative baselines. The learned attention weights also provide intuitive signals of cross-layer coupling patterns.

Future work will explore simulation-efficient supervision, more efficient alignment and attention computation strategies for large-scale multiplex networks, and more explicit set-level seed selection objectives. Another direction is to extend the framework to dynamic multiplex networks, content-driven diffusion, and cross-platform information spread by incorporating temporal features, user interests, and semantic content.

Acknowledgments. This work was supported in part by the National Key Research and Development Program of China (Research and Demonstration Application of Key Technologies for Personalized Learning Driven by Educational Big Data) under Grant 2023YFC3341200, in part by the Guangdong Basic and Applied Basic Research Foundation (No. 2026A1515011870), and in part by the Youth S&T Talent Support Programme of Guangdong Provincial Association for Science and Technology (GDSTA) under Grants SKXRC2025022 and SKXRC2025028.

References

1. Kivelä, M., Arenas, A., Barthelemy, M., Gleeson, J.P., Moreno, Y., Porter, M.A.: Multilayer networks. J. Complex Netw. **2**(3), 203–271 (2014)
2. De Domenico, M.: More is different in real-world multilayer networks. Nat. Phys. **19**(9), 1247–1262 (2023)

3. Kempe, D., Kleinberg, J., Tardos, É.: Maximizing the spread of influence through a social network. In: Proceedings of the Ninth ACM SIGKDD International Conference on Knowledge Discovery and Data Miningm pp. 137–146 (2003)
4. Tang, Y., Shi, Y., Xiao, X.: Influence maximization in near-linear time: a martingale approach. In: Proceedings of the 2015 ACM SIGMOD International Conference on Management of Data, pp. 1539–1554 (2015)
5. Freeman, L.C.: Centrality in social networks conceptual clarification. Soc. Netw. **1**(3), 215–239 (1978)
6. Kumar, S., Lohia, D., Pratap, D., Krishna, A., Panda, B.: MDER: modified degree with exclusion ratio algorithm for influence maximisation in social networks. Computing **104**(2), 359–382 (2022)
7. Zhang, H., Zhong, S., Deng, Y., Cheong, K.H.: LFIC: identifying influential nodes in complex networks by local fuzzy information centrality. IEEE Trans. Fuzzy Syst. **30**(8), 3284–3296 (2022). https://doi.org/10.1109/TFUZZ.2021.3112226
8. Qiu, J., Tang, J., Ma, H., Dong, Y., Wang, K., Tang, J.: DeepInf: social influence prediction with deep learning. In: Proceedings of the 24th ACM SIGKDD International Conference on Knowledge Discovery & Data Mining, pp. 2110–2119 (2018)
9. Li, H., Xu, M., Bhowmick, S.S., Rayhan, J.S., Sun, C., Cui, J.: PIANO: influence maximization meets deep reinforcement learning. IEEE Trans. Comput. Soc. Syst. **10**(3), 1288–1300 (2022)
10. Li, Y., Gao, H., Gao, Y., Guo, J., Wu, W.: A survey on influence maximization: from an ML-Based combinatorial optimization. ACM Trans. Knowl. Discov. Data **17**(9), 1–50 (2023)
11. Kuhnle, A., Alim, M.A., Li, X., Zhang, H., Thai, M.T.: Multiplex influence maximization in online social networks with heterogeneous diffusion models. IEEE Trans. Comput. Soc. Syst. **5**(2), 418–429 (2018)
12. K, V.R., Katukuri, M., Jagarapu, M.: CIM: clique-based heuristic for finding influential nodes in multilayer networks. Appl. Intell. **52**, 5173–5184 (2022). https://doi.org/10.1007/s10489-021-02656-0
13. Wang, S., Liu, W., Chen, L., Zong, S.: Influence maximization based on discrete particle swarm optimization on multilayer network. Inf. Syst. **127**, 102466 (2025). https://doi.org/10.1016/j.is.2024.102466
14. Do, N.H.K., Chowdhury, T., Ling, C., Zhao, L., Thai, M.T.: MIM-Reasoner: learning with theoretical guarantees for multiplex influence maximization. In: Proceedings of the 27th International Conference on Artificial Intelligence and Statistics. Proceedings of Machine Learning Research, vol. 238, pp. 2296–2304. PMLR (2024)
15. Wang, X., Ji, H., Shi, C., Wang, B., Ye, Y., Cui, P., Yu, P.S.: Heterogeneous graph attention network. In: Proceedings of the World Wide Web Conference (WWW 2019), pp. 2022–2032 (2019)
16. Fu, X., Zhang, J., Meng, Z., King, I.: MAGNN: metapath aggregated graph neural network for heterogeneous graph embedding. In: Proceedings of the Web Conference 2020, pp. 2331–2341 (2020)
17. Kitsak, M., Gallos, L.K., Havlin, S., Liljeros, F., Muchnik, L., Stanley, H.E., Makse, H.A.: Identification of influential spreaders in complex networks. Nat. Phys. **6**(11), 888–893 (2010)
18. Ling, C., Jiang, J., Wang, J., Thai, M.T., Xue, R., Song, J., Qiu, M., Zhao, L.: Deep graph representation learning and optimization for influence maximization. In: Proceedings of the 40th International Conference on Machine Learning (ICML), pp. 21350–21361. PMLR (2023)

19. Vaswani, A., Shazeer, N., Parmar, N., Uszkoreit, J., Jones, L., Gomez, A.N., Kaiser, Ł., Polosukhin, I.: Attention is all you need. Advances in Neural Information Processing Systems **30** (2017)
20. Veličković, P., Cucurull, G., Casanova, A., Romero, A., Liò, P., Bengio, Y.: Graph attention networks. In: International Conference on Learning Representations (2018)
21. Zhuang, Y., Yağan, O.: Information propagation in clustered multilayer networks. IEEE Trans. Netw. Sci. Eng. **3**(4), 211–224 (2016)
22. Kermack, W.O., McKendrick, A.G.: A contribution to the mathematical theory of epidemics. Proc. Royal Soc. London Ser. A Contain. Pap. Math. Phys. Charact. **115**(772), 700–721 (1927)
23. Pathak, N., Banerjee, A., Srivastava, J.: A generalized linear threshold model for multiple cascades. In: 2010 IEEE International Conference on Data Mining, pp. 965–970. IEEE (2010)
24. Oord, A.v.d., Li, Y., Vinyals, O.: Representation learning with contrastive predictive coding. arXiv preprint arXiv:1807.03748 (2018)
25. Xu, K., Hu, W., Leskovec, J., Jegelka, S.: How powerful are graph neural networks? In: International Conference on Learning Representations (2019)
26. Snijders, T.A.B., Pattison, P.E., Robins, G.L., Handcock, M.S.: New specifications for exponential random graph models. Sociol. Methodol. **36**(1), 99–153 (2006)
27. Nasiri, E., Berahmand, K., Li, Y.: A new link prediction in multiplex networks using topologically biased random walks. Chaos Solitons Fractals **151**, 111230 (2021)
28. Gautam, R.K., Kare, A.S., Durga Bhavani, S.: Centrality measures based heuristics for perfect awareness problem in social networks. In: International Conference on Multi-disciplinary Trends in Artificial Intelligence, pp. 91–100. Springer (2023)
29. Liu, Z., Ye, J., Zou, Z.: Closeness centrality on uncertain graphs. ACM Trans. Web **17**(4), 1–29 (2023)
30. Zhang, Q., Deng, R., Ding, K., Li, M.: Structural analysis and the sum of nodes' betweenness centrality in complex networks. Chaos Solitons Fractals **185**, 115158 (2024)
31. Chiranjeevi, M., Dhuli, V.S., Enduri, M.K., Hajarathaiah, K., Cenkeramaddi, L.R.: Quantifying node influence in networks: isolating-betweenness centrality for improved ranking. IEEE Access **12**, 93711–93722 (2024)
32. Kumar, S., Singhla, L., Jindal, K., Grover, K., Panda, B.S.: IM-ELPR: influence maximization in social networks using label propagation based community structure. Appl. Intell. **51**(11), 7647–7665 (2021)

HARP: Hub-Routed Attention with Linear-Complexity Cross-Stock Interaction for Large-Universe Stock Prediction

Zekai Chen(✉)

School of Business, Soochow University, Suzhou, Jiangsu, China
cy1onch3n@gmail.com

Abstract. Cross-sectional stock prediction must model rich and time-varying interactions among hundreds to thousands of stocks. Existing deep models face three intertwined limitations: pairwise cross-stock attention scales as $\mathcal{O}(N^2)$ and becomes prohibitive once the universe exceeds a few hundred names; dense global attention conflates the identification of information hubs with the routing of information through them, producing diffuse and uninformative interaction patterns; and deep temporal stacks tend to overfit the low signal-to-noise regime of daily returns. We present **HARP**, a stock trend predictor built around a router-mediated cross-stock attention module. HARP introduces three matched designs: $K \ll N$ learnable router tokens that act as information bottlenecks and reduce the cross-stock cost from $\mathcal{O}(N^2)$ to $\mathcal{O}(NK)$; a two-stage gather-then-scatter mechanism that decouples hub identification from information routing and yields a sparse, interpretable hub-spoke pattern; and a lightweight attention-pooled temporal head that replaces deep temporal encoders. On CSI300 and CSI800, HARP attains the best result on five of six standard metrics on both datasets, reaches Information Ratios of 2.15 and 1.74, and recovers a long-short cumulative net value of 2.37 on CSI300 against an equal-weight benchmark of 0.92.

Keywords: Stock trend prediction · Cross-stock attention · Router-based attention · Financial time series · Quantitative trading

1 Introduction

Stock trend prediction is a foundational task in quantitative finance: even small improvements in cross-sectional ranking accuracy translate into substantial portfolio returns. Modern formulations are not univariate; the daily returns of hundreds to thousands of stocks must be predicted jointly, exploiting the rich and time-varying network of inter-stock relations [1].

Early deep models treated each stock as an isolated time series. A first wave of multi-stock models added cross-sectional context via attention over peer stocks

L. Ding et al. (Eds.): APWeb-WAIM 2026, LNCS 16993, pp. 250–265, 2027.
https://doi.org/10.1007/978-981-92-5693-8_16

[2] and via market-level feature gating [3]; subsequent work added cross-time interaction to capture lagged relations between non-aligned segments [4]. These designs inherit pairwise attention from natural language processing [5], which scales quadratically in the number of tokens. Efficient-attention variants developed for general time-series forecasting [6–9] target the time axis rather than the stock axis, leaving cross-stock attention quadratic in N. A complementary line replaces attention with MLP mixers [10] or with dynamic relational graphs [11,12], but at the price of expressivity or auxiliary supervision.

Three intertwined challenges remain. ***C1: Quadratic cost on the stock axis***. Self-attention across N stocks costs $\mathcal{O}(N^2d)$ in time and memory, tolerable on CSI300 ($N \approx 300$) but exhausting a consumer GPU on CSI800 ($N \approx 760$) and infeasible on a global universe; sparsifying along the time axis [6,9] does not help, since the stock axis lacks an analogue of temporal locality. ***C2: Conflated hub identification and information routing***. Pairwise attention treats every pair of stocks as a candidate edge and learns one weight per pair, conflating two distinct operations—identifying which stocks act as information hubs on a given day, and routing information through them to peripheral names—so the resulting attention maps are diffuse and rarely correspond to recognizable sectoral structure [3]. ***C3: Depth overfitting on low-SNR returns***. Recent stock models stack deep cross-time encoders on top of cross-stock blocks [4, 9]; daily returns have low signal-to-noise ratio and an effective sample size of one per day, so additional temporal layers inflate parameter count without a corresponding gain in usable signal.

We propose **HARP**, a stock trend predictor centered on a router-mediated cross-stock attention module with three matched components: ❶ **Router-mediated cross-stock attention** introduces $K \ll N$ learnable router tokens as information bottlenecks, reducing the cross-stock cost from $\mathcal{O}(N^2)$ to $\mathcal{O}(NK)$ (addresses C1); ❷ **two-stage gather-then-scatter** decouples hub identification from information routing, producing a sparse hub-spoke pattern over the implied stock-stock interaction matrix (addresses C2); and ❸ **attention-pooled temporal head** replaces deep cross-time encoders with a single attention pool over an LSTM, eliminating parameter inflation while preserving short-horizon temporal dependence (addresses C3).

On CSI300 and CSI800 with Alpha158 features, HARP attains the best result on five of six standard metrics on both datasets, reaches Information Ratios of 2.15 and 1.74, and delivers a long-short cumulative net value of 2.37 on CSI300 against an equal-weight benchmark of 0.92.

The contributions of this paper are:

1. We reformulate cross-stock interaction as decoupling hub identification from information routing through a small set of bottleneck tokens, and identify three intertwined limitations of pairwise cross-stock attention in large-universe stock prediction.
2. We design a router-mediated cross-stock attention module whose two-stage gather-then-scatter mechanism reduces the asymptotic complexity from

$\mathcal{O}(N^2d)$ to $\mathcal{O}(NKd)$, and we show that the implied stock-stock interaction exhibits a clean hub-spoke pattern with time-varying sectoral leaders.
3. We introduce a lightweight attention-pooled temporal head that avoids the parameter inflation of deep cross-time encoders, reducing the model from 148K to 98K parameters while improving RankIC.
4. Across eleven competitive baselines on CSI300 and CSI800, HARP attains the best result on five of six metrics on both datasets, with relative gains of up to 25% on RankIC over the strongest baseline.

The remainder of the paper is organized as follows. Section 2 reviews related work; Sect. 3 states the preliminaries; Sect. 4 presents the HARP architecture; Sect. 5 reports experimental results; Sect. 6 concludes.

2 Related Work

2.1 Graph and Hypergraph Models for Stock Prediction

Graph neural networks emerged as the natural tool for cross-stock interaction once single-stock encoders proved limiting. The graph attention network [13] provides a flexible mechanism to weight neighbors by learned scores, and was rapidly adopted alongside graph-convolutional architectures imported from traffic forecasting [14]. Subsequent work extended this paradigm to heterogeneous graphs that distinguish multiple relation types [15], attribute-driven attention for momentum spillover [16], top-K ranking with bipartite graphs [17], and knowledge-graph-augmented attention with executive-level entities [18]. Hierarchical adaptive temporal-relational modeling [19] composes a stock graph with a temporal encoder, while relational graph convolution [20] and multi-scale temporal hypergraph learning [21] have recently been applied to stock ranking. A parallel thread uses hypergraphs to capture group-wise relations beyond pairwise edges, including spatiotemporal hypergraph convolution [22], hypergraph attention with a learning-to-rank objective [23], tri-attention over temporal-relational hypergraphs [24], and industry-relation hypergraph attention [25]. All of these methods require a pre-specified or learned adjacency at $\mathcal{O}(N^2)$ cost, and the underlying interaction kernel remains pairwise once the graph or hypergraph convolution is unrolled.

2.2 Time-Series Transformers

Long-horizon forecasting has motivated a rich literature on efficient Transformer variants. Autoformer replaces dot-product attention with auto-correlation [26]; FEDformer projects attention into the frequency domain for linear complexity [27]; FiLM combines Legendre memory with frequency enhancement to mitigate noise overfitting [28]. DLinear [29] questioned the necessity of Transformers altogether, motivating channel-independent patching [7] and inverted formulations that treat variates as tokens [8]. TimesNet [30] reframes the temporal axis as a 2D structure to capture multi-period variation, and Crossformer [9] introduces cross-dimension attention with router tokens that mediate inter-variable information flow. We adapt the router design of Crossformer to a different statistical regime: the original routers were designed for multivariate forecasting with few stationary variables, whereas we target N in the hundreds with a daily varying universe. The adaptation requires reconsidering what a router represents and whether a cross-time encoder is still warranted; the latter receives a negative answer in our setting (Sect. 5.5).

3 Preliminary

3.1 Problem Formulation

We consider a stock universe $\mathcal{U} = \{u_1, u_2, \ldots, u_N\}$ in which N varies day by day due to listing or delisting. On trading day t, each stock $u_i \in \mathcal{U}_t$ is associated with a feature matrix $\mathbf{X}_i^t \in \mathbb{R}^{T \times F}$, where T is the lookback window and F is the number of per-stock features. The objective is to predict the h-day cumulative return $y_i^t \in \mathbb{R}$ for each stock at time $t+h$. Following standard practice [3,4], we set $T = 8$, $F = 158$, and $h = 5$.

Given the daily input tensor $\mathbf{X}^t \in \mathbb{R}^{N_t \times T \times F}$, the model produces a score vector $\hat{\mathbf{y}}^t \in \mathbb{R}^{N_t}$ that is later used to rank stocks for top-K portfolio construction. We denote the trainable parameters by Θ and the model by f_Θ. The central challenge is that future returns of different stocks are highly correlated, especially within the same sector or factor exposure, yet N_t ranges from a few hundred (CSI300) to over a thousand (CSI800), making naive pairwise attention $\mathcal{O}(N^2)$ prohibitive. Our framework addresses this with a router-mediated cross-stock attention mechanism that scales linearly in N.

3.2 Stock-Token Embedding

For each stock i, we project the lookback window into a d-dimensional token sequence:

$$\mathbf{H}_i = \text{LayerNorm}(\mathbf{X}_i \mathbf{W}_e + \mathbf{b}_e) + \mathbf{P}, \tag{1}$$

where $\mathbf{X}_i \in \mathbb{R}^{T \times F}$ is the per-stock feature matrix, $\mathbf{W}_e \in \mathbb{R}^{F \times d}$ and $\mathbf{b}_e \in \mathbb{R}^d$ are linear projection parameters, and $\mathbf{P} \in \mathbb{R}^{T \times d}$ is a learnable positional encoding shared across stocks. The output $\mathbf{H}_i \in \mathbb{R}^{T \times d}$ is treated as a length-T token sequence describing the recent state of stock i. Stacking across stocks yields $\mathbf{H} \in \mathbb{R}^{N \times T \times d}$, the input to the cross-stock interaction module of HARP.

4 Methodology

HARP consists of two core modules that operate on the embedded tensor $\mathbf{H}$ defined in Sect. 3.2. The first module, *router-mediated cross-stock attention*, performs interaction along the stock axis through a small set of learnable bottleneck tokens, and is responsible for the linear complexity in N together with the sparse hub-spoke structure that characterizes HARP's predictions. The second module, *temporal aggregation and prediction*, collapses the per-stock token sequence into a scalar score with a lightweight attention-pooled head. The two modules are connected by a single residual stream and trained end-to-end. The overall pipeline is illustrated in Fig. 1.

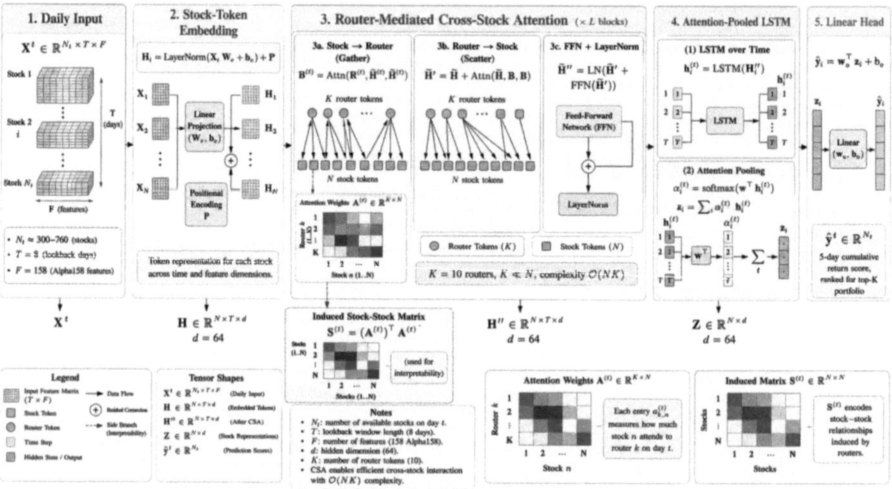

Fig. 1. Overall pipeline of HARP. The model takes a daily input tensor $\mathbf{X}^t \in \mathbb{R}^{N_t \times T \times F}$ (step 1) and produces a per-stock score vector $\hat{\mathbf{y}}^t \in \mathbb{R}^{N_t}$ (step 5) through five connected steps: stock-token embedding (step 2), router-mediated cross-stock attention with K bottleneck routers in a gather-then-scatter form (step 3), an attention-pooled LSTM head (step 4), and a linear regression head (step 5). The dashed side branch in step 3 highlights the induced stock-stock matrix $\mathbf{S}^{(t)} = (\mathbf{A}^{(t)})^\top \mathbf{A}^{(t)}$, used only for interpretability and not for prediction.

4.1 Router-Mediated Cross-Stock Attention

Stocks do not interact uniformly. On any given day, a small subset of bellwether names (index leaders, sector heads) absorbs most trading information and propagates it to peripheral names. A pairwise attention layer over N stocks computes a dense $N \times N$ map and conflates two distinct phenomena: identifying which stocks act as information hubs, and routing information through them. Decoupling these two phenomena yields a sparser, more interpretable, and substantially cheaper attention pattern.

We introduce $K \ll N$ learnable router tokens that act as information bottlenecks. Each router gathers signals from all stocks via one attention pass and redistributes them via a second attention pass. The resulting $\mathcal{O}(NK)$ complexity replaces the $\mathcal{O}(N^2)$ of naive cross-stock attention, while the small number of routers forces the model to compress cross-stock structure into a low-rank representation. As shown empirically (Sect. 5.7), this design produces a hub-spoke pattern in which the most influential stocks dominate the columns of the induced stock-stock attention matrix.

Let $\mathbf{R} \in \mathbb{R}^{T\times K\times d}$ denote the learnable router tokens, with the same number of segments T as the stock embeddings. We rearrange $\mathbf{H}$ into segment-major form $\widetilde{\mathbf{H}} \in \mathbb{R}^{T\times N\times d}$ so that within each time segment, all N stocks attend together.

Stock-to-Router (gather). The router tokens query the stocks:

$$\mathbf{B}^{(t)} = \mathrm{Attn}\Big(\mathbf{R}^{(t)}, \widetilde{\mathbf{H}}^{(t)}, \widetilde{\mathbf{H}}^{(t)}\Big), \quad t = 1, \ldots, T, \tag{2}$$

where $\mathrm{Attn}(\mathbf{Q}, \mathbf{K}, \mathbf{V})$ denotes multi-head scaled dot-product attention with h_a heads, and $\mathbf{B}^{(t)} \in \mathbb{R}^{K\times d}$ is the buffered representation at segment t. Each row of $\mathbf{B}^{(t)}$ aggregates a soft cluster of stocks weighted by their relevance to the corresponding router.

Router-to-Stock (scatter). Each stock then queries the router buffer:

$$\widetilde{\mathbf{H}}'^{(t)} = \widetilde{\mathbf{H}}^{(t)} + \mathrm{Attn}\Big(\widetilde{\mathbf{H}}^{(t)}, \mathbf{B}^{(t)}, \mathbf{B}^{(t)}\Big), \tag{3}$$

followed by layer normalization and a position-wise feed-forward network:

$$\widetilde{\mathbf{H}}''^{(t)} = \mathrm{LN}\Big(\widetilde{\mathbf{H}}'^{(t)} + \mathrm{FFN}(\widetilde{\mathbf{H}}'^{(t)})\Big). \tag{4}$$

The block is stacked L times. We rearrange back to $\mathbf{H}'' \in \mathbb{R}^{N\times T\times d}$ for the temporal head.

Induced Stock-Stock Attention. Although the model never instantiates a dense $N \times N$ matrix, the two-stage process induces an effective stock-stock interaction. Let $\mathbf{A}^{(t)} \in \mathbb{R}^{K\times N}$ be the attention weights of Eq. (2) averaged over heads. The implicit stock-stock relation at segment t is

$$\mathbf{S}^{(t)} = \big(\mathbf{A}^{(t)}\big)^{\top}\mathbf{A}^{(t)} \in \mathbb{R}^{N\times N}, \tag{5}$$

the extent to which two stocks are co-routed by the same set of routers. Column sums of $\mathbf{S}^{(t)}$ define a per-stock influence score that we use for the visualization in Fig. 5.

4.2 Temporal Aggregation and Prediction

After cross-stock interaction, each stock holds a sequence $\mathbf{H}''_i \in \mathbb{R}^{T\times d}$. We aggregate it into a single representation using an attention-pooled LSTM head. Let $\mathbf{h}_i^{(t)} \in \mathbb{R}^d$ denote the LSTM hidden state at segment t. The attention pool computes

$$\alpha_i^{(t)} = \frac{\exp(\mathbf{w}^{\top}\mathbf{h}_i^{(t)})}{\sum_{t'=1}^{T}\exp(\mathbf{w}^{\top}\mathbf{h}_i^{(t')})}, \qquad \mathbf{z}_i = \sum_{t=1}^{T}\alpha_i^{(t)}\mathbf{h}_i^{(t)}, \tag{6}$$

where $\mathbf{w} \in \mathbb{R}^d$ is a learnable query vector. The score is produced by a linear head

$$\hat{y}_i = \mathbf{w}_o^{\top}\mathbf{z}_i + b_o. \tag{7}$$

A natural alternative is to replace the attention pool with the segment-wise temporal encoder of Crossformer [9]. We deliberately do not adopt it. The look-back window is short ($T = 8$), and our ablation (Sect. 5.5) shows that this replacement reduces RankIC by approximately 4%. The attention pool of Eq. (6) captures the relevant temporal dependence at much lower cost: keeping the lightweight pool keeps the model at 98,561 parameters, whereas the cross-time encoder variant requires 148,545.

4.3 Training Objective

The model is trained with mean squared error against the realized h-day cumulative return:

$$\mathcal{L}(\Theta) = \frac{1}{|\mathcal{B}|} \sum_{(i,t)\in\mathcal{B}} \left(\hat{y}_i^t(\Theta) - y_i^t\right)^2, \tag{8}$$

where $\mathcal{B}$ is a mini-batch of (stock, day) pairs sampled day by day. We do not employ ranking-based losses or auxiliary regularizers: inductive bias should reside in the architecture rather than the objective.

4.4 Computational Complexity

For a single forward pass on day t with N_t stocks, the cost decomposes as follows. Token embedding is $\mathcal{O}(N_t TFd)$ and is shared across stocks. Router-mediated attention costs $\mathcal{O}(N_t TKd)$ per block (gather and scatter each $\mathcal{O}(N_t TKd)$). The temporal head is $\mathcal{O}(N_t Td^2)$. The overall per-day cost is

$$\mathcal{O}\big(N_t T(Fd + LKd + d^2)\big), \tag{9}$$

linear in N_t. By contrast, naive cross-stock self-attention requires $\mathcal{O}(N_t^2 Td)$ and becomes prohibitive once N_t exceeds several hundred. The savings are most pronounced on CSI800, where $N_t \approx 760$ and the naive variant fails to fit in 8GB of GPU memory under our training configuration.

5 Experiments

5.1 Datasets and Settings

We evaluate on the two most widely used Chinese A-share benchmarks: **CSI300**, the 300 largest and most liquid stocks, and **CSI800**, which extends the universe to roughly 760 stocks per day. Both datasets use Alpha158 features ($F = 158$), span the same time range, and share the test split from June 17, 2020 to December 30, 2022 (619 trading days). The label is the 5-day cumulative return. We split the time axis as in prior work [3,4], with a lookback of $T = 8$ days.

We train all methods with Adam, batch size of one trading day, and an early-stopping patience of 5 epochs evaluated on validation RankIC. The default HARP configuration uses $d = 64$, $K = 10$, $L = 1$, eight attention heads, and dropout 0.1, totaling 98,561 parameters. Each result is averaged over three seeds (2024, 2025, 2026). All experiments run on a single RTX 5070 Laptop GPU with 8GB memory.

We report six standard metrics: Information Coefficient (IC), risk-adjusted ICIR, rank-based RankIC and RankICIR, the annualized return AR of a top-30 equal-weight portfolio with 5-day rebalancing, and its Information Ratio IR. Higher is better for all six.

5.2 Baselines

We compare against eleven baselines covering three families. The first family contains general-purpose temporal models: LSTM, GRU, TCN, and DLinear [29]. The second contains attention-based time-series models: PatchTST [7], iTransformer [8], FiLM [28], and LightTS. The third contains finance-tailored sequence models with explicit cross-stock structure: a vanilla Transformer [5] applied per stock, GAT [13] for graph-based interaction, and DTML [2] for dual-level temporal modeling. All baselines are tuned with the same protocol as HARP.

5.3 Main Comparison

CSI300. Table 1 reports the comparison on CSI300. HARP achieves the best result on five of six metrics. The largest gain is on RankIC (0.0650 versus 0.052 from the second-best DTML, a relative improvement of 25%). The standard deviation of HARP is consistently among the smallest across all methods, indicating that the router-mediated attention not only improves accuracy but also stabilizes optimization. The annualized return of 0.204 is competitive with the strongest baselines (Transformer at 0.22, DTML at 0.21), and the IR of 2.147 is the highest in the table.

Table 1. Performance comparison on CSI300 with Alpha158 features. The best and **second-best** results in each column are highlighted.

Model	IC ↑	ICIR ↑	RankIC ↑	RankICIR ↑	AR ↑	IR ↑
FiLM	0.0349 ± 0.0058	0.230 ± 0.055	0.0319 ± 0.0082	0.198 ± 0.067	0.133 ± 0.045	1.377 ± 0.496
DLinear	0.0391 ± 0.0049	0.250 ± 0.036	0.0410 ± 0.0029	0.251 ± 0.022	0.133 ± 0.028	1.330 ± 0.297
LightTS	0.0420 ± 0.0026	0.276 ± 0.025	0.0407 ± 0.0017	0.255 ± 0.016	0.144 ± 0.019	1.474 ± 0.190
iTransformer	0.0430 ± 0.0030	0.279 ± 0.014	0.0419 ± 0.0020	0.256 ± 0.016	0.144 ± 0.036	1.536 ± 0.318
LSTM	0.0461 ± 0.0006	0.310 ± 0.005	0.0436 ± 0.0012	0.277 ± 0.006	0.134 ± 0.008	1.391 ± 0.102
GRU	0.0445 ± 0.0016	0.287 ± 0.020	0.0444 ± 0.0071	0.276 ± 0.055	0.151 ± 0.017	1.565 ± 0.203
PatchTST	0.0439 ± 0.0013	0.291 ± 0.034	0.0453 ± 0.0052	0.292 ± 0.061	0.166 ± 0.017	1.728 ± 0.114
TCN	0.0457 ± 0.0010	0.323 ± 0.028	0.0461 ± 0.0019	0.312 ± 0.036	0.156 ± 0.017	1.605 ± 0.216
Transformer	0.0472 ± 0.0071	**0.390 ± 0.041**	0.051 ± 0.002	**0.423 ± 0.045**	0.223 ± 0.068	**2.014 ± 0.417**
GAT	**0.054 ± 0.002**	0.362 ± 0.023	0.041 ± 0.002	0.252 ± 0.024	0.190 ± 0.035	1.313 ± 0.304
DTML	0.049 ± 0.006	0.335 ± 0.041	**0.052 ± 0.005**	0.334 ± 0.047	**0.218 ± 0.032**	1.714 ± 0.325
HARP	0.0573 ± 0.0017	0.399 ± 0.005	0.0650 ± 0.0032	0.450 ± 0.041	0.204 ± 0.010	2.147 ± 0.077

CSI800. Table 2 confirms the picture under a substantially harder setting where the universe roughly triples. HARP attains the best result on five of six metrics.

The advantage on RankIC (0.0579 versus 0.0481 from DTML, a relative gain of 20%) is preserved, and the gap on RankICIR widens to 15% over the runner-up. Methods that scale poorly in N degrade: PatchTST and iTransformer lose more than half of their CSI300 IR when moved to CSI800. The router-mediated design retains its advantage because its cost grows linearly in N, in line with the complexity analysis in Sect. 4.4.

Table 2. Performance comparison on CSI800 with Alpha158 features. The best and **second-best** results in each column are highlighted.

Model	IC ↑	ICIR ↑	RankIC ↑	RankICIR ↑	AR ↑	IR ↑
FiLM	0.0298 ± 0.0041	0.252 ± 0.038	0.0371 ± 0.0049	0.305 ± 0.054	0.082 ± 0.024	0.881 ± 0.286
DLinear	0.0310 ± 0.0033	0.269 ± 0.045	0.0397 ± 0.0035	0.331 ± 0.049	0.067 ± 0.038	0.679 ± 0.385
LightTS	0.0334 ± 0.0024	0.288 ± 0.027	0.0381 ± 0.0028	0.318 ± 0.031	0.094 ± 0.020	1.012 ± 0.215
iTransformer	0.0341 ± 0.0035	0.291 ± 0.041	0.0398 ± 0.0044	0.330 ± 0.052	0.108 ± 0.027	1.151 ± 0.298
LSTM	0.0363 ± 0.0019	0.333 ± 0.046	0.0399 ± 0.0061	0.353 ± 0.094	0.135 ± 0.033	1.437 ± 0.318
GRU	0.0365 ± 0.0033	0.323 ± 0.057	0.0460 ± 0.0042	0.398 ± 0.077	0.137 ± 0.036	1.448 ± 0.466
PatchTST	0.0352 ± 0.0021	0.305 ± 0.030	0.0428 ± 0.0040	0.362 ± 0.058	0.124 ± 0.018	1.328 ± 0.197
TCN	0.0315 ± 0.0017	0.278 ± 0.029	0.0440 ± 0.0038	0.378 ± 0.048	0.131 ± 0.011	1.424 ± 0.106
Transformer	0.0368 ± 0.0058	0.357 ± 0.044	0.0467 ± 0.0042	0.421 ± 0.031	0.142 ± 0.039	1.512 ± 0.354
GAT	0.0370 ± 0.0027	**0.339 ± 0.029**	0.0454 ± 0.0024	0.385 ± 0.022	0.149 ± 0.018	1.563 ± 0.247
DTML	0.0369 ± 0.0050	0.348 ± 0.039	**0.0481 ± 0.0048**	**0.412 ± 0.041**	**0.156 ± 0.029**	**1.621 ± 0.286**
HARP	0.0392 ± 0.0013	0.326 ± 0.007	0.0579 ± 0.0020	0.474 ± 0.023	0.160 ± 0.014	1.745 ± 0.161

Portfolio Backtest. Figure 2 translates ranking quality into realized portfolio returns. The figure reports the cumulative net value of a long-short strategy that buys the top-30 stocks and shorts the bottom-30 every five trading days on CSI300, with the shaded band showing the standard deviation across three seeds and the dashed line denoting the equal-weight market benchmark. HARP reaches a final net value of 2.37, exceeding the four baselines (LSTM, GRU, TCN, DLinear) shown in the figure and clearing the equal-weight benchmark of 0.92 by a wide margin. The same strategy on CSI800 reaches 2.11 over the same period against an equal-weight benchmark of 0.96, confirming that the ranking advantage extends to the larger universe. Consistent with this, the Information Ratios in Tables 1 and 2 reach 2.147 on CSI300 and 1.745 on CSI800, the highest among all eleven baselines on both datasets, and the standard deviation of HARP's IR on CSI300 is the smallest in the table.

5.4 Efficiency-Performance Trade-Off

A deployable stock predictor must be efficient in both parameters and computation, particularly as the universe size N grows. Figure 3 jointly visualizes predictive quality (RankIC, y-axis), wall-clock training cost (training time per epoch, x-axis), and parameter count (bubble area). All twelve models are trained in the same pipeline on the same hardware, so the comparison is direct.

Pareto frontier. HARP occupies the upper-left region of both panels. With 98.6K parameters and 32 seconds per epoch, HARP attains a RankIC of 0.0650

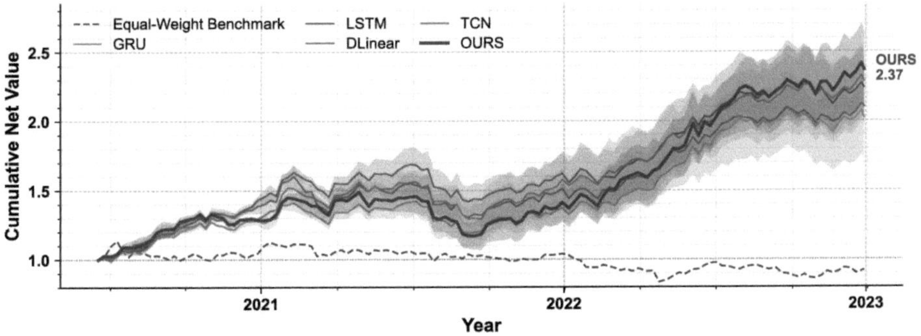

Fig. 2. Cumulative net value of long-short top/bottom-30 portfolios on CSI300, rebalanced every five trading days. Shaded bands denote one standard deviation over three seeds. The dashed line is the equal-weight market benchmark. HARP (dark blue) reaches a final net value of 2.37, the highest among all curves; the corresponding numbers on CSI800 and the Information Ratios on both datasets are reported in Tables 1 and 2.

on CSI300 and 0.0579 on CSI800, both higher than every competing baseline. The contrast against PatchTST is informative: PatchTST allocates the largest parameter budget (398.4K, four times that of HARP) and the longest training time per epoch (55 seconds), yet its RankIC on CSI300 is 30% lower than HARP (0.0453 versus 0.0650). FiLM exhibits a similar pattern with 209.7K parameters and the lowest RankIC of all twelve models on CSI300 (0.0319).
Capacity does not explain the gap. The strongest baselines—DTML, Transformer, and PatchTST—all carry larger parameter budgets and longer training times without achieving comparable RankIC. The natural reading is that pairwise cross-stock attention is a fundamentally limited mechanism that additional capacity does not rescue. The training-time advantage is consistent with the linear-complexity analysis of Sect. 4.4: the cross-stock cost is $\mathcal{O}(NK)$ rather than $\mathcal{O}(N^2)$, so HARP scales gracefully from CSI300 ($N \approx 300$) to CSI800 ($N \approx 760$) without the parameter inflation observed in pairwise-attention baselines.

5.5 Ablation Study

Table 3 isolates the contribution of HARP's two core modules on CSI300. Removing the router-mediated cross-stock attention module (*w/o Router-Mediated CSA*) is the most damaging change: RankIC drops from 0.0650 to 0.0507 (−22%), AR drops from 0.204 to 0.175 (−14%), and the parameter count falls only by 23%, ruling out a capacity-based explanation. Replacing the attention-pooled temporal head with a Crossformer-style cross-time encoder (*w/o Temporal Aggregation*) slightly degrades RankIC and IR while inflating the model from 98K to 148K parameters, confirming that within an eight-step window the lightweight attention pool already captures the relevant temporal dependence and a heavier temporal stack only adds redundant features. The complementary

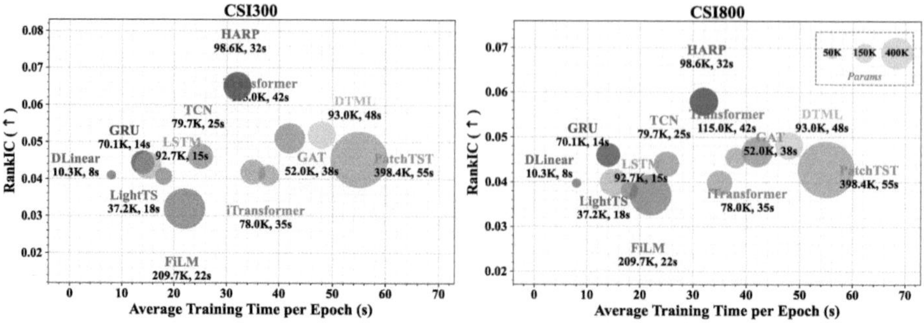

Fig. 3. Efficiency-performance trade-off on CSI300 (left) and CSI800 (right). Each bubble represents one of the twelve models. Bubble area is proportional to parameter count (see the dashed reference legend in the right panel: 50K, 150K, 400K). The colored label next to each bubble names the model; the second line gives "parameters, training time per epoch". HARP (dark red) attains the highest RankIC on both datasets while using fewer parameters and less training time than the strongest baselines (DTML, Transformer, PatchTST).

sweep over hidden width d, router count K, and encoder depth L is reported visually in the sensitivity analysis below (Fig. 4).

Table 3. Component ablation on CSI300. **HARP** is the default configuration. Each variant modifies one of HARP's two core modules: the router-mediated cross-stock attention (RM-CSA) is removed, or the attention-pooled temporal head is replaced with a Crossformer-style cross-time encoder. Reported values are mean ± std over 3 seeds.

Variant	Params	IC ↑	ICIR ↑	RankIC ↑	RankICIR ↑	AR ↑	IR ↑
HARP (default)	**98K**	**0.0573 ± 0.0017**	**0.399 ± 0.005**	**0.0650 ± 0.0032**	**0.450 ± 0.041**	**0.204 ± 0.010**	**2.147 ± 0.077**
w/o Router-Mediated CSA	76K	0.0492 ± 0.0046	0.383 ± 0.040	0.0507 ± 0.0057	0.383 ± 0.054	0.175 ± 0.030	1.805 ± 0.277
w/o Temporal Aggregation	148K	0.0563 ± 0.0032	0.402 ± 0.026	0.0627 ± 0.0026	0.438 ± 0.017	0.199 ± 0.011	2.081 ± 0.150

5.6 Sensitivity Analysis

Figure 4 provides a finer view of how each hyperparameter affects all six metrics. Each row corresponds to one hyperparameter (d, K, or L), each column to one metric. The red circle marks the HARP default and the gray band shades the suboptimal region. The default lies at the peak in twelve of eighteen panels and within one standard deviation of the peak in the remaining six. The most pronounced sensitivity is to encoder depth L: every metric in the bottom row drops sharply at $L = 2$ and partially recovers at $L = 3$, indicating that the loss with deeper encoders is not a smooth monotone effect but the onset of optimization difficulty. The middle row confirms that K is the least sensitive of the three knobs, with all six metrics nearly flat across $K \in [5, 20]$.

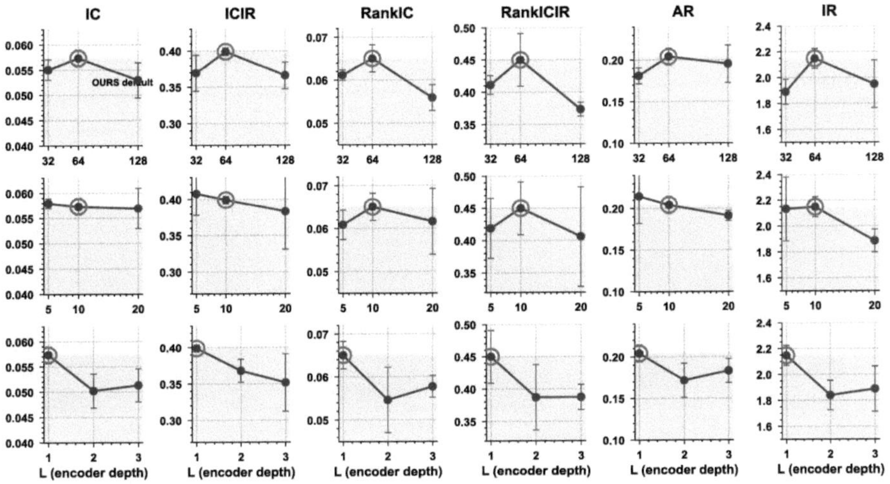

Fig. 4. Sensitivity of HARP on CSI300 to three hyperparameters (rows: d, K, L) across six evaluation metrics (columns). Error bars are one standard deviation over three seeds. The red circle marks the HARP default; the gray band shades the suboptimal region.

5.7 Case Study: Cross-Stock Attention Pattern

Figure 5 visualizes the induced stock-stock attention $\mathbf{S}^{(t)}$ defined in Eq. (5) on three representative trading days. The selection covers a bullish post-COVID rally (July 2020), a bearish phase during the early Russia-Ukraine conflict (April 2022), and a volatile period with sector rotation (October 2022). For each day, the main panel shows the top-50 most influential stocks ordered by their column sum of $\mathbf{S}^{(t)}$; the inset shows the full $N = 300$ matrix with a red box marking the zoomed region.

A consistent hub-spoke structure emerges across all three regimes: the top-left block is significantly brighter than the rest of the matrix, indicating that a small group of stocks accounts for most of the cross-stock information flow. The structure is not uniform. In the bullish regime the bright region is tight and concentrated around the top-10 stocks, consistent with momentum buying being narrowly led. In the bearish regime the bright band extends to the top-25 with a more distributed pattern, mirroring cross-sector contagion typical of risk-off episodes. In the volatile regime the bright region is laterally extended, suggesting that information flows from a small set of leaders to a broader periphery.

The identity of the hub stocks also varies with the regime. The most influential names on July 3, 2020 include vaccine-related companies, aligning with sector momentum during the post-COVID rally. On April 15, 2022 the leaders are dominated by financials and large-cap banks. On October 31, 2022 the leaders shift to technology firms listed on the STAR Market. The cross-stock attention is therefore neither static nor tied to market capitalization alone; it adapts to which sectors are driving information flow at each point in time. This dynamic, sparse, and interpretable interaction is what the router-mediated attention is designed to produce, and it is the structural reason behind the consistent ranking gains in Tables 1 and 2.

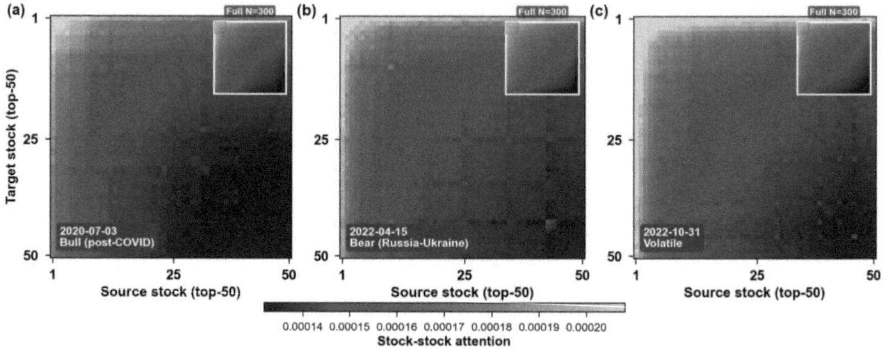

Fig. 5. Induced stock-stock attention $\mathbf{S}^{(t)}$ on three representative trading days. Stocks are sorted in descending order of column-sum influence; the main panel shows the top-50 region and the inset shows the full $N = 300$ matrix with the red box marking the zoomed area. A hub-spoke pattern is present in all three regimes, with the spread and identity of the leading hubs varying with the market state.

6 Conclusion

This paper proposes **HARP**, a router-mediated cross-stock attention model that addresses three intertwined limitations of pairwise cross-stock attention: a small set of router tokens reduces the cross-stock cost from $\mathcal{O}(N^2)$ to $\mathcal{O}(NK)$; a gather-then-scatter mechanism produces a sparse hub-spoke interaction pattern; and a lightweight attention-pooled temporal head avoids the overfitting of deep temporal stacks. On CSI300 and CSI800, HARP attains the best result on five of six metrics, with Information Ratios of 2.15 and 1.74, and a long-short cumulative net value of 2.37 on CSI300 against an equal-weight benchmark of 0.92. The learned routers automatically discover time-varying sectoral leaders, providing a degree of interpretability that pairwise attention does not afford. HARP achieves these results with 98,561 parameters and 32 seconds per training epoch on a single 8GB consumer GPU, fitting comfortably below the cost of every competing baseline. Two directions deserve further study: extending the routers to span multiple market segments so that information can flow across regional or asset-class boundaries, and combining HARP with a market-state controller so that the number and behavior of routers adapts to changing market regimes.

References

1. Feng, F., He, X., Wang, X., Luo, C., Liu, Y., Chua, T.-S.: Temporal relational ranking for stock prediction. ACM Trans. Inf. Syst. **37**(2), 1–30 (2019). https://doi.org/10.1145/3309547
2. Yoo, J., Soun, Y., Park, Y., Kang, U.: Accurate multivariate stock movement prediction via data-axis transformer with multi-level contexts. In: Proceedings of the 27th ACM SIGKDD Conference on Knowledge Discovery and Data Mining, Singapore, 2021, pp. 2037–2045. https://doi.org/10.1145/3447548.3467297
3. Li, T., Liu, Z., Shen, Y., Wang, X., Chen, H., Huang, S.: MASTER: market-guided stock transformer for stock price forecasting. Proc. AAAI Conf. Artif. Intell. **38**(1), 162–170 (2024). https://doi.org/10.1609/aaai.v38i1.27767
4. Cao, Z., Xu, J., Dong, C., Yu, P., Bai, T.: MATCC: a novel approach for robust stock price prediction incorporating market trends and cross-time correlations. In: Proceedings of the 33rd ACM International Conference on Information and Knowledge Management, Boise, ID, USA, 2024, pp. 187–196. https://doi.org/10.1145/3627673.3679715
5. Vaswani, A., Shazeer, N., Parmar, N., et al.: Attention is all you need. Proc. Adv. Neural Inf. Process. Syst. **30**, 5998–6008 (2017)
6. Zhou, H., Zhang, S., Peng, J., et al.: Informer: beyond efficient transformer for long sequence time-series forecasting. Proc. AAAI Conf. Artif. Intell. **35**(12), 11106–11115 (2021). https://doi.org/10.1609/aaai.v35i12.17325
7. Nie, Y., Nguyen, N.H., Sinthong, P., Kalagnanam, J.: A time series is worth 64 words: long-term forecasting with transformers. In: Proceedings of the International Conference on Learning Representations, Kigali, Rwanda (2023)
8. Liu, Y., Hu, T., Zhang, H., et al.: iTransformer: inverted transformers are effective for time series forecasting. In: Proceedings of the International Conference on Learning Representations, Vienna, Austria (2024)
9. Zhang, Y., Yan, J.: Crossformer: transformer utilizing cross-dimension dependency for multivariate time series forecasting. In: Proceedings of the International Conference on Learning Representations, Kigali, Rwanda (2023)
10. Fan, J., Shen, Y.: StockMixer: a simple yet strong MLP-based architecture for stock price forecasting. Proc. AAAI Conf. Artif. Intell. **38**(8), 8389–8397 (2024). https://doi.org/10.1609/aaai.v38i8.28681
11. Qian, H., Zhou, H., Zhao, Q., et al.: MDGNN: multi-relational dynamic graph neural network for comprehensive and dynamic stock investment prediction. Proc. AAAI Conf. Artif. Intell. **38**(13), 14642–14650 (2024). https://doi.org/10.1609/aaai.v38i13.29381
12. Zhu, P., Li, Y., Hu, Y., Liu, Q., Cheng, D., Liang, Y.: LSR-IGRU: stock trend prediction based on long short-term relationships and improved GRU. In: Proceedings of the 33rd ACM International Conference on Information and Knowledge Management, Boise, ID, USA, 2024, pp. 5135–5142. https://doi.org/10.1145/3627673.3680012
13. Veličković, P., Cucurull, G., Casanova, A., Romero, A., Liò, P., Bengio, Y.: Graph attention networks. In: International Conference on Learning Representations, Vancouver, Canada (2018)
14. Zhao, L., Song, Y., Zhang, C., et al.: T-GCN: a temporal graph convolutional network for traffic prediction. IEEE Trans. Intell. Transp. Syst. **21**(9), 3848–3858 (2020). https://doi.org/10.1109/TITS.2019.2935152

15. Xiang, S., Cheng, D., Shang, C., Zhang, Y., Liang, Y.: Temporal and heterogeneous graph neural network for financial time series prediction. In: Proceedings of the 31st ACM International Conference on Information and Knowledge Management, Atlanta, GA, USA, 2022, pp. 3584–3593. https://doi.org/10.1145/3511808.3557089.
16. Cheng, R., Li, Q.: Modeling the momentum spillover effect for stock prediction via attribute-driven graph attention networks. Proc. AAAI Conf. Artif. Intell. **35**(1), 55–62 (2021). https://doi.org/10.1609/aaai.v35i1.16077
17. Hsu, Y.-L., Tsai, Y.-C., Li, C.-T.: FinGAT: financial graph attention networks for recommending top-K profitable stocks. IEEE Trans. Knowl. Data Eng. **35**(1), 469–481 (2023). https://doi.org/10.1109/TKDE.2021.3079496
18. Zhao, Y., Du, H., Liu, Y., et al.: Stock movement prediction based on bi-typed hybrid-relational market knowledge graph via dual attention networks. IEEE Trans. Knowl. Data Eng. **35**(8), 8559–8571 (2023). https://doi.org/10.1109/TKDE.2022.3220520
19. Wang, H., Li, S., Wang, T., Zheng, J.: Hierarchical adaptive temporal-relational modeling for stock trend prediction. In: Proceedings of the 30th International Joint Conferences on Artificial Intelligence, Montreal, Canada, 2021, pp. 3691–3698. https://doi.org/10.24963/ijcai.2021/508
20. Zheng, Z., Shao, J., Zhu, J., Shen, H.T.: Relational temporal graph convolutional networks for ranking-based stock prediction. In: Proceedings IEEE 39th International Conference on Data Engineering, Anaheim, CA, USA, 2023, pp. 123–136. https://doi.org/10.1109/ICDE55515.2023.00017
21. Song, L., Li, H., Chen, S. et al.: Multi-scale temporal neural network for stock trend prediction enhanced by temporal hyperedge learnings. In: Proceedings of the 34th International Joint Conference on Artificial Intelligence, Montreal, Canada, 2025, pp. 3272–3280. https://doi.org/10.24963/ijcai.2025/364
22. Sawhney, R., Agarwal, S., Wadhwa, A., Shah, R.R.: Spatiotemporal hypergraph convolution network for stock movement forecasting. In: Proceedings of the IEEE International Conference on Data Mining, Sorrento, Italy, 2020, pp. 482–491. https://doi.org/10.1109/ICDM50108.2020.00057
23. Sawhney, R., Agarwal, S., Wadhwa, A., Derr, T., Shah, R.R.: Stock selection via spatiotemporal hypergraph attention network: a learning to rank approach. Proc. AAAI Conf. Artif. Intell. **35**(1), 497–504 (2021). https://doi.org/10.1609/aaai.v35i1.16127
24. Cui, C., Li, X., Zhang, C., Guan, W., Wang, M.: Temporal-relational hypergraph tri-attention networks for stock trend prediction. Pattern Recognit. **143**, 109759 (2023). https://doi.org/10.1016/j.patcog.2023.109759
25. Han, H., Xie, L., Chen, S., et al.: Stock trend prediction based on industry relationships driven hypergraph attention networks. Appl. Intell. **53**(24), 29448–29464 (2023). https://doi.org/10.1007/s10489-023-05035-z
26. Wu, H., Xu, J., Wang, J., Long, M.: Autoformer: decomposition transformers with auto-correlation for long-term series forecasting. Proc. Adv. Neural Inf. Process. Syst. **34**, 22419–22430 (2021)
27. Zhou, T., Ma, Z., Wen, Q., Wang, X., Sun, L., Jin, R.: FEDformer: frequency enhanced decomposed transformer for long-term series forecasting. In: Proceedings of the 39th International Conference on Machine Learning. Baltimore, MD, USA, 2022, vol. 162, pp. 27268–27286
28. Zhou, T., Ma, Z., Wang, X., et al.: FiLM: frequency improved Legendre memory model for long-term time series forecasting. Proc. Adv. Neural Inf. Process. Syst. **35**, 12677–12690 (2022)

29. Zeng, A., Chen, M., Zhang, L., Xu, Q.: Are transformers effective for time series forecasting? Proc. AAAI Conf. Artif. Intell. **37**(9), 11121–11128 (2023). https://doi.org/10.1609/aaai.v37i9.26317
30. Wu, H., Hu, T., Liu, Y., Zhou, H., Wang, J., Long, M.: TimesNet: temporal 2D-variation modeling for general time series analysis. In: Proceedings of the International Conference on Learning Representations, Kigali, Rwanda (2023)

HBCGNN: An Inductive GNN Framework for Predicting Historical Betweenness Centrality in Temporal Graphs

Zhenyu Mao[1], Ming Zhong[1(✉)], Yuanyuan Zhu[1], Tieyun Qian[1], Mengchi Liu[2], and Jeffrey Xu Yu[3]

[1] School of Computer Science, Wuhan University, Wuhan, China
{mzyyui,clock,yyzhu,qty}@whu.edu.cn

[2] South China Normal University, Guangzhou, China
liumengchi@scnu.edu.cn

[3] DSA Thrust, HKUST(GZ), Guangzhou, China
yu@se.cuhk.edu.hk

Abstract. Betweenness centrality is a fundamental metric for identifying critical intermediary nodes in graph analysis. Since most real-world networks carry temporal information, recent studies have proposed various temporal betweenness centralities (TBCs) based on time-respecting paths, which are ideal for sequential propagation scenarios. However, there are also many scenarios that involve a number of discrete subnetworks called snapshots at each timestamp. Research in this domain is still rather lacking. To bridge this gap, we propose historical betweenness centrality (HBC) for temporal networks, the first centrality metric designed to identify nodes that exhibit strong intermediation capabilities persistently within a given historical period. While exact computation of betweenness is expensive, learning-based approaches face challenges from extreme label skewness, where models tend to overfit to the zero-centrality majority, failing to identify truly central nodes. To address this, we develop HBCGNN, a scalable and inductive framework that integrates a Merged Graph structure with a path-time encoder and contrastive learning guided by bootstrap stability clustering. Extensive experiments demonstrate that HBC uniquely identifies essential persistent intermediaries, while HBCGNN consistently outperforms state-of-the-art baselines in both ranking correlation and predictive accuracy across massive, unseen networks.

Keywords: Temporal graph · Betweenness · GNN

1 Introduction

Network centrality metrics serve as fundamental instruments in graph analysis, with Betweenness Centrality (BC) standing out as a classical measure of a node's capacity for information control and behavioral dominance. While traditional BC

L. Ding et al. (Eds.): APWeb-WAIM 2026, LNCS 16993, pp. 266–281, 2027.
https://doi.org/10.1007/978-981-92-5693-8_17

focuses on static structures, modern systems—ranging from social platforms to urban infrastructures—are inherently dynamic. These systems are best modeled as temporal graphs, conceptually represented as a sequence of static subgraphs, or *snapshots*, evolving along a timeline (as depicted in Fig. 1(a)).

Extending BC to the temporal domain has led to Temporal Betweenness Centrality (TBC) [20,27], which requires paths to respect strict chronological ordering (i.e., time-respecting paths). While effective for modeling sequential propagation processes like epidemic spreading [7], TBC's strict temporal constraint often identifies paths spanning excessively long durations. Consequently, it falls short in scenarios that prioritize high-frequency, sustained interactions within a concentrated historical window.

In many real-world applications, the analytical goal is not to trace such long-range propagation, but to identify nodes that consistently maintain a critical intermediary role. For instance, in a city's traffic network modeled across 10-minute snapshots, identifying intersections that remain uncongested and critical across multiple intervals is vital for alleviating regional congestion. In such contexts, a node's value derives from its persistent presence on shortest paths throughout a specific period, necessitating a metric that aggregates structural persistence rather than mere sequential reachability.

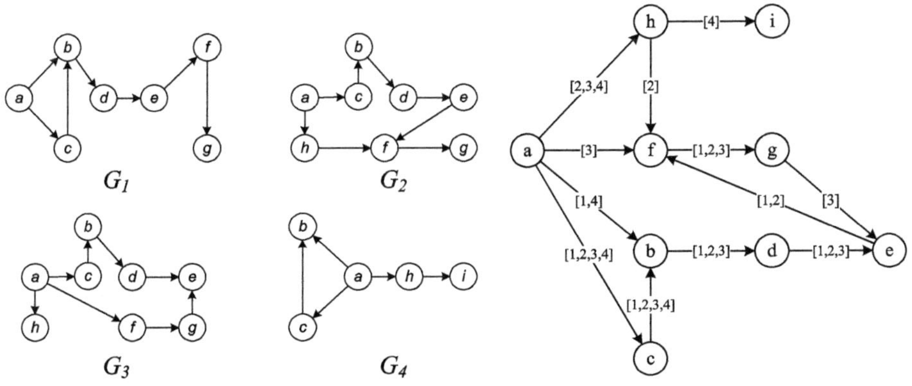

(a) The snapshots of G. (b) The Merged Graph of G.

Fig. 1. Two equivalent logical representations of an example temporal graph G.

To address these scenarios where sustained intermediation is critical, we propose a novel metric: **Historical Betweenness Centrality (HBC)**. Unlike TBC, HBC is built upon instantaneous path semantics, quantifying the importance of nodes that lie on a significant portion of historical shortest paths emerging across multiple snapshots. However, exact calculation of HBC incurs prohibitive computational redundancy due to the traversal-and-accumulation paradigm across multi-snapshot graphs. Consequently, data-driven approaches like Graph Neural Networks (GNNs) present a highly promising, scalable alternative for predicting centrality.

Nevertheless, applying GNNs to predict HBC is challenging due to the extreme class imbalance inherent in temporal centrality. HBC exhibits a severe heavy-tailed distribution: the vast majority of nodes possess zero centrality, while crucial intermediaries are exceptionally rare. This skewness causes model degeneration, where loss functions are overwhelmed by the majority class, leading the model to predict near-zero values for all nodes. Furthermore, standard data augmentation techniques (e.g., node dropping, edge perturbation) are inapplicable here: modifying the graph topology fundamentally alters the underlying shortest paths and distorts the ground-truth centrality values.

To overcome these obstacles without distorting the underlying topology, we propose **HBCGNN**, a novel inductive GNN framework tailored for the imbalanced regression of historical centrality. First, we introduce a *Merged Graph* structure (Fig. 1(b)) to integrate multiple snapshots, eliminating redundant topological processing while preserving temporal reachability. Second, a Representation Module employs a path-time encoder to extract robust spatio-temporal features. Finally, to tackle the extreme heavy-tailed distribution, we introduce a prediction strategy that partitions nodes into stable value tiers via K-means clustering evaluated by bootstrap resampling stability. Building upon this robust stratification, a re-weighted contrastive learning paradigm is implemented to pull nodes with similar values together while pushing apart those with significant gaps, effectively isolating rare high-value intermediaries from the overwhelming zero-value majority in the embedding space.

In brief, our contributions are summarized as follows:

- We formally define Historical Betweenness Centrality (HBC) to quantify a node's importance as persistent intermediaries over specific historical periods, effectively capturing sustained structural interaction that traditional TBC fails to identify.
- We propose HBCGNN, an efficient inductive learning framework. By integrating a Merged Graph structure with a path-time encoder and contrastive learning guided by bootstrap stability clustering, our model effectively handles extreme label skewness and generalizes to unseen networks.
- Extensive experiments demonstrate that HBC uniquely identifies essential persistent intermediaries overlooked by TBC. While baselines often collapse to trivial zero-value predictions on unseen large-scale networks, HBCGNN maintains superior ranking correlation and accuracy, proving its robust inductive generalization and scalability.

2 Related Work

Given the significance of centrality measurement for network analysis, many definitions and algorithms of centrality have been proposed in different application scenarios. In this section, we will focus on the scenarios that are most relevant to our work, grouped as follows.

Traditional BC computation methods. The computation of Betweenness Centrality (BC) has evolved from static foundations to complex temporal frameworks. For static graphs, Brandes' algorithm [3] remains the cornerstone for exact computation, while various sampling-based approximations [2,4,6,16,17] enhance scalability. In temporal domains, Temporal Betweenness Centrality (TBC) systematically evaluates time-respecting paths [5], with approximation techniques like ONBRA [20] or graph transformations [27] providing efficiency gains. However, TBC metrics strictly focus on sequential information propagation, failing to capture nodes that consistently serve as structural intermediaries across historical periods. To fill this gap, Historical Betweenness Centrality (HBC) was recently established to formalize structural persistence over snapshot sequences [12]. Yet, these graph-traversal algorithms remain bottlenecked on massive graphs, motivating a complementary learning-based paradigm for rapid, inductive prediction without exhaustive counting.

Graph neural network based model. As a scalable alternative, data-driven approaches using Graph Neural Networks (GNNs) have been developed to estimate centrality in static domains [15,29]. Recently, this methodology has been extended to temporal networks to capture temporal importance [28]. Specifically, DBGNN [8] models Temporal Betweenness Centrality (TBC) via a time-aware architecture, while Zhang [26] employs a contrastive learning framework on time-instance graphs to enhance TBC prediction. Despite their success in TBC, existing temporal models are primarily optimized for time-respecting path constraints—where information must flow through edges with increasing timestamps. In contrast, our proposed HBC is governed by structural persistence, identifying nodes that consistently serve as intermediaries across multiple historical snapshots, a property that goes beyond simple temporal sequencing. Furthermore, HBC exhibits a significantly more severe heavy-tailed distribution than traditional metrics, necessitating a more specialized treatment to effectively capture the exceptionally sparse set of persistent intermediaries.

3 Preliminaries

In this section, we formalize the concept of the Historical Betweenness Centrality (HBC) of nodes in temporal networks.

Definition 1 (Temporal Graph). *A temporal graph G is a sequence of snapshots $(G_1, \ldots, G_n)$, where each $G_t = (V_t, E_t)$ is a static directed graph at timestamp t. We denote the union of all nodes and edges as $V = \bigcup_{t=1}^{n} V_t$ and $E = \bigcup_{t=1}^{n} E_t$, respectively, and $n = |G|$ is the total number of snapshots in G.*

Definition 2 (Historical Shortest Path). *Given a temporal graph G and a subset of timestamps $T \subseteq [1, n]$, a historical path p from u to v at time $t \in T$ is a sequence of nodes $\langle v_1, \ldots, v_{k+1} \rangle$ where $(v_i, v_{i+1}) \in E_t$ for all $i \in [1, k]$. A path p is a historical shortest path if its length $|p|$ is minimal among all historical paths from u to v at time t.*

Different from "temporal paths" [23] that model time-respecting propagation (e.g., disease spreading), historical paths [21] represent instantaneous connectivity within a specific historical period T. To illustrate, consider the temporal graph in Fig. 1(a), the path $a \rightarrow c \rightarrow b$ is a historical path from a to b at $t = 1$, 2, 3, or 4, and the historical shortest path from a to b only at $t = 2$ or 3. When $t = 1$ or 4, the path $a \rightarrow b$ becomes the historical shortest path from a to b.

On top of the historical shortest path, we introduce the historical betweenness centrality of a node, which intuitively aggregates the fraction of historical shortest paths that pass through the node throughout the historical period.

Definition 3 (Historical Betweenness Centrality). *Given a temporal graph G and a subset $T \subseteq [1, n]$ of timestamps, the historical betweenness centrality of a node $v \in V$ is defined as*

$$HBC^T(v) = \frac{1}{|V|(|V|-1)} \sum_{t \in T} \sum_{s,z \in V, s \neq v \neq z} \frac{\sigma_{sz}^t(v)}{\sum_{t \in T} \sigma_{sz}^t} \tag{1}$$

where $|V|$ denotes the number of nodes, σ_{sz}^t denote the number of historical shortest paths from s to z at time t, and $\sigma_{sz}^t(v)$ denote the number of historical shortest paths that pass through v from s to z at time t.

To calculate exact HBC values, a basic approach (BA) executes a standard Single-Source Shortest Path (SSSP) algorithm for every node within each individual snapshot. By adapting Brandes' accumulation technique [5,27], we obtain the dependency of a node v across all snapshots. The final HBC is derived by aggregating these dependencies, effectively summing v's static contributions at each time step normalized by the total historical path count $\sum_{t \in T} \sigma_{sz}^t$.While conceptually simple, this method is computationally prohibitive for large-scale graphs. The complexity scales as $\mathcal{O}(|T| \cdot \overline{|V|} \cdot (\overline{|V|} + \overline{|E|}))$, where $\overline{|V|}$ and $\overline{|E|}$ represent the average number of nodes and edges per snapshot, rendering exact computation intractable for large-scale networks and underscoring the necessity for a scalable, learning-based solution.

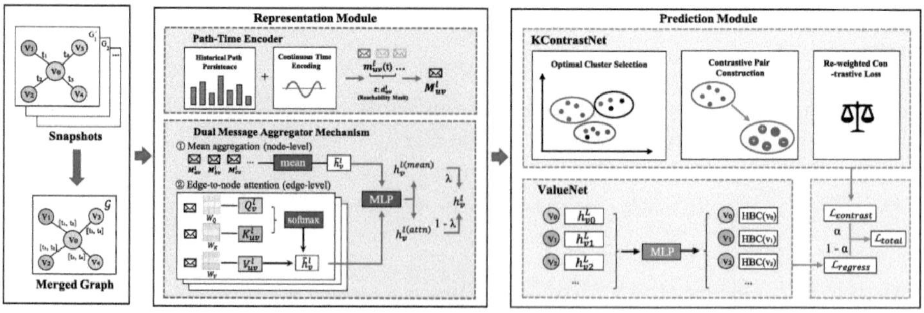

Fig. 2. Overview of the proposed model: HBCGNN.

4 Method

To efficiently predict HBC under extreme data imbalance, we propose HBCGNN (Fig. 2), shifting from exhaustive path counting to a learning-based framework. It comprises three core components: Merged Graph construction, a Spatiotemporal Representation Module, and an Imbalance-aware Prediction Module.

4.1 Merged Graph

As analyzed previously, executing independent SSSP algorithms across each snapshot leads to significant computational redundancy, as real-world temporal graphs often feature snapshots with substantial overlap in nodes and edges. To address this inefficiency and provide a unified input for our learning framework, we first introduce the Merged Graph structure, which integrates all snapshots into a single coherent representation. The Merged Graph is formally defined as follows, and Fig. 1(b) shows the Merged Graph of the snapshots in Fig. 1(a).

Definition 4 (Merged Graph). *Given a temporal graph* $G = (G_1, \cdots, G_n)$*, its Merged Graph is an edge-labeled directed graph* $\mathcal{G} = (V, \mathcal{E}, \mathcal{L})$*, where* $\mathcal{E} = \{(u, v) \mid \exists t \in [1, n], (u, v) \in E_t\}$*, and* $\mathcal{L}$ *is a mapping from the edges* (u, v) *to the labels* $\mathcal{L}(u, v) = \{t | (u, v) \in E_t\}$*.*

To process path information across multiple snapshots in parallel, our GNN framework utilizes the Merged Graph to learn the connectivity patterns among edges, thereby efficiently identifying the candidates of historical shortest paths to extract structural and temporal reachability features from the Merged Graph. The core principle of this temporal reachability relies on the intersection of edge labels. Specifically, for a path to exist at a given timestamp t, all its constituent edges must be present at t. When extending a path p with a new edge (v, w) to form an extended path p', the temporal presence of p' is determined by taking the intersection of the valid timestamps of p and the new edge: $\mathcal{L}(p') = \mathcal{L}(p) \cap \mathcal{L}(v, w)$. If this intersection is empty, the extended path does not exist in any snapshot. Our GNN implicitly captures this intersection logic to efficiently aggregate valid path features across the entire historical period.

As illustrated in Fig. 1(b), for a historical period $T = [1, 2, 3, 4]$, extending a path $p = \langle c, b \rangle$ with edge (b, d) recursively restricts the valid timestamp label from $[1, 2, 3, 4]$ to $[1, 2, 3]$ via chronological intersection.

4.2 Representation Module

The Representation Module transforms the Merged Graph into high-dimensional embeddings h_v^l by capturing and interleaving topological structure with temporal reachability.

Path-Time Encoder To identify historical intermediaries, the model must recognize which paths remain valid across various snapshots. We propose a Path-Time Encoder that couples temporal periodicity with path reachability.

- **Historical Reachability Mask**: We define a binary vector $d_{uv}^l \in \{0,1\}^{|T|}$ to track the "survival" of historical paths. For a path of length l, its validity at timestamp t is determined by the intersection of all constituent edge labels. We update this mask recursively, here $1_{\mathcal{L}(u,v)} \in \{0,1\}^{|T|}$ denotes the indicators of $\mathcal{L}(u,v)$ in the Merged Graph:

$$d_{uv}^l = d_u^{l-1} \odot 1_{\mathcal{L}(u,v)}, \quad d_v^l = \sum_{u \in N_{in}(v)} d_{uv}^l \tag{2}$$

where d_v^l represents the distribution of l-hop reachable paths arriving at v across the history. This mask ensures the model only considers "historically valid" connections.
- **Historical Path Persistence**: We quantify the strength of intermediation by the number of snapshots in which a path exists, $P_{uv}^l = \|d_{uv}^l\|_1$. To stabilize training against heavy-tailed path distributions, we apply a log-transformation:

$$\phi_{path}^l(u,v) = MLP_{path}^l(reshape(log(1 + P_{uv}^l))) \tag{3}$$

- **Continuous Time Encoding**: To capture the periodic nature of interactions, we map each timestamp t to a d_T-dimensional vector $\phi_{time}(t)$ using learnable frequency parameters:

$$\phi_{time}(t) = \sqrt{\frac{1}{d_T}}[cos(\omega_1 t), sin((\omega_1 t), \ldots, cos(\omega_d t), sin((\omega_d t))]^T \tag{4}$$

Message Function A key distinction of HBCGNN is that it does not favor a specific timestamp t. Instead, it aggregates messages from all valid snapshots in the history to form a holistic view of the node's importance. For an edge (u,v), we compute a comprehensive message M_{uv}^l by summing instantaneous representations across the entire reachability mask:

$$m_{uv}^l(t) = MLP_{msg}^l(h_u^{l-1} || \phi_{time}(t) || \phi_{path}^l(u,v)), \forall t \in \{\tau | d_{uv}^l[\tau] > 0\} \tag{5}$$

$$M_{uv}^l = \sum_{t: d_{uv}^l[t] > 0} m_{uv}^l(t) \tag{6}$$

This formulation ensures that if a node serves as a bridge at both $t = 1$ and $t = 100$, both contributions are equally preserved in the resulting edge-level representation.

Dual Message Aggregator Mechanism To capture both global neighborhood statistics and specific high-influence paths, we employ a dual aggregation strategy.

- **Mean Aggregation (Node-level)**: This ensures a stable baseline by treating all incoming neighbors equally:

$$\bar{h}_v^l = W_{mean}^l \cdot \Big(\frac{1}{|N_{in}(v)|} \sum_{u \in N_{in}(v)} M_{uv}^l \Big) \tag{7}$$

- **Edge-to-Node Attention (Edge-level)**: We use a multi-head attention mechanism to emphasize specific neighbors that provide more critical "shortcuts" in the historical shortest path structure. By measuring the compatibility between node v's query ($Q_v^l = h_v^{l-1} \cdot W_Q^l$) and each neighbor u's key ($K_{uv}^l = M_{uv}^l \cdot W_K^l$), we derive weights α_{uv} to aggregate edge-level messages $V_{uv}^l = M_{uv}^l \cdot W_V^l$ into a unified node representation $\tilde{h}_v^l$. This weighted sum effectively integrates messages from various neighbors, allowing the model to filter out less relevant connections and isolate the most influential structural paths:

$$\tilde{h}_v^l = \sum_{u \in N_{in}(v)} \alpha_{uv} V_{uv}^l, \quad \text{where} \quad \alpha_{uv} = \frac{\exp\left(\frac{Q_v^l \cdot (K_{uv}^l)^T}{\sqrt{d_h}}\right)}{\sum_{u' \in N_{in}(v)} \exp\left(\frac{Q_v^l \cdot (K_{u'v}^l)^T}{\sqrt{d_h}}\right)} \tag{8}$$

Embedding The final embedding h_v^l for the current layer is a weighted combination of the outputs of mean aggregation and edge-to-node attention:

$$h_v^{l(mean)} = \text{MLP}_{mean}^l \left(\bar{h}_v^l \parallel h_v^{l-1} \right) \tag{9}$$

$$h_v^{l(attn)} = \text{MLP}_{attn}^l \left(\tilde{h}_v^{l(0)} \parallel \tilde{h}_v^{l(1)} \parallel \cdots \parallel \tilde{h}_v^{l(k-1)} \parallel h_v^{l-1} \right) \tag{10}$$

$$h_v^l = \lambda \cdot h_v^{l(mean)} + (1 - \lambda) \cdot h_v^{l(attn)}, \tag{11}$$

Unlike traditional temporal GNNs where embeddings are time-dependent ($h_v^l(t)$), our resulting h_v^l is stationary for the historical period T. This design directly aligns the GNN's output with the definition of HBC, which seeks a single value representing the node's total intermediary capacity over a historical span.

4.3 Prediction Module

HBC typically exhibits a heavy-tailed distribution, where a small number of nodes possess extremely high centrality values while the majority have values close to 0. To address this severe data imbalance and improve the model's predictive accuracy, we design the prediction module with two components: KContrastNet and ValueNet.

KContrastNet KContrastNet utilizes a contrastive learning strategy to clearly separate the representation features of low-, medium-, and high-value nodes. To construct meaningful positive and negative pairs, we first partition the nodes into distinct clusters based on their HBC values.

Optimal Cluster Selection. To robustly group nodes across the heavily skewed heavy-tailed distribution, we employ a K-means clustering approach evaluated via *bootstrap resampling stability* [11]. Unlike standard metrics that fail on heavy-tailed data, this stability-based criterion ensures partitions reflect real structural tiers rather than noise. Specifically, for a given k, we repeatedly draw pairs of bootstrap subsets from the data, apply K-means to each, and measure the assignment difference on their overlapping nodes. By selecting the optimal cluster count k that minimizes this average clustering instability, we obtain a highly stable tier assignment ψ. This stable assignment robustly categorizes nodes into distinct value scales, providing a solid foundation for the subsequent contrastive pair construction.

Contrastive Pair Construction. To maintain structural and semantic consistency, we restrict the sampling of contrastive pairs to nodes within the same cluster. For a given node u, positive pairs are sampled from nodes with highly similar HBC values, while negative pairs are selected from those with significantly different values. Using the median HBC to ensure robustness against the heavy-tailed distribution, the positive candidate set $\mathcal{S}^+(u)$ and negative candidate set $\mathcal{S}^-(u)$ are defined as:

$$\mathcal{S}^+(u) = \{v \mid \psi(u) = \psi(v), 0 < |\Delta_{uv}| \leq \gamma_{pos} HBC_{median}\} \tag{12}$$

$$\mathcal{S}^-(u) = \{v \mid \psi(u) = \psi(v), |\Delta_{uv}| \geq \gamma_{neg} HBC_{median}\} \tag{13}$$

where $\Delta_{uv} = HBC(u) - HBC(v)$, and $\gamma_{pos}, \gamma_{neg}$ are scaling thresholds.

Re-weighted Contrastive Loss. To prioritize highly informative pairs and prevent gradient instability, we introduce adaptive value-gap weights that amplify the importance of near-positives and distant-negatives:

$$\beta_{uv} = \frac{\gamma_{pos} HBC_{median}}{|\Delta_{uv}|}, \beta_{uw} = \frac{|\Delta_{uw}|}{\gamma_{neg} HBC_{median}} \tag{14}$$

Let h_u^L and h_x^L denote the node embeddings from the final L-th layer of the representation module. We define the re-weighted similarity z_{ux} between node u and node $x \in \{v, w\}$ as $z_{ux} = \beta_{ux} \cdot \frac{sim(h_u^L, h_x^L)}{\tau}$. The final contrastive loss is computed across all k clusters, pulling close-valued nodes together while pushing apart nodes with larger value gaps:

$$\mathcal{L}_{contrast} = \sum_{i=1}^{k} \sum_{u \in \psi_i} -\log \frac{\sum_{v \in \mathcal{S}^+(u)} \exp(z_{uv})}{\sum_{v \in \mathcal{S}^+(u)} \exp(z_{uv}) + \sum_{w \in \mathcal{S}^-(u)} \exp(z_{uw})} \tag{15}$$

ValueNet After representation refinement via KContrastNet, ValueNet predicts the exact HBC values. Since the Merged Graph inherently integrates historical reachability, the L-th layer representation h_v^L captures the overall structural dependency of node v. Thus, we directly map this embedding to the global HBC value using a Multi-Layer Perceptron (MLP):

$$HBC(v) = MLP_{reg}(h_v^L) \tag{16}$$

The overall model is trained end-to-end by balancing the contrastive and regression objectives:

$$\mathcal{L}_{total} = \alpha \cdot \mathcal{L}_{contrast} + (1 - \alpha) \cdot \mathcal{L}_{regress} \tag{17}$$

where α controls the trade-off, and $\mathcal{L}_{regress}$ is the standard regression error (e.g., Mean Squared Error) between predicted and ground-truth HBC values.

Complexity Analysis The training cost per epoch is driven by the Representation and Prediction modules. Due to path-masking, the GNN processes only valid historical interactions, yielding a complexity of $O(L \cdot N_{valid} \cdot d^2)$, where N_{valid} is the number of valid paths in the Merged Graph, which is significantly lower than the sum of edges across all snapshots. The Prediction module involves K-means clustering and pair construction, adding a cost of $O(B \cdot k + P \cdot d)$, where B is the batch size and P is the number of sampled pairs. Notably, this cost is independent of the time window size $|T|$. During inference, clustering and contrastive components are deactivated, reducing the runtime complexity strictly to the backbone forward pass: $O(L \cdot N_{valid} \cdot d^2)$. Notably, the inductive nature of HBCGNN enables zero-shot inference on unseen networks without prior knowledge of their HBC distributions, confirming that our representation module captures universal, transferable spatiotemporal features.

5 Experiment Evaluation

5.1 Experimental Setup

Datasets. We adopt 9 real-world temporal graphs, as shown in Table 1. Hypertext, Highschool series, Primary School are from SocioPatterns.[1] EmailsKonect, Wikiedits-se, and Wikivoyage-it are from Konect.[2] Superuser is from the SNAP.[3] Our training dataset consists of 20 real-world temporal networks from Konect. For every dataset, we repeated each experiment 30 times, and we reported the mean and the standard deviation of all scores. All experiments were conducted on a workstation equipped with an NVIDIA GeForce RTX 4090 GPU, CUDA 12.2.

Compared Baselines. To evaluate the performance of HBCGNN, we benchmark it against the exact Basic Approach (BA) detailed in Sect. 3 to assess computational efficiency. For predictive effectiveness, we select representative

[1] SocioPatterns is available at http://www.sociopatterns.org/datasets/.
[2] Konect is available at http://konect.cc/.
[3] SNAP is available at https://snap.stanford.edu/data/.

Table 1. Statistics of the datasets.

Datasets	Properties				
	$\|V\|$	$\|E\|$	n	$\overline{\text{deg}}$	Granularity
Hypertext	113	20816	5244	184.21	20 s
Highschool2011	126	28559	5607	453.31	20 s
Highschool2012	180	45045	11271	500.51	20 s
EmailsKonect	167	82927	57791	993.13	1 day
Primaryschool	242	125771	3100	1039.43	20 s
Highschool2013	327	188506	7375	1152.94	20 s
Wikiedits-se	18055	261169	72	28.93	1 h
Wikivoyage-it	31501	419474	450	26.63	1 quarter
Superuser	194085	1443339	110	14.87	1 month

learning-based models to evaluate how well they capture HBC: (i) Static GNN: GNN-Bet [14], a supervised framework that predicts betweenness scores by learning node-level structural embeddings from static snapshots. (ii) Temporal GNN: DBGNN [8], the state-of-the-art temporal GNN specifically designed for centrality prediction, which captures dynamic dependencies through time-aware graph structures.

Evaluation Metrics. We mainly use two metrics to assess performance: mean absolute error (MAE) for prediction accuracy, Spearman correlation for ranking quality.

We seek to answer the following research questions:

RQ1 (Effectiveness of HBC Definition). How effectively does HBC identify persistent intermediaries in temporal graphs compared to traditional TBC?

RQ2 (Performance and Robustness). Does HBCGNN consistently outperform representative baselines in predictive accuracy and scalability across diverse temporal datasets?

RQ3 (Computational Efficiency). How much faster is HBCGNN compared with the exact method BA?

RQ4 (Stratified Performance). How does HBCGNN perform across discretized centrality ranges (zero, mid, and high values)?

RQ5 (Ablation Study). What are the individual contributions of the contrastive learning, path-time encoder, and optimal clustering to HBCGNN's overall performance?

5.2 Experimental Results

RQ1 (Effectiveness of HBC Definition). We evaluate HBC through a structural case study and a score distribution analysis.

- *Persistent vs. Transient Nodes*: Figure 3 compares node importance in Highschool2011 across two snapshots ($t = 5450, 5458$). HBC (green) accurately

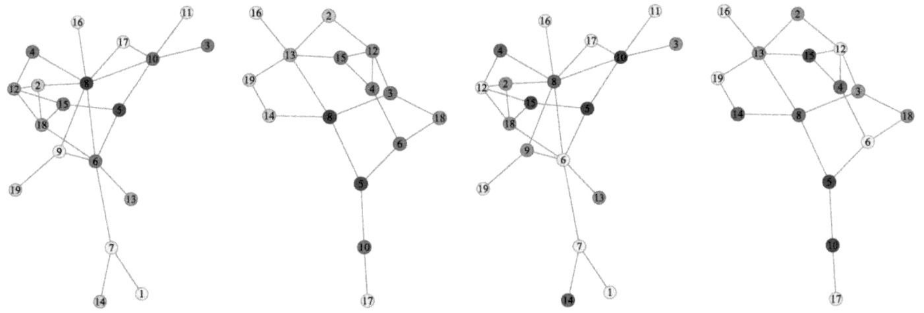

(a) G_{5450} with HBC. (b) G_{5458} with HBC. (c) G_{5450} with TBC. (d) G_{5458} with TBC.

Fig. 3. Case study comparing node centralities evaluated by HBC and TBC across two snapshots ($t = 5450$ and $t = 5458$) in the Highschool2011. Darker colors indicate higher centrality scores.

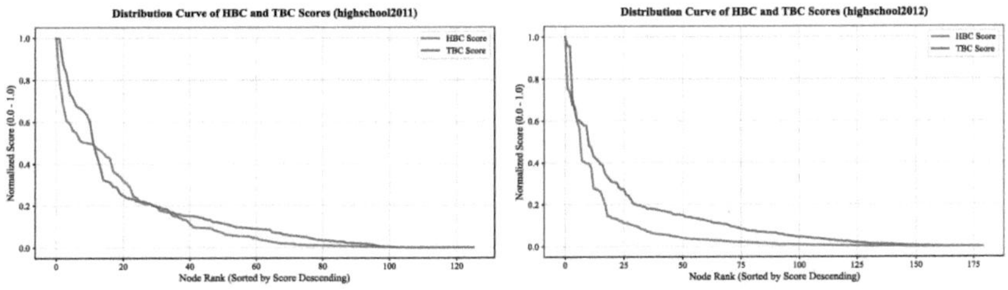

(a) Distribution on Highschool2011 (b) Distribution on Highschool2012

Fig. 4. Normalized score distributions of HBC and TBC.

assigns high importance (darker colors) to nodes 8, 5, 12, and 15, which consistently maintain critical intermediary positions across both timestamps. Conversely, TBC (purple) misjudges the structure by missing persistent intermediaries (e.g., node 12) and overvaluing transient nodes (e.g., node 14) that act as intermediaries in only a single snapshot.

- *Score Distribution*: The normalized score curves in Fig. 4 reveal a significantly steeper, heavily skewed drop-off for HBC compared to the flatter TBC curve. This structural difference confirms their distinct measurement goals: TBC calculates intermediaries along time-increasing temporal paths, distributing scores more broadly across nodes that bridge different timestamps. HBC, conversely, requires nodes to persistently act as structural intermediaries within multiple individual snapshots. This strict constraint naturally narrows the focus to a smaller subset of consistently central nodes, resulting in a more heavily skewed distribution.

RQ2 (Performance and Robustness). Table 2 shows HBCGNN leads in Spearman correlation across all datasets, outperforming baselines by up to 11.5×. Although GNN_bet shows lower MAE on small graphs, its poor Spearman scores indicate it fails to learn structural features and simply outputs uni-

Table 2. Performance comparison of HBCGNN against baselines. The best results in each metric are highlighted in **bold.** ↓ indicates lower is better, while ↑ indicates higher is better. 'OOM' stands for Out of Memory.

Dataset	MAE (↓)			Spearman (↑)		
	GNN_bet	DBGNN	HBCGNN	GNN_bet	DBGNN	HBCGNN
Hypertext	**2.9639**	103.4000	67.7101	0.2333	– 0.0853	**0.6648**
Highschool2011	**4.2283**	138.9000	123.2029	0.2309	0.4555	**0.7823**
Highschool2012	**2.2314**	168.1000	62.0058	0.1970	0.3700	**0.7390**
Highschool2013	**3.9820**	119.9000	55.3674	0.3345	0.0771	**0.7265**
EmailsKonect	**1.6036**	58.8000	16.5518	0.0593	0.0914	**0.6796**
Primaryschool	**2.3167**	58.3000	17.7827	0.3185	0.0608	**0.4070**
Wikiedits-se	2.6985	57.9000	**0.1620**	0.3517	0.1285	**0.6690**
Wikivoyage-it	2.0569	25.3000	**0.0700**	0.0712	– 0.1008	**0.4786**
Superuser	1.3469	OOM	**0.0284**	0.1698	OOM	**0.3196**

Table 3. Execution time (seconds) comparison between HBCGNN and the exact basic approach (BA) detailed in Sect. 3.

Method	Hypertext	Highschool2011	Highschool2012	EmailsKonect	Primaryschool	Highschool2013	Wikiedits-se	Wikivoyage-it	Superuser
BA(s)	12.044	11.679	27.075	25.684	27.328	31.169	1610.867	2786.668	43404.100
GNN(s)	1.6455	1.5647	2.2815	2.9330	3.3350	4.0011	51.0305	20.6484	317.6425

formly low values to minimize absolute error. Conversely, HBCGNN demonstrates superior scalability, reducing MAE by 47.4× on large-scale graphs (e.g., Superuser) while maintaining high ranking precision, proving its effectiveness in capturing true centrality patterns.

RQ3 (Efficiency). As shown in Table 3, HBCGNN achieves significant speedups ranging from 7.3× to 136.6× compared to the exact algorithm, with the efficiency gains becoming increasingly pronounced as the graph scale grows (e.g., on Superuser).

RQ4 (Stratified Performance). Table 4 demonstrates that HBCGNN maintains robust predictive accuracy across all centrality strata, effectively addressing the label skewness common in temporal graphs. The inclusion of Contrastive Learning (CL) serves as a key optimization, particularly on large-scale datasets like Superuser. Without CL, the error (MAE) increases sharply—especially in the Zero and High strata—indicating that CL provides essential structural constraints that prevent the model from generating noisy predictions for non-central nodes while ensuring the precise capture of top-tier intermediaries.

RQ5 (Ablation: Necessity of Components). Table 5 confirms the necessity of all three core modules: (i) *Path–Time Encoder*: Essential for capturing temporal and path cues. Its removal leads to a collapse in ranking precision, with Spearman correlation reversing from positive to negative (e.g., from 0.4 to – 0.1 in Primaryschool). (ii) *Contrastive Learning*: Filters tail noise and sta-

Table 4. Performance across centrality strata: Zero ($HBC = 0$), Median ($0 < HBC \leq HBC_{median}$), and High ($HBC > HBC_{median}$). Δ indicates the impact of removing Contrastive Learning (CL).

Dataset	Zero-value (MAE ↓)			Mid-value (MAE ↓)			High-value (MAE ↓)		
	HBCGNN	w/o CL	Δ (%)	HBCGNN	w/o CL	Δ (%)	HBCGNN	w/o CL	Δ (%)
emailKonect	0.3348	0.4458	+ 33.15	0.9252	1.4968	+ 61.78	79.3985	88.1250	+ 10.99
highschool2011	0.3167	0.4252	+ 34.26	14.4491	14.9116	+ 3.20	272.6570	274.6681	+ 0.74
highschool2012	0.3011	0.6275	+ 108.40	4.0056	4.6927	+ 17.15	135.4323	137.8649	+ 1.79
highschool2013	0.4253	0.0695	− 83.66	1.5788	1.3286	− 15.85	118.2447	122.5145	+ 3.61
hypertext	1.8087	0.6382	− 64.71	6.2104	8.0352	+ 29.38	137.8307	142.1402	+ 3.13
primaryschool	3.9337	0.9211	− 76.58	8.8693	1.1579	− 86.94	32.4634	39.1376	+ 20.56
wikise	0.0032	0.0119	+ 271.88	0.1607	0.2224	+ 38.40	9.3040	10.0020	+ 7.50
wikivoyageit	0.0026	0.0069	+ 165.38	0.1452	0.1888	+ 30.03	10.2486	10.7905	+ 5.29
superuser	0.0045	0.4358	+ 9584.4	0.0343	2.1587	+ 6193.6	2.7998	5.7749	+ 106.26

Table 5. Ablation study on HBCGNN components. Δ represents the relative performance degradation compared to the full model.

Dataset	w/o Contrastive learning				w/o Path-time encoder				w/o Optimal clustering			
	MAE	Spea.	ΔMAE (%)	ΔSpea. (%)	MAE	Spea.	ΔMAE (%)	ΔSpea. (%)	MAE	Spea.	ΔMAE (%)	ΔSpea. (%)
Hypertext	70.54 ± 0.45	0.63 ± 0.02	+ 4.18	− 5.23	70.16 ± 0.71	0.53 ± 0.03	+ 3.62	− 20.28	70.67 ± 0.58	0.58 ± 0.02	+ 4.37	− 12.76
Highschool2011	124.28 ± 0.82	0.60 ± 0.03	+ 0.87	− 23.30	123.94 ± 0.81	0.41 ± 0.02	+ 0.60	− 47.59	123.92 ± 0.65	0.50 ± 0.01	+ 0.58	− 36.09
Highschool2012	63.42 ± 0.55	0.43 ± 0.04	+ 2.28	− 41.81	62.98 ± 0.45	0.32 ± 0.02	+ 1.57	− 56.70	63.13 ± 0.51	0.15 ± 0.02	+ 1.81	− 79.70
Highschool2013	57.19 ± 0.42	0.49 ± 0.02	+ 3.29	− 32.55	57.11 ± 0.66	0.32 ± 0.01	+ 3.15	− 55.95	57.38 ± 0.73	0.21 ± 0.03	+ 3.63	− 71.10
EmailsKonect	16.25 ± 0.31	0.64 ± 0.01	− 1.82	− 5.83	16.48 ± 0.38	0.69 ± 0.02	− 0.43	+ 1.53	16.48 ± 0.42	0.58 ± 0.02	− 0.43	− 14.65
Primaryschool	14.14 ± 0.68	0.03 ± 0.02	− 20.48	− 92.63	12.73 ± 0.29	-0.10 ± 0.03	− 28.41	− 124.57	12.29 ± 0.35	0.13 ± 0.02	− 30.89	− 68.06
Wikiedits-se	0.15 ± 0.02	0.33 ± 0.04	− 7.41	− 50.67	0.15 ± 0.02	0.32 ± 0.01	− 7.41	− 52.17	0.15 ± 0.01	0.32 ± 0.01	− 7.41	− 52.17
Wikivoyage-it	0.08 ± 0.01	0.27 ± 0.02	+ 14.29	− 43.59	0.08 ± 0.01	0.09 ± 0.02	+ 28.58	− 56.12	0.08 ± 0.01	0.20 ± 0.01	+ 14.29	− 58.21
Superuser	0.49 ± 0.13	0.18 ± 0.04	+ 1625.35	− 43.68	0.38 ± 0.05	0.20 ± 0.02	+ 1238.03	− 37.42	0.52 ± 0.04	0.19 ± 0.02	+ 1730.99	− 40.55

bilizes ranking under structural skew. Without it, MAE increases sharply on massive graphs (e.g., + 1625% on Superuser). (iii) *Optimal Clustering*: Mitigates head-tail imbalance by effectively structuring samples. Its removal reduces Spearman by up to 79.7% on community-dense datasets (e.g., Highschool2012).

6 Conclusion

In this paper, we highlight the concept of Historical Betweenness Centrality (HBC) to effectively identify persistent intermediaries, distinguishing persistent intermediaries from transient noise. To overcome the severe computational bottlenecks of exact HBC algorithms on massive temporal graphs, we propose HBCGNN, a scalable and inductive representation learning framework, which can effectively capture complex spatio-temporal cues while mitigating severe head-tail label skewness. Extensive experiments on diverse real-world datasets demonstrate that HBCGNN achieves state of the art predictive accuracy, robust stratified performance, and significant computational speedups over exact methods. Crucially, its inductive nature enables effective generalization to unseen networks. Future work will explore optimizing HBCGNN for other complex temporal metrics.

References

1. Alsayed, A., Higham, D.J.: Betweenness in time dependent networks. Chaos, Solitons Fractals **72**, 35–48 (2015)
2. Borassi, M., Natale, E.: KADABRA is an ADaptive algorithm for betweenness via random approximation. ACM JEA **24**, 1.2:1–1.2:35 (2019)
3. Brandes, U.: A faster algorithm for betweenness centrality. J. Math. Sociol. **25**, 163–177 (2001)
4. Brandes, U., Pich, C.: Centrality estimation in large networks. Int. J. Bifurcat. Chaos **17**(07), 2303–2318 (2007)
5. Buß, S., Molter, H., Niedermeier, R., et al.: Algorithmic aspects of temporal betweenness. Netw. Sci. **12**(2), 160–188 (2024)
6. Cousins, C., Wohlgemuth, C., Riondato, M.: Bavarian: betweenness centrality approximation with variance-aware Rademacher averages. ACM TKDD **17**(6), 78 (2023)
7. Dekker, A.H.: Network centrality and super-spreaders in infectious disease epidemiology. In: MODSIM, pp. 113–119 (2013)
8. Heeg, F., Scholtes, I.: Using time-aware graph neural networks to predict temporal centralities in dynamic graphs. NIPS. Art 949 (2024)
9. Katz, L.: A new status index derived from sociometric analysis. Psychometrika **18**(1), 39–43 (1953)
10. Kim, H., Anderson, R.: Temporal node centrality in complex networks. Phys. Rev. E **85**, 026107 (2012)
11. Lange, T., Roth, V., Braun, M.L., et al.: Stability-based validation of clustering solutions. Neural Comput. **16**(6), 1299–1323 (2004)
12. Mao, Z., Zhong, M., Zhu, Y., et al.: Historical betweenness centrality and its computation. World Wide Web **29**(3), 25 (2026)
13. Makarov, V.V., et al.: Betweenness centrality in multiplex brain network during mental task evaluation. Phys. Rev. E **98**(6), 062413 (2018)
14. Maurya, S.K., Liu, X., Murata, T.: Fast approximations of betweenness centrality with graph neural networks. In: CIKM, pp. 2149–2152 (2019)
15. Maurya, S.K., Liu, X., Murata, T.: Graph neural networks for fast node ranking approximation. ACM TKDD **15**, 1–32 (2021)
16. Pellegrina, L., Vandin, F.: SILVAN: estimating betweenness centralities with progressive sampling and non-uniform Rademacher bounds. ACM TKDD **18**(3), 52 (2023)
17. Riondato, M., Upfal, E.: ABRA: approximating betweenness centrality in static and dynamic graphs with Rademacher averages. ACM TKDD **12**(5), 61 (2018)
18. Riondato, M., Kornaropoulos, E.M.: Fast approximation of betweenness centrality through sampling, pp. 413–422. WSDM (2014)
19. Rozenshtein, P., Gionis, A.: Temporal PageRank. In: ECML PKDD, pp. 674–689 (2016)
20. Santoro, D., Sarpe, I.: ONBRA: rigorous estimation of the temporal betweenness centrality in temporal networks, pp. 1579–1588. WWW (2022)
21. Semertzidis, K., Lili, K., Pitoura, E.: TimeReach: historical reachability queries on evolving graphs, pp. 121–132. EDBT (2015)
22. Tsalouchidou, I., Baeza-Yates, R., Bonchi, F., et al.: Temporal betweenness centrality in dynamic graphs. Int. J. Data Sci. Anal. **9**(3), 257–272 (2020)
23. Wu, H., Cheng, J., Huang, S., et al.: Path problems in temporal graphs. PVLDB **7**(9), 721–732 (2014)

24. Xu, W., Mao, H., Shao, H., et al.: An adaptive sampling algorithm for the Top-K group betweenness centrality. In: ICDE, pp. 170–182 (2025)
25. Zaoli, S., Mazzarisi, P., Lillo, F.: Betweenness centrality for temporal multiplexes. Sci. Rep. **11**(1), 4919 (2021)
26. Zhang, T., et al.: CLGNN: a contrastive learning-based GNN model for betweenness centrality prediction on temporal graphs. ArXiv abs/2506.14122 (2025)
27. Zhang, T., Gao, Y., Zhao, J.: Efficient exact and approximate betweenness centrality computation for temporal graphs, pp. 2395–2406. WWW (2024)
28. Zhang, T., Fang, J., Yang, Z.: TATKC: a temporal graph neural network for fast approximate temporal Katz centrality ranking, pp. 527–538. WWW (2024)
29. Zou, Y., Li, T., Luo, Z.: Node centrality approximation for large networks based on inductive graph neural networks (2024). ArXiv abs/2403.04977

Multi-modal Causal Transformers for Social Media Popularity Prediction

Mingzhu Wang, Dong Zhou(✉), Jianghao Lin, and Yongmei Zhou

School of Information Science and Technology, Guangdong University of Foreign Studies, Guangzhou 510006, Guangdong, China
dongzhou@gdufs.edu.cn

Abstract. Understanding and predicting the terminal popularity of social media content on a specific future target day is critical for digital marketing and recommendation systems. Existing methods often rely on static feature concatenation, which fails to capture the complex multi-modal interactions and strict causality inherent in long-term popularity evolution. To address these limitations, we propose the Multi-Modal Causal Transformer Framework (**MMCTF**) to enhance popularity prediction. Our framework extracts and refines key features from video covers, texts, category tags, and numerical statistics. We utilize a dynamic modality interaction module that adaptively fuses these inputs to establish a robust foundation for temporal relevance. Furthermore, a causal encoding module strictly maintains causality and prevents future information leakage during the sequence modeling phase. Extensive experiments on the public SMTPD and ICIP datasets utilizing a 30-day horizon as the primary evaluation setting for long-term forecasting demonstrate that MMCTF significantly outperforms strong baselines. Specifically, our model reduces Mean Absolute Error by 4.1% and 5.3% and improves Spearman Rank Correlation by 0.42% and 0.65% on the SMTPD and ICIP datasets respectively.

Keywords: Social Media Popularity · Terminal Prediction · Multi-Modal Causal Transformer Framework

1 Introduction

With the rapid development of social networks, massive amounts of User Generated Content (UGC) have emerged. A single piece of content can generate substantial social and commercial value, making accurate Social Media Popularity Prediction (SMPP) crucial for intelligent recommendation, targeted digital marketing, content optimization [29], and public opinion monitoring [6]. Early research focused on mining predictive patterns. For instance, the confirmation by Cao et al. [1] of the decisive role of early popularity initially revealed the key laws of content popularity evolution. In recent years, deep learning and multi-modal models such as HyFea [11] and MMF [15] have made significant progress in fusing heterogeneous information to predict popularity.

L. Ding et al. (Eds.): APWeb-WAIM 2026, LNCS 16993, pp. 282–296, 2027.
https://doi.org/10.1007/978-981-92-5693-8_18

However, existing research still faces challenges in translating complex social media UGC into stable and effective popularity predictions. UGC is highly multimodal, including visual, textual, audio information and rich metadata [27]. Most current methods adopt simple feature concatenation or static weighting strategies, which easily lose deep cross-modal semantic associations and cause cross-modal semantic inconsistency [9]. Although pre-trained models such as BLIP [13] and CLIP [17] have improved vision-language understanding, solving modality heterogeneity and effectively integrating such capabilities into popularity prediction still requires further exploration [8,26].

A central challenge of SMPP is accurately capturing the complex temporal dynamics behind popularity evolution to forecast the terminal state. Content popularity is a dynamic process driven by user behavior, social trends and information diffusion mechanisms [21]. Most existing temporal modeling methods only extract statistical spatio-temporal correlations. They treat popularity prediction as simple pattern matching and ignore the inherent causal logic that history determines the future. Without causal constraints models are easily misled by spurious correlations and cannot distinguish real driving factors from noise. Information diffusion involves complex long- and short-term temporal impacts [5], and even multi-scale time decomposition methods [21] still fail to capture the true evolutionary patterns of popularity without causal mechanism constraints.

The lack of temporal causality modeling makes existing models vulnerable in dynamic social environments. They suffer severe prediction drift [12] when new trends emerge or user behaviors change. AMCFG [12] and MMF [15] identify prediction drift as a key barrier to model robustness.Moreover, over-reliance on environment-specific non-causal features limits model generalization in cold-start, new content, and missing modality scenarios [3]. Insufficient causal interpretability and the high computational cost of fully fine-tuning large pre-trained models [4] limit the exploration of the fundamental drivers of popularity.

To address the aforementioned challenges caused by spurious correlations and simple modality fusion, this paper proposes the Multi-Modal Causal Transformer Framework (MMCTF). Rather than relying solely on traditional semantic alignment, the framework explicitly models temporal dynamics through causal mechanisms before extracting the terminal state. By integrating causal masking directly into the temporal attention network, our model ensures that sequence representations at any given intermediate time step rely exclusively on historical and current information for SMPP.

The core contributions of this work are summarized as follows.

(1) We designed a multi-modal key feature extraction module and a dynamic modality interaction module driven by multi-head attention. This approach adaptively fuses heterogeneous visual, textual, categorical, and numerical representations into a noise-reduced foundation for subsequent sequential modeling.
(2) We developed a causal temporal encoding module by embedding a $t \times t$ causal mask into self-attention layers to model long-term popularity evolution up to the target day t. This mechanism forces attention weights for future states to

zero, preventing information leakage and shielding predictions from spurious correlations common in bidirectional architectures.

(3) We integrated extraction, dynamic fusion, and temporal modeling into a cohesive framework with a terminal prediction head. Evaluations on the SMTPD and ICIP datasets utilizing a 30-day prediction horizon confirm that MMCTF significantly outperforms state-of-the-art baselines. Particularly in long-term forecasting, our model achieves lower Mean Absolute Error and higher Spearman's Rank Correlation, demonstrating its robustness in dynamic real-world environments.

2 Related Work

Early research on popularity prediction primarily relied on statistical models and social network topologies to model propagation dynamics or extract structural features [23]. While Szabo et al. [19] confirmed the decisive role of early popularity and Cheung et al. [7] clustered temporal evolutionary patterns, these methods depend heavily on early statistical features. Consequently, they struggle to handle the increasingly rich multi-modal content and long-term dynamic processes inherent in modern social media.

Modern social media content possesses significant multi-modal attributes, prompting research into integrating visual, textual, and metadata features using pre-trained models like ALBEF [24,31], ResNet, and BERT [30]. However, early methods [10,25] typically employed simple concatenation or static weighting, which limits their effectiveness [2]. Subsequent research introduced self-attention mechanisms [14] to adaptively allocate weights based on content semantics. Nevertheless, maintaining computational efficiency under large-scale inputs and ensuring strict temporal logical rules remains a major challenge [22].

Accurately forecasting long-term terminal dynamics requires handling distant historical dependencies and maintaining temporal causality. Early small-scale datasets limited to specific domains [16,18] or lacking temporal alignment [20] only supported static point prediction tasks. However, the emergence of large-scale, temporally aligned multi-modal benchmarks like SMTPD [29] now enables accurate prediction of long-term popularity dynamics.

Despite advancements in modeling dynamic content evolution, existing approaches exhibit critical shortcomings for terminal popularity prediction. They often rely on static fusion that fails to capture dynamic feature interactions. Furthermore, standard bidirectional Transformer architectures lack rigorous causal constraints. Because they process all inputs simultaneously, they are prone to implicitly utilizing future information within the internal states and fitting spurious correlations. This lack of strict unidirectional logic inevitably degrades the accuracy of the final target day prediction.

To address these limitations, MMCTF employs causality-oriented modeling with causal masking to prevent internal data leakage during the feature encoding phase. By restricting the intermediate multi-modal representations for any given day k to only attend to preceding states up to day k, the framework maintains directional integrity before extracting the target day t. This mechanism actively mitigates spurious correlations and enforces true causal logic, enabling an accurate and robust terminal popularity prediction in social networks.

3 Methodology

3.1 Problem Definition

Let the input be defined as a multimodal content set $X = \{X_v, X_t, X_c, X_n\}$, where the four distinct modalities are formally defined as follows. The visual features X_v are extracted solely from the video cover image. The textual features X_t are derived from the concatenation of the video title, description, and tags. The categorical features X_c comprise the discrete category and language classifications of the content. The numerical features X_n are continuous variables representing the video duration, follower count, and early popularity metrics. The primary objective is to output a single terminal popularity prediction for a specific future target day denoted as t. Let $\hat{p}_t$ represent the model prediction and p_t represent the corresponding ground truth popularity on the target day t. The model aims to minimize the discrepancy between $\hat{p}_t$ and p_t by mapping the heterogeneous initial inputs through a temporal evolution process of length t while strictly preserving temporal causality.

3.2 System Architecture

The MMCTF architecture is designed to map raw, multi-source heterogeneous inputs into a final terminal popularity prediction through a complete non-linear transformation. As illustrated in Fig. 1, the framework logically progresses through three primary stages.

(1) **Feature Extraction** independently learns representations and extracts key features for each specific modality through dedicated neural pathways.
(2) **Multimodal Fusion** takes these extracted modality feature vectors and feeds them into a Multi-Head Attention module. This step facilitates deep, dynamic feature interaction and aggregation across the heterogeneous inputs.
(3) **Temporal Modeling** replicates the aggregated multimodal representation across the time dimension, combines it with positional encodings, and processes it through a **Causal Transformer Encoder**. This module explicitly emphasizes the chronological progression by employing causal masking within its self-attention layers, effectively capturing causal dependencies while strictly preventing future information leakage prior to the target day.

The target prediction for the specific day t is generated through an output Multi-Layer Perceptron (MLP) by extracting the final encoded state. Throughout the entire architecture, residual connections and Layer Normalization are extensively deployed within the core computational blocks to ensure gradient-friendly training and maintain stable information flow across the deep network.

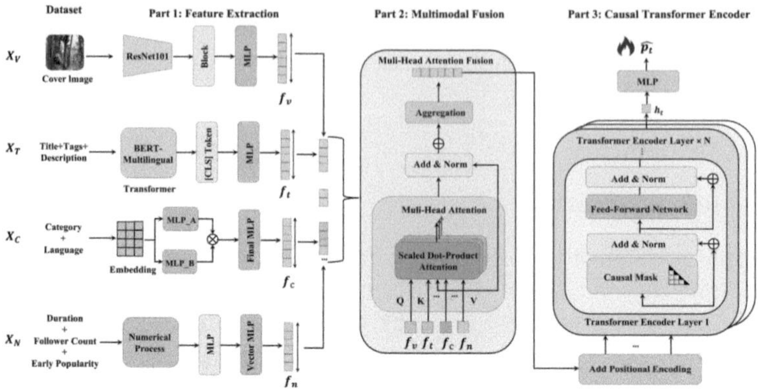

Fig. 1. The overall architecture of the proposed Multi-Modal Causal Transformer Framework.

3.3 Core Components

Multimodal Key Feature Extraction Module

This module aims to extract the core representations of the four modalities, reducing the dimensionality of high-dimensional heterogeneous inputs and uniformly mapping them into compact, dense feature vectors to facilitate subsequent fusion.

Visual Path. A pre-trained ResNet-101 processes the video cover images to extract high-level visual semantics, which are subsequently projected to a unified dimension through a MLP:

$$f_v = \text{MLP}(\text{ResNet}(X_v)). \tag{1}$$

Textual Path. We employ a pre-trained BERT-Multilingual model to encode the textual metadata. Specifically, the [CLS] token representation is extracted and projected through a MLP to capture the global semantic context:

$$f_t = \text{MLP}(\text{BERT}(X_t)_{[\text{CLS}]}). \tag{2}$$

Categorical Path. Discrete category and language features are mapped into dense continuous spaces via an Embedding layer. They are subsequently processed through parallel MLPs, integrated via element-wise multiplication, and passed through a final MLP:

$$f_c = \text{MLP}_f(\text{MLP}_A(\text{Embed}(X_c)) \otimes \text{MLP}_A(\text{Embed}(X_c))). \tag{3}$$

Numerical Path. Continuous numerical features undergo a numerical processing step (e.g., logarithmic transformation and standardization) before being mapped to the target dimension through a vector MLP:

$$f_n = \text{MLP}(\text{Process}(X_n)). \tag{4}$$

Dynamic Modality Interaction Module

To capture the complex, dynamic interactions between different modalities, the system utilizes a Multi-Head Attention mechanism [14]. The four distilled feature vectors (f_v, f_t, f_c, f_n) are projected to a unified hidden dimension d_{model} and concatenated to form a pre-attention sequence $X \in \mathbb{R}^{S \times d_{model}}$ (where the modality sequence length $S = 4$). Rather than relying on static weights, the module internally employs scaled dot-product attention across this sequence to adaptively compute cross-modal dependencies. The multi-head mechanism executes this interaction in parallel, allowing each modality to dynamically attend to relevant features in the others. This process is followed by a standard aggregation step and Add & Norm layers, effectively fusing the heterogeneous multimodal context into a unified representation.

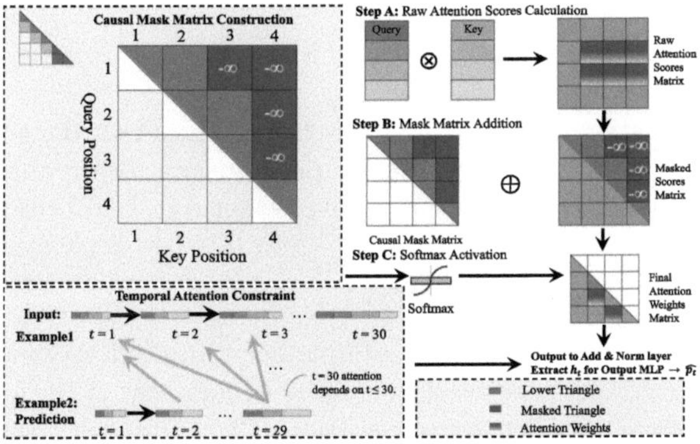

Fig. 2. Mechanism of directional transformer encoder module.

Causal Transformer Encoder Module

This module is specifically designed to capture the evolutionary dynamics and progression of video popularity up to the target day t. As illustrated in Fig. 2, because standard Transformer architectures process inputs in parallel and lack inherent sequential awareness, this module introduces two critical mechanisms to explicitly model the unidirectional flow of time.

The fused multimodal feature vector is replicated t times to establish the foundation of the temporal representation. It should be noted that while visual and textual features are extracted from static snapshots at the time of posting, they serve as a robust content prior that defines the intrinsic quality of the UGC. The dynamic evolutionary momentum is primarily injected through the Numerical Path, which encapsulates early popularity metrics. When these replicated representations are coupled with unique positional encodings for each specific day, the static content attributes are projected into a dynamic temporal space. This embeds the absolute chronological position, explicitly differentiating between historical, current, and future states, and simulates how initial engagement drives long-term popularity growth.

As popularity evolves along a strict timeline, the model must prevent future information leakage. To enforce a strict directional attention constraint within the N self-attention layers of the Transformer Encoder, a lower-triangular directional mask is applied. By adding a mask matrix where the upper triangular region is set to $-\infty$, the Softmax activation forces all attention weights pointing to unobserved future features to strictly zero. This ensures that the Transformer models the progression with strict directional integrity. When generating the intermediate hidden state h_i for a specific day i, the module dynamically weights only the historical data from day 1 to i, keeping the model completely blind to the future progression from day $i+1$ to the target day t.

Terminal State Readout and Prediction

To normalize the extreme long-tailed distribution and mitigate the impact of extreme outliers, we apply a logarithmic popularity score transformation. The ground truth terminal popularity p_t on the target day t is formulated as:

$$p_t = \log_2\left(\frac{c_t}{t} + 1\right) \tag{5}$$

where c_t denotes the view counts of a sample accumulated up to the target day t.

Correspondingly, the predicted terminal popularity $\hat{p}_t$ is formally derived from the model's final encoded representation. The framework explicitly extracts the target-day hidden state h_t from the Causal Transformer Encoder and projects it through an output mapping:

$$\hat{p}_t = \text{MLP}_{\text{out}}(h_t) \tag{6}$$

To map the temporally encoded hidden states to the final popularity prediction $\hat{p}_t$, the framework extracts the target-day hidden state h_t and employs the aforementioned Output MLP. By focusing the network's capacity strictly on this terminal state rather than an entire sequence, the model significantly reduces the redundant parameter space, mitigates the risk of overfitting to intermediate noise, and ensures consistent gradient propagation directed specifically at the target day.

The loss function of our framework is strictly optimized for the terminal forecasting objective. We employ a Smooth L1 Loss between the model's terminal output and the target. Unlike sequence-matching approaches that rely on complex derivative differences or peak alignments, which can introduce unnecessary noise for single-point forecasting, our formulation provides robust regularization against outliers in social media data. The overall loss function $\mathcal{L}$ for the target day is formulated as:

$$\mathcal{L} = \text{SmoothL1}(\hat{p}_t, p_t) = \begin{cases} 0.5(\hat{p}_t - p_t)^2/\beta, & \text{if } |\hat{p}_t - p_t| < \beta \\ |\hat{p}_t - p_t| - 0.5\beta, & \text{otherwise} \end{cases} \quad (7)$$

In this formulation, $\hat{p}_t$ and p_t represent the predicted and ground truth terminal popularity on the target day t, respectively, and β is a hyperparameter governing the transition between L1 and L2 loss behaviors. This robust estimator inherently captures the mapping dynamics while preventing exploding gradients from abnormal popularity spikes. We empirically evaluate the sensitivity and optimal setting of β in Sect. 4.5. During training, the learning rates and network weights are adjusted dynamically using a cosine annealing algorithm to ensure smoother convergence toward the target day's global minimum throughout the training process.

4 Experiments and Results

4.1 Experimental Setup

We implement our method using PyTorch on an NVIDIA GPU. Two datasets, SMTPD [29] and ICIP [28], are utilized for experimental evaluation. The SMTPD dataset comprises 282K samples across 15 categories, covering over 90 languages and 30 days of daily popularity data. The ICIP dataset contains unimodal data consisting of 21K images and their corresponding 30-day engagement metrics. Both datasets are partitioned using a 5-fold cross-validation scheme. The models are trained for a total of 40 epochs using the AdamW optimizer with a batch size of 64. The learning rate is initialized to 1×10^{-2} and dynamically adjusted at the end of each epoch using PyTorch's ReduceLROnPlateau scheduler.

To ensure a fair evaluation of the compared models, we employ both error-based and correlation-based metrics, reporting the results at the target day t milestone. The Mean Absolute Error (MAE) is defined as:

$$MAE = \frac{1}{n} \sum_{i=1}^{n} |\hat{p}_{t,i} - p_{t,i}| \,. \quad (8)$$

where n represents the total number of samples, and $p_{t,i}$ and $\hat{p}_{t,i}$ represent the ground truth and predicted popularity on the target day t, respectively. Lower MAE values indicate smaller prediction errors. For correlation-based metrics, we use Spearman's Rank Correlation (SRC) as:

$$SRC = \frac{1}{n-1} \sum_{i=1}^{n} \left(\frac{\hat{p}_{t,i} - \bar{\hat{p}}_t}{\sigma_{\hat{p}_t}} \right) \left(\frac{p_{t,i} - \bar{p}_t}{\sigma_{p_t}} \right) . \quad (9)$$

where $\bar{p}_t$ and σ_{p_t} denote the mean and standard deviation of the ground truth popularity on the target day t, respectively, while $\bar{\hat{p}}_t$ and $\sigma_{\hat{p}_t}$ represent the mean and standard deviation of the predicted popularity on the target day t. Higher SRC values indicate a stronger correlation between the predicted and actual trends.

4.2 Baseline Methods

To comprehensively assess our model's performance, we incorporate several baseline methods for comparison. By comparing results, we highlight the advantages of our approach in the SMPP task.

(1) **MLP** [29]: This method heavily relies on a stacked structure of multi-layer fully connected networks. It can only capture static correlations between input features and fails to model sequential dependencies in the temporal dimension.
(2) **LSTM** [29]: This method fully utilizes gating mechanisms to effectively alleviate the vanishing gradient problem in traditional RNNs. It integrates cell states and hidden states to accurately capture both long and short-term temporal dependencies in social media popularity sequences.
(3) **MTD** [21]: This method decouples popularity into user-item and time-sensitive contexts by extracting dual temporal variability features across multiple scales. It fuses user-item data with multi-scale sub-matrices to predict popularity through matrix norm error minimization.
(4) **HMMVED** [25]: This method hierarchically fuses user information with multi-modal video content by learning a coarse-grained popularity prior through a user encoder-decoder. It encodes a content posterior aligned with this prior using a video encoder-decoder to decode fine-grained popularity, while optimizing latent embeddings via a multi-modal variational information bottleneck to efficiently represent popularity.
(5) **MASSL** [30]: This multi-modal VAE regression model predicts micro-video popularity by performing feature extraction and Product of Experts fusion. It addresses multi-modal correlation mining and missing modality adaptation challenges within a variational autoencoder framework.
(6) **CBAN** [7]: This method utilizes a cross-modal bipolar attention mechanism to capture both positive and negative bidirectional semantic relationships. Building on ViT and BERT features, it fuses these multi-modal dependencies to enhance prediction accuracy.

4.3 Performance Comparison

In this section, we compare our model with various baseline methods and analyze the results presented in Table 1. The evaluation metrics comprise MAE and SRC.

(1) Traditional models like MLP and LSTM struggle with the 30-day horizon because they ignore evolutionary dynamics or lack sophisticated multi-modal fusion. While advanced models like MASSL perform better, they lack strict causal constraints and remain vulnerable to spurious spatio-temporal correlations. By enforcing a unidirectional causal mask, MMCTF prevents future data leakage during the encoding phase and significantly outperforms both basic and advanced approaches.

Table 1. Performance comparison of six baseline models and our MMCTF model using the SMTPD and ICIP datasets for the target day $t = 30$.

Dataset	Method	Target day $t = 30$	
		MAE ↓	SRC ↑
SMTPD	MLP	1.137	0.925
	LSTM	0.782	0.958
	MTD	0.775	0.960
	HMMVED	0.785	0.952
	MASSL	0.768	0.961
	CBAN	0.760	0.961
	MMCTF	**0.729**	**0.965**
ICIP	MLP	1.710	0.885
	LSTM	1.498	0.897
	MTD	0.850	0.908
	HMMVED	0.920	0.900
	MASSL	0.830	0.911
	CBAN	0.790	0.918
	MMCTF	**0.748**	**0.924**

(2) Compared to the strongest baseline CBAN, MMCTF delivers consistent gains for the terminal prediction task. On the SMTPD dataset, it achieves a 4.1% MAE reduction and a 0.4% SRC improvement. On the ICIP dataset, it secures a 5.3% MAE decrease and a 0.6% SRC increase. This demonstrates that effectively modeling multi-modal causal dependencies allows our framework to mitigate temporal information loss and maintain exceptional robustness in extended prediction scenarios.

To further justify the added architecture design, we conducted a brief efficiency analysis. Compared to the strongest baseline CBAN, MMCTF achieves superior performance without a significant increase in parameter scale. This is primarily due to our design of the Weight-Shared Output MLP, which restricts the parameter space by sharing weights across all sequence steps. Consequently, MMCTF maintains a favorable performance-complexity trade-off, delivering robust long-term forecasting accuracy while maintaining an inference latency comparable to standard multi-modal attention-based models.

4.4 Ablation Study

To evaluate the proposed causal Transformer, this section provides a multi-dimensional analysis including component ablation, hyperparameter sensitivity, and qualitative visualization of multi-modal attention.

Table 2. Ablation study of different components in our framework.

Configuration	MAE ↓	SRC ↑	ΔMAE (%)	ΔSRC (%)
No dynamic interaction (Simple concatenation)	0.776	0.960	+ 6.45	− 0.52
No causal encoding (Replace with LSTM)	0.764	0.962	+ 4.25	− 0.31
No causal mask (Future information leakage)	0.752	0.963	+ 3.16	− 0.21
Full framework	**0.729**	**0.965**		

To verify the effectiveness and necessity of each component, we conducted a comprehensive ablation study on the SMTPD dataset and uniform training settings for a fair comparison.

As detailed in Table 2, experimental results clearly reveal each module's specific contribution to the overall model performance. Removing the Dynamic Modality Interaction module causes the most severe degradation, increasing MAE by 6.45% and decreasing SRC by 0.52%. This proves that when handling complex social media data, simple feature concatenation cannot effectively align heterogeneous semantics, highlighting the interaction module's crucial role in adaptive cross-modal feature fusion.

The temporal modeling components are equally critical to the architecture. Replacing the causal Transformer encoder with a traditional LSTM worsens MAE by 4.25% and SRC by 0.31%, validating that causal self-attention better captures long-sequence temporal dependencies than traditional RNNs. Furthermore, disabling the causal mask increases MAE by 3.16%, empirically confirming the absolute necessity of maintaining strict temporal causality to prevent future data leakage in popularity evolution prediction.

Overall, the dynamic modality interaction and Causal Transformer Encoder modules yield performance gains of 3.1% and 4.5% respectively. Their integration achieves a synergistic 6.8% improvement, validating the rationality of our framework design.

4.5 Hyperparameter Sensitivity of β

To further investigate the impact of our target-optimized loss function on terminal popularity prediction, we conduct a sensitivity analysis on the hyperparameter β within the Smooth L1 Loss. As formulated in Eq. 6, β controls the transition threshold between L1 and L2 loss behaviors, making it crucial for handling the abnormal popularity spikes inherently present in social media data.

We vary β across a candidate set $\{0.1, 0.5, 1.0, 2.0\}$ and evaluate the model's performance on the SMTPD dataset. The results are summarized in Table 3.

As observed, when β is set too small (e.g., 0.1), the loss function predominantly behaves as an L1 loss. While this provides robustness against outliers,

Table 3. Impact of the loss hyperparameter β on model performance (SMTPD dataset).

Hyperparameter β	MAE ↓	SRC ↑
$\beta = 0.1$ (L1 dominant)	0.758	0.951
$\beta = 0.5$	0.738	0.963
$\beta = 1.0$ **(Optimal)**	**0.729**	**0.965**
$\beta = 2.0$ (L2 dominant)	0.751	0.958

it causes gradient oscillations near the convergence point, slightly degrading the MAE. Conversely, a large β (e.g., 2.0) shifts the behavior toward an L2 loss over a wider error range, making the model overly sensitive to terminal popularity spikes and leading to less stable gradients. The empirical results demonstrate that $\beta = 1.0$ achieves the optimal balance. It effectively smooths the gradients for minor prediction errors to facilitate steady convergence while capping the gradient penalty for extreme viral outliers, ultimately yielding the best MAE and SRC performance.

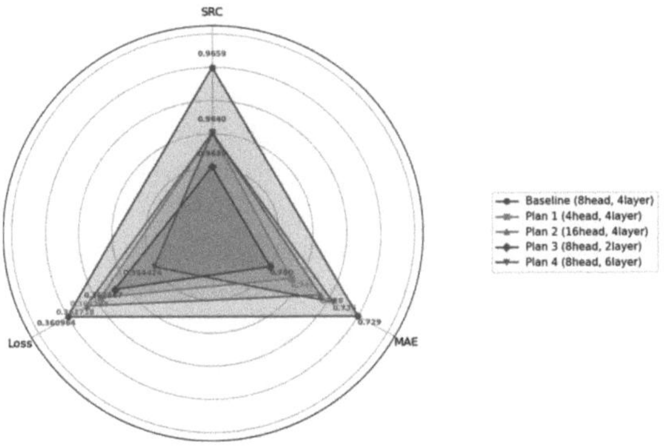

Fig. 3. Architecture tuning for the causal transformer. The radar chart compares the performance of different configurations across Loss, MAE, and SRC metrics. The baseline (8 heads, 4 layers) achieves the optimal balance.

4.6 Architecture Tuning

Next we focus on the number of attention heads and Transformer layers by using the SMTPD multi-modal long-sequences for the causal Transformer.

The radar chart in Fig. 3 compares performance across Loss, MAE, and SRC, showing that the baseline configuration of 8 attention heads and 4 layers achieves the optimal balance. Deviating from this setup leads to performance degradation as fewer heads or layers limit model capacity while excessive configurations yield diminishing returns and potential overfitting.

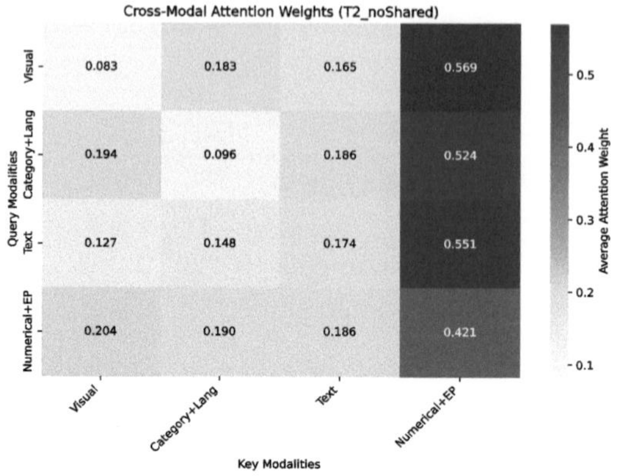

Fig. 4. Visualization of the average cross-modal attention weights learned by our optimal configuration in the dynamic modal interaction module.

4.7 Modality Interaction Visualization

To explore its internal logic of integrating multi-modal features, we visualize the average cross-modal attention weights learned by the dynamic modality interaction module under the optimal configuration.

As illustrated in Fig. 4, the combined Numerical and Early Popularity features act as the primary predictive anchor by regulating other modalities. The Visual, Text, and Category-Language modalities assign high attention weights of 0.569, 0.551, and 0.524 to these features respectively. This confirms that anchoring content to early performance maximizes information gain and verifies our framework's interpretability in capturing multi-modal dependencies.

5 Conclusion

This paper proposes an end-to-end Multi-Modal Causal Transformer Framework (MMCTF) for long-term social media popularity prediction. The framework adaptively fuses heterogeneous features via dynamic interaction and employs directional temporal encoding to maintain strict temporal directionality before extracting the final terminal prediction for the target day. Experiments on SMTPD and ICIP datasets demonstrate its effectiveness and robustness in long-term terminal forecasting. One limitation of the current study is the absence of underlying social graph topology, as the utilized datasets primarily provide content-centric engagement metrics. Therefore, future work includes integrating spatial-temporal graph neural networks to capture dynamic diffusion networks, integrating large language models for low-resource languages, and designing lightweight variants for efficiency.

Acknowledgements. This work was supported by the National Natural Science Foundation of China (No. 62376062), the Ministry of Education of Humanities and

Social Science Project (No. 23YJAZH220, No. 24YJAZH244), and the National Social Science Fund of China (No.24BXW047).

References

1. Cao, Q., Shen, H., Gao, J.: Popularity prediction on social platforms with coupled graph neural networks. In: Proceedings of the 13th International Conference on Web Search and Data Mining, pp. 70–78 (2020)
2. Chen, T., Guestrin, C.: XGBoost: a scalable tree boosting system. In: Proceedings of the 22nd ACM SIGKDD International Conference on Knowledge Discovery and Data Mining, pp. 785–794 (2016)
3. Cheng, Z., Lang, J., Zhong, T.: Seeing the unseen in micro-video popularity prediction: self-correlation retrieval for missing modality generation. In: Proceedings of the 31st ACM SIGKDD Conference on Knowledge Discovery and Data Mining, vol. 1, pp. 142–152 (2025)
4. Cheng, Z., Li, J., Lang, J.: In-context prompt-augmented micro-video popularity prediction. In: Proceedings of the AAAI Conference on Artificial Intelligence, pp. 11527–11535 (2025)
5. Cheng, Z., Ye, W., Liu, L.: Enhancing information diffusion prediction with self-supervised disentangled user and cascade representations. In: Proceedings of the 32nd ACM International Conference on Information and Knowledge Management, pp. 3808–3812 (2023)
6. Cheng, Z., Zhang, J., Xu, X.: Retrieval-augmented hypergraph for multimodal social media popularity prediction. In: Proceedings of the 30th ACM SIGKDD Conference on Knowledge Discovery and Data Mining, pp. 445–455 (2024)
7. Cheung, T., Lam, K.: Crossmodal bipolar attention for multimodal classification on social media. Neurocomputing **514**, 1–12 (2022)
8. Hou, W., Li, W.: Modality-aligned hierarchical attention network for multi-modal popularity prediction on social media. In: Proceedings of the 33rd ACM International Conference on Multimedia, pp. 14073–14078 (2025)
9. Hsu, C.C., Lee, C.M., Lin, Y.F.: Revisiting vision-language features adaptation and inconsistency for social media popularity prediction. In: Proceedings of the 32nd ACM International Conference on Multimedia, pp. 11464–11469 (2024)
10. Kang, P., Lin, Z., Teng, S.: Catboost-based framework with additional user information for social media popularity prediction. In: Proceedings of the 27th ACM International Conference on Multimedia, pp. 2677–2681 (2019)
11. Lai, X., Zhang, Y., Zhang, W.: HyFea: winning solution to social media popularity prediction for multimedia grand challenge 2020. In: Proceedings of the 28th ACM International Conference on Multimedia, pp. 4565–4569 (2020)
12. Lee, C.M., Qiu, B.C., Kang, C.J.: Anchoring trends: mitigating social media popularity prediction drift via feature clustering and expansion. In: Proceedings of the 33rd ACM International Conference on Multimedia, pp. 14094–14100 (2025)
13. Li, J., Li, D., Xiong, C., et al.: BLIP: bootstrapping language-image pre-training for unified vision-language understanding and generation. In: International Conference on Machine Learning, pp. 12888–12900 (2022)
14. Lin, H.H., Lin, J.D., Ople, J.J.M., et al.: Social media popularity prediction based on multi-modal self-attention mechanisms. IEEE Access **10**, 4448–4455 (2021)

15. Lin, Y.S., Lee, A.J.T.: MMF: winning solution to social media popularity prediction challenge 2024. In: Proceedings of the 32nd ACM International Conference on Multimedia, pp. 11445–11449 (2024)
16. Mazloom, M., Rietveld, R., Rudinac, S.: Multimodal popularity prediction of brand-related social media posts. In: Proceedings of the 24th ACM International Conference on Multimedia, pp. 197–201 (2016)
17. Radford, A., Kim, J.W., Hallacy, C.: Learning transferable visual models from natural language supervision. In: Proceedings of the International Conference on Machine Learning, pp. 8748–8763 (2021)
18. Sanjo, S., Katsurai, M.: Recipe popularity prediction with deep visual-semantic fusion. In: Proceedings of the 2017 ACM on Conference on Information and Knowledge Management, pp. 2279–2282 (2017)
19. Szabo, G., Huberman, B.A.: Predicting the popularity of online content. Commun. ACM **53**(8), 80–88 (2010)
20. Wu, B., Cheng, W.H., Liu, P.: SMP challenge: an overview of social media prediction challenge. In: Proceedings of the 27th ACM International Conference on Multimedia, pp. 2667–2671 (2019)
21. Wu, B., Mei, T., Cheng, W.H.: Unfolding temporal dynamics: predicting social media popularity using multi-scale temporal decomposition. In: Proceedings of the AAAI Conference on Artificial Intelligence, (2016)
22. Wu, J., Zhao, L., Li, D.: Deeply exploit visual and language information for social media popularity prediction. In: Proceedings of the 30th ACM International Conference on Multimedia, pp. 7045–7049 (2022)
23. Wu, L., Yi, L., Ren, X.L., et al.: Predicting the popularity of information on social platforms without underlying network structure. Entropy **25**(6), 916 (2023)
24. Xie, J., Zheng, X., Zheng, L.: Prototype-aware multimodal alignment for open-vocabulary visual grounding. arXiv preprint arXiv:2509.06291 (2025)
25. Xie, J., Zhu, Y., Chen, Z.: Micro-video popularity prediction via multimodal variational information bottleneck. IEEE Trans. Multim. **25**, 24–37 (2021)
26. Xu, K., Lin, Z., Zhao, J.: Multimodal deep learning for social media popularity prediction with attention mechanism. In: Proceedings of the 28th ACM International Conference on Multimedia, pp. 4580–4584 (2020)
27. Xu, K., Xu, Q., Luo, B., et al.: Higher-order vision-language fusion for video popularity prediction. In: Proceedings of the 33rd ACM International Conference on Multimedia, pp. 14086–14093 (2025)
28. Xu, X., Zhang, Y., Zhou, F.: Improving multimodal social media popularity prediction via selective retrieval knowledge augmentation. In: Proceedings of the AAAI Conference on Artificial Intelligence, pp. 932–940 (2025)
29. Xu, Y., Zheng, B., Zhu, W.: SMTPD: a new benchmark for temporal prediction of social media popularity. In: Proceedings of the Computer Vision and Pattern Recognition Conference, pp. 18847–18857 (2025)
30. Zhang, Z., Xu, S., Guo, L.: Multi-modal variational auto-encoder model for micro-video popularity prediction. In: Proceedings of the 8th International Conference on Communication and Information Processing, pp. 9–16 (2022)
31. Zhou, J., Wang, X., Liu, N.: Visual and linguistic double transformer fusion model for multimodal tweet classification. In: Proceedings of the 2023 International Joint Conference on Neural Networks, pp. 1–8 (2023)

Physics-Informed Chain-of-Thought Reasoning for Physical Field Prediction

Yuxin Bai[1,2], Xin Bi[1,2(✉)], Yuxin Feng[1], Qinghan Jin[1,2], Ben-guo He[1], Yongjiao Sun[2], and Zhen Zhang[3]

[1] State Key Laboratory of Intelligent Deep Metal Mining and Equipment, Northeastern University, Shenyang, China
bixin@mail.neu.edu.cn

[2] School of Computer Science and Engineering, Northeastern University, Shenyang, China

[3] Yingkou Institute of Technology, Yingkou, China

Abstract. Physical field prediction is a cornerstone in various scientific and engineering applications. Existing deep learning approaches typically require substantial domain expertise for physics loss formulation and parameter configuration, limiting their prediction accuracy and adaptability. Although large language models (LLMs) have demonstrated strong capabilities in natural language understanding, they struggle to construct physically consistent formulations for complex physical systems due to intricate interdependencies among physical parameters and strict constraints imposed by fundamental physical laws. To bridge this gap, we propose PhysCoT, a framework designed for physical scenario understanding and physical field prediction from natural language descriptions. PhysCoT consists of two core components, namely the Physical Scenario Interpreter (PSI) and the Physical Field Predictor (PFP). PSI utilizes chain-of-thought (CoT) prompting to guide LLMs in translating unstructured physical scenario descriptions into structured representations, including governing mechanisms and associated parameters. Building on this structured understanding, PFP constructs physics-informed loss functions for downstream model training and performs physical field prediction using neural solvers. PhysCoT is evaluated on four benchmark tasks in computational mechanics. Experimental results show that PhysCoT improves symbolic specification quality and provides a stronger overall balance between prediction accuracy and solver reliability than direct LLM-based baselines.

Keywords: Chain-of-Thought · LLM · Physics-informed learning

1 Introduction

The ability to accurately predict physical fields, such as stress distributions in mechanical components and fluid dynamics in aerospace design, is a cornerstone of modern scientific discovery and engineering innovation [11]. However, a key

L. Ding et al. (Eds.): APWeb-WAIM 2026, LNCS 16993, pp. 297–311, 2027.
https://doi.org/10.1007/978-981-92-5693-8_19

challenge underlies these capabilities: *the translation of a real-world problem into a computable representation.* Specifically, converting complex physical scenarios, typically described through unstructured modalities such as natural language, into formalized systems comprising partial differential equations (PDEs), boundary conditions (BCs), and domain-specific parameters remains a bottleneck [7]. Consequently, the power of physics-based computational tools remains largely confined to expert users, limiting broader scientific and engineering participation.

While scientific machine learning methods such as Physics-Informed Neural Networks (PINNs) and neural operators have demonstrated remarkable success in solving PDE-governed problems, they typically assume that the governing equations, boundary conditions, and physical parameters are already available. In practice, however, obtaining such formulations from real-world problem descriptions remains a labor-intensive and expertise-dependent process. Automating this modeling process using Large Language Models (LLMs) has emerged as an important research direction. LLMs possess remarkable capabilities in understanding, reasoning over, and generating complex natural language, making them natural candidates for bridging the gap between unstructured problem descriptions and formal mathematical representations.

However, current LLMs exhibit significant limitations in generating physically consistent formulations for complex systems. The fundamental challenge is not a lack of encoded scientific knowledge, but rather the insufficient capability of LLMs to perform *constraint-aware reasoning* across the multiple interdependent components of a physical model. Physical systems involve tightly coupled relationships among variables, equations, constitutive laws, and boundary conditions, making it difficult for LLMs to generate globally consistent physical models from natural language descriptions.

To address this challenge, **PhysCoT** is introduced, a framework that systematically guides LLMs to emulate the reasoning process of expert physicists. The framework consists of two core components: the *Physical Scenario Interpreter (PSI)* and the *Physical Field Predictor (PFP)*. (1) The PSI module translates natural language descriptions of physical scenarios into formal, machine-interpretable representations. It leverages a carefully crafted Chain-of-Thought (CoT) prompting strategy that progressively identifies relevant physical phenomena, selects appropriate governing equations, and specifies boundary and initial conditions. This process generates a structured model specification that encapsulates the key components required for physics-based modeling. (2) Building upon the output of PSI, the PFP module performs downstream model construction and field prediction. Specifically, it uses the structured formulations produced by PSI to instantiate a physics-informed loss function, which is then used to train a predictive model. Given the verified symbolic specification, a Physics-Informed Neural Network (PINN) [13,22,24] is used to solve the resulting physical field prediction problem. PINNs are particularly well-suited for this task, as they allow the symbolic equations and constraints generated by PSI to be directly integrated into the learning objective, thereby serving as an ideal platform for validating the physical coherence and utility of the generated model descriptions.

To summarize, the main contributions of this work are threefold. (1) Physical scenario understanding is formulated as a structured reasoning problem that bridges natural language descriptions and executable physical models. (2) PhysCoT, a physics-aware Chain-of-Thought framework, decomposes physical modeling into geometry identification, governing equation formulation, and boundary condition extraction, enabling the generation of physically consistent and mathematically well-formed model representations. (3) A symbolic verification mechanism is developed to improve the consistency of generated physical models, with comprehensive experiments demonstrating that PhysCoT improves symbolic consistency and provides a stronger overall balance between prediction accuracy and solver reliability than direct LLM-based approaches for physical scenario understanding and physical field prediction.

2 Related Work

2.1 LLMs for Scientific Reasoning

Large language models (LLMs) are increasingly being explored as assistants and collaborators in scientific discovery [4,9,30]. Their ability to process vast amounts of text and generate human-like responses has found applications across various domains, such as translating natural language to executable code [5], planning complex chemical synthesis pathways [3], and assisting in formal mathematical reasoning [20].

Recent studies have demonstrated the ability of LLMs to perform a variety of scientific reasoning tasks, including mathematical problem solving, code generation, and scientific question answering [1,14,26]. However, most existing approaches focus on solving predefined problems or producing a single output, whereas PhysCoT addresses the more challenging task of constructing a complete physical model from unstructured natural-language descriptions.

2.2 Chain-of-Thought

Standard LLM prompting often elicits direct answers, which can be unreliable for multi-step reasoning tasks. Chain-of-Thought (CoT) prompting [28] was a landmark development, showing that prompting a model to "think step by step" significantly improves its performance on tasks requiring logical or mathematical reasoning. This simple technique externalizes the model's reasoning process, making it more robust and interpretable.

The CoT paradigm has since been refined and extended. Methods like "Self-Consistency" improve reliability by sampling multiple reasoning paths and choosing the most frequent answer [6,8,27]. The "Tree of Thoughts" (ToT) framework generalizes this by allowing LLMs to explore and evaluate different reasoning branches in a tree structure [31]. Similarly, "Least-to-Most" prompting breaks down a complex problem into a sequence of simpler subproblems to be solved in order [32]. Unlike generic reasoning frameworks such as ToT or Least-to-Most prompting, PhysCoT incorporates domain-specific physical priors into the reasoning process. The reasoning chain explicitly follows the workflow adopted by human physicists, progressing from physical phenomenon identification to governing equation selection and finally to boundary and initial condition specification. This structured decomposition enables the model to better maintain consistency across the multiple interdependent components of a physical system.

2.3 Physics-Informed Learning

The field of scientific machine learning seeks to fuse domain knowledge, typically in the form of physical laws, with data-driven techniques [11,21]. This has led to a diverse ecosystem of powerful methods. Representative approaches include neural operators such as DeepONets [17] and FNOs [15], as well as physics-constrained learning methods that incorporate differential equations into the learning process [23].

A more recent line of research leverages neural networks that directly solve differential equations by parameterizing the solution with a neural network and minimizing the residuals. Physics-Informed Neural Networks (PINNs) [18,22] are a typical example of this approach [10]. By minimizing a loss function composed of the PDE residual and boundary/initial condition mismatches, PINNs can find solutions without mesh generation or labeled solution data. Variants have been developed to better enforce physical principles, such as Conservative PINNs (cPINNs) that ensure conservation laws are strictly satisfied.

Unlike these approaches, which assume the governing equations are already available, the present work focuses on constructing such formulations from natural language descriptions. A PINN is employed for model solving because the symbolic PDEs and boundary conditions extracted by the proposed framework can be naturally incorporated into the PINN loss function, making it an ideal testbed for validating the generated physical models.

3 Method

3.1 Framework Overview

PhysCoT is a framework that transforms natural-language descriptions of physical scenarios into structured physical models for physics-informed field prediction. The framework consists of two components: the Physical Scenario Interpreter (PSI) and the Physical Field Predictor (PFP). PSI employs a physics-aware Chain-of-Thought (CoT) reasoning process to convert textual descriptions into machine-interpretable physical representations, while PFP translates the resulting symbolic models into executable objectives for physical field prediction.

The overall workflow maps a natural-language description $\mathcal{D}$ to the predicted physical field u_{pred} through an intermediate structured representation $\mathcal{S}_{\text{structured}}$:

$$\mathcal{D} \xrightarrow{\text{PSI}} \mathcal{S}_{\text{structured}} \xrightarrow{\text{PFP}} u_{\text{pred}} \tag{1}$$

The structured representation is defined as

$$\mathcal{S}_{\text{structured}} = (G, E, C, P), \tag{2}$$

where G denotes the geometric domain, E represents the governing partial differential equations (PDEs), C contains the boundary and initial conditions, and P denotes the associated physical parameters.

As illustrated in Fig. 1, PSI generates a structured physical model comprising geometry, governing equations, boundary/initial conditions, and physical parameters. This symbolic model is subsequently processed by PFP, which automatically constructs a PINN loss function and performs physical field prediction.

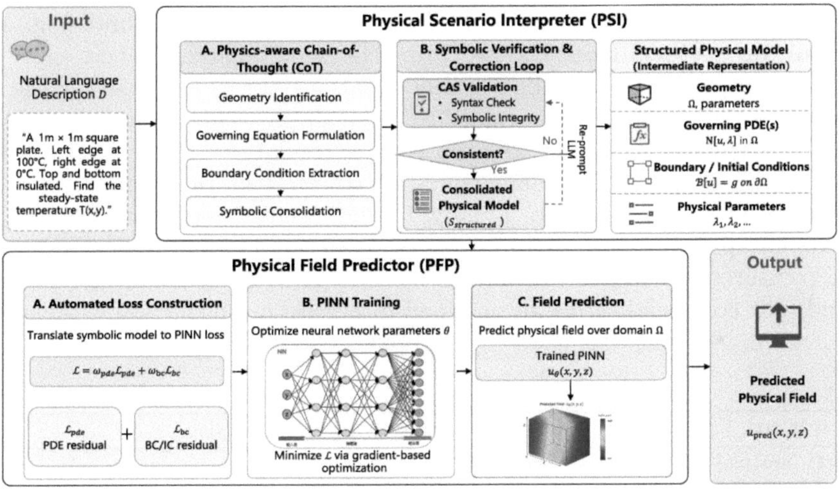

Fig. 1. Overview of PhysCoT. PSI transforms natural-language descriptions into structured physical models, and PFP predicts the target physical field.

3.2 Physical Scenario Interpreter (PSI)

The PSI converts the natural language description $\mathcal{D}$ into a structured, physically consistent, and machine-readable representation $\mathcal{S}_{\text{structured}}$ through CoT-guided parsing and a symbolic verification loop.

CoT-Guided Semantic Parsing. Directly translating unstructured language into a formal model using a single, monolithic prompt is inherently brittle. This approach often fails on complex problems, producing syntactically invalid or physically inconsistent outputs. To overcome this fragility, the PSI employs a

physics-aware Chain-of-Thought (CoT) strategy. This method programmatically guides the Large Language Model (LLM) through a sequence of logical steps that mirror an expert's systematic workflow, transforming the opaque, internal reasoning of the LLM into a transparent and verifiable dialogue.

As formalized in Algorithm 1, the PSI decomposes the complex modeling task into a series of focused, context-aware sub-tasks, with each step iteratively building upon the output of the preceding one.

1. **Geometry Identification**: The process begins by prompting the LLM to identify only the computational domain Ω and its parameters. For example, from "a 1-meter square plate," it extracts a `Rectangle` shape with `width=1.0` and `height=1.0`. This establishes the foundational spatial context.
2. **Governing Equation Formulation**: With the geometry established, this information is fed back to the LLM as context. The model is then tasked to infer the relevant governing PDEs in symbolic form, along with all dependent/independent variables (e.g., `T(x,y)`) and physical constants (e.g., `k`).
3. **Boundary Condition Extraction**: The accumulated context, now containing both geometry and governing equations, forms the basis for the final reasoning step. The LLM is guided to parse all physical constraints, mapping descriptive language (e.g., "the top edge is insulated") to its precise mathematical form (e.g., a Neumann condition `dT/dn=0` on the boundary `y=1`).
4. **Symbolic Consolidation**: Finally, the information extracted from all preceding steps is synthesized into a unified, structured format (e.g., JSON). This step ensures all components are organized logically for machine interpretation and that colloquial terms are mapped to precise mathematical expressions.

Algorithm 1. CoT-Guided Semantic Parsing within PSI

Input: Natural language description $\mathcal{D}$
Output: Initial structured semantic representation $\mathcal{S}_{\text{structured}}$

```
history ← [ ]
prompt_geo ← "From D, identify geometry. Output structured."
geometry ← LLM(prompt_geo)
history.append("Context: " + geometry)
prompt_pde ← history + " State the governing PDEs."
pdes ← LLM(prompt_pde)
history.append("Context: " + pdes)
prompt_bcs ← history + " Extract all BCs/ICs."
bcs_ics ← LLM(prompt_bcs)
S_structured ← ConsolidateToJSON(geometry, pdes, bcs_ics)
return S_structured
```

Symbolic Verification and Correction Loop. This stage is the PSI's critical quality assurance mechanism, designed to enforce mathematical self-consistency in the LLM-generated model. It operates on the principle that a valid model must not use any variables or parameters in its equations that it has not explicitly defined. The process, formalized in Algorithm 2, is an automated **Generate-then-Verify** cycle implemented with a Computer Algebra System (CAS) [19]:

1. **Syntactic Check**: The CAS first attempts to parse each symbolic equation string (e.g., 'diff(u, x, 2) + diff(u, y, 2) - f'). A failure indicates a malformed expression, such as unbalanced parentheses or invalid operators, and is immediately flagged.
2. **Symbolic Integrity Check**: If the syntax is valid, the CAS performs a deeper check. For each equation, it extracts the set of all "free symbols" (variables and parameters) present in the expression. It then compares this set against the comprehensive list of symbols explicitly defined by the LLM in the 'parameters' and 'variables' sections of $\mathcal{S}_{\text{structured}}$. An inconsistency is detected if any symbol is used but not defined (e.g., using a diffusion coefficient 'k' in the PDE without providing its value in the parameters list).
3. **Corrective Feedback Loop**: If any check fails, the PSI formulates a new, contextualized prompt for the LLM. This prompt includes the original problem, the flawed model, and a specific, machine-generated error message (e.g., "Error: The symbol 'k' was used in the PDE but not defined. Please correct the model."). The LLM is then tasked with providing a revised formulation. This loop iterates until a fully self-consistent model passes all checks, guaranteeing a valid input for the next stage.

Before the verified specification is passed to PFP, a deterministic normalization step canonicalizes executable-format details, such as derivative notation, numeric constants, and parameter containers, without changing the recovered PDEs, boundary/initial conditions, or physical parameters.

3.3 Physical Field Predictor (PFP)

The PFP ingests the verified structured representation $\mathcal{S}_{\text{verified}}$ generated by the PSI and performs the downstream tasks of loss construction, model training, and physical field prediction. In this work, a Physics-Informed Neural Network (PINN) is adopted as the implementation backend for translating the verified physical specifications into trainable loss functions and numerical field predictions.

Automated Loss Construction and Model Training. The PFP first automatically compiles the symbolic model in $\mathcal{S}_{\text{verified}}$ into a composite Physics-Informed Neural Network (PINN) loss function. The total loss $\mathcal{L}_\theta$ for a neural network u_θ that approximates the solution is a weighted sum of the residuals from the governing PDE, boundary conditions (BC), and initial conditions (IC) [2,25]:

Algorithm 2. Symbolic Verification and Correction in PSI

Input: Initial structured data $\mathcal{S}_{\text{current}}$, Original context $\mathcal{C}$
Output: Verified structured data $\mathcal{S}_{\text{verified}}$

```
is_valid ← false
attempts ← 0
while not is_valid and attempts < MAX_ATTEMPTS do
    attempts ← attempts + 1
    is_valid, errors ← ValidateWithCAS(S_current)
    if not is_valid then
        feedback ← GenerateFeedback(errors)
        prompt ← C + feedback
        S_current ← LLM(prompt)
    end if
end while
if not is_valid then
    raise VerificationFailedError
end if
S_verified ← S_current
return S_verified
```

$$\mathcal{L}_{\theta} = w_{\text{pde}}\mathcal{L}_{\text{pde}} + \sum_{c \in \mathcal{C}} w_c \mathcal{L}_c \tag{3}$$

The component of the loss is generated by translating the corresponding symbolic expression from $\mathcal{S}_{\text{verified}}$ into a differentiable function executable within a deep learning framework such as PyTorch. The residual loss of the PDE, $\mathcal{L}_{\text{pde}}$, is formed from the governing equation (e.g., $\mathcal{N}(u) - f = 0$) by computing the mean squared error of this expression over a set of collocation points [29] $\{\mathbf{x}_p^i\}_{i=1}^{N_p}$ sampled from the interior of the domain Ω:

$$\mathcal{L}_{\text{pde}} = \frac{1}{N_p} \sum_{i=1}^{N_p} \left| \mathcal{N}(u_{\theta}(\mathbf{x}_p^i)) - f(\mathbf{x}_p^i) \right|^2 \tag{4}$$

Similarly, the boundary and initial condition losses are constructed. For a boundary condition $\mathcal{B}(u) - g = 0$ on a boundary $\partial\Omega_k$, the PFP creates a loss term that penalizes the mean squared residual over points $\{\mathbf{x}_{b_k}^j\}$ sampled on that specific boundary. Any partial derivatives of the field variable u required in the operators $\mathcal{N}$ or $\mathcal{B}$ (e.g., $\frac{\partial u}{\partial x}$, $\frac{\partial^2 u}{\partial t^2}$) are computed using automatic differentiation on the neural network u_{θ}. This direct translation from symbolic representations to computational graphs enables end-to-end automation.

Once the total loss function $\mathcal{L}_{\theta}$ is defined, the PFP trains the neural network u_{θ} by minimizing this loss using standard gradient-based optimization. The process is generalized in Algorithm 3. After training, the optimized network u_{θ^*} serves as the final physics-based predictor, capable of evaluating the physical field at any point in the domain.

Algorithm 3. Automated Loss Construction and Training in PFP

Input: Verified structured data $\mathcal{S}_{\text{verified}}$, NN model u_θ
Output: Trained NN model u_{θ^*}

```
Initialize ℒ_total ← 0
Parse governing operator 𝒩 and source term f from 𝒮_verified[pde]
Sample collocation points x_p from domain Ω
ℒ_pde ← MSE(𝒩(u_θ(x_p)), f(x_p))
ℒ_total ← ℒ_total + w_pde · ℒ_pde
for condition in 𝒮_verified[conditions] do
    Parse condition operator ℬ and target value g
    Sample points x_c from the condition location
    ℒ_c ← MSE(ℬ(u_θ(x_c)), g(x_c))
    ℒ_total ← ℒ_total + w_c · ℒ_c
end for
Train u_θ by minimizing ℒ_total
return u_θ*
```

4 Experiments

4.1 Experimental Setup

PhysCoT is evaluated on four benchmark problems spanning three major PDE categories in scientific computing: Elliptic (Poisson, Kirsch), Hyperbolic (Wave), and Parabolic (Multiscale Heat). These benchmarks assess the ability to handle complex geometries, time-dependent dynamics, and multiscale physical parameters [10,18].

All experiments were conducted on a workstation equipped with an NVIDIA RTX 4090 GPU and an Intel i9-12900K CPU. DeepSeek-V3 [16] was used as the LLM backbone, and the downstream PINN was implemented in DeepXDE with six hidden layers of 128 neurons and Tanh activations. Training employed Adam [12] (1×10^{-3}, 8000 epochs) followed by L-BFGS. A fixed prompt template and temperature of 0 were used throughout all experiments.

4.2 Benchmark Scenarios

Case 1: 2D Poisson's Equation (Elliptic/Complex Geometry). A steady-state heat conduction process is simulated on a non-convex L-shaped domain $\Omega = [-1,1]^2 \setminus [0,1]^2$ (a square with the top-right quadrant removed). A uniform internal heat source $f = 1$ is applied, with zero Dirichlet boundary conditions on all boundaries. The model must correctly infer the Poisson equation $-\Delta u = 1$ (distinguishing it from the Laplace equation) and implement the Constructive Solid Geometry (CSG) logic for the L-shape.
Reference for MSE: High-fidelity Finite Element Method (FEM) solution generated via FreeFEM++ on a fine mesh. The MSE is computed for the temperature field u over the entire domain Ω.

Case 2: 2D Kirsch Problem (Linear Elasticity). This classic problem considers an infinite elastic plate with a circular hole of radius $r = 1$ subjected to uniform far-field tension $\sigma_\infty = 1$ in the x-direction. The material is isotropic with Young's modulus $E = 10$ and Poisson's ratio $\nu = 0.3$ (plane stress assumption). For numerical simulation, the infinite domain is truncated to a square region $[-10, 10] \times [-10, 10]$ with the hole at the center. The outer boundary is constrained using analytical far-field Kirsch boundary conditions, while the circular hole boundary is traction-free.

Reference for MSE: Analytical Kirsch solution. The MSE is computed as the average mean squared error of the stress components $(\sigma_{xx}, \sigma_{yy}, \sigma_{xy})$ over the computational domain excluding the circular hole, i.e., $r \geq 1 + \epsilon$.

Case 3: 1D Wave Equation (Hyperbolic/Time-Dependent). To test the handling of second-order time derivatives, a taut string ($L = 1$) vibrating over $t \in [0, 1]$ with wave speed $C = 2$ is simulated. The string is "released from rest" from an initial shape $u_0 = \sin(\pi x) + 0.5 \sin(4\pi x)$.

Reference for MSE: Analytical standing wave solution. The MSE is computed for the displacement u over the entire spacetime domain $[0, 1] \times [0, 1]$.

Case 4: 2D Multiscale Heat Equation (Parabolic/Anisotropic). This scenario evaluates the model's ability to handle extreme multiscale coefficients. The task is to model anisotropic heat diffusion on a unit square ($t \in [0, 5]$) with diffusivities $D_x = (500\pi)^{-2}$ and $D_y = \pi^{-2}$. The initial condition is defined as $u(x, y, 0) = \sin(20\pi x) \sin(\pi y)$, and homogeneous Dirichlet boundary conditions ($u = 0$) are imposed on all boundaries.

Reference for MSE: Analytical solution derived via separation of variables. The MSE is computed for the temperature u over the entire spacetime domain $[0, 1]^2 \times [0, 5]$.

4.3 Evaluation Metrics

A dual-layer evaluation system is employed to independently assess symbolic reasoning and numerical accuracy:

Interpretation Layer (Symbolic). The generated code is assessed to determine whether it captures the correct physics:

- **Equation Discovery Accuracy** (Acc_{PDE}): Measures correct inference of the governing equation topology (e.g., correct operator signs, derivative orders, and source terms).
- **BC Recall** ($Recall_{BC}$): The ratio of correctly identified boundary/initial condition components (type, geometric location, and value function).

- **Parameter Error** (Err_{param}): The relative error of extracted physical coefficients ($|p_{pred} - p_{gt}|/|p_{gt}|$), which is critical for the multiscale problem. For cases without explicit physical parameters, Err_{param} is reported as 0. Failed or non-verified symbolic outputs are reflected in Acc_{PDE} and $Recall_{BC}$, while Err_{param} is computed only when identifiable physical parameters are available.

Solver Layer (Numerical). The **Mean Squared Error (MSE)** of the predicted solution u_{pred} against the ground truth u_{ref} on uniformly sampled test points:

$$\mathrm{MSE} = \frac{1}{N}\sum_{i=1}^{N} \|u_{\mathrm{pred}}(\mathbf{x}_i) - u_{\mathrm{ref}}(\mathbf{x}_i)\|^2 \tag{5}$$

4.4 Results and Analysis

Symbolic Reasoning Performance. Table 1 compares the symbolic accuracy of the code generated by our PhysCoT framework against the direct LLM baseline over ten independent runs. The baseline exhibits notable limitations when faced with complex physical scenarios. In the Multiscale Heat equation, the extremely small diffusion coefficient introduces an additional challenge for symbolic interpretation. Across the benchmark cases, PhysCoT provides more reliable recovery of PDE topology and boundary/initial condition structure than the direct baseline.

Table 1. Interpretation layer results over ten independent runs.

Case	LLM-Direct			PhysCoT (ours)		
	Acc_{PDE} (%)	$Recall_{BC}$ (%)	Err_{param}	Acc_{PDE} (%)	$Recall_{BC}$ (%)	Err_{param}
Case 1: Poisson	80.00	90.00	0.000	**100.00**	**100.00**	**0.000**
Case 2: Kirsch	78.00	79.17	0.000	**90.00**	**90.00**	**0.000**
Case 3: Wave 1D	80.00	76.67	0.000	**100.00**	**100.00**	**0.000**
Case 4: Heat Multi	70.00	70.00	0.210	**100.00**	**100.00**	0.125

Table 2. Ablation study: mean Mean Squared Error (MSE) over successful PINN solver runs. The number in parentheses denotes successful solver runs out of ten independent runs.

Method	Case 1: Poisson	Case 2: Kirsch	Case 3: Wave 1D	Case 4: Heat Multi
LLM-Direct	2.888×10^{-6} (8/10)	3.134×10^{-4} (4/10)	1.020×10^{-1} (6/10)	1.794×10^{-6} (7/10)
PhysCoT (w/o CoT)	6.081×10^{-3} (10/10)	1.273×10^{-1} (10/10)	1.329×10^{-1} (10/10)	1.647×10^{-4} (10/10)
PhysCoT (w/o Verification)	3.669×10^{-6} (10/10)	9.780×10^{0} (4/10)	6.601×10^{-2} (4/10)	2.974×10^{-6} (10/10)
PhysCoT (Full)	2.800×10^{-6} (10/10)	1.676×10^{-4} (9/10)	7.011×10^{-2} (10/10)	1.270×10^{-6} (10/10)

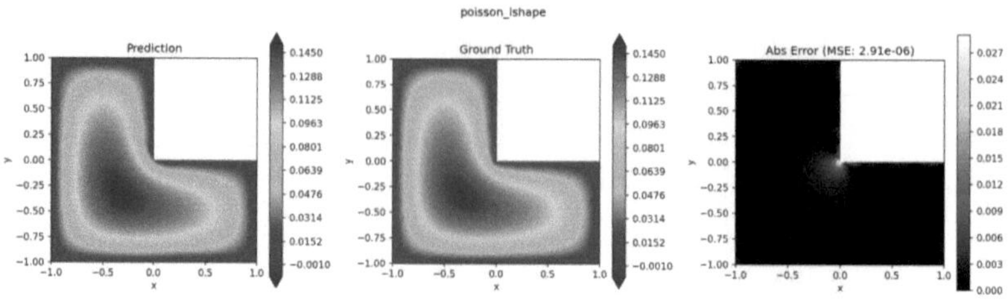

(a) Case 1: 2D Poisson Equation (Elliptic)

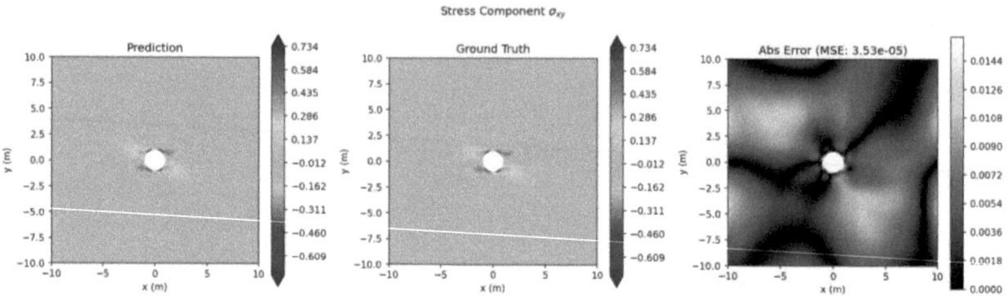

(b) Case 2: 2D Kirsch Problem (Linear Elasticity)

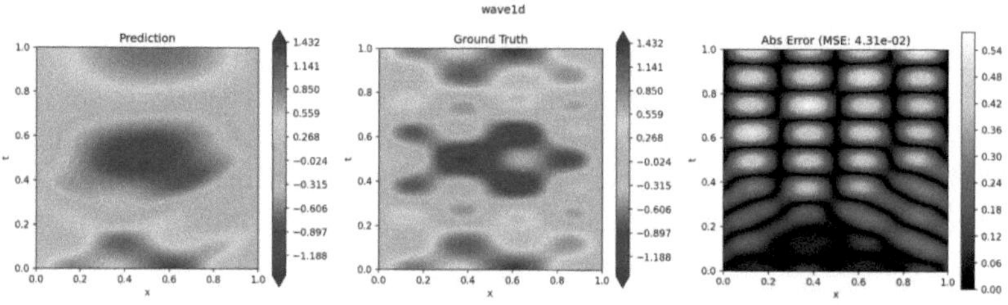

(c) Case 3: 1D Wave Equation (Hyperbolic)

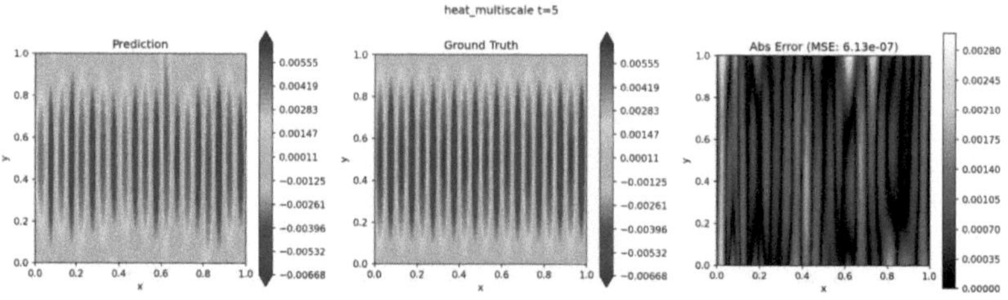

(d) Case 4: 2D Multiscale Heat Equation (Parabolic)

Fig. 2. Numerical prediction results for the four benchmarks. For each case, panels (left to right) show the predicted field, the reference solution, and the absolute error. Each subfigure is a representative successful run, so its MSE may differ from the averaged values in Table 2; Case 4 is shown at $t = 5$, while all reported MSE values are computed over the full spatiotemporal domain.

Numerical Solver Performance and Ablation Study. Table 2 reports the end-to-end MSE against reference solutions, validating the necessity of each PhysCoT component. Each value is the mean MSE over successful PINN solver runs, and the number in parentheses denotes successful solver runs out of ten independent runs. While the "LLM-Direct" baseline can handle relatively simple Poisson cases, its success rate decreases on the Kirsch, Wave, and Heat benchmarks due to incomplete or unstable physics extraction. Ablation studies confirm that removing CoT reasoning leads to significant degradation in the elasticity, wave, and multiscale heat problems, while disabling symbolic verification reduces executable robustness and makes the numerical outcomes more sensitive to the subset of runs that remain solvable. Overall, the full PhysCoT framework provides the strongest balance between prediction accuracy and solver reliability, demonstrating that structured reasoning and symbolic verification are indispensable for robust automated scientific computing.

Visual Comparison of Predicted Fields. Figure 2 illustrates the predicted physical fields for all four benchmarks. The results demonstrate that PhysCoT maintains stable predictive performance across diverse PDE types, capturing the re-entrant corner behavior in Case 1, stress concentration around the circular hole in Case 2, the dominant wave propagation trend in Case 3 (with limited high-frequency recovery), and anisotropic diffusion behavior in Case 4. Beyond point-wise accuracy, the model preserves the main physical structures under different geometric, temporal, and multiscale constraints. The remaining errors are mainly concentrated in regions with high gradients or multiscale sensitivity, which is consistent with the quantitative evaluation.

5 Conclusion

PhysCoT has been proposed as a framework that enables large language models to automatically comprehend natural language descriptions of physical scenarios and predict physical fields. PhysCoT comprises a Physical Scenario Interpreter (PSI) and a Physical Field Predictor (PFP), enabling the translation of natural language descriptions into executable physical models. Through a symbolic verification loop, PhysCoT improves mathematical self-consistency and executable-format consistency. PhysCoT is evaluated on four benchmark problems spanning elliptic, hyperbolic, and parabolic PDEs. Experimental results demonstrate that PhysCoT improves symbolic physical specification and provides a stronger overall balance between prediction accuracy and solver reliability than direct LLM-based baselines. By automating the translation from natural language to computable physical models, PhysCoT reduces the need for expert intervention and advances the accessibility of scientific computing.

Acknowledgements. This work was supported in part by Deep Earth Probe and Mineral Resources Exploration - National Science and Technology Major Project under Grant 2025ZD1011305, the National Natural Science Foundation of China under Grant U23A20297, and the Independent Research Project of State Key Laboratory of Intelligent Deep Metal Mining and Equipment (No. IDMEIRI2504).

References

1. Achiam, J., Adler, S., Agarwal, S., Ahmad, L., Akkaya, I., Aleman, F.L., Almeida, D., Altenschmidt, J., Altman, S., Anadkat, S.: GPT-4 technical report (2023). arXiv preprint arXiv:2303.08774
2. Bischof, R., Kraus, M.A.: Multi-objective loss balancing for physics-informed deep learning. Comput. Methods Appl. Mech. Eng. **439**, 117914 (2025)
3. Boiko, D.A., MacKnight, R., Kline, B., Gomes, G.: Autonomous chemical research with large language models. Nature **624**(7992), 570–578 (2023)
4. Bran, A.M., Cox, S., Schilter, O., Baldassari, C., White, A.D., Schwaller, P.: Chemcrow: augmenting large-language models with chemistry tools (2023). arXiv preprint arXiv:2304.05376
5. Chen, M., Tworek, J., Jun, H., Yuan, Q., Pinto, H.P.D.O., Kaplan, J., Edwards, H., Burda, Y., Joseph, N., Brockman, G.: Evaluating large language models trained on code (2021). arXiv preprint arXiv:2107.03374
6. Chen, W., Ma, X., Wang, X., Cohen, W.W.: Program of thoughts prompting: disentangling computation from reasoning for numerical reasoning tasks (2022). arXiv preprint arXiv:2211.12588
7. Cuomo, S., Di Cola, V.S., Giampaolo, F., Rozza, G., Raissi, M., Piccialli, F.: Scientific machine learning through physics-informed neural networks: where we are and what's next. J. Sci. Comput. **92**(3), 88 (2022)
8. Gao, L., Madaan, A., Zhou, S., Alon, U., Liu, P., Yang, Y., Callan, J., Neubig, G.: Pal: program-aided language models. In: International Conference on Machine Learning, pp. 10764–10799. PMLR (2023)
9. Ghafarollahi, A., Buehler, M.J.: SciAgents: automating scientific discovery through bioinspired multi-agent intelligent graph reasoning. Adv. Mater. **37**(22), 2413523 (2025)
10. Hao, Z., Yao, J., Su, C., Su, H., Wang, Z., Lu, F., Xia, Z., Zhang, Y., Liu, S., Lu, L., et al.: Pinnacle: a comprehensive benchmark of physics-informed neural networks for solving PDEs. Adv. Neural. Inf. Process. Syst. **37**, 76721–76774 (2024)
11. Karniadakis, G.E., Kevrekidis, I.G., Lu, L., Perdikaris, P., Wang, S., Yang, L.: Physics-informed machine learning. Nat. Rev. Phys. **3**(6), 422–440 (2021)
12. Kingma, D.P., Ba, J.: Adam: a method for stochastic optimization (2014). arXiv preprint arXiv:1412.6980
13. Lagaris, I.E., Likas, A., Fotiadis, D.I.: Artificial neural networks for solving ordinary and partial differential equations. IEEE Trans. Neural Netw. **9**(5), 987–1000 (1998)
14. Lewkowycz, A., Andreassen, A., Dohan, D., Dyer, E., Michalewski, H., Ramasesh, V., Slone, A., Anil, C., Schlag, I., Gutman-Solo, T., et al.: Solving quantitative reasoning problems with language models. Adv. Neural. Inf. Process. Syst. **35**, 3843–3857 (2022)
15. Li, Z., Kovachki, N., Azizzadenesheli, K., Liu, B., Bhattacharya, K., Stuart, A., Anandkumar, A.: Fourier neural operator for parametric partial differential equations (2020). arXiv preprint arXiv:2010.08895
16. Liu, A., Feng, B., Xue, B., Wang, B., Wu, B., Lu, C., Zhao, C., Deng, C., Zhang, C., Ruan, C.: Deepseek-v3 technical report (2024). arXiv preprint arXiv:2412.19437
17. Lu, L., Jin, P., Pang, G., Zhang, Z., Karniadakis, G.E.: Learning nonlinear operators via DeepONet based on the universal approximation theorem of operators. Nat. Mach. Intell. **3**(3), 218–229 (2021)

18. Lu, L., Meng, X., Mao, Z., Karniadakis, G.E.: DeepXDE: a deep learning library for solving differential equations. SIAM Rev. **63**(1), 208–228 (2021)
19. Meurer, A., Smith, C.P., Paprocki, M., Čertík, O., Kirpichev, S.B., Rocklin, M., Kumar, A., Ivanov, S., Moore, J.K., Singh, S., et al.: SymPY: symbolic computing in Python. PeerJ Comput. Sci. **3**, e103 (2017)
20. Polu, S., Han, J.M., Zheng, K., Baksys, M., Babuschkin, I., Sutskever, I.: Formal mathematics statement curriculum learning (2022). arXiv preprint arXiv:2202.01344
21. Quarteroni, A., Gervasio, P., Regazzoni, F.: Combining physics-based and data-driven models: advancing the frontiers of research with scientific machine learning (2025). arXiv preprint arXiv:2501.18708
22. Raissi, M., Perdikaris, P., Karniadakis, G.E.: Physics-informed neural networks: a deep learning framework for solving forward and inverse problems involving nonlinear partial differential equations. J. Comput. Phys. **378**, 686–707 (2019)
23. Sanchez-Gonzalez, A., Godwin, J., Pfaff, T., Ying, R., Leskovec, J., Battaglia, P.: Learning to simulate complex physics with graph networks. In: International Conference on Machine Learning, pp. 8459–8468 (2020) PMLR
24. Tancik, M., Srinivasan, P., Mildenhall, B., Fridovich-Keil, S., Raghavan, N., Singhal, U., Ramamoorthi, R., Barron, J., Ng, R.: Fourier features let networks learn high frequency functions in low dimensional domains. Adv. Neural. Inf. Process. Syst. **33**, 7537–7547 (2020)
25. Wang, S., Teng, Y., Perdikaris, P.: Understanding and mitigating gradient flow pathologies in physics-informed neural networks. SIAM J. Sci. Comput. **43**(5), A3055–A3081 (2021)
26. Wang, X., Hu, Z., Lu, P., Zhu, Y., Zhang, J., Subramaniam, S., Loomba, A.R., Zhang, S., Sun, Y., Wang, W.: SciBench: evaluating college-level scientific problem-solving abilities of large language models (2023). arXiv preprint arXiv:2307.10635
27. Wang, X., Wei, J., Schuurmans, D., Le, Q.V., Chi, E.H., Narang, S., Chowdhery, A., Zhou, D.: Self-consistency improves chain of thought reasoning in language models. In: The Eleventh International Conference on Learning Representations (2023)
28. Wei, J., Wang, X., Schuurmans, D., Bosma, M., Xia, F., Chi, E., Le, Q.V., Zhou, D., et al.: Chain-of-thought prompting elicits reasoning in large language models. Adv. Neural. Inf. Process. Syst. **35**, 24824–24837 (2022)
29. Wu, C., Zhu, M., Tan, Q., Kartha, Y., Lu, L.: A comprehensive study of non-adaptive and residual-based adaptive sampling for physics-informed neural networks. Comput. Methods Appl. Mech. Eng. **403**, 115671 (2023)
30. Xi, Z., Chen, W., Guo, X., He, W., Ding, Y., Hong, B., Zhang, M., Wang, J., Jin, S., Zhou, E., et al.: The rise and potential of large language model based agents: a survey. Sci. China Inf. Sci. **68**(2), 121101 (2025)
31. Yao, S., Yu, D., Zhao, J., Shafran, I., Griffiths, T., Cao, Y., Narasimhan, K.: Tree of thoughts: deliberate problem solving with large language models. Adv. Neural. Inf. Process. Syst. **36**, 11809–11822 (2023)
32. Zhou, D., Schärli, N., Hou, L., Wei, J., Scales, N., Wang, X., Schuurmans, D., Cui, C., Bousquet, O., Le, Q.: Least-to-most prompting enables complex reasoning in large language models (2022). arXiv preprint arXiv:2205.10625

LLM and NLP

AERO: Adaptive Evaluation for Reliable Optimization in RL-Based Automatic Prompt Optimization

Xiru Ma, Wei Wang(✉), Di Qiao, and Zhuobing Jiang

College of Computer Science and Technology, Harbin Engineering University, Harbin, China
{maxiru,w_wei,soduko,zbjiang}@hrbeu.edu.cn

Abstract. Reinforcement learning (RL)-based automatic prompt optimization (APO) provides an effective framework for searching discrete natural language prompts. However, under limited evaluation budgets, reward signals estimated from a target large language model (LLM) are vulnerable to small performance differences among candidates and finite-sample noise. This budget-constrained evaluation can lead to false positives among top-ranked prompts and undermine training stability. To address this, we propose Adaptive Evaluation for Reliable Optimization (AERO), which jointly models adaptive candidate evaluation and policy optimization under a fixed total budget. Specifically, AERO improves candidate selection through adaptive evaluation and stabilizes policy learning via evidence-aware calibration, enabling limited budgets to support both more reliable candidate ranking and better-calibrated policy updates. Extensive experiments show that, under the same budget, AERO reduces false-positive ranking errors and improves budget efficiency, with the clearest downstream gains appearing in low-budget and ranking-noise-sensitive settings.

Keywords: Automatic prompt optimization · Large language models · Reinforcement learning · Proximal policy optimization · Adaptive evaluation · Budget-constrained evaluation

1 Introduction

As pre-trained large language models (LLMs) have become increasingly capable across a broad range of natural language tasks, prompts have evolved from heuristic design choices into optimization targets because of their strong influence on model behavior and task performance [1,23]. In this setting, Automatic Prompt Engineering (APE) and Automatic Prompt Optimization (APO) aim to automatically discover high-quality prompts in discrete natural language spaces [10,11,23]. Because APO is fundamentally a black-box optimization problem over discrete text, where gradient-based optimization is not directly applicable, reinforcement learning (RL) has emerged as a natural approach [4].

L. Ding et al. (Eds.): APWeb-WAIM 2026, LNCS 16993, pp. 315–329, 2027.
https://doi.org/10.1007/978-981-92-5693-8_20

Prior work has demonstrated the promise of RL for discrete prompt search and extended it to online policy optimization for LLMs [4,9]. Yet as APO moves from static candidate selection to continual policy updates, training stability has become a central bottleneck. Existing methods mainly constrain the search space, restrict editing operations, or regulate policy updates with anchor models [4,9,10], while the role of feedback reliability in continual optimization remains underexplored.

This challenge is especially pronounced in budget-constrained RL-based APO [13,18]. Under limited target-model interaction budgets, reward estimates become more uncertain, while the true performance of LLM-generated candidate prompts is often tightly concentrated. As a result, finite-sample noise can easily distort candidate comparisons and weaken the reliability of the resulting feedback signals [13,22]. One direct consequence is false positives among top-ranked candidates, where prompts that are not truly superior receive spuriously high rewards [22]. For PPO, which updates the policy through advantage signals, such unreliable rewards can misdirect subsequent updates and eventually lead to training instability or even performance collapse [12,22].

Motivated by these observations, we propose **Adaptive Evaluation for Reliable Optimization (AERO)**, which jointly considers candidate evaluation and policy optimization under a fixed total budget. At a high level, AERO improves the reliability of candidate ranking through adaptive evaluation and stabilizes PPO updates through evidence-aware calibration. In this way, the same limited budget supports both more reliable candidate selection and more stable policy optimization.

Experimental results show that, under the same overall budget, AERO consistently improves reward-ranking reliability by reducing false positives among top-ranked candidates, and translates this reliability gain into better budget efficiency and downstream performance in the main low-budget and ranking-noise-sensitive settings. The benefits are most pronounced when small-sample noise strongly affects candidate ranking, while performance gains are more task-dependent on knowledge-intensive or semantically variable tasks. Taken together, these results suggest that feedback reliability is a key factor shaping optimization quality and training stability in RL-based APO and should be explicitly accounted for during optimization.

The main contributions of this paper are as follows:

- We identify a key source of instability in budget-constrained APO: small-sample noise amplified by uniform budget allocation leads to false positives among top-ranked prompts.
- We propose AERO, a unified framework combining adaptive evaluation with evidence-aware optimization under a fixed total budget.
- Experiments show that AERO improves reward-ranking reliability, budget efficiency, and downstream performance in the main low-budget and ranking-noise-sensitive settings, without increasing the overall evaluation budget.

2 Related Work

2.1 Automatic Prompt Optimization and RL-Based Approaches

Automatic Prompt Optimization (APO) aims to automatically discover high-quality prompts for large language models (LLMs) [11,19,21,23]. In most prior methods, candidate generation and refinement operate at the individual prompt level, without closed-loop feedback from downstream tasks.

To address the limitations of candidate-wise optimization, reinforcement learning (RL) has been increasingly applied to APO [4,9]. By framing discrete prompt search as a feedback-driven optimization problem, RL enables more structured exploration of high-dimensional prompt spaces. Representative methods include GrIPS [10], which improves task instructions through gradient-free edits, and PromptBoosting [8], which combines multiple weak prompt learners to enhance query efficiency and overall optimization performance. RLPrompt [4] further formulates discrete prompt generation as a policy learning problem. These methods demonstrate improved candidate selection and task performance. However, they typically assume downstream evaluation scores provide reliable rewards, leaving reward uncertainty under limited-budget evaluation largely unaddressed [4,9,22].

2.2 Positioning with Respect to StablePrompt

As APO becomes increasingly integrated with PPO-style optimization, recent work has begun to pay greater attention to training stability in RL-based prompt optimization. In particular, StablePrompt systematically formulates natural language prompt tuning as an online RL problem between a policy model and a target model, establishes a full PPO-style optimization pipeline, and uses an anchor model to adaptively regulate policy updates, thereby mitigating policy drift and training instability [9]. At the same time, StablePrompt mainly addresses stability at the level of the optimization process, and its effectiveness still depends heavily on the reliability of the reward signal itself. In budget-constrained settings, however, reliable reward estimation is often difficult to obtain, so instability may arise not only from the update mechanism but also from noisy and weakly supported reward feedback [13,18,22].

Compared with search-based or textual-gradient APO methods, AERO focuses on PPO-based RL optimization under fixed target-model evaluation budgets. Compared with StablePrompt, AERO does not replace the PPO optimization backbone; instead, it extends this backbone with a reliability-aware connection between target-model evaluation and policy optimization. This connection explicitly models the evidence behind adaptively estimated rewards and uses it to calibrate PPO updates, thereby addressing a fixed-budget reward-reliability problem that is not captured by optimizer-level stabilization alone.

3 Method

Figure 1 presents the overall pipeline of AERO. Unlike conventional prompt optimization methods that rely solely on point-estimate reward feedback, AERO

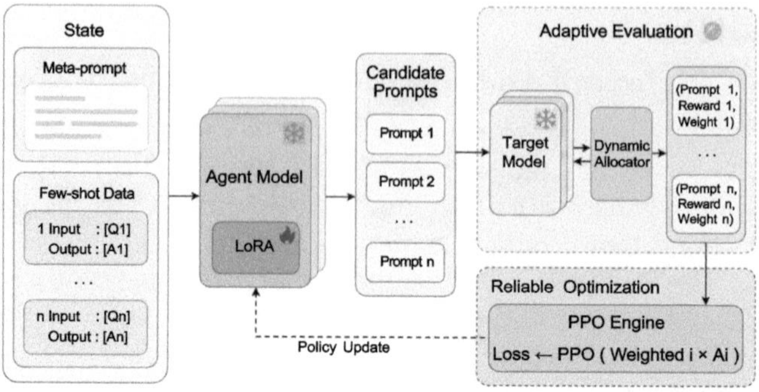

Fig. 1. Overview of AERO. At each training iteration, the agent policy generates candidate prompts, which are then evaluated under a fixed budget through an adaptive CR-based screening process. This process produces both empirical rewards and candidate-level evidence signals, which are subsequently used to calibrate the PPO update.

explicitly retains finite-sample evidence from the CR-based evaluation process and carries this evidence forward into policy optimization. This design tightly couples budget-constrained evaluation with PPO training.

3.1 Problem Formulation

Following StablePrompt, we formulate automatic prompt optimization as an on-policy reinforcement learning problem. Different from the standard setting, however, we explicitly consider a fixed target-model evaluation budget at each training iteration.

State, Action, and Reward. Given a target model M_T, a task dataset D, and a vocabulary $\mathcal{V}$, we aim to learn a policy π_θ that generates high-reward discrete prompts $z \in \mathcal{V}^L$. At training iteration t, the state is defined as $s_t = (m, E_t)$, where m is a task-level meta-prompt and E_t denotes the few-shot example set. Conditioned on s_t, the policy generates a set of K candidate prompts, $\mathcal{C}_t = \{z_t^{(1)}, \dots, z_t^{(K)}\}$, and each candidate prompt is treated as one RL sample.

Following StablePrompt, we use task-specific reward definitions. For generation tasks, both training rewards and final performance are computed using the benchmark-designated metric: exact match (EM), exact set (ES), F1, or Contains. For classification tasks, the reward from one evaluation on a validation minibatch $\mathcal{B}$ is defined as $r(z; \mathcal{B}) = c_a \,\mathrm{Acc}(z; \mathcal{B}) + c_s \, D(z; \mathcal{B})$, where Acc denotes minibatch accuracy and D is the softmax-difference term used to distinguish prompts with identical accuracy. If candidate z_i is evaluated N_i times in the current iteration, its empirical reward is $\hat{r}_i = \frac{1}{N_i} \sum_{n=1}^{N_i} r(z_i; \mathcal{B}_{i,n})$.

Baseline Optimization Backbone. For policy optimization, we follow the same StablePrompt backbone and adopt its APPO-style PPO training framework. Specifically, the policy and value function share a frozen pretrained language model backbone; the policy is updated through LoRA adapters, value estimation is performed by an additional value head, and training is regularized by a KL term with respect to an anchor policy.

Fixed-Budget Setting. Let B denote the total target-model evaluation budget available at each training iteration, where one unit of budget corresponds to one target-model evaluation interaction on a validation minibatch. This budget constraint is practically important because repeated target-model evaluations are costly for both proprietary API-based models and open-weight models. Accordingly, we study prompt optimization under a fixed evaluation budget.

3.2 Adaptive Candidate Evaluation Under a Fixed Budget

Given the candidate set $\mathcal{C}_t = \{z_t^{(1)}, \ldots, z_t^{(K)}\}$ generated at iteration t and the fixed evaluation budget B, deciding how to distribute target-model evaluations across candidates is naturally a fixed-budget pure-exploration problem. We therefore adopt Continuous Rejects (CR) [18] as the evaluation mechanism. In AERO, however, CR is not used merely to return a final winner; instead, it serves as an adaptive reward-evaluation procedure that allocates limited evaluation effort online across candidate prompts.

Adaptive Allocation via CR. Starting from the candidate set $\mathcal{C}_t$, AERO maintains an active set of prompts that are still under consideration. Rather than evaluating all candidates uniformly, it repeatedly assigns target-model evaluations online and progressively removes prompts whose empirical performance is already insufficiently supported by the current evidence, following the standard CR procedure. In this way, prompts that become clearly uncompetitive stop consuming additional evaluation budget, while prompts that remain competitive continue to receive further evaluation. As a result, under the same total budget, more target-model calls are devoted to the candidates whose relative ranking is most informative for subsequent optimization.

Retained Evidence Context. A key distinction from using CR solely for final prompt selection is that AERO retains the evaluation trajectory of each candidate. For every candidate prompt z_i, once its evaluation is finalized—either because it is eliminated early or because the total budget is exhausted—we retain not only its empirical reward $\hat{r}_i$, but also the associated evidence context (N_i, j_i, B_i). Here, N_i is the total number of evaluations received by z_i, j_i is the active-set size at its last evaluation, and B_i denotes the effective budget scale at that stage. Together, these quantities summarize how strongly the empirical reward of z_i is supported by the fixed-budget CR trajectory. This retained evidence is then passed to the policy optimization stage, where it is used to calibrate PPO updates. The resulting non-uniform evaluation trajectory is therefore explicitly retained as evidence of reward reliability rather than discarded after candidate scoring.

3.3 PPO Policy Calibration with Evidence Scores

After adaptive evaluation, each candidate prompt is associated with an empirical reward $\hat{r}_i$, but these rewards are not equally supported by evidence. This does not make the empirical rewards invalid for PPO; rather, it induces a non-uniform, selection-dependent estimation process that makes their reliability heterogeneous, because early-eliminated prompts receive fewer evaluation trials while retained prompts are evaluated more frequently. Accordingly, AERO does not aim to obtain uniformly unbiased reward estimates for all candidates, but to improve the reliability of optimization-relevant feedback under a fixed budget. Standard PPO can use these rewards through their estimated advantages, but it does not explicitly account for such evidence heterogeneity. AERO therefore uses the retained CR trajectory to calibrate sample-level policy contributions according to the strength of their supporting evidence.

Evidence Score. For each candidate prompt z_i, we first define a local evidence proxy

$$\tilde{\beta}_i = \mathrm{clip}\left(\frac{N_i \overline{\log}(j_i)}{B_i}, \epsilon_\beta, 1\right), \tag{1}$$

where N_i, j_i, and B_i are the retained evidence quantities from Sect. 3.2, and $\overline{\log}(\cdot)$ denotes the same smoothed logarithmic term used in the CR rejection condition. In CR, this budget-normalized quantity controls when an empirical gap is considered sufficiently supported, given the current active-set size and budget scale, for rejecting an arm. We transfer this role from candidate elimination to policy calibration: $\tilde{\beta}_i$ summarizes how much adaptive-evaluation support underlies the empirical reward $\hat{r}_i$, and is therefore used as a local reliability proxy rather than a reward-dependent weighting heuristic. We then convert it into a bounded evidence score

$$e_i = \frac{1}{1 + G(\tilde{\beta}_i)} = \sqrt{\tilde{\beta}_i}, \qquad e_i \in (0, 1]. \tag{2}$$

where $G(\beta) = 1/\sqrt{\beta} - 1$ follows the CR threshold function. The resulting square-root score preserves the monotonic relation between the CR-derived support quantity and reward reliability, while smoothing the scale to avoid overly aggressive amplification of heavily evaluated candidates.

Policy Weighting and Objective. To obtain relative sample weights within the current batch, we compute

$$\tilde{w}_i = \left(\frac{e_i}{\bar{e}}\right)^p, \qquad \bar{e} = \frac{1}{K}\sum_{i=1}^{K} e_i, \tag{3}$$

where $p > 0$ controls the sharpness of the relative scaling. The final weight is obtained by clipping and mean-normalizing $\tilde{w}_i$,

$$w_i = \mathrm{Normalize}\big(\mathrm{clip}(\tilde{w}_i, w_{\min}, w_{\max})\big), \tag{4}$$

so that $\frac{1}{K}\sum_{i=1}^{K} w_i = 1$. This preserves the overall scale of the PPO step while adjusting the relative influence of different samples.

AERO applies evidence-based weighting only to the policy term, while leaving the value loss and KL regularization unchanged. The resulting policy objective is

$$L_{\mathrm{policy}}^{\mathrm{AERO}} = \mathbb{E}_i[\min(\rho_i w_i A_i,\ \mathrm{clip}(\rho_i, 1 - \epsilon_c, 1 + \epsilon_c)\, w_i A_i)], \tag{5}$$

Algorithm 1 AERO: Adaptive Evaluation for Reliable Optimization

Input: π_θ, V_ϕ, π_{anchor}, K, B, T_{iter}
for $t = 1, 2, \ldots, T_{\text{iter}}$ **do**
    Construct state $s_t = (m, E_t)$
    Sample candidate prompts $\mathcal{C}_t \sim \pi_\theta(\cdot \mid s_t)$
    $(\{\hat{r}_i\}, \{(N_i, j_i, B_i)\}) \leftarrow \text{ADAPTIVEEVALUATE}(\mathcal{C}_t, B)$ // Sec. 3.2
    $\{w_i\} \leftarrow \text{COMPUTEEVIDENCEWEIGHTS}(\{(N_i, j_i, B_i)\})$ // Sec. 3.3
    Compute evidence-aware objective L_{AERO} from $\{\hat{r}_i, w_i\}$
    Update θ, ϕ using L_{AERO}
    Update π_{anchor}
end for

and the overall training objective becomes

$$L_{\text{AERO}} = L_v + L_{\text{policy}}^{\text{AERO}} + P. \tag{6}$$

Compared with standard PPO, the only modification is the evidence-calibrated scaling of the policy term. Consequently, candidate prompts whose rewards are supported by stronger evidence retain larger policy influence, whereas weakly supported samples are correspondingly attenuated. From a variance perspective, if $\hat{r}_i$ is averaged over N_i evaluations, its estimation variance typically decreases with N_i, e.g., $\text{Var}(\hat{r}_i) \approx \sigma_i^2/N_i$ under independent sampling. Thus, evidence-based weighting reduces the relative contribution of high-variance reward estimates to the policy gradient, while clipping and mean normalization keep the overall PPO step scale controlled. Since w_i is derived from the retained CR evidence rather than from reward magnitude itself, the update is calibrated by reward reliability rather than reward value alone.

3.4 Overall Algorithm

Algorithm 1 summarizes the overall training procedure of AERO. AERO unifies budget-aware candidate evaluation and evidence-aware policy optimization, allowing the evidence extracted during fixed-budget evaluation to directly calibrate subsequent policy learning.

Computational cost and overhead. In this setting, the dominant computational cost is target-model inference, measured by the number of target-model evaluation calls. AERO remains budget-neutral relative to the uniform-evaluation baseline: each training iteration still uses exactly B target-model evaluations. Its additional overhead only comes from CR bookkeeping, active-set updates, empirical reward updates, and evidence-weight computation. With K candidate prompts, these operations introduce lightweight scalar computation, at most $O(BK)$ under straightforward active-set scanning and $O(K)$ for evidence-weight computation, with $O(K)$ additional storage for the retained evidence context. Compared with target-model inference, this overhead is negligible in practice.

4 Experiments

We evaluate AERO along three axes: overall task performance, reward reliability and budget efficiency under constrained evaluation budgets, and the contribution of its core components. Unless otherwise specified, we use StablePrompt [9] as the baseline, instantiate both the agent model and the target model as Gemma-1.1-7B-it, and compare all methods under the same prompt generation pipeline, PPO training configuration, reward definition, and total target-model evaluation budget.

4.1 Main Results Across Tasks

Experimental Setup and Metrics. We evaluate AERO on three benchmark families while keeping the dataset setup identical to StablePrompt [9]. (1) **Few-shot Text Classification:** Following prior prompt tuning studies, we use subsets of GLUE [17] and SuperGLUE [16], including SST-2 [14], MRPC [5], MNLI [20], QNLI, SNLI [2], and RTE [3], covering sentiment analysis, paraphrase classification, and natural language inference. Following StablePrompt, inference is performed with predefined verbalizers, and model predictions are selected only from the corresponding verbalizer set. (2) **Instruction Induction:** We use Instruction Induction (II) [7] and BigBench-Instruction Induction (BBII) [7,15], covering both classification and generation tasks. (3) **Question Answering:** We evaluate MMLU [6] over 57 subjects grouped into STEM, Humanities, Social Sciences, and Other, using option letters as verbalizers.

We report two core metrics: *final_acc*, the highest test performance among the top-5 prompts selected according to their training-time rewards, which measures the optimization process's ability to discover its best result; and *final_mean_acc*, the average test performance of these top-5 prompts, which reflects the overall quality of the top-ranked prompt set.

Main Results. Table 1 shows that AERO achieves a modest but more stable improvement over the matched APPO baseline, increasing average *final_acc* from 76.9 ± 1.7 to 77.5 ± 0.5. AERO also exhibits lower variance across random seeds on multiple datasets, suggesting that adaptive evaluation and evidence-aware calibration can make prompt search more stable under the same evaluation budget.

Figure 2 reports the Instruction Induction results after grouping the 24 generation subtasks by evaluation metric. AERO improves the overall performance, raising the average *final_acc* over all 24 tasks from 58.24 to 62.42 and the average *final_mean_acc* from 49.89 to 54.00. The overall improvement is driven primarily by the EM group, where both top-1 and mean scores increase substantially. By contrast, ES declines markedly, F1 shows mixed behavior, and Contains improves. These results indicate that the gains of AERO are concentrated mainly in EM rather than being uniform across all evaluation groups.

Figure 3 shows BBII results, highlighting the contrast between text generation (tg) and classification (tc) subsets. On BBII-tg, AERO remains competitive: most tasks improve or remain near baseline, resulting in gains in both average

Table 1. Top-1 prompt performance (*final_acc*) on six few-shot text classification datasets. The upper block reports baseline results from StablePrompt for contextual comparison only. The lower block reports our direct matched-setting comparison between the reproduced APPO baseline and AERO under identical backbone, reward definition, PPO configuration, and total evaluation budget.

Cat.	Method	SST-2	MRPC	RTE	QNLI	MNLI	SNLI	Avg.
FT	Fine-tuning	71.9	59.6	55.7	63.1	41.1	64.8	59.3
	Soft prompt	78.3	57.1	51.6	**89.0**	34.9	55.8	61.1
Fixed	Manual	89.1	51.0	64.0	73.0	67.0	47.0	65.2
	Zero-shot CoT	57.9	38.4	**81.6**	75.2	**71.1**	66.3	65.1
	Few-shot	55.0	49.0	76.0	82.0	58.0	52.2	62.0
Rep.	GrIPS	84.7±4.6	55.6±2.6	60.9±3.5	28.9±1.2	44.4±1.1	63.5±2.3	59.4
	PromptBoost.	65.4±1.0	52.7±1.1	71.6±0.9	71.6±1.1	35.5±1.4	52.6±1.8	58.2
	APE	83.2±7.7	55.3±4.9	78.6±1.3	75.0±2.2	54.6±7.9	72.3±4.8	70.1
	ProTeGi	69.2±8.4	48.8±1.3	73.2±6.3	74.2±7.7	56.6±10.9	61.3±12.3	64.0
	RLPrompt	70.8±6.5	56.0±1.5	67.3±2.5	62.6±1.3	54.6±1.9	56.6±1.3	61.3
	StableP.	**92.5±1.3**	71.3±3.4	81.5±2.8	75.9±1.4	63.3±1.2	74.1±1.4	76.4
Matched	APPO	90.9±2.8	69.6±6.9	80.5±1.5	77.9±4.4	68.2±2.5	74.1±0.8	76.9±1.7
	AERO	92.0±0.7	**71.9±4.0**	80.9±2.0	79.6±0.4	65.9±2.2	**74.9±0.9**	**77.5±0.5**

final_acc and *final_mean_acc*, suggesting that adaptive evaluation enhances both the best prompt and the quality of the top-ranked prompt set. On BBII-tc, results are more mixed: the average *final_acc* decreases and several tasks underperform the baseline, but the average *final_mean_acc* still increases, indicating that AERO improves the quality of the top-ranked prompt set even when the highest-ranked prompt is not consistently better. Together, these results show that AERO is more consistent on generation tasks, while on classification tasks gains are mainly reflected in mean performance rather than top-1 accuracy.

Table 2 shows that AERO remains broadly comparable to the reproduced baseline, with a small gain in average top-1 accuracy (from 54.99 to 55.57) and no change in average mean accuracy (50.97). The gains are concentrated mainly in STEM and Other, while the remaining groups stay close to the baseline. This suggests that AERO offers more modest gains on knowledge-intensive QA, where the downstream benefits of improved ranking reliability may be partially constrained by the target model's underlying knowledge capacity.

4.2 Reward Reliability and Budget Efficiency Under Constrained Budgets

Experimental Setup. We evaluate reward reliability and budget efficiency on SST-2 under three per-prompt evaluation budgets: *low* (8), *medium* (12), and *standard* (16). With four examples per validation minibatch, these correspond to 2, 3, and 4 target-model calls per prompt, respectively. At each budget level,

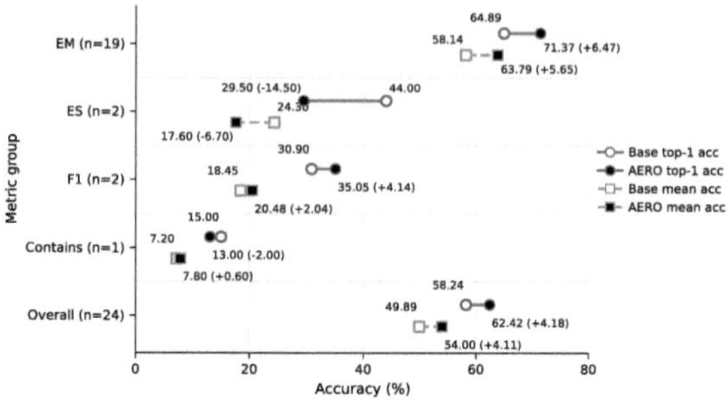

Fig. 2. Category-level results on Instruction Induction generation tasks, grouped by evaluation metric into EM (19 tasks), ES (2 tasks), F1 (2 tasks), and Contains (1 task), together with the overall average over all 24 tasks. Circles denote top-1 score and squares denote mean score; hollow markers indicate the reproduced baseline and filled markers indicate AERO. The numbers next to the filled markers show the AERO score and its absolute change relative to the baseline.

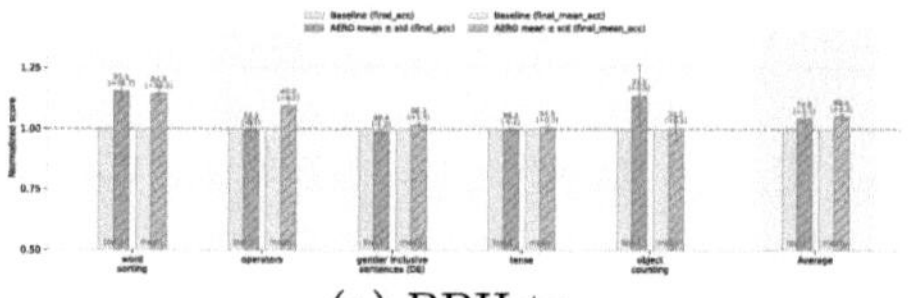

(a) BBII-tg.

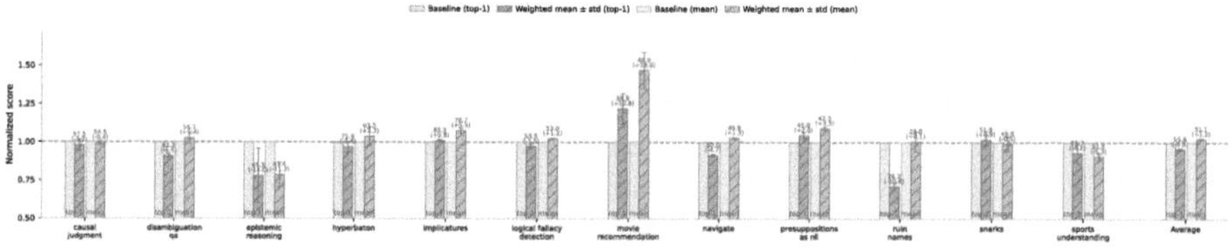

(b) BBII-tc.

Fig. 3. BBII-tg and BBII-tc results normalized to the reproduced baseline, with the red dashed line marking 1.0. Bars show seed means (five seeds for tg and three for tc), error bars denote standard deviations, and labels report raw scores and absolute changes. The rightmost group shows the task average.

Table 2. Results on MMLU, averaged over 57 subjects and grouped into STEM (18 tasks), social sciences (12 tasks), humanities (13 tasks), and other (14 tasks). We compare the reproduced baseline with the seed-matched AERO run under the same controlled setup, and report both top-1 accuracy and mean accuracy.

Metric	Method	STEM (18)	Soc. Sci. (12)	Hum. (13)	Other (14)	Avg. (57)
Top-1	Base	46.98	**61.63**	**58.58**	56.27	54.99
	AERO	**48.31**	61.34	57.93	**57.76**	**55.57**
Mean	Base	42.79	**57.90**	53.56	**53.15**	50.97
	AERO	**43.47**	56.87	**53.69**	53.01	50.97

AERO and the baseline use the same total evaluation budget, differing only in its allocation: adaptive for AERO and uniform for the baseline.

For offline analysis only, we re-evaluate the same candidate prompts on the full SST-2 validation set (872 examples) to obtain oracle rewards. We evaluate reward-estimation error, ranking consistency, top-ranked false positives, and downstream performance.

Results. Table 3 shows that AERO improves all four reward-reliability metrics across the three budget levels. The gains are largest under the *low* budget: *Gap* decreases by 39.8% (5.117 to 3.082), Spearman correlation increases from 0.259 to 0.509, inversion rate decreases from 0.424 to 0.314, and *FPR@5* drops from 1.000 to 0.600. Thus, under the same budget, AERO better preserves candidate ordering and suppresses noisy false positives in the top-ranked pool.

Table 3. Reward estimation quality and top-pool false-positive rates under different budget levels on SST-2. *Gap*: mean absolute error relative to oracle rewards; *Sp.*: Spearman correlation; *Inv.*: pairwise inversion rate; F5/F10: *FPR@5*/*FPR@10*; B/A: baseline/AERO.

Budget	Gap-B	Gap-A	Sp.-B	Sp.-A	Inv.-B	Inv.-A	F5-B	F5-A	F10-B	F10-A
low	5.117	3.082	0.259	0.509	0.424	0.314	1.000	0.600	0.600	0.433
medium	4.037	2.506	0.030	0.296	0.483	0.402	0.800	0.667	0.633	0.533
standard	2.811	1.897	0.092	0.275	0.472	0.401	0.867	0.600	0.667	0.533

Table 4a shows that AERO improves both *final_acc* and *final_mean_acc* under *low* and *medium* budgets. Under the *low* budget, the two metrics increase from 0.900 to 0.924 and from 0.846 to 0.888, respectively, with *final_acc* already matching the baseline under the *standard* budget (0.924 vs. 0.922). At the *standard* budget, *final_acc* is identical and *final_mean_acc* remains modestly higher, indicating that AERO's budget-efficiency gains are strongest when evaluation resources are limited.

Table 4. Additional analysis of AERO. (a) Final downstream performance under different budget levels on SST-2. (b) Ablation results on few-shot text classification averaged over six datasets.

(a) Budget levels

Budget	Acc (Base)	Acc (AERO)	Mean (Base)	Mean (AERO)
low	0.900	0.924	0.846	0.888
medium	0.914	0.925	0.842	0.888
standard	0.922	0.922	0.869	0.876

(b) Ablation

Metric	Baseline (APPO)	AERO (cr-only)	**AERO (full)**
final_acc	76.9±1.7	77.0±0.9	**77.5±0.5**
final_mean_acc	70.4±2.5	71.6±0.2	**72.4±0.8**

4.3 Ablation Study

Experimental Setup. We conduct ablations on the few-shot text classification benchmark to isolate the effects of adaptive evaluation and evidence-aware calibration in AERO. The main ablation compares three variants: the APPO baseline, a cr-only variant with adaptive evaluation but no weighting, and the full AERO model combining both components. A separate "weighted-only" variant is omitted because, without CR evidence, all candidates receive identical weights and the method reduces to the baseline. Results are averaged over six classification datasets and two random seeds.

We further compare calibration strategies through a task-level analysis under the same controlled setting. Besides the baseline and cr-only variants, we include SE-based weighting using inverse standard error, Bernstein-based weighting using inverse empirical-Bernstein confidence radius, and full AERO with CR-derived evidence weighting. As this analysis uses a single seed, its results may differ from the cross-seed aggregates.

Results and Analysis. Table 4b shows stepwise improvement from the APPO baseline to cr-only and full AERO. Cr-only raises average *final_acc* from 76.9 to 77.0 and *final_mean_acc* from 70.4 to 71.6. Adding evidence-aware calibration further improves performance, with full AERO reaching 77.5 and 72.4, the best overall results. Smaller standard deviations indicate improved stability across seeds. These results show that adaptive evaluation and evidence-aware calibration contribute complementarily: adaptive evaluation improves candidate assessment under a fixed budget, while evidence-aware calibration strengthens the final optimization outcome.

Figure 4 shows task-level differences in *final_mean_acc* across weighting strategies under the same controlled setting. Each cell reports the raw score and, in parentheses, its absolute change from the baseline; blue and yellow indicate degradation and improvement, respectively. SE- and Bernstein-based weighting show less consistent gains across tasks, with improvements on some datasets and drops on others. In contrast, full AERO achieves the highest average *final_mean_acc* across six datasets and a more balanced pattern. Although not outperforming all alternatives on every task, it improves most datasets and avoids the larger task-wise fluctuations of other schemes, suggesting that CR-derived evidence provides more consistent reliability signals under adaptive evaluation.

Hyperparameter sensitivity. To assess the sensitivity of AERO-specific calibration parameters, we vary the evidence-weight sharpness p and clipping range $[w_{\min}, w_{\max}]$ on SST-2 with Gemma-2B as a lightweight validation setting, while keeping other settings fixed. Table 5 shows that moderate weighting achieves the highest mean and final accuracy, outperforming the baseline by 4.4 and 2.8 points, respectively, whereas conservative weighting provides smaller gains and aggressive weighting degrades performance. We therefore use $p = 1.5$ and $[w_{\min}, w_{\max}] = [0.3, 3.0]$ throughout the main experiments.

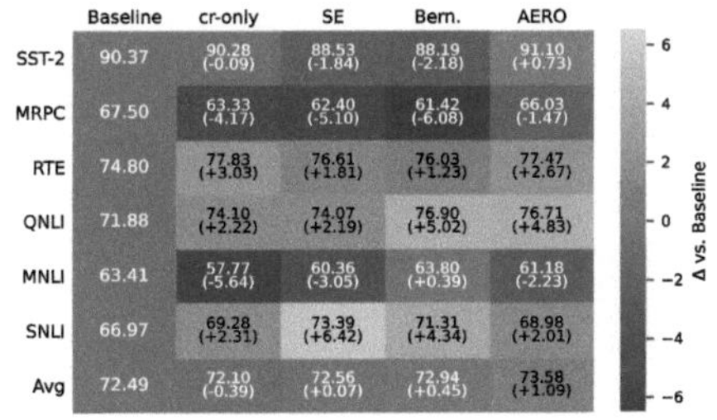

Fig. 4. Task-level changes in *final_mean_acc* across weighting strategies.

Table 5. Sensitivity analysis of AERO-specific weighting hyperparameters on SST-2 with Gemma-2B. We vary the evidence-weight sharpness p and clipping range $[w_{\min}, w_{\max}]$ while keeping all other settings fixed.

Setting	p	Clip	Wt. range	Mean	Final
Baseline	–	–	–	79.6	84.1
Conservative	0.5	$[0.5, 2.0]$	0.86–1.14	82.2	86.2
Moderate	1.5	$[0.3, 3.0]$	0.61–1.39	**84.0**	**86.9**
Aggressive	2.5	$[0.15, 5.0]$	0.40–1.60	80.2	85.3
Aggressive	3.0	$[0.1, 6.0]$	0.32–1.68	72.2	83.1

5 Conclusion

We proposed AERO, which combines fixed-budget adaptive evaluation with evidence-calibrated PPO updates for RL-based prompt optimization. Under the same target-model interaction budget, AERO improves reward fidelity, reduces false positives, and increases budget efficiency, with the clearest downstream gains observed in low-budget, ranking-noise-sensitive, and EM-type generation settings.

Limitations and Future Work. Our evaluation is limited by the number of random seeds and target-model families, primarily Gemma-1.1-7B-it. Future work will examine broader models and tasks and further analyze how heterogeneous reward evidence affects policy optimization dynamics.

References

1. Achiam, J., Adler, S., Agarwal, S., Ahmad, L., Akkaya, I., Aleman, F.L., Almeida, D., Altenschmidt, J., Altman, S., Anadkat, S., et al.: GPT-4 technical report. arXiv preprint arXiv:2303.08774 (2023). https://arxiv.org/abs/2303.08774
2. Bowman, S.R., Angeli, G., Potts, C., Manning, C.D.: A large annotated corpus for learning natural language inference. In: Proceedings of the 2015 Conference on Empirical Methods in Natural Language Processing, pp. 632–642. Association for Computational Linguistics, Lisbon, Portugal (2015). https://doi.org/10.18653/v1/D15-1075
3. Dagan, I., Glickman, O., Magnini, B.: The pascal recognising textual entailment challenge. In: Quiñonero-Candela, J., Dagan, I., Magnini, B., d'Alché Buc, F. (eds.) Machine Learning Challenges: Evaluating Predictive Uncertainty, Visual Object Classification, and Recognising Textual Entailment, Lecture Notes in Computer Science, vol. 3944, pp. 177–190. Springer (2006). https://doi.org/10.1007/11736790_9
4. Deng, M., Wang, J., Hsieh, C.P., Wang, Y., Guo, H., Shu, T., Song, M., Xing, E.P., Hu, Z.: RLPrompt: optimizing discrete text prompts with reinforcement learning. In: Proceedings of the 2022 Conference on Empirical Methods in Natural Language Processing. pp. 3369–3391. Association for Computational Linguistics, Abu Dhabi, United Arab Emirates (2022). https://doi.org/10.18653/v1/2022.emnlp-main.222

5. Dolan, W.B., Brockett, C.: Automatically constructing a corpus of sentential paraphrases. In: Proceedings of the Third International Workshop on Paraphrasing (IWP2005) (2005)
6. Hendrycks, D., Burns, C., Basart, S., Zou, A., Mazeika, M., Song, D., Steinhardt, J.: Measuring massive multitask language understanding. In: International Conference on Learning Representations (2021)
7. Honovich, O., Shaham, U., Bowman, S.R., Levy, O.: Instruction induction: from few examples to natural language task descriptions. In: Proceedings of the 61st Annual Meeting of the Association for Computational Linguistics (Volume 1: Long Papers), pp. 1935–1952. Association for Computational Linguistics, Toronto, Canada (2023). https://doi.org/10.18653/v1/2023.acl-long.108
8. Hou, B., O'Connor, J., Andreas, J., Chang, S., Zhang, Y.: Promptboosting: black-box text classification with ten forward passes. In: Proceedings of the 40th International Conference on Machine Learning. Proceedings of Machine Learning Research, vol. 202, pp. 13309–13324. PMLR (2023)
9. Kwon, M., Kim, G., Kim, J., Lee, H., Kim, J.: Stableprompt: automatic prompt tuning using reinforcement learning for large language model. In: Proceedings of the 2024 Conference on Empirical Methods in Natural Language Processing. pp. 9868–9884. Association for Computational Linguistics, Miami, Florida, USA (2024). https://doi.org/10.18653/v1/2024.emnlp-main.551
10. Prasad, A., Hase, P., Zhou, X., Bansal, M.: GrIPS: gradient-free, edit-based instruction search for prompting large language models. In: Proceedings of the 17th Conference of the European Chapter of the Association for Computational Linguistics, pp. 3845–3864. Association for Computational Linguistics, Dubrovnik, Croatia (2023). https://doi.org/10.18653/v1/2023.eacl-main.277
11. Pryzant, R., Iter, D., Li, J., Lee, Y., Zhu, C., Zeng, M.: Automatic prompt optimization with "gradient descent" and beam search. In: Proceedings of the 2023 Conference on Empirical Methods in Natural Language Processing, pp. 7957–7968. Association for Computational Linguistics, Singapore (2023). https://doi.org/10.18653/v1/2023.emnlp-main.494
12. Schulman, J., Wolski, F., Dhariwal, P., Radford, A., Klimov, O.: Proximal policy optimization algorithms (2017). arXiv preprint arXiv:1707.06347
13. Shi, C., Yang, K., Chen, Z., Li, J., Yang, J., Shen, C.: Efficient prompt optimization through the lens of best arm identification. Adv. Neural Inf. Process. Syst. **37** (2024)
14. Socher, R., Perelygin, A., Wu, J., Chuang, J., Manning, C.D., Ng, A., Potts, C.: Recursive deep models for semantic compositionality over a sentiment treebank. In: Proceedings of the 2013 Conference on Empirical Methods in Natural Language Processing, pp. 1631–1642. Association for Computational Linguistics, Seattle, Washington, USA (2013)
15. Srivastava, A., Rastogi, A., Rao, A., Shoeb, A., Abid, A., Fisch, A., Brown, A.R., Santilli, A., Gupta, A., Garriga-Alonso, A.: Beyond the imitation game: quantifying and extrapolating the capabilities of language models. Trans. Mach. Learn. Res. (2023)
16. Wang, A., Pruksachatkun, Y., Nangia, N., Singh, A., Michael, J., Hill, F., Levy, O., Bowman, S.R.: Superglue: a stickier benchmark for general-purpose language understanding systems. Adv. Neural Inf. Process. Syst. **32**, 3261–3275 (2019)
17. Wang, A., Singh, A., Michael, J., Hill, F., Levy, O., Bowman, S.R.: GLUE: a multitask benchmark and analysis platform for natural language understanding. In: Proceedings of the 2018 EMNLP Workshop BlackboxNLP: Analyzing and Interpreting

Neural Networks for NLP, pp. 353–355. Association for Computational Linguistics, Brussels, Belgium (2018). https://doi.org/10.18653/v1/W18-5446

18. Wang, P.A., Tzeng, R.C., Proutiere, A.: Best arm identification with fixed budget: a large deviation perspective. Adv. Neural Inf. Process. Syst. **36** (2023)
19. Wang, X., Li, C., Wang, Z., Bai, F., Luo, H., Zhang, J., Jojic, N., Xing, E.P., Hu, Z.: Promptagent: strategic planning with language models enables expert-level prompt optimization. In: International Conference on Learning Representations (2024)
20. Williams, A., Nangia, N., Bowman, S.: A broad-coverage challenge corpus for sentence understanding through inference. In: Proceedings of the 2018 Conference of the North American Chapter of the Association for Computational Linguistics: Human Language Technologies, Volume 1 (Long Papers), pp. 1112–1122. Association for Computational Linguistics, New Orleans, Louisiana (2018). https://doi.org/10.18653/v1/N18-1101
21. Yang, C., Wang, X., Lu, Y., Liu, H., Le, Q.V., Zhou, D., Chen, X.: Large language models as optimizers. In: The Twelfth International Conference on Learning Representations (2024)
22. Zhang, C., Shen, W., Zhao, L., Zhang, X., Xu, X., Dou, W., Bian, J.: Policy filtration for RLHF to mitigate noise in reward models. In: Proceedings of the 42nd International Conference on Machine Learning. Proceedings of Machine Learning Research, vol. 267, pp. 76023–76046. PMLR (2025)
23. Zhou, Y., Muresanu, A.I., Han, Z., Paster, K., Pitis, S., Chan, H., Ba, J.: Large language models are human-level prompt engineers. In: International Conference on Learning Representations (2023)

Budget-Constrained Preference-Aligned Prompt Optimization for Controllable Summarization

Yide Li(✉)

School of Computing and Artificial Intelligence, Southwest Jiaotong University, 611756Chengdu, China
gafeiguocha@qq.com

Abstract. Large language models (LLMs) have substantially improved summarization quality. Nevertheless, effective prompt optimization for summarization remains challenging when user preference modeling, explicit output constraints, and fair comparison under fixed search budgets must be considered simultaneously. This paper proposes a budget-constrained preference-aligned prompt optimization framework that formulates summarization prompt search as a multi-objective optimization problem under a fixed evaluation budget. The framework integrates structured prompt representation, operationally defined control-oriented scoring, and same-budget comparison across search strategies without modifying model parameters. In particular, the control signal combines a preference-alignment score computed from a fixed textual preference profile and a rule-verifiable compliance score based on length control, numeric preservation, avoidance of bullet structures, hedging reduction, and first-person avoidance. Experiments on CNN/DailyMail show that the proposed method improves preference-oriented and rule-verifiable utility while maintaining comparable ROUGE performance. Under the same prompt evaluation budget, the hybrid strategy achieves the best search-stage composite objective with $F = 0.583$ among the automatic search methods, and reaches $P = 82.67$ on the final test set. The main contributions are threefold: (1) a budget-constrained prompt optimization framework that jointly models task quality, preference alignment, and rule-verifiable compliance; (2) a structured prompt search scheme combined with same-budget comparison for fair evaluation of prompt optimization strategies; and (3) empirical evidence that the proposed method is effective for controllable summarization relative to unoptimized prompts and simple search baselines.

Keywords: Prompt optimization · Controllable summarization · Preference alignment · Budget-constrained search · Large language models

L. Ding et al. (Eds.): APWeb-WAIM 2026, LNCS 16993, pp. 330–343, 2027.
https://doi.org/10.1007/978-981-92-5693-8_21

1 Introduction

Summarization has become increasingly important in information access, news compression, document assistance, and question answering, and is now a core application scenario for large language models. High-quality summaries should not only compress content accurately, but should also satisfy practical requirements on length, style, and structure. Existing summarization paradigms, however, are still dominated by reference-summary similarity objectives [1,3,4,7]. As a result, they often provide limited support for modeling user preferences, output structure, and explicit constraints. For real-world controllable summarization, this limitation becomes more pronounced: a prompt may achieve acceptable task scores while still failing to satisfy requirements on brevity, compliance, or stylistic consistency.

The rapid development of LLMs has introduced strong capabilities in contextual understanding, semantic reasoning, and natural-language generation [20,21]. These advances create new opportunities for summarization from unstructured text. Compared with traditional summarization models, LLMs are more flexible in handling complex context dependencies and natural-language realization. In controlled generation settings, prompts influence not only what information is retained, but also how outputs are organized, what tone is used, and whether explicit output constraints are followed [8–11]. This makes prompt-based control a practical mechanism for generating summaries tailored to user requirements.

Despite this promise, prompt optimization for summarization still faces major challenges. First, many existing prompt optimization methods treat task quality as the only or dominant target, implicitly assuming that overlap-based metrics are sufficient to judge prompt quality [13–19]. In realistic summarization scenarios, however, users may require concise outputs, restrained factual expression, preservation of key numbers and named entities, and avoidance of speculative wording or unwanted structures [7,8,11]. Second, prompt optimization is inherently evaluation-driven: every candidate prompt must be executed by the model and scored. Prompt evaluation count is therefore an important computational resource. If competing methods are compared under inconsistent evaluation budgets, observed differences may partly reflect budget differences rather than actual search ability.

To address these issues, we propose a budget-constrained preference-aligned prompt optimization method for controllable summarization. The method formulates summarization prompt search as a multi-objective optimization problem under a fixed budget, with summary quality, preference alignment, and rule-verifiable compliance jointly forming the optimization target. We construct a structured discrete prompt space in which prompts are treated not as arbitrary free-form text, but as structured objects composed of role settings, stylistic requirements, generation guidelines, and output constraints. On top of this space, we introduce a same-budget comparison protocol, using manual prompts as a non-search reference baseline and comparing random search, hill-climbing search, genetic search, and hybrid evolutionary local-search strategies under aligned evaluation budgets.

We instantiate the proposed framework with Qwen2.5-1.5B-Instruct as the fixed backbone summarization model, abbreviated as Qwen2.5-1.5B hereafter, and evaluate it on CNN/DailyMail [2–4]. Task quality is measured by ROUGE-1, ROUGE-2, and ROUGE-L [1]. In addition, we report preference alignment, rule-verifiable compliance, and the composite objective. The experiments show that structured prompt search can improve overall prompt utility within a fixed evaluation budget without updating model parameters. Importantly, the observed gains should be interpreted primarily as improvements in preference-oriented controllability rather than as large improvements in lexical-overlap scores.

The contributions of this paper are as follows. First, we formalize summarization prompt optimization as a budget-constrained multi-objective search problem that unifies task quality, preference alignment, and rule-verifiable compliance. Second, we propose a structured prompt search framework together with same-budget comparison for fair evaluation of prompt optimization strategies. Third, experiments show that the proposed method improves composite utility for controllable summarization relative to unoptimized prompts and simple search baselines, while maintaining comparable ROUGE performance.

2 Related Work

Recent research on summarization and controllable summarization has developed along several lines. In content-control joint modeling, CTRLsum [8] unifies controllable summarization through keyword-driven prompting and supports multiple control scenarios, including entity control, length control, contribution-focused summaries, patent-use summaries, and QA-guided summaries. Controllable neural dialogue summarization with personal named entity planning [9] modulates attention focus in dialogue summarization and improves factual consistency and temporal coherence. Aspect-controllable opinion summarization [10] introduces aspect controllers so that summaries can focus on specified opinion dimensions. Readability-controllable summarization [11] addresses readability control through instruction design, reinforcement learning, and look-ahead decoding. For long-context settings, FRAME/SCOPE [12] reformulates meeting summarization as a fact- and personalization-oriented question-driven process. These studies show that summarization has shifted from generating merely readable outputs to generating outputs that satisfy explicit control requirements.

A parallel line of work studies automatic prompt optimization. Representative methods include APE [13], which casts instruction generation and selection as a search problem; ProTeGi [14], which views prompt revision as text-based gradient descent combined with beam search; OPRO [15], which treats the LLM itself as an optimizer; Promptbreeder [16], which introduces self-referential evolution of task prompts and mutation prompts; EvoPrompt [17], which combines evolutionary algorithms with LLMs for population-based discrete prompt search; RePrompt [19], which updates prompts using interaction history and intermediate feedback; and MAPO [18], which augments prompt optimization with momentum to reduce oscillation and improve efficiency.

Despite this progress, several gaps remain for summarization. Existing controllable summarization methods often focus on a single control dimension, such as keywords, entities, aspects, or readability. Existing prompt optimization methods have shown strong performance on classification, reasoning, and agent tasks, but their objectives still largely revolve around task performance; user preference and explicit rule constraints are less thoroughly modeled, and many comparisons do not strictly align evaluation budgets. These limitations are amplified in summarization: the outputs naturally involve style, length, information retention, and factual restraint, while prompt optimization requires repeated model calls whose number directly affects comparison fairness.

The proposed method is designed for this gap. Unlike methods that control only one summary attribute, our framework unifies summary quality, preference alignment, and rule-verifiable compliance within a single composite objective. Unlike prompt optimization methods that rely primarily on task scores, our method explicitly formulates prompt search as a fixed-budget multi-objective optimization problem and compares representative search strategies under the same prompt evaluation budget. The aim is not to claim a new general-purpose optimizer, but to provide a reproducible framework for identifying prompts that balance quality, user preference, and explicit rules under a fixed evaluation cost.

3 Problem Definition and Metrics

We define summarization prompt optimization as a budget-constrained search problem over a structured prompt space. Let the summarization dataset be $D = \{(x_i, y_i)\}_{i=1}^{N}$, where x_i is the source document and y_i is the reference summary. Let $\mathcal{P}$ denote the candidate prompt space and M denote a fixed summarization model. For any prompt $p \in \mathcal{P}$, the generated summary is written as $\hat{y}_i = M(x_i, p)$. Under this setting, the objective is to find a prompt p^* that maximizes a composite objective under a fixed evaluation budget B.

Instead of evaluating prompts only by task scores, we characterize prompt utility along three dimensions. The first is summary quality $Q(p)$, which measures reference-based task quality. The second is an embedding-based preference alignment signal $c_{\text{embed}}(p)$, which measures how well the candidate prompt matches a fixed textual preference profile. The third is rule-verifiable compliance $P_{\text{rule}}(p)$, which measures whether the generated output satisfies explicit requirements such as length limits, preservation of key numbers, avoidance of bullet structures, avoidance of speculative wording, and avoidance of first-person expression. These three signals correspond to content quality, semantic preference consistency, and output-level constraint satisfaction, respectively.

3.1 Operational Definition of the Scores

Summary Quality. During prompt search, task quality is computed on a fixed development subset. In the standard configuration used for paper reporting, $Q(p)$ is a weighted average of ROUGE-1, ROUGE-2, and ROUGE-L:

$$Q(p) = 0.33R_1(p) + 0.33R_2(p) + 0.34R_L(p), \tag{1}$$

where R_1, R_2, and R_L denote averaged ROUGE-1, ROUGE-2, and ROUGE-L F1 scores on the evaluation subset. In the final test stage, ROUGE-1, ROUGE-2, and ROUGE-L are reported separately rather than being replaced by Q.

Embedding-Based Preference Alignment. The target preference profile is represented by a fixed textual description of the desired summary behavior: conciseness, formal tone, factual expression, number preservation, and an explicit word limit. In our implementation, both the target preference profile and a candidate prompt are encoded as normalized 256-dimensional hashed lexical vectors for reproducibility and low computational cost. Let u be the preference-profile vector and $e(p)$ be the candidate prompt vector. The embedding-based alignment score is computed as

$$c_{\text{embed}}(p) = \sigma\left(\frac{\cos(u, e(p)) - \mu}{\tau}\right), \tag{2}$$

where $\sigma(\cdot)$ is the logistic sigmoid function. We set $\mu = 0$ and $\tau = 0.2$ in the formal experiments. This score is a soft proxy for whether the prompt explicitly expresses the desired preference profile. The automatic preference and compliance scores used in this work are reproducible proxy indicators for search; they are not intended to replace human preference evaluation.

Rule-Verifiable Compliance. Rule-verifiable compliance is computed from generated summaries and does not require human annotation. For each generated summary $\hat{y}_i$, we compute five component scores:

$$P_{\text{rule}}(\hat{y}_i, x_i) = \frac{S_{\text{num}} + S_{\text{len}} + S_{\text{bul}} + S_{\text{hed}} + S_{\text{fp}}}{5}. \tag{3}$$

Here S_{num} is numeric-token recall from the source document, S_{len} is a length-compliance score, S_{bul} is a binary score indicating absence of bullet or list markers, S_{hed} penalizes frequent hedging or speculative words, and S_{fp} is a binary score indicating absence of first-person pronouns. Length compliance is defined as

$$S_{\text{len}} = \begin{cases} 1, & \text{if } |\hat{y}_i| \le L, \\ \max(0, 1 - (|\hat{y}_i| - L)/L), & \text{otherwise,} \end{cases} \tag{4}$$

where L is the target word limit. Hedging compliance is computed as $S_{\text{hed}} = \max(0, 1 - 10r_{\text{hed}})$, where r_{hed} is the proportion of hedging tokens such as "may", "might", "could", "possibly", "likely", "probably", "unclear", "appears", and "suggests". The prompt-level rule score $P_{\text{rule}}(p)$ is the average of $P_{\text{rule}}(\hat{y}_i, x_i)$ over the evaluation subset. The final preference score P in Table 3 is reported on a 0–100 scale, i.e., $P = 100 \times P_{\text{rule}}(p)$.

3.2 Composite Objective Under a Fixed Budget

To combine soft preference alignment and explicit rule compliance into a single control-oriented component, we define the control utility score as

$$C(p) = \alpha c_{\text{embed}}(p) + (1 - \alpha) P_{\text{rule}}(p), \tag{5}$$

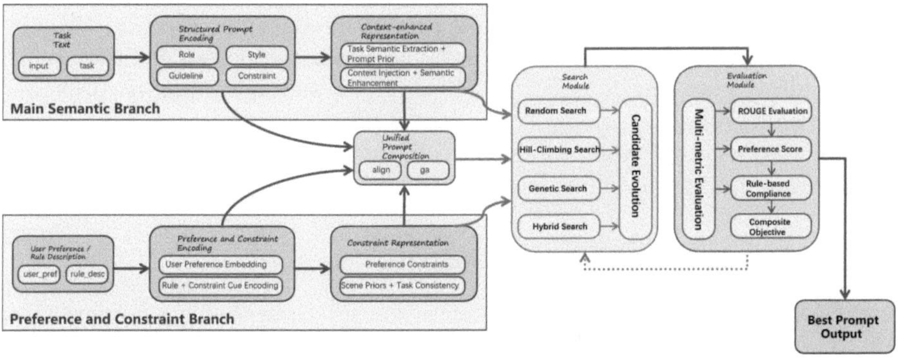

Fig. 1. Overview of the proposed framework for budget-constrained preference-aligned prompt optimization.

where $\alpha \in [0, 1]$ balances preference expression in the prompt and verifiable compliance in the generated output. In the formal experiments, $\alpha = 0.5$ unless otherwise stated. The overall optimization objective is then defined as

$$F(p) = Q(p) + \lambda C(p), \tag{6}$$

where λ controls the relative importance of control utility against task quality. In the formal experiments, $\lambda = 0.1$. Under these definitions, prompt optimization can be written as

$$p^* = \arg\max_{p \in \mathcal{P}} F(p) \quad \text{s.t.} \quad \text{EvalCount}(p) \leq B. \tag{7}$$

One prompt evaluation is defined as a complete execution-and-scoring cycle of one candidate prompt on the fixed evaluation subset. This formulation places budget, quality, alignment, and compliance within the same search framework and provides a basis for same-budget comparison.

4 Method

This section presents the proposed budget-constrained prompt optimization method for controllable summarization. The goal is not to update the parameters of the backbone language model, but to automatically search for prompts that balance summary quality, preference alignment, and rule-based compliance under a fixed prompt evaluation budget.

4.1 Overall Framework

Figure 1 illustrates the overall workflow of the proposed method. Given an input document and a predefined prompt space, the system first constructs candidate prompts from functional components, including role, style, generation guideline, and output constraint. Each candidate prompt is then executed by the fixed backbone model to generate a summary. The generated output is evaluated by a multi-objective scoring module, which combines summary quality, preference alignment, and rule-based compliance. Based on the obtained score, the search module updates candidate prompts and continues the optimization process until the evaluation budget is exhausted.

4.2 Structured Prompt Representation

We design a structured prompt representation for controllable summarization. Directly modifying prompts as free-form text can lead to unstable results, because small wording changes may affect role definition, output format, and constraint expression simultaneously. To reduce this uncertainty, we decompose a prompt into independent fields:

$$p = (r, s, g, k, o), \tag{8}$$

where r denotes the role instruction, s denotes the output style, g denotes the generation guideline, k denotes the explicit output constraint, and o denotes optional decoding or format-control settings. This decomposition allows each part of the prompt to be optimized more precisely and makes crossover, mutation, and local replacement easier to apply.

4.3 Prompt Execution and Evaluation

For each candidate prompt, the system uses the fixed backbone model to generate summaries. Given an input document x_i and a candidate prompt p, the generated summary is denoted as

$$\hat{y}_i = M(x_i, p), \tag{9}$$

where M represents Qwen2.5-1.5B. During this process, the model parameters are not updated. After generation, the output summary is evaluated using the scoring components defined in Sect. 3. This evaluation design is important because controllable summarization requires more than reference-summary similarity: a summary may obtain an acceptable ROUGE score but still fail to satisfy length, style, factual restraint, or formatting requirements.

4.4 Budget-Constrained Search

We compare random search, hill-climbing search, genetic search, and hybrid search. Random search samples prompts from the structured prompt space and provides a baseline for evaluating whether the prompt space itself is useful. Hill-climbing search performs local modifications around the current best prompt and keeps a modification if the score improves. Genetic search maintains a population of candidate prompts and updates them through selection, crossover, and mutation. Hybrid search combines population-level exploration with local refinement, aiming to improve both exploration ability and convergence efficiency.

For all automatic search methods, one prompt evaluation means executing one candidate prompt on the fixed evaluation subset and computing its score. The total number of prompt evaluations is limited by the budget B. This setting ensures that different search strategies are compared under the same cost, so observed performance differences reflect search behavior rather than the number of model calls.

4.5 Implementation Protocol

We implement the proposed framework using Qwen2.5-1.5B-Instruct as the fixed backbone model. The decoding configuration is fixed for all candidate prompts to reduce the influence of generation randomness. The maximum generation length is set to 80 words for CNN/DailyMail. For automatic search methods, the evaluation budget is set to 120 prompt evaluations. Each method is repeated with three random seeds, and we report mean and standard deviation. The manual prompt is reported separately as a non-search baseline and is not included in the budget-aligned optimization comparison.

5 Experimental Setup

We evaluate the proposed method on CNN/DailyMail, a widely used English news summarization benchmark [2–4]. This dataset consists of news articles paired with human-written highlight-style summaries. In the processed subsets used in our implementation, the CNN/DailyMail training subset contains 5,000 examples with an average source length of approximately 697 words and an average reference length of approximately 52 words; the validation subset contains 1,000 examples with an average source length of approximately 682 words and an average reference length of approximately 58 words; and the test subset contains 1,000 examples with an average source length of approximately 672 words and an average reference length of approximately 55 words. The dataset is suitable for evaluating factual information retention, length control, and preservation of entities and numbers. At the same time, CNN/DailyMail is relatively extractive, so it does not fully reflect more abstractive summarization scenarios.

To ensure comparability with standard summarization work, we also describe the original CNN/DailyMail split, which contains 287,113 training examples, 13,368 validation examples, and 11,490 test examples. Prompt search uses only a predefined evaluation subset and does not update model parameters on training data, which keeps the setting consistent with black-box prompt search on a fixed model.

We use Qwen2.5-1.5B-Instruct as the fixed backbone summarization model. This model is chosen because it provides stable instruction-following ability and reasonable summarization performance while allowing prompt optimization effects to be observed without parameter updates. Evaluation follows the standard summarization protocol. Summary quality is measured by ROUGE-1, ROUGE-2, and ROUGE-L [1]. In addition to task quality, we report the control

Table 1. Reproducibility details of the main experiment.

Item	Setting
Backbone model	Qwen2.5-1.5B-Instruct
Dataset	CNN/DailyMail
Processed subsets	5,000 train / 1,000 validation / 1,000 test examples
Search budget	120 prompt evaluations per automatic method
Repeated runs	3 random seeds
Max generation length	80 words
Search methods	random, hill-climbing, genetic, hybrid
Control weights	$\alpha = 0.5$, $\lambda = 0.1$
Reported metrics	ROUGE-1/2/L, Q, C, F, and P

Table 2. Search-stage performance on CNN/DailyMail. The control score c denotes $C(p)$ in Eq. (7), combining embedding-based preference alignment and rule-verifiable compliance.

Method	Budget	Q	c	F
hybrid search	120	0.506 ± 0.012	0.796 ± 0.021	0.583 ± 0.013
ga search	120	0.502 ± 0.010	0.774 ± 0.039	0.579 ± 0.011
hill search	120	0.504 ± 0.005	0.749 ± 0.014	0.578 ± 0.004
random search	120	0.501 ± 0.001	0.659 ± 0.038	0.567 ± 0.004
manual baseline	–	0.438	0.830	0.521

score C, the composite objective F, and the final rule-verifiable preference score P. The comparison includes manual prompting, random search, hill-climbing search, genetic search, and hybrid evolutionary local search (Table 1).

6 Results and Analysis

6.1 Search-Stage Results

Table 2 reports search-stage performance on CNN/DailyMail. Under the same search budget, hybrid search achieves the best search-stage composite score among the automatic search strategies, with $F = 0.583 \pm 0.013$, slightly higher than genetic search and hill-climbing search, and clearly better than random search. Hybrid search also attains the highest mean Q and c, indicating a stronger balance between summary quality and user-side control signals under the fixed budget.

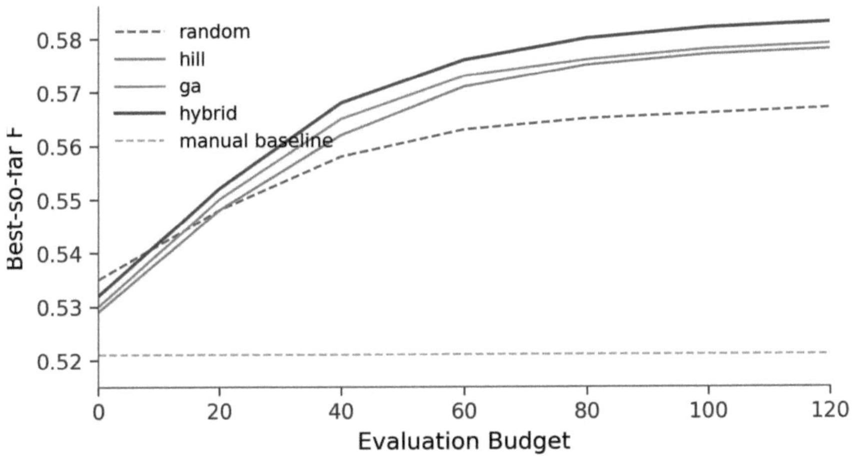

Fig. 2. Best-so-far composite score F under different prompt evaluation budgets on CNN/DailyMail.

Table 3. Final test results on CNN/DailyMail. P is reported on a 0–100 scale and corresponds to rule-verifiable preference compliance.

Method	ROUGE-1	ROUGE-2	ROUGE-L	P
hybrid search	29.23 ± 0.35	8.37 ± 0.32	18.45 ± 0.35	82.67 ± 0.46
random search	29.22 ± 0.52	8.39 ± 0.35	18.45 ± 0.34	79.60 ± 4.97
ga search	29.15 ± 0.46	8.36 ± 0.29	18.27 ± 0.24	78.23 ± 3.17
hill search	28.55 ± 0.39	8.02 ± 0.32	18.06 ± 0.22	75.08 ± 1.67
manual baseline	28.95	8.35	18.46	69.85

Figure 2 compares the best-so-far F as the evaluation budget increases. Random search gains some improvement early on but quickly enters a plateau, suggesting that pure random sampling is insufficient for continuously discovering better prompts. By contrast, hill-climbing, genetic search, and hybrid search show more stable improvement. Among them, hybrid search continues to improve in the middle and later stages and ultimately reaches the highest best-so-far F.

6.2 Final Test Results

Table 3 presents the final test results on CNN/DailyMail. The automatic search methods remain close to manual prompting on the ROUGE metrics, but show more pronounced improvements on P. Hybrid search obtains the highest

$P = 82.67 \pm 0.46$, which is 12.82 points higher than the manual baseline. At the same time, hybrid search reaches 29.23 in ROUGE-1, 8.37 in ROUGE-2, and 18.45 in ROUGE-L, indicating that the gain in control utility does not come at the cost of severe degradation in summary quality.

The ROUGE differences among methods are relatively small and should be interpreted cautiously. The main conclusion is therefore not that prompt search substantially improves lexical-overlap metrics, but that it improves preference-oriented controllability and rule-verifiable utility while maintaining comparable task quality. This interpretation is consistent with the motivation of controllable summarization: the practical value of a prompt is determined not only by overlap with reference summaries, but also by whether the generated output satisfies user-side constraints.

6.3 Sensitivity Analysis

Table 4. Sensitivity of the composite objective to λ on the development setting. Values are recomputed from the reported Q and C components to show how much the control term influences the ranking.

λ	random F_λ	hill F_λ	ga F_λ	hybrid F_λ
0.00	0.501	0.504	0.502	0.506
0.05	0.534	0.541	0.541	0.546
0.10	0.567	0.578	0.579	0.583
0.20	0.633	0.654	0.657	0.665
0.30	0.699	0.729	0.734	0.745

Table 4 addresses the sensitivity of the composite objective to the control weight λ. When $\lambda = 0$, the objective reduces to the ROUGE-based quality component and the differences among automatic methods are very small. As λ increases, the effect of preference alignment and rule-verifiable compliance becomes more visible. The ranking around $\lambda = 0.1$ remains consistent with the main results, and larger λ values further emphasize the same controllability-oriented differences. We therefore use $\lambda = 0.1$ as a bounded setting that gives control utility explicit influence without allowing it to dominate task quality. We set $\alpha = 0.5$ in the main experiment to give equal weight to embedding-based preference expression and rule-verifiable compliance; a fuller sweep over α is left for future work.

6.4 Qualitative Example

Table 5. Abridged qualitative example from CNN/DailyMail. The source excerpt and outputs are shortened for space while preserving the facts relevant to control evaluation.

Item	Text
Source excerpt	Maureen and Bob McDonnell were convicted in a joint trial of accepting more than $165,000 in gifts and loans from Jonnie Williams in exchange for promoting his company's nutritional supplements. Her attorneys argued that the conviction relied on an overly broad definition of bribery
Reference summary	Maureen McDonnell's attorneys argued that her corruption conviction should be overturned because it was based on an overly broad definition of bribery. The McDonnells were convicted of accepting more than $165,000 in gifts and loans
Manual prompt output	Maureen McDonnell requested a new trial, arguing that the conviction relied on an overly broad interpretation of an official act
Hybrid searched output	Maureen McDonnell challenged her corruption conviction after she and Bob McDonnell were convicted of accepting over $165,000 in gifts and loans from Jonnie Williams while promoting his nutritional supplement business
Observation	The searched prompt preserves the key monetary amount and the causal relation between gifts and promotion, while keeping a formal single-paragraph style without bullet markers. This helps explain why the improvement is more visible in the rule-verifiable preference score than in ROUGE

Table 5 gives an abridged example from the CNN/DailyMail test subset to contextualize the automatic scores. The source article concerns the corruption conviction of former Virginia first lady Maureen McDonnell and contains several verifiable facts, including the amount of gifts and loans and the relation between the gifts and the promotion of a supplement business.

7 Conclusion and Limitations

This paper presented a budget-constrained prompt optimization framework for controllable summarization. The framework unifies structured prompt construction, fixed-model execution, multi-objective scoring, and budget-constrained search within a reproducible pipeline. By explicitly combining task quality, embedding-based preference alignment, and rule-verifiable compliance, the framework evaluates prompt utility beyond reference-summary overlap alone. Experiments on CNN/DailyMail show that automatic prompt search can improve preference-oriented and rule-verifiable utility while maintaining comparable ROUGE performance under a fixed evaluation budget.

Several limitations remain. First, the current experiments are conducted on a single backbone model, Qwen2.5-1.5B, and broader validation on additional LLMs is needed. Second, the primary evaluation is conducted on CNN/DailyMail, which is a useful but relatively extractive news summarization benchmark. More abstractive datasets such as XSum, dialogue summarization datasets such as SAMSum, and long-document datasets such as Multi-News or GovReport would provide stronger evidence of generality. Third, the current comparison focuses on representative search strategies implemented in a unified structured prompt space. We do not directly compare against full public implementations of APE, OPRO, ProTeGi, PromptBreeder, or MAPO, because their search spaces, feedback mechanisms, and model-call accounting are not directly aligned with the current setup. Incorporating these methods under strictly matched budgets is an important direction for future work. Fourth, the preference and compliance scores are proxy indicators. Although they are deterministic and reproducible, they do not replace human preference evaluation.

Future work can proceed in several directions. The framework should be validated on more summarization backbones, more datasets, and more complex application settings to better assess generalization and stability. The current preference alignment and rule-verifiable compliance mechanisms can be extended to richer user-side signals, such as interactive feedback, usage history, or learned preference models. Beyond summarization, the framework may also be applied to other controlled generation tasks, such as report generation, long-document compression, and multi-turn information organization.

Acknowledgments. This work was supported by the Joint Fund of National Natural Science Foundation of China (No. 62576295), Chengdu Science and Technology Program (No. 2024-YF05-00340-SN).

Disclosure of Interests. The author has no competing interests to declare that are relevant to the content of this article.

References

1. Lin, C.-Y.: ROUGE: a package for automatic evaluation of summaries. In: Text Summarization Branches Out, pp. 74–81. Association for Computational Linguistics (2004)
2. Hermann, K.M., Kočiský, T., Grefenstette, E.: Teaching machines to read and comprehend. In: Advances in Neural Information Processing Systems (2015)
3. Nallapati, R., Zhou, B., dos Santos, C., Gülçehre, Ç., Xiang, B.: Abstractive text summarization using sequence-to-sequence RNNs and beyond. In: Proceedings of the 20th SIGNLL Conference on Computational Natural Language Learning, pp. 280–290 (2016)
4. See, A., Liu, P.J., Manning, C.D.: Get to the point: summarization with pointer-generator networks. In: Proceedings of ACL, pp. 1073–1083 (2017)

5. Narayan, S., Cohen, S.B., Lapata, M.: Don't give me the details, just the summary! Topic-aware convolutional neural networks for extreme summarization. In: Proceedings of EMNLP, pp. 1797–1807 (2018)
6. Wang, A., Cho, K., Lewis, M.: Asking and answering questions to evaluate the factual consistency of summaries. In: Proceedings of ACL, pp. 5008–5020 (2020)
7. Fabbri, A.R., Kryściński, W., McCann, B., et al.: SummEval: re-evaluating summarization evaluation. Trans. Assoc. Comput. Linguist. **9**, 391–409 (2021)
8. He, J., Kryściński, W., McCann, B., Rajani, N., Xiong, C.: CTRLsum: towards generic controllable text summarization. In: Proceedings of EMNLP, pp. 5988–6005 (2022)
9. Liu, Z., Chen, N.F.: Controllable neural dialogue summarization with personal named entity planning. In: Proceedings of EMNLP, pp. 92–106 (2021)
10. Amplayo, R.K., Angelidis, S., Lapata, M.: Aspect-controllable opinion summarization. In: Proceedings of EMNLP, pp. 6578–6593 (2021)
11. Ribeiro, L.F.R., Bansal, M., Dreyer, M.: Generating summaries with controllable readability levels. In: Proceedings of EMNLP, pp. 11579–11597 (2023)
12. Kirstein, F., Kumar, S., Ruas, T., Gipp, B.: Re-FRAME the meeting summarization SCOPE: fact-based summarization and personalization via questions. In: Findings of EMNLP (2025)
13. Zhou, Y., Muresanu, A.I., Han, Z.: Large language models are human-level prompt engineers. In: International Conference on Learning Representations (2023)
14. Pryzant, R., Iter, D., Li, J.: Automatic prompt optimization with "gradient descent" and beam search. In: Proceedings of EMNLP, pp. 7957–7977 (2023)
15. Yang, C., Wang, X., Lu, Y.: Large language models as optimizers. In: International Conference on Learning Representations (2024)
16. Fernando, C., Banarse, D., Michalewski, H.: Promptbreeder: self-referential self-improvement via prompt evolution. In: Proceedings of ICML (2024)
17. Guo, Q., Wang, R., Guo, J., et al.: Connecting Large Language Models with Evolutionary Algorithms Yields Powerful Prompt Optimizers. arXiv:2309.08532 (2023)
18. Cui, A., Nandyalam, P., Cheung, E., Zhu, K.: Introducing MAPO: Momentum-Aided Gradient Descent Prompt Optimization (2024). arXiv:2410.19499
19. Chen, W., Koenig, S., Dilkina, B.: RePrompt: Planning by Automatic Prompt Engineering for Large Language Models Agents (2024). arXiv:2406.11132
20. Brown, T.B., Mann, B., Ryder, N.: Language models are few-shot learners. In: Advances in Neural Information Processing Systems, vol. 33, pp. 1877–1901 (2020)
21. Ouyang, L., Wu, J., Jiang, X.: Training language models to follow instructions with human feedback. In: Advances in Neural Information Processing Systems, vol. 35, pp. 27730–27744 (2022)

TSP-LLM: A Unified Textual Serialization Framework for Multivariate Spatiotemporal Forecasting via Structured Prompting

Siyi Liu, Ziyi Lei, and Yunxuan Dong(✉)

School of Computer, Electronics and Information, Guangxi University, Nanning, China
{2413394018,2207310513}@st.gxu.edu.cn, dongyx@gxu.edu.cn

Abstract. Multivariate spatiotemporal forecasting systems that serve diverse variables and spatial aggregations often suffer from severe model redundancy and computational overhead, as dedicated models are maintained for each heterogeneous variable. Adapting pre-trained Large Language Models via a text-to-text paradigm offers a promising path toward a unified predictor, yet the core challenge lies in how to effectively serialize continuous numerical time series. Naive concatenation of raw values lacks task and temporal context and may leave the expected textual output format under-specified. To this end, we propose TSP-LLM, a unified textual serialization framework based on temporally structured prompting. The key idea is to employ a fixed natural-language template as the serialization interface, providing explicit semantic anchors for heterogeneous inputs. Using this structured prompt, we map 24-hour numerical observations into a unified semantic text space, enabling a single T5 model to accommodate eight meteorological factors and multiple spatial weighting schemes without architectural modifications. Experiments on a 43-year country-level benchmark show competitive performance against 11 dedicated neural baselines, particularly on variables with smooth, periodic dynamics. In controlled prompt ablations, removing the semantic anchors increases SMAPE on irradiance-related variables from single-digit values to more than 80%, although MAE and RMSE do not improve uniformly across all variables.

Keywords: Spatiotemporal Data Mining · Time Series Forecasting · Large Language Models · Structured Prompting · Textual Serialization

1 Introduction

Multivariate spatiotemporal forecasting is a fundamental task for meteorological data mining and complex dynamic modeling [10,21]. In practical deployments,

This research was supported by the School of Computer, Electronics and Information, Guangxi University under Grant No. 2606020162.

L. Ding et al. (Eds.): APWeb-WAIM 2026, LNCS 16993, pp. 344–359, 2027.
https://doi.org/10.1007/978-981-92-5693-8_22

target systems rarely serve an isolated forecasting objective; instead, they must concurrently process diverse meteorological factors, multiple spatial aggregation schemes, and varying forecasting horizons within a single pipeline. Under such settings, maintaining a dedicated numerical architecture, such as Informer [27], FEDformer [29], or iTransformer [13], for each variable or task variant introduces severe model redundancy, redundant tuning costs, and unnecessary deployment complexity.

Adapting pre-trained Large Language Models (LLMs) via a text-to-text paradigm offers an alternative path toward a unified predictor: by converting numerical histories into text and modeling the prediction as a conditional generation task, a single pre-trained language model can theoretically unify heterogeneous tasks through a shared vocabulary interface [7,8,23]. However, recent diagnostic analyses indicate that such gains are not automatic [18,26]. When raw continuous values are directly concatenated as plain text, the serialized sequence lacks sufficient structural constraints and can leave task identity, temporal scope, and the expected output form under-specified across variables with different scales and temporal patterns.

Therefore, the central question of this paper is not simply whether an LLM can forecast, but whether a properly structured textual interface can transform a single pre-trained language model into a robust, shared forecaster for highly heterogeneous spatiotemporal series. In our setting, overcoming the primary obstacle of cross-modal alignment requires mapping continuous meteorological observations into a discrete token space without losing task identity, temporal scope, or output-format constraints. An effective solution must standardize heterogeneous inputs and maintain competitive performance against specialized numerical baselines.

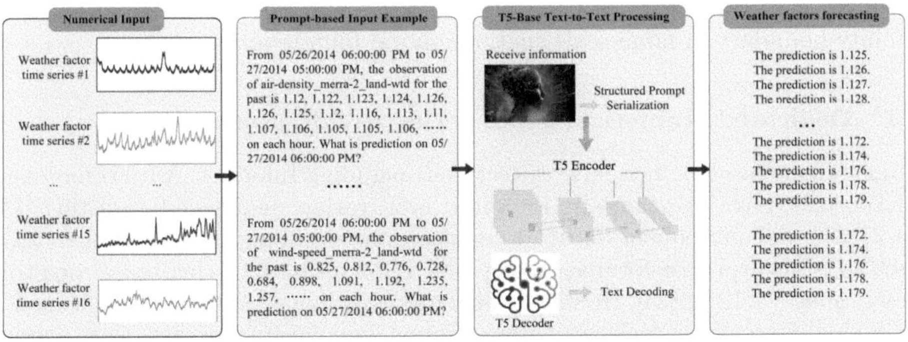

Fig. 1. Overview of the proposed TSP-LLM framework. Numerical weather histories are serialized into structured textual prompts, processed by a T5 encoder–decoder, and decoded as textual forecasts.

To address these challenges, we propose TSP-LLM, a unified forecasting framework based on temporally structured prompting (Fig. 1). Instead of relying on task-specific architectural modifications, TSP-LLM serializes each 24-hour observation window into a fixed natural-language template that explicitly encodes the temporal horizon, variable identity, and spatial weighting scheme, serving as a semantic anchor for a pre-trained T5 (Text-to-Text Transfer Transformer) backbone. This design enables a single shared predictor to concurrently handle eight distinct meteorological factors under both land-weighted (LW) and population-weighted (PW) aggregations without.

In summary, our contributions are delineated as follows:

- We propose TSP-LLM, a unified textual serialization framework that transforms continuous numerical sequences into fixed natural-language templates. Structured semantic anchors provide task, temporal, and output-format context for adapting the pre-trained T5-base backbone.
- We formulate a unified sequence modeling task that eliminates model redundancy in spatiotemporal forecasting, enabling a single shared predictor to concurrently handle eight distinct meteorological factors, two spatial weighting schemes, and multiple forecasting horizons without task-specific architectural modifications.
- We conduct extensive evaluations on a 43-year country-level benchmark and provide controlled ablations that quantify how structured textual serialization changes forecasting errors relative to prompt-free numerical.

2 Related Work

We organize the related literature around three directions directly relevant to our work: the model redundancy problem in dedicated numerical architectures, the cross-modal serialization challenge in LLM-based forecasting, and the applicability boundary of large-scale spatiotemporal foundation models.

2.1 Dedicated Numerical Time-Series Architectures

Transformer-based numerical architectures, including Informer, Autoformer, and FEDformer, have substantially improved multivariate sequence forecasting [19, 20,27,29], and subsequent linear, decomposition-based, and mixing-style models such as DLinear, iTransformer, Koopa, and TSMixer have further broadened this design space [4,12,13,24]. However, these methods remain dedicated solutions for individual forecasting tasks: in heterogeneous deployment settings, they require separate model instances or task-specific tuning across variables, horizons, and data regimes, leading to inevitable model redundancy. Our goal is not to propose another dedicated architecture, but to investigate whether these heterogeneous tasks can be unified by a single shared model.

2.2 Cross-Modal Serialization for LLM Forecasting

PromptCast and Time-LLM demonstrate that time series can be reformulated as text and processed by pre-trained language models [8,15,23]; zero-shot studies further suggest that tokenized sequences sometimes support useful extrapolation even without task-specific optimization [7,26]. However, recent diagnostic analyses reveal a key mechanistic limitation: when raw continuous values are directly concatenated as plain text, the serialized sequence lacks structural constraints and may leave variable identity, temporal scope, and the expected output form ambiguous [18,26]. Therefore, the unresolved issue is not merely whether serialization is feasible, but how continuous values should be serialized so that task identity is preserved within a shared model. We address this gap with a fixed temporal template that standardizes heterogeneous inputs.

Recent time-series foundation models further broaden this context. Chronos adapts T5-family architectures to quantized time-series tokens [1], TimesFM studies decoder-only pre-training for zero-shot forecasting [5], Lag-Llama develops probabilistic decoder-only forecasting with lag covariates [16], and Moirai investigates universal forecasting transformers trained across large-scale time-series archives [22]. TSP-LLM is complementary to these systems: rather than pre-training a new time-series foundation model, it evaluates whether a lightweight textual interface can consolidate heterogeneous meteorological forecasting tasks within a single fine-tuned sequence-to-sequence backbone.

2.3 Deep Models for Spatiotemporal Applications

Large spatiotemporal models such as Pangu-Weather, GraphCast, and Aurora have demonstrated remarkable progress in global atmospheric forecasting [2, 3,10], with related applications also emerging in energy-oriented environmental scenarios [21]. However, these systems are designed for massive 3D global dynamics or operational weather modeling [2,10], and their computational overhead and memory demands are excessive for regional, aggregated downstream forecasting tasks. Our problem scope is narrower but practically critical: multi-factor, multi-aggregation shared forecasting under strict deployment constraints. We therefore evaluate whether a lightweight textual serialization framework can provide a resource-efficient unified forecasting interface in such downstream settings.

3 The Proposed TSP-LLM Framework

Temporally Structured Prompting-based Large Language Model (TSP-LLM) reformulates highly heterogeneous multivariate spatiotemporal forecasting into a single text-conditioned generation task. The core idea is to employ a structured textual serialization mechanism that uses semantic anchoring to standardize diverse inputs. This approach bridges the cross-modal gap between continuous numerical time series and the discrete natural language space while providing explicit task and output-format constraints for the pre-trained language model.

3.1 Problem Definition

In aggregated multivariate spatiotemporal forecasting, the objective is to predict future meteorological states from historical observations under different spatial weighting schemes. Let $x_{t-w+1:t}^{(v,g)} \in \mathbb{R}^w$ denote a historical time-series window of length w for weather factor v under spatial aggregation scheme $g \in \{\text{land}, \text{population}\}$. The forecasting task is defined as learning a unified mapping function f that predicts the subsequent H steps:

$$\hat{x}_{t+1:t+H}^{(v,g)} = f\left(x_{t-w+1:t}^{(v,g)}, v, g, H\right), \tag{1}$$

where $H \in \{1, 3, 5\}$ denotes the forecasting horizon. In our implementation, the look-back window is fixed at $w = 24$, corresponding to 24 hourly observations. The primary challenge in this setting is that f must remain shared across variables with vastly different scales, periodicities, and volatility patterns, while simultaneously accommodating multiple weighting schemes and horizons. To address this, we reformulate f from an ensemble of task-specific numerical models into a unified sequence-to-sequence generation problem, evaluating the capacity of a pre-trained language model to approximate this highly non-linear mapping under a structured textual interface.

We use "multivariate" in the deployment sense that one shared predictor serves multiple meteorological variables and aggregation schemes. Each serialized instance targets a specified factor and aggregation mode; explicit joint vector prediction across variables is not claimed in the current implementation.

3.2 Framework Overview

As illustrated in Fig. 2, the pipeline consists of four functional stages: (1) a sliding-window extractor converts raw numerical series into fixed-length historical windows; (2) a textual serialization operator maps each numerical window into a structured prompt with explicit temporal and task metadata; (3) a pre-trained T5 encoder–decoder models the serialized prompt; and (4) an autoregressive decoder generates the future value sequence in a standardized textual format. This design keeps the model architecture invariant to meteorological factors and aggregation schemes, ensuring that data heterogeneity is handled through the prompt interface rather than task-specific network redesign.

3.3 Textual Serialization and Semantic Anchoring

Serialization operator. To adapt continuous time series for the language-model-oriented T5 backbone, we construct a cross-modal mapping from numerical windows to token sequences. Let $\mathcal{V}$ denote the vocabulary space of the language model. We define a serialization operator $f_{\text{prompt}} : \mathbb{R}^w \times \mathcal{M} \to \mathcal{V}^L$, where $\mathcal{M}$ denotes the metadata space containing the temporal identifier, variable identity v, weighting scheme g, and forecasting query.

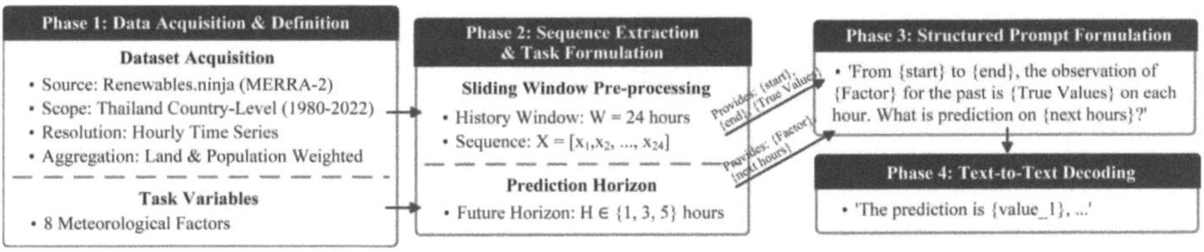

Fig. 2. The textual serialization pipeline of TSP-LLM. Phase 1: spatiotemporal series are extracted into 24-point sliding windows. Phase 2: numerical sequences are mapped into a fixed structured textual space. Phase 3: the T5-base backbone is fine-tuned. Phase 4: the decoder autoregressively generates the prediction.

Structured prompt template. Directly inputting raw numerical arrays creates a contextual void, because plain numeric sequences cannot convey task identity or temporal scope to the language model. To resolve this, the serialization operator wraps each window in a fixed natural-language template comprising three elements: a temporal window identifier that explicitly bounds the observation period, a spatiotemporal descriptor encoding the meteorological factor and aggregation mode, and the numerical sequence embedded as comma-separated tokens. This mechanism equips the decoder with stable lexical anchors prior to encountering the raw values, enabling a single model to process highly heterogeneous sequences. A serialized example is shown below:

Input sequence in vocabulary space: From 01/01/1980 12:00:00 AM to 01/01/1980 11:00:00 PM, the observation of temperature_land-wtd for the past is 25.1, 25.2, ... on each hour. What is prediction on 01/02/1980 12:00:00 AM?
Target output: The prediction is 24.9.

Prompt-free baseline design. To isolate the effect of structured serialization in ablation experiments, we design a prompt-free baseline that receives the identical 24 continuous values as a plain numeric string, devoid of the temporal and semantic wrapper. This control setting strictly separates the contribution of structured serialization from the inherent representational capacity of the T5 backbone.

3.4 Model Optimization and Output-Format Regularization

The model is trained using a standard conditional generation objective. Given a serialized input prompt P, the decoder generates the target textual sequence $S = \{s_1, s_2, \ldots, s_T\}$, and the optimization minimizes the negative log-likelihood:

$$\mathcal{L} = -\sum_{t=1}^{T} \log P(s_t \mid s_{<t}, P; \Theta), \tag{2}$$

where Θ denotes the parameters of the T5 backbone.

In this framework, the structured template serves a strictly operational rather than rhetorical role. Specifically, it performs three functions: regularizing the surface form of the input, preserving task identity within a shared parameter space, and specifying a consistent textual output pattern. The ablation study in Sect. 4.3 tests how removing these semantic anchors changes predictive errors; it is not a direct repeated-decoding variance experiment.

4 Experiments

Our empirical evaluation pursues two primary objectives. First, we benchmark TSP-LLM against 11 dedicated numerical forecasters to assess the competitiveness of a unified text-conditioned model across highly heterogeneous weather-series prediction tasks. Second, we conduct controlled ablations to isolate the effect of structured prompting relative to a prompt-free baseline.

4.1 Datasets and Experimental Setup

We conduct experiments on the country-level Thailand weather series derived from Renewables.ninja and built upon NASA MERRA-2 reanalysis data [6,14,17]. The benchmark spans continuous hourly records from 1980 to 2022. We study eight heterogeneous meteorological factors: air density (Air_dy, kg/m^3), cloud cover (Clc, [0,1]), specific humidity (Hum, kg/kg), surface irradiance (Irr, W/m^2), top-of-atmosphere irradiance (Irrto, W/m^2), precipitation (Pre, mm/h), temperature (Tem, °C), and wind speed (Wsp, m/s). To test the models on the original temporal dynamics rather than heavily curated inputs, preprocessing is kept strictly minimal without extra dataset-level imputation.

For comparison, we evaluate TSP-LLM against 11 established multivariate forecasting baselines: DLinear [24], FEDformer [29], FiLM [28], Informer [27], iTransformer [13], Koopa [12], LightTS [25], Pyraformer [11], Reformer [9], Transformer [19], and TSMixer [4]. All models follow a standardized evaluation protocol with author-recommended hyperparameters. The 43-year series is chronologically partitioned into training, validation, and testing sets at a 70:10:20 ratio.

TSP-LLM employs a pre-trained T5-base backbone fine-tuned via a sequence-generation objective. To account for natural data sparsity, such as zero-heavy precipitation intervals, all methods are evaluated under a unified masked-metric protocol. We report Mean Absolute Error (MAE), Root Mean Square Error (RMSE), Symmetric Mean Absolute Percentage Error (SMAPE), and the coefficient of determination (R^2); formal definitions are provided in the Appendix. For forecasting horizons $H \in \{1, 3, 5\}$, baseline comparisons emphasize the more demanding 3- and 5-step settings, while the 1-step horizon is reserved for prompt ablation studies.

4.2 Basic Results: Comparative Performance

Tables 1 and 2 report the detailed 3-step and 5-step results of TSP-LLM under land-weighted and population-weighted aggregations, respectively. Figures 3 and 4 provide a visual summary of the 12-model comparison. To make the head-to-head comparison numerically verifiable, Table 3 reports representative 5-step baseline results; the complete 12-model result matrices are provided in the supplementary workbook.

The main findings are as follows. First, TSP-LLM is competitive across most variables but not uniformly dominant. On smooth, periodic variables, especially temperature and irradiance-related series, the shared text-conditioned formulation remains close to or among the best dedicated baselines. For example, on Irrto, TSP-LLM maintains near-perfect $R^2 = 1.0000$ under both weighting schemes. On Irr, the 5-step R^2 reaches 0.9950 (LW) and 0.9926 (PW), with SMAPE at 6.34% and 7.37%, respectively. On temperature, the 5-step SMAPE is 0.64% (LW) and 0.68% (PW), ranking among the top three.

Second, performance degrades more visibly on highly volatile variables. Precipitation (Pre) shows 5-step SMAPE of 34.74% (LW) and 36.42% (PW), with R^2 dropping to 0.8195 and 0.7826, where specialized architectures, such as Koopa, retain a clearer advantage. Third, the performance gap between 3-step and 5-step settings widens more significantly on unstable variables than on periodic ones, suggesting that the robustness of textual serialization for longer horizons is related to the regularity of the underlying physical dynamics.

Table 1. Multi-step forecasting results of the TSP-LLM model (land-weighted).

Variable	3-step				5-step			
	MAE	RMSE	SMAPE	R^2	MAE	RMSE	SMAPE	R^2
Air_dy	0.0006	0.0009	0.0515	0.9962	0.0008	0.0012	0.0704	0.9934
Clc	0.0231	0.0368	4.4178	0.9672	0.0354	0.0568	6.7388	0.9217
Hum	0.0002	0.0004	1.3144	0.9746	0.0002	0.0005	1.5610	0.9696
Irr	10.4176	16.9562	5.4051	0.9977	14.7083	25.1552	6.3359	0.9950
Irrto	0.0458	0.2906	0.1405	1.0000	0.0389	0.2269	0.0799	1.0000
Pre	0.0357	0.0729	25.2471	0.8993	0.0503	0.0976	34.7350	0.8195
Tem	0.1122	0.2075	0.4341	0.9972	0.1680	0.2946	0.6445	0.9943
Wsp	0.0579	0.0904	4.0359	0.9770	0.0819	0.1248	5.6862	0.9561

Note. SMAPE values are percentages. Gold, silver, and copper indicate first, second, and third place.

Table 2. Multi-step forecasting results of the TSP-LLM model (population-weighted).

Variable	3-step				5-step			
	MAE	RMSE	SMAPE	R^2	MAE	RMSE	SMAPE	R^2
Air_dy	0.0007	0.0012	0.0568	0.9934	0.0009	0.0014	0.0776	0.9899
Clc	0.0301	0.0496	5.6302	0.9390	0.0445	0.0728	8.2680	0.8685
Hum	0.0002	0.0005	1.3891	0.9676	0.0003	0.0005	1.6619	0.9607
Irr	12.7914	20.9875	6.2067	0.9965	17.8516	30.4555	7.3716	0.9926
Irrto	0.0479	0.0848	0.0839	1.0000	0.0455	1.5318	0.0639	1.0000
Pre	0.0395	0.0871	26.2730	0.8749	0.0552	0.1148	36.4229	0.7826
Tem	0.1237	0.2107	0.4600	0.9966	0.1845	0.3097	0.6808	0.9927
Wsp	0.0873	0.1318	4.8595	0.9666	0.1238	0.1835	6.8816	0.9354

Note. SMAPE values are percentages. Gold, silver, and copper indicate first, second, and third place.

Table 3. Representative 5-step head-to-head baseline results. Values are reported as MAE/RMSE/SMAPE/R^2 and rounded to four decimals.

Aggregation	Variable	TSP-LLM	Baseline	Baseline result
LW	Irr	14.7083 / 25.1552 / 6.3359 / 0.9950	Pyraformer	18.4470 / 30.2042 / 24.2536 / 0.9872
			TSMixer	20.7755 / 32.7799 / 26.6851 / 0.9849
LW	Irrto	0.0389 / 0.2269 / 0.0799 / 1.0000	TSMixer	6.2967 / 14.8375 / 14.8145 / 0.9989
			LightTS	8.1662 / 16.6396 / 15.2379 / 0.9986
LW	Tem	0.1680 / 0.2946 / 0.6445 / 0.9943	Pyraformer	0.1684 / 0.2679 / 0.6539 / 0.9953
			Informer	0.1712 / 0.2730 / 0.6661 / 0.9951
LW	Pre	0.0503 / 0.0976 / 34.7350 / 0.8195	iTransformer	0.0462 / 0.0923 / 34.2003 / 0.8340
			Pyraformer	0.0465 / 0.0915 / 34.7198 / 0.8367
PW	Irr	17.8516 / 30.4555 / 7.3716 / 0.9926	Pyraformer	20.3434 / 32.9703 / 25.4796 / 0.9845
			TSMixer	23.4730 / 36.8988 / 27.1719 / 0.9806
PW	Pre	0.0552 / 0.1148 / 36.4229 / 0.7826	iTransformer	0.0539 / 0.1138 / 37.4307 / 0.7822
			Pyraformer	0.0545 / 0.1122 / 39.8760 / 0.7881

Note. SMAPE values are percentages. Gold, silver, and copper indicate first, second, and third place.

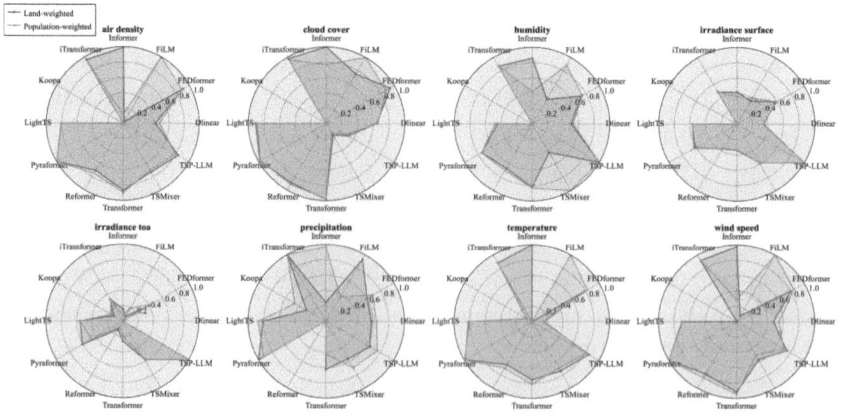

Fig. 3. Radar-chart summary of the 5-step multi-model comparison. Each subplot compares 12 models for one weather variable, with LW and PW profiles shown together. Smaller radial extent corresponds to lower normalized SMAPE.

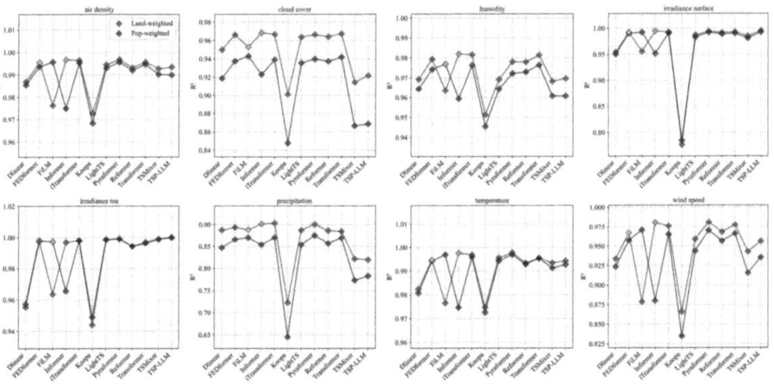

Fig. 4. R^2 comparison of the 5-step forecasting models. The two markers in each panel correspond to LW and PW evaluation.

4.3 Ablation Studies: The Efficacy of Textual Serialization

To isolate the effect of structured prompting, we compare TSP-LLM against a prompt-free baseline that processes the identical 24 continuous values as a raw numerical string, devoid of semantic anchors.

Tables 4 and 5 report the 1-step prompt ablation results, separately from the 3-step and 5-step results in Tables 1 and 2. Removing the template increases SMAPE on Irr from 4.3031% to 89.9620% (LW) and from 4.6411% to 90.6642% (PW); on Irrto, it increases from 0.2364% to 86.4115% (LW) and from 0.1574% to 87.0620% (PW). However, MAE and RMSE do not improve uniformly. Because near-zero irradiance values make SMAPE sensitive to small absolute deviations,

Table 4. 1-step prompt ablation: comparison of TSP-LLM and the prompt-free baseline (land-weighted).

Variable	Prompt-based TSP-LLM				Prompt-free			
	MAE	RMSE	SMAPE	R^2	MAE	RMSE	SMAPE	R^2
Air_dy	0.0004	0.0006	0.0314	0.9982	0.0004	0.0007	0.0358	0.9979
Clc	0.0096	0.0137	1.8429	0.9954	0.0107	0.0154	2.0660	0.9943
Hum	0.0001	0.0004	0.8936	0.9823	0.0002	0.0004	1.0937	0.9780
Irr	5.5481	8.1813	4.3031	0.9995	3.9026	7.3536	89.9620	0.9992
Irrto	0.0600	0.7105	0.2364	1.0000	0.5028	3.3103	86.4115	1.0000
Pre	0.0183	0.0433	13.2559	0.9642	0.0165	0.0429	20.5639	0.9636
Tem	0.0557	0.1192	0.2175	0.9991	0.0838	0.1503	0.3276	0.9985
Wsp	0.0282	0.0449	1.9950	0.9943	0.0404	0.0706	2.9311	0.9860

Note. SMAPE values are percentages. Gold, silver, and copper indicate first, second, and third place.

it should be interpreted together with MAE, RMSE, and R^2. Thus, structured prompting reduces relative error on irradiance-related series, but does not dominate every metric under every condition.

Table 5. 1-step prompt ablation: comparison of TSP-LLM and the prompt-free baseline (population-weighted).

Variable	Prompt-based TSP-LLM				Prompt-free			
	MAE	RMSE	SMAPE	R^2	MAE	RMSE	SMAPE	R^2
Air_dy	0.0004	0.0007	0.0336	0.9978	0.0004	0.0008	0.0381	0.9971
Clc	0.0134	0.0203	2.4981	0.9898	0.0143	0.0218	2.6997	0.9882
Hum	0.0001	0.0004	0.9073	0.9785	0.0002	0.0004	1.1062	0.9736
Irr	6.6953	10.1087	4.6411	0.9992	4.6294	9.1816	90.6642	0.9988
Irrto	0.0549	0.1253	0.1574	1.0000	0.5118	4.8408	87.0620	0.9999
Pre	0.0202	0.0525	13.7542	0.9534	0.0186	0.0512	21.2454	0.9549
Tem	0.0604	0.1219	0.2264	0.9989	0.0919	0.1523	0.3444	0.9982
Wsp	0.0413	0.0641	2.3095	0.9921	0.0602	0.1002	3.4571	0.9807

Note. SMAPE values are percentages. Gold, silver, and copper indicate first, second, and third place.

5 Discussion and Limitations

The present study focuses on a single 43-year Thailand meteorological benchmark. This design allows the proposed serialization interface to be evaluated under long historical coverage, multiple weather factors, and two spatial weighting schemes, but it does not by itself establish cross-domain generalization to traffic, electricity, finance, or other non-meteorological series. Accordingly, the term "unified" in this paper refers to unified multi-factor forecasting within the studied meteorological deployment setting, rather than a universal time-series foundation model.

The computational advantage of TSP-LLM is primarily a deployment-consolidation argument: one shared T5-base predictor (approximately 220 million parameters [15]) is used for multiple variables, aggregation schemes, and horizons, whereas dedicated baselines typically require separate task-specific model instances or repeated tuning. This reduces model-management redundancy. It does not imply that text serialization is always faster than lightweight numerical models at per-sample inference time. Tokenization and text decoding can introduce latency, especially in high-frequency deployments. Controlled wall-clock training and inference latency, hardware-specific memory and throughput, and a direct comparison against 16 separately fine-tuned T5 models were not conducted in this study and are therefore left as necessary future work.

T5-base was retained as a fixed backbone to isolate the effect of the serialization interface; the experiments do not establish that it is the strongest available language-model backbone. Similarly, the ablation pattern is consistent with reduced relative-error instability on irradiance-related variables, but it should not be interpreted as a direct stochastic decoding-variance measurement across repeated sampling runs. Future work will add explicit repeated-decoding experiments and direct comparisons with recent time-series foundation models.

6 Conclusion

We proposed TSP-LLM, a unified textual serialization framework based on temporally structured prompting, which transforms a single pre-trained language model into a shared forecaster for heterogeneous meteorological forecasting tasks. Experiments on a 43-year country-level benchmark demonstrate that TSP-LLM achieves competitive performance against 11 dedicated numerical baselines on temperature and irradiance series exhibiting smooth and periodic dynamics, while still underperforming on highly volatile variables such as precipitation. Ablation experiments further show that removing structured prompting causes SMAPE on irradiance-related variables to increase from single digits to over 80%, although MAE and RMSE do not improve uniformly across all variables. Future work will explore direct decoding-variance measurements, stronger time-series foundation baselines, and domain-specific physical constraints to improve robustness on non-stationary dynamics.

Acknowledgments. This research was supported by the School of Computer, Electronics and Information, Guangxi University under Grant No. 2606020162.

Disclosure of Interests. The authors have no competing interests to declare

A Supplementary Material

A.1 Evaluation Metrics

Four evaluation metrics are used in our experiments. Let n denote the number of evaluated test points, y_i the observed value, $\hat{y}_i$ the predicted value, and $\bar{y}$ the mean of the observed values. Their formal definitions are as follows:

$$\mathrm{MAE} = \frac{1}{n}\sum_{i=1}^{n}|y_i - \hat{y}_i|, \tag{3}$$

$$\mathrm{RMSE} = \sqrt{\frac{1}{n}\sum_{i=1}^{n}(y_i - \hat{y}_i)^2}, \tag{4}$$

$$\mathrm{SMAPE} = \frac{1}{n}\sum_{i=1}^{n}\frac{y_i - \hat{y}_i}{(y_i + \hat{y}_i)/2} \times 100\%, \tag{5}$$

$$R^2 = 1 - \frac{\sum_{i=1}^{n}(y_i - \hat{y}_i)^2}{\sum_{i=1}^{n}(y_i - \bar{y})^2}. \tag{6}$$

A.2 Dataset Profiling

Fig. 5 presents two complementary views of the preprocessed data. Subfigure (a) shows the marginal distributions of the eight meteorological factors under LW and PW aggregations. Subfigure (b) validates the data volume consistency of the 16 weighted spatiotemporal series via a heatmap of file sizes.

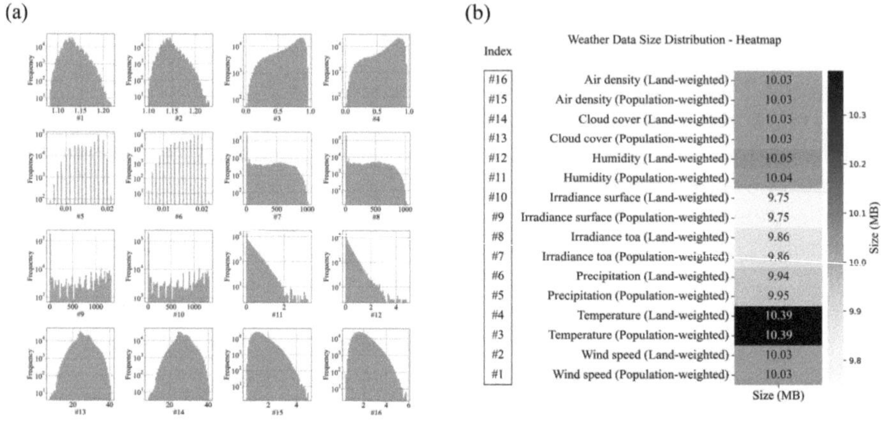

Fig. 5. Dataset profiling: (a) marginal distributions of eight meteorological factors under LW and PW aggregations; (b) heatmap of data file sizes for the 16 weighted spatiotemporal series.

A.3 Extended Ablation Results: 5-Step Forecasting

Tables 6 and 7 report the 5-step ablation results, comparing the structured prompt-based TSP-LLM against the prompt-free baseline. These results complement the ablation presented in the main text, confirming that semantic anchoring remains critically effective for longer forecasting horizons.

A.4 Supplementary Release Note

Due to space constraints, the exhaustive raw results matrices covering 12 models, 8 variables, 4 metrics, 2 aggregation schemes, and multiple forecasting horizons are provided as supplementary material rather than printed in full. The supplementary workbook includes the complete numerical baseline comparisons underlying the radar and scatter visualizations.

Table 6. 5-step ablation results under land-weighted aggregation.

Variable	Prompt-based (LW)				Prompt-free (LW)			
	MAE	RMSE	SMAPE	R^2	MAE	RMSE	SMAPE	R^2
Air_dy	0.0008	0.0012	0.0704	0.9934	0.0009	0.0014	0.0768	0.9921
Clc	0.0354	0.0568	6.7388	0.9217	0.0380	0.0612	7.2320	0.9092
Hum	0.0002	0.0005	1.5610	0.9696	0.0003	0.0005	1.7699	0.9647
Irr	14.7083	25.1552	6.3359	0.9950	8.9270	20.3401	90.9676	0.9943
Irrto	0.0389	0.2269	0.0799	1.0000	0.0310	0.1802	86.1238	1.0000
Pre	0.0503	0.0976	34.7350	0.8195	0.0434	0.0896	39.7332	0.8411
Tem	0.1680	0.2946	0.6445	0.9943	0.1782	0.3144	0.6863	0.9935
Wsp	0.0819	0.1248	5.6862	0.9561	0.0858	0.1306	5.9793	0.9520

Note. SMAPE values are percentages. Gold, silver, and copper indicate first, second, and third place.

Table 7. 5-step ablation results under population-weighted aggregation.

Variable	Prompt-based (PW)				Prompt-free (PW)			
	MAE	RMSE	SMAPE	R^2	MAE	RMSE	SMAPE	R^2
Air_dy	0.0009	0.0014	0.0776	0.9899	0.0009	0.0015	0.0829	0.9883
Clc	0.0445	0.0728	8.2680	0.8685	0.0465	0.0762	8.6896	0.8560
Hum	0.0003	0.0005	1.6619	0.9607	0.0003	0.0006	1.8511	0.9551
Irr	17.8516	30.4555	7.3716	0.9926	10.7659	24.5864	91.9794	0.9914
Irrto	0.0455	1.5318	0.0639	1.0000	0.0429	2.8562	86.8047	1.0000
Pre	0.0552	0.1148	36.4229	0.7826	0.0496	0.1093	41.8352	0.7942
Tem	0.1845	0.3097	0.6808	0.9927	0.1968	0.3256	0.7276	0.9919
Wsp	0.1238	0.1835	6.8816	0.9354	0.1310	0.1932	7.3562	0.9284

Note. SMAPE values are percentages. Gold, silver, and copper indicate first, second, and third place.

References

1. Ansari, A.F., Stella, L., Turkmen, C., Zhang, X., Mercado, P., Shen, H., et al.: Chronos: learning the language of time series. arXiv preprint arXiv:2403.07815 (2024)
2. Bi, K., Xie, L., Zhang, H., Chen, X., Gu, X., Tian, Q.: Accurate medium-range global weather forecasting with 3D neural networks. Nature **619**, 533–538 (2023). https://doi.org/10.1038/s41586-023-06185-3
3. Bodnar, C., Bruinsma, W.P., Lucic, A., Stanley, M., Allen, A., Brandstetter, J., et al.: A foundation model for the earth system. Nature **641**, 1180–1187 (2025). https://doi.org/10.1038/s41586-025-09005-y

4. Chen, S.A., Li, C.L., Yoon, J., Chan, J., Fu, D.Y., Song, Y.: TSMixer: An All-MLP Architecture for Time Series Forecasting, pp. 459–471. KDD (2023). https://doi.org/10.1145/3580305.3599793
5. Das, A., Kong, W., Sen, R., Zhou, Y.: A decoder-only foundation model for time-series forecasting. In: International Conference on Machine Learning, pp. 10148–10167 (2024)
6. Gelaro, R., McCarty, W., Suarez, M.J., Todling, R., Molod, A., Takacs, L., et al.: The modern-era retrospective analysis for research and applications, version 2 (MERRA-2). J. Clim. **30**(14), 5419–5454 (2017). https://doi.org/10.1175/JCLI-D-16-0758.1
7. Gruver, N., Finzi, M., Qiu, S., Wilson, A.G.: Large language models are zero-shot time series forecasters. NeurIPS 36 (2023)
8. Jin, M., Wang, S., Ma, L., Chu, Z., Zhang, J.Y., Shi, X.: Time-LLM: time series forecasting by reprogramming large language models, p. ICLR (2024)
9. Kitaev, N., Kaiser, L., Levskaya, A.: Reformer: The efficient transformer, p. ICLR (2020)
10. Lam, R., Sanchez-Gonzalez, A., Willson, M., Wirnsberger, P., Fortunato, M., Alet, F., et al.: Learning skillful medium-range global weather forecasting. Science **382**(6677), 1416–1421 (2023). https://doi.org/10.1126/science.adi2336
11. Liu, S., Yu, H., Liao, C., Li, J., Lin, W., Liu, A.X., Wang, S.: Pyraformer: low-complexity pyramidal attention for long-range time series modeling and forecasting. In: ICLR (2022)
12. Liu, X., Zhao, Y., Jin, Y., Zhang, Z., Wang, Y., Wang, Y., Wang, Z.: Koopa: learning non-stationary time series dynamics with Koopman predictors. In: ICLR (2024)
13. Liu, Y., Lin, M., Cao, Y., Wang, Z., Liu, S., Zhang, Y., Chen, T., et al.: iTransformer: inverted transformers are effective for time series forecasting. In: ICLR (2024)
14. Pfenninger, S., Staffell, I.: Long-term patterns of European PV output using 30 years of validated hourly reanalysis and satellite data. Energy **114**, 1251–1265 (2016). https://doi.org/10.1016/j.energy.2016.08.060
15. Raffel, C., Shazeer, N., Roberts, A., Lee, K., Narang, S., Matena, M., et al.: Exploring the limits of transfer learning with a unified text-to-text transformer. J. Mach. Learn. Res. **21**(140), 1–67 (2020)
16. Rasul, K., Ashok, A., Williams, A.R., Ghonia, H., Bhagwatkar, R., Khorasani, A.: Lag-Llama: towards foundation models for probabilistic time series forecasting (2023). arXiv:2310.08278 arXiv preprint
17. Staffell, I., Pfenninger, S.: Using bias-corrected reanalysis to simulate current and future wind power output. Energy **114**, 1224–1239 (2016). https://doi.org/10.1016/j.energy.2016.08.068
18. Tan, M., Merrill, M.A., Gupta, V., Althoff, T., Hartvigsen, T. Are language models actually useful for time series forecasting? In: NeurIPS, vol. 37 (2024)
19. Vaswani, A., Shazeer, N., Parmar, N., Uszkoreit, J., Jones, L., Gomez, A.N., Kaiser, L., Polosukhin, I.: Attention is all you need. In: NeurIPS, vol. 30 (2017)
20. Wu, H., Xu, J., Wang, J., Long, M.: Autoformer: decomposition transformers with auto-correlation for long-term series forecasting. In: NeurIPS, vol. 34 (2021)
21. Wu, T., Ling, Q.: STELLM: spatio-temporal enhanced pre-trained large language model for wind speed forecasting. Appl. Energy **375**, 124034 (2024). https://doi.org/10.1016/j.apenergy.2024.124034

22. Woo, G., Liu, C., Kumar, A., Xiong, C., Savarese, S., Sahoo, D.: Unified training of universal time series forecasting transformers. In: International Conference on Machine Learning, pp. 53140–53164 (2024)
23. Xue, H., Salim, F.D.: PromptCast: a new prompt-based learning paradigm for time series forecasting. IEEE Trans. Knowl. Data Eng. **36**(11), 6851–6864 (2024). https://doi.org/10.1109/TKDE.2023.3342137
24. Zeng, A., Chen, M., Zhang, L., Xu, Q.: Are transformers effective for time series forecasting? AAAI **37**(9), 11121–11128 (2023). https://doi.org/10.1609/aaai.v37i9.26317
25. Zhang, T., Zhang, Y., Cao, W., Bian, J., Yi, X., Zheng, S., Li, J. Less is more: fast multivariate time series forecasting with light sampling-oriented MLP structures. In: ICDM, pp. 131–140 (2022). https://doi.org/10.1109/ICDM54844.2022.00020
26. Zhang, X., Chowdhury, R.R., Gupta, R.K., Shang, J.: Large language models for time series: a survey. In: IJCAI, pp. 8335–8343 (2024). https://doi.org/10.24963/ijcai.2024/921
27. Zhou, H., Zhang, S., Peng, J., Zhang, S., Li, J., Xiong, H., Zhang, W.: Informer: beyond efficient transformer for long sequence time-series forecasting. AAAI **35**, 11106–11115 (2021). https://doi.org/10.1609/aaai.v35i12.17325
28. Zhou, T., Ma, Z., Wang, X., Wen, Q., Sun, L., Yao, T., Yin, W., Jin, R.: FiLM: frequency improved Legendre memory model for long-term time series forecasting. In: NeurIPS, vol. 35, pp. 12677–12690 (2022)
29. Zhou, T., Ma, Z., Wen, Q., Wang, X., Sun, L., Jin, R.: FEDformer: frequency enhanced decomposed transformer for long-term series forecasting. In: ICML, pp. 27268–27286 (2022)

AORS: Atomic Operator Driven Structured Reasoning Framework with Dual-Level Retrieval

Jingyu Zhang[1], Wenheng Li[1], Zhijie Zhu[1], Liqiang Xie[1], and Qianzhen Zhang[2](✉)

[1] School of Computer Science and Technology, Changsha University of Science and Technology, 410076 Changsha, China
{zhangzhang,24208051819,zhuzhijie920q,xlq}@csust.edu.cn
[2] National Key Laboratory of Information Systems Engineering, National University of Defense Technology, 410073 Changsha, China
zhangqianzhen18@nudt.edu.cn

Abstract. Recent advances in large language models (LLMs) have substantially improved their performance on complex question answering (QA), particularly in handling long contexts and sophisticated reasoning patterns. However, in open-domain multi-hop QA scenarios, small-scale models still face two fundamental challenges: (1) instability in reasoning planning across diverse entities, and (2) imbalance between semantic coverage and relational precision during retrieval. To bridge this gap, we propose the Atomic Operator Reasoning System (AORS). AORS introduces an atomic operator based reasoning navigation module that explicitly maps complex natural language questions into executable reasoning plans, thereby constraining reasoning steps and improving planning stability. Furthermore, the system integrates a unified execution framework synthesizing semantic retrieval, knowledge graph augmentation, and multi-round verification. This design aligns evidence retrieval with structured reasoning, maintaining high semantic coverage while enforcing relational constraints. Extensive experiments on open-domain multi-hop QA benchmarks compare AORS against existing mainstream reasoning and retrieval-augmented baselines. The results demonstrate that AORS achieves significantly superior stability and precision on small-scale models, proving that AORS can effectively reduce dependence on massive model parameters.

Keywords: Complex Question Answering · Retrieval Augmented Generation · Information Retrieval · Structured Reasoning

1 Introduction

In recent years, question answering (QA) has seen significant advances driven by large language models (LLMs) for natural language understanding and generation [3,13,14]. Despite this progress, stable and reliable reasoning remains

L. Ding et al. (Eds.): APWeb-WAIM 2026, LNCS 16993, pp. 360–375, 2027.
https://doi.org/10.1007/978-981-92-5693-8_23

challenging for small-scale models, particularly in open-domain and multi-hop QA. When queries require compositional reasoning across entities, relations, and intermediate facts, small models often fail to construct complete reasoning paths [10], leading to logical gaps, incorrect decomposition, and inconsistent intermediate results [22]. This issue stems not only from limited knowledge storage but also from constrained model parameters, which restricts structured reasoning and multi-step dependency modeling. As a result, maintaining coherent reasoning chains remains difficult.

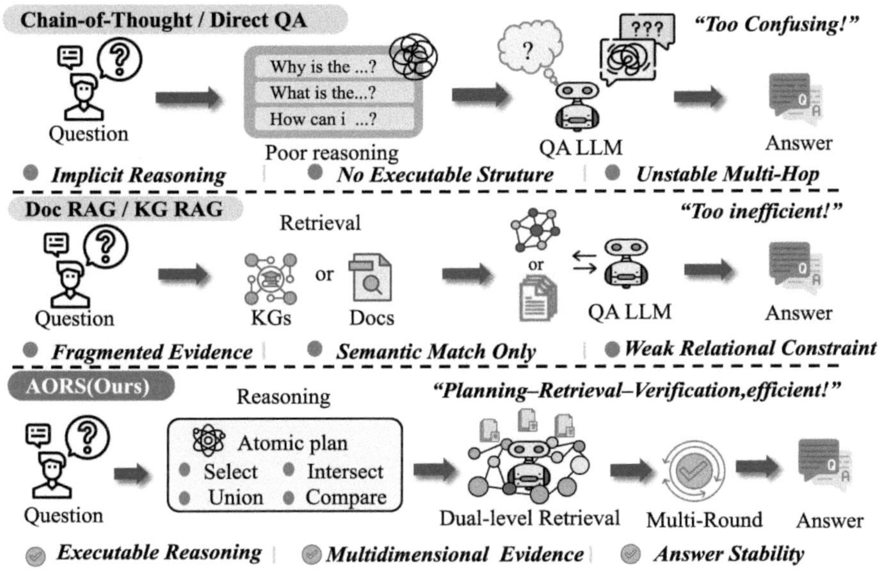

Fig. 1. Comparisons of reasoning paradigms for multi-hop QA.

To address these limitations, prior work has widely adopted Retrieval Augmented Generation (RAG) [9] to incorporate external knowledge. However, existing retrieval paradigms face challenges in multi-hop reasoning. Semantic retrieval provides broad coverage but lacks explicit structure, hindering precise relational reasoning and often producing fragmented evidence [7]. In contrast, knowledge graph-based retrieval offers structured relations but suffers from sparse coverage, entity linking errors, and high construction costs, limiting scalability. Moreover, current methods combining retrieval with reasoning prompts rely on unstructured natural language [21,27], lacking unified and executable semantics. This makes it difficult to align retrieved evidence with reasoning steps, reducing inference stability.

These challenges indicate that complex QA requires not only effective retrieval but also a unified framework that explicitly represents reasoning structures and aligns them with retrieval. To this end, as shown in Fig. 1, we propose the Atomic Operator Reasoning System (AORS), an end-to-end framework for complex QA. AORS uses atomic operators as intermediate representations to decompose queries into structured, executable reasoning plans. It integrates dual-level retrieval with multi-round verification to jointly support reasoning planning, evidence acquisition, and answer generation. The atomic operator module enforces structured reasoning constraints, while the dual-level design (combining semantic retrieval and graph enhancement) balances coverage and relational precision. Multi-round verification further improves robustness and stability. Overall, AORS provides a controllable, interpretable, and reliable solution for small-scale models in complex QA. Our contributions are as follows:

(1) We propose AORS, a unified framework for complex question answering that maps natural language questions into executable atomic reasoning plans and couples structured reasoning with evidence acquisition, thereby improving reasoning stability for small-scale language models.
(2) Within AORS, we design a dual-level retrieval and execution mechanism that integrates semantic retrieval, knowledge graph enhancement, and multi-round verification, enabling the framework to balance broad evidence coverage with precise relational constraints.
(3) Extensive experiments on open-domain multi-hop QA benchmarks demonstrate that AORS consistently improves the reasoning performance of small-scale models, showing that reliable complex reasoning can be achieved without relying solely on large model scale.

2 Related Work

2.1 Natural Language Reasoning

Existing work improves complex QA by explicitly modeling reasoning. Representative methods include Chain-of-Thought (CoT) [21] and Tree-of-Thought (ToT) [27], which guide step-by-step or multi-path reasoning. In open-domain QA, ReAct [28] and Self-Ask [15] combine reasoning with retrieval, iteratively acquiring evidence via sub-questions. Methods such as IRCoT [19] and HippoRAG [4] further explore reasoningretrieval interaction through multi-round retrieval and evidence aggregation.

However, these approaches rely on free-form natural language reasoning without unified, executable semantics. Consequently, aligning reasoning steps with retrieved evidence depends on implicit modeling, which is unstable for small-scale models. In contrast, AORS uses atomic operators with explicit set semantics to construct structured, executable reasoning plans, providing a unified basis for retrieval and evidence integration.

2.2 Knowledge-Augmented Retrieval

Retrieval Augmented Generation (RAG) addresses knowledge insufficiency in QA by incorporating external information. Semantic similaritybased retrieval achieves high recall [25] but often lacks explicit entity and relation structures, limiting its support for precise multi-hop reasoning. In contrast, knowledge graphbased methods model entities and relations explicitly, providing structured support, but suffer from limited coverage, entity linking errors, and high construction costs in open-domain settings.

Recent work integrates text retrieval with graph modeling. For example, GraphRAG builds relation graphs over retrieved evidence to enhance structural connections [8,23]. However, these methods focus on context-level enrichment and lack a unified, executable representation aligned with reasoning steps. In contrast, AORS employs structured atomic reasoning plans to unify retrieval and graph enhancement, ensuring alignment between evidence and reasoning while maintaining coverage and controllable relational constraints.

2.3 Reasoning of Small Language Models

Improving reasoning stability in small language models under constrained settings is an important research direction. Existing approaches rely on knowledge distillation [5], prompt tuning, or supervised training on natural language reasoning chains to transfer capabilities from large models. However, these methods treat free-form reasoning as the target, lacking explicit constraints on structure and step dependencies. As a result, small models often exhibit logical inconsistencies in multi-hop and set-based reasoning.

In contrast, AORS uses supervised fine-tuning to map natural language questions to structured atomic reasoning plans. This enables explicit modeling of dependencies and set semantics, improving reasoning stability and controllability. The plan-centered paradigm allows small models to generate executable reasoning plans and provides a unified structured interface for retrieval and verification.

3 Methodology

This section presents the AORS framework for complex QA. AORS begins with reasoning navigation, decomposing a question into an executable sequence of atomic operators. The system then performs semantic retrieval to obtain relevant evidence, followed by knowledge graph enhancement to introduce structured relations for multi-hop reasoning. Finally, multi-round answer verification ensures the stability and consistency of intermediate results. These steps form a unified planningretrievalverification process, as illustrated in Fig. 2.

3.1 Reasoning Navigation

To improve structured reasoning and retrieval in complex QA, inspired by knowledge graph logic, we propose a reasoning navigation module based on atomic operators and SQL-style execution templates. It represents the reasoning process

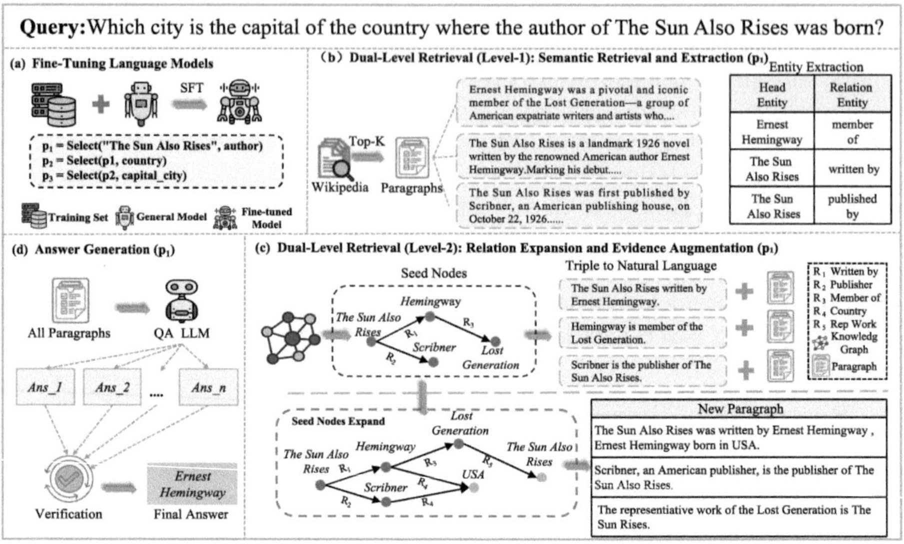

Fig. 2. Overview of our atomic operator reasoning system (AORS) framework.

as an ordered sequence of atomic operators with explicit dependencies, enabling small language models to generate structured steps with clear set semantics:

$$P = \{p_1, \ldots, p_t\}, \quad p_t \in \{Select, Intersect, Union, Compare\}, \tag{1}$$

Each step p_t corresponds to one of four operations: (1) one-hop projection on an entity or intermediate result (Select), (2) set operations over intermediate results (Intersect/Union), or (3) comparison across results on a shared attribute (Compare).

Training Data Construction. In an open-domain knowledge graph, facts are represented as triples (h,r,t) with set query properties similar to databases. Based on this, we map the relational structure to an executable logical sub-language with strict set semantics, defining four atomic operators: Select (e,r), Intersect (p_1,p_2), Union (p_1,p_2), and Compare (p_1,p_2,a,op). Unlike complex query languages such as SPARQL, this system targets structured reasoning in small-scale models by constraining reasoning through a representation consistent with SQL logic. It provides clear execution semantics and improves interpretability, controllability, and stability in multi-hop QA and combinatorial reasoning.

Instantiation. Given a knowledge graph KG, the system extracts relation patterns under the structural constraints of four atomic operators–Select, Intersect, Union, and Compare–and maps them into step-by-step atomic reasoning plans with set semantics. This process yields consistent and executable operator instances, serving as structured intermediate representations for reasoning plan learning and execution. We use Wikidata15k [2], a subset of Wikidata, as the knowledge graph source.

Table 1. Prompt for generating questions from atomic reasoning plans.

Prompt: Atomic Reasoning Plan to Natural Language Question
Context:
You are given a step-by-step **atomic reasoning plan** with explicit set semantics.
Operators:
(1) `Select(e, r)`: one-hop relation projection.
(2) `Intersect`(p_1, p_2) / `Union`(p_1, p_2): intersection / union of result sets.
(3) `Compare`(p_1, p_2, a, op): decision-making based on operator op and attribute a.
Task:
Convert the plan into a single natural language question reflecting its overall intent.
Requirements:
(1) Preserve all semantic constraints and dependencies.
(2) Express as a coherent question (not procedural steps).
(3) Do not introduce extra information or entities not in the plan.
Input: Atomic reasoning plan → **Output:** Semantically equivalent question.

Verbalization. Atomic operator sequences represent reasoning plans with explicit semantics. To build supervised fine-tuning data, we introduce a verbalization process that converts structured sequences into semantically equivalent natural language questions. Using prompt templates, as shown in Table 1, GPT-4o generates questions from reasoning plans, establishing a mapping between natural language and structured reasoning.

Via instantiation and verbalization, we construct a dataset of 7,000 samples:

$$D = \{(q_i, P_i)\}_{i=1}^{7000}, \tag{2}$$

where q_i is a natural language question and P_i is the corresponding atomic reasoning plan. Each atomic pattern contains 1,500 samples, while three compositional patterns total 1,000 samples. The dataset covers multi-step dependencies, deep Select operations, and multi-condition Intersect and Union. We randomly sample 200 instances for manual verification, achieving over 95% accuracy.

Model Fine-Tuning. Based on the training set D, we perform supervised fine-tuning on a small-scale language model to map a question q_i to its atomic operator plan P_i. Let the reasoning model be M_p, which learns the mapping $M_p(q_i) \to p_i$ under a standard autoregressive objective:

$$\max_{M_p} \mathbb{E}_{(q_i, p_i) \in \mathcal{D}} \sum_{t=1}^{|p_i|} \log p_{M_p}\left(p_i^{(t)} \mid q_i, p_i^{(<t)}\right), \tag{3}$$

The model learns basic atomic patterns and their compositions. We adopt LoRA/QLoRA for parameter-efficient training and mix sample types to ensure stable and consistent plan generation. At inference, given q_i, the model outputs

Table 2. Examples of atomic reasoning plans.

Query 1: What is the capital of the country where the author of The Sun Also Rises was born?	**Query 2:** What is the capital of the country where Ernest Hemingway was born and lived?
$\mathbf{p_1}$: Select("The Sun Also Rises", author) $\mathbf{p_2}$: Select(P1, country) $\mathbf{p_3}$: Select(P2, capital_city)	$\mathbf{p_1}$: select ("Ernest Hemingway", birthplace) $\mathbf{p_2}$: select ("Ernest Hemingway", country) $\mathbf{p_3}$: Intersect (P1, P2)
Query 3: What are the major works of Ernest Hemingway and William Faulkner?	**Query 4:** What is the larger country between the USA and Spain in terms of population?
$\mathbf{p_1}$: select ("Ernest Hemingway", works) $\mathbf{p_2}$: select ("William Faulkner", works) $\mathbf{p_3}$: Union (P1, P2)	$\mathbf{p_1}$: select ("USA", population) $\mathbf{p_2}$: select ("Spain", population) $\mathbf{p_3}$: Compare (P1, P2, population, greater)

the plan,as shown in Table 2:

$$P = \arg\max_{p_1,\ldots,p_T} \sum_{t=1}^{T} \log P_{\mathcal{M}_p}(p_t \mid q_{test}, \boldsymbol{p}_{<t}), \quad (4)$$

The plan is executed step by step by a downstream executor that caches intermediate results and applies set operations. For multi-hop queries, the model can generate placeholders (e.g., ANS_k) as intermediate variables filled during retrieval and QA, decoupling plan generation from execution.

The reasoning navigation module produces structured atomic plans, but final answers still depend on retrieval and execution. Accordingly, the QA stage follows the plan to perform evidence acquisition, relation expansion, and answer verification via three modules: semantic retrieval, knowledge graph enhancement, and multi-round answer verification. They form a closed-loop "planningretrievalverification" framework for executable and reliable reasoning in complex QA.

3.2 Semantic Retrieval

As the first layer of dual-level retrieval, the semantic retrieval module ensures broad evidence coverage. Unlike traditional RAG, which retrieves from the original question, it follows the structured atomic plan P and performs stepwise retrieval. To handle coreference and step dependencies, we introduce a dynamic instantiation mechanism that uses prior context and intermediate results to instantiate variables in $Select(e, r)$, producing clear sub-queries for vector-based retrieval. This aligns each step with the reasoning state and improves evidence precision for graph enhancement and verification.

We use Contriever-MSMARCO to encode sub-questions into dense vectors and build an approximate nearest neighbor index over a 21M Wikipedia corpus. For each sub-question, the top 3 paragraphs are selected as evidence, balancing recall and noise. This realizes an "atomic plantostepwise retrieval" process, supporting knowledge graph enhancement and enabling a transition from semantic matching to structured multi-hop reasoning [16].

3.3 Knowledge Graph Enhancement

Building on the first-layer retrieval, the knowledge graph enhancement module incorporates explicit entity relations and multi-hop connections to refine retrieved evidence, providing more structured and relationally precise support for reasoning.

Knowledge Graph Pre-Construction. We perform offline preprocessing to construct a knowledge graph for structured reasoning in AORS. Documents are segmented into sentences and paragraphs, then divided into fixed-length chunks to preserve semantic coherence. Entity recognition and relation extraction are applied using BERT-NER and REBEL to generate triples (h, r, t), each linked to its source chunk c_i, forming traceable quadruples. These are merged into a unified entity space to build a knowledge graph G that captures multi-hop relations and aligns with semantic retrieval:

$$G = \bigcup_{i=1}^{N} \{(h, r, t, c_i) \mid (h, r, t) = \text{Extract}(c_i)\}. \tag{5}$$

This graph forms a structured entityrelation network that reduces content fragmentation by linking related text segments. It also supports a transition from text-based retrieval to structured knowledge usage, enabling AORS to resolve entity relations and multi-hop dependencies during atomic operator execution.

Injecting Structured Relations. After constructing the knowledge graph, we inject fact-level relations into first-layer retrieval results to integrate textual and structured knowledge. For each retrieved paragraph d_j (top-3 from Contriever-MSMARCO), we extract core entities $\mathbb{E}_{d_j}$ (e.g., h and r) as anchors to match triples in G. The matched triples are converted into natural language via $\phi(\cdot)$ and appended to the paragraph:

$$d_j^{aug} = d_j \mid\mid \{\phi(h, r, t) \mid (h, r, t) \in G,\ h \in E_{d_j},\ r \in E_{d_j}\} \tag{6}$$

This augmentation improves context precision and traceability while providing relational constraints for atomic reasoning plans. For example, operations such as $Select(e, r)$ and $\text{Intersect}(p_1, p_2)$ can be consistently resolved in a unified entity space. It mitigates the imprecision of pure vector retrieval while preserving coverage, and supports subsequent relation network expansion.

Relation Expansion for Generating New Paragraphs. After relation injection, this step expands the knowledge graph to discover additional associations and generate supplementary paragraphs, improving context coverage.

As shown in Fig. 3, we use core entities from the previous subsection and their associated triples as seed nodes S, and traverse multi-hop paths in G to

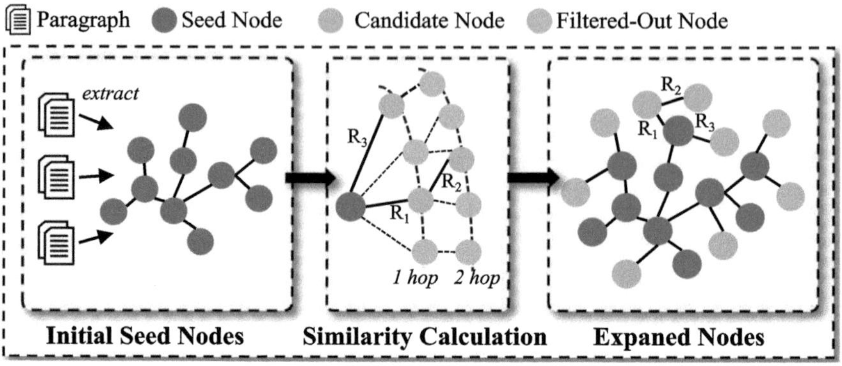

Fig. 3. Expansion of seed nodes based on knowledge graphs.

obtain the neighborhood $\mathcal{N}_k(S)$. This expands a relevant subgraph, capturing indirect relations and facts not covered by first-level retrieval.

The triples in the expanded subgraph are converted into natural language and organized into a new paragraph p_{new}. The process is defined as follows:

(1) Construction of the k-hop Neighborhood Entity Set:

$$\mathcal{N}_k(S) = \{e_j \in E \mid \exists R(e_i, e_j) \in R, e_i \in S, \text{hops}(R) \leq k\} \tag{7}$$

Here, $R(e_i, e_j)$ denotes a relational path from seed entity e_i to e_j, and hops(R) its length. For each $e_j \in \mathcal{N}_k(S)$, we compute a relevance score $\Omega(e_j)$ combining path confidence and semantic similarity with q_{sub}:

$$\Omega(e_j|S, q_{sub}) = \max_{\pi \in \{S \rightsquigarrow e_j\}} \left(\prod_{(u,r,v) \in \pi} \sigma(\mathbf{h}_u^\top \mathbf{W}_r \mathbf{h}_v) \right) \cdot \exp\left(\frac{\text{sim}(\mathbf{E}(e_j), \mathbf{E}(q_{sub}))}{\tau} \right) \tag{8}$$

where $\mathbf{E}(\cdot)$ denotes embeddings, $\mathbf{h}_u$ node representations, $\mathbf{W}_r$ relation projections, and $\sigma(\cdot)$ the sigmoid. The first term models structural confidence, and the second semantic relevance.

(2) Triples from $\mathcal{N}_k(S)$ are converted into natural language to form new paragraphs:

$$P_{\text{new}} = \{\phi(h, r, t) \mid \langle h, r, t \rangle \in \mathcal{N}_k(S)\} \tag{9}$$

(3) Retrieved paragraphs, injected relations, and P_{new} are integrated into the final context:

$$C_{\text{final}} = \bigcup_{j=1}^{k} \left[d_{\text{j}}^{\text{avg}} \cup P_{\text{new}} \right] \tag{10}$$

This integration improves coherence and expands initial retrieval into a richer, connected context, enabling a shift from semantic retrieval to structured multi-hop reasoning.

3.4 Multi-round Answer Verification

In AORS, complex questions are decomposed into atomic sub-questions whose outputs serve as intermediate states for subsequent reasoning. Thus, the stability of sub-question answers directly impacts the reliability of the overall reasoning chain. Although semantic retrieval and knowledge graph enhancement improve evidence quality, QA models may still produce inconsistent answers due to sampling randomness and contextual noise.

To address this, AORS introduces a multi-round answer verification mechanism [24]. For each sub-question, multiple independent samples are generated under a fixed context to form candidate answers. Invalid responses (e.g., empty, incomplete, or constraint-violating) are filtered out, and the final answer is selected based on frequency or semantic consistency.

Formally, let $\mathcal{A} = \{a_1, ..., a_M\}$ be candidate answers from M sampling rounds. The final answer a^* is selected by maximizing a joint consistency objective:

$$
\begin{aligned}
a^* = \arg\max_{a_i \in \mathcal{A}} \Bigg[& \frac{\lambda}{M} \sum_{j=1}^{M} \mathbb{I}(a_i = a_j) \\
& + \frac{1-\lambda}{M-1} \sum_{j \neq i} \mathcal{K}_{\text{sem}}(a_i, a_j) \cdot \Theta(\text{conf}_j) \Bigg]
\end{aligned} \tag{11}
$$

Here, $\mathbb{I}(\cdot)$ denotes exact match, $\mathcal{K}_{\text{sem}}$ semantic similarity (e.g., BERTScore), and $\Theta(\text{conf}_j)$ a confidence gate from retrieval probability. If no consensus is reached, a conservative strategy prevents error propagation. This process reduces noise in multi-hop reasoning and improves overall stability and consistency without altering the atomic reasoning structure.

4 Experiments

We address the following research questions: **RQ1**: How does AORS perform against baseline models on multi-hop QA, especially for small-scale language models? **RQ2**: Does each component of AORS contribute positively to the framework? **RQ3**: What is the error distribution across reasoning stages, and which stage remains the primary performance bottleneck?

4.1 Experimental Setup

Fine-Tuning. We perform supervised fine-tuning on small language models to generate structured atomic reasoning plans from natural language questions. Two models with different architectures, CodeQwen1.5-7B-Chat and Llama3-8B-Instruct, are selected as the reasoning module backbone.The training data consists of 7,000 structured samples from Sect. 3. Each sample pairs a question q_i with its atomic reasoning plan P_i, covering logic types: Select, Intersect, Union, and Compare.

We employ the LoRA [6] strategy for two epochs on 4× NVIDIA L20 GPUs, using a 5e-5 learning rate, the AdamW [12] optimizer, and a Cosine Decay [11] scheduler. Atomic operator formats and placeholder structures are strictly preserved to ensure compatibility with the reasoning execution stage.

Datasets. To evaluate the reasoning, retrieval, and QA effectiveness, we conduct experiments on three multi-hop QA datasets: HotpotQA [26], MuSiQue [18], and 2WikiMultiHopQA (2WikiMQA) [20]. HotpotQA features large-scale cross-document reasoning with implicit 2-hop bridge and comparison questions. MuSiQue focuses on realistic multi-hop scenarios with numerous distractor paragraphs, increasing retrieval and filtering difficulty. 2WikiMultiHopQA, built from Wikipedia entities and attributes, provides explicit 2-hop and 3-hop inference paths. Following prior work [1,17], we sample the first 500 examples from the test sets of each dataset.

Evaluation Metrics. To evaluate AORS, we adopt standard metrics for complex reasoning tasks. On the three multi-hop QA datasets, we report Exact Match (EM) and token-level F1 scores. EM measures if the output exactly matches the reference answer, while token-level F1 evaluates the overlap between predicted and ground-truth answers, providing a fine-grained assessment of answer quality.

Baselines. We compare AORS against representative baselines across five categories:

(1) **Direct & Chain-of-Thought (CoT):** Assess intrinsic capabilities via direct answering and step-by-step reasoning without retrieval.
(2) **Direct RAG & Graph RAG:** Enhance generation using semantic paragraph retrieval and structure-aware graph retrieval.
(3) **Iterative Reasoning (ReAct, Self-Ask, IRCoT):** Use tool-use interleaving, sub-question decomposition, and iterative retrieval updates.
(4) **Memory Augmented (HippoRAG & IRCoT + HippoRAG):** Leverage long-term memory for multi-hop reasoning, tested independently and with IRCoT.
(5) **AORS-NF (A.-NF):** AORS without fine-tuning, relying on in-context learning (ICL) [**30**] for reasoning plans. It employs only semantic retrieval, disabling the knowledge graph module, while retaining the multi-round verification for fair comparison.

Implementation Details. All baselines are reproduced using the GPT-3.5-turbo-1106 (GPT-3.5) API to ensure consistency. For the IRCoT + HippoRAG baseline, HippoRAG serves as a long-term memory module within the IRCoT framework. To ensure fairness, we decouple reasoning planning from answer generation: the reasoning model only produces plans, while final answers for all methods are uniformly generated by the same QA LLM. Specifically, we evaluate two configurations using GPT-3.5 and GPT-4o as the QA LLM, ensuring all methods share the same backend to eliminate model capability bias.

Table 3. Comparison of different methods under GPT-3.5/4o as QA-LLMs.

Method	GPT-3.5						GPT-4o					
	HotpotQA		MuSiQue		2WikiMQA		HotpotQA		MuSiQue		2WikiMQA	
	EM	F1	EM	F1	EM	F1	EM	F1	EM	F1	EM	F1
Direct	0.264	0.271	0.085	0.096	0.284	0.294	0.275	0.293	0.103	0.128	0.306	0.351
CoT	0.287	0.292	0.090	0.108	0.286	0.295	0.299	0.301	0.112	0.156	0.314	0.369
Direct RAG	0.293	0.326	0.087	0.097	0.230	0.243	0.311	0.372	0.107	0.131	0.245	0.269
Graph RAG	0.317	0.351	0.121	0.132	0.225	0.265	0.327	0.430	0.131	0.232	0.255	0.279
ReAct	0.215	0.282	0.060	0.112	0.216	0.291	0.243	0.307	0.087	0.123	0.234	0.337
Self-Ask	0.173	0.254	0.116	0.157	0.194	0.272	0.187	0.265	0.127	0.208	0.217	0.307
IRCoT	0.421	0.563	0.234	0.347	0.443	0.451	0.434	0.589	0.254	0.364	0.455	0.467
HippoRAG	0.407	0.526	0.292	0.356	0.463	0.468	0.421	0.561	0.312	0.389	0.472	0.483
IRCoT+HippoRAG	0.456	0.596	0.325	0.411	0.473	0.541	0.467	0.581	0.351	0.467	0.498	0.581
A.-NF(GPT-3.5)	0.352	0.446	0.252	0.298	0.344	0.387	0.367	0.412	0.263	0.347	0.355	0.392
A.-NF(GPT-4o-mini)	0.387	0.492	0.283	0.345	0.354	0.413	0.403	0.512	0.292	0.378	0.403	0.489
A.-NF(Qwen2.5-72B)	0.412	0.521	0.312	0.369	0.368	0.421	0.431	0.521	0.341	0.411	0.412	0.492
A.-NF(GLM-4-Plus)	0.418	0.523	0.324	0.371	0.381	0.463	0.442	0.529	0.347	0.413	0.433	0.521
A.-NF(GPT-4o)	0.442	0.536	0.403	0.489	0.443	0.517	0.462	0.578	0.412	0.512	0.493	0.571
AORS (Qwen1.5-7B)	0.398	0.503	0.297	0.354	0.365	0.417	0.419	0.517	0.327	0.398	0.409	0.499
AORS (Llama3-8B)	0.462	0.621	0.439	0.538	0.507	0.614	0.483	0.659	0.443	0.543	0.520	0.687

4.2 Experimental Results (RQ1)

As shown in Table 3, AORS achieves clear improvements over Direct, CoT, Direct RAG, and Graph RAG across all datasets. Implicit reasoning methods often struggle with multi-hop dependencies, while retrieval-based approaches lack tight alignment between evidence and reasoning. In contrast, AORS explicitly structures reasoning and enhances retrieval via semantic matching and relational augmentation, ensuring stable predictions. Compared with iterative methods like ReAct, Self-Ask, IRCoT, and HippoRAG, AORS maintains consistent advantages. While those methods improve reasoning through memory or iterative retrieval, they lack unified execution. By integrating structured reasoning, dual-level retrieval, and multi-round verification, AORS achieves superior alignment and performance.

Table 4.1 also reports results under different QA LLM settings. AORS consistently performs best across all datasets and metrics. While all methods benefit from stronger QA models, AORS shows more stable gains. Notably, although the fine-tuned CodeQwen (7B) and Llama3 (8B) models are substantially smaller than closed-source large models such as GPT-3.5, GPT-4o, and GLM-4-Plus, fine-tuned CodeQwen-7B and Llama3-8B under AORS match or surpass larger closed-source models (GPT-3.5, GPT-4o, GLM-4-Plus) using in-context learning. This indicates that improvements stem from the AORS framework rather than solely relying on model scale.

4.3 Ablation Studies (RQ2)

Based on Table 4 , AORS core components undergo systematic ablation. Results show performance gains stem from modular synergy, with structured reasoning planning as the primary driver. By replacing implicit natural language with explicit, executable atomic operators, structured reasoning planning constrains reasoning paths and maintains stability. Furthermore, the dual-level retrieval mechanism optimizes evidence quality: the semantic layer ensures broad coverage, while knowledge graph enhancement improves precision through relation injection and expansion. Finally, multi-round verification enhances robustness by mitigating sampling randomness and noise.

Table 4. Ablation and retrieval performance analysis of AORS.

Setting	HotpotQA (EM)	MuSiQue (EM)	2WikiMQA (EM)
Full AORS	**0.462**	**0.439**	**0.507**
w/o Multi-Round Verification	0.421	0.408	0.457
w/o Knowledge Graph Enhancement	0.413	0.403	0.424
w/o Reasoning Navigation	0.399	0.295	0.371
w/o KG-E & MR-V	0.376	0.265	0.352
w/o all	0.251	0.078	0.271
Retrieval Performance Analysis			
Setting	Paragraph-level Recall	Step-level Retrieval	Answer-bearing Passage Rate
Semantic only	0.67	0.78	0.75
w/ Relation Injection	0.67	0.82	0.79
w/ Relation Expansion	0.83	0.85	0.82
w/ Injection + Expansion	**0.83**	**0.91**	**0.87**

We assess knowledge graph enhancement via three metrics: Paragraph-level Recall, Answer-bearing Passage Rate, and Step-level Retrieval Success. Here, Paragraph-level Recall measures document retrieval, while Answer-bearing Passage Rate evaluates if the context contains the ground-truth answer. Step-level Retrieval Success measures alignment: a step is successful if its retrieved passages R_i contain information for intermediate answer a_i. As shown in Table 4 and Fig. 4(b), combining relation injection and expansion leads to significant improvements, proving AORS grounds multi-hop inference in evidence.

Finally, we conduct experiments on the number of rounds for the multi-round verification mechanism. As shown in Fig. 4(a), we select K=5 as performance plateaus and noise is neutralized. Further increasing K yields diminishing returns with significantly higher latency.

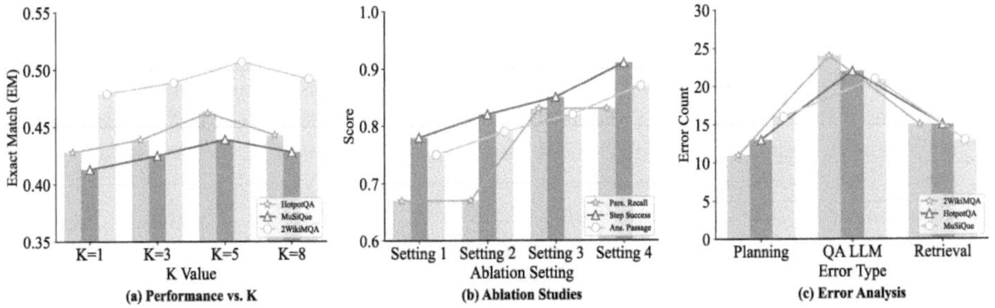

Fig. 4. Mechanism-level analysis of AORS: (a) effect of sampling rounds K in multi-round verification; (b) retrieval performance under knowledge graph enhancement; (c) error distribution.

4.4 Error Analysis (RQ3)

We randomly sample 50 error cases from each dataset (Fig. 4(c)). Across all datasets, errors primarily concentrate in the final answer generation stage, highlighting it as a key bottleneck despite structured reasoning and enhanced retrieval. Varying proportions of reasoning planning and retrieval errors across datasets reflect distinct challenges in question complexity and evidence acquisition. These findings suggest that performance depends on both execution mechanisms and dataset-specific optimization of planning and retrieval strategies.

5 Conclusion

This paper proposes AORS, which maps natural language questions into executable atomic reasoning plans to alleviate reasoning instability in small-scale language models. It integrates a dual-level retrieval mechanism that balances evidence coverage and relational precision, along with multi-round verification to enhance robustness. Experimental results show that AORS consistently improves multi-hop reasoning without relying on large model scales, providing an efficient paradigm for reliable reasoning in resource-constrained settings.

Acknowledgments. This work is supported by the National Natural Science Foundation of China (No. 62402064), the Hunan Provincial Key Research and Development Program (Nos. 2024JK2005 and 2026AQ2032), the Natural Science Foundation of Hunan Province, China, (Nos. 2023JJ30054 and 2026JJ81155), the Research Foundation of Education Bureau of Hunan Province, China, (No. 23B0303), the Postgraduate Practice Innovation Project of Changsha University of Science and Technology (No. CLSJCX25070).

References

1. Aksitov, R., Miryoosefi, S., Li, Z., Li, D., Babayan, S., Kopparapu, K., Fisher, Z., Guo, R., Prakash, S., Srinivasan, P., Zaheer, M., Yu, F.X., Kumar, S.: Rest meets react: self-improvement for multi-step reasoning LLM agent. CoRR (abs/2312.10003) (2023)
2. Chen, X., Song, D., Gui, H., Wang, C., Zhang, N., Jiang, Y., Huang, F., Lyu, C., Zhang, D., Chen, H.: Factchd: benchmarking fact-conflicting hallucination detection. In: Proceedings of the IJCAI, pp. 6216–6224 (2024)
3. Fang, Y., Zhan, J., Ai, Q., Mao, J., Su, W., Chen, J., Liu, Y.: Scaling laws for dense retrieval. In: Proceedings of the SIGIR, pp. 1339–1349 (2024)
4. Gutiérrez, B.J., Shu, Y., Gu, Y., Yasunaga, M., Su, Y.: Hipporag: neurobiologically inspired long-term memory for large language models. In: Proceedings of the NeurIPS, pp. 59532–59569 (2024)
5. Hsieh, C.Y., Li, C.L., Yeh, C.K., Nakhost, H., Fujii, Y., Ratner, A., Krishna, R., Lee, C.Y., Pfister, T.: Distilling step-by-step! outperforming larger language models with less training data and smaller model sizes. In: Proceedings of the ACL, pp. 8003–8017 (2023)
6. Hu, E.J., Shen, Y., Wallis, P., Allen-Zhu, Z., Li, Y., Wang, S., Wang, L., Chen, W.: Lora: low-rank adaptation of large language models. In: Proceedings of the ICLR (2022)
7. Huang, W., Lapata, M., Vougiouklis, P., Papasarantopoulos, N., Pan, J.Z.: Retrieval augmented generation with rich answer encoding. In: Proceedings of the IJCNLP, pp. 1012–1025 (2023)
8. Lan, L., Wang, P., Shi, R., Liu, T., Zeng, J., Sun, F., Ren, Y., Tao, J., Guan, X.: Grand: a fast and accurate graph retrieval framework via knowledge distillation. In: Proceedings of the SIGIR, pp. 1639–1648 (2024)
9. Lewis, P., Perez, E., Piktus, A., Petroni, F., Karpukhin, V., Goyal, N., Küttler, H., Lewis, M., Yih, W.t., Rocktäschel, T., Riedel, S., Kiela, D.: Retrieval-augmented generation for knowledge-intensive nlp tasks. In: Proceedings of the NeurIPS, pp. 9459–9474 (2020)
10. Li, Y., Yue, X., Xu, Z., Jiang, F., Niu, L., Lin, B.Y., Ramasubramanian, B., Poovendran, R.: Small models struggle to learn from strong reasoners. In: Proceedings of the ACL, pp. 25366–25394 (2025)
11. Loshchilov, I., Hutter, F.: SGDR: stochastic gradient descent with warm restarts. In: Proceedings of the ICLR (2017)
12. Loshchilov, I., Hutter, F.: Decoupled weight decay regularization. In: Proceedings of the ICLR (2019)
13. Ma, C., Chen, Y., Wu, T., Khan, A., Wang, H.: Large language models meet knowledge graphs for question answering: synthesis and opportunities. In: Proceedings of the EMNLP, pp. 24578–24597 (2025)
14. Ouyang, L., Wu, J., Jiang, X., Almeida, D., Wainwright, C., Mishkin, P., Zhang, C., Agarwal, S., Slama, K., Ray, A., et al.: Training language models to follow instructions with human feedback. Adv. Neural. Inf. Process. Syst. **35**, 27730–27744 (2022)
15. Press, O., Zhang, M., Min, S., Schmidt, L., Smith, N.A., Lewis, M.: Measuring and narrowing the compositionality gap in language models. In: Proceedings of the EMNLP, pp. 5687–5711 (2023)
16. Salemi, A., Zamani, H.: Evaluating retrieval quality in retrieval-augmented generation. In: Proceedings of the SIGIR, pp. 2395–2400 (2024)

17. Shao, Z., Gong, Y., Shen, Y., Huang, M., Duan, N., Chen, W.: Enhancing retrieval-augmented large language models with iterative retrieval-generation synergy. In: Proceedings of the EMNLP, pp. 9248–9274 (2023)
18. Trivedi, H., Balasubramanian, N., Khot, T., Sabharwal, A.: Musique: multihop questions via single-hop question composition. Trans. Assoc. Comput. Linguistics **10**, 539–554 (2022)
19. Trivedi, H., Balasubramanian, N., Khot, T., Sabharwal, A.: Interleaving retrieval with chain-of-thought reasoning for knowledge-intensive multi-step questions. In: Proceedings of the ACL, pp. 10014–10037 (2023)
20. Vrandecic, D., Krötzsch, M.: Wikidata: a free collaborative knowledgebase. Commun. ACM **57**(10), 78–85 (2014)
21. Wei, J., Wang, X., Schuurmans, D., Bosma, M., Ichter, B., Xia, F., Chi, E., Le, Q.V., Zhou, D.: Chain-of-thought prompting elicits reasoning in large language models. In: Proceedings of the NeurIPS, vol. 35, pp. 24824–24837 (2022)
22. Xiong, S., Payani, A., Kompella, R., Fekri, F.: Large language models can learn temporal reasoning. In: Proceedings of ACL, pp. 10452–10470. Association for Computational Linguistics (2024)
23. Xu, Z., Cruz, M.J., Guevara, M., Wang, T., Deshpande, M., Wang, X., Li, Z.: Retrieval-augmented generation with knowledge graphs for customer service question answering. In: Proceedings of the SIGIR, pp. 2905–2909 (2024)
24. Yang, D., Rao, J., Chen, K., Guo, X., Zhang, Y., Yang, J., Zhang, Y.: Im-rag: multi-round retrieval-augmented generation through learning inner monologues. In: Proceedings of the SIGIR, pp 730–740 (2024)
25. Yang, Y., Carlson, P., He, S., Qiao, Y., Yang, T.: Cluster-based partial dense retrieval fused with sparse text retrieval. In: Proceedings of the SIGIR, pp. 2327–2331 (2024)
26. Yang, Z., Qi, P., Zhang, S., Bengio, Y., Cohen, W.W., Salakhutdinov, R., Manning, C.D.: Hotpotqa: a dataset for diverse, explainable multi-hop question answering. In: Proceedings of the EMNLP, pp. 2369–2380 (2018)
27. Yao, S., Yu, D., Zhao, J., Shafran, I., Griffiths, T., Cao, Y., Narasimhan, K.: Tree of thoughts: deliberate problem solving with large language models. In: Proceedings of the NeurIPS, pp. 11809–11822 (2023)
28. Yao, S., Zhao, J., Yu, D., Du, N., Shafran, I., Narasimhan, K.R., Cao, Y.: React: synergizing reasoning and acting in language models. In: Proceedings of the ICLR (2023)

IteraTri: Detecting Hallucination of LLM in Knowledge-Intensive QA via Iterative Verification

Yunsong Wang[1], Junwei Zhang[2], Dongjin Yu[1](✉), and Xiaolin Li[2]

[1] Hangzhou Dianzi University, Zhejiang, China
yudj@hdu.edu.cn
[2] Hangzhou Institute of Medicine Chinese Academy of Sciences, Zhejiang, China

Abstract. Large Language Models (LLMs) frequently hallucinate when performing complex, multi-hop reasoning, as they lack a mechanism to ground their reasoning in verifiable facts. Existing solutions either rely on the model's internal consistency, which cannot correct parametric errors, or perform retrieval to provide contextual knowledge without explicit stepwise verification. To bridge this gap, we propose IteraTri, a novel **I**terative, **Tri**plet-Driven Knowledge Acquisition and Verification framework. IteraTri reformulates complex question answering into a dynamic process where an LLM planner iteratively decomposes the question, generating sequences of verifiable (subject, relation, object) triplets as its knowledge needs. A dedicated reflection agent then condenses these triplets into a coherent evidence chain, which is rigorously validated against a trusted knowledge graph. This creates a tight, explainable coupling between neural reasoning and symbolic fact-checking. We evaluate IteraTri on three challenging benchmarks (FactCHD, PathQuestion, MetaQA), where it consistently outperforms the baselines, achieving state-of-the-art factual accuracy. Further more, ablation studies confirm the critical role of both iterative extraction and knowledge reflection. Our work demonstrates that using structured triplets as a medium for planning and verification is a promising path towards more reliable and transparent LLMs for knowledge-intensive QA tasks.

Keywords: Large Language Model · Hallucination detection · Knowledge Graph · Explainable AI · IteraTri

1 Introduction

The remarkable ability of Large Language Models (LLMs) to comprehend and generate human-like text has propelled them to the forefront of knowledge-intensive question answering (QA) [1]. However, their propensity to produce convincing yet factually incorrect statements, which is a phenomenon known as hallucination[2,3], remains a critical barrier to reliable, real-world deployment, especially in domains requiring complex, multi-step reasoning over precise

L. Ding et al. (Eds.): APWeb-WAIM 2026, LNCS 16993, pp. 376–391, 2027.
https://doi.org/10.1007/978-981-92-5693-8_24

facts [4,5]. The challenge is exacerbated when models are required to synthesize answers from disparate pieces of knowledge [6], as they may fabricate plausible-sounding connections or entities not grounded in any credible source [7,8].

To combat hallucination, existing research has evolved along two primary paradigms. The first paradigm seeks to **ground LLMs in external knowledge sources** [9]. This includes Retrieval-Augmented Generation (RAG), which augments prompts with retrieved document passages, and Knowledge Graph-based QA (KGQA), which executes precise symbolic queries over structured graphs [10]. While promising, these methods face inherent trade-offs: RAG often yields **imprecise** evidence from unstructured text, complicating direct fact verification, while KGQA systems suffer from **inflexibility**, struggling to generalize to complex questions requiring dynamic, multi-hop reasoning paths. The second paradigm attempts to **elicit self-assessment from the LLM itself**, leveraging its inherent parametric knowledge and reasoning capability [11]. Methods in this vein, such as consistency sampling [12], self-interrogation [13], or multi-agent debate [14], detect hallucinations by analyzing the models own output variations or internal consistency. However, these approaches are fundamentally constrained by the model's **prior beliefs and systematic biases**; they may fail to correct errors that are consistently and confidently reproduced by the model itself, and they offer little insight into which specific fact is at fault when an error is detected.

In essence, a significant gap persists between **flexible but ungrounded self-verification** and **precise but rigid external knowledge access**. Current hybrid approaches that loosely combine these elements lack a tight, verifiable coupling between the iterative reasoning process and atomic factual evidence. This results in limited **explainability** and persistent **hallucination** in complex reasoning scenarios.

To bridge this gap, we introduce **IteraTri**, a novel framework for Iterative, Triplet-Driven Knowledge Acquisition and Verification. IteraTri reformulates complex reasoning as an iterative process that involves the generation and verification of structured knowledge needs through a three-stage pipeline. First, an LLM planner decomposes the question via multi-round deliberation, each step producing a natural language query andcriticallythe expected answer in the form of structured **(subject, relation, object)** triplets. Second, a distinct LLM reflection agent condenses this extracted knowledge, selecting only the triplets that form a minimal, coherent evidence chain. Third, each triplet in this chain is directly verified against a trusted Knowledge Graph, and a factuality judgment is made based on the verification rate. This methodology ensures that the final verdict is not only derived from a transparent reasoning trace but also built upon a verified factual foundation.

Our primary contributions are threefold:

- We propose **IteraTri**, a novel framework that uses structured triplets as the central medium for iterative reasoning planning and explicit fact verification, effectively bridging flexible neural reasoning with precise symbolic grounding for hallucination detection.

- We introduce a dedicated **knowledge reflection and condensation** step, which significantly enhances the relevance and precision of the evidence chain before verification, improving both efficiency and accuracy.
- We conduct comprehensive experiments on multiple hallucination detection benchmarks. Results demonstrate that IteraTri achieves superior detection accuracy compared to state-of-the-art baselines, while providing fully explainable judgment paths grounded in verified facts.

2 Relate Work

Our work sits at the intersection of hallucination detection in large language models, knowledge-augmented reasoning. We review the most relevant literature in these areas and highlight the distinctive position of our proposed IteraTri framework.

2.1 Hallucination Detection and Mitigation in LLMs

The problem of hallucination has spurred numerous detection and mitigation strategies. These can be broadly categorized by their core mechanism. **Internal Consistency** methods, such as SelfCheckGPT [12] and its variants, operate on the principle that a fact is less trustworthy if the LLM gives inconsistent answers across multiple samplings or prompt perturbations. Similarly, **Self-Interrogation** methods like InterrogateLM [13] and related dialogue-based probing techniques ask the model to explain or justify its own claims, detecting hallucination through the quality or consistency of the generated rationale. More recently, **Multi-Agent Debate** frameworks have been proposed, where multiple LLM agents reason collaboratively or adversarially to arrive at a more faithful conclusion, as seen in the TRUTH-TRIANGULATOR baseline [14].
Critical Analysis: While effective in many scenarios, introspective methods are fundamentally constrained by the model's parametric knowledge. They operate entirely within the model's internal representations, offering no mechanism to consult external, authoritative sources. Consequently, they may confidently reproduce systematic errors present in the training data, and when a hallucination is detected, they cannot pinpoint which specific fact is at fault. This lack of external grounding and fine-grained explainability limits their reliability for high-stakes applications. By contrast, our work shifts the paradigm from internal consistency checking to external factual verification.

2.2 Knowledge-Augmented Language Models

To ground LLMs in external knowledge, retrieval-augmented generation (RAG) has become the predominant paradigm. It can be categorized according to the form of the knowledge retrieved.[15] The classic and most common approach is **Textual RAG** [16], which enhances prompts with relevant passages retrieved from an unstructured or semi-structured corpus (e.g., Wikipedia). For more complex reasoning, **Iterative RAG** methods interleave retrieval and generation in multiple steps.

A significant advancement is the integration of structured knowledge, leading to **Knowledge Graph-enhanced RAG**. This line of work retrieves information from knowledge graphs, typically by sampling or linearizing relevant subgraphs or by using KG embeddings to find semantically related facts. The retrieved structured data is then serialized into text and fed into the LLM as context. This method aims to combine the precision of structured knowledge with the flexibility of LLMs. [17]

Critical Analysis: KG-enhanced RAG advances beyond pure introspection by incorporating structured knowledge. However, its core mechanism remains one of contextual supplementation: retrieved triples are linearized and fed to the LLM as additional context, with reasoning performed in a single, opaque forward pass. Although this can improve the accuracy of facts, it lacks a built-in mechanism to verify which specific retrieved fact supports which step of reasoning. The final answer, therefore, lacks a verifiable, stepwise link to atomic KG facts. In comparison, IteraTri addresses this by reframing retrieval as a targeted verification of each discrete reasoning step, ensuring full traceability.

Unlike iterative RAG (no step-wise verification), KG-enhanced QA (single-pass context injection), and multi-agent verification (internal debate only), IteraTri uniquely enables atomic triplet verification and full step-wise traceability by iteratively decomposing questions, filtering evidence via reflection, and validating each reasoning step against a trusted knowledge graph.

3 Methodology

We propose the **IteraTri** (Iterative Triplet-Driven Reasoning) framework to detect hallucination in complex knowledge reasoning. As illustrated in Fig. 1, IteraTri operates through three sequential stages: **Iterative Knowledge Extraction**, **Knowledge Reflection and Condensation**, and **Knowledge Verification and Factuality Judgment**. This structured approach ensures that the final answer is grounded in a verifiable chain of evidence.

3.1 Iterative Knowledge Extraction

This module decomposes a complex question into a series of verifiable sub-queries via a closed-loop Plan-Query-Extract process.

1. **Query Planning (Thought Generation).** Given a user question Q, the framework invokes a planner LLM, LLM_{plan}, to analyze the current reasoning state and determine the most critical piece of information required at next step. This generates a Thought that explicitly states the knowledge gap and the intent of the next query. The process at step t is formalized as:

$$\text{Thought}_t = LLM_{\text{plan}}(Q, \mathcal{H}_{t-1}),$$

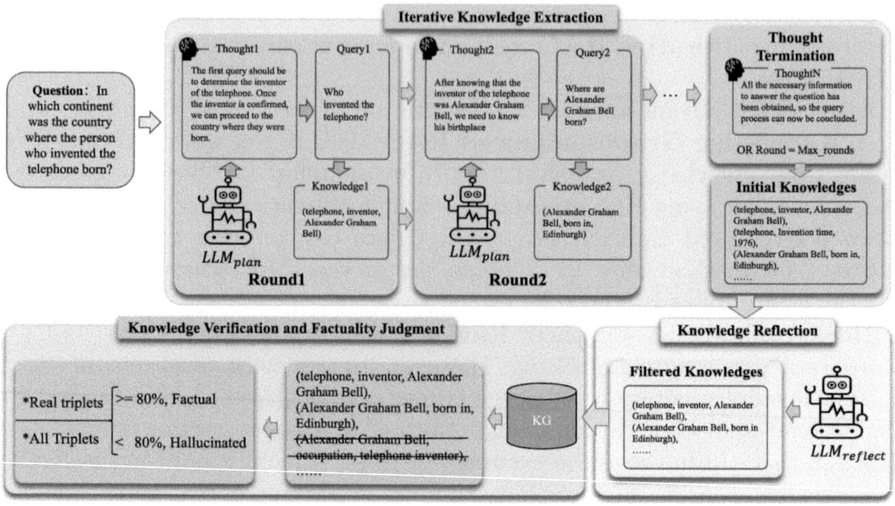

Fig. 1. The overall architecture of the IteraTri. The framework processes a user question through three core stages: (1) **Iterative Knowledge Extraction**, where an LLM planner decomposes the question across multiple rounds, generating structured knowledge triplets; (2) **Knowledge Reflection**, which condenses the extracted triplets into a coherent evidence chain; and (3) **Knowledge Verification**, where each triplet is checked against a trusted Knowledge Graph to produce a final, explainable factuality judgment.

where

$$\mathcal{H}_{t-1} = \bigcup_{i=1}^{t-1} \{(\text{Thought}_i, \text{Query}_i, \text{Knowledge}_i)\}$$

is the history of all prior steps.

2. **Targeted Query Formulation.** Based on Thought_t, LLM_{plan} formulates a precise, retrievable natural language query:

$$\text{Query}_t = LLM_{\text{plan}}(\text{Thought}_t).$$

3. **Structured Knowledge Extraction (Triplet Formation).** Upon receiving the textual answer Answer_t for Query_t,

$$\text{Answer}_t = LLM_{\text{plan}}(\text{Query}_t)$$

the framework does not adopt it directly. Instead, it prompts LLM_{plan} to distill the supporting facts into structured **knowledge triplets** $\mathcal{K}_t$. Each triplet is in the form $(subject, relation, object)$, transforming unstructured text into verifiable atomic facts:

$$\mathcal{K}_t = \{(s, r, o)\} = LLM_{\text{plan}}(\text{Query}_t, \text{Answer}_t).$$

4. **Iterative Loop.** The triplets $\mathcal{K}_t$ are appended to the history $\mathcal{H}_t$, triggering the next cycle. This loop continues until LLM_{plan} determines that sufficient information has been gathered to answer Q or a pre-defined maximum number of rounds is reached. The output is an initial knowledge set tailored to the original question:

$$\mathcal{K}_{\text{initial}} = \bigcup_{t=1}^{T} \mathcal{K}_t.$$

Prompt Design for Implementation. The iterative extraction process is governed by a structured prompt that is presented to LLM_{plan}. This prompt requires the model to output the four components (`Thought`, `Query`, `Answer`, `Knowledge`) in a strict cumulative format for each round t. The prompt operationalizes three key principles:

- **Single-focus querying:** Each query targets exactly one missing piece of information, **which prevents compound errors and simplifies subsequent verification of atomic facts.**
- **Cumulative triplet extraction:** All previously extracted triplets are carried forward in each `Knowledge` field.
- **Self-termination:** The model explicitly outputs "No further query needed" when sufficient information is gathered.

Prompt details: prompt follow a structured template with clear role definitions (planner agent), task instructions, and constraints on output format. The planner prompt enforces round-wise output of Thought Query Answer Triplets and cumulative triplet tracking

3.2 Knowledge Reflection

The set $\mathcal{K}_{\text{initial}}$ may contain redundancies or facts that are only peripherally related to the final answer. To enhance the efficiency and precision of subsequent verification, we introduce a **Reflection** stage, executed by a dedicated reflection agent LLM_{reflect}.

This agent takes the original question Q and the initial knowledge set $\mathcal{K}_{\text{initial}}$ as input. Its task is to **select the minimal and logically coherent subset of triplets that are essential and sufficient to answer Q directly and concisely**. The process is formalized as follows:

$$\mathcal{K}_{\text{condensed}} = LLM_{\text{reflect}}(Q, \mathcal{K}_{\text{initial}}),$$

where $\mathcal{K}_{\text{condensed}} \subseteq \mathcal{K}_{\text{initial}}$.

Rationale. The reflection step not only reduces the computational cost of verification but also mimics the human "rethinking" process. By filtering out noise and focusing on the evidence chain, it significantly improves the robustness and accuracy of the final reasoning step.**The resulting $\mathcal{K}_{\text{condensed}}$ serves as input**

to the verification module (Section 3.3), ensuring that only relevant facts are checked against the KG.

Prompt Design for Reflection. The reflection agent LLM_{reflect} operates based on a structured prompt that defines its core task: to filter the initial knowledge set $\mathcal{K}_{\text{initial}}$ by selecting only the triplets that are essential and sufficient for answering Q. The prompt provides explicit criteria for usefulness and mandates a strict output format that includes a justification for each triplet's categorization and final statistics. Key features include:

- **Binary usefulness classification:** Each triplet is judged as *Useful* or *Not Useful* based on its contribution to answering the question. **A triplet is considered useful if it directly participates in the reasoning chain or provides the necessary context without which the answer would be incomplete.**
- **Justification requirement:** For every triplet, a one-sentence reason must be provided, ensuring transparency.
- **Structured output:** The final output includes analysis, per-triplet categorization, statistics, and the condensed triplet list.

Prompt details: the reflection prompt follows a structured template with clear role definitions (reflection agent), task instructions, and constraints on output format. The reflection prompt enforces binary classification of triplets (Useful/Not Useful), requires one-sentence justification per triplet, and outputs a condensed, coherent evidence chain.

3.3 Knowledge Verification and Factuality Judgment

To ensure reliability, this module performs rigorous fact-checking on the condensed knowledge set $\mathcal{K}_{\text{condensed}}$ against a trusted Knowledge Graph (KG). The lexical gap between natural language phrases and KG identifiers is bridged by a neuralsymbolic matching procedure that treats each candidate triple as an atomic textual unit and performs holistic similarity comparison.

1. **KG Verification.** For each natural language triplet $(s, r, o) \in \mathcal{K}_{\text{condensed}}$, we determine whether it corresponds to an existing triplet in the KG through the following multi-step process.

Embedding Model and Precomputation. All KG triples are pre-encoded into dense vectors to enable efficient similarity search. For each triple (e_h, p, e_o) in the KG, we concatenate the textual labels of its components into a single string (e.g., e_h p e_o) and encode this string using a pretrained BERT model. All such embeddings are stored offline for fast cosine similarity computation during verification.

Head Entity Candidate Selection. For the subject phrase s:

- **Exact match check:** After applying caseinsensitive normalization and trimming whitespace, we search for any KG entity whose label exactly equals s. If such an entity exists, it is selected as the **sole candidate** $\mathcal{C}_s = \{e^*\}$, and we skip fuzzy matching.

- **Fuzzy match:** If no exact match is found, we encode s using the same SentenceBERT encoder to obtain its embedding $\mathbf{e}_s$. We then compute cosine similarity between $\mathbf{e}_s$ and all precomputed KG entity label embeddings. The **top2 entities** with the highest similarity scores are selected as the set of candidates $\mathcal{C}_s$.
- **Early termination:** If $\mathcal{C}_s = \varnothing$ (which can occur when no exact match exists and the top similarity scores are extremely low), we immediately conclude that no matching triple exists and set Verify$(s, r, o) = 0$ without proceeding further.

Holistic Triple Matching. For each candidate head entity $e_h \in \mathcal{C}_s$, we examine all outgoing triples from that entity in the KG:

- Retrieve all outgoing triples $\mathcal{T}_{e_h} = \{(e_h, p, e_o)\}$ from the KG.
- For each $(e_h, p, e_o) \in \mathcal{T}_{e_h}$, we have its precomputed embedding $\mathbf{t}_{e_h,p,e_o}$.
- The input triplet (s, r, o) is serialized into the same format (e.g., $s\ r\ o$) and encoded onthefly to obtain its embedding $\mathbf{q}$.
- Compute the cosine similarity between the query embedding and the KG triple embedding:

$$\text{sim} = \cos(\mathbf{q}, \mathbf{t}_{e_h,p,e_o}).$$

- If sim $\geq \theta$ (with $\theta = 0.96$), the candidate triple (e_h, p, e_o) is considered a **match** for (s, r, o).

Verification Decision. The triplet (s, r, o) is assigned Verify$(s, r, o) = 1$ (i.e., verified as factual) if and only if both of the following conditions are satisfied:

1. **Head entity found:** $\mathcal{C}_s \neq \varnothing$ (at least one candidate head entity was identified).
2. **Matching triple exists:** There exists at least one candidate head entity $e_h \in \mathcal{C}_s$ such that, for some triple $(e_h, p, e_o) \in \mathcal{T}_{e_h}$, the cosine similarity satisfies sim $\geq \theta$.

If either condition fails, Verify$(s, r, o) = 0$, indicating that the triplet could not be verified against the KG.

Threshold Selection. The similarity threshold $\theta = 0.96$ was empirically determined on a development set. Values below 0.94 introduce a high rate of false positives (semantically similar but factually different triples), while values above 0.98 cause false negatives due to minor surface variations (e.g., United States vs. USA). $\theta = 0.96$ provides the best accuracy for the verification step itself and is fixed for all experiments.

2. **Factuality Scoring and Judgment**. An overall factuality support score ρ for the condensed set is computed:

$$\rho = \frac{\sum_{(s,r,o)\in\mathcal{K}_{\text{condensed}}} \text{Verify}(s,r,o)}{|\mathcal{K}_{\text{condensed}}|}.$$

Given a predefined threshold τ, a final judgment on the factuality of the prospective answer is made:

$$\text{Judgment} = \begin{cases} \textbf{Factual}, & \text{if } \rho \geq \tau \\ \textbf{Hallucinated}, & \text{otherwise.} \end{cases}$$

If the judgment is *Factual*, the framework synthesizes the final answer based on the verified triplets in $\mathcal{K}_{\text{condensed}}$. If *Hallucinated*, the framework either refrains from answering or flags the response as having insufficient factual support.

4 Experiments

We conducted comprehensive experiments to evaluate the effectiveness of the proposed IteraTri framework. Our experiments are designed to answer the following research questions:

- **RQ1:** Does IteraTri outperform all baseline methods in reducing hallucination and improving factuality in complex QA?
- **RQ2:** How does each component (e.g., iterative extraction, reflection) contribute to the overall performance?
- **RQ3:** How does IteraTri perform under different backbone LLMs and resource settings (zero-shot vs. few-shot)?

4.1 Experimental Setup

Datasets. We evaluate our method on three challenging benchmarks that require structured knowledge and complex reasoning, with a focus on verifiable factuality:

- **FactCHD** [14]: A benchmark designed for evaluating fact-conflicting hallucinations in knowledge-grounded QA. It provides questions with KG-grounded evidence chains. To ensure a rigorous and consistent evaluation of retrieval-based verification methods like ours, we focus exclusively on its fully verifiable **Wikidata subset**. We curated a set of 1,889 samples that are both retrievable against Wikidata and equipped with complete categorical metadata for per-type evaluation, making it an ideal testbed for assessing fine-grained reasoning and hallucination mitigation.
- **PathQuestion** [18]: A knowledge base question answering (KBQA) dataset specifically designed to evaluate multi-hop reasoning capabilities over knowledge graphs. To adapt it for our task of hallucination detection, we process it into a balanced binary classification benchmark. The factual half retains the original questions and correct answers. The hallucinated half is constructed

by using prompt-guided LLM generation to produce answers that are semantically type-consistent but factually incorrect with respect to the knowledge base, which are then paired with the original questions. This transformation allows us to directly evaluate a model's ability to distinguish fact from hallucination in a multi-hop reasoning context.
- MetaQA [19]: A large-scale knowledge base question answering dataset in the **movie domain**, containing over 400,000 questions that require multi-hop reasoning over a dedicated knowledge graph of movies, actors, and directors. Similar to our adaptation of PathQuestion, we process MetaQA into a balanced hallucination detection benchmark. The factual portion uses the original questions and answers. For the hallucinated portion, we employ a similar prompt-guided generation strategy with a large language model to create plausible but factually incorrect answers based on the movie-domain KG, ensuring semantic type alignment (e.g., generating a different movie title or actor name). This enables a comprehensive evaluation of our framework's ability to handle domain-specific, multi-hop queries and identify hallucinations within a complex, structured domain.

The choice of these datasets allows us to assess IteraTri's capability across different reasoning complexities (e.g., multi-hop, comparison) and key tasks (i.e., accurate QA and explicit hallucination detection).
Baselines. We compare IteraTri against a comprehensive suite of competitive baselines. For a direct capability comparison, we evaluate the same suite of open-source LLMs (**GEMMA3-4B/12B** [20], **Llama3.1-8B** [21], and **Qwen3-8B** [22]) under both **Zero-shot** and **Few-shot** (with 4 in-context exemplars) CoT[23] prompting settings.

The few-shot prompt for baseline hallucination judgment follows a structured template with clear role definitions (judge agent), task instructions, and output format constraints. It provides four in-context QA-judgment examples, each demonstrating analysis steps and a binary factual/hallucinated verdict, guiding the model to produce a consistent judgment for the target question-answer pair.

We further compare against state-of-the-art specialized methods for hallucination detection and knowledge grounding:

- **TRUTH-TRIANGULATOR** [14]: Co-developed with FactCHD, this strong baseline employs a collaborative multi-agent architecture. It uses a *Truth-Guardian* for direct fact-checking and a *Truth-Seeker* for multi-hop evidential reasoning. A final arbitrator synthesizes their outputs for judgment.
- **SelfCheckGPT** [12]: This method detects hallucination via consistency checking. We generate five stochastic answers per question and use an NLI model to compute pairwise entailment, aggregating the scores into a final consistency signal.
- **InterrogateLM** [13]: This method first generates an answer, then uses the LLM to produce multiple follow-up questions about it. The consistency between the original answer and the LLM's answers to these new questions is used to assess factuality.

- **RAG + LLM Judge**: This retrieval-based baseline first embeds the KG and retrieves the top-K triples most similar to the query. A powerful judge LLM (Qwen3-70B) is then prompted to determine hallucination by reasoning over this retrieved evidence subgraph.

All baseline methods are implemented following their original papers, using the best-performing backbone models and hyperparameters reported in each respective work.

Our Method (IteraTri) is instantiated using the same backbone LLMs as above, ensuring a fair comparison that highlights the gains from our framework's architecture rather than base model capabilities.

Evaluation Metrics. The primary evaluation metric is the **Overall Accuracy** of factuality judgment. A claim (question-answer pair) is correctly judged if our framework's binary verdict (**Factual** or **Hallucinated**) matches the ground-truth label.

Table 1. Performance comparison between IteraTri and baseline methods in accuracy. **Bold** and underlined numbers denote the best and second-best values, respectively.

Methods		FactCHD	PathQuestion	MetaQA
Zero-shot	Gemma3-4B	0.518	0.514	0.413
	Llama3.1-8B	0.471	0.552	0.526
	Qwen3-8B	0.641	0.609	0.115
	Gemma3-12B	0.526	0.549	0.451
ICL(4-shot)	Gemma3-4B	0.542	0.524	0.315
	Llama3.1-8B	0.498	0.562	0.532
	Qwen3-8B	0.608	0.612	0.436
	Gemma3-12B	0.641	0.655	0.393
RAG + LLM		0.652	0.680	0.593
InterrogateLLM		0.615	0.627	0.615
SelfCheckGPT		0.640	0.661	0.627
TRUTH-TRIANGULATOR		<u>0.735</u>	0.686	0.628
IteraTri	Gemma3-4B	0.712	0.785	0.753
	Llama3.1-8B	0.717	<u>0.790</u>	<u>0.786</u>
	Qwen3-8B	0.734	0.785	0.762
	Gemma3-12B	**0.741**	**0.793**	**0.798**

Implementation Details. We implement IteraTri using the official APIs or checkpoints of the backbone LLMs. For the knowledge graph verification stage, we use **Wikidata** as the trusted KG for FactCHD and PathQuestion, and the dedicated movie KG for MetaQA. The factuality judgment threshold τ is set to 0.8 based on a held-out validation set. The iterative extraction is limited to a maximum of 5 rounds. All prompts for Thought generation, Query formulation, Triplet extraction, and Reflection are carefully designed and kept consistent across models. Experiments are conducted on two NVIDIA A40 GPUs (each with 48GB of memory) (Table 2).

Table 2. Ablation study on the IteraTri framework. 'w/o reflection' removes the knowledge reflection step; 'w/o iteration' performs single-round extraction.

Methods		FactCHD	PathQuestion	MetaQA
w/o reflection	Llama3.1-8B	0.694	0.776	0.768
	Gemma3-12B	0.723	0.781	0.776
w/o Iteration	Llama3.1-8B	0.672	0.732	0.736
	Gemma3-12B	0.634	0.754	0.746
IteraTri	Llama3.1-8B	0.717	0.790	0.786
	Gemma3-12B	0.741	0.793	0.798

Evaluation Protocol. For each dataset and model, we report the performance of: (1) The base LLM under zero-shot and few-shot settings; (2) The specialized hallucination detection and grounding baselines (TRUTH-TRIANGULATOR, SelfCheckGPT, InterrogateLM, RAG+LLM Judge); (3) Our full IteraTri framework. This protocol allows for a clear isolation of the performance gain attributable to our framework.

4.2 Main Results

Table 1 presents the overall performance comparison on FactCHD, PathQuestion, and MetaQA datasets. Our proposed **IteraTri** framework consistently achieves superior accuracy across all evaluation settings.

Performance against base LLMs. IteraTri demonstrates substantial and consistent improvements over the zero-shot and few-shot (4-shot ICL) prompting of the same backbone LLMs. For instance, on FactCHD, IteraTri lifts the performance of Llama3.1-8B from 0.471 (zero-shot) to **0.717**, and improves Qwen3-8B from 0.641 to **0.734**. This underscores that the performance gain is attributed to our framework's architecture rather than merely scaling the base model. **(This addresses RQ3 by showing IteraTri's gains across different backbone models.)**

Performance against specialized baselines. IteraTri outperforms all strong, specialized baselines across all datasets. It surpasses the retrieval-based **RAG+LLM Judge**, the self-consistency method **SelfCheckGPT**, and the self-interrogation method **InterrogateLM** by a considerable margin. Compared to the multi-agent **TRUTH-TRIANGULATOR**, IteraTri achieves higher average accuracy on FactCHD (0.741 vs. 0.735 with Gemma3-12B) and substantially better results on both PathQuestion and MetaQA. Notably, with the

Gemma3-12B backbone, IteraTri achieves the top scores of **0.741** on FactCHD, **0.793** on PathQuestion, and **0.798** on MetaQA, setting new state-of-the-art performance on these benchmarks. **(These results provide a strong affirmative answer to RQ1, demonstrating IteraTri's effectiveness in hallucination detection.)**

Model-scale analysis. The results within IteraTri show a positive correlation between backbone model scale and final accuracy, with larger models (Gemma3-12B) consistently outperforming smaller ones (Gemma3-4B). This indicates that our framework effectively leverages enhanced base capabilities. **(This further elucidates RQ3, showing a consistent scaling trend.)**

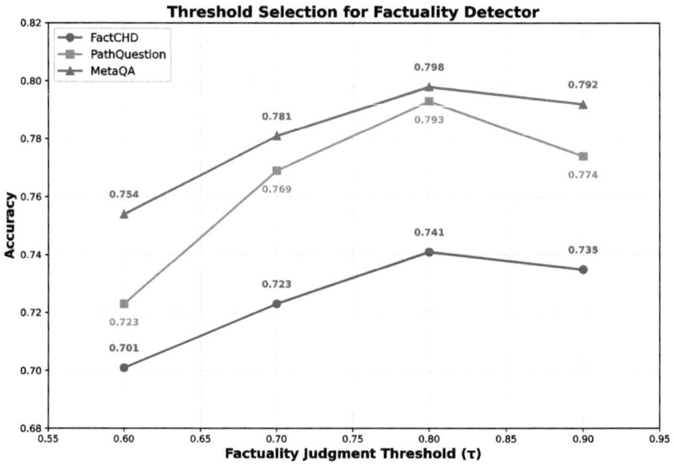

Fig. 2. Factuality judgment threshold analysis.

4.3 Ablation Study

To dissect the contribution of each core component, we conduct an ablation study on two representative backbones, with results detailed in Table 2.

Impact of Knowledge Reflection ('w/o reflection'). Removing the reflection module leads to a clear drop in performance across all datasets. For example, with Llama3.1-8B, the FactCHD average score decreases from 0.717 to 0.694, and the PathQuestion score falls from 0.790 to 0.776. This confirms that the reflection step is crucial for condensing the extracted knowledge into a more precise and relevant evidence chain, thereby improving the efficiency and focus of the subsequent verification stage.

Impact of Iterative Extraction ('w/o iteration'). Disabling the multi-round iterative extraction causes the most significant performance degradation. The FactCHD average for Llama3.1-8B drops to 0.672, and for Gemma3-12B, it falls sharply to 0.634. This substantial decline validates our core hypothesis: complex questions cannot be reliably answered through a single query. The iterative process of planning, querying, and acquiring verifiable triplets is **essential** for decomposing and solving multi-hop reasoning problems. The full IteraTri framework, integrating both iteration and reflection, reliably recovers and exceeds the performance of the ablated variants, demonstrating the synergistic effect of its designed components.

(The ablation study directly answers RQ2, the contribution of both the iterative extraction and knowledge reflection components to IteraTris overall performance.)

The threshold τ directly controls the framework's strictness in judging an answer as *Factual*. To determine its value, we conducted a cross-dataset sensitivity analysis on FactCHD, PathQuestion, and MetaQA, using the Gemma3-12B backbone. As shown in Fig. 2, accuracy improves consistently across all three datasets as τ increases from 0.6 to 0.8, indicating that requiring a higher proportion of verified triplets leads to more reliable judgments. Beyond $\tau = 0.8$, however, accuracy plateaus or begins to decrease slightly on all datasets, suggesting that an overly strict threshold may discard correct answers supported by largely valid but partially incomplete evidence chains. This consistent trend across different datasets confirms that $\tau = 0.8$ provides a robust and generalizable trade-off. Therefore, we select $\tau = 0.8$ as the optimal trade-off point for our experiments.

5 Limitations

While IteraTri achieves strong results on the evaluated benchmarks, several inherent limitations should be acknowledged.

Dependence on KG coverage. The verification module assumes that the target KG contains the necessary facts. For our datasets (FactCHD, PathQuestion, MetaQA), the associated KGs provide sufficient coverage; however, for domains with incomplete or rapidly evolving knowledge(e.g., newly released movies or recent events), false negatives may increase. This is an intrinsic limitation of any KGgrounded approach.

Computational cost. The iterative multiround process introduces higher latency than singlepass methods. In our offline evaluation setting this overhead is acceptable, but it currently limits deployment in latencysensitive applications. This tradeoff is a direct consequence of prioritizing verification depth over speed.

Reflection sensitivity. The condensation step relies on a single LLM call to identify relevant triplets. While we observe that the reflection agent consistently produces coherent evidence chains (as evidenced by the ablation study), occasional overfiltering or underfiltering can occur. This sensitivity is inherent to the use of a zeroshot LLM for semantic filtering.

6 Conclusion

We present **IteraTri**, a framework for hallucination detection in knowledge-intensive QA by iteratively acquiring and verifying structured knowledge triplets. Its three-stage pipelineiterative extraction, knowledge reflection, and KG-grounded verificationproduces explainable factuality judgments with full traceability. Extensive experiments on multiple benchmarks demonstrate that IteraTri consistently outperforms strong baselines in detection accuracy, while providing transparent reasoning chains.

Future Work. To extend IteraTris applicability, in the future we can incorporate multi-source verification (e.g., textual corpora, live APIs) to reduce reliance on a single KG, explore efficient prompting strategies to lower latency, and investigate learning-based relevance scoring to further improve reflection robustness. We believe that triplet-driven, verifiable reasoning opens a promising path toward more reliable and auditable LLMs for knowledge-intensive tasks.

Acknowledgments. This work was supported by National Natural Science Foundation of China under Grant 62372145, Natural Science Foundation of Zhejiang Province under Grant LZ25F020011, and Key Research and Development Program of Zhejiang Province under Grant 2025C01129. The authors would also like to thank the anonymous reviewers for their insightful comments.

References

1. Jason, W., Yi, T., Rishi, B.: Emergent abilities of large language models. Trans Mach Learn Res (2022)
2. Maynez, J., Narayan, S., et al.: On faithfulness and factuality in abstractive summarization. In Proceedings of the 58th Annual Meeting of the Association for Computational Linguistics, pp. 1906–1919, Online. Association for Computational Linguistics (2020)
3. Martindale, M., Carpuat, M., et al.: Identifying fluently inadequate output in neural and statistical machine translation. In: Proceedings of Machine Translation Summit XVII: Research Track, pp. 233–243, Dublin, Ireland (2019)
4. Ji, Z., Lee, N, Frieske, R., et al.: Survey of hallucination in natural language generation. ACM Comput Surv **55**(12), 1–38.653 (2023)
5. Yuxuan, X., et al.: Reasoning path generation for answering multi-hop questions over knowledge graph. In: Asia-Pacific Web (APWeb) and Web-Age Information Management (WAIM) Joint International Conference on Web and Big Data, pp. 195-209. Springer Nature Switzerland, Cham (2022)
6. Zhang, Y., Gibson, E., Davis, F.: Can language models be tricked by language illusions? Easier with syntax, harder with semantics. In: Proceedings of the 27th Conference on Computational Natural Language Learning (CoNLL), pp. 1–14, Singapore (2023)
7. Zhang, Y., Li, Y., Cui, L., et al.: Siren's song in the ai ocean: a survey on hallucination in large language models. Comput. Linguist. **51**(1), 1–45 (2025)
8. Rawte, V, Chakraborty, S., Pathak, A., et al.: The troubling emergence of hallucination in large language models—an extensive definition, quantification, and prescriptive remediations. In: Proceedings of the 2023 Conference on Empirical Methods in Natural Language Processing, pp. 2541–2573, Singapore (2023)

9. Gao, L., Dai, Z., Pasupat, P., et al.: Rarr: researching and revising what language models say, using language models. In: Proceedings of the 61st Annual Meeting of the Association for Computational Linguistics, vol. 1, pp. 16477–16508, Toronto, Canada (2023)
10. Chen, Y., Liu, H., Liu, Y., et al.: GraphCheck: breaking long-term text barriers with extracted knowledge graph-powered fact-checking. In: Proceedings of the 63rd Annual Meeting of the Association for Computational Linguistics (Volume 1: Long Papers), pp. 14976–14995, Vienna, Austria (2025)
11. Mündler, N., He, J., Jenko, S., Vechev, M.: Self-contradictory hallucinations of large language models: evaluation, detection and mitigation. In: The Twelfth International Conference on Learning Representations (2024)
12. Manakul, P., Liusie, A., Gales, M.: SelfcheckGPT: zero-resource black-box hallucination detection for generative large language models. In: The 2023 Conference on Empirical Methods in Natural Language Processing, Singapore (2023)
13. Yehuda, Y., Malkiel, I., Barkan, O., et al.: InterrogateLLM: zero-resource hallucination detection in LLM-generated answers. In: Proceedings of the 62nd Annual Meeting of the Association for Computational Linguistics, pp. 9333–9347, Bangkok, Thailand (2024)
14. Chen, X., Song, D., Gui, H., et al.: Factchd: benchmarking fact-conflicting hallucination detection. In: IJCAI, pp. 6216–6224. Jeju, South Korea (2024)
15. Ruize, A., et al.: Retrieval-based knowledge consistency validation for fake news detection. In: Asia-Pacific Web (APWeb) and Web-Age Information Management (WAIM) Joint International Conference on Web and Big Data, pp. 436-451. Springer Nature Singapore, Singapore (2025)
16. Guu, K., Lee, K., Tung, Z., et al.: Retrieval augmented language model pre-training. In Proceedings of the 37th International Conference on Machine Learning, pp. 3929–3938. Virtual (2020)
17. Vedula, N., Parthasarathy, S.: Face-keg: fact checking explained using knowledge graphs. In: Proceedings of the 14th ACM International Conference on Web Search and Data Mining, pp. 526–534 (2021)
18. Zhou, M., Huang, M., Zhu, X.: An interpretable reasoning network for multi-relation question answering. In: Proceedings of the 27th International Conference on Computational Linguistics, pp. 2010–2022, Santa Fe, New Mexico, USA (2018)
19. Puerto, H., Ahin, G., Gurevych, I.: Metaqa: combining expert agents for multi-skill question answering. In: Proceedings of the 17th Conference of the European Chapter of the Association for Computational Linguistics, pp. 3566–3580 (2023)
20. Team, G., Kamath, A., Ferret, J., Pathak, S.: Gemma 3 technical report (2025). arXiv:2503.19786 Preprint
21. Grattafiori, A., Dubey, A., Jauhri, A.: The llama 3 herd of models (2024). arXiv:2407.21783 Preprint
22. Yang, A., Li, A., Yang, B., et al.: Qwen3 technical report. arXiv preprint (2025)
23. Wei, J., Wang, X., et al.: Chain-of-thought prompting elicits reasoning in large language models. In: Advances in Neural Information Processing Systems, vol. 35, pp. 24824–24837. Inc, Curran Associates (2022)

Recommendation Systems

CARE: Cross-Domain Agent-Routed Expert Recommendation via Multi-agent Collaboration

Zi-Xuan Yuan[1], Chang-Dong Wang[2(✉)], Ping-Hua Chen[1], and Jian-Huang Lai[2]

[1] School of Computer Science, Guangdong University of Technology, Guangzhou, China
3878351848@mails.gdut.edu.cn, phchen@gdut.edu.cn

[2] School of Computer Science and Engineering, Sun Yat-sen University, Guangzhou, China
changdongwang@hotmail.com, stsljh@mail.sysu.edu.cn

Abstract. Cross-domain recommendation leverages multi-domain knowledge to alleviate data sparsity and cold-start issues in single-domain recommendation. Existing methods largely rely on neural representation alignment across domains, while large language model (LLM)-based approaches typically use a single model for all domains and therefore fail to capture domain heterogeneity explicitly. We observe that this problem can be naturally decomposed into three sub-tasks: preference understanding, domain selection, and candidate ranking, each of which is better handled by a specialized component. Based on this observation, we propose CARE, a multi-agent framework for cross-domain recommendation. CARE consists of an Analyst that produces structured user profiles, a Router that performs dynamic domain routing, and multiple LoRA-tuned domain experts for candidate ranking. On an Amazon dataset spanning 8 product domains, CARE achieves 31.2% HR@1, outperforming LLM zero-shot ranking (10.7%) and the untuned base 7B model (24.8%). Ablation results further show that both user preference modeling and dynamic domain routing are critical to the final performance.

Keywords: Cross-domain recommendation · Multi-agent collaboration · Large language models · Domain expert routing

1 Introduction

Recommender systems are a core technology in modern e-commerce, where the goal is to predict items a user is likely to prefer from historical behavior. As product ecosystems continue to expand, user behavior increasingly exhibits cross-domain structure: purchases in books, electronics, and household goods often reflect shared latent preferences. Traditional recommender systems, however, are usually built for a single domain and rely only on within-domain interaction

L. Ding et al. (Eds.): APWeb-WAIM 2026, LNCS 16993, pp. 395–410, 2027.
https://doi.org/10.1007/978-981-92-5693-8_25

data. As a result, they suffer from two persistent challenges: data sparsity, where each user has only a limited number of interactions in any given domain, and cold start, where the system has insufficient history when a user enters a new domain. Cross-Domain Recommendation (CDR) addresses these challenges by transferring information across domains and has therefore attracted substantial recent attention [3,9,11,15,18,23].

Existing CDR methods can be broadly grouped into three categories. The first includes representation-learning approaches that transfer information across domains through sequential modeling, collaborative filtering constraints, or heterogeneous graph integration, as exemplified by MAN, CUT, and HAGO [9,11,23]. The second includes LLM-based and foundation-style recommenders [5,6,17,24], which leverage semantic modeling to reduce reliance on collaborative signals. The third includes multi-agent methods, such as AgentCF [22] and MACRec [19]; recent surveys and benchmarks further document this trend [14,16]. Despite their differences, these methods share a common limitation: they do not explicitly model domain heterogeneity or dynamically select domain-specific knowledge. Representation-learning methods still depend on a unified transfer mechanism across domains; LLM-based methods use a single parameter space to process all domains; and existing multi-agent methods mainly target single-domain recommendation, without domain-aware routing or expert specialization for cross-domain settings. In practice, domains differ substantially in item characteristics, user decision logic, and interaction patterns. Users may focus on authors and topics when purchasing books, but prioritize brands and technical specifications when purchasing electronics. Existing approaches therefore struggle to produce genuinely differentiated recommendation strategies across domains.

To address these limitations, we revisit cross-domain recommendation from a task-decomposition perspective. We argue that it is not an indivisible end-to-end decision problem, but can be naturally decomposed into three sub-tasks. The first is preference understanding, which extracts user interests and behavioral patterns from multi-domain history. The second is domain selection, which determines which domain knowledge should be emphasized for the current recommendation instance. The third is candidate ranking, which ranks candidate items from the selected domain perspective. These sub-tasks require different capabilities: preference understanding requires cross-domain analysis, domain selection requires semantic discrimination, and candidate ranking requires domain-specific expertise. This decomposition motivates a multi-agent design in which different agents specialize in different sub-tasks and communicate through structured intermediate representations, rather than through a loosely coupled pipeline.

Based on this idea, we propose Cross-domain Agent-Routed Expert recommendation (CARE). CARE consists of three collaborative agents: an Analyst that summarizes users' multi-domain purchase histories into structured profiles, a Router that performs dynamic domain routing based on candidate semantics and user profiles, and a set of LoRA-tuned domain experts that produce the final ranking within their respective domains. On an Amazon dataset spanning 8 product domains, CARE substantially outperforms both LLM zero-shot methods and the untuned base 7B model. Ablation studies further show that user preference modeling and dynamic domain routing are both essential to the improvement.

Our main contributions are as follows:

1. We propose CARE, a multi-agent collaborative framework for cross-domain recommendation that models the task as three collaborative sub-tasks, namely preference understanding, domain selection, and domain-perspective candidate ranking, which achieves explicit modeling of domain heterogeneity.
2. We design an Analyst-Router-Expert three-stage collaboration mechanism, where Analyst and Router are implemented via LLM for cross-domain analysis and routing, and domain experts achieve differentiated candidate ranking through LoRA fine-tuning.
3. Through systematic comparative experiments, ablation studies, and routing behavior analysis, we reveal the critical roles of dynamic domain routing and user preference modeling in cross-domain recommendation, and analyze the relationship between routing accuracy and recommendation performance.

2 Related Work

2.1 Cross-Domain Recommendation

Cross-domain recommendation aims to transfer user preference information across domains to alleviate sparsity and cold start. Representative recent work spans sequential cross-domain modeling, target-aware collaborative filtering, heterogeneous graph integration, and language-model-based transfer [3,9,11,15,18,23]. Despite these differences, most methods still treat cross-domain transfer primarily as representation alignment or knowledge sharing, and therefore provide limited support for dynamically selecting domain-specific knowledge at recommendation time.

2.2 LLM-Based Recommendation

LLM-based recommendation typically uses large language models either as end-to-end recommenders or as semantic augmentation modules [2,10,17]. Representative recent studies include foundation-style recommenders such as Universal Recommendation Learners, RecLM, and RecBase, as well as contextual adaptation for conversational recommendation [5,6,8,24]. Recent work has also extended LLMs to cross-domain recommendation through prompting, memory, and transfer-oriented designs [1,12]. However, most of these approaches still rely on a single model space to serve multiple domains, which weakens explicit modeling of domain-specific decision logic.

2.3 Multi-agent Recommender Systems

Multi-agent systems have recently been introduced into recommendation to decompose complex workflows across specialized agents [14]. Representative work includes AgentCF and MACRec, which demonstrate the potential of agent-based recommendation pipelines [19,22]. More recent studies focus on agentic recommendation design and evaluation, such as iAgent, AgentRecBench, and RecZero [7,16,20]. These studies illustrate the promise of agent-based decomposition, but they are still largely designed for single-domain settings and do not explicitly address domain-aware routing or expert specialization for cross-domain recommendation.

3 The Proposed CARE Method

3.1 Problem Definition

Let $\mathcal{D} = \{d^{(1)}, d^{(2)}, \ldots, d^{(M)}\}$ be a set of M product domains. For user u, the purchase history is a time-ordered sequence $H_u = [(i_1, z_1, \mathbf{a}_1), \ldots, (i_n, z_n, \mathbf{a}_n)]$, where i_t is the item identifier, $z_t \in \mathcal{D}$ is the domain of the item, and $\mathbf{a}_t$ represents the item's structured and textual metadata (title, category, price, brand, etc.). Given a candidate set $C = \{c_1, c_2, \ldots, c_K\}$ containing K items, where each candidate $c_j = (i^c_j, z^c_j, \mathbf{a}^c_j)$ includes an item identifier, domain label, and metadata, and candidates come from multiple domains (i.e., $\{z^c_j\}_{j=1}^K$ need not be identical). The target item is $c^* \in C$, with its ground-truth domain label denoted as $d^{\text{gt}} = z^c_{c^*}$.

The task studied in this paper is **mixed-domain candidate ranking**: given H_u and C, identify c^* from C. Unlike traditional single-domain recommendation, the candidate set spans multiple domains, requiring the model to possess both cross-domain preference understanding and domain-specific ranking capabilities.

We decompose this task into two sub-problems:

- **Domain routing**: Predict the most likely domain $\hat{d}$ of the target item, formulated as a classification problem over H_u and C: $\hat{d} = \arg\max_{d \in \mathcal{D}_C} P(d \mid H_u, C)$, where $\mathcal{D}_C \subseteq \mathcal{D}$ is the subset of domains present in the candidate set. Routing is correct if and only if $\hat{d} = d^{\text{gt}}$.
- **Domain-perspective candidate ranking**: Guided by the routing result $\hat{d}$, rank items in C such that c^* is ranked as high as possible.

The primary evaluation metric is top-1 hit rate HR@1 $= P(\hat{y}_1 = c^*)$, where $\hat{y}_1$ is the top-ranked item. Since the Router is a non-differentiable LLM inference module, the system adopts staged construction rather than joint optimization: only domain experts are trained via supervised fine-tuning, while Analyst and Router operate as fixed LLM inference modules.

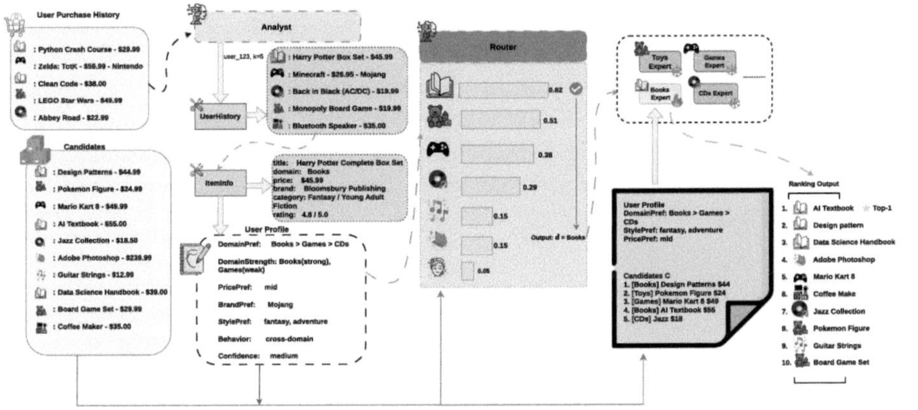

Fig. 1. Overview of the CARE framework. The Analyst generates structured profiles from user history, the Router performs domain routing based on profiles and candidates, and the selected domain expert completes the final ranking.

3.2 Framework Overview

The CARE framework completes the above task through three collaborative agents in sequence, as illustrated in Fig. 1.

Stage 1: Preference Modeling. The Analyst agent compresses user history H_u into a structured profile P_u, providing a compact user representation for downstream modules:

$$P_u = f_{\text{Analyst}}(H_u) \tag{1}$$

Stage 2: Domain Routing. The Router agent predicts the target domain based on profile P_u and candidate set C:

$$\hat{d} = f_{\text{Router}}(P_u, C), \quad \hat{d} \in \mathcal{D}_C \tag{2}$$

The Router directly outputs a domain label through LLM semantic reasoning, rather than explicitly computing probability distributions over domains.

Stage 3: Domain-Perspective Candidate Ranking. The selected domain expert $f_{\text{Expert}}^{(\hat{d})}$ outputs the ranking of candidate items:

$$\hat{\mathbf{y}} = f_{\text{Expert}}^{(\hat{d})}(P_u, C) \tag{3}$$

where $\hat{\mathbf{y}} = [\hat{y}_1, \hat{y}_2, \ldots, \hat{y}_K]$ is the ranked list of candidates. Note that the Expert receives the complete candidate set C rather than only the target domain subset, but ranks items from the perspective of domain $\hat{d}$'s decision logic.

The rationale for this decomposition is that the three sub-tasks require different capabilities: preference modeling requires cross-domain analysis, domain routing requires semantic discrimination, and candidate ranking requires domain-specific knowledge. Specialized modules therefore better match the underlying capability structure than a single end-to-end model with one shared decision process. Moreover, the Analyst compresses raw interaction history into a compact structured representation P_u. Since both the Router and the Expert take P_u rather than raw history H_u as input, the profile must preserve the preference information from H_u that is relevant to both routing and ranking, while reducing unnecessary redundancy. In this sense, P_u is not only a memory summary but also a shared interface that keeps downstream decisions grounded in the same user evidence.

3.3 Analyst Agent: Preference Modeling

The Analyst compresses the variable-length user history sequence H_u into a fixed-format structured profile P_u, which serves as a unified user representation for both the Router and the Expert.

Profile Schema. Profile P_u contains seven fields, each serving specific downstream decision needs.

Table 1. User profile schema and downstream usage

Field	Value space	Primary consumer
DomainPref	Ranked domain list	Router
DomainStrength	{Strong, medium, weak}/domain	Router
PricePref	{Low, mid, high, mixed}	Router + expert
BrandPref	Brand list or unknown	Router + expert
StylePref	Theme tags	Router + expert
Behavior	Behavioral pattern description	Router + expert
Confidence	{High, medium, low}	Router

DomainPref and DomainStrength provide the primary signals for routing, while price, brand, style, and behavior support both routing and downstream ranking. We implement the Analyst with Qwen-Plus in tool-use mode: it first reads the interaction sequence, then selectively queries metadata for historically interacted items when the history alone is insufficient to infer domain preference or consumption style, and finally produces a fixed-format profile that follows Table 1. The Analyst never accesses the candidate set C, thereby avoiding information leakage between preference summarization and final ranking. During training, the resulting profiles are cached and reused by all downstream modules; during inference, the same schema is generated online for each test user.

This structured profile forms the key interface between cross-domain preference understanding and downstream decision modules. For the Router, it converts sparse and heterogeneous user histories into compact domain-level evidence, making domain selection less sensitive to the raw order and length of user records. For the Expert, the same profile serves as a normalized preference summary that highlights price range, brand tendencies, and behavioral style cues relevant to fine-grained ranking within a routed domain. Using a shared schema also keeps the Router and Expert aligned on the same user representation, reducing inconsistencies that could arise if each module interpreted raw history independently.

In implementation, the Analyst only observes historical interactions and item metadata, and its output is constrained to a stable textual schema to simplify downstream parsing. Tool use is limited to a small number of steps so that profile generation remains efficient and focused on salient evidence rather than exhaustive retrieval. We use deterministic decoding to improve reproducibility across training and evaluation. This design makes the Analyst a lightweight preference abstraction module rather than an additional unconstrained reasoning stage. It also avoids passing long raw histories into every subsequent module, which would otherwise increase prompt length and amplify variance in downstream reasoning.

3.4 Router Agent: Domain Routing

The Router solves the domain routing sub-problem: given P_u and C, it predicts $\hat{d} \in \mathcal{D}_C$, where the ground-truth label is $d^{\text{gt}} = z^{c}_{c*}$. We use Qwen-Plus in single-turn inference mode to directly output one domain label from $\mathcal{D}_C$ rather than training a separate classifier. The prompt uses DomainPref as the primary signal and then incorporates price, brand, and style cues for candidate-profile matching; when profile confidence is low, it relies more heavily on candidate semantics. We adopt hard routing because each test instance contains a single target domain and invoking only one expert keeps inference practical. The effect of routing quality is analyzed through oracle-routing and ablation experiments.

The key motivation for using a Router rather than directly applying all experts is that domain selection in our setting depends on both user-side and candidate-side evidence. The profile captures long-range cross-domain preferences, while the candidate set provides local semantic clues about the domain in which the final click or purchase is most plausible. A prompt-based Router can jointly reason over these two signals without introducing an additional supervised classifier that would require separate training data and feature engineering. More importantly, the routing decision here is not a conventional static classification problem: the same user can be routed to different domains under different candidate sets, because the relevant decision depends on the interaction between personal preference and the semantics of the current recommendation context.

The Router follows a priority order consistent with the task structure. It first considers dominant domains in DomainPref and DomainStrength, and then checks whether candidate attributes such as price, brand, and style are consistent with these preferences. When profile confidence is low, the Router shifts more weight to candidate semantics to avoid overcommitting to weak historical patterns. We adopt hard routing because each constructed candidate set has a single ground-truth domain, and scoring with one selected expert is considerably cheaper than running all experts in parallel. This choice also matches the intended deployment pattern of CARE, in which the system makes one domain decision and then commits to the corresponding domain perspective for final ranking. Oracle routing in the experiments isolates the contribution of routing quality and provides an upper bound on downstream ranking under correct domain selection.

3.5 Domain Expert: Domain-Perspective Candidate Ranking

Domain experts rank candidate items from the perspective of the routed domain. Each expert is built from Qwen2.5-7B-Instruct [21] with LoRA [4] and trained independently on domain-specific ranking data using an instruction-tuning format [5]. The input concatenates the user profile and the candidate list, and the output is a ranking sequence whose supervision emphasizes placing the positive item first, consistent with HR@1. This formulation turns each expert into a domain-perspective ranker: it does not merely detect whether a candidate belongs to a domain, but learns how users typically make decisions within that domain once the routing perspective has been fixed.

We inject domain-specific guidance into prompts so that each expert follows domain-relevant ranking criteria and cross-domain transfer heuristics. For example, a Books-oriented expert is encouraged to focus on topic, author, and reading-interest continuity, while an Electronics- or Appliances-oriented expert is guided to attend more to function, specification, compatibility, and brand reliability. For low-resource domains with too few training samples, we fall back to the base model rather than training a separate expert.

This design differs from a single general ranker in that each expert is expected to apply domain-specific decision logic after routing has already narrowed the perspective. For example, the ranking criteria that matter in Books, such as topic and author affinity, differ qualitatively from those in Software or Appliances, where compatibility, function, or specification cues may dominate. Training one expert per domain allows the model to specialize in these patterns without forcing all domains into a single shared ranking behavior.

Table 2. Dataset statistics.

Domain	Train	Test	Proportion (%)
Books	15,132	3814	38.1
Toys and games	13,837	3446	34.5
Video games	2912	721	7.2
CDs and vinyl	2694	661	6.6
Software	2140	559	5.6
Musical instruments	1937	455	4.5
Appliances	1174	308	3.1
All beauty	174	36	0.4
Total	40,000	10,000	100

Training and test sample counts per domain with proportions

Domain-specific guidance further sharpens this specialization by making ranking preferences explicit in prompts used during training and inference. The guidance describes both within-domain ranking signals and plausible cross-domain transfer rules, allowing the expert to use the routed domain as a perspective rather than as a hard filter on candidate membership. When a domain has very limited data, falling back to the base model avoids overfitting a weak expert while preserving full system coverage. This fallback is especially useful because it keeps the framework extensible to new or sparse domains without forcing every domain to have enough data for a separately tuned expert.

3.6 Training and Inference Pipeline

CARE adopts a staged pipeline. During training, we first generate and cache user profiles, then split data by domain and fine-tune each expert separately, while the Router remains a fixed LLM module. During inference, CARE executes the Analyst, the Router, and the selected Expert in sequence. This design keeps the three components decoupled and makes it straightforward to extend the system to new domains by adding experts and the corresponding routing labels. The full workflow therefore follows a stable three-step order: profile generation, domain routing, and selected-expert ranking.

The staged design is important for both practicality and modularity. During training, cached profiles allow all domain experts to learn from a consistent user representation without repeatedly invoking the Analyst. During inference, the three-step sequence is fixed: the Analyst summarizes user history into P_u, the Router predicts the most likely target domain from P_u and C, and the selected Expert outputs the final ranking. This separation makes it possible to replace or improve one component without retraining the entire system, and it provides a natural path for adding new domains by expanding the routing label space and training only the corresponding expert. It also keeps the responsibilities of preference abstraction, domain selection, and ranking clearly separated, which makes CARE easier to analyze through ablations and easier to maintain as a modular recommendation pipeline.

4 Experiments

4.1 Experimental Setup

Dataset. We construct a cross-domain recommendation benchmark using the Amazon Review dataset [13]. The dataset contains real purchase records and review information from users on the Amazon platform, spanning multiple product domains. We select 8 domains: Books, Toys and Games, Video Games, Musical Instruments, CDs and Vinyl, All Beauty, Appliances, and Software.

The data construction process is as follows: for each user, the most recent purchase is selected as the target item c^*, with the remaining history serving as input H_u. The candidate set C contains 10 items: c^* and 9 negative samples, of which 4 share the same domain as c^* and 5 come from other domains.

This construction results in candidate sets averaging approximately 6 different domains, increasing recommendation difficulty. Table 2 presents detailed dataset statistics.

The dataset exhibits a pronounced long-tail distribution: Books and Toys and Games together account for over 70% of samples, while All Beauty comprises only 0.4%. This distribution poses additional challenges for cross-domain recommendation: the model must balance between data-rich head domains and data-scarce tail domains.

Figure 2 shows a heatmap of users' cross-domain purchasing behavior. Users' purchases indeed span multiple domains, with significant variation in association strength between different domains, further validating the necessity of introducing domain-aware routing mechanisms.

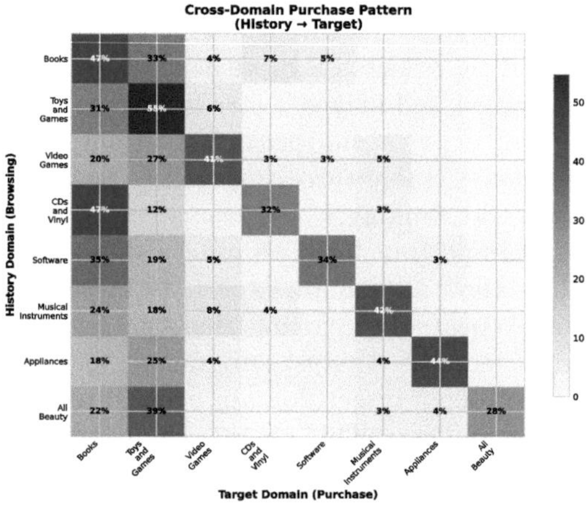

Fig. 2. Heatmap of cross-domain purchasing behavior. Color intensity represents the frequency of users purchasing target domain (horizontal axis) items from source domain (vertical axis).

Evaluation Metrics. We adopt the following metrics to evaluate recommendation performance: **HR@K** (Hit Rate at K), which measures whether the target item appears in the top-K positions of the ranking result for $K \in \{1, 3, 5\}$, and **Router Accuracy**, which measures the consistency between the Router's predicted domain label and the target item's true domain. HR@1 is the primary evaluation metric because it directly reflects the model's ability to identify the target item.

Baselines. We compare CARE with two groups of baselines. **Random** randomly orders candidate items and serves as a lower bound. **Pop** ranks items by their frequency in the training set and reflects a popularity-based heuristic baseline. We also construct several controlled LLM-based variants for our task setting. **LLM Zero-shot** directly uses Qwen-Plus to rank candidates without user profiles, testing general LLM zero-shot recommendation capability. **LLM +**

Profile augments the zero-shot setting with Analyst-generated user profiles to test the benefit of structured preference information. **Base 7B** uses Qwen2.5-7B-Instruct [21] to directly rank candidates without LoRA fine-tuning, testing the capability of the untuned base model. **CARE (Oracle)** replaces the Router's prediction with the target item's ground-truth domain label d^{gt} while keeping all other components unchanged, thereby serving as an upper bound that removes routing error.

Note that we do not include traditional CDR methods (e.g., EMCDR, CoNet, PPGN) in the baseline comparison. This is due to fundamental differences in task settings: traditional CDR methods typically target source-to-target domain rating prediction or single-domain ranking tasks relying on overlapping user embedding alignment, while our work studies mixed-domain candidate ranking with multi-domain candidate sets using natural language text as input. The two task types are incompatible in input format, candidate construction, and evaluation protocol, precluding fair direct comparison. We therefore select baselines covering different capability levels: Random and Pop as statistical baselines, LLM Zero-shot and LLM + Profile testing general LLM capability, and Base 7B testing unfine-tuned 7B model capability.

Implementation Details. Analyst and Router both use Qwen-Plus as the backbone language model with temperature set to 0. Domain experts are based on Qwen2.5-7B-Instruct [21], with LoRA [4] fine-tuning accelerated by the Unsloth framework, trained on a single NVIDIA RTX PRO 6000 Blackwell (96GB). Training time per domain expert ranges from 10–30 minutes depending on data volume. All experiments involving Expert training use 5 different random seeds, reporting mean and standard deviation.

4.2 Comparison Results

Table 3. Comparison results (mean ± std over 5 runs).

Method	HR@1 (%)	HR@3 (%)	HR@5 (%)
Random	9.8	29.7	49.6
Pop	16.9	35.1	53.0
LLM zero-shot	10.7	28.4	46.8
LLM + profile	11.2	31.0	50.9
Base 7B	<u>24.8</u>	<u>49.7</u>	<u>65.2</u>
CARE (oracle)	33.4 ± 0.6	60.1 ± 0.4	76.0 ± 0.3
CARE	**31.2 ± 0.7**	**57.3 ± 0.5**	**72.4 ± 0.4**

Best baseline results are underlined, and CARE results are shown in bold

Table 3 presents the recommendation performance of all methods on the test set. We draw four main observations. First, CARE outperforms all non-oracle baselines, indicating that the proposed multi-agent decomposition provides clear advantages over both simple heuristics and single-model baselines in our task setting. Second, LLM Zero-shot performs only slightly above random ranking, suggesting that general-purpose LLMs still struggle to solve mixed-domain recommendation without task-specific adaptation [17]. Third, adding user profiles to a zero-shot LLM brings only limited gains, which suggests that structured profiles are more effectively utilized by domain experts than by a general LLM used directly as the ranker. Finally, the remaining gap between CARE and CARE (Oracle) is relatively small, indicating that the Router captures most of the domain-selection signal under the current candidate construction protocol.

4.3 Ablation Study

To verify the contribution of each CARE component, we design the following ablation experiments: **w/o Analyst**, which removes the Analyst component and lets the Expert rank directly from raw user history without profiles; **w/o Router**, which removes the Router and uses a randomly selected domain expert for ranking; and **Rule Router**, which replaces the LLM Router with a simple rule-based strategy that directly selects the top-ranked domain from DomainPref in the user profile (Table 4).

Table 4. Ablation results (mean±std over 5 runs).

Configuration	HR@1 (%)	HR@3 (%)	HR@5 (%)	Δ HR@1 (%)
CARE (full)	31.2 ± 0.7	57.3 ± 0.5	72.4 ± 0.4	–
Rule router	27.2 ± 0.8	66.6 ± 0.6	79.6 ± 0.5	−4.0
W/O analyst	23.2 ± 0.9	57.3 ± 0.6	79.4 ± 0.5	−8.0
W/O router	22.4 ± 1.1	56.0 ± 0.8	77.0 ± 0.6	−8.8

Δ denotes HR@1 change relative to the full model

The ablation results reveal four findings. First, removing Analyst substantially degrades HR@1, showing that structured profiles provide essential user-preference information for downstream ranking. Second, removing Router leads to the largest decline, which confirms the critical role of domain-aware routing in cross-domain recommendation. Third, Rule Router performs better than random expert selection but remains clearly worse than the LLM Router, indicating that semantic routing benefits from using both user profiles and candidate-item information rather than relying only on historical domain preference. Finally, although the weakened variants can still maintain relatively high HR@5, their top-1 performance declines noticeably, suggesting that Analyst and Router primarily improve top-position precision rather than broad recall.

4.4 Router Analysis

To gain deeper understanding of Router's behavioral characteristics, we analyze its routing decisions from the CARE main experiment, examining routing accuracy and misclassification patterns. Table 5 presents per-domain routing accuracy. This analysis is based on 2000 randomly sampled test instances. Routing accuracy shows a loose tendency to be higher in data-rich domains: for example, Toys and Games and Video Games achieve 86 and 79% routing accuracy, respectively, while low-resource domains such as Appliances reach only 26%. All Beauty has relatively few test samples (52), so its routing accuracy and recommendation performance have limited statistical stability. Notably, Books, despite being the largest domain, achieves only 59% routing accuracy, possibly due to its high thematic diversity leading to semantic overlap with other domains.

Table 5. Per-domain routing accuracy and recommendation performance

Domain	Routing acc. (%)	HR@1 (%)	Test samples
Toys and games	86	22.5	690
Video games	79	26.3	144
Musical instruments	76	24.0	90
CDs and vinyl	72	25.0	132
Books	59	41.1	700
Software	53	36.8	96
Appliances	26	21.1	96
All beauty	12	23.0	52

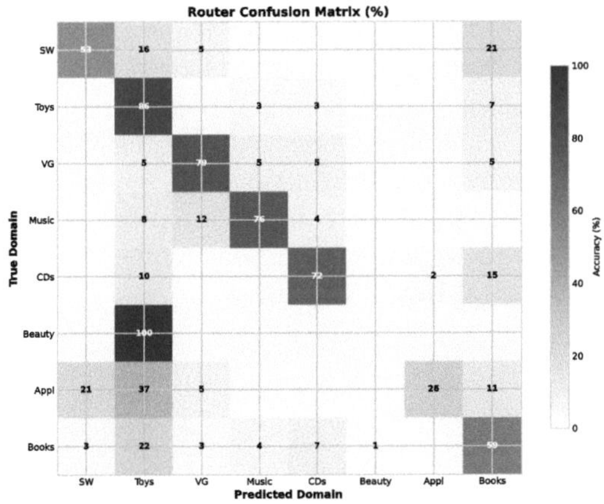

Fig. 3. Router confusion matrix. Diagonal entries represent correct routing proportions; color intensity is proportional to values.

Figure 3 shows Router's confusion matrix (axes use domain abbreviations: SW = Software, Toys = Toys and Games, VG = Video Games, Music = Musical Instruments, CDs = CDs and Vinyl, Beauty = All Beauty, Appl = Appliances). Key misclassification patterns include: (1) Toys and Games is the most common misclassification target, with samples from multiple domains incorrectly routed there, possibly due to its large proportion in training data; (2) Books and Software exhibit mutual misclassification, possibly because both contain technical and educational products. An interesting finding is that routing accuracy and HR@1 are not simply positively correlated. For example, Books has lower routing accuracy (59%) than Toys and Games (86%), yet achieves notably higher HR@1 (41.1%). This suggests that recommendation performance depends not only on routing correctness but also on the domain expert's intrinsic ranking capability. Books items typically have richer descriptions (including author, genre, theme, etc.), providing Expert with more exploitable ranking signals.

5 Conclusion

This paper proposes CARE, a multi-agent collaborative framework for cross-domain recommendation. CARE decomposes the task into preference modeling, domain routing, and domain-perspective candidate ranking, and assigns these sub-tasks to an Analyst, a Router, and domain-specific Experts, respectively. This design enables explicit modeling of domain heterogeneity while preserving modularity across components.

Experimental results show that CARE consistently outperforms general LLM baselines and the untuned base 7B model in our mixed-domain candidate ranking setting. Ablation studies further confirm that both preference modeling and dynamic domain routing are necessary for the framework, while router analysis indicates that final recommendation quality depends on both correct routing and the intrinsic ranking capability of domain experts.

Future work will explore the following directions: (1) investigating learnable routing mechanisms, such as contrastive learning-based domain classifiers, to replace the current prompt-driven routing; (2) studying multi-expert fusion strategies, such as top-k routing, to accommodate more open multi-domain candidate scenarios; (3) introducing knowledge sharing mechanisms between experts to alleviate data insufficiency in tail domains.

References

1. Liu, J., et al.: AgentCF++: Memory-enhanced LLM-based agents for popularity-aware cross-domain recommendations (2025). arXiv:2502.13843
2. Elmoghazy, S.S., Shouman, M.A., Elminir, H.K., Selim, G.E.I.: Comparative analysis of methodologies and approaches in recommender systems utilizing large language models. Artif. Intell. Rev. **58**, 207 (2025). https://doi.org/10.1007/s10462-025-11189-8

3. Hadad, G., Roitman, H., Eshel, Y., Shapira, B., Rokach, L.: X-cross: dynamic integration of language models for cross-domain sequential recommendation. In: SIGIR, pp. 1497–1507 (2025)
4. Hu, E.J., Shen, Y., Wallis, P., Allen-Zhu, Z., Li, Y., Wang, S., Wang, L., Chen, W.: LoRA: low-rank adaptation of large language models. In: ICLR (2022)
5. Jiang, Y., Yang, Y., Xia, L., Luo, D., Lin, K., Huang, C.: RecLM: Recommendation instruction tuning. In: Proceedings of the 63rd Annual Meeting of the Association for Computational Linguistics, pp. 15443–15459 (2025). https://doi.org/10.18653/v1/2025.acl-long.751
6. Jiang, J., Huang, Y., Liu, B., Kong, X., Xu, Z., Zhu, H., Xu, J., Zheng, B.: Large language models are universal recommendation learners. CoRR (2025)
7. Kong, X., Jiang, J., Liu, B., Xu, Z., Zhu, H., Xu, J., Zheng, B., Wu, J., Wang, X.: Think before recommendation: autonomous reasoning-enhanced recommender. In: NeurIPS (2025)
8. Li, C., Deng, Y., Hu, H., Ng, S.K., Kan, M.Y., Li, H.: CARE: contextual adaptation of recommenders for LLM-based conversational recommendation. CoRR (2025)
9. Li, H., et al.: Aiming at the Target: Filter collaborative information for cross-domain recommendation. In: SIGIR, pp. 794–803 (2024). https://doi.org/10.1145/3626772.3657713
10. Li, L., Zhang, Y., Liu, D., Chen, L.: Large Language Models for Generative Recommendation: A Survey and Visionary Discussions. In: Proceedings of the 2024 Joint International Conference on Computational Linguistics, Language Resources and Evaluation (LREC-COLING 2024), pp. 10146–10159 (2024). https://doi.org/10.63317/4pmv5q3r3yc5
11. Lin, G., et al.: Mixed Attention Network for Cross-domain Sequential Recommendation. In: WSDM, pp. 450–458 (2024). https://doi.org/10.1145/3616855.3635801
12. Liu, Q., Zhu, J., Lai, Y., Dong, X., Fan, L., Bian, Z., Dong, Z., Wu, X.M.: Assessing large language models (LLMs) as foundational recommenders: a multi-domain, multi-dataset benchmark. In: OpenReview (2025)
13. McAuley, J., Targett, C., Shi, Q., Van Den Hengel, A.: Image-based recommendations on styles and substitutes. In: SIGIR, pp. 43–52 (2015)
14. Peng, Q., Liu, H., Huang, H., Yang, J., Yang, Q., Shao, M.: A survey on llm-powered agents for recommender systems. In: EMNLP Findings, pp. 11574–11583 (2025)
15. Rahmatikargar, B., Khan, A.R., Zadeh, P.M., Kobti, Z.: Cross-domain recommendation: leveraging semantic alignment and user clustering to address data sparsity. Proced. Comput. Sci. **257**, 706–713 (2025). https://doi.org/10.1016/j.procs.2025.03.091
16. Shang, Y., Liu, P., Yan, Y., Wu, Z., Sheng, L., Yu, Y., Jiang, C., Zhang, A., Xu, F., Wang, Y., Zhang, M., Li, Y.: AgentRecBench: benchmarking LLM agent-based personalized recommender systems. In: NeurIPS D&B, Spotlight (2025)
17. Shehmir, S., Kashef, R.: LLM4Rec: a comprehensive survey on the integration of large language models in recommender systems—approaches, applications and challenges. Fut. Internet **17**(6), 252 (2025). https://doi.org/10.3390/fi17060252
18. Shyam, A., Kamani, R., Kagita, V.R., Kumar, V.: Cross-domain recommender systems via multimodal domain adaptation. Comput. Electr. Eng. **123**, 110300 (2025). https://doi.org/10.1016/j.compeleceng.2025.110300
19. Wang, Z., Yu, Y., Zheng, W., Ma, W., Zhang, M.: MACRec: A Multi-Agent Collaboration Framework for Recommendation. In: SIGIR, pp. 2760–2764 (2024). https://doi.org/10.1145/3626772.3657669

20. Xu, W., Shi, Y., Liang, Z., Ning, X., Mei, K., Wang, K., Zhu, X., Xu, M., Zhang, Y.: Iagent: LLM agent as a shield between user and recommender systems. In: ACL Findings, pp. 18056–18084 (2025). https://doi.org/10.18653/v1/2025.findings-acl.928
21. Yang, A., Yang, B., Zhang, B., Hui, B., Zheng, B., Yu, B., Li, C., Liu, D., Huang, F., Wei, H., et al.: Qwen2.5 Technical Report. arXiv:2412.15115 (2024)
22. Zhang, J., Hou, Y., Xie, R., Sun, W., McAuley, J., Zhao, W.X., Lin, L., Wen, J.R.: AgentCF: collaborative learning with autonomous language agents for recommender systems. In: WWW, pp. 3679–3689 (2024)
23. Zhang, H., et al.: Adaptive Graph Integration for Cross-domain Recommendation via Heterogeneous Graph Coordinators. In: SIGIR, pp. 1860–1869 (2025). https://doi.org/10.1145/3726302.3729886.
24. Zhou, S., Gan, W., Liu, Q., Lei, K., Zhu, J., Huang, H., Xia, Y., Tang, R., Dong, Z., Zhao, Z.: RecBase: generative foundation model pretraining for zero-shot recommendation. In: EMNLP, pp, 15587–15599 (2025). https://doi.org/10.18653/v1/2025.emnlp-main.786

Cross-Behavior Knowledge Modeling Based on Mixture-of-Experts for Multi-behavior Recommendation

Yan Wang, Shaoqing Wang(✉), Han Wang, Dongjie Yang, Lexin Han, and Fuzhen Sun

School of computer science and technology, Shandong University of Technology, Zibo 255049, Shandong, China
0816wangyan@gmail.com, {wsq0533,19811737215,hanlx2001}@163.com, wanghan011216@gmail.com, sunfuzhen@sdut.edu.cn

Abstract. Multi-behavior recommendation leverages multiple auxiliary user-item interactions to enhance target behavior prediction. Existing methods mainly employ graph neural networks to capture high-order interactions and utilize multi-task learning to jointly optimize prediction tasks. However, these methods often struggle to adequately model cross-behavior patterns during multi-behavior information aggregation. Moreover, current multi-task learning fails to effectively address distribution biases across behaviors and overlooks dynamic transitions in user preferences, which frequently lead to negative transfer. To overcome these limitations, we propose a novel framework named Cross-behavior Knowledge Modeling based on Mixture-of-Experts for Multi-behavior Recommendation (CKMME). Specifically, we design a Cross-behavior Cascade Graph Convolution Network (CCGCN) that holistically models sequential and leapfrogging behavior patterns via parallel cascading and cross-behavior chains. For target behavior prediction, we develop a Collaborative Fused Mixture-of-Experts Network (CFME) to optimize expert generation and aggregation. This network effectively mitigates feature and label distribution biases while capturing refined behavior-aware user preferences across behaviors. Experiments on three real-world datasets demonstrate that CKMME consistently outperforms state-of-the-art methods. Our code is available at https://github.com/0816wangyan-eng/CKMME.

Keywords: Multi-behavior recommendation · Multi-task learning · Graph convolution networks · Mixture-of-experts network

1 Introduction

Recommender systems aim to predict user preferences based on historical interactions [8] and have been widely applied in domains such as e-commerce [16], streaming services [15], and social platforms [24]. Although traditional collaborative filtering (CF) methods [4] remain fundamental, their reliance on a single

L. Ding et al. (Eds.): APWeb-WAIM 2026, LNCS 16993, pp. 411–426, 2027.
https://doi.org/10.1007/978-981-92-5693-8_26

dominant behavior limits recommendation performance. In real-world scenarios, user-item interactions are inherently diverse. Besides the target behavior (e.g., buy), users often exhibit multiple auxiliary behaviors (e.g., view, collect, and cart), which provide rich signals and alleviate data sparsity.

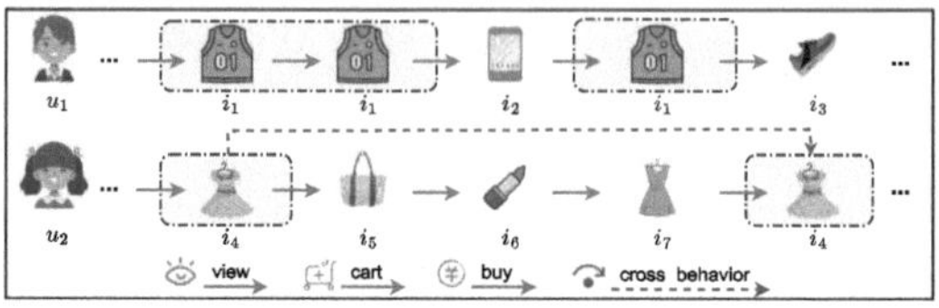

Fig. 1. Illustration of heterogeneous user-item interaction patterns. User u_1 follows a typical cascading sequence, while user u_2 exhibits a cross-behavior pattern with a direct view-to-buy transition.

To exploit heterogeneous useritem interactions, multi-behavior recommendation (MBR) has emerged as a prominent research direction. Existing MBR methods [10] enhance target behavior prediction by leveraging user preferences. Typical MBR frameworks integrate multi-behavior information aggregation with target behavior prediction [14]. The former commonly employs graph neural networks (GNNs) to model high-order dependencies in heterogeneous user-item graphs, while the latter utilizes multi-task learning (MTL) to jointly optimize multiple behavior prediction tasks.

Advances in deep neural networks [5,6], particularly GNNs [7,10], have driven significant progress in MBR. Early studies primarily rely on matrix factorization [23] to learn shared representations across behaviors. Subsequent approaches, such as MBGCN [10] and MB-HGCN [20], leverage graph structures to capture high-order useritem interactions. In practice, user behaviors often follow sequential patterns (e.g., view $\rightarrow$ add to cart $\rightarrow$ buy), where inter-behavior dependencies are critical for inferring user preferences (Fig. 1). Accordingly, CRGCN [18] introduces a residual GCN to model behavioral sequences and capture cascading dependencies. MB-CGCN [3] further incorporates feature transformation to alleviate information loss from direct residual connections. However, these methods focus on predefined cascading patterns and struggle to capture flexible behavior transitions, especially the prevalent leapfrogging behaviors in real-world scenarios (e.g., users directly leapfrog from viewing to buying).

For target behavior prediction, MTL [18,19] leverages signals from different behaviors to jointly learn multiple tasks. By sharing low-level representations, MTL alleviates data sparsity and improves generalization. To balance parameter sharing and mitigate task interference, MoE-based models have been explored. For example, MMoE [13] uses gating mechanisms to weight experts for each task. PKEF [14] incorporates PME to suppress task-irrelevant noise and negative transfer. AutoDCS [11] designs a bilateral gating mechanism to relax the rigid constraints imposed by user decision chains. Despite these advances, existing methods suffer from negative transfer and over-optimize target behavior at the expense of auxiliary behavior performance.

Although GCN-based and MTL-based multi-behavior recommendation methods have achieved progress in multi-behavior modeling and target behavior prediction, several critical challenges still remain:

(1) Insufficient modeling of cross-behavior dependencies. Existing methods either ignore inter-behavior dependencies and treat behaviors independently [10], or impose rigid cascading dependencies [3,18]. However, in reality, user behavior patterns are highly individualized and exhibit stochastic and leapfrogging transitions driven by external environmental fluctuations or internal cognitive changes (e.g., Fig. 1). Such purposeful behavior patterns cannot be adequately captured by predefined static behavioral patterns, which limits the model's ability to understand and predict true user intentions.

(2) Distribution biases in MTL [22]. At the feature level, the feature spaces of different behaviors exhibit inherent distributional heterogeneity. Although recent studies design behavior-specific learning pathways, misaligned feature distributions still lead to suboptimal aggregation of multiple expert outputs. At the label level, the data distribution between auxiliary and target behaviors is typically imbalanced, which disrupts gradient optimization in the shared parameter space and causes updates to be dominated by high-frequency auxiliary behaviors. Existing methods have not yet addressed the aforementioned biases.

(3) Inadequate modeling of user preferences. Direct knowledge transfer from auxiliary to target behaviors may introduce noise due to variations in user attention [19]. User preferences are inherently behavior-dependent. As shown in Fig. 1, user u_2 may focus on intrinsic item attributes (e.g., material) when viewing, while prioritizing external factors (e.g., price) when buying. However, most methods fail to capture refined behavior-aware preferences, relying on static shared embeddings or linear weighting for prediction. As a result, knowledge transfer lacks contextual specificity.

Motivated by these challenges, we propose a novel Cross-behavior Knowledge Modeling framework based on Mixture-of-Experts (CKMME) to address limitations in multi-behavior information aggregation and target behavior prediction. CKMME consists of the Cross-behavior Cascade Graph Convolution Network (CCGCN) and the Collaborative Fused Mixture-of-Experts Network (CFME). Specifically, CCGCN overcomes the reliance of conventional methods on sequential patterns by modeling sequential and leapfrogging behavioral dependencies via a dual-path structure with cascade and cross-behavior chains.

To mitigate negative transfer, CFME optimizes the MTL process. At the feature level, behavior-specific experts and contrastive learning align the representation spaces of multiple behaviors. To alleviate suboptimal aggregation, we design a Behavior-fused Expert to decouple effective information across behaviors via feature projection. At the label level, stop-gradient isolates interference from auxiliary behaviors in target behavior optimization and suppresses biased parameter learning. Additionally, CFME incorporates the Behavior-aware Refined Preference Network (BRPN) to refine behavior-aware preferences.

Briefly, our main contributions are as follows:

- We design a novel Cross-behavior Cascade Graph Convolution Network (CCGCN). It employs a dual-path structure integrating cascading and cross-behavior chains to holistically model sequential and leapfrogging behavior patterns, reducing over-reliance on cascading dependencies.
- We develop a Collaborative Fused Mixture-of-Experts Network (CFME), which introduces feature projection alignment and stop-gradient to jointly mitigate negative transfer in MTL at the feature and label levels, promoting effective knowledge transfer across behaviors.
- We construct a Behavior-aware Refined Preference Network (BRPN) within CFME to achieve the modeling of refined behavior-aware user preferences across behaviors and facilitate adaptive fusion of multi-expert knowledge based on behavioral context.
- Extensive experiments on three real-world datasets demonstrate that the proposed CKMME consistently outperforms existing state-of-the-art baselines, while additional results validate the effectiveness of the model.

2 Related Work

2.1 Multi-behavior Recommendation

Multi-behavior recommendation (MBR) aims to capture user preferences via heterogeneous useritem interactions, alleviating data sparsity. Early studies mainly rely on matrix factorization (MF) [23]. For instance, CMF [23] jointly decomposes multiple interaction matrices to learn user and item representations. In addition, negative sampling-based methods such as MF-BPR [12] improve optimization by designing behavior-aware sampling.

With the advancement of deep learning, deep neural networks (DNNs) and graph convolutional networks (GCNs) have become mainstream. DNN-based methods learn non-linear user and item representations. NMTR [5] models userit em interactions and sequentially propagates interaction scores. DIPN [6] learns implicit inter-behavior relationships by leveraging attention weights.

By modeling useritem interactions as heterogeneous graphs, GCN-based methods effectively aggregate high-order neighborhood information. MBGCN [10] builds independent subgraphs to learn behavior-specific representations. CRGCN [18] proposes a cascading residual GCN to capture behavior dependencies. MB-CGCN [3] adopts feature transformation to mitigate information loss. Recently, PKEF [14] uses parallel knowledge fusion to address behavioral imbalance. BCIPM [19] emphasizes target behavior information to learn item-aware user preferences. However, existing methods rely on predefined patterns and struggle to capture leapfrogging behaviors. To this end, the Cross-behavior Cascade Graph Convolution Network (CCGCN) models sequential and leapfrogging behavior patterns to alleviate over-reliance on such patterns.

2.2 Multi-task Learning

Multi-task learning (MTL) improves generalization and training efficiency by sharing representations across tasks and is widely used in MBR. Traditional MTL approaches [2] employ hard parameter sharing or regularization to learn shared representations. However, they often encounter parameter conflicts caused by task heterogeneity [18]. To address this issue, attention-based and gating-based frameworks have been proposed. For example, MoE [9] consists of multiple expert networks to capture diverse representations. MMoE [13] introduces task-specific gates to aggregate expert outputs.

Although MTL improves performance, negative transfer caused by task heterogeneity remains. For instance, PKEF [14] introduces PME to mitigate suboptimal expert aggregation and filter task-irrelevant noise. COPF [22] alleviates negative transfer by enhancing multi-expert generation and aggregation processes. Moreover, user preferences vary across behaviors. UIPL [21] aims to learn intrinsic user preferences from multiple behaviors. Existing MTL-based methods still suffer from negative transfer. Unlike previous works, the Collaborative Fused Mixture-of-Experts Network (CFME) optimizes expert generation and aggregation at the feature and label levels to mitigate distribution bias. Furthermore, the Behavior-aware Refined Preference Network (BRPN) within CFME captures refined behavior-aware preferences.

3 Problem Definition

Let $U = \{u_1, u_2, \ldots, u_{|U|}\}$ and $I = \{i_1, i_2, \ldots, i_{|I|}\}$ denote the user and item sets, respectively, where $|U|$ and $|I|$ are the numbers of users and items. Each user and item is associated with a learnable d-dimensional embedding, i.e., $\mathbf{e}_u \in \mathbb{R}^d$ and $\mathbf{e}_i \in \mathbb{R}^d$. Users interact with items via K behaviors $\{1, 2, \ldots, K\}$. Behavior-specific interactions are represented by binary adjacency matrices $\mathcal{B} = \{B_1, B_2, \ldots, B_K\}$, where $B_k = [b_{ui}^{(k)}]_{|U| \times |I|}$ and $b_{ui}^{(k)} \in \{0, 1\}$ indicates whether user u has interacted with item i under behavior k. To model heterogeneous interactions, we construct a multi-behavior bipartite graph $\mathcal{G} = (\mathcal{V}, \mathcal{E}, \mathcal{B})$, where $\mathcal{V} = U \bigcup I$ and $\mathcal{E} = \bigcup_{k=1}^{K} \mathcal{E}_k$. Behavior K is treated as the target behavior, and the goal is to predict user preferences for unobserved items and generate top-N recommendations.

4 Methodology

We propose a Cross-behavior Knowledge Modeling framework based on Mixture-of-Experts (CKMME), as illustrated in Fig. 2. CKMME consists of two modules: the Cross-behavior Cascade Graph Convolution Network (CCGCN) and the Collaborative Fused Mixture-of-Experts Network (CFME). Specifically, CCGCN holistically captures sequential and leapfrogging behavior patterns via a dual-path propagation structure; CFME mitigates feature and label distribution biases via feature-level alignment and label-level coordination to reduce negative transfer in MTL; and BRPN, integrated within CFME, further refines behavior-aware preferences via gating across behaviors.

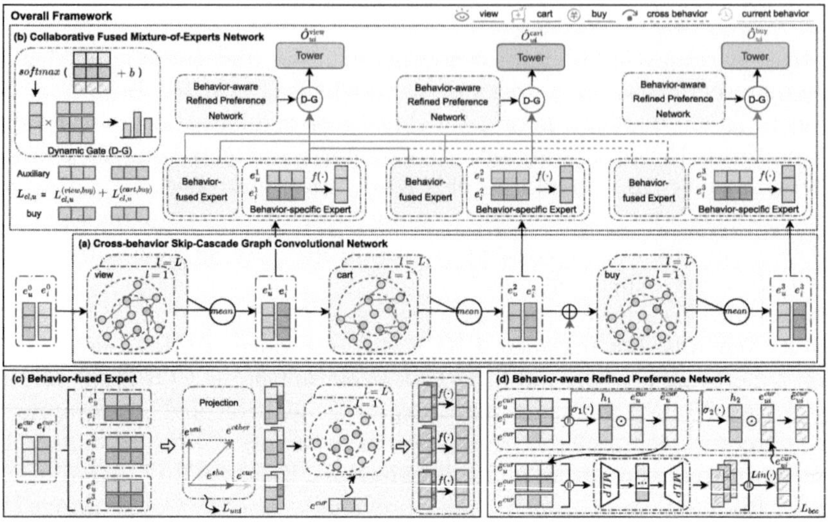

Fig. 2. Overview of CKMME. The upper part shows the overall framework, and the lowers illustrate the two core modules of CFME.

4.1 Cross-Behavior Cascade Graph Convolution Network

Most existing MBR methods assume rigid cascading patterns, making it difficult to model leapfrogging behaviors that reflect direct user preferences. To address this, we design the Cross-behavior Cascade Graph Convolution Network (CCGCN), which employs parallel cascading and cross-behavior chains to propagate information from qualified upstream to downstream behaviors.

Embedding Layer. Following standard GCN-based models, we initialize trainable embeddings for users and items. Let $\mathbf{E}_U^{(0)} \in \mathbb{R}^{|U| \times d}$ and $\mathbf{E}_I^{(0)} \in \mathbb{R}^{|I| \times d}$ denote the initial embedding matrices. For a user $u \in U$ and an item $i \in I$, their representations are obtained via embedding lookup of ID_u and ID_i:

$$\mathbf{e}_u^{(0)} = \mathbf{E}_U^{(0)} \cdot \mathrm{ID}_u, \quad \mathbf{e}_i^{(0)} = \mathbf{E}_I^{(0)} \cdot \mathrm{ID}_i, \tag{1}$$

where $\mathbf{e}_u^{(0)} \in \mathbb{R}^d$ and $\mathbf{e}_i^{(0)} \in \mathbb{R}^d$ are the initial embeddings of user u and item i.

Definition of the Cross-Behavior Chain. To model leapfrogging behavior patterns and mitigate noise from ineffective auxiliary behaviors, we construct cross-behavior chains based on sequence gaps, linking the target behavior with contextually relevant but non-adjacent predecessor behaviors.

Formally, given an ordered behavior sequence, if a user-item pair (u, i) appears under auxiliary behavior k and target behavior K with $|K - k| \geq 2$, we construct a leapfrogging chain. For example, in the sequence view $\rightarrow$ cart $\rightarrow$ buy, the gap between view and buy is 2, and thus a view $\rightarrow$ buy chain is constructed to capture the transition from initial interest to final decision. Finally, cross-behavior and cascading embeddings are fused via element-wise addition ($\oplus$) to enhance the target behavior embedding.

Graph Convolution. Existing studies have shown that GNNs are effective in modeling high-order interactions [7,10]. Through message passing, GCN-based methods can capture neighborhood information. For each behavior, we construct an interaction graph with the following adjacency matrix definition:

$$A_k = \begin{pmatrix} 0 & B_k \\ B_k^T & 0 \end{pmatrix}, \tag{2}$$

where A_k denotes the adjacency matrix corresponding to behavior k. Accordingly, the embedding matrices for users and items are defined as:

$$E_u = \left[\mathbf{e}_{u_1}, \ldots, \mathbf{e}_{u_{|U|}}\right], \quad E_i = \left[\mathbf{e}_{i_1}, \ldots, \mathbf{e}_{i_{|I|}}\right]. \tag{3}$$

Following [7,10], the embedding update at layer $l+1$ for behavior k is:

$$E^{k,l+1} = (D^{-1}A_k + I)\, E^{k,l}, \tag{4}$$

where D is the degree matrix and I is the identity matrix. The matrix $E^{k,l} = E_u^{k,l} \| E_i^{k,l}$, where $\|$ denotes concatenation and l indicates the l-th layer.

Since different layers capture neighborhood information of varying orders, we perform layer-wise fusion via weighted averaging:

$$\mathbf{e}_u^{k,*} = \sum_{l=0}^{L} a_l \mathbf{e}_u^{k,l}, \quad \mathbf{e}_i^{k,*} = \sum_{l=0}^{L} a_l \mathbf{e}_i^{k,l}, \tag{5}$$

where the weight coefficient $a_l = \frac{1}{l+1}$. $\mathbf{e}^{k,*}$ denotes the k-th final embedding.

To enable cross-behavior information propagation, we design a dual-path with cascading and cross-behavior chains. In the cascading chain, we adopt a progressive strategy, where behavior k initializes behavior $k+1$ embeddings:

$$E_u^{k+1,0} = E_u^{k,*}, \quad E_i^{k+1,0} = E_i^{k,*}, \tag{6}$$

where $E_u^{k,*}$ is the final user embedding under the behavior k, and $E_u^{k+1,0}$ is the initial embedding under the behavior $k+1$.

In the cross-behavior chain, we focus on the target behavior K, allowing information from qualified upstream behaviors to propagate directly to it. The aggregated embedding then initializes the target behavior, formulated as follows:

$$E_u^{K,0} = E_u^{K-1,*} \oplus \sum_{k \in \mathcal{S}} E_u^{k,L}, \quad E_i^{K,0} = E_i^{K-1,*} \oplus \sum_{k \in \mathcal{S}} E_i^{k,L}, \tag{7}$$

where $\mathcal{S} = \{\, k \in \{1, \ldots, K-2\} \mid |K-k| \geq 2 \,\}$, $E^{K-1,*}$ is the output of the last auxiliary behavior for users, and $E^{k,L}$ is the L-layer embedding of behavior k.

4.2 Collaborative Fused Mixture-of-Experts Network

Although MTL enhances performance, existing methods often suffer from negative transfer due to heterogeneous feature spaces and imbalanced label distributions. Moreover, dynamic transitions in user preferences cause interference. To address these issues, we propose the Collaborative Fused Mixture-of-Experts Network (CFME), which jointly optimizes expert generation and aggregation to mitigate feature- and label-level biases and model behavior-aware preferences.

Behavior-Specific Experts. To capture behavior-specific interactions and suppress interference from other behaviors, we introduce an independent expert for each behavior. For current behavior k, the expert specializes in modeling useritem interactions, which is formulated as:

$$\mathbf{e}^k = \mathbf{e}_u^{k,*} \circ \mathbf{e}_i^{k,*}, \tag{8}$$

where $\circ$ denotes the Hadamard product.

Furthermore, we apply contrastive learning to improve the learning quality of behavior-specific experts by aligning target and auxiliary behavior representations. The user-side contrastive loss is defined as:

$$\mathcal{L}_{\mathrm{cl},U}^{K,k} = \frac{1}{|U|} \sum_{u \in U} \left[-\ln \left(\frac{\exp\left(\varphi\left(\mathbf{e}_u^{K,*}, \mathbf{e}_u^{k,*}\right)/\tau\right)}{\sum_{u' \in U} \exp\left(\varphi\left(\mathbf{e}_u^{K,*}, \mathbf{e}_{u'}^{k,*}\right)/\tau\right)} \right) \right], \tag{9}$$

where τ is the temperature, and $\varphi(\cdot,\cdot)$ denotes the cosine similarity function.

Behavior-Fused Experts. As feature distribution biases across behaviors degrade performance, we introduce the Behavior-fused Expert to disentangle shared and unique information via projection. Specifically, behavior-specific embeddings from other behaviors k' are projected into the space of the current behavior k.

$$\mathbf{e}_{\mathrm{sha}}^{k',k} = \frac{\mathbf{e}^{k'} \cdot \mathbf{e}^k}{\| \mathbf{e}^k \|^2} \mathbf{e}^k, \quad \mathbf{e}_{\mathrm{uni}}^{k',k} = \mathbf{e}^{k'} - \mathbf{e}_{\mathrm{sha}}^{k',k}, \tag{10}$$

where $\mathbf{e}^{k'}$ and $\mathbf{e}^k$ are the embeddings under the behavior k' and k. $\mathbf{e}_{\mathrm{sha}}^{k',k}$ captures the shared information, while $\mathbf{e}_{\mathrm{uni}}^{k',k}$ retains the unique information of k'.

Based on the above disentangling, the shared embeddings are then concatenated and propagated via graph convolution:

$$\mathbf{e}_{\mathrm{in}}^{k',k} = \mathbf{e}_{u,\mathrm{sha}}^{k',k} \| \mathbf{e}_{i,\mathrm{sha}}^{k',k}, \quad \mathbf{e}_{\mathrm{out}}^{k',k} = f_{\mathrm{agg}}\left(\mathbf{e}_{\mathrm{in}}^{k',k}, A_k\right), \tag{11}$$

where $\mathbf{e}_{\mathrm{out}}^{k',k} = \mathbf{e}_{u,\mathrm{out}}^{k',k} \| \mathbf{e}_{i,\mathrm{out}}^{k',k}$. The aggregation operator $f_{\mathrm{agg}}(\cdot)$ follows the same design as Eq. (5). The graph convolution update is formulated as:

$$E^{k',k,l+1} = (D^{-1}A_k + I)(E^{k',k,l} \circ R^{k,l}), \quad R^{k,l} = W^l R^{k,l-1}, \tag{12}$$

where W^l is a layer-shared parameter matrix, and $R^{k,l}$ is a dynamically updated behavior embedding matrix.

Finally, to generate the fused expert representation for behaviors k' and k, we follow the same procedure as behavior-specific experts using Hadamard product:

$$\mathbf{e}^{k',k} = \mathbf{e}_{u,\text{out}}^{k',k} \circ \mathbf{e}_{i,\text{out}}^{k',k}. \tag{13}$$

Behavior-Aware Refined Preference Network. In MBR, effectively leveraging auxiliary behavior information is crucial for target behavior prediction. However, existing methods often overlook dynamic transitions in user preferences across behaviors. Thus, we construct the Behavior-aware Refined Preference Network (BRPN) to extract refined behavior-aware preferences.

We first introduce a learnable gating vector $\mathbf{h}_1 \in \mathbb{R}^d$ to incorporate behavioral awareness into user embeddings:

$$\mathbf{h}_1 = \sigma\left(W_1 \cdot \left(\mathbf{e}_u^{k,*} \| \mathbf{e}_i^{k,*} \| \mathbf{e}_k\right) + \mathbf{b}_1\right), \tag{14}$$

$$\tilde{\mathbf{e}}_u^{k,*} = \mathbf{h}_1 \circ \mathbf{e}_u^{k,*}, \tag{15}$$

where $\tilde{\mathbf{e}}_u^{k,*}$ denotes the enhanced embedding of user u for behavior k, σ is the sigmoid function. $W_1 \in \mathbb{R}^{d\times 3d}$ and $\mathbf{b}_1 \in \mathbb{R}^d$ are trainable parameters.

Next, to capture user preferences under behavior k, we employ an MLP:

$$\mathbf{e}_{ui}^{k,*} = f\left(\tilde{\mathbf{e}}_u^{k,*} \| \mathbf{e}_i^{k,*} \| \mathbf{e}_k\right), \tag{16}$$

where $\mathbf{e}_{ui}^{k,*}$ denotes the preliminary preference representation of user u for item i under behavior k.

To further refine the preliminary preference, an additional gating layer is employed to progressively filter irrelevant contextual noise:

$$\mathbf{h}_2 = \sigma\left(W_2 \cdot \left(\mathbf{e}_u^{k,*} \| \mathbf{e}_i^{k,*} \| \mathbf{e}_k\right) + \mathbf{b}_2\right), \tag{17}$$

$$\tilde{\mathbf{e}}_{ui}^{k,*} = \mathbf{h}_2 \circ \mathbf{e}_{ui}^{k,*}, \tag{18}$$

where $\tilde{\mathbf{e}}_{ui}^{k,*}$ is the refined behavior-aware preference representation.

Intuitively, when behavior-aware preferences are more strongly aligned with the item, the model can more effectively capture true user intentions. Therefore, BRPN is optimized using binary cross-entropy:

$$\mathcal{L}_{\text{bce}} = -\sum \left[y \cdot \log \sigma(y') + (1-y) \cdot \log\left(1-\sigma(y')\right)\right], \tag{19}$$

where $y \in \{0,1\}$ denotes the ground-truth interaction label, and $y' = (\tilde{\mathbf{e}}_{ui}^{k,*})^\top \mathbf{e}_i^{k,*}$ represents the predicted score.

Aggregation of Experts. To mitigate negative transfer, we design a gating function to adaptively weight experts for aggregation. Based on GCNs and behavior-aware preferences, it fuses multi-expert knowledge to alleviate label distribution bias. The gating weights are computed as:

$$\mathbf{g}^k = \text{Softmax}\left(W_g\left(\mathbf{e}_u^{k,*}\|\mathbf{e}_i^{k,*}\|\tilde{\mathbf{e}}_{ui}^{k,*}\right) + \mathbf{b}_g\right), \tag{20}$$

where $W_g \in \mathbb{R}^{K\times 3d}$ and $\mathbf{b}_g \in \mathbb{R}^{K\times 1}$ are learnable parameters, and $\mathbf{g}^k \in \mathbb{R}^{K\times 1}$ denotes the attention vector used to weight all experts.

We take the representations $\{\mathbf{e}^{j,k}\}_{j\neq k}$ of other behaviors and $\mathbf{e}^k$ as inputs to the k-th gate for task-specific aggregation. To mitigate the negative impact of label distribution bias between auxiliary and target behaviors, a stop-gradient operation is applied during shared-parameter optimization:

$$\mathbf{o}^k(j) = \begin{cases} g^k(j)\cdot \mathbf{e}^k, & j = k \\ g^k(j)\cdot \mathbf{e}^{j,k}, & j \neq k \text{ and } j < K \\ \text{sg}(g^k(j)\cdot \mathbf{e}^{j,k}), & j \neq k \text{ and } j = K \end{cases} \tag{21}$$

where $g^k(j)$ is the j-th component of $\mathbf{g}^k$, sg$(\cdot)$ denotes the stop-gradient operator.

The final prediction for task k is obtained by aggregating all expert outputs:

$$\hat{O}_{u,i}^k = h^k\left(\sum_{j=1}^{K}\mathbf{o}^k(j)\right), \tag{22}$$

where $h^k(\cdot)$ is the task-specific tower function implemented via average pooling. $\hat{O}_{u,i}^k$ denotes the predicted score for user u with item i under behavior k.

4.3 Joint Optimization

Unique Loss. To capture discriminative information in $\mathbf{e}_{\text{uni}}^{k',k}$, we design an auxiliary prediction task that leverages only the unique interaction information of behavior k'. The loss function is defined as follows:

$$\mathcal{L}_{\text{uni}} = -\sum_{k=1}^{K}\sum_{\substack{k'=1\\k'\neq k}}^{K}\sum_{(u,s,t)\in\mathcal{T}_{k',k}}\lambda_k\cdot\ln\sigma\left(\hat{O}_{us}^{k',k,\text{uni}} - \hat{O}_{ut}^{k',k,\text{uni}}\right), \tag{23}$$

where $\hat{O}_{ui}^{k',k,\text{uni}} = \mathbf{e}_{u,\text{uni}}^{k',k}\cdot\mathbf{e}_{i,\text{uni}}^{k',k}$ is the predicted score. The training triplets $\mathcal{T}_{k',k} = \{(u,s,t)\mid(u,s)\in O_{k'}^+\cap O_k^-,\ (u,t)\in O_k^-\cup(O_{k'}^+\cap O_k^+)\}$. O_k^+ and O_k^- denote observed and unobserved user-item interactions under behavior k, respectively. Thus, we utilize only the interactions of behavior k' via unique representations.

BPR Loss. We optimize the model using BPR over the predicted scores $\hat{O}^k_{u,i}$:

$$\mathcal{L}_{\text{bpr}} = -\sum_{k=1}^{K} \sum_{(u,s,t)\in\mathcal{O}_k} \lambda_k \cdot \ln\sigma\left(\hat{O}^k_{us} - \hat{O}^k_{ut}\right), \tag{24}$$

where $\mathcal{O}_k = \{(u,s,t) \mid (u,s) \in \mathcal{O}_k^+, (u,t) \in \mathcal{O}_k^-\}$ denotes the training triplets for behavior k, with $\mathcal{O}_k^+$ and $\mathcal{O}_k^-$ representing the observed and unobserved interactions, respectively. For each positive pair (u,s), the negative item t is randomly sampled from $\mathcal{O}_k^-$. BPR adopts behavior-specific negative sampling. λ_k is the coefficient of behavior k, and $\sigma(\cdot)$ is the sigmoid function.

The joint optimization objective is as follows:

$$\mathcal{L}(\Theta) = \mathcal{L}_{\text{bpr}} + \gamma_1\mathcal{L}_{\text{uni}} + \gamma_2\mathcal{L}_{\text{bce}} + \gamma_3 \sum_{k=1}^{K-1} \mathcal{L}_{\text{cl}}^{K,k} + \mu\|\Theta\|_2^2, \tag{25}$$

where γ_1, γ_2 and γ_3 weight different losses, and Θ denotes the set of all trainable parameters. μ regulates the strength of L_2 regularization.

5 Experiments

5.1 Experimental Setting

Dataset Description. Following MB-CGCN [3] and CRGCN [18], we conduct experiments on three real-world datasets (Beibei, Taobao, and Tmall). We follow standard preprocessing in prior studies [10], removing duplicate useritem interactions and retaining only the earliest record. This preprocessing is commonly adopted to avoid potential data leakage from repeated interactions and to align with the BPR training objective. Table 1 summarizes the three datasets.

Evaluation Metrics. To evaluate the performance of CKMME, we adopt two widely used evaluation metrics: Hit Rate (HR@N) and Normalized Discounted Cumulative Gain (NDCG@N). Besides, we utilize the leave-one-out validation method for evaluation and set $N = 10$ in all experiments.

Table 1. Statistics of evaluation datasets.

Dataset	#User	#Item	#Interaction	#Target interaction	#Interactive behavior type
Beibei	21,716	7977	3.3×10^6	282,860	{View, cart, buy}
Taobao	15,449	11,953	1.2×10^6	92,180	{View, cart, buy}
Tmall	41,738	11,953	2.3×10^6	255,586	{View, collect, cart, buy}

Baseline Models. To validate the effectiveness of CKMME, we compare it with three categories of baseline methods: (1) **Single-behavior methods**: MF-BPR

[12], NeuMF [8] and LightGCN [7], (2) **Multi-behavior methods without multi-task learning**: NMTR [5], MBGCN [10], KMCLR [17] and MB-CGCN [3], (3) **Multi-behavior methods with multi-task learning**: CRGCN [18], PKEF [14], BCIPM [19], AutoDCS [11] and UIPL [21].

Table 2. Overall performance comparison.

Dataset	Metric	Single-behavior			Multi-behavior without MTL				Multi-behavior with MTL						Impr. (%)
		MF-BPR	NeuMF	LightGCN	NMTR	MBGCN	KMCLR	MB-CGCN	CRGCN	PKEF	BCIPM	AutoDCS	UIPL	CKMME	
Beibei	HR@10	0.0191	0.0232	0.0391	0.0429	0.0470	0.0531	0.0579	0.0459	0.1130	0.0458	0.1295	0.0423	**0.1814**	40.08
	NDCG@10	0.0049	0.0135	0.0209	0.0198	0.0259	0.0263	0.0381	0.0324	0.0582	0.0221	0.0677	0.0202	**0.1022**	50.96
Taobao	HR@10	0.0076	0.0236	0.0411	0.0282	0.0509	0.1185	0.1233	0.0855	0.1385	0.1201	0.1522	0.1345	**0.1701**	11.76
	NDCG@10	0.0036	0.0128	0.0240	0.0137	0.0294	0.0659	0.0677	0.0439	0.0785	0.0656	0.0813	0.0822	**0.0891**	8.39
Tmall	HR@10	0.0230	0.0124	0.0393	0.0536	0.0549	0.0603	0.0984	0.0840	0.1277	0.1414	0.1432	0.1144	**0.1668**	16.48
	NDCG@10	0.0207	0.0062	0.0209	0.0286	0.0285	0.0310	0.0558	0.0442	0.0721	0.0741	0.0743	0.0784	**0.0918**	17.09

Boldface denotes the highest score, and underline indicates the best baseline.

Parameter Settings. The CKMME model is implemented in TensorFlow [1]. For fair comparison, we follow common parameter settings [3]. The embedding dimension is set to 64 for all methods, and the batch size is fixed at 256. Model parameters are initialized with Xavier and optimized using Adam with a learning rate of 10^{-3}. We conduct a grid search over $\{1, 2, 3, 4, 5\}$ for the number of GNN layers. Loss-weight coefficients are tuned over $\{0, 1/6, 2/6, 3/6, 4/6, 5/6, 1\}$, with the sum constrained to 1 for balanced behavior contributions.

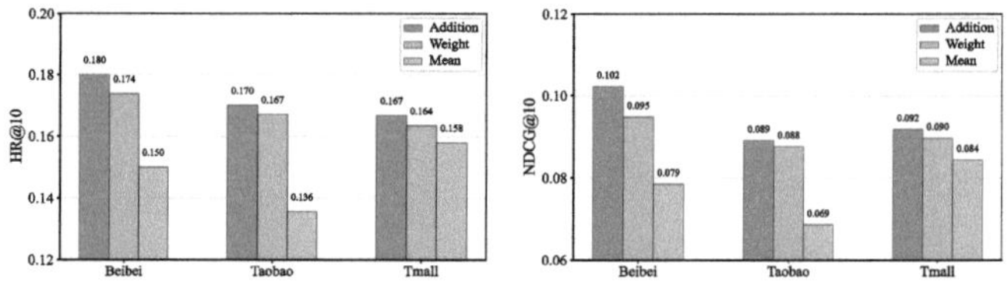

Fig. 3. The influence of the merge methods for two behavior chains.

5.2 Performance Comparison

Table 2 presents the performance of CKMME and baselines on three datasets in terms of HR@10 and NDCG@10. We summarize key observations as follows:

Analysis of the proposed CKMME: CKMME consistently outperforms all baselines across datasets, demonstrating its applicability and effectiveness. These gains are due to the effective modeling of cross-behavior dependencies and the optimization of the mixture-of-experts network. Compared with cascading models such as CRGCN and MB-CGCN, AutoDCS achieves competitive performance by adaptively constraining decision chains. Meanwhile, PKEF uses parallel knowledge fusion to learn user behavior patterns, while BCIPM relaxes constraints via behavior-specific modeling and emphasizes the target behavior.

Analysis of MBR-based Methods: Even the best single-behavior model, LightGCN, is outperformed by most multi-behavior methods, highlighting the value of auxiliary behaviors in alleviating data sparsity. GCN-based methods (e.g., MBGCN and MB-CGCN) further outperform MF-based and DNN-based models, as graph structures better capture high-order signals. Moreover, KMCLR also verifies the effectiveness of contrastive learning.

Analysis of MTL-based Methods: MTL-based models such as PKEF, BCIPM, and UIPL consistently surpass methods without MTL. For example, PKEF mitigates gradient conflicts and negative transfer via the PME module. However, direct knowledge transfer may introduce noise. BCIPM and UIPL further achieve improved performance by learning item-aware preferences and invariant preferences, respectively.

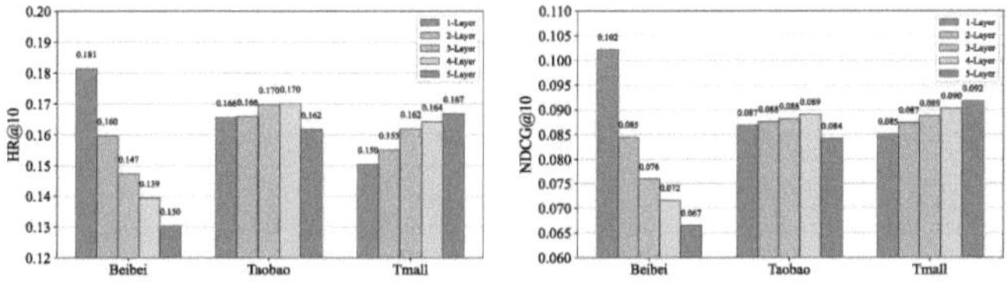

Fig. 4. Impact of GCN layers.

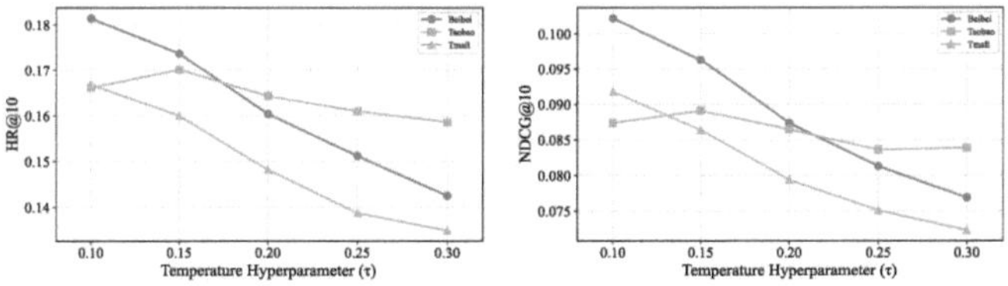

Fig. 5. Impact of temperature hyperparameter.

5.3 Effect of Aggregation Strategy on Dual-Behavior Chain

To explore the optimal aggregation strategy for dual-behavior chains, we compare element-wise addition (Addition), weighted addition (Weight), and averaging (Mean). As shown in Fig. 3, Addition consistently outperforms the others. This is because it preserves the distinct characteristics of each behavior chain. In contrast, Weight suffers from fluctuations due to unstable weight learning, while Mean causes information loss by compressing feature dimensions.

5.4 Parameter Analysis

Effect of the Number of GCN Layers. By varying the number of GCN layers $L \in \{1, 2, 3, 4, 5\}$, we assess the impact of high-order behavioral modeling on CKMME. Results (e.g., Fig. 4) show that the optimal L varies across datasets due to differences in the balance between noise and useful signals in high-order information. This reflects intrinsic differences in user decision patterns, and performance degrades with an inappropriate number of layers.

Effect of Temperature Hyperparameter. To examine the effect of temperature τ on contrastive learning, we vary τ over $\{0.10, 0.15, 0.20, 0.25, 0.30\}$. As shown in Fig. 5, lower τ values tend to yield better performance. As τ increases, performance gradually declines, especially when $\tau \geq 0.20$, due to weakened softmax discrimination. Taobao performs best at $\tau = 0.15$, indicating that a moderate τ helps balance auxiliary and target behaviors while mitigating bias.

6 Conclusion and Future Work

In this paper, we propose the Cross-behavior Knowledge Modeling based on Mixture-of-Experts (CKMME) to address limitations in multi-behavior information aggregation and target behavior prediction. Specifically, CCGCN employs a dual-path structure to model sequential and leapfrogging behavioral patterns. CFME optimizes expert generation and aggregation, mitigating distribution biases in MTL via feature projection and stop-gradient. Moreover, BRPN within CFME refines behavior-aware user preferences. Extensive experiments on three real-world datasets show that CKMME achieves superior performance. Future work will explore negative transfer and develop more generalizable models.

References

1. Abadi, M., Barham, P., Chen, J., Chen, Z., Davis, A., Dean, J., Devin, M., Ghemawat, S., Irving, G., Isard, M., et al.: TensorFlow: a system for large-scale machine learning. In: Proceedings of the 12th USENIX Symposium on Operating Systems Design and Implementation (OSDI 16), pp. 265–283 (2016)
2. Caruana, R.: Multitask learning. Mach. Learn. **28**(1), 41–75 (1997)
3. Cheng, Z., Han, S., Liu, F., Zhu, L., Gao, Z., Peng, Y.: Multi-behavior recommendation with cascading graph convolution networks. In: Proceedings of the ACM Web Conference 2023, pp. 1181–1189 (2023)
4. Dong, X., Zhu, L., Song, X., Li, J., Cheng, Z.: Adaptive Collaborative Similarity Learning for Unsupervised Multi-view Feature Selection. arXiv:1904.11228 (2019)
5. Gao, C., He, X., Gan, D., Chen, X., Feng, F., Li, Y., Chua, T.-S., Jin, D.: Neural multi-task recommendation from multi-behavior data. In: Proceedings of the 2019 IEEE 35th International Conference on Data Engineering (ICDE), pp. 1554–1557 (2019)
6. Guo, L., Hua, L., Jia, R., Zhao, B., Wang, X., Cui, B.: Buying or browsing? Predicting real-time purchasing intent using attention-based deep network with multiple behavior. In: Proceedings of the 25th ACM SIGKDD International Conference on Knowledge Discovery and Data Mining, pp. 1984–1992 (2019)

7. He, X., Deng, K., Wang, X., Li, Y., Zhang, Y., Wang, M.: Lightgcn: simplifying and powering graph convolution network for recommendation. In: Proceedings of the 43rd International ACM SIGIR Conference on Research and Development in Information Retrieval, pp. 639–648 (2020)
8. He, X., Liao, L., Zhang, H., Nie, L., Hu, X., Chua, T.-S.: Neural collaborative filtering. In: Proceedings of the 26th International Conference on World Wide Web, pp. 173–182 (2017)
9. Jacobs, R.A., Jordan, M.I., Nowlan, S.J., Hinton, G.E.: Adaptive mixtures of local experts. Neural Comput. **3**(1), 79–87 (1991)
10. Jin, B., Gao, C., He, X., Jin, D., Li, Y.: Multi-behavior recommendation with graph convolutional networks. In: Proceedings of the 43rd International ACM SIGIR Conference on Research and Development in Information Retrieval, pp. 659–668 (2020)
11. Liu, D., Xian, S., Wu, Y., Yang, C., Tang, X., He, X., Ming, Z.: AutoDCS: automated decision chain selection in deep recommender systems. In: Proceedings of the 47th International ACM SIGIR Conference on Research and Development in Information Retrieval, pp. 956–965 (2024)
12. Loni, B., Pagano, R., Larson, M., Hanjalic, A.: Bayesian personalized ranking with multi-channel user feedback. In: Proceedings of the 10th ACM Conference on Recommender Systems, pp. 361–364 (2016)
13. Ma, J., Zhao, Z., Yi, X., Chen, J., Hong, L., Chi, E.H.: Modeling task relationships in multi-task learning with multi-gate mixture-of-experts. In: Proceedings of the 24th ACM SIGKDD International Conference on Knowledge Discovery and Data Mining, pp. 1930–1939 (2018)
14. Meng, C., Zhai, C., Yang, Y., Zhang, H., Li, X.: Parallel knowledge enhancement based framework for multi-behavior recommendation. In: Proceedings of the 32nd ACM International Conference on Information and Knowledge Management, pp. 1797–1806 (2023)
15. Quan, Y., Ding, J., Gao, C., Li, N., Yi, L., Jin, D., Li, Y.: Alleviating video-length effect for micro-video recommendation. ACM Trans. Inform. Syst. **42**(2), 1–24 (2023)
16. Xu, W., Wu, Q., Wang, R., Ha, M., Ma, Q., Chen, L., Han, B., Yan, J.: Rethinking cross-domain sequential recommendation under open-world assumptions. In: Proceedings of the ACM Web Conference 2024, pp. 3173–3184 (2024)
17. Xuan, H., Liu, Y., Li, B., Yin, H.: Knowledge enhancement for contrastive multi-behavior recommendation. In: Proceedings of the Sixteenth ACM International Conference on Web Search and Data Mining, pp. 195–203 (2023)
18. Yan, M., Cheng, Z., Gao, C., Sun, J., Liu, F., Sun, F., Li, H.: Cascading residual graph convolutional network for multi-behavior recommendation. ACM Trans. Inform. Syst. **42**(1), 1–26 (2023)
19. Yan, M., Liu, F., Sun, J., Sun, F., Cheng, Z., Han, Y.: Behavior-contextualized item preference modeling for multi-behavior recommendation. In: Proceedings of the 47th International ACM SIGIR Conference on Research and Development in Information Retrieval, pp. 946–955 (2024)
20. Yan, M., Cheng, Z., Sun, J., Sun, F., Peng, Y.: MB-HGCN: A Hierarchical Graph Convolutional Network for Multi-behavior Recommendation. arXiv:2306.10679 (2023)
21. Yan, M., Cheng, Z., Liu, F., Lyu, Y., Han, Y.: User invariant preference learning for multi-behavior recommendation. ACM Trans. Inform. Syst. (2025)

22. Zhai, C., Meng, C., Yang, Y., Zhang, K., Zhao, X., Li, X.: Combinatorial Optimization Perspective Based Framework for Multi-behavior Recommendation. arXiv:2502.02232 (2025)
23. Zhao, Z., Cheng, Z., Hong, L., Chi, E.H.: Improving user topic interest profiles by behavior factorization. In: Proceedings of the 24th International Conference on World Wide Web, pp. 1406–1416 (2015)
24. Zhou, X., Qin, D., Lu, X., Chen, L., Zhang, Y.: Online social media recommendation over streams. In: Proceedings of the 2019 IEEE 35th International Conference on Data Engineering (ICDE), pp. 938–949 (2019)

Disentangled Representation Learning-Based Personalized Tag Recommendation

Shengwei Qian[1], Aoran Zhang[2], Rong Gao[3], Li Zhang[4], and Yonghong Yu[1,2(✉)]

[1] Tongda College of Nanjing University of Posts and Telecommunications, Yangzhou, Jiangsu 225100, China
wayneqian83@outlook.com
[2] State Key Laboratory of Novel Software Technology, Nanjing University, Nanjing, Jiangsu 210023, China
JUSTzhangaoran@gmail.com, yuyh@njupt.edu.cn
[3] Hubei University of Technology, Wuhan, Hubei 430068, China
gaorong@hbut.edu.cn
[4] Royal Holloway University of London, Egham, Surrey TW20 0EX, UK
Li.Zhang@rhul.ac.uk

Abstract. Personalized tag recommendation algorithms provide users with personalized tag recommendations by modeling the third-order interactions between users, items and tags. However, traditional personalized tag recommendation models are unable to effectively distinguish the multiple latent intents of users when annotating items, leading to sub-optimal personalized tag recommendation performance. To solve the above problems, we propose a disentangled representation learning-based personalized tag recommendation algorithm, namely DPTR. Specifically, DPTR utilizes the intent-aware module to explicitly model multiple latent intents of users, rather than iteratively refine intent-aware interaction graphs. Thus, DPTR is able to simultaneously enhance the representation capability of latent intents and reduce the computational overhead. Moreover, we integrate disentangled representation learning into graph neural networks and then utilize graph convolutional neural networks to capture the high-order collaborative signals among entities. We conduct extensive experiments on real-world datasets and the experimental results demonstrate that DPTR outperforms traditional personalized tag recommendation models.

Keywords: Tag recommendation algorithm · Disentangled representation learning · Graph neural network

1 Introduction

Personalized tag recommendation system (i.e. PTR) [5,6,8,16,18,20,28] is an important branch of recommendation systems, which generates lists of tags for

L. Ding et al. (Eds.): APWeb-WAIM 2026, LNCS 16993, pp. 427–442, 2027.
https://doi.org/10.1007/978-981-92-5693-8_27

users to annotate items by modeling the interaction among users, items and tags. Representative PTR models include HOSVD [20], RTF [16] and PITF [18]. These traditional PTR models only consider third-order interactions among entities, and ignore high-order collaborative signals hidden in the interaction behaviors, leading to insufficient representations of entities. In addition, some researchers propose to utilize graph neural networks (i.e. GNN) to rich the semantics of entities representations [2,4,19,25,27]. However, the decision making of choosing specific tags to annotate items is complicated and is affected by multiple latent intents. As shown in Fig.1, according to the genre of movies, user u_1 annotates "Matrix" and "Forrest Gump" with tags "Science Fiction" and "Comedy", respectively. Considering the actors of movies, user u_1 assigns "Morgan Freeman" and "Heath Ledger" to "The Shawshank Redemption" and "The Dark Knight", respectively. Since user u_2 is more concerned about the quality of the movies, she/he annotate movies with "Classic" or "Good story".

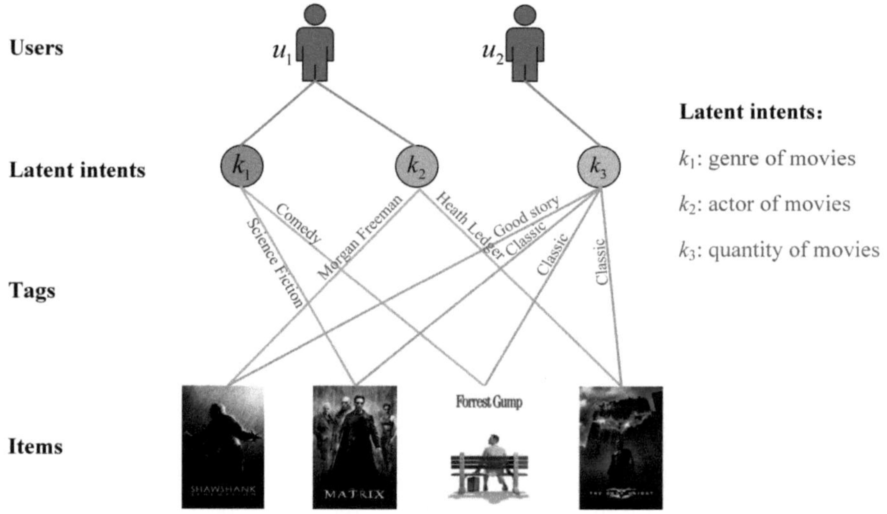

Fig. 1. An example of the diversity of latent user intents.

Recently, since disentangled representation learning [3,10,11,14,23,26] is able to reduce the association between different features and improve the robustness and interpretability of the models, it has achieved great success in the fields of natural language processing and computer vision. Inspired by the success of disentangled representation learning, some researchers [1,7,9,12,13,15,22,24,30] have proposed several disentangled representation learning-based recommendation models. However, existing disentangled representation learning-based models usually refine the intent-aware interaction graph in an iterative manner [7,22]. Specifically, they usually construct intent-aware interaction graphs for each latent intents and inject intents information via multiple iterations, which results in high training overhead. In addition, to learn the latent intent representations, it is necessary for personalized item recommendation to iteratively refine the intent-aware graph via splitting the embeddings [22]. This heuristic-based splitting scheme reduces the dimensionality of the latent intent representation, which may lead to insufficient intent-aware capability.

To address the above issues, we propose a disentangled representation learning-based personalized tag recommendation model, namely DPTR. Specifically, to disentangle latent intents of users, DPTR utilizes the intent-aware module to model latent intents of users. In this way, we avoid the extra computational overhead of repeatedly generating intent-aware graphs and ensure that each latent intent is sufficient encoded. In addition, we integrate disentangled representation learning into GNN, which not only extracts high-order collaborative signals among entities, but also utilizes disentangled representation learning to distinguish multiple latent intents of users. The main contributions of this paper are listed as follows:

- We utilize the intent-aware module to learn embeddings of latent intents, which is used to infer what factors affect the tagging decisions of users and the corresponding weights. Moreover, the usage of intent-aware module makes DPTR avoid the huge computational overhead incurred by iteratively refining the intent-aware graph.
- We integrate disentangled representation learning and GNN into a unified framework, endowing DPTR with the capability of capturing the high-order collaborative signals and modeling multiple latent intents.
- We conduct extensive experiments on real-world datasets to evaluate the performance of our proposed model. The experimental results demonstrate that our DPTR outperforms other traditional PTR models.

2 Related Work

2.1 Personalized Tag Recommendations

Classical tag recommendation algorithms include HOSVD [20], RTF [16], and PITF [18]. For instance, HOSVD [20] utilized the high-order singular value decomposition technique to factorize the third-order tensor of users-items-tags. However, HOSVD focuses on the users' ratings on tags and ignores the ranking among tags. To tackle this issue, Rendle et al. [16] proposed the RTF model. RTF learns the user preferences over tags from pairwise ranking constraints, improving the performance of tag recommendation. Although HOSVD and RTF are effective in some scenarios, they usually have high computational cost and are hard to scale to large datasets. To deal with this problem, Rendle et al. [18] proposed the pairwise interaction tensor factorization model, namely PITF. PITF explicitly models pairwise interactions among entities and its time complexity is linearly proportional to the embedding size. In addition, Fang et al. [5] proposed a nonlinear tensor factorization method, which employs the Gaussian radial basis function to capture the nonlinear interactions among users, items and tags. However, the above mentioned PTR methods only consider the first-order collaborative signals among entities and fail to capture the high-order collaborative signals. Recently, some researchers utilized deep learning techniques to improve the performance of PTR. For example, Yuan et al. [28] proposed a deep learning-based approach, namely ABNT. ABNT employs the multi-layer perceptron to model the nonlinear relationships of entities. In addition, Chen et al. [2] proposed the GNN-PTR, which utilizes GNN to capture high-order collaborative signals in interaction graphs. To reduce the training difficulty of PTR models, Yu et al. [27] removes the feature transformation and nonlinear activation components from GNN-PTR, and proposed the LNGTR model. To alleviate the problem of data sparsity, Zhang et al. [29] proposed the CLPTR, which utilizes contrastive learning module to extract self-supervised signals from interaction graphs. However, the above PTR models ignore the latent intents when users annotate the items with tags, causing the sub-optimal performance of personalized tag recommendation.

2.2 Disentangled Representation Learning

The purpose of disentangled representation learning is to reduce the association among different features, and it is widely used in the fields of computer vision and natural language processing. For instance, Ma et al. [14] proposed a multi-branch reconstruction structure to disentangle pose factors whin an image, and then fuse these factors into embedding features. Cheng et al. [3] introduced the disentangled representation learning technique into natural language processing, which explicitly reduces the correlation between style and content, and preserves sentence information in the latent space. In the field of item recommendation, disentangling the latent intents of user behaviors is vital to the recommendation performance. Some researchers proposed several disentangled representation learning-based item recommendation models. For example, Ma et al. [12] proposed a disentangle representation learning-based graph convolutional neural network, namely DisenGCN. Considering the diversity of user-item interactions, Wang et al. [22] proposed the DGCF. In order to better capture the semantic information hidden in user domain or item domain, Wang et al. [24] proposed a heterogeneous graph attention network-based disentangled representation learning method, namely DisenHAN. In the field of session-based recommendation, Li et al. [9] proposed a disentangled graph neural networks-based session recommendation model, namely Disen-GNN. Disen-GNN integrates the disentangled representation learning into gated graph neural networks to capture the main intents of users for the target session. Recently, the contrastive learning community also attempts to integrate disentangled representation learning into contrastive learning. For example, Li et al. [10] proposed DGCL. DGCL employs disentangled graph encoder to learn the disentangled graph representations by aggregating the features of latent factors, and utilizes factor-wise contrastive learning to capture multiple aspects of the graph. To alleviate the negative effect of interaction noise, Ren et al. [15] proposed the disentangled contrastive learning recommendation model with adaptive augmentation, namely DCCF.

Different from the above work, we focus on personalized tag recommendation. Specifically, We utilize the intent-aware module to learn embeddings of latent intents, which is used to infer what factors affect the tagging decisions of users and the corresponding weights.

3 Disentangled Representation Learning-Based Personalized Tag Recommendation

See Fig. 2.

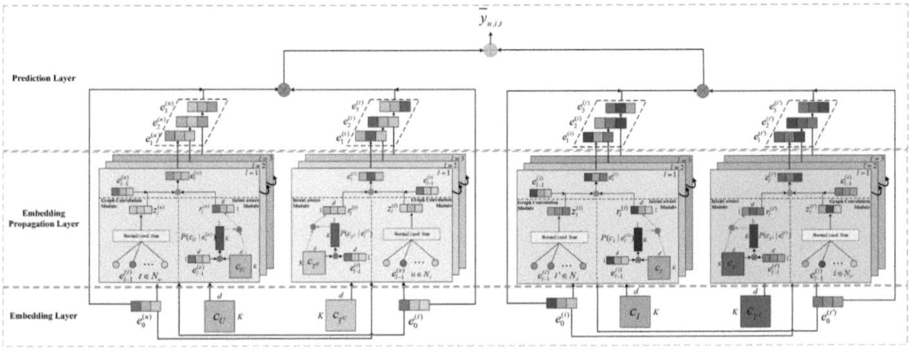

Fig. 2. The framework of disentangled representation learning based personalized tag recommendation model.

3.1 Problem Description

Unlike traditional item recommendation, PTR usually contains three different entities: the set of users U, the set of items I, and the set of tags T. The historical interactions S of all users is a subset of $U \times I \times T$. A ternary $(u, i, t) \in S$ denotes that user u assigns tag t to item i. Based on S, we can obtain a third-order tensor $Y \in \mathbb{R}^{|U| \times |I| \times |T|}$, where one element $y_{u,i,t} = 1$, if (u, i, t) is the positive feedback, otherwise 0. The aim of the PTR is to recommend a ranking list of tags to the user, which is able to help the user annotate an item.

3.2 Our Proposed Method

In this section, we detailedly describe the disentangled representation learning-based personalized tag recommendation model, namely DPTR. DPTR mainly contains two important modules, i.e., the intent-aware module and the graph convolution module. The framework of disentangled representation learning-based personalized tag recommendation model is presented in Fig. 2.

Embedding Layer. In the embedding layer, we map users, items and tags into the low dimensional space according to their IDs. Specifically, we perform a lookup operation over the corresponding feature matrices according to the indexes of the entities and obtain the embeddings of user u, item i and tag t. Formally,

$$\begin{aligned} e_0^{(u)} &= lookup(\mathbf{U}, u), e_0^{(i)} = lookup(\mathbf{I}, i), \\ e_0^{(t)} &= lookup\left(\mathbf{T}^U, t\right), e_0^{(t')} = lookup\left(\mathbf{T}^I, t\right), \end{aligned} \tag{1}$$

where $e_0^{(u)} \in \mathbb{R}^d, e_0^{(i)} \in \mathbb{R}^d, e_0^{(t)} \in \mathbb{R}^d, e_0^{(t')} \in \mathbb{R}^d$, and d denotes the dimension of embeddings. Note that $e_0^{(t)}$ is the user-specific embedding of tag t and $e_0^{(t')}$ is the item-specific embedding of tag t. $\mathbf{U} \in \mathbb{R}^{|U|\times d}$ is the latent user feature matrix, $\mathbf{I} \in \mathbb{R}^{|I|\times d}$ is the latent item feature matrix, $\mathbf{T}^U \in \mathbb{R}^{|T|\times d}$ is the latent user-specific tag feature matrix, $\mathbf{T}^I \in \mathbb{R}^{|T|\times d}$ is the latent item-specific tag feature matrix. We use the *lookup* $(\cdot)$ operation to retrieval the corresponding embeddings from the latent feature matrices.

In order to characterize the latent intents that affect users' tagging behaviors, we define K unique intent prototypes for each type of entities, including user intent prototypes $\left\{c_{\mathrm{U},k} \in \mathbb{R}^d\right\}_{k=1}^K$, item intent prototypes $\left\{c_{\mathrm{I},k} \in \mathbb{R}^d\right\}_{k=1}^K$, user-specific tag intent prototypes $\left\{c_{\mathrm{T}^U,k} \in \mathbb{R}^d\right\}_{k=1}^K$, and item-specific tag intent prototypes $\left\{c_{\mathrm{T}^I,k} \in \mathbb{R}^d\right\}_{k=1}^K$. We could regard the intent prototypes of items and tags as the contexts when annotating items.

Embedding Propagation Layer. In our proposed DPTR, the main goal of embedding propagation layer is to distinguish latent user intents via computing relevance score between latent intent prototypes and entities, and capture high-order collaborative signals on user-tag and item-tag interaction graphs by utilizing embedding propagation and aggregation mechanisms.

Graph Convolution Module: Generally, there are three types of interaction graph in PTR, i.e. user-item interaction graph, user-tag interaction graph and item-tag interaction graph. Inspired by works [2,18,27], to predict what tags the user would choose to annotate an item, we take user-tag interaction graph and item-tag interaction graph into consideration. On the user-tag interaction graph, we employ a light graph convolutional network to capture the high-order collaborative signals between users and tags.

At the lth layer, the high-order collaborative embeddings of user $z_l^{(u)}$ and the user-specific tag $z_l^{(t)}$ are defined as follows,

$$z_l^{(u)} = \sum_{t\in N_u} \tilde{M}_{ut}(u,\mathrm{t}) \cdot e_{l-1}^{(\mathrm{t})}, z_l^{(\mathrm{t})} = \sum_{u\in N_{\mathrm{t}}} \tilde{M}_{ut}(u,\mathrm{t}) \cdot e_{l-1}^{(u)}, \tag{2}$$

where $e_{l-1}^{(u)}$ and $e_{l-1}^{(t)}$ denote the user embeddings and the user-specific tag embeddings at the $(l-1)^{th}$ embedding propagation layer, respectively. N_u and N_t are the set of neighbor nodes of user u and tag t in the user-tag interaction graph, respectively. $\tilde{M}_{ut}$ is the normalized Laplacian matrix of the adjacency matrix of user-tag interaction graph. Formally,

$$\tilde{M}_{ut}(u,t) = D_u^{-\frac{1}{2}}(u) \cdot M_{ut}(u,t) \cdot D_t^{-\frac{1}{2}}(t), \tag{3}$$

where $M_{ut} \in \mathbb{R}^{(|U|+|T|)\times(|U|+|T|)}$ is the adjacency matrix of the user-tag interaction graph. $D_u \in \mathbb{R}^{(|U|+|T|)\times(|U|+|T|)}$ and $D_t \in \mathbb{R}^{(|U|+|T|)\times(|U|+|T|)}$ are the diagonal matrices derived from the adjacency matrix M_{ut}, $D_u(ii) = \sum_{j\in N_u} M_{ut}(i,j)$ is the sum of non-zero elements in the i-th row of M_{ut}, and $D_t(ii) = \sum_{j\in N_t} M_{ut}(j,i)$ is the sum of non-zero elements in i-th column of M_{ut}.

Intent-Aware Module: To disentangle the latent intents, we first employ the intent-aware module to compute the relevance score between latent intent prototypes and entities, and then generate the intent-aware embeddings of entities. A higher degree of similarity between an intent prototype and an embedding of an entity indicates that the interaction among entities is driven by this intent prototype with a large probability. Taking the user-tag interaction graph as an example, we inject the K latent intent prototypes into the embeddings of entities to generate intent-aware embeddings of users and tags at the l-th layer, formally,

$$\begin{aligned} r_l^{(u)} &= \sum_k^K c_{\mathrm{U},k} P\left(c_{\mathrm{U},k} \mid e_l^{(u)}\right), \\ r_l^{(t)} &= \sum_k^K c_{\mathrm{T}^U,k} P\left(c_{\mathrm{T}^U,k} \mid e_l^{(t)}\right), \end{aligned} \tag{4}$$

where $P(\cdot)$ is the relevance score between the entities and the latent intent prototypes,

$$\begin{aligned} P\left(c_{\mathrm{U},k} \mid e_l^{(u)}\right) &= \frac{\exp\left(sim\left(e_{l-1}^{(u)}, c_{\mathrm{U},k}\right)\right)}{\sum_{k'}^K \exp\left(sim\left(e_{l-1}^{(u)}, c_{\mathrm{U},k'}\right)\right)}, \\ P\left(c_{\mathrm{T}^U,k} \mid e_l^{(t)}\right) &= \frac{\exp\left(sim\left(e_{l-1}^{(t)}, c_{\mathrm{T}^U,k}\right)\right)}{\sum_{k'}^K \exp\left(sim\left(e_{l-1}^{(t)}, c_{\mathrm{T}^U,k'}\right)\right)}, \end{aligned} \tag{5}$$

where $sim(x,y)$ is the cosine similarity between x and y.

To simultaneously capture high-order collaborative signals and disentangle latent intents, we fuse the intent-aware embeddings and the high-order collaborative embeddings to generate the embeddings of user and user-specific tag at the lth layer, formally,

$$e_l^{(u)} = e_{l-1}^{(u)} + z_l^{(u)} + r_l^{(u)}, e_l^{(t)} = e_{l-1}^{(t)} + z_l^{(t)} + r_l^{(t)}. \tag{6}$$

For the item-tag interaction graph, we adopt the same scheme to generate the embeddings of item $e_l^{(i)}$ and item-specific tag $e_l^{(t')}$ at the l-th layer.

Prediction Layer. By stacking L embedding propagation layers, we obtain the sets of entities embeddings. To simultaneously capture user intents and high-order collaborative signals from entity interactions, we combine all elements to obtain the final entity embeddings,

$$\begin{aligned} e_*^{(u)} = e_0^{(u)}||e_1^{(u)}||\cdots||e_L^{(u)}, e_*^{(i)} = e_0^{(i)}||e_1^{(i)}||\cdots||e_L^{(i)}, \\ e_*^{(t)} = e_0^{(t)}||e_1^{(t)}||\cdots||e_L^{(t)}, e_*^{(t')} = e_0^{(t')}||e_1^{(t')}||\cdots||e_L^{(t')}, \end{aligned} \tag{7}$$

where $||$ denotes the concatenation operation.

Given a user-item pair (u, i), the main purpose of the prediction layer is to compute the relevance between the user-item pair and the candidate tags, and generate a list of tags for the user according to the predicted scores. For a given triplet (u, i, t), the predicted scores between user-item pair (u, i) and candidate tag t is defined as follows,

$$\bar{y}_{u,i,t} = e_*^{(u)} \odot e_*^{(t)} + e_*^{(i)} \odot e_*^{(t')}, \tag{8}$$

where $\odot$ denotes the dot product.

Objective Function. For the user-item pair (u, i), if user u has not assigned j' to item i and annotate item i with tag j, we assume that user u prefer tag j over tag j'. And the training set $D_S = \{(u, i, j, j') \mid (u, i, j) \in S \wedge (u, i, j') \notin S\}$.We adopt a widely used BPR [17] to compute the loss function as follows,

$$\mathcal{L} = \sum_{(u,i,j,j') \in D_S} - \ln \sigma \left(\bar{y}_{u,i,j} - \bar{y}_{u,i,j'} \right) + \lambda_1 \cdot \|\Theta_1\|_{\mathrm{F}}^2 + \lambda_2 \cdot \|\Theta_2\|_{\mathrm{F}}^2, \tag{9}$$

where $\Theta_1 = \{\mathbf{U}, \mathbf{I}, \mathbf{T}^U, \mathbf{T}^I\}$ and $\Theta_2 = \left\{ \{c_{\mathrm{U},k}\}_{k=1}^K, \{c_{\mathrm{I},k}\}_{k=1}^K, \{c_{\mathrm{T}^U,k}\}_{k=1}^K, \{c_{\mathrm{T}^I,k}\}_{k=1}^K \right\}$ are the trainable parameters of DPTR.

4 Complexity Analysis

In this section, we analyse the time and space complexity of DPTR and iterative disentangled representation learning(DRL)-based models. Firstly, we compute the time complexity of iterative DRL-based models. The embedding propagation layers of iterative DRL-based models involves L layers, leading to a time complexity is $O(L \cdot t \cdot K \cdot |S| \cdot d)$, where t is times of graph iterations and K is the number of latent intents. The space complexity of embedding propagation layer and intent-aware graphs is $O((|U| + |I| + 2 \cdot |T|) \cdot d + K \cdot |S|)$. Hence, the total time of iterative DRL-based models is $O(L \cdot t \cdot K \cdot |S| \cdot d)$, and the total space is $O((|U| + |I| + 2 \cdot |T|) \cdot d + K \cdot |S|)$.

Secondly, we analyse the time and space complexity of DPTR. Specifically, DPTR contains two important modules, i.e. the graph convolution module and the intent-aware module. For the graph convolution module, it captures high-order collaborative signals from entities interactions, thus the time complexity of the graph convolution module is $O(L \cdot |S| \cdot d)$ and an additional memory usage for storing the sparse adjacency matrices is $O(|S|)$. For the intent-aware module, it utilizes independent intent prototypes to model latent user intents, which introduces the time cost is $O(L \cdot (|U| + |I| + 2 \cdot |T|) \cdot K \cdot d)$. The space complexity of the embedding layer is $O((|U| + |I| + 2|T| + 4 \cdot K) \cdot d)$. Hence, the total time complexity of DPTR is $O(L \cdot |S| \cdot d + L \cdot (|U| + |I| + 2 \cdot |T|) \cdot K \cdot d)$ and the total space complexity is $O((|U| + |I| + 2|T| + 4 \cdot K) \cdot d + |S|)$.

5 Experiment

In this section, we describe the datasets, evaluation metrics and comparison methods. In addition, we conduct a series of experiments to analyze the impact of DPTR's parameters.

Table 1. The statistics of the datasets

Dataset	#Users	#Items	#Tags	#Interactions
lastfm-5	1348	6927	2132	162,047
lastfm-10	966	3870	1204	133,945
ml-10m-5	990	3247	2566	61,688
ml-10m-10	469	1524	1017	37,414

5.1 Datasets

To verify the effectiveness of DPTR, We conduct several groups of experiments on two public datasets (i.e. lastfm and ml-10m). Then, we pre-process each dataset and remove users, items and tags that appear less than p times for all datasets. We set p to 5 or 10 and obtain four datasets, i.e., lastfm-5, lastfm-10, ml-10m-5 and ml-10m-10. The statistics of the datasets are summarized in Table 1.

5.2 Evaluation Metrics and Baselines

To evaluate the performance of our proposed DPTR, we choose two broadly used rank-oriented metrics *Pre@N* and *Rec@N*. N is the length of the tag recommendation list. For these two metrics, we set $N = 3$, 5, and 10. In addition, we select the following baselines as comparison methods:

- PITF [18] explicitly models pairwise interactions among entities and utilizes low-dimensional feature vectors to represent users, items and tags.
- NLTF [5] employs Gaussian radial basis function to capture non-linear interactions among entities.

- ABNT [28] models the non-linear interactions among entities via multi-layer perceptron.
- NGCF [21] utilizes graph convolutional networks to boost the performance of item recommendation. In our experiment, we utilize user-tag interaction as input.
- GNN-PTR [2] employs the graph convolution module to capture high-order collaborative signals and injects them into the embeddings of entities.
- LNGTR [27] removes the feature transformation and nonlinear activation components from GNN-PTR to further improve the PTR performance.
- CLPTR [29] utilizes contrastive learning module to extract self-supervised signals from raw data.

Table 2. Performance comparison

Datasets	Metric	PITF	NLTF	ABNT	NGCF	GNN-PTR	LNGTR	CLPTR	**DPTR**
lastfm-5	Pre@3	0.2127	0.1949	0.1563	0.1679	0.2324	0.2789	0.3591	**0.3803**
	Pre@5	0.1789	0.1678	0.1353	0.1395	0.1913	0.2325	0.2918	**0.3086**
	Pre@10	0.1274	0.1191	0.1018	0.1023	0.1327	0.1596	0.1911	**0.1950**
	Rec@3	0.2571	0.2275	0.1569	0.2191	0.3244	0.3415	0.4490	**0.4878**
	Rec@5	0.3479	0.3239	0.2194	0.2907	0.4170	0.4511	0.5736	**0.6249**
	Rec@10	0.4814	0.4523	0.3298	0.4013	0.5454	0.5861	0.6990	**0.7411**
lastfm-10	Pre@3	0.2513	0.2443	0.1605	0.1739	0.2647	0.3240	0.4244	**0.4272**
	Pre@5	0.2088	0.2064	0.1367	0.1468	0.2143	0.2652	0.3371	**0.3455**
	Pre@10	0.1458	0.1249	0.0943	0.1140	0.1462	0.1833	0.2168	**0.2182**
	Rec@3	0.3204	0.2849	0.1579	0.2180	0.3479	0.3949	0.5250	**0.5357**
	Rec@5	0.4158	0.4017	0.2190	0.2878	0.4529	0.5208	0.6587	**0.6840**
	Rec@10	0.5654	0.5541	0.3034	0.4289	0.5874	0.6830	0.7998	**0.8023**
ml-10m-5	Pre@3	0.1398	0.1323	0.0822	0.0950	0.1455	0.1795	0.1929	**0.2194**
	Pre@5	0.1021	0.0972	0.0628	0.0683	0.1055	0.1388	0.1455	**0.1599**
	Pre@10	0.0641	0.0596	0.0400	0.0438	0.0672	0.0892	0.0908	**0.1037**
	Rec@3	0.3208	0.2974	0.2089	0.2463	0.3331	0.3819	0.4111	**0.4649**
	Rec@5	0.3910	0.3560	0.2538	0.2820	0.3965	0.4817	0.4992	**0.5476**
	Rec@10	0.4623	0.4270	0.3039	0.3495	0.4852	0.6008	0.6116	**0.7022**
ml-10m-10	Pre@3	0.1706	0.1436	0.0896	0.1244	0.1933	0.2267	0.2530	**0.2936**
	Pre@5	0.1245	0.1143	0.0759	0.0896	0.1390	0.1748	0.1833	**0.2027**
	Pre@10	0.0776	0.0714	0.0501	0.0571	0.0842	0.1064	0.1106	**0.1201**
	Rec@3	0.3628	0.3388	0.2210	0.3198	0.4602	0.4990	0.5795	**0.6593**
	Rec@5	0.4452	0.4334	0.3017	0.3837	0.5461	0.6319	0.6653	**0.7465**
	Rec@10	0.5615	0.5341	0.3858	0.4688	0.6398	0.7698	0.7775	**0.8654**

5.3 Experimental Settings

For all comparison methods, the embedding size d is tuned in $\{8, 16, 32, 64, 128, 256\}$, the batch size is set to 1024, the learning rate η is selected from $\{0.001, 0.005, 0.01\}$, the regularization coefficient λ_1 is chosen from $\{0.00001, 0.00005, 0.0001, 0.0005, 0.001, 0.005, 0.01\}$ and λ_2 varies in $\{0.00001, 0.00005, 0.0001, 0.0005, 0.001, 0.005, 0.01, 0.05\}$. For the GNN-based recommendation models, the number of layers L is selected from $\{1, 2, 3\}$. For DPTR, the number of latent intents K is tuned within $\{4, 8, 16, 32, 64, 128, 256, 512\}$. The parameters of all compared models are initialized via the Gaussian distribution with mean of 0 and standard deviation of 0.01. In addition, we utilize the Adam to optimize the parameters of all methods.

5.4 Performance Analysis

Table 2 demonstrates the performance of all comparison methods on different datasets. From Table 2, we have the following observations:

- PITF generally outperforms NGCF, NLTF and ABNT. It indicates that explicitly modelling the pairwise interactions among entities is significant for improving the performance of tag recommendation.
- The performance of GNN-PTR is superior to that of PITF. It demonstrates that utilizing the graph convolution module to capture high-order collaborative signals is beneficial for PTR.
- LNGTR performs better than GNN-PTR. One possible reason is that the light convolutional neural network is able to further improve the performance of tag recommendation models.
- CLPTR achieves better performance than LNGTR. This observation suggests that employing contrastive learning to extract self-supervised signals from interaction graphs is helpful to learn entities representations.
- Our proposed DPTR consistently outperforms other comparison methods, which indicates that integrating disentangled representation learning into PTR is effective. For instance, in terms of $Pre@5$ and $Rec@5$, DPTR outperforms CLPTR by 9.9 and 9.7% on the ml-10m-5. On the ml-10m-10, the improvements over CLPTR are 10.6 and 12.2%, respectively. The main reason is that DPTR not only employs the intent-aware module to model global intent-aware dependencies among different entities, but also utilizes the graph convolution module to capture the high-order collaborative signals.

5.5 Efficiency Analysis

In this section, we conduct experiment comparing the per-epoch runtime between iterative DRL-based models and our proposed DPTR model. As shown in Table 3, compared to the iterative DRL-based model, our DPTR achieves at least 3× speedup among all datasets and reaches up to the peak of 4.6× speedup on ml-10m-5, which demonstrates the efficiency of our proposed DPTR.

Table 3. Comparison of runtime (per epoch).

Datasets	Iterative DRL-based models	DPTR (ours)	Speedup
lastfm-5	8.3277s	2.6981s	3.1×
lastfm-10	6.6383s	2.2217s	3.0×
ml-10m-5	4.0533s	0.8851s	4.6×
ml-10m-10	2.4555s	0.6036s	4.1×

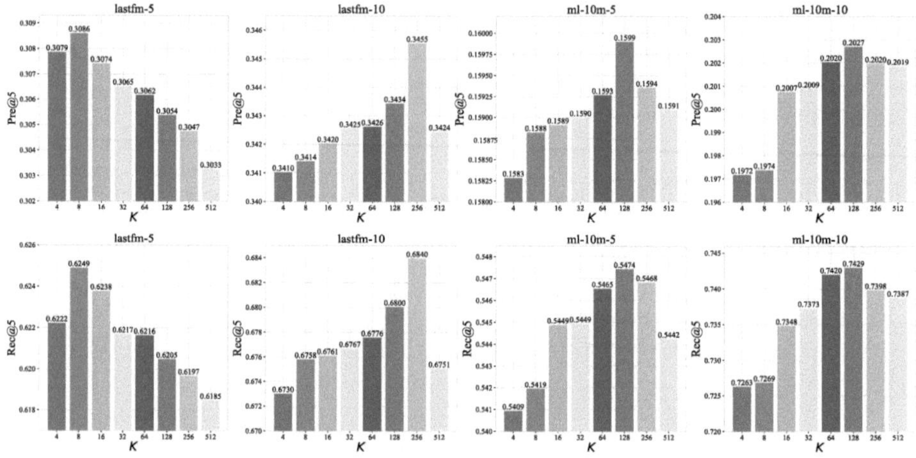

Fig. 3. The impact of K.

5.6 The Impact of K

For our proposed method, the number of latent intents K is a crucial parameter that affects the capability of disentangling latent intents. Therefore, we conduct a group of experiments to explore the impact of K. As shown in Fig. 3, with the increase of K from 4 to 512, the performance of DPTR reaches peak when K is 128 on the ml-10m. On the lastfm-5 and lastfm-10, DPTR achieves the best performance when K is 8 and 256, respectively. In addition, when the value of K reaches the threshold, further increase the value of K may be harmful to the performance. One possible reason is that much more fine-grained latent intents cause redundancy.

5.7 The Impact of d

To investigate the sensitivity of the embedding size d, we tune the value of d in $\{8, 16, 32, 64, 128, 256\}$ and keep the other parameters unchanged. The experimental results are plotted in Fig. 4. We can observe that DPTR exhibits the

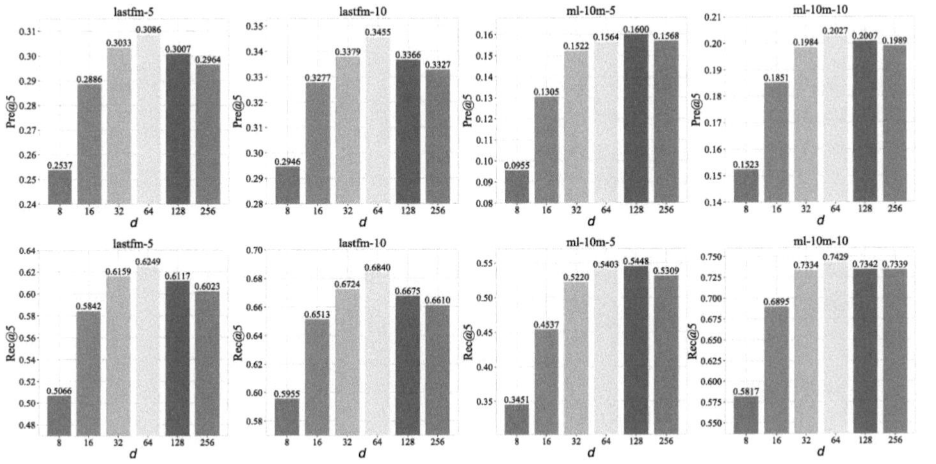

Fig. 4. The impact of d.

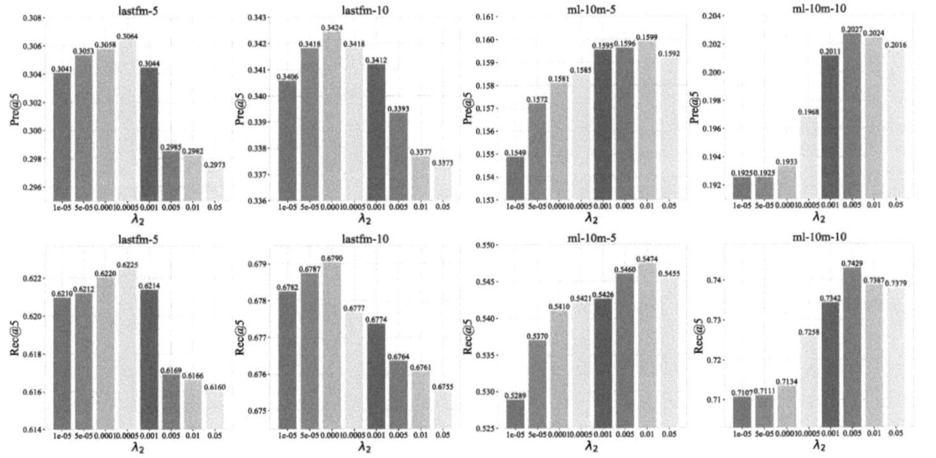

Fig. 5. The impact of λ_2.

poor performance on all datasets when d is relatively small. One possible reason is that the embedding of entities with small value of d is not able to accurately encode the latent intent information. Furthermore, when $d = 64$, the performance of DPTR reaches its peak on the lastfm-5, lastfm-10, and ml-10m-10. On the ml-10m-5, DPTR achieves the best performance when d is 128.

5.8 The Impact of λ_2

In this section, we conduct another group of experiments to investigate the impact of λ_2 on the performance of personalized tag recommendation. As shown in Fig. 5, the performance of DPTR achieves the best results on the lastfm-5, lastfm-10, ml-10m-5 and ml-10m-10 when $\lambda_2 = 0.0005$, 0.0001, 0.01 and 0.005, respectively. We observe that the values of λ_2 on the lastfm are smaller than those of on ml-10m when DPTR achieve the optimal performance. This indicates that the value of λ_2 should be carefully tuned for different datasets to ensure the effectiveness of intent-aware module.

6 Conclusion

In this paper, we propose a disentangled representation learning-based personalized tag recommendation. Specifically, we utilize the similarities between intent prototypes and entities to infer the latent intents of the tagging decisions of user. In addition, we integrate the intent-aware module into GNN. In this way, we utilize the intent-aware module to distinguish the latent user intents and employ graph convolution module to capture the high-order collaborative signals among entities. Extensive experiments on all datasets demonstrate that DPTR outperforms traditional PTR models.

Acknowledgments. This work is supported in part by the Open Foundation of State Key Laboratory for Novel Software Technology at Nanjing University of P.R. China (No. KFKT2025B18), the Future Network Scientific Research Fund Project (FNSRFP-2021-YB-54), Qing Lan Project of Jiangsu Province, and Tongda College of Nanjing University of Posts and Telecommunications (XK203XZ21001).

Disclosure of Interests. The authors declare that they have no known competing financial interests or personal relationships that could have appeared to influence the work reported in this paper.

References

1. Chen, H., Chen, Y., Wang, X., Xie, R., Wang, R., Xia, F., Zhu, W.: Curriculum disentangled recommendation with noisy multi-feedback. Nips **34**, 26924–26936 (2021)
2. Chen, X., Yu, Y., Jiang, F., Zhang, L., Gao, R., Gao, H.: Graph neural networks boosted personalized tag recommendation algorithm. In: IJCNN, pp. 1–8. IEEE (2020)
3. Cheng, P., Min, M.R., Shen, D., Malon, C., Zhang, Y., Li, Y., Carin, L.: Improving Disentangled Text Representation Learning with Information-theoretic Guidance. arXiv:2006.00693 (2020)
4. Fan, W., Ma, Y., Li, Q., He, Y., Zhao, E., Tang, J., Yin, D.: Graph neural networks for social recommendation. In: The World Wide Web Conference, pp. 417–426 (2019)

5. Fang, X., Pan, R., Cao, G., He, X., Dai, W.: Personalized tag recommendation through nonlinear tensor factorization using gaussian kernel. In: AAAI, vol. 29 (2015)
6. Hotho, A., Jäschke, R., Schmitz, C., Stumme, G.: Information retrieval in folksonomies: search and ranking. In: The Semantic Web: Research and Applications: 3rd European Semantic Web Conference, ESWC 2006 Budva, Montenegro, June 11–14, 2006 Proceedings 3, pp. 411—426. Springer (2006)
7. Hu, L., Xu, S., Li, C., Yang, C., Shi, C., Duan, N., Xie, X., Zhou, M.: Graph neural news recommendation with unsupervised preference disentanglement. In: ACL, pp. 4255–4264 (2020)
8. Jäschke, R., Marinho, L., Hotho, A., Schmidt-Thieme, L., Stumme, G.: Tag recommendations in folksonomies. In: PKDD, pp. 506–514. Springer (2007)
9. Li, A., Cheng, Z., Liu, F., Gao, Z., Guan, W., Peng, Y.: Disentangled graph neural networks for session-based recommendation. IEEE Trans. Knowl. Data Eng. **35**(8), 7870–7882 (2022)
10. Li, H., Wang, X., Zhang, Z., Yuan, Z., Li, H., Zhu, W.: Disentangled contrastive learning on graphs. Nips **34**, 21872–21884 (2021)
11. Liu, Y., Wang, X., Wu, S., Xiao, Z.: Independence promoted graph disentangled networks. In: AAAI, vol. 34, pp. 4916–4923 (2020)
12. Ma, J., Cui, P., Kuang, K., Wang, X., Zhu, W.: Disentangled graph convolutional networks. In: ICML, pp. 4212–4221. PMLR (2019)
13. Ma, J., Zhou, C., Cui, P., Yang, H., Zhu, W.: Learning disentangled representations for recommendation. Nips **32**, 54–98 (2019)
14. Ma, L., Sun, Q., Georgoulis, S., Van Gool, L., Schiele, B., Fritz, M.: Disentangled person image generation. In: CVPR, pp. 99–108 (2018)
15. Ren, X., Xia, L., Zhao, J., Yin, D., Huang, C.: Disentangled contrastive collaborative filtering. In: SIGIR, pp. 1137–1146 (2023)
16. Rendle, S., Balby Marinho, L., Nanopoulos, A., Schmidt-Thieme, L.: Learning optimal ranking with tensor factorization for tag recommendation. In: KDD, pp. 727–736 (2009)
17. Rendle, S., Freudenthaler, C., Gantner, Z., Schmidt-Thieme, L.: Bpr: Bayesian Personalized Ranking from Implicit Feedback. arXiv:1205.2618 (2012)
18. Rendle, S., Schmidt-Thieme, L.: Pairwise interaction tensor factorization for personalized tag recommendation. In: WSDM, pp. 81–90 (2010)
19. Scarselli, F., Gori, M., Tsoi, A.C., Hagenbuchner, M., Monfardini, G.: The graph neural network model. IEEE Trans. Neural Netw. **20**(1), 61–80 (2008)
20. Symeonidis, P., Nanopoulos, A., Manolopoulos, Y.: Tag recommendations based on tensor dimensionality reduction. RecSystem **19**, 43–50 (2008)
21. Wang, X., He, X., Wang, M., Feng, F., Chua, T.S.: Neural graph collaborative filtering. In: SIGIR, pp. 165–174 (2019)
22. Wang, X., Jin, H., Zhang, A., He, X., Xu, T., Chua, T.S.: Disentangled graph collaborative filtering. In: SIGIR, pp. 1001–1010 (2020)
23. Wang, X., Chen, H., Wu, Z., Zhu, W.: Disentangled representation learning. IEEE Trans. Pattern Anal. Mach. Intell. **4**, 1542 (2024)
24. Wang, Y., Tang, S., Lei, Y., Song, W., Wang, S., Zhang, M.: Disenhan: disentangled heterogeneous graph attention network for recommendation. In: CIKM, pp. 1605–1614 (2020)
25. Wu, S., Tang, Y., Zhu, Y., Wang, L., Xie, X., Tan, T.: Session-based recommendation with graph neural networks. AAAI **33**, 346–353 (2019)
26. Yang, Y., Feng, Z., Song, M., Wang, X.: Factorizable graph convolutional networks. Nips **33**, 20286–20296 (2020)

27. Yu, Y., Chen, X., Zhang, L., Gao, R., Gao, H.: Neural graph for personalized tag recommendation. IEEE Intell. Syst. **37**(1), 51–59 (2020)
28. Yuan, J., Jin, Y., Liu, W., Wang, X.: Attention-based neural tag recommendation. In: DASFAA, pp. 350–365. Springer (2019)
29. Zhang, A., Yu, Y., Li, S., Gao, R., Zhang, L., Gao, S.: Contrastive learning-based personalized tag recommendation. Sensors **24**(18), 6061 (2024)
30. Zhao, S., Wei, W., Zou, D., Mao, X.: Multi-view intent disentangle graph networks for bundle recommendation. AAAI **36**, 4379–4387 (2022)

LIPKE: Multi-behavior Recommendation Based on Long-Short Interest Perception and Knowledge Enhancement

Zihao Ma, Haibo Liu(✉), Xin Song, Liang Wang, and Bo Sun

School of Cyber Security and Computer, Hebei University, Baoding, China
mazihao@stumail.hbu.edu.cn, liuhaibo@hbu.edu.cn

Abstract. Multi-behavior recommendation improves target-behavior prediction by leveraging heterogeneous user feedback such as view, cart, and purchase. In this setting, two practical challenges often arise simultaneously. On the one hand, effective target prediction requires both relatively stable long-term preferences and rapidly changing short-term intent. On the other hand, indiscriminate sharing across behaviors may introduce conflicting signals and lead to negative transfer. To address these issues, we propose **LIPKE**, a unified framework for multi-behavior recommendation. Specifically, LIPKE employs a Cascade–Parallel Graph Encoder (CPG) to capture long-term preferences from multi-behavior interaction structures, a Mamba-based Temporal Module (MTM) to model recency-sensitive target intent, and a Projection-Based Multi-expert Decoder (PME) to enhance target-behavior representations with selectively filtered and target-aligned auxiliary knowledge while suppressing harmful cross-behavior interference. Experiments on three public datasets show that LIPKE consistently outperforms strong baselines. Additional ablation studies and diagnostic analyses further verify the effectiveness of long-short interest perception and selective cross-behavior knowledge enhancement.

Keywords: Multi-behavior recommendation · Long-short interest perception · Knowledge enhancement

1 Introduction

Recommender systems learn user preferences from interaction logs and are widely used in online platforms [3,12]. Classic collaborative filtering usually optimizes a single target action and often suffers from severe sparsity. In practice, users generate multiple behavior types such as view, add-to-cart, and purchase, which reflect different decision stages and provide complementary intent signals [5, 9]. Multi-behavior recommendation (MBR) leverages such auxiliary behaviors to improve target-behavior prediction under sparse supervision [15]. However, effective target prediction in MBR often depends on both relatively stable long-term preference and rapidly changing short-term intent, while heterogeneous auxiliary behaviors may also introduce negative transfer.

L. Ding et al. (Eds.): APWeb-WAIM 2026, LNCS 16993, pp. 443–459, 2027.
https://doi.org/10.1007/978-981-92-5693-8_28

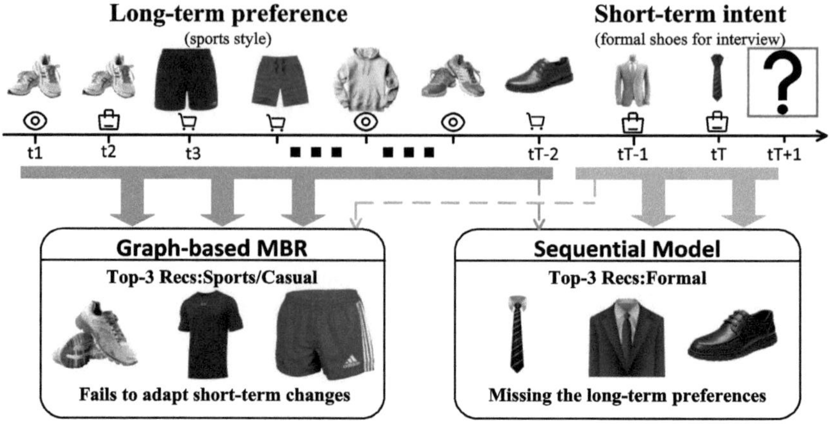

Fig. 1. Motivating example of long–short preference conflict in multi-behavior recommendation.

Existing MBR methods mainly improve recommendation through cross-behavior sharing, structural modeling, or dependency modeling [5,9,15,21]. Although they achieve strong results, temporal modeling and reliable cross-behavior transfer are often not handled together. We therefore focus on the following two coupled challenges.

Challenge 1: Long-Term Preference Versus Short-Term Target Intent . Graph-based MBR methods are effective at learning relatively stable structural preference, but may be less sensitive to recent target-intent shifts. Sequential models are better suited to temporal dynamics, yet they may underutilize long-range multi-behavior structural evidence. As illustrated in Fig. 1, jointly modeling long-term consistency and recency-sensitive intent remains challenging.

Challenge 2: Negative Transfer from Heterogeneous Auxiliary Behaviors . Auxiliary behaviors differ in semantics, noise, and frequency. Naive cross-behavior sharing may therefore introduce conflicting signals, and high-frequency behaviors may dominate representation learning, resulting in negative transfer.

To address these challenges, we propose **LIPKE** (*Multi-Behavior Recommendation based on Long-Short Interest Perception and Knowledge Enhancement*), a unified framework for multi-behavior recommendation. LIPKE consists of three components: a *Cascade–Parallel Graph Encoder* (CPG) for long-term multi-behavior structural modeling, a *Mamba-based Temporal Module* (MTM) for recency-sensitive target-intent modeling, and a *Projection-Based Multi-expert Decoder* (PME) for target-aligned auxiliary knowledge enhancement with reduced negative transfer. Rather than assuming that all aligned auxiliary signals are beneficial, we seek a target-biased transfer mechanism that retains target-consistent components while leaving behavior-specific residuals outside the shared prediction path.

Our main contributions are summarized as follows:

- We study two coupled challenges in multi-behavior recommendation, namely long-short interest perception and cross-behavior negative transfer, and propose a unified framework for target-behavior prediction.
- We develop three complementary components in LIPKE: CPG for long-term structural modeling, MTM for recency-sensitive target-intent modeling, and PME for target-aligned selective transfer from heterogeneous auxiliary behaviors.
- Experiments on three public datasets show that LIPKE consistently outperforms strong baselines, while ablation studies and diagnostic analyses support the effectiveness of long-short interest modeling and selective cross-behavior knowledge enhancement.

2 Related Work

Multi-behavior recommendation (MBR) exploits heterogeneous user actions such as view, cart, and purchase to alleviate target-behavior sparsity and improve recommendation quality [19]. Early studies mainly extend matrix factorization or multi-task learning to share information across behaviors, while more recent methods build behavior-specific user-item graphs and model cross-behavior dependencies through graph propagation or cascade-style designs, such as NMTR [5], MBGCN [9], and MB-CGCN [2]. Although these methods achieve strong results, they mainly focus on structural dependency modeling, while jointly handling long-term structural preference, short-term target intent, and reliable cross-behavior transfer remains challenging.

Sequential recommendation predicts future interactions from ordered user histories. Representative models include SASRec [10], BERT4Rec [17], and time-aware variants such as TiSASRec. For multi-behavior scenarios, MBSRec [4] further incorporates behavior types into sequence modeling. These methods are effective at capturing temporal dynamics and recent behavioral patterns, but they do not explicitly model long-range multi-behavior structural information. In addition, efficient temporal encoders such as state-space models have recently been explored in recommendation, e.g., Mamba4Rec [13].

Multi-task learning (MTL) improves recommendation by sharing supervision across related tasks. To reduce task conflicts caused by naive parameter sharing, expert-based models such as MMoE [14] and PLE [18] perform more selective sharing, while recent methods such as PKEF [15] and COPF [23] further suppress harmful transfer through projection or behavior filtering. However, in multi-behavior recommendation, auxiliary behaviors may differ substantially in semantics, frequency, and noise level, making negative transfer control still a challenging problem.

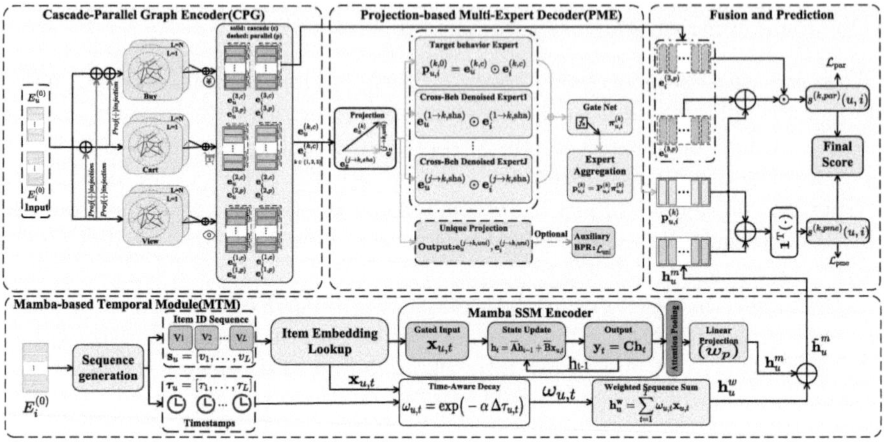

Fig. 2. Overview of LIPKE: Cascade–parallel graph encoder(CPG for long-term), Projection-based Multi-expert Decoder(PME for negative-transfer suppression), and Mamba-based Temporal Module (MTM for short-term intent).

3 Methodology

We propose **LIPKE**, a unified framework for multi-behavior recommendation, as illustrated in Fig. 2. LIPKE consists of three components: a *Cascade–Parallel Graph Encoder* (CPG) for long-term multi-behavior structural modeling, a *Projection-Based Multi-expert Decoder* (PME) for target-aligned auxiliary knowledge enhancement with reduced negative transfer, and a *Mamba-based Temporal Module* (MTM) for short-term target-intent modeling from target-behavior sequences. The resulting graph-based and temporal representations are fused for final prediction under the target behavior.

3.1 Problem Definition and Data Construction

We consider a multi-behavior recommendation setting with user set U and item set I, where $|U| = M$ and $|I| = N$. There are K behavior types, and we denote the behavior set by $\mathcal{B} = \{1, \ldots, K\}$. Each behavior $k \in \mathcal{B}$ is associated with a binary interaction matrix $\mathbf{R}^{(k)} \in \{0, 1\}^{M \times N}$. The K-th behavior is treated as the target behavior, and the goal is to learn a scoring function $s^{(K)}(u, i)$ for ranking items for user u under the target behavior. For any behavior pair (k, j), we define a cross-behavior unique interaction matrix $\mathbf{R}^{(k \setminus j)} = \mathbf{R}^{(k)} \odot (1 - \mathbf{R}^{(j)})$, which preserves interactions appearing in behavior k but not in behavior j and is used for behavior-specific residual supervision.

For temporal modeling, we precompute a fixed-length target-behavior sequence for each user, $s_u = [v_{u,1}, \ldots, v_{u,L}]$, with the corresponding ordered timestamps $\tau^u = [\tau_{u,1}, \ldots, \tau_{u,L}]$. We initialize trainable user and item embeddings as $\mathbf{E}_u^{(0)} \in \mathbb{R}^{M \times d}$ and $\mathbf{E}_i^{(0)} \in \mathbb{R}^{N \times d}$, which are shared by the graph and temporal modules.

3.2 Cascade–Parallel Graph Encoder (CPG)

For each behavior k, we construct a behavior-specific user-item bipartite graph and perform message passing with the normalized adjacency matrix $\tilde{\mathbf{A}}^{(k)}$. CPG captures long-term multi-behavior structural preference through two branches: a parallel branch for within-behavior structural modeling, and a cascade branch that propagates information along a predefined behavior order to exploit cross-behavior dependency. To reduce noisy accumulation during cascade propagation, only the target-aligned component from the parallel branch is injected.
Parallel Per-behavior Encoder. Let $\mathbf{E}^{(0)} = [\mathbf{E}_u^{(0)}; \mathbf{E}_i^{(0)}] \in \mathbb{R}^{(M+N) \times d}$. For behavior k, the parallel encoder applies L_k LightGCN-style layers:

$$\mathbf{E}^{(k,p,\ell+1)} = \tilde{\mathbf{A}}^{(k)} \mathbf{E}^{(k,p,\ell)} + \mathbf{E}^{(k,p,\ell)}, \tag{1}$$

and aggregates the layer-wise embeddings as $\mathbf{E}^{(k,p)} = \sum_{\ell=0}^{L_k} \mathbf{E}^{(k,p,\ell)}$.
Cascade Encoder with Projection-Based Denoising. Behaviors are processed sequentially with a cascade input $\mathbf{E}_{in}$ initialized as $\mathbf{E}^{(0)}$. At layer ℓ, the cascade branch first performs neighborhood aggregation $\mathbf{S}^{(k,\ell)} = \tilde{\mathbf{A}}^{(k)} \mathbf{E}^{(k,c,\ell)}$. Instead of directly injecting the parallel representation, we only retain the component aligned with the current cascade signal through a node-wise projection operator. Specifically, for two node embedding vectors $\mathbf{x}, \mathbf{y} \in \mathbb{R}^d$, we define

$$\mathrm{Proj}(\mathbf{x} \mid \mathbf{y}) = \frac{\langle \mathbf{x}, \mathbf{y} \rangle}{\|\mathbf{y}\|_2^2 + \epsilon} \mathbf{y}, \tag{2}$$

where the projection is applied row-wise when the input is a stack of node embeddings. The cascade embedding is then updated by

$$\mathbf{E}^{(k,c,\ell+1)} = \mathbf{S}^{(k,\ell)} + \mathbf{E}^{(k,c,\ell)} + \gamma \cdot \mathrm{Proj}\Big(\mathbf{E}^{(k,p,\ell+1)} \mid \mathbf{S}^{(k,\ell)}\Big). \tag{3}$$

Here, γ controls the strength of the injected aligned signal. When $\gamma = 0$, the update reduces to pure cascade propagation. After L_k layers, the final cascade output is added back to the running cascade input, $\mathbf{E}_{in} \leftarrow \mathbf{E}_{in} + \mathbf{E}^{(k,c,L_k)}$, and we obtain $\mathbf{E}^{(k,c)} = \sum_{\ell=0}^{L_k} \mathbf{E}^{(k,c,\ell)}$.

3.3 Projection-Based Multi-expert Decoder (PME)

Cascade embeddings $\mathbf{e}_u^{(k,c)}$ and $\mathbf{e}_i^{(k,c)}$ encode long-term structural preference under behavior k, but directly aggregating auxiliary behaviors may introduce misaligned evidence and lead to negative transfer. To address this issue, we design a *Projection-Based Multi-expert Decoder* (PME), which uses projection to separate target-aligned and behavior-specific components and an adaptive soft gate to select reliable experts for each user-item pair.

We note that projection is not intended to provide a strict semantic guarantee that the retained component is always beneficial. Instead, it serves as a target-biased filtering operator that emphasizes the component of auxiliary behavior embeddings aligned with the target-behavior representation under the learned space. To further reduce the risk of transferring spuriously aligned but unhelpful signals, PME does not directly inject all projected information into the final prediction path; instead, it combines projection decomposition with instance-wise gated aggregation, while keeping the orthogonal residual only for auxiliary supervision.

Projection Decomposition. Given the target behavior k and an auxiliary behavior $j \neq k$, PME decomposes behavior-j information into a shared component aligned with the target space and a unique residual preserving behavior-specific variations. For any node $x \in U \cup I$, we compute

$$\mathbf{e}_x^{(j \to k, sha)} = \eta \cdot \text{Proj}\Big(\mathbf{e}_x^{(j,c)} \mid \mathbf{e}_x^{(k,c)}\Big), \tag{4}$$

$$\mathbf{e}_x^{(j \to k, uni)} = \eta \cdot \Big(\mathbf{e}_x^{(j,c)} - \text{Proj}\Big(\mathbf{e}_x^{(j,c)} \mid \mathbf{e}_x^{(k,c)}\Big)\Big), \tag{5}$$

where $\text{Proj}(\cdot)$ denotes the projection operator, and η controls the transfer magnitude. Only the target-aligned shared component is used for cross-behavior fusion, while the residual component is reserved for auxiliary supervision.

Shared Experts and Gated Aggregation. For each behavior k, PME builds an expert set consisting of one target expert and $K-1$ denoised auxiliary experts. Given a user-item pair (u, i), the target expert is defined as $\mathbf{p}_{u,i}^{(k,0)} = \mathbf{e}_u^{(k,c)} \odot \mathbf{e}_i^{(k,c)}$, and each auxiliary behavior $j \in \mathcal{B} \setminus \{k\}$ provides a denoised expert $\mathbf{p}_{u,i}^{(k,j)} = \mathbf{e}_u^{(j \to k, sha)} \odot \mathbf{e}_i^{(j \to k, sha)}$. These experts are then aggregated with an instance-wise soft gate:

$$\boldsymbol{\alpha}_{u,i}^{(k)} = \text{softmax}\Big(g\Big([\mathbf{e}_u^{(k,c)}; \mathbf{e}_i^{(k,c)}]\Big)\Big), \quad \mathbf{p}_{u,i}^{(k)} = \sum_{m=0}^{K-1} \alpha_{u,i}^{(k,m)} \mathbf{p}_{u,i}^{(k,m)}. \tag{6}$$

This design makes transfer data-dependent, so that different users or items can rely on different auxiliary behaviors.

Unique Branch and Auxiliary Supervision. The unique residual $\mathbf{e}^{(j \to k, uni)}$ is not injected into the shared fusion path. Instead, it is used only for auxiliary training on the cross-behavior unique interactions $\mathbf{R}^{(k \setminus j)}$, providing complementary supervision without forcing behavior-specific noise into the target-aligned space. To further prevent auxiliary gradients from overwriting the target representation, we apply stop-gradient to the shared-path anchor $\mathbf{e}_x^{(k,c)}$ during this auxiliary optimization. Specifically, for each auxiliary behavior $j \neq k$, we define the unique-branch score as

$$s^{(k,j,uni)}(u,i) = \left\langle \mathrm{sg}\left(\mathbf{e}_u^{(k,c)}\right) + \mathbf{e}_u^{(j\to k,uni)}, \mathrm{sg}\left(\mathbf{e}_i^{(k,c)}\right) + \mathbf{e}_i^{(j\to k,uni)} \right\rangle, \quad (7)$$

where $\mathrm{sg}(\cdot)$ denotes the stop-gradient operator. This auxiliary score is optimized on $\mathbf{R}^{(k\backslash j)}$ and is used only during training, making cross-behavior learning more selective and less destructive. In this way, even if some auxiliary residual patterns are correlated with the target space, their optimization does not overwrite the target anchor representation through the shared path.

3.4 Mamba-Based Temporal Module (MTM)

To model recency-sensitive target intent, we introduce a *Mamba-Based Temporal Module* (MTM) over the fixed-length target-behavior sequence. MTM adopts a Mamba-style state-space backbone, while its key design lies in recency-aware temporal modeling rather than the backbone alone. For each user u, we use the target-behavior sequence $\mathbf{s}_u = [v_{u,1}, \ldots, v_{u,L}]$ with timestamps $\boldsymbol{\tau}^u = [\tau_{u,1}, \ldots, \tau_{u,L}]$, where each item $v_{u,t}$ is mapped to an embedding $\mathbf{x}_{u,t} \in \mathbb{R}^d$.

Time-Aware Decay. To reflect the diminishing influence of older interactions, we assign each step a continuous recency weight:

$$\omega_{u,t} = \exp(-\alpha(\tau_{u,\max} - \tau_{u,t})), \quad (8)$$

where $\tau_{u,\max} = \max_t \tau_{u,t}$ is the most recent timestamp, and α is a learnable coefficient controlling recency sensitivity.

Recency Shortcut. Before sequential encoding, we compute a lightweight weighted summary of the sequence: $\mathbf{h}_u^w = \sum_{t=1}^{L} \omega_{u,t}\mathbf{x}_{u,t}$, which preserves strong recent signals and serves as a stable shortcut when sequential patterns are noisy.

Mamba-Style Sequential Encoding. To inject recency bias into token-level dynamics, we first modulate each input with a time-aware gate:

$$\mathbf{g}_{u,t} = \sigma(\mathbf{x}_{u,t}\mathbf{W}_g + \delta_g \log(\omega_{u,t} + \epsilon)), \quad \mathbf{u}_{u,t} = \mathbf{g}_{u,t} \odot \mathbf{x}_{u,t}, \quad (9)$$

where $\sigma(\cdot)$ is the sigmoid function, $\mathbf{W}_g$ is a learnable projection, δ_g controls the recency effect in gating, and ϵ is a small constant for numerical stability. The gated input is then propagated through a state-space recurrence:

$$\mathbf{h}_{u,t} = \mathbf{h}_{u,t-1}\mathbf{A} + \mathbf{u}_{u,t}\mathbf{B}, \qquad \mathbf{y}_{u,t} = \mathbf{h}_{u,t}\mathbf{C}, \quad (10)$$

where $\mathbf{A}$, $\mathbf{B}$, and $\mathbf{C}$ are learnable SSM parameters. This design maintains a compact sequential state while explicitly biasing the model toward recent target-behavior evidence.

Recency-Aware Pooling and Output Fusion. The token-level outputs $\{\mathbf{y}_{u,t}\}$ are aggregated into a user-level short-term representation via attention pooling:

$$a_{u,t} = \mathrm{softmax}(\mathbf{y}_{u,t}\mathbf{w}_{att} + \delta_a \log(\omega_{u,t} + \epsilon)), \tag{11}$$

$$\tilde{\mathbf{h}}_u^m = \left(\sum_{t=1}^{L} a_{u,t}\mathbf{y}_{u,t}\right)\mathbf{W}_p, \tag{12}$$

where $\mathbf{w}_{att}$ and $\mathbf{W}_p$ are learnable parameters, and δ_a controls the recency bias in pooling. Finally, we combine the pooled sequential representation with the recency shortcut: $\mathbf{h}_u^m = \tilde{\mathbf{h}}_u^m + \mathbf{h}_u^w$. The resulting vector $\mathbf{h}_u^m$ serves as the short-term target-intent representation and is later fused with long-term graph representations for target-behavior prediction.

3.5 Fusion and Prediction

MTM produces a short-term target-intent vector $\mathbf{h}_u^m$, which complements the long-term graph representations in both prediction heads. We use two behavior-level heads to score each user-item pair under behavior k. The *long–short interest perception head* combines the parallel graph representation with short-term intent:

$$s^{(k,par)}(u,i) = D\langle \mathbf{e}_u^{(k,p)} + \mathbf{h}_u^m, \mathbf{e}_i^{(k,p)}\rangle, \tag{13}$$

where $D\langle\cdot,\cdot\rangle$ denotes the inner-product decoder. The *knowledge-enhanced head* scores the PME expert representation together with the short-term intent:

$$s^{(k,pme)}(u,i) = \mathbf{1}^\top\left(\mathbf{p}_{u,i}^{(k)} + \mathbf{h}_u^m\right), \tag{14}$$

where $\mathbf{1}$ is an all-one vector used to sum the representation dimensions into a scalar score. For inference on the target behavior K, we combine the two heads:

$$s(u,i) = s^{(K,par)}(u,i) + s^{(K,pme)}(u,i), \tag{15}$$

where $s(u,i)$ is the final ranking score of item i for user u under the target behavior. This design allows the final prediction to jointly exploit long-term structural preference, short-term target intent, and target-aligned auxiliary knowledge.

3.6 Objective Function

We optimize LIPKE with the Bayesian Personalized Ranking (BPR) objective, which maximizes the margin between a positive item i^+ and a sampled negative item i^- for each user u.

Specifically, the parallel-branch BPR loss is applied to the auxiliary behaviors to learn behavior-specific structural representations. For the target behavior, we optimize the PME head for the main prediction task, while the unique-branch loss provides complementary supervision on cross-behavior unique interactions. With ℓ_2 regularization, the overall objective is

$$\mathcal{L} = \sum_{k=1}^{K-1} \lambda_k \mathcal{L}_{\mathrm{BPR}}\left(s^{(k,par)}\right) + \lambda_K \mathcal{L}_{\mathrm{BPR}}\left(s^{(K,pme)}\right) + \lambda_K \mathcal{L}_{uni} + \mu\|\Theta\|_2^2, \quad (16)$$

where $\mathcal{L}_{uni} = \sum_{j=1}^{K-1} \mathcal{L}_{\mathrm{BPR}}\big(s^{(K,j,uni)}\big)$ is trained on $\mathbf{R}^{(K\setminus j)}$ with stop-gradient applied to the shared-path anchor. Here, λ_k balances the contributions of different loss terms.

4 Experiments

In this section, we conduct extensive experiments on three real-world datasets to comprehensively evaluate LIPKE. We aim to answer the following research questions:

RQ1: How does LIPKE perform compared with state-of-the-art baselines on overall recommendation accuracy?

RQ2: How do different components of LIPKE affect performance, and do they solve the above two challenges?

RQ3: How sensitive is LIPKE to the target-sequence truncation length in temporal modeling?

RQ4: How sensitive is LIPKE to key hyperparameters?

4.1 Experimental Settings

Datasets. Following PKEF [15] and COPF [23], we adopt the same three public multi-behavior datasets for evaluation: Beibei, Taobao, and Tmall. These datasets contain multiple user behaviors (e.g., View, Cart, Collect, and Buy) together with timestamps. Following prior work, we filter out users and items with fewer than 10 interactions and sort all interactions chronologically. In all datasets, the target behavior is *Buy*. For temporal modeling, we construct a fixed-length sequence for each user using only the most recent target-behavior interactions observed before the prediction timestamp, together with their timestamps. The detailed statistics are summarized in Table 1.

Evaluation Metrics. Following prior work [15,23], we evaluate the performance of LIPKE and all baselines on Top-K recommendation using two widely used metrics: Hit Ratio (H@K) and Normalized Discounted Cumulative Gain (N@K), where $K \in \{10, 20\}$.

Baselines. To comprehensively evaluate LIPKE, we compare it with representative baselines from four categories. **Single-behavior models**: MF-BPR [16], NeuMF [8], and LightGCN [7]. **Sequential models**: SASRec [10], Mamba4Rec [13], and MBSRec [4]. **Multi-behavior GNN-based models**: NMTR [5], MBGCN [9], S-MBRec [6], and MB-CGCN [2]. **Multi-behavior**

models with MTL/cascade training: CML [20], CRGCN [21], PKEF [15], BCIPM [22], and COPF [23]. All methods are evaluated under the same data split and ranking protocol.

Implementation Details. LIPKE is implemented in TensorFlow [1]. The embedding dimension is set to $d = 64$. All parameters are initialized with Xavier initialization and optimized by Adam [11] with learning rate 1×10^{-3} and batch size 2048. The ℓ_2 regularization coefficient is set to $\mu = 1 \times 10^{-2}$. For MTM, we use a Mamba state expansion factor of 2, and the target-behavior sequence is constructed from the most recent L target-behavior interactions of each user, with the default truncation length $L = 30$. For the cascade branch, the predefined behavior order follows the natural action dependency in each dataset, i.e., View → Cart → Buy on Beibei and Taobao, and View → Collect → Cart → Buy on Tmall. We tune the GCN depth in $\{1, 2, 3, 4\}$, the projection scale η in $\{0.0, 0.25, 0.5, 0.75, 1.0\}$, and the cascade injection coefficient γ in $\{0.0, 0.1, 0.3, 0.5, 0.7\}$. The behavior weights (λ_1, λ_2) for auxiliary behaviors are searched in $\{0, \frac{1}{6}, \ldots, 1\}$ under the constraint $\lambda_1 + \lambda_2 \leq 1$, and the target-behavior weight is set accordingly. The best configuration is selected on the validation set. Unless otherwise specified, all baselines are tuned following their original papers under the same experimental protocol, and all reported results are averaged over five runs. Hyperparameter sensitivity is further analyzed in Sect. 4.5.

Table 1. Statistics of evaluation datasets.

Dataset	#User	#Item	#Interaction	#Target Inter.	#Behavior Type
Beibei	21,716	7,977	3.3×10^6	282,860	{View, Cart, Buy}
Taobao	15,449	11,953	1.2×10^6	92,180	{View, Cart, Buy}
Tmall	41,738	11,953	2.3×10^6	255,586	{View, Collect, Cart, Buy}

4.2 Overall Performance Comparison (RQ1)

Table 2 reports the overall performance of LIPKE and all baselines on Beibei, Taobao, and Tmall. We summarize the main observations as follows.

Overall Performance. LIPKE achieves the best H@K and N@K on all three datasets. Compared with the strongest baseline, the relative improvements reach 16.47% on Beibei (H@20), 15.6% on Taobao (N@20), and 13.15% on Tmall (N@20). The gains are particularly notable on Taobao, where the target behavior is relatively sparse, and remain consistent on Tmall, suggesting that LIPKE is effective across datasets with different sparsity characteristics.

Table 2. Overall comparison on Beibei, Taobao, and Tmall.

Model	Beibei				Taobao				Tmall			
	H@10	N@10	H@20	N@20	H@10	N@10	H@20	N@20	H@10	N@10	H@20	N@20
MF-BPR	0.0191	0.0049	0.0427	0.0179	0.0076	0.0036	0.0221	0.0113	0.0230	0.0124	0.0316	0.0144
NeuMF	0.0232	0.0135	0.0736	0.0290	0.0236	0.0128	0.0493	0.0236	0.0124	0.0062	0.0311	0.0152
LightGCN	0.0391	0.0161	0.0478	0.0204	0.0411	0.0240	0.0603	0.0312	0.0393	0.0209	0.0538	0.0243
SASRec	0.0423	0.0352	0.0554	0.0384	0.0793	0.0391	0.1042	0.0673	0.0659	0.0465	0.1453	0.0742
Mamba4Rec	0.0561	0.0301	0.0935	0.0525	0.0792	0.0391	0.1034	0.0612	0.0838	0.0502	0.1321	0.0746
MBSRec	0.0732	0.0514	0.1103	0.0732	0.0841	0.0627	0.1423	0.0725	0.0744	0.0524	0.0851	0.0552
NMTR	0.0429	0.0198	0.0776	0.0296	0.0282	0.0137	0.0515	0.0242	0.0536	0.0286	0.0642	0.0303
MBGCN	0.0619	0.0297	0.1019	0.0397	0.0509	0.0294	0.0564	0.0342	0.1461	0.0770	<u>0.2072</u>	<u>0.0920</u>
S-MBRec	0.0489	0.0253	0.1059	0.0313	0.0498	0.0269	0.0811	0.0408	0.0694	0.0362	0.0958	0.0502
MB-CGCN	0.0579	0.0381	0.0972	0.0404	0.1233	0.0677	0.1497	0.0712	0.0984	0.0558	0.2007	0.0880
CML	0.0507	0.0292	0.0649	0.0310	0.0298	0.0150	0.0378	0.0171	0.0388	0.0127	0.0493	0.0138
CRGCN	0.0459	0.0324	0.0944	0.0361	0.0855	0.0439	0.1463	0.0717	0.0840	0.0442	0.1238	0.0540
PKEF	0.1130	0.0582	0.1321	0.0652	0.1385	0.0785	0.1482	0.0883	0.1277	0.0721	0.1487	0.0893
BCIPM	<u>0.1772</u>	<u>0.0925</u>	0.2024	<u>0.1105</u>	0.1292	0.0716	0.1594	0.0843	0.1414	0.0741	0.2049	0.0897
COPF	0.1694	0.0903	<u>0.2386</u>	0.1065	<u>0.1552</u>	<u>0.0838</u>	<u>0.1908</u>	<u>0.0981</u>	<u>0.1502</u>	<u>0.0846</u>	0.1902	0.0882
LIPKE	**0.1903***	**0.1027***	**0.2779***	**0.1248***	**0.1855***	**0.0902***	**0.2335***	**0.1134***	**0.1574***	**0.0884***	**0.2194***	**0.1041***
(Rel. Impr.)	7.39%	11.03%	16.47%	12.94%	19.52%	7.64%	22.38%	15.60%	4.79%	4.49%	5.89%	13.15%

Boldface denotes the best result, and <u>underlined</u> denotes the best baseline.
* indicates statistical significance ($p < 0.05$) compared with the best baseline

Single-Behavior Models. Among the target-only baselines, LightGCN achieves the strongest overall performance. However, single-behavior models do not leverage auxiliary behaviors, and are therefore more limited under sparse target supervision. By incorporating auxiliary signals through selective cross-behavior transfer, LIPKE achieves clear improvements over these baselines.

Sequential Models. Among the sequential baselines, MBSRec performs best by explicitly modeling behavior-aware transitions, while Mamba4Rec provides an efficient state-space sequential backbone. However, under our experimental setting, sequence-only models rely mainly on target-behavior histories and do not explicitly exploit global multi-behavior structural information. In contrast, LIPKE combines recency-sensitive temporal modeling with graph-based long-term representations, leading to consistently better results.

Multi-behavior GNN-Based Models. Graph-based MBR methods such as MBGCN and MB-CGCN effectively capture high-order structural dependencies from behavior-specific interaction graphs. However, they mainly emphasize structural propagation and may be less sensitive to recent target-intent shifts. LIPKE further benefits from the MTM module for recency-aware temporal modeling and the PME module for more selective cross-behavior transfer, which together improve target-behavior prediction.

MTL/Cascade Frameworks. Strong MTL/cascade baselines, including PKEF, BCIPM, and COPF, improve cross-behavior learning through cascade training, bias correction, or transfer filtering. Nevertheless, they do not explicitly model short-term target intent in the same framework. By combining long-term structural modeling, short-term temporal modeling, and target-aligned auxiliary knowledge enhancement, LIPKE achieves the best overall performance across all datasets.

4.3 Ablation Study and Diagnostic Analysis (RQ2)

Impact of the Key Components. To study the contribution of the main modules in LIPKE, we consider the following variants:

- **Base**. removes both MTM and PME, retaining only the cascade–parallel graph encoder.
- **w/o MTM**: removes the Mamba-Based Temporal Module and keeps only the graph-based branch.
- **w/o PME**: replaces the Projection-Based Multi-expert Decoder with a standard shared embedding layer.

Table 3. Performance of different LIPKE variants.

	Beibei		Taobao		Tmall	
Model	H@10	N@10	H@10	N@10	H@10	N@10
Base	0.0726	0.0384	0.0812	0.0441	0.0921	0.0478
w/o MTM	0.1428	0.0769	0.1567	0.0722	0.1325	0.0745
w/o PME	0.1327	0.0714	0.1602	0.0843	0.1032	0.0643
LIPKE	**0.1903**	**0.1027**	**0.1855**	**0.0902**	**0.1574**	**0.0884**

As shown in Table 3, removing either MTM or PME consistently degrades performance across all datasets, while the Base variant shows the largest drop. These results suggest that MTM and PME provide complementary benefits in LIPKE. In particular, MTM improves the modeling of recency-sensitive target intent, whereas PME improves the use of auxiliary behaviors by making cross-behavior transfer more selective.

Effect of Long-Short Interest Perception. To better understand the contribution of long-term and short-term signals, we compare three settings on Beibei: **Graph-only** (w/o MTM), **Seq-only** (removing the graph encoder and using only the temporal branch), and the full LIPKE. Figure 3 groups users by target-behavior sequence length. Under our experimental setting, Seq-only is more competitive on shorter sequences, where recent target-behavior interactions provide stronger local evidence, whereas Graph-only performs better on longer sequences, where richer structural history becomes more useful. LIPKE consistently outperforms both diagnostic variants across all groups, suggesting that combining graph-based long-term information with temporal short-term information is beneficial for target-behavior prediction.

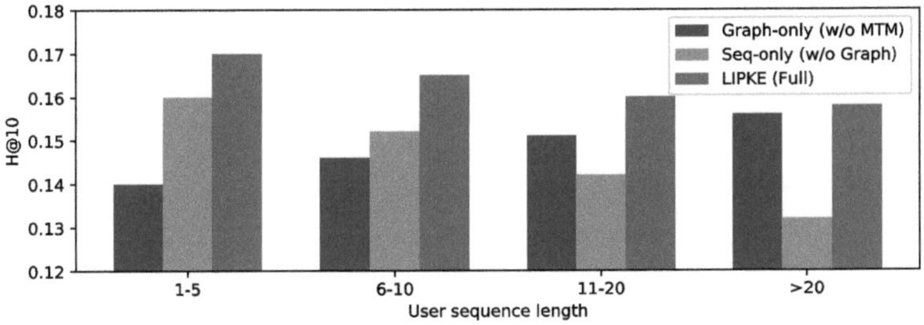

Fig. 3. Diagnostic comparison for long–short interest perception.

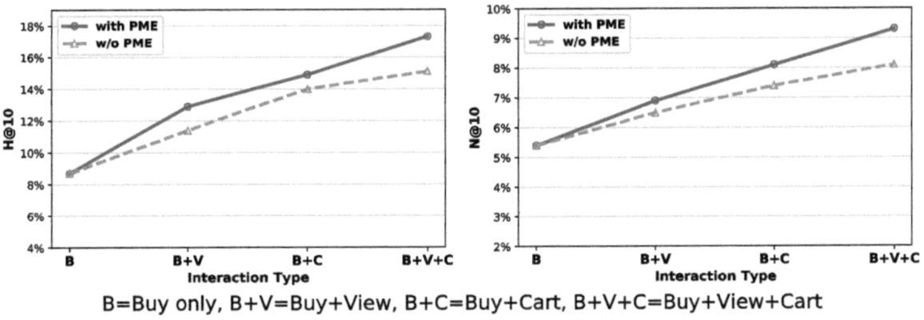

Fig. 4. Effect of PME under incremental auxiliary behaviors.

Effect of PME on Cross-Behavior Transfer. We further examine the role of PME when auxiliary behaviors are introduced on Beibei. Starting from the target behavior only, we progressively add auxiliary behaviors ($Buy \rightarrow Buy+View \rightarrow Buy+View+Cart$) and compare LIPKE with and without PME under the same training setting. As shown in Fig. 4, removing PME leads to less stable performance, and in some cases performance decreases after adding auxiliary behaviors. This suggests that naive incorporation of additional behaviors may introduce conflicting signals. In contrast, the full LIPKE improves more consistently as auxiliary behaviors are added, indicating that PME helps make cross-behavior transfer more selective.

We also note that the gain brought by PME is smaller on Taobao than on Beibei and Tmall, suggesting that the benefit of projection-based selective transfer depends on dataset-specific behavior overlap and supervision structure. When auxiliary behaviors are already relatively close to the target behavior or provide weaker complementary signals, PME still helps stabilize transfer, but its marginal gain may become smaller.

Overall, the ablation results suggest that MTM is helpful for incorporating short-term target intent, while PME improves the selectivity of cross-behavior transfer. Their combination leads to the strongest overall performance.

4.4 In-Depth Analysis (RQ3)

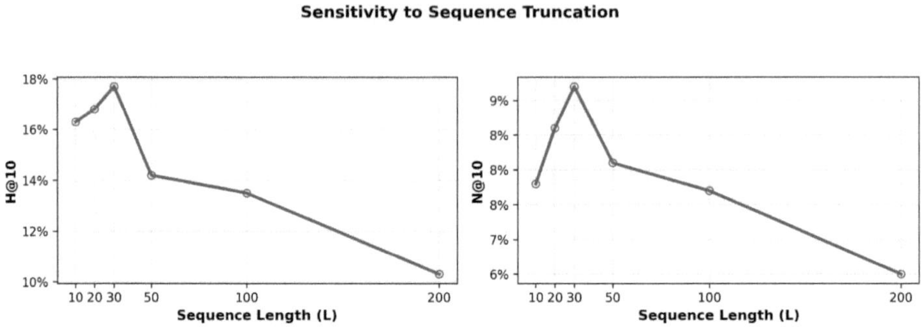

Fig. 5. Sensitivity to target-sequence truncation length.

Impact of Sequence Length. We study the sensitivity of LIPKE to the target-sequence truncation length L on Beibei. As shown in Fig. 5, both H@10 and N@10 improve as L increases from 10 to around 30, indicating that a moderate amount of recent target-behavior history provides useful context for temporal intent modeling. When L becomes larger (e.g., 50–200), performance gradually decreases under our MTM setting. This observation suggests that excessively long truncated histories may introduce less informative or less relevant interactions for the current target prediction task. Overall, LIPKE achieves the best performance at a moderate sequence length, which provides a reasonable balance between contextual information and recency.

4.5 Parameter Analysis (RQ4)

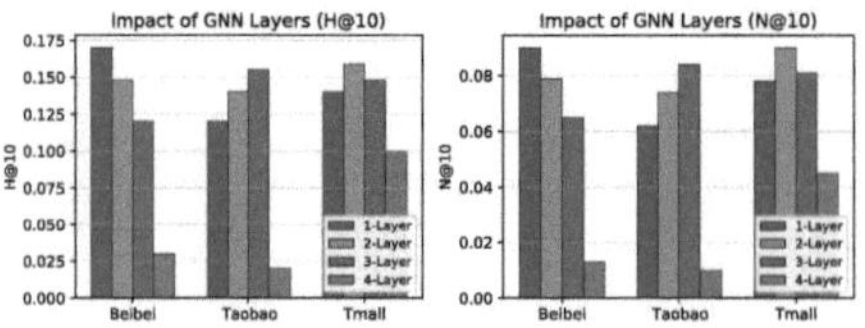

Impact of GCN depth.

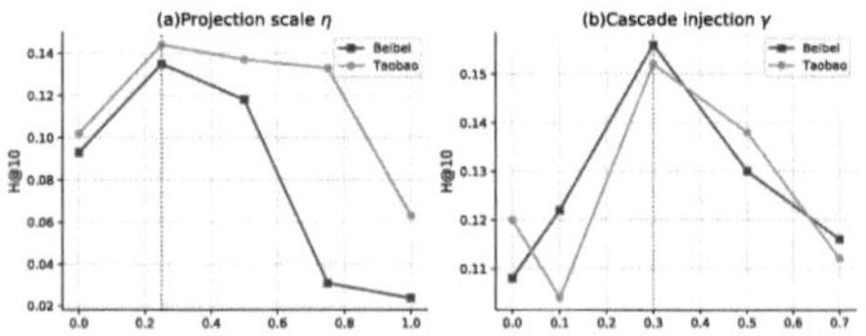

Projection scale η and cascade injection γ.

Fig. 6. Sensitivity of LIPKE to key hyperparameters.

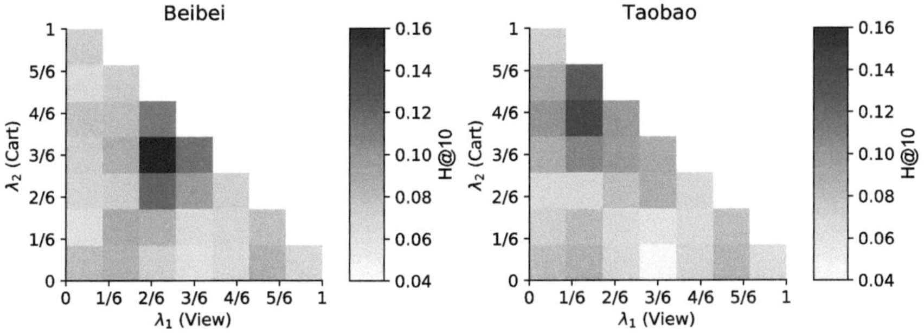

Fig. 7. Impact of behavioral coefficients.

We further analyze the sensitivity of LIPKE to several key hyperparameters, including the GCN depth in the graph encoder, the projection-related coefficients in the transfer path, and the behavioral coefficients that weight auxiliary supervision.

Impact of GCN Depth. As shown in Fig. 6a, the optimal GCN depth varies across datasets. Beibei prefers shallow propagation, Taobao benefits from moderate depth, and Tmall peaks at a small depth before becoming stable. We therefore tune the GCN depth within a small range and use a moderate setting by default.

Impact of Projection Scale η and Cascade Injection Coefficient γ. Figure 6b shows that both datasets achieve the best performance around $\eta = 0.25$ and $\gamma = 0.3$. Smaller values underuse auxiliary information, while larger values tend to introduce more interference into the target representation. Accordingly, we set $\eta = 0.25$ and $\gamma = 0.3$ as the default values in our experiments unless otherwise specified.

Impact of Behavioral Coefficients. Figure 7 shows the performance under different combinations of the auxiliary-behavior weights λ_1 and λ_2, subject to $\lambda_1 + \lambda_2 \leq 1$. The best regions are concentrated around intermediate combinations and generally assign a larger weight to Cart than to View. This observation suggests that Cart provides supervision that is more closely related to the target behavior, while overly extreme weighting is less effective.

5 Conclusion

This paper studies two key challenges in multi-behavior recommendation: long-short interest perception and negative transfer from behavioral heterogeneity. We propose LIPKE, a unified framework combining cascadeparallel graph encoding, longshort interest perception, and projection-based knowledge enhancement. PME disentangles shared signals from behavior-specific noise to reduce harmful transfer, while MTM captures short-term intent via an efficient Mamba-style temporal encoder and injects it into long-term graph representations. Experiments on three real-world datasets demonstrate LIPKE's effectiveness and robustness.

References

1. Abadi, M., Barham, P., Chen, J., Chen, Z., Davis, A., Dean, J., Devin, M., Ghemawat, S., Irving, G., Isard, M., et al.: {TensorFlow}: a system for {Large-Scale} machine learning. In: Proceedings of the 12th USENIX Symposium on Operating Systems Design and Implementation (OSDI 16), pp. 265–283 (2016)
2. Cheng, Z., Han, S., Liu, F., Zhu, L., Gao, Z., Peng, Y.: Multi-behavior recommendation with cascading graph convolution networks. In: Proceedings of the ACM Web Conference 2023, pp. 1181–1189 (2023)
3. Dang, Y., Zhang, J., Liu, Y., Yang, E., Liang, Y., Guo, G., Zhao, J., Wang, X.: Augmenting sequential recommendation with balanced relevance and diversity. In: Proceedings of the AAAI Conference on Artificial Intelligence, vol. 39, pp. 11563–11571 (2025)
4. Elsayed, S., Rashed, A., Schmidt-Thieme, L.: Multi-behavioral sequential recommendation. In: Proceedings of the 18th ACM Conference on Recommender Systems (RecSys), pp. 902–906 (2024)
5. Gao, C., He, X., Gan, D., Chen, X., Feng, F., Li, Y., Chua, T.S., Jin, D.: Neural multi-task recommendation from multi-behavior data. In: IEEE 35th International Conference on Data Engineering (ICDE), pp. 1554–1557. IEEE (2019)
6. Gu, S., Wang, X., Shi, C., Xiao, D.: Self-supervised graph neural networks for multi-behavior recommendation. IJCAI **14**, 2052–2058 (2022)
7. He, X., Deng, K., Wang, X., Li, Y., Zhang, Y., Wang, M.: Lightgcn: Simplifying and powering graph convolution network for recommendation. In: Proceedings of the 43rd International ACM SIGIR Conference on Research and Development in Information Retrieval, pp. 639–648 (2020)
8. He, X., Liao, L., Zhang, H., Nie, L., Hu, X., Chua, T.S.: Neural collaborative filtering. In: Proceedings of the 26th International Conference on World Wide Web, pp. 173–182 (2017)
9. Jin, B., Gao, C., He, X., Jin, D., Li, Y.: Multi-behavior recommendation with graph convolutional networks. In: Proceedings of the 43rd International ACM SIGIR Conference on Research and Development in Information Retrieval, pp. 659–668 (2020)
10. Kang, W.C., McAuley, J.: Self-attentive sequential recommendation. In: Proceedings of the IEEE International Conference on Data Mining (ICDM), pp. 197–206. IEEE (2018)
11. Kingma, D.P.: Adam: A Method for Stochastic Optimization. arXiv:1412.6980 (2014)
12. Li, X., Sheng, J., Cao, J., Zhang, W., Li, Q., Liu, T.: Cdrnp: cross-domain recommendation to cold-start users via neural process. In: Proceedings of the 17th ACM International Conference on Web Search and Data Mining, pp. 378–386 (2024)
13. Liu, C., Lin, J., Wang, J., Liu, H., Caverlee, J.: Mamba4rec: towards efficient sequential recommendation with selective state space models. In: Proceedings of the 1st International Workshop on Reliable Knowledge Discovery (RelKD '24), Held in Conjunction with the Web Conference 2024 (WWW '24) (2024)

14. Ma, J., Zhao, Z., Yi, X., Chen, J., Hong, L., Chi, E.H.: Modeling task relationships in multi-task learning with multi-gate mixture-of-experts. In: Proceedings of the 24th ACM SIGKDD International Conference on Knowledge Discovery and Data Mining, pp. 1930–1939 (2018)
15. Meng, C., Zhai, C., Yang, Y., Zhang, H., Li, X.: Parallel knowledge enhancement based framework for multi-behavior recommendation. In: Proceedings of the 32nd ACM International Conference on Information and Knowledge Management, pp. 1797–1806 (2023)
16. Rendle, S., Freudenthaler, C., Gantner, Z., Schmidt-Thieme, L.: Bpr: Bayesian Personalized Ranking from Implicit Feedback. arXiv:1205.2618 (2012)
17. Sun, F., Liu, J., Wu, J., Pei, C., Lin, X., Ou, W., Jiang, P.: BERT4Rec: sequential recommendation with bidirectional encoder representations from transformer. In: Proceedings of the 28th ACM International Conference on Information and Knowledge Management (CIKM), pp. 1441–1450 (2019)
18. Tang, H., Liu, J., Zhao, M., Gong, X.: Progressive layered extraction (ple): a novel multi-task learning (mtl) model for personalized recommendations. In: Proceedings of the 14th ACM Conference on Recommender Systems, pp. 269–278 (2020)
19. Tang, L., Long, B., Chen, B.C., Agarwal, D.: An empirical study on recommendation with multiple types of feedback. In: Proceedings of the 22nd ACM SIGKDD International Conference on Knowledge Discovery and Data Mining, pp. 283–292 (2016)
20. Wei, W., Huang, C., Xia, L., Xu, Y., Zhao, J., Yin, D.: Contrastive meta learning with behavior multiplicity for recommendation. In: Proceedings of the Fifteenth ACM International Conference on Web Search and Data Mining, pp. 1120–1128 (2022)
21. Yan, M., Cheng, Z., Gao, C., Sun, J., Liu, F., Sun, F., Li, H.: Cascading residual graph convolutional network for multi-behavior recommendation. ACM Trans. Inform. Syst. **42**(1), 1–26 (2023)
22. Yan, M., Liu, F., Sun, J., Sun, F., Cheng, Z., Han, Y.: Behavior-contextualized item preference modeling for multi-behavior recommendation. In: Proceedings of the 47th International ACM SIGIR Conference on Research and Development in Information Retrieval, pp. 946–955 (2024)
23. Zhai, C., Meng, C., Yang, Y., Zhang, K., Zhao, X., Li, X.: Combinatorial optimization perspective based framework for multi-behavior recommendation. In: Proceedings of the 31st ACM SIGKDD Conference on Knowledge Discovery and Data Mining (KDD), pp. 1891–1902. ACM (2025)

Query Processing

QAQ: Query-Adaptive Quantization for Large Language Model Inference

Shuxing Li[1], Shaowei Li[1], Tuchao Li[1], Zhaoyang Chen[1], Yu Yang[2], and Jiaxing Shen[3](✉)

[1] Guangzhou Vocational University of Science and Technology, Guangzhou, China
{li.shuxing.guangzhou,ltcnice184,chenchaoyang470}@gmail.com, lishaowei@gkd.edu.cn

[2] The Education University of Hong Kong, Hong Kong, Hong Kong SAR
yangyy@eduhk.hk

[3] Lingnan University, Hong Kong, Hong Kong SAR
jiaxingshen@LN.edu.hk

Abstract. Large language model (LLM) inference is often constrained by GPU memory and host-device transfer overhead, especially on edge devices. Static quantization methods employ offline-fixed bit-width configuration and therefore cannot dynamically adapt precision based on input complexity. Multi-precision representations enable multiple bit-width weight formats. However, without runtime mechanisms for on-demand residency/eviction and pipelined execution, such "dynamic precision" does not necessarily translate into lower peak memory usage. We propose Query-Adaptive Quantization (QAQ), which (i) routes each query to a block-wise bit-width map for MHA and MLP, (ii) materializes only the required LUTs/weight prefixes under a GPU budget via on-demand residency/eviction with optional CPU offloading, and (iii) overlaps transfers with computation via asynchronous prefetching and scheduling. Experiments demonstrate QAQ matches the quality of BF16 and static INT8 quantization while reducing peak end-to-end GPU memory from 15.28 GB to 9.02 GB, and further to 6.66 GB with weight offloading (on Qwen3-8B). The code is available in this repository: https://github.com/hingsli/query-adaptive-quantization.

Keywords: large language models · quantization · dynamic precision · GPU memory management · asynchronous prefetching

1 Introduction

As LLM inference is increasingly deployed in latency- and memory-constrained environments, cost-efficiency, throughput, and reliability are critical [22]. Quantization addresses these demands by lowering numerical precision, thereby reducing GPU memory footprint, bandwidth consumption, and arithmetic cost [3,8,17]. However, aggressive bit-width reduction can noticeably degrade quality [8,13,19]. This creates an inherent trade-off between efficiency and

L. Ding et al. (Eds.): APWeb-WAIM 2026, LNCS 16993, pp. 463–477, 2027.
https://doi.org/10.1007/978-981-92-5693-8_29

accuracy in LLM serving [11]. The efficiencyaccuracy trade-off is amplified on resource-constrained platforms (e.g., edge GPUs) with tight memory budgets and strong throughput requirements. Moreover, a small fraction of queries can trigger activation outliers and demand higher precision for reliable quality [21].

On a single GPU, peak VRAM is often primary bottleneck. Both model weights and the keyvalue (KV) cache typically stay resident in GPU memory during inference [18], which largely determines whether a model can be deployed. Although on-demand weight loading appears promising, serializing CPU→GPU transfers with computation leads to GPU stalls and increased end-to-end latency [16]. Meanwhile, mainstream post-training quantization (PTQ) pipelines determine offline-fixed precision configuration (global, layer-wise, or block-wise) and apply it to all queries at runtime [4,8]. Such static configurations cannot adapt to per-query difficulty. To remain robust under worst-case inputs, they conservatively allocate higher precision, incurring unnecessary memory and bandwidth overhead on the many "easy" queries that could execute at lower bit-widths. Because query difficulty is input-dependent, static precision must be conservative for worst-case robustness, wasting memory and bandwidth on the many queries that could run at lower bit-widths [1,17]. Recent work also explores co-locating multiple quantized weight variants on a single GPU, e.g., AnyPrecision [15]. However, since these methods implement weight overlays, highest remained precision stay resident in GPU memory, making peak VRAM determined by the maximum bit-width instead of the runtime-selected precision.

To resolve the tension between average efficiency and worst-case quality while minimizing peak GPU memory and I/O stalls, we propose **Query-Adaptive Quantization (QAQ)**. QAQ consists of three components: (1) A router predicts per-query, per-layer bit-widths and constructs a block-wise precision map, modeled separately for MHA and MLP blocks. (2) A budgeted on-demand residency/eviction mechanism materializes only the quantized artifacts needed by the current request on GPU, so peak memory scales with the *selected* bit-width set rather than the union of all supported bit-widths. (3) An asynchronous prefetching and scheduling pipeline overlaps host–device transfers quantized artifacts with compute to hide I/O latency.

Turning this idea into a practical end-to-end inference system is non-trivial: (i) router training lacks supervised labels for an "optimal" bit-width policy and must balance output quality with average bit-width; (ii) without on-demand residency/eviction, persistent multi-precision overlays fix peak VRAM to the union of all candidate precisions, so dynamic bit-widths do not reduce peak VRAM without on-demand residency/eviction; and (iii) on-demand materialization introduces CPU→GPU transfer and scheduling overhead, that can hurt throughput and tail latency unless overlapped with compute.

Contributions.

- **Query-adaptive routing and training:** We propose a block-wise bit-width router that outputs per-query precision maps. The router is trained with distillation signals and differentiable discrete selection, together with an average-bit-width constraint that encourages lower precision when quality is preserved (Table 1 and Fig. 5).

- **Budgeted on-demand residency/eviction:** We design a budgeted materialization and eviction mechanism that retains only the quantized artifacts required by the active request on GPU. On Qwen3-8B, this reduces peak end-to-end GPU memory from 15.28 GB to 9.02 GB, and further to 6.66 GB with weight offloading (Table 1).
- **Asynchronous prefetching and scheduling:** We develop a CUDA stream and event-based pipeline that overlaps the transfer of quantization lookup tables (LUTs) and weights with computation, mitigating I/O stalls and latency overhead under on-demand execution (Fig. 6).

2 Background and Motivation

We focus on post-training quantization (PTQ), which is widely adopted in deployment settings because it avoids full retraining and keeps engineering overhead low. In contrast, quantization-aware training (QAT) typically incurs additional training overhead and higher engineering complexity, which can be costly at LLM scale [14].

Static weight quantization. Static PTQ methods choose a **offline-fixed** bit-width configuration, and all queries share the same configuration at inference time. Representative approaches include weight-only GPTQ/AWQ [8,13] and outlier-aware methods such as SmoothQuant and LLM.int8 [3,17]. They improve quality without (or with minimal) retraining via error compensation, sensitivity estimation (e.g., second-order approximations), outlier handling, and static mixed-precision assignment. Comprehensive surveys and empirical analyses can be found in [1,9], alongside representative methods including OBQ [7], HAWQ [6], SpQR/SqueezeLLM [5,10], OWQ [12], and QuIP [2]. While these techniques improve accuracy with minimal retraining, they fundamentally assume fixed precision. Treating bit-width as a *query-dependent runtime decision*, and having peak GPU memory scale with the precision actually used, requires additional runtime mechanisms beyond static quantization.

Multi-precision weight representations. A related line of work explores multi-precision weight representations within a single model. Any-Precision DNN [20] introduces shared representations and execution mechanisms for arbitrary precision. Any-Precision LLM [15] organizes weights into bit-nested (bitplane) formats with overlay mechanisms, enabling multiple bit-width variants to coexist in memory while reading only the required bitplanes at runtime. However, because the overlays persist on GPU, peak VRAM is largely dominated by the highest retained precision and changes little with the runtime-selected bit-widths. We confirm this with a controlled static-precision and map-only ablation on Qwen3-8B using the AnyPrecision runtime (Table 3).

Motivation. In summary, static PTQ optimizes quality under offline-fixed precision configurations, whereas multi-precision representations enable multi-bit execution but remain constrained by persistent overlays and synchronous loading paths. In practical deployment, bit-width should become a per-query runtime decision while satisfying three objectives: (i) low average bit-width, (ii) peak GPU memory governed by the precision selected for the current request rather than the union of all candidates, and (iii) throughput preserved under on-demand materialization.

Achieving these objectives requires rethinking precision as a runtime resource rather than a static configuration. In particular, dynamic precision must (a) adapt to input-dependent difficulty without being overly conservative, (b) translate logical precision choices into actual physical memory savings, and (c) avoid placing additional I/O overhead on the critical path.

3 Method

QAQ elevates bit-width selection to a query-time decision and realizes this capability through three system-level components. (1) A router predicts per-layer precision distributions from the input and generates a block-wise precision map, separately modeling multi-head attention (MHA) and feed-forward (MLP) blocks. (2) A budget-aware residency and eviction mechanism materializes and retains on GPU only the lookup tables (LUTs) and prefixes of `qweight` required by the active request, ensuring that peak VRAM scales with the selected bit-width set rather than the maximum supported precision. (3) An asynchronous prefetching and scheduling pipeline overlaps I/O with computation, masking stalls introduced by on-demand loading.

Figure 1 summarizes the end-to-end workflow: an *offline* phase trains only the router via teacher–student distillation, while an *online* phase uses the router's precision map to drive budgeted on-demand materialization and an asynchronous CPU↔GPU pipeline that overlaps host-to-device transfers with GPU computation.

3.1 Router: balancing quality and average bit-width

Motivation. Queries are highly heterogeneous in difficulty and quantization sensitivity, making a single fixed bit-width suboptimal: it wastes precision on easy inputs while risking substantial degradation on hard ones. One could use rule-based policies (e.g., thresholds on confidence or activation/outlier statistics), but they require manual tuning and generalize poorly across models and datasets. We therefore adopt a trainable, query-conditioned router that predicts per-query distributions over candidate bit-widths. It can be optimized end-to-end to allocate higher precision selectively when necessary to preserve worst-case quality, while reducing the average bit-width to control cost. Figure 5(b) shows that the router makes non-uniform precision choices across layers, leading to different average bit-widths and a substantial fraction of low-bit selections per query.

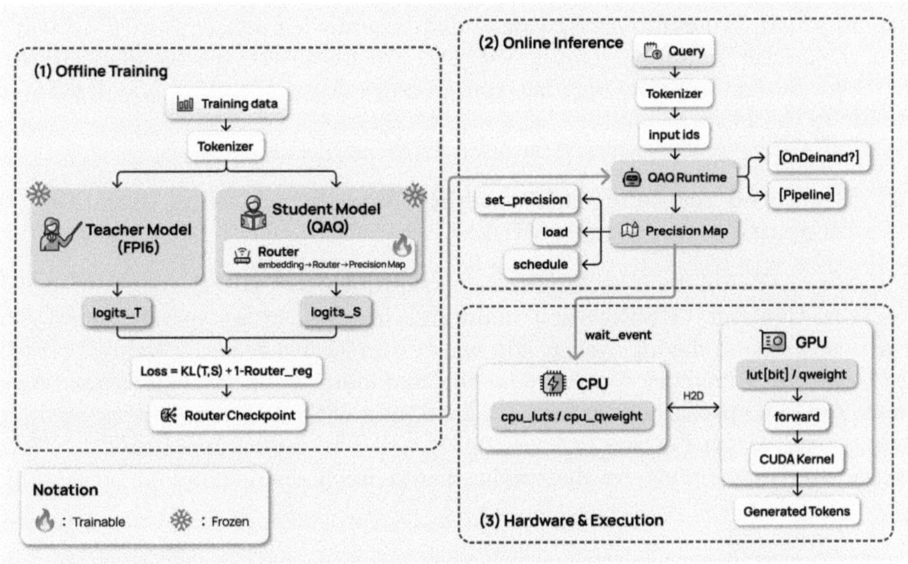

Fig. 1. System overview of QAQ. (1) Offline training distills a query-conditioned router using a frozen FP16 teacher and a frozen quantized student, producing a router checkpoint. (2) Online inference tokenizes each query, runs the router to generate a per-layer precision map, and triggers `set_precision`/`load`/`schedule` decisions in the QAQ runtime. (3) During execution, multi-precision LUTs and offloaded `qweight` reside on CPU; only the required LUTs and bitplane prefixes are transferred (H2D) to GPU and synchronized via CUDA events (e.g., `wait_event`) before kernels consume them.

However, we lack supervision labels for an optimal policy. In practice, constructing labels would require evaluating numerous candidate bit-width assignments, often across layers, for each query and measuring both quality and cost, which is prohibitively expensive and unlikely to remain stable across models or deployment settings. We therefore train the router via teacherstudent distillation, using the full-precision teacher's outputs as supervision instead of explicit bit-width labels.

Router design. We design a lightweight router as an MLP over the input token embeddings. Given hidden states $\mathbf{H} \in \mathbb{R}^{B \times N \times d}$ (batch size B, sequence length N, hidden dimension d) and an attention mask $\mathbf{m}$, we obtain a query representation $\mathbf{r} = g(\mathbf{H}, \mathbf{m})$ via masked mean pooling. The MLP outputs per-layer logits over candidate bit-widths, and we sample assignments with Gumbel-Softmax during training and use $\arg\max$ at inference. The resulting layer-wise choices are expanded into a block-wise map $\phi(\ell, u)$ that can assign different bit-widths to MHA vs MLP within the same layer.

We train the router without explicit bit-width labels by distilling from a full-precision (BF16/FP16) teacher. For each input, the teacher produces logits $\mathbf{y}^T$, while the student runs under the router-selected precision map ϕ and outputs $\mathbf{y}^S(\phi)$. We minimize KL-based distillation with temperature T (distinct from the router sampling temperature τ). We freeze the teacher and student model weights and update only the router, so we learn a routing policy without retraining the LLM.

3.2 Budgeted residency and weight offloading: making dynamic bit-width reduce peak VRAM

Motivation. We build on the AnyPrecision runtime to support dynamic bit-width selection. However, AnyPrecision maintains multi-precision quantized weights as a persistent on-device overlay for bit-widthselective reads, which effectively ties peak GPU memory footprint to the maximum supported precision. As a result, dynamic precision becomes a logical map without tangible peak-memory savings (e.g., larger batches or lower OOM risk). To unlock real benefits, multi-precision artifacts must be materialized and freed on demand under a GPU memory budget.

Approach. We replace persistent overlays with *budget-constrained on-demand residency.* Multi-precision LUTs are stored on the host, and for each request we materialize only the LUTs selected by the precision map $\phi(\ell, u)$ onto GPU, evicting when the LUT budget M would be exceeded. Let $m_{\ell,u}^{(k)}$ be the GPU bytes for layer ℓ and submodule $u \in \{\text{MHA}, \text{MLP}\}$ at bit-width k. Persistent overlays allocate $M_{\text{overlay}} = \sum_{\ell,u,k} m_{\ell,u}^{(k)}$, while on-demand residency allocates $M_{\text{on-demand}}(x) \approx \sum_{\ell,u} m_{\ell,u}^{(\phi(\ell,u;x))}$. When evicting, we preferentially remove higher-bit LUTs to keep low-bit LUTs resident for better reuse under tight budgets (Algorithm 1).

For further peak-memory reduction, we offload quantized weights (`qweight`) to CPU. We store `qweight` in a bitplane-prefix format and transfer only a prefix of w bitplanes to GPU, where w controls the memory/bandwidth–quality trade-off. When the `qweight` budget is exceeded, we apply a layer-level LRU policy and first trim higher bitplanes before evicting an entire layer's `qweight` back to CPU.

Figure 2 illustrates the role of our budget mechanism: it turns the router's precision choices into concrete peak-VRAM savings by caching only the requested precision artifacts and enforcing eviction policies that favor low-bit reuse (LUTs) and shrink-before-offload (qweight).

3.3 Asynchronous prefetching and scheduling: hiding LUT/`qweight` I/O

Motivation. On-demand materialization adds extra host→device transfers (LUTs and `qweight` prefixes) and CPU-side scheduling overhead. With a synchronous copy-then-compute pipeline, transfers serialize with kernels, causing GPU idle time and significant throughput loss (Fig. 6). In a dynamic-bit setting, frequent precision switches further increase transfer frequency and can push

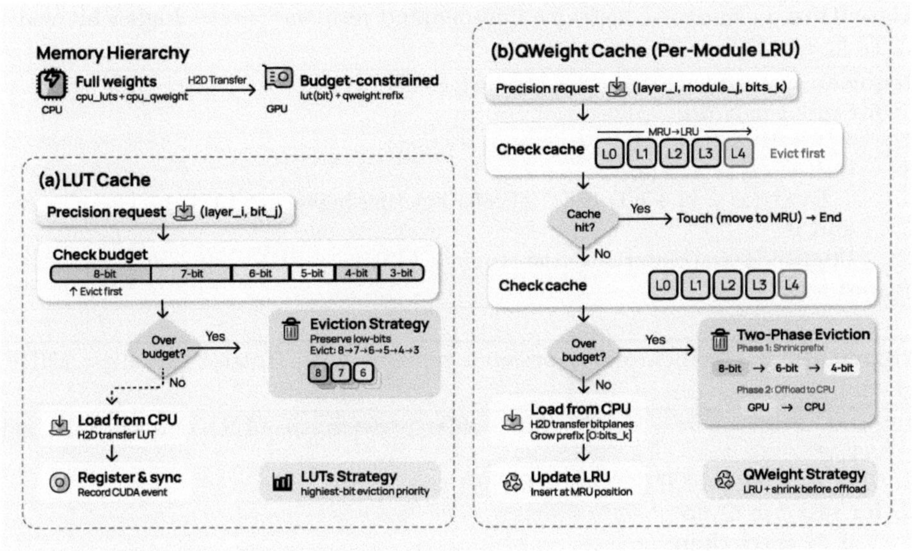

Fig. 2. Budgeted on-demand residency and eviction in QAQ. CPU stores full multi-precision LUTs and offloaded `qweight`, while GPU keeps only the LUTs and bitplane prefixes required by each precision request under a fixed budget. (a) LUT cache: on a per-layer precision request, the runtime checks the LUT budget and evicts higher-bit LUTs first (preserving low-bit reuse) before issuing H2D loads and recording CUDA events for synchronization. (b) `qweight` cache: a per-module LRU (least-recently-used; hits are moved to MRU, most-recently-used) serves requests when resident; on miss, the runtime loads the needed bitplane prefix if within budget, otherwise performs two-phase eviction by first shrinking prefixes and then offloading the module back to CPU.

scheduling overhead onto the critical path. We therefore aim to overlap I/O with compute and schedule tasks to maximize reuse and hide transfer latency.

Approach. We build an asynchronous I/O–compute pipeline. From the precision map, we construct prefetch tasks $\texttt{PipelineTask} = (\ell, u, k, f, b)$, where ℓ is layer, u is submodule, k is bit-width, f is estimated from recent runtime profiling, and b is LUT bytes. We then apply *Hottest Bit First (HBF)* scheduling, prioritizing tasks that are more frequent and more likely to be hidden by compute. Given per-bit profiles $\texttt{profile}[k] = (\texttt{comp}_k, \texttt{io}_k)$ estimating compute and I/O cost, we define a score

$$s(t) = f(t) \cdot \frac{\texttt{comp}_k}{\max(\texttt{io}_k, \epsilon)}. \tag{1}$$

At execution time, we enqueue non-blocking H2D copies of LUTs (and `qweight` prefixes) on a dedicated prefetch stream and record CUDA events. On the compute stream, the consumer site (linear layer forward) waits on the corresponding event only when the resource is actually used, enabling fine-grained synchronization and true overlap. Algorithm 2 shows the overall procedure.

Algorithm 1. Budget-constrained on-demand residency (evict higher bit-width LUTs first).

Require: planned load tasks $\mathcal{S}$, LUT budget M
for task t in $\mathcal{S}$ **do**
  $b(t) \leftarrow$ BYTES(t), $B \leftarrow$ RESIDENTBYTES()
  if $B + b(t) > M$ **then**
    EVICT($\Delta = B + b(t) - M$) {Prefer evicting higher-bit LUTs}
  end if
  LOADLUT(t) {Materialize the required LUT on GPU}
end for

Algorithm 2. Asynchronous prefetch pipeline with Hottest Bit First (HBF) scheduling.

Require: Precision map Π, bit-width profiles, prefetch stream $\mathcal{S}_{\text{io}}$, optional LUT budget M
$\mathcal{T} \leftarrow$ BUILDTASKS(Π), $\mathcal{Q} \leftarrow$ HBF($\mathcal{T}$)
for task t in $\mathcal{Q}$ **do**
  if M is set **then**
    BUDGETEVICTIFNEEDED(t, M)
  end if
  enqueue async copy of LUT/`qweight` for t on $\mathcal{S}_{\text{io}}$; **record** event $e(t)$
end for
compute stream: at consumer, **wait** on $e(t)$ only when resource is used

4 Experiments

We evaluate QAQ with (i) end-to-end `generate` comparisons against static quantization and multi-precision baselines, and (ii) component ablations and runtime breakdowns. We report quality (PPL and downstream zero-shot accuracy), peak GPU memory, and throughput/latency to quantify the trade-offs introduced by query-adaptive precision.

4.1 Experimental setup

Models and quantization. We report results primarily on Qwen3-8B and Llama-3.1-8B. The router selects from the candidate bit-width set $\{3, 4, 5, 6, 7, 8\}$ and outputs a block-wise precision map, which is executed in end-to-end `generate` with on-demand residency/eviction and the asynchronous pipeline.

Baselines. We compare against Full BF16/FP16, AnyPrecision with static 8-bit precision [15], and 8-bit weight-only PTQ baselines (GPTQ [8], AWQ [13]). We evaluate two QAQ modes: QAQ and QAQ + Offload, where offloading further reduces peak VRAM at the cost of additional transfers.

Metrics. We report (i) quality: perplexity (PPL) on WikiText-2 (WT2) and Penn Treebank (PTB), and downstream zero-shot accuracy on HellaSwag(HS), PIQA, ARC-E, ARC-C and Winogrande(WG); (ii) efficiency: throughput (tok/s) and latency (ms/token); and (iii) resources: peak VRAM during end-to-end `generate`. Throughput/latency are measured with fixed prompt lengths (64 tokens) after warmup (2 times); we repeat runs and report mean$\pm$std. Peak VRAM is the maximum observed GPU memory allocation during inference.

4.2 End-to-end results

Quality and peak GPU memory. Table 1 places the QAQ rows at the end of each model block, so the quality–memory comparison is easier to read. Against the quality-matched baselines, QAQ preserves the high-quality regime while lowering peak end-to-end GPU memory from 15.28 GB to 9.02 GB on Qwen3-8B and from 14.98 GB to 8.70 GB on Llama-3.1-8B; QAQ + Offload further reduces the peaks to 6.66 GB and 6.34 GB. On Qwen3-4B, QAQ remains close to the 8-bit baselines while reducing peak VRAM below static-8 (5.25 GB $\rightarrow$ 4.27 GB), and offloading further reaches 2.97 GB (Fig. 3).

Throughput–memory trade-off. Table 2 shows that under end-to-end `generate`, QAQ reduces peak VRAM from 15.28 GB (BF16) to 9.02 GB (41%). QAQ achieves throughput comparable to AnyPrecision with static 8-bit while using lower peak VRAM, and QAQ + Offload further reduces peak VRAM to 6.66 GB with a throughput drop. Figure 4 plots throughput versus peak VRAM for these methods.

4.3 Ablations and analysis

Router bit-width selection behavior. Figure 5 reports (a) the overall bit-width distribution and (b) the per-layer average bit-width. Across evaluation queries with candidate bits $\{3, 4, 5, 6, 7, 8\}$, the router achieves an average bit-width of $\sim$4.8 and assigns 3/4/5-bit to $\approx$72% (Qwen3-8B) and 69% (Llama-3.1-8B) of blocks. Combined with Table 1, this suggests the router frequently selects lower precision when quality is preserved.

From dynamic bit-widths to peak memory savings: static-precision ablation. Because QAQ builds on the AnyPrecision runtime, we run controlled ablations in the same stack. We evaluate (i) static precision (router off; fixed 8-bit across layers) and (ii) a QAQ map-only variant that applies the router's precision map but keeps persistent overlays (no on-demand residency/eviction). Table 3 shows that peak VRAM does not change without on-demand residency, but drops once on-demand materialization/eviction is enabled.

Table 1. Quality and peak VRAM on Qwen3-8B, Llama-3.1-8B, and Qwen3-4B. QAQ matches the quality of strong 8-bit baselines across perplexity and downstream tasks, while consistently achieving lower peak VRAM usage. Bold marks the best value within each model block (lower is better for WT2/PTB/Peak VRAM; higher is better for downstream accuracy).

Method	Peak VRAM (GB)	PPL		Downstream Tasks				
		WT2	PTB	HS	PIQA	ARC-E	ARC-C	WG
				Qwen3-8B				
BF16/FP16	15.28	9.72	13.54	**74.95**	77.80	80.89	56.48	67.72
AnyPrec-8	10.24	9.72	13.54	74.92	77.74	80.85	**56.57**	67.80
GPTQ-8	9.07	9.71	13.55	**74.95**	77.48	**81.02**	56.23	67.96
AWQ-8	11.34	**9.70**	**13.53**	74.77	**77.86**	80.68	56.14	**68.03**
QAQ	9.02							
QAQ + Offload	**6.66**	9.72	13.54	74.92	77.74	80.85	**56.57**	67.80
				Llama-3.1-8B				
BF16/FP16	14.98	**6.24**	**9.01**	78.90	81.18	81.10	53.50	73.48
AnyPrec-8	9.92	**6.24**	**9.01**	78.98	81.12	80.93	53.58	**73.56**
GPTQ-8	8.74	7.41	10.63	**80.38**	**81.28**	81.02	**57.51**	73.32
AWQ-8	10.68	**6.24**	9.02	79.01	81.23	**81.14**	53.24	73.16
QAQ	8.70							
QAQ + Offload	**6.34**	**6.24**	**9.01**	78.98	81.12	80.93	53.58	**73.56**
				Qwen3-4B				
BF16/FP16	7.51	**13.64**	18.74	68.42	74.97	**78.49**	53.92	66.06
AnyPrec-8	5.25	14.83	18.75	68.45	74.81	78.32	53.92	65.98
GPTQ-8	4.28	**13.64**	**18.71**	68.46	75.03	78.24	53.84	**66.30**
AWQ-8	4.97	13.74	18.83	**68.47**	75.08	78.32	**54.01**	66.22
QAQ	4.27							
QAQ + Offload	**2.97**	14.85	18.75	68.45	74.81	78.32	53.92	65.98

Effect of the I/O pipeline: asynchronous prefetching and bottleneck breakdown. Figure 6 breaks down end-to-end `generate` time into schedule construction, weight/LUT loading, precision-map application, and model forward. With on-demand enabled, the **synchronous** pipeline (Sync) drops throughput from 21.90 tok/s (Baseline) to 13.30 tok/s, while **asynchronous** LUT prefetching (Async) restores throughput to 40.93 tok/s. Async prefetching reduces blocking I/O in `apply` from $\sim$1.4 s to tens of milliseconds while keeping `forward` nearly unchanged, showing that I/O–compute overlap hides transfer stalls.

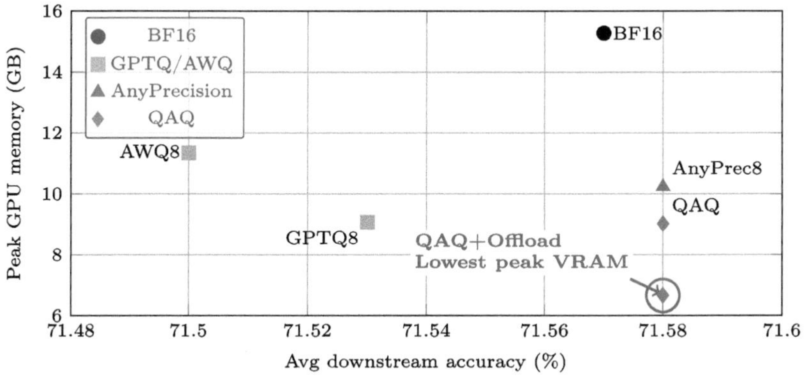

Fig. 3. Quality–memory trade-off on Qwen3-8B. Each point plots peak VRAM against average downstream accuracy (%) during end-to-end `generate` (data from Table 1), so memory differences are emphasized vertically when quality is matched.

Table 2. Throughput and peak VRAM on Qwen3-8B. End-to-end `generate` on a single NVIDIA RTX 5090 (fixed prompt/output lengths and batch size); mean±std. Bold marks the best value in each column (higher is better for tok/s; lower is better for ms/token and peak GPU memory).

Method	tok/s	ms/token	Peak GPU (GB)
Full BF16	**48.37±0.72**	**20.68±0.31**	15.28
GPTQ Int8	23.69±0.09	42.21±0.17	9.07
AWQ Int8 (W8A16)	23.60±0.02	42.37±0.03	11.34
AnyPrecision (static 8-bit)	44.22±0.08	22.62±0.04	10.24
QAQ	45.05±0.99	22.21±0.50	9.02
QAQ + weight offloading	38.68±0.73	25.86±0.50	**6.66**

4.4 Summary

Overall, QAQ reduces peak VRAM in end-to-end inference while maintaining quality close to static INT8 and sustaining usable throughput. On Qwen3-8B/Llama-3.1-8B, peak VRAM drops from 15.28 GB and 14.98 GB (BF16) to 9.02 GB and 8.70 GB, and further to 6.66 GB and 6.34 GB with offloading (Table 1). On Qwen3-8B, QAQ achieves throughput comparable to static-8 AnyPrecision while using lower peak VRAM (Table 2). Ablations confirm that the router often selects low bit-widths (Fig. 5), budgeted residency/eviction is required for peak-memory savings (Table 3), and asynchronous prefetching hides I/O stalls to restore throughput (Fig. 6).

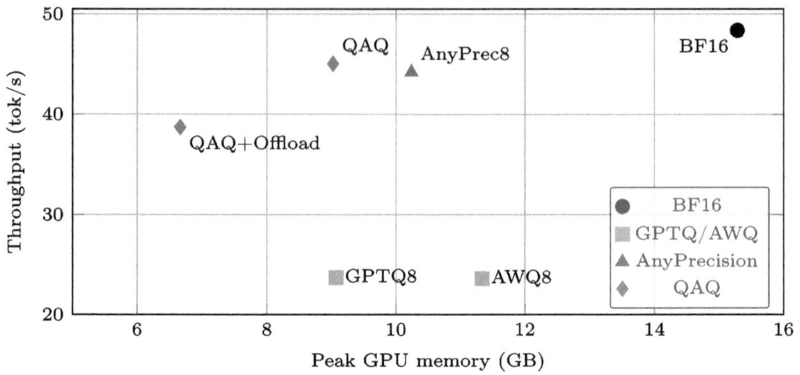

Fig. 4. Throughput–memory trade-off on Qwen3-8B under end-to-end **`generate`** (data from Table 2). QAQ+Offload trades lower peak VRAM for additional transfer overhead.

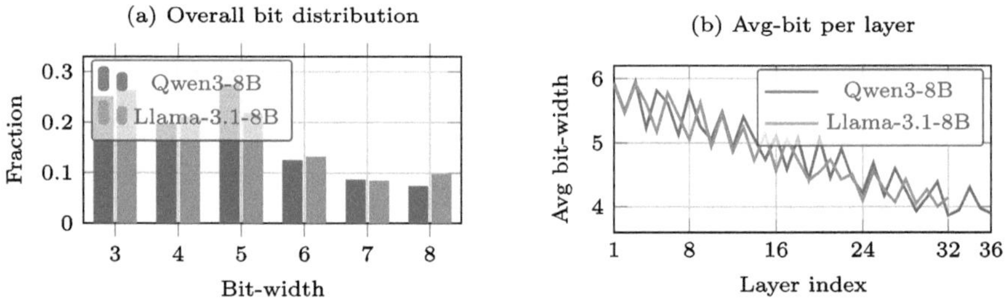

Fig. 5. Router bit-width selection statistics: (a) overall distribution; (b) per-layer average bit-width averaged across evaluation queries, highlighting frequent low-bit selections.

Table 3. Static-precision ablation (Qwen3-8B). End-to-end **`generate`**; mean±std.

Config	ms/token	tok/s	Peak GPU (GB)
Static 8-bit	22.62±0.04	44.22±0.08	10.24
QAQ (map-only)	22.49±0.07	44.46±0.14	10.24
QAQ	22.21±0.50	45.05±0.99	9.02
QAQ+Offload	25.86±0.50	38.68±0.73	6.66

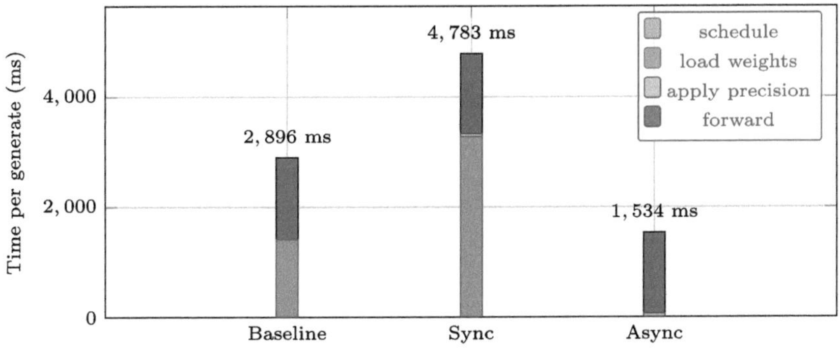

Fig. 6. Stacked breakdown of end-to-end `generate` time on Qwen3-8B (averaged). Baseline/Sync/Async denote on-demand execution with different (synchronous vs asynchronous) I/O pipelines. To avoid double counting I/O, we estimate "apply precision" as the total apply time minus explicit load time.

5 Conclusion

We show that QAQ enables query-adaptive bit-width inference that reduces peak VRAM in end-to-end LLM serving while preserving quality and usable throughput. By combining a learned routing policy, budgeted on-demand residency/eviction, and asynchronous prefetching/scheduling, QAQ achieves substantial memory savings with minimal quality loss (Section 4).

Our evaluation is limited to the current inference stack built on AnyPrecision and our custom pipeline. In some end-to-end settings, Full BF16 can be faster than quantized execution, likely because BF16/FP16 kernels and framework-level optimizations are more mature. As future work, we plan to integrate QAQ into widely used serving frameworks (e.g., vLLM and TensorRT-LLM) and optimize key kernels and scheduling/prefetch policies.

Acknowledgments. This work has benefited from the financial support of Lingnan University (102078) and EdUHK Seed Funding Grant (No. R4539).

Disclosure of Interests. The authors have no competing interests to declare that are relevant to the content of this article.

References

1. Bondarenko, Y., Nagel, M., Blankevoort, T.: Understanding and overcoming the challenges of efficient transformer quantization. In: Proceedings of the 2021 Conference on Empirical Methods in Natural Language Processing, pp. 8998–9010 (2021)
2. Chee, J., Cai, Y., Kuleshov, V., De Sa, C.: QuIP: 2-bit quantization of large language models with guarantees. In: Advances in Neural Information Processing Systems. NeurIPS '23 (2023)

3. Dettmers, T., Lewis, M., Belkada, Y., Zettlemoyer, L.: Llm.int8(): 8-Bit Matrix Multiplication for Transformers at Scale. arXiv preprint arXiv:2208.07339 (2022). https://doi.org/10.48550/arXiv.2208.07339, neurIPS 2022
4. Dettmers, T., Pagnoni, A., Holtzman, A., Zettlemoyer, L.: Qlora: Efficient Fine-tuning of Quantized llms (2023). arXiv preprint arXiv:2305.14314
5. Dettmers, T., Svirschevski, R., Egiazarian, V., Kuznedelev, D., Frantar, E., Ashkboos, S., Borzunov, A., Hoefler, T., Alistarh, D.: Spqr: a sparse-quantized representation for near-lossless llm weight compression. In: International Conference on Learning Representations (ICLR) (2024)
6. Dong, Z., Yao, Z., Gholami, A., Mahoney, M.W., Keutzer, K.: Hawq: Hessian aware quantization of neural networks with mixed-precision. In: Proceedings of the IEEE/CVF International Conference on Computer Vision (ICCV) (2019)
7. Frantar, E., Alistarh, D.: Optimal brain compression: a framework for accurate post-training quantization and pruning. Adv. Neural. Inf. Process. Syst. **35**, 4475–4488 (2022)
8. Frantar, E., Ashkboos, S., Hoefler, T., Alistarh, D.: Gptq: Accurate Post-training Quantization for Generative Pre-trained Transformers. arXiv preprint arXiv:2210.17323 (2022). https://doi.org/10.48550/arXiv.2210.17323, iCLR 2023
9. Gholami, A., Kim, S., Dong, Z., Yao, Z., Mahoney, M.W., Keutzer, K.: A Survey of Quantization Methods for Efficient Neural Network Inference (2021)
10. Kim, S., Hooper, C., Gholami, A., Dong, Z., Li, X., Shen, S., Mahoney, M.W., Keutzer, K.: SqueezeLLM: Dense-and-Sparse Quantization (2023). arXiv:2306.07629 arXiv preprint
11. Kurtic, E., Marques, A., Pandit, S., Kurtz, M., Alistarh, D.: Give me bf16 or Give Me Death"? Accuracy-Performance Trade-offs in llm Quantization. arXiv preprint arXiv:2411.02355 (2024)
12. Lee, C., Jin, J., Kim, T., Kim, H., Park, E.: OWQ: outlier-aware weight quantization for efficient fine-tuning and inference of large language models. Proceedings of the AAAI Conference on Artificial Intelligence **38**(12), 13355–13364 (2024). https://doi.org/10.1609/aaai.v38i12.29237
13. Lin, J., Tang, J., Tang, H., Yang, S., Chen, W.M., Wang, W.C., Xiao, G., Dang, X., Gan, C., Han, S.: Awq: Activation-Aware Weight Quantization for llm Compression and Acceleration. arXiv preprint arXiv:2306.00978 (2023). https://doi.org/10.48550/arXiv.2306.00978, mLSys 2024 Best Paper
14. Liu, Z., Oguz, B., Zhao, C., Chang, E., Stock, P., Mehdad, Y., Shi, Y., Krishnamoorthi, R., Chandra, V.: LLM-QAT: Data-Free Quantization Aware Training for Large Language Models (2023)
15. Park, Y., Hyun, J., Cho, S., Sim, B., Lee, J.W.: Any-precision llm: Low-Cost Deployment of Multiple (2024). arXiv:2402.10517 different-sized llms. arXiv preprint
16. Wang, H., Zhou, Q., Hong, Z., Guo, S.: D2moe: Dual routing and dynamic scheduling for efficient on-device moe-based llm serving. In: Proceedings of the 31st Annual International Conference on Mobile Computing and Networking, pp. 574–588 (2025)
17. Xiao, G., Lin, J., Seznec, M., Wu, H., Demouth, J., Han, S.: Smoothquant: Accurate and Efficient Post-training Quantization for Large Language Models. arXiv preprint arXiv:2211.10438 (2022). https://doi.org/10.48550/arXiv.2211.10438, iCML 2023
18. Xu, Y., Jie, Z., Dong, H., Wang, L., Lu, X., Zhou, A., Saha, A., Xiong, C., Sahoo, D.: Think: Thinner key cache by query-driven pruning. In: The Thirteenth Inter-

national Conference on Learning Representations (2025). https://openreview.net/forum?id=n0OtGl6VGb
19. Xu, Z., Liu, Z., Chen, B., Tang, Y., Wang, J., Zhou, K., Hu, X., Shrivastava, A.: Compress, then Prompt: Improving Accuracy-Efficiency Trade-off of llm Inference with Transferable Prompt (2023). arXiv preprint arXiv:2305.11186
20. Yu, H., Li, H., Shi, H., Huang, T.S., Hua, G.: Any-precision deep neural networks. In: Thirty-Fifth AAAI Conference on Artificial Intelligence, pp. 10763–10771. AAAI '21 (2021). https://doi.org/10.1609/AAAI.V35I12.17286
21. Zeng, B., Ji, B., Liu, X., Yu, J., Li, S., Ma, J., Li, X., Wang, S., Hong, X., Tang, Y.: Lsaq: Layer-Specific Adaptive Quantization for Large Language Model Deployment. arXiv preprint arXiv:2412.18135 (2024)
22. Zhou, Z., Ning, X., Hong, K., Fu, T., Xu, J., Li, S., Lou, Y., Wang, L., Yuan, Z., Li, X., et al.: A Survey on Efficient Inference for Large Language Models. arXiv preprint arXiv:2404.14294 (2024)

A Join Tree Approach for Efficient Distributed Query Processing on Large-Scale Knowledge Graphs

Shujun Sheng, Huajian Zhou, and Xiaofeng Ding(✉)

School of Computer and Technology, Huazhong University of Science and Technology, Wuhan, China

{sjsheng,hjzhou,xfding}@hust.edu.cn

Abstract. Knowledge graphs are structured semantic networks that represent real-world entities, concepts, and their relationships, enabling complex associative queries and semantic understanding of user intent. Given their massive scale and heterogeneous nature, distributed systems are essential for efficient storage and query processing. While existing research has primarily focused on optimizing distributed storage, significant challenges remain in achieving load balancing and efficient distributed join operations. This paper presents a distributed query system specifically designed for large-scale knowledge graphs. We introduce an elastic data structure for management nodes and an optimized intermediate data organization for computing nodes that facilitates efficient join processing. The system employs adaptive data partitioning, merging, and join operations to achieve fine-grained parallelism while maintaining intermediate results in memory to minimize I/O overhead. A key innovation is the join tree mechanism, constructed using dynamic programming and decomposed according to cluster load conditions to ensure balanced workload distribution. For inter-node communication, we implement asynchronous non-blocking data transmission with fixed-length encoding of RDF triples (subject-predicate-object) to reduce communication overhead. Experimental results demonstrate that our data-distribution-based join algorithm achieves superior parallelism and significantly reduced query latency compared to traditional distributed join approaches, while exhibiting strong scalability across varying workloads.

Keywords: Knowledge graph · Distributed graph processing platform · Distributed query · Join optimization

1 Introduction

In the big data era, the volume of collected data has reached the zettabyte scale (1 ZB = 10^6 PB). These data capture real-world events, describe diverse entities and phenomena, and encode complex relationships among them. Given such massive and heterogeneous data, efficiently retrieving information and discovering knowledge has become a critical challenge.

L. Ding et al. (Eds.): APWeb-WAIM 2026, LNCS 16993, pp. 478–492, 2027.
https://doi.org/10.1007/978-981-92-5693-8_30

Traditional search engines rely on keyword matching, which cannot comprehend user intent. For instance, a query for "Einstein Nobel Prize" may return documents merely containing these keywords rather than the structured fact that Albert Einstein received the Nobel Prize in Physics in 1921 for his work on the photoelectric effect. Knowledge graphs address this limitation by modeling entities and their relationships as a structured semantic network, enabling search systems to understand query intent and return precise answers.

A knowledge graph represents real-world entities (such as products, locations, and organizations) and their relationships as a directed labeled graph. The concept was popularized by Google in 2012 and has since become an indispensable component of modern search engines and question-answering systems. Fig. 1 illustrates an example knowledge graph centered on a textile product "Cotton T-Shirt A." Entities such as "SGS Lab," "GB 18401," and "Formaldehyde Excess" are represented as nodes, while predicates such as "testedBy," "compliesWith," and "hasRiskType" are represented as directed edges. Real-world knowledge graphs such as Wikidata and DBpedia contain billions of such triples. When a user asks "which markets recalled this product?", a query over this graph directly yields the answer "EU Market" without keyword-based document retrieval.

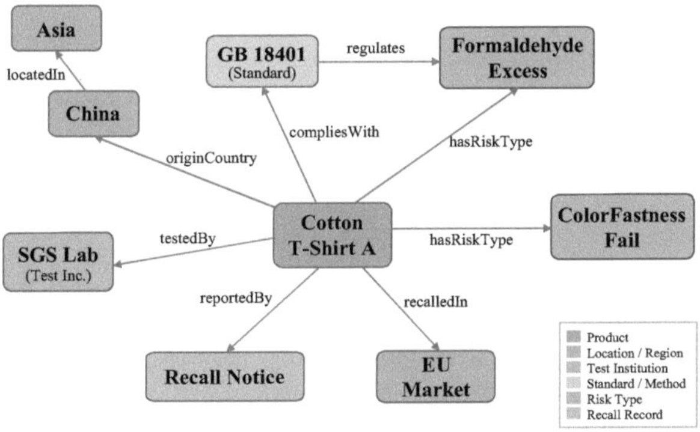

Fig. 1. An example of knowledge graph

The massive scale of knowledge graphs exceeds the processing capabilities of single nodes. Distributed query systems have therefore become the prevailing solution for handling knowledge graphs that surpass single-machine performance limits. Developing an effective distributed query system for knowledge graphs involves addressing four key challenges. First, graph partitioning: how to partition and distribute the knowledge graph across multiple machines to minimize intermediate data volume and network communication overhead. Second, query decomposition: how to decompose queries and distribute sub-queries to appropriate machines to improve query processing efficiency. Third, join plan optimization: after each node executes its sub-query, the returned intermediate results must be further processed. When multiple intermediate results exist, different join sequences incur varying costs, necessitating an optimal join plan with minimal execution time. Fourth, load balancing during joins: during the join process, data from one node is typically sent to another node for joining. It is essential to minimize machine idle time and balance workloads across machines to avoid the bottleneck effect that leads to resource waste.

This paper designs and implements a distributed join algorithm based on data distribution that finds the optimal join order using dynamic programming principles and allocates computation based on cluster load conditions, significantly improving cluster utilization and achieving load balancing. Our contributions can be summarized as follows:

- We review the popular hash join algorithm for single machines and three distributed join algorithms, providing detailed analysis and illustrative examples (Sect. 3).
- To achieve clear separation between the management and data layers, we design distinct data structures and operations for management nodes and data nodes. We create a global index for cardinality estimation and a range index to accelerate single-machine queries. We propose a novel distributed join algorithm based on data distribution, innovatively introducing a join tree structure and achieving load balancing through join tree generation and decomposition (Sect. 4).
- Based on the new data structures and distributed join algorithm, we design and implement a complete distributed query system. We present the overall system architecture, followed by detailed descriptions of the management layer and data layer architectures (Sect. 5).
- We implement traditional distributed join algorithms within our system and compare them with our newly proposed algorithm. Additionally, we evaluate system scalability with respect to both data volume and cluster size. Experimental results demonstrate that our algorithm achieves superior efficiency and scalability (Sect. 6).

2 Related Work

2.1 Distributed SPARQL Query Processing

Single-machine RDF engines such as RDF-3X [1] and gStore [2] established foundational paradigms. The transition to distributed architectures produced Trinity.RDF [3], Rya [4], Huang et al. [30], and Wukong [31], progressively improving scalability through native graph storage, key-value indexing, locality-based optimization, and RDMA-based exploration. Federated processing was advanced by FedX [5], FedUP [6], and Lothbrok [7]. Comprehensive surveys [8, 9] compare over 135 systems.

Among systems most relevant to our work, TripleBit [22] uses bit-matrix representations for efficient joins, AdPart [23] exploits hash-based locality, SemStore [24] applies semantic-preserving partitioning, TriAD [25] employs asynchronous message passing, and Wu et al. [26] develop path partitioning. Arnaout and Elbassuoni [32] extend queries with keyword ranking. While these systems optimize storage and communication, they rely on conventional join strategies without explicit workload balancing—a gap our join tree mechanism addresses.

2.2 Join Optimization and Cardinality Estimation

Veldhuizen [10] introduced worst-case optimal Leapfrog Triejoin. Subsequent work unified join paradigms: Free Join [11] reconciles binary hash joins with worst-case optimal algorithms, and Freitag et al. [12] demonstrated practical implementations. For join ordering, Moerkotte and Neumann [13] advanced dynamic programming-based join enumeration, Mancini et al. [14] proposed parallel optimization, and Leis et al. [33] showed that cardinality estimation errors dominate suboptimal orderings. Our work constructs join trees via dynamic programming at the management layer and decomposes them for load-balanced distributed execution.

Cardinality estimation underpins join optimization. The System R optimizer [15] established cost-based optimization. Recent learned approaches include graph neural networks [16], factor graphs [17], multi-set convolutional models [34], and cost-aware learned estimators [35]. Our system employs histogram-based statistical indices for lightweight prediction, trading precision for low overhead suitable for distributed management nodes.

2.3 Graph Partitioning and Load Balancing

The classical METIS algorithm [18] established multilevel graph partitioning. For RDF workloads, Peng et al. [19] proved NP-completeness of workload-aware parti-tioning; streaming approaches include CUTTANA [20] and Triparts [21]. Zeng et al. [36] proposed game-theoretic dynamic partitioning, and Sun and Luo [37] conduct-ed an in-depth study of in-memory subgraph matching. For large-scale computation, PowerGraph [27] and Pregel [28] established vertex-cut and vertex-centric paradigms respectively.

In the broader knowledge graph context, Qi et al. [38] proposed dual-store structures, Ji et al. [39] surveyed KG representation and applications, and Sun et al. [40] developed efficient subgraph matching on billion-node graphs. These methods focus on minimizing communication by co-locating data but do not account for varying join costs. Our approach complements partitioning by decomposing join trees according to predicted workload, balancing execution time rather than data volume alone.

3 Traditional Distributed Join Algorithms

Join processing is the performance bottleneck in distributed SPARQL query systems. The standard single-machine hash join builds an in-memory hash table from the smaller relation and probes it with tuples from the larger relation. Extending this to distributed settings yields three classical algorithms, each targeting different data scale regimes. We briefly review them below, as they serve as baselines in our experimental evaluation.

Broadcast Hash Join. When one join operand is small (typically$<$10 MB), it is broadcast to all nodes holding the larger table. Each node then performs a local hash join. This avoids data shuffling but becomes impractical when both operands are large, as broadcasting consumes excessive bandwidth and memory.

Shuffle Hash Join. Both operands are hash-partitioned on the join key so that matching records are co-located on the same node. Each node then performs a local hash join on its partition. While this handles larger tables than broadcast join, partitions can remain large under data skew, leading to memory pressure and load imbalance.

Sort Merge Join. Both operands are shuffled by join key and then locally sorted. A merge pass joins the two sorted streams on each node. This approach handles very large tables without requiring the entire hash table to fit in memory, but incurs the additional cost of sorting and remains sensitive to uneven key distributions across nodes.

Table 1 summarizes the three algorithms. All three balance data volumes across nodes but do not account for varying computational costs of join operations—a critical distinction for knowledge graph queries where result sizes follow power-law distributions.

Table 1. Comparison of traditional distributed join algorithms

Algorithm	Strategy	Best Scenario	Limitation
Broadcast Hash	Broadcast small table; local hash join	One operand $<$ 10 MB	Bandwidth/memory explosion for large tables
Shuffle Hash	Hash-partition by join key; local hash join	Medium-to-large tables	Memory pressure under data skew
Sort Merge	Shuffle, sort locally, merge-join streams	Very large tables	Sorting overhead; skew sensitivity

Our join tree approach, presented in Sect. 4, addresses this fundamental limitation by decomposing the join plan itself according to predicted execution costs, ensuring workload balance rather than mere data balance.

4 Distributed Join Algorithm Based on Data Distribution

4.1 Abstract Query Class and Operations

A key challenge in distributed query systems is enabling operations on queries as complete units to achieve true parallelism. We introduce two complementary abstractions: abstract query classes, which serve as lightweight metadata on the management node, and query instances, which hold materialized data on worker nodes. The two maintain a one-to-one correspondence.

Definition 1 (Abstract Query Class). A read-only logical data partition $Q = \langle ID, V, C, |R| \rangle$, where *ID* is a unique identifier, *V* is the set of query variables, *C* specifies conjunctive conditions on variables, and $|R|$ is predicted result cardinality estimated from histogram-based statistical indices.

Definition 2 (Query Instance). A physical data structure on a worker node corresponding to an abstract query class, containing materialized query results.

Abstract Query Classes Are Immutable and Support Four Operations that Form a Complete Algebra for Query Manipulation:

- Division: splits a class whose cardinality exceeds a threshold into two subclasses with non-overlapping condition ranges. The split boundary is determined by scanning the statistical index until half the parent's cardinality is reached, ensuring balanced subclasses even under skewed distributions.

- Merge: combines two classes with identical variables but different conditions into a single class. For overlapping conditions, the statistical index re-estimates cardinality to avoid over-counting.
- Join: produces a new class from two classes sharing at least one common variable. Join result cardinality is conservatively estimated as the minimum of the input cardinalities. If either input exceeds the division threshold, division is applied first to bound peak resource consumption.
- Creation: parses a SPARQL query to extract variables and conditions, then queries the statistical index for cardinality estimation.

These operations and classes naturally form a tree structure, the join tree, where leaf nodes are classes created from queries, intermediate nodes are results of division, merge, or join operations, and the root represents the final result. Figure 2 shows an example. The tree abstraction enables systematic optimization through dynamic programming-based construction (Sect. 4.2) and load-aware decomposition (Sect. 4.3).

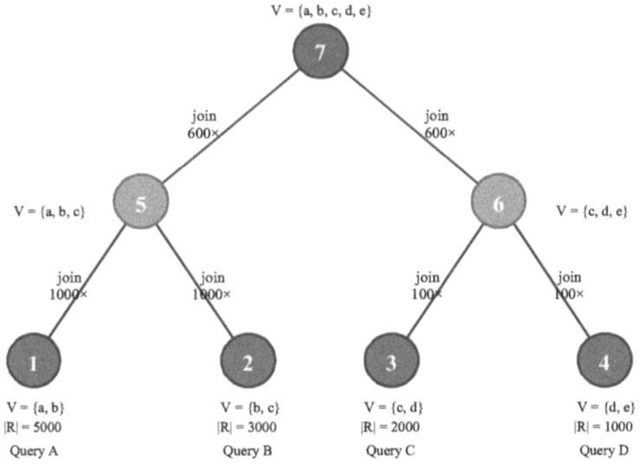

Fig. 2. A join tree

4.2 Join Tree Generation

The management node decomposes incoming queries using a star decomposition strategy: it iteratively selects the highest-degree node in the query graph, aggregates associated patterns into a sub-query, and distributes sub-queries to partitions. Each partition creates abstract query classes with cardinality estimates from local statistical metadata.

Since different join orderings can produce dramatically different execution costs, finding the minimum-cost join tree is critical. For example, given three sub-queries A, B, C with pairwise join costs, the sequence that joins the smallest intermediate result first can reduce total cost by over 10%. Algorithm 1 constructs the join tree using a greedy strategy guided by estimated cardinalities: it first divides any class exceeding the cardinality threshold, then iteratively selects the pair of classes whose join produces the smallest intermediate result, continuing until a single root class remains.

Algorithm 1. Greedy Join Tree Construction

Input: Set of abstract query classes *P*, cardinality threshold *Max*

Output: Join tree *T*

1: $T \leftarrow \emptyset; P^{'} \leftarrow \emptyset$

2: **for each** $s \in P$ **do**

3: **if** $s.$ Rcount $>$ *Max* **then**

4: $(s_l, s_r) \leftarrow d\text{ivision}(s)$

5: $P^{'} \leftarrow P^{'} \cup \{s_l, s_r\}$

6: **else** $P^{'} \leftarrow P^{'} \cup \{s\}$

7: $P \leftarrow P^{'}$

8: **while** $|P| > 1$ **do**

9: $(s_a, s^b) \leftarrow \text{argmin}\{s_i, s_j \in P, i < j\}(s_i \bowtie s_j).\text{Rcount}$

10: $s_k \leftarrow s_a \bowtie s^b$

11: $T \leftarrow T \cup \{(s_a, s^b, s_k)\}$

12: $P \leftarrow (P \setminus \{s_a, s^b\}) \cup \{s_k\}$

13: **return** *T*

For queries spanning multiple partitions, the management node first applies Algorithm 1 within each partition to build local subtrees, then merges the root nodes of local subtrees and applies Algorithm 1 again to construct the global join tree.

4.3 Join Tree Decomposition

Given the constructed join tree and a cluster of k execution nodes, the management node must decompose the tree into k subtrees for parallel execution. The goal is to minimize the maximum execution time across nodes, thereby achieving load balance. Fig. 3 illustrates this problem: a naïve decomposition can assign 1600 operations to one node and 100 to another (Fig. 3a), while a balanced decomposition assigns approximately 1000 and 700 operations respectively (Fig. 3c).

Algorithm 2 achieves this by recursively predicting the execution cost of each subtree and comparing the cost ratio of the left and right subtrees against the available node capacity ratio. When a subtree's cost proportion matches an available node's capacity within tolerance ε, that subtree is assigned to the node and removed from the tree.

Algorithm 2. Load-Balanced Join Tree Decomposition

Input: Join tree *T*, number of execution nodes *k*, tolerance ε

Output: Join forest *S*

1: $S \leftarrow \emptyset$

(continued)

(*continued*)

Decompose (T, k)
return S

function Decompose (t, m)

if $m = 1$ **then** $S \leftarrow S \cup \{t\}$; **return**

$c_l \leftarrow$ PredictCost(t. left)

$c_r \leftarrow$ PredictCost(t. right)

$r \leftarrow c_l/(c_l + c_r)$

$k_l \leftarrow \max(1, \text{round}(r \cdot m))$; $k_r \leftarrow m - k_l$
if $k_r < 1$ **then** $k_l \leftarrow m - 1$; $k_r \leftarrow 1$

Decompose(t. left, k_l)

Decompose(t. right, k_r)

The PredictCost function recursively sums the predicted cardinalities of all nodes in a subtree. By decomposing based on predicted execution cost rather than data volume, the algorithm ensures that nodes with more complex joins receive proportionally more resources, avoiding the load imbalance inherent in traditional data-partitioning approaches.

5 System Architecture

We implement the algorithms from Sects. 3 and 4 in a distributed query system with a clear management–data layer separation. The system uses TripleBit [22] as the single-node RDF storage engine on each data node and star decomposition for query graph resolution. Figure 4 presents the overall system architecture.

As shown in Fig. 4, a SPARQL query enters the management node, which processes it through a four-stage pipeline before distributing subtrees to worker nodes via the MPI communication layer. Each worker node executes its assigned subtree using local TripleBit storage, exchanges intermediate results with peers as needed, and returns final results to the management node. We detail each layer below.

5.1 Management Layer

The management node (Fig. 5) accepts SPARQL queries and outputs results in triple format. Its processing pipeline consists of four stages. First, the query resolver converts the query into a query graph and decomposes it via star decomposition by iteratively selecting the highest-degree node. Second, the query class generator creates abstract query classes on partitions where results are predicted to exist, using the statistical index for cardinality estimation. Third, the join tree manager constructs and optimizes the join tree using Algorithm 1, assigns unique IDs via pre-order traversal, and decomposes the tree using Algorithm 2 based on real-time cluster load. Finally, the partition generator maps each subtree to an execution node and creates a global ID-to-partition mapping so that cross-partition data requests can be routed correctly.

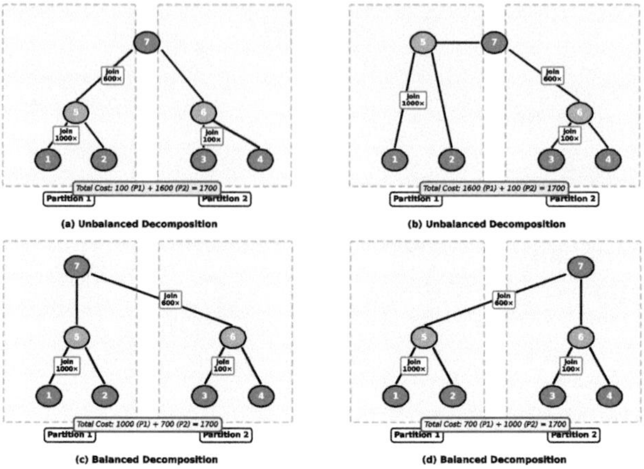

Fig. 3. Example of join tree decomposition

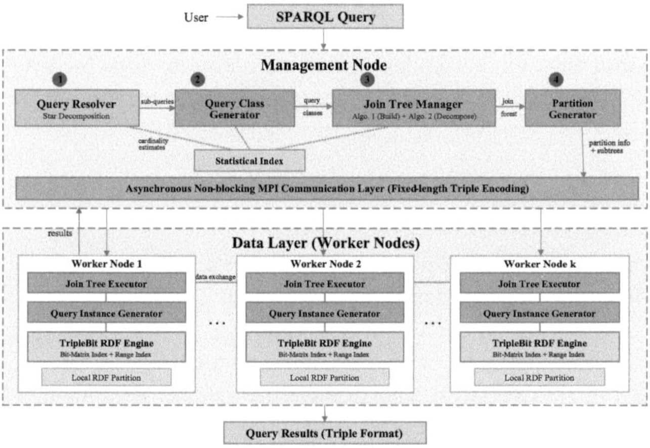

Fig. 4. System overview

5.2 Data Layer

Each data node (Fig. 6) receives its assigned subtree and the global ID-to-partition mapping from the management layer. The join tree executor first creates query instances for leaf nodes by querying the local TripleBit database, then executes the tree bottom-up: operations at the same level are parallelized across threads, and intermediate results are kept in memory to minimize I/O overhead. When a required query class resides on a remote partition, the communication layer fetches the data using asynchronous non-blocking MPI with fixed-length triple encoding to reduce transmission overhead. The final result is stored in the root node's query instance and returned to the management layer.

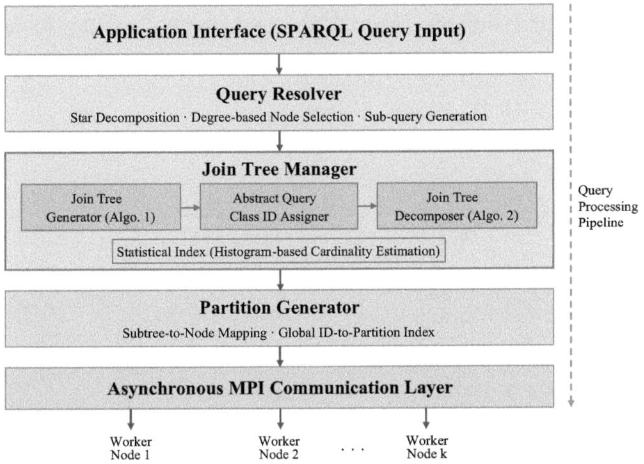

Fig. 5. Architecture of management node

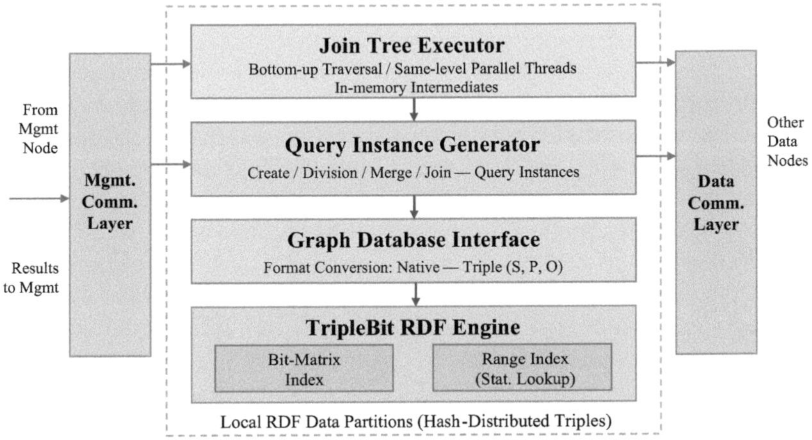

Fig. 6. Architecture of data node

6 Experiment

6.1 Experimental Setup

The system is deployed on a 13-node cluster (1 management node, 12 worker nodes) with identical configurations, using C++ on Linux. Each worker node runs TripleBit [22] as the local RDF engine. Nodes communicate via asynchronous non-blocking MPI with fixed-length triple encoding. We evaluate on the LUBM benchmark [29], using LUBM200M, LUBM500M, and LUBM1000M for performance tests, and LUBM1000M–LUBM10000M for scalability tests. Table 2 summarizes the dataset characteristics. During preprocessing, we hash-partition triples across data nodes and build statistical indices for cardinality estimation and range indices for accelerating local queries. All string-valued subjects, predicates, and objects are dictionary-encoded to IDs.

Table 2. LUBM dataset

Dataset	Triples	Subjects	Objects
LUBM200M	221,015,745	43,438,911	32,285,424
LUBM300M	400,512,826	65,155,053	48,423,840
LUBM500M	691,085,836	108,598,613	80,715,573
LUBM1000M	1,335,081,176	217,206,844	161,413,041
LUBM4000M	4,377,917,672	418,098,667	276,889,045
LUBM10000M	10,856,387,772	914,072,889	554,813,378

The LUBM benchmark, while drawn from the university domain, captures the structural characteristics shared by many real-world knowledge graphs: heavy-tailed cardinality distributions, star-shaped subgraph patterns, and multi-hop join paths. Such patterns are typical in domain knowledge graphs used for risk identification. For example, in import–export inspection scenarios, a subgraph query over a product knowledge graph, linking products, test institutions, applicable standards, risk types, and recall records, exhibits the same structural complexity that our join tree mechanism is designed to optimize. Our preliminary experiments on a real-world textile inspection dataset, which links products, test institutions, applicable standards, risk types and recall records, show consistent performance trends with those observed on LUBM, suggesting that the proposed method generalizes well to such application-driven workloads. Further tests on other product categories, including electrical and electronic products, toys, and hazardous chemicals, also exhibit similar trends.

We select seven multi-pattern queries (Q1–Q7) covering single-variable (Q1), cyclic (Q2–Q4), and acyclic (Q5–Q7) patterns. Each query is executed ten times; after removing the maximum and minimum, we report the arithmetic mean. We compare our Join Tree algorithm against Broadcast Hash Join, Shuffle Hash Join, and Sort Merge Join, all implemented within our system framework.

6.2 Performance

Table 3 reports results on LUBM1000M. For simple queries (Q1–Q3) with small result sets, all algorithms perform comparably. For complex queries (Q4–Q7), the Join Tree algorithm achieves 3–507× speedup over Broadcast Hash Join, 2–285× over Shuffle Hash Join, and 2–212× over Sort Merge Join. The advantage is most pronounced on Q7, where Join Tree completes in 5.06 s versus 1071s for Sort Merge Join (212× speedup). We observe consistent trends on LUBM200M and LUBM500M: on LUBM200M, Join Tree achieves up to 53× speedup on Q7; on LUBM500M, it achieves up to 154× on Q7. The speedup grows with data scale, confirming that our workload-aware decomposition becomes increasingly effective as intermediate result sizes grow.

Table 3. Query performance comparison on LUBM1000M (seconds)

	Broadcast Hash	Shuffle Hash	Sort Merge	Join Tree
Q1	1.98	2.06	1.99	0.56
Q2	3.07	3.76	3.98	1.56
Q3	7.89	8.91	8.82	3.06
Q4	167.13	106.08	121.89	50.08
Q5	421.96	272.12	302.23	81.87
Q6	1021.02	702.09	789.21	156.87
Q7	2561.91	1441.08	1071.09	5.06

6.3 Scalability

Varying cluster size. Fig. 7a shows query time ratios (normalized to single-node) on LUBM1000M with 1, 3, 6, 9, and 12 nodes. For simple queries (Q1–Q3), the single node outperforms distributed execution due to communication overhead. For complex queries (Q4–Q7), performance improves with more nodes but with diminishing returns—the largest gain occurs from 1 to 3 nodes, after which increasing data redundancy and communication costs offset parallelism benefits.

Varying data scale. Fig. 7b shows time ratios (normalized to LUBM200M) with 3 nodes across LUBM200M–LUBM10000M. Complex query time grows super-linearly with data scale due to larger intermediate results and increased communication. Simple queries (Q1–Q3) remain nearly constant, demonstrating that the system scales well for selective queries even at 10 billion triples.

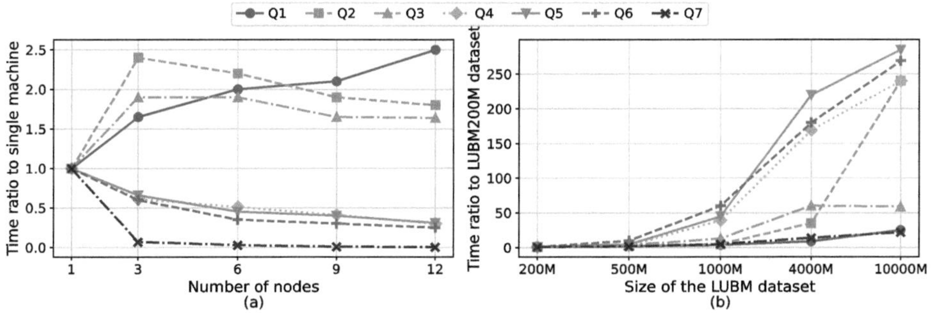

Fig. 7. Scalability evaluation: (a) time ratio with different cluster sizes; (b) time ratio with different data scales

6.4 Discussion

A fundamental limitation of traditional distributed joins is their reliance on data partitioning for parallelism, which inevitably degrades under the heavy data skew typical of knowledge graphs. Our Join Tree mechanism shifts the paradigm toward workload decomposition. By using the division operator to proactively fragment computationally expensive intermediate results based on cardinality predictions, we ensure that actual execution costs, rather than just data volumes, are balanced across nodes. This decouples load balancing from physical data distribution, offering robustness that key-based partitioning lacks.

7 Conclusion

This paper presented a distributed query system for large-scale knowledge graphs centered on a novel join tree mechanism. We introduced abstract query classes as lightweight metadata on the management node, supporting four algebraic operations (creation, division, merge, join) that separate query planning from physical data. The join tree is constructed using a greedy cardinality-guided strategy (Algorithm 1) and decomposed across cluster nodes according to predicted execution cost (Algorithm 2), ensuring workload balance rather than mere data balance.

Experiments on LUBM datasets up to 10.8 billion triples with a 13-node cluster demonstrate that the join tree algorithm achieves up to 212× speedup over Sort Merge Join on complex queries, with the advantage growing as data scale increases. Scalability tests confirm near-linear improvement from 1 to 3 nodes for complex queries, with diminishing returns beyond 6 nodes due to communication overhead.

Limitations of the current work include the use of only synthetic LUBM data and the absence of comparisons with external distributed RDF engines. Future work will evaluate on real-world knowledge graphs (e.g., DBpedia, Wikidata), incorporate learned cardinality estimation to improve join tree quality, and explore adaptive re-decomposition for dynamic workloads.

Acknowledgments. This study was funded by the National Key Research and Development Program of China (No. 2024YFF0618700).

Disclosure of Interests. The authors have no competing interests to declare that are relevant to the content of this article.

References

1. Neumann, T., Weikum, G.: The RDF-3X engine for scalable management of RDF data. VLDB J. **19**(1), 91–113 (2010)
2. Zou, L., Özsu, M.T., Chen, L., Shen, X., Huang, R., Zhao, D.: gStore: a graph-based SPARQL query engine. VLDB J. **23**(4), 565–590 (2014)
3. Zeng, K., Yang, J., Wang, H., Shao, B., Wang, Z.: A distributed graph engine for web scale RDF data. Proc. VLDB Endowment. **6**(4), 265–276 (2013)
4. Punnoose, R., Crainiceanu, A., Rapp, D.: SPARQL in the cloud using Rya. Inf. Syst. **48**, 181–195 (2015)
5. Schwarte, A., Haase, P., Hose, K., Schenkel, R., Schmidt, M.: FedX: optimization techniques for federated query processing on linked data. In: Aroyo, L., et al. (eds.) The Semantic Web—ISWC 2011 LNCS, vol. 7031, pp. 601–616. Springer, Heidelberg (2011)

6. Aimonier-Davat, J., Nédelec, B., Dang, M.-H., Molli, P., Skaf-Molli, H.: FedUP: querying large-scale federations of SPARQL endpoints. In: Proceedings of the ACM Web Conference 2024, pp. 2315–2324. ACM, New York (2024)
7. Aebeloe, C., Montoya, G., Hose, K.: Optimizing SPARQL queries over decentralized knowledge graphs. Semantic Web. **14**(6), 1121–1165 (2023)
8. Ali, W., Saleem, M., Yao, B., Hogan, A., Ngomo, A.-C.: A survey of RDF stores & SPARQL engines for querying knowledge graphs. VLDB J. **31**(3), 1–26 (2022)
9. Abdelaziz, I., Harbi, R., Khayyat, Z., Kalnis, P.: A survey and experimental comparison of distributed SPARQL engines for very large RDF data. Proc. VLDB Endowment. **10**(13), 2049–2060 (2017)
10. Veldhuizen, T.L.: Leapfrog Triejoin: a simple, worst-case optimal join algorithm. In: Proceedings of the 17th International Conference on Database Theory, pp. 96–106. ACM, New York (2014)
11. Wang, Y., Willsey, M., Suciu, D.: Free join: unifying worst-case optimal and traditional joins. Proc. ACM Manage. Data. **1**(2), 1–23 (2023)
12. Freitag, M., Bandle, M., Schmidt, T., Kemper, A., Neumann, T.: Adopting worst-case optimal joins in relational database systems. Proc. VLDB Endowment. **13**(11), 1891–1904 (2020)
13. Moerkotte, G., Neumann, T.: Dynamic programming strikes back. In: Proceedings of the 2008 ACM SIGMOD International Conference on Management of Data, pp. 539–552. ACM, New York (2008)
14. Mancini, R., Karthik, S., Chandra, B., Mageirakos, V., Ailamaki, A.: Efficient massively parallel join optimization for large queries. In: Proceedings of the 2022 ACM SIGMOD International Conference on Management of Data, pp. 122–135. ACM, New York (2022)
15. Selinger, P.G., Astrahan, M.M., Chamberlin, D.D., Lorie, R.A., Price, T.G.: Access path selection in a relational database management system. In: Proceedings of the 1979 ACM SIGMOD International Conference on Management of Data, pp. 23–34 (1979)
16. Schwabe, T., Acosta, M.: Cardinality estimation over knowledge graphs with embeddings and graph neural networks. Proc. ACM Manage. Data. **2**(1), 1–26 (2024)
17. Wu, Z., Negi, P., Alizadeh, M., Kraska, T., Madden, S.: FactorJoin: a new cardinality estimation framework for join queries. Proc. ACM Manage. Data. **1**(1), 1–27 (2023)
18. Karypis, G., Kumar, V.: A fast and high quality multilevel scheme for partitioning irregular graphs. SIAM J. Sci. Comput. **20**(1), 359–392 (1998)
19. Peng, P., Ji, S., Özsu, M.T., Zou, L.: Minimum motif-cut: a workload-aware RDF graph partitioning strategy. VLDB J. **33**(5), 1517–1542 (2024)
20. Hajidehi, M.R., Sridhar, S., Seltzer, M.: CUTTANA: scalable graph partitioning for faster distributed graph databases and analytics. Proc. VLDB Endowment. **18**(1), 14–27 (2024)
21. Bhoot, R., Khare, T., Agarwal, M., Jaiswal, S., Simmhan, Y.: Triparts: scalable streaming graph partitioning to enhance community structure. Proc. VLDB Endowment. **18**(9), 2992–3006 (2025)
22. Yuan, P., Liu, P., Wu, B., Jin, H., Zhang, W., Liu, L.: TripleBit: a fast and compact system for large scale RDF data. Proc. VLDB Endowment. **6**(7), 517–528 (2013)
23. Harbi, R., Abdelaziz, I., Kalnis, P., Mamoulis, N., Ebrahim, Y., Sahli, M.: Accelerating SPARQL queries by exploiting hash-based locality and adaptive partitioning. VLDB J. **25**(3), 355–380 (2016)
24. Wu, B., Zhou, Y., Yuan, P., Jin, H., Liu, L.: SemStore: a semantic-preserving distributed RDF triple store. In: Proceedings of the 23rd ACM International Conference on Information and Knowledge Management, pp. 509–518. ACM, New York (2014)
25. Gurajada, S., Seufert, S., Miliaraki, I., Theobald, M.: TriAD: a distributed shared-nothing RDF engine based on asynchronous message passing. In: Proceedings of the 2014 ACM SIGMOD International Conference on Management of Data, pp. 289–300 (2014)

26. Wu, B., Zhou, Y., Yuan, P., Liu, L., Jin, H.: Scalable SPARQL querying using path partitioning. In: Proceedings of the 31st IEEE International Conference on Data Engineering, pp. 795–806. IEEE, Piscataway (2015)
27. Gonzalez, J.E., Low, Y., Gu, H., Bickson, D., Guestrin, C.: PowerGraph: distributed graph-parallel computation on natural graphs. In: Proceedings of the 10th USENIX Symposium on Operating Systems Design and Implementation, pp. 17–30. USENIX Association, Berkeley (2012)
28. Malewicz, G., Austern, M.H., Bik, A.J.C., Dehnert, J.C., Leiser, N., Czajkowski, G.: Pregel: a system for large-scale graph processing. In: Proceedings of the 2010 ACM SIGMOD International Conference on Management of Data, pp. 135–146. ACM, New York (2010)
29. Guo, Y., Pan, Z., Heflin, J.: LUBM: a benchmark for OWL knowledge base systems. J. Web Semantics. **3**(2–3), 158–182 (2005)
30. Huang, J., Abadi, D.J., Ren, K.: Scalable SPARQL querying of large RDF graphs. Proc. VLDB Endowment. **4**(11), 1123–1134 (2011)
31. Shi, J., Yao, Y., Chen, R., Chen, H., Li, F.: Fast and concurrent RDF queries with RDMA-based distributed graph exploration. In: Proceedings of the 12th USENIX Symposium on Operating Systems Design and Implementation, pp. 317–332 (2016)
32. Arnaout, H., Elbassuoni, S.: Effective searching of RDF knowledge graphs. J. Web Semantics. **48**, 66–88 (2018)
33. Leis, V., Gubichev, A., Mirchev, A., Boncz, P., Kemper, A., Neumann, T.: How good are query optimizers, really? Proc. VLDB Endowment. **9**(3), 204–215 (2015)
34. Kipf, A., Kipf, T., Radke, B., Leis, V., Boncz, P., Kemper, A.: Learned cardinalities: estimating correlated joins with deep learning. 9th Biennial Conference on Innovative Data Systems Research (CIDR 2019), Online Proceedings. (2019)
35. Negi, P. et al.: Flow-loss: learning cardinality estimates that matter. Proc. VLDB Endowment. **14**(11), 2019–2032 (2021)
36. Zeng, Y., Li, Y., Zhou, X., Yang, J., Jiang, W., Li, K.: Efficient game theoretic approach to dynamic graph partitioning. Inf. Sci. **606**, 892–909 (2022)
37. Sun, S., Luo, Q.: In-memory subgraph matching: an in-depth study. In: Proceedings of the 2020 ACM SIGMOD International Conference on Management of Data, pp. 1083–1098. ACM, New York (2020)
38. Qi, Z., Wang, H., Zhang, H.: A dual-store structure for knowledge graphs. IEEE Trans. Knowl. Data Eng. **35**(2), 1104–1118 (2023)
39. Ji, S., Pan, S., Cambria, E., Marttinen, P., Yu, P.S.: A survey on knowledge graphs: representation, acquisition, and applications. IEEE Trans. Neural Networks Learn. Syst. **33**(2), 494–514 (2022)
40. Sun, Z., Wang, H., Wang, H., Shao, B., Li, J.: Efficient subgraph matching on billion node graphs. Proc. VLDB Endowment. **5**(9), 788–799 (2012)

Efficient GPU-Based Continuous Subgraph Matching on Batch Updates

Guanghua Li[1], Xibo Sun[2], Qiong Luo[1,2(✉)], and Lijun Chang[3]

[1] The Hong Kong University of Science and Technology (Guangzhou), Guangzhou, China
gli945@connect.hkust-gz.edu.cn

[2] The Hong Kong University of Science and Technology, Hong Kong, Hong Kong SAR
xsunax@connect.ust.hk, luo@cse.ust.hk

[3] The University of Sydney, Sydney, Australia
lijun.chang@sydney.edu.au

Abstract. Continuous subgraph matching (CSM) algorithms process edge updates (insertions and deletions) on the data graph and find new matches of the query graph that either appear or disappear as a result of each update. Existing CSM algorithms organize the matching process by the edge update to the data graph. We refer to this approach as update-oriented CSM (UO-CSM). While UO-CSM effectively handles single updates, directly applying it to a batch of updates can lead to redundant computations and duplicate results. To address this problem, existing work uses a deduplication technique based on update-edge ordering, which entails additional data structures to record whether an edge is an update-edge and an explicit duplication-removal step during the matching result enumeration. We propose a novel query-oriented CSM algorithm (QO-CSM), which avoids duplicate matches and ensures consistent results on dynamic graphs with batch updates, without additional data structures and the explicit de-duplication step. Our main idea is to put each update (insertion or deletion) edge to the data graph into its corresponding query edge delta relation ΔR, if any, and then process these ΔRs in order. Building on this paradigm, we develop a GPU-based CSM algorithm, GCSM-BU, which employs a two-level indexing mechanism for each ΔR and utilizes parallel breadth-first or depth-first search, based on runtime workload, for result enumeration. With the QO-CSM paradigm and effective GPU parallelism, GCSM-BU achieves correct query results on batch updates, while outperforming state-of-the-art CPU-based CSM methods by up to two orders of magnitude. It also outperforms existing GPU-based UO-CSM methods as well as their QO-CSM adaptations.

Keywords: Continuous Subgraph Matching · GPU Acceleration

G. Li and X. Sun: Equal Contribution

L. Ding et al. (Eds.): APWeb-WAIM 2026, LNCS 16993, pp. 493–510, 2027.
https://doi.org/10.1007/978-981-92-5693-8_31

1 Introduction

Subgraph matching (SM), which extracts all matches in a data graph G that are isomorphic to a query graph Q, is a common operation in various graph analytic tasks [9,25]. Since many real-life graphs are dynamic, with edges inserted and deleted over time, researchers have investigated the problem of continuous subgraph matching (CSM), which finds *incremental matches*, i.e., matches of the query graph Q in the data graph G that appear or disappear due to each edge update. Existing CSM algorithms [6,8,10,15,16,18,22] organize the matching process by the edge update to the data graph. We refer to this approach as update-oriented CSM (UO-CSM). While UO-CSM effectively handles single updates, directly applying it to a batch of updates can lead to redundant computations and duplicate results, resulting in efficiency and consistency issues. In this paper, we propose a consistent and efficient approach to CSM with batch updates, without requiring additional data structures or explicit steps for deduplication.

Most of the existing CSM algorithms process a single updated edge at a time and are designed for running with a single thread on the CPU. However, some real-world dynamic graphs evolve at an extremely high speed [2,28], e.g., 143,000 new tweets appear in the Twitter graph within a second [26]. In addition, batch updates are common in real-world graph analytics where updates are grouped and periodically processed [8,11,20]. Such high-rate and batch-based graph updates are challenging for single-update based algorithms to catch up with. To process batch updates efficiently, a recent GAMMA algorithm [24] parallelized the matching process on the GPU. GAMMA's matching speed was much faster than that of CPU-based single-update algorithms, but it must explicitly remove duplicates due to its direct application of UO-CSM to a batch of updates. This explicit de-duplication technique relies on additional data structures and a duplicate removal step during matching result enumeration, occupying additional GPU memory and degrading the overall performance. We will show that the UO-CSM framework is efficient only in the special case of single-update and subgraph isomorphism.

Table 1. Categorization of CSM algorithms. **UO** is for **U**pdate-**O**riented. **QO** is for **Q**uery-**O**riented.

Handle batches?	UO-CSM	QO-CSM
Yes	GAMMA [24]	GCSM-BU (ours)
No	SymBi [22], CaLiG [39], RapidFlow [32]	

Specifically, we first study the existing UO-CSM framework and identify its problem. We formulate the execution of algorithms based on the UO-CSM framework as the evaluation of relational algebra (RA) expressions, and explain why the existing framework is at risk of redundant computation and requires explicit duplicate removal. Based on our findings, we propose a new query-oriented CSM framework (QO-CSM) that can handle both single updates and batch updates correctly and efficiently.

Following our proposed QO-CSM framework, we implement GCSM-BU, a GPU-accelerated continuous subgraph matching algorithm for batch updates. Table 1 shows our GCSM-BU in comparison with existing work on the processing scheme and update size. One challenge of implementing such a QO-CSM algorithm on the GPU is the balance between parallelism and memory footprint. We adopt a dynamic strategy for searching matching results: we start with a parallel breadth-first-search and then switch to depth-first-search when the partial matches become sufficiently large. Another challenge is the load balance among GPU thread warps, which is caused by the skewness of vertex degree distribution in data graphs. The performance degradation due to load imbalance is prominent when we match the leaf vertices in the query graph. We introduce the backtracking flattening technique for leaf vertex matching to achieve a balanced workload distribution on the GPU. In summary, we make the following contributions.

- We study the existing UO-CSM framework and point out the problem in applying it directly to batch updates. To address this issue, we propose the QO-CSM framework that supports parallel CSM processing for batch updates.
- Based on the proposed framework, we implement our own CSM algorithm GCSM-BU, which runs on the GPU and processes batch updates efficiently.
- We adopt a dynamic search strategy for matching results, balancing the parallelism of the algorithm and the GPU memory footprint. We also propose the backtracking flattening technique for leaf vertex matching to avoid load imbalance.
- We conduct extensive experiments to demonstrate the overall efficiency of our algorithm, the efficiency of the QO-CSM framework, and the performance benefit of each individual technique.

2 Preliminaries

2.1 Problem Statement

This paper focuses on edge- and vertex-labeled undirected graphs denoted by $g = (V, E)$, where V is the set of vertices and E is the set of edges. We use $V(g)$ and $E(g)$ to denote the vertex set and edge set of the graph g, respectively. The notation $e(u_x, u_y)$ represents the edge connecting vertices u_x and u_y. For a given vertex $u \in V(g)$, $N(u)$ denotes the set of neighbors, i.e., the vertices adjacent to u, and $d(u) = |N(u)|$ is the degree of vertex u. Q represents the *query graph* and G is the *data graph*.

Definition 1. *Given graphs g and g', a subgraph isomorphism is a* ***injective mapping*** *M: $V(g) \to V(g')$ such that 1) $\forall u \in V(g), L(u) = L(M(u))$; 2) $\forall e(u, u') \in E(g), e(M(u), M(u')) \in E(g')$; and 3) $\forall e(u, u') \in E(g), L(e(u, u')) = L(e(M(u), M(u')))$.*

Subgraph matching (SM) finds all isomorphisms of Q in G. The set of all isomorphisms (matches) is denoted by $\mathcal{M}$.

In this paper, we consider a dynamic data graph G, which changes over time. $\Delta\mathcal{G}$ is a sequence of graph updates $\{(\oplus_1, \Delta G_1), (\oplus_2, \Delta G_2), \cdots)\}$ on G. Each $\oplus$ is a graph update operation that can be either insertion (+) or deletion (−). Each ΔG contains a set of update edges $\{e\}$. The data graph edges to be deleted must exist in G, whereas the edges to be inserted must not already exist in G. $|\Delta G|$ denotes the *batch size*. Usually, $|\Delta G| > 1$. When the update ΔG is applied to G, resulting in a modified graph G', we can identify the *incremental matches* $\Delta\mathcal{M}$, i.e., the differences between the matches $\mathcal{M}$ of Q in G and $\mathcal{M}'$ of Q in G'. We define the *continuous subgraph matching* problem in Definition 2.

Definition 2 (Problem Statement). *Given Q, G and $\Delta\mathcal{G}$, continuous subgraph matching (CSM) finds all incremental matches $\Delta\mathcal{M}$ for each $(\oplus, \Delta G) \in \Delta\mathcal{G}$.*

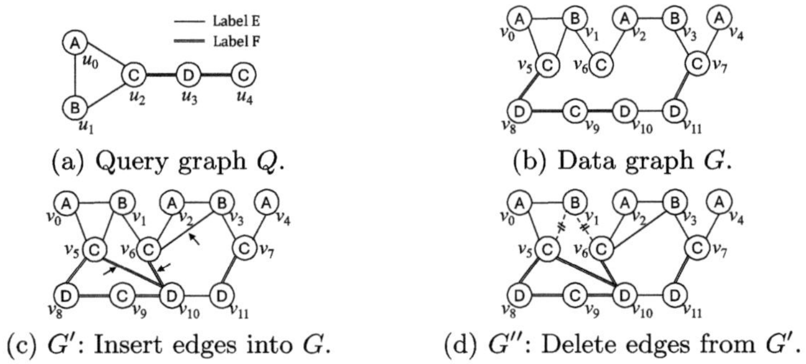

(a) Query graph Q.
(b) Data graph G.
(c) G': Insert edges into G.
(d) G'': Delete edges from G'.

Fig. 1. Example graphs.

We follow the practice in graph databases that data graph edges are grouped by their edge types. The *edge type* is defined as a 3-tuple (source-vertex label, edge label, destination-vertex label). Each edge group is considered a relation.

2.2 The Search Procedure in Subgraph Matching

Existing subgraph matching algorithms enumerate matching results with a backtracking search procedure, which maps each query vertex to a data graph vertex along a *matching order* φ. An order φ is a permutation of query vertices. We denote $u_x \prec_\varphi u_y$ if u_x appears before u_y in φ. $N_+^\varphi(u)$ (resp., $N_-^\varphi(u)$) denotes the neighbors of u positioned before (resp., after) u, namely the backward (resp., forward) neighbors. We use $\varphi[i]$ to represent the i-th query vertex (counting from 1) and $\varphi[i, j]$ is the subsequence of φ from position i to j (both ends included).

Algorithm 1 shows the matching result search procedure, commonly used in both SM and CSM [32]. A is an index of query edges to data edges. $A^u_{u'}$ contains

Algorithm 1: The Backtracking Search Procedure

1 **Procedure** ENUMERATE(φ, A, M, i)
2   **if** $i = |\varphi| + 1$ **then** Output M, **return**;
3   **else if** $i = 1$ **then** $u \leftarrow \varphi[1], C_M(u) \leftarrow \pi_{\varphi[1]} A_{\varphi[1]}^{\varphi[2]}$;
4   **else** $u \leftarrow \varphi[i]$, $C_M(u) \leftarrow \bigcap_{u' \in N_+^{\varphi}(u)} A_{u'}^{u}(M(u'))$;
5   **foreach** $v \in C_M(u)$ **do**
6   **if** v *is not visited* **then** `//remove "if" to find homomorphism`
7   Add (u, v) to M;
8   ENUMERATE($\varphi, A, M, i + 1$);
9   Remove (u, v) from M;

the candidate edges in the data graph for the query edge $e(u', u)$, $A_{u'}^{u}[v']$ is the set of v''s neighbors found in $A_{u'}^{u}$, with v' matching u' and neighbors matching u. i is the recursion depth (counting from 1) and M is a partial matching result that contains the mappings for $\varphi[1, i-1]$. $C_M(u)$ is the *enumeration candidate set* for query vertex u. At Lines 5-9 of Algorithm 1, we loop over vertices in $C_M(u)$ and extend M with one mapping for u inside each loop. Line 6 performs the isomorphism check. If all query vertices have been mapped, Line 2 outputs one matching result M. If the current recursion depth is 1, we generate the enumeration candidate set $C_M(u)$ by taking the candidates for u in the index $A_{\varphi[1]}^{\varphi[2]}$; otherwise, $C_M(u)$ is set to the intersection of the neighbor sets for all candidates that match the backward neighbors of u. In practice, the set intersection operation is usually implemented as a traversal of the neighbor set of one backward neighbor's match, followed by a check on whether each neighbor also belongs to the neighbor sets of other backward neighbors' matches. As previous work [31] has shown, if we view each $A_{u'}^{u}$ as a relation and remove the isomorphism check at Line 6, the ENUMERATE procedure in Algorithm 1 is equivalent to a multi-way join for relations $\{A_{u'}^{u} \in A \mid e(u', u) \in E(Q) \wedge u' \prec_{\varphi} u\}$.

3 Related Work

Subgraph Matching. Ullmann et al. [35] first proposed to solve subgraph matching with backtracking. Since then, extensive techniques have been proposed to improve the matching efficiency [4,7,14,17,27,29,30]. Recent work has started to utilize modern hardware, including GPU-based systems such as GunRockSM [36], GSI [40], and CuTS [38]. These methods enumerate results in BFS order. STMatch [37] adopted DFS, and EGSM [33] developed a DFS method optimized for GPU warps.

Continuous subgraph matching has been explored extensively on CPUs [6, 8,10,15,18]. Various CPU algorithms have been proposed, including SymBi [22], CaLiG [39], RapidFlow [32], and NewSP [19]. Most recently, Qiu et al. designed the GPU-based CSM method, GAMMA [24], to process batch updates, and it

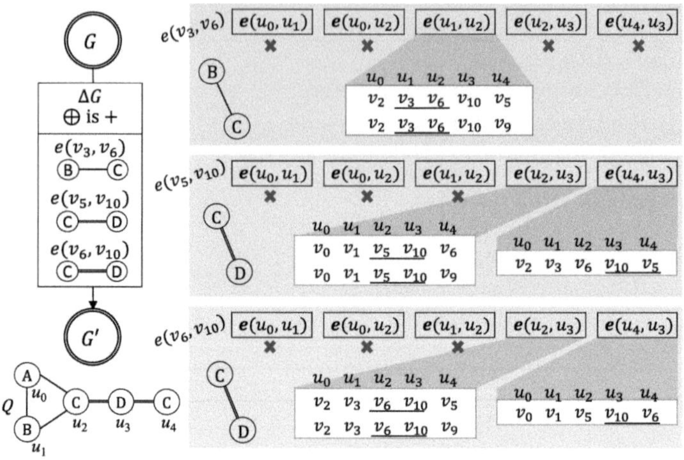

Fig. 2. Overview of the existing UO-CSM framework (w/o de-duplication).

significantly outperforms state-of-the-art CPU-based CSM methods that handle single updates. However, since GAMMA follows the existing UO-CSM algorithmic framework, it suffers from the memory and time cost of explicit de-duplication.

4 Framework Design

4.1 Foundation of an Efficient CSM Framework

Given the candidate relation for each query edge, subgraph isomorphism query processing is equivalent to performing a multi-way join as shown in Equation 1 [1,8,15,16,18,21,22].

$$\mathcal{M} = \sigma_{iso}(\bowtie_{e(u_x,u_y)\in E(Q)} R(u_x, u_y)) \tag{1}$$

Equation 1 can be decomposed as shown in Equation 2 [3,12,13,34].

$$\begin{aligned} \Delta\mathcal{M} &= \bigcup_i \Delta\mathcal{M}_i. \\ \Delta\mathcal{M}_1 &= \sigma_{iso}(\Delta R_1 \bowtie R_2 \bowtie \cdots \bowtie R_m), \\ \Delta\mathcal{M}_i &= \sigma_{iso}(R'_1 \bowtie \cdots \bowtie R'_{i-1} \bowtie \Delta R_i \bowtie R_{i+1} \bowtie \cdots \bowtie R_m), \\ \Delta\mathcal{M}_m &= \sigma_{iso}(R'_1 \bowtie \cdots \bowtie R'_{m-1} \bowtie \Delta R_m), \end{aligned} \tag{2}$$

We have the following proposition.

Proposition 1. *In Equation 2,* $\forall i, j \in [1, m]$ *and* $i \neq j, \Delta\mathcal{M}_i \cap \Delta\mathcal{M}_j = \emptyset$

If we decompose the CSM problem into subtasks corresponding to $\Delta\mathcal{M}_i$, there will be no duplicate results across subtasks.

Algorithm 2: Existing UO-CSM for Batch Updates

Input: query graph Q, initial data graph G, update stream $\Delta\mathcal{G}$
Output: incremental matches $\Delta\mathcal{M}$ for each $(\oplus, \Delta G) \in \Delta\mathcal{G}$

1 $I \leftarrow$ build an index based on Q and G;
2 **foreach** $(\oplus, \Delta G) \in \Delta\mathcal{G}$ **do**
3   **if** $\oplus$ *is* $+$ **then**
4         $G \leftarrow G \oplus \Delta G$ and update I;
5   **foreach** $e(v_a, v_b) \in \Delta G$ **do** `// parallel or sequential`
6   FindIncrementalMatchWithDuplicateRemoval$(Q, I, e(v_a, v_b))$;
7   **else** `//` $\oplus$ `is` $-$
8   `// Omitted.`
9 **Procedure** FindIncrementalMatchWithDuplicateRemoval$(Q, I, e(v_a, v_b))$
10     $\Delta\mathcal{M} \leftarrow \{\}$;
11   **foreach** $e(u_a, u_b) \in E(Q)$ **do** `// parallel or sequential`
12   **if** $e(v_a, v_b) \equiv e(u_a, u_b)$ **then**
13             $\varphi \leftarrow$ generate a matching order;
14             $A \leftarrow$ build a local index based on I (or just use I);
15             $M \leftarrow \{(u_a, v_a), (u_b, v_b)\}$;
16             $\Delta\mathcal{M}_{e(u_a,u_b)} \leftarrow$ EnumerateWithDuplicateRemoval$(\varphi, A, M, 3)$;
17   Add results in $\Delta\mathcal{M}_{e(u_a,u_b)}$ into $\Delta\mathcal{M}$;
18   Output $\Delta\mathcal{M}$;

4.2 Why is Explicit De-duplication Required in UO-CSM?

Algorithm 2 [34] presents the existing CSM framework. Figure 2 shows an example of using the existing framework to find incremental matches for the data graph in Fig. 1. In Algorithm 2, each iteration in the for-loop in the function FindIncrementalMatch corresponds to a select-join expression evaluation. Specifically, if we number the query edges in the order they appear in the for-loop at Line 13 in Algorithm 2, then collecting the results of the i-th loop (counting from 1) from each update edge in ΔG is equivalent to performing $\sigma_{iso}(R'_1 \bowtie \cdots \bowtie R'_{i-1} \bowtie \Delta R_i \bowtie R'_{i+1} \bowtie \cdots \bowtie R'_m)$. Note that all relations (except the i-th one) are updated versions, because before executing FindIncrementalMatch, we have updated both the data graph G (candidate relations) and the index I with the newly inserted edges in the current batch. ΔR_i contains the update edges that match the query edge e_i. In short, Algorithm 2 corresponds to Equation 3:

$$\begin{aligned}
\Delta\mathcal{M} &= \bigcup_i \Delta\mathcal{M}'_i. \\
\Delta\mathcal{M}'_1 &= \sigma_{iso}(\Delta R_1 \bowtie R'_2 \bowtie \cdots \bowtie R'_m), \\
\Delta\mathcal{M}'_i &= \sigma_{iso}(R'_1 \bowtie \cdots \bowtie R'_{i-1} \bowtie \Delta R_i \bowtie R'_{i+1} \bowtie \cdots \bowtie R'_m), \\
\Delta\mathcal{M}'_m &= \sigma_{iso}(R'_1 \bowtie \cdots \bowtie R'_{m-1} \bowtie \Delta R_m),
\end{aligned} \tag{3}$$

Note that all relations R in Equation 3 are updated versions. Proposition 1 does not hold for Eq. 3. As a result, explicit duplicate removal is required for Algorithm 2.

Example 1. In Fig. 2, the matches $(v_2, v_3, v_6, v_{10}, v_5)$, $(v_2, v_3, v_6, v_{10}, v_9)$, and $(v_0, v_1, v_5, v_{10}, v_6)$ are duplicated and must be explicitly removed.

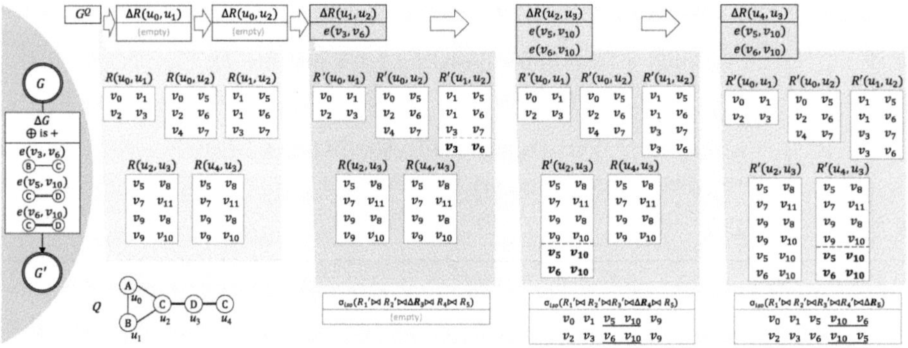

Fig. 3. Overview of the proposed QO-CSM framework.

4.3 Our Proposed QO-CSM Framework

Algorithm 3 shows our proposed QO-CSM framework. Figure 3 gives an example of using QO-CSM to find incremental matches for the data graph G in Fig. 1.

In Algorithm 3, we use G^Q to denote a collection of raw candidate relations for query Q. The difference between Algorithm 3 and Algorithm 2 is that, in Algorithm 3, we put each update edge into a ΔR according to its edge type. A ΔR corresponds to a query edge. A single update edge can be added to multiple ΔRs, because multiple query edges may share the same edge type. We update G^Q one ΔR at a time. FINDINCREMENTAL is interleaved with the ΔR updates. Inside FINDINCREMENTAL, we just use the ENUMERATE procedure as in the static subgraph matching, without the need to perform duplicate removal. For the iteration on ΔR_i at Line 6, the raw candidate relations for query edges

Algorithm 3: Proposed QO-CSM Framework

Input: query graph Q, a set of raw candidate relations $G^Q = \{R(u_a, u_b) | e(u_a, u_b) \in E(Q)\}$, update stream $\Delta\mathcal{G}$
Output: incremental matches $\Delta\mathcal{M}$ for each $(\oplus, \Delta G) \in \Delta\mathcal{G}$

$I \leftarrow$ build an index based on Q and G^Q;
foreach $(\oplus, \Delta G) \in \Delta\mathcal{G}$ **do**
  foreach $e(u_a, u_b) \in E(Q)$ **do**
    $\Delta R(u_a, u_b) \leftarrow \{e | e \in \Delta G \wedge e \equiv e(u_a, u_b)\}$;
  if $\oplus$ *is* $+$ **then**
    foreach $e(u_a, u_b) \in E(Q)$ **do** `// sequential`
      if $\Delta R(u_a, u_b) = \emptyset$ **then continue**;
      $R(u_a, u_b) \leftarrow R(u_a, u_b) \oplus \Delta R(u_a, u_b)$, update I;
      FindIncremental$(Q, I, e(u_a, u_b), \Delta R(u_a, u_b))$;
  else `// ⊕ is −`
    foreach $e(u_a, u_b) \in E(Q)$ **do** `// sequential`
      if $\Delta R(u_a, u_b) = \emptyset$ **then continue**;
      FindIncremental$(Q, I, e(u_a, u_b), \Delta R(u_a, u_b))$;
      $R(u_a, u_b) \leftarrow R(u_a, u_b) \oplus \Delta R(u_a, u_b)$, update I;
Procedure FindIncremental$(Q, I, e(u_a, u_b), \Delta R(u_a, u_b))$
  // Omitted.

of previous iterations $\Delta R_1, \ldots, \Delta R_{i-1}$, have been updated, and the updates $\Delta R_{i+1}, \ldots, \Delta R_m$ have not been applied. Hence, iteration i can be expressed as $\sigma_{iso}(R'_1 \bowtie \cdots \bowtie R'_{i-1} \bowtie \Delta R_i \bowtie R_{i+1} \bowtie \cdots \bowtie R_m)$, which is exactly $\Delta\mathcal{M}_i$ in Eq. 2. According to Proposition 1, no de-duplication is needed.

The QO-CSM framework also applies to edge deletions. The main difference lies in the order between enumeration and relation/index update. For an insertion batch, GCSM-BU first inserts the corresponding query-edge delta relation ΔR_i into R_i and updates the index, and then enumerates the newly generated matches anchored at ΔR_i. For a deletion batch, GCSM-BU performs these two steps in the reverse order: it first enumerates the matches that contain edges in ΔR_i, which are the matches that will disappear after the deletion, and then removes ΔR_i from R_i and updates the index. Therefore, deletion can be handled by the same query-oriented delta-relation processing principle, with the update operation placed after enumeration. Our experimental evaluation will focus on insertion streams, following the experimental settings of prior CSM studies [32].

5 Implementation

In this section, we describe the implementation of our GPU-based CSM algorithm GCSM-BU, following the proposed CSM framework in Algorithm 3. Figure 4 gives an overview.

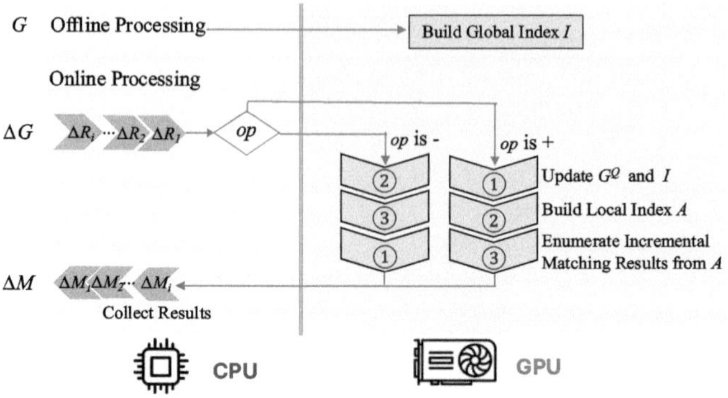

Fig. 4. Overview of GCSM-BU.

5.1 Data Structures

Given a data graph G and a query graph Q, our QO-CSM framework operates on a collection of raw candidate relations G^Q. We store a raw candidate relation $R(u_x, u_y)$ using two storage units, considering u_x and u_y as source vertices, respectively, to facilitate neighbor traversal in both directions. A storage unit is a data structure called a consecutive adjacency array, which consists of three arrays, namely *ptrs*, *capacities*, and *degrees*, indexed by source vertex IDs. These arrays maintain a dynamic array for each neighbor list.

5.2 Two-Level Indexing Mechanism

We utilize the two-level indexing mechanism following the CPU-based algorithm RapidFlow [32] , and apply it to the batch-update case, using a GPU implementation. When the query graph is dense, the time cost of local index building for a batch of update edges becomes significant. Hence, we decide to build the local index only when the query graph is acyclic or the average degree of the query graph is smaller than a threshold.

5.3 Search Strategy

We call the search strategy used by GCSM-BU for result enumeration *dynamic semi-BFS*, which takes advantage of both BFS and DFS search on the GPU. The execution of the ENUMERATE function as described in Algorithm 1 forms a search tree. Each pair of (an updated edge e, a query edge e_i that can be mapped to e) corresponds to one such search tree. In the case of depth-first-search (DFS), a search tree is assigned to a GPU warp, and the warp performs DFS on that tree. In contrast, breadth-first-search (BFS) performs the search layer by layer. At each layer, we assign a tree node to a GPU warp, which is responsible for enumerating the children of that tree node. BFS has a high GPU memory consumption and DFS may fail to fully utilize the parallelism of a GPU. In dynamic semi-BFS, we first perform the BFS until the size of the intermediate results reaches a pre-defined threshold. Then, we assign each intermediate matching result to a GPU warp and let that warp perform DFS.

We also adopt a backtracking flattening strategy. Given a query graph Q and a matching order $\varphi = u_0 u_1 u_2 ... u_l u_{l+1} ... u_n$. If u_l has more than one neighbor in Q and each query vertex positioned after u_l in φ has only a single neighbor, we call the latter vertices *tail leaf vertices.* For any tail leaf vertex u_p, its neighbor u_q cannot also be a tail leaf vertex, because if so, u_p and u_q are not connected with the other part of the query graph Q, which contradicts our basic assumption that Q is connected. Hence, there are no edges between any two tail leaf vertices, and each tail leaf vertex must be connected to a vertex that belongs to the non-leaf part of Q. We propose to use *backtracking flattening* to enumerate the matching results for the tail leaf vertices. We illustrate this technique in Example 2.

Example 2. Suppose u_p and u_q are the only two tail leaf vertices, $e(u_1, u_p), e(u_2, u_q) \in E(Q)$ and $u_p \prec_\varphi u_q$ (i.e. $p = l+1, q = n$). Given an intermediate result $(v_0, v_1, v_2, ..., v_l)$, suppose v_1 and v_2 have d_1 and d_2 neighbors that can map u_p and u_q, respectively. Then, this intermediate result can be extended to at most $d_1 * d_2$ final results. Given integers i, j, k, if $i \in [0, d_1 * d_2)$, $j = \lfloor i/d_1 \rfloor$ and $k = i \bmod d_2$, then in the i-th of the $d_1 \times d_2$ potential final results, v_p is mapped to j-th neighbor of v_1 and u_q is mapped to the k-th neighbor of v_2 (all counting from 0). Hence, we can use $d_1 * d_2$ GPU threads to extend the intermediate result $(v_0, v_1, v_2, ..., v_l)$. Inside each thread, we locate the corresponding potential final result using thread ID and perform the isomorphism check. If that potential result passes the isomorphism check, we count it as a match.

6 Experiments

6.1 Experimental Setup

We compare GCSM-BU with the three latest CPU-based single-update CSM algorithms, SymBi [22], RapidFlow [32] and NewSP [19], using their publicly available GitHub implementations[1,2,3]. We set the query-graph-average-degree threshold for GCSM-BU to adopt the two-level indexing mechanism to 3. We have implemented the GPU-based batch-update CSM algorithm GAMMA [24] because the original code is unavailable, denoted as GAMMA*. In our implementation, QO-GAMMA* and GAMMA* use the same graph data structure as GCSM-BU for a fair comparison. Experiments show that our GAMMA* implementation achieves better overall performance than that originally reported in the paper [24] on the same GPU hardware model (5–30 times faster). All methods under comparison are compiled with g++ 11.4.0 and cuda- 12.8. We conduct experiments on a Linux server with 256 GiB of RAM, two AMD EPYC 7302 CPUs, and one NVIDIA RTX 3090 GPU with 24 GiB of device memory.

---

[1] https://github.com/RapidsAtHKUST/ContinuousSubgraphMatching
[2] https://github.com/shixuansun/RapidFlow
[3] https://github.com/hnuGraph/NewSP

Table 2. Experimental statistics.

(a) Dataset statistics[a].

Datasets	$\|V\|$	$\|E\|$	$\|\Sigma_V\|$	$\|\Sigma_E\|$	d_{avg}	d_{max}	raw_size
LSBench (*lb*)	5.2M	20.3M	1	44	8.2	2.3M	443.74MB
Netflow (*nf*)	3.1M	2.9M	1	7	2.0	0.2M	83.64MB
LiveJournal (*lj*)	4.9M	42.9M	30	1	18.1	4.3M	819.57MB
Amazon (*az*)	0.4M	2.4M	6	1	12.2	0.2M	43.92MB

(b) Number of solved queries.

Queries	Tree				Sparse				Dense			
Datasets	*lb*	*nf*	*lj*	*az*	*lb*	*nf*	*lj*	*az*	*lb*	*nf*	*lj*	*az*
SymBi	88	55	96	**100**	96	88	**100**	**100**	**100**	**100**	**100**	**100**
NewSP	89	86	**100**	**100**	81	**100**	**100**	**100**	**100**	**100**	**100**	**100**
RapidFlow	89	86	**100**	**100**	97	**100**	**100**	**100**	**100**	**100**	**100**	**100**
GAMMA*	48	72	**100**	**100**	48	78	**100**	**100**	27	58	**100**	**100**
QO-GAMMA*	89	87	**100**	**100**	97	**100**	**100**	**100**	**100**	**100**	**100**	**100**
GCSM-BU	**92**	**90**	**100**	**100**	**98**	**100**	**100**	**100**	**100**	**100**	**100**	**100**

[a] d_{avg}: average vertex degree; d_{max}: maximum vertex degree; raw_size: total size of dataset files

Datasets We adopt four datasets frequently used in previous work, including LSBench [23], Netflow [5], LiveJournal, and Amazon. Table 2a lists the statistics of each dataset. Since all competing algorithms perform symmetric operations for edge insertions and deletions, we follow previous studies [19,24,32] and only report the results on the insertion stream for brevity. We split the edge set in a dataset into initial data graph edges and inserted edges. The insertion rate is set to 10%, following previous studies [32]. We group all update edges into a single batch by default.

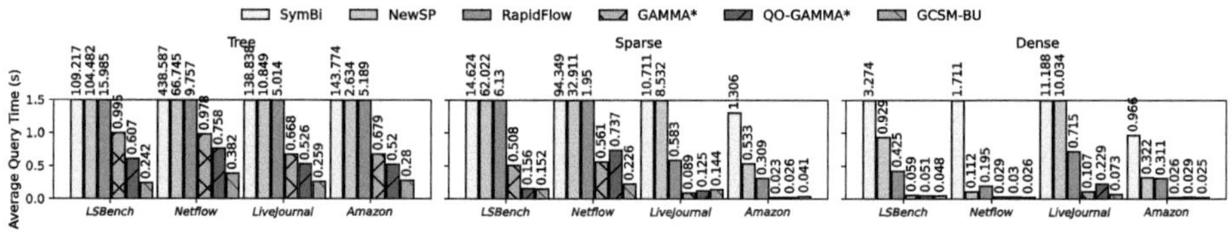

Fig. 5. Average query time of solved queries (in seconds).

Query Graphs and Metrics We use query graphs from previous studies [32], which were constructed by random walks in the data graph. For all datasets, we use query graphs with 6 vertices by default. We generate a set of 100 queries for each query type and size. We measure the elapsed time of the entire online processing as query time. We set the time limit for processing a query to 0.5 hours to complete our experiments in a reasonable amount of time. We call a query completed within the time limit a *solved query*; otherwise, we call it an *unsolved query*. We report the average query time over the set of queries that are solved by all compared methods.

6.2 Overall Evaluation

Table 2b lists the number of solved queries for all query graph shapes on the four datasets. Unsolved queries mainly occur for tree and sparse query graphs, especially with skewed label distribution, such as *lb* and *nf*. Our method, GCSM-BU, can solve more queries than all CPU- and GPU-based baselines in all cases. We measure the average query time on the four datasets. RapidFlow and NewSP are the top performers among existing CPU-based algorithms, and GCSM-BU consistently outperforms them. On tree queries, our method runs 111×, 25×, 20× and 9× faster than the best CPU-based method on *lb*, *nf*, *lj*, and *az*, respectively, and nearly 3–4× faster than GAMMA*. On sparse queries, this performance trend remains in comparison with CPU-based methods, and GCSM-BU is still faster than or on par with GPU-based GAMMA* and QO-GAMMA*. Dense queries are generally easier to solve because dense edges provide stronger pruning power. GCSM-BU achieves a speedup of up to 9× over the best CPU-based algorithm and is on par with GAMMA* and QO-GAMMA* on the dense queries.

6.3 Efficiency of QO-CSM Framework

We compare the query time of GAMMA* and QO-GAMMA* to evaluate the efficiency of our QO-CSM framework. Figure 6 shows that, in most cases, QO-GAMMA* runs faster than GAMMA*. The speedup ratio ranges from 1.2 to 2.1, which demonstrates the benefit of QO-CSM, which does not require explicit duplicate removal. For sparse and dense queries on *lj* and *az*, the query workload is small, so the update cost of QO-CSM outweighs the benefit of avoiding explicit de-duplication. We have seen in Fig. 5 that even in the cases where QO-GAMMA* runs slower than GAMMA*, by adopting optimizations such as the dynamic semi-BFS search strategy, our GCSM-BU still performs better than or on par with GAMMA*.

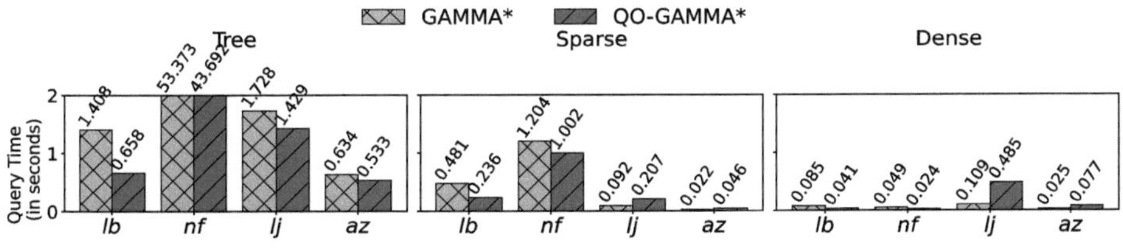

Fig. 6. Query time comparison between UO- & QO-CSM on solved queries. GAMMA* and QO-GAMMA* are different only in the framework they adopt, namely UO-CSM and QO-CSM, respectively.

6.4 Evaluation of Optimizations in Indexing and Enumeration

Table 3 shows the speedup achieved by the full-fledged GCSM-BU over two variants of our algorithm with backtracking flattening disabled (-Flatten) and with the dynamic semi-BFS strategy disabled (-semiBFS). The backtracking

Table 3. Average speedups of our optimizations.

Queries	Tree				Sparse				Dense			
Datasets	*lb*	*nf*	*lj*	*az*	*lb*	*nf*	*lj*	*az*	*lb*	*nf*	*lj*	*az*
-Flatten	1.3	4.7	1.8	4.5	1.0	1.9	1.3	2.6	1.1	0.8	1.0	1.2
-semiBFS	1.2	191.1	1.0	1.0	1.0	2.2	1.3	1.5	1.0	0.8	1.2	1.0

flattening mechanism improves the matching efficiency in all cases because it is common for a query graph to contain leaf vertices and these leaf vertices are often placed at the end of the matching order. The dynamic semi-BFS strategy shows its benefits mainly on the dataset nf, where the number of updated edges in each sub-batch is small.

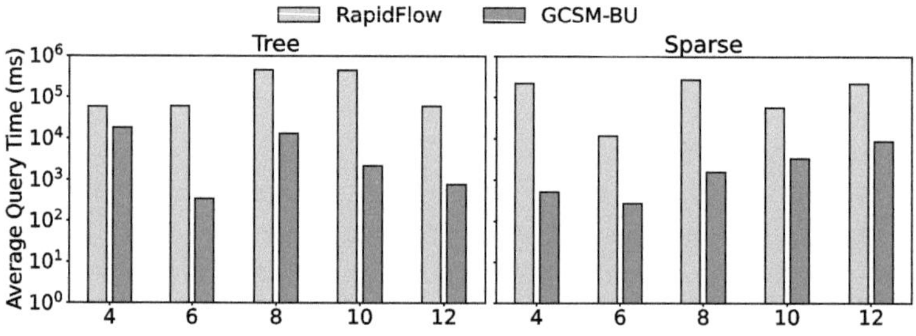

Fig. 7. Varying $|V(Q)|$.

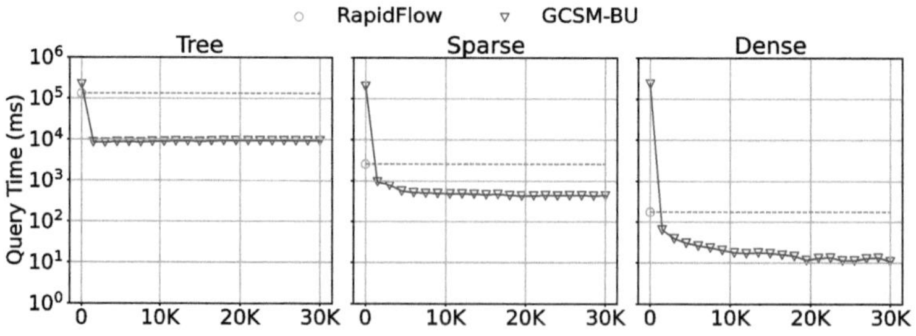

Fig. 8. Query time with various batch sizes.

6.5 Varying Query Graph Size and Batch Size

Query Size We first perform tree and sparse queries on the dataset ls with the query graph size varied from 4 to 12 in increments of 2. As shown in Fig.

7, GCSM-BU achieves speedups of around 99× and 136× over the best baseline method RapidFlow, on tree and sparse queries, respectively. The results indicate that our proposed techniques consistently show benefits under different query graph sizes.

Batch Size Finally, we run GCSM-BU with the batch size of the update stream varied from 1 to 30k in increments of 1,500. Then, we plot the average query time of GCSM-BU under various batch sizes and that of RapidFlow for single updates in Fig. 8. Given a batch size of 1, GCSM-BU underperforms RapidFlow since the matching workload caused by a single edge update is small and cannot fully utilize the parallel computing power of a GPU. The query time drops as the batch size increases. The performance gain becomes negligible when the batch size reaches 1500 in tree queries, 4500 in sparse queries, or 19500 in dense queries because, under these settings, the matching workload of a batch is sufficient to fully utilize the GPU.

7 Conclusion and Future Work

In this paper, we studied the problem of continuous subgraph matching for batch updates and proposed a query-oriented CSM framework, QO-CSM, which avoids duplicate query results automatically. Based on QO-CSM, we implemented a GPU-based CSM algorithm, GCSM-BU, which integrates various techniques and practical optimizations. Experiments show that GCSM-BU significantly outperforms the latest CPU-based CSM algorithms on batch updates and achieves better overall performance than the GAMMA* variants.

Although QO-CSM provides a hardware-independent framework for avoiding duplicate results in batch-update CSM, its performance benefit depends on the workload characteristics. When the matching workload is small, the additional update cost may outweigh the benefit of avoiding explicit duplicate removal. Future work could investigate an adaptive execution framework that chooses between QO-CSM and UO-CSM-style processing based on the estimated update cost, search cost, and duplicate-removal cost. GCSM-BU is designed primarily for GPU-friendly batch workloads. Its performance relies on exposing sufficient parallelism across update edges and search-tree nodes. For very small batches or highly selective queries, the GPU may not be fully utilized, and its advantage over CPU-based or simpler GPU-based methods can become less significant. To address this limitation, future work can explore adaptive CPU-GPU execution, where small or highly selective workloads can be routed to the CPU, while large and highly parallel workloads are executed on the GPU.

Acknowledgment. This work was supported by Grant 16209821 from the Hong Kong Research Grants Council.

References

1. Ammar, K., McSherry, F., Salihoglu, S., Joglekar, M.: Distributed evaluation of subgraph queries using worst-case optimal and low-memory dataflows. Proc. VLDB Endow. **11**(6), 691–704 (2018). https://doi.org/10.14778/3184470.3184473
2. Armstrong, T.G., Ponnekanti, V., Borthakur, D., Callaghan, M.: Linkbench: a database benchmark based on the facebook social graph. In: Proceedings of the ACM SIGMOD International Conference on Management of Data, SIGMOD 2013, New York, NY, USA, June 22–27, 2013, pp. 1185–1196. ACM (2013). https://doi.org/10.1145/2463676.2465296
3. Blakeley, J.A., Larson, P., Tompa, F.W.: Efficiently updating materialized views. In: Proceedings of the 1986 ACM SIGMOD International Conference on Management of Data, Washington, DC, USA, May 28–30, 1986, pp. 61–71. ACM Press (1986). https://doi.org/10.1145/16894.16861
4. Bonnici, V., Giugno, R., Pulvirenti, A., Shasha, D.E., Ferro, A.: A subgraph isomorphism algorithm and its application to biochemical data. BMC Bioinform. **14**(S-7), S13 (2013). https://doi.org/10.1186/1471-2105-14-S7-S13
5. CAIDA: The Caida ucsd Anonymized Internet Traces 2013 (2013). https://catalog.caida.org/details/dataset/passive_2013_pcap. Accessed Date: Mar 07, 2022
6. Choudhury, S., Holder, L.B., Jr., G.C., Agarwal, K., Feo, J.: A selectivity based approach to continuous pattern detection in streaming graphs. In: Proceedings of the 18th International Conference on Extending Database Technology, EDBT 2015, Brussels, Belgium, March 23–27, 2015, pp. 157–168. OpenProceedings.org (2015). https://doi.org/10.5441/002/edbt.2015.15
7. Cordella, L.P., Foggia, P., Sansone, C., Vento, M.: A (sub)graph isomorphism algorithm for matching large graphs. IEEE Trans. Pattern Anal. Mach. Intell. **26**(10), 1367–1372 (2004). https://doi.org/10.1109/TPAMI.2004.75
8. Dhulipala, L., Durfee, D., Kulkarni, J., Peng, R., Sawlani, S., Sun, X.: Parallel batch-dynamic graphs: algorithms and lower bounds. In: Proceedings of the 2020 ACM-SIAM Symposium on Discrete Algorithms, SODA 2020, Salt Lake City, UT, USA, January 5–8, 2020, pp. 1300–1319. SIAM (2020). https://doi.org/10.1137/1.9781611975994.79
9. Fan, W.: Graph pattern matching revised for social network analysis. In: 15th International Conference on Database Theory, ICDT '12, Berlin, Germany, March 26–29, 2012, pp. 8–21. ACM (2012). https://doi.org/10.1145/2274576.2274578
10. Fan, W., Li, J., Luo, J., Tan, Z., Wang, X., Wu, Y.: Incremental graph pattern matching. In: Proceedings of the ACM SIGMOD International Conference on Management of Data, SIGMOD 2011, Athens, Greece, June 12–16, 2011, pp. 925–936. ACM (2011). https://doi.org/10.1145/1989323.1989420
11. Farhan, M., Wang, Q., Koehler, H.: Batchhl: Answering distance queries on batch-dynamic networks at scale. In: SIGMOD '22: International Conference on Management of Data, Philadelphia, PA, USA, June 12–17, 2022, pp. 2020–2033. ACM (2022). https://doi.org/10.1145/3514221.3517883
12. Gao, J., Zhou, C., Yu, J.X.: Toward continuous pattern detection over evolving large graph with snapshot isolation. VLDB J. **25**(2), 269–290 (2016). https://doi.org/10.1007/S00778-015-0416-Z
13. Griffin, T., Libkin, L.: Incremental maintenance of views with duplicates. In: Proceedings of the 1995 ACM SIGMOD International Conference on Management of Data, San Jose, California, USA, May 22–25, 1995, pp. 328–339. ACM Press (1995). https://doi.org/10.1145/223784.223849

14. Han, M., Kim, H., Gu, G., Park, K., Han, W.: Efficient subgraph matching: Harmonizing dynamic programming, adaptive matching order, and failing set together. In: Proceedings of the 2019 International Conference on Management of Data, SIGMOD Conference 2019, Amsterdam, The Netherlands, June 30–July 5, 2019, pp. 1429–1446. ACM (2019). https://doi.org/10.1145/3299869.3319880
15. Idris, M., Ugarte, M., Vansummeren, S.: The dynamic yannakakis algorithm: compact and efficient query processing under updates. In: Proceedings of the 2017 ACM International Conference on Management of Data, SIGMOD Conference 2017, Chicago, IL, USA, May 14–19, 2017, pp. 1259–1274. ACM (2017). https://doi.org/10.1145/3035918.3064027
16. Kankanamge, C., Sahu, S., Mhedhbi, A., Chen, J., Salihoglu, S.: Graphflow: An active graph database. In: Proceedings of the 2017 ACM International Conference on Management of Data, SIGMOD Conference 2017, Chicago, IL, USA, May 14–19, 2017, pp. 1695–1698. ACM (2017). https://doi.org/10.1145/3035918.3056445
17. Kim, H., Choi, Y., Park, K., Lin, X., Hong, S., Han, W.: Versatile equivalences: Speeding up subgraph query processing and subgraph matching. In: SIGMOD '21: International Conference on Management of Data, Virtual Event, China, June 20–25, 2021, pp. 925–937. ACM (2021). https://doi.org/10.1145/3448016.3457265
18. Kim, K., Seo, I., Han, W., Lee, J., Hong, S., Chafi, H., Shin, H., Jeong, G.: Turboflux: A fast continuous subgraph matching system for streaming graph data. In: Proceedings of the 2018 International Conference on Management of Data, SIGMOD Conference 2018, Houston, TX, USA, June 10–15, 2018, pp. 411–426. ACM (2018). https://doi.org/10.1145/3183713.3196917
19. Li, Z., Li, Y., Chen, X., Zou, L., Li, Y., Yang, X., Jiang, H.: Newsp: a new search process for continuous subgraph matching over dynamic graphs. In: 40th IEEE International Conference on Data Engineering, ICDE 2024, Utrecht, The Netherlands, May 13–16, 2024, pp. 3324–3337. IEEE (2024). https://doi.org/10.1109/ICDE60146.2024.00257
20. Mariappan, M., Vora, K.: Graphbolt: dependency-driven synchronous processing of streaming graphs. In: Proceedings of the Fourteenth EuroSys Conference 2019, Dresden, Germany, March 25–28, 2019, pp. 25:1–25:16. ACM (2019). https://doi.org/10.1145/3302424.3303974
21. Mhedhbi, A., Salihoglu, S.: Optimizing subgraph queries by combining binary and worst-case optimal joins. Proc. VLDB Endow. **12**(11), 1692–1704 (2019). https://doi.org/10.14778/3342263.3342643
22. Min, S., Park, S.G., Park, K., Giammarresi, D., Italiano, G.F., Han, W.: Symmetric continuous subgraph matching with bidirectional dynamic programming. Proc. VLDB Endow. **14**(8), 1298–1310 (2021). https://doi.org/10.14778/3457390.3457395
23. Phuoc, D.L., Dao-Tran, M., Pham, M., Boncz, P.A., Eiter, T., Fink, M.: Linked stream data processing engines: facts and figures. In: The Semantic Web - ISWC 2012 - 11th International Semantic Web Conference, Boston, MA, USA, November 11–15, 2012, Proceedings, Part II. Lecture Notes in Computer Science, vol. 7650, pp. 300–312. Springer (2012). https://doi.org/10.1007/978-3-642-35173-0_20
24. Qiu, L., Chen, L., Jie, H., Ke, X., Gao, Y., Liu, Y., Zhang, Z.: Gpu-accelerated batch-dynamic subgraph matching. In: 40th IEEE International Conference on Data Engineering, ICDE 2024, Utrecht, The Netherlands, May 13–16, 2024, pp. 3204–3216. IEEE (2024). https://doi.org/10.1109/ICDE60146.2024.00248
25. Qiu, X., Cen, W., Qian, Z., Peng, Y., Zhang, Y., Lin, X., Zhou, J.: Real-time constrained cycle detection in large dynamic graphs. Proc. VLDB Endow. **11**(12), 1876–1888 (2018). https://doi.org/10.14778/3229863.3229874

26. Reichhold, J., Helder, D., Asemanfar, A., Molina, M., Harris, M.: New Tweets per Second Record, and How! https://blog.twitter.com/engineering/en_us/a/2013/new-tweets-per-second-record-and-how. Accessed Date: Jun 30th, 2023 (2013)
27. Rivero, C.R., Jamil, H.M.: Efficient and scalable labeled subgraph matching using SGMatch. Knowl. Inf. Syst. **51**(1), 61–87 (2016). https://doi.org/10.1007/s10115-016-0968-2
28. Sengupta, D., Sundaram, N., Zhu, X., Willke, T.L., Young, J.S., Wolf, M., Schwan, K.: Graphin: an online high performance incremental graph processing framework. In: Euro-Par 2016: Parallel Processing - 22nd International Conference on Parallel and Distributed Computing, Grenoble, France, August 24–26, 2016, Proceedings. Lecture Notes in Computer Science, vol. 9833, pp. 319–333. Springer (2016). https://doi.org/10.1007/978-3-319-43659-3_24
29. Shang, H., Zhang, Y., Lin, X., Yu, J.X.: Taming verification hardness: an efficient algorithm for testing subgraph isomorphism. Proc. VLDB Endow. **1**(1), 364–375 (2008). https://doi.org/10.14778/1453856.1453899
30. Sun, S., Luo, Q.: In-memory subgraph matching: an in-depth study. In: Proceedings of the 2020 International Conference on Management of Data, SIGMOD Conference 2020, online conference [Portland, OR, USA], June 14–19, 2020, pp. 1083–1098. ACM (2020). https://doi.org/10.1145/3318464.3380581
31. Sun, S., Sun, X., Che, Y., Luo, Q., He, B.: Rapidmatch: a holistic approach to subgraph query processing. Proc. VLDB Endow. **14**(2), 176–188 (2020). https://doi.org/10.14778/3425879.3425888
32. Sun, S., Sun, X., He, B., Luo, Q.: Rapidflow: an efficient approach to continuous subgraph matching. Proc. VLDB Endow. **15**(11), 2415–2427 (2022)
33. Sun, X., Luo, Q.: Efficient gpu-accelerated subgraph matching. Proc. ACM Manag. Data **1**(2), 181:1–181:26 (2023). https://doi.org/10.1145/3589326
34. Sun, X., Sun, S., Luo, Q., He, B.: An in-depth study of continuous subgraph matching. Proc. VLDB Endow. **15**(7), 1403–1416 (2022)
35. Ullmann, J.R.: An algorithm for subgraph isomorphism. J. ACM **23**(1), 31–42 (1976). https://doi.org/10.1145/321921.321925
36. Wang, L., Owens, J.D.: Fast Gunrock Subgraph Matching (GSM) on gpus (2020). CoRR abs/2003.01527
37. Wei, Y., Jiang, P.: Stmatch: accelerating graph pattern matching on GPU with stack-based loop optimizations. In: SC22: International Conference for High Performance Computing, Networking, Storage and Analysis, Dallas, TX, USA, November 13–18, 2022, pp. 53:1–53:13. IEEE (2022). https://doi.org/10.1109/SC41404.2022.00058
38. Xiang, L., Khan, A., Serra, E., Halappanavar, M., Sukumaran-Rajam, A.: Cuts: scaling subgraph isomorphism on distributed multi-gpu systems using trie based data structure. In: International Conference for High Performance Computing, Networking, Storage and Analysis, SC 2021, St. Louis, Missouri, USA, November 14–19, 2021, p. 69. ACM (2021). https://doi.org/10.1145/3458817.3476214
39. Yang, R., Zhang, Z., Zheng, W., Yu, J.X.: Fast continuous subgraph matching over streaming graphs via backtracking reduction. Proc. ACM Manag. Data **1**(1), 15:1–15:26 (2023). https://doi.org/10.1145/3588695
40. Zeng, L., Zou, L., Özsu, M.T., Hu, L., Zhang, F.: GSI: gpu-friendly subgraph isomorphism. In: 36th IEEE International Conference on Data Engineering, ICDE 2020, Dallas, TX, USA, April 20-24, 2020, pp. 1249–1260. IEEE (2020). https://doi.org/10.1109/ICDE48307.2020.00112

Just a "Hop" to Efficient Query of Optimal Temporal Paths: A Novel Labeling Approach

Yufei Sun[1], Ming Zhong[1(✉)], Yuanyuan Zhu[1], Tieyun Qian[1], and Mengchi Liu[2]

[1] School of Computer Science, Wuhan University, Wuhan, China
{sunyufeics,clock,yyzhu,qty}@whu.edu.cn
[2] South China Normal University, Guangzhou, China
liumengchi@scnu.edu.cn

Abstract. As a classical graph analysis task, the optimal path query has regained extensive research interests in the temporal graph scenarios. Among those researches, the two-hop labeling approaches are promising for real-time query processing. However, these approaches either cannot return all exact optimal paths or cannot scale to large graphs. In this paper, we propose a novel two-hop labeling approach. It both reuses a minimum set of components of existing labels to preserve the correctness of query processing and the scalability of indexing and introduces a new component, namely, "hop" to facilitate the search of exact paths. We theoretically prove the correctness and complexity of optimal path search base on our labels. We also design effective optimization techniques for index construction. Lastly, we conduct comprehensive experiments on fourteen real-world datasets to compare the performance of our approach with state-of-the-art approaches.

Keywords: Temporal graph · Reachability · Two-hop index · Optimal path · Query processing

1 Introduction

Recently, temporal graphs such as social networks [22], transaction networks [24], and transportation networks [23] have attracted intensive research interests. Generally, a temporal graph is a topological graph in which each edge is established at a specific moment and may last only for a period of time. For example, users in social networks follow each other from some dates until unfollowing, and airlines in transportation networks depart at scheduled times and arrive at other times later. The previous researches [30,31] suggest that, temporal information play a vital role in many real-world applications, for revealing time-related patterns. As a representative example, transportation networks can be naturally modeled as temporal graphs, where each vertex in the temporal graph represents a traffic station or place area, each temporal edge represents the departure time from a vertex, and there may be values on the temporal edges

L. Ding et al. (Eds.): APWeb-WAIM 2026, LNCS 16993, pp. 511–526, 2027.
https://doi.org/10.1007/978-981-92-5693-8_32

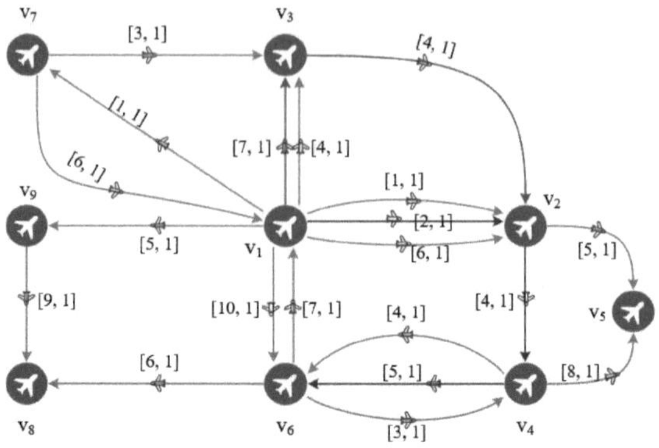

Fig. 1. Examples of temporal graph and time-ordered path.

indicating the time elapsed from that vertex to the target vertex. By temporal modeling of the traffic network, the trip planning problem in the traffic network can be solved and an optimal path can be automatically planned according to the user's demand. Consequently, the concept of a "path," a fundamental primitive for advanced tasks like centrality computation and graph clustering, has received renewed attention in the context of temporal graphs.

As a fundamental concept underlying many advanced graph analysis tasks (e.g., centrality computation, graph clustering, etc.), path also has a rebirth on temporal graphs. Current literature generally classifies temporal paths into two categories: *time-ordered paths* and *time-bounded paths*. Time-ordered paths (e.g., [1,3–7,19]) require a strictly non-descending order of edge timestamps. In contrast, time-bounded paths (e.g., [2,29,32]) constrain all edge timestamps within a user-specified interval. Both are pervasive in real-world scenarios. For example, Fig. 1 shows an example of transportation network, in which each vertex is a travel destination and each edge is a scheduled airline. The label on each edge denotes the departure time and duration of the airline. A time-ordered path from v_1 to v_6 (highlighted in purple) ensures that passengers arrive at an intermediate stop before the next departure. Conversely, the red path, though valid in a static sense, is infeasible due to temporal violations.

In this paper, we focus on the Time-Ordered Path Query (TOPQ) problems, the classic definitions of which are given by [1] as follows.

Definition 1 (Time-Ordered Path Query Problems). *Given a directed temporal graph G, a source vertex u, and a target vertex v, return*

1. ***(Reachability)*** *whether there exists any time-ordered path from u to v;*
2. ***(Optimal time)*** *the optimal value of a specific metric, such as the latest departure time, the earliest arrival time, or the fastest travel time, of all time-ordered paths from u to v;*
3. ***(Optimal path)*** *all the optimal time-ordered paths from u to v with a specific optimal time.*

Although path problems [8–12,15,20,21] have been studied extensively, new challenges arise from the interplay of topology and time in temporal path problems. To address the challenges, existing research works on TOPQ problems mainly exploit two methodologies, namely, transformed graph (e.g., [1,3]) or two-hop labeling (e.g., [2,5,19]). The vulnerability of transformed graph is that, since it preserves all complete temporal paths by a lossless compression, it could be hundreds times larger than the original graph, so that solving TOPQ problems by searching the transformed graph could be inefficient. In contrast, two-hop labeling can solve the problems by directly intersecting two intermediate vertex sets retrieved from labels in much less time.

However, two-hop labeling is a kind of lossy compression that neglects which edges comprise the result paths. TVL [5] does not preserve any intermediate edge on paths, which means it cannot decompress the labels to any path longer than one hop, and thus can only solve the reachability and optimal time problems. TTL [19] preserves a "pivot" in each label, and can use pivot to further decompress labels to only one of the optimal paths that only has vertex information. None existing two-hop labeling approach can solve the optimal path problem completely.

In practice, we usually need the airline (edges) information in a travel plan (path). Therefore, we propose a novel two-hop labeling approach for solving all three TOPQ problems. Especially for the optimal path problem, our approach introduces only a new component of label called "hop", namely, the number of edges of path represented by label. The reachability and optimal time problems can still be solved by other existing components of labels. Moreover, we develop an optimal path query algorithm to leverage the new component to solve the optimal path problem with different metrics.

In summary, our contributions are as follows.

- We propose a novel two-hop labeling approach that introduces a "hop" component to labels for supporting all three TOPQ problems. Moreover, our Temporal Hop Labeling (THL) index is space-efficient for only recording skyline time-ordered paths, and can be constructed faster than existing indexes for using a new pruning strategy.
- We design an efficient optimal path query algorithm based on THL, which exploits temporal and hop constraints to prune the search space.
- We conduct an extensive experimental study on fourteen real-world datasets. The results demonstrate that THL achieves an order-of-magnitude speedup in index construction over state-of-the-art TILL, improves query efficiency for reachability and optimal time by up to two orders of magnitude.

2 Related Work

Two-hop labeling is a classical technique for reachability and distance queries in static graphs [21]. The core principle entails assign each vertex two label sets, namely outgoing labels and incoming labels, such that reachability between any two vertices can be determined by intersecting their labels. Although computing an optimal two-hop labeling is NP-hard, practical heuristics have been shown to achieve high query efficiency.

In temporal graphs, Wu et al. [1] first formalized time-ordered path problems and proposed transformed-graph-based solutions. However, the transformed graph may become hundreds of times larger than the original graph, which limits its scalability.

Several labeling-based approaches have been proposed to address TOPQ problems more efficiently. TTL [19] extends two-hop labeling to temporal graphs by compressing time-ordered paths into tuples containing departure and arrival times. It further introduces a pivot vertex to partially reconstruct paths. However, TTL can only retrieve one optimal path and cannot enumerate all optimal paths. Moreover, preserving additional path information leads to significant space overhead.

In a different vein, TopChain [3] constructs two-hop labels over selected chains in the transformed graph, reducing index size while supporting temporal reachability and optimal time queries. TVL [5] further improves space efficiency by aggressively compressing temporal information on the original graph. However, both TopChain and TVL discard essential path structure and are unable to support optimal path retrieval.

To summarize, existing temporal labeling approaches either fail to retrieve complete optimal paths or incur excessive space overhead when preserving path information. In contrast, our proposed Temporal Hop Labeling (THL) introduces only a lightweight hop component to existing temporal labels. This innovation enables the efficient enumeration of all optimal time-ordered paths while ensuring a compact index size and superior query performance.

3 Preliminary

Let $G = (V, E)$ be a directed temporal graph, where V denotes the set of vertices and E denotes the set of edges. Each edge $e \in E$ can be represented by a quadruple $< u, v, t, \lambda >$ indicating that an event with the duration λ from u to v starts at time t and ends at time $t + \lambda$. Notably for two vertices, there may be multiple edges with different departure times, which is reasonable in a temporal graph. Without loss of generality, we assume that t is an integer and $\lambda = 1$ for all edges (Note that the assumption of $\lambda = 1$ is just for the sake of presentation; λ can be any non-negative value in the actual dataset chosen.).

For convenience, we denote the size of the vertex set by $n = |V|$ and the size of the edge set by $m = |E|$. For each vertex $u \in V$, we use $\Gamma_{out}(u)$ to denote all out-neighbors and $\Gamma_{in}(u)$ to denote all in-neighbors of vertex u. Similarly, we use $\Phi_{out}(u)$ to denote all outgoing edges and $\Phi_{in}(u)$ to denote all incoming edges of vertex u. We use $d_{out}(u) = |\Phi_{out}(u)|$ to denote the out-degree and $d_{in}(u) = |\Phi_{in}(u)|$ to denote the in-degree of vertex u.

A time-ordered path in temporal graphs is formally defined as follows.

Definition 2 (Time-Ordered Path). *In a temporal graph G, a path $p =< v_1, e_1, v_2, \cdots, v_k, e_k, v_{k+1} >$ (or $p =< e_1, e_2, \cdots, e_k >$), where $v_i \in V$ denotes the i-th vertex and $e_i =< v_i, v_{i+1}, t_i, \lambda_i >\in E$ denotes the i-th temporal edge in the path p with $1 \leq i \leq k$, is time-ordered if $t_i + \lambda_i \leq t_{i+1}$. Let $start(p) = t_1$, $end(p) = t_k + \lambda_k$, and $dura(p) = end(p) - start(p)$ be the start time, end time, and duration of p respectively. In addition, let $src(p)$ and $dest(p)$ be the source vertex and the destination vertex of p.*

Then, we give formal definitions of three kinds of Optimal Time-Ordered Paths (OTOP). Note that, the shortest time-ordered path proposed by [1] is not time-dependent and thus is not considered.

Definition 3 (Optimal Time-Ordered Path). *Given a temporal graph G, a source vertex u and a destination vertex v, let $p =< v_1, e_1, \cdots, v_k, e_k, v_{k+1} >$ be the set of time-ordered paths from u to v with the start time no earlier than ts and the end time no later than te in G. A path $p \in P(u, v)$ is an optimal time-ordered path if it can satisfy one of following conditions,*

- ***earliest-arrival:*** $end(p) = \min\{end(p') : p' \in P(u, v, [ts, te])\}$;
- ***latest-departure:*** $start(p) = \max\{start(p') : p' \in P(u, v, [ts, te])\}$;
- ***fastest-arrival:*** $dura(p) = \min\{dura(p') : p' \in P(u, v, [ts, te])\}$.

Example 1. In Fig. 1, the purple edges represent a time-ordered path where each departure occurs after the preceding arrival. Conversely, the red path is valid in a static graph but violates temporal constraints. Consider multiple paths from v_1 to v_3: $p_1 = \langle v_1, v_3, 7, 1\rangle$ achieves the **latest-departure** at $t = 7$; $p_2 = \langle v_1, v_7, 1, 1\rangle, \langle v_7, v_3, 3, 1\rangle$ provides the **earliest-arrival** at $t = 4$; while p_1 and $p_3 = \langle v_1, v_3, 4, 1\rangle$ both represent **fastest-travel** paths with $dura(p) = 1$.

In the rest of this paper, we will solve the problems in Definition 1 with respect to above definitions.

4 Approach

In this section, we present label definition, query processing, and index construction for the proposed labeling approach respectively.

4.1 Temporal Hop Labeling

Similar to traditional two-hop labeling [21], Temporal Hop Labeling (THL) precomputes two sets of labels, denoted by $L_{out}(u)$ and $L_{in}(u)$, for each vertex u in a temporal graph. Each label in $L_{out}(u)$ (or $L_{in}(u)$) is a quadruple $< v, ts, te, h >$ preserving the summary information of a time-ordered path from u to v (or from v to u), where v is any vertex other than u, ts and te are the departure time and arrival time of traveling through this path respectively, and h is the "hop" (namely, edge number) of path. The new component "hop" can help to address the optimal path problem efficiently.

Moreover, THL also exploits the following two concepts to compress labels.

Table 1. The temporal hop labeling index of example graph.

Rank	Vertex	$L_{in}(v)$	$L_{out}(v)$
1	v_1	$\emptyset$	$\emptyset$
2	v_2	$< v_1, 1, 2, 1 >$ $< v_1, 2, 3, 1 >$ $< v_1, 6, 7, 1 >$	$\emptyset$
3	v_6	$< v_1, 2, 6, 3 >$ $< v_1, 10, 11, 1 >$ $< v_2, 4, 6, 2 >$	$< v_1, 7, 8, 1 >$
4	v_4	$< v_1, 2, 5, 2 >$ $< v_2, 4, 5, 1 >$ $< v_6, 3, 4, 1 >$	$< v_1, 5, 8, 2 >$ $< v_6, 4, 5, 1 >$ $< v_6, 5, 6, 1 >$
5	v_3	$< v_1, 1, 4, 2 >$ $< v_1, 4, 5, 1 >$ $< v_1, 7, 8, 1 >$	$< v_2, 4, 5, 1 >$
6	v_7	$< v_1, 1, 2, 1 >$	$< v_1, 6, 7, 1 >$ $< v_2, 3, 5, 2 >$ $< v_3, 3, 4, 1 >$
7	v_5	$< v_1, 2, 6, 2 >$ $< v_2, 5, 6, 1 >$ $< v_6, 3, 9, 2 >$ $< v_4, 8, 9, 1 >$	$\emptyset$
8	v_8	$< v_1, 5, 10, 2 >$ $< v_2, 4, 7, 3 >$ $< v_6, 6, 7, 1 >$	$\emptyset$
9	v_9	$< v_1, 5, 6, 1 >$	$< v_8, 9, 10, 1 >$

Definition 4 (Vertex Rank). *Given a total order on vertices of a temporal graph, the rank of each vertex u, denoted by $rank(u)$, is the unique order of u in all vertices from the highest to the lowest.*

For example, we can rank vertices with respect to their degrees. Without loss of generality, we assume that rank(v) is an integer in $[1, |V|]$. Specifically, we have $rank(u) < rank(v)$ if $d_{out}(u) + d_{in}(u) > d_{out}(v) + d_{in}(v)$, and randomly determine the order of u and v if they have the same degree.

Definition 5 (Skyline Time-Ordered Path). *For a set of time-ordered paths $P(u, v)$ between vertices u and v, a path $p \in P(u, v)$ is a **Skyline Time-Ordered Path (STOP)** if there exists no other path $p' \in P(u, v)$ that dominates it. Formally, p is a STOP if there is no p' such that $start(p) \leq start(p')$, $end(p) \geq end(p')$, and $hop(p') < hop(p)$.*

Obviously, for each time-ordered path that is not a STOP, we can find a STOP that arrives earlier, departures later, and travels faster than it, which means it must not be an optimal path, or is longer than it if they departure and arrive at the same time.

With Definition 4 and 5, a THL index is eventually defined as follows.

Definition 6 (Temporal Hop Labeling Index). *Given a temporal graph, we assign two label sets $L_{out}(u)$ and $L_{in}(u)$ to each vertex u. Each label $< v, ts, te, h >$ in $L_{out}(u)$ (or $L_{in}(u)$) represents a STOP in $P(u, v)$ (or $P(v, u)$), where $rank(v)$ is the minimum among all vertices on this path.*

Table 1 illustrates the THL index for the example graph in Fig. 1. Consider the time-ordered path from v_4 to v_8 via v_6. Since $rank(v_6)$ is the minimum among the vertices on this path (i.e., $rank(v_6) < rank(v_4) < rank(v_8)$), we record the respective sub-paths $\langle v_6, 5, 6, 1\rangle \in L_{out}(v_4)$ and $\langle v_6, 6, 7, 1\rangle \in L_{in}(v_8)$.

4.2 Query Processing

In this subsection, we present the algorithm that uses the "hop" component of THL to solve the optimal path problem in Definition 1. Note that, the other two problems in Definition 1 can also be solved by using THL as follows.

Lemma 1. *Given a temporal graph, a source vertex u, and a target vertex v, there exists at least a time-ordered path from u to v (namely, $P(u,v) \neq \emptyset$), if one of following three cases is satisfied.*

1. $\exists < v, ts, te, h > \in L_{out}(u)$;
2. $\exists < u, ts, te, h > \in L_{in}(v)$;
3. $\exists < w, ts, te, h > \in L_{out}(u)$ *and* $< w, ts', te', h' > \in L_{in}(v)$ *such that* $te \leq ts'$.

Lemma 1 answers the reachability query directly. Moreover, no matter which of above cases is satisfied, the optimal time can also be evaluated. For example, the fastest travel time is $\min\{te' - ts| < w, ts', te', h' > \in L_{in}(v), < w, ts, te, h > \in L_{out}(u), te \leq ts'\}$ for the third case. In particular, the label (for the first two cases) or labels (for the third case) with the optimal value are called "optimal label", which actually represents optimal paths. For example, $< w, ts, te, h > \in L_{out}(u)$ and $< w, ts', te', h' > \in L_{in}(v)$ that lead to the optimal value (e.g., the maximum ts, the minimum te', or the minimum $te' - ts$) are both optimal labels.

The basic idea of our optimal path search algorithm is to perform Breadth-First Search (BFS) from the source vertex, and meanwhile use the THL index to prune paths during search with respect to the following observation.

Lemma 2 (Pruning Criterion). *Let $\langle u, ts, te, h\rangle$ (or its constituent labels) be the optimal label for a query from u to v. A time-ordered path p is a candidate for (or a sub-component of) an optimal path if and only if:*

1. *The first edge (u, w, t, λ) of p satisfies $t = ts$;*
2. *The last edge (w', v, t', λ') of p satisfies $t' + \lambda' = te$;*
3. *The total hop count of p does not exceed h.*

With Lemma 2, for an optimal path query, we firstly determine the reachability regarding Lemma 1, and then can prune paths during search regarding the optimal label for the first two cases. Moreover, if the reachability is determined by the third case, we divide the optimal path query into two sub-queries, namely, find the paths from u to w regarding $< w, ts, te, h > \in L_{out}(u)$ and from w to v regarding $< w, ts', te', h' > \in L_{in}(v)$ respectively. For each sub-query, we still address it as an independent query.

Specifically, the pseudo code of optimal path query processing based on THL is shown in Algorithm 1. Note that, Algorithm 1 is able to query all three kinds of optimal time-ordered paths in Definition 3, and for the same optimal time-ordered path, Algorithm 1 can solve for all optimal time-ordered paths with the same optimal time. In the main function, the algorithm first determines the reachability from the source vertex u to the target vertex v according to Lemma 1. If the reachability is established by Case 1 or Case 2, the optimal label $\langle v, ts, te, h\rangle$ (or $\langle u, ts, te, h\rangle$) is identified and used to guide the subsequent traversal. If the reachability is established by Case 3, the optimal path query is decomposed into two subqueries via an intermediate vertex w. In this case, paths from u to w and from w to v are traversed independently with their corresponding optimal labels, and the resulting subpaths are concatenated to form complete optimal paths.

Algorithm 1: Optimal Path Query

```
Input: temporal graph G, source vertex u, target vertex v, optimal path type
Output: the set of all optimal paths
P ← ∅;
determine the reachability from u to v by Lemma 1;
if case 1 or 2 in Lemma 1 is satisfied then
    obtain the optimal label < v, ts, te, h >∈ L_out(u) or < u, ts, te, h >∈ L_in(v) with
      respect to optimal path type;
    P ← traverse(G,u,v,ts,te,h);
else if case 3 in Lemma 1 is satisfied then
    obtain the optimal labels < w, ts, te, h >∈ L_out(u) and < w, ts', te', h' >∈ L_in(v)
      with respect to optimal path type;
    P1 ← traverse(G,u,w,ts,te,h);
    P2 ← traverse(G,w,v,ts',te',h');
    P ← concatenation of paths in P1 and P2;
return P;
Function traverse(G,u,v,ts,te,h):
    P, Q ← ∅;
    foreach e = (u, w, t, λ) ∈ Φ_out(u) do
        if t = ts then // case 1 in Lemma 2
            if w = v and t + λ = te then
                add the 1-hop path comprised of e to P;
            else
                add the 1-hop paths comprised of e to Q;
    for i ← 2 to h do // case 3 in Lemma 2
        size ← |Q|, Q' ← ∅;
        for j ← 1 to size do
            p ← Q.pop();
            e = (w, w', t, λ) ← the last edge of p;
            if v is unreachable from w' then // Lemma 1
                continue;
            foreach e' = (w', w'', t', λ') ∈ Φ_out(w') s.t. t' ≥ t + λ do
                if w'' = v and t' + λ' = te then // case 2 in Lemma 2
                    concatenate p and e' and add the new path to P;
                else if t' + λ' < te and w'' is not on p then
                    concatenate p and e' and add the new path to Q'.
        Q ← Q';
    return P;
```

The traverse() function implements a hop-bounded BFS guided by the optimal label. It first enumerates all outgoing edges from the source vertex whose departure time matches the optimal start time. Then, partial paths are recursively expanded by appending time-ordered edges, while ensuring that the total number of hops does not exceed the hop value recorded in the optimal label. During the traversal, THL-based reachability checking is applied to prune partial paths that cannot reach the target vertex. According to Lemma 2, only those paths that satisfy the temporal constraints and reach the target vertex with the optimal end time are added to the result set.

Example 2. Let us take v_1 as the source vertex and v_6 as the target vertex, and search the latest-departure path. We first prove the reachability of the two vertices according to lemma 1 and find the optimal label $l = < v_1, 2, 6, 3 >$.

We first visit all out-edges of v_1. Only $< v_1, v_2, 2, 1 >$ will be added to the queue Q. Next we only need to visit the edges of depth 2 and depth 3 again to obtain the latest-departure path (Line 20). We pop the last element in Q, i.e., $< v_1, v_2, 2, 1 >$. We use lemma 1 to determine that v_2, v_6 are reachable, and push out-neighbors of v_2 to Q. At this point there are two paths in Q $\{< v_1, v_2, 2, 1 >, < v_2, v_4, 4, 5 >\}, \{< v_1, v_2, 2, 1 >, < v_2, v_5, 5, 6 >\}$. Next we repeat the same operation and finally find the latest-departure path $\{< v_1, v_2, 2, 1 >, < v_2, v_4, 4, 5 >, < v_4, v_5, 5, 6 >\}$ from v_1 to v_6 .

Algorithm 1 is a scalable algorithm that can rapidly retrieve all specific optimal paths, and it can also accommodate additional constraints during the query process, such as retrieving optimal paths within a defined time interval $[t_1, t_2]$. In real-world datasets, Algorithm 1 boasts a commendable execution speed. Next, we present the time complexity of Algorithm 1.

Using d_{max} to denote the maximum number of outgoing edges of all vertices and *hop* to denote the number of intermediate vertices from vertex u to vertex v, we have the following theorem:

Theorem 1. *The time complexity of solving the optimal path algorithm is limited by* $O(d_{max}^2 \cdot (|L_{in}(u)| + |L_{out}(u)|))$.

Proof. The worst complexity of determining the reachability of two vertices using THL is $O(|L_{out}(u)| + |L_{in}(v)|)$ (Lines 23-24). We scan the out-neighbors of w if line 23 not holds (Line 25). This process requires at worst d_{max} cycles. In extreme cases, the *hop* value can become very large, in which case up to d_{max} cycles are required. Therefore, The time complexity of Algorithm 1 is limited by $O(d_{max}^2 \cdot (|L_{in}(u)| + |L_{out}(u)|))$.

4.3 Index Construction

For constructing a THL index, we extend the previous algorithm [2] by 1) maintaining the hop of enumerated paths and 2) applying an optimization with respect to the following observation.

Lemma 3. *When traversing paths from a vertex* u*, for two enumerated paths with labels* $< w, ts, te, h >$ *and* $< w, ts', te', h' >$ *respectively to a same vertex* w*, if we have* $< w, ts, te, h >$ *dominates* $< w, ts', te', h' >$*, namely, 1)* $ts > ts'$*, 2)* $te < te'$*, or 3)* $h > h'$*,* $ts = ts'$*, and* $te = te'$*, the path with label* $< w, ts', te', h' >$ *and the paths containing it as a sub-path to any other vertex* v *must not be the optimal path from* u *to* w *or* v.

The pseudo code of index construction algorithm is given in Algorithm 2. Compared with existing labeling approaches, Algorithm 2 explicitly maintains hop information for enumerated paths and incorporates an effective pruning strategy based on Lemma 3, which significantly reduces the number of candidate paths during index construction.

We enumerate the vertex u sequentially in an ordered list of vertices by rank. For each vertex, we use a priority queue, instead of using a normal queue for

Algorithm 2: THL-Index Construction Algorithm

Input: a temporal graph G, a ranking function of vertices
Output: $L_{in}(u)$ and $L_{out}(u)$ for each vertex u of G

1 **foreach** *vertex* u *of* G *in ascending order of* $rank(u)$ **do**
2 $\quad L_{in}(u), L_{out}(u), Q \leftarrow \emptyset$;
3 $\quad Q$.push($< u, +\infty, -\infty, 0 >$);
4 $\quad$ **while** Q *is not empty* **do**
5 $\quad\quad < w, ts, te, h > \leftarrow Q$.pop();
6 $\quad\quad$ **if** $w \neq u$ **then**
7 $\quad\quad\quad L_{in}(w) \leftarrow L_{in}(w) \cup \{< u, ts, te, hop >\}$;
8 $\quad\quad\quad$ remove non-STOP from $L_{in}(w)$;
9 $\quad\quad\quad$ remove paths dominated by $< w, ts, te, h >$ from Q ; // Lemma 3
10 $\quad\quad$ **foreach** *edge* $(w, v, t, \lambda) \in \Phi_{out}(w)$ **do**
11 $\quad\quad\quad$ **if** $rank(v) > rank(u)$ *and* $te \leq t$ **then**
12 $\quad\quad\quad\quad ts' \leftarrow \min(t, ts), te' \leftarrow t + \lambda$;
13 $\quad\quad\quad\quad Q$.push($< v, ts', te'$,the hop of $< w, ts, te, h >$+1>);
14 $\quad$ repeat lines 4-14 to symmetrically construct L_{out} by reversing edge directions;

storage. Then, we perform BFS from the current vertex w (Line 10). We add each enumerated vertex u to $L(w)$ and then remove non-STOP among them (Line 7-8). We simply traverse from back to front starting with the newly added vertex w' until $w' \neq w$. During the traversal we remove the dominated labels and remove paths dominated by $< w, ts, te, h >$ from Q. Then for $\forall(w, v, t, \lambda) \in \Phi_{out}(w)$, if the departure time t is greater than the arrival time of w and $rank(v) > rank(u)$, we add the label which contains v to Q.

Note that in Algorithm 2, according to lemma 3 we need to remove all the paths dominated by $< w, ts, te, h >$ from Q. When we remove the dominated labels, we keep the labels containing their neighbours in a label set L. We only need to remove all the labels in the set L from the queue Q to further speed up the index construction (Line 9).

The introduction and proof details of the complexity of Algorithm 2 have been given in [2], so only a brief introduction is given here. Let n_p be the number of all STOPs in the index and $n = |V|$. We use n_p represents the number of all indexed elements, or the index size of all vertices is capped by setting n_p. Let $n_q = max_{u \in V} \cdot max\{|L_{in}(u)|, |L_{out}(u)|\}$, and $d_{max} = max_{u \in V} \cdot max\{d_{in}(u), d_{out}(u)\}$. Therefore, the time complexity of the algorithm can be expressed by the following theorem:

Theorem 2. *The time complexity of the Algorithm 2 is bounded by* $O(n_p \cdot d_{max} \cdot (log(n_p \cdot d_{max}) + n_q))$.

Table 2. Statistics of datasets.

Dataset	Directed	$\|V\|$	$\|E\|$	d_{max}	n
DBLP	True	12,590	49,759	714	30
CollegeMsg	True	1899	59,835	1,546	58,911
Chess	True	7,301	65,053	280	100
Slashdot	True	51,083	140,778	3,357	90,345
MathOverflow	True	24,818	506,500	11,039	505,784
Facebook	False	63,731	817,035	1,098	333,924
AskUbuntu	True	159,316	964,437	12,316	960,866
Enron	True	87,273	1,148,072	38,785	220,364
Wikipedia talk (ar)	True	1,095,799	1,913,103	915,536	1,773,133
Wiktionary edits (ru)	False	1,274,165	8,349,235	1,569,395	7,979,905
movielens	False	80,555	10,000,054	34,864	7,096,905
YouTube	True	3,223,589	9,375,374	91,751	203
Epinions	False	876,252	13,668,320	162,169	501
Wikipedia edits (vi)	False	3,585,652	25,286,492	5,902,991	21,844,850

5 Experiment

In this section, we conduct extensive experiments to evaluate the performance of our proposed index and algorithms. All algorithms are implemented in Java and executed on a Windows machine with a 3.2 GHz CPU and 16 GB of RAM.

5.1 Dataset

We select fourteen publicly available real-world temporal graphs with different scales from SNAP and KONECT. Table 2 summarizes the statistical information of these datasets, where $|V|$ denotes the number of vertices, $|E|$ denotes the number of edges, d_{max} denotes the maximum degree of vertices, and n denotes the number of timestamps.

5.2 Algorithm

We compare the following three groups of algorithms in the evaluation.

- (Indexing) THL: Algorithm 2;
- (Indexing) TILL: The two-hop labeling index construction algorithm proposed by [2].
- (Optimal time) One-Pass: The optimal time query algorithm proposed by [1].
- (Optimal time) TopChain: The optimal time query algorithm proposed by [3].
- (Optimal path) One-Pass* : A BFS algorithm that uses One-Pass to determine reachability and uses the reachability to prune paths.

- (Optimal path) THL: Algorithm 1.
- (Optimal path) THL*: Algorithm 1 without using hop component.

Note that, since TTL [19] or TVL [5] based query processing cannot deal with the optimal path query problem and is equivalent to our approach on dealing with other two problems, we do not consider them in comparison.

5.3 Evaluation of Index Construction

We evaluate the performance of the index construction in this subsection. Firstly, we compare THL construction (Algorithm 2) with existing TILL construction on indexing time in Fig. 2a. Due to the optimization (Lemma 3), Algorithm 2 generates two-hop labels faster than TILL on almost all datasets, though Algorithm 2 computes the hops of paths additionally. Especially for some large datasets, the effect of optimization is significant, THL achieves approximately an **order-of-magnitude speedup**.

Then, we show the THL index sizes of all the datasets and compare them with the sizes of original datasets in Fig. 2b. We can see that, THL indexes are normally several times larger than original datasets. We do not compare THL with other two-hop labeling approaches on index size because the hop component only takes a limited space that is linear to the number of labels. Exceptionally, for some datasets such as *DBLP* and *Wiktionary*, the THL index sizes are even smaller than original dataset. A possible reason is that, a number of STOPs that have very short duration dominate the vast majority of time-ordered paths in the graph.

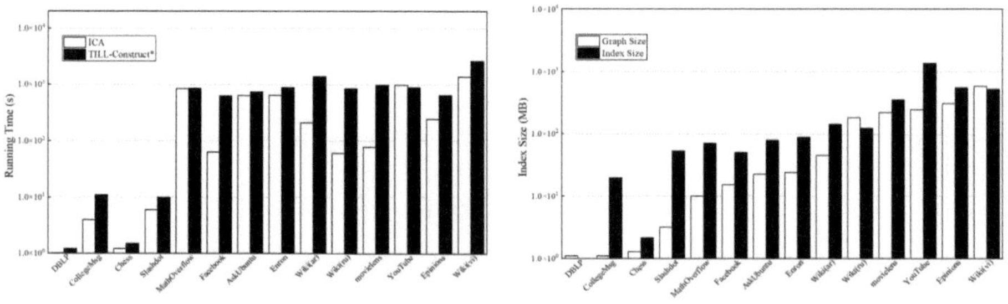

(a) Index construction time. (b) Index size.

Fig. 2. Evaluation of THL index construction.

5.4 Evaluation of Reachability and Optimal Time Query

Since THL can also be used to address reachability and optimal value queries and actually needs to do that firstly during optimal path search (Algorithm 1), we compare THL with other existing approaches (TopChain and One-Pass) that can solve optimal path problem on the efficiency of processing reachability and optimal value queries. To generate input queries, we randomly pick 100 vertex pairs in each graph G.

The experimental results are shown in Table 3. As expected, THL significantly outperforms TopChain and One-Pass. On the largest dataset, Wikipedia (vi), THL processes queries in less than **0.4 ms**, whereas TopChain and One-Pass require over 30 ms and 100 ms, respectively, representing a speedup of over **250**×.

Table 3. Average running time of reachability and optimal value queries (ms).

Dataset	Earliest-arrival			Latest-departure			Fastest		
	THL	TopChain	1-pass	THL	TopChain	1-pass	THL	TopChain	1-pass
DBLP	0.01	1.4	10	0.01	1.1	8	0.01	1.6	14
CollegeMsg	0.01	1.8	13	0.01	1.4	12	0.01	2.1	16
Chess	0.01	2.0	18	0.01	1.7	12	0.01	2.4	19
Slashdot	0.06	4.5	11	0.05	4.4	13	0.1	4.4	27
MathOverflow	0.04	24	101	0.05	15	23	0.1	20	33
Facebook	0.04	5.1	13	0.05	4.9	14	0.1	5.0	18
AskUbuntu	0.06	3.5	12	0.08	3.6	18	0.09	4.1	25
Enron	0.05	6.1	52	0.05	6	54	0.09	6.1	78
Wikipedia (ar)	0.06	11.2	33	0.05	10.4	31	0.08	16.3	56
Wiktionary (ru)	0.08	5.0	17	0.04	4.8	19	0.11	6.7	34
movielens	0.14	6.5	41	0.12	5.7	50	0.16	6.4	69
YouTube	0.27	10.8	56	0.21	10.7	61	0.32	12.6	83
Epinions	0.17	8.5	47	0.15	8.2	55	0.14	9.8	72
Wikipedia (vi)	0.24	36	108	0.25	38	117	0.37	44	145

5.5 Evaluation of Optimal Path Query

We randomly select 10 pairs of vertices from each dataset. The reported running time is the average running time of 10 queries for each datasdet.

For THL based approach (Algorithm 1), Fig. 3a shows the results of three different optimal path queries, namely, earliest arrival, latest departure, and fastest travel on several datasets. We can see that there is no significant difference in running time between queries for different optimal paths, though queries for the fastest path always take longer due to the complex reachability checks required to determine the accessibility of two vertices.

Moreover, we compare Algorithm 1 with other algorithms. The experimental results are shown in Fig. 3b. The BFS algorithm without any optimization is the slowest. One-Pass* is faster than BFS for pruning paths by reachability

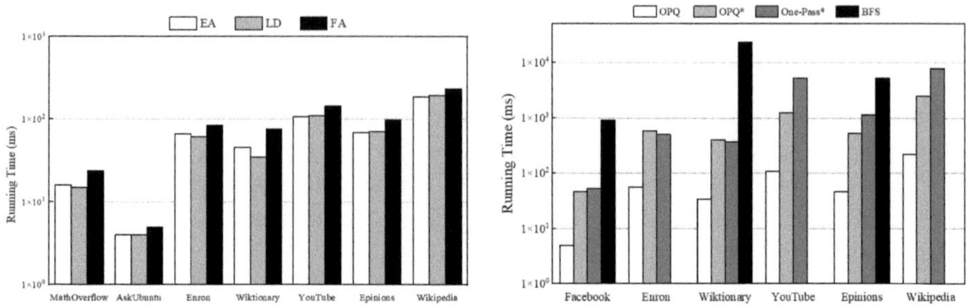

(a) Average running time of the TOPQ process.

(b) Query time for different algorithms.

Fig. 3. Time-ordered Optimal Path Query.

determined by One-Pass during BFS. THL* exploits the temporal information in optimal label to prune paths and thus is more efficient than existing approaches. Lastly, THL outperforms the ablation version THL* by at least **one order of magnitude**, which directly validates the effectiveness of incorporating the"hop" component for pruning the search space.

6 Conclusion

We propose a novel two-hop labeling approach (THL), which is suitable for solving TOPQ problems on all general temporal graphs. In addition, we present query algorithms that use THL to support three types of optimal path queries (i.e., earliest-arrival path, latest-departure path, fastest-arrival path) on temporal graphs. We provide some non-trivial lemmas that enable improved efficiency. We conduct comprehensive experiments on a number of real-world datasets to compare the performance of our approach and state-of-the-art labelling approaches. The experimental evaluation demonstrates that THL is a scalable index that has low query cost and low index construction overhead.

References

1. Wu, H., Cheng, J., Huang, S., Ke, Y., Lu, Y., Xu, Y.: Path problems in temporal graphs. Proc. VLDB Endow. **7**(9), 721–732 (2014). https://doi.org/10.14778/2732939.2732945
2. Wen, D., Yang, B., Zhang, Y., et al.: Span-reachability querying in large temporal graphs. VLDB J. 1–19 (2022)
3. Wu, H., Huang, Y., Cheng, J.: Reachability and time-based path queries in temporal graphs. In: IEEE 32nd International Conference on Data Engineering (ICDE), pp. 145–156. IEEE (2016)
4. Zhao, A., Liu, G., Zheng, B., et al.: Temporal paths discovery with multiple constraints in attributed dynamic graphs. World Wide Web **23**, 313–336 (2020)

5. Zhang, T., Gao, Y., Chen, L., Guo, W., Pu, S., Zheng, B., Jensen, C.S.: Efficient distributed reachability querying of massive temporal graphs. VLDB J. **28**(6), 871–896 (2019). https://doi.org/10.1007/s00778-019-00572-x
6. Yuan, Y., Lian, X., Wang, G., et al.: Constrained shortest path query in a large time-dependent graph. Proc. VLDB Endow. **12**(10), 1058–1070 (2019)
7. Liu, Z., Li, L., Zhang, M.: Efficient constrained shortest path query answering with forest hop labeling. In: 2021 IEEE 37th International Conference on Data Engineering (ICDE), pp. 1763–1774. IEEE (2021)
8. Rost, C., Gomez, K., Täschner, M., et al.: Distributed temporal graph analytics with GRADOOP. VLDB J. **31**(2), 375–401 (2022)
9. Sengupta, N., Bagchi, A., Ramanath, M.: Arrow: Approximating reachability using random walks over web-scale graphs. In: IEEE 35th International Conference on Data Engineering (ICDE), pp. 470–481. IEEE (2019)
10. Zhang, Y., Yu, J.X.: Hub labeling for shortest path counting. In: Proceedings of the 2020 ACM SIGMOD International Conference on Management of Data, pp. 1813–1828 (2020)
11. Fan, W., Wang, X., Wu, Y.: Performance guarantees for distributed reachability queries (2012). arXiv preprint arXiv:1208.0091
12. Gurajada, S., Theobald, M.: Distributed set reachability. In: Proceedings of the 2016 International Conference on Management of Data, pp. 1247–1261 (2016)
13. van Schaik, S.J., de Moor, O.: A memory efficient reachability data structure through bit vector compression. In: Proceedings of the 2011 ACM SIGMOD International Conference on Management of Data, pp. 913–924 (2011)
14. Xuan, B.B., Ferreira, A., Jarry, A.: Computing shortest, fastest, and foremost journeys in dynamic networks. Int. J. Found. Comput. Sci. **14**(02), 267–285 (2003)
15. Abraham, I., Delling, D., Goldberg, A.V.: Hierarchical hub labelings for shortest paths. In: European Symposium on Algorithms, pp. 24–35. Springer (2012)
16. Redmond, U., Cunningham, P.: Subgraph isomorphism in temporal networks (2016). arXiv:1605.02174 arXiv preprint
17. Abraham, I., Delling, D., Goldberg, A.V.: Hierarchical hub labelings for shortest paths. In: European Symposium on Algorithms, pp. 24–35. Springer (2012)
18. Akiba, T., Iwata, Y., Yoshida, Y.: Fast exact shortest-path distance queries on large networks by pruned landmark labeling. In: Proceedings of the 2013 ACM SIGMOD International Conference on Management of Data, pp. 349–360 (2013)
19. Wang, S., Lin, W., Yang, Y.: Efficient route planning on public transportation networks: A labelling approach. In: Proceedings of the 2015 ACM SIGMOD International Conference on Management of Data, pp. 967–982 (2015)
20. Akiba, T., Iwata, Y., Yoshida, Y.: Fast exact shortest-path distance queries on large networks by pruned landmark labeling. In: Proceedings of the 2013 ACM SIGMOD International Conference on Management of Data, pp. 349–360 (2013)
21. Cohen, E., Halperin, E., Kaplan, H., et al.: Reachability and distance queries via 2-hop labels. SIAM J. Comput. **32**(5), 1338–1355 (2003)
22. Raghavan, V., Ver Steeg, G., Galstyan, A., et al.: Modeling temporal activity patterns in dynamic social networks. IEEE Trans. Comput. Soc. Syst. **1**(1), 89–107 (2014)
23. Rost, C., Gomez, K., Täschner, M., et al.: Distributed temporal graph analytics with GRADOOP. VLDB J. **31**(2), 375–401 (2022)
24. Bai, Q., Zhang, C., Liu, N., et al.: Evolution of transaction pattern in Ethereum: a temporal graph perspective. IEEE Trans. Comput. Soc. Syst. **9**(3), 851–866 (2021)

25. Li, R.H., Su, J., Qin, L.: Persistent community search in temporal networks. In: IEEE 34th International Conference on Data Engineering (ICDE), pp. 797–808. IEEE (2018)
26. Lambiotte, R., Tabourier, L., Delvenne, J.C.: Burstiness and spreading on temporal networks. Eur. Phys. J. B **86**, 1–4 (2013)
27. Qin, H., Li, R.H., Wang, G.: Mining periodic cliques in temporal networks. In: IEEE 35th International Conference on Data Engineering (ICDE), pp. 1130–1141. IEEE (2019)
28. Pietilänen, A.K., Diot, C.: Dissemination in opportunistic social networks: the role of temporal communities. In: Proceedings of the 13th ACM International Symposium on Mobile Ad Hoc Networking and Computing, pp. 165–174 (2012)
29. Yang, Y., Li, H., Zhu, X., et al.: HR-index: an effective index method for historical reachability queries over evolving graphs. Proc. ACM Manag. Data **1**(2), 1–25 (2023)
30. Holme, P., Saramäki, J.: Temporal networks. Phys. Rep. **519**(3), 97–125 (2012)
31. Masuda, N., Lambiotte, R.: A Guide to Temporal Networks, World Scientific (2016)
32. Semertzidis, K., Pitoura, E., Lillis, K.: TimeReach: Historical Reachability Queries on Evolving Graphs, pp. 121–132. EDBT (2015)

Query-Aware Adaptive Weight Learning for Multimodal Search of Target Modality

Yikai Zhang[1], Liwei Wang[1(✉)], and Qing Xie[2]

[1] Wuhan University, Wuhan 430072, China
{yikaizhang,liwei.wang}@whu.edu.cn
[2] Wuhan University of Technology, Wuhan 430070, China
felixxq@whut.edu.cn

Abstract. Multimodal search of target modality aims to retrieve results in a specified target modality by jointly using target-modality inputs and auxiliary modalities. Existing global-weight methods, represented by MUST(Multimodal Search of Target Modality), provide an efficient fusion strategy by learning a single set of modality weights for all queries. However, such fixed weights mainly reflect average modality importance over the training workload, and are insufficient to capture query-specific user intent. To address this limitation, we propose a query-aware adaptive weight learning method for multimodal search of target modality. Using the global weights provided by an existing retrieval framework, our method obtains a stable candidate set and performs query-specific adaptation only within the recalled candidates. Specifically, we first construct query-level oracle weights by searching locally optimal modality weights in each candidate set. Then, a lightweight predictor is trained to estimate adaptive weights from candidate-score statistics, local ranking structures, and query-side features. During inference, the predicted weights are used to re-rank the retrieved candidates without modifying the underlying feature extractors or indexing pipeline. Experiments demonstrate that the proposed method consistently improves over the fixed global-weight baseline. The improvements are especially significant on fine-grained and product retrieval datasets, while the oracle results further reveal the potential of query-level modality adaptation.

Keywords: Multimodal Retrieval · Target Modality Search · Query-aware Learning · Adaptive Weight Learning

1 Introduction

In many real-world retrieval scenarios, a user's search intent cannot be fully expressed by a single modality [3,16]. For example, in face image retrieval, a user may provide a reference face and expect results that preserve the identity-related appearance while satisfying additional constraints such as "with eyeglasses", "wearing a hat", or "without sunglasses". In product search, a user may provide a shoe image and further specify a desired change in category, style, or attribute.

L. Ding et al. (Eds.): APWeb-WAIM 2026, LNCS 16993, pp. 527–542, 2027.
https://doi.org/10.1007/978-981-92-5693-8_33

In these cases, the system should not simply return the nearest neighbor of the reference image, but should infer the user's intent from both the target-modality input and auxiliary modalities.

This setting is closely related to multimodal search of target modality (MSTM), where the query can contain multiple modalities while the returned results are restricted to a specified target modality [19]. The key challenge is not merely how to represent different modalities in a common space, but how to determine their relative importance for the current query. The target modality usually provides the main semantic reference, whereas auxiliary modalities describe additional constraints or intended changes. Since some queries rely more on visual similarity and others are mainly determined by textual modifications or state constraints, applying the same fusion weights to all queries may fail to capture query-specific user intent.

Existing multimodal retrieval methods have made significant progress in jointly modeling visual, textual, and structured information [3]. From the perspective of modality fusion, two representative paradigms are multi-streamed retrieval and joint embedding retrieval. Multi-streamed retrieval first retrieves results within each modality and then fuses modality-specific rankings or scores [12,16]. In contrast, joint embedding retrieval maps different modalities into a shared representation space before retrieval [7,11]. Along this line, image-text matching and visual-semantic embedding methods improve cross-modal alignment between images and texts [6,13], while vision-language pre-training and large-scale visual-language models provide stronger transferable representations [5,15]. Beyond matching independent images and texts, composed image retrieval further considers queries formed by a reference image and textual modification, so as to model relative search intent [17,20]. Recent CLIP-based methods further improve conditioned and composed image retrieval by combining visual and textual features from pretrained vision-language models, often through feature composition or combiner networks [1,2,15]. However, these methods mainly focus on representation learning, CLIP-based feature combination, or fixed composition mechanisms. They pay relatively less attention to how the importance of different modalities should vary across queries in MSTM.

Compared with traditional multi-streamed retrieval and joint embedding retrieval paradigms, MUST provides one of the most mature and representative frameworks for MSTM by learning global modality weights and supporting efficient joint similarity search [19]. By assigning different weights to different modalities, MUST offers a system-level fusion strategy that is more flexible than treating all modalities equally, while keeping the retrieval process stable and scalable. However, the learned weights are still global. They mainly reflect average modality importance over the training workload and are shared by all queries. As a result, a globally effective weight configuration may still be suboptimal for individual queries. Learning query-specific weights is related to query-adaptive fusion and query-specific rank fusion [21,23,24], but it is non-trivial because query-level weight annotations are unavailable, full-database weight search is expensive, and replacing the global-weight retrieval pipeline may affect system stability.

To address this problem, we propose a query-aware adaptive weight learning method for MSTM. Given the global weights produced by an existing retrieval framework, our method retrieves a stable top-M candidate set and then performs query-specific adaptation within this local search space. For each query, we search the candidate set for an oracle weight vector that best improves the ground-truth ranking. In this paper, the term oracle refers to a candidate-level ideal upper-bound weight constructed with ground-truth information. This oracle weight is used only as supervision for training a lightweight adaptive predictor. During inference, the predictor estimates query-specific weight adjustments from candidate-level retrieval features and re-ranks candidates without full-database re-scoring, keeping the retrieval process efficient and compatible with existing global-weight retrieval frameworks.

We evaluate the proposed method on three multimodal retrieval datasets constructed from CelebA, CUB, and UT-Zap50K [14,18,22]. Evaluations show consistent improvements over the global-weight baseline. Specifically, our approach yields stable gains on large-scale generic data like CelebA+ with a 4.46% increase at Recall@50. On fine-grained and product retrieval tasks such as CUB+ and UT-Zap50K+, the method achieves substantial leaps especially for top-ranked retrieval, boosting Recall@1 by 198% and 301%, respectively. Oracle results further reveal the potential of query-level modality adaptation, while ablation studies validate the effectiveness of our feature design, nonlinear predictor, and re-ranking strategy.

The main contributions of this paper are summarized as follows:

- We formulate the query-insensitivity problem of fixed global modality weights and analyze it from the perspective of candidate-level re-ranking.
- We construct query-level oracle supervision by searching locally optimal modality weights within the recalled candidate set, enabling supervised learning of query-specific modality preferences without manual weight annotations.
- We design a lightweight adaptive weight predictor based on candidate-level retrieval features, and use the predicted weights for candidate re-ranking without modifying feature encoders or the indexing pipeline. Experiments on three datasets validate the effectiveness of the proposed method.

2 Preliminaries

In this section, we introduce the task setting and notation used throughout the paper. We first define multimodal search of target modality, and then describe a general multi-vector representation form for multimodal objects and queries. Based on this representation, we introduce the query and ground-truth construction used in our experiments, followed by a global-weight retrieval baseline that motivates the proposed adaptive method.

2.1 Multimodal Search of Target Modality

Multimodal search of target modality aims to retrieve results in a specified target modality by jointly using target-modality and auxiliary-modality information [19]. Let S denote the object collection. Each object $o \in S$ consists of m modalities and is written as $o = \{o_0, o_1, \ldots, o_{m-1}\}$, where o_i denotes the content of object o in the i-th modality. Similarly, a query is written as $q = \{q_0, q_1, \ldots, q_{t-1}\}$, where $1 \leq t \leq m$.

Following the MSTM setting, q_0 denotes the target-modality input, and $q_1, \ldots, q_{t-1}$ denote auxiliary-modality inputs. The retrieval system returns objects in the target modality from S, rather than returning all modalities jointly.

2.2 Multimodal Representation

We use a general vector representation form to describe multimodal objects and queries. A modality may correspond to image, text, audio, video, or structured attributes. For each modality, a selected encoder maps the original input into a vector representation. The key requirement is that object-side and query-side modality representations are aligned in order and semantic meaning.

For each modality, let $\phi_i(\cdot)$ denote its encoder. Given an object $o \in S$, the encoded vector of its i-th modality is $\phi_i(o_i)$. Suppose a global modality weight vector is available:

$$\omega_{\text{global}} = [\omega_0, \omega_1, \ldots, \omega_{m-1}], \quad \omega_i \geq 0, \quad \sum_{i=0}^{m-1} \omega_i = 1. \tag{1}$$

Then the weighted concatenated representation of object o is defined as

$$\hat{o}_\omega = [\omega_0\phi_0(o_0), \omega_1\phi_1(o_1), \ldots, \omega_{m-1}\phi_{m-1}(o_{m-1})]. \tag{2}$$

Similarly, for a query q with t available modalities, its weighted representation can be written as

$$\hat{q}_\omega = [\omega_0\phi_0(q_0), \omega_1\phi_1(q_1), \ldots, \omega_{t-1}\phi_{t-1}(q_{t-1})]. \tag{3}$$

This representation keeps modality-specific vectors separated before fusion, while allowing their contributions to be explicitly controlled by weights. The encoder $\phi_i(\cdot)$ can be a single-modality encoder or a multimodal encoder that produces a composed representation. Thus, the formulation does not restrict the framework to a fixed set of modalities or encoders.

2.3 Query and Ground-Truth Construction

To instantiate the proposed framework in our experiments, we follow the composed image retrieval setting and construct each query from a reference image and a relative semantic modification [17,20]. This is a task-specific implementation for image-target retrieval, while the proposed framework is not restricted to image inputs. Let r denote the reference image. Based on the original state of r, we construct a target state vector a_q, which represents the desired attribute, category, or structured state of the target object. A relative text description d_q is generated to describe the change from the reference image to the target state. Thus, a query is written as

$$q = (r, d_q). \tag{4}$$

For each query, we keep a unique ground-truth target t. Specifically, we first filter the object collection according to the target state a_q, obtaining a candidate set C_q. Then, within C_q, the object most consistent with the compositional semantics of the query is selected as the ground-truth target:

$$t = \arg \max_{o \in C_q,\ o \neq r} s_{\mathrm{comp}}(q, o), \tag{5}$$

where $s_{\mathrm{comp}}(q, o)$ measures the compositional semantic similarity between the query $q = (r, d_q)$ and a candidate object o, which can be estimated using vision-language representations such as CLIP [15]. This construction avoids simple self-retrieval and requires the target object to be consistent with both the target state and the relative semantic modification.

2.4 Global-Weight Retrieval Framework

A representative way to solve MSTM is to adopt a global-weight retrieval framework, as exemplified by MUST [19]. Its simplified workflow is shown in Fig. 1. In the offline stage, each object $o \in S$ is encoded into modality-specific vectors $\phi_i(o_i)$. Based on these vectors, the framework learns a global modality weight vector ω_{global}, as defined in Eq. (1), and builds an index structure over the object collection for efficient retrieval.

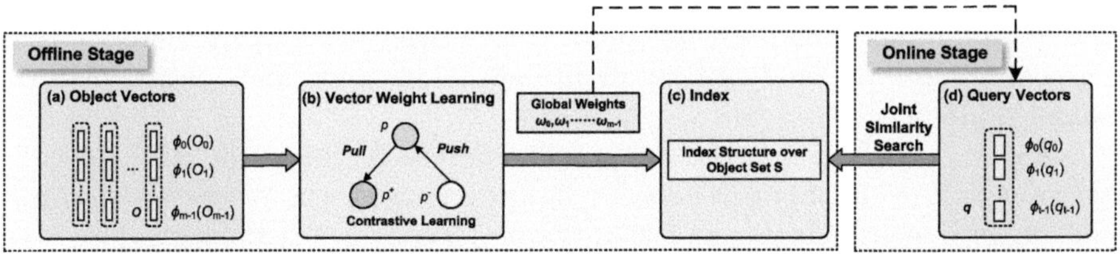

Fig. 1. Overview of the global-weight retrieval framework.

During global weight learning, training samples are constructed around an anchor object p. The corresponding ground-truth target is regarded as the positive sample p^+, while hard negative samples p^- are selected from objects that are similar to the anchor under the current weighted representation [4,9]. The learning objective encourages p to be closer to p^+ and farther from p^-. Through this process, the retrieval framework obtains a stable global weight vector that reflects average modality importance over the training data.

In the online stage, a query q is encoded into modality-specific vectors $\phi_i(q_i)$. For the i-th modality, we define the modality-specific similarity between query q and candidate object o as

$$s_i(q, o) = \mathrm{sim}\big(\phi_i(q_i), \phi_i(o_i)\big), \tag{6}$$

where $\mathrm{sim}(\cdot, \cdot)$ denotes the similarity function used in the corresponding representation space. The global-weight framework combines these modality-specific similarities using ω_{global}:

$$s_{\mathrm{base}}(q, o) = \sum_{i=0}^{m-1} \omega_i s_i(q, o). \tag{7}$$

The retrieval system performs joint similarity search over the indexed object collection and returns target-modality results according to $s_{\mathrm{base}}(q, o)$.

Although this global-weight retrieval framework provides a stable and efficient fusion strategy, the learned ω_{global} is shared by all queries. It reflects average modality importance over the training data, but cannot adapt to query-specific modality preferences. This limitation motivates the query-aware adaptive weight learning method introduced in the next section.

3 Methodology

This section presents the proposed query-aware adaptive weight learning method for multimodal search of target modality. As discussed in Sect. 2.4, existing global-weight retrieval frameworks can provide stable modality fusion by learning a shared weight vector for all queries. However, such shared weights mainly reflect average modality importance and make it difficult to capture query-specific modality preferences [12,24]. To address this limitation, we introduce a query-level adaptation layer on top of the existing retrieval framework, using its global weights for candidate recall and adapting the weights only within the recalled candidate set.

Based on this design, the proposed framework takes the global-weight retrieval result as the input to a local adaptation stage, where query-level supervision, feature construction, and adaptive re-ranking are performed. The overall framework is shown in Fig. 2. It consists of an offline stage and an online stage. In the offline stage, we retrieve candidate sets from the existing framework, construct query-level oracle supervision, extract query features, and train a lightweight adaptive predictor. In the online stage, the trained predictor generates query-specific modality weights for a new query, and the recalled candidates are re-ranked using the predicted adaptive weights.

3.1 Global Weight-Based Candidate Recall

The first stage relies on the global-weight retrieval result produced by the existing framework. As defined in Sect. 2.4, the baseline score $s_{\mathrm{base}}(q, o)$ combines

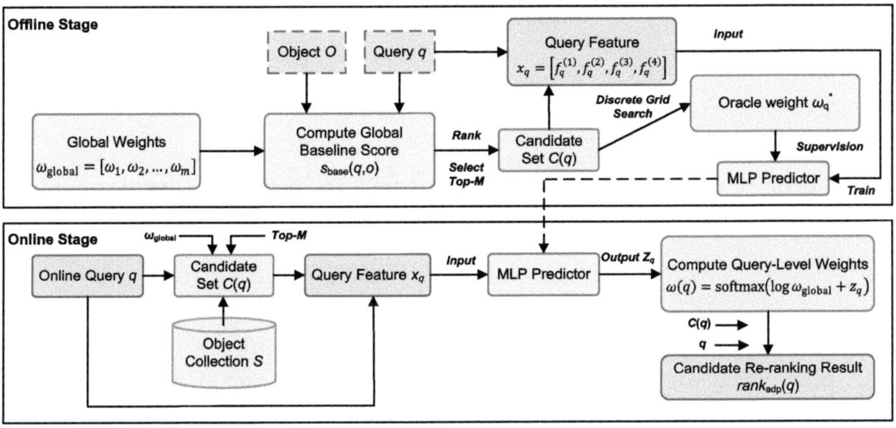

Fig. 2. Overview of the proposed query-aware adaptive weight learning framework.

modality-specific similarities with the global weights ω_{global}. In our method, this score is used to obtain a compact candidate set rather than as the final ranking criterion.

For each query q, we retrieve the top-M objects with the highest baseline scores from the whole object collection S:

$$C(q) = \text{TopM}_{o \in S}\ s_{\text{base}}(q, o), \tag{8}$$

where $C(q)$ denotes the candidate set of query q, and M is the candidate set size.

This step allows the proposed method to reuse the candidate recall results of the existing retrieval framework, while restricting oracle construction and adaptive re-ranking to a much smaller local search space. Therefore, query-aware adaptation can be performed without full-database re-scoring or re-indexing, which is important for scalable retrieval systems [8, 10].

3.2 Candidate-Level Oracle Weight Construction

A central challenge in query-aware modality weighting is that query-specific optimal weights are not manually annotated. To obtain supervision signals, we construct oracle weights within the retrieved candidate set. The oracle weight of a query is defined as the weight vector that produces the best local ranking performance for the ground-truth target among a finite set of valid weight candidates. This construction is performed only in the offline supervision stage and therefore does not introduce additional overhead during online inference.

Let Ω_δ denote a discrete simplex of modality weight vectors, where each vector satisfies non-negativity and normalization constraints. The step size δ controls the granularity of the search. For a weight vector $\omega \in \Omega_\delta$, the weighted score of object $o \in C(q)$ is computed as

$$s_\omega(q,o) = \sum_{i=0}^{m-1} \omega_i s_i(q,o). \tag{9}$$

The objects in $C(q)$ are ranked according to $s_\omega(q,o)$. Given the unique ground-truth target t of query q, the oracle weight is defined as

$$\omega_q^* = \arg\max_{\omega \in \Omega_\delta} \text{Recall@}k(\text{rank}(C(q);\omega), t), \tag{10}$$

where $\text{rank}(C(q);\omega)$ denotes the ranking of candidate objects under weight vector ω. Since each query has a unique ground-truth target, Recall@k indicates whether the target appears in the top-k results.

When multiple weight vectors achieve the same Recall@k, we use the weighted score of the ground-truth target $s_\omega(q,t)$ as a tie-breaking criterion. The resulting oracle weight ω_q^* reflects the locally optimal modality preference of query q within its candidate set, and also serves as an empirical upper bound for query-level weight adaptation.

3.3 Query Feature Construction

After constructing oracle weights, we learn a mapping from each query to its corresponding modality preference. Instead of feeding high-dimensional image or text embeddings into the predictor, we construct compact query features from the retrieval behavior of the candidate set. This keeps the predictor lightweight and focuses on how different modalities contribute to the current ranking.

For each query q, we construct a feature vector x_q by concatenating four types of features:

$$x_q = [f_q^{(1)}, f_q^{(2)}, f_q^{(3)}, f_q^{(4)}]. \tag{11}$$

The first part $f_q^{(1)}$ contains statistics of modality-specific scores, such as mean, standard deviation, extrema, top scores, and score gaps over the candidate set. The second part $f_q^{(2)}$ contains statistics of the baseline scores $s_{\text{base}}(q,o)$, which describe the ranking structure under global weights. The third part $f_q^{(3)}$ captures local information from top-ranked candidates, including their modality-specific scores and baseline scores. The fourth part $f_q^{(4)}$ contains query-side statistics derived from the reference visual features and target state. Together, these features describe both global candidate-score distribution and local ranking competition, enabling the predictor to infer query-specific modality preferences without retraining multimodal encoders.

3.4 Adaptive Weight Prediction

Given the query feature vector x_q and the oracle supervision ω_q^*, we train a lightweight predictor to estimate query-aware modality weights. The goal of this module is to learn a query-specific adjustment on top of the global-weight result, according to the local retrieval characteristics of the current query. The predictor is implemented as a two-hidden-layer multilayer perceptron:

$$z_q = \mathrm{MLP}(x_q), \tag{12}$$

where $z_q \in \mathbb{R}^m$ is a real-valued adjustment vector.

The predicted vector z_q is fused with the global weights ω_{global} to obtain the final query-aware weights:

$$\omega(q) = \mathrm{softmax}(\log \omega_{\text{global}} + z_q). \tag{13}$$

This formulation uses the global weights as a prior while allowing query-level adaptation. When $z_q = 0$, the predicted weights reduce to the global-weight result. Therefore, the model learns a residual-style correction rather than predicting modality weights from scratch.

For training, we use the oracle weight ω_q^* as supervision and optimize the predictor with a weighted mean squared error loss:

$$L = \frac{1}{|B|} \sum_{q \in B} \alpha_q \left\| \omega(q) - \omega_q^* \right\|_2^2, \tag{14}$$

where B is the mini-batch and α_q is a sample weight determined by the improvement of the oracle result over the baseline result. The training objective encourages the predicted weight $\omega(q)$ to approximate the oracle weight ω_q^*.

3.5 Candidate Re-Ranking

After training, the predictor can be used for online query-level adaptation. Given a new query q, the existing retrieval framework first returns the candidate set $C(q)$ using the global-weight score. Then, the query feature vector x_q is extracted from the candidate set, and the adaptive weight vector $\omega(q)$ is predicted by the trained model.

For each candidate object $o \in C(q)$, the adaptive score is computed as

$$s_{\text{adp}}(q, o) = \sum_{i=0}^{m-1} \omega_i(q) s_i(q, o). \tag{15}$$

The final ranking is obtained by sorting all candidates in $C(q)$ according to this adaptive score:

$$\mathrm{rank}_{\text{adp}}(q) = \mathrm{sort}_{o \in C(q)}\, s_{\text{adp}}(q, o). \tag{16}$$

The adaptive weights are applied only to the recalled candidate set. The method does not require re-indexing, modifying feature encoders, or re-scoring the entire object collection. Therefore, it can be integrated as a lightweight re-ranking layer on top of existing global-weight retrieval frameworks.

4 Experiments

In this section, we evaluate the proposed query-aware adaptive weight learning method. The experiments are designed to answer four questions: whether query-aware adaptive weighting improves over the fixed global-weight result, how the improvement varies across datasets and retrieval depths, whether the adaptive layer remains efficient during online inference, and whether the key components of the proposed framework are effective.

4.1 Experimental Setup

Datasets. We conduct experiments on three MSTM-style datasets constructed from public image datasets: CelebA, CUB, and UT-Zap50K [14,18,22]. Following Sect. 2.3, we organize them into CelebA+, CUB+, and UT-Zap50K+. In all datasets, the target modality is image, and each query is constructed from a reference image and auxiliary modalities with one unique ground-truth target.

The three datasets differ in scale, object type, and modality-dependency patterns, while sharing the same MSTM task format and modal representation. Table 1 summarizes their statistics.

Table 1. Statistics of the experimental datasets.

Dataset	Scenario	Base	Query	Modalities	GTs/query
CelebA+	Face attribute retrieval	191,549	17,163	4	1
CUB+	Fine-grained bird retrieval	11,788	3,000	4	1
UT-Zap50K+	Product shoe retrieval	40,020	5,000	4	1

Table 2. Four-modal representation used in this work.

Modality	Base object representation	Query object representation
Modality 0	CLIP image embedding of the candidate image	CLIP composition embedding of reference image r and relative text d_q
Modality 1	Attribute, category, or structured state vector	Target state vector a_q
Modality 2	ResNet18 visual feature of the candidate image	ResNet18 visual feature of reference image r
Modality 3	ResNet50 visual feature of the candidate image	ResNet50 visual feature of reference image r

Representation Setting. Following Sect. 2.2, all experiments use four modalities for fair comparison with the global-weight baseline. Table 2 gives the concrete implementation in our experiments.

Evaluation Metric. We use Recall@k as the evaluation metric. For each query, let R_k denote the top-k retrieved results, G denote the ground-truth set, and $k' = |G|$ denote the number of relevant targets. Then

$$\text{Recall@}k(k') = \frac{|R_k \cap G|}{k'}. \tag{17}$$

In our setting, each query has one unique ground-truth target, i.e., $k' = 1$, so Recall@k measures whether the target appears in the top-k results.

Compared Methods. We compare three types of results. **Baseline** uses the global modality weights learned by MUST [19], which is adopted because it provides explicit modality weights for MSTM, while traditional MR and JE methods are not designed for query-aware weight adaptation. **Adaptive** is the proposed method, which predicts query-specific weights and re-ranks the candidate set. **Oracle** uses the oracle weights obtained by candidate-level discrete search, and serves as an upper bound within the recalled candidate set.

4.2 Main Results

Table 3. Recall@k comparison on three datasets.

(a) CelebA+					
Method	**Recall@5**	**Recall@10**	**Recall@20**	**Recall@50**	**Recall@100**
Baseline	0.6326	0.6439	0.6565	0.6778	0.6998
Adaptive	0.6508 (+2.88%)	0.6626 (+2.90%)	0.6807 (+3.69%)	0.7080 (+4.46%)	0.7308 (+4.43%)
Oracle	0.6751	0.7002	0.7280	0.7651	0.7860
(b) CUB+					
Method	**Recall@1**	**Recall@5**	**Recall@10**	**Recall@20**	**Recall@50**
Baseline	0.0570	0.1687	0.2503	0.3453	0.4690
Adaptive	0.1700 (+198.25%)	0.3663 (+117.13%)	0.4617 (+84.46%)	0.5580 (+61.60%)	0.6453 (+37.59%)
Oracle	0.3550	0.5060	0.5977	0.6540	0.6937
(c) UT-Zap50K+					
Method	**Recall@1**	**Recall@5**	**Recall@10**	**Recall@20**	**Recall@50**
Baseline	0.0920	0.2346	0.3156	0.4067	0.5288
Adaptive	0.3692 (+301.30%)	0.6498 (+176.98%)	0.6884 (+118.12%)	0.7048 (+73.30%)	0.7318 (+38.39%)
Oracle	0.6650	0.6768	0.7172	0.7472	0.7694

We compare Baseline, Adaptive, and Oracle on three datasets. Table 3 reports Recall@k results and the relative improvement of Adaptive over Baseline.

Adaptive consistently outperforms Baseline on all three datasets and all reported values of k. This confirms that fixed global weights are stable but insufficient for query-specific modality preferences. By re-ranking only the candidate set, our method improves retrieval performance without modifying feature encoders or full-database retrieval.

The improvement differs across datasets. On CelebA+, the relative gains are moderate but stable, ranging from 2.88% to 4.46%, partly because the large base collection leads to a relatively strong baseline. On CUB+ and UT-Zap50K+, the gains are much larger, especially at smaller k, suggesting that adaptive weighting is more beneficial when fine-grained distinctions or structured constraints create stronger query-level modality differences.

The results also show a clear relationship between retrieval depth and improvement. On CUB+ and UT-Zap50K+, the relative gains decrease as k becomes larger. Small-k retrieval is more sensitive to the exact order of top-ranked candidates, while at larger k the baseline has a higher chance of already including the target in a broader result set.

Oracle results are consistently higher than both Baseline and Adaptive. This indicates that better query-specific weights can further improve the ranking within the recalled candidate set. The gap between Adaptive and Oracle shows that the predictor captures part of the query-level modality preference, while leaving room for improved feature design and weight prediction.

4.3 Online Efficiency

To further examine the efficiency of the proposed adaptive layer, we compare the online inference latency of Baseline and Adaptive on the test split. The same candidate-size settings as the main experiments are used for each dataset.

Table 4. Online inference latency comparison on the test split. The latency is reported as the average time per query after 50 warm-up queries using a single thread.

Dataset	Baseline (ms/query)	Adaptive (ms/query)	Latency Increase
CelebA+	71.29	74.09	+2.80 ms (+3.93%)
CUB+	3.01	3.76	+0.75 ms (+25.11%)
UT-Zap50K+	15.87	17.49	+1.62 ms (+10.19%)

Table 4 shows that the proposed adaptive layer introduces only a small absolute latency increase, ranging from 0.75 ms to 2.80 ms per query. On the largest CelebA+ dataset, Adaptive increases the latency by only 2.80 ms per query, corresponding to a 3.93% increase over Baseline. These results support that the proposed method remains lightweight in online inference, as it only performs candidate-level feature extraction, MLP prediction, and re-ranking within the recalled candidates.

4.4 Ablation Studies

To understand the key components of the proposed method, we conduct ablations on query feature design, predictor architecture, and candidate size. Recall@k measures the final retrieval effectiveness after re-ranking, while the prediction MSE is reported in feature and predictor ablations to evaluate how closely the adaptive predictor fits the oracle-weight supervision.

Effect of Query Features. The adaptive predictor relies on query features to infer modality preferences. We compare three input configurations: *full*, *stats_only*, and *top_only*. The *full* setting uses all feature groups introduced in Sect. 3.3, while *stats_only* and *top_only* keep only candidate-level statistics and top-ranked local information, respectively.

Effect of Predictor Architecture. We compare a linear predictor with the MLP predictor used in our method. Both models take the same query feature vector as input and predict adaptive weights based on the global-weight prior. The linear model captures simple linear relations, while the MLP introduces lightweight nonlinear modeling.

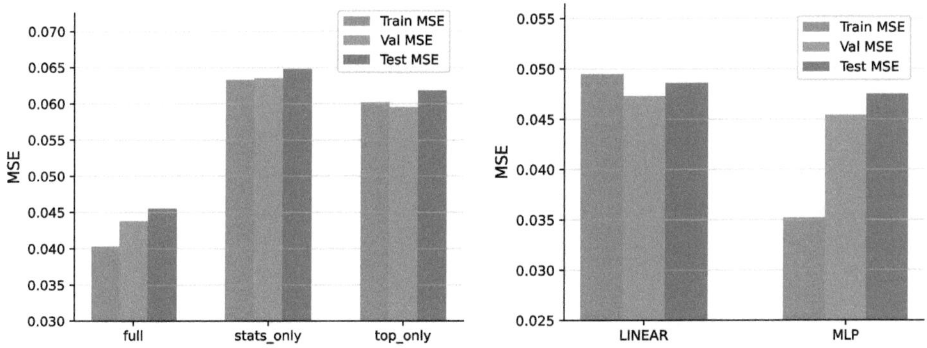

(a) Feature ablation (b) Predictor architecture

Fig. 3. Ablation results on query features and predictor architecture.

Figure 3(a) shows that the *full* feature configuration performs best, indicating that global score statistics and local candidate competition provide complementary cues for predicting modality preferences. The weaker performance of *stats_only* and *top_only* suggests that using only one part of the features may be insufficient when the baseline ranking is locally ambiguous. Figure 3(b) shows that the MLP outperforms the linear predictor, indicating that the mapping from query features to oracle weights is not purely linear and may depend jointly on global score distribution and top-candidate behavior.

Effect of Candidate Size. The candidate size M controls the local search space for oracle construction and adaptive re-ranking. A small M may miss the ground-truth target, while a large M may introduce more noisy candidates. Therefore, M reflects the trade-off between candidate coverage and local ranking complexity.

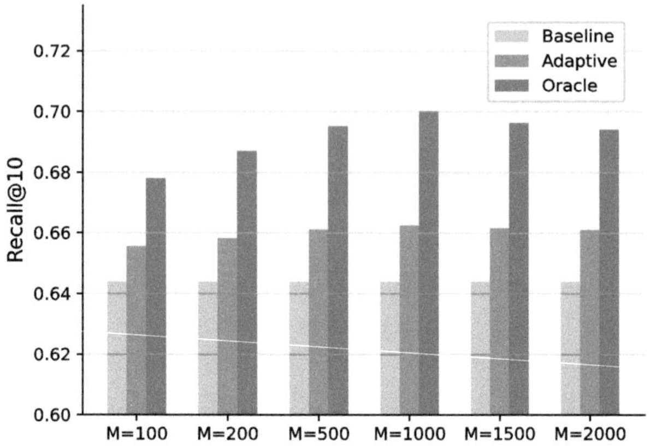

Fig. 4. Effect of candidate size M on CelebA+.

Figure 4 shows that candidate size affects Adaptive and Oracle more directly than Baseline, because both methods operate within the recalled candidate set. As M increases, target coverage improves and provides more opportunity for query-aware re-ranking. However, once M becomes sufficiently large, additional candidates mainly introduce noise and the gain tends to saturate. This confirms that a suitable candidate size should balance target coverage and re-ranking difficulty.

5 Conclusion

In this paper, we studied the query-insensitivity problem of fixed global modality weights in multimodal search of target modality. To address this problem, we proposed a query-aware adaptive weight learning method that can be integrated as a lightweight re-ranking layer on top of existing global-weight retrieval frameworks. The proposed method uses global-weight results for candidate recall, constructs candidate-level oracle supervision, and trains a lightweight predictor to estimate query-specific weights for candidate re-ranking.

Experiments on CelebA+, CUB+, and UT-Zap50K+ show that the proposed method consistently improves over the fixed global-weight baseline, especially on fine-grained and product retrieval datasets where query-level modality preferences are more diverse. Ablation studies further verify the effectiveness of the query features, nonlinear predictor, and candidate-level adaptation strategy.

The current framework can also be extended in future work. Since the proposed method operates within the recalled candidate set, its performance still depends on the coverage of first-stage retrieval. Future work may improve this stage through dynamic candidate expansion or multi-stage retrieval. More scalable oracle construction, stronger query-level predictors, and broader modality settings can also be explored to improve the generality and effectiveness of query-aware adaptive weighting.

References

1. Baldrati, A., Bertini, M., Uricchio, T., Del Bimbo, A.: Conditioned and composed image retrieval combining and partially fine-tuning CLIP-based features. In: Proceedings of the IEEE/CVF Conference on Computer Vision and Pattern Recognition (CVPR) Workshops, pp. 4959–4968 (2022)
2. Baldrati, A., Bertini, M., Uricchio, T., Del Bimbo, A.: Effective conditioned and composed image retrieval combining CLIP-based features. In: Proceedings of the IEEE/CVF Conference on Computer Vision and Pattern Recognition, pp. 21466–21474 (2022)
3. Baltrušaitis, T., Ahuja, C., Morency, L.P.: Multimodal machine learning: a survey and taxonomy. IEEE Trans. Pattern Anal. Mach. Intell. **41**(2), 423–443 (2019). https://doi.org/10.1109/TPAMI.2018.2798607
4. Chen, T., Kornblith, S., Norouzi, M., Hinton, G.: A simple framework for contrastive learning of visual representations. In: Proceedings of the 37th International Conference on Machine Learning. Proceedings of Machine Learning Research, vol. 119, pp. 1597–1607. PMLR (2020)
5. Chen, Y.-C., Li, L., Yu, L., El Kholy, A., Ahmed, F., Gan, Z., Cheng, Yu., Liu, J.: UNITER: universal image-text representation learning. In: Vedaldi, A., Bischof, H., Brox, T., Frahm, J.-M. (eds.) ECCV 2020. LNCS, vol. 12375, pp. 104–120. Springer, Cham (2020). https://doi.org/10.1007/978-3-030-58577-8_7
6. Faghri, F., Fleet, D.J., Kiros, J.R., Fidler, S.: VSE++: improving visual-semantic embeddings with hard negatives (2017)
7. Frome, A., Corrado, G.S., Shlens, J., Bengio, S., Dean, J., Ranzato, M., Mikolov, T.: DeViSE: a deep visual-semantic embedding model. In: Advances in Neural Information Processing Systems, vol. 26, Curran Associates, Inc (2013)
8. Gordo, A., Almazán, J., Revaud, J., Larlus, D.: Deep Image Retrieval: Learning Global Representations for Image Search. In: Leibe, B., Matas, J., Sebe, N., Welling, M. (eds.) ECCV 2016. LNCS, vol. 9910, pp. 241–257. Springer, Cham (2016). https://doi.org/10.1007/978-3-319-46466-4_15
9. Hadsell, R., Chopra, S., LeCun, Y.: Dimensionality reduction by learning an invariant mapping. In: 2006 IEEE Computer Society Conference on Computer Vision and Pattern Recognition (CVPR'06). vol. 2, pp. 1735–1742 (2006). https://doi.org/10.1109/CVPR.2006.100
10. Jégou, H., Douze, M., Schmid, C.: Product quantization for nearest neighbor search. IEEE Trans. Pattern Anal. Mach. Intell. **33**(1), 117–128 (2011). https://doi.org/10.1109/TPAMI.2010.57
11. Karpathy, A., Joulin, A., Fei-Fei, L.: Deep fragment embeddings for bidirectional image sentence mapping. In: Advances in Neural Information Processing Systems, vol. 27, Curran Associates, Inc (2014)

12. Kennedy, L., Chang, S.F., Natsev, A.: Query-adaptive fusion for multimodal search. Proc. IEEE **96**(4), 567–588 (2008). https://doi.org/10.1109/JPROC.2008.916345
13. Lee, K.H., Chen, X., Hua, G., Hu, H., He, X.: Stacked cross attention for image-text matching. In: Proceedings of the European Conference on Computer Vision (ECCV) (2018)
14. Liu, Z., Luo, P., Wang, X., Tang, X.: Deep learning face attributes in the wild. In: Proceedings of the IEEE International Conference on Computer Vision (ICCV) (2015)
15. Radford, A., Kim, J.W., Hallacy, C., Ramesh, A., Goh, G., Agarwal, S., Sastry, G., Askell, A., Mishkin, P., Clark, J., Krueger, G., Sutskever, I.: Learning transferable visual models from natural language supervision. In: Proceedings of the 38th International Conference on Machine Learning. Proceedings of Machine Learning Research, vol. 139, pp. 8748–8763. PMLR (2021)
16. Tautkute, I., Trzciński, T., Skorupa, A.P., Brocki, Ł, Marasek, K.: DeepStyle: multimodal search engine for fashion and interior design. IEEE Access **7**, 84613–84628 (2019). https://doi.org/10.1109/ACCESS.2019.2923552
17. Vo, N., Jiang, L., Sun, C., Murphy, K., Li, L.J., Fei-Fei, L., Hays, J.: Composing text and image for image retrieval - an empirical odyssey. In: Proceedings of the IEEE/CVF Conference on Computer Vision and Pattern Recognition (CVPR) (2019)
18. Wah, C., Branson, S., Welinder, P., Perona, P., Belongie, S.: The Caltech-UCSD birds-200-2011 dataset. Tech. rep, California Institute of Technology, Pasadena, CA (2011)
19. Wang, M., Ke, X., Xu, X., Chen, L., Gao, Y., Huang, P., Zhu, R.: MUST: An effective and scalable framework for multimodal search of target modality. In: 2024 IEEE 40th International Conference on Data Engineering (ICDE), pp. 4747–4759 (2024). https://doi.org/10.1109/ICDE60146.2024.00361
20. Wu, H., Gao, Y., Guo, X., Al-Halah, Z., Rennie, S., Grauman, K., Feris, R.: Fashion IQ: a new dataset towards retrieving images by natural language feedback. In: Proceedings of the IEEE/CVF Conference on Computer Vision and Pattern Recognition (CVPR), pp. 11307–11317 (2021)
21. Ye, C., Peng, T., Chang, T., Zhou, Z., Wang, F.: Query-aware multi-modal based ranking relevance in video search. In: Proceedings of the 2023 Conference on Empirical Methods in Natural Language Processing: Industry Track. pp. 322–330. Association for Computational Linguistics, Singapore (2023). https://doi.org/10.18653/v1/2023.emnlp-industry.31, https://aclanthology.org/2023.emnlp-industry.31/
22. Yu, A., Grauman, K.: Fine-grained visual comparisons with local learning. In: Proceedings of the IEEE Conference on Computer Vision and Pattern Recognition (CVPR) (2014)
23. Zhang, S., Yang, M., Cour, T., Yu, K., Metaxas, D.N.: Query specific rank fusion for image retrieval. IEEE Trans. Pattern Anal. Mach. Intell. **37**(4), 803–815 (2015). https://doi.org/10.1109/TPAMI.2014.2346201
24. Zheng, L., Wang, S., Tian, L., He, F., Liu, Z., Tian, Q.: Query-adaptive late fusion for image search and person re-identification. In: Proceedings of the IEEE Conference on Computer Vision and Pattern Recognition (CVPR) (2015)

Security and Privacy

A Preprocessing Defense for Adversarial Attacks Using Attention Residual U-Net

Minh-Tuan Thai, Tan-Sang Nguyen, and Duy-An Ha(✉)

Can Tho University, 3/2 Street - Ninh Kieu ward, Can Tho 900000, Viet Nam
{minhtuan,hdan}@ctu.edu.vn, sangm5123016@gstudent.ctu.edu.vn

Abstract. Adversarial attacks threaten deep learning models by causing misclassification with subtle changes. To address such an issue, this study introduces a preprocessing defense based on an improved U-Net with residual connections and CBAM attention. It removes adversarial noise and restores images before classification. Experiments on CIFAR-10 with FGSM and PGD attacks across different classifiers show the method raises classification accuracy, increasing average performance from 29.75%–54.30% (adversarial) to 76.60%–80.57% after denoising.

Keywords: Adversarial attacks · Adversarial perturbations · Convolutional neural networks (CNN) · Computer vision · Deep learning

1 Introduction

Digital images are essential to modern AI systems, powered by advances in deep learning. Yet, in real-world deployment, deep learning models confront formidable adversarial perturbations - intentional, subtle alterations that deceive predictions. These perturbations undermine local classification and jeopardize system reliability, especially in automated pipelines and integrated services. Despite numerous defense strategies, most are computationally demanding, attack-specific, and lack adaptability across environments. Consequently, developing an independent preprocessing module to mitigate adversarial effects before feeding data into deep learning models is a practical solution.

In practice, robust preprocessing delivers two main advantages. First, it reduces prediction errors under adversarial perturbations, thereby enhancing system reliability. Second, the denoising module can function as a flexible, model-agnostic defense layer that integrates smoothly with diverse architectures, without altering their structure or training. This flexibility is particularly valuable for systems with limited resources or those demanding swift, resilient deployment.

With advances in deep learning, image restoration models, including denoising networks, U-Net, autoencoders, and encoder–decoder architectures, can learn to map noisy images to clean versions guided by data distributions [1–3]. Unlike traditional filters, deep learning models discern adversarial patterns and reconstruct key features for recognition, upgrading input quality while preserving crucial details. Moreover, coupled with

L. Ding et al. (Eds.): APWeb-WAIM 2026, LNCS 16993, pp. 545–558, 2027.
https://doi.org/10.1007/978-981-92-5693-8_34

data augmentation, these models improve generalization and resilience against varied attack types.

This study proposes a preprocessing-based defense that uses a generative network to remove adversarial noise and restore images ahead of classification. The system leverages an enhanced U-Net architecture with residual blocks augmented with a Convolutional Block Attention Module (CBAM) [4] to preserve critical features during denoising. Experiments use the CIFAR-10 dataset with Fast Gradient Sign Method (FGSM) [5] and Projected Gradient Descent (PGD) [6] attacks, and are evaluated on classifiers including ResNet-56, MobileNetV2, VGG19_bn, ShuffleNetV2, and RepVGG-A2. Results reveal accuracy improves from 29.75%–54.30% on adversarial inputs to 76.60%–80.57% after denoising. The method also surpasses previous work [7], securing higher average accuracy (80.57% vs. 74.60%).

Main contributions of this study are:

1. Design a deep learning model to eliminate adversarial perturbations from images, producing outputs that closely resemble clean images.
2. Construct adversarial datasets from a standard benchmark (e.g., CIFAR-10) using widely adopted attack methods such as FGSM and PGD for training and evaluation.
3. Evaluate model performance using key metrics, including Clean Accuracy (CA), Adversarial Accuracy (AA), Defended Accuracy (DA), and Recovery Rate (RR), where RR quantifies the proportion of classification performance recovered from adversarial degradation.
4. Benchmark the proposed model against conventional preprocessing/denoising approaches to emphasize strengths, limitations, and effective operating conditions.
5. Introduce an application framework integrating the adversarial denoising model as a modular element within computer vision pipelines, targeting practical implementation and extensibility to related tasks.

2 Background and Related Works

2.1 Adversarial Vulnerabilities of Deep Vision Models

The rapid advancement of deep learning–based computer vision models has led to significant breakthroughs in real-world applications, including autonomous systems, medical diagnosis, and security surveillance. Despite these achievements, the widespread adoption of convolutional neural networks (CNNs) has revealed a critical vulnerability: susceptibility to intentionally crafted input perturbations. The phenomenon of adversarial examples, inputs modified with carefully designed perturbations to mislead models, was first highlighted by C. Szegedy and colleagues in 2014 [8]. To date, defending against such adversarial inputs remains a major challenge for the reliability of artificial intelligence systems.

To distinguish adversarial threats from natural distortions (e.g., noise or motion blur), note that adversarial perturbations are generated across optimization processes that exploit weaknesses in the model's feature space. Early work by Ian Goodfellow et al. [5] attributed this vulnerability to the linear behavior of neural networks in high-dimensional spaces. Recently, A. Ilyas et al. [9] provided a more in-depth explanation, suggesting that adversarial examples arise from exploiting non-robust features that are highly predictive yet fragile and misaligned with human perception.

2.2 Defense and Denoising Approaches

Given these challenges, a wide range of defense strategies has been proposed to improve model robustness against adversarial perturbations:

Restoration and noise-based defenses: Lee et al. [10] proposed a defense framework that combines traditional image restoration techniques, such as ROF and NL-means filtering, with stochastic noise injection during training. Experimental results demonstrate that this approach effectively mitigates performance degradation under attack and enhances robustness in black-box scenarios across various classification architectures.

Transformation-based preprocessing: Wang et al. [11] introduced a practical preprocessing layer that combines WebP image compression with geometric transformations (e.g., flipping) to weaken adversarial signals. This method significantly improves accuracy across multiple attack settings while maintaining acceptable performance on clean data, highlighting preprocessing as a cost-effective defense mechanism, albeit with sensitivity to the data domain.

Generative model–based restoration: T. D. Su et al. [7] proposed reconstructing clean images using an encoder–decoder architecture with a ResNet-based bottleneck. Their approach enables strong generalization across classifiers and serves as a model-agnostic purification module, eliminating the need for prior knowledge of specific attack patterns. Compared to optimization-based defenses, this method grants improved computational effectiveness through direct per-sample processing.

In addition, approaches leveraging generative adversarial networks (GANs) [12] and diffusion models [13] have been explored to map adversarial inputs back to the clean data distribution. While these methods provide strong denoising capabilities, they often incur high computational costs, increased latency, and the risk of introducing artifacts that may distort critical classification features.

2.3 Motivation for Proposing the Attention Residual U-Net Architecture

Despite promising results from prior studies [7, 10, 11] suggesting that preprocessing-based image purification is a viable approach for restoring classification accuracy under adversarial conditions, traditional filtering methods remain highly sensitive to parameter settings: excessive denoising can blur critical details, while insufficient filtering can fail to remove adversarial components. Meanwhile, deep learning–based approaches can learn direct mappings from corrupted to clean images, although their effectiveness may vary across different feature types.

Taking these considerations into account, we propose using the Attention Residual U-Net architecture for this problem to leverage three core advantages:

1. U-Net structure with skip connections: Preserves spatial information and edge features, thereby minimizing the loss of fine-grained details.
2. Residual blocks: Enable the model to focus on learning noise-induced differences, reducing over-smoothing commonly observed in conventional filtering methods.
3. Attention mechanism: Allows the model to prioritize regions and feature channels heavily affected by adversarial perturbations while suppressing irrelevant background information.

With this integrated design, we seek to build on prior empirical findings and provide a more effective denoising mechanism than handcrafted transformations, while preserving semantic content. Consequently, this architecture enhances the robustness and stability of classification models against complex adversarial attacks such as FGSM and PGD.

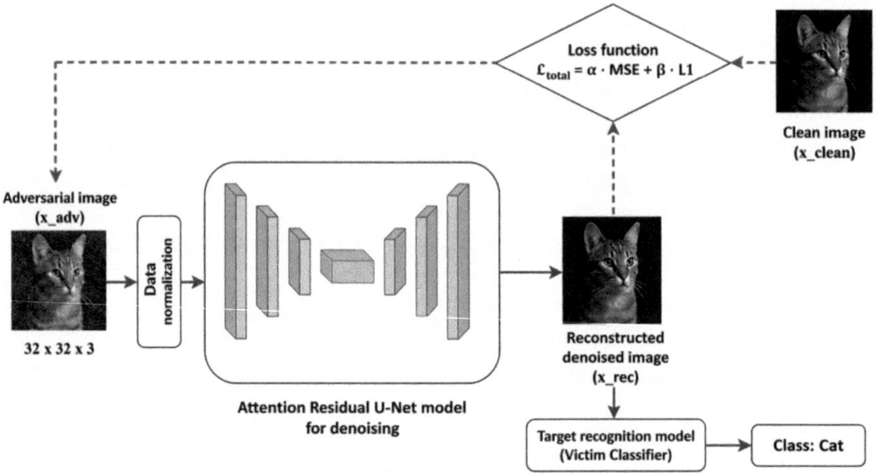

Fig. 1. General pipeline of the proposed adversarial noise removal approach

3 Method

3.1 Proposed Approach Overview

The overall processing pipeline for the proposed adversarial noise removal framework is illustrated in Fig. 1. The input is an adversarial image of size $32 \times 32 \times 3$, which is first normalized and then passed through the core component, which is an Attention Residual U-Net. This module learns to transform corrupted inputs into restored images that approximate clean data. The reconstructed image is subsequently fed into a victim classifier to evaluate label recovery.

Adversarial samples x_{adv} are generated from clean images x_{clean} using FGSM and PGD. Although visually similar to the original, these samples are designed to mislead classifiers. The resulting pairs (x_{adv}, x_{clean}) form the basis for supervised restoration. Before denoising, inputs are normalized to ensure stable learning and reduce variability unrelated to adversarial perturbations.

The Attention Residual U-Net serves as the central denoising module. Its encoder–decoder structure captures global context and reconstructs fine details via skip connections, while residual blocks enable the model to focus on perturbation components rather than full image reconstruction. The attention mechanism further enhances performance by prioritizing regions and feature channels most affected by adversarial noise. The output is a restored image x_{rec}, expected to preserve both visual fidelity and discriminative features.

After that, the pipeline branches into two objectives to jointly evaluate restoration quality and defensive effectiveness. In the first branch, x_{rec} is compared with x_{clean}, to compute reconstruction loss, ensuring structural fidelity and preventing the generation of artifacts or excessive smoothing. The resulting error signal is backpropagated, as illustrated by dashed lines in Fig. 1, to update the Attention Residual U-Net's parameters during training. In the second branch, x_{rec} is fed into the victim classifier, representing the target system to be protected. Without defense, adversarial inputs can significantly degrade prediction accuracy. Therefore, this step evaluates the study's central objective: whether denoising can effectively restore correct classification decisions.

3.2 Adversarial Dataset Construction

This study is based on the CIFAR-10 dataset, which consists of $32 \times 32 \times 3$ color images and was introduced by Alex Krizhevsky [14]. Since adversarial datasets are not publicly available, adversarial samples are generated using established attack methods applied to CIFAR-10.

Instead of generating adversarial examples on-the-fly during training, which incurs high computational cost due to repeated backpropagation through victim models, we adopt an offline data-generation strategy. Specifically, a static adversarial dataset is precomputed and stored, containing paired samples (x_{clean}, x_{adv}). This approach significantly accelerates training by eliminating repeated attack computations and ensuring consistency during evaluation, enabling fair comparison across model configurations.

The dataset construction pipeline consists of four main steps. First, the CIFAR-10 dataset is loaded, including 50,000 training images and 10,000 test images. Second, a diverse set of pre-trained victim models is initialized. Third, adversarial examples are generated by attacking each clean sample using these models. Finally, the resulting data are packaged and stored in an optimized binary format for efficient retrieval. The process is applied to both training and test sets, ensuring a clear separation between training and evaluation data.

Diverse Victim Model Strategy

Victim models are used to compute gradients for each input image, where each gradient indicates the direction and magnitude of perturbations that increase the loss. Adversarial attacks exploit this information to generate perturbations based on the gradient sign. To mitigate overfitting to architecture-specific noise and bolster generalization, an ensemble attack methodology is employed. Our approach utilizes a diverse set of five surrogate models, namely ResNet-56, VGG19, MobileNetV2, ShuffleNetV2, and RepVGG, to act as the victim architectures. During dataset generation, for each batch of input images, a victim model is selected either randomly or in a round-robin manner to perform the attack. This ensures that the resulting adversarial dataset contains diverse perturbation patterns arising from different architectures. Such diversity is crucial, as adversarial noise generated by different models exhibits distinct spatial and frequency characteristics. Training on this heterogeneous dataset enables the denoising model to learn more generalizable noise patterns, thereby improving robustness against unseen attacks.

Adversarial Perturbation Attack Methods

In this study, FGSM and PGD, which are two widely adopted and effective adversarial attack methods, are employed to generate perturbations of varying difficulty for the defense model. FGSM is a single-step attack designed for efficient data generation. It perturbs the input by adding a small noise component in the direction of the loss gradient. In this study, multiple perturbation levels ϵ are considered, with $\epsilon \in \{0.05, 0.10, 0.15, 0.25\}$, simulating attack strengths ranging from weak to strong. In contrast, PGD is a multi-step iterative attack and is widely regarded as a stronger adversarial method. Perturbations are generated through multiple update steps, with each step constrained to ensure the perturbation remains within a predefined bound. In our implementation, PGD is configured with 7 iterations, and the step size (α) is set proportionally to ϵ. This approach yields more challenging adversarial samples, requiring the denoising model to capture finer-grained structures to achieve effective image restoration.

Hybrid Dataset Structure

A key contribution of this study is the design of a hybrid adversarial dataset. Instead of training on a single attack type, the proposed dataset combines samples generated by both FGSM and PGD. Specifically, each batch contains a proportion of FGSM-generated samples with a given perturbation level, while the remaining samples are generated using PGD with different configurations. FGSM samples with larger ϵ introduce more noticeable perturbations, enabling the model to learn coarse noise patterns during early training stages. In contrast, PGD samples, typically generated with smaller ϵ but optimized iteratively, contain more subtle and challenging perturbations, facilitating fine-grained denoising capabilities. This combination promotes more stable convergence and improved overall performance compared to training on a single attack type. To prevent overfitting to data ordering, the entire hybrid dataset is randomly shuffled before storage.

3.3 Attention Residual U-Net Implementation

In this study, the adversarial denoising model is implemented using an Attention Residual U-Net architecture with a symmetric Encoder–Bottleneck–Decoder structure, as illustrated in Fig. 2. The model serves as an intermediate module that transforms adversarial inputs into restored images, which are then fed directly into pre-trained victim classifiers without modifying their architecture or retraining.

To ensure consistency across the pipeline, the model operates entirely in the normalized input space, aligned with the preprocessing used by CIFAR-10 and the victim models.

Architecturally, the Encoder extracts multi-scale features and encodes high-level semantic representations. The Bottleneck serves as the deepest processing stage, incorporating residual blocks enhanced with CBAM [4] to improve noise modeling and feature selection. The Decoder reconstructs the image at the original resolution by combining semantic information from the Bottleneck with spatial details from the Encoder via skip connections. The U-Net design is chosen for its ability to preserve fine-grained details, which is critical for image restoration tasks.

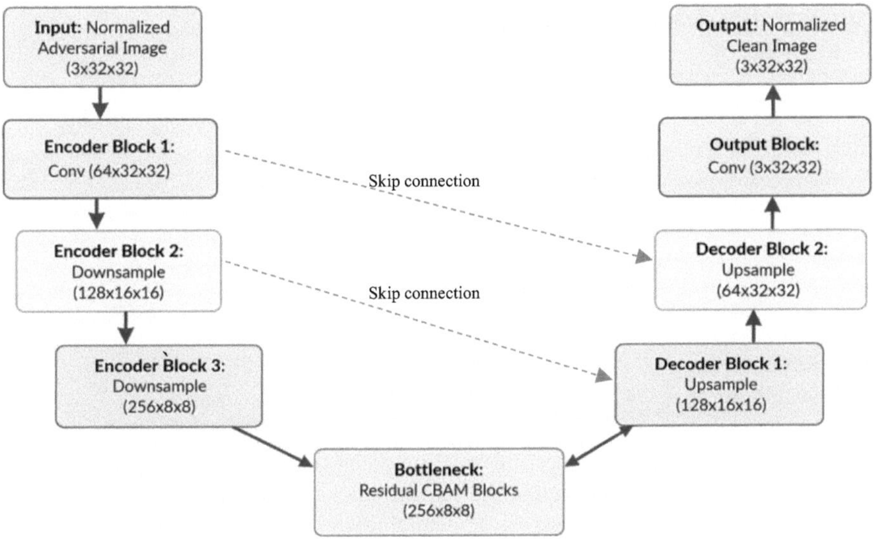

Fig. 2. The Attention Residual U-Net architecture used in the proposed method

Residual learning facilitates stable training of deeper networks and encourages the model to learn perturbation corrections rather than full image reconstruction. CBAM modules are integrated within residual blocks to emphasize informative feature channels and spatial regions affected by adversarial noise. The training process follows a supervised approach using paired image sets (x_{adv}, x_{clean}). A reconstruction loss is employed to steer the model toward the clean ground truth, enabling it to learn an efficient one-step transformation from corrupted adversarial data to restored images.

Training Strategy and Loss Function

To optimize the restoration of clean images from adversarial inputs, a hybrid loss function is employed that combines Mean Squared Error (MSE) and L1 Loss. This formulation balances global structure reconstruction and preservation of fine-grained details.

The formula for the MSE component is denoted in Eq. (1), which measures the average squared difference between the reconstructed image I_{rec} and the clean image I_{clean} over N pixels of size $H \times W \times C$. Due to its strong penalization of large errors, MSE effectively captures global structure and suppresses high-intensity perturbations. However, it may introduce over-smoothing and degrade high-frequency details.

To address this limitation, L1 Loss, denoted in Eq. (2), is incorporated as a complementary term. With its linear penalty, L1 maintains stable gradients and encourages sparsity in the error distribution, thereby preserving edges and fine details while reducing blurring artifacts.

The total loss L_{total} is defined as a weighted sum of these two components, as shown in Eq. (3). MSE contributes to global denoising, whereas L1 enhances local detail preservation. The weighting coefficients α and β are empirically determined to balance denoising performance and image sharpness, ultimately improving reconstruction quality and downstream classification accuracy.

$$\mathcal{L}_{\mathcal{MSE}} = \frac{1}{N}\sum_{i=1}^{N}\left(I_{rec}^{(i)} - I_{clean}^{(i)}\right)^2 \tag{1}$$

$$\mathcal{L}_{L1} = \frac{1}{N}\sum_{i=1}^{N}\left|I_{rec}^{(i)} - I_{clean}^{(i)}\right| \tag{2}$$

$$\mathcal{L}_{total} = \alpha \cdot \mathcal{L}_{MSE} + \beta \cdot \mathcal{L}_{L1} \tag{3}$$

Evaluation Metrics

The evaluation metrics used in our study include Clean Accuracy (CA), Adversarial Accuracy (AA), Defended Accuracy (DA), and Recovery Rate (RR). Specifically, CA measures the model's baseline performance on clean data, while AA quantifies accuracy under adversarial attacks, reflecting performance degradation. DA represents the accuracy after applying the defense mechanism, indicating its effectiveness. Finally, RR evaluates the proportion of classification performance recovered relative to the degradation caused by the attack, thereby measuring the defended model's restoration capability. RR is computed as defined in Eq. (4).

$$RR = \frac{DA - AA}{CA - AA} \times 100\% \tag{4}$$

4 Results

The adversarial denoising model is trained using a "train hard, test easy" strategy, where training is conducted on strongly perturbed data. At the same time, evaluation is performed on test sets with lower noise levels. Fig. 3 presents qualitative results on representative samples after applying the proposed denoising model.

Table 1 presents the results under FGSM attacks at different perturbation levels. At $\epsilon = 0.15$, the model performance degrades significantly (AA = 54.03%) but is substantially recovered after defense (DA = 76.60%), corresponding to RR = 56.2%. As ϵ decreases to 0.1 and 0.05, AA increases to 60.87% and 69.98%, respectively, while RR declines to 53.3% and 46.9%, indicating reduced relative effectiveness of the denoising mechanism under weaker perturbations. RepVGG_a2 consistently achieves the highest DA across all noise levels (79.11%, 80.90%, 83.51%), demonstrating strong stability and feature extraction capability. Overall, the proposed method is most effective under strong perturbations, with diminishing gains as noise intensity decreases.

Table 2 shows that PGD induces more severe degradation than FGSM, with AA dropping to 29.75% at $\epsilon = 0.15$. Nevertheless, the proposed method achieves substantial recovery (DA = 77.79%, RR = 74.6%). As ϵ decreases to 0.1 and 0.05, AA improves to 39.04% and 54.30%, while RR declines to 71.0% and 65.9%. RepVGG_a2 again attains the highest performance (DA = 80.86%, 81.21%, 82.98%), highlighting the importance of backbone architecture in leveraging denoised inputs. Empirical evidence demonstrates

Fig. 3. Qualitative results of the proposed denoising model on sample images. For each class, five samples are selected; from left to right: clean image, adversarial image, and the corresponding denoised output produced by the Attention Residual U-Net

Table 1. Experimental results under the FGSM adversarial attack, N/A: Not Available

ϵ	Metric	ResNet-56	MobileNetV2	VGG19_bn	ShuffleNetV2	RepVGG_a2	AVERAGE
N/A	CA	94.37	94.05	93.91	93.30	95.27	94.18
0.05	AA	68.29	68.03	72.34	68.58	72.64	69.98
	DA	80.53	79.17	82.29	81.10	83.51	81.32
	RR	46.90	42.80	46.10	50.60	48.00	46.90
0.10	AA	59.05	58.80	63.51	59.69	63.28	60.87
	DA	77.61	76.38	79.90	78.30	80.90	78.62
	RR	52.50	49.90	53.90	55.40	55.10	53.30
0.15	AA	52.59	52.41	56.55	51.98	56.61	54.03
	DA	75.56	74.65	77.42	76.28	79.11	76.60
	RR	55.00	53.40	55.90	58.80	58.20	56.20

the high efficacy of the proposed approach, even against sophisticated iterative attacks such as PGD.

The generative denoising approach (Model G) in [7] achieves an average accuracy of 74.60% across the same victim model architectures. In comparison, the proposed method improves performance by approximately 5.97 percentage points under PGD attacks with

Table 2. Experimental results under PGD adversarial attack, N/A: Not Available

ϵ	Metrics	ResNet-56	MobileNetV2	VGG19_bn	ShuffleNetV2	RepVGG_a2	AVERAGE
N/A	CA	94.37	94.05	93.91	93.30	95.27	94.18
0.05	AA	49.02	49.83	60.11	54.96	57.56	54.30
	DA	79.20	78.46	81.89	80.31	82.98	80.57
	RR	66.50	64.70	64.40	66.10	67.40	65.90
0.1	AA	32.53	33.54	47.53	41.56	40.03	39.04
	DA	76.24	75.55	79.70	78.18	81.21	78.18
	RR	70.70	69.40	69.40	70.80	74.50	71.00
0.15	AA	23.29	23.96	39.14	32.73	29.62	29.75
	DA	75.73	75.22	79.03	78.11	80.86	77.79
	RR	73.80	73.10	72.80	74.90	78.10	74.60

Table 3. Comparison of defended accuracy (DA) achieved by the proposed method and the generative denoising approach (Model G) in [7]

Method	ResNet-56	MobileNetV2	VGG19_bn	ShuffleNetV2	RepVGG_a2	AVERAGE
Our Method	79.20	78.46	81.89	80.31	82.98	80.57
Model G	77.00	70.00	77.00	77.00	72.00	74.60

$\epsilon = 0.05$. The most significant gains are observed for RepVGG_a2 (+10.98 percentage points) and MobileNetV2 (+8.46 percentage points), while ResNet-56 shows a more modest improvement (+2.20 percentage points). Detailed results are reported in Table 3.

However, this performance gap should be interpreted with caution due to differences in experimental settings. Specifically, the authors in [7] employed a Hybrid CIFAR-10 dataset with GAN-generated perturbations, mixed with increasing coefficients, and evaluated on a subset of 500 adversarial samples that successfully fooled all models, resulting in a more challenging benchmark. Therefore, the current results are better viewed as a reference for recovery capability after defense rather than definitive evidence of superiority.

Overall, the results indicate that classification accuracy degrades sharply as attack strength increases, especially for PGD (AA $= 29.75\%$ at $\epsilon = 0.15$). With the proposed denoising model, performance is consistently restored: FGSM achieves DA in the range of 76.60%–81.32%, while PGD reaches 77.79%–80.57%, as illustrated in Fig. 4. A general trend is observed: as ϵ increases, AA decreases while RR increases, indicating that the denoising mechanism is more effective under stronger perturbations. Conversely, under weaker noise, recovery gains diminish due to the trade-off between noise removal and feature preservation. Additionally, RepVGG_a2 consistently outperforms other models, underscoring the critical role of the classifier backbone in the overall defense framework.

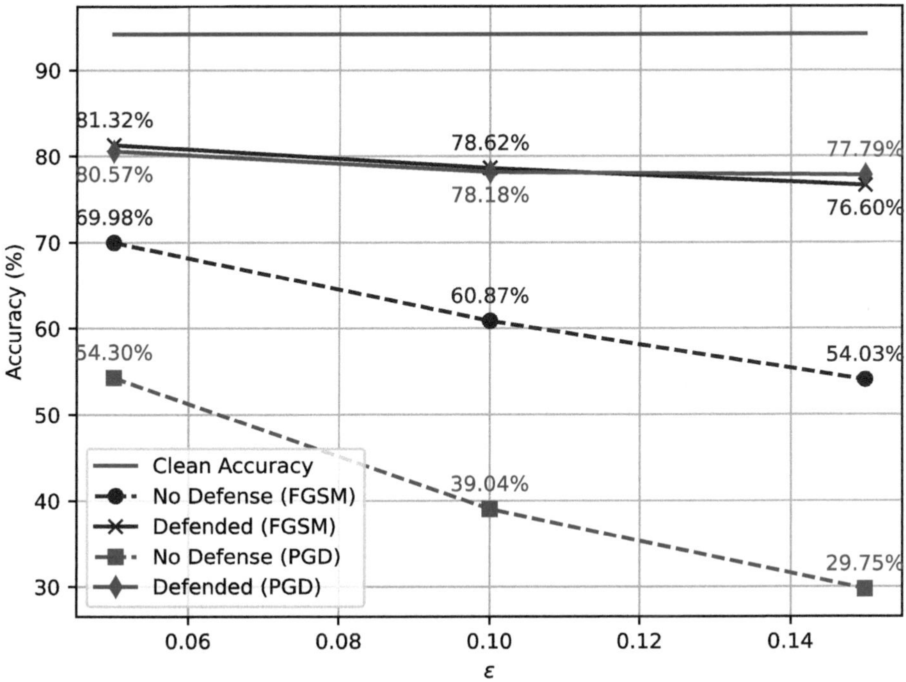

Fig. 4. Classification accuracy under FGSM and PGD attacks at varying perturbation levels (ϵ), comparing defended and undefended models

Class-wise analysis is necessary because adversarial perturbations and recovery performance vary across categories with distinct visual characteristics. Classes with fine-grained structures or high intra-class variability (e.g., bird, cat, deer) are generally more sensitive to perturbations; therefore, evaluation should be reported per class under three conditions: clean, adversarial, and denoised. Fig. 5 shows that PGD at $\epsilon = 0.1$ significantly degrades accuracy across all classes, with cat, bird, and deer being the most affected (AA <40%), while automobile, ship, and truck retain relatively higher accuracy. Fig. 6 illustrates class-wise gains, revealing clear variation in recovery performance. Airplane (+42.6%), ship (+37.8%), and horse (+36.5%) exhibit the largest improvements, indicating strong effectiveness on structurally distinctive objects. In contrast, the frog shows the lowest gain (+12.7%), highlighting limitations in recovering classes with subtle visual features. The remaining classes (cat, bird, deer) achieve moderate improvements, suggesting that defense effectiveness is closely tied to class-specific visual properties.

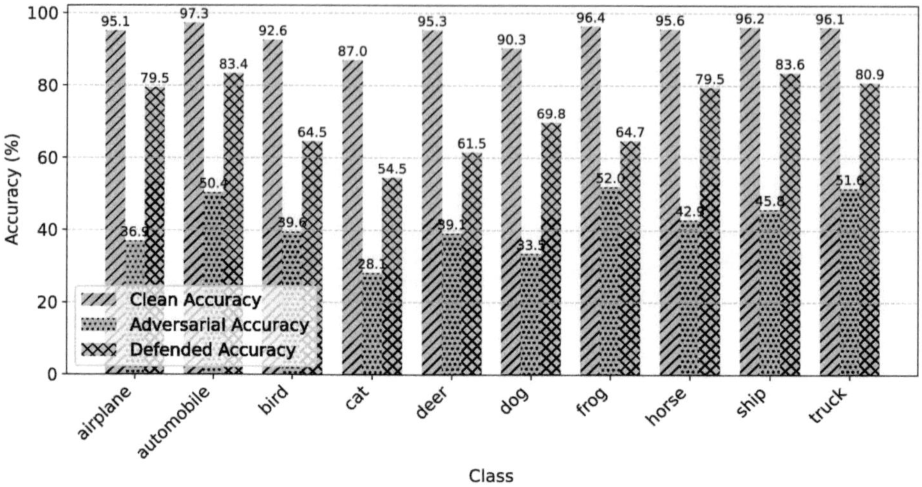

Fig. 5. Evaluation results by class with PGD and $\epsilon = 0.1$

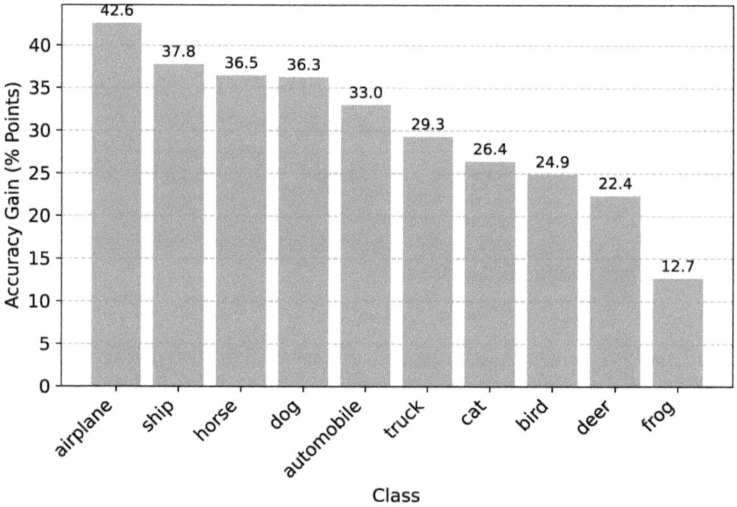

Fig. 6. Class-based resilience ranking (Accuracy Gain = DA − AA)

5 Conclusion

Experimental results demonstrate that the proposed Attention Residual U-Net effectively restores classification performance on adversarial data. Defended Accuracy remains consistently high ($\approx$69–81%) across attack types and perturbation levels, while Recovery Rate ranges from ~50% to over 70%, indicating that a substantial portion of performance degradation is recovered. These findings confirm the model's role as an effective preprocessing module for adversarial denoising, enabling performance to approach that of clean data.

The method exhibits relatively stable performance across different classifier backbones, although variations persist, reflecting differences in feature extraction capabilities. Moreover, defense effectiveness is sensitive to the noise distribution during evaluation, suggesting limited generalization when attack types or perturbation levels change.

In terms of computational cost, the model is moderately sized and suitable for deployment as a preprocessing layer. However, a trade-off between accuracy and inference latency must be considered; optimization strategies such as model compression or architectural simplification require further validation to avoid degrading recovery performance.

Several limitations remain. The evaluation is restricted to CIFAR-10, which limits the generalizability of the conclusions to larger and more complex datasets. Additionally, reliance on standard attacks (FGSM, PGD) does not fully rule out gradient masking, and adaptive attacks may reduce defense effectiveness. The observed sensitivity to noise distribution further indicates that the model has not yet learned a fully generalized denoising mechanism.

Future work should extend evaluation to more complex datasets (e.g., CIFAR-100, Tiny-ImageNet) and diverse real-world scenarios. Stronger attacks, such as AutoAttack, should be used alongside a broader range of perturbation levels to ensure a comprehensive assessment. Furthermore, integrating image quality metrics (e.g., SSIM, PSNR) and inference latency will provide a more complete evaluation of the trade-off between effectiveness and efficiency. Finally, combining the approach with advanced generative models, such as diffusion-based methods, is a promising direction for improving restoration quality and practical applicability.

References

1. Zhang, K., Zuo, W., Chen, Y., Meng, D., Zhang, L.: Beyond a Gaussian Denoiser: residual learning of deep CNN for image Denoising. IEEE Trans. Image Process. **26**, 3142–3155 (2017). https://doi.org/10.1109/TIP.2017.2662206
2. Vincent, P., Larochelle, H., Bengio, Y., Manzagol, P.-A.: Extracting and composing robust features with denoising autoencoders. In: Proceedings of the 25th International Conference on Machine Learning - ICML '08, pp. 1096–1103. Helsinki, Finland (2008). https://doi.org/10.1145/1390156.1390294
3. Ronneberger, O., Fischer, P., Brox, T.: U-Net: Convolutional Networks for Biomedical Image Segmentation. In: Medical Image Computing and Computer-Assisted Intervention – MICCAI 2015, pp. 234–241. Springer International Publishing, Cham (2015)

4. Woo, S., Park, J., Lee, J.-Y., Kweon, I.S.: CBAM: Convolutional Block Attention Module. In: Computer Vision – ECCV 2018: 15th European Conference, Part VII, pp. 3–19 (2018). https://doi.org/10.1007/978-3-030-01234-2_1
5. Goodfellow, I.J., Shlens, J., Szegedy, C.: Explaining and Harnessing Adversarial Examples. arXiv. (2014)
6. Mądry, A., Makelov, A., Schmidt, L., Tsipras, D., Vladu, A.: Towards Deep Learning Models Resistant to Adversarial Attacks. arXiv. (2017)
7. Sự, T.Đ., Dũng, N.T., Khanh, Đ.D.: Proposed method to remove adversarial perturbation using generative model based on deep learning. TNU J. Sci. Technol. **229**, 95–102 (2024). https://doi.org/10.34238/tnu-jst.11486
8. Szegedy, C. et al.: Intriguing properties of neural networks. arXiv. (2014)
9. Ilyas, A., Santurkar, S., Tsipras, D., Engstrom, L., Tran, B., Madry, A.: Adversarial Examples Are Not Bugs, They Are Features. arXiv. (2019)
10. Lee, S., Lee, J.: Defensive denoising methods against adversarial attack. In: Proceedings of the KDD Deep Learning Day, pp. 1–4. London, UK (2018)
11. Wang, H., Wang, J., Yin, Z.: An Efficient Pre-processing Method to Eliminate Adversarial Effects. arXiv. (2019)
12. Samangouei, P., Kabkab, M., Chellappa, R.: Defense-GAN: Protecting Classifiers Against Adversarial Attacks Using Generative Models. arXiv. (2018)
13. Nie, W., Guo, B., Huang, Y., Xiao, C., Vahdat, A., Anandkumar, A.: Diffusion Models for Adversarial Purification. arXiv. (2022). https://doi.org/10.48550/ARXIV.2205.07460
14. Krizhevsky, A.: Learning Multiple Layers of Features from Tiny Images. Master's thesis, University of Toronto (2009)

AT-M-GNN: Adversarial Adaptive GNN Fraud Detector with Multi-granularity Aggregation and Dynamic Threshold

Qianhui Zheng and Yindong Chen(✉)

Shantou University, Shantou, China
ydchen@stu.edu.cn

Abstract. In recent years, fraud has become increasingly rampant, causing huge economic losses to society. Although graph neural networks (GNN) significantly enhance node representation capabilities by aggregating neighborhood information, fraudsters often undermine the performance of traditional GNN in abnormal behavior identification by forging neighbor relationships and feature distributions. In addition, the highly unbalanced distribution of fraud samples in practical applications also limits the generalization ability and detection performance of the model. To address these problems, we propose a deep graph neural network model (AT-M-GNN), which integrates neighbor selection and aggregation, adversarial training, and optimal threshold retrieval. By introducing a multi-scale guide node in the multi-relational graph to guide the selection and aggregation of neighbors, the feature consistency constraint is also strengthened. In addition, the adversarial learning mechanism and the threshold optimization strategy is innovatively combined to ensure the robustness of the model against the imbalance of the data classes.

Keywords: Fraud detection · Adversarial learning · Reinforcement learning · Dynamic threshold optimization

1 Introduction

With the popularity of the Internet, various types of fraud have become increasingly prevalent in real scenarios [1], such as false comments, fake accounts, and malicious websites. To identify suspicious entities in such multi-relational graphs, graph-based algorithms are widely used. In recent years, Graph neural Network (GNN) has gained great attention as an effective method for deep learning of graph data, and has become the mainstream method for graph-based fraud detection.

Fraud detection technology based on the graph neural network constructs a heterogeneous graph representation by abstracting entities into nodes and mapping relationships into edges, so as to use the multi-modal information of node features and topology structure to identify fraud patterns. For example, GraphSAGE [2] achieves efficient node representation learning by sampling

L. Ding et al. (Eds.): APWeb-WAIM 2026, LNCS 16993, pp. 559–571, 2027.
https://doi.org/10.1007/978-981-92-5693-8_35

neighbor nodes in the Review-User-Review graph for classification of fraudulent reviews; GraphRNN [3] captures the complex relationship between accounts in the Account graph through a generative model to achieve fake account detection; CARE-GNN [4] combines sensing mechanisms and relational modeling to improve the accuracy and robustness of fraud detection.

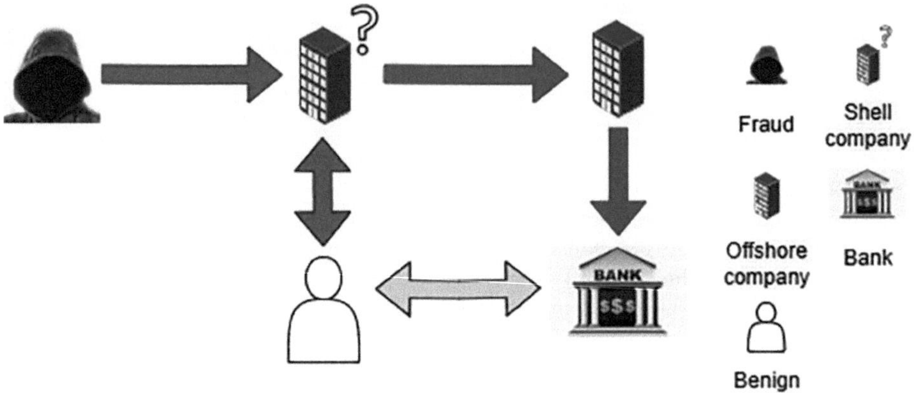

Fig. 1. Type II fraud camouflage: capital network relation disguise.

However, fraudsters often disguise themselves and mitigate suspicions by various means, such as blurring the characteristics and relationships of nodes in the graph to limit the effectiveness of fraud detectors. In financial transaction scenarios, fraudsters usually adopt two camouflage strategies to avoid risk detection. The first type is the disguise of transaction features. Fraudsters simulate normal transaction patterns, using high-frequency small transfers, time period dispersion operations, and even using generative adversarial networks (GAN) to synthesize transaction amounts and time intervals that conform to the normal distribution, resulting in temporal matching deviations between the transaction features of the nodes and risk labels. The second type is the disguise of capital network relationships(see Fig. 1). Fraudsters embed illegal capital flows into the normal enterprise trade network through methods such as nesting multiple shell companies and cross-border multi-hop settlement, forming a closed-loop transaction chain with topological structural camouflage, which leads to a mismatch between the capital flow and the embedding of the real business graph.

Adversarial learning is often seen as an effective way to improve the robustness of models. However, many defense methods can be bypassed by the corresponding attack strategies if the attacker has complete knowledge of the defense model [5,6]. According to recent research, robust graph neural networks are also vulnerable to adaptive attacks [7]. Adversarial modifications on graphs often destroy some inherent properties that real-world graphs possess, such as increasing heterogeneity [8] or focusing on graph embeddings [9]. Attackers can easily bypass defenses by imposing attribute constraints in the attack process. In addition, adversarial training on graph structures may cause the model to learn incorrect (feature, structure)-label mappings. In this context, [10] reexamines graph attacks and defenses from the perspective of OOD (Out-of-Distribution) and explores the trade-off between attack effectiveness and defensiveness.

The method of using adversarial example edge (OOD) to enhance the robustness of GNN has been considered as a promising fraud detection method. However, our theoretical analysis shows that it is difficult to effectively improve the robustness of GNN based only on adversarial edge detection. In actual attacks, the joint perturbation of the feature and structure is more common, and it is difficult to deal with complex attack scenarios by simply defending the structural perturbation. At the same time, in real applications, the distribution of normal edges and adversarial edges may overlap, which makes it difficult to accurately define the "normal distribution" boundary.

In order to improve the robustness of GNN, researchers have proposed other defense strategies. For example, RGCN [11] effectively captures the structural information in multi-relational graphs to improve the robustness by introducing relational graph convolution; SimPGCN [12] uses the similarity of node representations for smoothing to enhance the resistance of the model to disturbances; GNN-Jaccard [8] adjusts edge weights based on Jaccard similarity of node features to reduce the impact of adversarial edges; GNNGuard [13] effectively identifies and filters potential adversarial edges through a screening mechanism based on the consistency of neighbor node features; ElasticGNN [14] combines the sparsity and low-rank of the graph through elastic regularization to effectively alleviate the structural disturbance caused by adversarial attacks.

All of these methods are based on the inherent properties of graphs. Although it improves the robustness of GNN to some extent, these methods often rely on the inherent characteristics of graphs, so they are vulnerable to the threat of adaptive attacks and show great vulnerability. DiG-in-GNN [15] attempts to alleviate the problem of feature and structure inconsistency by introducing the neighbor selection strategy of multi-scale contrastive learning and reinforcement learning, and ACR [16] attempts to alleviate the problem of feature and structure inconsistency through neighbor aggregation and node reweighting learning. However, it is still lacking the ability to deal with feature and structure inconsistency and data class imbalance scenarios. In order to solve this problem, we design an improved model. Attempting to address the deficiency of complex fraud camouflage and dynamic environment, we design a more efficient neighbor aggregation, a confrontation training strategy, and an optimal classification threshold selection mechanism, which can significantly enhance the ability and robustness of the model to identify diversified fraud on imbalanced data sets. The main contributions of our work are as follows:

- Based on multi-scale contrastive learning (including contextual and local levels) guided node generation strategy and reinforcement learning (RL) neighbor selection strategy, we combine neighbor aggregation with attention head weight adaptive learning to enhance the aggregation of beneficial neighbors, so as to enhance the adaptation ability of the fraud detector to the changes in node characteristics and relationships.

- We have introduced adversarial training and multi-index optimal threshold optimization to effectively improve the robustness and generalization ability of the fraud detector in the environment of data class imbalance.
- The experimental results of the model are better than the existing methods on multiple public data sets, which fully reflects the effectiveness and practical value of the improvement.

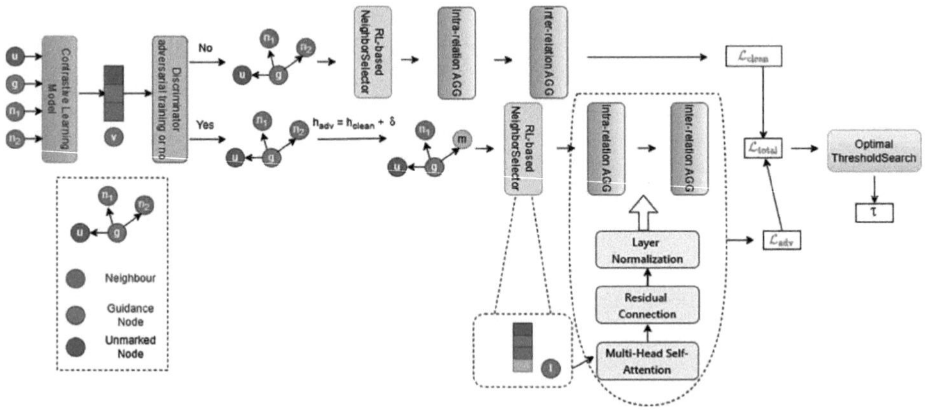

Fig. 2. The overall architecture of AT-M-GNN includes three core modules: neighbor aggregation, adversarial training, and optimal threshold retrieval.

2 Methodology

In this section, we introduce the proposed AT-M-GNN framework. We give an overview of the whole framework at the beginning. Then we introduce in detail the adversarial neighbor selection training process, the optimal threshold retrieval process, and the neighbor aggregation process, respectively.

2.1 Overview

This section describes our proposed AT-M-GNN in detail. The general structure of the framework is seen in Fig. 2 . As shown in the figure, it consists of the following parts: generation-guided node training, neighbor selection, neighbor aggregation, adversarial/normal training, and optimal threshold retrieval. To prevent the model from overly focusing on adversarial samples while neglecting normal ones, we adopt an alternating training approach, switching the training mode every F epochs and alternating between normal training and adversarial training to generate the total loss. That is,

$$\mathcal{L}_{\text{total}} = \mathcal{L}_{\text{clean}} + \lambda \cdot \mathcal{L}_{\text{adv}} \tag{1}$$

where λ is the weight of the adversarial loss. It is used to balance the proportion between standard training and adversarial training. We then automatically select the optimal classification threshold to achieve the best classification performance and robustness of the model in practical applications.

2.2 Neighbor Selection With Adversarial Learning

To address topology camouflage and feature disturbance issues in fraud detection, we design a neighbor selection framework integrated with adversarial learning. This framework aims to dynamically identify informative neighbors while improving the robustness of feature aggregation against adversarial perturbations. By introducing reward-guided neighbor selection and adversarial training in a unified optimization process, our model can suppress misleading camouflaged edges and maintain stable representation learning even under complicated fraudster interference.

Let the node embedding be $h \in \mathbb{R}^d$ (d is the embedding dimension) and the clean sample embedding be h_{clean}. The adversarial disturbance is $\delta \in \mathbb{R}^d$, and the constraint of the amplitude of the disturbance is satisfied $\|\delta\|_\infty \leq \epsilon$: ($\delta$ is the maximum disturbance range); The loss function of the classification of the model is $\mathcal{L}(h, y)$, where y denotes the node label. Adversarial examples are included as:

$$\text{h}_{adv} = \text{h}_{\text{clean}} + \delta \tag{2}$$

Firstly, normal forward propagation is performed on the original input node to obtain clean embedding and basis loss. Compute clean embeddings as $\text{h}_{\text{clean}}=$ Encoder(nodes) (where Encoder is the GNN embedding generation module, such as the inter1 aggregator in the code); The clean sample loss is calculated as:

$$\mathcal{L}_{clean} = \mathcal{L}_{gnn}(h_{clean}, y) + \alpha \cdot \mathcal{L}_{reward} \tag{3}$$

where $\mathcal{L}_{gnn}$ is the loss in the classification of the nodes, $\mathcal{L}_{reward}$ is the reward loss, and α is the reward loss weight.

To guide reinforced neighbor selection, the reward loss $\mathcal{L}_{reward}$ is defined as:

$$\mathcal{L}_{\text{reward}} = -\frac{1}{N}\sum_{i=1}^{N}\left(\text{Attn}_{\text{valid}}(i) \cdot \text{Sim}(h_i, \mathcal{N}_i) - \text{Attn}_{\text{invalid}}(i) \cdot \text{Sim}(h_i, \mathcal{N}_i)\right) \tag{4}$$

where $\text{Attn}_{\text{valid}}(i)$ and $\text{Attn}_{\text{invalid}}(i)$ denote the attention weights assigned to informative and camouflaged neighbors of node i, respectively, and $\text{Sim}(h_i, \mathcal{N}_i)$ measures the feature consistency between node i and its selected neighborhood.

The reward loss provides explicit supervision for the neighbor selection policy, encouraging the model to assign higher weights to discriminative neighbors while suppressing misleading edges. By jointly optimizing $\mathcal{L}_{gnn}$ and $\mathcal{L}_{reward}$, the model learns robust node embeddings that are resistant to topological perturbations and feature camouflage in adversarial training.

Then, projective gradient descent is used to generate adversarial perturbations, and the adversarial loss is maximized via multi-step iteration. The perturbation is initialized first and a random initial perturbation is added to the clean embedding, and use clip to ensure the initial perturbation is within the legal range:

$$\begin{aligned} \delta_0 &\sim U([-\epsilon, \epsilon]^d) \\ h_{\text{adv},0} &= h_{\text{clean}} + \text{clip}(\delta_0, -\epsilon, \epsilon) \end{aligned} \tag{5}$$

Then iteratively update the perturbation. For t = 1,2,... T (T is the number of iterations), calculate the loss gradient of the current adversarial sample (in the direction of loss increase): $\nabla_{\mathbf{h}} \mathcal{L}_{\text{gnn}}(h_{\text{adv},t-1}, y)$; Update the perturbation along the gradient direction (with a step size of ϵ/T):

$$\delta_t = \delta_{t-1} + \frac{\epsilon}{T} \cdot \text{sign}\left(\nabla_h \mathcal{L}_{\text{gnn}}(h_{\text{adv},t-1}, y)\right) \tag{6}$$

project the perturbation into the sphere:

$$\begin{aligned} \delta_t &= \text{clip}(\delta_t, -\epsilon, \epsilon) \\ h_{\text{adv},t} &= h_{\text{clean}} + \delta_t \end{aligned} \tag{7}$$

After that, the adversarial embedding $h_{\text{adv},t}$ obtained by the final iteration is used to calculate the adversarial loss:

$$\mathcal{L}_{\text{adv}} = \mathcal{L}_{\text{gnn}}(h_{\text{adv},T}, y) + \alpha \cdot \mathcal{L}_{\text{reward}} \tag{8}$$

then clean sample loss and adversarial sample loss are combined as the final training loss(see formula 1)(the model parameters are updated by minimizing gradient descent $\mathcal{L}_{\text{total}}$).

2.3 Neighbor Aggregation

We design a neighbor aggregation method based on multi-head attention mechanism. By introducing temperature parameter adjustment, adaptive learning of attention head weight and gating features, combined with residual connection and layer normalization, we achieve more accurate and robust neighbor feature aggregation, and improve the expressive power and discrimination of node representation.

Firstly, for a given input feature matrix $X \in \mathbb{R}^{B \times L \times d_q}$ (where B is the batch size, L is the sequence length of the node and d_q is the dimension of the input feature), EMHA(Extended Multi-Head Attention) first maps the input feature X into the query, key and value space by three sets of linear layers independently learnable. We generate $Q \in \mathbb{R}^{B \times L \times d_k}$, $K \in \mathbb{R}^{B \times L \times d_k}$, $V \in \mathbb{R}^{B \times L \times d_v}$, Q/K/V is the feature dimension, and satisfies $d_k = h \cdot d_{\text{head}}$, h is the number of attention heads, d_{head} is the single head dimension, $d_v$is the V feature dimension); Then, Q, K, V are split according to the number of heads h, and the dimension transpose is performed (the head dimension is advanced) to obtain the local features of each head $Q_i, K_i, V_i \in \mathbb{R}^{B \times h \times L \times d_{\text{head}}}$ to adapt to the multi-head parallel attention calculation.

Then, the operation of the dot product scaling is performed on the local characteristics of each head Q_i, K_i, and the temperature parameter τ is introduced to dynamically adjust the smoothness of the attention distribution, and the original attention score is calculated as:

$$S_i \in \mathbb{R}^{B \times h \times L \times L}$$
$$S_i = \frac{Q_i \cdot K_i^\top}{\sqrt{d_{\text{head}}} \cdot \tau} \tag{9}$$

If there are invalid neighbors, the score of invalid locations is set to -10^9through the mask matrix to avoid invalid associations interfering with attention allocation. The GELU function is applied to the original attention score S_i(gradient information is retained through a smooth non-linear transformation to alleviate the disappearance of gradients), and adaptive head weights α_i are combined as:

$$\alpha_i = \frac{\exp(w_i)}{\sum_{i=1}^{h} \exp(w_i)} \tag{10}$$

that is, weighted to generate weighted scores $\widehat{S}_i$. Subsequently, Softmax normalization is performed on the dimension of the sequence that runs along $\widehat{S}_i$ to obtain the final weight matrix of attention $Attn_i \in \mathbb{R}^{B \times h \times L \times L}$, which ensures that the sum of the weights of each of each weights.

Then, we perform matrix multiplication on the normalized attention weights $Attn_i$ and the value features V_i of the corresponding heads to achieve local value feature aggregation based on attention weights, obtaining the aggregated features $Z_i \in \mathbb{R}^{B \times h \times L \times d_{head}}$ of each head. We then perform dimension transposition and concatenation on Z_i across all heads, restore the feature dimension to $\mathbb{R}^{B \times L \times d_v}$, and project it onto the target dimension through the output linear layer to generate the global attention output $O \in \mathbb{R}^{B \times L \times d_v}$. Next, we construct a gating network composed of a linear layer and a Sigmoid activation function. Taking O as input, we learn the gating weight $G \in \mathbb{R}^{B \times L \times d_v}$, whose value range is $[0, 1]$. The gating weight is defined as:

$$G = \sigma(W_g \cdot O + b_g) \tag{11}$$

where W_g and b_g are the learnable parameters of the gating network, and $\sigma(\cdot)$ denotes the Sigmoid function. Based on the learned gating weight G, we perform element-wise weighted fusion of the global attention output O with the original input X. The fusion operation is formulated as:

$$Y = G \odot O + (1 - G) \odot X \tag{12}$$

where $\odot$ represents the element-wise product. This operation dynamically balances the information contribution ratio of the attention output to the original input, generating the intermediate features $Y \in \mathbb{R}^{B\times L\times d_v}$.

Finally, the original input X and intermediate feature Y were superimposed through the residual connection to construct an "input-output" direct gradient path to alleviate the problem of gradient disappearance in deep networks. Then, layer normalization is performed on the superposition results along the feature dimension, and the feature distribution is standardized to mean 0 and variance 1 to eliminate the influence of feature distribution offset on subsequent calculations. Finally, the EMHA aggregation output $Output_{EMHA} \in \mathbb{R}^{B\times L\times d_v}$ is generated, and the end-to-end neighbor feature aggregation process is completed.

Table 1. Details of the dataset

Datasets	Nodes	Edges	Feature dimension	Positive sample ratio (%)	Quantity of relationship types
Amazon	11,944	4,398,392	25	6.87	3
YelpChi	45,954	3,846,979	32	4.25	3
Tfinance	39,357	21,222,543	10	2.32	1

2.4 Multi-index Joint Threshold Optimization

To solve the problem of data class imbalance, we propose a multi-index joint threshold optimization strategy to automatically retrieve the optimal classification threshold. The specific process is as follows: traverse different thresholds on the validation set, jointly optimize F1-macro, G-mean and other indicators, and the threshold with the highest comprehensive score is used as the final classification threshold. This strategy can optimize the decision boundary of the model and improve the robustness of the model.

In the node classification task, let the positive class probability output by the model be $y_{prob}$and the true label be y_{true}. There are K evaluation metrics, namely $Metric_1$, $Metric_2$, $\ldots Metric_k$, whose weights are w_1, w_2, $\ldots$, w_k, satisfied $\sum_{k=1}^{K} w_k = 1$. For any threshold τ, the prediction label of the model is: $y_{\text{pred}}(\tau) = I(y_{\text{prob}} \geq \tau)$, where I() is the indicator function. The multi-metric weighted score is defined as:

$$\text{Score}(\tau) = \sum_{k=1}^{K} w_k \cdot \text{Metric}_k(y_{\text{true}}, y_{\text{pred}}(\tau)) \tag{13}$$

The final optimal threshold $\tau^*$is chosen as:

$$\tau^* = \arg\max_{\tau\in T} \text{Score}(\tau) \tag{14}$$

where T is the set of candidate thresholds.

By adjusting the classification threshold τ, the model achieved the best performance under the weighted combination of multiple performance indicators.

3 Experiment

In this section, we investigate the effectiveness of the proposed AT-M-GNN model through experiments to answer the following research questions:

- RQ1 Does AT-M-GNN outperform state-of-the-art fraud anomaly detection methods based on relational graphs?
- RQ2 Do the key features benefit the model's predictions?

3.1 Experimental Setup

Datasets. We selected three representative real datasets, namely YelpChi, Amazon and T-Finance, to comprehensively evaluate the performance of the model in multi-graph and single-graph scenarios. YelpChi: It contains users and review nodes and constructs three types of heterogeneous edges, R-U-R (user behavior correlation), R-S-R (rating similarity), and R-T-R (time correlation), which are suitable for review spam detection tasks. Amazon: The user relationship network is constructed by musical instrument product reviews, including U-P-U (common browsing), U-S-U (score synchronization), and U-V-U (feature similarity) edge types, reflecting the complex interactions of e-commerce users. T-Finance: The financial transaction network contains account nodes and transfer/device sharing relationships, with extreme class imbalance characteristics (positive and negative sample ratio 1:200), which is used to verify the robustness of financial fraud detection. The three datasets cover social network, e-Commerce and financial transaction scenarios, respectively, and contain multiple characteristics such as heterogeneous/homogeneous graph structure, balanced/unbalanced data distribution, which can comprehensively verify the generalization ability of the model in different application scenarios. The details of these three datasets are shown in Table 1.

Table 2. Performance comparison of different methods on three datasets. The underlined values denote the best results among all comparison experiments for the corresponding evaluation metric.

Method	Dataset	YelpChi			Amazon			T-Finance		
	Metric	AUC	F1-macro	Gmean	AUC	F1-macro	Gmean	AUC	F1-macro	Gmean
GCN (ICLR'17)		0.5983	0.5620	0.4365	0.8369	0.6408	0.5718	0.9176	0.8828	0.8402
GAT (ICLR'18)		0.5715	0.4879	0.1659	0.8102	0.6464	0.6675	0.9553	0.9059	0.8636
CARE-GNN (CIKM'20)		0.7619	0.6332	0.6791	0.9067	0.8890	0.8962	0.9014	0.8778	0.8038
RioGNN (TOIS'21)		0.8238	0.6526	0.7508	0.9558	0.8848	0.9012	0.9456	0.7945	0.8614
PC-GNN (WWW'21)		0.7987	0.6300	0.7160	0.9586	0.8956	0.9030	0.9272	0.8734	0.7967
AO-GNN (WWW'22)		0.8805	0.7042	0.8134	0.9640	0.8921	0.9096	–	–	–
GTAN (AAAI'23)		0.9108	0.8037	0.7768	0.9736	0.9230	0.9203	0.9641	0.9086	0.8720
GHRN (WWW'23)		0.8957	0.7622	0.7703	0.9649	0.9111	0.9002	0.9601	0.8942	0.8552
DiG-In-GNN (AAAI'24)		0.9348	0.8154	0.8407	0.9778	0.9251	0.9214	0.9651	0.9112	0.8916
ACR (ICASSP'25)		0.8662	0.7343	0.7207	–	–	–	0.9583	0.9175	0.8709
Ablation	AT-M-GNN$_{AT}$	0.9352	0.8110	0.8422	0.9792	0.9267	0.9207	0.9648	0.9170	0.8920
	AT-M-GNN$_{M}$	0.9359	0.8028	0.8475	0.9791	0.9266	0.9365	0.9646	0.9193	0.9155
Ours (AT-M-GNN)		0.9396	0.8223	0.8470	0.9838	0.9267	0.9372	0.9661	0.9194	0.9183

Comparison Method. We compare our model with classical models and several state-of-the-art graph neural network fraud detection models: GCN [17], GAT [18], CARE-GNN [4], RioGNN [19], PC-GNN [20], AO-GNN [21], GTAN [22], GHRN [23], DiG-In-GNN [15] and ACR [16]. AT-M-GNN$_{AT}$ removes adversarial training and AT-M-GNN$_{M}$ removes multi-index joint threshold optimization. This model comparison experiment method uses the code published by the author.

Experimental Parameter Setting and Implementation. Adam optimizer is used to update the parameters in all experiments, the base learning rate is set to 0.003, and the learning rate for the GNN backbone is 0.005. The node embedding dimension is unified to 128, the dataset is split according to the ratio of 40% training set, 20% validation set and 40% test set. To balance the models ability to learn normal features and resist perturbed samples, the two training methods of the model were carried out alternately, and the alternating period was set to 7 epochs. In the multi-index joint threshold optimization, F1-macro, G-mean and other indicators are used for weighted joint optimization on the validation set. The threshold search interval is set as [0.2, 0.8] with a step size of 0.005. Finally, the threshold with the highest comprehensive score is selected for the classification decision in the test phase. This strategy ensures that the model can obtain optimal performance under extreme imbalance of data categories.

Evaluation Index. Due to the imbalance of data classes, in this article three representative evaluation metrics are selected, which are the F1-macro, the G-mean, and the AUC.

Sensitivity Analysis. In order to verify the sensitivity of AT-M-GNN to hyperparameters ϵ and λ, we conducted experiments in YelpChi and Amazon datasets, as shown in Fig. 3. We perform hyperparameter selection on perturbation strength ϵ and adversarial loss weight λ by grid search, and the results show that AT-M-GNN is not highly sensitive to changes in ϵ and λ. AT-M-GNN achieves good AUC values when ϵ and λ are about 0.45 and 0.6 on Amazon and 0.6 and 0.5 on YelpChi, respectively. These results indicate that AT-M-GNN is insensitive to various hyperparameters.

3.2 Performance Comparison (RQ1)

Traditional graph neural network-based detection models suffer from limited performance because of severe data class imbalance, whereas adversarial training models specifically designed for fraud detection demonstrate superior effectiveness, highlighting the importance of adversarial training in this domain. However, existing adversarial training algorithms primarily defend against either structural or feature-based attacks in isolation, failing to account for fraudsters' simultaneous manipulation of both node features and relational patterns, which

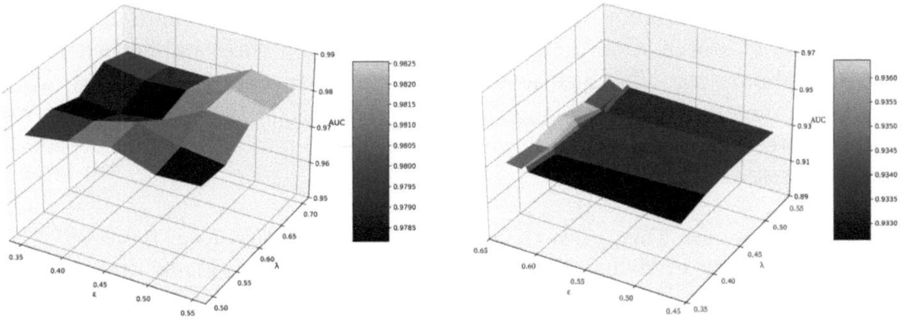

Fig. 3. Sensitivity analysis of AT-M-GNN on the hyperparameters ϵ and λ on the Amazon (left) and YelpChi (right) datasets.

limits their robustness in realistic scenarios. In contrast, AT-M-GNN integrates an adversarial training mechanism and a threshold optimization strategy into multi-scale guide node design and feature consistency enforcement, which solves the problem that the distribution of normal edges and adversarial edges overlap, which makes it difficult to accurately define the normal distribution boundary, so that the performance of the proposed method exceeds that of the previous state-of-the-art methods. Table 2 presents the comparison of AT-M-GNN performance with the baseline model, and the model achieves significantly improved performance across all metrics on all three datasets.

3.3 Ablation Experiment (RQ2)

To verify the effectiveness of AT + MMTO in the model, we designed two ablation studies for AT-M-GNN, AT-M-GNN$_{AT}$in Table 2 achieves the performance without the adversarial training module, and AT-M-GNN$_{M}$achieves that performance without the multi-index joint threshold optimization module. It can be seen that the two modules already achieve good performance when used individually, and combining the two modules together yields even better results. In the case of G-mean, AT-M-GNN achieves an improvement of 1.6% and 2.7% on the Amazon and T-Finance datasets, respectively. The above experiments show that adversarial training and threshold optimization can effectively improve the performance of fraud detector.

4 Conclusions

In this paper, we propose a dynamic graph adversarial multiple attention fraud detector for multiple relational graphs. AT-M-GNN effectively address the problems of structure-feature inconsistency and data sample imbalance via guided nodes, enhanced neighbor aggregation, adversarial learning, and multi-index joint threshold search. Comprehensive experiments on three public benchmark datasets validate the effectiveness of our proposed approach. For future work, integrating heterogeneous multimodal data into AT-M-GNN to improve the model's detection performance in complex fraud scenarios could be a promising future research direction.

Acknowledgments. This research was supported by the Key Research Platforms and Projects of Higher Education Institutions in Guangdong Province (No. 2024ZDZX1021), the Basic and Applied Basic Research Foundation of Guangdong Province, China (No. 2025A1515012156).

References

1. Jiang, M., Cui, P., Faloutsos, C.: Suspicious behavior detection: current trends and future directions. IEEE Intell. Syst. **31**(1), 31–39 (2016)
2. Hamilton, W.L., Ying, R., Leskovec, J.: Inductive representation learning on large graphs. In: Proceedings of the 31st International Conference on Neural Information Processing Systems, NeurIPS 2017, pp. 1025–1035. Curran Associates Inc (2017)
3. You, J., Ying, R., Ren, X., Hamilton, W., Leskovec, J.: GraphRNN: generating realistic graphs with deep auto-regressive models. In: Dy, J., Krause, A. (eds.) Proceedings of the 35th International Conference on Machine Learning, Volume 80 of Proceedings of Machine Learning Research, pp. 5708–5717. PMLR (2018)
4. Dou, Y., Liu, Z., Sun, L., Deng, Y., Peng, H., Yu, P.S.: Enhancing graph neural network-based fraud detectors against camouflaged fraudsters. In: Proceedings of the 29th ACM International Conference on Information and Knowledge Management (CIKM 2020) (2020)
5. Goodfellow, J., Shlens, J., Szegedy, C.: Explaining and harnessing adversarial examples. In: International Conference on Learning Representations. ICLR 2015, (2015)
6. Kurakin, A., Boneh, D., Tramèr, F., Goodfellow, I., Papernot, N., McDaniel, P.: Ensemble adversarial training: attacks and defenses. In: International Conference on Learning Representations. ICLR 2018 (2018)
7. Dai, H., Li, H., Tian, T., Huang, X., Wang, L., Zhu, J., Song, L.: Adversarial attack on graph structured data. In: Proceedings of the 35th International Conference on Machine Learning, ICML 2018, Stockholmsmässan, Stockholm, Sweden, July 10–15, 2018, Volume 80 of Proceedings of Machine Learning Research, pp. 1123–1132. PMLR (2018)
8. Zügner, D., Günnemann, S.: Adversarial attacks on graph neural networks via meta learning. In: 7th International Conference on Learning Representations. ICLR 2019, (2019)
9. Bojchevski, A., Günnemann, S.: Adversarial attacks on node embeddings via graph poisoning. In: Proceedings of the 36th International Conference on Machine Learning, ICML, Proceedings of Machine Learning Research. PMLR (2019)
10. Li, K., Chen, Y., Liu, Y., Wang, J., He, Q., Cheng, M., Ao, X.: Boosting the adversarial robustness of graph neural networks: an ood perspective. In: The Twelfth International Conference on Learning Representations. ICLR 2024 (2024)

11. Schlichtkrull, M., Kipf, T.N., Bloem, P., van den Berg, R., Titov, I., Welling, M.: Modeling relational data with graph convolutional networks. In: Gangemi, A., Navigli, R., Vidal, M.-E., Hitzler, P., Troncy, R., Hollink, L., Tordai, A., Alam, M. (eds.) ESWC 2018. LNCS, vol. 10843, pp. 593–607. Springer, Cham (2018). https://doi.org/10.1007/978-3-319-93417-4_38
12. Chen, M., Wei, Z., Huang, Z., Ding, B., Li, Y.: Simple deep graph convolutional networks. In: Proceedings of the 37th International Conference on Machine Learning, ICML 2020. JMLR.org (2020)
13. Zhang, X., Zitnik, M.: GNNguard: defending graph neural networks against adversarial attacks. In: NeurIPS 2020 (2020)
14. Liu, X., Jin, W., Ma, Y., Li, Y., Liu, H., Wang, Y., Yan, M., Tang, J.: Elastic graph neural networks. In: Proceedings of the 38th International Conference on Machine Learning, Proceedings of Machine Learning Research. PMLR (2021)
15. Zhang, J., Xu, Z., Lv, Zhan, D., Shi, Shen, D., Jin, J., Dong, F.: Dig-In-GNN: discriminative feature guided GNN-based fraud detector against inconsistencies in multi-relation fraud graph. In: AAAI Conference on Artificial Intelligence, AAAI 24, pp. 9323–9331. AAAI Press (2024)
16. Gao, J., Cao, J., Qian, S., Guan, W.: Enhancing graph-based fraud detection by adversarial confidence reweighting. In: 2025 IEEE International Conference on Acoustics, Speech and Signal Processing (ICASSP 2025), pp. 1–5 (2025)
17. Kipf, T.N., Welling, M.: Semi-supervised classification with graph convolutional networks. In: 5th International Conference on Learning Representations. ICLR 2017 (2017)
18. Veličković, P., Cucurull, G., Casanova, A., Romero, A., Liò, P., Bengio, Y.: Graph attention networks. In: 6th International Conference on Learning Representations. ICLR 2018 (2018)
19. Peng, H., Zhang, R., Dou, Y., Yang, R., Zhang, J., Philip, S.Y.: Reinforced neighborhood selection guided multi-relational graph neural networks. ACM Trans. Inf. Syst. **40**(4), 1–20 (2021)
20. Liu, Y., Ao, X., Qin, Z., Chi, J., Feng, J., Yang, H., He, Q.: Pick and choose: a GNN-based imbalanced learning approach for fraud detection. In: Proceedings of the Web Conference 2021, WWW 21, pp. 3168–3177 (2021)
21. Huang, M., Liu, Y., Ao, X., Li, K., Chi, J., Feng, J., Yang, H., He, Q.: AUC-oriented graph neural network for fraud detection. In: Proceedings of the ACM Web Conference 2022, WWW 22, pp. 1311–1321 (2022)
22. Xiang, S., Zhu, M., Cheng, D., Li, E., Zhao, R., Ouyang, Y., Chen, L., Zheng, Y.: Semi-supervised credit card fraud detection via attribute-driven graph representation. In: Proceedings of the AAAI Conference on Artificial Intelligence (2023)
23. Gao, Y., Wang, X., He, X., Liu, Z., Feng, H., Zhang, Y.: Addressing heterophily in graph anomaly detection: a perspective of graph spectrum. In: Proceedings of the ACM Web Conference, vol. 23, pp. 1528–1538. WWW (2023)

Efficient Revocable Identity-Based Inner Product Functional Encryption Based on SM9

Zinan Shen[1], Zhaoyu Chen[1], Wu Xin[1(✉)], Zhangti Li[2], Yahui Zhao[2], Cong Li[1(✉)], and Zhonghai Wu[1]

[1] Peking University, Beijing, China
{sznnzs,xinwu,li.cong,wuzh}@pku.edu.cn, chenzhaoyu@stu.pku.edu.cn
[2] Chinaunicom Software, Beijing, China
{lizt21,zhaoyh99}@chinaunicom.cn

Abstract. As a national and also ISO/IEC standard concerning identity-based cryptosystem, SM9 plays a significant role in numerous applications. Motivated by the fact that the decryption in SM9 merely offers all-or-nothing access to the plaintext, Li et al. proposed a hierarchical identity-based broadcast inner product functional encryption from SM9. It supports inner product operations and one-to-many access control mechanism simultaneously. Nevertheless, it cannot support scenarios in which user keys need to be revoked. Existing indirect revocation mechanisms based on periodic key and ciphertext updates suffer from severe scalability problems in large-scale cloud environments. To address this, we integrate TEE technology to replace the conventional time-slice-driven update mechanism, obtaining a user-revocable inner product functional encryption scheme, called HR-IP-SM9. We formalize security models for both schemes and prove their security under the (q, n)-DBDHI assumption in the random oracle model. Theoretical analysis and experimental results consistently show that HR-IP-SM9 outperforms existing SM9-based revocable encryption schemes in both encryption and decryption efficiency.

1 Introduction

Although SM9-based cryptography attracts growing attention, efficient user revocation remains challenging in large-scale data sharing and cloud storage. Indirect revocation [3,16] embeds timestamps into ciphertexts while the KGC periodically updates non-revoked users' keys, and ciphertext delegation [15] further lets servers update ciphertext timestamps to prevent historical data access. However, massive user and ciphertext scales render these periodic updates computationally and communicatively expensive.

Trusted Execution Environments (TEEs) offer a new solution by providing an isolated enclave on an untrusted host for secure execution without costly

Zinan Shen and Zhaoyu Chen have contributed equally to this work.

L. Ding et al. (Eds.): APWeb-WAIM 2026, LNCS 16993, pp. 572–588, 2027.
https://doi.org/10.1007/978-981-92-5693-8_36

cryptographic updates. Motivated by this, we introduce TEE into SM9-based identity-based inner product functional encryption, replacing traditional time-slice updates with a TEE-assisted revocation mechanism.

Given the constrained resources of TEEs and clients, we further incorporate a two-stage outsourced decryption technique [12]. As shown in Fig. 1, the user's private key is split into a transformation key, a helper key, and a decryption key. The cloud server performs the heavy operations (pairings, exponentiations) to produce a partially transformed ciphertext. The TEE then checks the revocation list; for a non-revoked user, it applies the helper key to produce a further transformed ciphertext. Finally, the user decrypts with the decryption key. This design offloads the main cost to the cloud, leaving only lightweight operations to the TEE and client, achieving efficiency and fine-grained revocation.

Our scheme differs from prior TEE-based revocable encryption in two aspects. First, legacy time-slice schemes [10,17] incur bandwidth proportional to user and ciphertext populations due to periodic updates; conversely, our scheme leverages the TEE as an online verifier checking membership via a compact sMHT root, eliminating per-interval re-encryption or broadcasts. Second, partitioning decryption into cloud, TEE, and client stages restricts enclave operations to a constant cost (two G_T exponentiations and one Merkle-path verification), ensuring practicality even on resource-constrained enclaves.

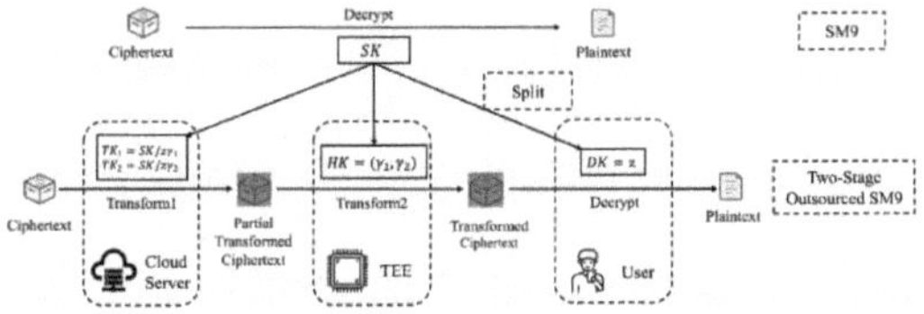

Fig. 1. Schematic comparison of SM9 and the two-stage outsourced decryption variant.

The main contributions of this paper are summarized as follows.

- We propose IP-SM9-2OD, an SM9-based inner product functional encryption scheme with two-stage outsourced decryption. We define its security model and prove security under the (q, n)-DBDHI assumption in the random oracle model.
- Using IP-SM9-2OD as a building block, we construct HR-IP-SM9, a TEE-based revocable inner product functional encryption based on SM9. Under fully trusted and semi-trusted TEE models, we define threat models and formally prove its security.
- We evaluate HR-IP-SM9 against two SM9-based revocation baselines [10,17] via theoretical analysis and C++ benchmarks (runtime, key size, ciphertext size). Results show that both its encryption and decryption efficiencies outperform the baselines.

2 Design of IP-SM9-2OD

2.1 Formal Definition

We give the formal definition of an identity-based inner product functional encryption scheme with two-stage outsourced decryption (IB-IPFE-2OD). The scheme consists of six algorithms: Setup, KeyGen, Encrypt, Transform1, Transform2, and Decrypt.

Setup$(1^\lambda, l) \rightarrow (PP, MSK)$. The setup algorithm takes a security parameter λ and a maximum vector length l as input. It outputs public parameters PP and a master secret key MSK. The public parameters are broadcast to all users, and the master secret key is kept secret by the KGC.

KeyGen$(PP, MSK, ID, \mathbf{u}) \rightarrow (TK, HK, DK)$. The key generation algorithm takes the public parameters PP, the master secret key MSK, a user identity ID, and a vector $\mathbf{u} = (u_1, \ldots, u_l)$ as input. It outputs a key triple (TK, HK, DK), where TK is the transformation key, HK is the helper key, and DK is the decryption key.

Encrypt$(PP, ID, \mathbf{v}) \rightarrow CT$. The encryption algorithm takes the public parameters PP, a user identity ID, and a plaintext vector $\mathbf{v}$ as input. It outputs a ciphertext CT associated with ID and $\mathbf{v}$.

Transform1$(PP, TK, CT) \rightarrow PTC/\perp$. The first-stage transformation algorithm takes the public parameters PP, a transformation key TK, and a ciphertext CT as input. If the decrypting user's identity is consistent with the identity embedded in CT, the algorithm outputs a partial transformed ciphertext PTC; otherwise it outputs $\perp$.

Transform2$(PP, HK, PTC) \rightarrow TC/\perp$. The second-stage transformation algorithm takes the public parameters PP, a helper key HK, and a partial transformed ciphertext PTC as input. It outputs a transformed ciphertext TC or $\perp$.

Decrypt$(PP, SK, TC) \rightarrow \langle \mathbf{u}, \mathbf{v} \rangle/\perp$. The decryption algorithm takes the public parameters PP, a decryption key SK, and a transformed ciphertext TC as input. It outputs the inner product $\langle \mathbf{u}, \mathbf{v} \rangle$ or $\perp$.

For any security parameter λ, an IB-IPFE-2OD scheme is required to satisfy decryption correctness and transformation correctness. Decryption correctness requires that for any vectors $\mathbf{u}, \mathbf{v}$ in the vector space,

$$\Pr\left[\mathsf{Dec}(PP, SK, TC) = \langle \mathbf{u}, \mathbf{v} \rangle \;\middle|\; \begin{array}{l} (PP, MSK) \leftarrow \mathsf{Setup}(1^\lambda, l) \\ (TK, HK, DK) \leftarrow \mathsf{KeyGen}(PP, MSK, ID, \mathbf{u}) \\ CT \leftarrow \mathsf{Encrypt}(PP, ID, \mathbf{v}) \\ PTC \leftarrow \mathsf{Transform1}(PP, TK, CT) \\ TC \leftarrow \mathsf{Transform2}(PP, HK, PTC) \end{array}\right] \geq 1 - \mathsf{negl}(\lambda).$$

Transformation correctness is implied by decryption correctness, and requires that for any valid key triple (TK, HK, DK),

$$\Pr[\mathsf{Transform2}(PP, HK, PTC) = \perp] \leq \mathsf{negl}(\lambda).$$

2.2 Construction

We now present the concrete construction of IP-SM9-2OD. For convenience, we write H_{ID} as shorthand for $H(ID\|hid, p)$.

Setup$(1^\lambda, l) \to (PP, MSK)$. The setup algorithm first calls a group generation algorithm $\mathcal{G}(1^\lambda)$ to obtain an asymmetric bilinear group $D = (p, \mathbb{G}_1, \mathbb{G}_2, \mathbb{G}_T, e)$. It then selects group generators $g \in \mathbb{G}_1$ and $g_2 \in \mathbb{G}_2$, and samples $\alpha, \beta_1, \ldots, \beta_n \in \mathbb{Z}_p^*$ at random, letting $\boldsymbol{\beta} = (\beta_1, \ldots, \beta_l)$. The algorithm also selects two collision-resistant hash functions $H\colon \{0,1\}^* \times \mathbb{Z}_p^* \to \mathbb{Z}_p^*$ and $G\colon \{0,1\}^* \times \mathbb{Z}_p^* \to \mathbb{Z}_p^*$, together with a suitable private-key-generation function identifier hid. It computes $g_1 = g^\alpha$ and $\{g_2^{\beta_i}\}_{i\in[l]}$, and outputs the master secret key and the public parameters:

$$MSK = (\alpha, \boldsymbol{\beta}), \quad PP = \big(D,\, g,\, g_1,\, g_2,\, \{g_2^{\beta_i}\}_{i\in[l]},\, H,\, l,\, hid\big).$$

KeyGen$(PP, MSK, ID, \mathbf{u}) \to (TK, HK, DK)$. The key generation algorithm parses $PP = (D, g, g_1, g_2, \{g_2^{\beta_i}\}_{i\in[l]}, H, l, hid)$, $MSK = (\alpha, \boldsymbol{\beta})$, and $\mathbf{u} = (u_1, \ldots, u_l)$. It samples $z, \gamma_1, \gamma_2 \in \mathbb{Z}_p^*$ at random, sets $DK = z$ and $HK = (\gamma_1, \gamma_2)$, and computes $TK_i = g_2^{\frac{\alpha\langle\boldsymbol{\beta}, \mathbf{u}\rangle}{z\cdot\gamma_i\cdot(\alpha + H_{ID})}}$, $i \in \{1, 2\}$. The algorithm outputs $(TK = (\mathbf{u}, TK_1, TK_2),\ HK,\ DK)$.

Encrypt$(PP, ID, \mathbf{v}) \to CT$. The encryption algorithm parses PP and the plaintext vector $\mathbf{v} = (v_1, \ldots, v_l)$. It samples $s \in \mathbb{Z}_p^*$ at random and computes

$$C_1 = g_1^s \cdot g^{s\cdot H_{ID}}, \qquad C_{2,i} = e(g, g_2)^{v_i} \cdot e(g_1, g_2^{\beta_i})^s, \quad i \in [l].$$

The ciphertext is $CT = (C_1,\ \{C_{2,i}\}_{i\in[l]})$.

Transform1$(PP, TK, CT) \to PTC/\perp$. The algorithm first checks whether the decrypting user's identity matches the identity embedded in CT; if not, it returns $\perp$. Otherwise it parses $TK = (\mathbf{u}, TK_1, TK_2)$ and $CT = (C_1, \{C_{2,i}\}_{i\in[l]})$, and computes

$$CP_1 = e(C_1, TK_1), \quad CP_2 = e(C_1, TK_2), \quad CP_3 = \prod_{i\in[l]} C_{2,i}^{u_i}.$$

It outputs the partial transformed ciphertext $PTC = (CP_1, CP_2, CP_3)$.

Transform2$(PP, HK, PTC) \to TC/\perp$. The algorithm parses $HK = (\gamma_1, \gamma_2)$ and $PTC = (CP_1, CP_2, CP_3)$. It first checks whether $CP_1^{\gamma_1} = CP_2^{\gamma_2}$; if not, it returns $\perp$. Otherwise it computes and outputs $TC = \big(T_1 = CP_1^{\gamma_1},\ T_2 = CP_3\big)$.

Decrypt$(PP, DK, TC) \to \langle\mathbf{u}, \mathbf{v}\rangle/\perp$. The algorithm parses $DK = z$ and $TC = (T_1, T_2)$, and computes $W = \frac{T_2}{T_1^z}$. It then searches in the inner product space for a value θ satisfying $e(g, g_2)^\theta = W$. If such a θ exists, the algorithm outputs θ; otherwise it outputs $\perp$.

Algorithm 1. Security game for the IND-sIDV-CDA model.

1: $\mathcal{A}$ outputs ID^* and two challenge vectors $\mathbf{v}_0^*, \mathbf{v}_1^* \in \mathbb{Z}^l$ to $\mathcal{C}$.
2: $\mathcal{C}$ runs $(PP, MSK) \leftarrow \mathsf{Setup}(1^\lambda, l)$, gives PP to $\mathcal{A}$, initializes $TB \leftarrow \emptyset$, and sets $k \leftarrow 1$.

Phase 1. $\mathcal{A}$ adaptively issues the following queries:
– **Hash query:** $\mathcal{C}$ returns a random value.
– **KeyGen query** $(ID_k, \mathbf{u}_k)$: $\mathcal{C}$ computes $(TK_k, HK_k, DK_k) \leftarrow \mathsf{KeyGen}(PP, MSK, ID_k, \mathbf{u}_k)$, stores $TB[k] = (ID_k, \mathbf{u}_k, TK_k, HK_k, DK_k)$, returns TK_k, and sets $k \leftarrow k+1$.
– **DK query** i: if $TB[i]$ is undefined, return $\perp$; otherwise return DK_i.
– **Transform2 query** (i, PTC): if $TB[i]$ is undefined, return $\perp$; otherwise parse $TB[i] = (ID_i, \mathbf{u}_i, TK_i, HK_i, DK_i)$ and return $\mathsf{Transform2}(PP, HK_i, PTC)$.
Challenge. $\mathcal{C}$ chooses $b \leftarrow \{0,1\}$, computes $CT^* \leftarrow \mathsf{Encrypt}(PP, ID^*, \mathbf{v}_b^*)$, and sends CT^* to $\mathcal{A}$.
Phase 2. $\mathcal{A}$ continues to issue queries as in Phase 1, except that for any Transform2 query on index i, $\mathcal{C}$ returns $\perp$ if $ID_i = ID^*$ and $\langle \mathbf{u}_i, \mathbf{v}_0^* - \mathbf{v}_1^* \rangle \neq 0$.
Guess. $\mathcal{A}$ outputs $b' \in \{0,1\}$ and wins iff $b' = b$.

Algorithm 2. Security game for the IND-sIDV-CHA model.

1: $\mathcal{A}$ outputs a challenge identity ID^* and two challenge vectors $\mathbf{v}_0^*, \mathbf{v}_1^* \in \mathbb{Z}^l$ to $\mathcal{C}$.
2: $\mathcal{C}$ runs $(PP, MSK) \leftarrow \mathsf{Setup}(1^\lambda, l)$, gives PP to $\mathcal{A}$, initializes $TB \leftarrow \emptyset$, and sets $k \leftarrow 1$.

Phase 1. $\mathcal{A}$ adaptively issues the following queries:
– **Hash query:** $\mathcal{C}$ returns a random value.
– **KeyGen query** $(ID_k, \mathbf{u}_k)$: $\mathcal{C}$ computes $(TK_k, HK_k, DK_k) \leftarrow \mathsf{KeyGen}(PP, MSK, ID_k, \mathbf{u}_k)$, stores $TB[k] = (ID_k, \mathbf{u}_k, TK_k, HK_k, DK_k)$, returns TK_k, and sets $k \leftarrow k+1$.
– **Auxiliary-key query** i: if $TB[i]$ is undefined, return $\perp$; otherwise parse $TB[i] = (ID_i, \mathbf{u}_i, TK_i, HK_i, DK_i)$ and return HK_i.
– **Decryption-key query** i: if $TB[i]$ is undefined, or $ID_i = ID^*$ and $\langle \mathbf{u}_i, \mathbf{v}_0^* - \mathbf{v}_1^* \rangle \neq 0$, return $\perp$; otherwise parse $TB[i] = (ID_i, \mathbf{u}_i, TK_i, HK_i, DK_i)$ and return DK_i.
Challenge. $\mathcal{C}$ chooses $b \leftarrow \{0,1\}$, computes $CT^* \leftarrow \mathsf{Encrypt}(PP, ID^*, \mathbf{v}_b^*)$, and sends CT^* to $\mathcal{A}$.
Phase 2.$\mathcal{A}$ continues to issue queries as in Phase 1.
Guess.$\mathcal{A}$ outputs $b' \in \{0,1\}$ and wins iff $b' = b$.

2.3 Security Analysis

We first define two formal security models called IND-sIDV-CDA and IND-sIDV-CHA in Algorithms 1 and 2, which indicates that attackers without HK or DK learn nothing of the plaintext. We conclude the security analysis with the following theorem.

Definition 1. (Knowledge of Exponent Assumption, KEA [2]) *For any adversary $\mathcal{A}$ that takes $(g^{1/x}, g^{1/y})$ as input and outputs a pair (u, v) satisfying $u^x = v^y$, there exists an extractor $\mathcal{E}$ such that, on the same input as $\mathcal{A}$, $\mathcal{E}$*

outputs a value t satisfying $g^{t/x} = u$ and $g^{t/y} = v$. Formally, let

$$\mathsf{Adv}^{\mathsf{KEA}}_{\mathcal{A},\mathcal{E}}(1^\lambda) = \Pr\left[\mathcal{E}(g^{1/x}, g^{1/y}, g^{t/x}, g^{t/y}) \neq t\right].$$

The KEA assumption holds if for every adversary $\mathcal{A}$ there exists an extractor $\mathcal{E}$ and a negligible function ν such that $\mathsf{Adv}^{\mathsf{KEA}}_{\mathcal{A},\mathcal{E}}(1^\lambda) \leq \nu(\lambda)$.

Definition 2 ((q, n)-DBDHI Assumption) *Let $\mathbb{G} = (\mathbb{G}_1, \mathbb{G}_2, \mathbb{G}_T, e, p)$ be a bilinear group with generators $g \in \mathbb{G}_1$ and $g' \in \mathbb{G}_2$,* and let *$a, b, c \in \mathbb{Z}_p^*$ be random.*

Given the group elements $c,\ g,\ g^b,\ g^a,\ g^{a^2}, \ldots, g^{a^{n+1}},\ g',\ g'^b,\ g'^a,\ g'^{a^2}, \ldots, g'^{a^q},\ g'^{1/(a+c)^2},\ g'^{1/(a+c)^3}, \ldots, g'^{1/(a+c)^n}$ *and an element $T \in \mathbb{G}_T$, deciding whether $T = e(g, g')^{b/(a+c)}$ or $T = R$* for a random *$R \in \mathbb{G}_T$ is computationally hard.*

Theorem 1. *Let H be a random oracle controlled by $\mathcal{B}$, and let the (q, n)-DBDHI assumption be the input to $\mathcal{B}$. If the (q, n)-DBDHI assumption and the KEA assumption both hold, then IP-SM9-2OD is IND-sIDV-CDA secure in the random oracle model.*

Proof. Suppose there exists an adversary $\mathcal{A}$ that breaks IP-SM9-2OD with non-negligible advantage ϵ in the IND-sIDV-CDA game. We construct a simulator $\mathcal{B}$ that interacts with $\mathcal{A}$ to solve the (q, n)-DBDHI problem.

Initialization. $\mathcal{A}$ first submits a challenge identity pattern ID^* together with two challenge vectors $\mathbf{v}_0^* = (v_{0,1}, \ldots, v_{0,l})$ and $\mathbf{v}_1^* = (v_{1,1}, \ldots, v_{1,l})$ to $\mathcal{B}$.

Setup. $\mathcal{B}$ sets $c = H_{ID^*}$ and samples random values $w_2, \ldots, w_q, \phi_1, \ldots, \phi_l \in \mathbb{Z}_p^*$ (assumed pairwise distinct). It sets $g_1 = g^a$ and $g_2 = g'^\beta = g'^{(a+w_2)\cdots(a+w_q)}$, so implicitly $\alpha = a$ and $\beta = (a + w_2)\cdots(a + w_q) \pmod p$. For each $i \in [l]$, it sets $\beta_i = \phi_i(a + c) + (v_{0,i}^* - v_{1,i}^*)$. $\mathcal{B}$ then sends the public parameters to $\mathcal{A}$:

$$PP = \big(D,\ g,\ g_1,\ g_2,\ \{g_2^{\beta_i}\}_{i \in [l]},\ H,\ l,\ hid\big).$$

Query Phase 1. $\mathcal{A}$ issues polynomially many adaptive queries, which $\mathcal{B}$ answers as follows.

For a hash query on identity ID_i, $\mathcal{B}$ maintains a list L_H of identity-hash pairs. If ID_i is already in L_H, $\mathcal{B}$ returns the stored value. Otherwise, if $ID_i = ID^*$, it returns $h_i = H_{ID^*} = c$; if $ID_i \neq ID^*$, it assigns $h_i = w_j$ for a fresh index j and records (ID_i, h_i) in L_H.

For a key generation query on $(ID, \mathbf{u})$, $\mathcal{B}$ proceeds in three cases. If $ID \neq ID^*$, then $H(ID) = w_i$ for some $i \in [2, n]$ and the term $g_2^{\alpha\langle\boldsymbol{\beta}, \mathbf{u}\rangle/(\alpha + H_{ID})}$ can be computed from the available (q, n)-DBDHI instances; $\mathcal{B}$ then executes the full KeyGen procedure to produce a valid triple. If $ID = ID^*$ and $\langle \mathbf{u},\ \mathbf{v}_0^* - \mathbf{v}_1^* \rangle = 0$, the unknown factor $g'^{1/(a+c)}$ cancels in the exponent, so the required group element is again computable from the given instances, and $\mathcal{B}$ produces a valid triple. If $ID = ID^*$ and $\langle \mathbf{u},\ \mathbf{v}_0^* - \mathbf{v}_1^* \rangle \neq 0$, $\mathcal{B}$ samples $z^*, \gamma_1, \gamma_2 \in \mathbb{Z}_p^*$ and $r \in \mathbb{G}_2$ at random (with r implicitly equal to $g_2^{\alpha\langle\boldsymbol{\beta}, \mathbf{u}\rangle/(z\cdot(\alpha + H_{ID^*}))}$ for an unknown z), and sets $TK = (\mathbf{u}, r^{1/\gamma_1}, r^{1/\gamma_2})$, $HK = (\gamma_1, \gamma_2)$, $DK = z^*$. Although z^* is a fake decryption key, the triple is computationally indistinguishable from a valid one from the adversary's view.

For a decryption key query on index i, $\mathcal{B}$ returns the DK component stored in its table, or $\perp$ if the entry does not exist.

For a second-stage transformation query on index i and partial transformed ciphertext PTC, if $ID_i \neq ID^*$ or $\langle \mathbf{u}_i, \mathbf{v}_0^* - \mathbf{v}_1^* \rangle = 0$, $\mathcal{B}$ executes Transform2 directly with the stored valid HK_i. Otherwise, $\mathcal{B}$ parses $PTC = (CP_1, CP_2, CP_3)$, verifies $CP_1^{\gamma_1} = CP_2^{\gamma_2}$, and uses the KEA extractor together with a self-generated reference ciphertext to derive $s \cdot t$, ultimately returning $TC = (T_1 = e(g_1, g_2)^{\langle \beta, \mathbf{u}_i \rangle \cdot s \cdot t \cdot z^*}, T_2 = CP_3)$.

Challenge Phase. $\mathcal{A}$ ends Query Phase 1. $\mathcal{B}$ chooses a random bit $\mu \in \{0, 1\}$ and implicitly sets the challenge randomness to $s^* = b/(a+c)$. It writes $a\beta/(a+c) = f(a) + W/(a+c)$, where f is a polynomial of degree $q-1$ with computable coefficients and $W \in \mathbb{Z}_p^*$ is non-zero. The challenge ciphertext is constructed as $C_1^* = g^{(a+c)\cdot s^*} = g^b$, which is directly available from the (q, n)-DBDHI instance. For each $i \in [l]$, $\mathcal{B}$ computes

$$C_{2,i}^* = e(g, g')^{\beta v_{\mu,i}^*} \cdot e\Big(g^b, g'^{\beta_i f(a)}\Big) \cdot e\big(g^b, g'^{\phi_i W}\big) \cdot T^{(v_{0,i}^* - v_{1,i}^*)W},$$

where all terms are computable from the given instances and the challenge T. $\mathcal{B}$ sends $CT^* = (C_1^*, \{C_{2,i}^*\}_{i \in [l]})$ to $\mathcal{A}$.

Query Phase 2. Same as Query Phase 1, except that second-stage transformation queries are rejected when $ID_i = ID^*$ and $\langle \mathbf{u}_i, \mathbf{v}_0^* - \mathbf{v}_1^* \rangle \neq 0$.

Guess. $\mathcal{A}$ outputs a guess $\mu' \in \{0, 1\}$. $\mathcal{B}$ outputs 1 if $\mu = \mu'$ and 0 otherwise.

The simulation is perfect when $T = e(g, g')^{b/(a+c)}$, since $C_{2,i}^*$ then equals $e(g, g_2)^{v_{\mu,i}^*} \cdot e(g_1, g_2^{\beta_i})^{s^*}$, a valid encryption of $v_{\mu,i}^*$. When T is a random element of $\mathbb{G}_T$, an extra factor $e(g, g_2)^{r(v_{0,i}^* - v_{1,i}^*)Wb}$ (with r uniform in $\mathbb{Z}_p^*$) is introduced, making the encrypted vector completely random and hiding all information about μ. Therefore,

$$\Pr[\mu = \mu' \mid T = e(g, g')^{b/(a+c)}] = \tfrac{1}{2} + \epsilon, \quad \Pr[\mu = \mu' \mid T \in_R \mathbb{G}_T] = \tfrac{1}{2},$$

and $\mathcal{B}$'s advantage in solving (q, n)-DBDHI equals ϵ. Since (q, n)-DBDHI is hard, ϵ must be negligible, so IP-SM9-2OD is IND-sIDV-CDA secure.

Theorem 2. *Let H be a random oracle controlled by $\mathcal{B}$, and let the (q, n)-DBDHI assumption be the input to $\mathcal{B}$. If the (q, n)-DBDHI assumption holds, then IP-SM9-2OD is IND-sIDV-CHA secure in the random oracle model.*

Proof. The challenger's responses in the IND-sIDV-CHA game are identical to those in the IND-sIDV-CDA game in all phases except the helper-key and decryption-key query phases. In the helper-key query phase, $\mathcal{B}$ can return the actual HK for all queries. In the decryption-key query phase, $\mathcal{B}$ returns $\perp$ only when $ID_i = ID^*$ and $\langle \mathbf{u}_i, \mathbf{v}_0^* - \mathbf{v}_1^* \rangle \neq 0$; in all other cases, the valid DK is returned. Each adversary query is answered with a correctly distributed response from the adversary's perspective, so the simulation is perfect, and IP-SM9-2OD is IND-sIDV-CHA secure.

3 Design of HR-IP-SM9

3.1 System Architecture

The framework for HR-IP-SM9 is shown in Fig. 2 and involves four types of entities:

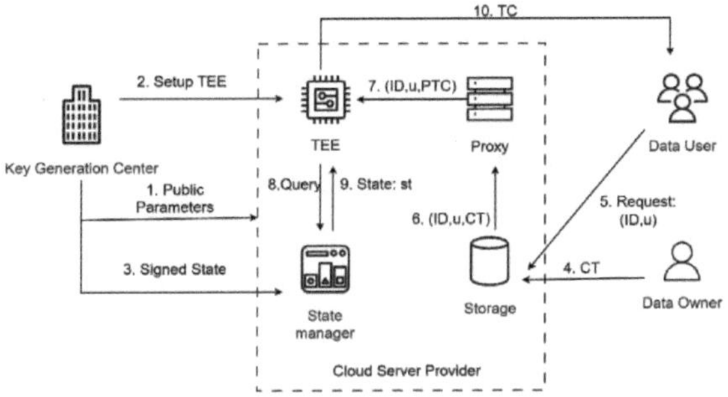

Fig. 2. System architecture of HR-IP-SM9.

The Key Generation Center (KGC) is responsible for system setup and user management. Every user in the system is associated with an identity ID and may apply to the KGC for a key triple associated with ID and a vector $\mathbf{u}$, consisting of a Transformation Key (TK), a Revocation Key (RK), and a Decryption Key (DK). The KGC maintains a User List (UL) and updates it whenever a user registers or is revoked. Concretely, the UL takes the form

$$UL = \{ID,\ \mathbf{u},\ TK_{ID,\mathbf{u}},\ \mathsf{Enc}_{K_{\mathsf{TEE}}}(RK_{ID,\mathbf{u}})\}_{ID \in \mathcal{U}},$$

where $\mathcal{U}$ denotes the set of legitimate data users in the system, and K_{TEE} is a symmetric key shared between the KGC and the TEE module via remote attestation.

The KGC operates in time intervals of length T. At the beginning of each interval it updates the UL. Let UL_i denote the UL updated during interval i. The KGC then generates a signed state $st_i = (\sigma, rt_i, i)$, where rt_i is the sMHT root committing to UL_i and σ is the KGC's signature over (rt_i, i), and stores st_i in the state module. The sparse Merkle hash tree (sMHT) is defined over a fixed identity space of size d. Let $\mathsf{idx}(\cdot)$ map an identity to its leaf position. For an active record $(ID, \mathbf{u}, TK_{ID,\mathbf{u}}, \mathsf{Enc}_{K_{\mathsf{TEE}}}(RK_{ID,\mathbf{u}}))$, the leaf at index $\mathsf{idx}(ID)$ stores the hash of this record; empty positions store a fixed empty value. The root rt_i is therefore a compact commitment to all active records in UL_i. For each active user, the state module stores the record and its Merkle authentication path $\pi_{ID,i}$, whose length is $O(\log d)$.

The Data Owner (DO) encrypts plaintext vectors and uploads the resulting ciphertexts to the storage module of the Cloud Service Provider.

The Cloud Service Provider (CSP) comprises four modules. The state module maintains the current signed state st_i. The storage module stores ciphertexts and, upon a data access request, forwards the requested ciphertext to the proxy module. The proxy module performs partial decryption: it retrieves st_i and $\pi_{ID,i}$ from the state module and verifies whether ID is active by verifying $\pi_{ID,i}$ against rt_i; if so, it uses $TK_{ID,u}$ to generate a partial transformed ciphertext (PTC) and forwards $(ID, u, \pi_{ID,i}, PTC)$ to the TEE module; otherwise, it rejects the request. The TEE module handles trusted transformation for non-revoked users: upon receiving $(ID, u, \pi_{ID,i}, PTC)$, it fetches st_i from the state module, verifies its freshness and signature validity, and checks if ID is active by verifying the same path against rt_i; if so, it uses $RK_{ID,u}$ to compute and forward the transformed ciphertext TC to the data user; otherwise, it rejects the request.

The Data User (DU) holds the decryption key $DK_{ID,\mathbf{u}}$ corresponding to their identity ID and uses it to perform the final decryption.

3.2 Security Models

Trust and Threat Model. In the HR-IP-SM9 framework, the KGC and DO are fully trusted. The CSP is a malicious party capable of launching active attacks, including rollback, collusion, and corrupted-TEE attacks. Data users comprise three types: revoked DUs; non-revoked but unauthorized DUs (who have not been revoked but cannot decrypt a ciphertext due to an identity mismatch); and non-revoked, authorized DUs. The first two types are treated as malicious parties that may collude with the CSP.

The TEE provides three standard hardware-enforced guarantees: (i) isolated execution, protecting enclave code and data from external software like a malicious OS or CSP; (ii) remote attestation, enabling the KGC to verify enclave identity and integrity before provisioning sensitive material; and (iii) sealed storage with trusted time or monotonic counters for rollback protection. Concretely, the KGC establishes a shared symmetric key K_{TEE} after a successful attestation handshake, provisioning it alongside programs $prog_1$ and $prog_2$ into the enclave. No other party, including the CSP, can learn K_{TEE} or decrypted revocation keys while the TEE remains uncompromised.

Our model considers three attack types. A rollback attack targets TEE freshness or integrity: the CSP may modify an intra-interval state or send an expired state to reset the system, enabling revoked DUs to decrypt illegally. Commercial TEE implementations, such as Intel SGX's trusted time service [7] and AMD SEV-SNP [1], already provide mechanisms to resist such threats. In a collusion attack, the CSP and revoked or unauthorized DUs jointly target HR-IP-SM9 confidentiality. For instance, the CSP can generate a valid PTC from a target ciphertext, request a second-stage TEE transformation under a non-revoked but unauthorized DU's identity, and decrypt the resulting TC using the colluding DU's key. In a corrupted-TEE attack, a malicious CSP exploits software vulnerabilities to breach enclave confidentiality, extracting internal secrets like K_{TEE} and revocation keys. Notably, if the TEE is fully compromised, the revocation guarantee collapses to that of the baseline IPFE scheme without revocation.

Formal Security Definitions. We define two formal security models corresponding to two TEE trust levels. The first, called Indistinguishability against Selective Identity and Vector and Collusion Attack (IND-sIDV-ColA), formalizes collusion attacks under a completely trusted TEE model. The second, called Indistinguishability against Selective Identity and Vector and Corrupted TEE Attack (IND-sIDV-CTA), formalizes corrupted-TEE attacks under a semi-trusted (transparent) TEE model [9]. The security games for IND-sIDV-ColA and IND-sIDV-CTA are defined in Algorithms 3 and 4, respectively.

3.3 Construction

HR-IP-SM9 is built on IP-SM9-2OD and a digital signature scheme. Let $\Pi_1 = (\mathsf{Setup}, \mathsf{KeyGen}, \mathsf{Encrypt}, \mathsf{Transform1}, \mathsf{Transform2}, \mathsf{Decrypt})$ denote the IP-SM9-2OD scheme, let $\Pi_{\mathsf{sig}} = (\mathsf{KeyGen}, \mathsf{Sign}, \mathsf{Verify})$ denote a digital signature scheme, and let Π_{AE} denote an authenticated encryption scheme. For convenience, we again write H_{ID} for $H(ID \| hid, p)$.

System Initialization. The initialization algorithm

$$\mathsf{Setup}(1^\lambda, l) \rightarrow (PP, MSK, st_0, UL)$$

takes a security parameter λ and a maximum vector length l as input and outputs public parameters PP, a master secret key MSK, an initial state st_0, and a user list UL.

The KGC first initializes the TEE and establishes a shared symmetric key K_{TEE} via remote attestation. During attestation, the KGC verifies the enclave's measurement and, upon success, provisions K_{TEE}, $prog_1$, and $prog_2$ over a secure channel established by the attestation protocol. It then loads programs $prog_1$ and $prog_2$ into the TEE via $\mathcal{G}.\mathsf{install}(prog_i)$ and invokes $prog_1$ to synchronize the time interval T via the interface $\mathcal{G}.\mathsf{resume}(\text{“Synchronize”}, T)$. The master secret key is set to $MSK = (MSK_1, sk, K_{\mathsf{TEE}})$ and the public parameters to $PP = (PP_1, vk)$, where (MSK_1, PP_1) are generated by $\Pi_1.\mathsf{Setup}(1^\lambda, l)$ and (sk, vk) are generated by $\Pi_{\mathsf{sig}}.\mathsf{KeyGen}(1^\lambda)$. Finally, the KGC calls $\mathsf{Update}(MSK, UL, 0) \rightarrow st_0$ to initialize the system state and outputs (PP, MSK, st_0, UL).

Encryption. The encryption algorithm $\mathsf{Encrypt}(PP, ID, \mathbf{v}) \rightarrow CT$ takes the public parameters, an identity ID, and a plaintext vector $\mathbf{v}$ as input. It calls $\Pi_1.\mathsf{Encrypt}(PP_1, ID, \mathbf{v})$ directly to generate the ciphertext. The DO then uploads the ciphertext to the CSP's storage module.

State Update. The state update phase consists of three algorithms: Join, Revoke, and Update.

$\mathsf{Join}(PP, MSK, UL, ID, \mathbf{u}) \rightarrow (UL', TK_{ID}, RK_{ID}, DK_{ID})$ registers a new user. The KGC calls $\Pi_1.\mathsf{KeyGen}(PP_1, MSK_1, ID, \mathbf{u})$ to generate the key triple, sets $RK_{ID,\mathbf{u}} = HK_{ID,\mathbf{u}}$, and outputs the updated list $UL' = UL \cup \{(ID, \mathbf{u}, TK_{ID,\mathbf{u}}, \mathsf{Enc}_{K_{\mathsf{TEE}}}(RK_{ID,\mathbf{u}}))\}$.

$\mathsf{Revoke}(UL, ID) \rightarrow UL'$ revokes a user. The KGC removes all records associated with ID from UL and outputs the updated list.

$\mathsf{Update}(PP, MSK, UL_i, i) \rightarrow st_i$ advances the system state. The KGC updates the sMHT according to the current UL_i: a join inserts or overwrites one non-empty leaf, and a revocation resets the corresponding leaf to the fixed empty value. Only the nodes on the affected root-to-leaf path are recomputed, so each state update performs $O(\log d)$ hash operations. Let rt_i be the resulting root. The KGC calls $\Pi_{\mathsf{sig}}.\mathsf{Sign}(sk, rt_i, i)$ to generate a signature σ, refreshes the affected authentication paths $\pi_{ID,i}$, and outputs $st_i = (\sigma, rt_i, i)$.

Decryption Phase. The decryption phase comprises three algorithms: Transform1, Transform2, and Decrypt.

$\mathsf{Transform1}(PP, st_i, \pi_{ID,i}, TK_{ID,\mathbf{u}}, CT) \rightarrow PTC$ is executed by the proxy module. It parses $st_i = (\sigma, rt_i, i)$ and verifies both $\Pi_{\mathsf{sig}}.\mathsf{Verify}(vk, rt_i, i, \sigma)$ and that $\pi_{ID,i}$ opens the leaf of ID's active record to rt_i. If both checks pass, it calls $\Pi_1.\mathsf{Transform1}(PP_1, TK_{ID,\mathbf{u}}, CT)$ to produce and output PTC; otherwise it aborts.

$\mathsf{Transform2}(PP, st_i, \pi_{ID,i}, RK_{ID,\mathbf{u}}, PTC) \rightarrow TC$ is executed inside the TEE module via the interface $\mathcal{G}.\mathsf{resume}(\text{“Transform2”}, K_{\mathsf{TEE}}, st_i, \pi_{ID,i}, ID, PTC)$, which invokes $prog_2$ loaded into the TEE. The TEE similarly verifies the freshness and signature of st_i and checks that $\pi_{ID,i}$ opens the active record to rt_i before producing TC.

$\mathsf{Decrypt}(PP, DK_{ID,\mathbf{u}}, \text{TC}) \rightarrow \langle \mathbf{u}, \mathbf{v} \rangle$ is executed by the data user, who calls $\Pi_1.\mathsf{Decrypt}(PP_1, DK_{ID,\mathbf{u}}, TC)$ to obtain the final decryption result.

3.4 Security Analysis

We define two formal security models, IND-sIDV-ColA and IND-sIDV-CTA, in Algorithms 3 and 4, describing the scenarios where CSP colludes with revoked and unauthorized DUs, and where TEE is corrupted separately. We conclude the security analysis with the following theorem.

In the IND-sIDV-ColA model, the TEE is fully trusted and its internal state (including K_{TEE} and all revocation keys) is never leaked to the adversary. In the IND-sIDV-CTA model, the TEE is semi-trusted: the adversary may have compromised the enclave and obtained K_{TEE} and all revocation keys. Consequently, the adversary can decrypt any $\mathsf{Enc}_{K_{\mathsf{TEE}}}(RK)$ ciphertext in the user list and issue revocation-key queries. The decryption-key queries are further restricted to prevent the trivial win.

Theorem 3. *Let H be a random oracle controlled by $\mathcal{C}$. If Π_1 is IND-sIDV-CDA secure, Π_{sig} is EUF-CMA secure, and Π_{AE} is CCA secure, then HR-IP-SM9 is IND-sIDV-ColA secure in the random oracle model.*

Proof. We define three games to bridge the gap between the original security game and the hardness assumption.

Game 0 is the original IND-sIDV-ColA game.

Game 1 is identical to Game 0, except that if the adversary submits a state $st_i^* = (\sigma^*, rt_i^*, i^*)$ that differs from the challenger's current state $st_i = (\sigma, rt_i, i)$, the challenger outputs a random bit and halts.

Algorithm 3. Security game for the IND-sIDV-ColA model.

1: $\mathcal{A}$ outputs a challenge identity ID^* and two challenge vectors $\mathbf{v}_0^*, \mathbf{v}_1^* \in \mathbb{Z}^l$ to $\mathcal{C}$.
2: $\mathcal{C}$ runs $(PP, MSK, st_0, UL) \leftarrow \mathsf{Setup}(1^\lambda, l)$, sends (PP, st_0) to $\mathcal{A}$, initializes $TB \leftarrow \emptyset$, and sets $k \leftarrow 1$.

Phase 1. $\mathcal{A}$ adaptively issues the following queries:
– **Hash query:** $\mathcal{C}$ returns a random value.
– **Registration query** $(ID_k, \mathbf{u}_k)$: $\mathcal{C}$ runs $(TK_k, RK_k, DK_k) \leftarrow \mathsf{Join}(PP, MSK, ID_k, \mathbf{u}_k)$, updates UL, stores $TB[k] = (ID_k, \mathbf{u}_k, TK_k, RK_k, DK_k)$, returns TK_k, and sets $k \leftarrow k + 1$.
– **Revocation query** ID: $\mathcal{C}$ runs $\mathsf{Rev}(UL, ID)$ and updates UL.
– **Update query** (i, st_{i-1}): $\mathcal{C}$ runs $st_i \leftarrow \mathsf{Update}(PP, st_{i-1}, i)$ and returns st_i.
– **Decryption-key query** j: if $TB[j]$ is undefined, return $\perp$; otherwise parse $TB[j] = (ID_j, \mathbf{u}_j, TK_j, RK_j, DK_j)$ and return DK_j.
– **Transform2 query** (j, PTC): if $TB[j]$ is undefined, return $\perp$; otherwise parse $TB[j] = (ID_j, \mathbf{u}_j, TK_j, RK_j, DK_j)$ and return $\mathsf{Transform2}(PP, st_i, RK_j, PTC)$.

Challenge. $\mathcal{A}$ submits a state st_i to $\mathcal{C}$. $\mathcal{C}$ removes from UL every entry with $ID_i = ID^*$, $\langle \mathbf{u}_i, \mathbf{v}_0^* - \mathbf{v}_1^* \rangle \neq 0$, and corrupted DK_i. $\mathcal{C}$ chooses $b \leftarrow \{0, 1\}$, computes $CT^* \leftarrow \mathsf{Encrypt}(PP, ID^*, \mathbf{v}_b^*)$, and sends CT^* to $\mathcal{A}$.

Phase 2. $\mathcal{A}$ continues to issue queries as in Phase 1, except that for any Transform2 query on index i, $\mathcal{C}$ returns $\perp$ if $ID_i = ID^*$ and $\langle \mathbf{u}_i, \mathbf{v}_0^* - \mathbf{v}_1^* \rangle \neq 0$.

Guess. $\mathcal{A}$ outputs $b' \in \{0, 1\}$ and wins iff $b' = b$.

Game 2 is identical to Game 1, except that all encrypted revocation keys $\mathsf{Enc}_{K_{\mathsf{TEE}}}(RK)$ in the UL are replaced by random ciphertexts.

Let E_j denote the event that the adversary wins Game j.

Lemma 1. *If Π_{sig} is EUF-CMA secure, then $|\Pr[E_0] - \Pr[E_1]|$ is negligible.*

Proof. The TEE's rollback-protection mechanism ensures that the signed sMHT root rt_i is always fresh. Games 0 and 1 are identical unless the adversary produces a forged signature σ^* on a modified root $rt_i^* \neq rt_i$. Hence there exists an adversary $\mathcal{F}$ such that

$$|\Pr[E_0] - \Pr[E_1]| = \mathsf{Adv}_{\mathcal{F}, \Pi_{\mathsf{sig}}}^{\mathsf{EUF\text{-}CMA}}.$$

Lemma 2. *If Π_{AE} is CCA secure, then $|\Pr[E_1] - \Pr[E_2]|$ is negligible.*

Proof. If there existed an adversary that distinguished Game 1 from Game 2 with non-negligible advantage, then that adversary could distinguish a real ciphertext from a random ciphertext, contradicting the CCA security of Π_{AE}. Thus there exists an adversary $\mathcal{F}$ such that

$$|\Pr[E_1] - \Pr[E_2]| = \mathsf{Adv}_{\mathcal{F}, \Pi_{\mathsf{AE}}}^{\mathsf{CCA}}.$$

Lemma 3. *If Π_1 is IND-sIDV-CDA secure, then $\Pr[E_2]$ is negligible.*

Algorithm 4. Security game for the IND-sIDV-CTA model.

$\mathcal{A}$ outputs a challenge identity ID^* and two challenge vectors $\mathbf{v}_0^*, \mathbf{v}_1^* \in \mathbb{Z}^l$ to $\mathcal{C}$.

$\mathcal{C}$ runs $(PP, MSK, st_0, UL) \leftarrow \mathsf{Setup}(1^\lambda, l)$, sends (PP, st_0) to $\mathcal{A}$, initializes $TB \leftarrow \emptyset$, and sets $k \leftarrow 1$.

Phase 1.$\mathcal{A}$ adaptively issues polynomially many queries, including hash, registration, revocation, update, revocation-key, and decryption-key queries. All queries are answered as in the IND-sIDV-ColA game, except for the following two queries.

– **Revocation-key query** j: if $TB[j]$ is undefined, return $\perp$; otherwise parse $TB[j] = (ID_j, \mathbf{u}_j, TK_j, RK_j, DK_j)$ and return RK_j.

– **Decryption-key query** j: if $TB[j]$ is undefined, or $ID_j = ID^*$ and $\langle \mathbf{u}_j, \mathbf{v}_0^* - \mathbf{v}_1^* \rangle \neq 0$, return $\perp$; otherwise parse $TB[j] = (ID_j, \mathbf{u}_j, TK_j, RK_j, DK_j)$ and return DK_j.

Challenge.$\mathcal{C}$ chooses $b \leftarrow \{0,1\}$, computes $CT^* \leftarrow \mathsf{Encrypt}(PP, ID^*, \mathbf{v}_b^*)$, and sends CT^* to $\mathcal{A}$.

Phase 2.$\mathcal{A}$ continues to issue queries as in Phase 1.

Guess.$\mathcal{A}$ outputs $b' \in \{0,1\}$ and wins iff $b' = b$.

Proof. Suppose an adversary $\mathcal{A}$ wins Game 2 with non-negligible advantage ϵ. We construct a simulator $\mathcal{B}$ that uses $\mathcal{A}$ to break Π_1.

In the initialization phase, $\mathcal{A}$ submits $(ID^*, \mathbf{v}_0^*, \mathbf{v}_1^*)$ and $\mathcal{B}$ forwards these to the Π_1 challenger.

In the setup phase, $\mathcal{B}$ receives PP_1 from the Π_1 challenger, generates a fresh symmetric key K_{TEE}, runs $\Pi_{\mathsf{sig}}.\mathsf{KeyGen}(1^\lambda) \rightarrow (vk, sk)$, and initializes $UL = \emptyset$. It sends (PP, st_0) to $\mathcal{A}$, where $PP = (PP_1, vk)$.

In query phase 1, $\mathcal{B}$ maintains tables T_B, T_{sat}, and T_{cor}, all initially empty. For a hash query, $\mathcal{B}$ queries the Π_1 hash oracle. For a registration query $(ID_k, \mathbf{u}_k)$, $\mathcal{B}$ forwards the query to the Π_1 key generation oracle to obtain TK_k, then queries the Π_1 decryption key oracle to obtain DK_k. It records $T_B[k] = (ID_k, \mathbf{u}_k, TK_k, \cdot, DK_k)$ (where the revocation key position is left blank as it is unknown), updates $UL \leftarrow UL \cup \{(ID_k, \mathbf{u}_k, TK_k, \mathsf{Enc}_{K_{\mathsf{TEE}}}(0))\}$ using a random ciphertext, and sends TK_k to $\mathcal{A}$. If $ID_k = ID^*$ and $\langle \mathbf{u}_k, \mathbf{v}_0^* - \mathbf{v}_1^* \rangle \neq 0$, $\mathcal{B}$ also updates $T_{\mathsf{sat}} \leftarrow T_{\mathsf{sat}} \cup \{T_B[k]\}$. For a revocation query on ID, $\mathcal{B}$ deletes all records associated with ID from UL. For an update query on index i, $\mathcal{B}$ signs the current sMHT root rt_i that commits to UL_i and returns $st_i = (\sigma, rt_i, i)$. For a decryption key query on index j, $\mathcal{B}$ returns DK_j and updates $T_{\mathsf{cor}} \leftarrow T_{\mathsf{cor}} \cup \{T_B[j]\}$. For a second-stage transformation query, if $ID \notin UL$, $\mathcal{B}$ returns $\perp$; otherwise it queries the Π_1 second-stage transformation oracle and returns the result.

In the challenge phase, $\mathcal{B}$ removes from UL all records in $T_{\mathsf{sat}} \cap T_{\mathsf{cor}}$, receives the challenge ciphertext CT^* from the Π_1 challenger, and forwards it to $\mathcal{A}$.

Query phase 2 is the same as Query phase 1, except that second-stage transformation queries with $ID_i = ID^*$ and $\langle \mathbf{u}_j, \mathbf{v}_0^* - \mathbf{v}_1^* \rangle \neq 0$ return $\perp$.

In the guess phase, $\mathcal{B}$ forwards $\mathcal{A}$'s output directly to the Π_1 challenger.

The simulation is perfect, so$\Pr[E_2] = \mathsf{Adv}_{\mathcal{B},\Pi_1}^{\mathsf{IND\text{-}sIDV\text{-}CDA}} + \frac{1}{2}$.

Combining the three lemmas,

$$\begin{aligned}\Pr[E_0] &\leq |\Pr[E_0] - \Pr[E_1]| + |\Pr[E_1] - \Pr[E_2]| + \Pr[E_2] \\ &= \mathsf{Adv}^{\mathsf{EUF\text{-}CMA}}_{\mathcal{F},\Pi_{\mathsf{sig}}} + \mathsf{Adv}^{\mathsf{CCA}}_{\mathcal{F},\Pi_{\mathsf{AE}}} + \mathsf{Adv}^{\mathsf{IND\text{-}sIDV\text{-}CDA}}_{\mathcal{B},\Pi_1} + \frac{1}{2}.\end{aligned}$$

Since all three advantages are negligible, the adversary's advantage in winning the IND-sIDV-ColA game is negligible, and HR-IP-SM9 is IND-sIDV-ColA secure.

Theorem 4. *Let H be a random oracle controlled by $\mathcal{C}$. If Π_1 is IND-sIDV-CHA secure, then HR-IP-SM9 is IND-sIDV-CTA secure in the random oracle model.*

Proof. In the IND-sIDV-CTA game, the challenger can forward all received responses from the Π_1 challenger directly at every phase. The proof is therefore straightforward, and HR-IP-SM9 is IND-sIDV-CTA secure.

4 Evaluation

Considering that existing SM9-based revocable encryption schemes [10,17] do not support inner product functional encryption (IPFE), to ensure comparability, we extend existing schemes to support IPFE and use them as baselines. We implement HR-IP-SM9 and the baseline schemes in standard C++ using the Pairing-Based Cryptography Library (PBC Library) [13], running in Intel SGX hardware mode. We simulate the BN curve specified in the SM9 standard by modifying the default parameters of the Type F elliptic curve [13]. The hardware environment consists of one server with 54 GB of memory, an Intel Xeon Silver 4314 CPU at 2.40 GHz with 32 physical cores, running 64-bit Ubuntu 20.04.6 LTS. All algorithms are executed single-threaded on a single CPU core. Each experiment is repeated 100 times and the reported value is the mean.

Table 1. Encryption time (ms) under different numbers of revoked users ($l = 20$)

Sch.	Number of Revoked Users						
	4	8	16	32	64	128	256
[10]	257.74	265.97	272.90	284.21	318.15	379.34	495.73
[17]	259.92	259.95	268.27	284.33	315.96	376.36	496.67
Ours	243.65	243.59	246.56	246.06	246.42	249.30	248.10

Tables 1 and 2 show encryption and decryption times (in milliseconds) as functions of the revocation list length at a fixed vector length $l = 20$. HR-IP-SM9 already matches or marginally outperforms [10,17] when the revocation list contains 4 users. The gap widens substantially as the list grows. At $n = 128$, HR-IP-SM9 achieves roughly 1.52× and 1.50× speedups over [10,17] in encryption, respectively. For decryption, the client-side speedups are approximately 73.91×

Table 2. Decryption time (ms) under different numbers of revoked users ($l = 20$)

Sch.		Number of Revoked Users						
		4	8	16	32	64	128	256
[10]		225.74	235.39	245.98	273.77	326.80	436.07	645.07
[17]		189.98	194.31	209.91	218.29	245.80	311.26	476.84
Ours	CSP	182.79	182.73	186.94	183.84	185.77	185.92	184.86
	TEE	19.41	19.32	19.34	19.41	19.32	19.42	19.33
	DU	5.88	5.93	5.94	5.88	6.01	5.93	5.96

and 52.48× over [10,17]. The decryption bottleneck in HR-IP-SM9 lies with the CSP (approximately 185.92 ms at $n = 128$), which nonetheless remains well below the costs of the comparison schemes and can be further reduced in a real cloud environment by scaling CSP resources.

Table 3. Revocation algorithm time (ms) under different total user counts.

Party	2^{10}	2^{12}	2^{14}	2^{16}	2^{18}
CSP	0.10	0.11	0.13	0.15	0.16
KGC	0.81	0.81	0.84	0.85	0.87

Table 3 shows the cost of the revocation algorithm as a function of total system user count, ranging from 2^{10} to 2^{18}. Because revocation requires only $O(\log d)$ hash operations to update the sMHT, the cost remains negligible even at large scale: at $d = 2^{18}$, the CSP's revocation cost is only 0.16 ms and the KGC's is only 0.87 ms.

Figure 3 compares the TEE-side computation time of HR-IP-SM9 against a baseline in which the entire transformation is executed inside the TEE. At $l = 20$ and $n = 128$, HR-IP-SM9's TEE cost is only 19.42 ms, compared to approximately 113.56 ms for the baseline, demonstrating that the two-stage outsourcing design substantially reduces TEE computational burden.

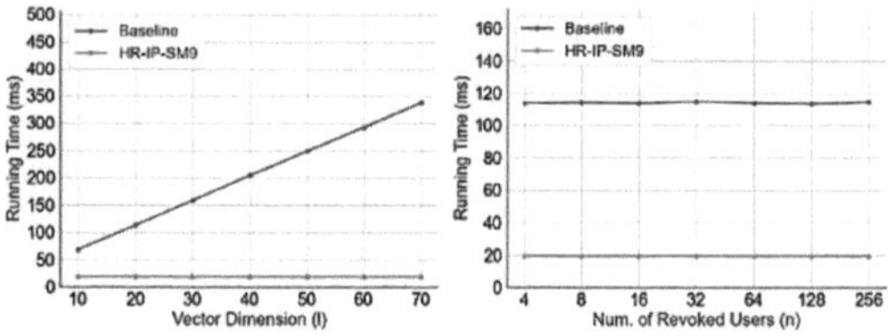

Fig. 3. TEE computation time of HR-IP-SM9 and the non-outsourced baseline under varying vector lengths and revocation list sizes.

Figures 4 and 5 evaluate the performance of HR-IP-SM9 under four elliptic curves selected according to NIST standards (224-bit to 512-bit security levels), with vector lengths from 10 to 70 and revocation list sizes from 4 to 256. Encryption and decryption times increase monotonically with the security parameter.

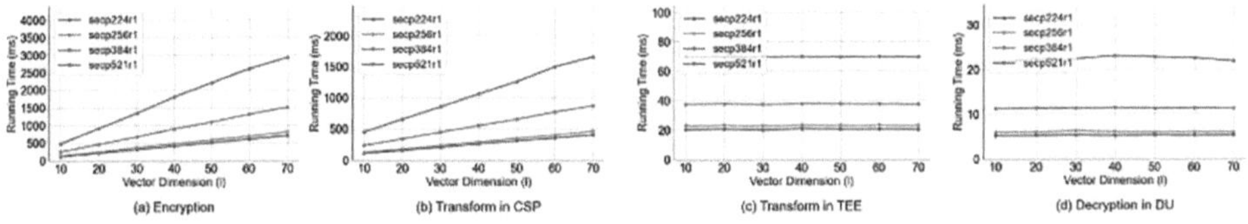

Fig. 4. Algorithm running time under $n = 128$ for different curves and vector lengths.

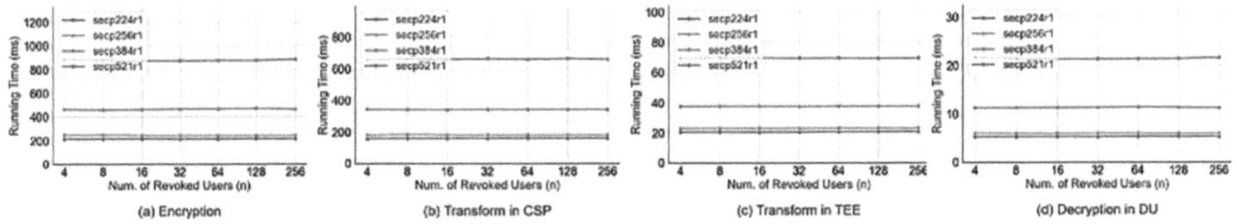

Fig. 5. Running time under $l = 20$ for different curves and revocation list sizes.

5 Conclusion

We have presented a two-stage outsourced decryption variant of SM9 identity-based inner product functional encryption, called IP-SM9-2OD. We formalized its security model and provided a formal proof under the (q, n)-DBDHI assumption in the random oracle model. Building on this, we integrated TEE technology to construct a user-revocable scheme, HR-IP-SM9, and proved its security under both a fully trusted and a semi-trusted TEE model. Theoretical analysis and experimental results consistently demonstrate that HR-IP-SM9 outperforms existing SM9-based user-revocable schemes in encryption and decryption efficiency.

Acknowledgments. This work was supported by China Unicom Software Research Institute and the Beijing Natural Science Foundation under Grant No. 4254081.

References

1. AMD: SEV-SNP: Strengthening VM isolation with integrity protection and more (2020). https://docs.amd.com/v/u/en-US/SEV-SNP-strengthening-vm-isolation-with-integrity-protection-and-more

2. Bellare, M., Palacio, A.: The knowledge-of-exponent assumptions and 3-round zero-knowledge protocols. In: Annual International Cryptology Conference, pp. 273–289. Springer Berlin Heidelberg, Berlin, Heidelberg (2004)
3. Boldyreva, A., Goyal, V., Kumar, V.: Identity-based encryption with efficient revocation. In: Proceedings of the 15th ACM Conference on Computer and Communications Security, pp. 417–426. ACM (2008)
4. Cash, D., Kiltz, E., Shoup, V.: The twin diffie-hellman problem and applications. J. Cryptol. **22**(4), 470–504 (2009)
5. Costan, V., Devadas, S.: Intel SGX explained. Cryptol. ePrint Arch (2016)
6. Fei, S., Yan, Z., Ding, W., et al.: Security vulnerabilities of SGX and countermeasures: a survey. ACM Comput. Surv. **54**(6), 1–36 (2021)
7. Intel Corporation: Trusted time and monotonic counters with intel®software guard extensions platform services (2017)
8. Kaplan, D., Powell, J., Woller, T.: AMD memory encryption (2016). https://docs.amd.com/api/khub/documents/ZcsCCmeL80dbtuf_VlGpvw/content
9. Kumar, N., Rathee, M., Chandran, N.: Cryptflow: secure tensorflow inference. In: 2020 IEEE Symposium on Security and Privacy, pp. 336–353. IEEE (2020)
10. Lai, J.C., Huang, X.Y., He, D.B., Chen, L.Q., Yang, S.J.: Revocation encryption scheme based on SM9. Ruan Jian Xue Bao/J. Softw. **35**(12), 5609–5620 (2024) (in Chinese)
11. Lewko, A., Sahai, A., Waters, B.: Revocation systems with very small private keys. In: 2010 IEEE Symposium on Security and Privacy, pp. 273–285. IEEE (2010)
12. Li, X., Yang, G., Xiang, T.: Make revocation cheaper: hardware-based revocable attribute-based encryption. In: 2024 IEEE Symposium on Security and Privacy (SP), pp. 3109–3127. IEEE (2024)
13. Lynn, B.: The pairing-based cryptography library. http://crypto.stanford.edu/pbc/
14. Murdock, K., Oswald, D., Garcia, F.D.: Plundervolt: software-based fault injection attacks against intel SGX. In: 2020 IEEE Symposium on Security and Privacy, pp. 1466–1482. IEEE (2020)
15. Sahai, A., Seyalioglu, H., Waters, B.: Dynamic credentials and ciphertext delegation for attribute-based encryption. In: Annual Cryptology Conference, pp. 199–217. Springer Berlin Heidelberg, Berlin, Heidelberg (2012)
16. Seo, J.H., Emura, K.: Revocable identity-based encryption revisited: security model and construction. In: International Workshop on Public Key Cryptography, pp. 216–234. Springer Berlin Heidelberg, Berlin, Heidelberg (2013)
17. Xie, Z.J., Zhang, W.L., Zhang, Y., et al.: Revocation encryption scheme based on domestic cryptographic algorithm sm9. J. Commun./Tongxin Xuebao **46**(5) (2025) (in Chinese)

MC-TCN: Multi-grain Cross-attention Temporal Convolutional Network for Web Attack Detection

Pan Deng and Yindong Chen(✉)

Shantou University, Shantou, Guangdong, China
ydchen@stu.edu.cn

Abstract. Existing deep learning methods for web attack detection, particularly LSTM-based models, often suffer from limited long-range dependency modeling and computational inefficiency. To address this, we propose MC-TCN (Multi-grain Cross-attention Temporal Convolutional Network). Our framework integrates a dual-channel embedding module to capture character- and subword-level representations, Temporal Convolutional Networks (TCN) for efficient long-range dependency modeling, and a Cross-Attention Fusion Module (CAFM) with multi-scale kernels for deep feature interaction. Extensive experiments on the CSIC-2010 and ATRDF-2023 datasets demonstrate MC-TCN's state-of-the-art-level performance and robust generalization. It achieves 99.77% accuracy and 99.72% F1-score on CSIC-2010, and 97.91% MCC and 98.19% F1-score on ATRDF-2023, outperforming strong baselines like HCLSTM, BCSP, and RoBERTa. Furthermore, TCN's parallel computing architecture enables approximately 1.4× faster inference compared to LSTM-based approaches.

Keywords: Web attack detection · Deep learning · Cross-attention mechanism · Network security

1 Introduction

The rapid proliferation of network applications has significantly widened the web attack surface, making robust security an urgent research challenge [1–4]. While Machine Learning (ML) automates network payload analysis, traditional methods rely on labor-intensive feature engineering and struggle to learn long-range dependencies [5,6].

Deep Learning (DL) overcomes these bottlenecks by automatically extracting complex features [7,8], yet existing approaches exhibit critical limitations. For instance, recent LSTM- and CNN-based methods [9,10] often overlook fine-grained character-level nuances, utilize fixed kernel sizes that limit varied receptive fields, or suffer from embedding sparsity. Furthermore, the inherent sequential dependency of LSTMs prevents full exploitation of GPU parallelization, causing computational inefficiencies. To address this, Temporal Convolutional

L. Ding et al. (Eds.): APWeb-WAIM 2026, LNCS 16993, pp. 589–604, 2027.
https://doi.org/10.1007/978-981-92-5693-8_37

Networks (TCN) [11] offer a compelling alternative, utilizing causal and dilated convolutions to efficiently capture long-range dependencies with strict parallelism.

In this paper, we propose the Multi-grain Cross-attention Temporal Convolutional Network (MC-TCN) for web attack detection. Our framework constructs a rich, dual-channel feature representation using character- and subword-level embeddings. It seamlessly integrates TCNs for efficient sequence modeling, a cross-attention module to fuse multi-grained features, and multi-scale CNNs to extract diverse local patterns.

Our main contributions are summarized as follows:

1. We propose the novel MC-TCN framework, which jointly exploits character- and subword-level payload representations through cross-attention fusion.
2. We utilize TCNs to overcome the computational bottlenecks of traditional LSTMs, enabling efficient long-range dependency modeling through highly parallelizable operations.
3. We design a comprehensive architecture combining TCNs and multi-scale CNNs to holistically capture both global sequential contexts and varied local patterns.
4. Extensive experiments on the CSIC-2010 and modern ATRDF-2023 datasets demonstrate that MC-TCN achieves state-of-the-art-level performance, robust generalization, and faster inference compared to existing baselines.

The rest of the paper is organized as follows. Section 2 introduces the related work. Sections 3 and 4 describe the design concept and construction of the MC-TCN. Section 5 shows the experimental results obtained for different datasets and compares our approach with state-of-the-art-level methods. Section 6 provides a discussion and the conclusions.

2 Related Work

2.1 Sequence Modeling-Based Approaches

Sequence modeling has formed the backbone of deep learning-based web attack detection, capturing temporal and contextual dependencies in web traffic [11–13]. Hao et al. [14] utilized a Bidirectional LSTM with subword embedding to detect malicious HTTP requests in the CSIC 2010 dataset, demonstrating the efficacy of bidirectional context modeling. Similarly, Liang et al. [3] employed LSTMs and GRUs for URL sequence modeling by integrating subword-level embeddings with rule-based feature extraction. More recently, Zhai et al. [15] leveraged CharBERT to capture joint subword and character-level features, achieving an accuracy exceeding 98%, while Nguyet Quang Do et al. [4] adopted Temporal Convolutional Networks (TCNs) coupled with Multi-Head Self-Attention for URL feature selection.

Limitations: Although these sequential methods effectively capture context, they suffer from inherent bottlenecks. Recurrent architectures (e.g., [3,14]) are hindered by sequential computation constraints, leading to low training and inference efficiency. While recent Transformer-based or TCN-based models [4,15] alleviate parallelization issues, they either incur massive computational overhead or fail to extract the fine-grained hierarchical syntax necessary to distinguish complex, obfuscated payloads. In contrast, our proposed MC-TCN addresses both efficiency and representation depth via parallel TCNs and hierarchical attention.

2.2 CNN-Based Approaches

Convolutional Neural Networks (CNNs) excel at capturing local spatial patterns and hierarchical structural features within web payloads [16,17]. Zhang et al. [18] tokenized HTTP requests into words and applied word embeddings, proving that structured embedding significantly enhances CNN feature extraction capabilities. To capture explicit token matrices, Tekerek et al. [19] employed a Bag-of-Words framework to extract vocabularies from URLs, constructing binary feature matrices for downstream CNNs. Furthermore, Liu et al. [9] proposed a Payload-based CNN that processes raw network payloads directly through stacked convolutional and max-pooling layers, successfully learning high-level semantic features from raw byte patterns.
Limitations: A major drawback of pure CNN-based approaches is their restricted receptive field. While effective at identifying localized malicious snippets (e.g., specific SQL keywords), they lack the capacity to model long-range, non-local sequential dependencies across an entire HTTP request. Furthermore, severe text cleaning or reliance on coarse word-level tokenization [18,19] inherently discards crucial fine-grained syntax, making them vulnerable to token-perturbation or obfuscation attacks. Our work fills this gap by coupling local TCN convolutions with a global hierarchical attention mechanism.

2.3 Generative and Data Augmentation Approaches

To mitigate data scarcity and class imbalance in web security, generative paradigms have gained traction. Aharon et al. [21] proposed a GAN-inspired framework leveraging a RoBERTa language model to synthesize domain-specific API requests, substantially boosting the robustness of downstream anomaly detection models.
Limitations: While data augmentation enhances training diversity, generative language models [21] require immense computational resources and risk introducing synthetic noise or hallucinated patterns that do not conform to strict protocol syntaxes. More importantly, these methods optimize data preparation rather than the core detection architecture. MC-TCN complements this line of research by fundamentally shifting the focus toward architectural efficiency and dual-granularity feature fusion, achieving robust generalization without relying on heavy generative components.

2.4 Hybrid Approaches

To harness the benefits of both local pattern extraction and global sequence modeling, recent studies have explored hybrid frameworks. Kim et al. [20] introduced the C-LSTM architecture for web traffic anomaly detection, utilizing a 1D-CNN for spatial feature extraction followed by an LSTM to capture temporal dependencies. Similarly, Luo et al. [1] proposed HCLSTM, which processes heterogeneous data across parallel branches and fuses features via an attention mechanism.
Limitations: Most existing hybrid models connect CNNs and RNNs in a rigid, sequential pipeline (e.g., [20]), creating a structural bottleneck where the recurrent layer restricts the throughput of the entire network. Furthermore, parallel hybrid structures like HCLSTM [1] rely heavily on recurrent units for their sequential branch, failing to achieve true end-to-end parallel acceleration during training and deployment.

2.5 Limitations and Motivation

A holistic review of the literature reveals three persistent challenges that motivate the design of MC-TCN:

1. **The Representation Dilemma**: Current models typically select either a character-level or subword-level representation. Character-level models capture precise syntax but suffer from excessively long sequence lengths, whereas subword/word-level models capture semantics but are blind to intra-token mutations and out-of-vocabulary (OOV) obfuscations. A systematic framework for dynamically fusing dual-granularity tokens is noticeably absent.
2. **The Efficiency-Dependency Trade-off**: Recurrent networks (LSTMs/GRUs) struggle with the extremely long sequence lengths typical of raw HTTP payloads, encountering vanishing gradients and a total lack of GPU parallelization. This makes them impractical for high-throughput, real-time Web Application Firewall (WAF) deployment.
3. **Static Feature Fusion**: Existing hybrid architectures often merge multi-source features via simple concatenation or static pooling, ignoring the dynamic interactions between fine-grained syntax and high-level semantics.

To overcome these boundaries, this paper introduces MC-TCN. By replacing recurrent structures with parallel TCNs, we break the sequential processing bottleneck, achieving a 1.73× training speedup over HCLSTM. Concurrently, our hierarchical cross-attention mechanism enables dynamic, bidirectional feature interactions between character and subword spaces, successfully combining the resilience of fine-grained tokenization with the high-level understanding of semantic modeling.

3 Method

3.1 Overall Framework

MC-TCN adopts a hierarchical processing approach: independent representation learning, cross-modal fusion, and multi-scale pattern extraction. As shown in

Fig. 1, the model comprises four modules: (1) Dual-Channel TCN Encoder, (2) Cross-Attention Fusion Module (CAFM), (3) Multi-Grain CNN Extractor, and (4) MLP-based Classifier.

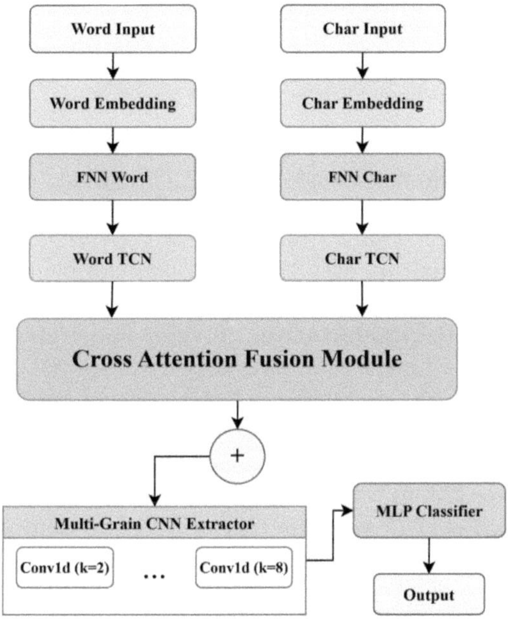

Fig. 1. Overall framework of MC-TCN.

The workflow proceeds: (1) Preprocessed character-level and subword-level sequences are fed into two TCN channels to capture long-range dependencies; (2) TCN outputs pass to CAFM for interaction to generate unified features; (3) Fused sequences are processed by multi-kernel CNN to extract multi-scale local patterns; (4) CNN features are pooled, concatenated, and fed through MLP classifier for final detection.

3.2 Input Representation and Embedding Layer

Preprocessing Strategy. We preprocess HTTP requests to extract features while mitigating overfitting. As shown in Fig. 2, HTTP requests contain metadata in headers and payloads for attack detection.

Raw header data presents challenges: (1)For CSIC2010, high cardinality fields like JSESSIONID may cause memorization rather than learning generalizable patterns; (2) Continuous numerical values like Content-Length create large sparse vocabularies lacking semantic value.

We apply normalization: (1) Cookie values replaced with placeholder <COOKIE_ID>; (2) Content-Length values converted to placeholder <CONTENT_LEN>.

Fig. 2. Example of an HTTP request.

Multi-Grain Tokenization. MC-TCN uses two complementary input granularities:

Character-Level Representation provides fine-grained views for detecting syntactic anomalies and attack payloads with special symbols (e.g., SQL Injection: ’, --, ;; XSS: $<, >$, ”). Character-level models handle Out-of-Vocabulary issues and obfuscated inputs.

Subword-Level Representation captures semantic information. We employ SentencePiece [23] to tokenize inputs into subword units, preserving common keywords (e.g., `SELECT`) as single tokens while decomposing rare strings.

Following preprocessing, each HTTP request is tokenized into two parallel integer sequences: $\mathbf{X}_c \in \mathbb{N}^{L_c}$ (character-level) and $\mathbf{X}_s \in \mathbb{N}^{L_s}$ (subword-level), where L_c and L_s denote the respective sequence lengths.

Embedding Layer. Two independent embedding layers transform discrete sequences into continuous representations. Let $|\mathcal{V}_c|$ and $|\mathcal{V}_s|$ denote vocabulary sizes:

$$\mathbf{E}_i = \text{Embed}_i(\mathbf{X}_i) \in \mathbb{R}^{L_i \times d_i}, \quad i \in c, s \tag{1}$$

A position-wise Feed-Forward Network refines embeddings:

$$\text{FFN}(\mathbf{x}) = \text{ReLU}(\mathbf{x}\mathbf{W}_1 + \mathbf{b}_1)\mathbf{W}_2 + \mathbf{b}_2 \tag{2}$$

3.3 Dual-Channel TCN Encoder

TCN captures temporal dependencies through three components:

Causal Convolution. TCN preserves temporal causality ensuring output at time t depends only on current and past inputs (Fig. 3):

$$y_t = \sum_{i=0}^{k-1} w_i \cdot x_{t-i} + b \tag{3}$$

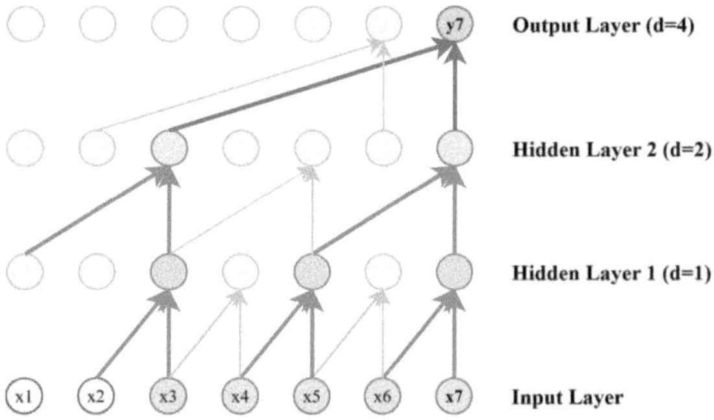

Fig. 3. Causal convolution.

Dilated Convolution. Dilated convolutions expand receptive field by introducing gaps controlled by dilation factor d:

$$h_t = \sum_{i=0}^{k-1} w_i \cdot x_{t-d \cdot i} \tag{4}$$

Using exponentially increasing dilation factors across n layers achieves receptive field:

$$\mathrm{RF} = 1 + 2(k-1)(2^n - 1) \tag{5}$$

Residual Connections. Each residual block processes input through main path and residual shortcut:

$$\mathbf{h}^{(l+1)} = \mathrm{ReLU}\left(\mathcal{F}(\mathbf{h}^{(l)}) + \mathbf{W}_s \mathbf{h}^{(l)}\right) \tag{6}$$

Dual-Channel Architecture. Two parameter-independent TCN encoders process character-level and subword-level sequences. Configurations are in Table 1.

Table 1. Configuration of dual-channel TCN encoders

Component	Char	Subword
Residual blocks	5	8
Kernel size	3	5
Dilation factors	$\{1, 2, 4, 8, 16\}$	$\{1, \ldots, 128\}$
Hidden dim	128	384
Dropout	0.2	0.2

For character-level features, the output shape of the final residual block is identical to that of the word-level features, thereby facilitating alignment.

3.4 Cross-Attention Fusion Module

The Cross-Attention Fusion Module is a CBAM-style attention module. It integrates dual-channel outputs $\mathbf{H}_c$ and $\mathbf{H}_s$ through two-stage attention (Fig. 4).

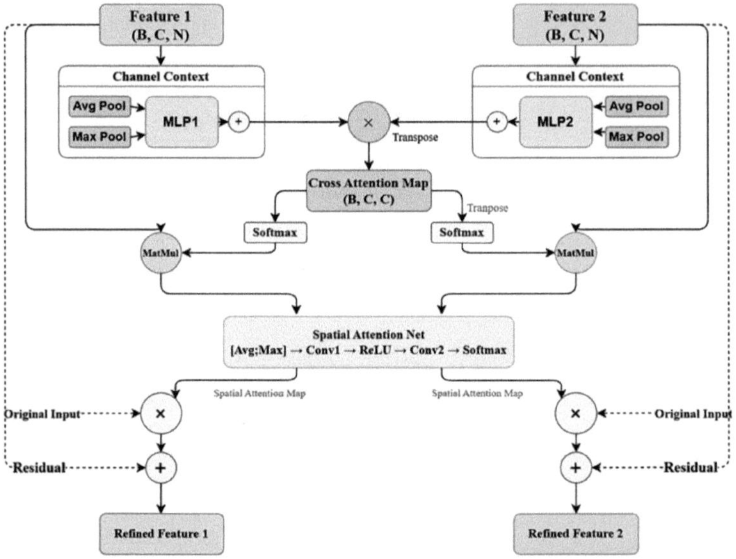

Fig. 4. Cross-Attention Fusion Module architecture.

Channel Cross-Attention. Global Average Pooling and Global Max Pooling generate channel descriptors:

$$\mathbf{z}_i^{\text{avg}} = \text{GAP}(\mathbf{H}_i) = \frac{1}{L_i}\sum_{t=1}^{L_i} \mathbf{H}_i[:, t, :] \in \mathbb{R}^{B\times d_h} \tag{7}$$

$$\mathbf{z}_i^{\max} = \text{GMP}(\mathbf{H}_i) = \max_{t=1}^{L_i} \mathbf{H}_i[:, t, :] \in \mathbb{R}^{B\times d_h} \tag{8}$$

Channel attention weights computed via MLPs:

$$\mathbf{M}_i = \text{MLP}_i^{\text{avg}}(\mathbf{z}_i^{\text{avg}}) + \text{MLP}_i^{\max}(\mathbf{z}_i^{\max}) \quad i \in \{c, s\} \tag{9}$$

Cross-attention matrix and feature reweighting:

$$\mathbf{M}_{\text{cross}} = \mathbf{M}_s \otimes \mathbf{M}_c, \quad \mathbf{H}_i' = \text{Softmax}(\mathbf{M}_{\text{cross}}) \cdot \mathbf{H}_i \quad i \in \{c, s\} \tag{10}$$

Temporal Attention and Fusion. Temporal attention maps computed via convolution:

$$\mathbf{M}_{T,i} = \text{Softmax}_L(\text{Conv}_T(\mathbf{D}_i)) \in \mathbb{R}^{B\times 1\times L_i} \quad i \in \{c, s\} \tag{11}$$

Final fusion with residual connection.

3.5 Multi-grain CNN Extractor

Multi-Kernel Convolutional Feature Extractor. Parallel multi-kernel convolution captures local dependencies, as shown in Fig. 5.

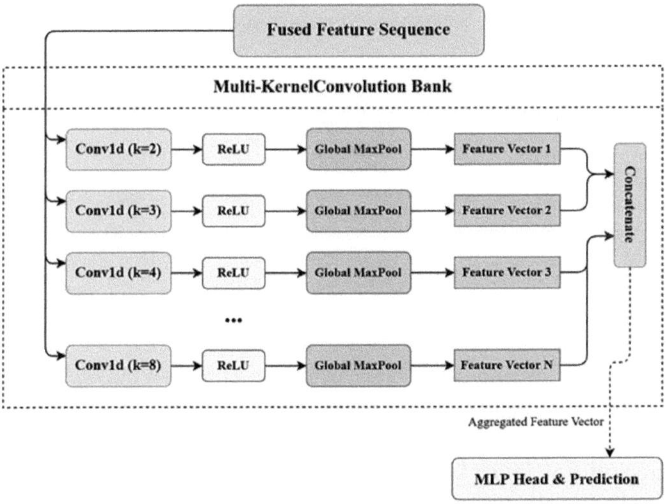

Fig. 5. Multi-kernel convolutional feature extraction.

For each kernel size:

$$\mathbf{C}_k = \text{ReLU}(\text{Conv1D}_k(\mathbf{H}_{fused})), \quad \hat{c}_k = \max_t(\mathbf{C}_k[:, :, t]) \tag{12}$$

Features concatenated:

$$\mathbf{v}_{final} = \text{Concat}(\hat{c}k_1, \hat{c}k_2, \ldots, \hat{c}k_N) \tag{13}$$

Prediction Layer. The final prediction is performed by an MLP which is composed of an input layer, an output layer, a hidden layer, and the ReLU activation function.

4 Experiments

4.1 Datasets and Evaluation Metrics

We evaluate our model using two distinct datasets: the classic CSIC-2010 benchmark [24] and the contemporary ATRDF framework (2023) [25]. While CSIC-2010 provides a stable foundation with over 97,000 HTTP requests covering traditional threats like SQLi and XSS, ATRDF introduces modern REST API traffic patterns and complex attacks such as Directory Traversal and BOLA. By combining these datasets, we ensure the model's robustness across both legacy web environments and high-dimensional, JSON-based modern API infrastructures. Detailed statistics for both are summarized in Table 2.

Table 2. Statistics of experimental datasets

Dataset	Subset	Benign	Malicious	Total
CSIC	Training	36,000	0	36,000
2010	Test (N)	36,000	0	36,000
	Test (A)	0	25,000	25,000
ATRDF	Overall	391,747	67,302	459,049

For the CSIC-2010 dataset, we pre-train the SentencePiece tokenizer exclusively on the official training set. To strictly prevent data leakage, the official test set is then partitioned into training, validation, and testing subsets at a 70:15:15 ratio. We evaluate using standard binary classification metrics: Accuracy, Precision, Recall, and F1-Score based on TP, TN, FP, and FN.

4.2 Baseline Models

We compare MC-TCN with five baseline models: PL-RNN [9] (RNN-based payload classification), CNN [19] (Bag-of-Words with CNN), CNN+LSTM [22] (hybrid local and sequential features), HCLSTM [1] (CNN with Bi-LSTM and self-attention), BCSP [15] (CharBERT with transformer and attention pyramid) and RoBERTa-GAN[21](RoBERTa-based with GAN).

4.3 Implementation Details

The dataset is split 70:15:15 for training, validation, and testing. HTTP requests are tokenized using parallel SentencePiece (vocab size 800) and character-level (vocab size 108) tokenizers, with sequences padded to 512 tokens. MC-TCN uses 384-dimensional subword and 128-dimensional character embeddings. The Cross-Attention Fusion Module employs [4] attention heads. The multi-kernel CNN utilizes filters of size $k \in \{2, 3, 4, 5, 6\}$ (128 filters each) with ReLU activation, and the MLP hidden dimension is 256. A dropout rate of 0.5 is applied to prevent overfitting. TCN configuration is shown in Table 1. Training uses the AdamW optimizer with Binary Cross-Entropy loss for a maximum of 100 epochs (early stopping patience of 4). Batch sizes are 64 (training) and 128 (validation/test), with an initial learning rate of 5×10^{-5}, weight decay of 1×10^{-5}, and a cosine annealing schedule with 10% warmup. Experiments run on Ubuntu 22.04, Intel i7-13700KF, NVIDIA RTX 5080, 48GB RAM, Python 3.10.16, and PyTorch 2.8.0.

4.4 Results and Analysis

Table 3 summarizes the performance of MC-TCN against baseline methods on the CSIC-2010 and ATRDF-2023 test sets. On the CSIC-2010 dataset, MC-TCN achieves state-of-the-art-level results across all metrics. MC-TCN improves 3.64% in accuracy and 3.65% in F1 over the best classical model, and exceeds HCLSTM by 0.31% accuracy and 0.35% F1. Compared to BCSP based with BERT, MC-TCN gains 1.48% accuracy and 0.41% F1. Furthermore, on the modern ATRDF-2023 dataset, MC-TCN demonstrates strong generalization capabilities. When compared to the RoBERTa baseline, our proposed model achieves an impressive 97.91% in MCC and 98.19% in F1-Score, yielding substantial improvements of 4.24% and 4.32%, respectively. Note that classical baselines are omitted for ATRDF-2023 in Table 3 due to the unavailability of their source codes for reliable reproduction.

Table 3. Performance comparison on CSIC-2010 and ATRDF

Method	CSIC-2010 (%)		ATRDF-2023(%)	
	ACC	F1	MCC	F1
PL-RNN	96.13	96.07	84.45	86.77
CNN	97.07	97.51	96.85	97.13
CNN+LSTM	95.50	94.40	93.91	94.19
BCSP	98.29	99.31	–	–
HCLSTM	99.46	99.37	–	–
RoBERTa	–	86.17	93.67	93.87
MC-TCN (ours)	99.77	99.72	97.91	98.19

Figure 6 shows both training and validation accuracy rapidly exceed 99% within the first 10 epochs, demonstrating efficient learning. The validation accuracy peaks at 99.84% at epoch 51. The small gap between training and validation losses indicates good generalization without overfitting. Figure 7 presents the ROC curve for MC-TCN. The model achieves an exceptional AUC of 0.9997. The ROC curve closely hugs the top-left corner, indicating that MC-TCN maintains a very high True Positive Rate across all operating points while keeping the False Positive Rate extremely low. Beyond classification accuracy, computational efficiency is crucial for practical deployment. Figure 8 compares the throughput of MC-TCN and HCLSTM in both training and inference phases. MC-TCN processes 461.44 samples/s (training) and 1408.0 samples/s (inference), achieving 1.73× and 1.39× speedups over HCLSTM. This computational advantage stems from TCN's parallelization capabilities, making MC-TCN more practical for large-scale deployment.

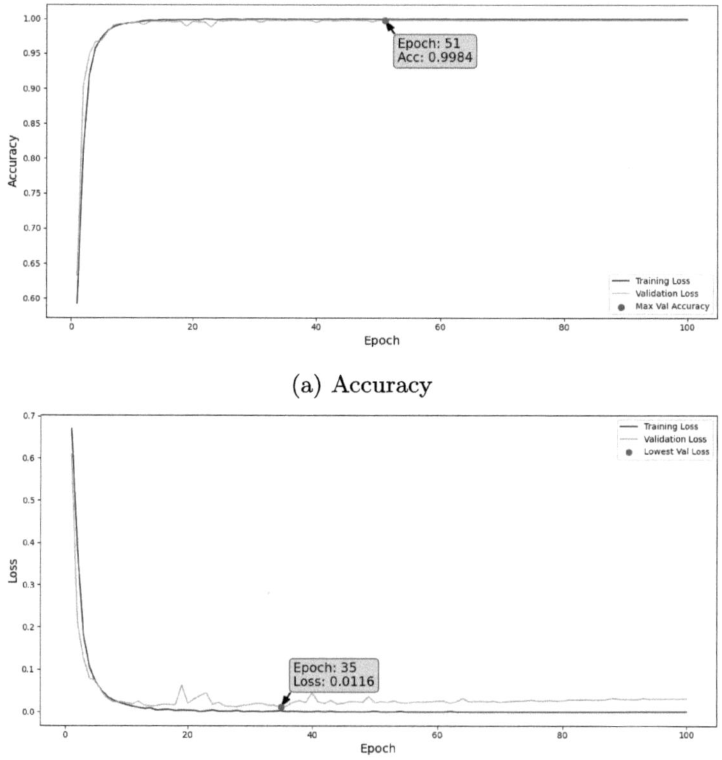

(a) Accuracy

(b) Loss

Fig. 6. Training and validation curves on CSIC-2010.

4.5 Ablation Study on CSIC-2010

We evaluate dual-granularity tokenization using three variants: Char-Only, Subword-Only, and Full Model. Table 4 shows Subword-Only achieves 99.12% F1, surpassing Char-Only (85.66% F1). The Full Model further improves F1 to 99.72% (+0.60%), with +1.22% recall gain, showing character features help detect attacks that subword tokenization might obscure, such as obfuscated attacks and OOV attack strings.

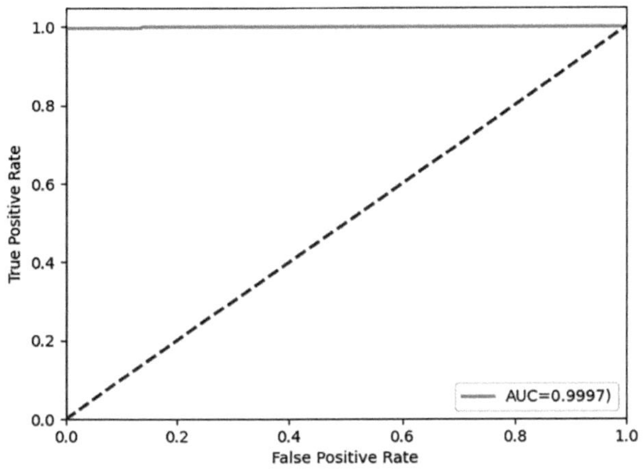

Fig. 7. ROC curve of MC-TCN (AUC = 0.9997) on CSIC-2010.

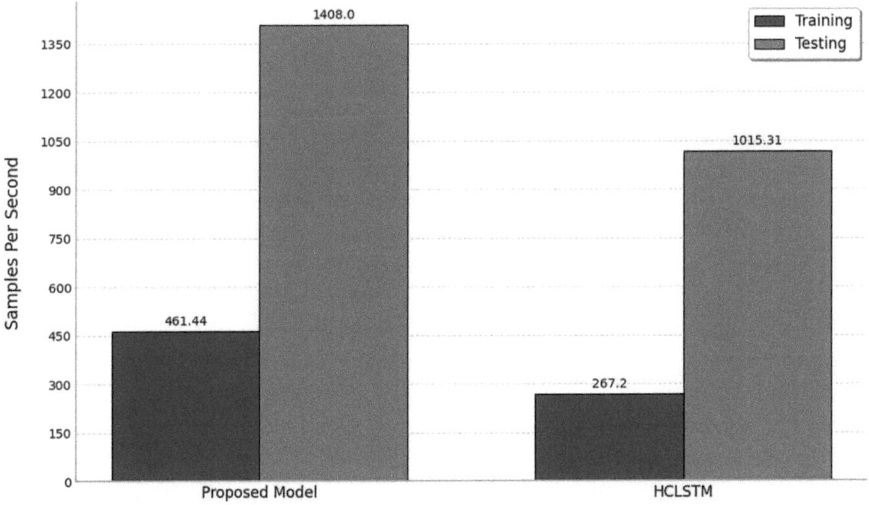

Fig. 8. Training and inference throughput comparison.

The "Baseline" refers to a minimal architecture consisting solely of multi-grain embeddings and the MLP classifier.Table 5 evaluates three components: TCN (A), CAFM (B), and Multi-Kernel CNN (C). TCN alone improves F1 by 6.73%, and CNN alone by 6.70%. Combining A+C yields 99.56% F1. Adding CAFM reaches 99.72% (+0.16%), confirming all components contribute to performance.

Table 4. Ablation study on tokenization granularity

Variant	ACC (%)	Prec (%)	Rec (%)	F1 (%)
Char-only	86.54	76.10	97.98	85.66
Subword-only	99.28	99.92	98.32	99.12
Full model	99.77	99.89	99.54	99.72

Table 5. Ablation study on architectural components

Configuration	ACC (%)	Prec (%)	Rec (%)	F1 (%)
Baseline	93.93	90.85	94.76	92.76
+ TCN (A)	99.59	99.87	99.12	99.49
+ CNN (C)	99.55	99.39	99.52	99.46
+ A + C	99.62	99.60	99.47	99.56
Full (A + B + C)	99.77	99.89	99.54	99.72

5 Conclusion

This paper presented MC-TCN, an efficient deep learning architecture for web attack detection. By integrating dual-granularity tokenization, parallel Temporal Convolutional Networks (TCN), and hierarchical attention, MC-TCN captures both fine-grained syntactic patterns and high-level semantic structures, enabling a more holistic understanding of malicious payloads than traditional sequence models.

Extensive experiments demonstrate the model's state-of-the-art-level performance and robust generalization across multiple benchmarks. On the CSIC-2010 dataset, MC-TCN achieves 99.77% accuracy, 99.89% precision, 99.54% recall, and 99.72% F1-Score, outperforming recent methods such as HCLSTM and BCSP. Furthermore, on the modern ATRDF-2023 dataset, the model maintains excellent detection capabilities, achieving 97.91% MCC and 98.19% F1-Score. Crucially, by replacing recurrent architectures with TCNs, MC-TCN achieves a 1.73× training speedup and a 1.39× inference speedup compared to HCLSTM while maintaining superior accuracy, making it highly practical for real-time deployment.

While MC-TCN demonstrates exceptional performance on benchmark datasets, transition to real-world deployment necessitates thriving under non-ideal conditions. Future work will primary focus on evaluating and enhancing the model's resilience against real-world noise and adversarial inputs, such as polymorphic payloads and deliberate obfuscation techniques. Additionally, we plan to investigate model interpretability to provide transparent security insights and develop lightweight variants via knowledge distillation for resource-constrained edge environments. Ultimately, MC-TCN's fusion of multi-grain representations and efficient sequence modeling establishes a robust foundation for practical, enterprise-grade web application firewalls.

Acknowledgments. This research was supported by the Key Research Platforms and Projects of Higher Education Institutions in Guangdong Province (No. 2024ZDZX1021), the Basic and Applied Basic Research Foundation of Guangdong Province, China (No. 2025A1515012156).

References

1. Luo, K., Chen, Y.: A novel hybrid neural network approach incorporating convolution and LSTM with a self-attention mechanism for web attack detection. Appl. Intell. **55**(2), 146 (2024)
2. Wang, K., Stolfo, S.J.: Anomalous payload-based network intrusion detection. In: Recent Advances in Intrusion Detection, pp. 203–222 (2004)
3. Liang, J., Zhao, W., Ye, W.: Anomaly-based web attack detection: a deep learning approach. In: Proceedings of ICNCC, pp. 80–85 (2017)
4. Do, N.Q., et al.: Detection of malicious URLs using temporal convolutional network and multi-head self-attention. Appl. Soft Comput. **169**, 112540 (2025)
5. Perdisci, R., et al.: McPAD: a multiple classifier system for accurate payload-based anomaly detection. Comput. Netw. **53**(6), 864–881 (2009)
6. Swarnkar, M., Hubballi, N.: OCPAD: one class naive Bayes classifier for payload based anomaly detection. Expert Syst. Appl. **64**, 330–339 (2016)
7. Baishya, D., Baruah, R.: Recent trends in deep learning for natural language processing. In: Proceedings of ICAISS, pp. 408–411 (2022)
8. Supriyono: Advancements in natural language processing: implications, challenges, and future directions. Telemat. Inform. Reports **16**, 100173 (2024)
9. Liu, H., et al.: CNN and RNN based payload classification methods for attack detection. Knowl. Based Syst. **163**, 332–341 (2019)
10. Jemal, I.: M-CNN: a new hybrid deep learning model for web security. In: Proceedings of IEEE/ACS AICCSA, pp. 1–7 (2020)
11. Bai, S., Kolter, J.Z., Koltun, V.: An empirical evaluation of generic convolutional and recurrent networks for sequence modeling (2018). arXiv:1803.01271
12. Zheng, S., et al.: A neural network framework for relation extraction: Learning entity semantic and relation pattern. Knowl. Based Syst. **114**, 12–23 (2016)
13. Vaswani, A.: Attention is all you need (2017). arXiv:1706.03762
14. Hao, S., Long, J., Yang, Y.: BL-IDS: detecting web attacks using Bi-LSTM model. In: Security and Privacy in New Computing Environments, pp. 551–563 (2019)
15. Zhai, J., et al.: Industrial IoT intrusion attack detection based on composite attention-driven multi-layer pyramid features. Comput. Netw. **263**, 111207 (2025)
16. Lee, G., et al.: Sentiment classification with word localization based on weakly supervised learning with CNN. Knowl. Based Syst. **152**, 70–82 (2018)
17. Agarwal, B., et al.: A deep network model for paraphrase detection in short text messages. Inform. Process. Manage. **54**(6), 922–937 (2018)
18. Zhang, M.: A deep learning method to detect web attacks using a specially designed CNN. In: Neural Information Processing, pp. 828–836 (2017)
19. Tekerek, A.: A novel architecture for web-based attack detection using CNN. Comput. Sec. **100**, 102096 (2021)

20. Kim, T.-Y., Cho, S.-B.: Web traffic anomaly detection using C-LSTM neural networks. Expert Syst. Appl. **106**, 66–76 (2018)
21. Aharon, U.: RoBERTa-augmented synthesis for detecting malicious API requests (2025). arXiv preprint arXiv:2405.11258
22. Kuang, X.: DeepWAF: Detecting web attacks based on CNN and LSTM models. In: Cyberspace Safety and Security, pp. 121–136 (2019)
23. Kudo, T., Richardson, J.: SentencePiece: a simple and language independent subword tokenizer (2018). arXiv preprint arXiv:1808.06226
24. HTTP dataset CSIC 2010: Spanish Research National Council (2010)
25. Lavian, S., Ariel University, Ariel Cyber Innovation Center (ACIC): The API Traffic Research Dataset Framework (ATRDF). GitHub Repository (2023)

Polynomial-Based Revocation for Attribute-Based Access Control in Secure Cloud Data Sharing

Yanyang Meng[1], Meng Wang[1], Zhibo Sun[2], Delei Wang[1], and Hong Zhang[1](✉)

[1] School of Cyber Security and Computer, Hebei University, Baoding 071032, Hebei, China
hzhang@hbu.edu.cn

[2] Department of Computer Science, College of Computing and Informatics, Drexel University, Philadelphia, USA

Abstract. With the widespread adoption of cloud computing, Ciphertext-Policy Attribute-Based Encryption (CP-ABE) has become a promising primitive for fine-grained access control over outsourced data. However, efficient attribute revocation remains a challenging issue in dynamic cloud data sharing, especially when a specific attribute of a user becomes invalid while the user's other attributes and the same attribute held by other users remain valid. Existing revocation mechanisms often require secret-key updates for non-revoked users, ciphertext re-encryption, or additional update metadata, which limits their scalability in practical cloud environments. In this paper, we propose PBER-ABE, a polynomial-based and efficiently revocable CP-ABE scheme for secure cloud data sharing. The proposed scheme associates each attribute with a selector polynomial over the authorized user set and defines revocation over user-attribute pairs. Using compact coefficient commitments, the cloud server can update only the affected ciphertext components during revocation and reactivation, without learning the plaintext or requiring non-revoked users to update their long-term secret keys. We also incorporate an attribute authentication mechanism to protect user identity privacy and prevent impersonation attacks. The security analysis shows that PBER-ABE achieves data confidentiality, forward and backward security, and resistance to collusion attacks. Theoretical analysis and experimental results demonstrate that PBER-ABE provides efficient revocation and low user-side decryption overhead, making it suitable for large-scale and fine-grained cloud data sharing.

Keywords: Access control · CP-ABE · attribute revocation · cloud computing · data sharing

1 Introduction

Cloud computing and the Internet of Things (IoT) have greatly promoted large-scale data outsourcing and sharing [19], enabling data owners to reduce local

L. Ding et al. (Eds.): APWeb-WAIM 2026, LNCS 16993, pp. 605–620, 2027.
https://doi.org/10.1007/978-981-92-5693-8_38

storage and computation costs while improving data accessibility [11]. However, once sensitive data are stored in the cloud, data owners lose direct control over data access, and an honest-but-curious cloud server may attempt to infer private information from outsourced ciphertexts and access requests [26]. Therefore, secure cloud data sharing requires cryptographic access control mechanisms that can provide confidentiality and fine-grained authorization without relying solely on trust in the cloud server.

Attribute-Based Encryption (ABE) is a promising primitive for fine-grained access control [21]. In Ciphertext-Policy Attribute-Based Encryption (CP-ABE), the data owner embeds an access policy into the ciphertext, and only users whose attributes satisfy the policy can decrypt the data [1,25]. This one-to-many encryption paradigm is suitable for cloud storage and cross-domain data sharing. Nevertheless, efficient attribute revocation remains a major challenge in dynamic cloud environments. When a user leaves a project, changes roles, or temporarily loses a privilege, the system should revoke only the affected attribute while preserving the user's other valid attributes and the same attribute held by other non-revoked users [10].

Existing revocation mechanisms often rely on key redistribution, time-based attributes, proxy-assisted ciphertext updates, or re-encryption of historical ciphertexts [4]. Although these methods can support revocation, they may introduce high communication, computation, or storage overhead, especially when non-revoked users are required to update their secret keys. The problem becomes more complicated in multi-authority settings, where different authorities manage different attribute domains and must coordinate key issuance, attribute authentication, and revocation-state updates [6,14]. Thus, it is desirable to design an efficient revocation mechanism that supports user-specific attribute-level revocation and reactivation while shifting most update costs to the cloud.

In this paper, we propose PBER-ABE, a polynomial-based and efficiently revocable CP-ABE scheme for secure cloud data sharing. The key idea is to associate each attribute with a selector polynomial over the authorized user set. Revocation is defined over a user-attribute pair rather than over an entire user or a globally removed attribute. When an attribute of a specific user is revoked, the corresponding authority updates the selector polynomial and its compact coefficient commitments, and the cloud server updates only the affected ciphertext components. The cloud server learns no plaintext information, and non-revoked users do not need to update their long-term secret keys. The same mechanism also supports efficient attribute reactivation.

The main contributions of this paper are threefold. First, we design a cloud-oriented revocable CP-ABE framework supporting user-specific attribute-level revocation and reactivation. Second, we propose a polynomial-based ciphertext update mechanism that enables cloud-side revocation without long-term key updates for non-revoked users. Third, we provide security analysis and performance evaluation, showing that PBER-ABE achieves data confidentiality, forward and backward security, resistance to collusion attacks, and efficient revocation with low user-side overhead.

2 Related Work

2.1 Attribute-Based Encryption

Attribute-Based Encryption (ABE) was introduced to support fine-grained access control by associating decryption capabilities with descriptive attributes rather than explicit identities [21]. Goyal et al. [9] proposed a key-policy ABE construction supporting monotonic access structures, while Bethencourt et al. [1] introduced Ciphertext-Policy ABE (CP-ABE), where access policies are embedded in ciphertexts. Waters [25] further presented an expressive and provably secure CP-ABE construction based on linear secret-sharing schemes. These works provide the foundation for one-to-many encrypted data sharing in cloud environments.

To improve expressiveness and privacy, subsequent studies extended ABE to support non-monotonic access structures, hidden policies, and outsourced decryption [18,24]. In addition, Multi-Authority ABE (MA-ABE) was proposed to reduce reliance on a single authority and allow different authorities to manage different attribute domains [2,12]. Recent MA-ABE schemes further consider decentralized authorization, cross-domain data sharing, and privacy-preserving authentication [8,22]. However, efficient revocation remains difficult when user attributes change frequently.

2.2 Attribute Revocation

Revocation is essential for practical CP-ABE systems because user memberships and attributes may change dynamically. Existing revocation mechanisms can be broadly divided into direct and indirect approaches [27]. Direct revocation embeds revocation information into ciphertexts or access policies, which enables immediate revocation but may increase ciphertext size as the revocation list grows [17]. Indirect revocation usually relies on periodic key updates, time-based attributes, or broadcast-style mechanisms, where update information is distributed to non-revoked users [20]. Although effective, such methods often require user-side key updates and introduce additional communication overhead.

To reduce user-side computation, proxy-assisted and cloud-assisted revocation mechanisms have been studied. Proxy re-encryption and attribute-based proxy re-encryption allow a semi-trusted proxy or cloud server to transform ciphertexts without learning plaintexts [29]. Puncturable ABE and update-key-based approaches have also been used to support flexible revocation, but they may require auxiliary update keys or local secret-key updates for non-revoked users [3]. More recent schemes also integrate blockchain or zero-knowledge proof techniques to improve auditability and verifiability [16,28]. Nevertheless, many existing solutions still incur high update costs or do not directly support efficient user-specific attribute-level revocation and reactivation. In contrast, our scheme uses selector polynomials and compact coefficient commitments to shift ciphertext updates to the cloud, while avoiding long-term key updates for non-revoked users.

3 Preliminaries

3.1 Bilinear Maps

Let $\mathbb{G}$ and $\mathbb{G}_T$ be two multiplicative cyclic groups of prime order p, and let g be a generator of $\mathbb{G}$. A bilinear map is an efficiently computable function $e : \mathbb{G} \times \mathbb{G} \to \mathbb{G}_T$ satisfying the following properties.

1. **Bilinearity**: For all $u, v \in \mathbb{G}$ and $\alpha, \beta \in \mathbb{Z}_p$, $e(u^\alpha, v^\beta) = e(u, v)^{\alpha\beta}$.
2. **Non-degeneracy**: There exist $u, v \in \mathbb{G}$ such that $e(u, v) \neq 1$.
3. **Computability**: For all $u, v \in \mathbb{G}$, there exists an efficient algorithm to compute $e(u, v)$.

3.2 Access Structures and LSSS

Let $\mathcal{U}$ denote the attribute universe. An access structure $\mathcal{A}$ is a collection of nonempty subsets of $\mathcal{U}$. It is monotone if, for any $B, C \subseteq \mathcal{U}$, $B \in \mathcal{A}$ and $B \subseteq C$ imply $C \in \mathcal{A}$. In this paper, an access policy is represented by a linear secret-sharing scheme (LSSS) matrix–label pair (M, ρ), where $M \in \mathbb{Z}_p^{\ell \times n}$ and ρ maps each row of M to an attribute. For a secret s, the share of row i is $\lambda_i = M_i \cdot \boldsymbol{v}$ with $\boldsymbol{v} = (s, v_2, \ldots, v_n)$. If an attribute set satisfies the policy, there exists an index set I and coefficients $\{\omega_i\}_{i \in I}$ such that $\sum_{i \in I} \omega_i \lambda_i = s$.

3.3 The q-BDHE Assumption

The security of our construction is based on the q-Bilinear Diffie-Hellman Exponent (q-BDHE) assumption. Let $s, a \in \mathbb{Z}_p$ be chosen uniformly at random. Given the tuple $\left(g, g^s, g^a, g^{a^2}, \ldots, g^{a^q}, g^{a^{q+2}}, \ldots, g^{a^{2q}}\right)$, the q-BDHE assumption states that no probabilistic polynomial-time adversary can distinguish $T = e(g, g)^{a^{q+1}s}$ from a random element $R \in \mathbb{G}_T$ with non-negligible advantage.

4 System Model and Algorithm Definition

4.1 System Model

The system model is illustrated in Fig. 1. The system consists of five entities: the certificate authority (CA), attribute authorities (AAs), data owners (DOs), data users (DUs), and the cloud server (CS). The CA is responsible for system initialization, user registration, and attribute authentication. Each AA manages a disjoint attribute domain and issues attribute secret-key components to authorized users. A DO encrypts data under an access policy and uploads the ciphertext to the CS. A DU obtains attribute secret keys from the corresponding AAs and requests encrypted data from the CS. The CS stores ciphertexts and performs cloud-side ciphertext updates during revocation and reactivation.

The CA is assumed to be fully trusted and communicates with other entities through authenticated and confidential channels. While a fully trusted CA is a

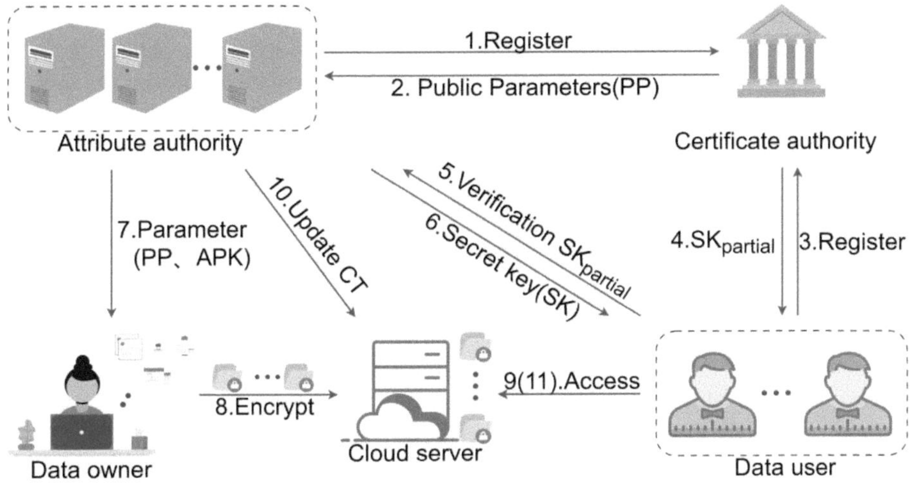

Fig. 1. System model of PBER-ABE.

common assumption in standard CP-ABE systems, a CA compromise would fundamentally undermine the entire system's security. In real-world cloud deployments, this single point of failure can be mitigated by adopting a decentralized or threshold CA architecture, which we leave as an important direction for future work. AAs are assumed to behave honestly during normal operation, while possible authority corruption and collusion are discussed in the security analysis. The CS is modeled as honest-but-curious: it follows the prescribed protocols for storage and ciphertext updating, but may attempt to infer plaintexts, user attributes, or access information from stored ciphertexts and update metadata. Users may be malicious and collude with other users or authorities. The scheme should prevent such collusion from producing unauthorized decryption capabilities. For each attribute x, the corresponding AA maintains an authorized node set $\widehat{\Omega}_x$. Revoking attribute x from user γ removes only the user-attribute pair (u_γ, x) from authorization, without removing x from the global attribute universe or affecting other non-revoked users holding x. The main design objective is to achieve confidentiality, user-specific attribute-level revocation, forward and backward security, collusion resistance, and low user-side overhead under the above threat model.

4.2 Algorithm Definition

The proposed scheme consists of the following algorithms.

System Initialization $(1^\lambda, \mathcal{U}) \rightarrow (PP, MSK)$. Given the security parameter 1^λ and the global attribute universe $\mathcal{U}$, the CA generates the bilinear group parameters, public hash functions, global public elements, and authentication keys. It outputs the public parameters PP and keeps the master secret key MSK private.

AASetup $(PP) \rightarrow (ASK_j, APK_j)$. Each attribute authority AA_j independently generates its local secret key ASK_j and public key APK_j for the attributes under its management. For each attribute x, the authority initializes the authorized node set $\widehat{\Omega}_x$ and the corresponding selector polynomial.

KeyGen $(PP, APK, ASK, UID_\gamma, S_\gamma) \rightarrow SK_\gamma$. User γ registers with the CA using identity UID_γ and requested attribute set S_γ. The CA issues identity-bound partial key materials and attribute authentication signatures. After verifying the signatures, the corresponding AAs generate attribute secret-key components and add u_γ to the authorized node sets of the approved attributes. The user combines all received components as SK_γ.

Encrypt $(PP, \mathcal{M}, \mathcal{A}) \rightarrow CT$. Given a plaintext $\mathcal{M}$ and an access policy $\mathcal{A}$ represented by an LSSS matrix–label pair (M, ρ), the DO encrypts the plaintext and embeds the access structure into the ciphertext. The ciphertext also contains the coefficient commitments associated with the attributes appearing in the policy.

Decrypt $(PP, SK_\gamma, CT) \rightarrow \mathcal{M}/\perp$. User γ decrypts the ciphertext using SK_γ. Decryption succeeds only if the current effective attribute set S_γ satisfies the access policy and the selector-polynomial evaluations confirm that u_γ remains authorized for the participating attributes. Otherwise, the algorithm outputs $\perp$.

Revoke $(PP, CT, x, u_\gamma) \rightarrow CT'$. To revoke attribute x from user γ, the responsible AA removes u_γ from $\widehat{\Omega}_x$, updates the selector polynomial and coefficient commitments, and sends the update information to the CS. The CS updates only the ciphertext components associated with attribute x and outputs the updated ciphertext CT'. Reactivation follows the same workflow by adding u_γ back to $\widehat{\Omega}_x$.

5 Proposed Scheme

In this section, we present the proposed PBER-ABE scheme. The main idea is to use a selector polynomial to encode the authorized user set of each attribute. During revocation, only the polynomial and the ciphertext components related to the revoked attribute are updated, while the long-term secret keys of non-revoked users remain unchanged.

5.1 Selector Polynomial

Let $\Omega = \{u_0, u_1, \ldots, u_{n-1}\} \subseteq \mathbb{Z}_p$ be a set of user nodes, where each node is derived from a user identity by $u_\gamma = H_1(UID_\gamma)$. For each attribute x, the corresponding authority maintains an authorized node set $\widehat{\Omega}_x \subseteq \Omega$. The selector polynomial $F_{\widehat{\Omega}_x}(u)$ is defined such that

$$F_{\widehat{\Omega}_x}(u) = \begin{cases} 1, & u \in \widehat{\Omega}_x, \\ 0, & u \in \Omega \setminus \widehat{\Omega}_x. \end{cases} \tag{1}$$

Let $G_\Omega(u) = \prod_{u_\gamma \in \Omega}(u - u_\gamma)$ be the vanishing polynomial over Ω. For each $u_\gamma \in \Omega$, the Lagrange basis polynomial is

$$f_\gamma(u) = \frac{G_\Omega(u)}{(u - u_\gamma)G'_\Omega(u_\gamma)}. \tag{2}$$

Then the selector polynomial for attribute x is constructed as

$$F_{\widehat{\Omega}_x}(u) = \sum_{u_\gamma \in \widehat{\Omega}_x} f_\gamma(u) = \sum_k c_{x,k} u^k. \tag{3}$$

For each attribute x, the authority publishes compact coefficient commitments

$$Coe_x = \left\{ g^{\frac{z_x}{\theta_x} c_{x,k}} \right\}_k, \tag{4}$$

where $z_x, \theta_x \in \mathbb{Z}_p$ are attribute-specific secret values. These commitments allow a user to derive a gating value associated with its node u_γ without revealing the polynomial coefficients.

5.2 System Initialization

Given the security parameter 1^λ and the attribute universe $\mathcal{U}$, the CA generates bilinear group parameters $(\mathbb{G}, \mathbb{G}_T, p, g, e)$ and selects hash functions $H_1 : \{0,1\}^* \to \mathbb{Z}_p$ and $H_2 : \{0,1\}^* \to \mathbb{G}$. It samples $a, \alpha, CSK \leftarrow \mathbb{Z}_p$ and sets $CPK = g^{CSK}$. For each attribute $x \in \mathcal{U}$, it samples $h_x \leftarrow \mathbb{Z}_p$ and computes $Q_x = g^{h_x} H_2(x)$. The public parameters are

$$PP = \{g, g^a, g^\alpha, H_1, H_2, \{g^{h_x}, Q_x\}_{x \in \mathcal{U}}, CPK\}, \tag{5}$$

and the master secret key is $MSK = \{a, \alpha, CSK\}$.

5.3 Authority Setup

Each attribute authority AA_j manages an attribute domain $S_j \subseteq \mathcal{U}$. It samples $\beta_j \leftarrow \mathbb{Z}_p$. For each attribute $x \in S_j$, it samples $\theta_x, z_x \leftarrow \mathbb{Z}_p$, initializes $\widehat{\Omega}_x = \emptyset$, and sets $F_{\widehat{\Omega}_x}(u) \equiv 0$. The public key and secret key of AA_j are

$$\begin{cases} APK_j = \{e(g,g)^{\beta_j}, \{g^{1/\theta_x}, Q_x^{z_x}\}_{x \in S_j}\}, \\ ASK_j = \left\{\beta_j, \{\theta_x, z_x, \widehat{\Omega}_x, F_{\widehat{\Omega}_x}(u)\}_{x \in S_j}\right\}. \end{cases} \tag{6}$$

5.4 Key Generation

User γ submits (UID_γ, S_γ) to the CA, where S_γ is the requested attribute set. The CA computes $u_\gamma = H_1(UID_\gamma)$ and samples $t_\gamma \leftarrow \mathbb{Z}_p$. For each requested attribute $x \in S_\gamma$, the CA generates the partial key materials

$$sk_{partial} = \{g^{t_\gamma}, g^{\alpha t_\gamma}, \{g^{h_x t_\gamma}, Q_x^{t_\gamma}\}_{x \in S_\gamma}\}. \tag{7}$$

To authenticate the attribute request, the CA computes

$$m_{\gamma,x} = H_2(u_\gamma \| x \| T_x \| T_{sig}), \quad \sigma_{\gamma,x} = m_{\gamma,x}^{CSK}, \tag{8}$$

where T_x is the validity period of attribute x and T_{sig} is the signature expiration time. The user sends the authentication materials to the corresponding AAs. Upon receiving them, each AA_j verifies $e(\sigma_{\gamma,x}, g) \stackrel{?}{=} e(m_{\gamma,x}, CPK)$.

If the verification succeeds, AA_j adds u_γ to $\widehat{\Omega}_x$, updates $F_{\widehat{\Omega}_x}(u) = \sum_k c_{x,k} u^k$, and publishes the updated commitment vector Coe_x. It then samples $\mu_\gamma \leftarrow \mathbb{Z}_p$ and generates the attribute secret-key component

$$SK_{\gamma,j,x} = \left\{K_{\gamma,j} = g^{\beta_j} g^{\alpha\mu_\gamma t_\gamma},\ L_{\gamma,j} = g^{\mu_\gamma t_\gamma},\ R_{\gamma,j,x} = Q_x^{\theta_x \mu_\gamma t_\gamma}\right\}. \tag{9}$$

The complete secret key of user γ is $SK_\gamma = \bigcup_{j,x} SK_{\gamma,j,x}$.

5.5 Encryption

Given a plaintext $\mathcal{M}$ and an access policy represented by an LSSS matrix–label pair (M, ρ), the data owner samples $\boldsymbol{v} = (s, v_2, \ldots, v_n) \leftarrow \mathbb{Z}_p^n$ and $\boldsymbol{r} = (r_1, \ldots, r_\ell) \leftarrow \mathbb{Z}_p^\ell$. For each row $i \in [\ell]$, it computes $\lambda_i = M_i \cdot \boldsymbol{v}$. Let $j = auth(\rho(i))$ be the authority managing attribute $\rho(i)$, and let J be the set of authorities involved in the policy. The ciphertext is

$$CT = \left\{C_0, C_1, \{C_{i,1}, C_{i,2}, Coe_{\rho(i)}\}_{i \in [\ell]}\right\}, \tag{10}$$

where

$$\begin{cases} C_0 = \mathcal{M} \cdot e(g,g)^{\sum_{j \in J} \beta_j s}, & C_1 = g^s, \\ C_{i,1} = g^{r_i/\theta_{\rho(i)}}, & C_{i,2} = g^{\alpha\lambda_i} Q_{\rho(i)}^{-(r_i + z_{\rho(i)})}. \end{cases} \tag{11}$$

The data owner uploads $((M, \rho), CT)$ to the cloud server.

5.6 Decryption

Given CT and SK_γ, user γ first checks whether its current effective attribute set satisfies the access structure. If not, the algorithm outputs $\perp$. Otherwise, the user computes reconstruction coefficients $\{\omega_i\}_{i \in I}$ such that $\sum_{i \in I} \omega_i \lambda_i = s$. For each participating attribute $\rho(i)$, the user evaluates the commitment vector with u_γ and obtains

$$Res_{\rho(i)} = \prod_k \left(g^{\frac{z_{\rho(i)}}{\theta_{\rho(i)}} c_{\rho(i),k}}\right)^{u_\gamma^k} = g^{\frac{z_{\rho(i)}}{\theta_{\rho(i)}} F_{\widehat{\Omega}_{\rho(i)}}(u_\gamma)}. \tag{12}$$

If user γ is authorized for attribute $\rho(i)$, then $F_{\widehat{\Omega}_{\rho(i)}}(u_\gamma) = 1$ and $Res_{\rho(i)} = g^{z_{\rho(i)}/\theta_{\rho(i)}}$. Otherwise, the required pairing cancellation fails. For each authority AA_j, the user computes

$$CT'_j = \frac{e(C_1, K_{\gamma,j})}{\prod_{i \in U_j} \left(e(C_{i,2}, L_{\gamma,j}) \cdot e(C_{i,1} Res_{\rho(i)}, R_{\gamma,j,\rho(i)})\right)^{\omega_i}}, \tag{13}$$

where $U_j = I \cap \{i : \rho(i) \in S_j\}$. Finally, the plaintext is recovered as

$$\mathcal{M} = \frac{C_0}{\prod_{j \in J} CT_j'}. \tag{14}$$

5.7 Revocation and Reactivation

To revoke attribute x from user $\hat{\gamma}$, the responsible authority removes $u_{\hat{\gamma}}$ from $\widehat{\Omega}_x$ and updates the selector polynomial. Let the original selector polynomial be

$$F_{\widehat{\Omega}_x}(u) = \sum_k c_{x,k} u^k. \tag{15}$$

After revocation, the updated polynomial is

$$F_{\widehat{\Omega}_x'}(u) = F_{\widehat{\Omega}_x}(u) - \frac{G_{\Omega_x}(u)}{(u - u_{\hat{\gamma}}) G'_{\Omega_x}(u_{\hat{\gamma}})} = \sum_k c'_{x,k} u^k. \tag{16}$$

The authority samples a new $z_x' \leftarrow \mathbb{Z}_p$ and computes the updated commitment vector $Coe_x' = \left\{ g^{\frac{z_x'}{\theta_x} c'_{x,k}} \right\}_k$. Let $\Delta z_x = z_x' - z_x$. The authority sends $(Coe_x', \Delta z_x)$ to the cloud server. For each ciphertext row satisfying $\rho(i) = x$, the cloud updates

$$C_{i,2}' = C_{i,2} \cdot Q_x^{-\Delta z_x}, \tag{17}$$

and replaces Coe_x with Coe_x'. This operation disables only the user-attribute pair $(u_{\hat{\gamma}}, x)$ and does not affect other attributes of $\hat{\gamma}$ or other users holding x. Reactivation follows the same procedure by adding $u_{\hat{\gamma}}$ back to $\widehat{\Omega}_x$ and updating the corresponding polynomial commitments.

6 Security Analysis

In this section, we analyze the security of PBER-ABE. The analysis covers data confidentiality, revocation security, attribute authentication, and resistance to collusion attacks.

6.1 Data Confidentiality

Theorem 1. *If the q-BDHE assumption holds, then PBER-ABE achieves selective IND-CPA security against polynomial-time adversaries.*

Proof. We prove the theorem by reduction. Assume that there exists a probabilistic polynomial-time adversary $\mathcal{A}$ that can distinguish the encryption of two equal-length messages under a challenge access structure with non-negligible advantage. We construct a simulator $\mathcal{B}$ that uses $\mathcal{A}$ to solve the q-BDHE problem.

At the beginning of the game, $\mathcal{A}$ commits to a challenge access structure (M^*, ρ^*). The simulator embeds the q-BDHE instance into the public parameters and programs the attribute-related public elements according to (M^*, ρ^*). For any secret-key query whose attribute set does not satisfy the challenge access structure, the LSSS property guarantees the existence of a vector orthogonal to all rows associated with the queried attributes. Using this vector, $\mathcal{B}$ can simulate valid secret-key components without knowing the hidden BDHE exponent. These simulated keys are distributed identically to real keys from the view of $\mathcal{A}$.

In the challenge phase, $\mathcal{B}$ uses the BDHE target element to construct the ciphertext header. If the target element is $e(g, g)^{a^{q+1}s}$, the challenge ciphertext is a valid encryption of the selected message. Otherwise, the header is masked by a random element in $\mathbb{G}_T$ and reveals no information about the challenge bit. Therefore, any non-negligible advantage of $\mathcal{A}$ in distinguishing the challenge ciphertext can be converted into a non-negligible advantage of $\mathcal{B}$ in solving the q-BDHE problem, contradicting the assumption. Note that our current proof achieves selective IND-CPA security, where the adversary is required to commit to the challenge access structure prior to viewing the public parameters. Achieving adaptive IND-CPA security, a stronger standard where the adversary can dynamically choose the challenge access structure after interacting with the system, remains a challenging open problem for this construction and will be explored in our future work.

6.2 Revocation Security

PBER-ABE supports user-specific attribute-level revocation through selector-polynomial updates. For each attribute x, the corresponding authority maintains a selector polynomial $F_{\widehat{\Omega}_x}(u)$ over the authorized user-node set $\widehat{\Omega}_x$. If user γ is authorized for x, then $F_{\widehat{\Omega}_x}(u_\gamma) = 1$, and the user can derive the correct gating value $Res_x = g^{z_x/\theta_x}$. This value cancels the corresponding attribute-related term in the decryption equation.

When attribute x is revoked from user $\hat{\gamma}$, the authority removes $u_{\hat{\gamma}}$ from $\widehat{\Omega}_x$ and updates the selector polynomial to $F_{\widehat{\Omega}'_x}(u)$. After the update, we have $F_{\widehat{\Omega}'_x}(u_{\hat{\gamma}}) = 0$. Thus, the revoked user can no longer derive the required gating value for attribute x. Even if the user keeps previously issued long-term key components, the updated ciphertext component and the new coefficient commitments prevent the pairing terms from being correctly canceled. Therefore, the revoked user cannot use the revoked attribute in decryption.

Forward security follows because ciphertexts generated after revocation use the updated revocation state and updated attribute-related components. The revoked user cannot obtain the post-revocation gating value for the revoked attribute. Backward security follows because previously generated ciphertexts stored in the cloud can be updated according to the new selector polynomial and re-randomized attribute component. After the update, the revoked user cannot decrypt these ciphertexts through the revoked attribute.

6.3 Attribute Authentication and Privacy

The CA generates an authentication signature $\sigma_{\gamma,x} = m_{\gamma,x}^{CSK}$ for each authorized user-attribute pair, where $m_{\gamma,x} = H_2(u_\gamma \| x \| T_x \| T_{sig})$. An AA issues the corresponding attribute key component only if

$$e(\sigma_{\gamma,x}, g) = e(m_{\gamma,x}, CPK) \tag{18}$$

holds. Since only the CA knows CSK, an adversary cannot forge a valid attribute authentication signature for an unauthorized user-attribute pair under standard hardness assumptions for pairing-based signatures. Therefore, unauthorized users cannot impersonate legitimate users during key issuance.

The use of identity-derived nodes and attribute authentication also helps protect user identity information from unrelated authorities. Each AA verifies only the authentication materials related to its own attribute domain. It cannot derive the user's complete attribute set from the information submitted to other authorities. In addition, attribute-related values appear as randomized group elements in public parameters, keys, and ciphertexts, thereby preventing external adversaries from directly recovering attribute information.

6.4 Resistance to User Collusion

PBER-ABE binds each user's secret key components to user-specific randomness. In KeyGen, the CA samples t_γ, while each AA samples μ_γ when generating attribute key components. The key components contain terms such as $g^{\alpha\mu_\gamma t_\gamma}$ and $g^{\mu_\gamma t_\gamma}$. Therefore, secret-key components issued to different users are associated with different randomness values.

Suppose several users collude and combine their attribute key components. Since their components are bound to different pairs (μ_γ, t_γ), the pairing cancellations required in the decryption equation cannot be completed consistently. As a result, key shares from different users cannot be combined to produce a valid decryption factor for an access policy that no individual user is authorized to satisfy. Hence, PBER-ABE resists user collusion attacks.

6.5 Resistance to Authority and User-Authority Collusion

Each AA holds only local secret parameters for its own attribute domain, including β_j, θ_x, z_x, and the selector polynomial for attributes under its management. It cannot derive the secret parameters of attributes managed by other authorities. Moreover, valid user secret keys require both CA-issued identity-bound materials and AA-issued attribute-specific components. Since the global secret α and the authentication secret CSK are known only to the CA, colluding authorities cannot independently generate valid complete secret keys for arbitrary users.

Even if malicious users collude with one or more authorities, they still cannot obtain valid key components for unauthorized attributes without valid CA-generated authentication signatures. Therefore, the separation between CA-issued authentication materials and AA-issued attribute keys restricts the power of colluding users and authorities, preventing them from obtaining unauthorized decryption capabilities.

Table 1. Functionality comparison

Scheme	Attribute revocation	Revocation type	Updating secret key	Immediate revocation
[13]	Yes	Per-file direct revocation	Needed	Yes
[7]	Yes	Proxy re-encryption	Not needed	Yes
[5]	Yes	KEK-tree revocation	Needed	Yes
[23]	Yes	Time-tree key/CT update	Needed	Yes
[15]	Yes	Blockchain ZK-proof	Not needed	No
[3]	Yes	Update-key based revocation	Needed	Yes
PBER-ABE	Yes	Polynomial-encoding based	Not needed	Yes

7 Performance Evaluation

We evaluate the performance of PBER-ABE and compare it with several representative revocable ABE schemes [3,5,7,13,15,23]. The comparison focuses on functionality, computational complexity, storage overhead, and experimental running time.

7.1 Theoretical Comparison

Table 1 compares the functionality of PBER-ABE with existing schemes. Most existing schemes support attribute revocation, but they differ in revocation type and whether non-revoked users need to update their secret keys. In contrast to schemes based on key updates, proxy re-encryption, time trees, or blockchain-assisted verification, PBER-ABE supports polynomial-encoding-based revocation and does not require long-term secret-key updates for non-revoked users. Furthermore, compared to blockchain-based revocation approaches, there exists a fundamental trade-off in the trust model. While blockchain approaches provide decentralized, verifiable audit trails often at the cost of consensus delays, PBER-ABE relies on a trusted CA but achieves immediate revocation and significantly lower runtime overhead.

Let $|\mathcal{U}|$ be the size of the attribute universe, $|S|$ be the number of attributes owned by a user, ℓ be the number of rows in the LSSS access matrix, k be the degree of the selector polynomial, E be one exponentiation, and P be one pairing operation. In PBER-ABE, the setup cost is $(|\mathcal{U}| + 2)E + P$, the key generation cost is $(2|S|+1)E$, the encryption cost is $(2\ell+2)E$, the decryption cost is $E+2\ell P$, and the revocation cost is $(k+1)E$. Therefore, the revocation overhead depends mainly on the selector polynomial degree k, rather than on the total number of users or the entire attribute universe. This makes PBER-ABE suitable for dynamic cloud data sharing scenarios with frequent attribute changes. However, it is worth noting a scalability consideration regarding the selector polynomial: for extremely large-scale deployments, the polynomial degree up to $|\hat{\Omega}_x|-1$ could lead to prohibitive ciphertext expansion. To mitigate this, a large user set can be systematically partitioned into smaller, manageable attribute sub-domains, thereby strictly bounding the maximum polynomial degree and ensuring system scalability.

The storage overhead of PBER-ABE is also lightweight. The public parameters require $(2|\mathcal{U}|+4)|\mathbb{G}|+2|\mathbb{G}_T|$, the user secret key requires $(2|S|+2)|\mathbb{G}|$, the ciphertext requires $(k+3)\ell|\mathbb{G}|+|\mathbb{G}_T|$, and each revocation operation requires only $(k+1)|\mathbb{G}|$ additional update material. Since the revocation material is sent to the cloud server and non-revoked users do not update their long-term keys, the communication cost on the user side remains low.

7.2 Experimental Results

We implement PBER-ABE using the Charm-Crypto framework. All experiments are conducted on an Ubuntu desktop machine equipped with an Intel(R) Core(TM) i7-10700 CPU @ 2.90GHz and 16 GB RAM. The number of user attributes $|S|$ varies from 25 to 100. Each experiment is repeated 20 times, and the average running time is reported.

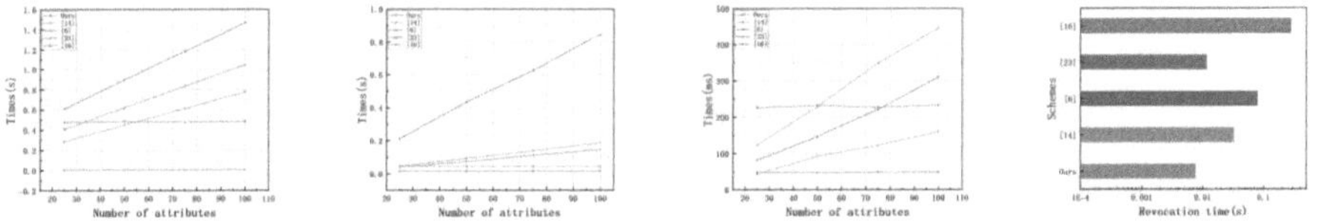

(a) KeyGen (b) Encryption (c) Decryption (d) Revocation

Fig. 2. Comparison of operation time.

Figure 2(a) shows that the KeyGen time of PBER-ABE increases almost linearly with the number of attributes, which is consistent with the theoretical complexity $(2|S|+1)E$. When $|S|$ increases from 25 to 100, the KeyGen time grows from 0.287 s to 0.775 s, indicating that the additional cost introduced by attribute authentication and polynomial maintenance remains moderate.

Figure 2(b) reports the encryption time. Since each row in the LSSS access matrix requires corresponding ciphertext components, the encryption cost increases with $|S|$. PBER-ABE is slightly slower than schemes with less expressive ciphertext structures, but it is significantly more efficient than [5], especially when the number of attributes becomes large. This shows that PBER-ABE achieves a practical balance between expressive access policies and encryption efficiency.

Figure 2(c) shows the decryption time. The decryption cost of PBER-ABE grows moderately because pairing operations are required for satisfied LSSS rows. Although its decryption time is slightly higher than that of [15], it remains lower than several other compared schemes and supports user-specific attribute-level revocation with expressive access policies.

Figure 2(d) compares the revocation time. PBER-ABE achieves the lowest revocation overhead among the compared schemes. When $|S| = 100$, its revocation time is only 7.562 ms, reducing the overhead by approximately 76.7%, 90.5%, 34.6%, and 97.3% compared with [5,13,23], and [15], respectively. This improvement comes from the selector-polynomial update mechanism, which updates only the affected coefficient commitments and ciphertext components.

Overall, the experimental results are consistent with the theoretical analysis. PBER-ABE keeps the computational overhead of KeyGen, Encrypt, and Decrypt within a practical range, while achieving particularly efficient revocation. The main reason is that the proposed polynomial-encoding mechanism shifts the update burden to the cloud server and avoids long-term secret-key updates for non-revoked users. Therefore, PBER-ABE achieves a favorable balance among policy expressiveness, revocation efficiency, and user-side computation cost.

8 Conclusion

In this paper, we proposed PBER-ABE, a polynomial-based and efficiently revocable CP-ABE scheme for secure cloud data sharing. The proposed scheme supports user-specific attribute-level revocation and reactivation by associating each attribute with a selector polynomial over the authorized user set. With compact coefficient commitments, the cloud server can update only the ciphertext components affected by a revoked user-attribute pair, without learning the plaintext or requiring non-revoked users to update their long-term secret keys. We also introduced an attribute authentication mechanism to protect user identity privacy and prevent impersonation attacks during key issuance. Security analysis shows that PBER-ABE provides data confidentiality, forward and backward security, and resistance to collusion attacks. Theoretical analysis and experimental results demonstrate that the proposed scheme achieves efficient revocation and low user-side decryption overhead, making it suitable for large-scale and dynamic cloud data sharing scenarios.

References

1. Bethencourt, J., Sahai, A., Waters, B.: Ciphertext-policy attribute-based encryption. In: IEEE Symposium on Security and Privacy (SP), pp. 321–334. IEEE (2007)
2. Chase, M.: Multi-authority attribute based encryption. In: Theory of Cryptography Conference, pp. 515–534. Springer (2007)
3. Chen, L., Xu, S., Jin, C., Zhang, H., Weng, J.: Partially hidden policy attribute-based multi-keyword searchable encryption with verification and revocation. IEEE Trans. Mob. Comput. (2025)

4. Cui, J., Chen, Y., Zhong, H., He, D., Wei, L., Bolodurina, I., Liu, L.: Lightweight encryption and authentication for controller area network of autonomous vehicles. IEEE Trans. Veh. Technol. **72**(11), 14756–14770 (2023)
5. Dai, Y., Xue, L., Yang, B., Wang, T., Zhang, K.: A traceable and revocable decentralized attribute-based encryption scheme with fully hidden access policy for cloud-based smart healthcare. Comput. Stand. Interfaces **92**, 103936 (2025)
6. Duan, P., Ma, Z., Gao, H., Tian, T., Zhang, Y.: Multi-authority attribute-based encryption scheme with access delegation for cross blockchain data sharing. IEEE Trans. Inf. Forensics Secur. (2024)
7. Ge, C., Susilo, W., Liu, Z., Baek, J., Luo, X., Fang, L.: Attribute-based proxy re-encryption with direct revocation mechanism for data sharing in clouds. In: Proceedings of the ACM Turing Award Celebration Conference-China 2023, pp. 164–165. (2023)
8. Ghopur, D., Ma, J., Ma, X., He, F., Liu, K., Jiang, T., Wang, X.: Decentralized multi-authority attribute-based searchable encryption for e-health cloud. IEEE Internet Things J. (2025)
9. Goyal, V., Pandey, O., Sahai, A., Waters, B.: Attribute-based encryption for fine-grained access control of encrypted data. In: Proceedings of the 13th ACM Conference on Computer and Communications Security, pp. 89–98 (2006)
10. Hao, J., Tang, W., Huang, C., Liu, J., Wang, H., Xian, M.: Secure data sharing with flexible user access privilege update in cloud-assisted IoMT. IEEE Trans. Emerg. Top. Comput. **10**(2), 933–947 (2021)
11. Lan, C., Liu, L., Wang, C., Li, H.: An efficient and revocable attribute-based data sharing scheme with rich expression and escrow freedom. Inf. Sci. **624**, 435–450 (2023)
12. Lewko, A., Waters, B.: Decentralizing attribute-based encryption. In: Annual International Conference on the Theory and Applications of Cryptographic Techniques, pp. 568–588. Springer (2011)
13. Li, J., Chen, S., Lu, Y., Ning, J., Shen, J., Zhang, Y.: Revocable registered attribute-based encryption with user deregistration. IEEE Internet Things J. (2025)
14. Li, J., Yan, H., Koe, A.S.V., Deng, W., Zhong, Z.: Secure and revocable multi-authority CP-ABE for mobile cloud computing. In: International Conference on Algorithms and Architectures for Parallel Processing, pp. 75–84. Springer (2024)
15. Li, X., Xie, Y., Peng, C., Luo, E., Li, X., Zhou, Z.: Eprear: an efficient attribute-based proxy re-encryption scheme with fast revocation for data sharing in AIoT. IEEE Trans. Mobile Comput. (2025)
16. Li, Z., Shi, G.: A CCA-secure puncturable attribute-based proxy re-encryption scheme. IEEE Internet Things J. (2025)
17. Liu, J.K., Yuen, T.H., Zhang, P., Liang, K.: Time-based direct revocable ciphertext-policy attribute-based encryption with short revocation list. In: International Conference on Applied Cryptography and Network Security, pp. 516–534. Springer (2018)
18. Luo, F., Wang, H., Yan, X., Wu, J.: Key-policy attribute-based encryption with switchable attributes for fine-grained access control of encrypted data. IEEE Trans. Inf. Forensics Secur. (2024)
19. Rasori, M., La Manna, M., Perazzo, P., Dini, G.: A survey on attribute-based encryption schemes suitable for the internet of things. IEEE Internet Things J. **9**(11), 8269–8290 (2022)

20. Sahai, A., Seyalioglu, H., Waters, B.: Dynamic credentials and ciphertext delegation for attribute-based encryption. In: Annual Cryptology Conference, pp. 199–217. Springer (2012)
21. Sahai, A., Waters, B.: Fuzzy Identity-Based Encryption. In: Cramer, R. (ed.) EUROCRYPT 2005. LNCS, vol. 3494, pp. 457–473. Springer, Heidelberg (2005). https://doi.org/10.1007/11426639_27
22. Shuangxi, Y.: BDAE: a blockchain-based and decentralized attribute-based encryption scheme for secure data sharing. Wuhan Univ. J. Nat. Sci. **29**(3), 228–238 (2024)
23. Sun, J., Bao, Y., Qiu, W., Lu, R., Zhang, S., Guan, Y., Cheng, X.: Privacy-preserving fine-grained data sharing with dynamic service for the cloud-edge IoT. IEEE Trans. Dependable Secure Comput. (2024)
24. Wang, X., Yu, M., Wang, Y., Pi, Y., Xu, P., Wang, S., Jin, H., Han, M.: Attribute-based access control encryption. IEEE Trans. Dependable Secure Comput. (2024)
25. Waters, B.: Ciphertext-policy attribute-based encryption: an expressive, efficient, and provably secure realization. In: International Workshop on Public Key Cryptography, pp. 53–70. Springer (2011)
26. Xiong, H., Zhang, H., Sun, J.: Attribute-based privacy-preserving data sharing for dynamic groups in cloud computing. IEEE Syst. J. **13**(3), 2739–2750 (2018)
27. Yu, K., Tan, L., Aloqaily, M., Yang, H., Jararweh, Y.: Blockchain-enhanced data sharing with traceable and direct revocation in IIoT. IEEE Trans. Industr. Inf. **17**(11), 7669–7678 (2021)
28. Zhai, Y., Yang, H., Yao, J., Wang, T., Zhou, Y., Zhu, F., Yang, B.: Cr^2-abe: a blockchain-assisted coercion-resistant and revocable attribute-based encryption for IoMT. IEEE Internet Things J. **12**(9), 13075–13096 (2025)
29. Zhang, Q., Fu, Y., Cui, J., He, D., Zhong, H.: Efficient fine-grained data sharing based on proxy re-encryption in IIoT. IEEE Trans. Dependable Secure Comput. **21**(6), 5797–5809 (2024)

Semantic Issues

Align and Adjudicate: Structured Semantic Validation for NL2SQL

Junyan He, Xuhua Huang, Xinyu Xiang, and Rong Zhang(✉)

East China Normal University, Shanghai, China
{jyhe,xhhuang,xyxiang}@stu.ecnu.edu.cn, rzhang@dase.ecnu.edu.cn

Abstract. NL2SQL systems allow users to query relational databases through natural language, making semantic validation critical for ensuring that generated SQL queries faithfully reflect user intent. While existing LLM-based non-execution validators are flexible, they typically depend on unstructured semantic comparisons between natural language questions and SQL queries. This approach lacks the capability to explicitly reason over fine-grained semantic elements–such as targets, aggregation functions, and filtering constraints–resulting in suboptimal error detection accuracy and inconsistent behavior across different LLMs. This paper presents a structured semantic validation framework for NL2SQL that reformulates validation as structured alignment between user intent and SQL semantics, followed by question-aware adjudication. The framework identifies fine-grained semantic inconsistencies while distinguishing them from semantically equivalent SQL variants. Experiments show that our method outperforms representative LLM-based validators in semantic consistency judgment and achieves stronger cross-model stability.

Keywords: NL2SQL · Semantic validation · Large language models

1 Introduction

Natural Language to SQL (NL2SQL), also known as Text-to-SQL, aims to translate natural language questions into executable SQL queries, enabling non-expert users to interact with relational databases through natural language. Recent large language model (LLM)-based NL2SQL systems have achieved strong performance on public benchmarks [1–4]. However, despite substantial progress in SQL generation accuracy, practical deployment of NL2SQL systems still faces a critical reliability challenge: a generated SQL query may be syntactically valid and executable while failing to faithfully capture the user's actual intent.

Such semantic inconsistencies are often subtle yet practically harmful. A query may omit necessary filtering conditions, apply incorrect aggregation granularity, use semantically irrelevant tables, or introduce spurious predicates. Since these queries can usually pass syntax checking and execute successfully, they may silently mislead downstream analysis and decision-making. Recent studies further show that semantic inconsistency remains a persistent problem under realistic schemas, enterprise workflows, and implicit business logic constraints [5–7].

L. Ding et al. (Eds.): APWeb-WAIM 2026, LNCS 16993, pp. 623–638, 2027.
https://doi.org/10.1007/978-981-92-5693-8_39

These observations suggest that semantic validation should be treated as an essential post-generation component in practical NL2SQL systems.

Existing semantic validation approaches include execution-based validation, trained semantic detectors, and LLM-based non-execution validators [7–9,11–15]. Execution-based methods validate SQL through runtime behavior or execution consistency (i.e., verifying if different SQL queries yield identical results on the same database), but they typically depend on database instances and execution permissions, while execution consistency itself does not necessarily imply semantic consistency. Trained semantic detectors provide stronger structured discrimination, yet they often require additional supervision, negative sample construction, or model-specific adaptation. More recently, LLM-based non-execution validators have emerged as highly flexible and easily deployable alternatives. By leveraging holistic reasoning, SQL-to-text explanations, or clause-level reviews, these methods bypass the costly requirements of dedicated model training and live database execution environments. However, the reliability of these LLM-driven approaches is often hindered by fundamental issues that affect their accuracy and cross-model stability. Existing methods face three critical challenges:

C1: Heterogeneous Semantic Representation. NL2SQL semantic validation suffers from a semantic gap between natural language intent and executable SQL semantics. Natural language questions express implicit user intent and business-oriented semantics, whereas SQL queries encode explicit schema-grounded relational operations. Directly comparing questions with raw SQL therefore forces validators to reason across heterogeneous semantic representations. They struggle to map free-form text directly to rigid database constraints, which often leads to unstable or incomplete semantic judgments.

C2: Structural-Semantic Non-Isomorphism. Structural differences between SQL queries do not necessarily imply semantic inconsistencies. SQL admits multiple semantically equivalent formulations, including alternative join paths, aggregation rewritings, and equivalent top-k implementations. For example, to retrieve the maximum value, one query might use an `ORDER BY ... LIMIT 1` structure, while another uses a subquery with the `MAX()` function; structurally they are vastly different, but semantically they are equivalent. Existing validators often rely heavily on surface-level string matching (e.g., checking if SQL keywords directly appear in the text) or clause-wise mismatch detection (e.g., independently comparing the `SELECT` or `WHERE` clauses without considering the global context). Consequently, these methods may over-penalize structurally different yet semantically valid SQL variants.

C3: Context-Dependent Semantic Correctness. Semantic correctness often depends on schema semantics and business rules beyond the database structure itself. Enterprise queries frequently involve implicit metric definitions, aggregation conventions, and domain-specific constraints. As a result, semantic validation requires context-aware intent grounding rather than schema-level matching alone.

To address these challenges, we reformulate NL2SQL semantic validation as structured semantic alignment between heterogeneous user intents and SQL queries based on a shared semantic template. By mapping both inputs into this predefined template, we ground the validation process in explicit semantic slots rather than unstable raw text comparison. Specifically, on the natural language side, we derive a structured intent representation by populating the template via schema- and rule-guided intent narrowing; on the SQL side, we extract a structured SQL representation by filling the identical template slots through AST-based semantic structuring. Together, these two processes populate the same semantic template with core semantic elements, including query targets, required tables, constraints, and query structures, thereby enabling precise semantic alignment.

Based on these dual-side abstractions, the framework performs fine-grained semantic alignment along target, table, constraint, and query-structure dimensions. To further address the non-equivalence between structural variation and semantic inconsistency, we introduce a question-aware adjudication stage that revisits the original question, schema semantics, and business rules to distinguish true semantic deviations from semantically equivalent SQL variants.

The contributions of this paper are summarized as follows:

1. We propose a structured semantic validation framework for NL2SQL that reformulates semantic validation as intent-level semantic alignment between natural language questions and executable SQL semantics.
2. To address heterogeneous semantic representations (*C1*), structural-semantic non-isomorphism (*C2*), and context-dependent semantic correctness (*C3*), we propose a unified validation framework that integrates dual-side structured semantic abstraction, schema- and rule-guided semantic grounding, and question-aware adjudication.
3. Experiments on the NL2SQL-BUGs benchmark demonstrate that our method outperforms representative LLM-based non-execution validators and achieves stronger cross-model robustness and stability.

2 Related Work

Semantic validation in NL2SQL aims to ensure that a syntactically correct SQL query faithfully reflects the user's true natural language intent. Based on their dependency on a real database execution environment, existing validation methods can be broadly categorized into execution-based approaches and non-execution approaches. Non-execution approaches can be further divided into trained semantic detectors and LLM-based validators.

Execution-based semantic validation. Execution-based methods validate generated SQL by using runtime behavior as feedback. CycleSQL [8] grounds validation in data-based self-explanations generated from SQL execution results and query operations. SQLDriller [9] checks execution consistency by constructing counterexample database instances to distinguish non-equivalent SQL queries.

These methods can expose semantic errors that are difficult to detect statically, but they usually depend on database instances, execution permissions, and additional execution or counterexample-generation procedures. More importantly, execution consistency does not necessarily imply semantic consistency. Two semantically different SQL queries may return the same result under a particular database state, and execution-based judgments can also be affected by instance-level details such as empty results or unordered outputs [10,11]. Therefore, execution-based validation mainly checks result-level behavioral consistency, rather than explicitly aligning the candidate SQL with the user's original intent. In contrast, our work focuses on non-execution validation and models the alignment between user intent and SQL semantics directly.

Trained semantic validation. Another line of work trains dedicated models or critics for semantic error detection in Text-to-SQL. Chen et al. [11] propose a parser-independent error detector using structural features of natural language questions and SQL queries. SQLens [12] performs fine-grained semantic error detection and correction in LLM-generated SQL by integrating database and LLM signals. SQLCritic [13] introduces a clause-wise critic that provides structured feedback for SQL correction. These methods improve error localization and correction, but typically require additional training data, weak supervision, negative sample construction, or model-specific adaptation. In contrast, our method uses structured representations to constrain LLM-based validation without training a dedicated detector.

LLM-based non-execution validation. Recent studies use LLMs as flexible non-execution validators. NL2SQL-BUGs [7] formulates semantic error detection as an independent task and evaluates LLMs with a two-level fine-grained error taxonomy. This taxonomy covers 9 first-level types, such as Attribute-, Table-, and Value-related Errors, which are further decomposed into 31 specific sub-types including Join Condition Mismatch and Value Mismatch. GBV-SQL [14] introduces SQL2Text back-translation validation to compare generated SQL with the original question. SQLFixAgent [15] uses a multi-agent framework in which a SQLReviewer inspects SQL components and identifies semantic mismatches. Although these methods are easy to integrate, many still rely on holistic natural language comparison or free-form explanations, which may obscure clause-level deviations and make judgments sensitive to LLM reasoning styles. Our framework addresses this issue by transforming both the question and SQL into comparable structured representations and introducing question-aware adjudication to distinguish true errors from equivalent SQL variants.

3 Problem Formulation

We formalize NL2SQL semantic validation as follows. Given a natural language question q, a database schema s, optional business rules $\mathcal{B}$, and a candidate SQL query c, NL2SQL semantic validation aims to determine whether c is semantically consistent with the user intent expressed by q. Here, business rules refer to domain-specific knowledge beyond the database schema, such as explicit mappings, formulas, aggregation conventions, or other evidence that constrains how the question should be interpreted. In this work, we assume that the candidate SQL query is syntactically valid, since our focus is on semantic inconsistencies that cannot be detected by SQL parsers or database syntax checkers.

Formally, the validation function can be defined as:

$$f(q, s, \mathcal{B}, c) \rightarrow (y, r), \tag{1}$$

where $y \in \{\textsc{Consistent}, \textsc{Inconsistent}\}$ denotes the final semantic consistency label, and r denotes the explanation or rationale supporting the decision. A candidate SQL query is considered CONSISTENT if it captures the intended query targets, required tables, constraints, and query structures expressed by the natural language question under the given schema and business rules. Otherwise, it is considered INCONSISTENT.

4 Method

4.1 Framework Overview

To reduce the semantic gap between natural language questions and SQL queries, we propose a structured semantic validation framework, as shown in Fig. 1. Instead of directly comparing the original question with the raw SQL query, we first define a unified semantic template–a shared intermediate structure that standardizes the comparison between heterogeneous representations. This template is strategically designed with four explicit semantic slots–targets, tables, constraints, and query structures (such as `GROUP BY`, `ORDER BY`, and `LIMIT`)–to cover the comprehensive taxonomy of semantic errors proposed in NL2SQL-BUGs [7], ensuring that semantic validation is grounded along four corresponding semantic dimensions. The framework maps both sides into the template and then performs staged semantic alignment and adjudication. Specifically, intent narrowing, structured alignment, and question-aware adjudication are carried out by the LLM under schema and rule constraints, while SQL semantic structuring is implemented through AST-based parsing. This framework keeps SQL-side analysis deterministic while constraining LLM reasoning to these predefined slots. The framework consists of four main stages:

Schema- and rule-guided intent narrowing. On the natural language side, the LLM interprets the natural language question q under the constraints of the database schema s and business rules $\mathcal{B}$ to populate the predefined slots of the semantic template. The output is a structured intent representation (I) that turns open-ended natural language semantics into a schema-grounded form suitable for semantic alignment.

SQL semantic structuring. On the SQL side, the candidate query c is parsed via abstract syntax tree analysis to populate the predefined slots of the semantic template. The output is a structured SQL representation (S) that abstracts

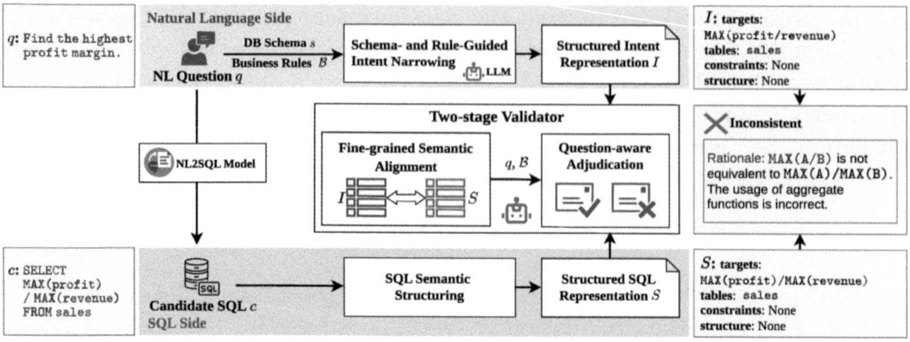

Fig. 1. Overview of our structured semantic validation framework, illustrated using a candidate SQL with a function-related error. Driven by the database schema and explicit business rules, the framework populates the identical slots of a unified semantic template to derive the structured intent and SQL representations (I and S). Next, template-based semantic alignment isolates a target-level structural deviation. Finally, the question-aware adjudication module evaluates this deviation, explicitly condemning it due to the mathematical inequivalence between the row-level calculation (`MAX(A/B)`) and the intended global aggregation (`MAX(A)/MAX(B)`).

away raw syntactic variations–such as aliases and equivalent structural forms–providing a comparable basis for semantic alignment.

Fine-grained semantic alignment. Given the dual-side representations I and S, this stage performs alignment along the four dimensions defined in the template. It produces structured deviation evidence indicating which specific dimensions of the user's intent may be misaligned with the candidate SQL.

Question-aware adjudication. Since structural differences do not always imply semantic errors, the LLM further revisits the original question and business rules to evaluate the detected deviations. Through explicit pardon and condemnation logic, the framework distinguishes true semantic inconsistencies from acceptable SQL variants to produce the final consistency adjudication and rationale.

Overall, the framework decomposes semantic validation into a sequence of constrained subtasks. By replacing direct natural-language-to-SQL comparison with template-based alignment, it provides explicit fine-grained evidence for semantic inconsistencies and reduces the dependence on unconstrained holistic LLM reasoning. The complete execution procedure of the proposed structured semantic validation framework is formalized in Algorithm 1.

4.2 Schema and Rule-Guided Intent Narrowing

Natural language questions are often open-ended, ambiguous, and underspecified, while SQL queries express semantics through rigid database structures. Directly comparing the original question with the raw SQL query therefore forces the LLM to bridge a large semantic gap. To reduce this gap, we introduce an

Algorithm 1. Structured Semantic Validation for NL2SQL

Require: question q, schema s, business rules $\mathcal{B}$, candidate SQL c
Ensure: label $y \in \{\text{Consistent}, \text{Inconsistent}\}$, rationale r

$\mathcal{K} \leftarrow \{\text{target}, \text{table}, \text{constraint}, \text{structure}\}$ ▷ semantic slots
$(C_{global}, I) \leftarrow \textsc{NarrowIntent}(q, s, \mathcal{B}, \mathcal{K})$ ▷ structured intent
$S \leftarrow \textsc{StructureSQL}(c, \mathcal{K})$ ▷ structured SQL
$D \leftarrow \textsc{SemanticAlign}(I, S, \mathcal{K})$ ▷ semantic deviations
$(C, r) \leftarrow \textsc{QuestionAwareAdjudicate}(D, q, s, \mathcal{B}, C_{global}, I, S)$ ▷ condemned deviations
if $C = \emptyset$ **then**
  $y \leftarrow$ Consistent
else
  $y \leftarrow$ Inconsistent
end if
return (y, r)

intent narrowing stage that converts the natural language question into a structured intent representation under the database schema and business rules.

We first rely on the LLM's schema-linking capability to associate entities, attributes, values, and conditions mentioned in the question with candidate tables and columns in the database schema. Recent studies suggest that strong LLMs are capable of identifying and utilizing relevant schema elements when the schema fits within the context window [16]. Based on this observation, we use the schema and business rules as contextual constraints for intent narrowing.

Given a question q, a database schema s, and optional business rules $\mathcal{B}$, this stage prompts the LLM to generate a global semantic context C_{global} and a structured intent representation I. The global semantic context C_{global} contains two auxiliary fields, both described in natural language: a summary of the query target serving as an interpretive context, and an unrepresented semantics field that captures any remaining intent from the natural language question that failed to be formally represented within the structured slots, ensuring the preservation of complex semantics critical for downstream adjudication. The structured intent representation I is derived by populating the explicit slots of the semantic template. It contains four specific semantic elements:

$$I = \langle T_I, R_I, C_I, G_I \rangle, \tag{2}$$

where T_I denotes the targets, R_I denotes the required tables, C_I denotes the constraints, and G_I denotes query structures.

More specifically, each target records the target column, aggregation function, and distinctness requirement. Required tables specify the database tables that are necessary for answering the question. Constraints describe atomic predicates, including the constrained column, operator, value, and logical connector. Query structures record explicit requirements such as `GROUP BY`, `ORDER BY`, and `LIMIT`. This representation does not aim to regenerate the full SQL query. Instead, it extracts the semantic components that are necessary for validating whether a candidate SQL query answers the original question.

Guided by the definitions above, the intent narrowing process follows four principles: schema grounding, priority of explicit business rules, atomic decomposition of constraints, and preservation of unrepresented semantics that cannot be safely encoded in fixed slots. These principles prevent unsupported schema elements, preserve rule-defined semantics, expose fine-grained constraints for later alignment, and avoid discarding complex semantics that exceed fixed fields.

4.3 AST-Based SQL Semantic Structuring

On the SQL side, the goal is to extract semantic elements from the candidate query and represent them in a form comparable to the structured intent. A raw SQL query may contain aliases, nested expressions, equivalent syntactic variants, and dialect-specific forms. Directly feeding the raw SQL into an LLM may cause the validation result to depend heavily on the model's ability to parse and normalize SQL. Therefore, we use abstract syntax tree (AST) analysis to derive a structured SQL representation.

Given a candidate SQL query c, we parse it with SQLGlot [17] and populate the predefined slots of the semantic template to derive the structured SQL representation S:

$$S = \langle T_S, R_S, C_S, G_S \rangle, \tag{3}$$

During extraction, we apply targeted normalizations: for **target items** (T_S), complex expressions (e.g., `CASE WHEN`) are preserved intact to prevent over-decomposition, ensuring the holistic target information is not lost; for **tables** (R_S) and **constraint items** (C_S), all aliases are rigorously resolved to physical names to accurately attach predicates; lastly, **query structures** (G_S) explicitly record `GROUP BY`, `ORDER BY`, and `LIMIT` clauses.

This SQL-side structuring stage makes SQL semantics explicit by mapping the raw query into the identical template slots used to construct the intent representation I, thereby enabling precise semantic alignment.

4.4 Fine-Grained Semantic Alignment

After obtaining the structured intent representation I and the structured SQL representation S, the framework performs template-based semantic alignment through a constrained LLM-based reasoning paradigm. Since both I and S are instantiations of the same semantic template, this stage aligns the values populated in each corresponding slot. Instead of asking the LLM for a single holistic judgment, we decompose semantic validation into four alignment dimensions: target alignment, table alignment, constraint alignment, and query-structure alignment, which provides theoretical completeness by explicitly covering the main semantic error types identified in the NL2SQL-BUGs taxonomy [7].

Target alignment. This dimension evaluates the consistency between the targets of I and S. It compares target columns, aggregation functions, distinctness requirements, and complex target expressions. It effectively detects **Attribute-related Errors** (e.g., target column mismatch) and **Function-related Errors** (e.g., incorrect aggregations). A deviation in this dimension indicates that the SQL may answer a different question, even if other clauses are correct.

Table alignment. This dimension checks whether the SQL representation S involves the tables required by the table slot of I. Missing necessary tables may indicate incomplete semantic coverage, while clearly irrelevant tables may introduce incorrect filtering effects. This alignment ensures the detection of **Table-related Errors**, including table omissions and redundancies.

Constraint alignment. This dimension aligns the constraint items defined in the template. It checks constrained columns, operators, values, and logical connectors between I and S. This fine-grained mapping is specifically designed to uncover **Condition-related Errors** (missing or extraneous filters), **Value-related Errors** (incorrect literal values), and **Operator-related Errors** (faulty comparison or logical operators).

Query-structure alignment. This dimension examines the slots dedicated to structural requirements. These structures are essential for questions involving aggregation, ranking, top-k selection, or grouped statistics. By explicitly validating these slots, the framework prevents **Clause-related Errors** (e.g., missing `GROUP BY`) and **Subquery-related Errors**. If the structured intent representation I explicitly requires a structure that is absent or mismatched in the SQL query, the framework records a structure-level deviation.

The output of this stage is a set of structured deviation records:

$$D = \{d_1, d_2, \ldots, d_n\}, \tag{4}$$

where each deviation d_i is associated with an alignment dimension and a brief explanation. These records provide explicit evidence for the final adjudication stage and improve the interpretability of the validation process.

4.5 Question-Aware Adjudication

Although template-based semantic alignment effectively isolates fine-grained structural deviations (D), not every structural mismatch constitutes a true semantic error. This discrepancy arises from the fundamental challenge of **structural-semantic non-isomorphism**: structural differences between SQL queries do not necessarily imply semantic inconsistencies. Conversely, rigid template slots may occasionally be over-strict or fail to encode highly irregular constraints. To bridge this critical gap between strict structural deviation and actual semantic equivalence, we introduce a question-aware adjudication stage.

This stage acts as the final judge by revisiting the original natural language question q, the business rules $\mathcal{B}$, and the global semantic context C_{global} preserved in the intent-narrowing stage. To explicitly address the non-isomorphism challenge and prevent the framework from over-penalizing structurally different yet semantically valid SQL variants, it applies two complementary types of rules.

Pardon rules. A detected deviation can be pardoned if it stems from valid structural variance rather than a semantic violation, preventing false positives caused by SQL's inherent syntactic flexibility. We categorize these cases into three types: (1) Semantic-preserving structural variations, such as using alternative join paths, varying top-k implementations (e.g., `LIMIT 1` vs. a `MAX` subquery), or combining multiple intent targets into valid arithmetic or conditional expressions; (2) Defensive SQL constructs, where safety mechanisms like `NULLIF` or `IS NOT NULL` introduce structural deviations but strictly preserve intended core semantics; (3) Intent over-extraction, where the strict slot-filling mechanism occasionally populates the template with implicit constraints not strictly mandated by the original question.

Condemnation rules. A deviation is condemned if it strictly changes the intent of the original question. Condemned deviations are grouped into target, table, constraint, and query-structure inconsistencies, corresponding to the four alignment dimensions.

Finally, the adjudicator outputs the final semantic consistency label:

$$y = \begin{cases} \textsc{Consistent}, & \text{if all detected deviations are pardoned :} \\ \textsc{Inconsistent}, & \text{if at least one deviation is condemned.} \end{cases} \tag{5}$$

Together with the label, the framework produces a concise rationale that summarizes the accepted equivalences or the condemned semantic inconsistencies. This two-stage design allows the validator to retain the fine-grained evidence provided by structured alignment while avoiding overly rigid exact matching.

5 Experiments

This section evaluates the effectiveness of the proposed structured semantic validation framework. We aim to answer the following research questions: (1) whether the proposed method improves semantic consistency judgment compared with representative LLM-based non-execution validators; (2) whether structured validation improves stability across different LLMs; (3) how much each component contributes to the overall performance; and (4) whether the structured design helps fine-grained semantic error localization.

5.1 Experimental Setup

Dataset. We conduct experiments on the NL2SQL-BUGs benchmark [7], a benchmark specifically designed for semantic error detection in NL2SQL translation. Unlike general text-to-SQL benchmarks that mainly evaluate execution or exact-match accuracy, NL2SQL-BUGs directly annotates whether a candidate SQL query is semantically consistent with the original natural language question. Each instance contains a natural language question, a database schema, a candidate SQL query, evidence that provides additional semantic context, and a semantic correctness annotation. For semantically incorrect SQL queries, it further provides fine-grained error labels. These properties make the benchmark particularly suitable for evaluating our framework, which aims to detect semantic inconsistencies and localize fine-grained semantic deviations without relying on costly query execution.

Baselines. We compare our method with three representative LLM-based non-execution validators. **NL2SQL-BUGs** [7] directly prompts the LLM to judge semantic consistency and classify semantic errors according to a predefined error taxonomy. **SQL2TextValidator** is a core validation module in GBV-SQL [14]; it performs semantic validation by translating the candidate SQL back into natural language and then checking whether the back-translated explanation aligns with the original question. **SQLReviewer** is an auxiliary agent in SQLFix-Agent [15]; it inspects SQL components step by step and identifies semantic inconsistencies between the SQL query and the user question.

Models and metrics. We use DeepSeek-V3.2 [18] as the main LLM for semantic validation and use GLM-4.7 [19] for cross-model stability analysis. For binary semantic consistency judgment, we report accuracy, positive precision (PP), positive recall (PR), negative precision (NP), and negative recall (NR). Here, positive samples denote semantically consistent SQL queries, and negative samples denote semantically inconsistent SQL queries. For fine-grained error classification, we report type-specific accuracy (TSA), which measures whether a method correctly identifies each semantic error type among erroneous samples.

5.2 Main Results

Table 1 reports the overall semantic consistency validation performance on the full NL2SQL-BUGs benchmark using DeepSeek-V3.2. Our method achieves the best accuracy and positive recall (PR) among all compared methods. In particular, the improvement in PR shows that our method is better at recognizing semantically correct SQL variants, while its competitive negative recall (NR) indicates that this gain is not obtained by simply accepting more queries as correct. These results suggest that structured alignment and question-aware adjudication help reduce false alarms while preserving the ability to detect semantic errors.

Table 1. Semantic consistency validation performance on NL2SQL-BUGs.

Method	Accuracy	PP	PR	NP	NR
NL2SQL-BUGs	0.7572	0.8206	0.6644	0.7133	0.8519
SQL2TextValidator	0.7443	0.8367	0.6133	0.6900	**0.8779**
SQLReviewer	0.7175	0.8193	0.5653	0.6631	0.8729
Ours	**0.7894**	**0.8383**	**0.7223**	**0.7518**	0.8579

The results show that purely holistic LLM judgments tend to be conservative toward semantically correct SQL queries, resulting in lower positive recall. SQL2TextValidator obtains a high negative recall, but its positive recall is lower, suggesting that back-translation may over-penalize valid SQL variants when the generated explanation differs from the original question wording. SQLReviewer performs step-by-step inspection, but it still relies heavily on direct natural-language-to-SQL comparison. By contrast, our method constrains comparison through structured representations and then uses question-aware adjudication to distinguish true semantic deviations from acceptable structural variations.

5.3 Cross-Model Stability

To evaluate whether the proposed framework reduces sensitivity to the underlying LLM, we compare validation methods under DeepSeek-V3.2 and GLM-4.7. The motivation is that LLM-based validators inherently exhibit model-specific preferences: some default to strict rejection, while others are overly permissive of potential semantic inconsistencies. Such implicit biases lead to unstable validation behavior when the underlying LLM is changed.

As shown in Fig. 2, three baseline validators exhibit large fluctuations between the two LLMs, especially in positive and negative recall, indicating a severe shift in decision preference. In contrast, our method maintains a balanced performance across accuracy, positive recall, and negative recall under both models. This robust stability is achieved by decomposing semantic validation into constrained subtasks across the four main stages. Instead of leaving the LLM to perform an unconstrained holistic comparison, each stage operates over explicit semantic elements, making the final adjudication highly controllable and effectively neutralizing the influence of model-specific reasoning styles.

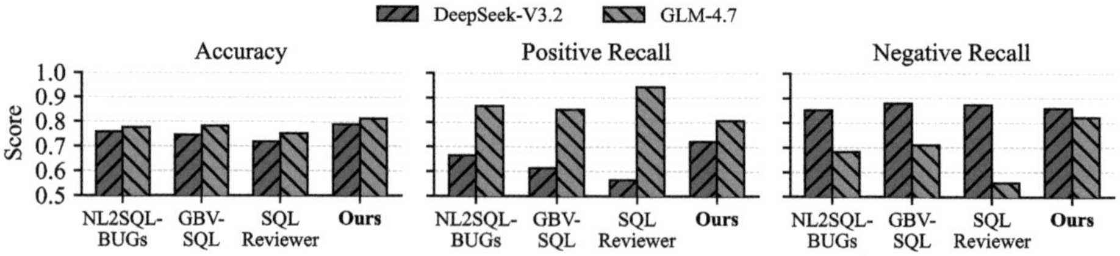

Fig. 2. Cross-model stability comparison under DeepSeek-V3.2 and GLM-4.7.

5.4 Ablation Study

To quantify the contribution of each component of our framework, we conduct an ablation study by independently removing three core modules: (1) the question-aware adjudication stage, (2) the AST-based SQL semantic structuring, and (3) the schema- and rule-guided structured intent representation.

Table 2. Ablation results of the proposed semantic validation method.

Method	ACC	PP	PR	NP	NR
Ours	**0.7894**	0.8383	**0.7223**	**0.7518**	0.8579
w/o question-aware adjudication	0.7735	**0.8495**	0.6703	0.7232	**0.8789**
w/o SQL semantic structuring	0.7825	0.8380	0.7056	0.7414	0.8609
w/o structured intent representation	0.7582	0.8234	0.6634	0.7135	0.8549

As shown in Table 2, all three components contribute to the final performance. Removing question-aware adjudication increases negative recall but substantially reduces positive recall, indicating that the validator becomes overly strict and tends to misclassify semantically valid SQL variants as incorrect. Removing SQL semantic structuring also degrades performance, showing that explicit SQL-side semantic elements are useful for stable comparison. Among the three variants, removing the structured intent representation causes the largest accuracy drop, which further confirms that schema- and rule-guided intent narrowing is essential for reducing the semantic gap between natural language questions and SQL queries.

5.5 Fine-Grained Error Analysis

In addition to binary consistency judgment, we evaluate whether the proposed structured design helps fine-grained semantic error localization. For erroneous samples, the LLM is asked to identify the corresponding semantic error types. Figure 3 reports the type-specific accuracy (TSA) of different methods on the 9 main semantic error types defined in the NL2SQL-BUGs taxonomy [7].

As shown in Fig. 3, our method achieves better localization ability on most structural error types, including attribute-, table-, condition-, function-, and clause-related errors. This improvement is consistent with the design of the proposed framework: the template-based alignment exposes deviations in targets, tables, constraints, and structures, providing the validator with deterministic structural evidence rather than relying on unstructured inference.

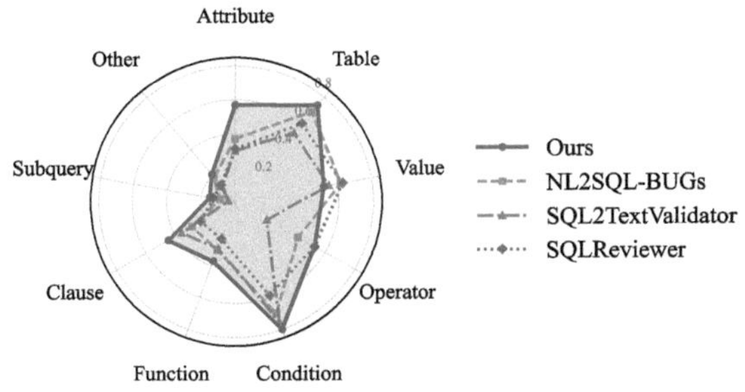

Fig. 3. Type-specific accuracy on main semantic error types.

However, our method is less effective on value-related errors due to the inherent trade-offs of structured abstraction. While optimizing for template-based alignment improves overall error localization, abstracting natural language into predefined slots inadvertently weakens fine-grained literal value details. Consequently, the model tends to conflate specific value mismatches with broader condition-related errors.

6 Discussion and Limitations

The results indicate that the main benefit of our framework comes from converting unconstrained natural-language-to-SQL comparison into structured representation alignment and question-aware adjudication. However, the framework is still a non-execution validator and does not inspect database instance values. Therefore, it may fail when correctness depends on domain-specific value conventions, abbreviations, aliases, or database contents that cannot be inferred from schema information and business rules alone. Future work will explore lightweight data probing and retrieval-enhanced evidence to better handle instance-level value semantics.

7 Conclusion

This paper studies semantic validation for NL2SQL, focusing on executable SQL queries that are syntactically valid but semantically inconsistent with user intent. We propose a structured non-execution validation framework that reformulates the task as template-based representation alignment followed by question-aware adjudication. Experiments on NL2SQL-BUGs show that our method outperforms representative LLM-based validators and achieves stronger cross-model stability, while ablation studies confirm the importance of structured intent representation, SQL semantic structuring, and question-aware adjudication. These results suggest that structured validation is a practical direction for improving the reliability and interpretability of NL2SQL systems.

Disclosure of Interests. The authors have no competing interests to declare that are relevant to the content of this article.

References

1. Liu, X., Shen, S., Li, B., Ma, P., Jiang, R., Zhang, Y., Fan, J., Li, G., Tang, N., Luo, Y.: A survey of text-to-SQL in the era of LLMs: where are we, and where are we going? IEEE Trans. Knowl. Data Eng. **37**(10), 5735–5754 (2025)
2. Hong, Z., Yuan, Z., Zhang, Q., Chen, H., Huang, J., Dong, F., Huang, X.: Next-generation database interfaces: a survey of LLM-based text-to-SQL. IEEE Trans. Knowl. Data Eng. **37**(12), 7328–7345 (2025)

3. Yu, T., Zhang, R., Yang, K., Yasunaga, M., Wang, D., Li, Z., Ma, J., Li, I., Yao, Q., Roman, S., Zhang, Z., Radev, D.: Spider: a large-scale human-labeled dataset for complex and cross-domain semantic parsing and text-to-SQL task. In: Proceedings of the 2018 Conference on Empirical Methods in Natural Language Processing, pp. 3911–3921. Association for Computational Linguistics (2018)
4. Li, J., Hui, B., Qu, G., Yang, B., Li, B., Li, B., Wang, B., Qin, B., Cao, R., Geng, N., Huo, X., Zhou, J., Ma, C., Zhang, G., Wang, J., Zhou, J., Li, J., Li, T., Yu, T., Zhang, S., Chen, C., Li, G., Chang, K.C.-C., Huang, F., Cheng, R., Li, Y.: Can LLM already serve as a database interface? A big bench for large-scale database grounded text-to-SQLs. In: Advances in Neural Information Processing Systems 36, Datasets and Benchmarks Track (2023)
5. Chang, S., Wang, J., Dong, M., Pan, L., Zhu, H., Li, A.H., Lan, W., Zhang, S., Jiang, J., Lilien, J., Ash, S., Wang, W.Y., Wang, Z., Castelli, V., Ng, P., Xiang, B.: Dr. Spider: a diagnostic evaluation benchmark towards text-to-SQL robustness. In: Proceedings of the Eleventh International Conference on Learning Representations (ICLR) (2023)
6. Lei, F., Chen, J., Ye, Y., Cao, R., Shin, D., Su, H., Suo, Z., Gao, H., Hu, W., Yin, P., Zhong, V., Xiong, C., Sun, R., Liu, Q., Wang, S., Yu, T.: Spider 2.0: evaluating language models on real-world enterprise text-to-SQL workflows. In: Proceedings of the Thirteenth International Conference on Learning Representations (ICLR) (2025)
7. Liu, X., Shen, S., Li, B., Ma, P., Jiang, R., Zhang, Y., Fan, J., Li, G., Tang, N., Luo, Y.: NL2SQL-BUGs: a benchmark for detecting semantic errors in NL2SQL translation. In: Proceedings of the 31st ACM SIGKDD Conference on Knowledge Discovery and Data Mining. ACM (2025)
8. Fan, Y., Ren, T., Huang, C., Li, G., Chai, C., Li, N.: Grounding natural language to SQL translation with data-based self-explanations. In: Proceedings of the 41st IEEE International Conference on Data Engineering (ICDE). IEEE (2025)
9. Yang, Y., Wang, Z., Xia, Y., Wei, Z., Ding, H., Piskac, R., Chen, H., Li, J.: Automated validating and fixing of text-to-SQL translation with execution consistency. Proc. ACM Manage. Data **3**(3), 1–28 (2025)
10. Zhong, R., Yu, T., Klein, D.: Semantic evaluation for text-to-SQL with distilled test suites. In: Proceedings of the 2020 Conference on Empirical Methods in Natural Language Processing (EMNLP), pp. 396–411. Association for Computational Linguistics (2020)
11. Chen, S., Chen, Z., Sun, H., Han, X., Xia, T., Kim, T., Hwang, S.: Error detection for text-to-SQL semantic parsing. In: Findings of the Association for Computational Linguistics: EMNLP 2023, pp. 11730–11743. Association for Computational Linguistics (2023)
12. Gong, Y., Lei, C., Qin, X., Vaidya, K., Narayanaswamy, B., Kraska, T.: SQLens: an end-to-end framework for error detection and correction in text-to-SQL. In: Advances in Neural Information Processing Systems, p. 39. (2025)
13. Chen, J., Gan, L., Zhao, Z., Chen, Y., Wang, J., Zhang, Z.: SQLCritic: correcting text-to-SQL generation via clause-wise critic. arXiv preprint arXiv:2503.07996 (2025)
14. Chen, D., Wang, X., Ren, S., Ma, Q., Zhao, P., Liu, A.: GBV-SQL: guided generation and SQL2Text back-translation validation for multi-agent Text2SQL, (2025). arXiv preprint arXiv:2509.12612
15. Cen, J., Liu, J., Li, Z., Wang, J.: SQLFixAgent: towards semantic-accurate text-to-SQL parsing via consistency-enhanced multi-agent collaboration. In: Proceedings of the Thirty-Ninth AAAI Conference on Artificial Intelligence. AAAI Press (2025)

16. Maamari, K., Abubaker, F., Jaroslawicz, D., Wu, J., Katsis, Y., Balazinska, M., Kraska, T., Tan, W.C.: The death of schema linking? Text-to-SQL in the age of well-reasoned language models, (2024). arXiv preprint arXiv:2408.07702
17. Mao, T.: SQLGlot: python SQL parser and translator. GitHub repository. https://github.com/tobymao/sqlglot. Accessed 27 Apr 2026
18. DeepSeek-AI: DeepSeek-V3.2: Pushing the Frontier of Open Large Language Models. arXiv preprint arXiv:2512.02556 (2025)
19. Z.AI: GLM-4.7—Overview. https://docs.z.ai/guides/llm/glm-4.7. Accessed 27 Apr 2026

Improving Multimodal Entity Linking by Cross-Modality Semantic Consistency

Lei Wang, Richong Zhang(✉), Junfan Chen, and Jaein Kim

School of Computer Science and Engineering, Beihang University, Beijing 100191, China
{wanglei24,zhangrichong,chenjf91,jaein}@buaa.edu.cn

Abstract. Multimodal Entity Linking (MEL) aims to resolve ambiguity in linking mentions to entities in multimodal knowledge graphs. It plays a key role in massive applications. Including images to entity linking is demonstrated effective, but the visual information brings two cross-modal semantic inconsistency problems to MEL, which introduce noise to MEL and restrict its performance. To address these issues, we propose a semantic consistency based method for MEL. Concretely, to deal with irrelevant visual information introduced by intra-mention cross-modal semantic inconsistency, we propose an intra-mention image-word consistency indicator (IICI) that determines whether to include the visual similarity for MEL prediction by cross-modal distance comparison. Meanwhile, to rectify the entity type error caused by mention-entity cross-modal semantic inconsistency, we propose a novel mention-entity semantic consistency (MSC) between the mention's multimodal information and the entity's descriptive information. Experimental results on three real-world benchmarks demonstrate the proposed method outperforms various MEL state-of-the-art methods. The code and data of this paper is available at https://github.com/ultrawalle/IMELCSC

Keywords: entity linking · multimodal alignment · semantic consistency

1 Introduction

Entity linking (EL) aims to identify mentions (named entities) in unstructured text and link them to their corresponding entities in a structured knowledge graph (KG). The goal of EL is to bridge the web content with a knowledge graph, enriching the down-stream application with external knowledge. It is an important task that supports numerous of application such as searching engine [7], question answering [20,28] and recommender systems [26]. Similar entities with diverse abbreviations and variants make resolving ambiguous mentions challenging. In multimodal entity linking, images accompanying the mention's sentence serve as an additional source of information to aid disambiguation. Abundant multimodal entity linking (MEL) approaches have proven the significance

L. Ding et al. (Eds.): APWeb-WAIM 2026, LNCS 16993, pp. 639–654, 2027.
https://doi.org/10.1007/978-981-92-5693-8_40

of including images to resolve ambiguous mentions. However, a new challenge arises with the inclusion of images in MEL. Since the mention sentence may originate from various sources, such as news articles or Wikipedia, it may include accompanying images that do not directly correspond to the mention word.

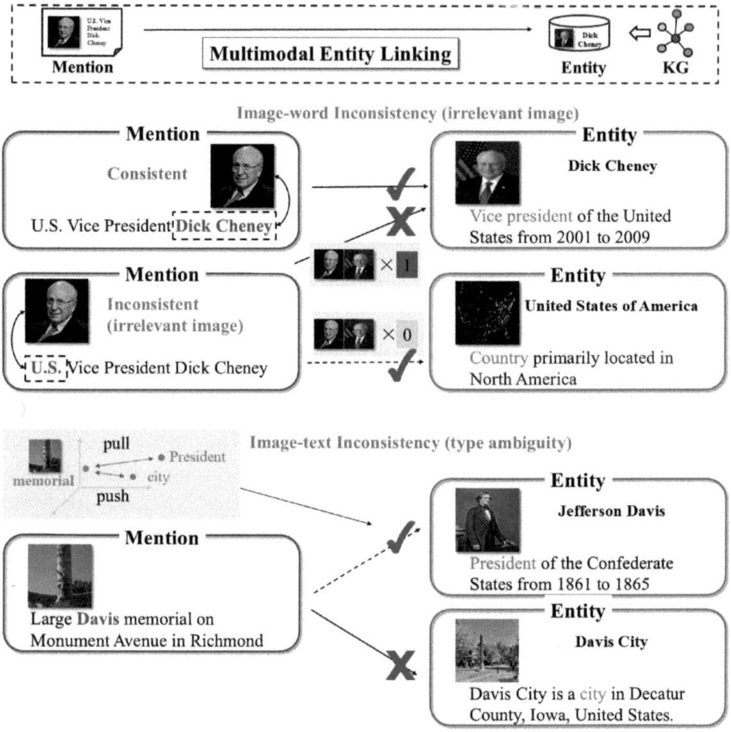

Fig. 1. Examples of two semantic inconsistency problems in MEL.

Since the mention sentence may originate from various sources, such as news articles or Wikipedia, it may include accompanying images that describe the mention sentence rather than the mention word. For example, consider the multimodal mention in the upper part of Fig. 1. For the same set of sentences and accompanying images crawled from web pages, the images may be useful information or noise depending on the candidate mention words. Such inconsistencies between images and textual mentions introduce noise, ultimately degrading MEL performance.

In this work, we address this intra-mention semantic inconsistency challenge by introducing an intra-mention image-word consistency indicator (IICI). In particular, this indicator measures the relevance between the mention image and the mention word by comparing image-to-word and image-to-sentence similarities within mentions, and determining whether the image similarity should part in MEL ranking for each mention. This indicator mitigates the noise introduced by image-word inconsistencies, enhancing the robustness and accuracy of MEL.

Another significant challenge is the mention-entity semantic inconsistency . For instance, in Fig. 1, the mention image of "Davis" presents a statue on the street, which differs significantly from its corresponding entity image–a portrait of "Jefferson Davis". Although the image of the Davis statue undoubtedly represents "Davis" and provides useful information (e.g., his appearance), it may be erroneously linked to the "Davis city" entity due to incorporating the street scene, finally resulting in wrongly predicted entity type (link a person to city). Mirroring issues occur in text for diversity of entity name (e.g., aliases, nicknames, or abbreviations). This issue exists in SOTA MEL methods, even these with fine-grained alignment. To address this mention-entity semantic inconsistency problem , we propose a Mention-entity Semantic Consistency (MSC) that enables the embedding of entity type and description to capture the potential visual variations and name variants of the entity. The main difference between our semantic consistency and existing cross-modal similarity measures (e.g., [16]) is the removal of entity names from the entity description. This design choice enables the entity embedding to collect diverse information of entity's variant while compelling the model to focus on aligning the mention's image with the entity's semantics and type, rather than relying solely on entity names. By doing so, our approach enhances disambiguation, particularly for entities with similar names and different types.

Our contributions can be summarized as follows:

- We propose an intra-mention image-word consistency indicator to weigh image similarities to address the intra-mention semantic inconsistency problem.
- We introduce an approach to measure the semantic consistency between the mention and entity's multimodal information to mitigate the mention-entity semantic inconsistency.
- We conduct experiments on three public MEL benchmarks. The experimental results demonstrate that our method outperforms various SOTA MEL baselines on three public MEL benchmarks.

2 Related Work

Text-based Entity linking The core challenge of Entity linking lies in modeling appropriate similarity between mentions and entities to resolve these ambiguities effectively. Early works utilize similarities based on statistical features [3] or document-level coherence [29] to disambiguate entities. As the neural network developing, different network architecture such as word2vec [2], LSTM [8] are employed for learning entity and mention representations for entity disambiguation. [4] utilize BART [12] to generate unique entity names for retrieval. [1] frame EL as a text extraction problem. Some researchers [11] exploring the use of Large Language Models (LLMs) for EL tasks.

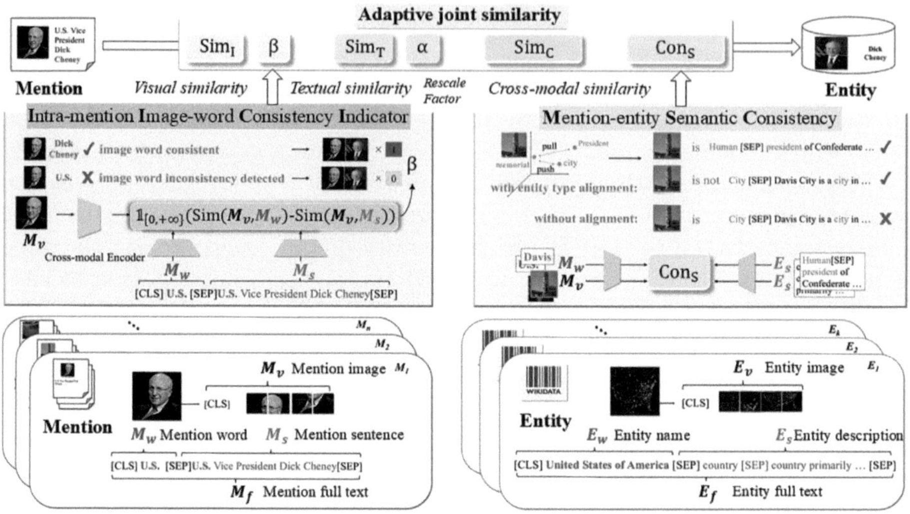

Fig. 2. Overall architecture of the proposed method.

<u>**Multimodal Entity Linking**</u> With the increasing presence of multimodal information online, MEL has gained attention. Various approaches have been proposed: [18] use multimodal attention to handle polysemous and incomplete mentions. One study [6] formulates MEL as a graph matching problem, another extended with embedding matching [31]. [32] incorporates scene graph features. A co-attention mechanism has been used to capture fine-grained inter-modal correlations [25], while [17] address cross-modal inconsistencies with multi-grained units. Some studies [15,22] attempt to enhance MEL using large language models.

While MEL research has demonstrated the effectiveness of images in disambiguation, issues related to semantic inconsistencies have not been thoroughly explored. VELML [30] identifies intra-mention semantic inconsistency but relies on cosine similarity from a pre-trained model without fine-tuning, which may lead to suboptimal embeddings. To address this, we fine-tune the cross-modal CLIP model and introduce a consistency indicator based on similarity comparison. MIMIC [16] attempts to resolve cross-semantic inconsistency through patch and sub-token alignment but can misclassify entity types due to coarse-grained labels; a semantic similarity measure is proposed to refine this. MELOV [24] tackles text-image inconsistency using generated visual features for denoising, but experimental results in ablation study suggest that the proposed modules outperform MELOV in handling semantic inconsistencies more effectively.

3 Problem Formulation

<u>**Notations**</u> A multimodal knowledge base (without relations of KG, which are not used in this task) can be represented as $\mathbb{KB} = \{\mathcal{E}\}$, where $\mathcal{E} = \{E^i\}_{i=1}^N$ is a set

of N entities. Each entity E consists of an entity name e_w, an entity description e_s, an entity attribute (type) e_a, and an entity image e_v, formulated as $E = \{e_w, e_s, e_a, e_v\}$. Additionally, a multimodal mention M consists of a sentence m_s, a mention word m_w, and an image m_v associated with M, formulated as $M = \{m_s, m_w, m_v\}$.

MEL Task Given a mention M, the task of MEL aims to find the corresponding entity E_n from the knowledge base $\mathbb{KB}$ that best matches the mention M by ranking the similarities $f(.)$ between them:

$$E_n = \arg\max_{E^i \in \mathcal{E}} f(E^i|M). \tag{1}$$

4 Methodology

4.1 Overall Architecture

We propose an adaptive joint similarity to disambiguate mentions for MEL. The joint similarity is the weighted sum of: textual, visual, cross-modal similarities, and the mention-entity semantic consistency to address the mention-entity semantic inconsistency problem. The intra-mention consistency indicator is proposed as the factor for visual similarity to address the intra-mention semantic inconsistency problem.

4.2 Multimodal Input and Similarities

Multimodal Input: The details of textual input M_w, M_s, M_f, E_w, E_s, E_f are shown in Fig. 2, where token [CLS]" are introduced to begin a textual input and "[SEP]" token are introduced for semantic separation. Visual input M_v, Ev is the sequence of 2D patches preprocessed following ViT [5] (Fig. 2). We input them to cross-modal encoder pre-trained CLIP [21] to generate cross-modal embeddings $M_W, M_S, M_F, E_W, E_S, E_F, M_V, E_V \in \mathbb{R}^{d_v}$, respectively. Additionally, to better capture contextual dependencies, we also feed the M_f, E_f into textual encoder pre-trained RoBETa [14], then project them to obtain the textual embedding M_T, $E_T \in \mathbb{R}^{d_v}$.

Textual Similarity: Text morphology and context provide the foundational and essential information for EL. Different from other works, to better capture this information, we compute text similarity using projected language model embeddings rather than vision-language model embeddings. Given a mention M and a candidate entity E the textual similarity computed as:

$$f_T(M, E) = h(M_T, E_T), \tag{2}$$

where $h(\cdot, \cdot)$ is the similarity function, we adopt dot production for time complexity

Visual Similarity: Images offer valuable intuitive visual context that can help resolve ambiguities in textual EL, particularly in challenging cases, by leveraging visual cues. We compute visual similarity using the vision-language model embeddings of images. Given a mention M and a candidate entity E visual similarity is computed as:

$$f_I(M, E) = h(M_V, E_V). \tag{3}$$

Cross-modal Similarity: Cross-modal similarity is designed to capture the global connections between mentions and entities across different modalities. Given a mention M and candidate entity E, the cross-modal similarity is computed as:

$$f_C(M, E) = \frac{1}{2}(h(M_V, E_F) + h(E_V, M_F)). \tag{4}$$

4.3 Intra-Mention Image-Word Consistency Indicator

To address the intra-mention cross-modal semantic inconsistency problem, we propose an intra-mention image-word consistency indicator (**IICI**). In MEL application scenarios, a mention image may describe an entire mention sentence rather than a specific mention word, in which case the mention image is regarded as irrelevant information (see examples in Fig. 1). Therefore, the purpose of the IICI is to disable the visual similarity when the similarity between the image-to-word similarity is lower than the image-to-sentence similarity. Intuitively, We propose this consistency indicator by comparing the image-to-word and image-to-sentence similarities within mentions and adopt this indicator in the computation of joint similarity (cf. Eq. 7) for inference, effectively filtering out irrelevant visual information or missing pictures (Please see the effect of other IICI computing methods in 5.11).

Given a mention M with image embedding M_V, we compute its similarity to the mention sentence embedding M_S and mention word embedding M_W from the same mention. If the mention image embedding is more similar to the sentence embedding than to the word embedding, the intra-mention image-word consistency indicator β is learned to **0**; otherwise, it is calculated to **1**. Formally,

$$\beta = \mathbb{1}_{[0,+\infty)}(h(M_V, M_W) + \theta - h(M_V, M_S)), \tag{5}$$

where $\mathbb{1}_{[0,+\infty)}(\cdot)$ is an indicator function whose value is 1 when input belongs to $[0, +\infty)$, and is 0 otherwise. θ is a threshold. To adjust the similarity optimized by the MEL task to measure semantic consistency, we add a threshold θ to the similarity between the mention image and mention word. This enables us to control the involvement of the IICI based on the quality of the MEL's mention image source. The lower the quality of the mention image, the lower the threshold θ should be set (Table 1).

4.4 Mention-Entity Semantic Consistency

Existing MEL methods suffer from the mention-entity cross-modal semantic inconsistency problem caused by the visual semantic diversity and textual variant. The fine-grained aliment approaches [17,25,30] fail to solve this problem,

Table 1. Comparison of multimodal entity linking results in three benchmarks.

Model	Wikidiverse				WikiMEL				RichpediaMEL			
	H@1	H@3	H@5	MRR	H@1	H@3	H@5	MRR	H@1	H@3	H@5	MRR
CLIP [21]	61.21	79.63	85.18	71.69	83.23	92.10	94.51	88.23	67.78	85.22	90.04	77.57
ALBEF [13]	60.59	75.59	81.30	69.93	78.64	88.93	91.75	84.56	65.17	82.84	88.28	75.29
GHMFC [25]	60.27	79.40	84.74	70.99	76.55	88.40	92.01	83.36	72.92	86.85	90.60	80.76
DWE [23]	–	–	–	–	72.80	–	97.50	–	–	–	–	–
MIMIC [17]	63.51	81.04	86.43	73.44	87.98	95.07	96.37	91.82	81.02	91.77	94.38	86.95
MELOV [24]	67.32	83.69	87.54	76.57	88.91	95.61	96.58	92.32	84.14	92.81	94.89	88.80
OT-MEL [31]	66.07	82.82	87.39	75.43	88.97	95.63	96.96	92.59	83.30	92.39	94.83	88.27
M^3MEL [9]	74.06	86.57	90.04	81.29	88.84	95.20	96.71	92.30	82.82	92.73	95.34	88.26
$\text{DEMEL}_{\text{basic}}$ [10]	74.25	87.87	91.34	81.84	89.65	95.84	97.14	93.02	83.13	92.63	94.86	88.31
MMoE+DME [9]	77.57	89.12	92.94	84.32	90.77	96.27	97.41	91.75	85.51	93.43	95.31	89.86
GEMEL [22]	–	–	–	–	82.6	–	–	–	–	–	–	–
BGMEL [15]	–	–	–	–	87.89	95.36	–	92.02	–	–	–	–
$\text{DEMEL}_{\text{MLLM}}$ [10]	78.64	90.04	**92.16**	**84.85**	92.24	96.77	97.52	94.69	86.10	93.68	95.34	90.34
Ours	**79.02***	**88.74**	91.00*	84.35*	**92.34***	**97.04***	**98.12***	**94.88***	**88.91***	**94.95***	**96.52***	**92.34***

"*" denotes the p-value of t-test compared with MIMIC is lower than 0.05

which leads to catastrophic wrong predictions with entity type error. This issue is rooted in misunderstanding of the semantics of the image and the mention word. To address this, we ensure the consistency between entity attributes e_s and descriptions e_s with the mention word m_w or image m_v to maintain cross-modal semantic consistency between mentions and entities. Specifically, Mention-entity Semantic Consistency (**MSC**) is employed to disambiguate the entity type. MSC focuses on semantic consistency between mentions and entities without impacting entity name matching.

Given a mention M with visual embedding M_V and word embedding M_W, as well as a candidate entity E with semantic embedding E_S as input, the MSC is:

$$\text{Con}_S(M, E) = \frac{1}{2}(h(M_V, E_S) + h(M_W, E_S)). \tag{6}$$

4.5 Adaptive Joint Similarity

To benefit from the RoBERTa's context understanding capabilities, we introduce a learnable scalar factor α to rescale the textual similarity's magnitude to cross-modal similarities'. In addition, the IICI β computed in 5 determines whether to include the visual similarity in the computation of adaptive joint similarity. Then, the adaptive joint similarity is a dynamic weighted sum of all other similarities, and formulated as:

$$f_J(M, E) = \frac{\sum_{K \in \{I,T,C,S\}} W_K \cdot f_K(M, E)}{\sum_{K \in \{I,T,C,S\}} W_K}, \tag{7}$$

where $W_I = \beta$, $W_T = \alpha$, $W_C = W_S = 1$, and α is initialized as 1, $f_S = \text{Con}_S$. During inference, we use the joint similarities between the given mention and candidate entities as the basis for ranking. In the training phase, we optimize a contrastive loss function to learn each individual similarity and the joint similarity, which is formulated as

$$\mathcal{L} = \sum_{k\in\{I,T,C,S,J\}} -\log\frac{\exp(f_K(M, E_a))}{\sum_{E^i\in\mathcal{E}}\exp(f_K(M, E_i,))}, \tag{8}$$

where the negative samples $E_i, i \neq a$ are sampled from the knowledge base, according to the batch size.

5 Experiments

5.1 Datasets

Table 2. The statistics of three datasets.

Datasets	WikiDiverse	WikiMEL	RichpediaMEL	Datasets	WikiDiverse	WikiMEL	RichpediaMEL
Mens	15,093	25,846	17,805	Ents	132,460	109,976	160,935
Sentences	74,05	22,070	17,724	Ents w img	58,733	67,795	86,769
Men imgs	6,697	22,136	15,853	Ents w attr	23,419	63,354	63,354
Mens in train	11,351	18,092	12,463	Ents w desc	116,503	105,438	151,0154
Mens in valid	1,664	2,585	1,780				
Mens in test	2,078	5,169	3,562				

We conduct experiments on the three most-widely used public datasets in MEL task, which are WikiDiverse [27], WikiMEL [25] and Richpedia [25]. The statistic is shown in Table 2. The entity types of WikiDiverse covers various topics, and the main entity type in WikiMEL and RichpedaiMEl is persons.method performs.

5.2 Implementation Details

The textual encoder is initialized with a pre-trained RoBERTa [14], and the dimensions of textual embeddings d_t is 768. The cross-modal encoder is initialized by a pre-trained CLIP-Vit-Base-Patch32 [21], and the dimensions of textual embeddings d_t is 512. All input images are rescaled into 224 × 224 resolution and zeros padding is used to initialize patches for the mentions and entities with no images or unavailable images. The batch size is set to 32. We optimize the method by AdamW with a learning rate of 1e-5. We implement our code using the Pytorch [19] and run all experiments on a single NVIDIA Tesla V100 GPU. We train this model for 10 epochs.

5.3 Metrics

During evaluation, given a mention, we rank all candidate entities in KB by their joint similarities with this mention in descending order. Then we calculate the H@1,3,5, MRR by the rank of the answer entities for every mention. H@k denotes the hit rate of answer entities while considering top k candidate entities. MRR denotes the mean reciprocal rank of all the answer entities respectively.

Table 3. Ablation study (β denotes the intra-mention image-word consistency indicator.

	Wikidiverse				WikiMEL				RichpediaMEL			
Model	H@1	H@3	H@5	MRR	H@1	H@3	H@5	MRR	H@1	H@3	H@5	MRR
ours	**79.02**	**88.74**	**91.00**	**84.35**	**92.34**	**97.04**	**98.12**	**94.88**	**88.91**	**94.95**	**96.52**	**92.34**
w/o IMG	71.13	86.43	89.94	79.51	79.20	90.15	93.05	85.39	78.07	89.95	93.12	84.69
w/o TXT	8.42	12.51	14.92	11.68	28.05	32.37	34.20	31.65	22.21	26.98	29.42	26.04
w/o Con_s	77.38	87.54	90.81	83.41	90.71	96.13	97.52	93.74	80.71	92.45	94.83	87.07
w/o β	74.83	85.51	88.40	81.16	92.28	97.18	98.08	94.88	87.37	94.83	96.52	91.46
RoBERTa*	69.15	84.12	88.16	77.55	74.70	86.57	90.13	81.62	63.00	83.24	88.04	74.12
CLIP*	61.21	79.74	85.32	71.68	83.25	91.64	94.23	88.07	66.76	83.66	88.24	76.24
R+C*	69.15	82.44	86.24	76.90	90.63	96.22	97.43	93.70	82.45	92.05	94.53	87.87

"*" denotes fine-tuned models, "R+C" denotes RoBETa as textual encoder and CLIP as multimodal encoder

5.4 Baselines

We compare with the **vision language pre-trained models** include CLIP [21], ALBEF [13] , and various **pre-trained model based SOTA MEL methods** include GHMFC [25], DWE [23], MIMIC [17], MELOV [24], OT-MEL [31] and M^3MEL [9], MMoE [9], DEMEL [10] and **Large Language Models (LLMs) based MEL methods** GEMEL [22], BGMEL [15], DEMEL [10].

5.5 Performance Comparison

We test the proposed method in three MEL benchmark datasets and compare its performance with several SOTA methods. Most results of baseline are taken from the reproduction of [17], which is also reproduced and checked by us. Other results are from their original paper. It's worth mentioning that GEMEL [22], BGMEL [15] use different datasets settings in Wikidiverse and the constrained decoding mechanism for LLMs make it hard to reproduce them for fair comparison, so we only report their comparable results in WikiMEL. The experimental results suggest that our proposed method achieves superior performance in all three datasets at all evaluation metrics, except H@10 and MRR in WikiDiverse.

DEMEL achieves performance comparable to ours in these two evaluation metrics due to the effective utilization of additional training data derived from Multimodal LLMs (MLLMs). We still achieve better performance without introducing LLMs. Moreover, we train models with random seed to get 15 MEL result examples of hit@1/3/5 and MRR index in 3 datasets. The t-tests results show that the proposed method outperforms MIMIC in all these indexes with p-value$\leq$0.05 except hit@3 in WikiDiverse. The proposed methods significantly outperform the text-based baselines and vision-language pre-trained model baselines, highlighting the importance of incorporating multimodal information. The substantial improvement over the state-of-the-art method demonstrates the necessity of addressing both types of semantic inconsistency problems, as well as the effectiveness of the proposed modules in resolving them within MEL. Moreover, the superior performance compared to some LLM-based methods further validates the approach of integrating pre-trained models, rather than relying solely on LLMs.

5.6 Ablation Study

We conducted an ablation study and presented the results in Table 3. The comparison with methods without using any visual or textual input $w/o\,IMG$ and $w/o\,TXT$ shows the importance of information from different modalities. The experiments without MSC w/o Sim_S and IICI $w/o\ \beta$ state the validity of the proposed module. The experimental results compared with the fine-tuned pre-trained models RoBETa*,CLIP* emphasizes the necessity of selecting different models and coefficients to constitute adaptive joint similarity. It's worth mentioning that the mention type in WikiMEL and Richpedia is all human, so their mention images are all portraits. The high association between the mention image and word in these two datasets masks the effect of IICI, which leads to little performance decrease. But in the more open WikiDiverse, whose mentions include more types (such as human, city, film, team, sport,...), the performance without IICI drops severely. This phenomenon suggests the proposed IICI is sensitive to image quality, which meets our design expectations.

5.7 Semantic Error Statistic

Existing MEL methods like MIMIC are committed to align the mention and entity image in a fine-granularity way (such as aligning the "US flag" image patch in motivation to entity "U.S."), but the experimental results suggest that they even wrongly predict the mentions type (such as linking a "person" to a "street") for some examples. This is known as a type error. The experiment in Fig. 3 shows that our proposed method reduces both the number and proportion of type errors in all errors (TE/AE) by MSC (Fig. 4).

5.8 Hyper Parameter Analysis

In IICI , we conduct the threshold θ to control the degree of included visual similarity based on the images' overall quality in the dataset. The θ is set as

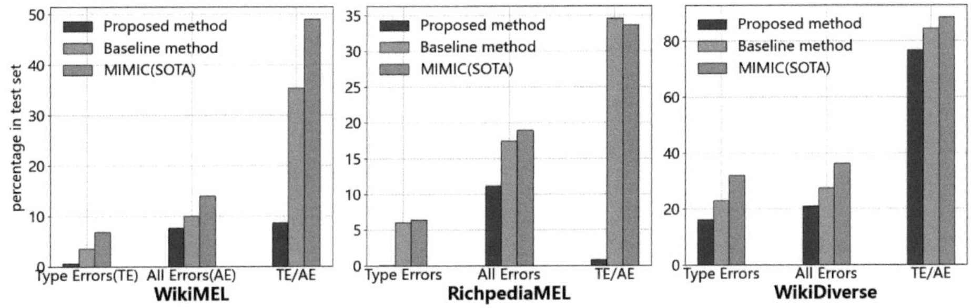

Fig. 3. The statistic of type error predicted by the fine-tuned baseline "$RoBERTa + CLIP*$", the "MIMIC" (SOTA), and our proposed model.

Mention	MIMIC		RoBERTa+CLIP*		Proposed method		
	Predicted entity	GD rank	Predicted entity	GD rank	Predicted entity	GD rank	α
 Soviet division commander Vladimir Kirpichnikov as prisoner of war in 1941 lights a cigarette for Oesch...	Solomon Asch Polish-American psychologist (1907-1996)	6	Oesho deitiy of the Kushan dynasty	3	Karl Lennart  Finnish general and war criminal (1892-1978)	1	1
 Corbett training for his fight with Jeffries	Corbett v Corbett 1969 English case on transgender marriage	3	Corbett v Corbett 1969 English case on transgender marriage	2	James J. Corbett  American boxer (1866-1933)	1	1
 Chinese dairy products are removed from a supermarket in China as a result of the scandal.	2008 Chinese milk scandal  Food safety crisis	13	2008 Chinese milk scandal  Food safety crisis	3	People's Republic of China 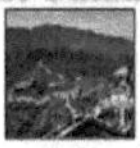 country in East Asia	1	0

Fig. 4. "Case study for MEL. "GD" represents ground truth, "*" represents fine-tuned, β is the intra-mention image-word consistency indicator (IICI).

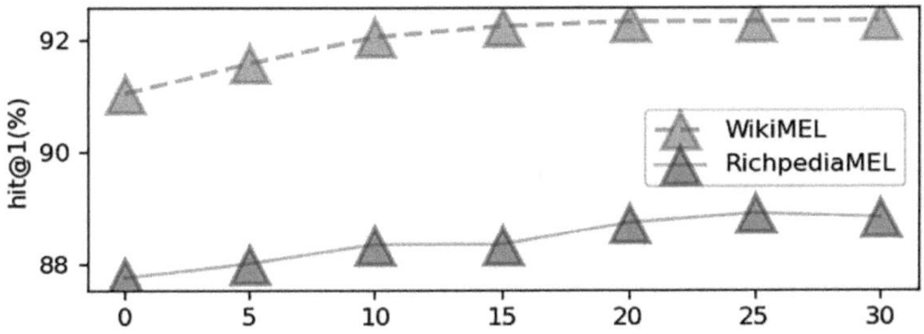

Fig. 5. Results of hyper-parameter analysis experiments on WikiMEL and RichpediaMEL (All results are average Top-1 accuracies).

within the range of ±10% of the average similarity of the pre-trained model. We performed a bi-direction grid search to optimize θ with a step size of 5, starting from 0. A negative value of -50 was used for WikiDiverse due to its weaker image-text correlation, while a positive value of 25 was used for the other two datasets. Here are the details of hyper parameter sensitivity in Fig. 5. The experimental results suggest that in WikiMEL and RichpediaMEL the higher θ bring better hit1 index overall, but the curve is not monotonous increasing. So, a choice of suited θ can control the included proportion of visual similarities.

Table 4. Time and space analysis.

		Wikidiverse	WikiMEL	RichpediaMEL
Ours	train time/s	2197	15178	8934
	inference time/s	1531	1010	1347
	#Params	341.3M	341.3M	341.3M
OT-MEL	train time/s	3170	21421	24088
	inference time/s	1842	3029	2176
	#Params	610.9M	610.9M	610.9M

The time statistics include the entire dataset

5.9 Case Study

We conduct a case study between the SOTA MEL method MIMIC as a baseline to illustrate how the proposed methods address two inconsistency problems in MEL. There is no inconsistency problem in the first line, IICI β is learned to be 1, making full use of image similarity to outperform SOTA and baselines. Due to the different gestures of the characters, the second line of mention image has a serious problem of mention-entity semantic inconsistency. In this case, IICI confirms the mention image is relevant, and MSC aligns the mention image with "boxer" instead of "case", avoiding outputting an answer with a type error. In the third line, the mention's image describes the mention's sentence "scandal affair" instead of mention word "Chinese", resulting in an intra-mention semantic inconsistency. The proposed method makes the correct prediction by finding β as 0.

5.10 Time and Space Analysis

To assess the accessibility and scalability of the proposed method, we analyze its time and space complexity. Table 4 summarizes the results. Considering both implementation simplicity and performance, we compare against the state-of-the-art method OT-MEL [31]. By omitting optimal transport, our method uses approximately half as many parameters as OT-MEL while achieving up to a 19% improvement in predictive accuracy. Moreover, it exhibits faster inference and substantially reduced training time due to quicker convergence. Overall, the proposed method is more parameter-efficient, faster to train and infer, and significantly more accurate than prior state-of-the-art MEL approaches.

Table 5. Hit@1 performance for different methods of calculating IICI θ on WikiDiverse and WikiMEL.

	Wikidiverse		WikiMEL	
Baseline	72.71		90.00	
+CP	77.38	(+4.67)	90.71	(+0.71)
+SIM	79.02	(+6.31)	90.19	(+0.19)
+RANK	72.08	(-0.63)	88.78	(+1.22)
+CLIP	70.21	(-2.50)	90.97	(+0.97)

5.11 Various Techniques to Compute IICI

The proposed work alleviates intra-mention semantic inconsistency by introducing IICI, which compares image-to-word and image-to-sentence similarities within mentions (**CP**). While intuitive, this method is relatively simple. We fine-tuned RoBETA and CLIP with a learnable scalar factor α as baseline. We further explore several alternatives for computing this metric: (1) **SIM**, which employs a classifier over mention images and words to estimate IICI, supervised by the normalized similarity between the mention image and the ground-truth entity image; (2) **RANK**, which replaces the similarity label in SIM with the reciprocal rank of the ground-truth entity within the batch; and (3) **CLIP**, which directly uses in-batch normalized similarities from a frozen CLIP model as IICI. Table 5 reports the best Hit@1 results on two datasets for all four methods. The results indicate that the simplest approach, **CP**, consistently yields the best overall performance, and we therefore adopt it for its strong generalization ability.

Table 6. Performance comparison with single encoder based MEL method.

	Wikidiverse				WikiMEL				RichpediaMEL			
Model	H@1	H@3	H@5	MRR	H@1	H@3	H@5	MRR	H@1	H@3	H@5	MRR
Ours with CLIP	**68.86**	**84.07**	**87.73**	**77.40**	**88.53**	**95.69**	**97.33**	**92.41**	**83.66**	**92.45**	**94.81**	**88.58**
MIMIC	63.51	81.04	86.43	73.44	87.98	95.07	96.37	91.82	81.02	91.77	94.38	86.95
CLIP*	61.21	79.74	85.32	71.68	83.25	91.64	94.23	88.07	66.76	83.66	88.24	76.24

"*" denotes the reproduced method

5.12 Performance with Single Encoder

Our method employs two pretrained encoders, RoBERTa and CLIP. To better capture long-text dependencies, we incorporate two complementary encoders, whereas methods such as MIMIC rely on a single encoder. Although our approach outperforms MEL methods with larger encoders (e.g., EMEL [22], BGMEL [15]), we also provide a fair comparison with single-encoder state-of-the-art methods such as MIMIC (Table 6).

The results show that our CLIP-based model consistently outperforms baselines with comparable parameter sizes, indicating that the gains are not solely attributable to increased model capacity.

6 Conclusion

In conclusion, we propose a multimodal entity linking method with adaptive joint similarity to address two semantic inconsistency problems. The first is the inconsistency between image and word in mentions. To address this, we propose a visual similarity indicator to filter irrelevant visual information. The second is the inconsistency between mention images and entity descriptions. We address this with a novel method to measure mention-entity semantic consistency which focuses on the semantic alignment rather than the entity name alignment. Empirical studies on MEL datasets show our significant improvements over the SOTA models. Our method even outperforms LLM-based MEL baselines without introducing LLMs. The ablation study and type error analysis experiment further demonstrate the effectiveness of the proposed modules.

Acknowledgments. This work was supported by the National Natural Science Foundation of China (No. U2433212), and supported by Beijing Advanced Innovation Center for Big Data and Brain Computing.

References

1. Barba, E., Procopio, L., Navigli, R.: ExtEnD: extractive entity disambiguation. In: ACL 2022, pp. 2478–2488 (2022). https://doi.org/10.18653/v1/2022.acl-long.177, https://aclanthology.org/2022.acl-long.177
2. Cao, Y., Huang, L., Ji, H., Chen, X., Li, J.: Bridge text and knowledge by learning multi-prototype entity mention embedding. In: ACL 2017, pp. 1623–1633 (2017). https://doi.org/10.18653/v1/P17-1149, https://aclanthology.org/P17-1149
3. Cucerzan, S.: Large-scale named entity disambiguation based on wikipedia data. EMNLP-CoNLL, pp. 708–716 (2007)
4. De Cao, N., Izacard, G., Riedel, S., Petroni, F.: Autoregressive entity retrieval. In: ICLR 2021, vol. 2021, (2020)
5. Dosovitskiy, A.: An image is worth 16×16 words: transformers for image recognition at scale, (2020). arXiv preprint arXiv:2010.11929

6. Gan, J., Luo, J., Wang, H., Wang, S., He, W., Huang, Q.: Multimodal entity linking: a new dataset and a baseline. In: MM 2021, pp. 993–1001. MM '21 (2021). https://doi.org/10.1145/3474085.3475400, https://doi.org/10.1145/3474085.3475400
7. Gerritse, E.J., Hasibi, F., de Vries, A.P.: Entity-aware transformers for entity search. In: SIGIR 2022, pp. 1455–1465. SIGIR '22 (2022). https://doi.org/10.1145/3477495.3531971, https://doi.org/10.1145/3477495.3531971
8. Gupta, N., Singh, S., Roth, D.: Entity linking via joint encoding of types, descriptions, and context. In: EMNLP 2017, pp. 2681–2690 (2017). https://doi.org/10.18653/v1/D17-1284, https://aclanthology.org/D17-1284
9. Hu, Z., Gutiérrez-Basulto, V., Li, R., Pan, J.Z.: Multi-level matching network for multimodal entity linking. In: SIGKDD 2025, pp. 508–519. (2025)
10. Huang, J., Wang, D., Li, S., Peng, Y., Jin, R.: Enhancing multimodal entity linking via distillation and multimodal large language models. In: CIKM 2025, pp. 960–969. (2025)
11. Kandpal, N., Deng, H., Roberts, A., Wallace, E., Raffel, C.: Large language models struggle to learn long-tail knowledge. In: ICML 2023, pp. 15696–15707. (2023)
12. Lewis, M., Liu, Y., Goyal, N., Ghazvininejad, M., Mohamed, A., Levy, O., Stoyanov, V., Zettlemoyer, L.: Bart: denoising sequence-to-sequence pre-training for natural language generation, translation, and comprehension. In: ACL 2020 (2020)
13. Li, J., Selvaraju, R., Gotmare, A., Joty, S., Xiong, C., Hoi, S.C.H.: Align before fuse: vision and language representation learning with momentum distillation. NeuraIPS **2021**(34), 9694–9705 (2021)
14. Liu, Y., Ott, M., Goyal, N., Du, J., Joshi, M., Chen, D., Levy, O., Lewis, M., Zettlemoyer, L., Stoyanov, V.: Roberta: A Robustly Optimized Bert Pretraining Approach, (2019). arXiv preprint arXiv:1907.11692
15. Luo, P., Xu, T., Liu, C., Zhang, S., Xu, L., Li, M., Chen, E.: Bridging gaps in content and knowledge for multimodal entity linking. In: MM 2024, pp. 9311–9320 (2024)
16. Luo, P., Xu, T., Wu, S., Zhu, C., Xu, L., Chen, E.: Multi-grained multimodal interaction network for entity linking. In: Proceedings of the 29th ACM SIGKDD Conference on Knowledge Discovery and Data Mining, pp. 1583–1594. KDD '23 (2023). https://doi.org/10.1145/3580305.3599439, https://doi.org/10.1145/3580305.3599439
17. Luo, P., Xu, T., Wu, S., Zhu, C., Xu, L., Chen, E.: Multi-grained multimodal interaction network for entity linking. In: SIGKDD 2023, pp. 1583–1594 (2023)
18. Moon, S., Neves, L., Carvalho, V.: Multimodal named entity disambiguation for noisy social media posts. In: ACL 2018, pp. 2000–2008 (2018). https://doi.org/10.18653/v1/P18-1186, https://aclanthology.org/P18-1186
19. Paszke, A., Gross, S., Massa, F., Lerer, A., Bradbury, J., Chanan, G., Killeen, T., Lin, Z., Gimelshein, N., Antiga, L., et al.: Pytorch: an imperative style, high-performance deep learning library. NeuraIPS **2019**, 32 (2019)
20. Qiu, J., Madotto, A., Lin, Z., Crook, P.A., Xu, Y.E., Damavandi, B., Dong, X.L., Faloutsos, C., Li, L., Moon, S.: Snapntell: enhancing entity-centric visual question answering with retrieval augmented multimodal LLM. In: Findings of EMNLP 2024, pp. 247–266. (2024)
21. Radford, A., Kim, J.W., Hallacy, C., Ramesh, A., Goh, G., Agarwal, S., Sastry, G., Askell, A., Mishkin, P., Clark, J.: Learning transferable visual models from natural language supervision, pp. 8748–8763. ICLR (2021)
22. Shi, S., Xu, Z., Hu, B., Zhang, M.: Generative multimodal entity linking. In: LREC-COLING 2024, pp. 7654–7665. (2024)

23. Song, S., Zhao, S., Wang, C., Yan, T., Li, S., Mao, X., Wang, M.: A dual-way enhanced framework from text matching point of view for multimodal entity linking. In: AAAI 2024. vol. 38, pp. 19008–19016 (2024)
24. Sui, X., Zhang, Y., Zhao, Y., Song, K., Zhou, B., Yuan, X.: Melov: multimodal entity linking with optimized visual features in latent space. In: Findings of ACL 2024, pp. 816–826. (2024)
25. Wang, P., Wu, J., Chen, X.: Multimodal entity linking with gated hierarchical fusion and contrastive training. In: SIGIR 2022, pp. 938–948. SIGIR '22 (2022). https://doi.org/10.1145/3477495.3531867, https://doi.org/10.1145/3477495.3531867
26. Wang, X., Liu, K., Wang, D., Wu, L., Fu, Y., Xie, X.: Multi-level recommendation reasoning over knowledge graphs with reinforcement learning. In: WWW 2022, pp. 2098–2108. WWW '22 (2022). https://doi.org/10.1145/3485447.3512083
27. Wang, X., Tian, J., Gui, M., Li, Z., Wang, R., Yan, M., Chen, L., Xiao, Y.: WikiDiverse: A multimodal entity linking dataset with diversified contextual topics and entity types. In: ACL 2022, pp. 4785–4797 (2022). https://doi.org/10.18653/v1/2022.acl-long.328, https://aclanthology.org/2022.acl-long.328
28. Wu, J., Lu, J., Sabharwal, A., Mottaghi, R.: Multi-modal answer validation for knowledge-based VQA. Proceedings of the AAAI Conference on Artificial Intelligence **36**(3), 2712–2721 (2022). https://doi.org/10.1609/aaai.v36i3.20174, https://ojs.aaai.org/index.php/AAAI/article/view/20174
29. Yang, Y., Irsoy, O., Rahman, K.S.: Collective entity disambiguation with structured gradient tree boosting. In: ACL 2018, pp. 777–786 (2018). https://doi.org/10.18653/v1/N18-1071, https://aclanthology.org/N18-1071
30. Zhang, L., Li, Z., Yang, Q.: Attention-Based Multimodal Entity Linking with High-Quality Images. In: Jensen, C.S., Lim, E.-P., Yang, D.-N., Lee, W.-C., Tseng, V.S., Kalogeraki, V., Huang, J.-W., Shen, C.-Y. (eds.) DASFAA 2021. LNCS, vol. 12682, pp. 533–548. Springer, Cham (2021). https://doi.org/10.1007/978-3-030-73197-7_35
31. Zhang, Z., Sheng, J., Zhang, C., Liang, Y., Zhang, W., Wang, S., Liu, T.: Optimal transport guided correlation assignment for multimodal entity linking. arXiv preprint arXiv:2406.01934 (2024)
32. Zheng, Q., Wen, H., Wang, M., Qi, G.: Visual entity linking via multi-modal learning. Data Intell. **4**(1), 1–19 (2022). https://doi.org/10.1162/dint_a_00114

LLM-Guided Semantic Profiling for Personalized Diversity Movie Re-ranking

Baofeng Ren[1(✉)], Tianyuan Yang[1], Boxuan Ma[2], and Shin'ichi Konomi[2]

[1] Graduate School of Information Science and Electrical Engineering, Kyushu University, 744 Motoka, Nishi-ku, Fukuoka 819-0395, Japan
{ren.baofeng.817,yang.tianyuan.791}@s.kyushu-u.ac.jp

[2] Faculty of Arts and Science, Kyushu University, 744 Motoka, Nishi-ku, Fukuoka 819-0395, Japan
{boxuan,konomi}@artsci.kyushu-u.ac.jp

Abstract. Recommender systems have achieved remarkable success in content consumption domains. However, over-reliance on historical interactions and coarse-grained item attributes often leads to popularity bias and reduced diversity, limiting user exploration. This paper addresses the challenge of enhancing *personalized diversity* in recommendations. Focusing on the movie domain, we leverage large language models (LLMs) to extract fine-grained semantic attributes across five expert-defined dimensions derived from film theory: Narrative Pacing, Emotional Tone, Visual Aesthetics, Sonic Identity, and Thematic Symbols. We propose the *Semantic Interest Spectrum* (SIS) structure to quantify user preferences by combining *personal preference* and *semantic uniqueness*, and design the *Spectrum-Modulated Re-ranking* (SMR) algorithm to produce recommendations that achieve a superior balance between accuracy and diversity tailored to each user. Experiments on two public movie datasets demonstrate that our LLM-enhanced approach significantly outperforms baselines in delivering personalized diversity while maintaining competitive accuracy, validating the effectiveness of Semantic Interest Spectrum (SIS) and the utility of LLM-derived features.

Keywords: Recommender systems · Large language models · Personalized diversity

1 Introduction

Modern recommender systems have achieved remarkable success in predictive accuracy and have become core engines for information distribution in domains such as e-commerce, streaming platforms, and news services [30]. These systems primarily learn user preferences by mining historical interaction data, with the central objective of maximizing predictive accuracy. However, this emphasis on

L. Ding et al. (Eds.): APWeb-WAIM 2026, LNCS 16993, pp. 655–670, 2027.
https://doi.org/10.1007/978-981-92-5693-8_41

accuracy introduces a significant side effect: systems tend to recommend popular items or those highly similar to a user's historical behavior, leading to the homogenization of recommendation lists and thus limiting diversity. This phenomenon not only restricts users' opportunities to broaden their horizons and discover new interests but can also confine them to so-called "filter bubbles" that reinforces existing viewpoints and preferences, which in the long term can narrow their perspectives and even entrench cognitive biases [18,21].

To address this lack of diversity, re-ranking the initial candidate list has become a mainstream and effective method [32,40,47]. Such approaches reorder items to enhance list-wise coverage and novelty while seeking to preserve relevance. Although these re-ranking strategies have partly mitigated the homogenization problem, they share a critical limitation: dependence on coarse-grained item attributes (e.g., a movie's genre or director) for diversity modeling, while lacking the capacity for deep, fine-grained semantic understanding of the content itself.

This limitation creates two critical issues: a lack of personalization and weak interpretability. For instance, a user might love the philosophical sci-fi of *2001: A Space Odyssey* but dislike the action-comedy of *Guardians of the Galaxy*, a nuance lost when both are simply labeled "science fiction." This black box logic erodes user trust and fails to satisfy personalized exploration needs.

In parallel, the rapid advancement of Large Language Models (LLMs) has spurred explorations into their application as end-to-end recommenders [5,11,22,41,42]. While promising, such approaches remain limited. The reasoning process of LLMs is inherently opaque, making the trade-off between accuracy and diversity difficult to control. We propose an alternative perspective: positioning LLMs as efficient semantic feature extractors. By constructing fine-grained semantic representations of both items and users, LLMs can provide a structured, controllable and interpretable foundation for personalized and diverse recommendations.

Specifically, we leverage an LLM to extract nuanced movie features across five expert-defined dimensions from film theory: *Narrative Pacing*, *Emotional Tone*, *Visual Aesthetics*, *Sonic Identity*, and *Thematic Symbols*. Based on these features, we introduce the *Semantic Interest Spectrum* (SIS) to build fine-grained user profiles and propose the *Spectrum-Modulated Re-ranking* (SMR) algorithm to deliver recommendations that are both relevant and personally diverse. Our approach introduces a comprehensive framework that systematically translates the latent knowledge of LLMs into a structured semantic space, enabling a novel approach to personalized diversity in recommendations.

Our key contributions are: **(1) LLM-Powered Semantic Profiling**: We are the first to combine LLM-driven feature extraction with expert-defined cinematic dimensions to create a rich semantic foundation for recommendations, from which we construct the Semantic Interest Spectrum (SIS), a novel user profile that captures nuanced tastes. **(2) Personalized Diversity Framework**: We propose the Spectrum-Modulated Re-ranking (SMR) algorithm, a method guided by the Semantic Interest Spectrum (SIS) to explicitly optimize for personalized diversity. Accompanying this, we introduce new metrics (SWD, SCB, and SCD) to quantify how well a recommendation list aligns with a user's unique spectrum of interests. **(3) Empirical Validation**: We conduct extensive experiments demonstrating that our framework significantly outperforms baselines in delivering personalized diversity while maintaining competitive accuracy.

2 Related Work

2.1 Re-ranking in Recommender Systems

Re-ranking is a crucial post-processing step in recommender systems, aiming to optimize recommendation lists toward specific objectives beyond initial accuracy [32]. A primary focus of re-ranking research has been to improve diversity [1,32, 40,47]. Classic diversification methods like MMR, DPP, and xQuAD primarily focus on item-to-item dissimilarity based on coarse features (e.g., genre) [4,6,8, 11,20,32]. While these methods improve list-wise variety, they share a critical limitation: diversity is typically modeled at a coarse granularity (e.g., genre) and often fails to account for users' personalized preferences [18,21,40].

Our work addresses this gap by explicitly modeling users' fine-grained semantic preferences through the *Semantic Interest Spectrum* (SIS). By quantifying preference intensities across multiple semantic dimensions, our *Spectrum-Modulated Re-ranking* (SMR) algorithm enables a more nuanced and interpretable re-ranking process that adapts to personalized notions of diversity.

2.2 Large Language Models in Recommender Systems

The integration of large language models (LLMs) has become a frontier research topic in recommender systems [10,17,23]. Research has explored several roles for LLMs. One prominent direction uses LLMs directly as recommenders or re-rankers, leveraging their world knowledge and reasoning abilities in zero-shot or few-shot settings [5,10,11,17,22,23,42]. Another line of research employs LLMs as feature encoders, using their language understanding capabilities to extract rich semantic representations that can alleviate cold-start and data sparsity issues [15,16,37,43]. LLMs have also been used to derive natural language user profiles from historical interactions, enhancing recommendation explainability [34,41].

In contrast to these directions, our work does not use LLMs as end-to-end recommenders or generic encoders. Instead, we integrate LLMs' world knowledge with domain expertise, distilling cinematic content into a structured, five-dimensional semantic space. This enables us to build quantifiable, fine-grained user profiles (SIS) that support our novel re-ranking algorithm (SMR), providing a more controllable and interpretable framework for personalized diversity.

3 Methodology

3.1 Problem Formulation

Our goal is to generate a personalized recommendation list $L_u = [i_1, i_2, \ldots, i_K]$ for each user u. Moving beyond traditional accuracy-focused tasks, we formulate this as a multi-objective re-ranking problem that jointly optimizes for *relevance* and *personalized diversity*.

Our framework (Fig. 1) addresses this through three stages: First, we use an LLM to extract semantic features for each item across predefined dimensions. From these, we construct a multi-dimensional Semantic Interest Spectrum (SIS) for each user. Finally, our Spectrum-Modulated Re-ranking (SMR) algorithm reorders an initial candidate list to balance relevance and alignment with the user's SIS.

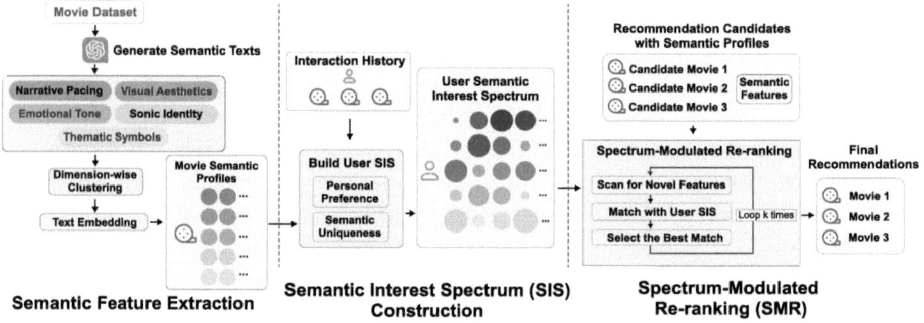

Fig. 1. Our three-stage framework.

3.2 LLM-Based Semantic Feature Extraction for Movies

We focus on the movie domain, whose rich cultural and aesthetic attributes are ideal for capturing fine-grained user needs. Recent successes in using LLMs as recommenders [10,11,17] highlight that modern LLMs encode extensive world knowledge, enabling us to treat LLMs as virtual movie experts to uncover nuanced semantic features embedded in movies. To ensure consistent and structured output, our prompts required the model to generate five concise keywords for each of five dimensions, outputting the results in a predefined JSON schema for reliable downstream analysis.

Model Selection and Quality Assessment The quality of extracted semantic features is paramount. We conducted a preliminary qualitative study comparing GPT-4o, GPT-4o mini, and a local 8B Gemma 3 model on selected classic movies. Expert evaluation revealed that GPT-4o consistently provided superior semantic depth and reliability. For instance, it generated nuanced themes for Toy Story ("identity crisis") where other models provided generic ("Friendship and loyalty" from 4o mini) or inaccurate labels ("parallel storytelling" from Gemma 3). Given its superior performance in generating high-fidelity features, GPT-4o was selected for all feature extraction tasks.

Semantic Feature Layers To systematically extract deep semantic features, our framework is grounded in established film studies literature. It employs five foundational dimensions that are widely used in cinematic research to deconstruct and summarize a film's deep information from multiple perspectives: **Narrative Pacing**, which examines a film's temporal structure and rhythm [3,9,31]; **Emotional Tone**, capturing its dominant emotional atmosphere [28,35,38]; **Visual Aesthetics**, evaluating its visual language and stylistic expression [12,25,39]; **Sonic Identity**, analyzing its complete *soundscape* [2,7,19]; and **Thematic Symbols**, uncovering its deeper socio-cultural meanings [26,27,36]. Together, these expert-defined dimensions form a multifaceted semantic representation that surpasses the expressive limitations of coarse-grained *genre* metadata.

Semantic Embedding and Clustering We first embed the extracted semantic keywords into dense vectors using OpenAI's text-embedding-3-large model. However, the LLM often generates semantically similar but lexically distinct phrases (e.g., "reflective self-discovery" vs. "introspective reflection"), which can fragment the semantic space and dilute interest representations. To create a standardized vocabulary of semantic concepts, we perform dimension-wise clustering on these embeddings, optimizing the number of clusters for recommendation performance. Each item's profile is then defined by its assigned cluster features–the "Movie Semantic Profile" in Fig. 1. Finally, by aggregating these features from a user's interaction history, we construct their Semantic Interest Spectrum (SIS), our novel, multi-dimensional representation of their fine-grained preferences.

3.3 Semantic Interest Spectrum (SIS) Construction

To capture personalized preferences, we propose the *Semantic Interest Spectrum* (SIS), a model that quantifies a user's affinity for fine-grained semantic clusters. Moving beyond the coarse-grained categories of traditional profiles, SIS constructs a multi-dimensional user spectrum based on two pillars: *Personal Preference* and *Semantic Uniqueness*.

Formally, for a given user u, a semantic dimension $d \in \mathcal{D}$, and a semantic cluster $c \in \mathcal{C}_d$ (where $\mathcal{C}_d$ is the set of all clusters in dimension d), we define its **Spectrum Intensity** $\sigma(u, c, d)$ as:

$$\sigma(u, c, d) = \alpha(u, c, d) \cdot \upsilon(c, d) \tag{1}$$

Personal Preference To construct a personalized profile, we first estimate the user's interest intensity for each semantic cluster. **Personal Preference** measures the relative strength of a user's interest in a specific semantic cluster within a given dimension. Let $\mathcal{I}_{u,c,d}$ denote the set of items associated with cluster c in dimension d that user u has interacted with. The preference is computed as the proportion of interactions for that cluster relative to all of the user's interactions within that dimension:

$$\alpha(u, c, d) = \frac{|\mathcal{I}_{u,c,d}|}{\sum_{c' \in \mathcal{C}_d} |\mathcal{I}_{u,c',d}|} \tag{2}$$

A high α value indicates that the cluster plays a key role in shaping the user's preference for that dimension.

Semantic Uniqueness Relying solely on personal preference risks overemphasizing mainstream preferences, thereby reinforcing popularity bias. To counter this, we introduce **Semantic Uniqueness** $v(c, d)$, which measures the rarity of a semantic cluster across the entire user population. This helps identify features that define a user's distinctive taste. Let $\mathcal{U}$ be the total set of users, and let $\mathcal{U}_{c,d}$ be the set of users who have interacted with at least one item in cluster c of dimension d. In this part, we define uniqueness as:

$$v(c, d) = \log\left(1 + \frac{|\mathcal{U}|}{|\mathcal{U}_{c,d}|}\right) \tag{3}$$

A high v value indicates non-mainstream, discriminative taste markers.

Combined Spectrum By integrating personal preference and semantic uniqueness, Semantic Interest Spectrum (SIS) balances alignment with a user's individualized taste against the promotion of diversity. Clusters with high Spectrum Intensity $\sigma(u, c, d)$ represent features that are both highly relevant to the user and distinctive across the population. This yields a profile that differentiates between *mass-market appeal* and *personal favorites*, providing a robust foundation for personalized re-ranking.

3.4 Spectrum-Modulated Re-ranking (SMR)

Given a user's Semantic Interest Spectrum (SIS), our **Spectrum-Modulated Re-ranking (SMR)** algorithm iteratively builds the final recommendation list. It employs a greedy process to select items that optimally balance initial relevance with personalized novelty, guided by the user's Semantic Interest Spectrum (SIS).

At each step, SMR appends the item that offers the best balance between initial relevance and personalized novelty. The core selection criterion is to choose the item i^* that maximizes a joint objective function:

$$i^* = \arg \max_{i \in \mathcal{C}_u \setminus \mathcal{L}_u} \left[(1 - \lambda) \cdot r(i, u) + \lambda \cdot \mathcal{N}(i, \mathcal{L}_u, u)\right] \tag{4}$$

where $\mathcal{L}_u$ is the list of already selected items, $\mathcal{C}_u$ is the full candidate set, and λ is the trade-off parameter.

Relevance Score The relevance score, $r(i, u)$, is a normalized representation of the initial item quality predicted by the base model. We use min-max normalization over the candidate set $\mathcal{C}_u$ for a given user u. Let $s_{u,i}$ be the raw score from the base model:

$$r(i, u) = \begin{cases} \dfrac{s_{u,i} - \min_{j \in \mathcal{C}_u} s_{u,j}}{\max_{j \in \mathcal{C}_u} s_{u,j} - \min_{j \in \mathcal{C}_u} s_{u,j}}, & \text{if den.} > 0, \\ 1, & \text{otherwise.} \end{cases} \tag{5}$$

Personalized Novelty Score The personalized novelty score, $\mathcal{N}(i, \mathcal{L}_u, u)$, quantifies the marginal contribution of item i to the list $\mathcal{L}_u$, personalized through the user's Semantic Interest Spectrum (SIS). Let $\Gamma(i)$ be the set of all semantic clusters associated with item i across all dimensions, and let $\Gamma(\mathcal{L}_u) = \bigcup_{j \in \mathcal{L}_u} \Gamma(j)$ be the set of clusters already covered by the list $\mathcal{L}_u$.

First, we compute the *raw novelty gain* $g(i, \mathcal{L}_u, u)$ for an item i as the sum of Spectrum Intensities of the new clusters it introduces:

$$g(i, \mathcal{L}_u, u) = \sum_{c \in \Gamma(i) \setminus \Gamma(\mathcal{L}_u)} \sigma(u, c) \tag{6}$$

Finally, to ensure a fair trade-off at each step, we normalize the raw novelty gains over the set of remaining candidates, $\mathcal{C}_u \setminus \mathcal{L}_u$. This per-iteration normalization yields the final *personalized novelty score*:

$$\mathcal{N}(i, \mathcal{L}_u, u) = \begin{cases} \dfrac{g(i, \mathcal{L}_u, u)}{\max\limits_{j \in \mathcal{C}_u \setminus \mathcal{L}_u} g(j, \mathcal{L}_u, u)}, & \text{if den.} > 0, \\ 0, & \text{otherwise.} \end{cases} \tag{7}$$

4 Experiments

4.1 Experimental Settings

To rigorously evaluate our framework, our experiments are designed to answer three research questions: **RQ1: Overall Performance.** How does our framework compare to established baselines in balancing accuracy and personalized diversity? **RQ2: Hyperparameter Sensitivity Analysis.** How sensitive is the Spectrum-Modulated Re-ranking (SMR) algorithm's performance to its key hyperparameters? **RQ3: Case Study and Interpretability.** Can a qualitative case study demonstrate that Spectrum-Modulated Re-ranking (SMR) improves recommendation quality by uncovering relevant, niche items aligned with a user's latent tastes?

Datasets We evaluate our framework on two widely-used movie recommendation datasets. The first is **MovieLens-1M** [13], which contains 999,611 interactions from 6040 users on 3416 movies. The second is **Douban Movie** [45,46], a denser dataset with 878,813 interactions from 2518 users on 18,383 movies. For both, we adopt the 5-core setting to ensure data quality, retaining only users and items with more than five interactions, and partition the data into 8:1:1 for training, validation, and testing.

Baselines To comprehensively evaluate our framework, we first generate top-200 candidate lists for each user–a standard size in the literature that balances high relevance coverage with computational efficiency for re-ranking. These lists are generated using four widely adopted base recommenders: a classic collaborative filtering method (ItemCF) [24,33], a matrix factorization model (BPRMF) [29], a state-of-the-art graph neural network (LightGCN) [14], and a diversity-aware graph-based model (DGCN) [44].

These candidate lists are then processed by our method and compared against three representative re-ranking baselines known for enhancing diversity: the relevance-dissimilarity greedy approach (MMR) [4], an efficient approximation of Determinantal Point Processes (FastDPP) [6], and an aspect-based diversification method (xQuAD) [32].

Evaluation Metrics Our evaluation focuses on accuracy (NDCG@K, Recall@K) and *personalized diversity*, for which we propose three novel metrics to measure alignment with a user's Semantic Interest Spectrum (SIS).

Traditional diversity metrics, such as Intra-List Distance (ILD) or genre coverage [8,40], are user-agnostic or operate at a coarse granularity. They fail to measure whether the diversity presented aligns with an individual's unique interests. To address this limitation, we propose three novel metrics designed to quantify the alignment between a recommendation list and a user's Semantic Interest Spectrum (SIS) profile.

Let $\mathcal{L}_u$ be the recommendation list for user u, $\Gamma(i)$ be the set of semantic clusters for item i, and $\sigma(u, c)$ be the user's Spectrum Intensity for cluster c.

Spectrum-Weighted Distance (SWD): This metric extends the concept of intra-list distance by weighting the dissimilarity between items according to the user's personal interest spectrum. The pairwise distance $\delta_u(i, j)$ between two items i and j is defined as a weighted Jaccard distance, where items sharing high-intensity clusters for user u are considered closer:

$$\delta_u(i, j) = 1 - \frac{\sum_{c \in \Gamma(i) \cap \Gamma(j)} \sigma(u, c)}{\sum_{c \in \Gamma(i) \cup \Gamma(j)} \sigma(u, c)} \tag{8}$$

The SWD for the list $\mathcal{L}_u$ is the average of all pairwise distances. For a list of size K, it is calculated as:

$$\text{SWD}(\mathcal{L}_u) = \frac{2}{K(K-1)} \sum_{i,j \in \mathcal{L}_u, i<j} \delta_u(i, j) \tag{9}$$

A higher SWD indicates that the list presents items that are distinct from each other from the user's perspective.

Spectrum Coverage Breadth (SCB): This metric measures how well the recommendation list reflects the breadth and balance of a user's diverse interests. It is calculated as the ratio of the entropy of the Semantic Interest Spectrum (SIS) distribution covered by the list to the entropy of the user's full Semantic Interest Spectrum (SIS) profile. Let $\Gamma(\mathcal{L}_u) = \bigcup_{i \in \mathcal{L}_u} \Gamma(i)$ be the set of clusters covered by the list, and let Γ_u be the set of all clusters in the user's complete profile. The entropy for a set of clusters $\mathcal{C}$ is given by $H(u, \mathcal{C}) = -\sum_{c \in \mathcal{C}} p(c) \log p(c)$, where $p(c) = \sigma(u, c) / \sum_{c' \in \mathcal{C}} \sigma(u, c')$. The SCB is then:

$$\text{SCB}(\mathcal{L}_u) = \frac{H(u, \Gamma(\mathcal{L}_u))}{H(u, \Gamma_u)} \tag{10}$$

A value closer to 1 indicates that the recommendations mirror the proportional balance of the user's full spectrum of interests.

Spectrum Coverage Depth (SCD): This metric quantifies how deeply the recommendation list covers the user's core, high-intensity interests. It is defined as the fraction of the user's total spectrum intensity that is covered by the unique semantic clusters present in the list:

$$\text{SCD}(\mathcal{L}_u) = \frac{\sum_{c \in \Gamma(\mathcal{L}_u)} \sigma(u, c)}{\sum_{c \in \Gamma_u} \sigma(u, c)} \tag{11}$$

A higher SCD value signifies that the recommendation list successfully incorporates items that align with the user's most distinctive and cherished preferences.

4.2 Overall Performance (RQ1)

Table 1 compares Spectrum-Modulated Re-ranking (SMR) against baseline re-rankers, focusing on the trade-off between accuracy and our personalized diversity metrics, with all results reported at top-10.

Personalized Diversity (SCB, SCD, SWD) Our Spectrum-Modulated Re-ranking (SMR) algorithm consistently demonstrates superior performance in personalized diversity. Across almost all settings, SMR achieves the highest or second-highest Spectrum Coverage Breadth (SCB), indicating it effectively mirrors the breadth of a user's interests. More importantly, SMR achieves the highest Spectrum Coverage Depth (SCD) in every single case, often by a significant margin (e.g., over 10% improvement on MovieLens-1M with LightGCN). This highlights SMR's unique strength in identifying and recommending items that align with a user's core, high-intensity niche interests. While MMR sometimes yields a higher Spectrum-Weighted Distance (SWD) due to its explicit dissimilarity objective, this often comes at the cost of covering a user's actual interests, as reflected in its lower SCB and SCD scores. In contrast, SMR delivers diversity aligned with the user's personal taste profile.

Table 1. Comprehensive performance comparison.

Reranker	MovieLens-1M					Douban Movie				
	NDCG	Recall	SWD	SCB	SCD	NDCG	Recall	SWD	SCB	SCD
Base Model: LightGCN										
Original	0.1798	0.0758	0.8343	0.9624	0.4032	0.1273	0.0252	0.9093	0.8846	0.3014
XQUAD	0.1764	0.0750	0.8205	0.9635	0.4152	0.1255	0.0238	0.8069	**0.9574**	0.4226
FAST-DPP	**0.1803**	**0.0760**	0.8383	0.9640	0.4058	**0.1274**	0.0253	0.9217	0.8786	0.2883
MMR	0.1775	0.0736	**0.8433**	0.9662	0.4095	0.1246	0.0249	**0.9670**	0.8250	0.2056
Ours	0.1776	0.0740	0.8399	**0.9664**	**0.4568**	0.1260	**0.0261**	0.8528	0.9520	**0.4432**
Base Model: BPRMF										
Original	0.1679	0.0645	0.8389	0.9625	0.3719	0.1366	0.0234	0.8849	0.9309	0.3381
XQUAD	0.1642	0.0642	0.8271	0.9648	0.3880	0.1358	0.0209	0.8148	0.9596	0.4093
FAST-DPP	0.1693	0.0655	0.8428	0.9642	0.3748	0.1366	0.0238	0.9002	0.9261	0.3237
MMR	0.1683	0.0656	**0.8475**	0.9665	0.3784	**0.1392**	**0.0254**	**0.9615**	0.8792	0.2281
Ours	**0.1707**	**0.0670**	0.8439	**0.9667**	**0.4270**	0.1282	0.0215	0.8369	**0.9624**	**0.4691**
Base Model: ItemCF										
Original	0.1630	0.0684	0.8334	0.9613	0.3656	0.0856	0.0193	0.9008	0.9248	0.3232
XQUAD	0.1596	0.0673	0.8222	0.9646	0.3839	0.0797	0.0167	0.8041	0.9579	0.4124
FAST-DPP	0.1637	0.0692	0.8383	0.9637	0.3693	0.0862	**0.0195**	0.9239	0.9158	0.2997
MMR	0.1637	0.0689	**0.8437**	0.9664	0.3742	**0.0869**	0.0195	**0.9805**	0.8407	0.1841
Ours	**0.1667**	**0.0696**	0.8400	**0.9664**	**0.4259**	0.0841	0.0168	0.8382	**0.9648**	**0.5002**
Base Model: DGCN										
Original	0.1561	0.0615	0.8331	0.9619	0.4033	0.0524	0.0110	0.9308	0.8885	0.2792
XQUAD	0.1511	0.0592	0.8204	0.9631	0.4150	**0.0573**	0.0114	0.8091	0.9573	0.4226
FAST-DPP	**0.1575**	**0.0624**	0.8370	0.9637	0.4061	0.0520	0.0115	0.9417	0.8817	0.2650
MMR	0.1564	0.0615	**0.8420**	0.9658	0.4097	0.0534	**0.0122**	**0.9797**	0.8116	0.1740
Ours	0.1561	0.0609	0.8387	**0.9659**	**0.4560**	0.0564	**0.0125**	0.8473	**0.9618**	**0.5020**

Results are grouped by the base recommendation model. For each base model, we present a side-by-side comparison of re-ranker performance on the two datasets. Within each column of a block, the best result is in **bold** and the second best is underlined.

Accuracy-Diversity Trade-off The results show that Spectrum-Modulated Re-ranking (SMR) achieves a superior trade-off between accuracy and diversity. While re-ranking baselines like FastDPP occasionally edge out other methods in NDCG or Recall, they typically do so without enhancing, and sometimes even hurting, personalized diversity (SCD). Our SMR method, while achieving these substantial gains in personalized diversity, maintains highly competitive accuracy. In several cases, such as with the BPRMF and ItemCF base models on MovieLens-1M, SMR even achieves the highest NDCG and Recall among all re-rankers. This demonstrates that by personalizing diversity, we can often enhance relevance simultaneously. The slight decreases in accuracy observed in

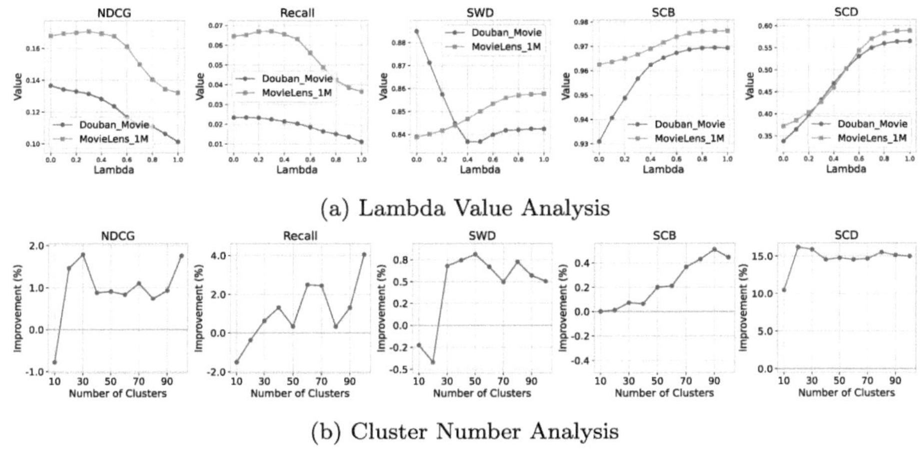

Fig. 2. Hyperparameter sensibility experiment results.

some other scenarios are modest when weighed against the major improvements in SCB and SCD.

To validate the significance of our model's diversity improvements, we performed a paired, two-tailed t-test. For each key diversity metric, we compared the list of per-user scores produced by SMR against those produced by the strongest competing re-ranker under the same base model and dataset setting. The test results indicate that the improvements on our personalized diversity metrics where our model excels are statistically significant ($p < 0.05$), suggesting that the observed gains are not due to random choice.

In summary, Spectrum-Modulated Re-ranking (SMR) consistently and substantially improves personalized diversity, uniquely excelling in enhancing both the breadth (SCB) and depth (SCD) of user interest coverage. Crucially, these gains are achieved without significant sacrifices in accuracy, establishing SMR as a highly effective and balanced re-ranking solution.

4.3 Hyperparameter Sensibility (RQ2)

We use BPRMF as the base model here to ensure clear observation of hyperparameter impacts, avoiding potential confounding factors from complex baselines.

Effect of Trade-off Parameter λ. As shown in Fig. 2a, increasing λ boosts personalized diversity metrics (SCB, SCD), as expected. On MovieLens-1M, this initially improves accuracy before a decline, while on Douban, accuracy shows a slight decrease. This confirms that λ effectively controls the accuracy-diversity trade-off, allowing us to find a sweet spot that enhances personalized diversity with minimal or no accuracy loss.

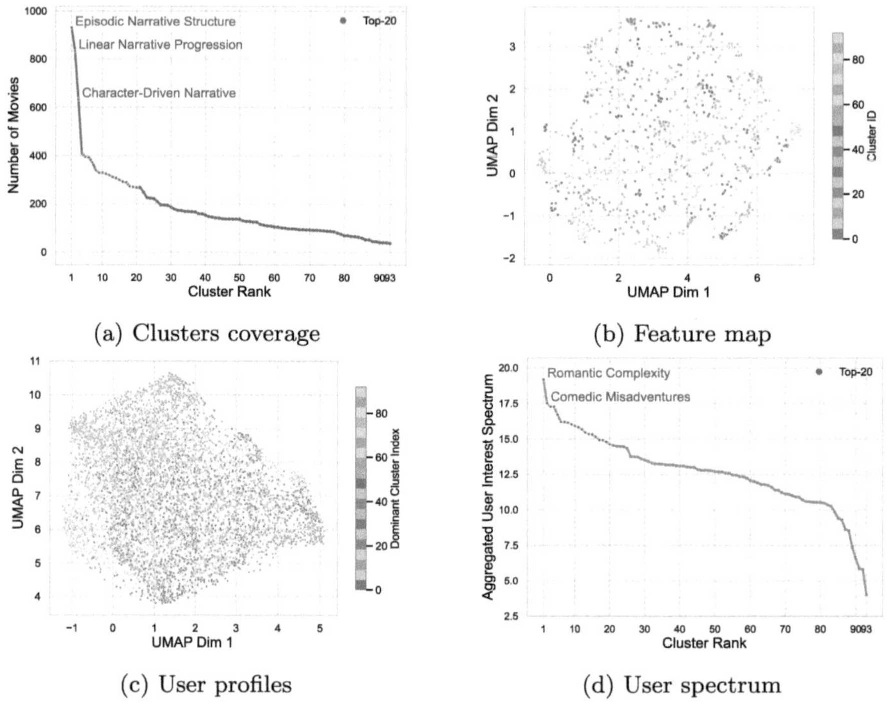

(a) Clusters coverage (b) Feature map

(c) User profiles (d) User spectrum

Fig. 3. Visual analysis of the *Narrative Pacing* dimension.

Effect of Maximum Cluster Count. We also analyzed the impact of semantic cluster granularity (Fig. 2b). Performance suffers when the cluster count is too low (insufficient semantic discriminability) or too high (interest spectrum becomes sparse). Both accuracy and diversity improvements plateau or decline beyond a certain point. Based on this analysis, we set the maximum cluster count to 100 in our main experiments to achieve a robust balance.

4.4 Visual Analysis of Semantic Space and User Spectrum

A visual analysis of the *Narrative Pacing* dimension validates our approach. We observe that item features follow a long-tail distribution (Fig. 3a), a source of popularity bias. However, our clustering effectively groups semantically similar features into coherent regions (Fig. 3b). Crucially, the aggregated user interest spectrum (Fig. 3c) is far more dispersed than the item distribution, revealing that user tastes are more diverse than what popular items suggest. UMAP projection of user profiles (Fig. 3d) further shows that users form distinct communities based on their dominant semantic interests. This confirms the existence of a personalized diversity space that traditional models overlook but our framework successfully captures.

4.5 Ablation Study on LLM Choice

To validate the effectiveness of our proposed semantic profiling pipeline and overall framework, we further conducted a comparison using a local open-source model, Gemma 3 8B, for semantic feature extraction. The results show that, compared with features extracted by GPT-4o, using Gemma 3 8B leads to inferior re-ranking performance on both accuracy and personalized diversity(approximate 10% improvements with 4o and 4% improvements with Gemma 3). Nevertheless, the re-ranked lists based on Gemma 3 8B features still achieve clear diversity improvements over the original (non-re-ranked) lists. These findings indicate that our extraction protocol and SIS-based user modeling remain effective even when using a local open-source LLM, supporting the robustness of our framework and the validity of the proposed user profiling method.

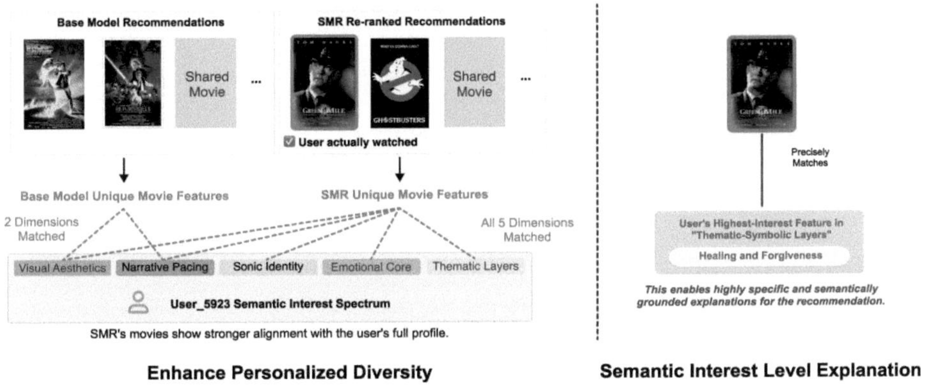

Fig. 4. Case study for user 5923.

4.6 Case Study (RQ3)

A case study on a random user (`User_5923`) demonstrates Spectrum-Modulated Re-ranking (SMR)'s effectiveness (Fig. 4). SMR replaced two popular but misaligned movies from the base list with *The Green Mile* and *Ghostbusters. The Green Mile*, an actual item in the user's history, perfectly aligned with the user's high-intensity Semantic Interest Spectrum (SIS) profile across all five dimensions. Specifically, it matched the user's top niche interest in the *Thematic Symbols* dimension: *Healing and Forgiveness.* This type of semantic match not only improves relevance but also enables precise, interpretable explanations (e.g., "We recommend this because you enjoy films about healing and forgiveness"), confirming that SMR enhances both personalized diversity and explainability.

5 Conclusion

In this work, we proposed a novel framework that leverages LLMs and domain expertise to enhance personalized diversity in recommender systems. Our approach uniquely guides this process using five expert-defined cinematic dimensions, allowing us to model users' fine-grained preferences through our *Semantic Interest Spectrum*. The resulting *Spectrum-Modulated Re-ranking* algorithm delivers recommendations that achieve a superior trade-off between competitive accuracy, significant gains in personalized diversity, and fine-grained interpretability.

While effective, our framework has limitations that guide our future research. The quality of semantic features is model-dependent, and our reliance on a proprietary LLM affects reproducibility. Furthermore, the Semantic Interest Spectrum profiles are static. Future work will therefore investigate open-source LLMs, develop methods for modeling dynamic user interests, and conduct user studies to assess the real-world acceptance of the personalized diversity it generates and the framework's generalizability to other domains.

Acknowledgments. This work was supported by JSPS KAKENHI Grant Number JP25K03230 and JP23K02469.

References

1. Agrawal, R., Gollapudi, S., Halverson, A., Ieong, S.: Diversifying search results. In: Proceedings of the Second ACM International Conference on Web Search and Data Mining, pp. 5–14 (2009)
2. Altman, R.: The material heterogeneity of recorded sound. In: Altman, R. (ed.) Sound Theory, Sound Practice, pp. 15–31. Routledge, New York (1992)
3. Bordwell, D.: The art cinema as a mode of film practice. Film Crit. **4**(1), 56–64 (1979)
4. Carbonell, J., Goldstein, J.: The use of MMR, diversity-based reranking for reordering documents and producing summaries. In: Proceedings of the 21st Annual International ACM SIGIR Conference on Research and Development in Information Retrieval, pp. 335–336 (1998)
5. Carraro, J., Bridge, D.: Enhancing recommendation diversity by re-ranking with large language models (2024). arXiv preprint arXiv:2403.14033
6. Chen, L., Zhang, G., Zhou, E.: Fast greedy map inference for determinantal point process to improve recommendation diversity. Adv. Neural Inf. Process. Syst. 5627–5638 (2018)
7. Chion, M.: The acousmêtre. In: The Voice in Cinema, pp. 17–29. Columbia University Press, New York (1999)
8. Clarke, C.L.A., Kolla, M., Cormack, G.V., Vechtomova, O., Ashkan, A., Büttcher, S., MacKinnon, I.: Novelty and diversity in information retrieval evaluation. In: Proceedings of the 31st Annual International ACM SIGIR Conference on Research and Development in Information Retrieval, pp. 659–666 (2008)
9. Cutting, J.E., DeLong, J.E., Nothelfer, C.E.: Attention and the evolution of Hollywood film. Psychol. Sci. **21**(3), 432–439 (2010)

10. Fan, W., Zhao, Z., Li, J., Liu, Y., Mei, X., Wang, Y., Tang, J., Li, Q.: Recommender systems in the era of large language models (LLMs). arXiv preprint arXiv:2307.02046 (2023)
11. Geng, S., Liu, S., Fu, Z., Ge, Y., Zhang, Y.: Recommendation as language processing (rlp): A unified pretrain, personalized prompt and predict paradigm (p5). In: Proceedings of the 16th ACM Conference on Recommender Systems, pp. 299–315 (2022)
12. Gunning, T.: The cinema of attractions: early film, its spectator and the avant-garde. Wide Angle **8**(3–4), 63–70 (1986)
13. Harper, F.M., Konstan, J.A.: The movielens datasets: history and context. ACM Trans. Interact. Intell. Syst. **5**(4), 19 (2015)
14. He, X., Deng, K., Wang, X., Li, Y., Zhang, Y., Wang, M.: Lightgcn: Simplifying and powering graph convolution network for recommendation. In: Proceedings of the 43rd International ACM SIGIR Conference on Research and Development in Information Retrieval, pp. 639–648 (2020)
15. Hou, Y., He, Z., McAuley, J., Zhao, W.X.: Learning vector-quantized item representation for transferable sequential recommenders. In: Proceedings of the ACM Web Conference 2023, pp. 1162–1171 (2023)
16. Hou, Y., Mu, S., Zhao, W.X., Li, Y., Ding, B., Wen, J.R.: Towards universal sequence representation learning for recommender systems. In: Proceedings of the 28th ACM SIGKDD Conference on Knowledge Discovery and Data Mining, pp. 585–593 (2022)
17. Hou, Y., Zhang, J., Lin, Z., Lu, H., Xie, R., McAuley, J., Zhao, W.X.: Large language models for generative recommendation: a survey and visionary outlook. arXiv preprint arXiv:2306.10843 (2023)
18. Kotkov, D., Wang, S., Veijalainen, J.: A survey of serendipity in recommender systems. Knowl.-Based Syst. **111**, 180–192 (2016)
19. Kozloff, S.: Narrative, narration, and the new film melodrama. J. Film Video **43**(1–2), 69–82 (1991)
20. Kulesza, A., Taskar, B.: Determinantal point processes for machine learning. Found. Trends. Machine Learn.**5**(2–3), 123–286 (2012)
21. Kunaver, M., Požrl, T.: Diversity in recommender systems—a survey. Knowl.-Based Syst. **132**, 154–162 (2017)
22. Li, Z., Du, Z., Wang, T., Wang, R., He, Q., Wang, M.: LLM-enhanced reranking in recommender systems: a survey. arXiv preprint arXiv:2405.13051 (2024)
23. Lin, T., Zhao, W.X., Wen, J.R., Wang, X.: A survey of large language models for recommendation (2023). arXiv preprint arXiv:2305.19860
24. Linden, G., Smith, B., York, J.: Amazon.com recommendations: item-to-item collaborative filtering. IEEE Internet Comput. **7**(1), 76–80 (2003)
25. Manovich, L.: What is digital cinema? In: Lunenfeld, P. (ed.) The Digital Dialectic: New Essays on New Media, pp. 173–192. MIT Press, Cambridge, MA (1999)
26. Metz, C.: The imaginary signifier. Screen **16**(2), 14–76 (1975)
27. Mulvey, L.: Visual pleasure and narrative cinema. Screen **16**(3), 6–18 (1975)
28. Plantinga, C.: The scene of empathy and the human face on film. In: Plantinga, C., Smith, G.M. (eds.) Passionate Views: Film, Cognition, and Emotion, pp. 239–255. Johns Hopkins University Press, Baltimore, MD (1999)
29. Rendle, S., Freudenthaler, C., Gantner, Z., Schmidt-Thieme, L.: BPR: Bayesian personalized ranking from implicit feedback. In: Proceedings of the Twenty-Fifth Conference on Uncertainty in Artificial Intelligence, pp. 452–461 (2009)

30. Ricci, F., Rokach, L., Shapira, B.: Recommender systems: introduction and challenges. In: Recommender Systems Handbook, 3 edn., pp. 1–35. Springer, New York (2021)
31. Salt, B.: Statistical style analysis of motion pictures. Film Q. **28**(1), 13–22 (1974)
32. Santos, R.L.T., Peng, J., Macdonald, C., Ounis, I.: Explicit search result diversification through sub-queries. Adv. Inf. Retrieval, pp. 87–99. Springer (2010)
33. Sarwar, B., Karypis, G., Konstan, J., Riedl, J.: Item-based collaborative filtering recommendation algorithms. In: Proceedings of the 10th International Conference on World Wide Web, pp. 285–295 (2001)
34. Shang, F., Liu, J., Tan, W., Peng, H.: Personalized recommendation systems powered by large language models: integrating semantic understanding and user preferences. Int. J. Innov. Res. Eng. Manag. **11**(4), 39–49 (2024)
35. Smith, G.M.: Local emotions, global moods, and film structure. In: Plantinga, C., Smith, G.M. (eds.) Passionate Views: Film, Cognition, and Emotion, pp. 103–126. Johns Hopkins University Press, Baltimore, MD (1999)
36. Stam, R., Spence, L.: Colonialism, racism, and representation: an introduction. Screen **24**(2), 2–20 (1983)
37. Sun, F., Liu, J., Wu, J., Pei, C., Lin, X., Ou, W., Jiang, P.: Bert4rec: sequential recommendation with bidirectional encoder representations from transformer. In: Proceedings of the 28th ACM International Conference on Information and Knowledge Management, pp. 1441–1450 (2019)
38. Tan, E.S.: Emotion, art, and the humanities. In: Forgas, J.P. (ed.) Feeling and Thinking: The Role of Affect in Social Cognition, pp. 99–114. Cambridge University Press, Cambridge (2000)
39. Thompson, K.: The concept of cinematic excess. Ciné-Tracts **1**(2), 54–63 (1977)
40. Vargas, S., Castells, P.: Rank and relevance in novelty and diversity metrics for recommender systems. In: Proceedings of the 5th ACM Conference on Recommender Systems, pp. 109–116 (2011)
41. Wang, W., Lin, X., Feng, F., He, X., Chua, T.S.: Generative recommendation: towards next-generation recommender paradigm. arXiv preprint arXiv:2304.03516 (2023)
42. Yang, F., Chen, Z., Jiang, Z., Cho, E., Huang, X., Lu, Y.: PALR: personalization aware LLMs for recommendation. arXiv preprint arXiv:2305.07622 (2023)
43. Zhang, Q., Li, J., Chen, Q., Zhou, J., Li, J., Tang, H., Hua, X.S.: UNBERT: user-news matching BERT for news recommendation. In: Proceedings of the Thirtieth International Joint Conference on Artificial Intelligence, pp. 3356–3362 (2021)
44. Zheng, Y., Gao, C., Chen, L., Jin, D., Li, Y.: DGCN: diversified recommendation with graph convolutional networks. In: Proceedings of The Web Conference 2021, pp. 401–412 (2021)
45. Zhu, F., Chen, C., Wang, Y., Liu, G., Zheng, X.: DTCDR: a framework for dual-target cross-domain recommendation. In: Proceedings of the 28th ACM International Conference on Information and Knowledge Management, pp. 1533–1542 (2019)
46. Zhu, F., Wang, Y., Chen, C., Liu, G., Zheng, X.: A graphical and attentional framework for dual-target cross-domain recommendation. In: Proceedings of the Twenty-Ninth International Joint Conference on Artificial Intelligence, pp. 3001–3008 (2020)
47. Ziegler, C.N., McNee, S.M., Konstan, J.A., Lausen, G.: Improving recommendation lists through topic diversification. In: Proceedings of the 14th International Conference on World Wide Web, pp. 402–411 (2005)

Column Type Annotation Based on Adaptive Decision Boundary

Changlong Wang, Wenhao Zhao(✉), Zhixiong Yin, Pengjuan Lu, and Huimei Tian

Northwest Normal University, Lanzhou, China
wchlong@nwnu.edu.cn, zwenhao12345@163.com

Abstract. Column type annotation has become an important task in table understanding and data integration. Its goal is to assign semantic type labels to table columns, thereby supporting downstream applications such as retrieval and data integration. In practice, table data often come from diverse sources, and the boundaries between semantic types can be highly similar. Moreover, annotations are typically constructed automatically, making noisy labels in the training data unavoidable. This further aggravates confusion between similar types and leads to unstable predictions near the decision boundary. To address this issue, we propose AdaDB, an adaptive decision boundary method for improving column type annotation performance. Specifically, AdaDB consists of two complementary modules. The type-adaptive module estimates type difficulty based on confusion-matrix statistics, where the confusion matrix is dynamically updated during training and smoothed with an exponential moving average, and then assigns larger classification margins to easily confused types. The sample-adaptive module measures the proximity of a sample to the decision boundary using the score gap between the ground-truth type and the highest-scoring candidate type, and enlarges the margin only for semi-hard samples near the boundary. These two modules capture boundary information at the type level and the sample level, respectively, and further map type-level margins into sample-level margins, which are then integrated with a reweighted training strategy for boundary-adjacent samples. Experimental results on the WebTables dataset show that the proposed method effectively improves column type annotation performance, achieving a weighted F1 score of 91.64%.

Keywords: Table understanding · Column type annotation · Adaptive decision boundary · Decisive vector learning · Noisy labels

1 Introduction

As the scale of tabular data continues to grow in web and data lake scenarios, how to extract computable semantic information from tables has become a fundamental problem in data management and knowledge organization. Column Type Annotation (CTA) aims to assign a semantic type label to each column

L. Ding et al. (Eds.): APWeb-WAIM 2026, LNCS 16993, pp. 671–686, 2027.
https://doi.org/10.1007/978-981-92-5693-8_42

in a table, thereby supporting tasks such as semantic retrieval, table integration, entity alignment, and downstream analysis. The type vocabulary is usually derived from predefined ontologies or schema vocabularies, such as the type systems in public knowledge bases [1].

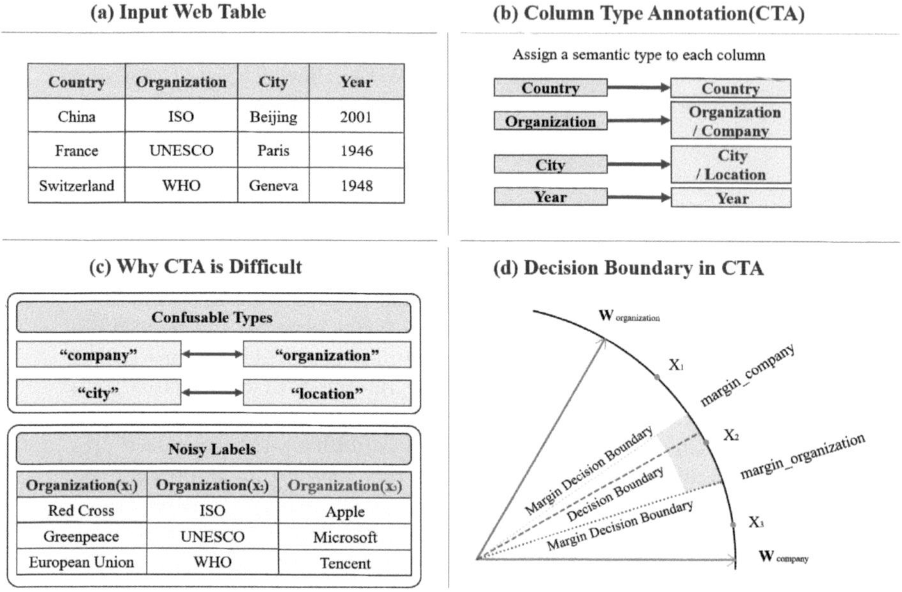

Fig. 1. Illustration of the Column Type Annotation task and its challenges.

As illustrated in Fig. 1, CTA aims to assign a semantic type label to each column in a web table according to its header and cell values. Figure 1a gives a simple web table example, and Fig. 1b shows the annotation objective. The main challenge, as shown in Fig. 1c, is that some semantic types are highly similar in meaning, such as "company" and "organization" or "city" and "location". Meanwhile, training labels are usually obtained through automatic construction or alignment, and therefore may contain errors. As a result, type confusion and noisy labels are often intertwined in real CTA scenarios.

Figure 1d provides a simplified illustration in the normalized angular space to explain the decision boundary between similar semantic types. It should be noted that this figure is not a complete visualization of the original high-dimensional feature space, but a local projection after normalizing column representations and classifier weights. In this illustration, $\boldsymbol{W}_{\text{organization}}$ and $\boldsymbol{W}_{\text{company}}$ denote two type prototypes, and $\boldsymbol{X}_1$, $\boldsymbol{X}_2$, and $\boldsymbol{X}_3$ denote representative column samples with different boundary positions. $\boldsymbol{X}_1$ is far from the boundary and can be regarded as an easy sample, $\boldsymbol{X}_2$ lies near the boundary and is more likely to cause unstable predictions, while $\boldsymbol{X}_3$ is closer to the company side and may correspond to a noisy or hard sample.

Such type confusion can directly affect downstream applications. For example, in enterprise information or open data lake scenarios, a column containing values such as "Apple", "Amazon", and "Microsoft" may be interpreted as "company", but may also be annotated as "organization" in some ontologies. If such labels are mixed during automatic alignment, semantic search may miss relevant tables, and table integration or entity alignment may fail to match columns that actually describe the same kind of entities. Similarly, values such as "Paris", "London", and "Tokyo" may lead to confusion between "city" and "location", thereby affecting geographic table retrieval and analysis.

Therefore, CTA is not merely a standard classification task. The model needs to distinguish semantically similar types while learning from labels that may be noisy. Existing methods usually apply the same boundary scale to all types and all samples, which does not fully match the characteristics of CTA data. In practice, different types have different levels of confusion, and samples within the same type may also lie at different distances from the decision boundary. This motivates us to design an adaptive decision boundary that adjusts the classification margin according to both type-level confusion and sample-level boundary proximity.

The main contributions of this paper are as follows:

- We propose AdaDB, an adaptive decision boundary method for CTA. Built upon a normalized cosine classifier and a margin-based learning framework, AdaDB dynamically adjusts the decision boundary at both type level and sample level.
- We design a type-level adaptive boundary module. By assigning different margins to different semantic types, this module enables the model to adjust the decision boundary according to type-specific difficulty, thereby improving the discrimination of closely related types.
- We design a sample-level adaptive boundary module. This module characterizes the proximity of a sample to the decision boundary using the score gap between the ground-truth type and competing candidate types, and performs more targeted boundary adjustment for semi-hard samples near the boundary. It is further combined with a reweighted training strategy to make more effective use of these decisive samples.
- We extensively evaluate the proposed method on the WebTables benchmarks.Experimental results show that AdaDB effectively improves overall performance on the CTA task and exhibits stronger robustness in the presence of noisy labels.

2 Related Work

2.1 Column Type Annotation and Semantic Type Detection in Tables

CTA aims to assign a semantic type label to each column in a table, and serves as a key step in semantic table understanding and data preparation. Early studies on web tables typically addressed this problem from the perspective of jointly modeling entities, types, and relations, laying the foundation for subsequent column-level semantic annotation [1]. With the development of learning-based methods, semantic type detection has gradually evolved from rule-based and feature-engineering approaches to data-driven representation learning methods.

In this line of research, Sherlock [5] is one of the most representative studies. It combines statistical features of column values, character distribution features, and textual representations, and uses deep neural networks to model column semantics, demonstrating the effectiveness of deep learning for semantic type detection. Building on this, SATO [6] further emphasizes the importance of table context for column semantic recognition. It shows that the semantic type of a column depends not only on its own values, but also on adjacent columns and the overall semantic environment of the table, and further improves type prediction through context modeling and structured prediction.

Overall, existing CTA and semantic type detection methods have gradually evolved from early joint annotation frameworks to learning paradigms that combine column content with table context. However, in real web-table scenarios, training data are often obtained through automatic construction or weak supervision, and therefore inevitably contain incorrect labels. Meanwhile, semantically similar types are also prone to inter-class confusion. These factors can substantially affect the model's type prediction performance. Motivated by this issue, subsequent studies have begun to investigate CTA under noisy-label settings, with particular attention to how to better handle critical samples near the decision boundary.

2.2 Column Type Annotation Under Noisy Labels

In real web-table scenarios, CTA training data are often constructed through automatic alignment, distant supervision, or rule-based matching, making noisy labels difficult to avoid. Once incorrect labels are introduced, the learned classification boundary can become unstable, especially for samples near the decision boundary, thereby degrading type prediction performance. To address this issue, prior studies on learning with noisy labels have proposed representative strategies such as sample selection, robust loss design, semi-supervised optimization, and adaptive reliable-sample mining [7–10]. These methods improve robustness from different perspectives, but they are mostly designed for general classification problems rather than the specific discriminative characteristics of CTA.

Compared with these general-purpose methods, DVGL [2] is more closely aligned with the CTA task. It analyzes the impact of noisy labels on CTA learning and proposes a decisive-vector-guided training strategy, which partitions samples into easy, semi-hard, and hard regions based on a margin-based decision boundary, with particular emphasis on semi-hard samples near the boundary. This line of research suggests that, for CTA, the selection and utilization of boundary-adjacent samples can directly affect the final discriminative performance of the model.

2.3 Margin-Based Discriminative Learning and Adaptive Decision Boundaries

Margin-based discriminative learning improves model discriminability by increasing the separation between different classes. Representative methods such as CosFace [3] and ArcFace [4] show that introducing margins in the normalized feature space can yield clearer decision boundaries and enhance class separability. Subsequent studies have further explored adaptive margin adjustment strategies. For example, CurricularFace [11] dynamically adjusts the relative importance of easy and hard samples at different training stages from the perspective of curriculum learning, while AdaFace [12] adaptively adjusts the classification margin according to image quality. These studies indicate that a fixed margin is not necessarily suitable for all cases. Dynamically adjusting the boundary strength according to sample conditions or data characteristics is an important direction for improving discriminative learning.

However, most existing adaptive margin methods are designed for visual recognition tasks such as face recognition. Their adaptivity is mainly derived from the training stage, sample difficulty, or image quality, without directly considering semantic type confusion and noisy labels in CTA. Unlike visual recognition tasks, the boundary difficulty in CTA mainly arises from the ambiguity between closely related semantic types and the noise introduced by automatically constructed labels. Therefore, directly applying adaptive strategies based on the training stage or image quality cannot fully capture the imbalanced type-confusion structure and the substantial variation in sample-boundary proximity in CTA. Motivated by this observation, we design adaptive decision boundaries from the perspective of the CTA task itself, considering both type confusion degree and sample boundary proximity, so as to more effectively handle column type annotation scenarios where closely related semantic types and noisy labels coexist.

3 Method

3.1 Preliminaries

Input and Column Representation. Let the input table be denoted by $\mathcal{T}$, where the i-th column is denoted by col_i. After serializing the target column together with its context columns, we obtain the input sequence $\boldsymbol{x}_i$. Let the encoder be denoted by $f_\phi(\cdot)$, and let its output column representation be $\boldsymbol{h}_i \in \mathbb{R}^d$, where d denotes the representation dimension.

$$\boldsymbol{h}_i = f_\phi(\boldsymbol{x}_i) \in \mathbb{R}^d. \tag{1}$$

Type Set and Normalized Classifier. Let the semantic type set be $\mathcal{Y} = \{\tau_1, \tau_2, \ldots, \tau_C\}$, where τ_k denotes the k-th semantic type and C denotes the total number of semantic types. Let the ground-truth type of the i-th column be denoted by $y_i \in \mathcal{Y}$. For any type $\tau_k \in \mathcal{Y}$, let its learnable weight vector be $\boldsymbol{W}_k$. After normalization, we obtain the normalized classifier weight vector $\boldsymbol{w}_k$.

Similarly, by normalizing the column representation vector $\boldsymbol{h}_i$, we obtain the normalized column representation vector $\boldsymbol{v}_i$. Together, they form a normalized cosine classifier:

$$\boldsymbol{w}_k = \frac{\boldsymbol{W}_k}{\|\boldsymbol{W}_k\|_2}, \qquad \boldsymbol{v}_i = \frac{\boldsymbol{h}_i}{\|\boldsymbol{h}_i\|_2}, \qquad k \in \{1, \ldots, C\}. \tag{2}$$

Similarity, Classification Score, and Classification Loss. Let $\cos\theta_{i,\tau_k}$ denote the cosine similarity between the i-th column and type τ_k, which is used to measure the matching degree between the current column sample and different semantic types. The cosine similarity between the i-th column and type τ_k is defined as $\cos\theta_{i,\tau_k} = \boldsymbol{v}_i^\top \boldsymbol{w}_k$. Let z_{i,τ_k} denote the classification score of type τ_k, i.e., the unnormalized score before softmax, where z_{i,y_i} denotes the classification score corresponding to the ground-truth type. Let $\mathcal{L}_{\text{soft}}(i)$ denote the standard softmax classification loss for the i-th column. Accordingly, the softmax loss can be written as follows:

$$\mathcal{L}_{\text{soft}}(i) = -\log \frac{e^{z_{i,y_i}}}{e^{z_{i,y_i}} + \sum_{\tau_k \neq y_i}^{C} e^{z_{i,\tau_k}}}. \tag{3}$$

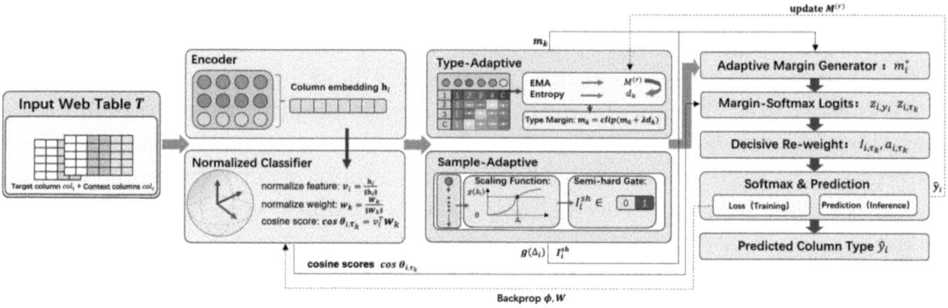

Fig. 2. The overall framework of AdaDB.

3.2 Overall Framework and the Dual-Adaptive Decision Boundary Model

Considering that different semantic types exhibit different confusion patterns and that different column samples may lie at substantially different distances from the decision boundary, we propose AdaDB, a dual-adaptive decision boundary method that dynamically adjusts the classification margin at both type level and sample level. The overall framework is illustrated in Fig. 2.

Input Representation and Normalized Classification. Given an input table $\mathcal{T}$, we first extract the target column together with its context columns and serialize them into an input sequence $\boldsymbol{x}_i$. The encoder $f_\phi(\cdot)$ then performs representation learning over the input and produces the corresponding column representation vector $\boldsymbol{h}_i$. On this basis, we adopt a normalized classifier, where both the column representation and the type weights are normalized, and the cosine similarity between the current column and each semantic type is computed. This similarity reflects the matching relationship between the current column sample and different semantic types, and also serves as the basis for the subsequent type-level and sample-level boundary adjustment.

Type-Adaptive Boundary Module. A fixed classification margin implicitly assumes that all semantic types have the same discrimination difficulty. However, in real CTA data, the degree of confusion varies substantially across different types. To address this issue, the Type-Adaptive module in Fig. 2 dynamically updates type confusion information based on the model's current predictions and estimates the confusion difficulty of each type via an exponential moving average, thereby generating type-level classification margins.

During training, we progressively update the type confusion statistics according to the current model predictions. For ease of matrix representation, we use indices u and v to denote the row and column positions of semantic types τ_u and τ_v in the confusion matrix, respectively. Specifically, at the r-th statistics update, let $S_{u,v}^{(r)}$ denote the number of samples whose ground-truth type is τ_u but are predicted as type τ_v. By normalizing each row, we obtain the conditional distribution estimate of the current statistics:

$$P_{u,v}^{(r)} = \frac{S_{u,v}^{(r)}}{\sum_{v'=1}^{C} S_{u,v'}^{(r)} + \varepsilon}. \tag{4}$$

Here, v' is the summation index, and $\varepsilon > 0$ is a smoothing term used to avoid a zero denominator. $P_{u,v}^{(r)}$ can be interpreted as the estimated probability, at the r-th statistics update, that a sample with ground-truth type τ_u is predicted as type τ_v.

We then smooth the confusion statistics using exponential moving averaging and obtain the confusion matrix $\boldsymbol{M}^{(r)}$:

$$\boldsymbol{M}^{(r)} = (1-\beta)\boldsymbol{M}^{(r-1)} + \beta\boldsymbol{P}^{(r)}, \qquad \beta \in (0, 1]. \tag{5}$$

Here, β is the update coefficient that balances the current statistics and the historical estimate.

To characterize the confusion difficulty between type τ_k and other types,we further construct its misclassification distribution. For convenience, we continue to use indices k and v to denote the row and column positions of types τ_k and τ_v in the confusion matrix, respectively. Note that the diagonal term $M_{k,k}^{(r)}$ represents correctly classified samples whose ground-truth and predicted types are the same, whereas the off-diagonal term $M_{k,v}^{(r)}$ represents samples whose ground-truth type is τ_k but are misclassified as τ_v. After removing the diagonal term and renormalizing the remaining entries, we obtain the misclassification distribution of type τ_k:

$$q_k(v) = \frac{M_{k,v}^{(r)}}{\sum_{\substack{v'=1 \\ v' \neq k}}^{C} M_{k,v'}^{(r)} + \varepsilon}, \qquad v \in \{1, \ldots, C\},\ v \neq k. \tag{6}$$

Here, $q_k(v)$ denotes the relative proportion of cases in which type τ_k is misclassified as type τ_v among all misclassification cases of τ_k. This distribution reflects the specific confusion pattern of type τ_k and provides the basis for subsequent type-difficulty estimation.

Next, we use normalized entropy to quantify the difficulty of type τ_k. If the misclassification distribution of a type is more dispersed, it indicates that this type is more likely to be confused with multiple other types and is therefore harder to classify. Based on this intuition, we define the difficulty of type τ_k as

$$d_k = -\frac{\sum_{\substack{v=1 \\ v \neq k}}^{C} q_k(v) \log\big(q_k(v) + \varepsilon\big)}{\log(C-1)} \in [0, 1]. \tag{7}$$

Here, d_k denotes the difficulty coefficient of type τ_k. A larger d_k indicates that the misclassification distribution of this type is more dispersed, meaning that it is more easily confused with multiple other types.

Finally, we map the type difficulty to a type-level classification margin:

$$m_k = \text{clip}(m_0 + \lambda d_k,\ m_{\min},\ m_{\max}), \tag{8}$$

where m_0 is the base classification margin, λ controls the strength of adaptive adjustment, and clip$(\cdot)$ constrains the margin to the interval $[m_{\min}, m_{\max}]$ to ensure training stability. In this way, the type-adaptive module generates for each semantic type a type-level classification margin that changes dynamically during training.

Intuitively, the type difficulty d_k measures the confusion difficulty faced by the model when distinguishing type τ_k from other types. If type τ_k is mostly predicted as a single closely related type, its confusion direction is relatively concentrated. In contrast, if it is frequently predicted as multiple different types, the model's prediction for this type is less stable, and its decision boundary is more difficult to learn. Therefore, we use normalized entropy to quantify this uncertainty, and assign larger classification margins to types with higher uncertainty. This encourages the model to reserve a larger separation space for easily confused types during training.

Sample-Adaptive Boundary Module. Beyond the confusion differences across semantic types, different samples within the same type may also lie at substantially different distances from the decision boundary. The sample-adaptive module in Fig. 2 characterizes the boundary proximity of each sample using cosine scores and applies stronger margin adjustment to critical samples near the boundary.

Specifically, we use the score gap between the ground-truth type and the highest-scoring competing type to describe the boundary proximity of a sample:

$$\Delta_i = \cos\theta_{i,y_i} - \max_{\tau_k \neq y_i} \cos\theta_{i,\tau_k}. \tag{9}$$

Here, $\max_{\tau_k \neq y_i} \cos\theta_{i,\tau_k}$ denotes the maximum cosine similarity among all non-ground-truth types, i.e., the classification score of the highest-scoring negative type. A smaller Δ_i indicates that the sample is closer to the decision boundary and that the competition among candidate types is more intense.

To this end, we design the following scaling function:

$$g(\Delta_i) = 1 + \rho \cdot \sigma\left(\frac{\mu - \Delta_i}{\gamma}\right), \qquad \sigma(u) = \frac{1}{1+e^{-u}}, \tag{10}$$

where ρ controls the maximum amplification strength, μ is the central threshold, and γ controls the smoothness of the transition. This function assigns a larger amplification factor to samples that are closer to the boundary.

However, directly enlarging the margin for all samples may impose overly strong constraints on extremely hard samples. Therefore, following the boundary partitioning idea of DVGL [2], we activate sample-level amplification only when a sample falls into the semi-hard region. The sample-level semi-hard indicator is defined as

$$I_i^{\text{sh}} = \mathbb{I}\left(\cos\theta_{i,y_i} - m_{y_i} \leq \max_{\tau_k \neq y_i} \cos\theta_{i,\tau_k} < \cos\theta_{i,y_i}\right), \tag{11}$$

where $\mathbb{I}(\cdot)$ is the indicator function, which equals 1 if the condition holds and 0 otherwise, and m_{y_i} denotes the type-level classification margin corresponding to the ground-truth type y_i.

Accordingly, the sample-adaptive module generates the sample-level classification margin within the Adaptive Margin Generator module in Fig. 2 based on the type-level margin m_{y_i}, the boundary score gap Δ_i, and the semi-hard indicator I_i^{sh}:

$$m_i^* = \text{clip}\left(m_{y_i} \cdot \left(1 + I_i^{\text{sh}} \cdot (g(\Delta_i) - 1)\right), m_{\min}, m_{\max}\right). \tag{12}$$

This means that when a sample does not fall into the semi-hard region, its margin reduces to the type-level margin of its ground-truth type. In contrast, when the sample lies near the boundary, its margin is further amplified according to its boundary proximity, thereby yielding a sample-level adaptive boundary.

This scaling function can be interpreted as a smooth sample-aware weighting mechanism. When the score of the ground-truth type is substantially higher than those of the other candidate types, the model is already confident about the semantic type of the sample, and thus there is no need to significantly enlarge the margin. In contrast, when the score of the ground-truth type is very close to that of the highest-scoring candidate type, the model has difficulty clearly distinguishing the ground-truth type from the competing candidate types, and the sample is also closer to the decision boundary. In this case, the scaling function gradually increases the sample-level margin according to the degree of boundary proximity, encouraging training to focus more on such semi-hard samples near the boundary. This strengthens the constraint on boundary-adjacent samples while maintaining a smooth and stable training process.

Adaptive Margin Generation and Training Objective. After obtaining the sample-level margin m_i^* through the joint effect of the type-level and sample-level classification margins in the previous two modules, we replace the fixed margin m with the sample-level margin m_i^* in the Margin-Softmax Logits module in Fig. 2, thereby obtaining the adaptive classification scores:

$$z_{i,\tau_k} = \begin{cases} s\left(\cos\theta_{i,y_i} - m_i^*\right), & \tau_k = y_i, \\ s\cos\theta_{i,\tau_k}, & \tau_k \neq y_i. \end{cases} \tag{13}$$

On top of this, we integrate the adaptive boundary into the decisive reweighting module of DVGL [2]. Specifically, when determining whether a candidate type falls into the semi-hard region, we use the sample-level boundary m_i^* instead of a fixed margin, and define

$$I_{i,\tau_k} = \mathbb{I}(\cos\theta_{i,y_i} - m_i^* \leq \cos\theta_{i,\tau_k} < \cos\theta_{i,y_i}), \qquad \tau_k \neq y_i. \tag{14}$$

Based on this indicator, the reweighting coefficient is computed as

$$\alpha_{i,\tau_k} = h(t, I_{i,\tau_k}), \tag{15}$$

where t denotes the training progress. We adopt the same reweighting function $h(\cdot)$ as in DVGL, which gradually increases the weight assigned to decisive types as training proceeds.

Accordingly, the training objective corresponding to the Decisive Re-weight module and the Softmax & Prediction module in Fig. 2 can be written as

$$\mathcal{L}_{\text{AdaDB}}(i) = -\log \frac{e^{z_{i,y_i}}}{e^{z_{i,y_i}} + \sum_{\tau_k \neq y_i} \alpha_{i,\tau_k} e^{z_{i,\tau_k}}}. \tag{16}$$

During training, the model updates the confusion matrix $\boldsymbol{M}^{(r)}$ according to the predictions and ground-truth labels within the current batch or statistics window, and jointly optimizes the encoder parameters ϕ and the classifier parameters $\boldsymbol{W}$ through backpropagation. During inference, the confusion statistics are no longer updated, and no ground-truth-based reweighting is involved. Instead, the predicted type is directly obtained from the softmax output:

$$\hat{y}_i = \arg\max_{\tau_k \in \mathcal{Y}} \text{softmax}(\boldsymbol{z}_i)_{\tau_k}. \tag{17}$$

Table 1. Summary of datasets adopted in the experiments.

Dataset	#Classes	#Tables	#Training	#Testing
WebTables	78	80K	64K	16K
WebTables$_{\text{multi}}$	78	~33K	~26.5K	~6.5K

4 Experiments

4.1 Datasets and Evaluation Metrics

Datasets. We evaluate the proposed method on two public CTA benchmarks, namely WebTables and WebTables$_{\text{multi}}$. Both are derived from the WebTables portion of the VizNet corpus and follow the data processing protocols of Sherlock and SATO [5,6]. Specifically, WebTables was constructed and processed by Sherlock from the original WebTables corpus. It contains 78 semantic types and approximately 80K tables, including about 64K for training and 16K for testing. WebTables$_{\text{multi}}$ is a public derivative benchmark further filtered by SATO on top of WebTables. It mainly removes single-column tables that lack inter-column contextual information and is therefore more suitable for evaluating methods that exploit table context for column type prediction. This dataset contains approximately 33K tables, including about 26.5K for training and 6.5K for testing. Compared with WebTables, WebTables$_{\text{multi}}$ is smaller in scale but places higher demands on context modeling because it relies more heavily on inter-column co-occurrence information. Table 1 summarizes the statistics of the two datasets.

Noise Label Generation. To simulate annotation noise in real-world scenarios, we synthesize two classical types of label noise on the training set: Pairflip noise and Symmetric noise. Let C denote the number of semantic types, y the clean label, $\widetilde{y}$ the noisy label, and η the noise rate. The label corruption process can be described by a noise transition matrix T, where $T_{ij} = P(\widetilde{y} = j \mid y = i)$.

(1) **Pairflip noise:** with probability η, the clean label y is flipped to its paired type $p(y)$; otherwise, it remains unchanged:

$$P(\widetilde{y} \mid y) = \begin{cases} 1-\eta, & \widetilde{y} = y, \\ \eta, & \widetilde{y} = p(y), \\ 0, & \text{otherwise}. \end{cases} \tag{18}$$

Here, $p(\cdot)$ denotes a predefined type-pairing function.

(2) **Symmetric noise:** with probability η, the clean label y is uniformly flipped to one of the other $C-1$ types; otherwise, it remains unchanged:

$$P(\widetilde{y} \mid y) = \begin{cases} 1-\eta, & \widetilde{y} = y, \\ \frac{\eta}{C-1}, & \widetilde{y} \neq y. \end{cases} \tag{19}$$

In this paper, we mainly report results under two high-noise settings, namely Pairflip = 0.45 and Symmetric = 0.5, together with the noise-free setting. These settings are used to compare the performance of different methods under severe label noise and under clean annotations. Due to space limitations, results under other noise rates are omitted.

Evaluation Metrics. Similar to prior work [2,6], we evaluate different methods by computing the F1 score for each target semantic type. Since the semantic type distribution in WebTables is imbalanced, we report two averaging schemes: Macro-F1 and Weighted-F1. Specifically, Weighted-F1 computes the weighted average of per-type F1 scores using the number of test instances (support) of each type as weights and therefore better reflects overall performance. In contrast, Macro-F1 computes the unweighted average of per-type F1 scores and treats all types equally, making it more sensitive to low-frequency types with fewer samples than Weighted-F1.

Table 2. Main comparison results.

Noise type and rate	Method	WebTables		$\text{WebTables}_{\text{multi}}$	
		Macro F1	Weighted F1	Macro F1	Weighted F1
Pairflip = 0.45	Sherlock	0.3629	0.6148	0.3351	0.6159
	SATO	0.3765	0.6228	0.3722	0.6206
	DivideMix	0.3978	0.6379	0.3816	0.6386
	BARE	0.4012	0.6423	0.3870	0.6479
	DVGL	0.4262	0.6635	0.3910	0.6556
	AdaDB	**0.4708**	**0.7746**	**0.4289**	**0.7183**
Symmetric = 0.5	Sherlock	0.5075	0.7815	0.4210	0.7697
	SATO	0.4319	0.7501	0.3646	0.7304
	DivideMix	0.5234	0.7987	0.4390	0.7909
	BARE	0.5387	0.8012	0.4497	0.8023
	DVGL	0.5421	0.8127	0.4684	0.8147
	AdaDB	**0.5706**	**0.8295**	**0.4956**	**0.8380**
Noise-free	Sherlock	0.7159	0.8753	0.6446	0.8803
	SATO	0.7852	0.9086	0.7469	0.9273
	DVGL	0.8016	0.9080	0.7550	0.9221
	AdaDB	**0.8155**	**0.9164**	**0.7719**	**0.9292**

4.2 Results

We denote our method as AdaDB and compare it with representative baselines, including Sherlock, SATO, DivideMix, BARE and DVGL. Table 2 reports the main comparison results of AdaDB and representative baseline methods on WebTables and $\text{WebTables}_{\text{multi}}$. All results are averaged over five runs with different random seeds. The compared methods include the classical column type annotation model Sherlock [5], the context-enhanced method SATO [6], the general noisy-label learning method DivideMix [9] and BARE [10], and the most closely related method DVGL [2]. Sherlock performs semantic type detection mainly using column-level features, such as statistical properties, character distributions, word-level representations, and paragraph vectors. SATO further incorporates table context, topic modeling, and structured prediction based on column value representations. DivideMix and BARE represent general noise-robust learning methods, while DVGL improves the robustness of column annotation under noisy labels by mining semi-hard samples as decisive vectors. Overall, these baselines cover traditional CTA methods, context-enhanced methods, general noisy-label learning methods, and boundary-sample modeling methods, thereby providing a comprehensive evaluation of AdaDB under type confusion and noisy-label conditions.

Extreme Noise Settings. We focus on two severe noise settings, namely Pairflip = 0.45 and Symmetric = 0.5, to evaluate the robustness of different methods under noisy labels. As shown in Table 2, AdaDB achieves the best performance on both WebTables and $\text{WebTables}_{\text{multi}}$ under the two noise settings.

Under Pairflip = 0.45, where noise mainly occurs between paired similar types, AdaDB obtains the most significant improvement. Compared with DVGL, AdaDB improves Weighted-F1 by 11.11% points on WebTables and 6.27 percentage points on $\text{WebTables}_{\text{multi}}$. This indicates that the proposed adaptive decision boundary is particularly effective when label noise is closely related to semantic type confusion.

Under Symmetric = 0.5, AdaDB also consistently outperforms the baselines on both datasets. Since symmetric noise randomly perturbs labels across different types, this result suggests that AdaDB is not limited to handling pairwise type confusion, but can also maintain robust type discrimination under more dispersed label noise. Overall, the results under both extreme noise settings show that jointly adapting the boundary at the type level and the sample level can effectively alleviate boundary distortion caused by noisy labels.

Noise-Free Setting. In the noise-free setting, AdaDB still achieves the best results on both datasets, reaching 0.9164 Weighted-F1 on WebTables and 0.9292 Weighted-F1 on $\text{WebTables}_{\text{multi}}$. This shows that the proposed method does not rely solely on noisy-label scenarios, but can also improve the discrimination of similar semantic types under clean annotations through more appropriate boundary adjustment.

Label-Level Analysis. As shown in Fig. 3, under both Pairflip = 0.45 and Symmetric = 0.5, AdaDB achieves higher F1 scores than DVGL on most semantic labels. These gains are observed not only on high-frequency labels, but also on many medium- and low-frequency ones. This result is consistent with our design: the type-adaptive module strengthens boundary separation for easily confused types, while the sample-adaptive module focuses on critical samples near the decision boundary. As a result, AdaDB improves label-level discrimination more consistently across different semantic types.

Computational Complexity Analysis. The additional overhead of AdaDB mainly comes from confusion matrix maintenance and adaptive margin computation. Let C denote the number of semantic types and B denote the batch size. The type-adaptive module maintains a $C \times C$ confusion matrix, resulting in an additional space complexity of $\mathcal{O}(C^2)$. For each batch, updating the confusion statistics according to the ground-truth and predicted labels takes $\mathcal{O}(B)$ time, while computing the type-level margins takes $\mathcal{O}(C^2)$ time. The sample-adaptive module mainly computes the score gap between the ground-truth type and the strongest competing type based on the logits, and then generates sample-level margins. Its time complexity is $\mathcal{O}(BC)$, and it introduces no additional neural network layers or learnable parameters. Therefore, the overall additional time complexity of AdaDB is $\mathcal{O}(B + C^2 + BC)$, and the additional space complexity is $\mathcal{O}(C^2)$. Since these computations are performed only at the level of type statistics and classification scores, their cost is relatively small compared with the forward propagation of the column encoder. During inference, the confusion matrix is no longer updated, and the ground-truth-label-based reweighting process is not performed. Thus, AdaDB does not significantly increase inference cost.

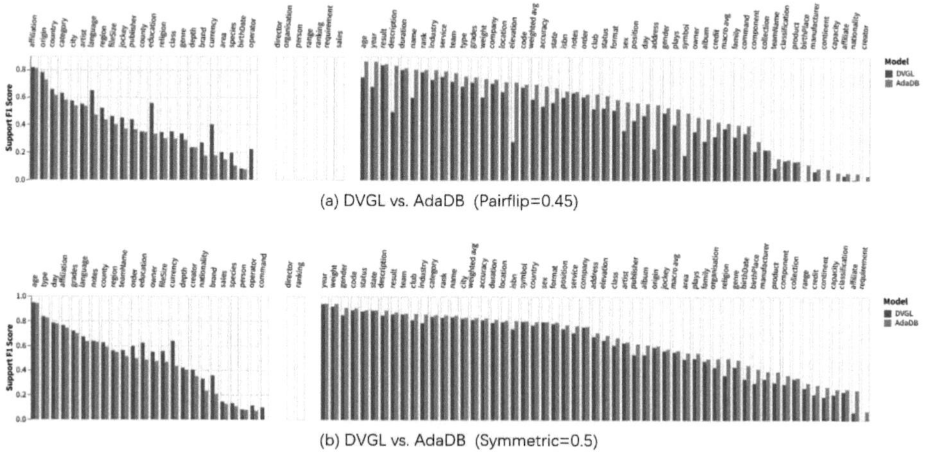

Fig. 3. Label-level comparison between DVGL (blue) and **AdaDB** (orange) on WebTables, where the y-axis denotes the F1 score of each semantic label. (a) Pairflip=0.45; (b) Symmetric=0.5. It can be observed that **AdaDB** improves performance on most semantic labels and consistently outperforms DVGL.

4.3 Ablation Study

To verify the effectiveness of the two adaptive modules, we separately evaluate the model with only the type-adaptive module (AdaDB-type), the model with only the sample-adaptive module (AdaDB-sample), and the full model that combines both modules (AdaDB). The results are reported in Table 3.

Table 3. Ablation results.

Noise type and rate	Method	WebTables		$WebTables_{multi}$	
		Macro F1	Weighted F1	Macro F1	Weighted F1
Pairflip = 0.45	Sherlock	0.3629	0.6148	0.3351	0.6159
	SATO	0.3765	0.6228	0.3722	0.6206
	DivideMix	0.3978	0.6379	0.3816	0.6386
	BARE	0.4012	0.6423	0.3870	0.6479
	DVGL	0.4262	0.6635	0.3910	0.6556
	AdaDB	**0.4708**	**0.7746**	**0.4289**	**0.7183**
Symmetric = 0.5	Sherlock	0.5075	0.7815	0.4210	0.7697
	SATO	0.4319	0.7501	0.3646	0.7304
	DivideMix	0.5234	0.7987	0.4390	0.7909
	BARE	0.5387	0.8012	0.4497	0.8023
	DVGL	0.5421	0.8127	0.4684	0.8147
	AdaDB	**0.5706**	**0.8295**	**0.4956**	**0.8380**
Noise-free	Sherlock	0.7159	0.8753	0.6446	0.8803
	SATO	0.7852	0.9086	0.7469	0.9273
	DVGL	0.8016	0.9080	0.7550	0.9221
	AdaDB	**0.8155**	**0.9164**	**0.7719**	**0.9292**

Analysis. The ablation results in Table 3 show that the two adaptive modules contribute differently under different noise patterns. Under Pairflip = 0.45, AdaDB-type is highly effective, indicating that type-level confusion is important when labels are flipped between similar semantic types. Under Symmetric = 0.5, AdaDB-sample performs best on both datasets, suggesting that focusing on boundary-adjacent samples is more useful when label noise is random and dispersed. In the noise-free setting, the full AdaDB achieves the best overall results, showing that type-level and sample-level adaptation can form a more stable complement when labels are clean. These results indicate that the two modules do not simply lead to additive improvements under all conditions, but play different roles depending on the noise pattern.

5 Conclusion and Future Work

In this paper, we proposed AdaDB, an adaptive decision boundary method for Column Type Annotation. Built upon a normalized cosine classifier and a margin-based learning framework, AdaDB dynamically adjusts the decision boundary at both type level and sample level, and further combines this mechanism with a reweighted training strategy for decisive samples near the boundary, thereby improving the model's ability to discriminate between easily confused types. Experimental results on the WebTables benchmark show that AdaDB consistently outperforms the baseline methods on the main evaluation metrics.

In future work, we plan to further incorporate structural dependencies in table context and extend AdaDB to larger-scale and cross-domain datasets, so as to analyze the behavior of boundary adaptation under long-tail type distributions. Meanwhile, we will further investigate the effects of hyperparameters such as λ, β, and the lower and upper bounds of the margin under different noise types and datasets, and further improve the training and inference efficiency of the model.

Acknowledgments. This work was supported by the National Natural Science Foundation of China under Grant Nos. 62362060 and 72364033.

References

1. Limaye, G., Sarawagi, S., Chakrabarti, S.: Annotating and searching web tables using entities, types and relationships. Proc. VLDB Endow. **3**(1–2), 1338–1347 (2010)
2. Wang, X., Wang, S., Liang, Y., et al.: Decisive vector guided column annotation. Pattern Recognit. **158**, 110958 (2025)
3. Wang, H., Wang, Y., Zhou, Z., et al.: CosFace: large margin cosine loss for deep face recognition. In: Proceedings of the IEEE Conference on Computer Vision and Pattern Recognition (CVPR), pp. 5265–5274 (2018)
4. Deng, J., Guo, J., Xue, N.: ArcFace: additive angular margin loss for deep face recognition. In: Proceedings of the IEEE/CVF Conference on Computer Vision and Pattern Recognition (CVPR), pp. 4690–4699 (2019)
5. Hulsebos, M., Hu, K., Bakker, M., et al.: Sherlock: a deep learning approach to semantic data type detection. In: Proceedings of the 25th ACM SIGKDD International Conference on Knowledge Discovery and Data Mining, pp. 1500–1508 (2019)
6. Zhang, D., Suhara, Y., Li, J., et al.: SATO: contextual semantic type detection in tables. Proc. VLDB Endow. **13**(11), 2685–2698 (2020)
7. Han, B., Yao, Q., Yu, X.: Co-teaching: Robust training of deep neural networks with extremely noisy labels. In: Advances in Neural Information Processing Systems (NeurIPS), p. 31 (2018)
8. Zhang, Z., Sabuncu, M.: Generalized cross entropy loss for training deep neural networks with noisy labels. In: Advances in Neural Information Processing Systems (NeurIPS), p. 31 (2018)
9. Li, J., Socher, R., Hoi, S.C.H.: DivideMix: learning with noisy labels as semi-supervised learning. In: International Conference on Learning Representations (ICLR) (2020)
10. Patel, D., Sastry, P.S.: Adaptive sample selection for robust learning under label noise. In: Proceedings of the IEEE/CVF Winter Conference on Applications of Computer Vision (WACV), pp. 3932–3942 (2023)
11. Huang, Y., Wang, Y., Tai, Y.: CurricularFace: adaptive curriculum learning loss for deep face recognition. In: Proceedings of the IEEE/CVF Conference on Computer Vision and Pattern Recognition (CVPR), pp. 5901–5910 (2020)
12. Kim, M., Jain, A.K., Liu, X.: AdaFace: quality adaptive margin for face recognition. In: Proceedings of the IEEE/CVF Conference on Computer Vision and Pattern Recognition (CVPR), pp. 18750–18759 (2022)

Logical Structure Aware Multi-relation Extraction for Materials Scientific Literature

Mingqian Li[1], Jinguo You[1(✉)], Xingrui Huang[1], Jialin Xu[1], Chuhan Zhang[1], Jingmei Tao[2], Caiju Li[2], and Jianhong Yi[2]

[1] Faculty of Information Engineering and Automation, Kunming University of Science and Technology, 650500 Kunming, Yunnan Province, China
jgyou@kust.edu.cn

[2] Faculty of Materials Science and Engineering, Kunming University of Science and Technology, 650093 Kunming, Yunnan Province, China

Abstract. Artificial intelligence is emerging as a new paradigm for materials computing and development, particularly within a data-driven context. Nevertheless, most current deep learning methodologies face significant challenges due to the high costs associated with data acquisition in the field of materials science. A promising approach to address this issue is the extraction of relevant data from the extensive body of open access scientific literature. However, the complex nature of multiple entities and their overlapping relationships within materials complicates the direct application of general entity relationship extraction techniques to this literature. In this paper, we introduce LOSAMRE, a Logical Structure-Aware Multi-Relationship Extraction method. This approach leverages the inherent logical relationships, such as $m{:}n{:}l$ relationships among key material data, which usually encompass various material entities, their performances, and performance values within a single sentence. Our methodology first involves identifying different types of entities within a sentence, followed by segmenting the sentence into clauses while normalizing the positions of the entities. Subsequently, we establish multiple relationships among these entities in a manner akin to a Cartesian product. In our experimental evaluation, we extracted 1217 sentences from a corpus of 55,850 articles, resulting in the construction of 1415 relationships between materials entities and their corresponding performances. We conducted a comparative analysis of metrics such as F1-Score against state-of-the-art methodologies, revealing that our approach surpasses supervised models by 6.2% and the Large Language models by 3.3%.

Keywords: Artificial intelligence · Literature mining · Entity relationship extraction · Multi-relationship · Logical structure-aware

L. Ding et al. (Eds.): APWeb-WAIM 2026, LNCS 16993, pp. 687–701, 2027.
https://doi.org/10.1007/978-981-92-5693-8_43

1 Introduction

In recent years, a new paradigm in materials computation has emerged, harnessing the capabilities of artificial intelligence (AI). This transformation has fundamentally altered the research process, shifting from conventional trial-and-error methodologies to data-driven approaches. Consequently, researchers have increasingly turned to machine learning to accelerate the development of new materials [1,2]. Scientific data is derived primarily from two sources: (1) experimental and computational results generated within research laboratories [3] and (2) data published in research papers. However, laboratories often encounter challenges in sharing their data due to factors such as the high costs of experimentation, project confidentiality, and other constraints. As a result, individual laboratories are typically unable to provide the extensive datasets necessary for training machine learning algorithms, in contrast to industries such as finance and e-commerce. To address this issue, the Materials Genome Project (MGP) has been established with the aim of creating comprehensive open-source databases that encompass materials' properties, compositions, and behaviors. This initiative also seeks to facilitate platforms for researchers, industry professionals, and academic institutions to share and access data, simulations, and models. Recently, peer-reviewed scientific literature has emerged as a crucial source of data at the intersection of materials science and artificial intelligence. By extracting information from a substantial number of high-quality publications, researchers can obtain the requisite data to foster innovation within this domain.

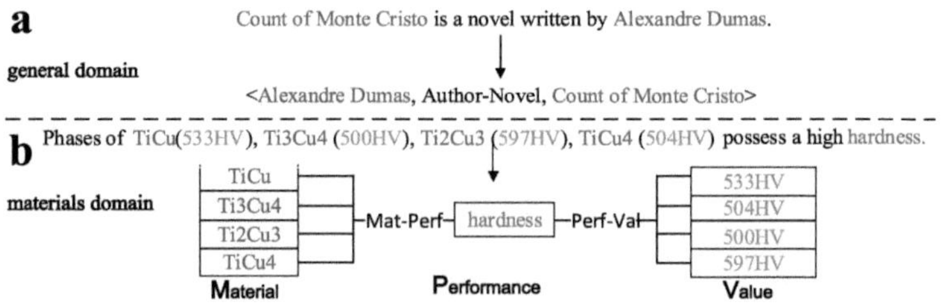

Fig. 1. Comparison of entity relationship extraction in the general domain and materials domain

The key work in materials science is to establish fundamental connections among process, structure, property, and performance (PSPP linkages). This involves designing microstructures that fulfill the performance requirements of materials, as well as optimizing their composition and processing in accordance with these linkages to achieve "material design on demand." However, these PSPP data relevant to this endeavor is often dispersed throughout various segments of the scientific literature. Collecting and structuring them as the needed information and knowledge is essential for advancing material computation and its integration with AI4Science.

A comprehensive review of the scientific literature pertaining in materials computation reveals that numerous statements encompass multiple material entities, each exhibiting diverse performance values across various metrics. Typically, these entities are expected to correspond in a one-to-one manner with their respective performance values, reflecting a Cartesian product-like relationship where the total number of entities multiplied by the number of performance values yields the total number of performance values. For example, the performance value associated with the first performance metric of the material mentioned in a sentence is also presented first, in accordance with the logical structure of human communication. This logical consistency is crucial; deviations from it can lead to confusion and poor clarity in expression. Consequently, once the pertinent entities are identified within sentences, their inherent logical relationships facilitate a more precise understanding of the connections among material composition, performance, and performance values. Traditional machine learning techniques, as well as contemporary deep learning approaches, often necessitate extensive annotated data and struggle to capture such logical relationships effectively.

In contrast to the sentence depicted in Fig. 1a, the entity relationships present in materials science literature typically consist of multiple sets. These relationships are predominantly characterized as single-entity overlap relationships, necessitating the utilization of more sophisticated models to effectively address this issue, as illustrated in Fig. 1b. However, when compared to general domains, specialized domains such as materials science are often deficient in labeled datasets of comparable scale, which adversely affects the performance of current AI-driven relationship extraction methodologies within these specialized fields. An alternative approach for data extraction involves the use of regular expressions. While this method alleviates the dependency on labeled data, it requires the careful development of complex regular expressions, which demands specialized computational expertise. Nonetheless, its applicability may be constrained by its inherent lack of generalizability. To tackle the aforementioned challenges, this paper introduces a relation extraction algorithm that is predicated on the quantity and spatial arrangement of entities, ensuring that the extraction outcomes from materials science literature are both logically structured and semantically coherent. The principal contributions of this study are as follows:

1. We propose a novel framework that extracts diverse entity relationships from materials science literature by modeling the logical patterns of entity combinations based on their quantity and position. It employs a large language model for entity recognition, which removes the need for crafting complex regular expressions and improves the framework's usability and scalability. Complex or lengthy sentences are decomposed into simpler clauses based on the identified quantity and positions of material, property, and value entities. This process reconstructs the intrinsic logical relationships, ultimately extracting the target relationships.

2. On a dataset of 485 copper-based materials papers, our method extracted 1415 relations. In F1-Score, it surpasses the state of art (SOTA) models by 6.2% and the Large Language models by 3.3%.

2 Related Work

The field of relationship extraction has seen rapid development in recent years, with existing methods primarily falling into two categories: traditional approaches and deep learning-based techniques. In this section, we briefly review the methods recently used by relevant researchers.

Han et al. [4] proposed ROMGCJE, a model with joint entity relationship extraction, which applied the attention mechanism to perceive the relationship between entities and used the relationship information to guide named entity recognition. Finally, the minimum risk training mechanism is introduced to train the model jointly. Experiments on NYT and WebNLG datasets show that the model can effectively extract overlapping triples.

Wang et al. [5] constructed a model based on pre-trained BERT and attention mechanisms to solve the problem that extracting multiple relationships from natural language requires multiple encodings of inputs. The scheme only needs to encode the input corpus once to complete the multi-entity relationship extraction task, and the accuracy reaches 83.9% in the ACE 2005 dataset.

Effective data extraction from the material scientific literature is a hot research topic. But most current work focuses on material entity recognition.

Ghadbeigiet et al. [6] manually extracted data on electrode materials for lithium-ion batteries from about 200 publications, and an extensive database of lithium-ion battery materials was established based on this work, which provided significant help for the research of battery materials researchers. Using machine learning, Kim et al. [7] successfully extracted data on oxide materials from 76,000 scientific papers containing oxides. Liu et al. [8] used active learning to extract data and successfully expand the 8845 material entities manually marked to 16,677. Wei et al. [9] constructed a Bi-GRU-GNN-CRF joint extraction method of material entity relationships. This work successfully automatically extracts material data such as materials entity, relationship, and process flow from patents and literature. The experimental results show that this work has better accuracy and recall rate in Chinese data and can effectively improve the knowledge coverage of the materials knowledge graph, which reaches 80%.

These machine learning models all have good results but have a weakness: they need labeled data.

In addition to machine learning approaches, traditional methods based on regular expressions have also been employed recently. Wang et al. [10] argue that the application of machine learning in the extraction of data from material science literature is challenging due to the scarcity of effectively annotated data in the domain. Recognizing the distinctive characteristics of specific domains, they developed a method utilizing a regular algorithm for identifying material entities and a distance algorithm for data extraction from materials science literature. This research validates the feasibility of regular data extraction from articles. Machine learning models need labeled data, which is scarce. Rule-based methods do not address overlapping entity relationships.

Recently, LLMs have been applied to scientific data extraction. Schilling-Wilhelm et al. [11] reviewed LLM-based chemical extraction, covering prompting and fine-tuning. Foppiano et al. [12] evaluated GPT models on superconductor NER (Named Entity Recognition) and relation extraction, finding that zero-shot LLMs underperform task-specific models and fine-tuning is necessary. However, both approaches still require careful prompt engineering or annotated data, and they do not handle multi-to-multi entity relations (e.g., Cartesian product links) common in materials science.

3 Our Model

In the absence of labeled data, we employed a large language model for entity relationship extraction in the materials science literature. In contrast to traditional methods, we reformulated the intricate regular relations into simpler logic units, which we refer to as clauses, to ensure that the classification of relationships is coherent and to prevent the overlap of single-entity relationships.

3.1 Formalization

In this paper, we assume that entity relationship extraction can be completed when all relevant entities are in the same sentence. Under this assumption, here are some definitions.

In this work, the term "logical structure" is operationalized as the positional order and count distribution of entities within a sentence. Scientific writing in materials science typically follows a predictable linear pattern: materials, properties, and their corresponding values are presented in a consistent sequence (e.g., materials are listed first, followed by their properties and associated values). This positional regularity constitutes a discourse-level logic that our method directly exploits.

Definition 1. (*Entity, E*) The data unit in the relation triple. The number of entities is defined as $|E|$. This paper has three kinds of entities: Materials Entity M, Performance Entity P, and Value Entity V.

Definition 2. (*Entity Sequence, ESQ*) An entity sequence is formed by ordering entities in the materials science literature by their position. As shown in Fig. 3a, the ESQ of the sample sentence can be expressed as $ESQ = (p_1, p_2, v_1, v_2, m_1, v_3, v_4, m_2)$.

Definition 3. (*Entity Set, ES*) A Set of the same type of entities, such as the Material Set ($MS = m_1, m_2, \ldots, m_n$).

Definition 4. (*Clause, C*) A clause is the minimum data extraction unit that includes the material entity, the performance entity, and the performance value entity. In this paper, we consider that entities follow the following rule:

$$|V| = |M| \times |P| \tag{1}$$

$$|M| = 1 \vee |P| = 1 \tag{2}$$

Definition 5. (*Clause Set, CS*) A Set of Clause is $(CS = c_1, c_2, \ldots, c_n)$.

Definition 6. (*Cartesian Product Link*) The direct product operation on the set $X = (x_1, x_2)$ and $Y = (y_1, y_2)$, which is formally expressed as follows:

$$X \times Y = \{(x_1, y_1), (x_1, y_2), (x_2, y_1), (x_2, y_2)\} \tag{3}$$

Definition 7. (*Direct Join Link*) The direct join operation on the set $X = (x_1, x_2)$ and $Y = (y_1, y_2)$, which is formally expressed as follows:

$$X \times Y = \{(x_1, y_1), (x_2, y_2)\} \tag{4}$$

3.2 Named Entity Recognition

To extract structured knowledge from scientific literature, this work employs a Large Language Model (LLM)-based Named Entity Recognition (NER) approach. We utilize GPT4o-mini as the core model, leveraging its strong natural language understanding and demonstrated proficiency in scientific texts to accurately identify diverse and complex domain-specific entities in materials science.

As illustrated in Fig. 2, our pipeline operates as follows: an original sentence (e.g., *"Phases of TiCu (533 HV), Ti_3Cu_4 (500 HV), Ti_2Cu_3 (597 HV), $TiCu_4$ (504 HV) possess a high hardness"*) serves as the input. Through carefully structured prompts, such as "You are an expert in material science entity recognition.", GPT4o-mini is guided to perform the targeted NER task. The prompt defines three entity types: Material (e.g., "TiCu"), Property (e.g., "hardness"), and Value (e.g., "533 HV").

3.3 Clause Splitting

In materials science, the literature often comprises texts that include multiple clauses, as illustrated in Fig. 1b. In this study, we segment the sentence into individual clauses. Initially, we create a sequence of entities based on their respective positions. Subsequently, we cut the entity sequence into clauses according to the definition of clauses. But the following algorithm presents only one case of the ESQ sequence; other combinations that conform to the literature syntax are also acceptable. The specific cutting algorithm is presented in Algorithm 1.

In this algorithm, the entity sequence will be divided into clauses according to lines 4–10. However, when traversing to the last element of the sequence, if the current sequence of elements does not constitute a clause, we will also force push this sequence into the clause set temporarily at line 11.

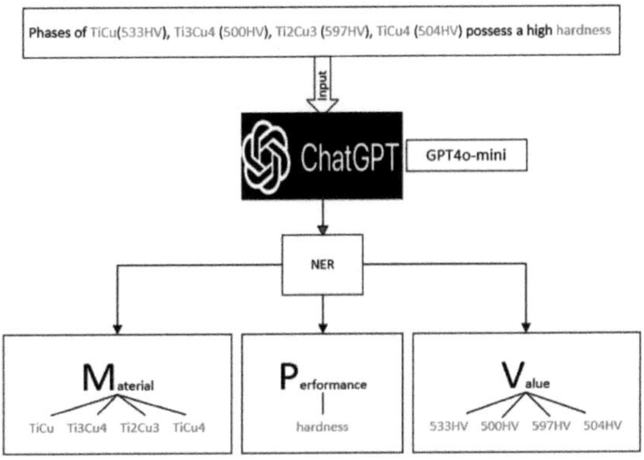

Fig. 2. Named entity recognition by LLM

Algorithm 1. Clause Splitting Algorithm

Input: Entity sequence(ESQ)
$ESQ = < m_1, m_2, p_1, v_1, v_2, p_2, v_3, v_4 >$
Output: Clauses Set(CS)
$CS = [< m_1, m_2, p_1, v_1, v_2 >, < p_2, v_3, v_4 >]$

```
1: function MAIN
2:     Clause List Set CS = [ ]
3:     Clause c = [ ]
4:     for i in ESQ do
5:         Push i into c
6:         if |V| = |M| × |P| then
7:             Push c into Clause Set CS
8:             Empty the Clause to [ ]
9:         end if
10:    end for
11:    Push c into Clause Set CS
12: end function
```

In this normalization algorithm, the clauses with missing information rely heavily on the first clause as a template to fill in the information. Lines 4–15 of the algorithm are the process of filling in the information. Here, we demonstrate a more sophisticated example. $ESQ = \langle m_1, m_2, p_1, v_1, v_2, p_2, v_3, v_4, p_3, v_5, v_6, \dots \rangle$. After the first step, We can get two clauses $C = [\langle m_1, m_2, p_1, v_1, v_2 \rangle, \langle p_2, v_3, v_4, p_3, v_5, v_6, \dots \rangle]$ from the ESQ. The first clause is a standard clause, but the second clause missing the material entity (M). After normalizing the second clause, we can get a new clause $C = \langle m_1, m_2, p_2, v_3, v_4, p_3, v_5, v_6, \dots \rangle$. In this clause $|M| = 2$ and $|P| = n{-}1$ which do not meet the definition $|M| = 1 \vee |P| = 1$, so we will re-split and re-normalize the second clause until all clauses fit the definition. Final the normalizing clause set will be like $C = [\langle m_1, m_2, p_1, v_1, v_2 \rangle, \langle m_1, m_2, p_2, v_3, v_4 \rangle, \langle m_1, m_2, p_3, v_5, v_6 \rangle, \dots]$.

3.4 Clause Normalizing

After cutting the clauses to obtain a set of clauses, the second step is to normalize the clauses in this set. The specific normalizing algorithm is shown in Algorithm 2.

Algorithm 2. Clause Normalizing Algorithm

```
Input: Clause sequence(CS)
       CS = [ < m1, m2, p1, v1, v2 >,< p2, v3, v4 >]
Output: Clauses Set(CS)
       CS = [ < m1, m2, p1, v1, v2 >,< m1, m2, p2, v3, v4 > ]
function MAIN(Clause Set CS)
    Main Clause MC = CS[0]
    for c in CS do
        if c.length != MC.length then
            Clause NC = MC
            for i=0→ NC.length do
                for j=0→ c.length do
                    if NC[i].type == c[j].type then
                        NC[i] = c[j]
                        Break
                    end if
                end for
            end for
        end if
    end for
    Clause Set.append(Clause)
end function
```

3.5 Relation Extraction

After establishing all clauses, this paper constructs the relationship between entities in each clause, similar to the Cartesian Product and Join operations. The specific algorithm is shown in Algorithm 3

Algorithm 3. Relation Extraction Algorithm

```
Input: Clauses Set(CS)
       CS = [ < m1, m2, p1, v1, v2 >,< m1, m2, p2, v3, v4 > ]
Output: Relation Set(RS)
       RS = [ < m1, p1, v1 >,< m2, p1, v2 >,< m1, p2, v3 >,< m2, p2, v4 > ]
function MAIN(Clause Set CS)
    Relation Set RS= [ ]
    for c in CS do
        Material Set MS= [ ]
        Performance Set PS= [ ]
        Value Set VS= [ ]
        Temp Set TS= [ ]
        Push all materials entity in c to MS
      such as m1
        Push all Performance entity in c to PS
      such as p1
        Push all Value entity in c to VS
      such as v1
        TS=Cartesian Product Link(MS,PS)
        TS=Direct Join Link(TS,VS)
        RS.append(TS)
    end for
end function
```

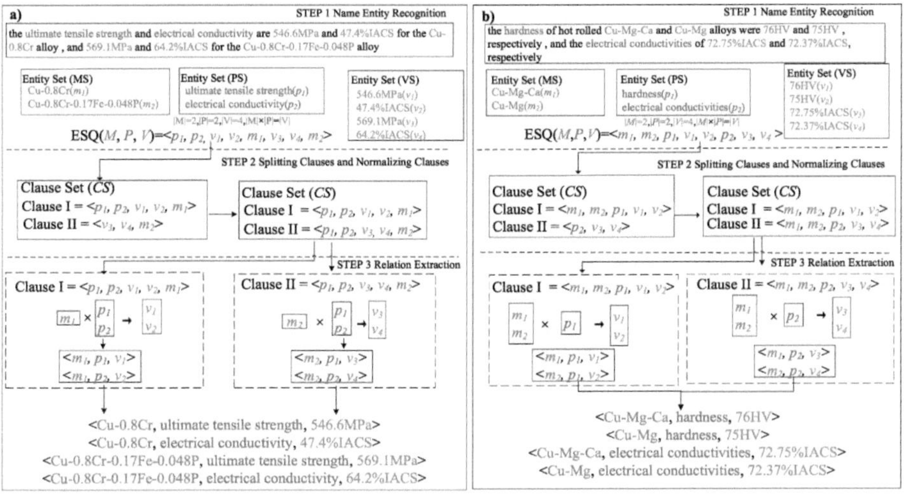

Fig. 3. Two samples of entity relationship extraction process

To avoid SEO problems in relationship classification as demonstrated in Fig. 1b. We consider the performance entity directly as the relationship between the material entity and the value entity. Therefore, the relational classification problem is transformed into a table-filling problem, where the row names of the table are the performance entities and the column names are the materials entities. To construct this table, the materials entities are first combined with the performance entities by the Cartesian product link which has been shown in the algorithm 3 line 11. If the materials set $MS = \{m_1, m_2\}$, performance set $PS = \{p_1\}$, after the Cartesian product link, we can get a temp set $TS = \{\langle m_1, p_1\rangle, \langle m_2, p_2\rangle\}$. At this point, it is only necessary to make a direct join between this combination and the performance entity in order to complete the table-filling task. If the value set $VS = \{v_1, v_2\}$, after Direct Join Link the TS and VS, the result will be $TS = \{\langle m_1, p_1, v_1\rangle, \langle m_2, p_2, v_2\rangle\}$. A more visual example can be found in Fig. 3, step 3.

As a consequence of dividing complex sentences into clauses, the entities in each clause are unique. Therefore, when combining relationships in a single clause, there will be no overlap of entity relationships.

4 Performance Evaluation

4.1 Experimental Settings

Datasets

- Open dataset: the open dataset used in Weston [13]'s report, which contains 278 copper-based materials entities can be used for materials named entity identification.

- manually annotated mixed relationship dataset: 1217 sentence containing materials entities, property names, and property value entities are extracted from 50000 materials science literature from 2011–2022 by the model of this paper.

4.2 Baseline

In this section, we outline several prominent baseline models in the field of relation extraction and named entity recognition.

(1) CasRel [14]: modeling relations and entities by a binary labeling framework (CasRel) while using Bert [15] as the underlying encoder.
(2) LSTM Joint Extraction [16]: proposes a new annotation method combined with LSTM [17] to solve the joint extraction task, converting the joint extraction problem into an annotation problem to avoid building complex feature engineering and using the traditional One-Hot word vector model in the underlying encoding.
(3) SuperAlloyDigger [10]: using the regular algorithm to identify materials entities and construct relational triples by the distance between entities to extract materials data from articles.
(4) BERT_{EM} [18]: investigates how to represent entity pairs in text and constructs a BERT-based relationship extraction model with inputs that work best on BERT, and then gives a pre-trained model that can be used for relationship extraction based on the best labels.
(5) Mre-In-One [5]: a model based on pre-trained BERT and attention mechanism. This model is proposed by experts from IBM and Tencent AI Joint Lab, which is arm to solve the problem of multiple encoding of inputs when extracting multivariate relations from natural language. The model only needs to encode the input corpus once and achieves an accuracy of 83.9% on the ACE 2005 dataset.
(6) SpERT [19]: SpERT is a joint entity and relationship extraction method that trains both entity and relationship in the same process. The idea is to first form all the spans from a sentence, and second, classify these spans to confirm if they are entities. Finally, match all spans that are entities in pairs for relationship classification. This baseline can effectively solve the problem of overlapping relationships.
(7) W2NER [20]: this model accomplishes the named entity recognition task by establishing word-to-word relationships. This feature can also be used for entity relationship extraction. This baseline algorithm achieves SOTA performance on 14 datasets.
(8) Llama3 [21]: Large language model adaptable to various NLP tasks including NER and relation extraction, achieving SOTA on several benchmark datasets.
(9) DeepSeekV3 [22]: Utilizes novel architecture optimized for efficiency and accuracy in NER, also applicable to relation extraction, achieving SOTA on multiple NER benchmarks.

(10) DeepSeekR1 [23]: Addresses NER through advanced reasoning capabilities and instruction following, also suitable for relation extraction with competitive performance.
(11) GPT4oMini [24]: Handles NER with optimized performance and reduced computational footprint, also applicable to relation extraction with strong performance.
(12) Qwen3 [25]: Accomplishes NER through multilingual capabilities and strong contextual understanding, also used for relation extraction, achieving SOTA on Chinese and English NER datasets.

4.3 Performance Metrics

To evaluate the performance of LOSAMRE, we use three different metrics: Precision, Recall, and F1-score.

$$Precision = \frac{TP}{TP + FP} \tag{5}$$

$$Recall = \frac{TP}{TP + FN} \tag{6}$$

$$F1\text{-}score = 2 \times \frac{Precision \times Recall}{Precision + Recall} \tag{7}$$

4.4 Experimental Results

Table 1 shows the results of the entity recognition comparison experiments under the three datasets, where BERT_{EM} and BERT_{SP} are not involved in the entity recognition experiments because they mainly focus on relationship extraction, from the experimental results. Our method uses GPT4o-mini as NER core.

Table 1. NER experiment

Model	Open dataset			Manual dataset		
	Precision (%)	Recall (%)	F1-score (%)	Precision (%)	Recall (%)	F1-score (%)
CasRel	0	0	0	64.2	45.5	53.3
SuperAlloyDigger	63.6	14.9	48.2	53.4	35.5	42.6
LSTM Joint Extraction	47.0	40.0	43.0	25.3	16.0	19.4
SpERT	13.8	27.9	15.5	**88.4**	72.7	79.7
W2NER	0	0	0	78.7	75.6	77.1
GPT4o-mini	**72.3**	**74.6**	**73.4**	84.3	**77.8**	**80.9**

The GPT4o-mini proposed in this paper scores higher than 70% overall stability in several metrics on all datasets. However, it does not achieve the best in all datasets. The Precision score of the SpERT model is the highest in the public dataset because the amount of annotated data is more than the two datasets that are manually annotated. Still, its overall score F1 is not good due to its low number of predictions with a lower check-all rate, and also because the coding layer of the model is Bert, it can be found by comparison that if the corpus is not used in advance, The coding layer of Joint Extraction adopts the One-Hot coding method, so the coding layer of the algorithm needs to be constructed using the existing corpus. The SuperAlloyDigger algorithm does not require training, but because it uses regular expressions to extract data, its regular coverage is incomplete, resulting in a lack of accuracy in entity recognition in other directions.

On the hand-labeled single-relationship dataset, the Joint Extraction model is unable to predict entities on the hand-labeled single-relationship dataset, although it is able to identify entities on the public dataset, mainly because the algorithm adopts the encoding method of One-Hot vector, so the content of the corpus influences the extraction effect on different datasets fluctuates greatly. This is mainly because the training set of this dataset is small. Still, the algorithm has a low completion rate, resulting in the same low overall F1-score. The performance of SuperAlloyDigger on this dataset is stronger than that of the public dataset because its regularity covers more material entities in this dataset and enough regular expressions should be written. From this level, writing reasonable regular expressions is the core of the algorithm.

Table 2. Relation extraction results by model category

Model	Precision (%)	Recall (%)	F1-score (%)
Supervised models			
Mre-In-One	66.5	57.7	61.8
W2NER	63.3	63.5	63.4
$BERT_{EM}$	62.6	54.4	58.2
SpERT	53.6	57.8	55.7
CasRel	49.1	27.7	35.4
LSTM joint extraction	23.2	13.9	17.1
Rule-based models			
SuperAlloyDigger	18.9	18.9	18.9
Large language models			
Llama3	58.2	72.7	64.7
GPT-4o-mini	56.3	**75.3**	64.5
Qwen3	54.1	66.9	59.9
DeepSeek-R1	52.2	66.9	58.6
DeepSeek-V3	44.7	63.5	52.7
Proposed method (label-free)			
LOSAMRE	**70.1**	66.1	**68.0**

From the result in Table 2, it can be seen that compared to other baselines, the proposed LOSAMRE performs better than other models. Among them, Super Alloy Digger is a rule-based entity relationship extraction method. As can be seen from the Table 2, the method can only be used for the superalloys mentioned in the original paper. The method has a lower overall score regarding the extracted content. CasRel, LSTM Joint Extraction, the $BERT_{EM}$ and $BERT_{SP}$ are four machine learning schemes for entity-relationship extraction, respectively. In the field of materials, LLM's accuracy of literature relationship extraction is not as good as that of the method we proposed. It can be seen from the Table 2 that CasRel and LSTM Joint Extraction perform poorly due to the small amount of data in the training set. $BERT_{SP}$ is 0.7% higher than this paper in terms of accuracy rate, but the overall F1 score is not as good as the $BERT_{SP}$, as a machine learning model, requires pre-annotated data, which is costly to use in the absence of public datasets in the current materials data extraction field. In contrast, the proposed extraction scheme can complete data extraction without annotated data. From another aspect, the results of $BERT_{SP}$ also illustrates that the content extracted by the invention can also be used as the input of a machine learning model, so the data extracted by the invention can also be used as a scheme to build a dataset for a materials science literature data extraction model.

5 Conclusion and Future Work

This paper further summarizes the logical structure of sentences in scientific literature, discovers certain characteristics of data in materials science literature, and proposes a method using LLM as entity recognition and a relationship construction algorithm using word position to improve the accuracy of entity recognition and relationship construction in materials science literature. The data extracted in this paper can be directly used for machine learning without further cleaning, providing a solution for expanding the data set of materials science literature information extraction.

The relationship construction method based on logical structure awareness proposed in this paper cannot analyze semantics and therefore cannot analyze special semantics in materials science literature, such as comparative semantics (the performance of material entity 1 is X% more than material entity 2), with percentage (the performance of material entity 1 is X% of material entity 2), etc. These special semantics usually involve multiple material entities and implicitly represent the performance of a material entity. The performance value of a materials entity needs to be inferred and calculated through semantics. However, the LOSAMRE entity recognition scheme cannot solve this problem. Therefore, in future work, we can consider using deep learning-based solutions or large language models to solve this problem, thereby improving the quantity and quality of data extraction in materials science literature.

References

1. Zhang, H., Fu: Machine learning assisted composition effective design for precipitation strengthened copper alloys. Acta Mater. **215**, 117118 (2021)
2. Butler, K.T., Davies, D.W., Cartwright, H., Isayev, O., Walsh, A.: Machine learning for molecular and materials science. Nature **559**, 547–555 (2018)
3. Hafner, J.: Ab-initio simulations of materials using vasp: density-functional theory and beyond. J. Comput. Chem. **29**(13), 2044–2078 (2008)
4. Han, H., Wang: A relation-oriented model with global context information for joint extraction of overlapping relations and entities. Front. Neurorobot. **16**, 914705 (2022)
5. Wang, H., Tan: Extracting multiple-relations in one-pass with pre-trained transformers. arXiv:1902.01030 (2019)
6. Ghadbeigi, L., Harada: Performance and resource considerations of Li-ion battery electrode materials. Energy Environ. Sci. **8**(6), 1640–1650 (2015)
7. Kim, E., Ming, J.: Machine-learned and codified synthesis parameters of oxide materials. Sci. Data **4**, 170127 (2017)
8. Liu, Y., Yao, C., Niu, C.: Text mining of hypereutectic Al-Si alloys literature based on active learning. Mater. Today Commun. **26**, 102032 (2021)
9. Wei, X., Wang: Constructing a material-domain knowledge graph based on natural language processing. Shanghai Univ. J. Nat. Sci. 386–398 (2022)
10. Wang, W., Jiang, X., Tian, S.: Automated pipeline for superalloy data by text mining. NPJ Comput. Mater. (2022)
11. Schilling-Wilhelmi, M., Ríos-García, M., Shabih, S., Gil, M.V., Miret, S., Koch, C.T., Márquez, J.A., Jablonka, K.M.: From text to insight: large language models for chemical data extraction. Chem. Soc. Rev. **54**, 1125–1150 (2025)
12. Foppiano, L., Lambard, G., Amagasa, T., Ishii, M.: Mining experimental data from materials science literature with large language models: an evaluation study. Sci. Technol. Adv. Mater. Methods **4**(1), 2356506 (2024)
13. Weston, L., Tshitoyan, V.: Named entity recognition and normalization applied to large-scale information extraction from the materials science literature. J. Chem. Inf. Model. **59**(9), 3692–3702 (2019)
14. Wei, Z., Su, J., Wang: A novel cascade binary tagging framework for relational triple extraction. In: Proceedings on 58th Annual Meeting of the Association for Computational Linguistics, pp. 1476–1488 (2020)
15. Devlin, J., Chang, M.-W., Lee, K., Toutanova, K.: Bert: pre-training of deep bidirectional transformers for language understanding. arXiv:1810.04805 (2018)
16. Zheng, S., Wang, F., Bao: Joint extraction of entities and relations based on a novel tagging scheme. In: Proceedings of the 55th Annual Meeting of the Association for Computational Linguistics, pp. 1227–1236 (2017)
17. Hochreiter, S., Schmidhuber, J.: Long short-term memory. Neural Comput. **9**(8), 1735–1780 (1997)
18. Soares, L.B., FitzGerald, N., Ling, J., Kwiatkowski, T: Matching the blanks: distributional similarity for relation learning. arXiv:1906.03158 (2019)
19. Eberts, M., Ulges, A.: Span-based joint entity and relation extraction with transformer pre-training. In: Proceedings of the 24th European Conference on Artificial Intelligence, vol. 325, pp. 2006–2013 (2020)
20. Li, J., Fei: Unified named entity recognition as word-word relation classification. In: Proceedings of the AAAI Conference on Artificial Intelligence, vol. 36, pp. 10965–10973 (2022)

21. Meta AI. Llama 3 model card. https://github.com/meta-llama/llama3 (2024)
22. DeepSeek AI. Deepseek-v3 technical report. https://github.com/deepseek-ai/DeepSeek-V3 (2024)
23. DeepSeek AI. Deepseek-r1: Reasoning-optimized language model. https://www.deepseek.com/r1 (2024)
24. OpenAI. Gpt-4o mini: Advanced multimodal model. https://openai.com/index/gpt-4o-mini-advancing-cost-efficient-intelligence/ (2024)
25. Qwen Team. Qwen2.5 technical report. arXiv:2412.15115 (2024)

Author Index

L. Ding et al. (Eds.): APWeb-WAIM 2026, LNCS 16993, pp. 703–705, 2027.
https://doi.org/10.1007/978-981-92-5693-8

MIX
Papier aus verantwortungsvollen Quellen
Paper from responsible sources
FSC® C105338

If you have any concerns about our products,
you can contact us on
ProductSafety@springernature.com

In case Publisher is established outside the EU,
the EU authorized representative is:
Springer Nature Customer Service Center GmbH
Europaplatz 3, 69115 Heidelberg, Germany

Printed by Libri Plureos GmbH
in Hamburg, Germany